THE BEST 361 COLLEGES

THE PRINCETON REVIEW

THE BEST 361 COLLEGES

2006 Edition

By Robert Franek,
Tom Meltzer, Christopher Maier, Carson Brown,
Julie Doherty, and Andrew Friedman

Random House, Inc.
New York
www.PrincetonReview.com

The Princeton Review, Inc.
2315 Broadway
New York, NY 10024
E-mail: bookeditor@review.com

ISBN 0-375-76483-6

Publisher: Robert Franek
Editors: Robert Franek and Erik Olson
Production Editor: Christine LaRubio
Production Manager: Scott Harris

Manufactured in the United States of America on partially recycled paper

9 8 7 6 5 4 3 2 1

2006 Edition

FOREWORD

Every year, about two million high school graduates go to college. To make sure they end up at the *right* school, they spend several billion dollars on the admissions process. This money pays for countless admissions officers and counselors, a bunch of standardized tests (and preparation for them), and many books similar to—but not as good as—this one.

It's expensive because most admissions professionals have a thing about being in control. As a group, colleges resist almost every attempt to standardize or otherwise simplify the process. Admissions officers want you to believe that every admissions decision that they render occurs within systems of weights, measures, and deliberations that are far too complex for you to comprehend. They shudder at the notion of having to respond to students and their parents in down-to-earth language that might reveal the arbitrary nature of a huge percentage of the admissions and denials that they issue during each cycle. That would be admitting that good luck and circumstance play a major part in many successful applications. So, in flight from public accountability, they make the process a lot more mysterious than it needs to be.

Even the most straightforward colleges hide the information you would want to know about the way they'll evaluate your application: What grades and SATs are they looking for? Do their reported SAT averages include minority students, athletes, and legacies (kids whose parents went to their school)? Exactly how much do extracurricular activities count? What percentage of the aid that they give out is in loans and what percentage is in grants?

We couldn't get answers to these questions from many colleges. In fact, we couldn't get answers to *any* questions from some schools. Others who supplied this information to us for earlier editions of this guide have since decided that they never should have in the first place. After all, knowledge is power.

Colleges seem to have the time and money to create beautiful brochures that generally show that all college classes are held under a tree on a beautiful day. Why not just tell you what sort of students they're looking for, and what factors they'll use to consider your application?

Until the schools demystify the admissions process, this book is your best bet. It's not a phone book containing every fact about every college in the country. And it's not a memoir written by a few graduates describing their favorite dining halls or professors. We've given you the facts you'll need to apply to the few hundred best schools in the country and enough information about them—which we gathered from more than 100,000 current college students—to help you make a smart decision about which school to attend.

One note: We don't talk a lot about majors. This is because most high school students really don't know what they want to major in—and the ones who do almost always change their minds by the beginning of junior year. Choosing a school because of the reputation of a single department is often a terrible idea. But if you're interested in learning about majors and the colleges that offer them, pick up our *Guide to College Majors*, or visit our website, www.PrincetonReview.com, where we explain majors and list the colleges that offer them.

As complicated and difficult as the admissions process is, we think you'll love college itself—especially at the schools listed in this book.

Good luck in your search.

John Katzman
June 2005

Acknowledgments

Each year we assemble an awe inspiringly talented group of colleagues who work together to produce our guidebooks; this year is no exception. Everyone involved in this effort—authors, editors, data collectors, production specialists, and designers—gives so much more than is required to make *The Best 361 Colleges* an exceptional student resource guide. This new edition yields the essentials of what prospective college students really want: the most honest, accessible, and pertinent information on the colleges they are considering attending for the next four years of their lives. My sincere thanks go to the many who contributed to this tremendous project. I am proud to note here that we have again successfully provided an uncompromising look into the true nature of each profiled college or university based on the opinions of each institution's current students. I know our readers will benefit from our cumulative efforts.

A special thank you goes to our authors, Tom Meltzer, Christopher Maier, Carson Brown, Julie Doherty, and Andrew Friedman for their dedication in sifting through tens of thousands of surveys to produce the essence of each school profiled. Very special thanks go to Erik Olson, Editorial Director, Lisa Marie Rovito and Spencer Foxworth, Editors, for their editorial commitment and vision. Erik deserves special thanks for the managerial role he took in working directly with our student survey team, establishing protocol with an unblinking eye on providing balanced narrative profiles. Lisa Marie and Spencer have quickly become assets to our editorial department. They met the challenges of this book head on; I am grateful for their thoughtful and careful reading.

Michael Palumbo, Student Survey Manager, has been a dedicated TPR staffer since 1999. This is Michael's second year at the helm of the student survey process, and we have all profited from his presence. Michael is a gifted communicator, he understands our survey/collection process and works exceptionally well with school administrators and students alike. A warm and special thank you goes to our Student Surveyor Administrators, Jen Adams and Chaitra Ramanathan. Jen and Chaitra are in the trenches everyday, their spirit never wavers, and their work—consistently excellent.

My continued thanks go to our data collection pros, Ben Zelevansky and Perry Medina, for their successful efforts in collecting and accurately representing the statistical data that appear with each college profile. A sincere thank you goes to Ben Zelevansky for all the needed work he completed for data generation and his competence in book pours.

The enormity of this project and its deadline constraints could not have been realized without the calm presence of our production team, Scott Harris, Production Manager; Christine LaRubio, Production Editor; and Ricky Marson, Copy Editor. Their unconditional dedication, focus, and most importantly, careful eyes, continue to inspire and impress me. They deserve great thanks for their flexible schedules and uncompromising efficiency.

Special thanks also go to Jeanne Krier, our Random House publicist, for the work she has done on this book and the overall series since its inception. Jeanne continues to be my trusted colleague, media advisor, and friend. I would also like to make special mention of Tom Russell, our Random House publisher, for his continuous investment and faith in our ideas.

Lastly, I thank John Katzman, Mark Chernis, and Young Shin for their steadfast confidence in this book and our publishing department, and for always being the champions of student opinion. It is a pleasure to work with each of you.

Again, to all who contributed so much to this publication, thank you for your efforts; they do not go unnoticed.

Robert Franek
VP—Publisher
Lead Author—*The Best 361 Colleges*

CONTENTS

PART 1: **INTRODUCTION** 1

A Parent's Guide to the College Search 3

Ap_lic_t_o_. 7

How We Produce This Book 9

How This Book is Organized 13

Glossary 23

About Those College Rankings 25

PART 2: **SCHOOLS RANKED BY CATEGORY** 29

PART 3: **THE BEST 361 COLLEGES** 45

PART 4: **"MY ROOMMATE'S FEET REALLY STINK."** 769

PART 5: **INDEXES** 785

Index of College Counselors 786

Index of Schools 801

Index of Schools by Location 805

About the Authors 810

DOONESBURY
By Garry Trude
SEEN THE PRINCETON REVIEW, THORNBERG?
YES, SIR. WE'RE THE NUMBER 7 PARTY SCHOOL IN THE NATION.
UP THREE TICKS. HOW DO YOU SUPPOSE THAT HAPPENED?
WELL, SIR, MAYBE IT WAS ABOLISHING THE 8-DRINK LIMIT AT COLLEGE FUNCTIONS.
WELL, IT DOESN'T SEEM TO BE HURTING US AT THE ADMISSIONS OFFICE. AFTER THE RIGORS OF HIGH SCHOOL, KIDS TODAY ARE LOOKING FOR A PLACE WHERE THEY CAN UNWIND FOR A FEW YEARS!
YES, SIR.
OF COURSE, I DON'T IMAGINE THE ALUMNI ARE TOO THRILLED.
NO, SIR. NOR THE FACULTY..
THEY'RE STARTING TO COMPLAIN ABOUT THE SPILLOVER.
SPILLOVER?
OKAY, JUST CURIOUS—HOW MANY OF YOU ARE DRUNK THIS MORNING?

PART 1

INTRODUCTION

A Parent's Guide to the College Search: Why It Ought To Be An Enjoyable Year

By Dan Lundquist, Vice President of Admissions and Financial Aid; and Peter Blankman, Director of Communications and Publications; Union College, Schenectady, NY. Reprinted with their permission from the Union College brochure of the same name.

There are some 3,500 colleges and universities in the United States, and by the time you leave your son or daughter at new student orientation, you may feel that you've seen every one of them—or at least received mail from most of them!

We hope that by sharing a college's perspective, we can shed some light on the search process and help you understand it better. We hope these "educated insights" will help you approach the process in the most positive and productive way.

The college search process ought to be a positive, educational experience in itself, not just something to be "survived." At this point—the bridge between high school and college, adolescence and young adulthood—students have a remarkable range of options in front of them, and it's a shame when the excitement of this situation becomes anxiety.

While there's no sure-fire way to eliminate anxiety, we believe proper planning, combined with a realistic and appropriate attitude, can go a long way toward minimizing anxiety.

And that's a laudable goal in itself.

Getting started

The college search needn't be that overwhelming—not if you start early, plan ahead, and take things one step at a time.

No question, you're facing a big change in your family's life. So how do you find a compass? How do you begin to sort through all the information and begin to make some choices that will make sense for you and your child?

There are a couple of first steps. One is to take a self-inventory. You and your child should ask yourselves realistic, sometimes tough, person-centered questions about interests, skills, values, and aspirations. Soon it will be appropriate to begin thinking about externally oriented issues like college size, location, and cost. And it's okay to admit that trepidation and uncertainty exist, even among "veteran" families.

Alongside the self-inventory is the gathering of objective information about colleges themselves—the kind of details that will help you narrow that list from 3,500 to perhaps a handful. This can be daunting. One of the overwhelming aspects of the college search is that there's so much information available. Sometimes it's hard to distinguish between what is and what isn't valuable.

One of the resources that too often is not used properly is your school counseling office. Nearly everything you need to start doing some preliminary sorting is here—an experienced college counseling staff, publications from colleges, guidebooks of all kinds, and electronic databases.

Along with the experiences of friends—students and adults—your own child's "instincts" are also resources to draw on. These anecdotal resources should not drive the search process, but you should feel free to start the preliminary list of colleges with some sentimental favorites.

As a goal begins to come into focus, sometimes working backward from that goal makes great sense. If your goal is to get to a small, liberal arts college in the northeast, for example, start with a group of schools and work backward, applying increasingly personal, student-oriented questions to make distinctions and winnow the list.

Let the student lead

It's important that the student take the lead in thinking critically to get down to the shortlist. Ultimately a student who's been spoon-fed is the one who's going to be disappointed in college when he or she discovers that other people's interests and values drove the college search.

One of your best strategies is to ask questions, keep your eyes open, and evaluate information and impressions. In the end, it's a question and answer process between family and college, parent and child.

Determining the fit between student and college depends on how you want to define the outcome of your child's college education. If you want to define it vocationally, you might look purely at statistics. To the extent that cost will be a factor, you will need to research tuition prices and/or financial aid policies. And if you want to define it as an academic, intellectual, personal, and cultural experience—and you are attuned to those values and clues that give you insights into a college's "character"—then your child's college years will be all the richer for that.

No such thing as a perfect fit

Happily, for most students there is no one perfect fit. In fact, against the backdrop of so many fine options, your child certainly has the talent and flexibility to succeed at a number of colleges. Strange as it may sound now, some of the students who turn out the happiest, in fact, are the ones who thought they had lost the "admissions sweepstakes" at the end of their senior year. Hence the old college counseling truism: The vast majority of students are at their first-choice college by Halloween of their first year.

Even though your child could be happy at a number of colleges, you still have to focus the search. Rankings, objective data, and reputation are necessary, but not sufficient, to judge the correctness of the fit between the individual and institution.

In short, it's time to hit the road.

Make those visits

Visiting a college is really the only way you're going to get a sense of the reality or the personality of the place—its strengths, its surprises, its life in and outside the classroom. From the time you first walk on campus, you will start picking up messages, from the quality of the facilities to the friendliness of the students, to the physical care of the campus grounds.

A prospective student ought to ask, "Can I see myself here?" Look at the students; look at the announcements on the bulletin boards; feel comfortable asking questions about any issue, from housing and campus safety to graduate school placement. Try to get a handle on the tone of the campus, what the students care about and pay attention to, and help your child compare that with her needs and "comfort zone."

The same goes for an interview. Treat it as a conversation, not an inquisition. Who does well in an interview? A relaxed student armed with good questions and ready to speak articulately about his interests and aspirations.

Will you get straight answers to your questions? In the overwhelming number of cases, yes. Sure, we're recruiters—salespeople—but we're also counselors. We want to enroll students who are going to be happy at our college. Maybe that's one reason we're an admissions office, not a rejection office. An overarching goal of ours is that the college search process be a positive educational experience in itself.

The "heart quotient"

A lot of people do a great job with the analytical part of the search, but they leave out the heart component, if you will. They are transfer students in the making!

When students are asked how they came to choose Union, they almost always cite the "smart," cognitive factors, such as academic program, size, and post-graduate placement.

That's fine. But we always discover that, as they narrowed it down, the answers come much more from the heart and describe how they felt when they first visited campus, or how much they liked the students and professors they met. If someone doesn't have a reasonable measure of that "heart quotient," then college's general educational value, as a total experience, is going to be lessened.

How we choose

At a certain point this whole process becomes more of an art than a science for you.

It's the same for us.

We have a parallel, shared process and goal. You are choosing a college, we are selecting students, and our goal—the best "match"—is the same.

Just like you, we begin by looking at the objective criteria (grades, quality of courses, and test scores) to see if there is an initial fit between your son or daughter and our college.

And like your college search, assembling a class is not a purely objective process. We want to bring together young men and women who have enough in common so that they're going to be good roommates, study partners, and friends, and support each other as they take the "prudent risks" that are an important part of the educational experience. We also want enough differences so they're going to educate each other in some subtle ways. That's the richness of a residential, undergraduate college.

Being a selective college means having a large enough applicant pool to select the students we think will be appropriate for our institution. It's important for parents to understand that at selective colleges the process is going to be just that—selective. And it is important to acknowledge that selective judgements based upon subjective evaluations are, to some extent, going to be "unfair." Coming to terms with that reality early on will help put any disappointments, if they come, into perspective later on.

A good rule of thumb

From the start of the process, you should keep this thought in mind:

What is a realistic pool for my child?

Most counselors are going to recommend that you have four schools that look likely to admit your child, have a reach or two (based on the objective data), and have a sure bet or two. That rule of thumb has been around all these decades because it's based on experience and realism.

A positive experience

We hope that some of these comments help you approach the college search process from a positive, productive perspective. College counselors—admissions officers, recruiters, and guidance personnel—believe that it ought to be an enjoyable, educational experience, one guided by concerns for what's best for the student at this pivotal point between late adolescence and young adulthood.

Assaying one's options at this time of life ought to be exciting and fun—at least most of the time. It's true that choosing a college is a serious business, but that does not mean one must be deadly serious about it.

Best wishes, good luck, and don't forget, Halloween is just around the corner!

For more than 20 years Dan Lundquist has worked at small, liberal arts colleges and Ivy League universities. He is now Vice President of Admissions and Financial Aid at Union College in Schenectady, NY.

A former reporter, Peter Blankman is the College's Director of Communications and Publications.

A P _ LIC _ T _ O_.

What's *that*?!?!

It's APPLICATION with P-A-I-N removed from the process.

We removed the paper, too.

With PrincetonReview.com's Online College Applications there are no endless piles to shuffle. No leaky pens, no hand cramps, no trying to figure out how many stamps to stick on that envelope.

The process is so painless, online applications practically submit themselves for you. Watch . . .

Type in your main contact information just once in our application profile and every subsequent application you file from our database—picking from hundreds of top schools—is automatically filled in with your information.

Not only are online applications:

- Faster to fill out
- Completely safe and secure
- Instantly trackable (check your application status online!)
- And . . . impossible to lose in the mail (they reach schools instantly)

But also: On PrincetonReview.com, there's no extra fee to submit your application online—our technology is totally FREE for you to use. In fact, some colleges even *waive* the application fee if you apply online.

Still have questions?

- Can I start an application now and finish it later?
- Are there easy-to-use instructions or someone I can call if I have a question? If I get stuck, are there application instructions?
- Do schools *really* want to receive applications online?

Yes, yes, and yes!

It's easy to see the advantages of online applications. Almost as easy as actually applying.

Just log on and apply. It's that easy.

PrincetonReview.com—Applications without the pain.

How We Produce This Book

When we first began work on this project in 1991, there was a void in the world of college guides (hard to believe, but true!). No one publication provided prospective college students with in-depth statistical data from the colleges on admission, financial aid, student body demographics, and academics, as well as narrative descriptions of college academic and social life on each campus based on the opinions of the very students who attend them. Thus *Best Colleges* was born. There wasn't then—and there still isn't now—any other college guide quite like this one.

The differences start right on the cover with the name—*The Best 361 Colleges*. Why not *The Best 300 Colleges*? Or just *The Best Colleges*? And how did we arrive at 361? Well, to be honest, the original plan back at the beginning was to produce a guide entitled *The Best 300 Colleges*. An initial list of colleges to be included was compiled, and the authors got to work arranging for on-campus student surveys to be conducted. Since student feedback is such an integral part of the individual college entries and several other aspects of the guide, it was absolutely imperative that every campus intended for inclusion be surveyed by academic year's end. Alas, Mother Nature and other forces kept our surveyors off of many campuses that year, and a number of colleges could not be included in the first edition. Thus it was simply called *The Best Colleges*, sans number.

The guide enjoyed some early success, but it really needed a number in its title in order to help position it in relation to other guides on the shelves of your friendly neighborhood book superstore. The second edition was referred to as *The Best 286 Colleges*, and it's all history from there.

To determine which colleges and universities are included in *The Best Colleges*, we have avoided using any sort of mathematical calculations or formulas. The initial list was built through consultation with a variety of expert sources, including 50 independent educational consultants from throughout the nation. From that point, new institutions have been added annually; a few have been dropped. A careful review of the guide will reveal a wide representation of colleges in terms of geography and enrollment size. Inside, you will read about public and private schools, historically black colleges and universities, science and technology-focused institutions, nontraditional colleges, highly selective schools and those with virtually open-door admissions policies, great buys, and the wildly expensive. We've added 11 schools to the guide this year: Berea College, Chapman University, Hillsdale College, Lynchburg College, Mills College, Monmouth University, Saint Michael's College, Transylvania University, University of Central Florida, University of South Florida, and Xavier University of Louisiana. Like the other schools in this guide, all are institutions well worth considering. Though not every college included will appeal to every student, this guide represents our version of the cream of the crop—comprising the top 10 percent of all colleges in the nation—and our best 361.

In addition to closely monitoring the statistical data we collect annually on nearly 2,000 colleges, we meet with dozens of admissions officers and college presidents and keep abreast of college news 24/7 throughout each year. As a result, we are able to maintain a working list of colleges to consider adding to or deleting from the guide for each subsequent edition. Any college we consider adding to the guide must agree to allow anonymous student surveys to be completed on campus; it is difficulty with this issue alone that explains, why some schools are conspicuously absent from *Best Colleges*.

Hundreds of thousands of students in total have been surveyed on the various campuses that comprise the best 361. Recent editions includes information based on the opinions of more than 100,000 students; we've surveyed anywhere from 20-odd men at Deep Springs College in the California desert to thousands of collegians at places like Clemson University and Louisiana State University. It's a mammoth undertaking, but the launch a few years ago of our online student survey (http://survey.review.com), available 24/7, has made it possible for students to complete a survey anytime and anywhere an Internet-enabled computer can be found. In fact, the majority of our student surveys are now collected with the online survey.

So how do we do it? Early on we surveyed at all of the included colleges and universities on our own, marshalling resources through our network of dozens of Princeton Review offices nationwide. Once we'd gone through a few editions, we switched to a two-to-three-year cycle for revisiting each campus. (The reality is that, unless there's been some grand upheaval at a campus, we've found that there's little change in student opinion from one year to the next.) Thus, each year we target 100 to 125 campuses for resurveying. Colleges that wish to be resurveyed prior to their regular survey cycle are accommodated with an earlier visit if at all possible. It should also be noted that online surveys submitted by students outside of schools' normal survey cycle and independent of any solicitation on our part are factored into the subsequent year's various calculations.

All colleges and universities we plan to visit are notified through established campus contacts that we wish to arrange a survey; we depend upon these contacts for assistance in either notifying the student body of our online survey, or, if the school opts for the paper survey, in identifying common, high-traffic areas on-campus in which to survey, and to help us make any necessary arrangements as required by campus policies. At colleges in the New York metropolitan area (we call it home), we most often send our own team to conduct the typically day-long surveys; at colleges that are further afield, we hire current students to conduct the surveys if at all possible. In recent years, many schools have chosen to send an e-mail to the entire student body notifying it of the availability of the online survey, which in some cases has yielded astonishing response rates.

The survey itself is extensive, divided into four sections—"About Yourself," "Your School's Academics/Administration," "Students," and "Life at Your School"—that collectively include more than 60 questions. We ask about all sorts of things, from "How many out-of-class hours do you spend studying each day?" to "How widely used is beer?" Most questions are multiple-response in nature, but seven offer students the opportunity to expand on their answers with narrative responses. These narrative responses are the sources of the student quotations that appear throughout each entry in *Best 361 Colleges*.

Once the surveys have been completed and the responses stored in our database, each college is given a grade point average (GPA) for its students' answers to each individual multiple-response question. It is these GPAs that enable us to compare student opinions from college to college, and to gauge which aspects of the complete experience at each college rate highest and lowest according to the institution's own students. Once we have this information in hand, we write the individual college entries. Student quotes expressed within the entries are not chosen for their extreme nature, humor, or singular perspective—in all cases the intention is that they represent closely the sentiments expressed by the majority of survey respondents from the college or that they illustrate one side or another of a mixed bag of student opinion, in which case one should also find a counterpoint within the text. And, of course, if they accomplish this *and* are noteworthy for their wittiness, they'll definitely make it into the guide.

The entries in general seek to accomplish that which a college admissions viewbook by its very nature can never really hope to achieve—to provide a (relatively) uncensored view of life at a particular college, and acknowledge that even the best of the best of America's 3,500 or so colleges have their drawbacks. Though some college administrators find this book hard to accept, most have come to recognize that college officials no longer enjoy the luxury of controlling every word that students hear or read about their institutions and that the age of consumerism in the college search process is here to stay.

Our survey is qualitative and anecdotal rather than quantitative. While this approach sometimes means we blow a result—such as when we surveyed at Stephens College during the week the administration was debating the abolition of women's studies as a major at that small women's college, and (*suprise!*) the survey results indicated an unhappy student body—most of our results are confirmed by feedback we get from alums, current students, counselors, and prospective students who visit the campuses. In order to help guard against the likelihood that we produce an entry that's way off the mark for any particular college, we send administrators at each school a copy of the entry we intend to publish prior to its actual publication date, with ample opportunity to respond with corrections, comments, and/or outright objections. In every case in which we receive a reply, we take careful steps to ensure that we review their suggestions and make appropriate changes when warranted.

Far more important than what college administrators think is what YOU think. Take our information on colleges as you should take information from all sources—as input that reflects the values and opinions of others, which may be helpful to you as you *form your own opinions* about the colleges you're considering. This guide is not an end point from which you should cull your list of colleges to apply to without referencing any other source or visiting any of the colleges covered here. Rather, it's a starting point, a tool that can help you to probe the surface and get a sense of the college experience. You simply must do your own investigation and develop your own list of best colleges. Only then will this book be the useful tool that it is intended to be.

How This Book Is Organized

Each of the colleges and universities listed in this book has its own two-page spread. To make it easier to find information about the schools of your choice, we've used the same format for every school. Look at the sample pages below:

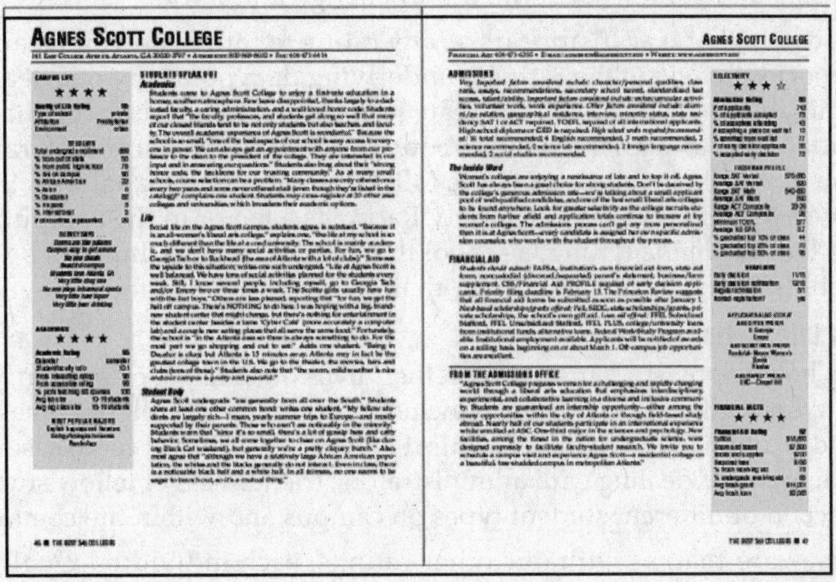

Each spread has nine major components. First, at the very top of the spread you will see the school's address, telephone, and fax numbers for the admissions office, the telephone number for the financial aid office, and the school's website and/or e-mail address. Second, there are two sidebars (the narrow columns on the outside of each page, which consist mainly of statistics) divided into the categories of Campus Life, Academics, Selectivity, and Financial Facts. Third, there are four headings in the main body text or "write-up" called "Students Speak Out," "Admissions," "The Inside Word," "Financial Aid," and "From the Admissions Office." Here's what each part contains:

The Sidebars

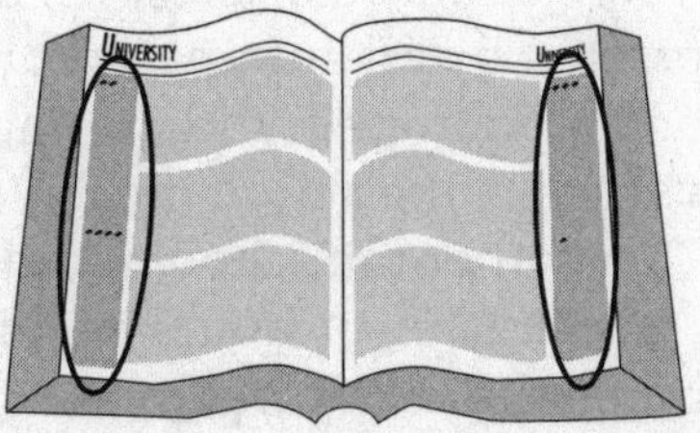

The sidebars contain various statistics culled from our own student surveys and from questionnaires school administrators fill out. Keep in mind that not every category will appear for every school, since in some cases the information is not reported or not applicable.

Here is what each statistical heading tells you:

Nota Bene

Our six ratings were determined using the results from our student surveys as well as institutionally-reported data. Six ratings are on a scale of 60–99. Each individual rating places each college on a continuum for purposes of comparing all colleges within this edition only. Although they are similar, *these ratings are not intended to be compared directly to those within any prior edition*, as our ratings computations are somewhat refined and change annually.

Please also note that if a **60*** appears as any rating for any school, it means that the school reported so few of the rating's underlying data points by our deadline that we were unable to calculate an accurate rating for it. In such cases the reader is advised to follow up with the school about the specific measures each rating takes into account, which are outlined in the following ratings explanations. Be advised that because the Admissions Selectivity Rating is a factor in the computation that produces the Academic Rating, a school that has **60*** as its Admissions Selectivity Rating will have an Academic Rating that is lower than it should be.

Quality of Life Rating

This rates how happy students are with their lives outside the classroom, on a scale of 60–99. We weighed several factors, including students' overall happiness; beauty, safety, and location of the campus; comfort of dorms; quality of food; ease of getting around campus and dealing with administrators; friendliness of fellow students; and the interaction of different student types on campus and within the community.

Please be aware that, as with our other ratings, each individual Quality of Life rating places the college that receives it on a continuum for purposes of comparing all colleges within this edition only. Although similar, *these ratings are not intended to be compared directly with those within any prior edition*, as our ratings computations are somewhat refined and change annually.

Fire Safety Rating

This rating measures how well prepared a school is to prevent or respond to campus fires, specifically in residence halls, on a scale of 60–99.

We asked all the schools we annually collect data from to answer several questions about their efforts to ensure fire safety for campus residents. Each school's responses to eight of those questions were considered when calculating its Fire Safety Rating. The questions were developed in consultation with the Center for Campus Fire Safety (www.campusfire.org <http://www.campusfire.org>) and cover: 1) the percentage of residence hall rooms protected by an automatic sprinkler system, 2) the percentage of residence hall rooms equipped with a smoke alarm that is connected to a supervised fire alarm system, 3) the action most often taken when a residence hall fire alarm is activated, 4) whether the school requires fire-resistance ratings on dorm room furniture, 5) the number of hours per student per year of fire prevention/evacuation training the school provides, 6) whether the school requires all students living in on-campus residences to receive fire extinguisher training, 7) whether certain fire-unsafe items or activities(e.g., candles, smoking) are banned in dorm rooms and 8) how often fire safety rules-compliance inspections are conducted in the school's residence halls.

Schools that did not report answers to any of the questions receive a Fire Safety Rating of 60*. The schools have an opportunity to update their fire safety data every year and will have their fire safety ratings re-calculated and published annually.

Each individual rating places a college on a continuum for purposes of comparing all colleges within this academic year only. Though similar, these ratings are not intended to be compared directly to those that appeared on PrincetonReview.com in any prior academic year or within any Princeton Review print publication, except for *Complete Book of Colleges, 2006 Edition* and *The Best Northeastern Colleges, 2006 Edition*, as our ratings computations are refined and change somewhat annually.

Type of school
Whether the school is public or private.

Affiliation
Any religious order with which the school is affiliated.

Environment
Whether the campus is located in an urban, suburban, or rural setting.

Total undergrad enrollment
The total number of degree-seeking undergraduates who attend the school.

"% male/female" through "# countries represented"
The demographic breakdown of the full-time undergraduate student body and what percentages of the student body live on campus, belong to Greek organizations, and, finally, the number of countries represented by the student body.

Survey Says
Summarizes the results of our survey. This list shows what the students we surveyed felt unusually strongly about, both positively and negatively, at their schools (see the end of the introduction for a more detailed explanation of items on the list).

Academic Rating
On a scale of 60–99, how hard students work at the school and how much they get back for their efforts. The ratings are determined based on results from our surveys of students and administrators. Factors weighed included how many hours students reported studying, and the quality of students the school attracts as measured by admissions statistics; we also considered students' assessments of their professors' abilities and helpfulness. This individual rating places each college on a continuum for purposes of comparing all colleges within this edition only. Though similar, *these ratings are not intended to be compared directly to those within any prior edition,* as our ratings computations are refined and change somewhat annually.

Calendar
The school's schedule of academic terms. A "semester" schedule has two long terms, usually starting in September and January. A "trimester" schedule has three terms, one usually beginning before Christmas and two after. A "quarterly" schedule has four terms, which go by very quickly: the entire term, including exams, usually lasts only nine or ten weeks. A "4-1-4" schedule is like a semester schedule, but with a month-long term in between the fall and spring semesters. (Similarly, a 4-4-1 has a short term following two longer semesters.) When a school's academic calendar doesn't match any of

these traditional schedules, we note that by saying "other." For schools that have "other" as their calendar, it is best to call the admissions office for details.

Student/faculty ratio

The ratio of full-time undergraduate instructional faculty members to all undergraduates.

Profs interesting rating

Based on student responses to the statement on the student survey: "Your instructors are good *teachers*."

Profs accessible rating

Based on student responses to the statement on the student survey: "Your instructors are available outside the classroom."

% profs teaching UG courses

This category shows the percentage of professors who teach undergraduates and eliminates any faculty whose focus is solely on research.

% classes taught by TAs

Many universities that offer graduate programs use graduate students as teaching assistants (TAs). They teach undergraduate courses, primarily at the introductory level. This category reports on the percentage of classes that are taught by TAs instead of regular faculty.

Most common lab size; Most common regular class size

College-reported figures on class size averages for regular courses and for labs/discussion sections.

Most Popular Majors

The three majors with the highest enrollment at the school.

Admissions Selectivity Rating

How competitive admission is at the school, on a scale of 60–99. This rating is determined by several factors, including the class rank of entering freshmen, test scores, and percentage of applicants accepted. By incorporating all these factors (and a few others), our admissions selectivity rating adjusts for "self-selecting" applicant pools. University of Chicago, for example, has a very high admissions selectivity rating, even though it admits a surprisingly large proportion of its applicants. Chicago's applicant pool is self-selecting; that is, nearly all the school's applicants are exceptional students. This individual rating places each college on a continuum for purposes of comparing all colleges within this edition. Though similar, *these ratings are not intended to be compared directly to those within any prior edition,* as our ratings computations are refined and change somewhat annually.

% of applicants accepted

The percentage of applicants to which the school offered admission.

% of acceptees attending

The percentage of those who were accepted who eventually enrolled.

 # accepting a place on wait list

The number of students who decided to take a place on the wait list when offered this option.

% admitted from wait list

The percent of applicants who opted to take a place on the wait list and were subsequently offered admission. These figures will vary tremendously from college to college, and should be a consideration when deciding whether to accept a place on a college's wait list.

# of early decision applicants

The number of students who applied under the college's early decision or early action plan.

% accepted early decision

The percentage of early decision or early action applicants who were admitted under this plan. By the nature of these plans, the vast majority who are admitted wind up enrolling. (See the early decision/action description that follows in this section for more detail.)

Range/Average SAT Verbal, Range/Average SAT Math

The average and the middle 50 percent range of test scores for entering freshmen. Don't be discouraged from applying to the school of your choice even if your combined SAT scores are 80 or even 120 points below the average, because you may still have a chance of getting in. Remember that many schools emphasize other aspects of your application (e.g., your grades, how good a match you make with the school) more heavily than test scores.

TPR (The Princeton Review) Projected Range SAT Writing

As of March 2005 the College Board has added a writing section to the SAT exam, inherently changing its structure. This addition will affect each prospective college bound student considering admission for fall 2006 and beyond, and we at The Princeton Review thought it important for students to have an idea of how new test scores would be used by each college profiled in this guide and on our website, www.PrincetonReview.com. However, the students taking the March 2005 SAT were the first to sit for the new exam, and will be the first applying to schools in fall 2006 with new scores. This makes it impossible for school administrators to report new scores for typical student applicants until the beginning of the fall 2006 semester. (We know this is confusing! Bear with us; it'll all make sense in a second.) Not to be alarmists, but the unfortunate fact is that students applying to schools this academic year, for admission to the entering class in fall 2006 (and some students entering in fall 2007) will be left without the useful guide of the full range of SAT scores for schools on their list of possible application considerations. Schools themselves are not at fault, as noted above they don't have the averages to report—at least not yet. As the SAT is the expertise of The Princeton Review, we believe we can remedy this problem, providing current students these needed benchmark scores for each school they're considering.

Here's what we did:

* Created an algorithm based on the middle 50 percent range of SAT scores reported back to The Princeton Review from students completing the new March 2005 exam. Our algorithm gave us the ability to create a middle 50 percent range for the new Writing section of the SAT. You will see this range generated for each school profiled in this guide and on our website.

The new SAT Writing Range is listed in the right-hand sidebar on each page in this guide under the heading: **TPR Projected Range SAT Writing.*

To be clear, these estimated scores are based on research conducted by The Princeton Review only, not information supplied to us by individual schools. We believe they offer benchmark guidance, not guarantees. You will only see this **TPR Projected Range SAT Writing* section this year and next. After that point, the aggregate scores of actual student applicants will be available to The Princeton Review from schools themselves.

In addition to the **TPR Projected Range SAT Writing,* you will see additional text added to the *From The Admissions Office* section for each school included in this book. This spring, we reached out to all schools included in this guide, giving them the opportunity to explain their admissions policies towards the new SAT, old SAT, SAT Subject Tests, etc. As there seemed to be some student and parent confusion around which exam submissions are acceptable and appropriate for admission to the fall 2006 entering class, we gave school admissions pros a chance to offer clarity to interested students. Each school's entry was limited to 50 words; we believe this text gives real clarity to the individual school's policies.

Minimum TOEFL
The minimum test score necessary for entering freshmen who are required to take the TOEFL (Test of English as a Foreign Language). Most schools will require all international students or non-native English speakers to take the TOEFL in order to be considered for admission.

Average HS GPA
We report this on a scale of 1–4 (occasionally colleges report averages on a 100 scale, in which case we report those figures). This is one of the key factors in college admissions. Be sure to keep your GPA as high as possible straight through until graduation from high school.

% graduated top 10%, top 25%, top 50% of class
Of those students for whom class rank was reported, the percentage of entering freshmen who ranked in the top tenth, quarter, and half of their high school classes.

Early decision/action deadlines
The deadline for submission of application materials under the early decision or early action plan. Early decision is generally for students for whom the school is a first choice. The applicant commits to attending the school if admitted; in return, the school renders an early decision, usually in December or January. If accepted, the applicant doesn't have to spend the time and money applying to other schools. In most cases, students may apply for early decision to only one school. Early action is similar to early decision, but less binding; applicants need not commit to attending the school and in some cases may apply early action to more than one school. The school, in turn, may not render a decision, choosing to defer the applicant to the regular admissions pool. Each school's guidelines are a little different, and the policies of a few of the most selective colleges in the country have changed quite dramatically recently. Some colleges offer more than one early decision cycle, so it's a good idea to call the school and get full details if you plan to pursue one of these options.

Early decision, early action, priority, and regular admission deadlines

The dates by which all materials must be postmarked (we'd suggest "received in the office") in order to be considered for admission under each particular admissions option/cycle for admission for the fall term.

Early decision, early action, priority, and regular admission notification

The dates by which you can expect a decision on your application under each admissions option/cycle.

Nonfall registration

Some schools will allow incoming students to matriculate at times other than the fall term—the traditional beginning of the academic calendar year. Other schools will only allow you to register for classes if you can begin in the fall term. A simple "yes" or "no" in this category indicates the school's policy on nonfall registration.

Applicants also look at

These lists are based on information solicited directly from the colleges. Admissions officers are given the opportunity to annually review and suggest alterations to these lists for their schools, as most schools track as closely as they can other schools to which applicants they accepted applied, and whether the applicants chose their school over the other schools, or vice versa.

Financial Aid Rating

Based on school-reported data on financial aid and awards to students and students' satisfaction (as collected through our student survey) with the financial aid they receive. Again, this is on a scale of 60–99. This individual rating places each college on a continuum for purposes of comparing all colleges within this edition only. Though similar, *these ratings are not intended to be compared directly to those within any prior edition,* as our ratings computations are refined and change somewhat annually.

Annual tuition, In-state tuition

The tuition at the school, or for public colleges, for a resident of the school's state. Usually much lower than out-of-state tuition for state-supported public schools.

Annual out-of-state tuition

For public colleges, the tuition for a nonresident of the school's state. This entry appears only for public colleges, since tuition at private colleges is generally the same regardless of state of residence.

Required fees

Any additional costs students must pay beyond tuition in order to attend the school. These often include fitness center fees and the like. A few state schools may not officially charge in-state students tuition, but those students are still responsible for hefty fees.

Tuition and fees

In cases where schools do not report separate figures for tuition and required fees, we offer this total of the two.

Comprehensive fee

A few schools report one overall fee that reflects the total cost of tuition, room and board, and required fees. If you'd like to see how this figure breaks down, we recommend contacting the school.

Room & board

Estimated annual room and board costs.

Books and supplies

Estimated annual cost of necessary textbooks and/or supplies.

% frosh receiving need-based aid

According to the school's financial aid department, the percentage of all degree-seeking freshmen who applied for financial aid, were determined to have financial need, and received any sort of aid, need-based or otherwise.

% UG receiving need-based aid

According to the school's financial aid department, the percentage of all degree-seeking undergrads who applied for financial aid, were determined to have financial need, and received any sort of aid, need-based or otherwise.

Avg frosh grant

The average grant or scholarship given to freshmen who receive either or both.

Avg frosh loan

The average amount of loans disbursed to freshmen.

Independent 529

Many private colleges have agreed to participate in the Independent 529 Plan, which allows parents or other family members to pay future tuition at any participating college at less than today's prices. It's a very novel way to approach the problem of financing college, especially given that in recent years private college tuition has been going up at least six percent a year. Visit www.independent529plan.org to learn more about the program. If a school participates in the plan, a simple "Yes" will appear in this field.

Students Speak Out

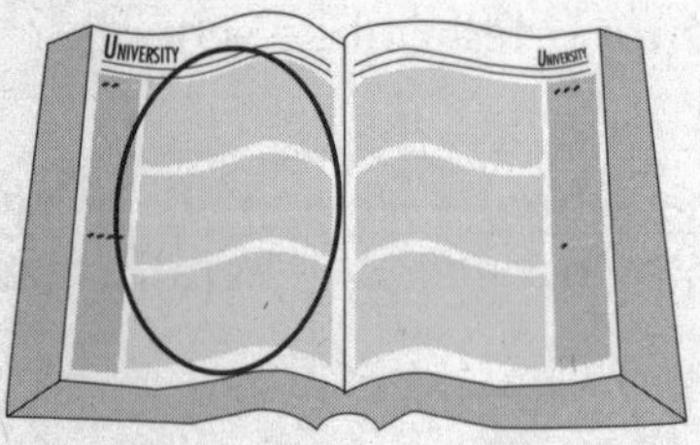

This section summarizes the results of the surveys we distributed to students at the school. When appropriate, it also incorporates statistics provided by the schools themselves. It is divided into three subheadings: Academics, Life, and Student Body. The Academics section reports how hard students work and how satisfied they are with the education they are getting. It also often tells you which academic departments our respondents rated favorably. Student opinion regarding administrative departments often works its way into this section. The Life section describes life outside the classroom and addresses questions ranging from "How nice is the campus?" and "How comfortable are the dorms?" to "How popular are fraternities and sororities?" The Student Body section tells you about what type of student the school attracts and how the students view the level of interaction between various groups, including those of different ethnic origins.

All quotations in these sections are from students' open-ended responses to our survey. We choose quotations based on the accuracy with which they reflect our survey results. Those students who wrote entertaining but nonrepresentative essays will find excerpts of their work in Part 4 of the book, a section entitled "My Roommate's Feet Really Stink."

Admissions

This section tells you what aspects of your application are most important to the school's admissions officers. It also lists the high school curricular prerequisites for applicants, which standardized tests (if any) are required, and special information about the school's admissions process (e.g., Do minority students and legacies, for example, receive special consideration? Are there any unusual application requirements for applicants to special programs?).

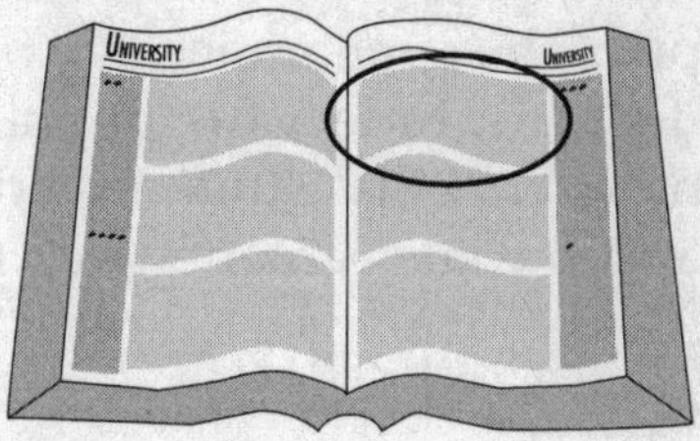

The Inside Word

This section contains our own insights about each school's admissions process.

Financial Aid

This section summarizes the financial aid process at the school: What forms you need and what types of merit-based aid and loans are available. Information about need-based aid is contained in the financial aid sidebar. While this section

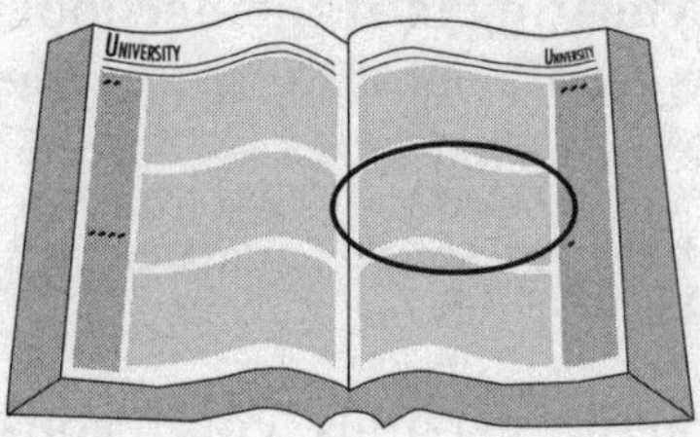

includes specific deadline dates for submission of materials as reported by the colleges, we strongly encourage students seeking financial aid to file all forms—federal, state, and institutional—as soon as they become available. In the world of financial aid, the early birds almost always get the best worms (provided, of course, that they're eligible for a meal!).

From the Admissions Office

This section contains text supplied by the colleges in response to our invitation that they use this space to speak directly to the readers of our guide. For schools that did not respond, we usually excerpted an appropriate passage from the school's catalog, website, or other admissions literature.

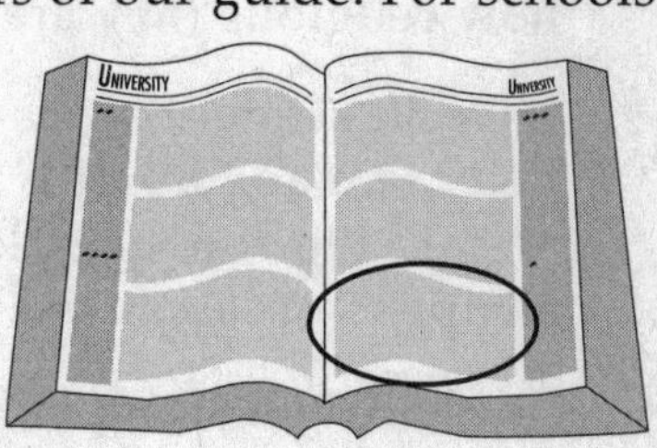

Survey Says

Our Survey Says list, located in the Campus Life sidebar on each school's two-page spread, is based entirely on the results of our on-campus surveys. In other words, the items on this list are based on the opinions of the students we surveyed at those schools (*not* on any numerical analysis of library size, endowment, etc.). Items are defined as those that are popular or unpopular on a campus. The appearance of a Survey Says item in the sidebar for a particular school does not reflect the popularity of that item relative to its popularity amongst other schools' student bodies. For relative popularity of certain items, see the appropriate ranking (e.g., for the Survey Says item "Library needs improving," see the "This is a Library?" ranking). Some of the terms that appear on the list are not entirely self-explanatory; these terms are defined below.

Different types of students interact: We asked students whether students from different class and ethnic backgrounds interacted frequently and easily. When students' collective response is "yes," the heading "Different types of students interact" appears on the list. When student response indicates there are not many interactions between different students from different class and ethnic backgrounds, the heading "Students are cliquish" appears on the list.

No one cheats: We asked students how prevalent cheating is at their school. If students reported cheating to be rare, "No one cheats" shows up on the list.

Students are happy: This category reflects student responses to the question "Overall, how happy are you?"

TAs teach lots of upper-level classes: At some large universities, you'll continue to be taught by teaching assistants even in your upper-level courses. It is safe to assume that when "TAs teach lots of upper-level courses" appears on the list, TAs also teach a disproportionate number of intro courses.

Students are very religious or Students aren't religious: We asked students how religious they are. Their responses are reflected in this category.

Diverse student types on campus: We asked students whether their student body is made up of a variety of ethnic groups. This category reflects their answers to this question. This heading shows up as "diversity lacking on campus" or "diverse student types on campus."

Students get along with local community: We asked students whether they got along with local residents; their answers are reflected by this category.

If you have any questions, comments, or suggestions, please contact us at Editorial Department, Admissions Services, 2315 Broadway, New York, NY 10024, or e-mail us at bookeditor@review.com. We appreciate your input and want to make our books as useful to you as they can be.

Glossary

ACT: Like the SAT I but less tricky. Many schools accept either SAT or ACT scores; if you consistently get blown away by the SAT, you might want to consider taking the ACT instead.

College-prep curriculum: 16 to 18 academic credits (each credit equals a full year of a high school course), usually including: 4 years of English, 3 to 4 years of social studies, and at least 2 years each of science, mathematics, and foreign language.

Core curriculum: Students at schools with core curricula must take a number of required courses, usually in such subjects as world history, western civilization, writing skills, and fundamental math and science.

CSS/Financial Aid PROFILE: The College Scholarship Service PROFILE, an optional financial aid form required by some colleges in addition to the FAFSA.

Distribution or general education requirements: Students at schools with distribution requirements must take a number of courses in various subject areas, such as foreign language, humanities, natural science, and social science. Distribution requirements do not specify which courses you must take, only which types of courses.

FAFSA: The Free Application for Federal Student Aid. Schools participating in federal student aid programs (not all so—see Hillsdale College) are required by law to accept the FAFSA; some require that applicants complete at least one other form (usually a CSS/Financial Aid PROFILE or the college's own form) to be considered for financial aid.

GDI: "Goddamned independents," a term frequently used by students in fraternities and sororities to describe those not in fraternities and sororities.

Greek system, Greeks: Fraternities and sororities.

Humanities: These include such disciplines as art history, drama, English, foreign languages, music, philosophy, and religion.

Merit-based grant: A scholarship (not necessarily full) given to students because of some special talent or attribute. Artists, athletes, community leaders, and geniuses are typical recipients.

Natural sciences: These include such disciplines as astronomy, biology, chemistry, genetics, geology, mathematics, physics, and zoology.

Need-based grant: A scholarship (not necessarily full) given to students because they would otherwise be unable to afford college. Student need is determined on the basis of the FAFSA. Some schools also require the CSS PROFILE and/or institutional applications.

Priority deadline: Some schools will list a deadline for admission and/or financial aid as a "priority deadline," meaning that while they will accept applications after that date, all applications received prior to the deadline are assured of getting the most thorough, in some instances potentially more generous, appraisal possible.

RA: Residence assistant (or residential advisor). Someone, usually an upperclassman or graduate student, who supervises a floor or section of a dorm, usually in return for free room and board. RAs are responsible for enforcing the drinking and noise rules.

SAT I: A college entrance exam required by many schools; most schools will accept either the ACT or the SAT I.

SAT Subject Tests: Subject-specific exams (previously called SAT IIs) administered by the Educational Testing Service (the SAT people). These tests are required by some, but not all, admissions offices.

Social sciences: These include such disciplines as anthropology, economics, geography, history, international studies, political science, psychology, and sociology.

Tuition GPA: The competitiveness of the total cost of attending a college for one year as a resident undergrad with a meal plan, on a scale of 0.00 to 4.00. We calculate the average tuition and room and board costs actually paid by each student attending the college by subtracting both need-based and non-need-based gift aid (grants and scholarships) awarded to undergraduates from the college's sticker price. We don't incorporate self-help aid (loans and work-study) in the GPA formula because these costs are ultimately the student's responsibility to meet. We only use the Tuition GPA in the formula that determines the schools on the Best Bargains lists; you won't see it reported in this edition of the book. The lower the average tuition, the higher the Tuition GPA, which works to schools' favor in the rankings.

Work-study: A government-funded financial aid program that provides assistance to financial aid recipients in return for work in the school.

About Those College Rankings

We've shed some light on how we conduct our student survey and produce the entries and ratings that make up *Best Colleges*, as well as a sense of why we publish the guide; now we'd like to discuss how to use the information that we've compiled—specifically the rankings.

Perhaps no single element of our guide to *The Best 361 Colleges* gets more attention than the section entitled "Schools Ranked By Category." Since it's become an annual subject addressed by the media, and subsequently college presidents, admission directors, public relations officers, students, and their parents, we want to share our own thoughts about it with the students and parents who have chosen this guide.

The "Schools Ranked By Category" section of *Best Colleges* includes 62 different rankings. (An additional "ranking" focuses on a single institution, Deep Springs College, the only two-year college ever included in the guide. Deep Springs is assigned its own "Honor Roll" list that includes all categories in which it placed highly, thus eliminating perpetual "apples and oranges" comparisons between it and the four-year colleges in the rankings.) All of the rankings are broad-based in their intent, designed to generally illustrate environmental considerations at the colleges across a wide variety of categories.

Fifty-eight of these lists are based entirely on either individual questions from our student surveys or are compiled from responses to several student survey questions. The other six lists include computations based on both student survey responses and statistical data provided by the colleges. Each list, even those entitled in a somewhat tongue-in-cheek manner, covers one of many aspects of a college's character that can be helpful in deciding if it's the right or wrong place for an individual student.

The rankings are often misconstrued; many in the media and general public think that The Princeton Review annually deems colleges "party schools" or places where the "students never stop studying." Actually, the vast majority of the rankings are based directly upon what students on each campus tell us about their college. Besides inquiring about where else they applied for admission, we ask them only about the college they attend. No students are asked to rate other colleges comparatively in terms of any of the items the lists rank. And compound rankings are just that—compound calculations based on responses to multiple questions. There's no individual "party school" question on the survey.

In case you haven't heard by now, the party school ranking draws lots of attention every year. It's even been the subject of a *Doonesbury* cartoon (which appears on the frontispiece of this book). Calls, e-mail, and letters begin to arrive in our offices as soon as the first word of our rankings hits the media. Some contacts are from students who complain that their college didn't make the list, while others are from those who are irate because their college did. A *Washington Post* writer challenged WVU's number-one ranking in the 1998 edition as undeserved, contending that it's nothing like the good old days when he attended the university. Local media have touted the fact that nearby colleges didn't make the list when they aren't even in the guide in the first place, and thus were not surveyed at all. Many incorrectly assume that an institution that shows up on the party school ranking is a lousy college to attend—when the basic premise of the guide is to highlight colleges that The Princeton Review feels are among the top 10 percent of colleges and universities in the U.S. and Canada.

Best Colleges begins with the best as its basis. Rankings that are among the less flattering of the 62 categories are not lists of bad schools—colleges on all of these lists are still among the best in the nation. This holds equally true for those on the party school list in particular. Remember our earlier comments about these rankings reflecting environmental considerations; broad categorizations of the college experience on each campus. Even schools placed at the top of the party school list are excellent places to pursue one's college career, and offer not only an exuberant social atmosphere but also a wide range of high-quality academic programs, as does every college or university that has ever appeared on this list in *Best Colleges*.

With few notable exceptions, no one should make the mistake of assuming that the colleges and universities that don't show up on the party school rankings are in any way insulated from the influences of alcohol and drugs on their student bodies and campuses. While a student who has little self-discipline or is easily led might be best off on a campus with a more distinctly academic emphasis, a glance at recent research reveals that such considerations aren't often useful benchmarks.

The gaps aren't large in this regard, and tragedy is not exclusive. A Harvard University study has revealed that 44 percent of undergraduates in general binge drink (consume five or more alcoholic beverages in one sitting for men, four drinks or more for women). These facts are sobering, as they should be. Fingers can be pointed in many directions as concerns campus drinking and partying. "Dry campus" policies drive drinking off-campus, make it even more dangerous, and only exacerbate the problem by removing any opportunity to influence student behavior in this regard. If you're going off campus to drink, don't drive back drunk—get a designated driver. Wherever you're going to drink, do it safely, smartly, responsibly, and within the law. Don't let a peer situation (fraternity rush, etc.) put you in jeopardy—it's simply not worth it. Don't use alcohol or drugs as a badge of your coolness—there's not much of a fine line between someone who's socially engaging and someone who's totally disengaging because he or she has performed a chemical auto-lobotomy. Lastly, don't simply take responsibility for yourself; remember to keep an eye on your friends, and never leave them passed out and alone.

We believe that little is more useful to students choosing a college than the opinions of current college students about their campuses? College is an incredible growth experience, one that covers a significant portion of the full spectrum of life's lessons. It's much more than classrooms, books, and professors—it's a complete experience that you're bound never to forget. College—there's nothing like it.

PART 2

Schools Ranked by Category

One of the great things about a multiple-choice survey administered to more than 100,000 college students is that the results give you lots of numbers. We wanted to present those numbers to you in a fun and informative way; hence, the following rankings of schools in 62 categories. In the following lists, the top 20 schools in each category appear in descending order. Remember, of course, that our survey included only students at *The Best 361 Colleges*, and that all schools appearing on negative lists have many assets that counterbalance their various deficiencies.

Simply put, our ranking lists are unique. They can be used to help you clarify some of the choices you have to make in picking the right college. College bound students, their parents, and counselors searching for substantive, easy to understand information will benefit from these kind of rankings because they are based on the opinions of tens of thousands of in-the-trenches college experts—students. As you read through them, focus on those categories that are important to you: Do you want to go to a school where discussion takes up most of class time? Would you prefer only to be lectured to? Do you care? Do you want to go to a school where students party nonstop? Or would you rather go somewhere with a subdued social scene? By looking through these lists, you should be able to get a good idea of what are and are not important considerations to you.

We've broken the rankings down into nine categories: Academics; Administration; Quality of Life; Politics; Demographics; Social Life; Extracurriculars; Parties;

and Schools by Type. Under each list heading, we tell you the survey question or assessment that we used to tabulate the list. For the Schools by Type rankings, we combined student responses to several questions to determine whether a school was a "jock" school, a "party" school, and so on. These lists have changed considerably since the first edition of this book, as we have had time to rethink what truly defines a school's character. For instance, we now factor students' answers to the question "How many hours a day do you study?" into our party-school calibrations. After all, as some of our readers have pointed out, at some schools students drink and do drugs to relieve the stress of their demanding curricula. And, in some cases, statistical data reported by the colleges is also factored in.

Be aware that all of these lists are based on our survey results. Therefore, they do not reflect our opinions, nor do they perfectly reflect reality; that is to say, we can't tell you at which schools registration is actually the biggest hassle. What we can tell you is the schools at which students are most pissed off about registration hassles. Our feeling is that students' self-perceptions are quite valuable. After all, what better way is there to judge a school than by how its students feel about it?

ACADEMICS

Best Overall Academic Experience For Undergraduates

Based on The Princeton Review ACADEMIC RATING (page 15)

1. Reed College
2. Marlboro College
3. St. John's College (NM)
4 Swarthmore College
5. Williams College
6. Middlebury College
7. Carleton College
8. Franklin W. Olin College of Engineering
9. Wellesley College
10. Washington and Lee University
11. Haverford College
12. United States Air Force Academy
13. Amherst College
14. St. John's College (MD)
15. Whitman College
16. Wabash College
17. United States Military Academy
18. Pomona College
19. Yale University
20. Davidson College

The Toughest to Get Into

Based on The Princeton Review ADMISSIONS RATING (page 16)

1. Massachusetts Institute of Technology
2. Yale University
3. Princeton University
4. Harvard College
5. Franklin W. Olin College of Engineering
6. California Institute of Technology
7. Columbia University—Columbia College
8. University of Pennsylvania
9. Stanford University
10. Brown University
11. Washington University in St. Louis
12. Pomona College
13. Amherst College
14. Duke University
15. Georgetown University
16. Williams College
17. Dartmouth College
18. Cooper Union
19. Webb Institute
20. Middlebury College

Their Students Never Stop Studying

How many out-of-class hours do you spend studying each day?

1. Reed College
2. Webb Institute
3. California Institute of Technology
4. Franklin W. Olin College of Engineering
5. Harvey Mudd College
6. St. John's College (NM)
7. Wabash College
8. Marlboro College
9. Middlebury College
10. Massachusetts Institute of Technology
11. Carleton College
12. Grinnell College
13. United States Military Academy
14. Haverford College
15. Swarthmore College
16. Bryn Mawr College
17. Davidson College
18. United States Air Force Academy
19. Rice University
20. Whitman College

Their Students (Almost) Never Study

How many out-of-class hours do you spend studying each day?

1. University of Mississippi
2. Ohio University—Athens
3. St. Bonaventure University
4. University of Idaho
5. State University of New York at Albany
6. Emerson College
7. Florida State University
8. Louisiana State University
9. University of Massachusetts—Amherst
10. Auburn University
11. University of Rhode Island
12. Manhattanville College
13. Suffolk University
14. The University of Texas—Austin
15. George Mason University
16. University of Central Florida
17. University of Maryland—College Park
18. University of Georgia
19. Hampton University
20. University of Louisiana at Lafayette

Professors Get High Marks

Are your instructors good teachers?

1. St. John's College (NM)
2. Marlboro College
3. Wabash College
4. Washington and Lee University
5. Wellesley College
6. Middlebury College
7. Davidson College
8. Franklin W. Olin College of Engineering
9. Reed College
10. Sewanee—The University of the South
11. Hendrix College
12. Knox College
13. Hampden-Sydney College
14. Harvey Mudd College
15. Sarah Lawrence College
16. Albertson College of Idaho
17. Amherst College
18. Centre College
19. Hillsdale College
20. University of Dallas

Professors Get Low Marks

Are your instructors good teachers?

1. California Institute of Technology
2. Stevens Institute of Technology
3. New Jersey Institute of Technology
4. Georgia Institute of Technology
5. United States Merchant Marine Academy
6. Rutgers, The State University of New Jersey—New Brunswick/Piscataway
7. Rensselaer Polytechnic Institute
8. State University of New York at Stony Brook
9. St. John's University (NY)
10. State University of New York at Albany
11. Illinois Institute of Technology
12. University of Hawaii—Manoa
13. Cooper Union
14. University of California—Los Angeles
15. University of Rhode Island
16. CUNY—Brooklyn College
17. Drexel University
18. State University of New York at Buffalo
19. University of Toronto
20. University of California—Riverside

Professors Make Themselves Accessible

Are your instructors accessible outside the classroom?

1. United States Air Force Academy
2. Franklin W. Olin College of Engineering
3. United States Naval Academy
4. Wabash College
5. Harvey Mudd College
6. St. John's College (NM)
7. Washington and Lee University
8. Davidson College
9. Webb Institute
10. College of the Atlantic
11. Sweet Briar College
12. United States Military Academy
13. Marlboro College
14. Haverford College
15. Wellesley College
16. Lawrence University
17. Rhodes College
18. Cornell College
19. Sewanee—The University of the South
20. Hampden-Sydney College

Professors Make Themselves Scarce

Are your instructors accessible outside the classroom?

1. State University of New York at Albany
2. New Jersey Institute of Technology
3. CUNY—Brooklyn College
4. University of North Dakota
5. University of Toronto
6. University of Hawaii—Manoa
7. University of Utah
8. Drexel University
9. State University of New York at Stony Brook
10. University of Rhode Island
11. University of California—Los Angeles
12. Stevens Institute of Technology
13. Illinois Institute of Technology

14. Rutgers, The State University of New Jersey—New Brunswick/Piscataway
15. State University of New York at Binghamton
16. St. John's University (NY)
17. State University of New York at Buffalo
18. University of California—Riverside
19. University of New Mexico
20. Georgia Institute of Technology

Class Discussions Encouraged

How much of your overall class time is devoted to discussion as opposed to lectures?

1. Eugene Lang College
2. St. John's College (NM)
3. St. John's College (MD)
4. Sarah Lawrence College
5. Marlboro College
6. Hampshire College
7. Reed College
8. Bard College
9. Wesleyan College
10. Simon's Rock College of Bard
11. Sweet Briar College
12. Bennington College
13. Wells College
14. Rhodes College
15. Stephens College
16. College of the Atlantic
17. Millsaps College
18. Oglethorpe University
19. Cornell College
20. Knox College

Class Discussions Rare

How much of your overall class time is devoted to discussion as opposed to lectures?

1. Georgia Institute of Technology
2. Colorado School of Mines
3. University of Toronto
4. University of Missouri—Rolla
5. McGill University
6. California Institute of Technology
7. University of Idaho
8. University of California—Davis
9. Clarkson University
10. University of California—San Diego
11. New Mexico Institute of Mining & Technology
12. State University of New York at Buffalo
13. Illinois Institute of Technology
14. Colorado State University
15. Stevens Institute of Technology
16. Worcester Polytechnic Institute
17. Grove City College
18. Virginia Tech
19. Texas A&M University—College Station
20. Xavier University of Louisiana

Teaching Assistants Teach Too Many Upper-Level Courses

What percentage of upper-level courses is taught by teaching assistants?

1. University of Illinois at Urbana-Champaign
2. Purdue University—West Lafayette
3. University of Florida
4. University of Tennessee—Knoxville
5. University of California—Riverside
6. University of Iowa
7. University of Michigan—Ann Arbor
8. University of Washington
9. Ohio State University—Columbus
10. University of New Mexico
11. Michigan State University
12. University of Minnesota—Twin Cities
13. Florida State University
14. Rutgers, The State University of New Jersey—New Brunswick/Piscataway
15. State University of New York at Binghamton
16. University of Connecticut
17. University of California—Los Angeles
18. University of Nebraska—Lincoln
19. State University of New York at Buffalo
20. University of Kentucky

Best College Library

Based on students' assessment of library facilities

1. Harvard College
2. Princeton University
3. University of Chicago
4. Brigham Young University (UT)
5. Whitman College
6. Stanford University
7. Oberlin College
8. Illinois Wesleyan University
9. Saint Olaf College
10. United States Air Force Academy
11. Cornell University
12. The University of Texas—Austin
13. Mount Holyoke College
14. Auburn University
15. Columbia University—Columbia College
16. Dartmouth College
17. Dickinson College
18. Emory University
19. West Virginia University
20. University of California—Berkeley

This is a Library?

Based on students' assessment of library facilities

1. Clarkson University
2. University of Dallas
3. Duquesne University
4. United States Coast Guard Academy
5. Bennington College
6. Wells College
7. Kalamazoo College
8. Bradley University
9. College of the Atlantic
10. Spelman College
11. The Catholic University of America
12. American University
13. Loyola College in Maryland
14. Eckerd College
15. Xavier University of Louisiana
16. Stevens Institute of Technology
17. Fisk University
18. Illinois Institute of Technology
19. Bard College
20. Wagner College

Students Happy with Financial Aid

Based on students' assessments of how satisfied they are with their financial aid package.

1. Princeton University
2. Lake Forest College
3. Knox College
4. Claremont McKenna College
5. Truman State University
6. Williams College
7. Pomona College
8. Wabash College
9. Cornell College
10. Agnes Scott College
11. Beloit College
12. New College of Florida
13. Amherst College
14. Alfred University
15. Berea College
16. Ripon College
17. Wittenberg University
18. St. Lawrence University
19. College of the Atlantic
20. Denison University

Students Dissatisfied with Financial Aid

Based on students' assessments of how satisfied they are with their financial aid package.

1. New York University
2. University of Mary Washington
3. University of Massachusetts—Amherst
4. Penn State University Park
5. University of Tennessee—Knoxville
6. Emerson College
7. University of Maryland—College Park
8. Hofstra University
9. State University of New York at Binghamton
10. Spelman College
11. Hampton University
12. State University of New York College at Geneseo
13. Elon University
14. State University of New York College at Purchase
15. Xavier University of Louisiana
16. Quinnipiac University
17. State University of New York at Albany
18. James Madison University
19. Flagler College
20. University of Oregon

School Runs Like Butter

Overall, how smoothly is your school run?

1. Princeton University
2. Whitman College
3. Wabash College
4. Middlebury College
5. Claremont McKenna College
6. Davidson College
7. Elon University
8. Pomona College
9. Carleton College
10. Stanford University
11. Williams College
12. Washington and Lee University
13. Rose-Hulman Institute of Technology
14. Amherst College
15. Haverford College
16. Washington University in St. Louis
17. Brigham Young University (UT)
18. Rhodes College
19. Bowdoin College
20. University of Notre Dame

Long Lines and Red Tape

Overall, how smoothly is your school run?

1. Fisk University
2. CUNY—Hunter College
3. University of Massachusetts—Amherst
4. Wells College
5. State University of New York College at Purchase
6. University of Hawaii—Manoa
7. Eugene Lang College
8. Cooper Union
9. University of Mary Washington
10. State University of New York at Albany
11. Drexel University
12. Hampton University

13. Bennington College
14. Illinois Institute of Technology
15. Seton Hall University
16. The Catholic University of America
17. Loyola University of Chicago
18. Hampshire College
19. Howard University
20. New Jersey Institute of Technology

QUALITY OF LIFE

Happiest Students

Overall, how happy are you?

1. Stanford University
2. Whitman College
3. Brown University
4. Southern Methodist University
5. Rhodes College
6. The College of New Jersey
7. St. John's College (NM)
8. University of North Carolina—Chapel Hill
9. The University of Tulsa
10. Haverford College
11. Amherst College
12. Brigham Young University (UT)
13. St. Mary's College of Maryland
14. William Jewell College
15. Clemson University
16. Princeton University
17. St. John's College (MD)
18. Yale University
19. Claremont McKenna College
20. Williams College

Least Happy Students

Overall, how happy are you?

1. Colorado School of Mines
2. United States Coast Guard Academy
3. University of Mary Washington
4. State University of New York at Stony Brook
5. New Jersey Institute of Technology
6. Clarkson University
7. University of Hawaii—Manoa
8. United States Merchant Marine Academy
9. State University of New York at Albany
10. Hampton University
11. Rensselaer Polytechnic Institute
12. Illinois Institute of Technology
13. Seton Hall University
14. St. John's University (NY)
15. Drexel University
16. Fisk University
17. Georgia Institute of Technology
18. Hofstra University
19. Case Western Reserve University
20. CUNY—Brooklyn College

Most Beautiful Campus

Based on students' rating of campus beauty

1. Pepperdine University
2. Agnes Scott College
3. Sweet Briar College
4. College of the Atlantic
5. Mercer University—Macon
6. Flagler College
7. Rhodes College
8. Sewanee—The University of the South
9. Mount Holyoke College
10. Swarthmore College
11. Loyola Marymount University
12. Kenyon College
13. Wellesley College
14. Colgate University
15. Princeton University
16. St. Mary's College of Maryland
17. Scripps College
18. Washington and Lee University
19. Vassar College
20. University of Richmond

Campus is Tiny, Unsightly, or Both

Based on students' rating of campus beauty

1. State University of New York at Albany
2. Drexel University
3. State University of New York College at Purchase
4. CUNY—Hunter College
5. Illinois Institute of Technology
6. New Jersey Institute of Technology
7. University of Dallas
8. Cooper Union
9. Massachusetts Institute of Technology
10. Xavier University of Louisiana
11. Rochester Institute of Technology
12. Rider University
13. University of New Orleans
14. University of Tennessee—Knoxville
15. Georgia Institute of Technology
16. Clarkson University
17. State University of New York at Binghamton
18. North Carolina State University
19. Harvey Mudd College
20. University of Massachusetts—Amherst

Best Campus Food

Based on students' rating of campus food

1. Bowdoin College
2. Franklin W. Olin College of Engineering
3. Saint Olaf College
4. Cornell University
5. Wheaton College (IL)
6. James Madison University
7. Colby College
8. Washington University in St. Louis
9. Virginia Tech
10. Middlebury College
11. Dartmouth College
12. University of Notre Dame
13. Bryn Mawr College
14. Miami University
15. Tufts University
16. Gustavus Adolphus College
17. Bates College
18. Claremont McKenna College
19. Scripps College
20. University of Georgia

Is It Food?

Based on students' rating of campus food

1. St. Bonaventure University
2. Colorado School of Mines
3. United States Merchant Marine Academy
4. Hampton University
5. State University of New York at Albany
6. Catawba College
7. Carnegie Mellon University
8. Seton Hall University
9. Fordham University
10. New Mexico Institute of Mining & Technology
11. Johns Hopkins University
12. Fisk University
13. Wells College
14. Guilford College
15. Flagler College
16. New College of Florida
17. Cornell College
18. Centenary College of Louisiana
19. Illinois Institute of Technology
20. Hiram College

Dorms Like Palaces

Based on students' rating of dorm comfort

1. Loyola College in Maryland
2. Franklin W. Olin College of Engineering
3. Smith College
4. Scripps College
5. Bryn Mawr College
6. Claremont McKenna College
7. Pepperdine University
8. Webb Institute
9. Pomona College
10. Whitman College
11. Agnes Scott College
12. New College of Florida
13. Washington University in St. Louis
14. Sweet Briar College
15. Williams College
16. Bowdoin College
17. Rhodes College
18. Mount Holyoke College
19. Trinity University
20. Skidmore College

Dorms Like Dungeons

Based on students' rating of dorm comfort

1. United States Coast Guard Academy
2. University of Hawaii—Manoa
3. University of New Orleans
4. United States Merchant Marine Academy
5. University of Oregon
6. United States Military Academy
7. Colorado School of Mines
8. State University of New York at Albany
9. Hampton University
10. University of Idaho
11. University of Louisiana at Lafayette
12. University of Kentucky
13. Flagler College
14. Xavier University of Louisiana
15. State University of New York College at Purchase
16. University of Washington
17. Georgia Institute of Technology
18. University of Florida
19. The University of South Dakota
20. Illinois Institute of Technology

Best Quality of Life

Based on The Princeton Review's QUALITY OF LIFE RATING (page 14)

1. Franklin W. Olin College of Engineering
2. Stanford University
3. Rice University
4. Saint Olaf College
5. Whitman College
6. Washington University in St. Louis
7. Rhodes College
8. Claremont McKenna College
9. Princeton University
10. The University of Tulsa
11. Haverford College
12. Middlebury College
13. Agnes Scott College
14. Brigham Young University (UT)

15. Seattle University
16. Webb Institute
17. Macalester College
18. Barnard College
19. Carleton College
20. Dartmouth College

POLITICS

Students Most Nostalgic for Ronald Reagan

Based on students' assessment of their personal political views

1. Hillsdale College
2. Grove City College
3. Brigham Young University (UT)
4. United States Air Force Academy
5. Hampden-Sydney College
6. College of the Ozarks
7. United States Naval Academy
8. University of Dallas
9. Wheaton College (IL)
10. United States Merchant Marine Academy
11. United States Military Academy
12. Samford University
13. Baylor University
14. Texas A&M University—College Station
15. Mercer University—Macon
16. Auburn University
17. Clemson University
18. University of Mississippi
19. Wofford College
20. Southern Methodist University

Students Most Nostalgic for Bill Clinton

Based on students' assessment of their personal political views

1. Mills College
2. Bard College
3. New College of Florida
4. Hampshire College
5. Warren Wilson College
6. Sarah Lawrence College
7. Pitzer College
8. Reed College
9. Marlboro College
10. Earlham College
11. Macalester College
12. The Evergreen State College
13. Vassar College
14. Oberlin College
15. Wesleyan University
16. College of the Atlantic
17. Bennington College
18. University of California—Santa Cruz
19. Grinnell College
20. Simon's Rock College of Bard

Most Politically Active Students

How popular are political/activist groups?

1. New College of Florida
2. United States Air Force Academy
3. Eugene Lang College
4. Macalester College
5. Lewis & Clark College
6. Columbia University—Columbia College
7. Harvard College
8. The George Washington University
9. Pitzer College
10. Princeton University
11. Oberlin College
12. University of Chicago
13. Hampden-Sydney College
14. United States Naval Academy
15. Wesleyan University
16. Mills College
17. Claremont McKenna College
18. Hampshire College
19. University of Mary Washington
20. Georgetown University

Election? What Election?

How popular are political/activist groups?

1. University of Idaho
2. Mercer University—Macon
3. Rose-Hulman Institute of Technology
4. Worcester Polytechnic Institute
5. University of Delaware
6. Quinnipiac University
7. Bradley University
8. Siena College
9. University of South Carolina—Columbia
10. Illinois Wesleyan University
11. Bellarmine University
12. State University of New York at Stony Brook
13. The College of New Jersey
14. Bentley College
15. Ohio Wesleyan University
16. Stevens Institute of Technology
17. Manhattanville College
18. College of Saint Benedict/ Saint John's University (MN)
19. Salisbury University
20. Eckerd College

DEMOGRAPHICS

Diverse Student Population

Is your student body made up of diverse social and ethnic types?

1. George Mason University
2. Temple University
3. CUNY—Hunter College
4. Mount Holyoke College
5. Stanford University
6. State University of New York at Buffalo
7. Massachusetts Institute of Technology
8. Wellesley College
9. Agnes Scott College
10. University of Maryland—Baltimore County
11. Wesleyan College
12. New Jersey Institute of Technology
13. University of Miami
14. State University of New York at Stony Brook
15. University of Southern California
16. University of San Francisco
17. Manhattanville College
18. University of South Florida
19. DePaul University
20. McGill University

Homogeneous Student Population

Is your student body made up of diverse social and ethnic types?

1. Flagler College
2. Grove City College
3. University of Mary Washington
4. Providence College
5. Saint Anselm College
6. Washington and Lee University
7. Loyola College in Maryland
8. Ohio Northern University
9. Fairfield University
10. Samford University
11. University of New Hampshire
12. College of the Holy Cross
13. St. Bonaventure University
14. Bucknell University
15. Lehigh University
16. Hampden-Sydney College
17. University of Richmond
18. Miami University
19. Hillsdale College
20. University of Denver

Lots of Race/Class Interaction

Do different types of students (black/white, rich/poor) interact frequently and easily?

1. Franklin W. Olin College of Engineering
2. Rice University
3. United States Air Force Academy
4. Webb Institute
5. Stanford University
6. St. John's College (MD)
7. St. John's College (NM)
8. Massachusetts Institute of Technology
9. Pitzer College
10. Mount Holyoke College
11. Austin College
12. Whitman College
13. The University of Tulsa
14. New College of Florida
15. McGill University
16. Eugene Lang College
17. St. Mary's College of Maryland
18. Carleton College
19. Hendrix College
20. United States Naval Academy

Little Race/Class Interaction

Do different types of students (black/white, rich/poor) interact frequently and easily?

1. University of Denver
2. College of the Holy Cross
3. Washington and Lee University
4. Vanderbilt University
5. University of New Hampshire
6. Duke University
7. Trinity College (CT)
8. Syracuse University
9. Southern Methodist University
10. University of Mary Washington
11. University of Richmond
12. Wake Forest University
13. Miami University
14. Rollins College
15. University of Virginia
16. State University of New York at Binghamton
17. Lafayette College
18. Saint Anselm College
19. Xavier University of Louisiana
20. Fairfield University

Gay Community Accepted

Is there very little discrimination against homosexuals?

1. New College of Florida
2. Macalester College
3. Wellesley College
4. Eugene Lang College
5. Mount Holyoke College
6. St. John's College (MD)
7. Bryn Mawr College
8. Lawrence University
9. Emerson College
10. Harvey Mudd College
11. St. John's College (NM)
12. Franklin W. Olin College of Engineering
13. Wesleyan University
14. Marlboro College
15. Carleton College
16. Smith College
17. Haverford College
18. Reed College
19. Bard College
20. Oberlin College

Alternative Lifestyles Not an Alternative*

Is there very little discrimination against homosexuals?

1. Hampden-Sydney College
2. University of Notre Dame
3. Baylor University
4. Wheaton College (IL)
5. Grove City College
6. University of Tennessee—Knoxville
7. Texas A&M University—College Station
8. College of the Holy Cross
9. Samford University
10. Brigham Young University (UT)
11. Seton Hall University
12. Valparaiso University
13. Pepperdine University
14. Washington and Lee University
15. Trinity College (CT)
16. Vanderbilt University
17. Wake Forest University
18. University of Utah
19. Providence College
20. Southern Methodist University

* Each of the five military academies were excluded from this list because of current, "Don't ask, don't tell" policies.

Students Pray on a Regular Basis

Are students very religious?

1. Brigham Young University (UT)
2. Wheaton College (IL)
3. Grove City College
4. University of Notre Dame
5. Samford University
6. University of Dallas
7. Hillsdale College
8. College of the Ozarks
9. University of Utah
10. Baylor University
11. United States Air Force Academy
12. William Jewell College
13. Texas A&M University—College Station
14. Calvin College
15. Furman University
16. Pepperdine University
17. Valparaiso University
18. The Catholic University of America
19. Auburn University
20. Brandeis University

Students Ignore God on a Regular Basis

Are students very religious?

1. Reed College
2. Bard College
3. Eugene Lang College
4. Hampshire College
5. Lewis & Clark College
6. Sarah Lawrence College
7. Simon's Rock College of Bard
8. Bennington College
9. New College of Florida
10. Emerson College
11. Mills College
12. Marlboro College
13. Oberlin College
14. Macalester College
15. Wesleyan University
16. Vassar College
17. Skidmore College
18. Grinnell College
19. Carleton College
20. Pomona College

SOCIAL LIFE

Great College Towns

Based on students' assessment of the surrounding city or town

1. Eugene Lang College
2. Barnard College
3. DePaul University
4. Southern Methodist University
5. Columbia University—Columbia College
6. McGill University
7. Lewis & Clark College
8. Suffolk University
9. University of San Francisco
10. Simmons College
11. New York University
12. Boston University
13. The University of Texas—Austin
14. Georgetown University
15. Emerson College
16. Northeastern University
17. Cooper Union
18. American University
19. The George Washington University
20. College of Charleston

More to Do on Campus

Based on students' assessment of the surrounding city or town

1. United States Military Academy
2. Rensselaer Polytechnic Institute
3. Union College (NY)
4. New Mexico Institute of Mining & Technology
5. New Jersey Institute of Technology
6. Lehigh University
7. Albion College
8. Trinity College (CT)
9. United States Coast Guard Academy
10. University of the Pacific
11. Earlham College
12. University of Notre Dame
13. Duke University
14. Wheaton College (MA)
15. DePauw University
16. Bennington College
17. Vassar College
18. University of Connecticut
19. State University of New York at Binghamton
20. Beloit College

Town-Gown Relations are Great

Do students get along well with members of the local community?

1. Saint Olaf College
2. William Jewell College
3. Texas A&M University—College Station
4. Franklin W. Olin College of Engineering
5. The University of Tulsa
6. Rhodes College
7. Wheaton College (IL)
8. Brigham Young University (UT)
9. Auburn University
10. College of the Ozarks
11. Eugene Lang College
12. Saint Michael's College
13. United States Naval Academy
14. Samford University
15. Wesleyan College
16. Clemson University
17. Agnes Scott College
18. Rice University
19. Davidson College
20. Sweet Briar College

Town-Gown Relations are Strained

Do students get along well with members of the local community?

1. Sarah Lawrence College
2. Trinity College (CT)
3. Lehigh University
4. Bennington College
5. Duke University
6. Union College (NY)
7. Northwestern University
8. Rensselaer Polytechnic Institute
9. Vassar College
10. Colorado College
11. College of the Holy Cross
12. University of New Hampshire
13. Simon's Rock College of Bard
14. State University of New York at Binghamton
15. University of Pennsylvania
16. Howard University
17. New Jersey Institute of Technology
18. DePauw University
19. New Mexico Institute of Mining & Technology
20. Illinois Institute of Technology

EXTRACURRICULARS

Students Pack the Stadiums

How popular are intercollegiate sports?

1. University of Maryland—College Park
2. University of Notre Dame
3. University of Florida
4. Penn State University Park
5. University of North Carolina—Chapel Hill
6. University of Georgia
7. Gonzaga University
8. University of Arizona
9. University of Tennessee—Knoxville
10. The University of Texas—Austin
11. Auburn University
12. United States Air Force Academy
13. Boston College
14. The University of Alabama—Tuscaloosa
15. Duke University
16. University of Southern California
17. University of Miami
18. University of Connecticut
19. Clemson University
20. Ohio State University—Columbus

Intercollegiate Sports Unpopular or Nonexistent

How popular are intercollegiate sports?

1. New College of Florida
2. Eugene Lang College
3. Franklin W. Olin College of Engineering
4. College of the Atlantic
5. St. John's College (NM)
6. Bennington College
7. Hampshire College
8. Marlboro College
9. St. John's College (MD)
10. Emerson College
11. Reed College
12. Sarah Lawrence College
13. New York University
14. University of Chicago
15. Simon's Rock College of Bard
16. Oberlin College
17. Bard College
18. California Institute of Technology
19. Cooper Union
20. University of California—Santa Cruz

Everyone Plays Intramural Sports

How popular are intramural sports?

1. University of Notre Dame
2. United States Air Force Academy
3. Whitman College
4. Wabash College
5. Carleton College
6. United States Naval Academy
7. Penn State University Park
8. North Carolina State University
9. University of Tennessee—Knoxville
10. College of Saint Benedict/ Saint John's University (MN)
11. University of Florida
12. United States Military Academy
13. Brigham Young University (UT)
14. Iowa State University
15. United States Coast Guard Academy
16. Baylor University
17. Samford University
18. Texas A&M University—College Station
19. University of Connecticut
20. St. Bonaventure University

Nobody Plays Intramural Sports

How popular are intramural sports?

1. Eugene Lang College
2. Emerson College
3. Marlboro College
4. Bennington College
5. Sarah Lawrence College
6. New York University
7. Simon's Rock College of Bard
8. New College of Florida
9. Stephens College
10. Cooper Union
11. Hollins University
12. Hampshire College
13. Bryn Mawr College
14. Spelman College
15. College of the Atlantic
16. Suffolk University
17. Barnard College
18. Pitzer College
19. Agnes Scott College
20. New Jersey Institute of Technology

Best College Radio Station

How popular is the radio station?

1. Emerson College
2. St. Bonaventure University
3. Ithaca College
4. DePauw University
5. Siena College

6. Guilford College
7. Oberlin College
8. Knox College
9. Brown University
10. Carleton College
11. Seton Hall University
12. University of Puget Sound
13. Whitman College
14. Howard University
15. Skidmore College
16. Bates College
17. Grinnell College
18. Alfred University
19. Reed College
20. The Evergreen State College

Best College Newspaper

How popular is the newspaper?

1. University of Arizona
2. Howard University
3. University of North Carolina—Chapel Hill
4. Yale University
5. University of Pennsylvania
6. University of Georgia
7. University of Maryland—College Park
8. Duke University
9. Indiana University—Bloomington
10. West Virginia University
11. Syracuse University
12. Northwestern University
13. Harvard College
14. Louisiana State University
15. The University of Texas—Austin
16. Penn State University Park
17. University of Minnesota—Twin Cities
18. Rice University
19. University of California—Los Angeles
20. University of Wisconsin—Madison

Best College Theater

How popular are college theater productions?

1. Wagner College
2. Stephens College
3. Emerson College
4. Catawba College
5. Drew University
6. Sarah Lawrence College
7. Yale University
8. Wesleyan University
9. Vassar College
10. Whitman College
11. State University of New York College at Purchase
12. Oberlin College
13. Skidmore College
14. Ithaca College
15. Bennington College
16. Northwestern University
17. Franklin W. Olin College of Engineering
18. Muhlenberg College
19. Kenyon College
20. Lawrence University

PARTIES

Lots of Beer

How widely used is beer?

1. Indiana University—Bloomington
2. Providence College
3. University of Wisconsin—Madison
4. University of Dayton
5. University of New Hampshire
6. Lehigh University
7. University of Florida
8. University of Iowa
9. Penn State University Park
10. University of California—Santa Barbara
11. Union College (NY)
12. Washington and Lee University
13. Colgate University
14. Ohio University—Athens
15. Dartmouth College
16. West Virginia University
17. University of Tennessee—Knoxville
18. Tulane University
19. The University of Texas—Austin
20. Loyola University New Orleans

Got Milk?

How widely used is beer?

1. Brigham Young University (UT)
2. Wheaton College (IL)
3. CUNY—Queens College
4. College of the Ozarks
5. United States Air Force Academy
6. Grove City College
7. CUNY—Brooklyn College
8. Spelman College
9. Wesleyan College
10. Howard University
11. Wellesley College
12. CUNY—Hunter College
13. Fisk University
14. Xavier University of Louisiana
15. Calvin College
16. Samford University
17. Berea College
18. Seattle University
19. United States Naval Academy
20. Franklin W. Olin College of Engineering

Lots of Hard Liquor

How widely used is hard liquor?

1. Tulane University
2. Washington and Lee University
3. University of Wisconsin—Madison
4. University of North Dakota
5. Loyola University New Orleans
6. St. Bonaventure University
7. University of Iowa
8. University of Georgia
9. Providence College
10. Sewanee—The University of the South
11. Trinity College (CT)
12. Lehigh University
13. Randolph-Macon College
14. Penn State University Park
15. Indiana University—Bloomington
16. Ohio University—Athens
17. University of California—Santa Barbara
18. Hampden-Sydney College
19. West Virginia University
20. University of Tennessee—Knoxville

Scotch and Soda, Hold the Scotch

How widely used is hard liquor?

1. Brigham Young University (UT)
2. Wheaton College (IL)
3. CUNY—Queens College
4. United States Air Force Academy
5. College of the Ozarks
6. Grove City College
7. CUNY—Brooklyn College
8. Wesleyan College
9. Calvin College
10. Samford University
11. CUNY—Hunter College
12. Wellesley College
13. Webb Institute
14. Seattle University
15. Spelman College
16. Berea College
17. United States Naval Academy
18. William Jewell College
19. United States Coast Guard Academy
20. Saint Olaf College

Reefer Madness

How widely used is marijuana?

1. Hampshire College
2. University of Vermont
3. Bard College
4. Oberlin College
5. Pitzer College
6. Colorado College
7. University of Wisconsin—Madison
8. New York University
9. University of California—Santa Cruz
10. New College of Florida
11. Ithaca College
12. Wesleyan University
13. University of Massachusetts—Amherst
14. University of California—Santa Barbara
15. Sarah Lawrence College
16. State University of New York at Albany
17. Vassar College
18. The Evergreen State College
19. West Virginia University
20. Emerson College

Don't Inhale

How widely used is marijuana?

1. United States Air Force Academy
2. Brigham Young University (UT)
3. United States Naval Academy
4. United States Coast Guard Academy
5. United States Military Academy
6. United States Merchant Marine Academy
7. Wheaton College (IL)
8. College of the Ozarks
9. Grove City College
10. CUNY—Queens College
11. Webb Institute
12. University of Notre Dame
13. Samford University
14. William Jewell College
15. Calvin College
16. Rose-Hulman Institute of Technology
17. Wesleyan College
18. Agnes Scott College
19. Hillsdale College
20. Wellesley College

Major Frat and Sorority Scene

How popular are fraternities/sororities?

1. DePauw University
2. Washington and Lee University
3. Birmingham-Southern College
4. Wofford College
5. Elon University
6. Sewanee—The University of the South
7. Bucknell University
8. Wabash College
9. Southern Methodist University
10. Texas Christian University
11. Fisk University
12. University of Illinois at Urbana-Champaign
13. Dartmouth College
14. Transylvania University

15. Vanderbilt University
16. Lehigh University
17. University of Mississippi
18. Randolph-Macon College
19. Centre College
20. Gettysburg College

SCHOOL BY TYPE

Party Schools

Based on a combination of survey questions concerning the use of alcohol and drugs, hours of study each day, and the popularity of the Greek system

1. University of Wisconsin—Madison
2. Ohio University—Athens
3. Lehigh University
4. University of California—Santa Barbara
5. State University of New York at Albany
6. Indiana University—Bloomington
7. University of Mississippi
8. University of Iowa
9. University of Massachusetts—Amherst
10. Loyola University New Orleans
11. Tulane University
12. University of Georgia
13. Penn State University Park
14. West Virginia University
15. The University of Texas—Austin
16. University of Tennessee—Knoxville
17. University of New Hampshire
18. University of Florida
19. Louisiana State University
20. University of Maryland—College Park

Stone-Cold Sober Schools

Based on a combination of survey questions concerning the use of alcohol and drugs, hours of study each day, and the popularity of the Greek system

1. Brigham Young University (UT)
2. United States Air Force Academy
3. Wheaton College (IL)
4. College of the Ozarks
5. United States Naval Academy
6. United States Coast Guard Academy
7. Webb Institute
8. United States Military Academy
9. Grove City College
10. Wesleyan College
11. Calvin College
12. CUNY—Queens College
13. Wellesley College
14. Franklin W. Olin College of Engineering
15. Saint Olaf College
16. Seattle University
17. Agnes Scott College
18. Berea College
19. California Institute of Technology
20. Bryn Mawr College

Jock Schools

Based on a combination of survey questions concerning intercollegiate and intramural sports and the popularity of the Greek system

1. University of Florida
2. Penn State University Park
3. United States Air Force Academy
4. Wabash College
5. University of Tennessee—Knoxville
6. University of Notre Dame
7. Clemson University
8. United States Naval Academy
9. University of Connecticut
10. University of Nebraska—Lincoln
11. University of Georgia
12. Florida State University
13. Colgate University
14. Duke University
15. Wake Forest University
16. University of North Carolina—Chapel Hill
17. Auburn University
18. North Carolina State University
19. The University of Texas—Austin
20. Iowa State University

Dodge-Ball Targets

Based on a combination of survey questions concerning intercollegiate and intramural sports and the popularity of the Greek system

1. Eugene Lang College
2. Bennington College
3. Marlboro College
4. Emerson College
5. Sarah Lawrence College
6. New College of Florida
7. Hampshire College
8. Simon's Rock College of Bard
9. New York University
10. College of the Atlantic
11. Reed College
12. Bard College
13. St. John's College (NM)
14. State University of New York College at Purchase
15. Oberlin College
16. Franklin W. Olin College of Engineering
17. Suffolk University
18. Hollins University
19. The Evergreen State College
20. St. John's College (MD)

Future Rotarians and Daughters of the American Revolution

Based on a combination of survey questions concerning political persuasion, the use of marijuana and hallucinogens, the prevalence of religion, the popularity of student government, and the students' level of acceptance of the gay community on campus

1. Brigham Young University (UT)
2. Grove City College
3. Wheaton College (IL)
4. Hillsdale College
5. United States Air Force Academy
6. College of the Ozarks
7. Samford University
8. University of Notre Dame
9. United States Naval Academy
10. University of Dallas
11. William Jewell College
12. United States Military Academy
13. Texas A&M University—College Station
14. Baylor University
15. Calvin College
16. United States Coast Guard Academy
17. Pepperdine University
18. United States Merchant Marine Academy
19. Clemson University
20. Furman University

Birkenstock-Wearing, Tree-Hugging, Clove-Smoking Vegetarians

Based on a combination of survey questions concerning political persuasion, the use of marijuana and hallucinogens, the prevalence of religion, the popularity of student government, and the students' level of acceptance of the gay community on campus

1. Hampshire College
2. Bard College
3. Sarah Lawrence College
4. The Evergreen State College
5. Oberlin College
6. Reed College
7. New College of Florida
8. Mills College
9. Simon's Rock College of Bard
10. Bennington College
11. Eugene Lang College
12. University of California—Santa Cruz
13. Wesleyan University
14. Vassar College
15. Pitzer College
16. Warren Wilson College
17. Lewis & Clark College
18. Macalester College
19. Marlboro College
20. Emerson College

Deep Springs Honor Roll

Since Deep Springs is a two-year college—the only one of its kind in The Best 361 Colleges—we've decided to remove it from the body of our individual rankings in order to avoid comparing "apples and oranges." Instead we've created this "honor roll," which includes all categories in which Deep Springs ranks high (or low, as it were) among the best colleges

Best Overall Academic Experience for Undergraduates
The Toughest to Get Into
Professors Make Themselves Accessible
Their Students Never Stop Studying
Class Discussions Encouraged
This is a Library?
School Runs Like Butter
Beautiful Campus
Great Food on Campus
Dorms Like Palaces
Best Quality of Life
Students Most Nostalgic for Bill Clinton
Most Politically Active
Students from Different Backgrounds Interact
Town-Gown Relations are Good
Intercollegiate Sports Unpopular or Nonexistent
Got Milk?
Scotch and Soda, Hold the Scotch
Don't Inhale
Stone Cold Sober Schools
Dodge-Ball Targets

A Final Note

The following schools have been excluded from our ranking lists dealing with financial aid:

College of the Ozarks
Cooper Union
Franklin W. Olin College of Engineering
United States Air Force Academy
United States Coast Guard Academy
United States Merchant Marine Academy
United States Military Academy
United States Naval Academy
Webb Institute

The reason—they're free!
We would like to commend each of these schools on their ability to do the seemingly impossible—not charge tuition. However, we thought it less than fair to include each of these schools in our financial lists, since each would have an unfair advantage over schools that charged even a moderate tuition.

PART 3

THE BEST 361 COLLEGES

Agnes Scott College

141 East College Avenue, Decatur, GA 30030-3797 • Admissions: 404-471-6285 • Fax: 404-471-6414

CAMPUS LIFE

Quality of Life Rating	**98**
Fire Safety Rating	**68**
Type of school	private
Affiliation	Presbyterian
Environment	metropolis

STUDENTS

Total undergrad enrollment	857
% male/female	0/100
% from out of state	46
% from public high school	70
% live on campus	87
% African American	22
% Asian	6
% Caucasian	53
% Hispanic	4
% international	7
# of countries represented	29

SURVEY SAYS

Small classes
No one cheats
Lab facilities are great
Diverse student types on campus
Great off-campus food
Frats and sororities are unpopular or nonexistent

ACADEMICS

Academic Rating	**89**
Calendar	semester
Student/faculty ratio	10:1
Professors interesting rating	88
Professors accessible rating	89
% professors teaching UG courses	98
% classes taught by TAs	0
Most common lab size	10-19 students
Most common regular class size	10-19 students

MOST POPULAR MAJORS

English language and literature
psychology

STUDENTS SPEAK OUT

Academics

"Beautiful walkways, crazy traditions, and lots of papers and presentations" are what it's all about at Agnes Scott College, a small women's liberal arts school where "intelligent and determined women live, work, play, and study with each other in an environment that is perfectly designed to foster female ambition and achievement of that ambition." Students agree that "the academic environment, although challenging and rigorous, is also supportive and not competitive," both because of professors who "truly love their jobs and [who] want to help us" and the school's strong sense of community, reinforced by the college's age-old and revered honor code. Size, location, and a sizable endowment combine to offer ASC students a number of enriching academic opportunities such as a study abroad program "that is highly popular, with about 50 percent of the class of 2003 participating." Easy access to a superb career planning office is another benefit of the school's size, and internship opportunities are plentiful "both because of ASC's location and the incredible alumnae network." Most of all, students appreciate how their fellow students embrace their studies and new ideas 24/7; one student explains, "The classrooms are busy with new ideas and tough concepts, and outside classroom conversations are very intellectually stimulating."

Life

During the week, the ASC campus is a bustle of activity, with students devoting themselves to "classes, work, studying, and participating in various organizations." When they can make the time, many Scotties attend the "numerous cultural events on campus, like international fashion shows featuring our many international students, coffeehouse series with bands and poets, music, theater, and [much] more." They also immerse themselves in the college's many traditions such as Black Cat, a weeklong event that involves competitions, pranks, a bonfire, and a formal dance. Or, they simply hang out in their "absolutely amazing dorms with high ceilings and hardwood floors" and stare out at the "beautiful campus with large trees, flowers, a gorgeous quad, historic buildings, and an easy design." However, "the campus is dead" on weekends because students head off to the many enticing destinations available in Atlanta. Some students seek parties at Emory and Georgia Tech, which "are right down the street," while other students board the MARTA for the "fifteen-minute ride to good ole Hotlanta." (That's Atlanta to you Yankees.) Major attractions in the South's most metropolitan metropolis include "the High Museum, the Fox Theatre, the Westin Hotel, the Atlanta Zoo," and "tons of restaurants serving anything you'd want from all around the world."

Student Body

ASC's highly motivated students "spend a lot of time focused on class work. Then they spend more time in the library in group-study sessions and catching up on computer things, and, instead of sleeping, they do extracurricular activities." The population itself, students adamantly tell us, "is very diverse when it comes to religions, sexual orientation, race, ethnicity, and cultural background. No two students are alike. This is what makes the campus interesting." As one student puts it, "We have everything from debutantes who wash their hair with bottled water to anime junkies to militant hippies. But everyone seems to work nicely together." Of the many groups on campus, "the two most visible are the outspoken, left-wing lesbians and the right-wing, frat-partying straight girls. And both of these groups get along and interact." What unites this smorgasbord of personalities is a shared devotion to their alma mater. One student adds, "We will argue [about] our differences all day amongst ourselves, but if an outsider were to say something negative about Agnes Scott, we defend each other to the death."

Agnes Scott College

Financial Aid: 404-471-6395 • E-mail: admission@agnesscott.edu • Website: www.agnesscott.edu

ADMISSIONS

Very important factors considered include: Character/personal qualities, class rank, essays, recommendations, secondary school record, standardized test scores, talent/ability. *Important factors considered include:* Extracurricular activities, volunteer work, work experience. *Other factors considered include:* Alumni/ae relation, geographical residence, interview, minority status, state residency. SAT Reasoning or ACT required. TOEFL required of all international applicants. High school diploma is required, and GED is accepted. *Academic units recommended:* 4 English, 3 math, 2 science (2 lab), 2 foreign language, 2 social studies.

The Inside Word

Women's colleges are enjoying a renaissance of late and to top it off, Agnes Scott has always been a great choice for strong students. Don't be deceived by the college's generous admission rate—we're talking about a small applicant pool of well-qualified candidates and one of the best small liberal arts colleges to be found anywhere. Look for greater selectivity as the college recruits students from farther afield and application totals continue to increase at top women's colleges. The admissions process can't get any more personalized than it is at Agnes Scott—every candidate is assigned her own specific admission counselor, who works with the student throughout the process.

FINANCIAL AID

Students should submit: FAFSA, institution's own financial aid form, state aid form. Regular filing deadline is 5/1. The Princeton Review suggests that all financial aid forms be submitted as soon as possible after 1/1. *Need-based scholarships/grants offered:* Pell, SEOG, state scholarships/grants, private scholarships, the school's own gift aid. *Loan aid offered:* FFEL Subsidized Stafford, FFEL Unsubsidized Stafford, FFEL PLUS, college/university loans from institutional funds. Applicants will be notified of awards on a rolling basis beginning on or about 3/1. Federal Work-study Program available. Institutional employment available. Off-campus job opportunities are excellent.

FROM THE ADMISSIONS OFFICE

"Agnes Scott College prepares women for a challenging and rapidly changing world through a liberal arts education that emphasizes interdisciplinary, experiential, and collaborative learning in a diverse and inclusive community. Students are guaranteed an internship opportunity—either among the many opportunities within the city of Atlanta or through field-based study abroad. Nearly half of our students participate in an international experience while enrolled at ASC. One-third major in the sciences and psychology. New facilities, among the finest in the nation for undergraduate science, were designed expressly to facilitate faculty-student research. We invite you to schedule a campus visit and experience Agnes Scott—a residential college on a beautiful, tree-studded campus in metropolitan Atlanta.

"Students applying for admission are required to submit score results from the new SAT with the Writing section or the ACT, with the Writing section recommended. We will allow students to submit scores from the old version of the SAT or ACT and will use the student's best scores from either test."

SELECTIVITY

Admissions Rating	**91**
# of applicants	1,252
% of applicants accepted	59
% of acceptees attending	35
# accepting a place on wait list	78
% admitted from wait list	4
# of early decision applicants	22

FRESHMAN PROFILE

Range SAT Verbal	540-680
Average SAT Verbal	611
Range SAT Math	500-620
Average SAT Math	563
**TPR Projected Range SAT Writing*	*590-680*
Range ACT Composite	22-28
Average ACT Composite	25
Minimum Paper TOEFL	577
Minimum Computer Based TOEFL	250
Average HS GPA	3.62
% graduated top 10% of class	50
% graduated top 25% of class	82
% graduated top 50% of class	94

DEADLINES

Early decision application deadline	11/15
Early decision notification	12/15
Regular notification	within 3 weeks of completion of file
Nonfall registration?	yes

APPLICANTS ALSO LOOK AT

AND OFTEN PREFER
University of Georgia, Wellesley College

AND SOMETIMES PREFER
Bryn Mawr College, Sewanee—The University of the South, Smith College

AND RARELY PREFER
Randolph—Macon Woman's College

FINANCIAL FACTS

Financial Aid Rating	**93**
Annual tuition	$22,050
Room & Board	$8,200
Books and supplies	$700
Required fees	$160
% frosh rec. need-based scholarship or grant aid	73
% UG rec. need-based scholarship or grant aid	63
% frosh rec. need-based self-help aid	63
% UG rec. need-based self-help aid	56
% frosh rec. any financial aid	99
% UG rec. any financial aid	88
Avg. frosh grant	$14,343
Avg. frosh loan	$2,560
Independent 529 member?	Yes

Albertson College

2112 Cleveland Boulevard, Caldwell, ID 83605 • Admissions: 208-459-5305 • Fax: 208-459-5757

CAMPUS LIFE

Quality of Life Rating	**74**
Fire Safety Rating	**82**
Type of school	private
Environment	town

STUDENTS

Total undergrad enrollment	777
% male/female	45/55
% from out of state	26
% live on campus	52
% in (# of) fraternities	7 (3)
% in (# of) sororities	7 (4)
% African American	1
% Asian	3
% Caucasian	74
% Hispanic	4
% Native American	1
% international	2
# of countries represented	12

SURVEY SAYS

Small classes
Great computer facilities
Students are friendly
Student publications are popular
Lots of beer drinking

ACADEMICS

Academic Rating	**88**
Calendar	13-week fall and spring semesters, 6-week winter term
Student/faculty ratio	13:1
Professors interesting rating	98
Professors accessible rating	90
% professors teaching UG courses	100
% classes taught by TAs	0
Most common regular class size	10-19 students

MOST POPULAR MAJORS

Biology/biological sciences
business administration/management
psychology

STUDENTS SPEAK OUT

Academics

Albertson College's chief distinguishing characteristic is its location; the school has many peer institutions on the ivy-covered coasts, but precious few among the proverbial potato fields of Idaho. Like its peer schools, "the single greatest strength of Albertson is the undying commitment of our faculty to the cause of their students' education." As one student put it, "The professors are phenomenal. Many go by their first names, which breaks down the hierarchical barrier between student and professor. They treat each student as a soon-to-be colleague rather than an uneducated child." Students here undergo a rigorous program that "teaches writing across the curriculum; you write papers for every class, and each one comes back with extensive comments, suggestions, and criticisms." Freshmen commence their work with the First Year Experience, a two-day mountain retreat followed by a sequence of special seminars and core courses. The goal is to rev recent high school grads up to college speed. "The First Year Experience can be a pain, but it gets you in touch with a lot of people and provides a good way to make friends," notes one undergrad. Asked to cite a weakness of ACI, many here finger the administration, however a new president and leadership style have helped. When all is said and done, students tell us that "when I look back on my days at Albertson College, I'm not going to remember the problems I had with deans, registrars, or the administration. Instead, I'm going to remember the professors."

Life

Students make clear from the get-go that Albertson is no party school. Simply put, "There is a lot of homework, and the teachers expect a lot from you." When students do take some time to cut loose, they enjoy "lots of theme parties at the fraternities. They are immensely popular; just about everyone parties it up together." Students are also deeply involved in athletics, playing "flag football and volleyball intramurals, ultimate Frisbee, and basketball" regularly, as well as engaging in outdoor activities; many here report favorably on the "awesome trips to Idaho's unique areas (deserts, mountains, sand dunes, hot springs), and activities (stargazing, backpacking, rafting, mountain biking) run by the outdoor program." The student-run Program Council works hard to "put on events like Spring Fling, midnight movies, bowling nights, and they're all free." All this helps make up for the fact that hometown Caldwell "is really boring." Fortunately, "Boise is only 30 minutes away, and there is generally plenty to do there. There are great restaurants, theaters, clubs, bars, sports venues, and anything else you could ever want. It's a great mix of rural and urban life." Faith-related activity plays a large role in many students' lives. Late Night, a weekly worship service, and Bible study groups help fill many students' extracurricular calendars. Albertson undergrads' biggest gripe: "Over half the campus goes home on weekends."

Student Body

"The student body of Albertson College is very homogeneous: almost exclusively white, Republican, upper-middle-class Idahoans," concede most Albertson undergraduates. "We can be like a herd of sheep in that respect. But, hey, we all get along!" Students typically "fall into four overlapping categories to which they gravitate socially: bookish, artsy, jocks (almost everyone here plays sports), or party-oriented." While the student body consists of "definite groups, it's not like high school cliques. Just groups of people who have common interests." Undergrads report that "the school has worked hard to lure foreign and minority students with attractive aid packages. However, overall lack of diversity is obvious and very much a detraction." Financial aid has certainly helped to diversify the economic backgrounds of students: "A number of us come from rich families, but there are a number that are on scholarship as well," reports one student.

FINANCIAL AID: 208-459-5308 • E-MAIL: ADMISSION@ALBERTSON.EDU • WEBSITE: WWW.ALBERTSON.EDU

ADMISSIONS

Very important factors considered include: Character/personal qualities, extracurricular activities, recommendations, secondary school record. *Important factors considered include:* Essays, interview, standardized test scores, volunteer work. *Other factors considered include:* Alumni/ae relation, class rank, geographical residence, talent/ability, work experience. SAT Reasoning or ACT required. TOEFL required of all international applicants. High school diploma is required, and GED is accepted. *Academic units required:* 4 English, 3 math, 2 science, 3 history, 3 academic electives. *Academic units recommended:* 3 science, 2 foreign language, 2 social studies.

The Inside Word

Albertson's open doors are a quirk of location. The college offers a challenging, high-quality academic program best suited to those who are intellectually curious and serious about their studies. The application process is relatively stress-free. (Note: For now, enrollment is on the rise. If Albertson were closer to the nation's population centers, admission would be even more selective.) As it is, the admissions committee is no less thorough than those at the highly selective level; its makeup consists of several deans and directors as well as faculty members. Students seeking to attend a small college in a rural setting near a small metropolitan area owe it to themselves to take a look. The admissions office points out that "although this college has a rolling admissions policy, it is to the applicant's advantage to apply by February 15 to be eligible for many scholarships."

FINANCIAL AID

Students should submit: FAFSA, institution's own financial aid form. The Princeton Review suggests that all financial aid forms be submitted as soon as possible after 1/1. *Need-based scholarships/grants offered:* Pell, SEOG, state scholarships/grants, private scholarships, the school's own gift aid. *Loan aid offered:* FFEL Subsidized Stafford, FFEL Unsubsidized Stafford, FFEL PLUS, Federal Perkins, alternative loans. Applicants will be notified of awards on or about 3/1. Off-campus job opportunities are good.

FROM THE ADMISSIONS OFFICE

"While the mission of Albertson College is traditional in that it remains committed to the teaching of the liberal arts, many of the approaches to accomplishing this goal are unique. Within the campus community is the creativity to create classroom opportunities for students that span the globe—both technologically and geographically. Here, students are just as apt to attend a biology class on campus as they are to hike in the nearby Owyhee or Sawtooth Mountains to carry out field research. And during the college's six-week winter term, more than 30 percent of the students are emailing friends and family from such locales as Australia, Israel, France, Ireland, England, Peru, or Mexico while taking part in faculty-led, multidisciplinary trips. Students are invited to visit the campus and the admissions counselors, either in person or through the website at www.albertson.edu.

"ACI requires all admission candidates (who have not reached sophomore status in college) to submit either the new SAT or the ACT with the Writing component. ACI will consider all scores, including the old SAT without Writing. There is no SAT Subject Test requirement, but scores will be considered as part of a holistic evaluation."

SELECTIVITY

Admissions Rating	**89**
# of applicants	634
% of applicants accepted	82
% of acceptees attending	37

FRESHMAN PROFILE

Range SAT Verbal	520-640
Average SAT Verbal	584
Range SAT Math	500-630
Average SAT Math	567
**TPR Projected Range SAT Writing*	*570-660*
Range ACT Composite	21-25
Average ACT Composite	24
Minimum Paper TOEFL	550
Minimum Computer Based TOEFL	213
Average HS GPA	3.58
% graduated top 10% of class	56
% graduated top 25% of class	87
% graduated top 50% of class	100

DEADLINES

Regular application deadline	5/1
Regular notification	ongoing
Nonfall registration?	yes

APPLICANTS ALSO LOOK AT AND OFTEN PREFER

Gonzaga University
Linfield College
University of Puget Sound
Whitman College
Willamette University

AND SOMETIMES PREFER

Carroll College (MT)
University of Idaho
Whitworth College

AND RARELY PREFER

Boise State University
Northwest Nazarene University

FINANCIAL FACTS

Financial Aid Rating	**74**
Annual tuition	$15,200
Room & Board	$6,475
Books and supplies	$700
Required fees	$690
% frosh rec. need-based scholarship or grant aid	70
% UG rec. need-based scholarship or grant aid	63
% frosh rec. need-based self-help aid	55
% UG rec. need-based self-help aid	51
% frosh rec. any financial aid	71
% UG rec. any financial aid	65
Avg. frosh grant	$13,407
Avg. frosh loan	$3,512
Independent 529 member?	No

Albion College

611 East Porter, Albion, MI 49224 • Admissions: 517-629-0321 • Fax: 517-629-0569

CAMPUS LIFE

Quality of Life Rating	**68**
Fire Safety Rating	**73**
Type of school	private
Affiliation	Methodist
Environment	village

STUDENTS

Total undergrad enrollment	1,853
% male/female	45/55
% from out of state	9
% from public high school	75
% live on campus	93
% in (# of) fraternities	42 (6)
% in (# of) sororities	46 (7)
% African American	4
% Asian	2
% Caucasian	88
% Hispanic	1
% international	1
# of countries represented	19

SURVEY SAYS

Small classes
Lab facilities are great
Great computer facilities
Students are friendly
Low cost of living
Frats and sororities dominate social scene
Lots of beer drinking

ACADEMICS

Academic Rating	**84**
Calendar	semester
Student/faculty ratio	13:1
Professors interesting rating	85
Professors accessible rating	94
% professors teaching UG courses	100
% classes taught by TAs	0
Most common lab size	10-19 students
Most common regular class size	10-19 students

MOST POPULAR MAJORS

Biology/biological sciences
economics
psychology

STUDENTS SPEAK OUT

Academics

A strong sense of community is among Albion College's strongest selling points, according to the students we surveyed. Many here mention "an immediate feeling of comfort when you come to this campus," that is reinforced over time by a school that "is truly dedicated to its students and their futures. The academics are excellent, the faculty top-notch, and the opportunities are amazing." Undergrads here love the strong pre-professional programs, which include "awesome pre-med and pre-dental institutes with very high acceptance rates at medical/dental schools" and a "strong business program." There's less unanimity over the school's liberal arts core curriculum; its champions laud the "multidimensional academic experience in a variety of departments" the core provides, while naysayers tell us that "it doesn't work, because most students just don't care about learning anything other than their major." Professors earn high marks here; students describe them as "very brilliant and having much to offer in regards to academia. They teach all of their courses as well as engage in research." They are also active in the campus community, "attending sporting, service, visual arts, Greek and other events hosted by different clubs and organizations on campus. They are an active faculty and involved with the campus." So, too, is the school's president, who "is rare in a sense that he is visible to students on a regular basis, dances with the dance team at half-time, sits in dunk tanks for philanthropic events, hosts dinner and dessert parties at his home, is always smiling, and knows the majority, if not all, of the students' names."

Life

Albion, Michigan, is a "small town that has nothing to offer a college student. The movie theater is really the only reason why anyone from the school would walk to downtown. There's not even a Wal-Mart here!" How big a problem this poses depends on the student. Some here tell us that "There are so many things to get involved in that the town we are in isn't that big of a deal." They cite athletic teams–the small student population means a relatively large proportion of students participate in intercollegiate sports–"meetings for various organizations, which are easy to start," "working with the community," and, of course, Greek life, which is "huge" here. Others feel that the campus doesn't make up for the dearth of opportunities in town; they tell us that "there's not a whole lot to do on campus that doesn't involve fraternity life in some way, so parties are obviously popular. Unfortunately, the school really doesn't have much else to offer." Adds one student, "Life is just like high school. There are your same basic drama, Greek, athletic, and 'alternative' groups. People usually have small parties or get-togethers, go to frat parties, or see movies at the movie theater. Otherwise, there's not much." As a result, "Leaving campus is popular on weekends. We are in close proximity to a lot of larger schools." Students generally "escape 20 minutes to a bigger town," such as Lansing, Ann Arbor, or Kalamazoo, "and a very high percentage goes home every weekend and/or every other weekend."

Student Body

Typical Albion undergrads "strive to do well in classes, study hard, are involved in extracurricular activities, and still finds time to relax and enjoy themselves." Students here usually "take on many extracurricular responsibilities: clubs, campus groups, community service organizations, athletic teams, intramural sports, and Greek life, to name a few of the possibilities. Everyone is here for academics first, however." Observes one student, "We have high goals for ourselves and others. We are hard-working and motivated." Students are also "outgoing and friendly, for the most part." The majority here "are white, suburban, upper-middle-class, and mostly conservative. Most are incredibly sheltered, too. It sometimes seems that a good number of students here have never stepped foot outside of suburbia."

FINANCIAL AID: 517-629-0440 • E-MAIL: ADMISSIONS@ALBION.EDU • WEBSITE: WWW.ALBION.EDU

ADMISSIONS

Very important factors considered include: Character/personal qualities, extracurricular activities, interview, secondary school record, talent/ability, volunteer work. *Important factors considered include:* Alumni/ae relation, essays, geographical residence, minority status, recommendations, standardized test scores. *Other factors considered include:* Class rank, work experience. SAT Reasoning or ACT required. TOEFL required of all international applicants. High school diploma is required, and GED is accepted. *Academic units required:* 4 English, 3 math, 3 science (1 science lab), 3 foreign language, 3 social studies. *Academic units recommended:* 4 English, 3 math, 3 science, 3 foreign language, 3 social studies, 3 history.

The Inside Word

Albion's approach to admissions is typical of many small colleges. Although the school has a very high admit rate, candidates can expect to undergo a thorough review, as matchmaking plays a strong part in the evaluation process. Your personal side and extracurricular involvements count a great deal when an admissions committee is engaged in community building. Though the college is on a rolling admission schedule, we encourage you to apply early to have the best shot at both admission and financial aid. Albion will waive the application fee for candidates who apply online.

FINANCIAL AID

Students should submit: FAFSA. The Princeton Review suggests that all financial aid forms be submitted as soon as possible after 1/1. *Need-based scholarships/grants offered:* Pell, SEOG, state scholarships/grants, private scholarships, the school's own gift aid. *Loan aid offered:* FFEL Subsidized Stafford, FFEL Unsubsidized Stafford, FFEL PLUS, Federal Perkins, state loans. Applicants will be notified of awards on a rolling basis beginning on or about 3/15. Federal Work-study Program available. Institutional employment available. Off-campus job opportunities are fair.

FROM THE ADMISSIONS OFFICE

"Albion offers a purposeful blend of a classical foundation in the liberal arts with a strong emphasis on professional development through highly selective institutes in environmental science, public policy and service, professional management, pre-medical and health care studies, honors and education, world-class internships, and study abroad opportunities. *Yahoo! Internet Life* ranks Albion the "7th Most Wired College in America" for integrating technology into academic, professional, and cocurricular programs; and a recent study conducted by the Council on Undergraduate Research ranked Albion among the top four colleges in the nation for the percentage of students engaged in original, funded undergraduate research. Albion is among the top eighty-five private, liberal arts colleges for the number of alumni who are corporate executives, including top executives and CEOs of *Newsweek*, the Lahey Clinic (MA), The Wharton School (University of Pennsylvania), PricewaterhouseCoopers, Dow Corning, Avon, the NCAA, and the Federal Accounting Standards Board (FASB). Albion's places over 95 percent of graduates into law, dental and medical schools including Harvard, Michigan, Columbia, Northwestern, Notre Dame, Vanderbilt, and Wisconsin. A full-service equestrian center opens August 2004 for all students, including the IHSA equestrian team. Campus organizations include Model United Nations, Fellowship of Christian Athletes, Canoe Club, Black Student Alliance, Equestrian Club, Ecological Awareness Club and Greek life. Of particular note are Albion's athletics (Britons), often dominating Division III football, women's basketball and soccer, and men's and women's golf and swimming. Five varsity teams have recently earned the highest grade point average in the MIAA conference, NCAA Division III, or any division nationwide

"Applicants for fall 2006 must submit the results from the SAT or ACT (with or without the Writing components from either test)."

SELECTIVITY

Admissions Rating	**83**
# of applicants	1,818
% of applicants accepted	86
% of acceptees attending	36

FRESHMAN PROFILE

Range SAT Verbal	512-640
Average SAT Verbal	562
Range SAT Math	520-660
Average SAT Math	582
**TPR Projected Range SAT Writing*	*570-660*
Range ACT Composite	22-27
Average ACT Composite	25
Minimum Paper TOEFL	550
Minimum Computer Based TOEFL	270
Average HS GPA	3.53
% graduated top 10% of class	34
% graduated top 25% of class	61
% graduated top 50% of class	89

DEADLINES

Regular application deadline	7/1
Regular notification	rolling
Nonfall registration?	yes

APPLICANTS ALSO LOOK AT

AND OFTEN PREFER
Grinnell College
University of Michigan—Ann Arbor

AND SOMETIMES PREFER
DePauw University
Hope College
Kalamazoo College
Kenyon College
Michigan State University

AND RARELY PREFER
Adrian College
Alma College
Calvin College
Olivet College

FINANCIAL FACTS

Financial Aid Rating	**90**
Annual tuition	$24,012
Room & Board	$6,928
Books and supplies	$700
Required fees	$284
% frosh rec. need-based scholarship or grant aid	64
% UG rec. need-based scholarship or grant aid	63
% frosh rec. need-based self-help aid	42
% UG rec. need-based self-help aid	49
% frosh rec. any financial aid	98
% UG rec. any financial aid	98
Avg. frosh grant	$16,890
Avg. frosh loan	$3,297
Independent 529 member?	Yes

ALFRED UNIVERSITY

ALUMNI HALL, ONE SAXON DRIVE, ALFRED, NY 14802-1205 • ADMISSIONS: 607-871-2115 • FAX: 607-871-2198

CAMPUS LIFE

Quality of Life Rating	**85**
Fire Safety Rating	**82**
Type of school	private
Environment	rural

STUDENTS

Total undergrad enrollment	1,971
% male/female	51/49
% from out of state	35
% African American	6
% Asian	2
% Caucasian	76
% Hispanic	4
% international	2

SURVEY SAYS

Small classes
Campus feels safe
Frats and sororities are unpopular or nonexistent

ACADEMICS

Academic Rating	**83**
Calendar	semester
Student/faculty ratio	12:1
Professors interesting rating	83
Professors accessible rating	84
% professors teaching UG courses	100
% classes taught by TAs	0
Most common lab size	10-19 students
Most common regular class size	10-19 students

MOST POPULAR MAJORS

Business administration/management
ceramic sciences and engineering
fine/studio arts

STUDENTS SPEAK OUT

Academics

Alfred University is a private school with a twist. The School of Engineering and the School of Art and Design receive state funding, resulting in reduced tuition for both New Yorkers and out-of-state students (although state residents receive a larger discount for the art school). The state-funded programs are "what Alfred is known for." The School of Engineering is famous for its glass and ceramics program and is, in fact, one of the few schools in the nation offering a degree in ceramic engineering. Students don't attend Alfred only for the art and engineering programs; they are also drawn to the business and English departments. Alfred provides a cozy community that students, professors, and administrators enjoy. One student says, "There is excellent interaction between students and professors; and with small classes, the faculty can devote more time to each individual student." Alfred is the kind of place where "about half our professors, maybe more, want to go by first name." One student reports, "Within a few months of being here, I had met the president of the university and the chairman of the board of trustees. I am now on a first-name basis with the president and the dean of students. I babysit the dean of students' kids." No wonder students tell us that "the level of personal connection here, all across the board, is exceptional."

Life

Small-town life can be a rough go for college students, especially in the wintry landscape of upstate New York, but fortunately "Alfred provides desperately needed entertainment. The school seems to realize that its position in the world (an hour away from civilization) requires some extra effort as far as keeping the students from going stir-crazy, and they really pull through." The school "is really good about bringing different performers and movies into town every weekend," while "art shows, visiting lecturers in every division," and "over a hundred clubs and activities" help round out the schedule. There are also activities that students enjoy in the snow, since "[they] get enough of it." One student explains, "Traying, or stealing dining hall trays and riding them down the dangerously steep hill between upper and lower campus, is a perennial favorite. I've seen [people do it in the] nude, in subzero weather, too." Even with all these activities, the small-town experience does occasionally get to people. One student writes, "Alfred is not without its small-town quirks. One of our theater professors, who has lived several places but is a devoted Alfred-ite, is throwing the town's one stoplight a thirtieth birthday party this summer." Students with cars remind us that "within thirty to sixty minutes' radius are most of the major entertainments you could want—movies, a mall or two, bowling, places to volunteer if you're so inclined, restaurants, and places to cut loose and dance."

Student Body

Alfred University, students tell us, "is like a bizarro high school where the artsy kids outnumber the football players. There are so many different social groups here. You have sporty kids, walking tapestries (dreaded neo-hippies), artsy indie rock kids, D&D [Dungeons and Dragons] kids, intellectuals, [and] engineering nerds. They tend to be somewhat cliquey, but everyone can find their place in Alfred." While some may say "it's not all artsy here," there are plenty of art students, and they tend to stick out in the crowd—when they're anywhere near the crowd, that is. "You don't always see a lot of them because they keep really strange hours," explains one nonartsy student. "Minorities and LGBT kids are well-represented on campus and in campus leadership positions," and "there's even peaceful coexisting with (neighboring) Alfred State. We rib them, and they probably rib us, but we have [Alfred] State kids in some of our extracurricular groups, and until I was told they weren't [Alfred] University kids, I would never have known the difference."

FINANCIAL AID: 607-871-2159 • E-MAIL: ADMWWW@ALFRED.EDU • WEBSITE: WWW.ALFRED.EDU

ADMISSIONS

Very important factors considered include: Character/personal qualities, class rank, extracurricular activities, recommendations, secondary school record. *Important factors considered include:* Essays, standardized test scores, volunteer work, work experience. *Other factors considered include:* Interview, minority status, talent/ability. SAT Reasoning or ACT required. TOEFL required of all international applicants. High school diploma is required, and GED is accepted. *Academic units required:* 4 English, 2 math, 2 science (2 science lab), 2 social studies. *Academic units recommended:* 4 math, 3 science (3 science lab), 3 social studies.

The Inside Word

There's no questioning the high quality of academics at Alfred, especially in their internationally known ceramics program. Still, the university's general lack of name recognition and relatively isolated campus directly affect both the applicant pool and the number of admitted students who enroll, and thus keeps selectivity relatively low for a school of its caliber. (The exception is clearly in ceramic arts, where candidates will face a very rigorous review.) If you're a back-to-nature type looking for a challenging academic environment, Alfred could be just what the doctor ordered. And if you're a standout academically, you may find that they're generous with financial aid, too—they are serious about competing for good students.

FINANCIAL AID

Students should submit: FAFSA, institution's own financial aid form, state aid form, noncustodial (divorced/separated) parents' statement, business/farm supplement. The Princeton Review suggests that all financial aid forms be submitted as soon as possible after 1/1. *Need-based scholarships/grants offered:* Pell, SEOG, state scholarships/grants, private scholarships, the school's own gift aid. *Loan aid offered:* FFEL Subsidized Stafford, FFEL Unsubsidized Stafford, FFEL PLUS, Federal Perkins, college/university loans from institutional funds, private alternative loans. Applicants will be notified of awards on a rolling basis beginning on or about 2/15. Federal Work-study Program available. Institutional employment available. Off-campus job opportunities are poor.

FROM THE ADMISSIONS OFFICE

"The admissions process at Alfred University is the foundation for the personal attention that a student can expect from this institution. Each applicant is evaluated individually and can expect genuine, personal attention at Alfred University.

"Alfred University requires that freshman applicants for fall 2006 submit scores from either the new SAT or the ACT (with Writing component)."

SELECTIVITY

Admissions Rating	**74**
# of applicants	2,243
% of applicants accepted	73
% of acceptees attending	31
# of early decision applicants	45
% accepted early decision	74

FRESHMAN PROFILE

Range SAT Verbal	500-610
Average SAT Verbal	565
Range SAT Math	500-610
Average SAT Math	572
**TPR Projected Range SAT Writing*	*560-640*
Range ACT Composite	20-26
Average ACT Composite	24
Minimum Paper TOEFL	550
Minimum Computer Based TOEFL	213
% graduated top 10% of class	15
% graduated top 25% of class	47
% graduated top 50% of class	84

DEADLINES

Early decision application deadline	12/1
Early decision notification	12/15
Regular notification	rolling
Nonfall registration?	yes

APPLICANTS ALSO LOOK AT

AND OFTEN PREFER

SUNY College at Geneseo

AND SOMETIMES PREFER

SUNY at Buffalo

Syracuse University

FINANCIAL FACTS

Financial Aid Rating	**92**
Annual tuition	$20,150
Room & Board	$9,600
Books and supplies	$850
Required fees	$810
% frosh rec. need-based scholarship or grant aid	80
% UG rec. need-based scholarship or grant aid	80
% frosh rec. need-based self-help aid	72
% UG rec. need-based self-help aid	74
% frosh rec. any financial aid	92
% UG rec. any financial aid	90
Independent 529 member?	No

ALLEGHENY COLLEGE

OFFICE OF ADMISSIONS, ALLEGHENY COLLEGE, MEADVILLE, PA 16335 • ADMISSIONS: 814-332-4351 • FAX: 814-337-0431

CAMPUS LIFE

Quality of Life Rating	**76**
Fire Safety Rating	**86**
Type of school	private
Affiliation	United Methodist
Environment	town

STUDENTS

Total undergrad enrollment	1,929
% male/female	48/52
% from out of state	34
% from public high school	83
% live on campus	75
% in (# of) fraternities	26 (5)
% in (# of) sororities	28 (4)
% African American	1
% Asian	3
% Caucasian	93
% Hispanic	1
% international	1
# of countries represented	31

SURVEY SAYS

Small classes
Lab facilities are great
Athletic facilities are great
Students are friendly
Students are happy
Lots of beer drinking

ACADEMICS

Academic Rating	**88**
Calendar	semester
Student/faculty ratio	13:1
Professors interesting rating	90
Professors accessible rating	88
% professors teaching UG courses	100
% classes taught by TAs	0
Most common regular class size	10-19 students

MOST POPULAR MAJORS

Biology/biological sciences
political science and government
psychology

STUDENTS SPEAK OUT

Academics

For students ready to hit the books hard, Allegheny College offers great rewards; explains one undergrad, "We have a huge workload here, with a lot of reading and a ton of writing. It really prepares you for graduate school and taking many upper-level courses at one time." The experience also benefits those looking to move directly into the business world after graduation because of its "great opportunities in experiential learning." As one student puts it, "Allegheny's strengths are its ample amounts of opportunity to excel both in and out of the classroom. The college provides numerous internship opportunities in addition to solid career services." Before they can reap the rewards of their degrees, though, Allegheny undergrads must complete a rigorous curriculum, one they praise for its "openness to individuality. It gave me the option of self-designing a major." Professors at Allegheny "are not only personally interested in you as a student, but in your personal well-being as well. You can't skip a class without a professor noticing and worrying about you, and you can be sure that they will go out of their way to help you whether or not you fall behind in class or are having a personal problem." Students say a larger school could not provide this kind of "professor–student connection." Administrators also integrate themselves wholly into the school community. Notes one undergrad, "Students will greet the dean or president from across campus and there is a great deal of interaction between administrators and students. No one is too important to make personal connections with students."

Life

A heavy workload keeps Allegheny students very busy during the week, so much so that, come the weekend, most look for a way "to relieve the stress caused by the demands of the school." Sometimes that involves drinking, sometimes not. Students report that "provisions by the school to crack down on off-campus parties in the past year have made social life pretty dull," making it harder–though certainly not impossible–to blow off some steam with a brew or four. Because of the new policy enforcement, "the greater portion of the campus community is more secluded from one another, with smaller groups of friends forming." This is especially true in the winter months, "when many students seem to hibernate," or hole up in the coffee house, "a hotspot for concerts, open mic nights, and general chillin,' the school's newly renovated and expanded campus center has also increased late night programming." The campus is considerably more active "in the early fall and late spring months, during which campus-wide activities from sports to college-run activities become much more common." Hometown Meadville—which some describe as "a bit backward"—is a quiet, low- to middle-income town, some of whose locals "resent the students who pay all this money to go to school and drive around in nice cars and wear nice clothes," according to Allegheny undergrads. As a result, students "band together to fight boredom" and "head up to Erie to go shopping or to Port Erie's Bayfront district for nightlife." Pittsburgh is an occasional destination, "but only for concerts or other big events."

Student Body

"Everyone is involved in a variety of activities" at Allegheny, students report. "No one is just involved in religious life or just involved in Greek life. Therefore, it's not hard to fit in somewhere." Agrees one undergrad, "We have athletes, sorority and fraternity members, very religious people, very artsy dreadlocked students, students heavily involved with the radio station and music department, etc. There are so many things to get involved in that it's hard to classify students." A common thread is that on this "politically opinionated campus, people can get pretty heated. Political and philosophical debates randomly occur." When not involved in a hot-button conversation, just about everyone "is studious to the point that it nags them during the week."

FINANCIAL AID: 800-835-7780 • E-MAIL: ADMISSIONS@ALLEGHENY.EDU • WEBSITE: WWW.ALLEGHENY.EDU

ADMISSIONS

Very important factors considered include: Class rank, secondary school record. *Important factors considered include:* Character/personal qualities, extracurricular activities, interview, recommendations, standardized test scores. *Other factors considered include:* Alumni/ae relation, essays, geographical residence, minority status, talent/ability, volunteer work, work experience. SAT Reasoning or ACT required. TOEFL required of all international applicants. High school diploma is required, and GED is accepted. *Academic units required:* 4 English, 3 math, 3 science, 2 foreign language, 3 social studies, 1 academic elective.

The Inside Word

Don't be deceived by the fairly high admit rate here—Allegheny draws a strong pool of academically well-qualified applicants, and candidate evaluation is rigorous and personalized. The admissions staff strongly recommends campus visits and interviews; students who visit the campus prior to Allegheny's application deadline receive application fee waivers. Given the highly personalized nature of candidate evaluation, we'd suggest both the visit and taking the most challenging courses in high school to be as competitive in the applicant pool as possible.

FINANCIAL AID

Students should submit: FAFSA. The Princeton Review suggests that all financial aid forms be submitted as soon as possible after 1/1. *Need-based scholarships/grants offered:* Pell, SEOG, state scholarships/grants, private scholarships, the school's own gift aid. *Loan aid offered:* FFEL Subsidized Stafford, FFEL Unsubsidized Stafford, FFEL PLUS, Federal Perkins, state loans, private loans from commercial lenders. Applicants will be notified of awards on a rolling basis beginning on or about 3/1. Federal Work-study Program available. Institutional employment available. Off-campus job opportunities are excellent.

FROM THE ADMISSIONS OFFICE

"We're proud of Allegheny's beautiful campus and cutting-edge technologies. And we know that our professors are leading scholars who pride themselves even more on being among the best teachers in the United States. But it's our students who make Allegheny the unique and special place that it is.

"Allegheny attracts students with unusual combinations of interests, skills, and talents. How do we characterize them? Although it's impossible to label our students, they do share some common characteristics. You'll find an abiding passion for learning and life, a spirit of camaraderie, and shared inquiry that spans across individuals as well as areas of study. And you'll see over and over again such a variety of interests and passions and skills that, after a while, those unusual combinations don't seem so unusual at all.

"Allegheny is not for everybody. If you find labels reassuring, if you're looking for a narrow technical training, if you're in search of the shortest distance between point A and point B, then perhaps another college will be better for you.

"But, if you recognize that everything you experience between points A and B will make you appreciate point B that much more; if you've noticed that when life gives you a choice between two things, you're tempted to answer both or simply yes; if you start to get excited because you sense there is a college willing to echo the resounding YES then we look forward to meeting you.

"Applicants for fall 2006 are required to take the new version of the SAT (we also accept the ACT; the new ACT Writing section is recommended but not required). We will allow students to submit scores from the old version of the SAT (prior to March 2005) and will use the student's best scores from either test."

SELECTIVITY

Admissions Rating	**89**
# of applicants	3,279
% of applicants accepted	74
% of acceptees attending	27
# accepting a place on wait list	122
% admitted from wait list	20
# of early decision applicants	72
% accepted early decision	77

FRESHMAN PROFILE

Range SAT Verbal	550-650
Average SAT Verbal	605
Range SAT Math	560-650
Average SAT Math	608
**TPR Projected Range SAT Writing*	*600-670*
Range ACT Composite	23-28
Average ACT Composite	26
Minimum Paper TOEFL	550
Minimum Computer Based TOEFL	213
Average HS GPA	3.74
% graduated top 10% of class	43
% graduated top 25% of class	72
% graduated top 50% of class	94

DEADLINES

Early decision application deadline	11/15
Early decision notification	11/30
Regular application deadline	2/15
Regular notification	4/1
Nonfall registration?	yes

APPLICANTS ALSO LOOK AT

AND OFTEN PREFER

Bucknell University, Carnegie Mellon University, Dickinson College

AND SOMETIMES PREFER

Denison University, Gettysburg College, Penn State University Park

AND RARELY PREFER

The College of Wooster, Miami University

FINANCIAL FACTS

Financial Aid Rating	**87**
Annual tuition	$26,650
Room & Board	$6,550
Books and supplies	$800
Required fees	$300
% frosh rec. need-based scholarship or grant aid	72
% UG rec. need-based scholarship or grant aid	72
% frosh rec. need-based self-help aid	58
% UG rec. need-based self-help aid	60
% frosh rec. any financial aid	98
% UG rec. any financial aid	96
Avg. frosh grant	$15,500
Avg. frosh loan	$3,230
Independent 529 member?	Yes

AMERICAN UNIVERSITY

4400 Massachusetts Avenue, NW, Washington, DC 20016-8001 • Admissions: 202-885-6000 • Fax: 202-885-1025

CAMPUS LIFE

Quality of Life Rating	**85**
Fire Safety Rating	**78**
Type of school	private
Affiliation	Methodist
Environment	metropolis

STUDENTS

Total undergrad enrollment	5,731
% male/female	38/62
% from out of state	95
% live on campus	68
% in (# of) fraternities	17 (10)
% in (# of) sororities	18 (13)
% African American	6
% Asian	5
% Caucasian	63
% Hispanic	5
% international	7
# of countries represented	118

SURVEY SAYS

Small classes
Students love Washington, DC
Great off-campus food
Campus feels safe
Political activism is popular
(Almost) everyone smokes

ACADEMICS

Academic Rating	**84**
Calendar	semester
Student/faculty ratio	15:1
Professors interesting rating	77
Professors accessible rating	79
% professors teaching UG courses	95
% classes taught by TAs	5
Most common regular class size	10-19 students

MOST POPULAR MAJORS

Business administration/management
international relations and affairs
mass communications/media studies

STUDENTS SPEAK OUT

Academics

"So many academic and social opportunities" await one at American University, thanks in large part to its location in northwest Washington, DC. Students have to be self-starters to take advantage of those opportunities, however; no one will hold your hand and accompany you to the threshold of learning here. "If you know what you want out of American University (AU), you will get it," explains one student. Professors ("about half are brilliant, and half are just okay," reports one undergrad) often have multiple commitments beyond campus. "We have lots of adjuncts who have super-professional experiences, but who are inaccessible outside class," warns one student. Adds another, "Professors are not always approachable. Some have an attitude with students if they ask for help [or] if students do not agree with their views." Students don't feel completely ignored on the matter of their instructors, though, as "the school really takes the students' feedback on the professors very seriously," which means bad teachers often quietly and mysteriously disappear. And the faculty has plenty of bright lights, dedicated teachers who "are really amicable and cordial and are willing to help students. And many are leaders in their fields." Students generally dislike the administration, perceiving it as "much more concerned with the outward appearance of the school" than with current students' concerns. Some are willing to concede, however, "Although our president rules the school like a banana republic, he has brought about much-needed improvements in the community." The business department draws kudos, though science facilities reportedly need some TLC. The study abroad program and internship opportunities earn students' universal praise.

Life

"DC is a great city to go to school," AU students agree. "The city is the school's most valuable asset; it's got a life of its own, in contrast to many college towns. It really makes going to school here exciting." Students love Dupont Circle and the nearby neighborhood of Adams Morgan ("a big attention drawer because there are so many restaurants, clubs, bars, and poetry places") but find plenty to do all over town. As one student told us, "There are so many other things to do in DC! There are dozens of clubs and hundreds of unique restaurants, many of which specialize in cultural goods." Another enthusiastic undergraduate adds, "It is not possible to go a single day without experiencing at least one aspect of a different culture." The city picks up the slack for the AU campus, which is often dormant: "Campus life itself isn't as exciting as a Big Ten school or something," concedes one student, "but that's because we're in a big city that actually has places to go [to] and hang out [in]." The campus is officially dry, a fact that further encourages this outwardly oriented student body to look for gathering places beyond the campus gates. With DC at the university's doorstep, partying away from school is a no-brainer. Students note that this is the type of campus where "we're more likely to attend Election Night parties than Super Bowl parties."

Student Body

The "idealistic, smart, concerned" students at American University are "extremely politically involved. People here are passionate about various issues, due in no small part to our location." Most are to the left end of the political spectrum; one disaffected undergrad writes, "The typical student is a liberal tree-hugger who thinks he/she has an open mind but actually doesn't." A large international population ("lots of diplomats' kids"), along with smaller minority populations, engenders a diversity that is "wonderful; it makes political science classes quite invigorating!" When we asked what the typical American University student was like, we typically got one of two responses. Some balked at the request: "This school is way too diverse to pinpoint the typical student," while others described a white kid from the "middle to upper middle class, interested in international relations, [who] likes trying new things [and is] interested in community service."

FINANCIAL AID: 202-885-6100 • E-MAIL: AFA@AMERICAN.EDU • WEBSITE: WWW.AMERICAN.EDU

ADMISSIONS

Very important factors considered include: Secondary school record, standardized test scores. *Important factors considered include:* Class rank, essays, extracurricular activities, recommendations, volunteer work. *Other factors considered include:* Alumni/ae relation, character/personal qualities, geographical residence, interview, minority status, talent/ability, work experience. SAT Reasoning or ACT required. TOEFL required of all international applicants. High school diploma is required, and GED is accepted. *Academic units required:* 4 English, 3 math, 2 science (2 science lab), 2 foreign language, 2 social studies, 3 academic electives. *Academic units recommended:* 4 English, 4 math, 4 science (2 science lab), 3 foreign language, 4 social studies, 1 academic elective.

The Inside Word

Washington, DC, is indeed a tremendous attraction for students who aspire to careers in government, politics, and other areas of public service. Georgetown skims most of the cream of the crop off the top of this considerable pool of prospective students, but American does quite nicely. Because the university is nationally known, it also has formidable competition outside its own backyard, and, as a result, its yield of admits who enroll is on the low side. This necessitates a higher admit rate than one might expect at a school with considerable academic strength and an impressively credentialed faculty. If you're an active leadership type with a strong academic record the admissions process should be fairly painless—American offers a great opportunity for a quality educational experience without having to plead for admission.

FINANCIAL AID

Students should submit: FAFSA, institution's own financial aid form. Regular filing deadline is 2/15. The Princeton Review suggests that all financial aid forms be submitted as soon as possible after 1/1. *Need-based scholarships/grants offered:* Pell, SEOG, state scholarships/grants, private scholarships, the school's own gift aid, Academic merit scholarships: Presidential scholarships, dean's scholarships, leadership scholarships, Phi Theta Kappa scholarships (transfers only), tuition exchange scholarships, United Methodist scholarships, and other private/restricted scholarships are awarded by the Undergraduate Admissions Office. Most scholarships do not require a separate application and are renewable for up to 3 years if certain criteria are met. *Loan aid offered:* Direct Subsidized Stafford, Direct Unsubsidized Stafford, Direct PLUS, FFEL PLUS, Federal Perkins, college/university loans from institutional funds. Applicants will be notified of awards on or about 4/1. Federal Work-study Program available. Institutional employment available. Off-campus job opportunities are excellent.

FROM THE ADMISSIONS OFFICE

"Ideas, action, and service—at AU, you interact regularly with decision makers and leaders in every profession and corner of the globe. You'll be academically challenged in a rich multicultural environment. Our expert teaching faculty provide a strong liberal arts education, characterized by small classes, the use of cutting-edge technology, and an interdisciplinary curriculum in the arts, education, humanities, social sciences, and sciences. Not just a political town, Washington, DC offers a variety of research, internship, and community service opportunities in every field. Our AU Abroad Program, with over 50 international locations, lets you expand your studies into international settings. The Princeton Review selected AU for the 2005 edition of America's Best Value Colleges. AU was one of 77 schools, and the only one from DC, selected as a 'best value' for its combination of outstanding academics, moderate tuition, and financial aid packages.

"AU requires all applicants graduating from high school in, or after, 2006 to take the new SAT or the ACT with the Writing section. Fall 2006 applicants are allowed to submit scores from the old versions of both tests as their best scores will be used in making admissions decisions."

SELECTIVITY

Admissions Rating	**93**
# of applicants	12,211
% of applicants accepted	53
% of acceptees attending	19
# of early decision applicants	227
% accepted early decision	61

FRESHMAN PROFILE

Range SAT Verbal	580-690
Average SAT Verbal	620
Range SAT Math	570-660
Average SAT Math	603
**TPR Projected Range SAT Writing*	*620-690*
Range ACT Composite	25-29
Average ACT Composite	27
Minimum Paper TOEFL	550
Minimum Computer Based TOEFL	213
Average HS GPA	3.47
% graduated top 10% of class	44
% graduated top 25% of class	82
% graduated top 50% of class	97

DEADLINES

Early decision application deadline	11/15
Early decision notification	12/31
Regular application deadline	1/15
Regular notification	4/1
Nonfall registration?	yes

APPLICANTS ALSO LOOK AT

AND OFTEN PREFER
Boston College, Boston U., Georgetown U., The George Washington U., N.Y.U., Syracuse U.

AND SOMETIMES PREFER
Columbia U.—Columbia College, University of California—Santa Barbara, U. of Delaware, U. of Southern California, U.

AND RARELY PREFER
The Catholic U. of America, Fordham U., George Mason U.

FINANCIAL FACTS

Financial Aid Rating	**80**
Annual tuition	$27,552
Room & Board	$10,700
Books and supplies	$600
Required fees	$467
% frosh rec. need-based scholarship or grant aid	39
% UG rec. need-based scholarship or grant aid	37
% frosh rec. need-based self-help aid	46
% UG rec. need-based self-help aid	43
% frosh rec. any financial aid	81
% UG rec. any financial aid	69
Avg. frosh grant	$15,813
Avg. frosh loan	$5,722
Independent 529 member?	Yes

AMHERST COLLEGE

CAMPUS BOX 2231, PO BOX 5000, AMHERST, MA 01002 • ADMISSIONS: 413-542-2328 • FAX: 413-542-2040

CAMPUS LIFE

Quality of Life Rating	**97**
Fire Safety Rating	**60**
Type of school	private
Environment	town

STUDENTS

Total undergrad enrollment	1,638
% male/female	52/48
% from out of state	87
% from public high school	59
% live on campus	98
% African American	9
% Asian	13
% Caucasian	46
% Hispanic	7
% international	6
# of countries represented	31

SURVEY SAYS

Small classes
Athletic facilities are great
Campus feels safe
Students are happy

ACADEMICS

Academic Rating	**98**
Calendar	semester
Student/faculty ratio	8:1
Professors interesting rating	98
Professors accessible rating	95
% professors teaching UG courses	100
% classes taught by TAs	0
Most common lab size	10-19 students
Most common regular class size	10-19 students

MOST POPULAR MAJORS

Economics
English language and literature
political science and government

STUDENTS SPEAK OUT

Academics

Amherst College goes against the national trend of imposing a regimented undergraduate curriculum and does not make its students take a single required course. Students approvingly say, "The requirement-free curriculum has been wonderful. Nearly everyone experiments in a range of departments on their own anyhow, and except in a few large introductory classes, the students are always there by choice." It takes a special type of student body to handle this large amount of academic freedom, but fortunately Amherst has just such an undergraduate population. As one student explains, "There is no such thing as 'too intellectual' here. I came to college dreaming of late-night intellectual discussions that would degenerate into fantastical idealism or dramatic fanatical stances, and I got them." Students enjoy a close academic community with "insanely accessible professors. They live across the street from the dorm and have students over on a regular basis. In fact, there is a program in which you can take them out for a meal financed by the school." Professors "do an excellent job [of] balancing their outside research and projects with their teachings. Their priority seems to be with the students." Amherst also boasts an "amazing alumni network." One student adds, "All my friends have gotten jobs doing what they want, where they want."

Life

Amherst is an "awesome college town" in "an area full of education and culture," especially since there are many colleges and universities nearby. Course work can be grueling: "Generally, people work during the week and party on the weekends. But partying comes in all forms. You can go to a keg party, or you can go to a coffeehouse. There's something for everyone and always something that doesn't involve drinking." Because Amherst lacks a Greek scene, "Social life is much more varied than at most other schools. Parties are always happening at different locations with different themes and sources of entertainment, and everyone's always welcome." Campus activities include "movies, plays, a cappella concerts (we are the singing school!), lectures, and meetings. There's also a movie theater nearby that people go to a lot." Also, "most people participate in team or club sports," and extracurricular clubs are popular. One undergraduate says, "With so many clubs and activities and [an] overall accepting atmosphere here at Amherst, it's hard not to fit in." Students love that Amherst "is a very close-knit campus. There is only one dining hall and everyone has to purchase a meal plan, so everyone pretty much eats every meal there. This allows you to see and interact with people every day." They're less pleased with the local weather. Students warn, "It can get pretty cold in the winter, so it takes more willpower to go out."

Student Body

Amherst is home to "two different types of students. One [type of student] is rich, white, and preppy. The other [type of student] is just a normal, funky, smart kid." Both groups are very bright. At Amherst "[students] are surrounded by the future leaders of the country and benefit from their ideas in class discussion[s], during lab[s], or over tea at the local coffee shop. There's always someone to debate with and always someone to help you out." The population boasts "a lot of racial diversity, and everyone interacts well together." One student agrees, "Students of different backgrounds tend to mix a lot more here than elsewhere." Politically, "most students are moderate-left wingers. However, there is a noticeable conservative contingent on campus." Many are "surprised to find how many student athletes there are. It seems that nearly everyone is on one of our varsity, club, or intramural teams or played in high school."

FINANCIAL AID: 413-542-2296 • E-MAIL: ADMISSION@AMHERST.EDU • WEBSITE: WWW.AMHERST.EDU

ADMISSIONS

Very important factors considered include: Character/personal qualities, essays, extracurricular activities, recommendations, secondary school record, standardized test scores, talent/ability. *Important factors considered include:* Alumni/ae relation, class rank, volunteer work. *Other factors considered include:* Geographical residence, state residency, work experience. SAT Reasoning and SAT Subject Tests or ACT required. TOEFL required of all international applicants. High school diploma or equivalent is not required. *Academic units recommended:* 4 English, 4 math, 3 science (1 science lab), 4 foreign language, 2 social studies, 2 history.

The Inside Word

Despite an up-and-down fluctuation in application totals at most highly selective colleges over the past couple of years, Amherst remains a popular choice and very competitive. You've got to be a strong match all-around, and given their formidable applicant pool, it's very important that you make your case as direct as possible. If you're a special-interest candidate such as a legacy or recruited athlete, you may get a bit of a break from the admissions committee, but you'll still need to show sound academic capabilities and potential. Those without such links have a tougher task. On top of taking the toughest courses available to them and performing at the highest of their abilities, they must be strong writers who demonstrate that they are intellectually curious self-starters who will contribute to the community and profit from the experience. In other words, you've got to have a strong profile and a very convincing application to get admitted.

FINANCIAL AID

Students should submit: FAFSA, CSS/Financial Aid PROFILE, noncustodial (divorced/separated) parents' statement, business/farm supplement, income tax and W-2 forms (submitted through IDOC). The Princeton Review suggests that all financial aid forms be submitted as soon as possible after 1/1. *Need-based scholarships/grants offered:* Pell, SEOG, state scholarships/grants, private scholarships, the school's own gift aid. *Loan aid offered:* Direct Subsidized Stafford, Direct Unsubsidized Stafford, Direct PLUS, Federal Perkins, college/university loans from institutional funds. Applicants will be notified of awards on or about 4/1. Federal Work-study Program available. Institutional employment available. Off-campus job opportunities are good.

FROM THE ADMISSIONS OFFICE

"Amherst College looks, above all, for men and women of intellectual promise who have demonstrated qualities of mind and character that will enable them to take full advantage of the college's curriculum. . . . Admission decisions aim to select from among the many qualified applicants those possessing the intellectual talent, mental discipline, and imagination that will allow them most fully to benefit from the curriculum and contribute to the life of the college and of society. Whatever the form of academic experience—lecture course, seminar, conference, studio, laboratory, independent study at various levels—intellectual competence and awareness of problems and methods are the goals of the Amherst program, rather than the direct preparation for a profession.

"Applicants must submit scores from the new SAT plus two SAT subject exams, or the old SAT I plus three SAT Subject Tests. Students may substitute the ACT with the Writing component (as of Spring 2005) or without Writing if the test was taken prior to Spring 2005."

SELECTIVITY

Admissions Rating	**98**
# of applicants	5,489
% of applicants accepted	21
% of acceptees attending	38
# accepting a place on wait list	1,023
% admitted from wait list	8
# of early decision applicants	127
% accepted early decision	38

FRESHMAN PROFILE

Range SAT Verbal	680-770
Average SAT Verbal	722
Range SAT Math	680-780
Average SAT Math	721
**TPR Projected Range SAT Writing*	*680-740*
Range ACT Composite	30-33
Average ACT Composite	31
Minimum Paper TOEFL	600
Minimum Computer Based TOEFL	250
% graduated top 10% of class	87
% graduated top 25% of class	99
% graduated top 50% of class	100

DEADLINES

Early decision application deadline	11/15
Early decision notification	12/15
Regular application deadline	12/31
Regular notification	4/2
Nonfall registration?	no

APPLICANTS ALSO LOOK AT AND OFTEN PREFER

Harvard College
Princeton University
Yale University

AND SOMETIMES PREFER

Brown University
Dartmouth College
Stanford University
Williams College

AND RARELY PREFER

Tufts University
University of Virginia
Vassar College

FINANCIAL FACTS

Financial Aid Rating	**99**
Annual tuition	$30,780
Room & Board	$8,160
Books and supplies	$900
Required fees	$584
% frosh rec. need-based scholarship or grant aid	44
% UG rec. need-based scholarship or grant aid	44
% frosh rec. need-based self-help aid	41
% UG rec. need-based self-help aid	43
Avg. frosh grant	$25,727
Avg. frosh loan	$1,839
Independent 529 member?	Yes

ARIZONA STATE UNIVERSITY

BOX 870112, TEMPE, AZ 85287-0112 • ADMISSIONS: 480-965-7788 • FAX: 480-965-3610

CAMPUS LIFE

Quality of Life Rating	**80**
Fire Safety Rating	**85**
Type of school	public
Environment	city

STUDENTS

Total undergrad enrollment	38,117
% male/female	48/52
% from out of state	23
% live on campus	14
% in (# of) fraternities	10 (28)
% in (# of) sororities	9 (22)
% African American	4
% Asian	5
% Caucasian	70
% Hispanic	12
% Native American	2
% international	3
# of countries represented	118

SURVEY SAYS

Great computer facilities
Athletic facilities are great
Students love Tempe, AZ
Great off-campus food
Students are happy
Student publications are popular
Lots of beer drinking
Hard liquor is popular
(Almost) everyone smokes

ACADEMICS

Academic Rating	**71**
Calendar	semester
Student/faculty ratio	23:1
Professors interesting rating	64
Professors accessible rating	64
% professors teaching UG courses	71
% classes taught by TAs	0
Most common lab size	20-29 students
Most common regular class size	10-19 students

MOST POPULAR MAJORS

Business administration/management
journalism
psychology

STUDENTS SPEAK OUT

Academics

With "500-plus student organizations, 364 days a year of sunshine, strong academics, and an incredible social life," Arizona State University (ASU) offers something for everyone. As one student puts it, "If you can't find someone or something that lights your fire here, you won't find it anywhere." Academically, the school is a rising star in the world of research. Undergraduates approvingly report that "the university is getting a face-lift and the high-quality facilities are becoming superb. The new administration has got a real vision and is making changes quickly, changes that are actually helping students right now." Among ASU's many assets are "a nationally ranked Honors College" and offerings in engineering, business, design, education, and journalism. Students point out that other areas, "while not as competitive, are smaller and easier to get help for (in regards to classes, registration, and advising)." The school uses introductory courses to separate the student body's wheat and chaff. One undergraduate explains, "The lower-division courses seem to treat the students like weeds: Get rid of 'em if you don't think they're beneficial. The upper-division courses are where the professors really take time to prepare students for the future." To bypass the weeding process, you need to enter the Honors College, which is "particularly strong." One student adds, "The ability to take small seminars and to write a thesis is good preparation for my educational pursuits beyond undergrad, and it adds an extra challenge and excitement to the learning experience."

Life

"Most people find that perfect balance between fun and school at ASU," students tell us, adding that "it all comes down to what you are looking for. If you are looking to go out every night to a bar, club, or party, you will find that. If you want to pursue a good education, you can find that as well. That's the best part of ASU: You can get whatever you want." Most underclassmen want to party, but once they become upperclassmen, most students settle down. One student explains, "Many students pay more attention to the college lifestyle and partying more so than studying, at least for the first year or two. As they get older, they take their studies more seriously and seek internships and professional development." Regardless of their lifestyles, ASU undergraduates enjoy the double benefit of having a large campus (and access to clubs, bars, and parties) and nearby Phoenix; "downtown is ten minutes away, so students can enjoy our four professional sports teams, a symphony, an opera, theater, and great eats." On campus, "student involvement is high. There are tons of academic clubs, social clubs, frats, and sororities to get involved in." Furthermore, "ASU athletic events are a huge part of many students' leisure time." Understandably, students "love to take advantage of the great weather, so outdoor activities are popular," as are intramural sports.

Student Body

Arizona State University "is known as a very image-conscious campus," a place where "almost everyone is beautiful: tall, blond, skinny, and bronzed." Students say, "Everyone works out and takes care of their bodies, but at the same time [they know] how to have a good time." As one student puts it, "It is rare to find an academically oriented soul on campus, as most students choose ASU for its social opportunities, even if they won't admit it." Obviously, with such a large student body, "there are a lot of 'atypical' students, and they seem to have no problem fitting in." Among the atypical kids are "some who are ultra-involved and very liberal. They have little patience for more politically conservative students or students who stray outside of their opinion paradigm." There are also "a lot of Hispanic students at ASU," as well as a considerable international population.

FINANCIAL AID: 480-965-3355 • E-MAIL: UGRADINQ@ASU.EDU • WEBSITE: WWW.ASU.EDU

ADMISSIONS

Very important factors considered include: Class rank, secondary school record, standardized test scores. *Important factors considered include:* State residency. *Other factors considered include:* Essays, extracurricular activities, interview, recommendations, talent/ability. SAT Reasoning or ACT required. TOEFL required of all international applicants. High school diploma is required, and GED is accepted. *Academic units required:* 4 English, 4 math, 3 science (3 science lab), 2 foreign language, 1 social studies, 1 history, 1 fine arts.

The Inside Word

A college preparatory curriculum and solid grades should lead to hassle-free admission. ASU uses a formula and cutoff admission process. Candidates who don't fit the bill through the formula can appeal their denial and submit additional information for consideration.

FINANCIAL AID

Students should submit: FAFSA. The Princeton Review suggests that all financial aid forms be submitted as soon as possible after 1/1. *Need-based scholarships/grants offered:* Pell, SEOG, state scholarships/grants, private scholarships, the school's own gift aid, Federal Nursing scholarships. *Loan aid offered:* Direct Subsidized Stafford, Direct Unsubsidized Stafford, Direct PLUS, FFEL PLUS, Federal Perkins. Applicants will be notified of awards on a rolling basis beginning on or about 3/15. Federal Work-study Program available. Institutional employment available. Off-campus job opportunities are good.

FROM THE ADMISSIONS OFFICE

"ASU is a place where students from all 50 states and abroad come together to live and study in one of the nation's premier collegiate environments. Situated in Tempe, ASU boasts a physical setting and climate second to none. ASU offers more than 150 academic programs of study leading to the BS and BA in eight undergraduate colleges and schools. Many of these programs have received national recognition for their quality of teaching, innovative curricula, and outstanding facilities. ASU's Barrett Honors College, the only Honors College in the Southwest that spans all academic disciplines, provides unique and challenging experiences for its students and was recently named one of eight 'best buys' in honors education by *Money* magazine.

"ASU requires the submission of either ACT or SAT scores in order to be reviewed for undergraduate admission. Presently, the essay portions of either exam are not required in order to be admitted."

SELECTIVITY	
Admissions Rating	**79**
# of applicants	20,789
% of applicants accepted	86
% of acceptees attending	40
FRESHMAN PROFILE	
Range SAT Verbal	490-600
Average SAT Verbal	547
Range SAT Math	500-620
Average SAT Math	559
**TPR Projected Range SAT Writing*	*550-630*
Range ACT Composite	21-26
Average ACT Composite	23
Minimum Paper TOEFL	500
Minimum Computer Based TOEFL	173
Average HS GPA	3.34
% graduated top 10% of class	27
% graduated top 25% of class	54
% graduated top 50% of class	83
DEADLINES	
Regular notification	rolling
Nonfall registration?	yes
FINANCIAL FACTS	
Financial Aid Rating	**69**
Annual in-state tuition	$3,973
Annual out-of-state tuition	$12,828
Room & Board	$6,574
Books and supplies	$838
Required fees	$91
% frosh rec. need-based scholarship or grant aid	37
% UG rec. need-based scholarship or grant aid	36
% frosh rec. need-based self-help aid	24
% UG rec. need-based self-help aid	33
% frosh rec. any financial aid	41
% UG rec. any financial aid	43
Avg. frosh grant	$5,370
Avg. frosh loan	$3,694
Independent 529 member?	No

AUBURN UNIVERSITY

202 MARY MARTIN HALL, AUBURN, AL 36849-5149 • ADMISSIONS: 334-844-4080 • FAX: 334-844-6179

CAMPUS LIFE

Quality of Life Rating	**88**
Fire Safety Rating	**86**
Type of school	public
Environment	town

STUDENTS

Total undergrad enrollment	18,879
% male/female	52/48
% from out of state	32
% from public high school	86
% live on campus	16
% in (# of) fraternities	17 (31)
% in (# of) sororities	31 (18)
% African American	7
% Asian	2
% Caucasian	87
% Hispanic	1
% Native American	1
% international	1
# of countries represented	91

SURVEY SAYS

Great library
Students are friendly
Students are happy
Everyone loves the Tigers
Lots of beer drinking

ACADEMICS

Academic Rating	**72**
Calendar	semester
Student/faculty ratio	16:1
Professors interesting rating	73
Professors accessible rating	74
% professors teaching UG courses	72
% classes taught by TAs	14
Most common lab size	10-19 students
Most common regular class size	20-29 students

MOST POPULAR MAJORS

Business administration/management
education
engineering

STUDENTS SPEAK OUT

Academics

Although many people at Auburn University feel that "the athletic program and the alumni program are the biggest strengths" of the school, the academics are nothing to be bashful about. Excellent programs in business, agriculture, engineering, nursing, and architecture are the most popular choices. Students are largely satisfied with Auburn's academics, although they are happily surprised by the academic excellence—they choose Auburn not for its academic reputation but for the allure of its "old Southern values and traditions." Some students attend simply because it's where everyone in their family has attended. Once at the school, however, most students quickly conclude that the faculty has "many good teachers who are easy to find" as well as "some duds." The ratio of good-to-bad professors improves as students ascend the ranks. Upper-level classes usually feature the best professors, who "are excited about teaching, give you one-on-one attention, and [answering] questions." As any Auburn watcher knows, the school has had administrative troubles in recent years. Presidents have come and gone with alarming frequency, and the Southern Association of Colleges and Schools (SACS) put the school on probation as a result of administrative policy issues in 2004, though it was later removed following a complete review. Fortunately for students, "this does not adversely affect the academic atmosphere on campus, [and] any potential student can rest assured that while times are currently tough, the Auburn family will weather it together and always be open to new members."

Life

"Auburn is a big school in a small town," students say, adding that "there's always someone new to meet, but you always see someone you know too. It's a truly laid-back atmosphere, and we have a lot of love for the town and school." The size of the student body means "there are a great deal of things to get involved with," while the small-town atmosphere means that very often "fun is really just hanging out. Be it drinking, church-related, going on road trips, playing cards, hiking at Chewacla State Park, or a game of Frisbee in the Ag Field, this is a small town, and the only thing to do is really to hang out with other people and make some fun happen." Traditions run deep, and students proudly take part in them. They love Hey Day (everyone on campus wears nametags and makes an effort to be extra friendly), tailgating before football games, and T.P.-ing Toomer's Corner (Auburn's main traffic intersection) following Auburn victories, to name just a few. Auburn athletics is "the most popular topic around town. It is always on everyone's mind." Greek life is also huge. When students need some big-city entertainment, they head for Birmingham or Atlanta, "each less than two hours away and great for shopping, concerts, and other big-city life."

Student Body

"The typical student at Auburn is the white, Protestant (most often Baptist), Republican, Southern person," students tell us, noting also that "there is a good-sized African-American population, but that's about it for minorities." We found an Auburn student who "has grown up with the same group of friends since kindergarten. He doesn't meet any new people unless, of course, they are in their fraternity, which in turn makes them cool by association." This same student also "grew up hearing about Auburn and probably had family members that went here," which accounts in part for the "unique sense of pride and unity on campus that you feel the very first time you visit." Our style correspondents say, "You would have to look really hard to find an ugly girl here. All the guys look like they stepped out of a frat house."

FINANCIAL AID: 334-844-4367 • E-MAIL: ADMISSIONS@AUBURN.EDU • WEBSITE: WWW.AUBURN.EDU

ADMISSIONS

Very important factors considered include: Secondary school record, standardized test scores. *Important factors considered include:* State residency. *Other factors considered include:* Alumni/ae relation, class rank, extracurricular activities, geographical residence, minority status, recommendations, talent/ability, volunteer work. SAT Reasoning or ACT required. TOEFL required of all international applicants. High school diploma is required, and GED is accepted. *Academic units required:* 4 English, 3 math, 2 science, 3 social studies. *Academic units recommended:* 4 English, 3 math, 3 science, 2 foreign language, 4 social studies.

The Inside Word

Auburn is another "follow the numbers" admission institution—if you have what they require, you're in with little sweat.

FINANCIAL AID

Students should submit: FAFSA, institution's own financial aid form. The Princeton Review suggests that all financial aid forms be submitted as soon as possible after 1/1. *Need-based scholarships/grants offered:* Pell, SEOG, state scholarships/grants, private scholarships, the school's own gift aid. *Loan aid offered:* FFEL Subsidized Stafford, FFEL Unsubsidized Stafford, FFEL PLUS, Federal Perkins, college/university loans from institutional funds. Federal Work-study Program available. Off-campus job opportunities are good.

FROM THE ADMISSIONS OFFICE

"Auburn University is a comprehensive land-grant university serving Alabama and the nation. The university is especially charged with the responsibility of enhancing the economic, social, and cultural development of the state through its instruction, research, and extension programs. In all of these programs, the university is committed to the pursuit of excellence. The university assumes an obligation to provide an environment of learning in which the individual and society are enriched by the discovery, preservation, transmission, and application of knowledge; in which students grow intellectually as they study and do research under the guidance of competent faculty, and in which the faculty develop professionally and contribute fully to the intellectual life of the institution, community, and state. This obligation unites Auburn University's continuing commitment to its land-grant traditions and the institution's role as a dynamic and complex, comprehensive university.

"Applicants for fall 2006 must submit scores from the SAT or ACT (with or without the Writing components from either test)."

SELECTIVITY

Admissions Rating	**83**
# of applicants	12,838
% of applicants accepted	84
% of acceptees attending	33
# accepting a place on wait list	488
% admitted from wait list	69
# of early decision applicants	587
% accepted early decision	89

FRESHMAN PROFILE

Range SAT Verbal	500-600
Average SAT Verbal	553
Range SAT Math	510-610
Average SAT Math	569
**TPR Projected Range SAT Writing*	*560-630*
Range ACT Composite	22-26
Average ACT Composite	24
Minimum Paper TOEFL	550
Minimum Computer Based TOEFL	213
Average HS GPA	3.53
% graduated top 10% of class	35
% graduated top 25% of class	57
% graduated top 50% of class	85

DEADLINES

Early decision application deadline	11/1
Regular application deadline	8/1
Regular notification	continuous
Nonfall registration?	yes

APPLICANTS ALSO LOOK AT AND SOMETIMES PREFER

Clemson University
Florida State University
Georgia Institute of Technology
Louisiana State University
The University of Alabama—Tuscaloosa
University of Florida
University of Georgia
University of Mississippi
University of Tennessee—Knoxville

FINANCIAL FACTS

Financial Aid Rating	**65**
Annual in-state tuition	$4,610
Annual out-of-state tuition	$13,830
Room & Board	$6,686
Books and supplies	$900
Required fees	$218
% frosh rec. need-based scholarship or grant aid	25
% UG rec. need-based scholarship or grant aid	24
% frosh rec. need-based self-help aid	22
% UG rec. need-based self-help aid	29
% frosh rec. any financial aid	55
% UG rec. any financial aid	53
Avg. frosh grant	$4,222
Avg. frosh loan	$3,718
Independent 529 member?	No

AUSTIN COLLEGE

900 NORTH GRAND AVENUE, SUITE 6N, SHERMAN, TX 75090-4400 • ADMISSIONS: 903-813-3000 • FAX: 903-813-3198

CAMPUS LIFE

Quality of Life Rating	**85**
Fire Safety Rating	**64**
Type of school	private
Affiliation	Presbyterian
Environment	town

STUDENTS

Total undergrad enrollment	1,281
% male/female	45/55
% from out of state	8
% from public high school	88
% live on campus	72
% in (# of) fraternities	30 (9)
% in (# of) sororities	30 (7)
% African American	4
% Asian	10
% Caucasian	75
% Hispanic	8
% Native American	1
% international	2
# of countries represented	20

SURVEY SAYS

Small classes
Great library
Athletic facilities are great
Students are friendly
Campus feels safe
Students are happy

ACADEMICS

Academic Rating	**89**
Calendar	4-1-4
Student/faculty ratio	12:1
Professors interesting rating	96
Professors accessible rating	92
% professors teaching UG courses	100
% classes taught by TAs	0
Most common lab size	fewer than 10 students
Most common regular class size	10-19 students

MOST POPULAR MAJORS

Business administration/management
psychology

STUDENTS SPEAK OUT

Academics

Austin College (AC), a small liberal arts school located an hour north of Dallas, has long been known for its excellent pre-med program. "Most students are pre-med" here, and one in eight proceeds to medical school upon graduation. Biology and chemistry aren't the only star attractions here, however; offering a "high standard of academic integrity in a liberal, laid-back, personal environment," AC excels in all pre-professional areas, leading some boosters to dub it "The 'hidden' Ivy League school of the South." Unlike many Ivies, though, AC offers its students lots of individual attention. Professors "are very helpful and encouraging, and they promote a very casual atmosphere," particularly in the mentoring program, which "helps students get used to the school in their first year, and after that the mentor (an on-campus professor) becomes like a friend that you can talk to about anything, from personal matters to what classes to register for. I have enjoyed every minute of it." Students also praise AC's "holistic" approach to education. "Instead of forcing you to choose a path the first day of school, they make us take many compulsory subjects, which allow us to experience different parts of the spectrum," writes one undergrad. The popular study abroad program can send "AC students to study virtually anywhere in the world. Personally, I went to New Zealand for a semester. It was one of the best things that I have done in my life." Sums up one satisfied student, "This college has all of the perks of a large university within a small, intimate environment."

Life

AC students agree on two things: While hometown Sherman "does not have much to offer," the school "does a pretty good job of finding things for us to do" on campus. "We have movie nights, bowling nights, and lots of performances, some by Austin College students and some brought in," explains one student. An active Greek scene keeps the parties hopping; notes one undergrad, "There are theme parties usually every weekend, so people focus more on costumes than drinking." Students admit, "If our football team wasn't so lame, maybe the student population would be more enthusiastic about being [Kanga]Roos," but add that "the soccer teams are growing in popularity. Intramural sports are always fun to watch, too." Immediately beyond campus, however, the pickings quickly grow slim. As one student put it, "For fun? Ha. Ha. We go to the local Wal-Mart or the deserted mall." Agrees another, "The only problem with AC is the location. The city of Sherman is small and does not have much to offer, but Dallas is only an hour away." Fortunately, "Dallas kicks ass. It has plenty of things to do: museums, clubs, restaurants, as well as three new Starbucks and a movie theater."

Student Body

Austin undergrads pride themselves on their independence; writes one, "Individuality itself prospers in this environment, fostering an atmosphere that is considerably accepting and open." Students are "a very diverse crop from many different cultures and backgrounds," including economic. "While it is quite an expensive school, there is so much scholarship [money] that many different economic classes can come here," explains one undergrad. These predominantly pre-professional students are serious about work without getting all pointy-headed about it; as one undergrad put it, "Students here don't exactly ponder the meaning of life, but we have engaging discussions because everyone is pretty much on the same academic level. There's no 'super jock' group or 'super intellectual' group." While "the typical student is a conservative Southerner," particularly from Texas, there are also "many gays and lesbians, and they all fit into the social atmosphere fine."

FINANCIAL AID: 903-813-2900 • E-MAIL: ADMISSION@AUSTINCOLLEGE.EDU • WEBSITE: WWW.AUSTINCOLLEGE.EDU

ADMISSIONS

Very important factors considered include: Secondary school record. *Important factors considered include:* Character/personal qualities, class rank, essays, extracurricular activities, recommendations, standardized test scores, talent/ability. *Other factors considered include:* Alumni/ae relation, geographical residence, interview, minority status, religious affiliation/commitment, state residency, volunteer work, work experience. SAT Reasoning or ACT required. TOEFL required of all international applicants. High school diploma is required, and GED is accepted. *Academic units required:* 4 English, 3 math, 3 science (2 science lab), 2 foreign language, 2 social studies, 1 academic elective, 1 fine arts. *Academic units recommended:* 4 English, 4 math, 4 science (3 science lab), 3 foreign language, 3 social studies, 2 fine arts.

The Inside Word

Austin continues to be a prize find among lesser-known colleges, but it isn't as much of a secret anymore. Freshman enrollment saw a major surge last year, which could translate into a somewhat tougher admissions committee. The college's emphasis on academic quality and its very sincere approach to recruitment of students has paid off handsomely. Efforts to increase minority representation on campus have been a big success—few small colleges have as impressive a level of diversity. Out-of-state students will continue to be appealing to the admissions committee, as their number is still rather low.

FINANCIAL AID

Students should submit: FAFSA, institution's own financial aid form. The Princeton Review suggests that all financial aid forms be submitted as soon as possible after 1/1. *Need-based scholarships/grants offered:* Pell, SEOG, state scholarships/grants, private scholarships, the school's own gift aid. *Loan aid offered:* FFEL Subsidized Stafford, FFEL Unsubsidized Stafford, FFEL PLUS, Federal Perkins, state loans, college/university loans from institutional funds. Applicants will be notified of awards on a rolling basis beginning on or about 3/1. Federal Work-study Program available. Institutional employment available. Off-campus job opportunities are good.

FROM THE ADMISSIONS OFFICE

"Students visiting Austin College immediately sense something different about the campus community. People look you in the eye. They call you by name. They want to see you succeed.

"That success comes from a strong academic foundation in the liberal arts and sciences, plus added opportunities like international study, January Term, and close involvement with committed faculty who become your partners in learning.

"The comments on these pages from students make it clear that there is no 'typical' student at Austin College. Students can retain their individuality and still fit in. Our students value and respect differences of background, style, and belief. Campus organizations offer activities for all interests.

"Austin College prepares you to do more than make a living. It prepares you to make a difference in the place you work, in the community you call home, in the friends you make, and in the way you live. Service to others is an important part of campus life.

"Visit and discover Austin College's legacy of learning, leadership, and lasting values for yourself.

"Applicants for fall 2006 must submit Writing scores from the new SAT or ACT."

SELECTIVITY

Admissions Rating	**89**
# of applicants	1,475
% of applicants accepted	69
% of acceptees attending	36
# accepting a place on wait list	56
% admitted from wait list	4
# of early decision applicants	27
% accepted early decision	84

FRESHMAN PROFILE

Range SAT Verbal	570-670
Average SAT Verbal	622
Range SAT Math	570-670
Average SAT Math	621
**TPR Projected Range SAT Writing*	*610-680*
Range ACT Composite	23-28
Average ACT Composite	26
Minimum Paper TOEFL	550
Minimum Computer Based TOEFL	213
Average HS GPA	3.51
% graduated top 10% of class	46
% graduated top 25% of class	77
% graduated top 50% of class	96

DEADLINES

Early decision application deadline	12/1
Early decision notification	1/10
Regular application deadline	5/1
Regular notification	4/1 and on space available basis thereafter
Nonfall registration?	yes

APPLICANTS ALSO LOOK AT

AND OFTEN PREFER

Southwestern U., Trinity U.

AND SOMETIMES PREFER

Baylor U., Rice U., Southern Methodist U., Texas A&M U.—College Station, Texas Christian U.

AND RARELY PREFER

Hendrix College, U. of Dallas

FINANCIAL FACTS

Financial Aid Rating	**97**
Annual tuition	$20,310
Room & Board	$7,376
Books and supplies	$800
Required fees	$160
% frosh rec. need-based scholarship or grant aid	61
% UG rec. need-based scholarship or grant aid	59
% frosh rec. need-based self-help aid	44
% UG rec. need-based self-help aid	48
% frosh rec. any financial aid	61
% UG rec. any financial aid	60
Avg. frosh grant	$13,227
Avg. frosh loan	$5,093
Independent 529 member?	Yes

Babson College

Mustard Hall, Babson Park, MA 02457 • Admissions: 781-239-5522 • Fax: 781-239-4135

CAMPUS LIFE

Quality of Life Rating	**79**
Fire Safety Rating	**88**
Type of school	private
Environment	village

STUDENTS

Total undergrad enrollment	1,697
% male/female	60/40
% from out of state	62
% live on campus	83
% in (# of) fraternities	10 (3)
% in (# of) sororities	10 (2)
% African American	3
% Asian	8
% Caucasian	44
% Hispanic	5
% international	17
# of countries represented	59

SURVEY SAYS

Small classes
Great computer facilities
Great library
Great off-campus food
Campus feels safe
Lots of beer drinking
Hard liquor is popular

ACADEMICS

Academic Rating	**88**
Calendar	semester
Student/faculty ratio	13:1
Professors interesting rating	89
Professors accessible rating	89
% professors teaching UG courses	100
% classes taught by TAs	0
Most common lab size	10-19 students
Most common regular class size	30-39 students

MOST POPULAR MAJORS

Business administration/management

STUDENTS SPEAK OUT

Academics

Entrepreneurship is the name of the game at Babson College. The college has strengths in other areas, surely, but most students arrive here hoping to learn the secret of establishing America's next Jiffy Lube or Continental Polymers (both of whose founders teach here). Babson stresses "hands-on experience" with a curriculum that "really plunges you into the real world, rather than teaching you theories. During [the] first year, you actually start a business and then learn how to manage it." (A few naysayers dismiss the freshman project as "small time. The businesses tends to be more of peddle-shops than anything.") Starting a business is only part of a rigorous freshman year that students uniformly refer to as "business boot camp." Warns one undergrad, "Free time is very hard to come by at Babson. You'll always have a business plan to write, a group meeting to go to, or reading to do for a class." Professors are admired for their experience and expertise ("They are typically seasoned businessmen and businesswomen who have a genuine desire to teach students how to be successful in the real world"). While some here complain that "at times Babson can focus too much on 'street smarts' at the expense of 'book smarts'" and others assert that "Babson needs to improve the quality and quantity of the liberal arts curriculum," most here believe the school's assets far outweigh its drawbacks. As one student put it, "From great speakers, like the head of the NYSE, to programs like the Rocket Pitch Event, Business Plan Competition, and entrepreneurship conferences . . . Babson students get what they pay for."

Life

Even though the Babson campus offers "tons of sports events, plays, concerts," and numerous active organizations (including Babson Dance Ensemble, the Babson Players, Student Government, and the Campus Activities Board), most students here agree that "There's lots of stuff offered on campus, but with such a diverse [international] population, it's hard to please everyone. Babson students are so spoiled in so many ways; we get very whiny and complain about things a lot, even though we have it so amazingly good." Some blame the situation on the school's small size; others finger the "super anal" campus police; still others say it's the grueling academic schedule ("Being both happy and successful at Babson requires 36 hours a day"). Fortunately, the school is "not quite in Boston, but close enough to all the action," at least for the majority of students who have cars (For those who don't, the college offers a weekend shuttle service). "Boston is the choice destination for partying," students tell us, warning that "clubs can set you back $100 in one night with cover charges, drinks, and shared cab fare." Students praise Babson's "small, beautiful campus" and the "extremely safe, lovely neighborhood" surrounding it.

Student Body

The typical Babson undergrad is either "a white suburbanite from an East Coast private school" or "an international who smokes, is always on his/her cell phone, and wears designer threads." Students are "very conservative" and "extremely competitive," leading some to complain that "there are too many unfriendly people here. No one says hello when you walk by them, and if you initiate a greeting, it is seldom returned." Reports one undergrad, "Many students are individualistic in nature. They could happily survive on a deserted island with a computer, a cell phone, and caffeine." Given the school's focus on entrepreneurship, it is unsurprising that many here are also very materialistic. "If you want to be criticized for not ordering every new gadget in *Maxim* magazine or for not having more than one car on campus, this is the place for you," is how one sardonic student here puts it.

FINANCIAL AID: 781-239-4219 • E-MAIL: UGRADADMISSION@BABSON.EDU • WEBSITE: WWW.BABSON.EDU

ADMISSIONS

Very important factors considered include: Secondary school record, standardized test scores. *Important factors considered include:* Class rank, essays, recommendations. *Other factors considered include:* Alumni/ae relation, character/personal qualities, extracurricular activities, geographical residence, interview, minority status, state residency, talent/ability, volunteer work, work experience. SAT Reasoning or ACT required. SAT Subject Tests recommended. High school diploma is required, and GED is accepted. *Academic units required:* 4 English, 3 math, 3 science (2 science lab), 2 foreign language, 2 social studies, 1 history. *Academic units recommended:* 4 English, 4 math, 3 science (2 science lab), 4 foreign language, 3 social studies, 1 precalculus.

The Inside Word

Minority representation, including that of women, remains low, which makes for a very advantageous situation for such candidates. In this age of corporate "downsizing," it has become much more commonplace for students to pursue college programs that lead directly to career paths, and Babson has benefited handsomely from this trend. When this trend and the college's fine reputation are combined, the result is a relatively challenging admissions process despite a relatively modest freshman academic profile. On top of this, the college is also recruiting further afield than in the past. Be wary of overconfidence when applying.

FINANCIAL AID

Students should submit: FAFSA, CSS/Financial Aid PROFILE, noncustodial (divorced/separated) parents' statement, business/farm supplement, federal tax returns, W-2 forms, and verification worksheet. Regular filing deadline is 2/15. The Princeton Review suggests that all financial aid forms be submitted as soon as possible after 1/1. *Need-based scholarships/grants offered:* Pell, SEOG, state scholarships/grants, the school's own gift aid. *Loan aid offered:* FFEL Subsidized Stafford, FFEL Unsubsidized Stafford, FFEL PLUS, Federal Perkins, state loans. Applicants will be notified of awards on or about 4/1. Federal Work-study Program available. Institutional employment available. Off-campus job opportunities are good.

FROM THE ADMISSIONS OFFICE

"In addition to theoretical knowledge, Babson College is dedicated to providing its students with hands-on business experience. The Foundation Management Experience (FME) and Management Consulting Field Experience (MCFE) are two prime examples of this commitment. During the FME, all freshmen are placed into groups of 30 and actually create their own businesses that they operate until the end of the academic year. The profits of each FME business are then donated to the charity of each group's choice.

"MCFE offers upperclassmen the unique and exciting opportunity to work as actual consultants for private companies and/or nonprofit organizations in small groups of three to five. Students receive academic credit for their work as well as invaluable experience in the field of consulting. FME and MCFE are just two of the ways Babson strives to produce business leaders with both theoretical knowledge and practical experience.

"Babson College requires freshman applicants to submit scores from either the new SAT or the ACT with Writing component. The school recommends that students also submit results from SAT Subject Tests."

SELECTIVITY	
Admissions Rating	**93**
# of applicants	3,064
% of applicants accepted	37
% of acceptees attending	38
# accepting a place on wait list	532
# of early decision applicants	119
% accepted early decision	52
FRESHMAN PROFILE	
Range SAT Verbal	560-640
Average SAT Verbal	597
Range SAT Math	600-690
Average SAT Math	655
**TPR Projected Range SAT Writing*	*600-660*
Range ACT Composite	26-28
% graduated top 10% of class	53
% graduated top 25% of class	83
% graduated top 50% of class	98
DEADLINES	
Early decision application deadline	11/15
Early decision notification	12/15
Regular application deadline	1/15
Regular notification	4/1
Nonfall registration?	no
FINANCIAL FACTS	
Financial Aid Rating	**95**
Annual tuition	$28,832
Room & Board	$10,376
Books and supplies	$856
% frosh rec. need-based scholarship or grant aid	42
% UG rec. need-based scholarship or grant aid	40
% frosh rec. need-based self-help aid	46
% UG rec. need-based self-help aid	45
% frosh rec. any financial aid	46
% UG rec. any financial aid	45
Avg. frosh grant	$20,589
Avg. frosh loan	$2,686
Independent 529 member?	No

BARD COLLEGE

OFFICE OF ADMISSIONS, ANNANDALE-ON-HUDSON, NY 12504 • ADMISSIONS: 845-758-7472 • FAX: 845-758-5208

CAMPUS LIFE

Quality of Life Rating	**76**
Fire Safety Rating	**80**
Type of school	private
Environment	rural

STUDENTS

Total undergrad enrollment	1,458
% male/female	45/55
% from out of state	76
% from public high school	67
% live on campus	81
% African American	3
% Asian	5
% Caucasian	70
% Hispanic	4
% international	5
# of countries represented	51

SURVEY SAYS

Small classes
Students aren't religious
Campus feels safe
Frats and sororities are unpopular or nonexistent
Political activism is popular
(Almost) everyone smokes

ACADEMICS

Academic Rating	**95**
Calendar	4-1-4
Student/faculty ratio	9:1
Professors interesting rating	89
Professors accessible rating	85
% professors teaching UG courses	100
% classes taught by TAs	0
Most common regular class size	10-19 students

MOST POPULAR MAJORS

English language and literature
social sciences
visual and performing arts

STUDENTS SPEAK OUT

Academics

Bard College, a Hudson Valley school that puts the "liberal" in "liberal arts," is a bastion of nonconformity and intellectualism. Professors and academics, students tell us, "are both pretty amazing. All the professors seem willing to bend over backward for the students while being respectable members of academia in general." Undergrads may also love the faculty because "the professors are a reflection of the student body: a combination of above-it-all artists, leftist intellectuals, and downright nerds." Students here love the school's "general looseness, which makes it easy to do things—start a club, get a tutorial, make your own major, whatever." Recounts one student, "I wanted to transfer credits so I walked into the registrar's office and was out in five minutes. I wanted a Hebrew tutorial, I found the professor in his office, and he arranged it. . . . Every time I've needed anything, people have graciously given me their time and their advice, minus formality and bureaucracy." According to students, the only exception to the rule is course registration, "which is a nightmare. Professors sit in their offices, and it's first come, first served. Registration opens at noon. People camp out outside the offices up to six hours ahead of time. It's like a *Star Wars* premiere."

Life

Because Bard "isn't really on top of any town—you have to drive 5 to 10 [miles] to hit anything more than a fruit stand," the school "tries to be its own entertainment." The campus scene is enjoyable, if subdued, according to most; explains one undergrad, "For fun we have intellectual conversations, go to the movies, go to campus events, go to see bands, hang out in the library, drive around, go to thrift stores or to Wal- Mart, hang out in the campus center . . . and surf the Internet." There are "always movies at the theatre on weekends, and there are often theatrical productions, art openings, concerts, and lectures" as well. Even so, "It's the party/music scene that runs the place." There "are a lot of herbal activities" here, though "for the most part, people respect themselves and one another and do not overuse." Many traditional college diversions are absent here; as one student puts it, "These are things people are not into: football, television, dating, and fast food. Things people are into: dance parties, leftist politics, New York City, organic vegetables, and doing their own thang."

Student Body

When conservatives complain about PC campuses and ultraliberal students, they might well be specifically describing Bard. It's the kind of place where students tell you that "we are more concerned with the terrorism for which our government is responsible than the terrorism that targets the United States," and mean it. "There is no typical Bard student" undergrads tell us, but most feel right at home here among the "leftist white woman who goes to Green Party rallies weekly" and the "friendly white guys with dreadlocks . . . whose joys include learning, music, and getting stoned with close friends." Bard students describe themselves as cerebral, telling us that "a certain level of intellectualism prevails here, and you really feel that the people you are talking to know what they are talking about, and have done research on these topics. Debates get heated, but that's essential to really get to the depth of an issue anyway." Undergrads appreciate the fact that "There is a really high percentage of international students, which gives the Americans a different perspective of the world."

FINANCIAL AID: 845-758-7526 • E-MAIL: ADMISSION@BARD.EDU • WEBSITE: WWW.BARD.EDU

ADMISSIONS

Very important factors considered include: Character/personal qualities, essays, extracurricular activities, recommendations, secondary school record, talent/ability, volunteer work. *Important factors considered include:* Work experience. *Other factors considered include:* Alumni/ae relation, class rank, geographical residence, interview, minority status, religious affiliation/commitment, standardized test scores, state residency. TOEFL required of all international applicants. High school diploma is required, and GED is accepted. *Academic units recommended:* 4 English, 4 math, 4 science, 4 foreign language, 4 social studies, 4 history.

The Inside Word

Applicants tend to be cerebral sorts. Bard is highly selective, but the match counts more than having the right numerical profile.

FINANCIAL AID

Students should submit: FAFSA, CSS/Financial Aid PROFILE, state aid form, noncustodial (divorced/separated) parents' statement, business/farm supplement. Regular filing deadline is 2/15. The Princeton Review suggests that all financial aid forms be submitted as soon as possible after 1/1. *Need-based scholarships/grants offered:* Pell, SEOG, state scholarships/grants, private scholarships, the school's own gift aid. *Loan aid offered:* FFEL Subsidized Stafford, FFEL Unsubsidized Stafford, FFEL PLUS, Federal Perkins, college/university loans from institutional funds, college/university loans from institutional funds (for international students only). Applicants will be notified of awards on or about 4/1. Federal Work-study Program available. Institutional employment available. Off-campus job opportunities are good.

FROM THE ADMISSIONS OFFICE

"An alliance with Rockefeller University, the renowned graduate scientific research institution, gives Bardians access to Rockefeller's professors and laboratories and to places in Rockefeller's Summer Research Fellows Program. Almost all our math and science graduates pursue graduate or professional studies; 90 percent of our applicants to medical and health professional schools are accepted.

"The Globalization and International Affairs (BGIA) Program is a residential program in the heart of New York City that offers undergraduates a unique opportunity to undertake specialized study with leading practitioners and scholars in international affairs and to gain internship experience with international-affairs organizations. Topics in the curriculum include human rights, international economics, global environmental issues, international justice, managing international risk, and writing on international affairs, among others. Internships/tutorials are tailored to students' particular fields of study.

"Student dormitory and classroom facilities are in Bard Hall, 410 West 58th Street, a newly renovated 11-story building near the Lincoln Center District in New York City.

"Bard College does not require SAT scores, new or old, to be submitted for admissions consideration. Students may choose to submit scores, and, if submitted, we will consider them in the context of the overall application."

SELECTIVITY

Admissions Rating	**96**
# of applicants	3,603
% of applicants accepted	36
% of acceptees attending	31
# accepting a place on wait list	267
% admitted from wait list	4

FRESHMAN PROFILE

Range SAT Verbal	650-750
Average SAT Verbal	690
Range SAT Math	590-690
Average SAT Math	630
**TPR Projected Range SAT Writing*	*670-730*
Minimum Paper TOEFL	600
Minimum Computer Based TOEFL	250
Average HS GPA	3.5
% graduated top 10% of class	64
% graduated top 25% of class	90
% graduated top 50% of class	99

DEADLINES

Regular application deadline	1/15
Regular notification	4/1
Nonfall registration?	yes

APPLICANTS ALSO LOOK AT

AND OFTEN PREFER

Amherst College
Brown University
Harvard College
Yale University

AND SOMETIMES PREFER

Boston University
New York University
Oberlin College
Reed College
Vassar College

AND RARELY PREFER

Hampshire College
Ithaca College
Macalester College
Sarah Lawrence College

FINANCIAL FACTS

Financial Aid Rating	**85**
Annual tuition	$31,850
Room & Board	$9,310
Books and supplies	$750
Required fees	$906
% frosh rec. need-based scholarship or grant aid	53
% UG rec. need-based scholarship or grant aid	58
% frosh rec. need-based self-help aid	48
% UG rec. need-based self-help aid	52
% frosh rec. any financial aid	65
% UG rec. any financial aid	68
Avg. frosh grant	$21,464
Avg. frosh loan	$3,434
Independent 529 member?	Yes

BARNARD COLLEGE

3009 BROADWAY, NEW YORK, NY 10027 • ADMISSIONS: 212-854-2014 • FAX: 212-854-6220

CAMPUS LIFE

Quality of Life Rating	**97**
Fire Safety Rating	**77**
Type of school	private
Environment	metropolis

STUDENTS

Total undergrad enrollment	2,287
% male/female	0/100
% from out of state	66
% from public high school	52
% live on campus	90
% African American	5
% Asian	17
% Caucasian	67
% Hispanic	7
% Native American	1
% international	3
# of countries represented	40

SURVEY SAYS

No one cheats
Great library
Students love New York, NY
Great off-campus food
Campus feels safe

ACADEMICS

Academic Rating	**94**
Calendar	semester
Student/faculty ratio	10:1
Professors interesting rating	91
Professors accessible rating	89
% professors teaching UG courses	100
% classes taught by TAs	0
Most common lab size	fewer than 10 students
Most common regular class size	10-19 students

MOST POPULAR MAJORS

Economics
English language and literature
psychology

STUDENTS SPEAK OUT

Academics

Barnard College, the all-women's liberal arts school associated with Columbia University, "offers students the best of both worlds: the seclusion and intimacy of a small liberal arts college within a tremendous research university and one of the greatest cities in the world." Women here explain that "because Barnard students have complete cross-registration privileges at Columbia, full access to all of its resources and libraries, and upon graduation receive a degree from the University, we enjoy the full benefits of an Ivy League education, without the punishment of having to take Columbia's core curriculum, pass a swim test, or eat at the lousy Columbia dining room." Students here also get more of a small-college experience than do their Columbia peers; explains one student, "While the Columbia professors can be arrogant and pompous, most of the Barnard professors are really nice, down-to-earth people." Administrators are "unequivocally dedicated to finding rapid, individualized solutions to students' problems." Because the school is in New York City, "there are amazing opportunities here; the city really is our learning lab!" In short, "Barnard is really great as a small school to act as your home base. From here, you can explore the university and the city as much as you want. You have to take the initiative, but if you do, you can find a way to do anything you want. And Barnard is so supportive, you'll be able to find someone on campus who's willing to help."

Life

"Life at school is dominated by studies." Undergraduates agree that "most students here spend at least 60 percent of their week on schoolwork." Still, to the degree allowed by their academic workload, "most undergraduates make a conscious effort to take advantage of NYC through internships, nightlife, museums, and exhibits. Many of us love to just spend an afternoon walking down Broadway and shopping." The campus is a magnet for high-powered speakers and prestigious events; reports one student, "There are always rallies or lectures going on that are highly attended. In the past year, Janeane Garofalo, John Edwards, Anna Quindlen, and Alice Walker have spoken on campus, to name a few." Barnard is located in Morningside Heights, "a neighborhood that thrives very much on the college community." Students here miss out a bit on the classic college experience, but they don't mind; explains one undergrad, "Barnard feels that, since we are in the city, they don't need to create a community for us. Therefore, occasionally I feel like I'm just living in the city and taking classes. It's definitely worth it, though, and my friends and I make our own college touch!" Women here also warn that "Barnard's facilities could use drastic remodeling. With the exception of a few recently renovated lecture spaces, the classrooms are in need of major technological and aesthetic updates. New resident halls need to be built because many of the existing buildings are too old."

Student Body

Barnard, like its hometown, is a magnet for the idiosyncratic. Explains one student, "New York is a place that allows people to be anyone they want to be. You can wear a zebra-striped bikini in the middle of winter on a snow covered street here and people would hardly look twice… [but] because we go to school in such an eclectic place, I don't think it's possible to describe a 'typical' Barnard student." Some here try all the same; they tell us that Barnard students are "driven, intelligent, cosmopolitan young women who come from every corner of the country and throughout the world, from different socioeconomic backgrounds, and varying life experiences." Because of a dual degree program with the Jewish Theological Seminary, "there are many Orthodox Jews here" who "typically socialize only with other Orthodox Jews." There's also a large, less insular Asian population. There are "many feminists and lesbians, too, but fewer than one might expect."

FINANCIAL AID: 212-854-2154 • E-MAIL: ADMISSIONS@BARNARD.EDU • WEBSITE: WWW.BARNARD.EDU

ADMISSIONS

Very important factors considered include: Essays, recommendations, secondary school record, standardized test scores. *Important factors considered include:* Class rank, extracurricular activities, talent/ability, volunteer work. *Other factors considered include:* Alumni/ae relation, character/personal qualities, geographical residence, interview, minority status, state residency, work experience. SAT Reasoning and SAT Subject Tests or ACT required. TOEFL required of all international applicants. High school diploma or equivalent is not required. *Academic units recommended:* 4 English, 3 math, 3 science (2 science lab), 3 foreign language, 3 history.

The Inside Word

As at many top colleges, early decision applications have increased at Barnard—although the admissions standards are virtually the same as for their regular admissions cycle. The college's admissions staff is open and accessible, which is not always the case at highly selective colleges with as long and impressive a tradition of excellence. The admissions committee's expectations are high, but their attitude reflects a true interest in who you are and what's on your mind. Students have a much better experience throughout the admissions process when treated with sincerity and respect—perhaps this is why Barnard continues to attract and enroll some of the best students in the country.

FINANCIAL AID

Students should submit: FAFSA, institution's own financial aid form, CSS/Financial Aid PROFILE, state aid form, noncustodial (divorced/separated) parents' statement, business/farm supplement, parents' individual, corporate, and/or partnership federal income tax returns. Regular filing deadline is 2/1. The Princeton Review suggests that all financial aid forms be submitted as soon as possible after 1/1. *Need-based scholarships/grants offered:* Pell, SEOG, state scholarships/grants, private scholarships, the school's own gift aid. *Loan aid offered:* FFEL Subsidized Stafford, FFEL Unsubsidized Stafford, FFEL PLUS, Federal Perkins, state loans, college/university loans from institutional funds. Applicants will be notified of awards on or about 4/1. Federal Work-study Program available. Institutional employment available. Off-campus job opportunities are excellent.

FROM THE ADMISSIONS OFFICE

"Barnard College, a small, distinguished liberal arts college for women that is affiliated with Columbia University, and located in the heart of New York City. The college enrolls women from all over the United States, Puerto Rico, and the Caribbean. More than thirty countries, including France, England, Hong Kong, and Greece, are also represented in the student body. Students pursue their academic studies in over 40 majors and are able to cross-register at Columbia University.

"Applicants for the fall 2006 entering class must submit scores from the SAT Reasoning Test and two SAT Subject Tests of their choice, or the ACT with the Writing component. For the old SAT I, students must submit results from three SAT Subject Tests (one of these must be Writing or Literature)."

SELECTIVITY

Admissions Rating	**97**
# of applicants	4,380
% of applicants accepted	27
% of acceptees attending	46
# accepting a place on wait list	931
% admitted from wait list	5
# of early decision applicants	167
% accepted early decision	41

FRESHMAN PROFILE

Range SAT Verbal	650-730
Average SAT Verbal	690
Range SAT Math	620-700
Average SAT Math	660
**TPR Projected Range SAT Writing*	*670-720*
Range ACT Composite	28-31
Average ACT Composite	30
Minimum Paper TOEFL	600
Minimum Computer Based TOEFL	250
Average HS GPA	3.93
% graduated top 10% of class	72
% graduated top 25% of class	93
% graduated top 50% of class	100

DEADLINES

Early decision application deadline	11/15
Early decision notification	12/15
Regular application deadline	1/1
Regular notification	4/1
Nonfall registration?	yes

APPLICANTS ALSO LOOK AT

AND OFTEN PREFER

Brown U., Columbia U.—Columbia College, Cornell ., U. of Chicago, Wellesley College

AND SOMETIMES PREFER

Boston College, Northwestern U., Tufts U., Vassar College

AND RARELY PREFER

Boston U., Brandeis U., Fordham U.,

FINANCIAL FACTS

Financial Aid Rating	**94**
Annual tuition	$27,064
Room & Board	$10,800
Books and supplies	$1,000
Required fees	$1,276
% frosh rec. need-based scholarship or grant aid	41
% UG rec. need-based scholarship or grant aid	38
% frosh rec. need-based self-help aid	44
% UG rec. need-based self-help aid	41
% frosh rec. any financial aid	55
% UG rec. any financial aid	56
Avg. frosh grant	$24,902
Avg. frosh loan	$3,382
Independent 529 member?	No

BATES COLLEGE

23 CAMPUS AVENUE, LINDHOLM HOUSE, LEWISTON, ME 04240 • ADMISSIONS: 207-786-6000 • FAX: 207-786-6025

CAMPUS LIFE

Quality of Life Rating	**87**
Fire Safety Rating	**60**
Type of school	private
Environment	town

STUDENTS

Total undergrad enrollment	1,743
% male/female	49/51
% from out of state	89
% from public high school	55
% live on campus	90
% African American	2
% Asian	4
% Caucasian	83
% Hispanic	3
% international	6
# of countries represented	72

SURVEY SAYS

Small classes
Great library
Students are friendly
Frats and sororities are unpopular or nonexistent
Lots of beer drinking

ACADEMICS

Academic Rating	**93**
Calendar	4-4-1
Student/faculty ratio	10:1
Professors interesting rating	88
Professors accessible rating	95
% professors teaching UG courses	100
% classes taught by TAs	0
Most common lab size	10-19 students
Most common regular class size	10-19 students

MOST POPULAR MAJORS

Economics
political science and government
psychology

STUDENTS SPEAK OUT

Academics

Those seeking "a high-paced rigorous academic college with a low-key, laid-back, and fun student body and campus life" should consider Maine's Bates College, a small liberal arts school that "focuses on students becoming critically and creatively thinking citizens of the world" through first-year seminars, mandatory senior projects, and a range of departmental, interdisciplinary, and student-designed majors. Undergrads report that departments in economics, biology, chemistry, religion, philosophy, and English are all "very good," with academics that "are challenging indeed, but not to the point where they interfere with all the other enjoyable aspects of life here." Professors are exemplars of exclusive, small-school pedagogy; they "are always willing to chat about classes, internship possibilities, future jobs, graduate school, further readings to be done and just about life." This is because "teaching is their main priority, and as a result they have an invested interest in their students that facilitates meaningful and personal relationships." Another adds student, "The feeling of community fostered at Bates is unparalleled. The students are truly welcoming, and the professors seem to really enjoy their jobs. The administration really gives the students a say in what happens at their college."

Life

"You can really develop into a complete person at Bates, through involvement in athletics, community service, and supportive relationships with faculty and staff. At Bates you don't have to choose between activities; you can do it all if you decide that is what you want." Adds another undergrad, "I can't think of a single person who isn't busy 24 hours a day, but by choice. People fill up their lives with things that are important to them, whether it be academics, sports, student government, political activism, outdoor activities, or clubs. Many people can't choose just one." "Student organizations are easy to become involved in here. For instance, anyone, regardless of experience or major, may try out for a play, and most likely will land a part." Students also love outdoor activities, especially "skiing at Sunday River in the winter," but also "varsity or club sports, which even those who aren't quite athletic enjoy. Bates really emphasizes an overall sort of health of mind and body." Parties "are quite common on the weekends, especially in the wood-frame houses that serve as one housing option." And while "there isn't much to do in the Lewiston-Auburn area," that hardly matters because "Bates does an excellent job of providing entertainment on the weekends for students." As one undergrad puts it, "Students rarely leave campus for the weekends; no one wants to leave because there is so much going on here!" When students feel they just have to get away, "Bates pays for buses to nearby cities like Freeport, Portland and Boston."

Student Body

Far from big-city pressures, Bates students can afford the luxury of being "laid-back and willing to take time to chat with friends over coffee, read the newspaper, go to plays, become engaged in the community and be active politically. Students value not only the academic experience they are offered at Bates, but take advantage of other fashions of learning." The student body includes "a lot of pseudo-hippies who cruise around campus pedaling their junkyard bikes with their Birkenstock-ed feet while toting their Nalgenes, who then spend their holidays in palatial mansions," and also has its share of "New Englander Ralph Lauren-wearing preppies." One student explains, "Bates combines hippies with Cape Cod kids, athletes with intellectuals. Everyone is a dork in his or her own way, and everyone's passionate about something ridiculous, and totally unpredictable." Students speculate that "Bates has one of the more vocal gay/bisexual populations out there," and proudly report that "straight students (even those who might come in with some prejudices in this regard) interact with them freely and openly. This is one instance where one really sees Bates overcoming prejudice."

FINANCIAL AID: 207-786-6096 • E-MAIL: ADMISSIONS@BATES.EDU • WEBSITE: WWW.BATES.EDU

ADMISSIONS

Very important factors considered include: Character/personal qualities, class rank, essays, extracurricular activities, interview, recommendations, secondary school record, talent/ability. *Other factors considered include:* Alumni/ae relation, geographical residence, minority status, standardized test scores, volunteer work, work experience. TOEFL required of all international applicants. High school diploma is required, and GED is not accepted. *Academic units required:* 4 English, 3 math, 2 science (1 science lab), 2 foreign language, 3 social studies, 3 history. *Academic units recommended:* 4 English, 4 math, 3 science (1 science lab), 4 foreign language, 3 social studies, 3 history.

The Inside Word

With or without test scores, the admissions office will weed out weak students who show little or no intellectual curiosity. Students with high SAT scores should always submit them. If you are curious about Bates, it is important to have solid grades in challenging courses; without them, you are not a viable candidate for admission. Tough competition for students between the college and its New England peers has intensified greatly over the past couple of years; Bates is holding its own. It remains a top choice among its applicants, and as a result selectivity is on the rise.

FINANCIAL AID

Students should submit: FAFSA, CSS/Financial Aid PROFILE, noncustodial (divorced/separated) parents' statement, business/farm supplement. Regular filing deadline is 2/1. The Princeton Review suggests that all financial aid forms be submitted as soon as possible after 1/1. *Need-based scholarships/grants offered:* Pell, SEOG, state scholarships/grants, private scholarships, the school's own gift aid. *Loan aid offered:* FFEL Subsidized Stafford, FFEL Unsubsidized Stafford, FFEL PLUS, Federal Perkins, state loans, alternative loans. Applicants will be notified of awards on or about 4/1. Federal Work-study Program available. Institutional employment available. Off-campus job opportunities are good.

FROM THE ADMISSIONS OFFICE

"Bates College is widely recognized as one of the finest liberal arts colleges in the nation. The curriculum and faculty challenge students to develop the essential skills of critical assessment, analysis, expression, aesthetic sensibility and independent thought. Founded by abolitionists in 1855, Bates graduates have always included men and women from diverse ethnic and religious backgrounds. Bates highly values its study abroad programs, unique calendar (4-4-1), and the many opportunities available for one-on-one collaboration with faculty through seminars, research, service-learning, and the capstone experience of senior thesis.

"Co-curricular life at Bates is rich; most students participate in club or varsity sports; many participate in performing arts; and almost all students participate in one of more than 90 student-run clubs and organizations. About 40 percent of students participate in career internships, and more than two-thirds of alumni enroll in graduate study within 10 years.

"The Bates College admissions staff reads applications very carefully; the high school record and the quality of writing are of particular importance. Applicants are strongly encouraged to have a personal interview, either on campus or with an alumni representative. Students who choose not to interview may place themselves at a disadvantage in the selection process. Bates offers tours, interviews and information sessions throughout the summer and fall. Drop-ins are welcome for tours and information sessions. Please call ahead to schedule an interview.

"At Bates, the submission of standardized testing (the SAT, SAT Subject Tests, and the ACT) is not required for admission."

SELECTIVITY

Admissions Rating	**96**
# of applicants	4,098
% of applicants accepted	30
% of acceptees attending	38
# accepting a place on wait list	1,055
% admitted from wait list	10
# of early decision applicants	216
% accepted early decision	54

FRESHMAN PROFILE

Range SAT Verbal	630-710
Average SAT Verbal	670
Range SAT Math	640-710
Average SAT Math	672
**TPR Projected Range SAT Writing*	*650-700*
Minimum Paper TOEFL	200
Minimum Computer Based TOEFL	40
% graduated top 10% of class	65
% graduated top 25% of class	92
% graduated top 50% of class	100

DEADLINES

Early decision application deadline	11/15
Early decision notification	12/20
Regular application deadline	1/1
Regular notification	4/1
Nonfall registration?	yes

APPLICANTS ALSO LOOK AT

AND OFTEN PREFER
Amherst College
Dartmouth College
Middlebury College

AND SOMETIMES PREFER
Bowdoin College
Brown University
Colby College

AND RARELY PREFER
Connecticut College
Hamilton College
Trinity College (CT)

FINANCIAL FACTS

Financial Aid Rating	**93**
Comprehensive fee	$39,900
Books and supplies	$1,750
% frosh rec. need-based scholarship or grant aid	40
% UG rec. need-based scholarship or grant aid	40
% frosh rec. need-based self-help aid	37
% UG rec. need-based self-help aid	39
% frosh rec. any financial aid	40
% UG rec. any financial aid	40
Avg. frosh grant	$21,983
Avg. frosh loan	$3,230
Independent 529 member?	No

Baylor University

One Bear Place #97056, Waco, TX 76798-7056 • Admissions: 254-710-3435 • Fax: 254-710-3436

CAMPUS LIFE

Quality of Life Rating	**72**
Fire Safety Rating	**62**
Type of school	private
Affiliation	Baptist
Environment	city

STUDENTS

Total undergrad enrollment	11,521
% male/female	42/58
% from out of state	16
% live on campus	34
% in (# of) fraternities	15 (18)
% in (# of) sororities	17 (15)
% African American	7
% Asian	6
% Caucasian	74
% Hispanic	8
% Native American	1
% international	1
# of countries represented	90

SURVEY SAYS

Small classes
Lab facilities are great
Great computer facilities
Great library
Athletic facilities are great
Intramural sports are popular
Frats and sororities dominate social scene

ACADEMICS

Academic Rating	**79**
Calendar	semester
Student/faculty ratio	16:1
Professors interesting rating	80
Professors accessible rating	82
% professors teaching UG courses	90
% classes taught by TAs	6
Most common lab size	20-29 students
Most common regular class size	20-29 students

MOST POPULAR MAJORS

Biology/biological sciences
Business administration/management
psychology

STUDENTS SPEAK OUT

Academics

"Even though we're in the Big Twelve, you don't feel like just a number here because people really reach out and try to make you feel welcome," writes one of the 11,000-plus undergraduates at Baylor University, the nation's biggest and most prominent Baptist academic institution. "Personal attention" is one of the surprise perks of attending this large school; less surprising, but no less welcome, is Baylor's emphasis on Christian values, which "are instilled in almost every class, but in a way that doesn't pressure kids to be religious. It's pretty effective too, presenting one path to kids and letting them choose on their own without forcing anything on them." The resulting atmosphere is one in which "most people on campus take spirituality seriously, whatever their beliefs or lack thereof. It creates an environment where people are much more free to explore their own beliefs than at many universities that lack a religious affiliation, because faith is something that is so openly and fully discussed." Undergrads also praise Baylor's "amazing facilities in the classrooms and labs," including "top-of-the-line technology and wireless connections." Those facilities are only bound to get better, as the school is in the midst of "an ambitious plan that will take it into the top tier of schools by 2012." Outstanding programs here include premedical and pre-dental offerings, nursing, engineering, business, pre-law, and the seminary.

Life

Usually by choice but always by school regulation, religion is central to life at Baylor University. "You have to attend chapel for two semesters twice a week, and freshmen have to go to chapel Fridays, which is a Bible study," students explain. The curriculum also includes two required religion courses. Many students seek more faith-related activity, participating in "ministry, community outreach and service, and involvement within and outside of the university." There are plenty of other things for students to do here besides explore their faith; in fact, "students can find something to be involved in no matter what their interests. There is an organization for everyone, from those interested in sororities and fraternities to those interested in video games or anime." This being Texas, "sports are huge," with the school boasting strong teams in tennis, women's basketball, and track. The football team, unfortunately, "is not highly skilled," to the great vexation of many. Also, "A lot of students like to party, whether or not school policy permits any drinking or use of drugs," and Baylor's popular Greek scene is happy to accommodate them. Students love Baylor's "terrific campus," with "its great overall layout and beautiful landscaping and architecture." The campus is so homey, in fact, that the academic community tends to get isolated here, resulting in an effect known as the "Baylor Bubble." One student explains, "We close ourselves off from the rest of Waco. A block in any direction from campus will take you to some of the poorest areas in town."

Student Body

"There are generally two types of students at Baylor," students here tell us, because "the fact that Baylor is a pricey private school attracts students that come from wealthy families; these students wear trendy clothes and drive expensive cars. However, Baylor is also a Christian university, and that attracts students who are interested in growing in the Lord while they are working toward earning a degree." While "there are not many other types of students," the student body does include "the occasional non-Christian student. We wonder why they chose Baylor. They fit in okay, but definitely stick out at a university that upholds Christianity in the classroom, in the dorms, and pretty much all other areas." Traditionally, "Baylor students tend to be conservative, socially conscious, and hard-working. They are also self-confident and friendly, with friendliness being one of Baylor's biggest strengths."

FINANCIAL AID: 254-710-2611 • E-MAIL: ADMISSIONS_SERV_OFFICE@BAYLOR.EDU • WEBSITE: WWW.BAYLOR.EDU

ADMISSIONS

Very important factors considered include: Class rank, secondary school record, standardized test scores. *Other factors considered include:* Alumni/ae relation, character/personal qualities, essays, extracurricular activities, geographical residence, interview, recommendations, religious affiliation/commitment, talent/ability, volunteer work. SAT Reasoning or ACT required. TOEFL required of all international applicants. High school diploma is required, and GED is accepted. *Academic units required:* 4 English, 3 math, 2 science (2 science lab), 2 foreign language, 1 social studies, 1 history, 3 academic electives.

The Inside Word

A largely self-selected applicant pool and the need for a fairly large freshman class each year makes for a high admit rate. If your values reflect those of the community at Baylor, the chances are you will be offered admission.

FINANCIAL AID

Students should submit: FAFSA. The Princeton Review suggests that all financial aid forms be submitted as soon as possible after 1/1. *Need-based scholarships/grants offered:* Pell, SEOG, state scholarships/grants, the school's own gift aid. *Loan aid offered:* FFEL Subsidized Stafford, FFEL Unsubsidized Stafford, FFEL PLUS, Federal Perkins, Federal Nursing, state loans, college/university loans from institutional funds, alternative lender. Applicants will be notified of awards on a rolling basis beginning on or about 3/1. Off-campus job opportunities are excellent.

FROM THE ADMISSIONS OFFICE

"Baylor University is a Christian university in the Baptist tradition and is affiliated with the Baptist General Convention of Texas. As the oldest institution of higher learning in the state, Baylor's founders sought to establish a college dedicated to Christian principles, superior academics, and a shared sense of community. Students come from all 50 states and some 90 foreign countries. Baylor's nationally recognized academic divisions offer 141 undergraduate degree programs, 71 master's degree programs, and 20 doctoral degree programs. Baylor ranks in the top 15 percent of colleges and universities participating in the National Merit Scholarship program. Baylor is one of the select 11 percent of U.S. colleges and universities with a Phi Beta Kappa chapter. The Templeton Foundation repeatedly names Baylor as one of America's top character-building colleges. Baylor's undergraduate programs emphasize the central importance of vocation (calling) and service in students' lives, helping them explore their value and role in society. Baylor is a charter member of the Independent 529 Tuition Plan, a prepaid college tuition plan. Baylor's tuition is one of the lowest of any major private university in the Southwest and one of the least expensive in the nation. Approximately 75 percent of Baylor students receive student financial assistance. The 508-acre main campus adjoins the Brazos River near downtown Waco, a Central Texas city of 110,000 people. By 2012, Baylor intends to enter the top tier of American universities while reaffirming its distinctive Christian mission. This bold 10-year Vision, Baylor 2012, is well underway benefiting students entering Baylor now.

"Baylor University requires applicants for admission into the fall 2006 freshman class to take the new version of the SAT or the ACT with the Writing section. Students may also choose to submit scores from the old version of the SAT or ACT (prior to March 2005) as their best scores (old/new) will be used when making admissions decisions."

SELECTIVITY

Admissions Rating	**83**
# of applicants	10,971
% of applicants accepted	72
% of acceptees attending	35

FRESHMAN PROFILE

Range SAT Verbal	530-640
Average SAT Verbal	589
Range SAT Math	550-650
Average SAT Math	601
**TPR Projected Range SAT Writing*	*580-660*
Range ACT Composite	22-27
Average ACT Composite	25
Minimum Paper TOEFL	540
Minimum Computer Based TOEFL	207
% graduated top 10% of class	39
% graduated top 25% of class	67
% graduated top 50% of class	91

DEADLINES

Regular notification	rolling
Nonfall registration?	yes

APPLICANTS ALSO LOOK AT

AND OFTEN PREFER
Texas A&M University—College Station
Texas Christian University
The University of Texas—Austin

AND SOMETIMES PREFER
Southern Methodist University
Texas Tech University
Trinity University

AND RARELY PREFER
Pepperdine University
Tulane University
Vanderbilt University

FINANCIAL FACTS

Financial Aid Rating	**70**
Annual tuition	$19,050
Room & Board	$6,485
Books and supplies	$1,382
Required fees	$2,020
% frosh rec. need-based scholarship or grant aid	56
% UG rec. need-based scholarship or grant aid	46
% frosh rec. need-based self-help aid	46
% UG rec. need-based self-help aid	38
% frosh rec. any financial aid	94
% UG rec. any financial aid	90
Avg. frosh grant	$10,128
Avg. frosh loan	$6,553
Independent 529 member?	Yes

BELLARMINE UNIVERSITY

2001 NEWBURG ROAD, LOUISVILLE, KY 40205 • ADMISSIONS: 502-452-8131 • FAX: 502-452-8002

CAMPUS LIFE

Quality of Life Rating	**78**
Fire Safety Rating	**60**
Type of school	private
Affiliation	Roman Catholic
Environment	village

STUDENTS

% from out of state	17
% from public high school	50
% live on campus	36
% in (# of) fraternities	2 (1)
% in (# of) sororities	2 (1)

SURVEY SAYS

Small classes
Great library
Students are friendly
Students love Louisville, KY
Great off-campus food
Lots of beer drinking
(Almost) everyone smokes

ACADEMICS

Academic Rating	**80**
Calendar	semester
Student/faculty ratio	13:1
Professors interesting rating	89
Professors accessible rating	88
% professors teaching UG courses	100
% classes taught by TAs	0
Most common regular class size	20-29 students

STUDENTS SPEAK OUT

Academics

Bellarmine University, "a small, liberal arts college, designed to cater to the needs of its students," provides its predominantly Catholic, pre-professional student body with "small classes, a friendly staff, and students who all contribute to the university's unique atmosphere." Students brag about "excellent programs in accounting, education, and nursing," delivered through classes "small enough that you get to personally know your professors and fellow classmates." Although "academically, Bellarmine is challenging," most here are confident that "with the tutoring services and the willingness to help that our professors have, there is no reason one shouldn't succeed." Professors earn high grades here because they are "enthusiastic about their field, which truly sets a positive learning atmosphere in the classroom," and are also "most willing to help at any time." Students also appreciate the fact that all "classes are taught by professors; TAs are basically just gophers here." They are less complimentary of the administration, griping that it "is completely inaccessible. It is like pulling teeth to get anything done. It seems as if we have to break down a brick wall to even get to the red tape."

Life

"There is just a laid-back atmosphere" at Bellarmine, where a tame Greek scene and a large percentage of students who go home each weekend all contribute to the quiet. Although the entire campus was once dry, beginning in the 2004–2005 academic year, residential students who are of legal drinking age may opt to live in housing that permits limited alcohol consumption. Most feel that "the school could work harder at trying to keep students here for the weekends" by "adding more social activities at school." Fortunately hometown Louisville makes up for the campus's shortcomings. According to those who live here, "Louisville is a great town. We go to bars to play pool and to clubs to dance and let loose. There are a lot of parks to go to when the weather is nice, and the art scene downtown is alive with new galleries. The city has lots of good restaurants, too. Bardstown Road is the place to go; there are tons of cool shops, bars, and clubs, all within walking distance." And, of course, "There's always [the Kentucky] Derby, the greatest day in Louisville, and the month before Derby there is always a festival going on. And by the way, we always get out of school before Derby (first Saturday in May), so that is definitely a plus!" For those few college students who relish quiet, "Dorm life is almost the best part of school. We like to watch movies or just sit around in the lobby or lounge and talk to the people passing by." A few undergrads complain about the school's strict social regulations: "They should allow alcohol on campus, allow 24-hour visitation in the dorms, and basically allow adult students to make grown-up decisions."

Student Body

Bellarmine draws a predominantly local crowd. "I think that the student body is three-quarters white, upper-middle-class students from [within] an hour-and-a-half radius of Louisville," explains one student. Adds another, "Our typical student went to Assumption, Sacred Heart, St. X, or Trinity. They are people who have gone to Catholic schools all of their lives and have lived in Louisville all of their lives. They come to Bellarmine and attend school with all of their old high school classmates. Most drive either a Volvo or a BMW. They are very rich, and they know it." Recent changes in the curriculum have helped the student body shed some of its "cookie-cutter" image; as one told us, "There are many 'atypical' students due to Louisville's growing creative/art movement. They fit into Bellarmine's environment easily but are sometimes looked down upon for not participating in university functions." There are also "tons more girls than guys—about [2:1] ratio the last I heard."

FINANCIAL AID: 502-452-8124 • E-MAIL: ADMISSIONS@BELLARMINE.EDU • WEBSITE: WWW.BELLARMINE.EDU

ADMISSIONS

Very important factors considered include: Essays, recommendations, secondary school record, standardized test scores. *Important factors considered include:* Character/personal qualities. *Other factors considered include:* Alumni/ae relation, class rank, extracurricular activities, interview, talent/ability, volunteer work, work experience. SAT Reasoning or ACT required. TOEFL required of all international applicants. High school diploma is required, and GED is accepted. *Academic units required:* 4 English, 3 math, 2 science, 2 social studies. *Academic units recommended:* 4 math, 3 science, 2 foreign language.

The Inside Word

Bellarmine's admissions process follows the typical small liberal arts college approach fairly closely—solid grades, test scores, and course selection from high school combined with a broad complement of extracurriculars generally will add up to acceptance. The applicant pool is very regional here; students who hail from outside the university's normal markets may benefit from the appeal that their relative scarcity brings to their candidacies.

FINANCIAL AID

Students should submit: FAFSA. The Princeton Review suggests that all financial aid forms be submitted as soon as possible after 1/1. *Need-based scholarships/grants offered:* Pell, SEOG, state scholarships/grants, the school's own gift aid. *Loan aid offered:* FFEL Subsidized Stafford, FFEL Unsubsidized Stafford, FFEL PLUS, Federal Perkins, college/university loans from institutional funds. Applicants will be notified of awards on or about 4/1. Federal Work-study Program available. Institutional employment available. Off-campus job opportunities are excellent.

FROM THE ADMISSIONS OFFICE

"Bellarmine University is known for providing students with outstanding personal attention in the classroom. For many out-of-town students, however, Bellarmine's location makes the difference. Just five miles from downtown Louisville, Bellarmine is at the heart of the cultural and recreational offerings of the nation's sixteenth largest city. The 135-acre campus is set in a safe, historic neighborhood that features an executive golf course, indoor and outdoor tennis courts, a fitness center, sand volleyball court, and athletic fields.

"Recent additions to the campus reflect the university's academic emphasis on a liberal arts core curriculum surrounded by competitive graduate and professional schools. The state-of-the-art Norton Health Sciences Center and a Service Learning Clinic offer real-life, hands-on experience for nursing and physical therapy students, while the campus library houses the largest collection of works by and about internationally-renowned author and Trappist monk Thomas Merton.

"With over 50 clubs and organizations on campus and 18 NCAA Division II athletic teams, Bellarmine offers a variety of recreational opportunities for all students. Beginning in 2004–2005 Bellarmine will field a Division I men's lacrosse team. Countless internships and study abroad programs offer additional opportunities for students to expand their horizons outside the classroom.

"Students who live on campus will also find a Bellarmine difference, namely the living arrangements. From the traditional college residence hall layout to apartment-style and suite living arrangements, students have many housing options. All residence halls offer amenities such as laundry facilities, computer labs, study rooms, and air conditioning.

"As of this book's publication, Bellarmine University did not have information available about their policy regarding the new SAT."

SELECTIVITY

Admissions Rating	**79**
# of applicants	1,485
% of applicants accepted	82
% of acceptees attending	37

FRESHMAN PROFILE

Range SAT Verbal	480-620
Average SAT Verbal	576
Range SAT Math	480-610
Average SAT Math	576
**TPR Projected Range SAT Writing*	*540-650*
Range ACT Composite	21-26
Average ACT Composite	24
Minimum Paper TOEFL	550
Minimum Computer Based TOEFL	213
Average HS GPA	3.51
% graduated top 10% of class	18
% graduated top 25% of class	51
% graduated top 50% of class	81

DEADLINES

Regular application deadline	8/15
Regular notification	rolling
Nonfall registration?	yes

APPLICANTS ALSO LOOK AT AND OFTEN PREFER

Butler University
Centre College
Transylvania University
University of Dayton
Xavier University (OH)

AND SOMETIMES PREFER

University of Kentucky
University of Louisville
Western Kentucky University

AND RARELY PREFER

Spalding University

FINANCIAL FACTS

Financial Aid Rating	**60**
Annual tuition	$17,820
Room & Board	$5,690
Books and supplies	$750
Required fees	$670
Avg. frosh grant	$6,200
Avg. frosh loan	$2,600
Independent 529 member?	No

BELOIT COLLEGE

700 College Street, Beloit, WI 53511 • Admissions: 608-363-2500 • Fax: 608-363-2075

CAMPUS LIFE

Quality of Life Rating	**78**
Fire Safety Rating	**60**
Type of school	private
Environment	metropolis

STUDENTS

Total undergrad enrollment	1,301
% male/female	41/59
% from out of state	80
% from public high school	80
% live on campus	93
% in (# of) fraternities	15 (3)
% in (# of) sororities	5 (2)
% African American	3
% Asian	3
% Caucasian	78
% Hispanic	3
% international	5
# of countries represented	54

SURVEY SAYS

Small classes
Students are friendly
Campus feels safe
Low cost of living
Lots of beer drinking

ACADEMICS

Academic Rating	**89**
Calendar	semester
Student/faculty ratio	11:1
Professors interesting rating	92
Professors accessible rating	91
% professors teaching UG courses	100
% classes taught by TAs	0
Most common regular class size	10-19 students

MOST POPULAR MAJORS

Anthropology
creative writing
psychology

STUDENTS SPEAK OUT

Academics

"Beloit seriously is about inventing yourself," writes one student, echoing the unofficial motto of this small, southern Wisconsin liberal arts school. "Come to this school if you have initiative and motivation to do creative things of your own design. If you build it . . . they will pay for it to be done. I love it here." Agrees another undergrad, "Beloit College is a bombardment of opportunities, and if you are lucky and smart, you will take the opportunities that are best for you as a person and academically." Students especially love the school's "multidisciplinary approach, which allows you to view events from the perspectives of different disciplines." They also appreciate the little things, from the academic advising to the uncommon sense of community that students, faculty, and administrators share. ("Last weekend, all sophomores and a number of professors and administrators were treated to a weekend away from campus at a resort," reports a typical student.) Students also approvingly declare, "Beloit College runs based on the desires of the student body. Money is allotted to groups by student funding boards so that there isn't any discrepancy between the interests of the students and college bureaucracy about distribution of funds." Profs here, by all accounts, "are amazing. They will all take the time to talk to anybody about anything. They all really care about making the students interested in the material. Seriously."

Life

Explains one student, "If you're okay with staying on campus all the time, Beloit's your school. If seeing the same places and the same people day after day after day bothers you, you might want to think over your decision to apply here." Given the situation, it's fortunate that "Beloit students are resourceful. Since there's not much to do in town, we learn to entertain ourselves and each other. We love theme parties ('Come As Another Beloit Student,' 'Dress Like Your Celebrity Look-Alike'), and ultimate Frisbee has a cult-like participation and following." "Clubs and student organizations thrive on this campus," and "besides the many student clubs, there are establishments such as the Coughy-Haus (which serves alcohol, allows smoking, and features loud bands) and the Java Joint (quiet music, no smoking, no alcohol, good for studying or playing board games) that one can go to for fun." There are also "sporting events, theater choir and band performances, intramurals, talks, lectures, discussions, Greek-sponsored events, all-campus activities, and movies at the cinema for additional entertainment. There's definitely always something going on at Beloit College." Students appreciate the school alcohol policy, which is "to treat us like adults unless we give them a reason to do differently." Those with cars occasionally escape to "Rockford and Janesville, which are 20 minutes away. Also, Milwaukee, Madison, and Chicago are all within 90 minutes, so there's always chances for breaking out of the bubble."

Student Body

Undergraduates insist, "There really is no 'typical student' at Beloit. People here are free to be whomever they want to be and definitely exercise that freedom." Most would concede, however, that the majority is a little on the nerdy side: "Beloit College is like high school, only now the misfits are the popular cliques, and they exclude people that seem too normal," notes one student. Many here are "always overly involved. I don't know anyone on campus that isn't involved in more than one club, sport, philanthropy, or Greek organization." The few conservative students warn, "A Beloit student will open his arms and celebrate just about any kind of person so long as that person is a liberal passionate activist who says he is open-minded. Oh yeah, and dreadlocks help." Beloit is also home to "a large, vocal international population [that] provides a worldview not available at most schools."

FINANCIAL AID: 608-363-2500 • E-MAIL: ADMISS@BELOIT.EDU • WEBSITE: WWW.BELOIT.EDU

ADMISSIONS

Very important factors considered include: Essays, recommendations, secondary school record. *Important factors considered include:* Class rank, interview, standardized test scores. *Other factors considered include:* Alumni/ae relation, character/personal qualities, extracurricular activities, talent/ability, volunteer work, work experience. SAT Reasoning or ACT required. TOEFL required of all international applicants. High school diploma is required, and GED is accepted. *Academic units recommended:* 4 English, 4 math, 3 science, 2 foreign language, 4 social studies, 4 history.

The Inside Word

Beloit expects to find evidence of intellectual curiosity and a concern for the common good in successful candidates. There is tough competition for students among colleges in the Midwest, which gives those Beloit applicants who don't show consistent strength a bit of a break.

FINANCIAL AID

Students should submit: FAFSA, institution's own financial aid form, state aid form, CSS/Financial Aid PROFILE accepted. Regular filing deadline is 3/1. The Princeton Review suggests that all financial aid forms be submitted as soon as possible after 1/1. *Need-based scholarships/grants offered:* Pell, SEOG, state scholarships/grants, private scholarships, the school's own gift aid. *Loan aid offered:* FFEL Subsidized Stafford, FFEL Unsubsidized Stafford, FFEL PLUS, Federal Perkins, college/university loans from institutional funds. Applicants will be notified of awards on a rolling basis beginning on or about 4/1. Federal Work-study Program available. Institutional employment available. Off-campus job opportunities are fair.

FROM THE ADMISSIONS OFFICE

"While Beloit students clearly understand the connection between college and career, they are more apt to value learning for its own sake than for the competitive advantage that it will afford them in the workplace. As a result, Beloit students adhere strongly to the concept that an educational institution, in order to be true to its own nature, must imply and provide a context in which a free exchange of ideas can take place. This precept is embodied in the mentoring relationship that takes place between professor and student and the dynamic, participatory nature of the classroom experience.

"Beloit College requires that all students applying for the fall of 2006 submit scores from the SAT or ACT. Applicants who have taken the old version of the SAT or ACT may submit those scores and are not required to take the new SAT or ACT with the Writing section."

SELECTIVITY

Admissions Rating	**89**
# of applicants	1,875
% of applicants accepted	70
% of acceptees attending	25
# accepting a place on wait list	41
% admitted from wait list	10

FRESHMAN PROFILE

Range SAT Verbal	590-700
Average SAT Verbal	640
Range SAT Math	570-660
Average SAT Math	610
**TPR Projected Range SAT Writing*	*620-700*
Range ACT Composite	24-29
Average ACT Composite	27
Minimum Paper TOEFL	525
Minimum Computer Based TOEFL	197
Average HS GPA	3.46
% graduated top 10% of class	36
% graduated top 25% of class	64
% graduated top 50% of class	92

DEADLINES

Regular notification	rolling
Nonfall registration?	yes

APPLICANTS ALSO LOOK AT

AND OFTEN PREFER

Carleton College
Colorado College
Kenyon College
Northwestern University
Oberlin College

AND SOMETIMES PREFER

Grinnell College
Lawrence University
Macalester College

AND RARELY PREFER

Gustavus Adolphus College
Lewis & Clark College
Ripon College
University of Illinois at Urbana-Champaign

FINANCIAL FACTS

Financial Aid Rating	**99**
Annual tuition	$26,664
Room & Board	$5,924
Books and supplies	$800
Required fees	$220
% frosh rec. need-based scholarship or grant aid	89
% UG rec. need-based scholarship or grant aid	68
% frosh rec. need-based self-help aid	77
% UG rec. need-based self-help aid	67
% frosh rec. any financial aid	94
% UG rec. any financial aid	93
Avg. frosh grant	$12,956
Avg. frosh loan	$2,920
Independent 529 member?	No

BENNINGTON COLLEGE

OFFICE OF ADMISSIONS AND FINANCIAL AID, BENNINGTON, VT 05201 • ADMISSIONS: 800-833-6845 • FAX: 802-440-4320

CAMPUS LIFE

Quality of Life Rating	**69**
Fire Safety Rating	**86**
Type of school	private
Environment	village

STUDENTS

Total undergrad enrollment	621
% male/female	34/66
% from out of state	96
% live on campus	97
% African American	1
% Asian	2
% Caucasian	86
% Hispanic	3
% international	4
# of countries represented	18

SURVEY SAYS

Small classes
Students aren't religious
Campus feels safe
Intercollegiate sports are unpopular or nonexistent
Frats and sororities are unpopular or nonexistent
Theater is popular
(Almost) everyone smokes

ACADEMICS

Academic Rating	**87**
Calendar	15-week fall and spring terms, 7-week winter work term
Student/faculty ratio	8:1
Professors interesting rating	84
Professors accessible rating	76
% professors teaching UG courses	100
% classes taught by TAs	2
Most common lab size	10-19 students
Most common regular class size	10-19 students

MOST POPULAR MAJORS

English language and literature
social sciences
visual and performing arts

STUDENTS SPEAK OUT

Academics

Bennington College has long been committed to "honoring individuality and the power to create your own education." Students at this unconventional school "don't ever officially declare majors," nor do they take final exams. "We do final projects instead," explained one undergrad. "I got to do a project imitating the style of my favorite poet and a psychological study about student drinking on campus. I feel so involved with my classes!" Instead of grades, most students receive written evaluations of their work, however, all students have the option to receive grades in addition. Bennington's curriculum "is really dependent on the makeup of the faculty" because "there are not a lot of professors" and also because "the teachers 'teach what keeps them up at night.'" Profs here are "brilliant, amazing people who deeply care about their students;" undergrads also praise the Field Work Term ("a great program of going out for eight weeks to intern or work in your field or a field that you're interested in learning more about"). The visual arts program is one of the school's undisputed strengths. The VAPA (Visual and Performing Arts) center is "open 24/7, and every studio, work space, or lab is open to everyone." Music and language arts instruction also receive praise; the sciences, on the other hand, are considered relatively weak. Many here worry that the student body is growing too rapidly ("We have 200 more students here this year than we had last year") without a proportionate increase in the faculty. "We need more professors," writes a typical student. "If the school is going to continue to accept more students, the college is going to change. Normalization is beginning, and that's sad."

Life

Bennington's "small and secluded" campus is "absolutely beautiful. Imagine the most beautiful haven you have ever been to; that is Bennington in early May. Imagine Norman Rockwell paintings; that is our winter and fall." Students enjoy the luxury of living in actual houses rather than dormitories. "We have both colonial-style houses built in the 1930s and modern houses that were built in 2001 and were featured in architecture magazines," writes one student. All the same, because of the school's remote location, "most people have a really hard time adjusting to life, myself included. If you stick it out, it gets better. There's a positive side to it: if I were in a larger city I would not be devoting as much time to my academics, which is the reason I came here." Bennington is "very isolated from the town, so there are a lot of on-campus events to keep one interested." Students mention "people screening independent films, stand-up comedy shows, and bands playing" as entertainment options. And "students are very supportive about attending others' performances." Undergrads also "tend to have small parties in their rooms, and every weekend, a house always throws a party." Because "constantly being on campus can get claustrophobic," "people with cars try to leave for the weekend." Many head to the Williams College campus, about a half-hour drive to the south.

Student Body

Bennington students range from "vegan, environmentally conscious punks that pretend to be hippies to a significant group of students extremely passionate about their work." The tiny student body "gets oppressive at times, but is very comforting at others. You can say 'I was with Patrick,' and everyone will know who you are talking about." Students tend to subdivide into cliques: "I have a small but very lovable group of friends; that's the tendency here, to form cliques of friends . . . it's just the nature of a small school like this," explains one student. The atmosphere here is politically and socially liberal; "sexuality, religion, social class—none of that matters. I swear, it's like a hippie commune utopia or at least another dimension from *The Matrix*," is how one student describes it.

FINANCIAL AID: 802-440-4325 • E-MAIL: ADMISSIONS@BENNINGTON.EDU • WEBSITE: WWW.BENNINGTON.EDU

ADMISSIONS

Very important factors considered include: Character/personal qualities, class rank, essays, interview, recommendations, secondary school record, standardized test scores, talent/ability, volunteer work. *Important factors considered include:* Extracurricular activities. *Other factors considered include:* Alumni/ae relation, minority status, work experience. SAT Reasoning or ACT required. SAT Subject Tests recommended. TOEFL required of all international applicants. High school diploma is required, and GED is accepted. *Academic units recommended:* 4 English, 3 math, 3 science, 3 foreign language, 3 social studies.

The Inside Word

For intellectually curious students Bennington can be a godsend, but for those who lack self-motivation it can represent a sidetracking of progress toward a degree. Admissions standards remain rigorous, and enrollment is on an upswing. Candidates will encounter a thorough review process that places great emphasis on matchmaking, which means that strong essays and solid interviews are a must. Intellectual types whose high school grades are inconsistent with their potential will find an opportunity for forgiveness if they can write well and demonstrate self-awareness and a capacity to thrive in the college's self-driven environment. Minority students are rarities in the applicant pool and thus enjoy "most-favored candidate" status—provided they fit Bennington's profile.

FINANCIAL AID

Students should submit: FAFSA, institution's own financial aid form, CSS/Financial Aid PROFILE, noncustodial (divorced/separated) parents' statement, parent and student federal tax returns and W-2 forms. CSS/Financial Aid PROFILE for early decision applicants only. Regular filing deadline is 2/15. The Princeton Review suggests that all financial aid forms be submitted as soon as possible after 1/1. *Need-based scholarships/grants offered:* Pell, SEOG, state scholarships/grants, private scholarships, the school's own gift aid. *Loan aid offered:* FFEL Subsidized Stafford, FFEL Unsubsidized Stafford, FFEL PLUS, college/university loans from institutional funds. College/university loans from institutional fund for international students only. Applicants will be notified of awards on or about 4/1. Federal Work-study Program available. Institutional employment available. Off-campus job opportunities are good.

FROM THE ADMISSIONS OFFICE

"The educational philosophy of Bennington is rooted in an abiding faith in the talent, imagination, and responsibility of the individual; thus, the principle of learning by practice underlies every major feature of a Bennington education. We believe that a college education should not merely provide preparation for graduate school or a career, but should be an experience valuable in itself and the model for lifelong learning. Faculty, staff, and students at Bennington work together in a collaborative environment based upon respect for each other and the power of ideas to make a difference in the world. We are looking for intellectually curious students who have a passion for learning, are willing to take risks, and are open to making connections.

"Scores from either the new SAT Reasoning Test or the "old" SAT (administered prior to March 2005) are required from applicants for fall 2006. Students are permitted to substitute the ACT in lieu of the SAT. SAT Subject Tests are recommended, but not required."

SELECTIVITY

Admissions Rating	**87**
# of applicants	842
% of applicants accepted	73
% of acceptees attending	33
# of early decision applicants	39
% accepted early decision	71

FRESHMAN PROFILE

Range SAT Verbal	580-690
Average SAT Verbal	640
Range SAT Math	510-610
Average SAT Math	560
**TPR Projected Range SAT Writing*	*620-690*
Range ACT Composite	23-27
Average ACT Composite	25
Minimum Paper TOEFL	550
Minimum Computer Based TOEFL	213
Average HS GPA	3.29
% graduated top 10% of class	23
% graduated top 25% of class	61
% graduated top 50% of class	86

DEADLINES

Early decision application deadline	11/15
Early decision notification	12/1
Regular application deadline	1/1
Regular notification	4/1
Nonfall registration?	yes

APPLICANTS ALSO LOOK AT

AND OFTEN PREFER

Brown University
Smith College
Wesleyan University

AND SOMETIMES PREFER

Bard College
Hampshire College
New York University
Sarah Lawrence College

AND RARELY PREFER

Marlboro College
Skidmore College

FINANCIAL FACTS

Financial Aid Rating	**70**
Annual tuition	$30,270
Room & Board	$7,710
Books and supplies	$800
Required fees	$800
% frosh rec. need-based scholarship or grant aid	64
% UG rec. need-based scholarship or grant aid	65
% frosh rec. need-based self-help aid	62
% UG rec. need-based self-help aid	63
% frosh rec. any financial aid	72
% UG rec. any financial aid	79
Avg. frosh grant	$19,163
Avg. frosh loan	$2,980
Independent 529 member?	No

BENTLEY COLLEGE

175 FOREST STREET, WALTHAM, MA 02452-4705 • ADMISSIONS: 781-891-2244 • FAX: 781-891-3414

CAMPUS LIFE

Quality of Life Rating	**87**
Fire Safety Rating	**86**
Type of school	private
Environment	city

STUDENTS

Total undergrad enrollment	4,250
% male/female	58/42
% from out of state	45
% from public high school	71
% live on campus	80
% African American	4
% Asian	7
% Caucasian	69
% Hispanic	4
% international	8
# of countries represented	78

SURVEY SAYS

Small classes
Great computer facilities
Great library
Campus feels safe
Lots of beer drinking
Hard liquor is popular

ACADEMICS

Academic Rating	**83**
Calendar	semester
Student/faculty ratio	13:1
Professors interesting rating	79
Professors accessible rating	84
% professors teaching UG courses	100
% classes taught by TAs	0
Most common regular class size	20-29 students

MOST POPULAR MAJORS

Business administration/management
finance
marketing/marketing management

STUDENTS SPEAK OUT

Academics

Bentley College, a business-focused school just outside Boston, "is all about making sure you have a career when you graduate, not just a job. They don't teach you useless textbook information just to impress people with how much you know. Most of what you learn is something that will help you advance, either as a business professional or as a person." Students agree that this practical approach is what makes Bentley special. One student writes, "It's like what my marketing professor taught me, 'Mass customization: You get what you need.' This school focuses on knowledge to take with you in life and gives you limitless options as to where you want it to go." Bentley professors are "really good in terms of teaching and [providing] assistance outside the classroom" and they make sure there is "a good balance between class work and homework." As one student puts it, "The overall academic environment is challenging but not rigorous. There is no need to study on Friday and Saturday night." Add "technological resources that are some of the best," an administration that "is very open to student suggestion and input," and the school's "connections with companies so you can get a job or an internship," and people are left asking themselves what else they could possibly need. Oh, yeah: "proximity to Boston."

Life

With an active campus set near a big college town, Bentley College offers its students the best of all possible social worlds. One undergraduate says, "Life here is great; not only is the campus fifteen minutes from Harvard Square by an hourly shuttle, but [also] there is a very active party scene at Bentley." Students "love to have fun, but never at the expense of grades. People who party even a little too hard tend to drop out very quick." Although many students drink, those who choose to abstain "are respected for it and have fun on campus as well." That fun includes involvement in Bentley's intramural and intercollegiate athletic programs. "There are also many extracurricular activities to participate in, so students are rarely bored. There's always a school-sponsored event every night of the week, generally more on weekends. There is a pub and [a] coffeehouse, which host weekly events such as movies, comedians, and musicians." Students who decide to just chill at home think "the dorms are outstanding, so living conditions after you are a freshman are nice." Beyond campus is the city of Boston, which is "a great college city. Going into the city to eat, shop, or just hang out is great for the weekends. [There are] great museums, lots of culture, and, of course, all the other colleges."

Student Body

There are plenty of "cookie-cutter business students" at Bentley; they're the type of kids who are "hardworking, Type A personality individuals [who are] looking for a predominantly business education and who are very career-focused." Many students who attend the school come from money. One student agrees and adds, "Typical Bentley student[s have] heavy wallet[s] in their Abercrombie pants, although [they are] sometimes [kept] in the center console[s] of their BMW[s]." A huge international population means "the campus is very diverse," but many wish the gender demographic would change. One male student complains, "There are a lot more males on the campus than females." The student body can be somewhat cliquish. One undergraduate explains, "There are three types of students at Bentley College: the jock, the Greek, and neither of the above. Everyone knows their group and is happy with it because you end up with people like yourself."

FINANCIAL AID: 781-891-3441 • E-MAIL: UGADMISSION@BENTLEY.EDU • WEBSITE: WWW.BENTLEY.EDU

ADMISSIONS

Very important factors considered include: Secondary school record, standardized test scores. *Important factors considered include:* Character/personal qualities, class rank, essays, extracurricular activities, interview, recommendations, talent/ability, volunteer work, work experience. *Other factors considered include:* Alumni/ae relation, geographical residence, minority status, state residency. SAT Reasoning, SAT Subject Tests, or ACT required. TOEFL required of all international applicants. High school diploma is required, and GED is accepted. *Academic units recommended:* 4 English, 4 math, 3 science (3 science lab), 3 foreign language, 3 social studies.

The Inside Word

If you're a solid B student, there's little challenge to encounter in the admissions process here. The college's appealing greater Boston location and career-oriented academic strengths account for a sizable applicant pool and the moderate selectivity that it enjoys.

FINANCIAL AID

Students should submit: FAFSA, CSS/Financial Aid PROFILE, noncustodial (divorced/separated) parents' statement, business/farm supplement. Regular filing deadline is 2/1. The Princeton Review suggests that all financial aid forms be submitted as soon as possible after 1/1. *Need-based scholarships/grants offered:* Pell, SEOG, state scholarships/grants, private scholarships, the school's own gift aid. *Loan aid offered:* FFEL Subsidized Stafford, FFEL Unsubsidized Stafford, FFEL PLUS, Federal Perkins, state loans. Applicants will be notified of awards on a rolling basis beginning on or about 3/25. Federal Work-study Program available. Institutional employment available. Off-campus job opportunities are excellent.

FROM THE ADMISSIONS OFFICE

"Bentley, a business university, blends the breadth and technological strength of a large university with the values and student focus of a small college. Students who are interested in business professions can choose from a wide variety of programs, including accountancy, finance, marketing, and management—all with a strong foundation in information technology. A Bentley education includes outstanding preparation in the arts and sciences, a faculty of dynamic teachers with real-world research and consulting experience, and a vibrant campus teeming with athletic, social, and cultural opportunities. Ethics and social responsibility are woven throughout the school's curriculum; Bentley's Service-Learning program is ranked among the top 20 in the United States. Students also study abroad and pursue internships at leading companies in the U.S. and overseas.

"Concepts and theories that students learn in the classroom come alive in several hands-on, high-tech learning laboratories—each among the first of its kind in higher education: the financial Trading Room, Center for Marketing Technology, Accounting Center for Electronic Learning and Business Measurement, Center for Languages and International Collaboration and the Design and Usability Testing Center. The Mobile Computing program provides all Bentley freshmen with a fully-loaded, network-ready laptop computer.

"New athletic and recreation facilities complement the 22 varsity teams in Division I and II, and the extensive intramural and recreational sports programs. Boston and Cambridge, just minutes from campus, are accessible via the school's free shuttle. Both cities are great resources for internships, job opportunities, cultural events, and social life.

"Students applying for freshman admission are required to take the new version of the SAT or the ACT with the Writing section. Students may also submit scores from the old version of the SAT or ACT (prior to March 2005) as their best scores (old/new) will be used. The SAT Subject Tests are not required."

SELECTIVITY

Admissions Rating	**89**
# of applicants	5,865
% of applicants accepted	45
% of acceptees attending	36
# accepting a place on wait list	936
% admitted from wait list	2
# of early decision applicants	111
% accepted early decision	63

FRESHMAN PROFILE

Range SAT Verbal	540-620
Average SAT Verbal	576
Range SAT Math	580-660
Average SAT Math	623
**TPR Projected Range SAT Writing*	*590-650*
Range ACT Composite	23-27
Minimum Paper TOEFL	550
Minimum Computer Based TOEFL	213
% graduated top 10% of class	35
% graduated top 25% of class	76
% graduated top 50% of class	97

DEADLINES

Early decision application deadline	11/15
Early decision notification	12/27
Regular application deadline	2/1
Regular notification	4/1
Nonfall registration?	yes

APPLICANTS ALSO LOOK AT

AND OFTEN PREFER
Babson College
Boston College
Boston University

AND SOMETIMES PREFER
New York University
Villanova University

AND RARELY PREFER
Bryant University
Northeastern University
University of Massachusetts—Amherst

FINANCIAL FACTS

Financial Aid Rating	**78**
Annual tuition	$25,330
Room & Board	$9,860
Books and supplies	$920
Required fees	$214
% frosh rec. need-based scholarship or grant aid	53
% UG rec. need-based scholarship or grant aid	48
% frosh rec. need-based self-help aid	48
% UG rec. need-based self-help aid	48
% frosh rec. any financial aid	75
% UG rec. any financial aid	70
Avg. frosh grant	$17,258
Avg. frosh loan	$4,570
Independent 529 member?	No

BEREA COLLEGE

CPO 2220, BEREA, KY 40404 • ADMISSIONS: 859-985-3500 • FAX: 859-985-3512

CAMPUS LIFE

Quality of Life Rating	**71**
Fire Safety Rating	**60**
Type of school	private
Environment	village

STUDENTS

Total undergrad enrollment	1,514
% male/female	41/59
% from out of state	64
% live on campus	84
% African American	19
% Asian	1
% Caucasian	69
% Hispanic	2
% Native American	1
% international	7
# of countries represented	71

SURVEY SAYS . . .

Small classes
Great computer facilities
Great library
Athletic facilities are great
Diverse student types on campus
Low cost of living
Frats and sororities are unpopular or nonexistent

ACADEMICS

Academic Rating	**88**
Calendar	4-1-4
Student/faculty ratio	11:1
Profs interesting rating	80
Profs accessible rating	78
% profs teaching UG courses	100
% classes taught by TAs	0
Most common reg class size	10-19 students

MOST POPULAR MAJORS

Business administration/management
family and consumer sciences/human sciences
industrial production technologies/technicians

STUDENTS SPEAK OUT

Academics

Among a handful of schools nationwide that allow students to earn the cost of their tuition by working on campus, Berea College lets undergrads "learn as much at work and in work training as [they] do in the classroom." But this is not to say that academics are a walk in the park; reports one junior, "you study, study, study." A sophomore adds, "The classes definitely are not easy. The professors expect you to show up for class and try your hardest." You're likely to find professors who are "down-to-earth, accessible, [and] willing to spend time outside of class with students." A sophomore tells us, "I have often enjoyed dinners at their houses or lunches with them around town." While there may be a few bad apples in the bunch, the profs overall encourage undergrads "to think in ways you never would have imagined." Be aware, though, that one of these ways is "liberal"—a term that tends to characterize the college's faculty, to the chagrin of some members of the largely conservative student body. Because Berea was founded in 1855 by abolitionists, students have little reason to be surprised that their ideas will be "challenged" here. The college's administration earns both cheers and jeers from the student body. Many hail the "free laptops" that all students receive and write that "the administration is agreeable and willing to help students;" yet others complain that "decisions are made on the basis of what is cheapest, what will look best, and what will make them look progressive." Overall, "Berea College students, faculty, and staff are committed to using their knowledge to leave the world a little better than they found it through learning, labor, and service."

Life

"We work at Berea," writes a sophomore, "either with our labor or school work." Between the "mandatory" work-study program and the "demanding" academics, students find plenty to keep them busy. And this is a good thing, because the "small, dry town" of Berea in central Kentucky offers few distractions, with the exception of—you guessed it—"Wal-mart!" Though cars on campus are heavily restricted, "one can get on the school shuttle and go to the Richmond Mall on Fridays, or sign up for the Lexington Mall shuttle on Saturdays. But if you spend most of your time on campus, it can quickly get really boring," warns a sophomore. Not everyone feels this way: "During the academic year, there is lots of stuff on campus other than classes," writes a French-econ double major. Many praise the Campus Activities Board for keeping the campus "always buzzing with activities." In their free time, students like to "think about life, society, classes, work, the world, food, contra dance, swing dance, bible study, partying, sex, drugs, and Christian rock. We also like to knit and hike." The college's 8,000-acre forest provides plenty of space for Berea's outdoor adventurers. Self-identified as a Christian school, Berea does put limits on the indoor "adventures" in which students are allowed to participate. While "campus policies are restrictive"—with a zero-tolerance alcohol regulations and prohibited overnighters by members of the opposite sex—some remark that they're also "inconsistently enforced."

Student Body

While the largest crop of students come "from the Appalachian area and low-income families," students are quick to remind us that the college's "diversity" includes "international, independent, nontraditional, married, and students of many colors, religions, and backgrounds;" Berea also has a huge (almost 60 percent of the student body) out-of-state constituency. There are some students here who claim that groups "do not really mix very well"; but overall these undergrads give each other props for being "very tolerant and open-minded." Considering all these differences, what's the "typical" undergrad here like? A junior muses, "This creature is a sleep-deprived individual that spends most of its time studying."

KH

olor atlas of emergency trauma / Diku P.
triades
als: wang Entry Date: Feb 8, 2006 12:54:29 PM

: intervention / [edited by] Susan L.

als: wang Entry Date: Feb 6, 2006 4:12:47 PM

ildren
r children
ration center
il
 action : community service learning projects,
from Alice Yang
als: wang Entry Date: Feb 7, 2006 3:44:23 PM

FINANCIAL AID: 859-985-3310 • E-MAIL: ADMISSIONS@BEREA.EDU • WEBSITE: WWW.BEREA.EDU

ADMISSIONS

Very important factors considered include: Class rank, essays, geographical residence, minority status, secondary school record, standardized test scores. *Important factors considered include:* Character/personal qualities, extracurricular activities, interview, talent/ability, volunteer work. *Other factors considered include:* Recommendations, state residency, work experience. SAT Reasoning or ACT required; TOEFL required of all international applicants. High school diploma is required and GED is accepted. *Academic units recommended:* 4 English, 3 math, 2 science, 2 foreign language, 1 social studies, 1 history.

Inside Word

The full tuition scholarship every entering student receives understandably entices lots of applicants, so competition among candidates is intense. To make matters worse, you may be too wealthy to get in here: Berea won't admit students whose parents can afford to send them to a school with comparable educational quality. In 2001, a family of four had to earn less than $51,000 to send a child here.

FINANCIAL AID

Students should submit: FAFSA. The Princeton Review suggests that all financial aid forms be submitted as soon as possible after January 1. *Need-based scholarships/grants offered:* Pell, SEOG, state scholarships/grants, private scholarships, the school's own gift aid. *Loan aid offered:* FFEL Subsidized Stafford, FFEL Unsubsidized Stafford, FFEL PLUS, Federal Perkins, state loans, college/university loans from institutional funds. Applicants will be notified of awards on a rolling basis beginning or about April 15.

FROM THE ADMISSIONS OFFICE

"Founded in 1855 by ardent abolitionists, Berea College was the first racially integrated coeducational college in the South. Over the past 150 years, Berea's has evolved into one of the most distinctive colleges in the United States. Serving students primarily from the Appalachian region, Berea College seeks to serve students who possess great academic promise but have access to limited financial resources. Berea provides an inviting and personal educational experience, evidenced in part by an 11:1 student to faculty ratio and extensive, faculty-led advising and orientation programs.

"In support of students with limited financial resources, every enrolling student receives a full-tuition scholarship, a laptop computer, as well as a paid on-campus job. Students pay room, board, and fee charges to the extent that they are able as determined by their FAFSA results. Any remaining room, board, and fee charges are covered through scholarships and grant-based aid. Students may use earnings from their job to assist with their portion of room, board, and fee charges; books and supplies; and other personal expenses.

"As a result of this combination of academic reputation and generous financial assistance, Berea attracts many more applicants than are able to be accepted and thus admission is competitive. The best means of improving the chances for admission is to complete the application process as early as possible, preferably by November 30 of the senior year.

"Applicants for fall 2006 must submit scores from the SAT or ACT (with or without the Writing components from either test)."

SELECTIVITY	
Admissions Rating	**91**
# of applicants	2,110
% of applicants accepted	27
% of acceptees attending	71
FRESHMAN PROFILE	
Range SAT Verbal	490-615
Average SAT Verbal	557
Range SAT Math	510-615
Average SAT Math	565
**TPR Projected Range SAT Writing*	*550-650*
Range ACT Composite	21-26
Average ACT Composite	24
Minimum Paper TOEFL	500
Minimum Computer Based TOEFL	173
Average HS GPA	3.6
% graduated top 10% of class	27
% graduated top 25% of class	64
% graduated top 50% of class	92
DEADLINES	
Regular application deadline	4/30
Regular notification	rolling
Nonfall registration?	yes
FINANCIAL FACTS	
Financial Aid Rating	**83**
Annual tuition	$21,600
Room & Board	$4,980
Required fees	$516
% frosh rec. need-based scholarship or grant aid	100
% UG rec. need-based scholarship or grant aid	100
% frosh rec. need-based self-help aid	100
% UG rec. need-based self-help aid	100
% frosh rec. any financial aid	100
% UG rec. any financial aid	100
Avg. frosh grant	$24,500
Independent 529 member?	No

BIRMINGHAM-SOUTHERN COLLEGE

900 ARKADELPHIA ROAD, BIRMINGHAM, AL 35254 • ADMISSIONS: 205-226-4696 • FAX: 205-226-3074

CAMPUS LIFE

Quality of Life Rating	**93**
Fire Safety Rating	**60**
Type of school	private
Affiliation	Methodist
Environment	metropolis

STUDENTS

Total undergrad enrollment	1,356
% male/female	42/58
% from out of state	26
% from public high school	65
% live on campus	79
% in (# of) fraternities	48 (6)
% in (# of) sororities	65 (7)
% African American	6
% Asian	3
% Caucasian	90
% Hispanic	1

SURVEY SAYS

Small classes
Lab facilities are great
Campus feels safe
Frats and sororities dominate social scene
Lots of beer drinking

ACADEMICS

Academic Rating	**87**
Calendar	4-1-4
Student/faculty ratio	12:1
Professors interesting rating	95
Professors accessible rating	90
% professors teaching UG courses	100
% classes taught by TAs	0
Most common lab size	10-19 students
Most common regular class size	10-19 students

MOST POPULAR MAJORS

Business administration/management
health/medical preparatory programs

STUDENTS SPEAK OUT

Academics

"Birmingham-Southern college is the best school in Alabama" students at this small, academically intense college in the state's largest city insist. Undergrads praise how the school achieves a "happy medium between well-rounded education and focused concentration on one's major," reporting that "BSU does a great job of preparing students for graduate, law, and medical schools." It also has "a good education program… and an excellent dance department that offers a top notch dance faculty with a focus on ballet." Students tell us that "the overall academic experience is challenging, yet very rewarding" and that "classroom discussion is not only encouraged, but is a necessity, since much of the grades are derived from participation." Experiential learning is paramount; one student reports, "I have not had a class yet that didn't provide some sort of hands-on experience. I have participated in everything from labs at the Cahaba River in my population ecosystem course to observations at a local Montessori school in my human growth and development class." The small classes mean "teachers get to know you by name, and many are willing to spend countless hours working with you individually on school matters and helping you plan [your] future. They take an interest in you as a person, not just as a student." Some here point out that "while being small is a benefit, it is also sometimes a downfall. Most classes are available every year, but you must be careful to schedule courses that only occur every other year or once a year carefully in order to graduate on time."

Life

"Most people live on campus because BSC is a smaller college," students here tell us, and "this allows for an attractive community-like atmosphere." Campus life includes "many student organizations, a very strong Greek system,[and] many different shows throughout the year, from dance to theater to music to art, all produced by the performing arts departments." Youth groups and religious organizations "are also big at the school. Many people attend chapel services and UCF [University Christian Fellowship]." There's fun to be had off campus as well, as "Birmingham is a rockin' city. There is always a concert or something off campus." Exploring Birmingham "is very easy [because] the school is located downtown, although it doesn't feel that way. You can go out to the middle of the academic quad at 11:00 P.M. and feel safe." There's "plenty to do off campus, including shopping, visiting the zoo, or going to see a show at one of the many theatres in town." Sums up one student, "Fun is either a night out in Birmingham—that's what you do if you have money: you go out to eat, then to the bars, a movie, or a small off-campus party at someone's apartment—or, if you're broke and you want to have fun, you usually end up on Fraternity Row. At least one of the fraternities is usually having a party, and there are always people down there."

Student Body

BSC undergrads "typically come from the Alabama, Mississippi, Tennessee, and Georgia areas," although "there are some students here from elsewhere." Many "are involved in Greek life, probably about 60 percent. Many more girls go Greek than guys, and the independents are still like their own Greek group," as they "find their own groups in which to socialize, such as the ultimate Frisbee team or service clubs such as Triangle Club or Students Offering Support." Most here agree that "the school could do better at attracting minorities and people of color," but point out that "with the size of our school you can only expect so much."

FINANCIAL AID: 205-226-4688 • E-MAIL: ADMISSION@BSC.EDU • WEBSITE: WWW.BSC.EDU

ADMISSIONS

Very important factors considered include: Essays, recommendations, secondary school record, standardized test scores. *Important factors considered include:* Character/personal qualities. *Other factors considered include:* Extracurricular activities, interview, state residency, talent/ability, volunteer work, work experience. SAT Reasoning or ACT required. TOEFL required of all international applicants. High school diploma is required, and GED is accepted. *Academic units required:* 4 English. *Academic units recommended:* 4 math, 4 science, 2 foreign language, 2 social studies, 2 history, 10 academic electives.

The Inside Word

Birmingham-Southern's lack of widespread national recognition by students and parents results in a small applicant pool, the majority of whom are admitted. Most of the admits are looking for a quality southern college, recognize a good situation here, and decide to enroll. Our impression is that few regret their decision. In a reflection of the entire administration, the admissions staff is truly personal and very helpful to prospective students.

FINANCIAL AID

Students should submit: State aid form. Regular filing deadline is 5/1. The Princeton Review suggests that all financial aid forms be submitted as soon as possible after 1/1. *Need-based scholarships/grants offered:* Pell, SEOG, state scholarships/grants, private scholarships, the school's own gift aid, United Negro College Fund. *Loan aid offered:* FFEL Subsidized Stafford, FFEL Unsubsidized Stafford, FFEL PLUS, Federal Perkins, college/university loans from institutional funds. Applicants will be notified of awards on a rolling basis beginning on or about 2/1.

FROM THE ADMISSIONS OFFICE

"Respected publishers continue to recognize Birmingham-Southern College as one of the top-ranked liberal arts colleges in the nation. One guide highlights our small classes and the fact that we still assign each student a 'faculty-cum-mentor,' to assure individualized attention to our students. One notable aspect of our academic calendar is our January interim term, a four-week period in which students can participate in special projects in close collaboration with faculty members, either on or off campus. One dimension of Birmingham-Southern's civic focus is the commitment to volunteerism. In fact, former President George Bush visited the campus to present our conservancy group with one of his 'Points of Light' volunteer service awards. The Center for Leadership Studies assists students in realizing their leadership potential by combining the academic study of leadership with significant community service.

"Freshman applicants must present acceptable scores on the SAT or the ACT; they must also submit an original essay and a satisfactory recommendation from the high school."

SELECTIVITY

Admissions Rating	**85**
# of applicants	1,157
% of applicants accepted	83
% of acceptees attending	37

FRESHMAN PROFILE

Range SAT Verbal	550-670
Average SAT Verbal	608
Range SAT Math	540-640
Average SAT Math	589
**TPR Projected Range SAT Writing*	*600-680*
Range ACT Composite	24-29
Average ACT Composite	27
Minimum Paper TOEFL	500
Minimum Computer Based TOEFL	173
Average HS GPA	3.38
% graduated top 10% of class	31
% graduated top 25% of class	64
% graduated top 50% of class	88

DEADLINES

Regular notification	rolling
Nonfall registration?	yes

APPLICANTS ALSO LOOK AT AND OFTEN PREFER

Rhodes College
Vanderbilt University

AND SOMETIMES PREFER

Auburn University
Furman University
Samford University
Sewanee—The University of the South
The University of Alabama—Tuscaloosa

AND RARELY PREFER

Louisiana State University
Tulane University

FINANCIAL FACTS

Financial Aid Rating	**80**
Annual tuition	$20,810
Room & Board	$7,080
Books and supplies	$800
Required fees	$630
% frosh rec. need-based scholarship or grant aid	44
% UG rec. need-based scholarship or grant aid	32
% frosh rec. need-based self-help aid	47
% UG rec. need-based self-help aid	42
% frosh rec. any financial aid	95
% UG rec. any financial aid	95
Avg. frosh grant	$8,800
Avg. frosh loan	$3,736
Independent 529 member?	Yes

BOSTON COLLEGE

140 COMMONWEALTH AVE., DEVLIN HALL 208, CHESTNUT HILL, MA 02467-3809 • ADMISSIONS: 617-552-3100 • FAX: 617-552-0798

CAMPUS LIFE

Quality of Life Rating	**94**
Fire Safety Rating	**99**
Type of school	private
Affiliation	Roman Catholic
Environment	city

STUDENTS

Total undergrad enrollment	9,059
% male/female	47/53
% from out of state	72
% from public high school	60
% live on campus	78
% African American	6
% Asian	9
% Caucasian	74
% Hispanic	7
% international	2
# of countries represented	94

SURVEY SAYS

Great library
Students love Chestnut Hill, MA
Campus feels safe
Everyone loves the Eagles
Frats and sororities are unpopular or nonexistent
Lots of beer drinking

ACADEMICS

Academic Rating	**88**
Calendar	semester
Student/faculty ratio	13:1
Professors interesting rating	84
Professors accessible rating	83
% professors teaching UG courses	100
% classes taught by TAs	0
Most common regular class size	10-19 students

MOST POPULAR MAJORS

Communications and media studies
English language and literature
finance

STUDENTS SPEAK OUT

Academics

Students praise the strong academics, the competitive athletic teams, the lively social scene, and the premium location that all combine to create a remarkable all-around college experience at Boston College. For many, though, BC's greatest asset is the "strong spiritual presence [that] shows how positive an influence religion can have on one's life." Don't worry; "They don't try to make anybody be Catholic" here. Rather, the school "simply reflects the Jesuit ideals of community, spirituality, and social justice," and these ideals pervade both the curriculum and the academic community. True to the Jesuit ideal of "educating the entire person," BC requires a thorough core curriculum "including philosophy, theology, and language requirements" rounded out by "strong [but optional] programs, such as internships and studying abroad." Beyond the core curriculum, "BC offers something for everyone. If you go here, you are with business students, nursing students, education majors, and arts and science majors." And even though this is a fairly large school, students insist that "you never feel like a number here. Yes, you have to be independent and seek out your professors. But when you do seek them out, you get incredible individualized attention." One undergrad sums it up like this: "BC's strength is a mix of everything. It may not be an Ivy League school in academics or win national championships everywhere in NCAA athletics, but it is a 'jack of all trades' when it comes to academics, athletics, art, and social activity."

Life

There is a "real spirit of volunteerism and giving back to the community [that] is one of BC's greatest strengths," many students here tell us, reporting that "there are about a million volunteer groups on campus, as well as a bunch of immersion trips to different places, the most renowned of which is the Appalachia group trip." Students here "really care about the world outside of Chestnut Hill. In a way, even the notion of studying abroad has turned into a question of 'How can I help people while there?' BC's Jesuit mission is contagious." Not all extracurricular life at BC is so altruistic, however; students here love to have fun in "the greatest location of any college ever! We are on the T [train] so we can get into the city of Boston whenever we like, but we are in suburbia so we can relax without all of the gimmicks of city life." Undergrads love to explore Boston, a city with "tons of great museums, historical sights, restaurants and a lot of great concerts," that also happens to be "such a big college town. It's easy to meet kids that go to BU, Harvard, Emerson, Northeastern or any of the other universities in the area." Closer to campus, BC has "great sports. Our football team has won five bowl games in a row and basketball is, at this writing, ranked 9th in the nation. The ice hockey team is consistently ranked high nationally," and students turn out to support their Eagles in both men's and women's athletics.

Student Body

Boston magazine once described the BC student body as "a J. Crew catalogue with a slight hangover," and while students protest that "there are a number of students who do not conform to such a vision of the student body," they also admit that "there are a lot of preppy people at our school. Girls usually wear skirts and Uggs (unless it's freezing out, but it has to be very, very cold), and boys usually wear jeans and t-shirts or collared cotton shirts." And yes, "the typical BC student is white, Catholic, usually from the Northeast, who probably had family that went to BC," but with 9,000 undergrads, "we have students from all sorts of backgrounds, religions, sexual orientations." BC students tend to be extremely ambitious; they are "those super-involved people in high school who were three-season team captains, class president, and straight-A students. [They] have carried over that focus and determination into college."

FINANCIAL AID: 800-294-0294 • E-MAIL: UGADMIS@BC.EDU • WEBSITE: WWW.BC.EDU

ADMISSIONS

Very important factors considered include: Secondary school record, standardized test scores. *Important factors considered include:* Alumni/ae relation, character/personal qualities, class rank, essays, extracurricular activities, recommendations, religious affiliation/commitment, talent/ability, volunteer work. *Other factors considered include:* Minority status, work experience. SAT Reasoning and SAT Subject Tests or ACT required. TOEFL required of all international applicants. High school diploma is required, and GED is accepted. *Academic units recommended:* 4 English, 4 math, 4 science (4 science lab), 4 foreign language.

The Inside Word

While applications to BC in general have increased over the past couple of years, early action applications have risen more dramatically. Standards remain high, and we more than recommend a strong college-preparatory curriculum in high school—it's a must to have a shot. With a large percentage of its students coming from Catholic high schools such applicants are treated well, but there is little room for relaxation in the process. Applicants need to show strong SAT reasoning and SAT subject scores, but keep the tests in perspective—BC is interested in the whole package.

FINANCIAL AID

Students should submit: FAFSA, CSS/Financial Aid PROFILE, noncustodial (divorced/separated) parents' statement, business/farm supplement, parent and student tax returns and W-2 forms. The Princeton Review suggests that all financial aid forms be submitted as soon as possible after 1/1. *Need-based scholarships/grants offered:* Pell, SEOG, state scholarships/grants, private scholarships, the school's own gift aid. *Loan aid offered:* FFEL Subsidized Stafford, FFEL Unsubsidized Stafford, FFEL PLUS, Federal Perkins, Federal Nursing, state loans. Applicants will be notified of awards on or about 4/1. Federal Work-study Program available. Off-campus job opportunities are excellent.

FROM THE ADMISSIONS OFFICE

"Boston College students achieve at the highest levels with honors last year including two Rhodes scholarship winners, nine Fulbrights, and one each for Marshall, Goldwater, Madison, and Truman Post-Graduate Fellowship Programs. Junior Year Abroad and Scholar of the College Program offer students flexibility within the curriculum. Facilities opened in the past 10 years include: the Merkert Chemistry Center, Higgins Hall (housing the Biology and Physics departments), three new residence halls, the Yawkey Athletics Center, the Vanderslice Commons Dining Hall, the Hillside Cafe, and a state-of-the-art library. Students enjoy the vibrant location in Chestnut Hill with easy access to the cultural and historical richness of Boston.

"Boston College requires freshman applicants for fall 2006 to take the new SAT (or the ACT with the Writing exam required). Students may submit scores from the old SAT as their best scores from either test will be used in admissions decisions. Two SAT Subject Tests are required; students are encouraged to take Subject Tests in fields in which they excel."

SELECTIVITY

Admissions Rating	**96**
# of applicants	22,451
% of applicants accepted	32
% of acceptees attending	32
# accepting a place on wait list	5,000
% admitted from wait list	3

FRESHMAN PROFILE

Range SAT Verbal	610-700
Average SAT Verbal	650
Range SAT Math	630-710
Average SAT Math	667
**TPR Projected Range SAT Writing*	*640-700*
Minimum Paper TOEFL	600
Minimum Computer Based TOEFL	250
% graduated top 10% of class	74
% graduated top 25% of class	95
% graduated top 50% of class	99

DEADLINES

Regular application deadline	1/2
Regular notification	4/15
Nonfall registration?	yes

APPLICANTS ALSO LOOK AT

AND OFTEN PREFER

Columbia University—Columbia College, Harvard College, Princeton University, Stanford University, Yale University

AND SOMETIMES PREFER

Boston University, Georgetown University, New York University, University of Notre Dame, University of Virginia

AND RARELY PREFER

College of the Holy Cross, Fairfield University, Northeastern University, Providence College, Villanova University

FINANCIAL FACTS

Financial Aid Rating	**93**
Annual tuition	$28,940
Room & Board	$10,580
Books and supplies	$650
Required fees	$456
% frosh rec. need-based scholarship or grant aid	36
% UG rec. need-based scholarship or grant aid	37
% frosh rec. need-based self-help aid	36
% UG rec. need-based self-help aid	38
% frosh rec. any financial aid	70
% UG rec. any financial aid	70
Avg. frosh grant	$17,638
Avg. frosh loan	$4,104
Independent 529 member?	No

BOSTON UNIVERSITY

121 BAY STATE ROAD, BOSTON, MA 02215 • ADMISSIONS: 617-353-2300 • FAX: 617-353-9695

CAMPUS LIFE

Quality of Life Rating	**82**
Fire Safety Rating	**60**
Type of school	private
Environment	metropolis

STUDENTS

Total undergrad enrollment	15,953
% male/female	40/60
% from out of state	77
% from public high school	70
% live on campus	74
% in (# of) fraternities	3 (8)
% in (# of) sororities	5 (10)
% African American	2
% Asian	13
% Caucasian	58
% Hispanic	5
% international	7
# of countries represented	103

SURVEY SAYS

Students love Boston, MA
Great off-campus food
Campus feels safe
Students are happy
Student publications are popular
Lots of beer drinking
(Almost) everyone smokes

ACADEMICS

Academic Rating	**85**
Calendar	semester
Student/faculty ratio	15:1
Professors interesting rating	72
Professors accessible rating	74
% professors teaching UG courses	75
% classes taught by TAs	6
Most common lab size	20-29 students
Most common regular class size	10-19 students

MOST POPULAR MAJORS

Business administration/management
communications and media studies
engineering

STUDENTS SPEAK OUT

Academics

Boston University (BU), "an intense academic school in the perfect, fun, intense college city" of Boston, knows how to wring the most out of its premier location. "Professors utilize the city [by] leading field trips to the Museum of Fine Arts, the Museum of Science, and a French film festival at Coolidge Corner, to name a few." Internships abound, aided by the school's "enormous alumni network" in its hometown. And of course, the allure of a world-class city helps BU attract luminaries to the faculty, including poet Robert Pinsky, physicist and Nobel laureate Sheldon Glashow, and biomedical engineer and MacArthur Grant recipient Jim Collins. Students say, "We have an amazing faculty and [amazing] resources. BU is very good about getting world-renowned writers, philosophers, and political figures to teach or engage in programs here at BU." Of course, not every class is taught by a Nobel laureate or even by a full professor; in fact, "the classes are too often taught by graduate students. Plus, there are too few sections of each class." Although this problem exists, most agree that their instructors "seem like really nice people. They all have office hours and encourage the students to come and visit." One student offers prospective undergraduates advice: "Go into this college as an 'undeclared' major. There is no changing majors without major paperwork and a high GPA."

Life

Boston University does not offer the classic campus-focused college experience because life "is very much centered [in] the city. Attending school is just part of your life at BU. There are so many other things going on in the area that you could go weeks without attending a BU party." The Boston club scene is a huge draw for BU students, as are the city's many bars, restaurants, stores, museums, theaters, concert halls, and ballets. There's a ton of colleges in town, so there's always a party—many parties—to be found. One place where students won't find parties is in BU dorms; the school's strict visitation policies ensure that. Many students complain that "the rules are way too strict," but others appreciate that the rules show "how focused our administration is on stressing academics to the students here." Campus is a term students rarely use since "Boston University doesn't really have a closed campus; the entire school is basically integrated with the city." However, the campus does offer "great fitness facilities with a swimming pool, ice-skating rink, weight rooms, cardio rooms, and classes in things from yoga to aerobics to Zen meditation to ice skating." You'll also find "lots of quiet places to read." Boston University's big intercollegiate sport is men's hockey, which some students follow religiously.

Student Body

Because "BU is huge," "there are all types of people here." Students say, "The school is so large that fitting in is not really an issue." The university's reputation as a haven for Louis Vuitton-toting rich girls may be undeserved; one student says, "These people are the loud stereotypes. BU is so large that the atypical people dominate my social life rather than the bland Abercrombie types that dominate the sidewalk on the way to class." While "most of the students at this school are from wealthy American families, there is a fair percentage of minority students, particularly Asians and Indians/Pakistanis." "Everyone gets along," although "there may not be too much interaction between the majority and minority." A lopsided female-to-male ratio means that "guys get along quite easily with each other because there is no competition." Students also report that "sexual orientation is not a big issue on this campus. Many people are openly homosexual, and they are accepted."

FINANCIAL AID: 617-353-2965 • E-MAIL: ADMISSIONS@BU.EDU • WEBSITE: WWW.BU.EDU

ADMISSIONS

Very important factors considered include: Secondary school record. *Important factors considered include:* Class rank, essays, recommendations, standardized test scores. *Other factors considered include:* Alumni/ae relation, character/personal qualities, extracurricular activities, volunteer work, work experience. SAT Reasoning and SAT Subject Tests or ACT required. TOEFL required of all international applicants. High school diploma is required, and GED is accepted. *Academic units required:* 4 English, 3 math, 3 science (3 science lab), 2 foreign language, 3 social studies. *Academic units recommended:* 4 English, 4 math, 4 science (4 science lab), 4 foreign language, 4 social studies.

The Inside Word

Boston is one of the nation's most popular college towns, and BU benefits tremendously. The university's last few entering classes have been chock-full of high-caliber students; despite a general decline in applications at colleges in the Northeast, it will continue to be competitive to gain admission to BU, as applications keep a steady upward trend and entering class size is kept in check. Those who aren't up to traditional standards are sometimes referred to the less selective College of General Studies, which allows students to continue on to other divisions of the university once they prove themselves academically—but standards here are rising.

FINANCIAL AID

Students should submit: FAFSA, CSS/Financial Aid PROFILE, state aid form, noncustodial (divorced/separated) parents' statement, business/farm supplement. Regular filing deadline is 2/15. The Princeton Review suggests that all financial aid forms be submitted as soon as possible after 1/1. *Need-based scholarships/grants offered:* Pell, SEOG, state scholarships/grants, private scholarships, the school's own gift aid. *Loan aid offered:* Direct Subsidized Stafford, Direct Unsubsidized Stafford, Direct PLUS, Federal Perkins, state loans. Applicants will be notified of awards on a rolling basis beginning on or about 3/15. Federal Work-study Program available. Institutional employment available. Off-campus job opportunities are excellent.

FROM THE ADMISSIONS OFFICE

"Boston University (BU) is a private teaching and research institution with a strong emphasis on undergraduate education. We are committed to providing the highest level of teaching excellence, and fulfillment of this pledge is our highest priority. Boston University has 11 undergraduate schools and colleges offering 250 major and minor areas of concentration. Students may choose from programs of study in areas as diverse as biochemistry, theater arts, physical therapy, elementary education, broadcast journalism, international relations, business, and computer engineering. BU has an international student body, with students from every state and more than 100 countries. In addition, opportunities to study abroad exist through 44 semester-long programs, spanning 26 cities and 18 countries on six continents.

"BU requires freshman applicants for fall 2006 to take the new version of the SAT. Two SAT Subject Tests are required; students are encouraged to take Subject Tests in fields in which they excel. Students may submit the results of the ACT (with the Writing section) in lieu of the SAT and SAT Subject Tests."

SELECTIVITY

Admissions Rating	**94**
# of applicants	28,240
% of applicants accepted	55
% of acceptees attending	28
# accepting a place on wait list	1,738
% admitted from wait list	3
# of early decision applicants	219
% accepted early decision	47

FRESHMAN PROFILE

Range SAT Verbal	600-690
Average SAT Verbal	643
Range SAT Math	610-700
Average SAT Math	656
**TPR Projected Range SAT Writing*	*630-690*
Range ACT Composite	26-30
Average ACT Composite	28
Minimum Paper TOEFL	550
Minimum Computer Based TOEFL	215
Average HS GPA	3.5
% graduated top 10% of class	60
% graduated top 25% of class	92
% graduated top 50% of class	100

DEADLINES

Early decision application deadline	11/1
Early decision notification	12/15
Regular application deadline	1/1
Regular notification	late March through mid-April
Nonfall registration?	yes

APPLICANTS ALSO LOOK AT

AND OFTEN PREFER
Cornell U., N.Y.U., U. of Southern California

AND SOMETIMES PREFER
Boston College, The George Washington U., Syracuse U.

AND RARELY PREFER
Northeastern U., SUNY at Buffalo, U. of Massachusetts—Amherst

FINANCIAL FACTS

Financial Aid Rating	**86**
Annual tuition	$31,530
Room & Board	$10,080
Books and supplies	$754
Required fees	$436
% frosh rec. need-based scholarship or grant aid	47
% UG rec. need-based scholarship or grant aid	43
% frosh rec. need-based self-help aid	43
% UG rec. need-based self-help aid	42
% frosh rec. any financial aid	70
% UG rec. any financial aid	66
Avg. frosh grant	$18,844
Avg. frosh loan	$3,656
Independent 529 member?	Yes

BOWDOIN COLLEGE

5000 College Station, Bowdoin College, Brunswick, ME 04011-8441 • Admissions: 207-725-3100 • Fax: 207-725-3101

CAMPUS LIFE

Quality of Life Rating	**95**
Fire Safety Rating	**60**
Type of school	private
Environment	village

STUDENTS

Total undergrad enrollment	1,665
% male/female	51/49
% from out of state	86
% from public high school	53
% live on campus	93
% African American	5
% Asian	11
% Caucasian	72
% Hispanic	6
% Native American	1
% international	3
# of countries represented	29

SURVEY SAYS

Small classes
Great food on campus
Lots of beer drinking

ACADEMICS

Academic Rating	**94**
Calendar	semester
Student/faculty ratio	10:1
Professors interesting rating	89
Professors accessible rating	94
% professors teaching UG courses	100
% classes taught by TAs	0
Most common lab size	10-19 students
Most common regular class size	10-19 students

MOST POPULAR MAJORS

Biology/biological sciences
economics
political science and government

STUDENTS SPEAK OUT

Academics

Bowdoin College offers an intensive liberal arts education in "an incredibly friendly, supportive, and challenging learning environment." This is "a beautiful place where students work hard at the things they love, not because they are competing with someone but because they want to do well." The school is especially "strong in the sciences, with great lab facilities and research opportunities;" few departments don't garner raves from students. Throughout the school, professors "are first-class teachers who are here because they want to teach. They go out of their way to have study groups and sessions that prepare the students well. They also unobtrusively go out of their way to make sure that each student is successful and comfortable." Regarding administrations, students say, "[They] do a great job of letting us know that the reason they're there is for us, and they really follow through on that. Every single one, from secretaries to the president of the college, is receptive and very visible on campus." Add "excellent internship and study abroad resources, willingness of alumni to stay in touch and help current students, and the dedication the school has for increasing diversity," and what more could a prospective freshman ask for from an undergraduate institution? Perhaps a "great outreach program; the school gets every student in touch with at least one faculty member who knows them well, so every student has a way out, a person to vent to in times of discomfort."

Life

Students describe Bowdoin as "a work-hard, play-hard type of place. Classes are really hard, and the students really like to wind down come Friday night. It's easy to get alcohol, but there's never a ton of abuse here." Students needn't drink for lack of things to do; our survey respondents describe an active campus outside of class. There is an unusually "high involvement in sports at Bowdoin, which keeps students active and well-rounded." Many undergraduates claim that "most students play a varsity sport." For entertainment, "the Campus Activities Board has a budget of $120,000-plus exclusively for booking acts at the school, [which] averages to about one event per week: theater groups, musical groups, and comedians." The school also "brings a lot of speakers and lecturers." Parties take place mostly in the social houses. One student says, "[Social houses] are basically frats without the exclusivity. [They] usually have a cool theme or band, but most everyone is downstairs at the keg. I don't drink, but I still go to these parties." Hometown Brunswick "is charming, with great restaurants, two movie theaters, a coffeehouse," and a few other student-friendly establishments. But "town-gown relations aren't the greatest as a result of the parties and noise." The school is conveniently located "fifteen to twenty minutes from Freeport, and if you're a shopper, this is heaven. Burberry, Coach, The North Face, Starbucks, Bath and Body Works, Abercrombie and Fitch outlet, Banana Republic, Gap outlet, they're all there." A little farther away is Portland, of which at least one student writes, "I'd take this city over Manhattan anyday: cobblestone streets, cute shops, great restaurants, and good parking. It's fabulous and right on the water!"

Student Body

Students proudly tell us that at Bowdoin, "everyone seems to be the kid in high school who played three varsity sports: ran the yearbook, newspaper, or student government: and worked hard to get good grades." These "intelligent, funny, socially active, and motivated" students are "primarily concerned with their academic success, putting academics before everything else." This explains why "they're so stressed out." The preppy contingent is large; an undergraduate explains, "There is definitely a certain J. Crew/Abercrombie and Fitch look to the majority of students." However, the student body "varie[s] socioeconomically." Although "mostly white," the student body "has become much more diverse in the past four years."

Financial Aid: 207-725-3273 • E-mail: admissions@bowdoin.edu • Website: www.bowdoin.edu

ADMISSIONS

Very important factors considered include: Character/personal qualities, class rank, essays, extracurricular activities, recommendations, secondary school record, talent/ability. *Important factors considered include:* Alumni/ae relation, geographical residence, minority status, volunteer work, work experience. *Other factors considered include:* Interview, standardized test scores, state residency. TOEFL required of all international applicants. High school diploma is required, and GED is not accepted. *Academic units recommended:* 4 English, 4 math, 4 science (3 science lab), 4 foreign language, 4 social studies.

The Inside Word

This is one of the 20 or so most selective colleges in the country. Virtually everyone who applies is well-qualified academically, which means criteria besides grades and test scores become critically important in candidate review. Who you are, what you think, where you are from, and why you are interested in Bowdoin are the sorts of things that will determine whether you get in, provided you meet their high academic standards.

FINANCIAL AID

Students should submit: FAFSA, institution's own financial aid form, CSS/Financial Aid PROFILE, noncustodial (divorced/separated) parents' statement, business/farm supplement. Regular filing deadline is 2/15. The Princeton Review suggests that all financial aid forms be submitted as soon as possible after 1/1. *Need-based scholarships/grants offered:* Pell, SEOG, state scholarships/grants, private scholarships, the school's own gift aid. *Loan aid offered:* FFEL Subsidized Stafford, FFEL Unsubsidized Stafford, FFEL PLUS, Federal Perkins, state loans, college/university loans from institutional funds. Applicants will be notified of awards on or about 4/5. Federal Work-study Program available. Institutional employment available. Off-campus job opportunities are good.

FROM THE ADMISSIONS OFFICE

"Each year Bowdoin sponsors myriad events, including performances by bands, comedians, artists, and dancers as well as lectures and film series, community service events, and the occasional scavenger hunt. Performers who have appeared at the college recently include Savion Glover, Dar Williams, Guster, Wynton Marsalis, and Mos Def. Speakers have included David Sedaris, Adrienne Rich, Robert Reich, Spike Lee, Nobel Laureate Thomas Cech, and playwright Tony Kushner. The college has more than 100 active student organizations. About 70 percent of students participate in community service during their time at Bowdoin, and the college's many volunteer programs allow students to interact with the Brunswick community. Club and intramural sports and the Outing Club enable students to get involved in physical fitness without having to be star athletes. Bowdoin is determined to be a place that brings together people from widely diverse ethnic and economic backgrounds, from different parts of the country and the world, and with divergent political beliefs, a full range of religious identities, and broad academic interests.

"Submission of the SAT or the ACT is optional for students applying to Bowdoin. Both the old and new versions of the SAT and ACT are acceptable. For candidates electing to submit them, the scores will be reviewed along with other indicators of academic achievement and potential."

SELECTIVITY

Admissions Rating	**98**
# of applicants	4,853
% of applicants accepted	24
% of acceptees attending	40
# of early decision applicants	189
% accepted early decision	30

FRESHMAN PROFILE

Range SAT Verbal	640-740
Average SAT Verbal	690
Range SAT Math	650-720
Average SAT Math	690
**TPR Projected Range SAT Writing*	*660-720*
Minimum Paper TOEFL	600
Minimum Computer Based TOEFL	250
% graduated top 10% of class	82
% graduated top 25% of class	96
% graduated top 50% of class	100

DEADLINES

Early decision application deadline	11/15
Early decision notification	12/31
Regular application deadline	1/1
Regular notification	4/5
Nonfall registration?	no

APPLICANTS ALSO LOOK AT

AND OFTEN PREFER
Brown University
Williams College
Yale University

AND SOMETIMES PREFER
Amherst College
Dartmouth College
Middlebury College

AND RARELY PREFER
Bates College
Colby College
Tufts University
Wesleyan University

FINANCIAL FACTS

Financial Aid Rating	**97**
Annual tuition	$30,944
Room & Board	$8,054
Books and supplies	$880
Required fees	$682
% frosh rec. need-based scholarship or grant aid	42
% UG rec. need-based scholarship or grant aid	46
% frosh rec. need-based self-help aid	37
% UG rec. need-based self-help aid	42
% frosh rec. any financial aid	45
% UG rec. any financial aid	49
Avg. frosh grant	$24,041
Avg. frosh loan	$3,275
Independent 529 member?	No

BRADLEY UNIVERSITY

1501 WEST BRADLEY AVENUE, PEORIA, IL 61625 • ADMISSIONS: 309-677-1000 • FAX: 309-677-2797

CAMPUS LIFE

Quality of Life Rating	**71**
Fire Safety Rating	**66**
Type of school	private
Environment	city

STUDENTS

Total undergrad enrollment	5,111
% male/female	47/53
% from out of state	11
% from public high school	87
% live on campus	70
% in (# of) fraternities	31 (16)
% in (# of) sororities	26 (12)
% African American	6
% Asian	3
% Caucasian	87
% Hispanic	2
% international	1
# of countries represented	37

SURVEY SAYS

Small classes
Students are friendly
Frats and sororities dominate social scene
Lots of beer drinking
Hard liquor is popular
(Almost) everyone smokes

ACADEMICS

Academic Rating	**68**
Calendar	semester
Student/faculty ratio	14:1
Professors interesting rating	69
Professors accessible rating	75
% professors teaching UG courses	100
% classes taught by TAs	0
Most common regular class size	20-29 students

MOST POPULAR MAJORS

Communications studies/speech communication and rhetoric
elementary education and teaching
mechanical engineering

STUDENTS SPEAK OUT

Academics

Who says size isn't important? According to the students at Bradley University, the school's size is its greatest asset. "If you like smaller schools, it is great," writes one undergraduate. "I haven't had a single TA or class larger than twenty-five." And yet the school is large enough to host standout programs in engineering, chemistry, math, education, physical therapy, music, and theater. Students also appreciate that "the opportunity for involvement at Bradley is better than any medium or small-sized university. Bradley is incredibly supportive in the creation of new organizations on campus." Academics "are very competitive," and "there can [be] a lot of jumping through hoops to get good grades;" however, students are highly satisfied with the academic experience. They warn that professors are a mixed bag. One student says, "Many of my teachers are very knowledgeable people, but I do not feel like they know how to actually teach the material to the students." Other students agree that the vast majority of the professors "are available both inside and outside of class and are willing to help and advise whenever possible."

Life

Athletics are a huge part of student life at Bradley. As one happy jock puts it, "If you like to play sports, Bradley offers a variety of sports [at] a variety of levels. At the bottom are intramurals, with A, B, and C levels. Then there are club sports, [which] are intercollegiate with less time commitment. Finally, Bradley is a Division I school" in terms of varsity sports. The fraternity and sorority houses, which are located just off campus, also occupy a good deal of students' time. One sophomore writes, "Greek life is a huge part of our campus's social scene, so sometimes if you don't want to party with the Greeks, there's not a lot to do socially." Some upperclassmen drift out of the Greek social scene, though, telling us "I grew out of it as I got older, as seems to be the case with a lot of people." Students not into Greek life find "clubs and resources available for any interest, "although some students complain that their peers are too "apathetic" to get involved. Many students seek fun in Peoria and get mixed results. One student says, "[While] some people complain about a lack of things to do in Peoria, I think they're crazy. My friends and I go out to eat a lot. There are movie theaters with really good discounts compared to home. There is a country line dance club not too far from campus that is really fun. There are also bands at bars, minor league baseball and hockey games, an art fair, and parks to hike. There is a lot to do if students just look a little."

Student Body

Bradley has increased its draw outside its immediate region in recent years, so while it's still true that many students are "from the Chicago suburbs or the St. Louis area," that characterization grows less true every year. Undergraduates note that "Bradley has been recruiting from all around the world. Every year we are a greater representation of the world and the cultures from nearly all continents." Students are generally laid-back; writes one, "Typical Bradley students are backpack-toting, flip-flop-wearing, eighteen- to twenty-two-year-olds who trudge across the quad several times a day, smiling at people they know along the way, and holding doors open for everyone, whether they know them or not." The student body can also be a bit cliquish, "kind of like high school. There are several large and smaller cliques going on. There are, of course, the Greeks, the loners who stay in the dorms all four years, the theater people, the smokers, the Christians, the Indians who only hang out with each other, the confused freshmen girls, the horny freshmen guys, the engineer majors who are never not studying if they know what's good for them, the baseball people, and the speech [writers]."

FINANCIAL AID: 309-677-3089 • E-MAIL: ADMISSIONS@BRADLEY.EDU • WEBSITE: WWW.BRADLEY.EDU

ADMISSIONS

Very important factors considered include: Secondary school record. *Important factors considered include:* Class rank, standardized test scores. *Other factors considered include:* Alumni/ae relation, character/personal qualities, essays, extracurricular activities, interview, minority status, recommendations, talent/ability, volunteer work, work experience. SAT Reasoning or ACT required. TOEFL required of all international applicants. High school diploma is required, and GED is accepted. *Academic units required:* 4 English, 3 math, 2 science (2 science lab), 2 social studies. *Academic units recommended:* 5 English, 4 math, 3 science (3 science lab), 2 foreign language, 3 social studies, 2 history.

The Inside Word

Though students come here from far and wide, Bradley is best known within the Midwest and its reach is primarily regional. As a result, the admission process at Bradley is not super competitive; combined with solid academic quality and a broad range of offerings, this makes Bradley a worthwhile choice for those seeking to attend a strong school without running a grueling admissions gauntlet.

FINANCIAL AID

Students should submit: FAFSA. The Princeton Review suggests that all financial aid forms be submitted as soon as possible after 1/1. *Need-based scholarships/grants offered:* Pell, SEOG, state scholarships/grants, private scholarships, the school's own gift aid. *Loan aid offered:* Direct Subsidized Stafford, Direct Unsubsidized Stafford, Direct PLUS, FFEL PLUS, Federal Perkins, Federal Nursing. Federal Work-study Program available. Institutional employment available. Off-campus job opportunities are good.

FROM THE ADMISSIONS OFFICE

"Does the size of a college make a difference? Bradley's 5,000 undergraduates and 1,000 graduates think so. They like the opportunities, choices, and technologies of a larger university and the quality, personal attention, and challenge of a small, private college. Bradley's size makes so many things possible—recognition instead of anonymity, accessibility instead of bureaucracy, and academic choices instead of limits. Bradley students choose from more than 100 programs of study in the Foster College of Business Administration, Slane College of Communications and Fine Arts, College of Education and Health Sciences, College of Engineering and Technology, and Liberal Arts and Sciences. Clearly, size does make a difference.

"Bradley requires freshman applicants to submit scores from either the old or the new SAT. Students may also choose to submit scores from the ACT, with or without the Writing component, in lieu of the SAT."

SELECTIVITY

Admissions Rating	**81**
# of applicants	5,753
% of applicants accepted	64
% of acceptees attending	27
# accepting a place on wait list	261
% admitted from wait list	24

FRESHMAN PROFILE

Range SAT Verbal	510-620
Average SAT Verbal	552
Range SAT Math	530-650
Average SAT Math	564
**TPR Projected Range SAT Writing*	*570-650*
Range ACT Composite	23-28
Average ACT Composite	25
Minimum Paper TOEFL	500
Minimum Computer Based TOEFL	197
% graduated top 10% of class	29
% graduated top 25% of class	61
% graduated top 50% of class	91

DEADLINES

Regular application deadline	rolling
Regular notification	rolling
Nonfall registration?	yes

APPLICANTS ALSO LOOK AT

AND OFTEN PREFER

Illinois Wesleyan University
Purdue University—West Lafayette
University of Illinois at Urbana-Champaign

AND SOMETIMES PREFER

DePaul University
Loyola University of Chicago
Marquette University

AND RARELY PREFER

Eastern Illinois University
Illinois State University
Northern Illinois University

FINANCIAL FACTS

Financial Aid Rating	**87**
Annual tuition	$17,600
Room & Board	$6,150
Books and supplies	$500
Required fees	$130
% frosh rec. need-based scholarship or grant aid	74
% UG rec. need-based scholarship or grant aid	70
% frosh rec. need-based self-help aid	54
% UG rec. need-based self-help aid	56
% frosh rec. any financial aid	96
% UG rec. any financial aid	87
Avg. frosh grant	$10,612
Avg. frosh loan	$3,680
Independent 529 member?	Yes

BRANDEIS UNIVERSITY

415 SOUTH STREET, MS003, WALTHAM, MA 02454 • ADMISSIONS: 781-736-3500 • FAX: 781-736-3536

CAMPUS LIFE

Quality of Life Rating	**84**
Fire Safety Rating	**60**
Type of school	private
Environment	village

STUDENTS

Total undergrad enrollment	3,158
% male/female	44/56
% from out of state	75
% from public high school	70
% live on campus	82
% African American	3
% Asian	8
% Caucasian	67
% Hispanic	3
% international	7
# of countries represented	54

SURVEY SAYS

Great library
Students are friendly
Great off-campus food
Campus feels safe
Students are happy

ACADEMICS

Academic Rating	**90**
Calendar	semester
Student/faculty ratio	9:1
Professors interesting rating	87
Professors accessible rating	83
% professors teaching UG courses	100
% classes taught by TAs	0
Most common regular class size	10-19 students

MOST POPULAR MAJORS

Computer and information sciences and support services
political science and government
psychology

STUDENTS SPEAK OUT

Academics

"Big enough [so you can] always meet new people, [yet] small enough [so you can] always see a friend," is how one English major describes Brandeis University. Most students agree that Brandeis gives them a taste of the research-oriented life usually found at a large university while letting them enjoy the comforts of a small liberal arts college. Students give rave reviews of their professors. One undergraduate writes, "Brandeis professors aren't just given a list of their students' names at the beginning of the semester. They're also given their pictures. And many of them, even in large lecture classes, make an effort to study those pictures and learn students' names. I think that's a statement on the relative involvement professors here have with students." Many of the faculty members at Brandeis are "illustrious professors who are often experts and distinguished people in their fields," but they also bring a sense of humor to the classroom. For example, a music and psychology double major recommends that newcomers look out for one of her music theory professors because he "balances a piano bench on his head." Another excellent benefit at Brandeis is that students are encouraged to take classes from a wide variety of disciplines. A third-year biology major boasts, "I've managed to take theater, neuroscience, music, and philosophy courses without conflict." But don't think that fun is the same as easy. Academics at Brandeis are "very competitive," and "students need to be highly motivated to succeed."

Life

"If you're looking for a big party school with outstanding sports, don't come here," warns a junior. "But if you're looking for a small liberal arts university with an intelligent, inquisitive student body [who balances] work and fun, this is the place for you." Students have long complained that the opportunities for fun at Brandeis are limited, but in recent years there's been "an amazing initiative taking place by students and administrators to make Brandeis more fun." Many students like to take a shuttle into Boston so they can get a little crazy; however, there are other diversionary outlets available. One undergraduate says, "In the time that I've been here, I've gotten to go skydiving, learn[ed] how to knit, learn[ed] to work a state-of-the-art sound system, [paid] $5.00 to see musical acts like Ben Folds, walk[ed] around an on-campus art museum, edit[ed] my own literary magazine, and participate[d] in all kinds of cool events in Boston and on campus, all because of the opportunities provided by the school." Performance groups are very popular— "a cappella groups are huge on campus!"—but there are also plenty of events and clubs that appeal to other interests. One student adds, "And if there isn't an activity that satisfies you, then charter your own club!" Students even report that the campus's "boxlike architecture and drab décor are undergoing some improvements." Students also do their best to take advantage of the New England winters. A senior says, "We sled down Library Hill on cafeteria trays."

Student Body

"While most people like to say they can define the typical Brandeis student (Jewish, from a suburb, upper-middle class), so many of my friends don't fit that stereotype," reports one student. It's true that "the university was established on Jewish ideals" and that "there is a decent Jewish population" at Brandeis, but "you can find anyone into anything, I promise," writes a junior. She continues, "I've done everything from pagan rituals to orthodox services to cutting friends' hair to dressing guys in drag." While one English major is exaggerating when she says, "The typical Brandeis student is a George W. Bush-loathing, wannabe gangsta that enjoys philosophy, tofu, and Birkenstocks," she's hinting at something that holds much of this student body together: Even when the wind's not blowing, the student body leans to the left politically. And regarding the political thing, Brandeis boasts "a pretty strong activist community."

FINANCIAL AID: 781-736-3700 • E-MAIL: SENDINFO@BRANDEIS.EDU • WEBSITE: WWW.BRANDEIS.EDU

ADMISSIONS

Very important factors considered include: Class rank, secondary school record. *Important factors considered include:* Character/personal qualities, essays, extracurricular activities, recommendations, standardized test scores, talent/ability, volunteer work, work experience. *Other factors considered include:* Alumni/ae relation, interview, minority status. SAT Reasoning and SAT Subject Tests or ACT required. TOEFL required of all international applicants. High school diploma is required, and GED is accepted. *Academic units recommended:* 4 English, 3 math, 1 science (1 science lab), 3 foreign language, 1 history, 4 academic electives.

The Inside Word

While the university has a reputation for quality, the low yield of admits who actually choose to attend Brandeis results in a higher acceptance rate than one might expect. Weak students will still find it difficult to gain admission. The option of submitting ACT scores instead of SAT and SAT Subject Test: Subject Test scores should be the hands-down choice of any candidate who doesn't have to take SAT Subject Tests for any other reason.

FINANCIAL AID

The Princeton Review suggests that all financial aid forms be submitted as soon as possible after 1/1.

FROM THE ADMISSIONS OFFICE

"Education at Brandeis is personal, combining the intimacy of a small liberal arts college and the intellectual power of a large research university. Classes are small and are taught by professors, 98 percent of whom hold the highest degree in their fields. They give students personal attention in state-of-the-art resources, giving them the tools to succeed in a variety of post-graduate endeavors.

"This vibrant, freethinking, intellectual university was founded in 1948. Brandeis University reflects the values of the first Jewish Supreme Court Justice Louis Brandeis, which are passion for learning, commitment to social justice, respect for creativity and diversity, and concern for the world.

"Brandeis has an ideal location on the commuter rail nine miles west of Boston; state-of-the-art sports facilities; and internships that complement interests in law, medicine, government, finance, business, and the arts. Brandeis offers generous university scholarships and need-based financial aid that can be renewed for four years.

"Brandeis requires that students send official scores for the new SAT and two SAT Subject Tests, or the ACT with Writing in place of all SATs. Students for whom English is not their first language should take the TOEFL (Test of English as a Foreign Language)."

SELECTIVITY

Admissions Rating	**96**
# of applicants	5,831
% of applicants accepted	40
% of acceptees attending	33
# accepting a place on wait list	874
% admitted from wait list	4
# of early decision applicants	222
% accepted early decision	67

FRESHMAN PROFILE

Range SAT Verbal	630-720
Average SAT Verbal	660
Range SAT Math	630-720
Average SAT Math	670
**TPR Projected Range SAT Writing*	*650-710*
Range ACT Composite	28-33
Minimum Paper TOEFL	600
Minimum Computer Based TOEFL	250
Average HS GPA	3.85
% graduated top 10% of class	71
% graduated top 25% of class	89
% graduated top 50% of class	100

DEADLINES

Early decision application deadline	1/1
Regular application deadline	1/31
Regular notification	4/15
Nonfall registration?	yes

APPLICANTS ALSO LOOK AT

AND OFTEN PREFER

Brown University
Columbia University—Columbia College
Cornell University
Dartmouth College
University of Pennsylvania

AND SOMETIMES PREFER

New York University
Tufts University
Washington University in St. Louis

AND RARELY PREFER

Boston College
Boston University
SUNY at Binghamton

FINANCIAL FACTS

Financial Aid Rating	**60**
Annual tuition	$30,159
Room & Board	$8,656
Books and supplies	$700
Required fees	$911
% frosh rec. need-based scholarship or grant aid	56
% frosh rec. need-based self-help aid	46
Avg. frosh grant	$15,825
Avg. frosh loan	$3,002
Independent 529 member?	No

BRIGHAM YOUNG UNIVERSITY (UT)

A-153 ASB, PROVO, UT 84602-1110 • ADMISSIONS: 801-422-2507 • FAX: 801-422-0005

CAMPUS LIFE

Quality of Life Rating	**98**
Fire Safety Rating	**75**
Type of school	private
Affiliation	Church of Jesus Christ of Latter-day Saints
Environment	city

STUDENTS

Total undergrad enrollment	30,847
% male/female	51/49
% from out of state	76
% live on campus	20
% Asian	3
% Caucasian	82
% Hispanic	3
% Native American	1
% international	4
# of countries represented	125

SURVEY SAYS

Great library
Students are very religious
Very little beer drinking
Very little hard liquor
(Almost) no one smokes
Very little drug use

ACADEMICS

Academic Rating	**82**
Calendar	semester
Student/faculty ratio	21:1
Professors interesting rating	85
Professors accessible rating	79
% classes taught by TAs	0
Most common regular class size	20-29 students

MOST POPULAR MAJORS

English language and literature
family and consumer sciences/human sciences
psychology

STUDENTS SPEAK OUT

Academics

Students at Brigham Young University in Provo, the flagship campus of the BYU system, love the amenities their big school provides. They praise the "great research opportunities for undergraduates, [the] amazing library with its great resources," and the availability of "lots of classes and almost every major imaginable." The school is also committed to "keeping ahead technologically and keeping current on world events." What they love most about their school, however, is "the opportunity to receive a religious education at the same time as you receive your academic education, and the opportunity for those to mingle. In classes that are not religion-based, there are often discussions of how religion fits into the subject area of that course. It is nice to be able to discuss those things thoughtfully in a university atmosphere." Incoming students should prepare for a big-school experience; one undergrad explains, "It's initially overwhelming to pour into your classrooms with hundreds of other students," and freshmen are well advised to "take advantage of the Freshman Academy or Honors programs." One student writes, "As you accrue credits, you will personally get to know some fabulous teachers…the key is that you have to take the initiative" in introducing yourself to them. Students praise the required curriculum, which they believe "helps [them] to be well-rounded individuals."

Life

"Religion defines what BYU is and why it is such a great school," students agree, frequently reminding us that "We don't have to worry about a lot of things that other schools worry about. At the holidays we don't have 'don't drink and drive' campaigns… we don't have to worry about the drug and alcohol abuse." BYU's honor code sets the tone; it "prohibits drinking, drugs, cheating and other dishonest actions. It also requires men to be clean shaven (no beards)." In short, "students are expected to keep high standards at BYU, and this helps the students to be better people." Undergrads find plenty of ways to have fun without intoxicants, they assure us; reports one, "There is never a night when something isn't happening on campus, whether it's an athletic event, or a play, or a smaller social event planned by some section of the student council." There are "tons of events like movies, dance performances, museums, lots of student clubs and organizations, and good restaurants" to choose from on campus, and then, of course, there's also all that Provo has to offer. Students especially love the outdoors; many "enjoy skiing and snowboarding, and there are others that love to hike." Dating is also a major focal point of social life. Explains one student, "BYU is a school where people come to get married. Due to the fact that BYU is owned by the LDS church and the Law of Chastity that they live by, people pretty much go to BYU to meet people with their same standards, and get married."

Student Body

The vast majority of BYU undergrads are members of the Church of Jesus Christ of Latter-day Saints, which results in a high comfort level for the majority; "It's nice to know that over 90 percent of the student body shares your morals and beliefs," explains one student. There are also "international students and ethnic minorities, and there is a fairly large Islamic community within BYU, and atypical students seem to fit in pretty well. Those who are not of our faith are still respected and encouraged to practice their own faith." Writes one student, "The greatest strength of BYU lies in its unity, unity that comes through diversity, not homogeneity. BYU students come from all over the world but are mostly people who have very high religious standards and come to BYU for that reason. This is a great strength because in unity we can address concerns with greater strength than [in] places that are torn with strife."

FINANCIAL AID: 801-378-4104 • E-MAIL: ADMISSIONS@BYU.EDU • WEBSITE: WWW.BYU.EDU

ADMISSIONS

Very important factors considered include: Character/personal qualities, interview, religious affiliation/commitment, secondary school record, standardized test scores. *Important factors considered include:* Essays, extracurricular activities, minority status, recommendations, volunteer work. *Other factors considered include:* Talent/ability, work experience. ACT required. TOEFL required of all international applicants. High school diploma is required, and GED is accepted. *Academic units required:* 4 English, 3 math, 2 science (2 science lab), 2 foreign language, 2 history, 2 literature or writing. *Academic units recommended:* 4 English, 4 math, 3 science (3 science lab), 4 foreign language.

The Inside Word

Despite the high acceptance rate, this is a rigorous application process that will quickly and efficiently eliminate candidates who make a poor match. Most eliminate themselves by not applying to begin with, as the matchmaking places the greatest weight on the ideological fit.

FINANCIAL AID

Students should submit: FAFSA. The Princeton Review suggests that all financial aid forms be submitted as soon as possible after 1/1. *Need-based scholarships/grants offered:* Pell, state scholarships/grants, private scholarships, the school's own gift aid. *Loan aid offered:* FFEL Subsidized Stafford, FFEL Unsubsidized Stafford, FFEL PLUS, college/university loans from institutional funds. Applicants will be notified of awards on or about 4/20. Federal Work-study Program available. Institutional employment available. Off-campus job opportunities are good.

FROM THE ADMISSIONS OFFICE

"The mission of Brigham Young University—founded, supported, and guided by the Church of Jesus Christ of Latter-day Saints—is to assist individuals in their quest for perfection and eternal life. That assistance should provide a period of intensive learning in a stimulating setting where a commitment to excellence is expected and the full realization of human potential is pursued. All instruction, programs, and services at BYU, including a wide variety of extracurricular experiences, should make their own contribution toward the balanced development of the total person. Such a broadly prepared individual will not only be capable of meeting personal challenge and change but will also bring strength to others in the tasks of home and family life, social relationships, civic duty, and service to mankind.

"Freshman applicants for fall 2006 class are required to take either the new ACT (with or without the optional Writing section) or the new version of the SAT. Students may also submit scores from the old (prior to the March 2005) version of either test. Their highest composite score will be used in admissions decisions."

SELECTIVITY

Admissions Rating	**84**
# of applicants	6,960
% of applicants accepted	134
% of acceptees attending	60

FRESHMAN PROFILE

Range SAT Verbal	550-660
Average SAT Verbal	587
Range SAT Math	570-670
Average SAT Math	592
**TPR Projected Range SAT Writing*	*600-670*
Range ACT Composite	25-29
Average ACT Composite	27
Minimum Paper TOEFL	500
Minimum Computer Based TOEFL	173
Average HS GPA	3.74
% graduated top 10% of class	48
% graduated top 25% of class	82
% graduated top 50% of class	98

DEADLINES

Regular application deadline	2/15
Regular notification	approximately 3 weeks from submission date
Nonfall registration?	yes

APPLICANTS ALSO LOOK AT AND AND SOMETIMES PREFER

Brigham Young University—Idaho
University of Utah

FINANCIAL FACTS

Financial Aid Rating	**78**
Annual tuition	$3,280
Room & Board	$5,570
Books and supplies	$1,240
% frosh rec. need-based scholarship or grant aid	14
% UG rec. need-based scholarship or grant aid	30
% frosh rec. need-based self-help aid	6
% UG rec. need-based self-help aid	16
% frosh rec. any financial aid	28
% UG rec. any financial aid	42
Avg. frosh grant	$2,383
Avg. frosh loan	$713
Independent 529 member?	No

BROWN UNIVERSITY

BOX 1876, 45 PROSPECT STREET, PROVIDENCE, RI 02912 • ADMISSIONS: 401-863-2378 • FAX: 401-863-9300

CAMPUS LIFE

Quality of Life Rating	**95**
Fire Safety Rating	**60**
Type of school	private

STUDENTS

Total undergrad enrollment	5,772
% male/female	46/54
% from out of state	96
% from public high school	60
% live on campus	85
% in (# of) fraternities	15 (10)
% in (# of) sororities	5 (3)
% African American	7
% Asian	13
% Caucasian	51
% Hispanic	7
% Native American	1
% international	6
# of countries represented	72

SURVEY SAYS

No one cheats
Students are friendly
Great off-campus food
Students are happy
Political activism is popular

ACADEMICS

Academic Rating	**83**
Calendar	semester
Student/faculty ratio	9:1
Professors interesting rating	84
Professors accessible rating	88
% professors teaching UG courses	100
% classes taught by TAs	13

MOST POPULAR MAJORS

History
international relations and affairs

STUDENTS SPEAK OUT

Academics

"It's like the school has a motto," writes a typical Brown University undergrad, "and that motto is: 'It's your money. Why should we choose your classes?'" Thanks to the school's open curriculum, "being at Brown means you will never again have to take a class if you don't want to." Students who flock here are the type who yearn for such academic freedom; they "love the open curriculum and the chance it gives us to really invest ourselves in what we're most interested in. Brown allows you to explore academically without punishing you for it." Brown also "allows students to choose how we are evaluated in our classes by choosing to take any class S/NC (Satisfactory/No Credit). This says a lot about the learning philosophy of the school, which is mainly focused on the process of learning rather than simply the results." Brown professors "are engaging, challenging us as students and as participants in the learning process," and are "very accessible, dedicated to undergraduate students and usually pretty funny outside the classroom." Students appreciate that "a lot of the introductory classes are taught by brilliant professors. The concentration is truly on the undergraduates." Administrators, "as strange as it seems, are also incredibly accessible." Sums up one student, "Everything is at your fingertips, but you have to reach out for it. At Brown, very few things will simply come to you, but you can be sure that if you want it, it will be there."

Life

"The social scene is a lot like the academic scene" at Brown "in that there is a huge variety of options, and people tend to experience most of them. From hanging out to cocktail parties, from hippies partying in their co-ops to kids studying in the library, from fraternity parties to watching a movie, everything you can imagine doing for fun happens." Students agree that "Brown is a school that definitely parties, and Wednesday night through Sunday students here are partying," but not until they get their schoolwork done. Academics are demanding and students here work hard, but "aside from exams and major assignments, life is laid-back. That isn't to say the students lack passion or drive— quite the opposite—but there's a marked lack of nervous tension." Undergrads find plenty of time for extracurriculars, populating "over 150 extracurricular clubs and activities," including "great theater and music" opportunities. They also enjoy "free lectures by everyone from Spike Lee to Mikhail Gorbachev, free concerts, free comedy show, plays. We have anything and everything. There is almost too much going on." And then there's Providence, "a nice location with all sorts of cool night clubs and restaurants that don't make it easy to be bored on a Saturday night. There are hot spots like Fish Company, where people drink and dance, and there's Thayer Street, with anything a college student could ever need, from groceries, books, and clothes to videos, bikes, and clubs." Brown undergrads also take advantage of the fact that "Boston and New York City are relatively close by."

Student Body

Most Brown undergrads are "individual, free-thinking, and eager to learn." They are "very smart, have a keen knowledge of current affairs, and can talk about Plato, FDR, or biology," but "they don't have swelled heads. They're generally pretty well-grounded, open to new ideas, and fun." Like the New Englanders who surround them, "they tend to be very liberal and very politically active. It is a necessity to be up-to-date on current events, as discussions and debates take place from dorm rooms to the gym to the cafeteria." The "typically small 'outsider' communities (e.g. GLBT students) here have a lot of support on campus and generally hang out together." While "Brown has a reputation as a hippie school, it really isn't: There are people who fit into every social niche, and although it's not always easy to find the right people right away, they're out there."

FINANCIAL AID: 401-863-2721 • E-MAIL: ADMISSION_UNDERGRADUATE@BROWN.EDU • WEBSITE: WWW.BROWN.EDU

ADMISSIONS

Very important factors considered include: Character/personal qualities, secondary school record, talent/ability. *Important factors considered include:* Class rank, essays, extracurricular activities, recommendations. *Other factors considered include:* Alumni/ae relation, geographical residence, interview, minority status, standardized test scores, state residency, volunteer work, work experience. SAT Reasoning and SAT Subject Tests or ACT required. TOEFL required of all international applicants. High school diploma is required, and GED is not accepted. *Academic units required:* 4 English, 3 math, 3 science (2 science lab), 3 foreign language, 2 history, 1 academic elective. *Academic units recommended:* 4 English, 4 math, 4 science (3 science lab), 4 foreign language, 2 history, 1 academic elective.

The Inside Word

The cream of just about every crop applies to Brown. Gaining admission requires more than just a superior academic profile from high school. Some candidates, such as the sons and daughters of Brown graduates (who are admitted at virtually double the usual acceptance rate), have a better chance for admission than most others. Minority students benefit from some courtship, particularly once admitted. Ivies like to share the wealth and distribute offers of admission across a wide range of constituencies. Candidates from states that are overrepresented in the applicant pool, such as New York, have to be particularly distinguished in order to have the best chance at admission. So do those who attend high schools with many seniors applying to Brown, as it is rare for several students from any one school to be offered admission.

FINANCIAL AID

Students should submit: FAFSA, CSS/Financial Aid PROFILE, noncustodial (divorced/separated) parents' statement, business/farm supplement. Regular filing deadline is 2/1. The Princeton Review suggests that all financial aid forms be submitted as soon as possible after 1/1. *Need-based scholarships/grants offered:* Pell, SEOG, state scholarships/grants, private scholarships, the school's own gift aid. *Loan aid offered:* Direct Subsidized Stafford, Direct Unsubsidized Stafford, Direct PLUS, Federal Perkins, state loans, college/university loans from institutional funds. Applicants will be notified of awards on or about 4/1. Federal Work-study Program available. Institutional employment available. Off-campus job opportunities are excellent.

FROM THE ADMISSIONS OFFICE

"It is our pleasure to introduce you to a unique and wonderful place of learning: Brown University. Founded in 1764, Brown is a private, coeducational, Ivy League university in which the intellectual development of undergraduate students is fostered by a dedicated faculty on a traditional New England campus.

"Applicants will be required to submit results of the SAT Reasoning Test and any two SAT Subject Tests (except for the SAT Subject Test Writing). Students may substitute any SAT tests with the ACT with the Writing component."

SELECTIVITY

Admissions Rating	**99**
# of applicants	15,286
% of applicants accepted	17
% of acceptees attending	58
# accepting a place on wait list	1,400
% admitted from wait list	6
# of early decision applicants	551
% accepted early decision	29

FRESHMAN PROFILE

Range SAT Verbal	650-760
Average SAT Verbal	690
Range SAT Math	660-760
Average SAT Math	700
**TPR Projected Range SAT Writing*	*670-740*
Range ACT Composite	27-32
Average ACT Composite	29
Minimum Paper TOEFL	600
Minimum Computer Based TOEFL	250
% graduated top 10% of class	90
% graduated top 25% of class	98
% graduated top 50% of class	100

DEADLINES

Early decision application deadline	11/1
Early decision notification	12/15
Regular application deadline	1/1
Regular notification	4/1
Nonfall registration?	no

APPLICANTS ALSO LOOK AT AND OFTEN PREFER

Harvard College, Princeton University, Stanford University, Yale University

AND SOMETIMES PREFER

Amherst College, Massachusetts Institute of Technology, Smith College, Williams College

AND RARELY PREFER

Bowdoin College, Georgetown University, Oberlin College, Tufts University

FINANCIAL FACTS

Financial Aid Rating	**96**
Annual tuition	$30,672
Room & Board	$8,474
Books and supplies	$2,300
Required fees	$901
% frosh rec. need-based scholarship or grant aid	39
% UG rec. need-based scholarship or grant aid	37
% frosh rec. need-based self-help aid	38
% UG rec. need-based self-help aid	39
Avg. frosh grant	$21,600
Avg. frosh loan	$4,000
Independent 529 member?	No

BRYANT UNIVERSITY

1150 Douglas Pike, Smithfield, RI 02917 • Admissions: 401-232-6100 • Fax: 401-232-6741

CAMPUS LIFE

Quality of Life Rating	**84**
Fire Safety Rating	**91**
Type of school	private
Environment	town

STUDENTS

Total undergrad enrollment	3,030
% male/female	60/40
% from out of state	83
% from public high school	80
% live on campus	84
% in (# of) fraternities	11 (6)
% in (# of) sororities	7 (3)
% African American	3
% Asian	3
% Caucasian	84
% Hispanic	3
% international	2
# of countries represented	28

SURVEY SAYS

Small classes
Great computer facilities
Great library
Athletic facilities are great
Campus feels safe
Lots of beer drinking
Hard liquor is popular

ACADEMICS

Academic Rating	**77**
Calendar	semester
Student/faculty ratio	16:1
Professors interesting rating	79
Professors accessible rating	82
% professors teaching UG courses	100
% classes taught by TAs	0
Most common lab size	30-39 students
Most common regular class size	30-39 students

MOST POPULAR MAJORS

Business administration/management
finance
marketing/marketing management

STUDENTS SPEAK OUT

Academics

Bryant University offers some majors outside of business and management, but students tell us that pursuing one of those majors would be like ordering a dinner salad at a steakhouse. Students report that "every class, including the liberal arts classes...will involve business in one way or another." Another trumpets, "All my sociology, psychology, even ecology classes somehow discussed the business world within them!" Technologically, the school goes all-out, with "an enormous amount of resources on campus, including a simulated trading floor of the NYSE. Also, the entire campus is now wireless, so students can connect to the Internet with their laptops anywhere." Studying in such technologically advanced facilities means that "students can relate classes to the real world. We really do live in a business environment." The school's "student-centered" approach distinguishes it as well; "Everything on campus is designed to help out the student body, from the student programming, to the facilities, to the faculty. It is a very nurturing environment," explains one undergrad. Students also appreciate the "strong alumni relations, which help with internships and job placement." Solid programs in accounting, finance, marketing, and management have earned Bryant "a strong academic reputation. The school challenges its students to think creatively, both alone and in group settings, to reach goals."

Life

Because many "students at Bryant have—on top of a full course load—a job and/or internship, are members of a minimum of two organizations and/or sports, and hold some type of position of leadership," undergraduates "have little free time during the week." The campus is a very work-friendly environment, students tell us; "The abundance of technology on our campus—television monitors in almost every corner that you look, VOIP phones in the dorm rooms, wireless internet connectivity all over campus—creates an environment where students can work hard, relax a little, and work some more." The "very clean and well-landscaped [campus] is basically in the middle of the woods," providing "peace to study," but with the benefit "of a great city not far away." While weekdays are devoted to work and clubs, "Thursday through Sunday there are parties, or people going out to Providence who you can catch a ride with, with more studying on the weekends at intermittent times."

Student Body

"Since it's a business school with all serious business students for the most part, it excludes a wide diversity of people and their quirks," Bryant students observe. "Every day, either you're dressing in a business suit or you're in your daily clothing (mainly Abercrombie and Fitch and North Face and other high-end brand names, such as Burberry, Gucci, Seven, etc)." In other words, "idiosyncrasy is not encouraged; business etiquette and manners are a must at most times in this school." Most here are "preppy and financially stable. There are not many people who come from non-wealthy backgrounds." They can be cliquish; explains one student, "people rarely leave their own groups and the drama caused by much of it can get annoying by senior year." The school "has a sizeable population of international students, including students from China, India, Spain, South Africa, Turkey, and Italy. These students, many of whom belong to the Multicultural Student Union, are among the most active members of the Bryant community and take part in a number of events to educate Bryant students and faculty about different races and cultures."

FINANCIAL AID: 401-232-6020 • E-MAIL: ADMISSION@BRYANT.EDU • WEBSITE: WWW.BRYANT.EDU

ADMISSIONS

Very important factors considered include: Character/personal qualities, class rank, essays, recommendations, secondary school record, standardized test scores. *Important factors considered include:* Alumni/ae relation, extracurricular activities, talent/ability. *Other factors considered include:* Geographical residence, interview, minority status, volunteer work, work experience. SAT Reasoning or ACT required. TOEFL required of all international applicants. High school diploma is required, and GED is accepted. *Academic units required:* 4 English, 4 math, 3 science (2 science lab), 2 foreign language, 2 history/social sciences. *Academic units recommended:* 4 history/social sciences.

The Inside Word

If you're a solid student you should meet little trouble getting into Bryant. The university's admissions effort has brought in qualified applicants from across the country, but the heaviest draw remains from New England. Students attending Bryant will receive a solid business education as well as precious connections in the corporate worlds of Providence and Boston.

FINANCIAL AID

Students should submit: FAFSA. Regular filing deadline is 2/15. The Princeton Review suggests that all financial aid forms be submitted as soon as possible after 1/1. *Need-based scholarships/grants offered:* Pell, SEOG, state scholarships/grants, private scholarships, the school's own gift aid. *Loan aid offered:* Direct Subsidized Stafford, Direct Unsubsidized Stafford, FFEL PLUS, Federal Perkins. Applicants will be notified of awards on or about 3/24. Federal Work-study Program available. Institutional employment available. Off-campus job opportunities are good.

FROM THE ADMISSIONS OFFICE

"Bryant is a student-centered University that provides the resources that students need to acquire knowledge, develop character, and achieve success—as they define it. In addition to a first-class faculty, state-of-the-art facilities, and advanced technology, Bryant offers stimulating classroom dynamics; internship opportunities at more than 300 companies; 60 student clubs and organizations; varsity, intramural, and club sports for men and women; and many opportunities for community service and leadership development.

"Bryant is the right choice for individuals seeking the best combination of a business and liberal arts education and offers degrees in Applied Psychology, Business Administration, Communication, Information Technology, International Business, and Liberal Studies. All of our academic programs blend the theoretical with the practical to make our graduates uniquely prepared to excel. Bryant's rigorous academic standards have been recognized and accredited by NEASC and AACSB International.

"Technology is a fundamental component of the learning process at Bryant. Every entering freshman is provided with an IBM laptop for personal use. Students exchange their laptop for a new one in their junior year, which they will own upon graduation. Bryant University was ranked 2nd of the "Top 25 Most Connected Campuses," by The Princeton's Review in October 2004 on Forbes.com.

"Bryant is situated on 392 acres of beautiful New England countryside and offers an array of cultural, social, and co-curricular educational activities right on campus. Bryant is only 15 minutes from Providence, one hour from Boston, and three hours from New York City and all of the attractions and opportunities available in these major metropolitan areas.

"Bryant requires that students enrolling in fall 2006 take the new SAT with the Writing component, or the ACT with the writing section. (We are not accepting the old SAT and we do not require the SAT Subject Tests.)"

SELECTIVITY

Admissions Rating	**84**
# of applicants	3,879
% of applicants accepted	63
% of acceptees attending	31
# accepting a place on wait list	541
% admitted from wait list	24
# of early decision applicants	48
% accepted early decision	75

FRESHMAN PROFILE

Range SAT Verbal	490-580
Average SAT Verbal	535
Range SAT Math	530-610
Average SAT Math	569
**TPR Projected Range SAT Writing*	*550-620*
Range ACT Composite	22-25
Average ACT Composite	24
Minimum Paper TOEFL	550
Minimum Computer Based TOEFL	213
Average HS GPA	3.2
% graduated top 10% of class	13
% graduated top 25% of class	47
% graduated top 50% of class	88

DEADLINES

Early decision application deadline	11/15
Early decision notification	12/15
Regular application deadline	2/15
Regular notification	3/15
Nonfall registration?	yes

APPLICANTS ALSO LOOK AT AND OFTEN PREFER

Bentley College, Northeastern University, Quinnipiac University

AND SOMETIMES PREFER

Amherst College, University of Massachusetts—Amherst, University of New Hampshire

AND RARELY PREFER

Assumption College, Roger Williams University, University of Rhode Island

FINANCIAL FACTS

Financial Aid Rating	**70**
Annual tuition	$24,762
Room & Board	$9,568
Books and supplies	$1,000
% frosh rec. need-based scholarship or grant aid	57
% UG rec. need-based scholarship or grant aid	48
% frosh rec. need-based self-help aid	60
% UG rec. need-based self-help aid	58
% frosh rec. any financial aid	81
% UG rec. any financial aid	88
Avg. frosh grant	$11,274
Avg. frosh loan	$4,231
Independent 529 member?	No

BRYN MAWR COLLEGE

101 North Merion Avenue, Bryn Mawr, PA 19010-2859 • Admissions: 610-526-5152 • Fax: 610-526-7471

CAMPUS LIFE

Quality of Life Rating	**95**
Fire Safety Rating	**89**
Type of school	private
Environment	metropolis

STUDENTS

Total undergrad enrollment	1,313
% male/female	2/98
% from out of state	80
% from public high school	60
% live on campus	97
% African American	5
% Asian	11
% Caucasian	45
% Hispanic	3
% international	8
# of countries represented	44

SURVEY SAYS

Small classes
No one cheats
Dorms are like palaces
Frats and sororities are unpopular or nonexistent

ACADEMICS

Academic Rating	**90**
Calendar	semester
Student/faculty ratio	8:1
Professors interesting rating	93
Professors accessible rating	90
% professors teaching UG courses	100
% classes taught by TAs	0
Most common regular class size	10-19 students

MOST POPULAR MAJORS

English language and literature
political science and government

STUDENTS SPEAK OUT

Academics

"In order to excel at Bryn Mawr, you need to be willing to do more work than you've ever done in your life," undergrads at this small, prestigious all-women's college warn. Most are. They "challenge themselves, always doing their individual best" to meet the demands of the school's "insanely rigorous, but rewarding, academics." Why? One student writes, "I feel that the hours and hours of work are worthwhile. The students know that their work isn't just busy work and that there are high standards; that pushes us to improve and learn in a way that wouldn't otherwise be possible." Bryn Mawr's "great track record for sending students to medical school" attests to the success of the school's approach; students' devotion to the school does likewise. Undergrads here especially appreciate the important role they play in running the school. Explains one student, "With the oldest self-governing association in the entire country, Bryn Mawr prides itself on the close communication between everyone in the community, from the president of the college to the incoming freshmen, each year." A student-administered honor code, one of the school's many treasured traditions, "makes taking final exams incredibly easy. Almost all exams are self-scheduled, so you can take them when you're ready, not when they're assigned." Additionally, "The student curriculum committee is very active in fulfilling the students' needs and desires for the academic process." Academic partnerships with Haverford, Swarthmore, and U Penn heavily supplement the "sometimes pitiful course selection" here.

Life

"Because Bryn Mawr is all women, the social life is different from the traditional college experience," students here explain. "When you're a freshman, traditions like Lantern Night, Hell Week, and Parade Night really make you feel like a part of 'the sisterhood' of Bryn Mawr." Undergrads also point out that except for the aforementioned traditions, "you really have to go off campus if you want to party. Fortunately there are so many colleges in such close proximity, including Villanova, Haverford, Swarthmore, and Penn, that you can always go out to a party if you want to, and you get to come home to a clean and quiet dorm." Many here report that "we spend most weekends in Philadelphia." For those who stick around campus on weekends, activities "usually include watching a movie and ordering out or going to some campus activity." The surrounding town, students agree, "is pretty boring." On a more positive note, "the campus is gorgeous. Imagine a Welsh castle," one undergrad suggests.

Student Body

"The only really common feature to Bryn Mawr women is an intense commitment to our studies. Other than that, everyone here really does their own thing," students agree. Even so, they see some dominant strains within their ranks; they detect, for example, a strong contingent of women who are "preppy, liberal, and open to homosexuality. Because it is an all-girls school, there are a lot of gay students, and those who aren't gay are accepting of the gay community." There are also conspicuous minorities of "high school misfits who come here to fit in, as well as students who take Harry Potter a little too seriously. They wear capes every day." Women here agree that "the community is overwhelmingly liberal politically, and the more moderate or conservative approaches or viewpoints of an issue can get lost in the majority at times. It would be nice to see more diversity of political opinion at Bryn Mawr." Otherwise, Bryn Mawr students "run the gamut from the well-groomed New Jersey girl, to the vegan Girl Scout, to the hairy rugby player."

BRYN MAWR COLLEGE

FINANCIAL AID: 610-526-5245 • E-MAIL: ADMISSIONS@BRYNMAWR.EDU • WEBSITE: WWW.BRYNMAWR.EDU

ADMISSIONS

Very important factors considered include: Essays, recommendations, secondary school record. *Important factors considered include:* Extracurricular activities. *Other factors considered include:* Class rank, interview, standardized test scores, talent/ability, volunteer work, work experience. SAT Reasoning and SAT Subject Tests or ACT required. TOEFL required of all international applicants. High school diploma is required, and GED is accepted. *Academic units required:* 2 academic electives. *Academic units recommended:* 4 English, 3 math, 2 science (1 science lab), 3 foreign language, 2 social studies, 2 history.

The Inside Word

Do not be deceived by Bryn Mawr's admit rate; its student body is among the academically best in the nation. Outstanding preparation for graduate study draws an applicant pool that is well prepared and intellectually curious. The admissions committee includes eight faculty members and four seniors. Each applicant is reviewed by four readers, including at least one faculty member and one student.

FINANCIAL AID

Students should submit: FAFSA, CSS/Financial Aid PROFILE, noncustodial (divorced/separated) parents' statement, business/farm supplement, student and parent federal tax returns. Regular filing deadline is 2/4. The Princeton Review suggests that all financial aid forms be submitted as soon as possible after 1/1. *Need-based scholarships/grants offered:* Pell, SEOG, state scholarships/grants, the school's own gift aid. *Loan aid offered:* FFEL Subsidized Stafford, FFEL Unsubsidized Stafford, FFEL PLUS, Federal Perkins. Applicants will be notified of awards on or about 3/23. Off-campus job opportunities are excellent.

FROM THE ADMISSIONS OFFICE

"One wouldn't ordinarily assume that a small institution could offer as diverse a range of opportunities as many large universities, or that a campus that looks like the English countryside could exist within 20 minutes of downtown Philadelphia, but Bryn Mawr is far from ordinary. Prepare to be surprised. Innovative, creative, and purposeful, the students at Bryn Mawr inspire their peers as much and as often as any faculty member. Spirited intellectual inquiry, a commitment to academic excellence, and a desire to impact the world in a meaningful way are the hallmarks of this community of equals. Students at Bryn Mawr learn by doing and lead by example. They take full advantage of all that Bryn Mawr has to offer, including internship opportunities, an active Alumnae Association, a lively Community Service office and a consortium of schools that includes Haverford, Swarthmore, and the University of Pennsylvania. Bryn Mawr's Student Government Association is the oldest in the country and students participate in every aspect of the college's decision-making process, serving as representatives to Admissions, The Honor Board, The Curriculum Committee, and even The Board of Trustees. Bryn Mawr is a demanding and caring place where both ideas and individuals matter.

"The new SAT and two SAT Subject Tests are required for admission. Students may choose SAT Subject Tests. Students may submit the ACT in lieu of the SAT and SAT Subject Tests. We recommend that students also take the optional ACT Writing Test."

SELECTIVITY

Admissions Rating	**95**
# of applicants	1,926
% of applicants accepted	47
% of acceptees attending	40
# accepting a place on wait list	288
% admitted from wait list	5
# of early decision applicants	97
% accepted early decision	73

FRESHMAN PROFILE

Range SAT Verbal	620-720
Average SAT Verbal	668
Range SAT Math	600-690
Average SAT Math	645
**TPR Projected Range SAT Writing*	*650-710*
Average ACT Composite	28
Minimum Paper TOEFL	600
Minimum Computer Based TOEFL	250
% graduated top 10% of class	66
% graduated top 25% of class	93
% graduated top 50% of class	100

DEADLINES

Early decision application deadline	11/15
Early decision notification	12/15
Regular application deadline	1/15
Regular notification	4/15
Nonfall registration?	no

APPLICANTS ALSO LOOK AT

AND OFTEN PREFER
Brown University, Harvard College, University of Pennsylvania

AND SOMETIMES PREFER
Haverford College, Mount Holyoke College, Scripps College, Smith College, Swarthmore College, Wellesley College

AND RARELY PREFER
Oberlin College, Vassar College

FINANCIAL FACTS

Financial Aid Rating	**97**
Annual tuition	$27,900
Room & Board	$9,700
Books and supplies	$1,000
Required fees	$730
% frosh rec. need-based scholarship or grant aid	52
% UG rec. need-based scholarship or grant aid	53
% frosh rec. need-based self-help aid	42
% UG rec. need-based self-help aid	45
% frosh rec. any financial aid	57
% UG rec. any financial aid	59
Avg. frosh grant	$22,406
Avg. frosh loan	$3,472
Independent 529 member?	No

BUCKNELL UNIVERSITY

FREAS HALL, BUCKNELL UNIVERSITY, LEWISBURG, PA 17837 • ADMISSIONS: 570-577-1101 • FAX: 570-577-3538

CAMPUS LIFE

Quality of Life Rating	**82**
Fire Safety Rating	**75**
Type of school	private
Environment	rural

STUDENTS

Total undergrad enrollment	3,419
% male/female	50/50
% from out of state	68
% from public high school	68
% live on campus	88
% in (# of) fraternities	35 (11)
% in (# of) sororities	38 (7)
% African American	3
% Asian	6
% Caucasian	84
% Hispanic	2
% international	3
# of countries represented	41

SURVEY SAYS

Small classes
Great library
Athletic facilities are great
Campus feels safe
Frats and sororities dominate social scene
Lots of beer drinking

ACADEMICS

Academic Rating	**91**
Calendar	semester
Student/faculty ratio	11:1
Professors interesting rating	87
Professors accessible rating	89
% professors teaching UG courses	100
% classes taught by TAs	0
Most common lab size	10-19 students
Most common regular class size	10-19 students

MOST POPULAR MAJORS

Biology/biological sciences
Business administration/management
economics

STUDENTS SPEAK OUT

Academics

Among an elite tier of small East Coast schools, Bucknell University prides itself on providing plenty of attention to its undergraduates. "Professors are always accessible and willing to help," confirms a junior. "I once missed a week of classes because I was sick—my professor called me in and spent three hours catching me up on everything I missed." But this isn't a simple case of babysitting. An accounting major explains, "The faculty challenge you on so many levels, and their commitment to our education is clear." This competitive student body of 3,000-plus can choose from over 50 majors and over 60 minors. Students say, "The academics are outstanding." Their review of the administration isn't as good, due in large part to recent anti-alcohol policies that have upset many students. But other students remind us that not everything is foul in the administrative wings. Online registration, a recent project, "makes things much easier," a sophomore says. The administration also makes sure that the "gorgeous campus" doesn't lose its luster. One theater major describes Bucknell as "a country club on the Susquehanna River."

Life

Bucknell is "located in the heart of central Pennsylvania," and it boasts a huge Greek scene. The student body's motto is "work hard, play hard," and much of the hard playing takes place "on frat row." As one student puts it, Bucknell students are "fratastically fun." A freshman adds that "for those who don't drink, there are tons of activities available." One of his classmates says, "The school works hard to bring in comedians, have concerts, or [provide] other recreational activities." The school just completed a $32 million expansion and renovation of its athletic facilities, and exercise enthusiasts report that "they are well used." Other on-campus perks include a poetry center, an observatory, and an eighteen-hole golf course. Although it may not be the most exciting place in the world, Lewisburg, Bucknell's host community, "is beautiful, quaint, and safe." But the social life at Bucknell provides enough excitement. Besides, these students don't need any more distractions. One student reminds us that the first part of the Bucknell creed is to work hard: "Lots of time spent studying," she says.

Student Body

"I've never been to a place with such a large percentage of cool and attractive people," raves a junior from New Jersey. A number of students corroborate this opinion and describe their classmates as look-alikes for models in "a J. Crew catalog." While this student body hails from all over the United States and more than 40 foreign countries, an education major tells us that you'll find a large number of students from "New Jersey, Pennsylvania, or California." No matter where they come from, those who arrive in Lewisburg find themselves in what students affectionately refer to as the "Bucknell Bubble." A student explains the bubble as a place where students are "disconnected from the real problems of the world." One business management major claims, "There could be more diversity here at Bucknell;" however, another undergraduate adds, "Each freshman class seems to be a bit more diversified."

ADMISSIONS

Very important factors considered include: Character/personal qualities, class rank, secondary school record, standardized test scores, talent/ability. *Important factors considered include:* Extracurricular activities, minority status, recommendations, volunteer work. *Other factors considered include:* Alumni/ae relation, essays, geographical residence, interview, religious affiliation/commitment, work experience. SAT Reasoning or ACT required. TOEFL required of all international applicants. High school diploma is required, and GED is accepted. *Academic units required:* 4 English, 3 math, 2 science, 2 foreign language, 2 social studies, 2 history, 1 academic elective. *Academic units recommended:* 4 English, 4 math, 3 science, 4 foreign language, 2 social studies, 2 history, 1 academic elective.

The Inside Word

Each application is read by two admissions officers. If you are serious about attending Bucknell, you'll need to take the most competitive courses available at your high school and have strong grades and test scores. Still, overconfidence or a so-so match can throw a wrench in the plans of some; recent trends show larger numbers on the university's wait list and a track record of increased competitiveness for admission.

FINANCIAL AID

Students should submit: FAFSA, CSS/Financial Aid PROFILE, noncustodial (divorced/separated) parents' statement. Regular filing deadline is 1/1. The Princeton Review suggests that all financial aid forms be submitted as soon as possible after 1/1. *Need-based scholarships/grants offered:* Pell, SEOG, state scholarships/grants, private scholarships, the school's own gift aid. *Loan aid offered:* FFEL Subsidized Stafford, FFEL Unsubsidized Stafford, FFEL PLUS, Federal Perkins. Applicants will be notified of awards on or about 4/1. Federal Work-study Program available. Off-campus job opportunities are poor.

FROM THE ADMISSIONS OFFICE

"Bucknell combines the personal experience of a small residential liberal arts college and the wide choices offered by a larger university. The College of Arts and Sciences and College of Engineering offer 53 majors and 64 minors. A college-like university enrolling 3,350 undergraduates and 150 graduate students. Bucknell offers many opportunities for learning in and out of the classroom. Engineering students take part in music ensembles, theater productions, and poetry readings. Arts and sciences students enroll in engineering courses. With a student/faculty ratio of 12:1, students gain exceptional first-hand experience by collaborating with faculty on serious research projects. Students complement their classroom experience with more than 150 student organizations, including competition in the prestigious Division I Patriot League. Together, these opportunities allow Bucknell students to learn how to think critically and to develop their leadership skills, preparing them to make a difference in their local communities and in the world.

"Applicants graduating from high school in—or after—2006 are required to take the new SAT or the ACT with the Writing section. Fall 2006 applicants are allowed to submit scores from the old versions of both tests as their best scores (old/new) will be used in making admissions decisions."

SELECTIVITY

Admissions Rating	**95**
# of applicants	8,324
% of applicants accepted	36
% of acceptees attending	30
# accepting a place on wait list	1,862
% admitted from wait list	4
# of early decision applicants	332
% accepted early decision	49

FRESHMAN PROFILE

Range SAT Verbal	600-670
Average SAT Verbal	636
Range SAT Math	630-710
Average SAT Math	666
**TPR Projected Range SAT Writing*	*630-680*
Range ACT Composite	27-31
Average ACT Composite	29
Minimum Paper TOEFL	550
Minimum Computer Based TOEFL	213
% graduated top 10% of class	64
% graduated top 25% of class	93
% graduated top 50% of class	99

DEADLINES

Early decision application deadline	11/15
Early decision notification	12/15
Regular application deadline	1/1
Regular notification	4/1
Nonfall registration?	no

APPLICANTS ALSO LOOK AT AND OFTEN PREFER

Boston College, Cornell U., Duke U., Middlebury College, Princeton U.

AND SOMETIMES PREFER

Carnegie Mellon U., Colgate U., College of William and Mary, U. of Richmond, Wake Forest U.

AND RARELY PREFER

Dickinson College, Franklin & Marshall College, Gettysburg College, Hamilton College

FINANCIAL FACTS

Financial Aid Rating	**96**
Annual tuition	$32,592
Room & Board	$6,872
Books and supplies	$750
Required fees	$196
% frosh rec. need-based scholarship or grant aid	46
% UG rec. need-based scholarship or grant aid	45
% frosh rec. need-based self-help aid	48
% UG rec. need-based self-help aid	51
% frosh rec. any financial aid	49
% UG rec. any financial aid	51
Avg. frosh grant	$17,300
Avg. frosh loan	$4,000
Independent 529 member?	No

CAL POLY—SAN LUIS OBISPO

1 GRAND AVENUE, SAN LUIS OBISPO, CA 93407 • ADMISSIONS: 805-756-2311 • FAX: 805-756-5400

CAMPUS LIFE

Quality of Life Rating	**88**
Fire Safety Rating	**60**
Type of school	public
Environment	town

STUDENTS

Total undergrad enrollment	16,565
% male/female	57/43
% from out of state	7
% from public high school	91
% live on campus	22
% in (# of) fraternities	10 (25)
% in (# of) sororities	8 (10)
% African American	1
% Asian	12
% Caucasian	64
% Hispanic	10
% Native American	1

SURVEY SAYS

Small classes
Great computer facilities
Athletic facilities are great
Students are friendly
Students love San Luis Obispo, CA
Great off-campus food
Students are happy
Student publications are popular

ACADEMICS

Academic Rating	**77**
Calendar	quarter
Student/faculty ratio	19:1
Professors interesting rating	86
Professors accessible rating	86
% classes taught by TAs	0
Most common lab size	20-29 students
Most common regular class size	30-39 students

MOST POPULAR MAJORS

Architecture (BArch, BA/BS, MArch, MA/MS, PhD)
Business administration/ management
psychology

STUDENTS SPEAK OUT

Academics

"Hands-on learning by doing is Cal Poly's philosophy, and they actually follow it," report students at this selective state school located about halfway between Los Angeles and San Francisco. California employers are aware of the benefits of Cal Poly's approach. They "know that a graduate from Poly is well prepared and well rounded, has worked in [his or her] field (most of the time extensively), and is hardworking and intelligent." The school demonstrates academic strength in areas ranging from business to architecture. Even its off-the-beaten-path course offerings are well regarded; its graphic communications major, for example, "is [a unique] program that provides students with a completely hands-on education [on] all the facets of printing, digital media, design, and management of the graphic communications industry." Cal Poly is large, but "within our majors, we feel like part of a small community. Everyone is very nice and helpful." Students also say that "the class sizes are small, and a lot of professors truly love teaching." On the down side, "many of the facilities could be improved. However, [because of] the budget issues in California, that's not too likely to happen."

Life

"There's an overwhelming amount of things to partake in" at Cal Poly, students inform us. "The Rec Sports program has better teams than the NCAA teams," some students claim, "and the women's field hockey team is headed to state championships." There's also the San Luis Obispo (SLO, pronounced "slow") region, which "offers many attractions, including a Farmers' Market every Thursday night, which is always a blast." Notes one student, "We have a really small downtown, but it's a lot of fun and has great places to eat. But if you're looking for a big city with tons of things to do every night, don't come here. It's called the 'SLO life' for a reason." Students also point out that "being as it is on the coast, the beach is always a great getaway. Whether it's a day trip or camping overnight on the sand with your closest friends, it's always a blast to be able to drive less than ten miles and be at the ocean. Cal Poly is definitely located in one of the best places in California." When it's time to socialize, "SLO is the right mix—hard-core academics and plenty of intellectuals in a good college town [who] love [their] beer and parties." Partying at Cal Poly "isn't as big as it is at other schools. There are a lot of people here that are very dedicated to their schoolwork and not interested in partying. But if you want to, you can find the parties." One student says, "One thing is for sure: Students in SLO drink for recreation and for fun, not to chase boredom or misery."

Student Body

The typical student at Cal Poly "is white, Christian, and Republican." However, students say that "the campus is diverse in people's backgrounds, beliefs, life experiences, lifestyles, and so on." That's why "walking through Cal Poly's campus is like taking a shopping trip: You have your cowboy boots (aggies), business suits (business majors), ink-clad jeans and T-shirts (GRC [graphic communications] majors), athletic apparel (kinesiology students)—a little mix of everything. Typical apparel is a Cal Poly sweatshirt and jeans, California casual." "Religion is big," especially for a state school, "but there are plenty of nonfanatics to hang out with." Geographically speaking, "everybody is either from the Bay Area or So Cal (Orange County or San Diego)." Because it's such a large school, "people mostly interact with those in their major or college."

Financial Aid: 805-756-2927 • E-mail: admissions@calpoly.edu • Website: www.calpoly.edu

ADMISSIONS

Very important factors considered include: Secondary school record, standardized test scores. *Other factors considered include:* Extracurricular activities, talent/ability, volunteer work, work experience. SAT Reasoning or ACT required. TOEFL required of all international applicants. High school diploma is required, and GED is accepted. *Academic units required:* 4 English, 3 math, 3 science (1 science lab), 2 foreign language.

The Inside Word

While it's tough to get admitted, Cal Poly doesn't spend much time on frills in the admissions process. Satisfy the formulas or else! As with all California public institutions, the banning of affirmative action will continue to roil the application process for the near future.

FINANCIAL AID

Students should submit: FAFSA, institution's own financial aid form. Regular filing deadline is 6/30. The Princeton Review suggests that all financial aid forms be submitted as soon as possible after 1/1. *Need-based scholarships/grants offered:* Pell, SEOG, state scholarships/grants, private scholarships, the school's own gift aid. *Loan aid offered:* FFEL Subsidized Stafford, FFEL Unsubsidized Stafford, FFEL PLUS, Federal Perkins, college/university loans from institutional funds, alternative loans. Applicants will be notified of awards on or about 4/15. Federal Work-study Program available. Institutional employment available. Off-campus job opportunities are excellent.

FROM THE ADMISSIONS OFFICE

"From row crops to computers, Cal Poly believes the best way for someone to learn something is to do it. That's been the school's philosophy since it began in 1901: Learn by Doing. Cal Poly students gain invaluable firsthand experience both on campus and off. On-campus opportunities such as the daily student-run newspaper and real world agricultural projects such as the organic farm, thoroughbred breeding project, ranch horse training project, test bull project, and market beef, sheep, and swine projects, as well as engineering opportunities like the Cal Poly CubeSat satellite-building project, make hands-on learning a daily reality, not just a catchphrase. Off-campus work with government agencies and major national corporations for both academic credit and a salary is available through various programs, including the largest cooperative education program in the western United States. With its successful, no-nonsense approach to education, Cal Poly has built a solid statewide and national reputation.

"Applicants for fall 2006 must submit the results of scores from the SAT or ACT (with or without the Writing components from either test)."

SELECTIVITY

Admissions Rating	**92**
# of applicants	22,551
% of applicants accepted	38
% of acceptees attending	33
# of early decision applicants	701
% accepted early decision	24

FRESHMAN PROFILE

Range SAT Verbal	540-640
Average SAT Verbal	594
Range SAT Math	580-680
Average SAT Math	639
**TPR Projected Range SAT Writing*	*590-660*
Range ACT Composite	24-28
Average ACT Composite	28
Minimum Paper TOEFL	550
Minimum Computer Based TOEFL	213
Average HS GPA	3.7
% graduated top 10% of class	42
% graduated top 25% of class	79
% graduated top 50% of class	97

DEADLINES

Early decision application deadline	10/31
Early decision notification	12/15
Regular application deadline	11/30
Regular notification	rolling
Nonfall registration?	yes

APPLICANTS ALSO LOOK AT AND SOMETIMES PREFER

Santa Clara University
University of California—Berkeley
University of California—Davis
University of California—Irvine
University of California—Los Angeles
University of California—San Diego
University of California—Santa Barbara
University of Southern California

FINANCIAL FACTS

Financial Aid Rating	**64**
Annual in-state tuition	$0
Annual out-of-state tuition	$226 per unit
Room & Board	$8,146
Books and supplies	$1,260
Required fees	$3,804
% frosh rec. need-based scholarship or grant aid	23
% UG rec. need-based scholarship or grant aid	24
% frosh rec. need-based self-help aid	22
% UG rec. need-based self-help aid	26
% frosh rec. any financial aid	65
% UG rec. any financial aid	69
Avg. frosh grant	$1,490
Avg. frosh loan	$6,643
Independent 529 member?	No

CALIFORNIA INSTITUTE OF TECHNOLOGY

1200 East California Blvd., Mail Code 328-87, Pasadena, CA 91125 • Admissions: 626-395-6341 • Fax: 626-683-3026

CAMPUS LIFE

Quality of Life Rating	**83**
Fire Safety Rating	**84**
Type of school	private
Environment	metropolis

STUDENTS

Total undergrad enrollment	896
% male/female	69/31
% from out of state	64
% from public high school	81
% live on campus	90
% African American	1
% Asian	31
% Caucasian	52
% Hispanic	7
% Native American	1
% international	7
# of countries represented	31

SURVEY SAYS

Small classes
No one cheats
Lab facilities are great
Great computer facilities
Great library
Students are friendly
Students love Pasadena, CA
Campus feels safe

ACADEMICS

Academic Rating	**89**
Calendar	quarter
Student/faculty ratio	3:1
Professors interesting rating	61
Professors accessible rating	65
% classes taught by TAs	0
Most common lab size	10-19 students
Most common regular class size	fewer than 10 students

MOST POPULAR MAJORS

Electrical, electronics, and communications engineering
physics

STUDENTS SPEAK OUT

Academics

Students arrive at Caltech knowing what to expect—namely, academic boot camp—and few graduate disappointed. The school's "grueling" demands "prepare students to face far more challenges than they ever thought possible." The school operates on the quarter system, which means "classes go by quickly." Warns one student, "Stay on top of things because before you know it, it's midterms. Then finals. Rinse and repeat two times. Then you have a complete school year. Good luck, you'll be fine. Don't worry. Too much." The first two freshman quarters "are pass/fail, which is extremely helpful in learning to adjust to the workload at Tech and to college life in general." First year is also when students immerse themselves in core courses that "consist of roughly three lectures a week (taught by a professor to the entire freshman class, some 215 people) and then one or two recitation sections, in which Teaching Assistants (graduate students, or occasionally undergraduates or other professors) go over the material covered in lecture and answer questions. The system works, I guess, but there is a lot (and I do mean a lot) of homework involved." Students note, "The core professors aren't always the best around, but once you get into the more specialized major-specific or elective courses, the classes become much smaller and the professors are generally excellent teachers who genuinely care about the educational experiences of the students." Caltech's rigors are softened by the fact that "the environment is a very supportive one. Students here work together in many subjects and general activities."

Life

"There is not a lot of time for extra activities" at Caltech. "A lot of people get beat down by the extreme workload." Writes one student, "Life is work. On an average day, the average Techer probably spends eight to ten hours on academic matters." As one undergrad joked, "We're not like MIT, where students take homework with them on dates. We generally bring our dates to work on our homework in group sessions." Social life "revolves around the housing system. All students join one of the seven Houses—they're kind of hybrids between dorms and frats—at the beginning of freshman year. The system is a real blessing." Once they've found their cohort, "Techers enjoy a random life filled with random events that just happen. One day they may build a giant jungle gym on the lawn of the faculty club building. Another day they may pull a prank by sneaking a girl into a group of high school students and parents visiting Caltech, then 'kidnapping' the girl and yelling, 'We got one! We got one!'" Beyond campus, "Old Pas, Pasadena's shopping district, is a short walk away, is one of LA's 'destinations' with good restaurants [and] movie theaters, and is just fun to walk around. If they get out, most students go there."

Student Body

Techers may debate whether they are technically geeks or nerds, but nearly all agree that theirs is a truly odd lot. Reports one from the "geek" camp: "The typical student here is a geek. I'm a geek. You're probably a geek too, if you're considering Tech. Of course, the list of things we do in our 'spare time' is diverse. You get geeks who play musical instruments, geeks who play sports, geeks who drink beer and smoke pot, and geeks who run around in winged monkey suits saying 'Whee!' (I kid you not), but we're all geeks." Within these parameters, "There are a lot people here who are interested in art, music, or literature, philosophy, history, and all manner of supposed humanities." As at most tech schools, "The guy-to-girl ratio is ridiculous. It creates an environment where guys can turn into infatuated/stalker types for a girl that would never get a second glance at her high school."

CALIFORNIA INSTITUTE OF TECHNOLOGY

FINANCIAL AID: 626-395-6280 • E-MAIL: UGADMISSIONS@CALTECH.EDU • WEBSITE: ADMISSIONS.CALTECH.EDU

ADMISSIONS

Very important factors considered include: Character/personal qualities, essays, recommendations, secondary school record, standardized test scores. *Other factors considered include:* Class rank, extracurricular activities, minority status, talent/ability, volunteer work, work experience. SAT Reasoning and SAT Subject Tests or ACT required. High school diploma or equivalent is not required. *Academic units required:* 3 English, 4 math, 2 science (1 science lab), 1 social studies, 1 history. *Academic units recommended:* 4 English.

The Inside Word

A mere glance at Caltech's freshman profile can discourage all but the most self-confident of high school seniors. It should. The impact of grades and test scores on the admissions process is minimized significantly when virtually every freshman was in the top fifth of his or her high school class and has a 1400 SAT. The admissions office isn't kidding when they emphasize the personal side of their criteria. Six students are on the admissions committee; every file is read at least twice. The process is all about matchmaking, and the Tech staff is very interested in getting to know you. Don't apply unless you have more than high numbers to offer.

FINANCIAL AID

Students should submit: FAFSA, CSS/Financial Aid PROFILE, state aid form, noncustodial (divorced/separated) parents' statement, business/farm supplement, noncustodial parents' statement and business/farm supplement forms are required only when applicable. Regular filing deadline is 1/15. The Princeton Review suggests that all financial aid forms be submitted as soon as possible after 1/1. *Need-based scholarships/grants offered:* Pell, SEOG, state scholarships/grants, private scholarships, the school's own gift aid. *Loan aid offered:* Direct Subsidized Stafford, Direct Unsubsidized Stafford, Direct PLUS, Federal Perkins, college/university loans from institutional funds. Applicants will be notified of awards on or about 4/15.

FROM THE ADMISSIONS OFFICE

"Admission to the freshman class is based on many factors—some quantifiable, some not. What you say in your application is important! And, because we don't interview students for admission, your letters of recommendation are weighed heavily. High school academic performance is very important, as is a demonstrated interest in math, science, and/or engineering. We are also interested in your character, maturity, and motivation. We are very proud of the process we use to select each freshman class. It's very individual, it has great integrity, and we believe it serves all the students who apply. If you have any questions about the process or about Caltech in general, write us a letter or give us a call. We'd like to hear from you!

"Freshman applicants must submit scores from either the new or old SAT (or ACT Writing section optional). In addition, students must submit the results of two SAT Subject Tests: Mathematics IIC and one of the following; Biology (Ecological or Molecular), Chemistry, or Physics."

SELECTIVITY

Admissions Rating	**99**
# of applicants	2,761
% of applicants accepted	20
% of acceptees attending	37
# accepting a place on wait list	156
% admitted from wait list	28

FRESHMAN PROFILE

Range SAT Verbal	700-770
Range SAT Math	750-800
**TPR Projected Range SAT Writing*	*700-740*
% graduated top 10% of class	93
% graduated top 25% of class	100
% graduated top 50% of class	100

DEADLINES

Regular application deadline	1/1
Regular notification	4/1
Nonfall registration?	no

APPLICANTS ALSO LOOK AT

AND OFTEN PREFER
Harvard College
Princeton University
Stanford University

AND SOMETIMES PREFER
Harvey Mudd College
Massachusetts Institute of Technology
University of California—Berkeley

AND RARELY PREFER
Rensselaer Polytechnic Institute
Virginia Tech

FINANCIAL FACTS

Financial Aid Rating	**98**
Annual tuition	$27,309
Room & Board	$8,814
Books and supplies	$1,047
% frosh rec. need-based scholarship or grant aid	56
% UG rec. need-based scholarship or grant aid	57
% frosh rec. need-based self-help aid	36
% UG rec. need-based self-help aid	41
% frosh rec. any financial aid	62
% UG rec. any financial aid	56
Avg. frosh grant	$23,545
Avg. frosh loan	$1,421
Independent 529 member?	No

CALVIN COLLEGE

3201 BURTON STREET SE, GRAND RAPIDS, MI 49546 • ADMISSIONS: 616-526-6106 • FAX: 616-526-6777

CAMPUS LIFE

Quality of Life Rating	**89**
Fire Safety Rating	**65**
Type of school	private
Affiliation	Christian Reformed
Environment	metropolis

STUDENTS

Total undergrad enrollment	4,028
% male/female	45/55
% from out of state	39
% from public high school	42
% live on campus	56
% African American	1
% Asian	3
% Caucasian	85
% Hispanic	1
% international	8
# of countries represented	51

SURVEY SAYS

Small classes
Great computer facilities
Great library
Students are happy
Frats and sororities are unpopular or nonexistent

ACADEMICS

Academic Rating	**83**
Calendar	4-1-4
Student/faculty ratio	12:1
Professors interesting rating	89
Professors accessible rating	89
% professors teaching UG courses	100
% classes taught by TAs	0
Most common lab size	20-29 students
Most common regular class size	20-29 students

MOST POPULAR MAJORS

Business administration/management
elementary education and teaching
engineering

STUDENTS SPEAK OUT

Academics

"The greatest strength of Calvin is the emphasis on becoming a better person," undergraduates at this Christian Reformed school tell us, observing that "every accredited college or university offers education, but not every school prepares students for the real world as Calvin does." Calvin accomplishes this feat through "great study-abroad opportunities, chapel services, group discussions, community service, and an emphasis on 'taking ownership' of one's faith," which "encourages students to think about how their faith integrates with all other parts of their life, including academics." The goal is to "equip students to engage and serve the world from a compassionate and professional Christian viewpoint." Students are quick to point out, however, that religious education and indoctrination are not synonymous here; on the contrary, "Calvin puts an emphasis on making your own choices—'responsible freedom'" is a key phrase. They also warn that "this school is one tough cookie. But it's the kind of cookie you love. Academics here are rigorous, to say the least, but they're interesting and led by the most wonderful professors." Students appreciate Calvin's demanding core curriculum, which "forces students to get out of their comfort zone by requiring them to take classes they wouldn't choose to. This ensures that graduates are well-rounded and well-prepared for the real world." Best of all, perhaps, Calvin "provides a fantastic Christian education for little money, compared to other private schools."

Life

"There's a lot to do without really leaving campus, [including] sporting activities like hockey and basketball, movies shown on campus, and the Dance Guild, which produces a show every semester." The school does a great job of bringing in "state-of-the-art musicians," including (in the last four years) John Mayer, Jason Mraz, Indigo Girls, Jimmy Eat World, The Calling, Michelle Branch, Ladysmith Black Mambazo, and Emmylou Harris. With all these options, "Your time at Calvin can be whatever you decide. You can be on a national championship team, you can use lab equipment that many graduate students don't even have, you can be part of an awesome Christian community, or if you really want, you can hide in your room all day and only come out for midterms and finals." (Those who choose the last option benefit from "dorms that are really beautiful, with huge rooms and nice furniture.") While "you can get involved in religious activities if you want, if you don't want to, you don't have to. There's not a lot of pressure even though it is a Christian school." Calvin is officially a dry campus, "and pretty strict rules about getting caught under the influence of controlled substances are enforced, but there is an average amount of off-campus drinking, and it's really not that big of a deal. You drink if you want to; you don't drink if you don't want to." You can also head into downtown Grand Rapids, a town that "can hold its own" even though "it's not a big metropolitan city. There are great restaurants here too, excellent movie complexes, malls, and extracurricular seasonal stuff, so you won't be bored unless you decide to be."

Student Body

Because of Calvin's affiliation with the Christian Reformed Church, "the Van, Vander and Sma last names are somewhat dominant in the directory. This can't really be helped because this school is in the middle of Dutch country. However, there are several students from other areas, states, and countries. There are a lot of African and Asian international students." Many here reckon that CRC members make up about half the student body and that "the typical student is tall and blond." Calvin undergrads tend to be conservative; writes one, "Bolt Hall (one of the residence halls) had about seventy Bush-Cheney posters in windows and one Kerry-Edwards poster in 2004." The school is home to "a smaller, but very active liberal group of students," and students point out that "people are pretty much accepting of the different political views."

Financial Aid: 616-957-6134 • E-mail: admissions@calvin.edu • Website: www.calvin.edu

ADMISSIONS

Very important factors considered include: Religious affiliation/commitment, secondary school record, standardized test scores. *Important factors considered include:* Character/personal qualities, essays, extracurricular activities, recommendations. *Other factors considered include:* Class rank, volunteer work, work experience. SAT Reasoning or ACT required. TOEFL required of all international applicants. High school diploma is required, and GED is accepted. *Academic units required:* 3 English, 3 math, 2 science, 2 social studies, 3 academic electives. *Academic units recommended:* 4 English, 3 math, 2 science (1 science lab), 2 foreign language, 3 social studies, 3 academic electives.

The Inside Word

Calvin's applicant pool is highly self-selected and small. Nearly all candidates get in, and over half choose to enroll. The freshman academic profile is fairly solid, but making a good match with the college philosophically is much more important for gaining admission than anything else.

FINANCIAL AID

Students should submit: FAFSA, institution's own financial aid form. The Princeton Review suggests that all financial aid forms be submitted as soon as possible after 1/1. *Need-based scholarships/grants offered:* Pell, SEOG, state scholarships/grants, private scholarships, the school's own gift aid. *Loan aid offered:* Direct Subsidized Stafford, Direct Unsubsidized Stafford, Direct PLUS, Federal Perkins, state loans, college/university loans from institutional funds, private alternative. Applicants will be notified of awards on a rolling basis beginning on or about 3/15. Federal Work-study Program available. Institutional employment available. Off-campus job opportunities are good.

FROM THE ADMISSIONS OFFICE

"Calvin's well-respected faculty, innovative core curriculum, and inquiring student body come together in an environment that links intellectual freedom with a heart for service. Calvin's 400-acre campus is home to more than 4,300 students and 300 professors who chose Calvin because of its national reputation for academic excellence and faith-shaped thinking. Calvin encourages students to explore all things and offers nearly 100 academic options to choose from, including accredited professional programs.

"Quality teaching and accessibility to students are considered top priorities by faculty members. More than 80 percent of Calvin professors hold the highest degree in their field, the student/faculty ratio is 12:1, and the average class size is 22. The college's 4-1-4 calendar offers opportunities for off-campus and international study, while service-learning projects draw Calvin students into the local community. Internships allow students to try their individual gifts in the workplace while gaining professional experience. In a recent survey, 96 percent of Calvin graduates reported that they had either secured a job or begun graduate school within six months of graduation. Calvin is among the top 3 percent of four-year private colleges in the number of graduates who go on to earn a PhD.

"Students applying for admission into the fall 2006 freshman class are required to submit scores from either the SAT or the ACT college entrance exam. Calvin does not require the Writing section of either test."

SELECTIVITY

Admissions Rating	**82**
# of applicants	1,721
% of applicants accepted	98
% of acceptees attending	53

FRESHMAN PROFILE

Range SAT Verbal	540-670
Average SAT Verbal	599
Range SAT Math	540-670
Average SAT Math	605
**TPR Projected Range SAT Writing*	*590-680*
Range ACT Composite	23-29
Average ACT Composite	26
Minimum Paper TOEFL	550
Minimum Computer Based TOEFL	213
Average HS GPA	3.56
% graduated top 10% of class	28
% graduated top 25% of class	57
% graduated top 50% of class	81

DEADLINES

Regular application deadline	8/15
Regular notification	rolling
Nonfall registration?	yes

APPLICANTS ALSO LOOK AT

AND OFTEN PREFER
Hope College

AND SOMETIMES PREFER
Grand Valley State University
University of Michigan—Ann Arbor
Wheaton College (IL)

AND RARELY PREFER
Michigan State University
Michigan Technological University

FINANCIAL FACTS

Financial Aid Rating	**77**
Annual tuition	$17,770
Room & Board	$6,185
Books and supplies	$700
% frosh rec. need-based scholarship or grant aid	68
% UG rec. need-based scholarship or grant aid	65
% frosh rec. need-based self-help aid	59
% UG rec. need-based self-help aid	59
% frosh rec. any financial aid	95
% UG rec. any financial aid	93
Avg. frosh grant	$10,415
Avg. frosh loan	$4,335
Independent 529 member?	No

CARLETON COLLEGE

100 South College Street, Northfield, MN 55057 • Admissions: 507-646-4190 and 800-995-2275 • Fax: 507-646-4526

CAMPUS LIFE

Quality of Life Rating	**97**
Fire Safety Rating	**60**
Type of school	private
Environment	village

STUDENTS

Total undergrad enrollment	1,932
% male/female	48/52
% from out of state	73
% from public high school	73
% live on campus	91
% African American	6
% Asian	9
% Caucasian	75
% Hispanic	4
% Native American	1
% international	5
# of countries represented	30

SURVEY SAYS

Small classes
Students are friendly
Intramural sports are popular
Frats and sororities are unpopular or nonexistent

ACADEMICS

Academic Rating	**99**
Calendar	trimester
Student/faculty ratio	10:1
Professors interesting rating	97
Professors accessible rating	93
% professors teaching UG courses	100
% classes taught by TAs	0
Most common lab size	10-19 students
Most common regular class size	10-19 students

MOST POPULAR MAJORS

Economics
political science and government

STUDENTS SPEAK OUT

Academics

"There is a sense of community that's hard to find elsewhere" at Carleton College, a small, academically demanding liberal arts school whose "greatest strengths lie in the natural sciences and mathematics." One undergraduate explains, "You'll find yourself striking up conversations with complete strangers at the post office, in town, and along sidewalks in the middle of a snowy night. New friends are found everywhere." This is true even from among the faculty; "Carleton is not a research college, so while professors do some research, they are much more focused on students. All classes are taught by professors, and professors have plenty of time for students to meet with them." Adds one student, "Know those special teachers you had in high school, the ones you will actually remember after graduation? That's what Carleton professors are like." Carleton operates on a unique trimester calendar, which students endorse. "It's nice to be only taking three classes, though more intensely, rather than spreading yourself over four or five." Students also love the "great study abroad office," which has provided at least one student here with "opportunities to travel to Hong Kong, China, Thailand, Spain, and, soon, Africa." But most of all, they love this Midwestern school's "intellectually stimulating environment. People are not afraid to work hard and get engrossed in what they study. At the same time, no one takes themselves too seriously, and we're always ready for a good time."

Life

Carleton's hometown of Northfield—also home to the Malt-O-Meal factory—"isn't much to get excited about. Besides some quaint shops and great food, there's nothing to do." One freshman told us that for fun she "makes a smoothie run to the Sayles-Hill Student Center" then later stops by the "Dacie Moses House, a place where students gather to bake cookies." However, "the school more than makes up for it: an evening doesn't go by without some kind of event, whether it be musical, artistic, theatrical, or political." "During the week everyone is studying, and there is little going on socially, but come Friday and Saturday, things get pretty lively." The notoriously heavy workload here can make students a little whacky, to the point that "eventually some people lose it. This comes more in the form of weird, creative outlets than it does self-destructive behavior, though. There are a lot of Naked Winter Olympics, pranks, tradition, and general goofing off." Students are proud of this "little bit of eccentricity [that] makes everything fun." Intramurals "are really hot at Carleton; the people who aren't playing them are much fewer and far between than the people who are." Ultimate Frisbee and broomball are the games of choice. "Don't know how to play broomball?" queries one student. "It's easy to pick up. And if you're really horrible at it, don't worry. That doesn't stop anyone from playing." There are also "plenty of parties" here, and while "a third of the student body will be drunk on a typical weekend," there is "absolutely no pressure to drink if you don't want to." Plus, Carleton is "conveniently close to Minneapolis and St. Paul" for urban getaways. No car? The school runs a shuttle bus on Fridays and Saturdays.

Student Body

The "creative, warm, compassionate, and helpful" undergrads of Carleton are "super smart and nerdy, but fun-nerdy, not scary-nerdy." We're told that "no one here pays a great deal of attention to socioeconomic background, race, gender, sexual orientation, or anything else that can define a group. Instead, we pay attention to the fact that somebody rides unicycles around campus, or can play strange instruments we've never heard of, or can do circular breathing, or collects anything shaped like a pair of lips, or skips down the sidewalk between classes. The extraordinary is ordinary at Carleton, in a positive way." Basically, you'll find the campus to be "a place where energy, creativity, and a good sense of humor get you really far." Students tend to be "liberal and very political" and very compatible. "There's a rumor that 60 percent of Carleton grads marry another Carl," students tell us.

Financial Aid: 507-646-4138 • E-mail: admissions@acs.carleton.edu • Website: www.carleton.edu

ADMISSIONS

Very important factors considered include: Secondary school record. *Important factors considered include:* Character/personal qualities, class rank, essays, extracurricular activities, minority status, recommendations, standardized test scores, talent/ability, volunteer work, work experience. *Other factors considered include:* Alumni/ae relation, geographical residence, interview, state residency. SAT Reasoning or ACT required. SAT Subject Tests recommended. TOEFL required of all international applicants. High school diploma is required, and GED is accepted. *Academic units recommended:* 4 English, 3 math, 3 science (1 science lab), 3 foreign language, 3 social studies and history.

The Inside Word

Admission to Carleton would be even more difficult if the college had more name recognition. Current applicants should be grateful for this because standards are already rigorous. Only severe competition with the best liberal arts colleges in the country prevents an even lower admit rate.

FINANCIAL AID

Students should submit: FAFSA, CSS/Financial Aid PROFILE, noncustodial (divorced/separated) parents' statement, business/farm supplement. Regular filing deadline is 2/15. The Princeton Review suggests that all financial aid forms be submitted as soon as possible after 1/1. *Need-based scholarships/grants offered:* Pell, SEOG, state scholarships/grants, private scholarships, the school's own gift aid. *Loan aid offered:* FFEL Subsidized Stafford, FFEL Unsubsidized Stafford, FFEL PLUS, Federal Perkins, state loans, college/university loans from institutional funds, Minnesota SELF Loan program. Applicants will be notified of awards on or about 4/1. Federal Work-study Program available. Institutional employment available. Off-campus job opportunities are fair.

FROM THE ADMISSIONS OFFICE

"In an annual college freshmen survey, Carleton students identify themselves as everything from conservatives to liberals, with a majority of them falling in the moderate to liberal range. Although individualistic and energetic Carls take their academics seriously, they don't take themselves seriously. Participation in athletics, theater, or music, religious events, or dining hall discussion over hearty fare marks the Carleton experience. Cool fact: More snow fell in the northeast than did here in the past five years. Carleton opened a new recreation center with indoor track and fitness center in 2000 and a new language and dining center in 2001 along with nine town house complexes providing some apartment-style living for students.

"With nearly three-fifths of the student body receiving need-based grant aid, there is a broad socioeconomic representation across the student body. Five percent of all students are international, and nearly 20 percent come from traditionally underrepresented groups. A look at majors in the past decade shows that graduates cover all areas, with about one-third of them in each of the following: math/science, humanities and arts, and social sciences. Typically, over two-thirds of all students will spend time studying off-campus; Carleton participates in programs worldwide from Asia to Africa. You can scuba dive off the Greater Barrier Reef or walk the Great Wall of China.

"Five years after graduating, between 65 percent and 75 percent of alumni pursue graduate or professional degrees. More Carleton graduates have pursued their doctorates in the sciences in the past twenty years than have graduates of other small, comparable liberal arts colleges.

"2006 high school graduates must take the new SAT or ACT with Writing component. Carleton will not accept results from the old format of the SAT for 2006 applicants. In addition the school recommends, but does not require, that candidates submit results from SAT Subject Tests, formerly called Achievement Tests."

SELECTIVITY

Admissions Rating	**97**
# of applicants	4,898
% of applicants accepted	29
% of acceptees attending	35
# accepting a place on wait list	273
% admitted from wait list	3
# of early decision applicants	209
% accepted early decision	45

FRESHMAN PROFILE

Range SAT Verbal	650-750
Range SAT Math	650-730
**TPR Projected Range SAT Writing*	*670-730*
Range ACT Composite	28-32
Minimum Paper TOEFL	600
Minimum Computer Based TOEFL	250
% graduated top 10% of class	73
% graduated top 25% of class	92
% graduated top 50% of class	98

DEADLINES

Early decision application deadline	11/15
Early decision notification	12/15
Regular application deadline	1/15
Regular notification	4/15
Nonfall registration?	no

APPLICANTS ALSO LOOK AT

AND OFTEN PREFER
Williams College
Yale University

AND SOMETIMES PREFER
Bowdoin College
Grinnell College
Washington University in St. Louis
Wesleyan College

AND RARELY PREFER
Macalester College
Oberlin College

FINANCIAL FACTS

Financial Aid Rating	**99**
Annual tuition	$30,501
Room & Board	$6,309
Books and supplies	$600
Required fees	$165
% frosh rec. need-based scholarship or grant aid	54
% UG rec. need-based scholarship or grant aid	57
% frosh rec. need-based self-help aid	51
% UG rec. need-based self-help aid	56
Independent 529 member?	Yes

Carnegie Mellon University

5000 Forbes Avenue, Pittsburgh, PA 15213 • Admissions: 412-268-2082 • Fax: 412-268-7838

CAMPUS LIFE

Quality of Life Rating	**66**
Fire Safety Rating	**71**
Type of school	private
Environment	metropolis

STUDENTS

Total undergrad enrollment	5,389
% male/female	61/39
% from out of state	76
% live on campus	84
% in (# of) fraternities	14 (13)
% in (# of) sororities	11 (5)
% African American	5
% Asian	23
% Caucasian	42
% Hispanic	5
% Native American	1
% international	12
# of countries represented	93

SURVEY SAYS

Registration is a breeze
Lab facilities are great
Great computer facilities
Diverse student types on campus
Lots of beer drinking

ACADEMICS

Academic Rating	**91**
Calendar	semester
Student/faculty ratio	10:1
Professors interesting rating	75
Professors accessible rating	79
% classes taught by TAs	0
Most common lab size	20-29 students
Most common regular class size	fewer than 10 students

MOST POPULAR MAJORS

Business administration and management
computer engineering
computer science

STUDENTS SPEAK OUT

Academics

The students of Carnegie Mellon University proudly report that their school fulfills the fundamental mission of the university: to offer excellent instruction in a wide variety of fields while also promoting cutting-edge research. "Of all the schools I've seen, no other is as well known in so many different fields: architecture, engineering, drama, science, design, music, and business, just to name a few," is how one undergrad put it, adding, "If you couldn't decide what path to take in life, you could still come to Carnegie Mellon and have a world-class education in almost any interest." Students warn, "Academically, this school will push you to your limit." As one puts it, "Carnegie Mellon is a very research-oriented university. . . . It has truly opened doors for me that I did not know were available. The professors are actively involved in the topics in which they teach. There is no such thing as a 'basic' course at Carnegie Mellon." The school does a good job of recognizing the demands it makes, however, and "in many departments, professors actually coordinate their tests and papers so that there is very little overlap in workloads between classes." It's just such little touches that so endear Carnegie Mellon to its students. Another example: "The Business School's administration loves to send us notes about various types of opportunities for internships, jobs, and lectures through email." Students are also unanimous in their praise for online services: "You can register online, check your grades online, often get assignments online, and even check what movie is playing at school online," reports an undergrad.

Life

Because of Carnegie Mellon's intense academic demands, "people here think about school 90 percent of the time. The other 10 percent is divided among when they're going to sleep next [and] how they're going to blow off some stress." Fortunately, there are lots of options for that scant 10 percent. Hometown Pittsburgh "is a great city if you let it be. There are many theaters, museums, and sporting events. Shops and great restaurants are all really close, and we get bus passes as students, so you can get anywhere." There are also many nearby bars, "most of which don't card." On campus, "people go to the fraternities on weekends." Also popular are one-dollar movies ("shown from Thursday to Sunday, which are a real great getaway from work, and they get good, recent movies") and student-produced plays. Student clubs and organizations also have their boosters; writes one student, "Carnegie Mellon has a lot of really fun, quirky organizations. My two favorites are the Kiltie Band and KGB. The Kiltie Band is our band for nonmajors. As The Band Without Pants, we wear our kilts proudly, cheer giddily, click our heels, and beep when we back up. Talent for music and/or marching is not a requirement. KGB stands for Keeping Geeks Busy. Each semester, they host Capture the Flag with Stuff, a game that always attracts a large crowd." Although "there are sports games going on, no one ever knows when or cares to go."

Student Body

"There are a few types that are typical," at Carnegie Mellon; identifiable factions include: "a large number of tech, math, and computer geeks . . . strange art students, loud drama students, and many Asian student groups." Most are "hardworking, bright, ambitious," and shy. Reports one undergrad, "Students here would be considered very friendly if they weren't so reserved. You'll find that the person who sits next to you in lecture is always really nice if either of you ever overcomes your shyness enough to say hello." Politically "there is a large minority of very left-wing, extremely active students who are responsible for most of what occurs on campus. Most students, however, are apathetic and very absorbed in their studies."

FINANCIAL AID: 412-268-2068 • E-MAIL: UNDERGRADUATE-ADMISSIONS@ANDREW.CMU.EDU • WEBSITE: WWW.CMU.EDU

ADMISSIONS

Very important factors considered include: Secondary school record, standardized test scores. *Important factors considered include:* Alumni/ae relation, character/personal qualities, class rank, extracurricular activities, recommendations, talent/ability, volunteer work, work experience. *Other factors considered include:* Essays, interview, minority status. SAT Reasoning or ACT required. TOEFL required of all international applicants. High school diploma is required, and GED is accepted. *Academic units required:* 4 English, 4 math, 3 science (3 science lab), 2 foreign language, 3 academic electives. *Academic units recommended:* 4 English, 4 math, 3 science (3 science lab), 2 foreign language, 4 academic electives.

The Inside Word

The Office of Admission reports that it uses "no cutoffs [and] no formulas" in assessing its applicant pool. Don't get too excited—that doesn't necessarily mean that applicants are looked at in a more personal fashion. Applications have seesawed here over the past couple of years, and to temper the effects of a decline in application totals on selectivity, Carnegie Mellon maintains a huge wait list. A very low yield of admits who enroll keeps selectivity moderate, but you've got to have strong numbers to gain admission.

FINANCIAL AID

Students should submit: FAFSA, institution's own financial aid form, parent and student federal tax returns, parent W-2 forms. Regular filing deadline is 5/1. The Princeton Review suggests that all financial aid forms be submitted as soon as possible after 1/1. *Need-based scholarships/grants offered:* Pell, SEOG, state scholarships/grants, private scholarships, the school's own gift aid. *Loan aid offered:* FFEL Subsidized Stafford, FFEL Unsubsidized Stafford, FFEL PLUS, Federal Perkins, Gate Student Loan. Applicants will be notified of awards on or about 3/15. Federal Work-study Program available. Institutional employment available.

FROM THE ADMISSIONS OFFICE

"Carnegie Mellon is a private, coeducational university with approximately 5,100 undergraduates; 3,300 graduate students; and 778 full-time faculty members. The university's 103-acre campus is located in the Oakland area of Pittsburgh, five miles from downtown. The university is composed of seven colleges: the Carnegie Institute of Technology (engineering), the College of Fine Arts, the College of Humanities and Social Sciences (combining liberal arts education with professional specializations), the Tepper School of Business (undergraduate business and industrial management), the Mellon College of Science, the School of Computer Science, and the H. John Heina III School of Public Policy and Management.

"Freshman applicants for fall 2006 must take the new SAT plus two SAT Subject Tests, or the old SAT plus three Subject Tests (including Writing). Students may take the ACT in lieu of the SAT. An applicant's best scores will be used in admissions decision-making."

SELECTIVITY

Admissions Rating	**96**
# of applicants	14,114
% of applicants accepted	42
% of acceptees attending	23
# accepting a place on wait list	2,709
% admitted from wait list	4
# of early decision applicants	179
% accepted early decision	53

FRESHMAN PROFILE

Range SAT Verbal	610-710
Average SAT Verbal	657
Range SAT Math	680-770
Average SAT Math	718
**TPR Projected Range SAT Writing*	*640-700*
Range ACT Composite	27-32
Average ACT Composite	30
Minimum Paper TOEFL	600
Minimum Computer Based TOEFL	250
Average HS GPA	3.6
% graduated top 10% of class	72
% graduated top 25% of class	95
% graduated top 50% of class	100

DEADLINES

Early decision application deadline	11/15
Early decision notification	12/15
Regular application deadline	1/1
Regular notification	4/15
Nonfall registration?	no

FINANCIAL FACTS

Financial Aid Rating	**76**
Annual tuition	$31,650
Room & Board	$8,916
Books and supplies	$925
Required fees	$584
% frosh rec. need-based scholarship or grant aid	52
% UG rec. need-based scholarship or grant aid	48
% frosh rec. need-based self-help aid	51
% UG rec. need-based self-help aid	49
% frosh rec. any financial aid	70
% UG rec. any financial aid	66
Avg. frosh grant	$17,446
Avg. frosh loan	$6,200
Independent 529 member?	Yes

CASE WESTERN RESERVE UNIVERSITY

103 TOMLINSON HALL, 10900 EUCLID AVENUE, CLEVELAND, OH 44106-7055 • ADMISSIONS: 216-368-4450 • FAX: 216-368-5111

CAMPUS LIFE

Quality of Life Rating	**64**
Fire Safety Rating	**75**
Type of school	private
Environment	metropolis

STUDENTS

Total undergrad enrollment	3,424
% male/female	60/40
% from out of state	41
% from public high school	70
% live on campus	78
% in (# of) fraternities	31 (16)
% in (# of) sororities	23 (6)
% African American	5
% Asian	15
% Caucasian	69
% Hispanic	2
% international	4
# of countries represented	28

SURVEY SAYS

Lab facilities are great
Great computer facilities
Great library
Diverse student types on campus
Low cost of living

ACADEMICS

Academic Rating	**83**
Calendar	semester
Student/faculty ratio	7:1
Professors interesting rating	71
Professors accessible rating	73
% professors teaching UG courses	72
% classes taught by TAs	5
Most common lab size	10-19 students
Most common regular class size	10-19 students

MOST POPULAR MAJORS

Biology/biological sciences
biomedical/medical engineering
business administration/management

STUDENTS SPEAK OUT

Academics

Case has long been perceived as a school that "is all about hardcore, technology-enhanced learning," and tech-related areas—particularly engineering and the sciences certainly remain the school's greatest strengths, but Case has worked hard to broaden its offerings in recent years. One student reports, "The focus [has] come off of engineering a little, as the school has spent (or received in donations) large sums of money to both Arts & Sciences and especially the Weatherhead School of Management." As a result, the picture at Case has grown more complex. For tech-oriented students, the school remains a place where "a lot of what you learn you must teach yourself and you receive most of your help from TAs and fellow students." Students in other areas tell a different story; they report that "professors here generally show a genuine interest in their students. They have tons of office hours and have review sessions set up to help students get the most out of the material as possible." Students in all disciplines agree that "The administration is just that—administration. There are often a lot of hoops to jump through when dealing with paying tuition, financial aid and similar paperwork issues. There is a definite need for more and better undergraduate advising. Class registration, however, is easy."

Life

"Day-to-day student life isn't the greatest" at Case, "simply because it's an urban campus, it doesn't have that tight-knit college feel," explains one student. The heavy workload–"life here is very studious, and there is rarely free time available"–is another factor. A third is the lopsided male/female ratio, which "makes it impossible for guys to get dates." Jokes one student, "This place is about remaining a virgin until you're 22." Greek life is one option students pursue in an effort to avoid "spending all your free time sitting in front of a computer bored out of your mind." Those who choose the latter at least benefit from the fact that "the campus is really wired and everyone pretty much relies on the Internet. Download speeds are amazing. A lot of classes post homework assignments, grades, and syllabi online, and most of my labs require you to download and read lab instructions online." There is a third way, however: Greater Cleveland offers lots of options, including "great clubbing in the Flats or Lakewood; theater, movies, museums, the botanical gardens, and Severance Hall where the Cleveland Orchestra plays," and three other area schools, Cleveland State University, the Cleveland Institute of Music, and the Cleveland Institute of Art, with more lively social scenes. The only problem, according to some, is that "it's hard to get around town if you don't have a car—some of us find public transportation pretty scary—and if you do have a car, trying to find a place to park will make your life miserable."

Student Body

"Typical students at Case spend the majority of their time studying and engrossing themselves in their courses," explains one student. Or, as another puts it, "The typical Case student is a nerd who is obsessed with his computer. But there are lots of other types too. They're only in love with their computers, not obsessed." Students are proud of who they are; explains one, "It's great to be at a school where everyone is like you and is as focused on academics as you are. I know that's why I chose to come here!" Some study too hard, we're told; writes one undergrad, "The typical student is hard to define because you rarely see him or her. Students become so focused on schoolwork that they lose track of the fact that there is more to college than simply studying." Case undergrads consider the student body diverse, in part because of the mix of "foreign students from all over Europe and especially Asia."

Case Western Reserve University

Financial Aid: 216-368-4530 • E-mail: admission@case.edu • Website: www.case.edu

ADMISSIONS

Very important factors considered include: Extracurricular activities, secondary school record, talent/ability, volunteer work, work experience. *Important factors considered include:* Alumni/ae relation, character/personal qualities, class rank, essays, interview, minority status, recommendations, standardized test scores. SAT Reasoning or ACT required. TOEFL required of all international applicants. High school diploma is required, and GED is accepted. *Academic units required:* 4 English, 3 math, 3 science (1 science lab), 2 foreign language, 3 social studies. *Academic units recommended:* 4 math, 2 science lab, 3 foreign language, 4 social studies.

The Inside Word

Case faces tough competition, and they handle it very well. The university received a record number of applications last year, and as a result it's quite a bit tougher to get admitted. Even if you solidly meet the academic profile, don't be complacent—Case Western's freshman profile reflects well on the academic preparedness of its candidates, and due to their good fortune they've got an opportunity to be significantly more choosy about who gets an offer.

FINANCIAL AID

Students should submit: FAFSA, institution's own financial aid form, noncustodial (divorced/separated) parents' statement, business/farm supplement, parent and student income tax returns and W-2 forms. The Princeton Review suggests that all financial aid forms be submitted as soon as possible after 1/1. *Need-based scholarships/grants offered:* Pell, SEOG, state scholarships/grants, private scholarships, the school's own gift aid. *Loan aid offered:* FFEL Subsidized Stafford, FFEL Unsubsidized Stafford, FFEL PLUS, Federal Perkins, Federal Nursing, state loans, college/university loans from institutional funds. Applicants will be notified of awards on a rolling basis beginning on or about 2/15. Federal Work-study Program available. Institutional employment available. Off-campus job opportunities are good.

FROM THE ADMISSIONS OFFICE

"An important part of Case's philosophy is that education is best accomplished through experience. We've begun a new undergraduate program called SAGES that strives to blur the distinctions between learning and life. In SAGES, all students engage with faculty, peers, and the larger Cleveland community through small seminars, research projects, internships, and community service. Their seminar professors serve as mentors, helping them design their educational plan. The opportunities Case students have to work with some of the top curators, scientists, musicians, educators, and professionals (to name a few) are truly exciting.

"Applicants for fall 2006 are required to take the new SAT (or the ACT with the Writing section), but we will allow students to submit scores from the old (prior to March 2005) version of the SAT (or ACT) as well, and will use the student's best scores from either test."

SELECTIVITY

Admissions Rating	**91**
# of applicants	5,493
% of applicants accepted	71
% of acceptees attending	20
# accepting a place on wait list	585
% admitted from wait list	26

FRESHMAN PROFILE

Range SAT Verbal	580-700
Range SAT Math	620-720
**TPR Projected Range SAT Writing*	*620-700*
Range ACT Composite	26-31
Minimum Paper TOEFL	550
Minimum Computer Based TOEFL	213
% graduated top 10% of class	68
% graduated top 25% of class	91
% graduated top 50% of class	99

DEADLINES

Regular application deadline	1/15
Regular notification	4/1
Nonfall registration?	yes

APPLICANTS ALSO LOOK AT

AND OFTEN PREFER
Cornell University
Duke University
Northwestern University

AND SOMETIMES PREFER
Johns Hopkins University
Ohio State University—Columbus
Rensselaer Polytechnic Institute

AND RARELY PREFER
Purdue University—West Lafayette
University of Pittsburgh—Pittsburgh Campus

FINANCIAL FACTS

Financial Aid Rating	**92**
Annual tuition	$28,400
Room & Board	$8,482
Books and supplies	$1,025
Required fees	$278
% frosh rec. need-based scholarship or grant aid	71
% UG rec. need-based scholarship or grant aid	57
% frosh rec. need-based self-help aid	49
% UG rec. need-based self-help aid	40
% frosh rec. any financial aid	93
% UG rec. any financial aid	87
Avg. frosh grant	$18,052
Avg. frosh loan	$3,506
Independent 529 member?	Yes

CATAWBA COLLEGE

2300 WEST INNES STREET, SALISBURY, NC 28144 • ADMISSIONS: 704-637-4402 • FAX: 704-637-4222

CAMPUS LIFE

Quality of Life Rating	**80**
Fire Safety Rating	**60**
Type of school	private
Affiliation	United Church of Christ
Environment	town

STUDENTS

Total undergrad enrollment	1,365
% male/female	47/53
% from out of state	30
% from public high school	80
% live on campus	45
% African American	15
% Asian	1
% Caucasian	79
% Hispanic	2
% Native American	1
% international	2
# of countries represented	12

SURVEY SAYS

Small classes
Students are friendly
Everyone loves the Indians
Frats and sororities are unpopular or nonexistent
Theater is popular

ACADEMICS

Academic Rating	**81**
Calendar	semester
Student/faculty ratio	16:1
Professors interesting rating	93
Professors accessible rating	88
% professors teaching UG courses	100
% classes taught by TAs	0
Most common lab size	fewer than 10 students
Most common regular class size	10-19 students

MOST POPULAR MAJORS

Business administration/management
drama and dramatics/theater arts
sports and fitness administration/management

STUDENTS SPEAK OUT

Academics

Catawba College is a small private school that offers "a strong, well-rounded education" bolstered by exceptional programs in theater, environmental science, and athletic training. Catawba's theater department "offers excellent training in a variety of areas," students tell us, reporting that "you can get fairly specialized degrees, including Bachelor's of Fine Arts in Performance, Musical Theatre, Directing, or Technical Theatre. The department is also very good about encouraging students to try areas outside their concentration so that they are well-rounded and have a better appreciation for what it takes to put on a theater production." Environmental science offerings benefit from "an entirely environmentally conscious building, plus an entire preserve protected and dedicated to studying and preserving wildlife." Athletic training reaps the benefits of the school's active intercollegiate sports programs. The business program here is also strong. Undergrads tell us that "the administration and professors at Catawba are awesome. They are there for you for any problem you have, whether it's school-related or personal." On the downside, "some of the facilities, like the theater labs and performance areas, have very out-of-date equipment" and the offline "registration process can get confusing."

Life

"Life at Catawba is generally enjoyable, although sometimes a little boring" due to the school's small-town location and the sometimes-strict rules enforced by the administration. Fortunately, "the student activity board, Wigwam Productions, usually has some activity planned for the weekend such as Late Nights with food and games, casino nights, laser tag, carnival rides, and big screen movies, free for any student." Also, "there are many places for fun within 45 minutes' driving distance from the school, including malls, clubs, and the entirety of downtown Charlotte, North Carolina," so students have options. The school's active theater department mounts regular productions, and Catawba's seventeen NCAA Division II intercollegiate athletic teams draw a lot of support. Hunting and fishing are popular with one subset of students, and most everyone enjoys being outdoors; reports one student, "In spring and fall it's really warm, so everyone will go outside and lay on blankets and do their homework. A lot of times students will toss around a Frisbee or get a pick-up game of football together." Because "there are no sororities or fraternities," there are "no big parties, but there are usually smaller room parties" that "never get out of hand." The food on campus, students agree, "is terrible, and the most frequently complained about aspect of campus life. Plan to spend at least $20 a week eating out, ordering pizza, or buying frozen dinners." Word to the wise: Lexington, the state barbecue Mecca, is just twenty miles up the road. The tea is sweet, the slaw goes on the sandwich, and yes, hush puppies come with that.

Student Body

"I'd love to see more diversity on campus," writes one Catawba undergrad, observing that "we have a sizable African American presence on campus, but other than a handful of individuals of other minorities, it's somewhat monotone, ethnically and religiously speaking." The "two main groups on campus are the athletes and the theater majors," and "although the theater kids are not all best friends with the jocks, there seems to be more camaraderie between the two groups than would stereotypically be expected." A "fairly large population of homosexuals [is] occasionally mistreated by athletes" but "otherwise very understood and accepted by the majority of the campus."

FINANCIAL AID: 704-637-4416 • E-MAIL: ADMISSION@CATAWBA.EDU • WEBSITE: WWW.CATAWBA.EDU

ADMISSIONS

Very important factors considered include: Class rank, essays, recommendations, secondary school record, standardized test scores. *Important factors considered include:* Character/personal qualities, extracurricular activities, interview, talent/ability, volunteer work. *Other factors considered include:* Alumni/ae relation, minority status, work experience. SAT Reasoning or ACT required. TOEFL required of all international applicants. High school diploma is required, and GED is accepted. *Academic units required:* 4 English, 2 math, 2 science, 2 social studies, 6 academic electives. *Academic units recommended:* 4 English, 3 math, 3 science (3 science lab), 2 foreign language, 3 social studies, 2 academic electives.

The Inside Word

Catawba's applicant pool is mainly from the Southeast, which tends to give candidates from far afield some extra appeal. There is serious competition for students among similar colleges in this neck of the woods, and the admissions staff here has to work hard to bring in the freshman class each year. They succeed because they are truly friendly and personal in their dealings with students and their families, and the college seems to have carved a worthwhile niche for itself amid the myriad choices available in the area.

FINANCIAL AID

Students should submit: FAFSA, state aid form. The Princeton Review suggests that all financial aid forms be submitted as soon as possible after 1/1. *Need-based scholarships/grants offered:* Pell, SEOG, state scholarships/grants, private scholarships, the school's own gift aid. *Loan aid offered:* FFEL Subsidized Stafford, FFEL Unsubsidized Stafford, FFEL PLUS, Federal Perkins, college/university loans from institutional funds, TERI Loans, Nellie Mae Loans, Advantage Loans, alternative loans. Applicants will be notified of awards on a rolling basis beginning on or about 2/15. Federal Work-study Program available. Institutional employment available. Off-campus job opportunities are excellent.

FROM THE ADMISSIONS OFFICE

"Catawba College prepares students for rewarding lives and careers in the liberal arts tradition. This attractive campus is centrally located in Salisbury, North Carolina, a short drive away from the mountains and Atlantic beaches. The community possesses a rich past and commitment to preserving its cultural and historic charm. In contrast, just 45 minutes away is the much faster pace of Charlotte, North Carolina where shopping, transportation, and entertainment of all kinds are readily available.

"On campus, students study and socialize in a small college setting that offers strong traditions, excellent facilities, and beautiful surroundings. The high standards of quality set by Catawba's academic programs are matched by equally demanding sports and cocurricular programs. Students describe the community as caring and personable. They also exhibit a high rate of involvement in campus activities ranging form the performing arts to homecoming and travel abroad. Faculty and staff are described by students as being important mentors. Whether in a state-of-the-art environmental science facility, attractive music and theatrical performance center, classroom, or one of the college's first-class athletic facilities, students report they feel as if they are among family when on campus.

"Perhaps the most important testimony to the attractiveness of Catawba is found in the words of its graduates who report numerous successful careers and rich memories of their time at school.

"Students applying for admission into the fall 2006 class are required to take the new version of the SAT (or the ACT with the writing section), but we will allow students to submit scores from the old (prior to March 2005) version of the SAT (or ACT) as well, and will use the student's best scores from either test."

SELECTIVITY

Admissions Rating	**79**
# of applicants	842
% of applicants accepted	63
% of acceptees attending	49

FRESHMAN PROFILE

Range SAT Verbal	460-570
Average SAT Verbal	526
Range SAT Math	470-570
Average SAT Math	524
**TPR Projected Range SAT Writing*	*530-610*
Range ACT Composite	19-23
Average ACT Composite	21
Minimum Paper TOEFL	525
Minimum Computer Based TOEFL	197
Average HS GPA	3.33
% graduated top 10% of class	14
% graduated top 25% of class	37
% graduated top 50% of class	71

DEADLINES

Regular notification	rolling
Nonfall registration?	yes

AND SOMETIMES PREFER

Appalachian State University
University of North Carolina—Chapel Hill
University of North Carolina—Charlotte

AND RARELY PREFER

Elon University
North Carolina State University
University of North Carolina—Greensboro
University of North Carolina—Wilmington

FINANCIAL FACTS

Financial Aid Rating	**70**
Annual tuition	$17,600
Room & Board	$5,900
Books and supplies	$800
% frosh rec. need-based scholarship or grant aid	61
% UG rec. need-based scholarship or grant aid	44
% frosh rec. need-based self-help aid	54
% UG rec. need-based self-help aid	55
% frosh rec. any financial aid	96
% UG rec. any financial aid	96
Avg. frosh grant	$6,905
Avg. frosh loan	$3,730
Independent 529 member?	Yes

THE CATHOLIC UNIVERSITY OF AMERICA

OFFICE OF ENROLLMENT SERVICES, WASHINGTON, DC 20064 • ADMISSIONS: 202-319-5305 • FAX: 202-319-6533

CAMPUS LIFE

Quality of Life Rating	**67**
Fire Safety Rating	**85**
Type of school	private
Affiliation	Roman Catholic
Environment	metropolis

STUDENTS

Total undergrad enrollment	2,871
% male/female	44/56
% from out of state	93
% from public high school	50
% live on campus	68
% in (# of) fraternities	1 (1)
% in (# of) sororities	1 (1)
% African American	7
% Asian	3
% Caucasian	71
% Hispanic	5
% international	2
# of countries represented	80

SURVEY SAYS

Small classes
Students are friendly
Frats and sororities are unpopular or nonexistent
Lots of beer drinking
Hard liquor is popular

ACADEMICS

Academic Rating	**73**
Calendar	semester
Student/faculty ratio	9:1
Professors interesting rating	76
Professors accessible rating	75
% professors teaching UG courses	66
% classes taught by TAs	11
Most common lab size	20-29 students
Most common regular class size	10-19 students

MOST POPULAR MAJORS

Architecture (BArch, BA/BS, MArch, MA/MS, PhD)
engineering
political science and government

STUDENTS SPEAK OUT

Academics

The Catholic University of America (CWA) is "a spiritual place with an excellent academic setting" where "the professional schools—engineering, architecture, and nursing—are outstanding." The school successfully combines the best aspects of a large university and a small liberal arts college. The university's Washington, DC setting provides access to government research projects, which in turn drive the school's cutting-edge School of Engineering. In all CUA schools, undergraduates are provided ample opportunity to participate in research. Music, theater, media studies, and theology are among the other departments praised by students. All undergraduates must complete CUA's core curriculum, which demonstrates "a deep respect for the classics." One student tells us, "This is one of the few places where Aristotle is always right, and Saint Thomas Aquinas is spoken of on a first-name basis." The university's professors provide "individual attention that allows each student to find a personal niche" and "will go above and beyond the call of duty to help you turn your dream into reality." The administration, however, "has a communication problem with the students, is too slow, [and] leaves much room for improvement." Undergraduates appreciate the fact that "the school is extremely strong in promoting its religious ideals and beliefs. There are many opportunities to get involved religiously."

Life

Students at CUA enjoy a campus that has "so much to do," and a hometown that's "the best city in the world." Students extol the campus's endless "dance lessons, vocal/instrumental lessons, student government, special-interest clubs, service organizations, sports, dances, open-mic nights, choirs, club-sponsored activities, literary contests, movie nights, [and] stimulating lectures." Of special note is the school's "outstanding music program. Students perform musical plays, showcases, and concerts free or [for a low] admission. [Both students and] people from the area come to see these students perform." The campus itself "is so beautiful and really easy to take walks at any time of the year. Everything is not too spread out, so you can easily walk across campus just to spend time with friends." Moreover, DC "provides a wealth of opportunities, especially since the Metro is right next to the campus. Just a few Metro stops away is Union Station with restaurants and shopping, the Capitol, and tons of museums. With Dupont Circle, Adams Morgan, Chinatown, and Capitol Hill, there's plenty to do and 10,000 places to eat." That's especially good to know since "the university food is gross."

Student Body

Undergraduates at CUA "are very similar to one another. Pretty much everyone is white, Catholic, from a middle- or upper-middle-class family somewhere in the Northeast. Most come from Maryland, Pennsylvania, New York, New Jersey, and Massachusetts." The great number of Irish Catholics leads one student to quip that they "look like Conan O'Brien's offspring. It's 'Irish Catholic extreme with a little Italian flavor.'" It "seems almost as if there is a dress code at CUA, since everyone wears pretty much the same thing: jeans always, sweatpants and hooded sweatshirts when the weather gets colder, and flip-flops are a requirement, even into November." Although the school has a religious affiliation and places a general emphasis on faith, one student reports, "Not everyone is religious. The people who are seem to be trying to make up for those of us heathens and then some." The student body is nearly politically homogeneous; writes one student, "It tries to be the Catholic University, but it should be called the Conservative Republican University."

THE CATHOLIC UNIVERSITY OF AMERICA

FINANCIAL AID: 202-319-5307 • E-MAIL: CUA-ADMISSIONS@CUA.EDU • WEBSITE: WWW.CUA.EDU

ADMISSIONS

Very important factors considered include: Character/personal qualities, essays, recommendations, secondary school record, standardized test scores, volunteer work. *Important factors considered include:* Class rank, extracurricular activities, interview, talent/ability. *Other factors considered include:* Alumni/ae relation, minority status, work experience. SAT Reasoning or ACT required. SAT Subject Tests recommended. TOEFL required of all international applicants. High school diploma is required, and GED is not accepted. *Academic units recommended:* 4 English, 3 math, 3 science (1 science lab), 2 foreign language, 4 social studies, 1 history.

The Inside Word

This is not the place to try radical approaches to completing your admissions application: smooth sailing for solid students and even friendlier for candidates from distant states or unique high schools.

FINANCIAL AID

Students should submit: FAFSA. Regular filing deadline is 2/1. The Princeton Review suggests that all financial aid forms be submitted as soon as possible after 1/1. *Need-based scholarships/grants offered:* Pell, SEOG, state scholarships/grants, private scholarships, the school's own gift aid, Federal Nursing scholarships. *Loan aid offered:* FFEL Subsidized Stafford, FFEL Unsubsidized Stafford, FFEL PLUS, Federal Perkins, Federal Nursing, commercial loans. Applicants will be notified of awards on a rolling basis beginning on or about 4/1. Federal Work-study Program available. Institutional employment available. Off-campus job opportunities are excellent.

FROM THE ADMISSIONS OFFICE

"The Catholic University of America's friendly atmosphere, rigorous academic programs, and emphasis on time-honored values attract students from most states and more than 30 foreign countries. Its 144-acre, tree-lined campus is only 10 minutes from the nation's capital. Distinguished as the national university of the Catholic Church in the United States, CUA is the only institution of higher education established by the U.S. Catholic bishops; however, students from all religious traditions are welcome.

"CUA offers undergraduate degrees in more than 60 major areas in six schools of study. Students enroll into the School of Arts and Sciences, Architecture, Nursing, Engineering, Music, or Philosophy. Additionally, CUA students can concentrate in areas of pre-professional study including law, dentistry, medicine, or veterinary studies.

"With Capitol Hill, the Smithsonian Institution, NASA, the Kennedy Center, and the National Institutes of Health among the places students obtain internships, firsthand experience is a valuable piece of the experience that CUA offers. Numerous students also take the opportunity in their junior year to study abroad at one of Catholic's 17 country program sites. Political science majors even have the opportunity to do a Parliamentary Internship in either England or Ireland. With the campus just minutes away from downtown via the Metrorail rapid transit system, students enjoy a residential campus in an exciting city of historical monuments, theaters, festivals, ethnic restaurants, and parks.

"Freshman applicants for fall 2006 must take the new SAT or ACT. Additionally, students may submit scores from the old SAT, and the best scores from either test will be used. Matriculating students should submit the SAT Subject Test: Foreign Language exam if they plan to continue studying that language at CUA."

SELECTIVITY

Admissions Rating	**85**
# of applicants	2,744
% of applicants accepted	82
% of acceptees attending	32
# of early decision applicants	85
% accepted early decision	65

FRESHMAN PROFILE

Range SAT Verbal	520-640
Average SAT Verbal	590
Range SAT Math	510-620
Average SAT Math	577
**TPR Projected Range SAT Writing*	*570-660*
Range ACT Composite	21-27
Average ACT Composite	24
Minimum Paper TOEFL	560
Minimum Computer Based TOEFL	220
Average HS GPA	3.37
% graduated top 10% of class	22
% graduated top 25% of class	57
% graduated top 50% of class	88

DEADLINES

Regular application deadline	2/1
Regular notification	3/15
Nonfall registration?	yes

APPLICANTS ALSO LOOK AT

AND OFTEN PREFER

Boston College
University of Maryland University College
University of Notre Dame

AND SOMETIMES PREFER

University of Virginia

AND RARELY PREFER

American University
Fordham University
The George Washington University
Saint Joseph's University (PA)

FINANCIAL FACTS

Financial Aid Rating	**69**
Annual tuition	$24,800
Room & Board	$9,838
Books and supplies	$1,000
Required fees	$1,200
% frosh rec. need-based scholarship or grant aid	40
% UG rec. need-based scholarship or grant aid	25
% frosh rec. need-based self-help aid	47
% UG rec. need-based self-help aid	42
% frosh rec. any financial aid	98
% UG rec. any financial aid	91
Avg. frosh grant	$10,231
Avg. frosh loan	$6,585
Independent 529 member?	Yes

CENTENARY COLLEGE OF LOUISIANA

PO BOX 41188, SHREVEPORT, LA 71134-1188 • ADMISSIONS: 318-869-5131 • FAX: 318-869-5005

CAMPUS LIFE

Quality of Life Rating	**76**
Fire Safety Rating	**84**
Type of school	private
Affiliation	Methodist
Environment	metropolis

STUDENTS

Total undergrad enrollment	891
% male/female	37/63
% from out of state	35
% from public high school	80
% live on campus	68
% in (# of) fraternities	26 (4)
% in (# of) sororities	28 (2)
% African American	8
% Asian	3
% Caucasian	85
% Hispanic	2
% Native American	1
% international	2
# of countries represented	12

SURVEY SAYS

Small classes
Athletic facilities are great
Musical organizations are popular

ACADEMICS

Academic Rating	**85**
Calendar	4-4-1
Student/faculty ratio	8:1
Professors interesting rating	87
Professors accessible rating	85
% professors teaching UG courses	100
% classes taught by TAs	0
Most common regular class size	10-19 students

MOST POPULAR MAJORS

Biology/biological sciences
Business administration/management
communications, journalism, and related fields

STUDENTS SPEAK OUT

Academics

The old saying that dynamite comes in small packages holds true when it comes to Centenary College, at least according to its students. With an enrollment of 900 undergraduates, the academic experience here is nothing if not personal. "Just the other night, I had dinner with the President and Provost," writes one typical senior. "They both know me by my first name. They, as well as the professors, are always available by appointment to meet with students." One fast-moving freshman brags that already "I have the cell phone numbers of my professors and have visited several of their homes." A small enrollment means small class sizes, which allow for learning to assume the form of a dialogue between teacher and student, rather than the former spitting out facts in a lecture hall and the latter parroting it back on tests. Students agree that professors "don't expect us to merely regurgitate onto paper later" what they say in classes. "In our First Year Experience classes, we are taught to question everything," and this questioning, which should lead students to learn how to come to their own conclusions, is an integral part of the undergraduate experience and is continually developed through the subsequent three years. But the small size also has its drawbacks. For instance, students wish "there were more class options available." Major offerings are heavy on the liberal arts, though the few pre-professional programs draw a fair number of students.

Life

First thing's first: This is not Mardi Gras country. In fact, the drive from Centenary to New Orleans takes about twice as long as it takes to drive to Dallas, which itself is almost 200 miles away. But distance doesn't deter students from thinking about the attractions of these other big cities; despite the fact that hometown area SMSA has a population of 400,000, students gripe that it's not the best college town. This sentiment seems tied to the strict door policies at most of the bars off-campus. "Shreveport is a great town for fun if you are 21. But most college students are not 21," and as a result many students turn to the Greeks to create opportunities to socialize. They visit "fraternity houses every weekend. There is some drinking going on, but no one pressures anyone." However, "once you are 21," you most likely spend quality time with friends in the local watering holes, and if you are feeling particularly adventurous, "the casinos are very fun (but expensive)." During the week, "most people are involved in an activity on campus, whether it's the newspaper, choir, sorority, fraternity," intramural sports, or "working out in our wonderful fitness center." The school also plays host to many "plays, concerts, [and] sports" events. The food on campus is universally despised. One thing that students would absolutely hate to see change, however, is the choir, which is the pride of the campus.

Student Body

Despite the influence of the Greeks, "the students on campus are not your typical party-all-night, football-playing frat boys and girls." Instead, Centenary students form a community based primarily on strong ethics and sharp intellects. As one student puts it, this is a "friendly and academically driven" environment. While Centenary is not the most culturally or geographically diverse campus on earth, "there are students here with different belief systems and alternative lifestyles," and "they are accepted with open arms." That said, there are few students who "thought there would be a good number of genuine Christians here—big mistake on that one." In general, there's a liberal breeze in the air in this little corner of Shreveport. "Although we are in a conservative, southern area," writes a freshman, "campus (known as the "Centenary Bubble" in the community) is surprisingly liberal, both with students and faculty." Since the school is so small, "everybody knows everybody, [so] rumors get around very quickly."

Centenary College of Louisiana

Financial Aid: 318-869-5137 • E-mail: admissions@centenary.edu • Website: www.centenary.edu

ADMISSIONS

Very important factors considered include: Extracurricular activities, secondary school record. *Important factors considered include:* Character/personal qualities, class rank, interview, recommendations, standardized test scores, talent/ability, volunteer work. *Other factors considered include:* Alumni/ae relation, essays, geographical residence, minority status, religious affiliation/commitment, work experience. SAT Reasoning or ACT required. TOEFL required of all international applicants. High school diploma is required, and GED is accepted. *Academic units recommended:* 4 English, 3 math, 3 science (2 science lab), 2 foreign language, 3 social studies.

The Inside Word

Centenary has historically had a small applicant pool, and thus has had to admit the majority to meet its freshman enrollment goals. Currently, the school has attracted a larger applicant pool and become noticeably more strict in its admit rate. Its reputation, though regional, is quite solid, and the college does a good job of enrolling its admits. A very friendly and efficient admissions office no doubt contributes to such success.

FINANCIAL AID

Students should submit: FAFSA, institution's own financial aid form. The Princeton Review suggests that all financial aid forms be submitted as soon as possible after 1/1. *Need-based scholarships/grants offered:* Pell, SEOG, state scholarships/grants, private scholarships, the school's own gift aid. *Loan aid offered:* FFEL Subsidized Stafford, FFEL Unsubsidized Stafford, FFEL PLUS, Federal Perkins. Applicants will be notified of awards on or about 3/15. Federal Work-study Program available. Institutional employment available. Off-campus job opportunities are good.

FROM THE ADMISSIONS OFFICE

"Centenary students work closely with a gifted faculty and inquisitive peers. Challenging classes and interactive learning keep our students coming back after class to ask that extra question . . . or working a little longer to produce their very best. Our students were the leaders of their schools and communities. We know college should not be an end to their activities, but a furthering of their experiences. Centenary College provides ample and varied opportunities to further leadership experiences in an atmosphere of integrity and honesty encouraged by the Honor Code. Our students come for experiential learning through our service-learning program. They participate in a global classroom through our intercultural and study abroad programs. They develop their career paths with the help of dedicated faculty, staff, and internship mentors. Come visit Centenary College, get the facts, and find out if we are best for you.

"First-year applicants for fall 2006 must submit either ACT or SAT examination scores. If either exam was taken before the recently revised version (February 2005 for ACT and March 2005 for the SAT), those scores can be submitted. We recommend, but do not require, the ACT Writing exam."

SELECTIVITY

Admissions Rating	**87**
# of applicants	1,166
% of applicants accepted	70
% of acceptees attending	35
# of early decision applicants	53
% accepted early decision	80

FRESHMAN PROFILE

Range SAT Verbal	530-650
Range SAT Math	550-650
**TPR Projected Range SAT Writing*	*580-670*
Range ACT Composite	23-28
Average ACT Composite	23
Minimum Paper TOEFL	550
Minimum Computer Based TOEFL	220
Average HS GPA	3.36
% graduated top 10% of class	35
% graduated top 25% of class	65
% graduated top 50% of class	88

DEADLINES

Early decision application deadline	12/1
Early decision notification	1/1
Regular notification	3/15
Nonfall registration?	yes

APPLICANTS ALSO LOOK AT

AND OFTEN PREFER
Rhodes College

AND SOMETIMES PREFER
Louisiana State University
Millsaps College

AND RARELY PREFER
Northwestern State University

FINANCIAL FACTS

Financial Aid Rating	**82**
Annual tuition	$16,750
Room & Board	$6,070
Books and supplies	$1,000
Required fees	$610
% frosh rec. need-based scholarship or grant aid	67
% UG rec. need-based scholarship or grant aid	61
% frosh rec. need-based self-help aid	38
% UG rec. need-based self-help aid	37
% frosh rec. any financial aid	98
% UG rec. any financial aid	96
Avg. frosh grant	$12,052
Avg. frosh loan	$3,025
Independent 529 member?	Yes

CENTRE COLLEGE

600 WEST WALNUT STREET, DANVILLE, KY 40422 • ADMISSIONS: 800-423-6236 • FAX: 859-238-5373

CAMPUS LIFE

Quality of Life Rating	**87**
Fire Safety Rating	**60**
Type of school	private
Affiliation	Presbyterian
Environment	village

STUDENTS

Total undergrad enrollment	1,060
% male/female	48/52
% from out of state	30
% from public high school	79
% live on campus	94
% in (# of) fraternities	38 (5)
% in (# of) sororities	39 (4)
% African American	2
% Asian	3
% Caucasian	93
% Hispanic	1
% international	2
# of countries represented	12

SURVEY SAYS

Small classes
No one cheats
Students are friendly
Students are happy
Frats and sororities dominate social scene
Lots of beer drinking
Hard liquor is popular

ACADEMICS

Academic Rating	**91**
Calendar	4-1-4
Student/faculty ratio	10:1
Professors interesting rating	98
Professors accessible rating	96
% professors teaching UG courses	100
% classes taught by TAs	0
Most common lab size	10-19 students
Most common regular class size	10-19 students

MOST POPULAR MAJORS

Economics
English language and literature
history

STUDENTS SPEAK OUT

Academics

Many schools offer opportunities for major-related internships and study abroad. Few, however, guarantee both. Centre College, a small liberal arts school in Kentucky, does. Under "The Centre Commitment," Centre not only ensures an internship and international study, it also guarantees graduation in four years and offers up to an additional year of tuition-free study to those who cannot graduate on time. Undergrads here praise the "awesome study abroad programs," reporting that "a wide variety of CentreTerm (i.e. January term) and long-term programs promises that there is something to study abroad that everyone will enjoy. It's a great way to get a break from campus and to see the world (and it really isn't that expensive)." They are even more impressed, however, with the amount of personal attention lavished on each student by faculty and administration. "Centre's greatest strength is that no one can slip through the figurative cracks, since nearly every person at Centre seems genuinely concerned about the students," writes one student. "Even the president of the college tries to get to know each student by name." Not only that, but "where else would your college president have you over for a BBQ, teach a class, and perform in a concert? Only at Centre." All this support helps students handle Centre's "strong academic program" that requires that "either you work hard or you flunk out." As one student puts it, "Classes, as a rule, are difficult, but we learn to push ourselves and achieve more." The entire experience leaves many here concluding that "Centre is just perfect. The small school environment lends itself so well to the liberal arts education platform, and Centre excels at everything it does."

Life

Centre "is academics-driven during the week, but on the weekend the school knows how to have fun," with a lively Greek scene occupying center (no pun intended) stage. Writes one student, "The 'Centre Experience' is all about being a part of the Centre community. We all work hard but we all know how to party hard as well. Weekends are filled with frat parties, the 'running of the flame' (streaking from a dorm to the statue in front of the library and back to the dorm), and playing pool at the Warehouse (i.e,. the student center)." Students must devote some extracurricular time to fulfilling Centre's convocation requirement, which mandates attendance at 30 convocation-designated events per year; such events typically include lectures and performances. Many fulfill their obligations at the Norton Center for the Arts, which "brings in many musicals, operas, ballets, plays, speakers, orchestras, etc. that would normally cost quite a bit to go see, but students get to go for free." Because "there isn't much to do in Danville," a lot of free time is spent "hanging out in each other's rooms, listening to music or watching shows." Students have discovered that "although Danville is a small town, Centre is a revitalizing, dynamic force in this community." And "the occasional jaunt to Lexington or Louisville helps to throw in some variety."

Student Body

"Most Centre students are from upper-middle class families in the South" and are "quite friendly and usually willing to go to great extents to help out other students." They tend to be "Christian, moderately conservative, and very enthusiastic about Greek life." Writes one student, "The boys have that Southern gentleman quality about them, and the girls are pretty and outgoing." Beyond the mainstream crowd, "there is a fair amount of atypical students. For example, there are many active liberals on campus as well as conservatives, and Greek life is big but you can have fun without it. Since everyone is pretty well-acquainted with everyone else on such a small campus, it's easy to fit in." Most everyone "works very hard but leaves room in their schedule to participate in sports and clubs and to just hang out with friends."

FINANCIAL AID: 859-238-5365 • E-MAIL: ADMISSION@CENTRE.EDU • WEBSITE: WWW.CENTRE.EDU

ADMISSIONS

Very important factors considered include: Class rank, secondary school record. *Important factors considered include:* Essays, standardized test scores. *Other factors considered include:* Alumni/ae relation, character/personal qualities, extracurricular activities, interview, recommendations, talent/ability. SAT Reasoning or ACT required. TOEFL required of all international applicants. High school diploma or equivalent is not required. *Academic units required:* 4 English, 4 math, 2 science (2 science lab), 2 foreign language, 2 history. *Academic units recommended:* 3 science (3 science lab).

The Inside Word

Centre's small but very capable student body reflects solid academic preparation from high school, and it's no surprise that this is exactly what the admissions committee expects from applicants. If you're ranked in the top quarter of your graduating class and have taken challenging courses throughout your high school career, you should have smooth sailing through the admissions process. Those who rank below the top quarter or who have inconsistent academic backgrounds will find entrance here more difficult, and may benefit from an interview.

FINANCIAL AID

Students should submit: FAFSA, institution's own financial aid form. Regular filing deadline is 3/1. The Princeton Review suggests that all financial aid forms be submitted as soon as possible after 1/1. *Need-based scholarships/grants offered:* Pell, SEOG, state scholarships/grants, private scholarships, the school's own gift aid. *Loan aid offered:* FFEL Subsidized Stafford, FFEL Unsubsidized Stafford, FFEL PLUS, Federal Perkins, college/university loans from institutional funds. Applicants will be notified of awards on or about 3/25. Federal Work-study Program available. Institutional employment available. Off-campus job opportunities are fair.

FROM THE ADMISSIONS OFFICE

""Centre provides its students with a personal education that enables them to achieve extraordinary success in advanced study and their careers. Centre teachers, virtually all of whom hold the highest degree available in their field, challenge their students and give them the individual attention and support they need to meet those challenges. The end result is highly capable graduates with a can-do attitude and the ability to accomplish their goals.

"Centre offers a multitude of advantages like, a National top 50 academic reputation, 'majors' options, and exposure to the internationally known artists and scholars, (Center hosted the U.S. Vice Presidential Debate in 2000); benefits like these produce extraordinary success. For example: entrance to top graduate and professional schools; the most prestigious post-graduate scholarships (Rhodes, Fulbright, Goldwater); interesting, rewarding jobs (96 percent of graduates are either employed or engaged in advance study within nine months of graduation).

"How do alumni respond? They express their customer satisfaction by leading the U.S. in their percentage of annual financial support. How much does all this cost? Because of our nation-leading alumni support, Centre is the most affordable of America's top 50 national liberal arts colleges.

"Centre's admissions policies have not been affected by the new SAT, and we will not consider a student's scores from the new Writing section."

SELECTIVITY

Admissions Rating	**92**
# of applicants	1,604
% of applicants accepted	69
% of acceptees attending	27
# accepting a place on wait list	94
% admitted from wait list	4

FRESHMAN PROFILE

Range SAT Verbal	600-700
Average SAT Verbal	612
Range SAT Math	580-680
Average SAT Math	603
**TPR Projected Range SAT Writing*	*630-700*
Range ACT Composite	25-30
Average ACT Composite	27
Minimum Paper TOEFL	580
Average HS GPA	3.7
% graduated top 10% of class	61
% graduated top 25% of class	85
% graduated top 50% of class	98

DEADLINES

Regular application deadline	2/1
Regular notification	3/15
Nonfall registration?	no

APPLICANTS ALSO LOOK AT

AND OFTEN PREFER

Davidson College
Washington and Lee University

AND SOMETIMES PREFER

Furman University
Kenyon College
Rhodes College

AND RARELY PREFER

Transylvania University
University of Kentucky
University of Louisville

FINANCIAL FACTS

Financial Aid Rating	**83**
Annual tuition	$21,800
Room & Board	$7,300
Books and supplies	$800
% frosh rec. need-based scholarship or grant aid	62
% UG rec. need-based scholarship or grant aid	62
% frosh rec. need-based self-help aid	41
% UG rec. need-based self-help aid	46
Avg. frosh grant	$14,000
Avg. frosh loan	$2,600
Independent 529 member?	Yes

CHAPMAN UNIVERSITY

ONE UNIVERSITY DRIVE, ORANGE, CA 92866 • ADMISSIONS: 714-997-6711 • FAX: 714-997-6713

CAMPUS LIFE

Quality of Life Rating	**78**
Fire Safety Rating	**60**
Type of school	private
Affiliation	Disciples of Christ
Environment	metropolis

STUDENTS

Total undergrad enrollment	3,708
% male/female	42/58
% from out of state	20
% from public high school	70
% live on campus	38
% in (# of) fraternities	14 (5)
% in (# of) sororities	17 (5)
% African American	2
% Asian	8
% Caucasian	65
% Hispanic	10
% Native American	1
% international	3
# of countries represented	37

SURVEY SAYS . . .

Small classes
Great computer facilities
Great off-campus food
Frats and sororities dominate social scene

ACADEMICS

Academic Rating	**80**
Calendar	4-1-4
Student/faculty ratio	16:1
Profs interesting rating	80
Profs accessible rating	84
% profs teaching UG courses	100
% classes taught by TAs	0
Most common lab size	10-19 students
Most common reg class size	20-29 students

MOST POPULAR MAJORS

Advertising
Business administration/management
cinematography and film/video production

STUDENTS SPEAK OUT

Academics

When you hear the word "university" it's easy to imagine an educational sprawl where class sizes grow into the hundreds and students are just a number. That's hardly the case at Chapman University, the California home of around 3,100 undergrads. One student explains, "The school is small enough that it is possible to build one-on-one relationships with your professors and administrators that will last for your four years, and maybe even longer." Most Chapman undergrads agree that the professors here are "highly intelligent, inspiring, compassionate, and genuinely interested in each and every person." Of course, you'll find "junk" professors here, as you will at any school. To save yourself the frustration of a bad class or poor professor, simply ask "friends and classmates what they thought of their classes and teachers." Some of the most popular academic offerings are found in the nationally-competetive School of Film and Television. "I think the film school is a real strength," opines one student who's taken several of its courses. Another fine attribute is that "the emphasis on 'global citizenship' [something particular to Chapman] permeates all aspects of Chapman's curriculum, from study abroad programs to this 'global responsibility' that is held by all faculty members."

Life

Life at Chapman is "pretty easygoing." Orange, Chapman's host town, "has such a small-town feel" that many students find local life safe and comfortable, if perhaps a bit dull. "But it's close to everything."—nearby "Anaheim is a goldmine when it comes to entertainment, and LA and the beach aren't very far either." Let's not forget that "Disneyland, the Block, the Arrowhead Pond, and a dance club" are "all within 10 driving minutes." The party scene at Chapman is quite dismal, largely thanks to "the insanely strict alcohol policy and campus safety's enthusiasm to bust innocent kids that are just trying to have a good time." And "fraternities and sororities are not allowed to own group houses in the city of Orange," which means it's unlikely you'll stumble upon any Animal House-style keg parties at Chapman. Nonetheless, students here still manage to "drink way too much." A wealthy community, Orange County teems with malls and movie theatres, where many students while away a lot of their time. The university's "global citizenship" emphasis ensures that the students interact with the community—and the world at large—in more substantive ways, as well. "Chapman is always doing something for abused women and children, or raising awareness about gay rights, or money for a school in Africa," writes one student.

Student Body

Studying and partying are many Chapman students' preeminent concerns, and many have struck a healthy balance between the two. "They know when it is time to hit the books and when a night out on the town is called for," remarks one. Despite the schools religious ties, the student body is not a wholly pious bunch, either. Students do have similarities, though. "Most of the students who go here are upper-class kids from Orange County who have never been out of California," reports one student. "The true lack of ethnic diversity" is an oft-heard complaint at Chapman, but most undergrads find their classmates to be tolerant of the diversity that does exist and overwhelmingly friendly toward everyone. "One of the main reasons I chose to attend Chapman University," comments an undergrad, was "the students' extreme hospitality and enthusiasm." In such an amiable environment, most students feel as if "the student body is more like a family than a competing group of students." Still, there are quite a few among the Chapman fold that can be "cliquey, conceited, [and] self-centered." If you find this to be the case, do as one student has: "I've found the people that I want to be friends with, and I just stay away from everyone else. It's fine that way."

FINANCIAL AID: 714-997-6741 • E-MAIL: ADMIT@CHAPMAN.EDU • WEBSITE: WWW.CHAPMAN.EDU

ADMISSIONS

Very important factors considered include: Character/personal qualities, class rank, essays, secondary school record, standardized test scores. *Important factors considered include:* Extracurricular activities, interview, talent/ability, volunteer work. *Other factors considered include:* Alumni/ae relation, minority status, recommendations, work experience. SAT Reasoning or ACT required; SAT Subject Tests recommended. TOEFL required of all international applicants. High school diploma is required and GED is accepted. *Academic units required:* 2 English, 2 math, 2 science, (1 science lab), 2 foreign language, 3 social studies.

Inside Word

As Chapman's reputation grows, so too does its applicant pool: the number of freshman candidates has increased by 150 percent over the past five years. Incoming class sizes, meanwhile, have held steady at 900, with no plans for expansion in the near future. Serious candidates should visit the school and interview with an admissions officer.

FINANCIAL AID

Students should submit: FAFSA, state aid form. The Princeton Review suggests that all financial aid forms be submitted as soon as possible after January 1. *Need-based scholarships/grants offered:* Pell, SEOG, state scholarships/grants, private scholarships, the school's own gift aid. *Loan aid offered:* FFEL Subsidized Stafford, FFEL Unsubsidized Stafford, FFEL PLUS, Federal Perkins, college/university loans from institutional funds. Applicants will be notified of awards on a rolling basis beginning or about March 15. Federal Work-Study Program available. Institutional employment available. Off-campus job opportunities are excellent.

FROM THE ADMISSIONS OFFICE

"During our 144 year history, Chapman has evolved from a small, church-related liberal arts college into a vibrant and comprehensive mid-sized liberal arts and sciences university distinguished for an eclectic group of nationally recognized programs including athletic training, film and television production, business and economics, dance, music, theatre, writing, and teacher education. Our Orange County, California location was recently rated by Places Rated Almanac as "the number one place to live in North America" citing superior climate, cultural, recreational, educational, and career entry opportunities.

"Chapman's environment is involving, and we seek students who are willing to enter an atmosphere of healthy competition where their talents will be nurtured and manifest to the fullest—whether it is in the classroom, on the stage, or the athletic field. We challenge prospective students to thoroughly investigate our fine balance of liberal and professional learning so they may make a fully informed decision about "fit" with regard to their personalities and that of the university.

"Students applying for freshman admission to Chapman University for spring and fall 2006 will be required to submit scores from the new SAT or the ACT including the Writing section. Fall 2006 applicants are allowed to submit scores from the old versions of both tests as their best scores (old/new) will be used in making admissions decisions. "

SELECTIVITY

Admissions Rating	**90**
# of applicants	3,463
% of applicants accepted	58
% of acceptees attending	41
# accepting a place on wait list	109
% admitted from wait list	22

FRESHMAN PROFILE

Range SAT Verbal	539-652
Average SAT Verbal	595
Range SAT Math	543-655
Average SAT Math	598
**TPR Projected Range SAT Writing*	*590-670*
Range ACT Composite	23-28
Average ACT Composite	26
Minimum Paper TOEFL	500
Minimum Computer Based TOEFL	173
Average HS GPA	3.6
% graduated top 10% of class	43
% graduated top 25% of class	76
% graduated top 50% of class	97

DEADLINES

Regular application deadline	1/31
Regular notification	rolling
Nonfall registration?	yes

FINANCIAL FACTS

Financial Aid Rating	**97**
Annual tuition	$28,050
Room & Board	$9,628
Required fees	$688
% frosh rec. need-based scholarship or grant aid	49
% UG rec. need-based scholarship or grant aid	47
% frosh rec. need-based self-help aid	33
% UG rec. need-based self-help aid	26
% UG rec. any financial aid	79
Avg. frosh grant	$20,045
Avg. frosh loan	$2,095
Independent 529 member?	Yes

City University of New York—Brooklyn College

2900 Bedford Avenue, Brooklyn, NY 11210-2889 • Admissions: 718-951-5001 • Fax: 718-951-4506

CAMPUS LIFE

Quality of Life Rating	**65**
Fire Safety Rating	**60**
Type of school	public
Environment	metropolis

STUDENTS

Total undergrad enrollment	10,789
% male/female	40/60
% from out of state	1
% from public high school	60
% in (# of) fraternities	2 (4)
% in (# of) sororities	2 (6)
% African American	29
% Asian	10
% Caucasian	43
% Hispanic	11
% international	6
# of countries represented	82

SURVEY SAYS

Small classes
Great computer facilities
Great library
Diverse student types on campus
Very little drug use

ACADEMICS

Academic Rating	**70**
Calendar	semester
Student/faculty ratio	15:1
Professors interesting rating	62
Professors accessible rating	61
% professors teaching UG courses	80
% classes taught by TAs	2
Most common regular class size	20-29 students

MOST POPULAR MAJORS

Business administration/ management
education
psychology

STUDENTS SPEAK OUT

Academics

It's "all about getting a quality, low-cost education" at Brooklyn College, a New York City school that serves a large undergraduate population of both traditional and nontraditional students. About 16 percent of undergraduates here major in business. Computer and information sciences, boosted by "very up-to-date technology," attract a sizable percentage of students, too. Psychology, education, and pre-medical studies are also popular programs. Undergrads report that it's rough going at first at BC; frequent griping by students has led to a change in the core requirements that have been deemed "too numerous," and "the professors who teach core courses are not the greatest." Things get much better once students find an area of specialization; explains one, "Until I found a program that I could tailor to my needs, I found BC to be a cold place lacking interest in its students. Now I realize that once students find their key supporting office or department, we actually have a chance to accomplish wonderful things." Professors here include "everything from a former truck driver to a top experienced CPA.... There are also professors from every background and religion." Although some teachers in the sciences and technology "don't really speak much English," students generally are impressed with the quality of the faculty, telling us that instructors "push us to do our best" and "foster a great environment for academic quality and success." Undergrads also appreciate the "great tutors" and "helpful writing center"; they complain, however, that "the school needs to do a better job helping students find jobs when they graduate;" the college has recently responded to these complaints with the creation of a Career Development Center. Those in the honors program tell us that "courses are compelling and challenging, fully preparing you to be at the top of your grad-school class."

Life

Brooklyn College "does not have too much of a social life outside of fraternities and sororities," in large part because there is no residential life here. The school's location in Midwood, a quiet, unhip neighborhood, also stifles extracurricular life. Students tell us that "there are basketball games, parties, and fashion shows, but relative to the number of students here, they are not that well attended." Perhaps the most popular extracurricular outlets on campus are the many interest- and background-related clubs and organizations, which "get together frequently and are very accepting no matter what your race, gender, or ethnicity." Students also like the student center, which "has fun games, sports, and other activities." Otherwise, undergrads visit campus to attend classes and study, then typically head home or off to another part of New York City for diversion. Manhattan and other areas are, fortunately, easy to reach by subway. Undergrads note that the BC campus is "quite beautiful" and that "library facilities are great." Sports facilities, on the other hand, "must improve," and improve they will when the college's West Quad Building opens its doors in 2007.

Student Body

The "busy, hurried" undergrads of Brooklyn College are "generally mature and look forward to earning their degrees." They are "very street-smart" and typically "in a rush to graduate, so they focus more on receiving their credentials than on participating in student life." Notes one student, "As a commuter college, BC is merely a brief stopping point for most of us." Students here "represent the plurality of ethnicities that make up Brooklyn," the most populous, and by some accounts, diverse of the Big Apple's five boroughs. As one student puts it, "There are so many different types of students in terms of race, ethnicity, and religion. In addition, the day students differ from the night students who all tend to be working full-time jobs." Undergrads here are impressed that "Brooklyn College graduates go on to do great things," like Eugene Shenderov, a 2005 Rhodes Scholar, who is the second BC student to win the prestigious award. "Perhaps it's that tough Brooklyn attitude they help us build."

CITY UNIVERSITY OF NEW YORK—BROOKLYN COLLEGE

FINANCIAL AID: 718-951-5051 • E-MAIL: ADMINQRY@BROOKLYN.CUNY.EDU • WEBSITE: WWW.BROOKLYN.CUNY.EDU

ADMISSIONS

Very important factors considered include: Secondary school record, standardized test scores. *Other factors considered include:* Recommendations. SAT Reasoning Test and ACT required. TOEFL required of all international applicants. High school diploma is required, and GED is accepted. *Academic units recommended:* 4 English, 3 math, 3 science, 3 foreign language, 4 social studies, 4 academic electives.

The Inside Word

Like other CUNY schools, Brooklyn College provides easy access to a college education for students who want one. Brooklyn raises the bar, however, with superior offerings in the arts and sciences. You don't have to have a spotless academic record to get into Brooklyn College, but once there you will receive a solid and respected education.

FINANCIAL AID

Students should submit: FAFSA, state aid form. The Princeton Review suggests that all financial aid forms be submitted as soon as possible after 1/1. *Need-based scholarships/grants offered:* Pell, SEOG, state scholarships/grants, private scholarships, the school's own gift aid. *Loan aid offered:* Direct Subsidized Stafford, Direct Unsubsidized Stafford, Direct PLUS, Federal Perkins. Applicants will be notified of awards on or about 5/1.

FROM THE ADMISSIONS OFFICE

"Brooklyn College, a premier public liberal arts college founded in 1930, ranked sixth this year in the Princeton Review's *America's Best Value Colleges.* In the 2003 edition of the Princeton Review's *The Best 351 Colleges* the college ranked first in the country for its "Beautiful Campus," and fifth for providing the "Best Academic Bang for Your Buck" and for its friendly diversity on the "Students from Different Backgrounds Interact" list. It again placed among the top five in the guide's 2004 edition.

"Brooklyn College's 15,000 undergraduate and graduate students represent the ethnic and cultural diversity of the borough. And the college's accessibility by subway or bus allows students to further enrich their educational experience through New York City's many cultural events and institutions.

"The college continues on an ambitious program of expansion and renewal. The dazzling new library is the most technologically advanced educational and research facility in the CUNY system. A state-of-the-art student services and physical education building, currently under construction, is scheduled to be completed in 2007.

"Respected nationally for its rigorous academic standards, the college takes pride in such innovative programs as its award-winning Freshman Year College; the Honors Academy, which houses nine programs for high achievers, and the core curriculum. Brooklyn College's strong academic reputation has attracted an outstanding faculty of nationally renowned teachers and scholars. Among the awards they have won are Pulitzers, Guggenheims, Fulbrights, and National Institutes of Health grants. Brooklyn College students also receive such prestigious honors as Fulbright Scholarships, the Beinecke Memorial Scholarship, and the Paul and Daisy Soros Fellowships for New Americans.

"As of this book's publication, Brooklyn College did not have information available about their policy regarding the new SAT."

SELECTIVITY

Admissions Rating	**82**
# of applicants	7,083
% of applicants accepted	33
% of acceptees attending	51

FRESHMAN PROFILE

Range SAT Verbal	450-570
Average SAT Verbal	515
Range SAT Math	490-600
Average SAT Math	544
**TPR Projected Range SAT Writing*	*520-610*
Minimum Paper TOEFL	500
Minimum Computer Based TOEFL	173
Average HS GPA	3.0
% graduated top 10% of class	14
% graduated top 25% of class	35
% graduated top 50% of class	77

DEADLINES

Regular notification	rolling
Nonfall registration?	yes

APPLICANTS ALSO LOOK AT

AND OFTEN PREFER

New York University

AND SOMETIMES PREFER

SUNY at Albany

SUNY at Stony Brook

AND RARELY PREFER

Long Island University—Brooklyn

Saint Francis College (NY)

FINANCIAL FACTS

Financial Aid Rating	**93**
Annual in-state tuition	$4,000
Annual out-of-state tuition	$8,640
Books and supplies	$800
Required fees	$353
% frosh rec. need-based scholarship or grant aid	75
% UG rec. need-based scholarship or grant aid	71
% frosh rec. need-based self-help aid	74
% UG rec. need-based self-help aid	70
% frosh rec. any financial aid	67
% UG rec. any financial aid	65
Avg. frosh grant	$4,000
Avg. frosh loan	$2,800
Independent 529 member?	No

City University of New York—Hunter College

695 Park Avenue, New York, NY 10021 • Admissions: 212-772-4490 • Fax: 212-650-3336

CAMPUS LIFE

Quality of Life Rating	**67**
Fire Safety Rating	**94**
Type of school	public
Environment	metropolis

STUDENTS

Total undergrad enrollment	14,109
% male/female	30/70
% from out of state	4
% from public high school	70
% live on campus	4
% in (# of) fraternities	1 (2)
% in (# of) sororities	1 (2)
% African American	16
% Asian	17
% Caucasian	39
% Hispanic	21
% international	7
# of countries represented	150

SURVEY SAYS

Diverse student types on campus
Students love New York, NY
Great off-campus food
Political activism is popular
(Almost) everyone smokes

ACADEMICS

Academic Rating	**66**
Calendar	semester
Student/faculty ratio	15:1
Professors interesting rating	74
Professors accessible rating	65
% professors teaching UG courses	100
% classes taught by TAs	0
Most common lab size	20-29 students
Most common regular class size	20-29 students

MOST POPULAR MAJORS

English language and literature
psychology
sociology

STUDENTS SPEAK OUT

Academics

Students describe Hunter College, a branch of the City University of New York located on Manhattan's Upper East Side, as "overcrowded [and having] too much paperwork, [but] the professors are top of the line, which is unexpected because of the low tuition." Don't expect much hand-holding or one-on-one instruction. City bureaucracy and the school being "terribly underfunded translate to poor services for students and huge class sizes." That's not to say that affordability is Hunter's only asset. On the contrary, the school has many tremendous assets, including its New York City location. Hunter provides fantastic learning opportunities ("One of my evolution labs is held at the American Museum of Natural History, which is neat," reports one undergraduate) and a stellar faculty. Many students commend the selective Honors College, and believe that "it gives you a ton back in return for your sacrifice of a 'normal' college experience, as well as saving you huge amounts of money." It can still be difficult to navigate through a school where administrative bureaucrats "always tell you that, whatever your problem, it's up to someone else to fix it, but recent changes in administration are working on new initiatives to counter this." One nontraditional undergraduate observes, "Hunter is a good environment for mature or older students who have a sense of their future goals, both career and otherwise. However, this is not the place for someone who needs a large network of support from career counselors or other students in order to make major decisions about their college track or career."

Life

Hunter is a commuter school. Even the relatively few students who live in dorms essentially live "off-campus," since the dormitories are located on Hunter's downtown campus, where the Health Professions school is located. Accordingly, "many people go straight home after classes," which stymies campus life. The physical facilities also present an obstacle because of the layout, which "offers nothing to do during three-hour breaks between classes except study." Although there are setbacks, one student says, "Many people are involved in on-campus activities apart from classes, including the large amounts of clubs we have, the student-faculty senate, student government, and just hanging out in the hallways waiting for class." Of course, New York City offers myriad things to do and draws away students who might otherwise remain on campus. Explains one undergraduate, "Living in New York City is incomparable. The city is alive with culture. There is so much to do and see that it can be overwhelming. There are shows, concerts, comedy clubs, various universities, and many other activities to keep the students busy." The school itself is "located in a decent neighborhood near many world-renowned cultural institutions: Carnegie Hall, the Metropolitan [Museum of Art], Central Park, Sotheby's. If you have time to kill, there are also lots of boutiques and little restaurants to eat in. And, in the warm months, you can go to Central Park between classes." The city also offers job seekers "endless networking opportunities, which are extremely helpful."

Student Body

It's not a surprise that Hunter is filled with a wide assortment of people; among the part-timers, full-timers, traditional students, nontraditional students (students who return to school after decades), there are individuals from every possible race and ethnicity, faith, and sexual orientation. "This school is extremely ethnically diverse," students tell us, noting that "all cultures are respectful of one another, and this is very interesting in the classroom." Many students "are first-generation college students, first-generation Americans, or both. Many of them go to outstanding lengths to achieve excellence in academics while supporting families and working part- or full-time jobs." The school is also home to "openly gay and lesbian groups," and according to one student, "they are not treated any differently. That's mostly because we are located in NYC, so most of the students grew up accepting difference." Conservatives warn that "Hunter can be a very hostile place to those on the political right."

FINANCIAL AID: 212-772-4820 • E-MAIL: ADMISSIONS@HUNTER.CUNY.EDU • WEBSITE: WWW.HUNTER.CUNY.EDU

ADMISSIONS

Very important factors considered include: Secondary school record, standardized test scores. SAT Reasoning or ACT required. TOEFL required of all international applicants. High school diploma is required, and GED is accepted. *Academic units required:* 2 English, 2 math, 1 science (1 science lab). *Academic units recommended:* 4 English, 3 math, 2 science (2 science lab), 2 foreign language, 4 social studies, 1 visual and performing arts.

The Inside Word

Like other City University of New York (CUNY) schools, Hunter College provides easy access to a college education for students who want one. Hunter raises the bar, however, with its superior offerings in the arts and sciences. You don't have to have a spotless academic record to get into Hunter College; but once you are there, you will receive a solid and respected education.

FINANCIAL AID

Students should submit: FAFSA, state aid form, institutional direct loan request form from direct loan applicants. The Princeton Review suggests that all financial aid forms be submitted as soon as possible after 1/1. *Need-based scholarships/grants offered:* Pell, SEOG, state scholarships/grants, private scholarships, the school's own gift aid. *Loan aid offered:* Direct Subsidized Stafford, Direct Unsubsidized Stafford, Direct PLUS, Federal Perkins, alternative loans. Applicants will be notified of awards on a rolling basis beginning on or about 5/15. Federal Work-study Program available. Institutional employment available. Off-campus job opportunities are good.

FROM THE ADMISSIONS OFFICE

"Located in the heart of Manhattan, Hunter offers students the stimulating learning environment and career-building opportunities you might expect from a college that's been a part of the world's most exciting city since 1870. The largest college in the City University of New York, Hunter pulses with energy. Hunter's vitality stems from a large, highly diverse faculty and student body. Its schools—Arts and Sciences, Education, the Health Professions, and Social Work—provide an affordable first-rate education. Undergraduates have extraordinary opportunities to conduct high-level research under renowned faculty, and many opt for credit-bearing internships in such exciting fields as media, the arts, and government. The College's high standards and special programs ensure a challenging education. The Block Program for first-year students keeps classmates together as they pursue courses in the liberal arts, pre–health science, pre-nursing, pre-med, or honors. A range of honors programs is available for students with strong academic records, including the highly competitive tuition-free Hunter CUNY Honors College for entering freshmen and the Thomas Hunter Honors Program, which emphasizes small classes with personalized mentoring by the most outstanding faculty. Qualified students also benefit from Hunter's participation in minority science research and training programs, the prestigious Andrew W. Mellon Minority Undergraduate Program, and many other passports to professional success.

"Applicants for the fall 2006 entering class are required to take either the SAT or the ACT. We will accept scores from the new SAT and scores from the old (prior to March 2005) version of the SAT. We will use the student's best scores from any of these tests."

SELECTIVITY

Admissions Rating	**86**
# of applicants	12,776
% of applicants accepted	30
% of acceptees attending	49

FRESHMAN PROFILE

Range SAT Verbal	470-570
Average SAT Verbal	520
Range SAT Math	500-590
Average SAT Math	545
**TPR Projected Range SAT Writing*	*530-610*
Minimum Paper TOEFL	500
Minimum Computer Based TOEFL	173
Average HS GPA	2.9
% graduated top 10% of class	21
% graduated top 25% of class	48
% graduated top 50% of class	78

DEADLINES

Regular application deadline	3/15
Regular notification	rolling
Nonfall registration?	yes

APPLICANTS ALSO LOOK AT AND OFTEN PREFER

New York University

AND SOMETIMES PREFER

Fordham University
SUNY at Binghamton
SUNY at Stony Brook

FINANCIAL FACTS

Financial Aid Rating	**92**
Annual in-state tuition	$4,000
Room & Board	$2,600
Books and supplies	$798
Required fees	$329
% frosh rec. need-based scholarship or grant aid	58
% UG rec. need-based scholarship or grant aid	50
% frosh rec. need-based self-help aid	10
% UG rec. need-based self-help aid	19
% frosh rec. any financial aid	78
% UG rec. any financial aid	52
Avg. frosh grant	$6,158
Avg. frosh loan	$2,309
Independent 529 member?	No

City University of New York—Queens College

65-30 Kissena Boulevard, Flushing, NY 11367 • Admissions: 718-997-5000 • Fax: 718-997-5617

CAMPUS LIFE

Quality of Life Rating	**67**
Fire Safety Rating	**60**
Type of school	public
Environment	metropolis

STUDENTS

Total undergrad enrollment	11,859
% male/female	38/62
% from out of state	1
% from public high school	67
% in (# of) fraternities	1 (3)
% in (# of) sororities	1 (2)
% African American	10
% Asian	19
% Caucasian	48
% Hispanic	17
% international	6
# of countries represented	140

SURVEY SAYS

Small classes
Great library
Diverse student types on campus
Very little beer drinking
Very little hard liquor
Very little drug use

ACADEMICS

Academic Rating	**71**
Calendar	semester
Student/faculty ratio	17:1
Professors interesting rating	67
Professors accessible rating	63
% professors teaching UG courses	90
% classes taught by TAs	3
Most common regular class size	20-29 students

MOST POPULAR MAJORS

Accounting
psychology
sociology

STUDENTS SPEAK OUT

Academics

The appeal of Queens College can be summed up in four words: "Great education, cheap price." Students say their college has "the best academic reputation of all the CUNY schools." Academic requirements place "a strong emphasis on the liberal arts, intended to create a well-rounded student." The faculty "encourages students to excel and seek their help." An evenhanded senior writes, "Although professors don't spoon-feed you, they really care about you as an individual and make you feel like you matter." Instructors set a rigorous academic standard and "sometimes expect too much from you, which can be stressful." Undergraduates typically encounter "a mix of great teachers and awful ones;" to sort it out, "you just need to ask around." Tight city and state budgets mean lab equipment better suited as museum pieces and "a few academic departments where it is virtually impossible for students to register for classes." An upperclassman writes, "Many students have to delay graduation because they cannot get in to the classes they need on time." Despite these snags, students believe that "you can get an amazing education if you try." The abundant resources of New York City are "used to enrich classes" and to compensate for any outdated or limited campus resources. Although students say "the administration is kind and cooperative," several people agree that Queens is "not a student-friendly school, although [they] see signs that it is slowly changing."

Life

Because a large percentage of Queens College students commute, people may expect a dismal campus social scene. It's true that "once classes are over, most students don't spend a lot of time on campus." However, as part of the "growing student life," midday "free hour" events bring everyone together for parties, speakers, discussion groups, or food before they head for home. One student says, "Free hour is the best thing that happened to collegiate education because it forces you to slow down and appreciate life." Students also commonly congregate in the cafeteria or student union. Another student explains that "clubs provide a viable substitute for residential life at Queens." People get "very active in clubs and after-school activities" to forge a sense of social connection. Many extracurricular activities reflect the international flavor of the campus, such as the popular dance performances put on by the Hindi Student Council. Some organizations "exist only in theory" and need to be revived by some fresh blood. A casual crew of Frisbee enthusiasts can typically be found on the lawn against the backdrop "of the spectacular midtown Manhattan skyline."

Student Body

In today's higher education landscape, Queens College stands out as a paragon of diversity. In fact, "it's one of the most diverse student populations of all campuses nationwide." Pick an ethnicity, culture, nation of origin, or religion, and you will most likely find it at the school. The student body "reflects the global population and the population of the great city [that] it is located in." Most students appreciate the resulting atmosphere. One student agrees, "The diversity is a great benefit to anyone who comes here. It opens up your eyes and mind to new cultures and customs." This "eclectic group" shows more signs of internal intermingling than other campuses that claim to have similar student body demographic numbers. "For the most part, different groups mix both in class and out of it." Intercultural exchange happens naturally: "All the students are glad to share with you something about their culture." With such a degree of heterogeneity, it's hardly surprising that "very few people feel left out." Students "on both extremes, from overachievers to slackers," come together in this "friendly and cheerful environment."

Financial Aid: 718-997-5101 • E-mail: admissions@qc.edu • Website: www.qc.edu

ADMISSIONS

Very important factors considered include: Secondary school record, standardized test scores. SAT Reasoning or ACT required. TOEFL required of all international applicants. High school diploma is required, and GED is accepted. *Academic units required:* 4 English, 3 math, 2 science (2 science lab), 3 foreign language, 4 social studies. *Academic units recommended:* 4 English, 3 math, 3 science (3 science lab), 3 foreign language, 4 social studies.

The Inside Word

Applicants to Queens follow the usual CUNY application procedures, which have gotten tougher with the implementation of updated high school curriculum requirements. Candidates for the Aaron Copeland School of Music must also successfully pass through a rigorous audition process. CUNY admissions requirements are currently undergoing close scrutiny; beware of the possibility of further changes.

FINANCIAL AID

Students should submit: FAFSA, state aid form. The Princeton Review suggests that all financial aid forms be submitted as soon as possible after 1/1. *Need-based scholarships/grants offered:* Pell, SEOG, state scholarships/grants, private scholarships, the school's own gift aid. *Loan aid offered:* Direct Subsidized Stafford, Direct Unsubsidized Stafford, Direct PLUS, Federal Perkins. Applicants will be notified of awards on a rolling basis beginning on or about 5/1. Federal Work-study Program available. Off-campus job opportunities are excellent.

FROM THE ADMISSIONS OFFICE

"New York State Governor George Pataki calls Queens College "the jewel of the City University of New York system" for two good reasons: its faculty and its students. Faculty members, who have received prestigious awards such as the Emmy, Guggenheim, and Fulbright, are renowned for their commitment to scholarship and teaching. Interaction among students, who come from 140 nations, and a fast-growing student life program also create a dynamic learning environment.

"Queens College, ranked as the 6th "Best Bargain Public College" by The Princeton Review in 2005, offers nationally recognized programs in many fields, including the Aaron Copland School of Music. In fall 2003, a Bachelor of Business Administration degree was introduced, providing business career preparation grounded in the liberal arts and sciences. A Bachelor of Science degree in graphic design was added in fall 2004. Aspiring teachers benefit from the Education Division's innovative programs (Queens College educates more teachers than any college in the tri-state area). Queens College also participates in the CUNY Honors College and offers its own Honors programs in the arts and humanities, sciences, and social sciences to qualified students. It is also the only CUNY college that participates in Division II sports.

"A commuter college with a residential feel, Queens boasts a beautiful, 77-acre campus lined with trees surrounding grassy open spaces and a traditional quad. In 2003, the completely renovated Powdermaker Hall, the major classroom building, reopened with state-of-the-art technology throughout. In fact, in an Intel survey that ranks the top 100 schools for wireless computing access, Queens College places #13 in the nation

"Applicants for fall 2006 can submit either the new SAT comprising the Critical Reading, Writing, and Math, or the old SAT. Pending further research on the merits of the Writing section, students will continue to be assessed based on their highest Math and Critical Reading scores."

SELECTIVITY	
Admissions Rating	**80**
# of applicants	6,518
% of applicants accepted	42
% of acceptees attending	51
FRESHMAN PROFILE	
Range SAT Verbal	440-550
Average SAT Verbal	500
Range SAT Math	490-580
Average SAT Math	535
**TPR Projected Range SAT Writing*	*510-600*
Minimum Paper TOEFL	500
Minimum Computer Based TOEFL	200
Average HS GPA	3.2
% graduated top 10% of class	15
% graduated top 25% of class	30
% graduated top 50% of class	82
DEADLINES	
Regular notification	rolling
Nonfall registration?	yes
FINANCIAL FACTS	
Financial Aid Rating	**88**
Annual in-state tuition	$4,000
Annual out-of-state tuition	$10,800
Required fees	$356
% frosh rec. need-based scholarship or grant aid	69
% UG rec. need-based scholarship or grant aid	47
% frosh rec. need-based self-help aid	56
% UG rec. need-based self-help aid	35
% frosh rec. any financial aid	95
% UG rec. any financial aid	95
Avg. frosh grant	$5,000
Avg. frosh loan	$2,500
Independent 529 member?	No

CLAREMONT MCKENNA COLLEGE

890 COLUMBIA AVENUE, CLAREMONT, CA 91711 • ADMISSIONS: 909-621-8088 • FAX: 909-621-8516

CAMPUS LIFE

Quality of Life Rating	**98**
Fire Safety Rating	**60**
Type of school	private
Environment	village

STUDENTS

Total undergrad enrollment	1,050
% male/female	55/45
% from out of state	51
% from public high school	73
% live on campus	96
% African American	4
% Asian	16
% Caucasian	67
% Hispanic	10
% Native American	1
% international	3

SURVEY SAYS

Small classes
Dorms are like palaces
Frats and sororities are unpopular or nonexistent
Lots of beer drinking

ACADEMICS

Academic Rating	**86**
Calendar	semester
Student/faculty ratio	8:1
Professors interesting rating	95
Professors accessible rating	97
% professors teaching UG courses	100
% classes taught by TAs	0

MOST POPULAR MAJORS

Economics
international relations and affairs
political science and government

STUDENTS SPEAK OUT

Academics

"Determined, intellectual pre-professionals in government, business, law, and medicine" fill the classrooms of Claremont McKenna College, where students who pursue less pragmatic disciplines (e.g., philosophy, religious studies) should "be prepared for a lot of 'What are you going to do with that?' from fellow students." The "amazing economics and government programs" are top draws thanks to high-profile professors and an excellent DC internship program. All programs benefit from CMC's strong ties to the community; explains one student, "There are many CMC companies in downtown LA that start with one alumnus and slowly absorb more CMCers. Since all the Claremont Colleges intermingle, alumni from the other colleges are often as nice as CMC alumni. There are many five-college alumni groups that foster 5-C interaction after college." CMC's proximity to LA also helps feed the Athenaeum, "a Monday through Thursday speaker series that is amazing, attracting many well-known academics and celebrities, authors, musicians, and comedians!" No kidding; Fall 2004 Athenaeum speakers included former senator Phil Gramm, academic and author Cornel West, and journalist Seymour Hersh. Further enhancing the experience here are "13 research institutes that give undergraduates the ability to do graduate-level research." The only drawback is that "CMC is small, so some of the less popular majors are really small," but even that isn't too big a deal, since the Claremont Colleges Consortium allows CMC students to supplement their curricula with classes at the other four consortium schools.

Life

"Some say CMC should stand for Club Med College, because it's fun in the sun and a great place to learn," but the nickname probably puts too much emphasis on "Club Med" and too little on "College." Students here work hard; they "focus intently on school work Monday through Thursday, plus they usually have jobs on-campus doing anything from research to tutoring to technology assistance. People also work diligently to find great internships and jobs during the summers." They also know how to kick back and relax, though, often with the help of the administration, which "is very lenient in its alcohol policy, as long as we're all responsible with what we do." The laid-back party atmosphere helps create a strong sense of campus community, as does the fact that "almost everyone at Claremont lives on campus. It's a very healthy scene, people carve out their niches for all four years on campus, and there's a stronger sense of tradition when different class years are always rubbing shoulders." Campus life also "provides awesome concerts two or three times a year" and "a bunch of different clubs on campus to get involved with." Still, "If there isn't anything going on at Claremont McKenna, chances are there is something going on at one of the other colleges, to which we have access," writes one student.

Student Body

Undergraduates are "very driven to succeed. We genuinely work hard and have large goals that we wish to achieve." The result is a friendly but competitive atmosphere "in which most people seem to thrive." Most here "are from middle- to upper-class families, which cause many to come to school with a sheltered perspective on the world, but through the Athenaeum and study abroad, undergrads develop informed views and diverse thoughts." The school's popular programs in political science, government, international relations, and economics mean that most undergrads are "very politically astute" and "willing to debate political issues frequently, but never to the point of anger. It is hardly a rarity to see a liberal and conservative sharing some beers over discussion, and it's a beautiful thing." Nearly everyone fits the CMC mold "because the admissions office does a good job of making sure that students are a good match for the college" and because the school is so small.

Claremont McKenna College

Financial Aid: 909-621-8356 • E-mail: admission@claremontmckenna.edu • Website: www.claremontmckenna.edu

ADMISSIONS

Very important factors considered include: Character/personal qualities, essays, extracurricular activities, secondary school record, standardized test scores. *Important factors considered include:* Recommendations, talent/ability. *Other factors considered include:* Alumni/ae relation, class rank, geographical residence, interview, minority status, state residency, volunteer work, work experience. SAT Reasoning or ACT required. TOEFL required of all international applicants. High school diploma is required, and GED is accepted. *Academic units required:* 4 English, 3 math, 2 science, 3 foreign language, 2 social studies, 1 history. *Academic units recommended:* 4 English, 4 math, 3 science, 3 foreign language, 2 social studies, 2 history.

The Inside Word

Although applicants have to possess solid academic qualifications to gain admission to Claremont McKenna, the importance of making a good match should not be underestimated. Colleges of such small size and selectivity devote much more energy to determining whether the candidate as an individual fits than they do to whether a candidate has the appropriate test scores.

FINANCIAL AID

Students should submit: FAFSA, CSS/Financial Aid PROFILE. Regular filing deadline is 2/1. The Princeton Review suggests that all financial aid forms be submitted as soon as possible after 1/1. *Need-based scholarships/grants offered:* Pell, SEOG, state scholarships/grants, private scholarships, the school's own gift aid. *Loan aid offered:* Direct Subsidized Stafford, Direct Unsubsidized Stafford, Direct PLUS, Federal Perkins, college/university loans from institutional funds. Applicants will be notified of awards on or about 4/1. Federal Work-study Program available. Institutional employment available. Off-campus job opportunities are excellent.

FROM THE ADMISSIONS OFFICE

"CMC's mission is clear: to educate students for meaningful lives and responsible leadership in business, government, and the professions. While many other colleges champion either a traditional liberal arts education with emphasis on intellectual breadth or training that stresses acquisition of technical skills, CMC offers a clear alternative. Instead of dividing the liberal arts and working world into separate realms, education at CMC is rooted in the interplay between the world of ideas and the world of events. By combining the intellectual breadth of liberal arts with the more pragmatic concerns of public affairs, CMC students gain the vision, skills, and values necessary for leadership in all sectors of society.

"Applicants for fall 2006 must take the new SAT (or ACT with Writing). Scores from the old (before March 2005) SAT (or ACT) will not be accepted for admission application purposes. We will use the highest scores from the SAT (or ACT). SAT Subject Tests are recommended."

SELECTIVITY

Admissions Rating	**97**
# of applicants	2,892
% of applicants accepted	29
% of acceptees attending	34
# accepting a place on wait list	317
# of early decision applicants	55
% accepted early decision	30

FRESHMAN PROFILE

Range SAT Verbal	650-730
Average SAT Verbal	690
Range SAT Math	660-730
Average SAT Math	700
**TPR Projected Range SAT Writing*	*670-720*
Range ACT Composite	28-33
Average ACT Composite	30
Minimum Paper TOEFL	600
Minimum Computer Based TOEFL	250
% graduated top 10% of class	83
% graduated top 25% of class	95
% graduated top 50% of class	100

DEADLINES

Early decision application deadline	11/15
Early decision notification	12/15
Regular application deadline	1/2
Regular notification	4/1
Nonfall registration?	yes

APPLICANTS ALSO LOOK AT

AND OFTEN PREFER
Harvard College
Stanford University

AND SOMETIMES PREFER
Georgetown University
Pomona College
Princeton University

AND RARELY PREFER
Berkeley College
Occidental College
University of Chicago

FINANCIAL FACTS

Financial Aid Rating	**99**
Annual tuition	$29,010
Room & Board	$9,780
Books and supplies	$1,850
Required fees	$200
% frosh rec. need-based scholarship or grant aid	50
% UG rec. need-based scholarship or grant aid	55
% frosh rec. need-based self-help aid	46
% UG rec. need-based self-help aid	51
% frosh rec. any financial aid	65
% UG rec. any financial aid	72
Avg. frosh grant	$24,000
Avg. frosh loan	$3,500
Independent 529 member?	Yes

Clark University

950 Main Street, Worcester, MA 01610-1477 • Admissions: 508-793-7431 • Fax: 508-793-8821

CAMPUS LIFE

Quality of Life Rating	**71**
Fire Safety Rating	**96**
Type of school	private
Environment	city

STUDENTS

Total undergrad enrollment	2,082
% male/female	39/61
% from out of state	60
% from public high school	70
% live on campus	77
% African American	3
% Asian	4
% Caucasian	64
% Hispanic	3
% international	7
# of countries represented	56

SURVEY SAYS

Small classes
Frats and sororities are unpopular or nonexistent
Lots of beer drinking
Hard liquor is popular

ACADEMICS

Academic Rating	**82**
Calendar	semester
Student/faculty ratio	10:1
Professors interesting rating	76
Professors accessible rating	80
% professors teaching UG courses	100
% classes taught by TAs	0
Most common lab size	10-19 students
Most common regular class size	10-19 students

MOST POPULAR MAJORS

English language and literature
political science and government
psychology

STUDENTS SPEAK OUT

Academics

"Clark is geared toward providing every student with the opportunity for personal growth," students at this prestigious liberal arts school report. The school achieves this goal "by offering a wide and fascinating variety of courses, programs, travel opportunities, and events that inform and intrigue." The solid academic community on campus is key to the Clark experience; a "group of mentors (your professors, the administration, and your peers)" is "always willing to help" students deal with the "extremely challenging classes" that make up the Clark curriculum. Writes a typical undergrad, "I know all my professors and all my professors know me (even in my larger classes)." Classes that are "usually small in size" are "intimate enough to give you a chance to connect with professors" who "really do want their students to actually understand the material, not just know it to succeed on tests. They also take a personal interest in the students; several friends have gone to their professors' houses for dinner (as first-year students)." This closeness between professors and students encourages "opportunities to get involved with research," a real boon to students' curriculum vitaes. Research is further promoted by Clark's constant efforts at self-improvement; students tell us that the school "keeps adding new facilities that are up-to-date so that learning can be more hands-on." Psychology and the hard sciences are standout offerings here; political science, government, and history are all also reportedly strong.

Life

"Clark is a small school with a very strong sense of community" where "you can sit down at a random table in the cafeteria and the odds are that you'll know at least one other person at the table." Writes one undergrad, "I can count on one hand the number of meals I've eaten alone this semester." Students love how Clark "retains its community feel without feeling cramped. The opportunities for community service, studying abroad, and internships provide plenty of opportunities to broaden oneself socially, and there are other ways to get away from people if one wants to be alone or lose oneself." Otherwise, "If you leave your room at all, ever, you will have a social life here, and that doesn't have to mean drinking or drugs, since there's a lot more to life here. There's also very little pressure to drink if you don't." If you do drink, you'll find plenty of company, as "people party a good amount. Going to local bars after parties is very popular. Hard liquor and beer is always around and never cheap beer or hard liquor, always good stuff." Other diversions include "sports, movies, theatre performances, comedy sketches, and lectures. Mostly indoor stuff, because Worcester gets really cold in the winter." Hometown Worcester has other problems; it "isn't the best city to go to school in, despite having eight colleges here. There's very little to do off campus on weekends unless you go to Boston."

Student Body

"We have a really unique combination of preppy, hippie, artsy, jock and everything in between" at Clark, students tell us, "most people fit into more than one category." Asked which category is represented with the greatest frequency, most here will tell you that "it's the student who looks like he's just returning from Woodstock: Birkenstocks, bandanas, grubby-looking, loose clothing, reeking of weed." Everyone is welcome, we're told; writes one outlier, "I myself am a practicing Republican ROTC cadet who abstains from nearly every vice, and I have no trouble fitting in." Clark undergrads appreciate that "students are focused more on learning than on competition with one another, so there are very few cutthroats about grades." Students tend to be bright and curious, so "it's easy to get involved in a very long conversation about some class topic, which is how a recent study session was extended from three to seven hours."

FINANCIAL AID: 508-793-7478 • E-MAIL: ADMISSIONS@CLARKU.EDU • WEBSITE: WWW.CLARKU.EDU

ADMISSIONS

Very important factors considered include: Character/personal qualities, recommendations, secondary school record, standardized test scores. *Important factors considered include:* Essays, extracurricular activities, talent/ability, volunteer work. *Other factors considered include:* Alumni/ae relation, class rank, geographical residence, interview, minority status, work experience. SAT Reasoning and SAT Subject Tests or ACT required. TOEFL required of all international applicants. High school diploma is required, and GED is accepted. *Academic units recommended:* 4 English, 3 math, 3 science (2 science lab), 2 foreign language, 2 social studies, 2 history.

The Inside Word

Clark is surrounded by formidable competitors, and its selectivity suffers because of it. Most B students will encounter little difficulty gaining admission. Given the university's solid academic environment and access to other member colleges in the Worcester Consortium, it can be a terrific choice for students who are not up to the ultra-competitive admission expectations of "top-tier" universities.

FINANCIAL AID

Students should submit: FAFSA, CSS/Financial Aid PROFILE. The Princeton Review suggests that all financial aid forms be submitted as soon as possible after 1/1. *Need-based scholarships/grants offered:* Pell, SEOG, state scholarships/grants, the school's own gift aid. *Loan aid offered:* FFEL Subsidized Stafford, FFEL Unsubsidized Stafford, FFEL PLUS, Federal Perkins, state loans, college/university loans from institutional funds. Applicants will be notified of awards on or about 3/31. Federal Work-study Program available. Institutional employment available. Off-campus job opportunities are good.

FROM THE ADMISSIONS OFFICE

"At Clark University, you are respected for challenging convention, for trying out new ideas and skills, and for inspiring new ways of thinking. You learn how social change is made, and you get to be a part of it. Individual development is nurtured by a dedicated faculty who encourages hands-on learning. Founded in 1887, Clark is home to students from more than 57 countries and 44 states.

"Clark requires that students submit scores from the SAT. Pending further examination of the virtues of the new Writing section, students will be judged by their performance in Critical Reading and Math. Clark does ask for writing samples as part of the application process."

SELECTIVITY

Admissions Rating	**89**
# of applicants	4,239
% of applicants accepted	62
% of acceptees attending	20
# accepting a place on wait list	91
% admitted from wait list	12
# of early decision applicants	75
% accepted early decision	83

FRESHMAN PROFILE

Range SAT Verbal	540-660
Average SAT Verbal	593
Range SAT Math	540-645
Average SAT Math	588
**TPR Projected Range SAT Writing*	*590-670*
Range ACT Composite	22-28
Average ACT Composite	25
Minimum Paper TOEFL	550
Minimum Computer Based TOEFL	213
Average HS GPA	3.4
% graduated top 10% of class	31
% graduated top 25% of class	72
% graduated top 50% of class	99

DEADLINES

Early decision application deadline	11/15
Early decision notification	12/15
Regular application deadline	2/1
Regular notification	4/1

APPLICANTS ALSO LOOK AT AND OFTEN PREFER

Boston College, Boston U., Brandeis U., Tufts U., Vassar College

AND SOMETIMES PREFER

Connecticut College, Ithaca College, Northeastern U., Skidmore College, Syracuse U., U. of New Hampshire

AND RARELY PREFER

Goucher College, U. of Connecticut, U. of Massachusetts—Amherst, U. of Vermont, Wheaton College (MA)

FINANCIAL FACTS

Financial Aid Rating	**89**
Annual tuition	$29,300
Room & Board	$5,400
Books and supplies	$800
Required fees	$265
% frosh rec. need-based scholarship or grant aid	58
% UG rec. need-based scholarship or grant aid	58
% frosh rec. need-based self-help aid	54
% UG rec. need-based self-help aid	54
% frosh rec. any financial aid	78
% UG rec. any financial aid	77
Avg. frosh grant	$17,630
Avg. frosh loan	$3,633
Independent 529 member?	Yes

Clarkson University

Box 5605, Potsdam, NY 13699 • Admissions: 315-268-6479 • Fax: 315-268-7647

CAMPUS LIFE

Quality of Life Rating	**62**
Fire Safety Rating	**78**
Type of school	private
Environment	village

STUDENTS

Total undergrad enrollment	2,717
% male/female	77/23
% from out of state	25
% from public high school	86
% live on campus	77
% in (# of) fraternities	15 (11)
% in (# of) sororities	12 (2)
% African American	2
% Asian	2
% Caucasian	92
% Hispanic	2
% international	2
# of countries represented	41

SURVEY SAYS

Class discussions are rare
Students are friendly
Low cost of living
Lots of beer drinking
Hard liquor is popular

ACADEMICS

Academic Rating	**70**
Calendar	semester
Student/faculty ratio	16:1
Professors interesting rating	64
Professors accessible rating	74
% professors teaching UG courses	85
% classes taught by TAs	1
Most common lab size	10-19 students
Most common regular class size	20-29 students

MOST POPULAR MAJORS

Civil engineering
mechanical engineering
multi/interdisciplinary studies

STUDENTS SPEAK OUT

Academics

"Academics and hockey are the greatest strengths at Clarkson University," a tech-heavy school in upstate New York where it sometimes seems that "99 percent of us are here for business, engineering, or science." For many here, Clarkson's chief appeal is the way it opens doors for graduates; explains one student, "Clarkson has a very good name… alumni have gone on to become CEOs or own their own company. Employers come here to recruit because they know the Clarkson student is likely to be successful." This is because Clarkson grads have conquered a curriculum that "is challenging even for people who are skilled in math, science, and engineering." It's so challenging, in fact, that "teamwork is essential here. It is the only way we can successfully learn all the material." Undergrads appreciate Clarkson's "interdisciplinary approach to all learning, as well as the emphasis on leadership" in the curriculum. They're less enamored of the liberal arts offerings, noting that the departments are small and classes are few. Professors get wildly mixed reviews, which actually puts them in the upper stratum of tech instructors, whose marks are usually quite low. Students warn that "the school often has new professors teaching classes in which they are unprepared to teach. Most of the time they are very well-qualified individuals but do not yet have the ability to properly teach a classroom full of students." Better teachers here "have a genuine interest in their students' succeeding, and enjoy their jobs."

Life

Located in Potsdam, NY, Clarkson "is in the middle of nowhere." Some see that as an asset; one such student explains, "It forces you to meet people and make friends to have fun. And since it is in the middle of nowhere, it is easier to get work done...there are fewer things to distract you from doing your work." Others see a downside; "Unless you are an avid hunter/fisherman, your options for not getting bored doing the same exact thing week after week are very poor. Remember the movie Groundhog Day? Life here is comparable." Compounding the challenges of extracurricular life here are the heavy workload and the fact that "it's freezing up there for about half of the school year," which drives many students "to bars, Canada, dinner, or hockey games. Or we stay in, playing video games or hanging out with friends." Some feel the school could do more to improve things; one undergrad observes, "There isn't enough money spent on bringing events to campus. Every year they bring the same comedians, the same small bands. The only event that seems to be any good is the spring concert, but that's about it." As a result, "Most of the students spend their free time hanging with friends and drinking." Sums up one student, "When I'm not working…I drink. We are a technical school that certainly knows how to party. There isn't much else to do up here."

Student Body

"There are typically two groups at Clarkson," students tell us. There are "those focused on learning and interested in having a good time; and, there are those solely focused on learning." Most Clarkson students share "a drive to succeed, an ability to learn in multi-disciplinary environments, and a strong career/graduate study focus." This focus can be overwhelming at times; "Even in party atmospheres you will find numerous conversations regarding nothing but academic-related topics. Not enough separation between 'business and pleasure,' so to speak." Like many tech-oriented schools, "Clarkson needs more women. The ratio is so completely horrible that it is probably the top of every male student's list of what needs improving here." Scattered among the student population are "a number of athletes and quite a few outdoorsy people."

FINANCIAL AID: 315-268-7699 • E-MAIL: ADMISSION@CLARKSON.EDU • WEBSITE: WWW.CLARKSON.EDU

ADMISSIONS

Very important factors considered include: Interview, secondary school record. *Important factors considered include:* Class rank, extracurricular activities, recommendations, standardized test scores, volunteer work. *Other factors considered include:* Alumni/ae relation, character/personal qualities, essays, talent/ability, work experience. TOEFL required of all international applicants. High school diploma is required, and GED is accepted. *Academic units required:* 4 English, 3 math, 2 science. *Academic units recommended:* 4 math, 3 science.

The Inside Word

Clarkson's acceptance rate is too high for solid applicants to lose much sleep about gaining admission. Serious candidates should interview anyway. If you are particularly solid and really want to come here, it could help you get some scholarship money. Women and minorities will encounter an especially friendly admissions committee.

FINANCIAL AID

Students should submit: FAFSA, institution's own financial aid form, state aid form. The Princeton Review suggests that all financial aid forms be submitted as soon as possible after 1/1. *Need-based scholarships/grants offered:* Pell, SEOG, state scholarships/grants, private scholarships, the school's own gift aid, HEOP. *Loan aid offered:* Direct Subsidized Stafford, Direct Unsubsidized Stafford, Direct PLUS, Federal Perkins, college/university loans from institutional funds, Gate. Applicants will be notified of awards on or about 3/23.

FROM THE ADMISSIONS OFFICE

"Clarkson is an independent, coeducational university with a strong focus on technology-based fields. It offers innovative programs in business, engineering, science, liberal arts, and health sciences. Clarkson is known for having a friendly, personal campus where professors are accessible. The academic environment is highly collaborative and interdisciplinary. A rigorous curriculum emphasizes team project-based learning and creative problem solving. Students develop collaboration, communication, and leadership skills along with versatility and hands-on management experience. They also enjoy opportunities for faculty-mentored research experience. Health sciences (including physical therapy) and health-oriented engineering are increasing in emphasis at Clarkson. With input from leading corporations, the business curriculum has been recently redesigned to develop skills needed in today's changing, global marketplace.

"Clarkson is nationally recognized for the effectiveness of its team, project-based learning programs. The university has won the Boeing Outstanding Educator Award and the Corporate and Foundation Alliance Award for team project-based learning and the IBM Linux Scholar Challenge (an international, open-source, computer programming competition). In business, Clarkson was a finalist for the National Undergraduate Entrepreneurship Education Award, and the program in Supply Chain Management is ranked in the nation's top 20 by *U.S. News and World Report*.

"Applicants for fall 2006 are required to take the ACT with Writing section optional, or the new version of the SAT. We will allow students to submit scores from the old (prior to March 2005) version of the SAT (or ACT) as well, and will use the student's best scores from either test. SAT Subject Tests are recommended but not required."

SELECTIVITY

Admissions Rating	**86**
# of applicants	2,473
% of applicants accepted	86
% of acceptees attending	31
# of early decision applicants	153
% accepted early decision	89

FRESHMAN PROFILE

Range SAT Verbal	520-630
Average SAT Verbal	574
Range SAT Math	570-660
Average SAT Math	619
**TPR Projected Range SAT Writing*	*570-650*
Range ACT Composite	23-28
Average ACT Composite	25
Minimum Paper TOEFL	500
Minimum Computer Based TOEFL	213
Average HS GPA	3.51
% graduated top 10% of class	33
% graduated top 25% of class	73
% graduated top 50% of class	93

DEADLINES

Early decision application deadline	12/1
Early decision notification	12/30
Regular application deadline	3/15
Regular notification	continuous
Nonfall registration?	yes

APPLICANTS ALSO LOOK AT AND OFTEN PREFER
Penn State University Park, Rensselaer Polytechnic Institute, Rochester Institute of Technology, SUNY College at Buffalo, University of Vermont

AND SOMETIMES PREFER
Alfred University, Lehigh University, University of Connecticut, University of Rochester

AND RARELY PREFER
Syracuse University

FINANCIAL FACTS

Financial Aid Rating	**90**
Annual tuition	$25,185
Room & Board	$9,345
Books and supplies	$1,000
Required fees	$400
% frosh rec. need-based scholarship or grant aid	69
% UG rec. need-based scholarship or grant aid	66
% frosh rec. need-based self-help aid	72
% UG rec. need-based self-help aid	75
% frosh rec. any financial aid	86
% UG rec. any financial aid	87
Avg. frosh grant	$13,680
Avg. frosh loan	$6,225
Independent 529 member?	No

Clemson University

106 Sikes Hall, Box 345124, Clemson, SC 29634-5124 • Admissions: 864-656-2287 • Fax: 864-656-2464

CAMPUS LIFE

Quality of Life Rating	**96**
Fire Safety Rating	**60**
Type of school	public
Environment	rural

STUDENTS

Total undergrad enrollment	13,808
% male/female	55/45
% from out of state	33
% from public high school	89
% live on campus	47
% in (# of) fraternities	17 (25)
% in (# of) sororities	31 (15)
% African American	7
% Asian	2
% Caucasian	82
% Hispanic	1

SURVEY SAYS

Great computer facilities
Students are friendly
Campus feels safe
Students are happy
Everyone loves the Tigers

ACADEMICS

Academic Rating	**79**
Calendar	semester
Student/faculty ratio	16:1
Professors interesting rating	78
Professors accessible rating	80
% professors teaching UG courses	95
% classes taught by TAs	7
Most common lab size	20-29 students
Most common regular class size	20-29 students

MOST POPULAR MAJORS

Business administration/management
engineering
secondary education and teaching

STUDENTS SPEAK OUT

Academics

One of the top public universities in the country, Clemson University offers the caliber of academics that prompts its students to declare, "If I didn't know better, I would think I were at a private Ivy League school." The university's president, who is "determined to get things accomplished and change some things here," receives serious kudos from undergraduates. Writes one satisfied student, "I am currently enrolled in a Presidential Seminar Class, and I think that it is amazing that he takes time out to do this. On a campus with over 17,000 students, it is unreal that the president knows my name." Students report that the "extremely attentive" administration "makes a daily effort to be approachable." Students also praise professors, calling them "enthusiastic, knowledgeable, caring, genuine, and passionate about teaching." One undergraduate gushes, "The students are treated respectfully, and most professors will go above and beyond to help any student who truly desires to excel." The coursework is typically "challenging, but interesting and very fair." Respondents single out the engineering, biology, and math departments as some of the strongest. Several students note problems with the registration system, while others gripe about many professors' attendance policies that "remind us of middle school." The recent tuition hike doesn't sit well with students, either. But generally, undergraduates agree, "Clemson is bliss because the school is focused on teaching the students the skills they need to succeed in the job market."

Life

If you want the short version, it's that "Clemson is a great academic school with [an] even better social life." When they are not studying, Clemson undergraduates can most often be found at football and baseball games or Greek events. During the season, "Clemson football becomes everything. An entire culture revolves around it." While certain contrarians consider such behavior "an annoying abundance of school spirit," the vast majority of students faithfully don orange on game days and fill Death Valley (Clemson's stadium, so called because opposing teams enter it to get killed) to capacity. Tailgaters convene well before kick-off, but several students assert, "Clemson students are not the hardcore partiers that our reputation has deemed us." Some undergrads wish for "more alcohol-free options" amid the sorority- and fraternity-dominated social scene, but others focus on the "billions of ways to get involved," including popular community service programs. The town of Clemson, set amid "the beauty of the South Carolina foothills," is so small and quiet that "you can even see a tumbleweed roll through the streets of 'downtown.'" On school grounds, "We have a bowling alley and pool hall that really keep the campus connected." In general, comments abound describing the "wonderful feel of the campus" and the "laid-back southern fun" the students create for themselves. Bottom line: "Everyone here seems to be having the time of [his] life."

Student Body

Clemson students describe their peers as generally southern, Christian, white, middle class, and conservative. "There are, however, other valuable members of the student body who do not fit this description and contribute greatly to the Clemson experience." At first glance, the population may appear to be a "cookie cutter" group of "preppy dressers." But upon closer inspection, you'll find that even "atypical students can always find someone to get along with here." Perhaps this welcoming atmosphere has something to do with the fact that most Clemson students are "just damn funny and likable." But don't be fooled by the southern savoir faire: though students "may not seem like they're working hard all the time, they are." Several survey respondents also observe, "Though it is not the most diverse school around, Clemson has a commitment to increasing diversity and a president who is very dedicated to fulfilling that commitment." Many students emphasize the "caring community" of the "Clemson family" that fosters "a pride in treating others as you would want to be treated."

CLEMSON UNIVERSITY

FINANCIAL AID: 864-656-2280 • E-MAIL: CUADMISSIONS@CLEMSON.EDU • WEBSITE: WWW.CLEMSON.EDU

ADMISSIONS

Very important factors considered include: Class rank, secondary school record, standardized test scores, state residency. *Important factors considered include:* Alumni/ae relation. *Other factors considered include:* Essays, recommendations, talent/ability. SAT Reasoning or ACT required. TOEFL required of all international applicants. High school diploma is required, and GED is accepted. *Academic units required:* 4 English, 3 math, 3 science (3 science lab), 3 foreign language, 3 social studies, 1 history, 2 academic electives, 1 physical education or ROTC. *Academic units recommended:* 4 math, 4 science lab.

The Inside Word

Admission by formula. Out-of-state students are in abundance; such applicants will find little difference in admissions standards from those for state residents.

FINANCIAL AID

Students should submit: FAFSA. The Princeton Review suggests that all financial aid forms be submitted as soon as possible after 1/1. *Need-based scholarships/grants offered:* Pell, SEOG, state scholarships/grants, private scholarships, the school's own gift aid, Federal Nursing scholarships. *Loan aid offered:* FFEL Subsidized Stafford, FFEL Unsubsidized Stafford, FFEL PLUS, Federal Perkins, state loans, college/university loans from institutional funds. Applicants will be notified of awards on a rolling basis beginning on or about 4/1. Federal Work-study Program available. Institutional employment available. Off-campus job opportunities are good.

FROM THE ADMISSIONS OFFICE

"One of the country's most selective public research universities, Clemson University was founded with a mission to be a high seminary of learning dedicated to teaching, research, and service. Nearly 120 years later, these three concepts remain at the heart of this university and provide the framework for an exceptional educational experience for Clemson students.

"At Clemson, professors take the time to get to know students and to explore innovative ways of teaching. Exceptional teaching is one reason Clemson's retention and graduation rates rank among the highest in the country among public universities.

"Exceptional teaching is also why Clemson continues to attract an increasingly talented student body. The class rank and SAT scores of Clemson's incoming freshman are among the highest of the nation's public research universities.

"Clemson offers over 250 student clubs and organizations; the spirit that students show for this university is unparalleled.

"Midway between Charlotte, North Carolina and Atlanta, Georgia, Clemson University is located on 1,400 acres of beautiful rolling hills within the foothills of the Blue Ridge Mountains and along the shores of Lake Hartwell.

"Applicants for fall 2006 are required to take either the new version of the SAT or the ACT with the Writing section. Scores from the old version of the SAT (prior to March 2005) will be accepted as well, and the best combined scores from either SAT test will be used in the admission process. We do not however, combine sub scores from the ACT in order to create a new composite score."

SELECTIVITY

Admissions Rating	**89**
# of applicants	10,620
% of applicants accepted	69
% of acceptees attending	42
# accepting a place on wait list	129
% admitted from wait list	15

FRESHMAN PROFILE

Range SAT Verbal	540-640
Average SAT Verbal	587
Range SAT Math	570-660
Average SAT Math	617
**TPR Projected Range SAT Writing*	*590-660*
Range ACT Composite	24-28
Average ACT Composite	26
Minimum Paper TOEFL	550
Minimum Computer Based TOEFL	213
Average HS GPA	3.9
% graduated top 10% of class	42
% graduated top 25% of class	72
% graduated top 50% of class	92

DEADLINES

Regular application deadline	5/1
Regular notification	rolling
Nonfall registration?	yes

APPLICANTS ALSO LOOK AT

AND OFTEN PREFER
Duke University
University of Georgia
University of North Carolina—Chapel Hill

AND SOMETIMES PREFER
Furman University
Vanderbilt University
Wake Forest University

AND RARELY PREFER
Auburn University
University of Florida

FINANCIAL FACTS

Financial Aid Rating	**68**
Annual in-state tuition	$7,840
Annual out-of-state tuition	$16,404
Room & Board	$5,292
Books and supplies	$798
Required fees	$234
% frosh rec. need-based scholarship or grant aid	13
% UG rec. need-based scholarship or grant aid	18
% frosh rec. need-based self-help aid	25
% UG rec. need-based self-help aid	29
% frosh rec. any financial aid	86
% UG rec. any financial aid	81
Avg. frosh grant	$6,598
Avg. frosh loan	$4,056
Independent 529 member?	No

COE COLLEGE

1220 FIRST AVENUE NE, CEDAR RAPIDS, IA 52402 • ADMISSIONS: 319-399-8500 • FAX: 319-399-8816

CAMPUS LIFE

Quality of Life Rating	**86**
Fire Safety Rating	**60**
Type of school	private
Affiliation	Presbyterian
Environment	city

STUDENTS

Total undergrad enrollment	1,250
% male/female	44/56
% from out of state	31
% from public high school	90
% live on campus	84
% in (# of) fraternities	25 (5)
% in (# of) sororities	19 (3)
% African American	2
% Asian	1
% Caucasian	91
% Hispanic	2
% international	4
# of countries represented	15

SURVEY SAYS

Small classes
Great library
Lots of beer drinking

ACADEMICS

Academic Rating	**86**
Calendar	semester
Student/faculty ratio	13:1
Professors interesting rating	86
Professors accessible rating	89
% professors teaching UG courses	100
% classes taught by TAs	0
Most common lab size	fewer than 10 students
Most common regular class size	10-19 students

MOST POPULAR MAJORS

Biology/biological sciences
business administration and management
psychology

STUDENTS SPEAK OUT

Academics

Coe College, a small liberal arts school in Iowa, "encompasses everything someone would want out of a college: close relationships between students and faculty, a supportive surrounding community, and a curriculum that is flexible to fit each student." With just over 1,300 undergraduates, Coe is "small enough that if you have a real problem, they can work with you." Notes one student, "The personal attention you get from your teachers makes you feel like they have an investment in your future." Central to the Coe educational experience is the Coe Plan, which requires community service of freshmen and a practicum—"an internship, study abroad experience, or research," among a few other possibilities—of upperclassmen. Many students use the Coe Plan to stretch themselves; one such undergrad writes, "Since coming to Coe, I've had three internships and completed research for my honors thesis." Coe is small, so "don't come here if you're expecting a huge number of classes. Some of the departments are very limited as far as offered classes go." In its most popular departments, though, Coe "gives you the resources you need to develop your own critical-thinking abilities and effectively learn what you need to know." Students tell us that the math and science departments here are excellent; "We have one of the best physics programs in the country," one physics major brags. Across disciplines, undergraduates claim academics "are challenging, leaving students more prepared when they graduate than students from other schools."

Life

Coe "gives students of all interests opportunities to have fun on and off campus, whether it's through free movie nights at a local theater, concerts of any musical style, or pretty much anything else one could imagine," which is a good thing, because "Cedar Rapids is a boring town" that offers little in the way of diversion. Iowa City, only 20 minutes away by car, is much better, students assure us, with "plenty of clubs that students enjoy." When the weekend rolls around, "Coe students party a lot," but "if you don't like to party, there are always weekend activities that students can participate in, and sometimes these activities draw a bigger crowd than parties do!" The biggest party of the year is Flunk Day, a "day where people skip classes and drink all day," though there is "a canoe trip that day for non-drinkers, but space is limited." When the weather is nice, "Coe is almost park-like. During spring and fall, there are always games going and people gathered on the quads." When the weather turns cold, students generally stay indoors; "Many students get involved with some type of activity, either intramurals or a club or group." They also pass the time with your standard small-group quiet activities, "watching movies, playing cards [or] just hanging out and talking."

Student Body

Students can be "somewhat cliquish" at Coe College, students tell us. Reports one, "It seems as though students who do not fit into one of the 'categories' (categories: students with high socioeconomic status, students who are involved in the religious group on campus, homosexual/bisexual students, minority/exchange students, students in sports, etc.) seem to get lost and left behind." While "most students are from Iowa, [Coe] does try to mix it up and prides itself on having many foreign exchange students and people from different states, though most of them are still from the Midwest." Internationals here "are mostly from Japan." Many students play sports, and "everyone here has something they are passionate about, whether it is athletics, academics, research, clubs, or community involvement."

FINANCIAL AID: 319-399-8540 • E-MAIL: ADMISSION@COE.EDU • WEBSITE: WWW.COE.EDU

ADMISSIONS

Very important factors considered include: Secondary school record, standardized test scores. *Important factors considered include:* Class rank, essays, recommendations. *Other factors considered include:* Alumni/ae relation, character/personal qualities, extracurricular activities, interview, minority status, talent/ability, volunteer work. SAT Reasoning or ACT required. TOEFL required of all international applicants. High school diploma is required, and GED is accepted. *Academic units recommended:* 4 English, 3 math, 3 science (1 science lab), 2 foreign language, 3 social studies, 2 academic electives.

The Inside Word

Coe's admissions process places a very high level of importance on your numbers. Candidates who don't have at least a 2.75 high school GPA and at least a 22 on the ACT may find tough going with the admissions committee. As is true of nearly all small liberal arts colleges, Coe conducts a thorough application review that also considers your personal background and involvements, but an emerging national reputation enables them to keep their focus upon academic achievement as the primary gatekeeper.

FINANCIAL AID

Students should submit: FAFSA. The Princeton Review suggests that all financial aid forms be submitted as soon as possible after 1/1. *Need-based scholarships/grants offered:* Pell, SEOG, state scholarships/grants, private scholarships, the school's own gift aid. *Loan aid offered:* Direct Subsidized Stafford, Direct Unsubsidized Stafford, Direct PLUS, Federal Perkins, college/university loans from institutional funds. Applicants will be notified of awards on a rolling basis beginning on or about 3/15. Federal Work-study Program available. Institutional employment available. Off-campus job opportunities are excellent.

FROM THE ADMISSIONS OFFICE

"A Coe education begins to pay off right away. In fact, 98 percent of last year's graduating class was either working or in graduate school within six months of graduation. One reason our graduates do so well is the Coe Plan—a step-by-step sequence of activities designed to prepare our students for life after Coe. This required sequence stretches from the first-year seminar to community service, issue dinners, career planning seminars, and the required hands-on experience. The hands-on component may be satisfied through an internship, research, practicum, or study abroad. One student lived with a Costa Rican family while she studied the effects of selective logging on rain forest organisms. Others have interned at places like Warner Brothers in Los Angeles and the Chicago Board of Trade. Still others combine travel with an internship or student teaching for an unforgettable off-campus experience. Coe College is one of the few liberal arts institutions in the country to require hands-on learning for graduation.

"For fall 2006, Coe will continue to focus on the Critical Reading/Verbal and Math sub sections of the SAT. Coe admission counselors believe it is best to learn about the new Writing component at the same time as students and parents, and we want to know more before deciding to use them in our admission decision-making."

SELECTIVITY

Admissions Rating	**86**
# of applicants	1,177
% of applicants accepted	72
% of acceptees attending	37

FRESHMAN PROFILE

Range SAT Verbal	550-650
Average SAT Verbal	581
Range SAT Math	540-650
Average SAT Math	571
**TPR Projected Range SAT Writing*	*600-670*
Range ACT Composite	22-27
Average ACT Composite	24
Minimum Paper TOEFL	500
Minimum Computer Based TOEFL	173
Average HS GPA	3.58
% graduated top 10% of class	25
% graduated top 25% of class	57
% graduated top 50% of class	93

DEADLINES

Regular application deadline	3/1
Regular notification	3/15
Nonfall registration?	yes

AND SOMETIMES PREFER

Beloit College
Cornell College
Grinnell College
Knox College
University of Iowa

FINANCIAL FACTS

Financial Aid Rating	**80**
Annual tuition	$23,570
Room & Board	$6,260
Books and supplies	$600
Required fees	$360
% frosh rec. need-based scholarship or grant aid	84
% UG rec. need-based scholarship or grant aid	80
% frosh rec. need-based self-help aid	69
% UG rec. need-based self-help aid	71
% frosh rec. any financial aid	98
% UG rec. any financial aid	96
Avg. frosh grant	$14,940
Avg. frosh loan	$5,745
Independent 529 member?	No

Colby College

4000 Mayflower Hill, Waterville, ME 04901-8848 • Admissions: 207-872-3168 • Fax: 207-872-3474

CAMPUS LIFE

Quality of Life Rating	**83**
Fire Safety Rating	**69**
Type of school	private
Environment	town

STUDENTS

Total undergrad enrollment	1,820
% male/female	47/53
% from out of state	87
% from public high school	58
% live on campus	93
% African American	1
% Asian	5
% Caucasian	83
% Hispanic	3
% Native American	1
% international	7
# of countries represented	66

SURVEY SAYS

Small classes
Great food on campus
Frats and sororities are unpopular or nonexistent
Lots of beer drinking

ACADEMICS

Academic Rating	**92**
Calendar	4-1-4
Student/faculty ratio	10:1
Professors interesting rating	89
Professors accessible rating	86
% professors teaching UG courses	100
% classes taught by TAs	0
Most common lab size	10-19 students
Most common regular class size	10-19 students

MOST POPULAR MAJORS

Biology/biological sciences
economics
English language and literature

STUDENTS SPEAK OUT

Academics

This small, close-knit liberal arts college draws praise from students for its rigorous but caring approach to academics. It's a place where devoted professors "invite students to dinner" and learning happens "for learning's sake." Small classes are one of Colby's biggest draws. "It's all about personal attention from professors," writes a freshman. One junior warns, "But watch out. If you've screwed up in one class, future profs will know." Professors get high grades for their teaching and accessibility, which together foster a "love for learning" in undergraduates. "What stands out about the professors is that most are the rare combination of brilliant mind and brilliant teacher," writes one student. "I know most of my professors and the deans on a personal level, and I have felt challenged by every course that I have taken," adds another student. This makes Colby an intense place to go to school, and students work a lot and study hard. Students must not only complete their major requirements but also fulfill a hefty load of distribution requirements to graduate. The popular "Jan Plan" lets students take an extra month long term of focused or independent study in January, often accompanied by an internship. The administration, however, is often criticized for being unresponsive to student concerns and input. "While they want to do what's best for the campus, their goals and ideals are antiquated," writes one senior.

Life

"Friends and a sense of community drive life at Colby," writes one senior. Students live together in coed, mixed-class dorms. Everything centers around the campus, which is "constructed on a gorgeous wooded hill near the Kennebec River in Central Maine." And since "there isn't a ridiculous amount to do" in these remote environs, "Colby works hard to fill the day with countless events, lectures, discussions, and concerts. People can study hard, party, take advantage of the beautiful outdoors, and most do all three." Students go hiking in autumn and spring, skiing in winter, and participate in traditional outdoor sports like lacrosse. Writes one senior, "People like to unwind after our incredibly stressful weeks with movies, skiing, and partying." Booze flows freely and drug use is not unheard of at Colby. The "alcohol-centered social scene" usually takes place at small dorm parties or at the few local pubs. Students make sure to add that they not only play hard but also they work hard. But drinkers beware: "This school is too small to have a private life," and "if you do something, everyone will know the details in a day or two."

Student Body

While the prototypical Colby student may be "white and from 20 minutes outside of Boston," undergrads are quick to point out that their "campus is very open to diversity and ready to embrace it." The administration recently launched a major push for diversity and it appears to have gained some initial success. "The diversity has increased a lot since my freshman year," notes a senior. "There are also a lot more international students." A junior adds, "We have students here that dress in business suits and bow ties while others walk around in capes." Most students, however, settle for the more general description of "preppy students who enjoy the outdoors and enjoy having a good time." Although this means that the student body can often look like a small army of "J. Crew models," students assure us that there is "an abundance of clubs on campus for all kinds of people. It's easy to find your niche." Both intellectual and adventurous, Colby students for the most part are "enthusiastic, gregarious, and well balanced."

FINANCIAL AID: 207-872-3168 • E-MAIL: ADMISSIONS@COLBY.EDU • WEBSITE: WWW.COLBY.EDU

ADMISSIONS

Very important factors considered include: Character/personal qualities, secondary school record. *Important factors considered include:* Class rank, essays, extracurricular activities, interview, minority status, recommendations, standardized test scores, talent/ability. *Other factors considered include:* Alumni/ae relation, geographical residence, state residency, volunteer work, work experience. SAT Reasoning or ACT required. TOEFL required of all international applicants. High school diploma or equivalent is not required. *Academic units recommended:* 4 English, 3 math, 2 science (2 science lab), 3 foreign language, 2 social studies, 2 academic electives.

The Inside Word

Colby continues to be both very selective and successful in converting admits to enrollees, which makes for a perpetually challenging admissions process.

FINANCIAL AID

Students should submit: FAFSA, Either institutional application or CSS/Financial Aid PROFILE and institutional supplement. Regular filing deadline is 2/1. The Princeton Review suggests that all financial aid forms be submitted as soon as possible after 1/1. *Need-based scholarships/grants offered:* Pell, SEOG, state scholarships/grants, private scholarships, the school's own gift aid. *Loan aid offered:* Direct Subsidized Stafford, Direct Unsubsidized Stafford, Direct PLUS, FFEL Subsidized Stafford, FFEL Unsubsidized Stafford, FFEL PLUS, Federal Perkins, state loans, college/university loans from institutional funds, alternative loans. Applicants will be notified of awards on or about 4/1. Off-campus job opportunities are fair.

FROM THE ADMISSIONS OFFICE

"Colby offers world-class academic programs, a supportive community atmosphere, and rich opportunities after graduation. Colby prepares students by giving them a broad foundation of knowledge and intellectual tools, experience as active participants in a diverse community of scholars, and opportunities to engage the world. The depth of student-faculty interaction and collaboration is extraordinary, and the college is recognized as a national leader in undergraduate research and project-based learning. Colby's commitment to global reach earned the college a 2005 Senator Paul Simon Award for internationalizing the campus. The award recognizes the international content of the curriculum, the college's emphasis on study abroad, and the international diversity of the student body and faculty. Colby's strong commitment to environmental stewardship was recognized in 2004 with an EPA Environmental Merit Award and a Maine Governor's Award for Environmental Excellence. The challenging academic experience is complemented by an active community life featuring 100 student-run organizations, more than 50 athletic and recreational choices, and many leadership and volunteer opportunities—all on one of the nation's most beautiful campuses. Colby graduates succeed, finding their places at the finest medical and other graduate schools, top Wall Street firms, and in the arts, government service, social service, education, and nonprofit organizations.

"Students applying for admission in the fall of 2006 may submit scores from either the old or the new SAT or ACT test. Beginning with applicants for admission in the fall of 2007, all candidates must submit SAT or ACT results with a Writing section."

SELECTIVITY

Admissions Rating	**96**
# of applicants	4,065
% of applicants accepted	37
% of acceptees attending	34
# accepting a place on wait list	604
% admitted from wait list	9
# of early decision applicants	197
% accepted early decision	40

FRESHMAN PROFILE

Range SAT Verbal	640-720
Average SAT Verbal	676
Range SAT Math	640-710
Average SAT Math	678
**TPR Projected Range SAT Writing*	*660-710*
Range ACT Composite	27-31
Average ACT Composite	29
Minimum Paper TOEFL	600
Minimum Computer Based TOEFL	240
% graduated top 10% of class	66
% graduated top 25% of class	92
% graduated top 50% of class	98

DEADLINES

Early decision application deadline	11/15
Early decision notification	12/15
Regular application deadline	1/1
Regular notification	4/1
Nonfall registration?	yes

APPLICANTS ALSO LOOK AT

AND OFTEN PREFER

Amherst College, Brown University, Dartmouth College, Middlebury College, Williams College

AND SOMETIMES PREFER

Bowdoin College, Colgate University, Tufts University

AND RARELY PREFER

Bates College, Connecticut College, Hamilton College, Trinity College (CT), Wellesley College

FINANCIAL FACTS

Financial Aid Rating	**94**
Comprehensive fee	$41,770
Books and supplies	$600
% frosh rec. need-based scholarship or grant aid	38
% UG rec. need-based scholarship or grant aid	37
% frosh rec. need-based self-help aid	32
% UG rec. need-based self-help aid	32
% frosh rec. any financial aid	39
% UG rec. any financial aid	39
Avg. frosh grant	$23,348
Avg. frosh loan	$2,984
Independent 529 member?	No

COLGATE UNIVERSITY

13 OAK DRIVE, HAMILTON, NY 13346 • ADMISSIONS: 315-228-7401 • FAX: 315-228-7544

CAMPUS LIFE

Quality of Life Rating	**83**
Fire Safety Rating	**82**
Type of school	private
Environment	rural

STUDENTS

Total undergrad enrollment	2,800
% male/female	48/52
% from out of state	65
% from public high school	70
% live on campus	90
% in (# of) fraternities	37 (7)
% in (# of) sororities	30 (4)
% African American	4
% Asian	6
% Caucasian	75
% Hispanic	4
% Native American	1
% international	5
# of countries represented	37

SURVEY SAYS

Small classes
Everyone loves the Raiders
Lots of beer drinking
Hard liquor is popular

ACADEMICS

Academic Rating	**93**
Calendar	semester
Student/faculty ratio	10:1
Professors interesting rating	92
Professors accessible rating	93
% professors teaching UG courses	100
% classes taught by TAs	0
Most common lab size	10-19 students
Most common regular class size	10-19 students

MOST POPULAR MAJORS

Economics
English language and literature
history

STUDENTS SPEAK OUT

Academics

Colgate University is the type of undergraduate institution that inspires fierce loyalty among students and alumni; as one undergrad puts it, "From the student athletes, professors, artists, political activists, to the maintenance people and administration, the majority of Colgate loves the school. People go into Colgate with numerous loves and passions and leave the University with Colgate as a newfound passion." A combination of factors spur this devotion: a beautiful campus, an accomplished and caring faculty, a bright and goal-oriented student body, and a strong sense of community forged at least in part by the school's geographic isolation. Students here report that "the academics are intense, but not overwhelming because the students are intelligent enough to handle the workload," and they praise the liberal arts core curriculum and distribution requirements that "serve as an excellent base for students to pursue other academic interests." They also love the "great study abroad opportunities; if you want to go anywhere in the world you generally can, and the trips are quite affordable." The Outdoor Education Program, through which "nearly 70 percent of students participate in physical education classes, Back Yard Adventures or the Pre-Orientation trip, Wilderness Adventure," is popular, too. Most of all, students love how Colgate prepares them for success in the real world. "Colgate fosters the education of students outside the classroom as well as inside the classroom. Therefore, when students leave Colgate they have great interpersonal skills," explains one student. Another goes on to say, "The 'Colgate Connection' is probably one of the school's greatest benefits, as alumni are very helpful in finding and offering careers for graduates."

Life

Colgate's hometown of Hamilton is a "small town that, without Colgate students, has only around 3,000 people." The good news is that "administrators recognize that our location in a small rural community may be construed as a weakness, so they do a great job to make up for this with a profusion of programs on campus. There is always something to do, and if you leave Hamilton for even one day, you feel you've missed out on incredible things." Colgate's geographic isolation is also tempered by the school's "ridiculously beautiful campus, like a country club," its "awesome dorms," and its "clean and comfortable facilities." Intercollegiate sports are big here; "Good Division I athletics are also a rarity among liberal arts colleges, but unlike larger schools, the athletes here are also some of the best students," brags one undergrad. The school is well known for its lively party scene, but students point out that "Colgate has something for just about everyone, including special events, newly opened restaurants, dance halls and the improved movie theater." And "although people party, they know how to keep up with their schoolwork and do well academically." Overall, Colgate undergrads "work hard in school, but also look to have a good time outside the classroom. Whether that means joining groups, playing sports, or going out with their friends, Colgate students like to have fun."

Student Body

Colgate draws an accomplished student body; "the typical Colgate student was captain of a sports team, homecoming king or queen, president of the class, and an excellent student at his or her high school. At Colgate, this translates to a student body of incredibly bright, talented and congenial students," explains one student. Undergrads tell us that "while everyone is really smart, people aren't pretentious about it. You don't feel lower than anyone else, but rather challenged to expand your mind and develop your knowledge and talents." Undergrads tend to be on the preppy side and are typically athletic; it's no surprise, then, that "the gym is one of the hot spots on campus." Colgate "has a reputation as a conservative school, but in fact the bent of the campus is moderately liberal, if anything. While there is a very vocal, organized conservative element, most people seem to be either moderate or left-of-center."

FINANCIAL AID: 315-228-7431 • E-MAIL: ADMISSION@MAIL.COLGATE.EDU • WEBSITE: WWW.COLGATE.EDU

ADMISSIONS

Very important factors considered include: Class rank, secondary school record. *Important factors considered include:* Character/personal qualities, essays, extracurricular activities, recommendations, standardized test scores, talent/ability, volunteer work, work experience. *Other factors considered include:* Alumni/ae relation, geographical residence, minority status. SAT Reasoning or ACT required. TOEFL required of all international applicants. High school diploma is required, and GED is accepted. *Academic units required:* 4 English, 3 math, 3 science (2 science lab), 3 foreign language, 2 social studies, 1 history. *Academic units recommended:* 4 English, 4 math, 4 science (3 science lab), 4 foreign language, 2 social studies, 3 history.

The Inside Word

Like many colleges, Colgate caters to some well-developed special interests. Athletes, minorities, and legacies (the children of alums) are among the most special of interests and benefit from more favorable consideration than applicants without particular distinction. Students without a solid, consistent academic record, beware—the university's wait list leans toward jumbo size.

FINANCIAL AID

Students should submit: FAFSA, CSS/Financial Aid PROFILE, noncustodial (divorced/separated) parents' statement, business/farm supplement. Regular filing deadline is 1/15. The Princeton Review suggests that all financial aid forms be submitted as soon as possible after 1/1. *Need-based scholarships/grants offered:* Pell, SEOG, state scholarships/grants, the school's own gift aid. *Loan aid offered:* FFEL Subsidized Stafford, FFEL Unsubsidized Stafford, FFEL PLUS, Federal Perkins. Applicants will be notified of awards on or about 4/1. Federal Work-study Program available. Off-campus job opportunities are good.

FROM THE ADMISSIONS OFFICE

"Students and faculty alike are drawn to Colgate by the quality of its academic programs. Faculty initiative has given the university a rich mix of learning opportunities that includes a liberal arts core, 51 academic concentrations, and a wealth of Colgate faculty-led, off-campus study programs in the United States and abroad. But there is more to Colgate than academic life, including more than 100 student organizations, athletics and recreation at all levels, and a full complement of living options set within a campus described as one of the most beautiful in the country. A new center for community service builds upon the tradition of Colgate students interacting with the surrounding community in meaningful ways. Colgate students become extraordinarily devoted alumni, contributing significantly to career networking and exploration programs on and off campus. For students in search of a busy and varied campus life, Colgate is a place to learn and grow.

"All admission candidates must submit the results of standardized testing from one of two sources: the SAT Reasoning Test (Writing, Critical Reading, and Mathematics), or the American College Testing Program (ACT, optional Writing exam not required)."

SELECTIVITY

Admissions Rating	**97**
# of applicants	6,551
% of applicants accepted	33
% of acceptees attending	34
# accepting a place on wait list	889
% admitted from wait list	5
# of early decision applicants	282
% accepted early decision	60

FRESHMAN PROFILE

Range SAT Verbal	630-710
Average SAT Verbal	666
Range SAT Math	640-720
Average SAT Math	675
**TPR Projected Range SAT Writing*	*650-700*
Range ACT Composite	28-32
Average ACT Composite	29
Minimum Paper TOEFL	600
Minimum Computer Based TOEFL	250
Average HS GPA	3.6
% graduated top 10% of class	73
% graduated top 25% of class	95
% graduated top 50% of class	100

DEADLINES

Early decision application deadline	11/15
Early decision notification	12/15
Regular application deadline	1/15
Regular notification	4/1
Nonfall registration?	no

APPLICANTS ALSO LOOK AT

AND OFTEN PREFER

Cornell U., Dartmouth College, Middlebury College, Williams College, Yale U.

AND SOMETIMES PREFER

Boston College, Bowdoin College, Georgetown U., Tufts U.

AND RARELY PREFER

Boston U., Colby College, Lafayette College, Trinity College (CT)

FINANCIAL FACTS

Financial Aid Rating	**98**
Annual tuition	$31,230
Room & Board	$7,620
Books and supplies	$830
Required fees	$210
% frosh rec. need-based scholarship or grant aid	36
% UG rec. need-based scholarship or grant aid	42
% frosh rec. need-based self-help aid	30
% UG rec. need-based self-help aid	34
% frosh rec. any financial aid	36
% UG rec. any financial aid	44
Avg. frosh grant	$29,338
Avg. frosh loan	$2,296
Independent 529 member?	No

COLLEGE OF THE ATLANTIC

105 EDEN STREET, BAR HARBOR, ME 04609 • ADMISSIONS: 207-288-5015 • FAX: 207-288-4126

CAMPUS LIFE

Quality of Life Rating	**95**
Fire Safety Rating	**87**
Type of school	private
Environment	rural

STUDENTS

Total undergrad enrollment	262
% male/female	37/63
% from out of state	80
% from public high school	69
% live on campus	36
% international	19
# of countries represented	36

SURVEY SAYS

Small classes
No one cheats
Students are friendly
Campus feels safe
Intercollegiate sports are unpopular or nonexistent
Frats and sororities are unpopular or nonexistent
Student government is popular

ACADEMICS

Academic Rating	**90**
Calendar	trimester
Student/faculty ratio	9:1
Professors interesting rating	96
Professors accessible rating	98
% professors teaching UG courses	100
% classes taught by TAs	0
Most common regular class size	10-19 students

MOST POPULAR MAJORS

Ecology

STUDENTS SPEAK OUT

Academics

"It is all about being a better citizen in the world," say the environmentally and politically conscious undergrads of College of the Atlantic, a tiny college whose "strengths include environmental sciences, biology, social sciences, philosophy, and psychology, as well as a tight community [that promotes] intellectual stimulation." COA fosters community spirit and responsibility through its administration, which "is mainly done by committees consisting of students, faculty, and staff, where everyone's opinion counts in decision making." Students love feeling plugged in to the deliberative process and say that the one-for-all approach here also engenders a pervasive feeling of "trust—we don't have locks on our mailboxes, and you can leave your laptop unattended for hours, and it will still be there when you get back." The school allows students "lots of freedom—freedom to take the classes we want, and freedom in those classes to direct our own studies." As one student tells us, "there is so much flexibility here. COA has very few requirements, and they really aren't a big deal." Students praise profs as "energetic and enthusiastic and constantly involved in the students' lives and their learning." Reports one undergrad, "There are posters by each phone on campus, which list the on-campus extension as well as the home phone number of each faculty and staff member. We can call them whenever we need to regarding school, campus committees, and/or personal matters."

Life

Bar Harbor, COA's hometown, may be the perfect antithesis of a college town; during the summer it's a hopping vacation resort, but during the school year "almost all the stores close up" and students "need to find their own entertainment." Bar Harbor is famous for its bracing winters: "It is gray and miserable," notes one undergrad who wishes she were somewhere else. Many here, though, are winter-philes who tout the range of available snow-related activities, which include "skating, cross-country skiing, and snowshoeing." The dearth of in-town options and the small student body combine to create a very subdued campus social scene; "this is not the place for those looking to party, drink, or do lots of drugs (or slack off, for that matter)," explains one student. For fun, "people like cooking together, playing cards, hanging out, going to contra dances, watching movies," and spending as much time outside as they can. Everyone here praises nearby Acadia National Park, "the best backyard a college student could ask for. Finding favorite beautiful hikes, walks, or study spots has become a four-year goal," reports one student. Students party on Tuesdays ("There are no classes on Wednesdays, so Tuesday night is the big social period," explains one student) and on weekends. "Parties are never big, but often fun." Students also want the world to know that "the food is SOOOOO good here! There's no corporate 'food service'—it's just people that work in the kitchen and concoct really tasty (and healthy) food."

Student Body

"Some people think this school is a bunch of granola-eating, flower-child, pot-smoking hippies, but that's not the way it is," reports one COA undergrad. "The typical COA student has a lot of individuality. We're not all cookie-cutter Rastafarians. We're all atypical." Agrees another student, "The COA student tries to be different . . . just like everyone else. There is no 'in' to fit into, just a lot of cliques." Those cliques, students tell us, include "hippies, lobstermen, city kids, trendy people . . . just about every category one could imagine." Students do, on the whole, tend to be "environmentally and socially sensitive" and "liberal in political thought," the type who attend "protests and drive an ancient Volvo or VW with a political bumper sticker and a Darwin fish." "There are quite a few international students, especially from Europe and Asia," at COA, and "they get along well with the rest of the students, but most tend to hang out [primarily] with each other."

Financial Aid: 207-288-5015 • E-mail: inquiry@ecology.coa.edu • Website: www.coa.edu

ADMISSIONS

Very important factors considered include: Essays, extracurricular activities, interview, recommendations, secondary school record, volunteer work. *Important factors considered include:* Character/personal qualities, talent/ability. *Other factors considered include:* Alumni/ae relation, class rank, minority status, standardized test scores, work experience. TOEFL required of all international applicants. High school diploma is required, and GED is accepted. *Academic units required:* 4 English, 3 math, 2 science (2 science lab), 2 social studies. *Academic units recommended:* 4 English, 4 math, 3 science (2 science lab), 2 foreign language, 2 social studies, 2 history, 1 academic elective.

The Inside Word

COA's academic emphasis results in a highly self-selected applicant pool. Fortunately for the college, its focus on human ecology strikes a chord that is timely in its appeal to students. Enrolling here is definitely opting to take an atypical path to higher education. Admissions evaluations emphasize what's on your mind over what's on your transcript, which makes thoughtful essays and an interview musts for serious candidates. It also makes the admissions process a refreshing experience in the relatively uniform world of college admission. The admissions committee includes a few current students who have full voting rights as members.

FINANCIAL AID

Students should submit: FAFSA, institution's own financial aid form, noncustodial (divorced/separated) parents' statement, business/farm supplement. Regular filing deadline is 2/15. The Princeton Review suggests that all financial aid forms be submitted as soon as possible after 1/1. *Need-based scholarships/grants offered:* Pell, SEOG, private scholarships, the school's own gift aid. *Loan aid offered:* FFEL Subsidized Stafford, FFEL Unsubsidized Stafford, FFEL PLUS, Federal Perkins. Applicants will be notified of awards on or about 4/1.

FROM THE ADMISSIONS OFFICE

"College of the Atlantic was created three decades ago at a time when it was becoming evident that conventional education was inadequate for citizenship in our increasingly complex and technical society. The growing interdependence of environmental and social issues and the limitations of academic specialization demanded a wider vision. COA's founders created a pioneering institution dedicated to the interdisciplinary study of human ecology, a college in which students overcome narrow points of view and integrate knowledge across traditional academic lines.

"College of the Atlantic does not require standardized testing as part of the application process. Learning and intelligence can be gauged in many ways; standardized test scores are just one of many measures. If an applicant chooses to submit standardized test scores for consideration, the SAT (either version), SAT Subject Tests, or ACT scores are all acceptable."

SELECTIVITY

Admissions Rating	**88**
# of applicants	255
% of applicants accepted	67
% of acceptees attending	40
# accepting a place on wait list	12
% admitted from wait list	33
# of early decision applicants	25
% accepted early decision	76

FRESHMAN PROFILE

Range SAT Verbal	550-680
Average SAT Verbal	624
Range SAT Math	510-620
Average SAT Math	586
**TPR Projected Range SAT Writing*	*600-680*
Range ACT Composite	23-31
Average ACT Composite	28
Minimum Paper TOEFL	550
Minimum Computer Based TOEFL	217
Average HS GPA	3.3
% graduated top 10% of class	29
% graduated top 25% of class	69
% graduated top 50% of class	87

DEADLINES

Early decision application deadline	12/1
Early decision notification	12/15
Regular application deadline	2/15
Regular notification	4/1
Nonfall registration?	yes

APPLICANTS ALSO LOOK AT

AND OFTEN PREFER
Bowdoin College, Colby College, Reed College

AND SOMETIMES PREFER
Bates College, Cornell University, Hampshire College, Marlboro College, University of Vermont

AND RARELY PREFER
Eckerd College, Oberlin College, University of Maine

FINANCIAL FACTS

Financial Aid Rating	**94**
Annual tuition	$24,870
Room & Board	$6,732
Books and supplies	$500
Required fees	$375
% frosh rec. need-based scholarship or grant aid	84
% UG rec. need-based scholarship or grant aid	81
% frosh rec. need-based self-help aid	83
% UG rec. need-based self-help aid	77
% frosh rec. any financial aid	87
% UG rec. any financial aid	90
Avg. frosh grant	$15,427
Avg. frosh loan	$2,625
Independent 529 member?	No

College of Charleston

66 George Street, Charleston, SC 29424 • Admissions: 843-953-5670 • Fax: 843-953-6322

CAMPUS LIFE

Quality of Life Rating	**92**
Fire Safety Rating	**87**
Type of school	public
Environment	city

STUDENTS

Total undergrad enrollment	9,479
% male/female	36/64
% from out of state	35
% from public high school	80
% live on campus	29
% in (# of) fraternities	13 (14)
% in (# of) sororities	15 (11)
% African American	8
% Asian	1
% Caucasian	84
% Hispanic	1
% international	2
# of countries represented	75

SURVEY SAYS

Small classes
Great library
Students love Charleston, SC
Great off-campus food
Students are happy
Lots of beer drinking
(Almost) everyone smokes

ACADEMICS

Academic Rating	**80**
Calendar	semester
Student/faculty ratio	14:1
Professors interesting rating	81
Professors accessible rating	82
% professors teaching UG courses	94
% classes taught by TAs	2
Most common lab size	20-29 students
Most common regular class size	20-29 students

MOST POPULAR MAJORS

Business administration/management
communications studies/speech communication and rhetoric
psychology

STUDENTS SPEAK OUT

Academics

Students interested in classroom experiences that are heavy on personal attention should take a closer look at the College of Charleston; "Classes at C of C are small enough that you actually get to know your teachers and they get to know you, providing a very different atmosphere and [more] caring environment than that at larger universities," writes a junior. And students are pleased to report that this quality education is getting even better. One sophomore boasts that the college "is clearly on a mission to become very competitive academically," in part due to the new administration's "Fourth Century Initiative" to raise the level of C of C's education. An example of the campus's academic growth is the new library, which provides students "a more interesting and stimulating meeting point, as well as more books, more collections, [and] better computer access." Incomers in search of a particularly rigorous curriculum—and a little special treatment—should take a look at the college's Honors Program; an honors student boasts, "The Honors Program has spoiled me with great discussion classes and extra perks (like priority registration)." Students do have a few complaints, however. For instance, "the laid-back beach attitude seeps into the school bureaucracy a little too much" and you occasionally "come across professors who aren't so hot."

Life

"The College of Charleston has a reputation around South Carolina as being a party school," and undergraduates are the first to admit that the reputation is well deserved. "Charleston has many places where the beer and liquor flow," including "off-campus parties," Greek shindigs, "hundreds of nightclubs . . . millions of bars . . . okay, I'm exaggerating," admits a freshman. But there are watering holes aplenty, including "a few 'chill' bars and clubs for those who desire a little more than drinking themselves into oblivion." While chugging beers is a fairly common phenomenon at C of C, these undergrads assure us that campus life achieves a healthy sense of balance. A freshman says, "The same person that I ran into doing a keg stand Thursday night can be found nestled in a private corner of the library studying the next day." There are also "a ton of community service and activist opportunities," as well as campus clubs, the wildly popular C of C basketball games, and a healthy array of Frisbee-related activities. Plus, there's the city of Charleston itself. Downtown Charleston—where most upperclassman land apartments—"is only one block away" from campus, and offers "numerous museums, innumerable little art galleries, an aquarium, an ice rink, and a handful of large cinemas." And "if none of that floats your boat, we're 15 minutes away from the beach."

Student Body

While it's true that "the vast majority" of the students at C of C are "white Southerners, mostly from South Carolina," "a growing segment of the student[s] are out-of-staters who come for the liberal arts reputation (and the weather)." Because this is a college with a distinctly Southern flavor, these undergrads sometimes look curiously—even critically—on their Northern classmates. But a senior says that Northerners tend to adopt the Southern way of life fairly quickly: "Most Northerners that come down here quickly pick up on things that are unacceptable and for the most part attempt to be more respectful and patient." Geography aside, most undergrads fit into two categories: the "preppies" (or "collar-poppers") and the "hippies." A freshman expands on this: "So basically you have a Lacoste-clad sorority girl hopping out of her SUV with a Bush/Cheney '04 sticker on it, or your dreadlocked, bearded guy in the Ford Festiva lighting up a joint and listening to a jam band." Among and beyond these groups, you'll also find the "Greeks, artists, theater folks, Christian groups, environmentalists, and kids just trying to make it." One final note, for the guys out there: At C of C, there are about two females for every male, and reportedly many of them are "gorgeous girls . . . Southern belles."

Financial Aid: 843-953-5540 • E-mail: admissions@cofc.edu • Website: www.cofc.edu

ADMISSIONS

Very important factors considered include: Secondary school record, standardized test scores. *Important factors considered include:* Character/personal qualities, class rank, essays, geographical residence, state residency, talent/ability. *Other factors considered include:* Extracurricular activities, minority status, recommendations, volunteer work, work experience. SAT Reasoning or ACT required. TOEFL required of all international applicants. High school diploma is required, and GED is accepted. *Academic units required:* 4 English, 3 math, 3 science (3 science lab), 2 foreign language, 3 social studies, 4 academic electives. *Academic units recommended:* 4 math, 4 science, 3 foreign language, 2 history.

The Inside Word

Although the admissions process is pretty straightforward at the College of Charleston—solid grades and test scores, as at most state schools, will serve you well—it's important to know that the college reviews applications with a private-school touch. Charleston's programs in the sciences, math, languages, and the classics are particularly competitive.

FINANCIAL AID

Students should submit: FAFSA. The Princeton Review suggests that all financial aid forms be submitted as soon as possible after 1/1. *Need-based scholarships/grants offered:* Pell, SEOG, state scholarships/grants, private scholarships, the school's own gift aid. *Loan aid offered:* Direct Subsidized Stafford, Direct Unsubsidized Stafford, Direct PLUS, Federal Perkins. Applicants will be notified of awards on a rolling basis beginning on or about 4/10. Federal Work-study Program available. Institutional employment available. Off-campus job opportunities are excellent.

FROM THE ADMISSIONS OFFICE

"The College of Charleston is a student-centered public liberal arts and sciences university located on South Carolina's coast. The oldest institution of higher learning in the state, the college offers an exceptional undergraduate experience—one that emphasizes intellectual growth through a combination of challenging coursework, study abroad, and cocurricular activities, such as service-learning programs and internships. Due to the college's small class sizes, students work closely with nationally recognized faculty and also have the opportunity to collaborate with them on faculty-student research projects—an experience usually reserved only for graduate students at other universities.

"The college stresses student involvement as an integral part of the educational experience. Students are encouraged to attend the many events on campus—from dramatic performances to thought-provoking guest lectures—and to take part in the diverse student organizations, volunteer groups, and academic clubs. Music, art, and culture thrive both within the confines of campus and throughout the greater Charleston community. Students can also participate in outdoor sports year round as well as enjoy the excitement of NCAA Division I athletics.

"The college provides traditional residence hall living and a variety of residential learning communities that bring students who wish to focus on specialized themes (such as leadership, wellness, or language immersion).

"Students receive valuable preparation for further academic study or entry into the professional world. The college furnishes a creative and intellectually stimulating environment led by a committed and caring faculty within a superb setting and at an incredible value.

"Freshman applicants for fall 2006 and thereafter are required to submit scores of the Writing section of the SAT or the ACT. Applicants may also submit scores from the old versions of both tests, and their best scores (old/new) will be used in making admissions decisions."

SELECTIVITY

Admissions Rating	**88**
# of applicants	8,076
% of applicants accepted	65
% of acceptees attending	37
# accepting a place on wait list	355
% admitted from wait list	20

FRESHMAN PROFILE

Range SAT Verbal	570-640
Average SAT Verbal	607
Range SAT Math	570-640
Average SAT Math	601
**TPR Projected Range SAT Writing*	*610-660*
Range ACT Composite	22-25
Average ACT Composite	24
Minimum Paper TOEFL	550
Minimum Computer Based TOEFL	213
Average HS GPA	3.78
% graduated top 10% of class	30
% graduated top 25% of class	65
% graduated top 50% of class	93

DEADLINES

Regular application deadline	4/1
Regular notification	rolling
Nonfall registration?	yes

APPLICANTS ALSO LOOK AT

AND OFTEN PREFER
University of Georgia
University of North Carolina—Chapel Hill

AND SOMETIMES PREFER
Clemson University
Furman University
James Madison University
University of South Carolina—Columbia

AND RARELY PREFER
Appalachian State University
Coastal Carolina University
Winthrop University,
Wofford College

FINANCIAL FACTS

Financial Aid Rating	**71**
Annual in-state tuition	$6,202
Annual out-of-state tuition	$14,140
Room & Board	$6,506
Books and supplies	$910
% frosh rec. need-based scholarship or grant aid	26
% UG rec. need-based scholarship or grant aid	24
% frosh rec. need-based self-help aid	26
% UG rec. need-based self-help aid	33
% frosh rec. any financial aid	51
% UG rec. any financial aid	50
Avg. frosh grant	$3,190
Avg. frosh loan	$2,315
Independent 529 member?	No

College of the Holy Cross

Admissions Office, 1 College Street, Worcester, MA 01610-2395 • Admissions: 508-793-2443 • Fax: 508-793-3888

CAMPUS LIFE

Quality of Life Rating	**65**
Fire Safety Rating	**60**
Type of school	private
Affiliation	Roman Catholic
Environment	city

STUDENTS

Total undergrad enrollment	2,718
% male/female	46/54
% from out of state	64
% from public high school	52
% live on campus	88
% African American	3
% Asian	5
% Caucasian	77
% Hispanic	5
% international	2
# of countries represented	18

SURVEY SAYS

Small classes
Frats and sororities are unpopular or nonexistent
Lots of beer drinking
Hard liquor is popular

ACADEMICS

Academic Rating	**89**
Calendar	semester
Student/faculty ratio	11:1
Professors interesting rating	85
Professors accessible rating	86
% professors teaching UG courses	100
% classes taught by TAs	0
Most common lab size	fewer than 10 students
Most common regular class size	10-19 students

MOST POPULAR MAJORS

Economics
English language and literature
psychology

STUDENTS SPEAK OUT

Academics

"Academics are very difficult, but very worth the effort" at College of the Holy Cross (HC), a small liberal arts school with "a total sense of community—almost family—just like the admissions propaganda claims." Professors pile on so much work that the school allows students to take only four classes per semester. Even with this limit, "the work is by all means tough. There's a lot of studying, but it really pays off in the real world." The grading system is equally demanding. Fortunately, HC's stringent standards are well known to the outside world. "A hiring manager from one of the big accounting firms told me the company considers a 3.0 at Holy Cross [equal to] a 3.5 at other schools," explained one student. Students gripe, but they appreciate the results. Wrote one, "I may hate actually being at school, but having Holy Cross on my resume has gotten me a great summer internship, is allowing me to intern in DC for the spring semester, and will even indirectly lead into being accepted [by] a reputable law school." They also appreciate the "close personal attention you can receive from professors. I have never had a problem getting extra help from a professor on papers or assignments." This is due in part to the "exclusively undergraduate environment. There are no grad students teaching the classes, and the 'good' professors are also available to everyone, not just upper-level or graduate students." "Active alumni support" further sweetens the deal.

Life

At HC, "everyone works their butt off, but also needs to let off steam. It's a really hard school with very high expectations. The stress can be too much at times." Students "work like mad Sunday through Wednesday" and then start letting off that steam on Thursday, usually at a kegger ("HC is a keg school," students tell us). Alternatives are few. "While the student programming people may put on events that try to bring students together, these events rarely draw many (Spring Weekend and the Opportunity Knocks dance are the exceptions)." Hometown Worcester "does not offer a lot despite the high number of colleges in the area. The city is also not very fond of college students." Nonetheless, a few intrepid souls venture out into the city and report that "dining in Worcester is amazing—many great restaurants. There are usually many choices of things to do here between film series, music performances, theatre, and varsity sports." They warn those who'd follow in their footsteps not to reveal their status as HC students. Undergrads praise their "absolutely gorgeous" campus but warn that its famous picturesque hill "is a real pain in the ass, especially in winter." Intercollegiate athletics, "especially men's and women's basketball teams, are hugely popular," as are intramurals. When escape is essential, students head to Boston or Providence.

Student Body

"There are no surprises" in the Holy Cross student body. "It is a small, private, liberal arts college with a Jesuit identity in New England. Therefore, the population is mostly white, middle class, Irish or Italian Catholics." As one student puts it, "A certain type of person, I believe, looks at Holy Cross. This type of person wants a small school in a suburb, with preppy students, small classes, and religion. I am not sure why minorities don't choose Holy Cross; I believe it is because this school just isn't what they want. It is nobody's fault." HC has made some inroads into minority populations through its outreach programs, students here report. The typical HC undergrad is "friendly, outgoing" and conservative. "Religion is big, sports are bigger, and drinking is the biggest." Students like that fact that HC "is a small community, which is nice because you can generally say 'Hi' to anyone and you know them."

FINANCIAL AID: 508-793-2265 • E-MAIL: ADMISSIONS@HOLYCROSS.EDU • WEBSITE: WWW.HOLYCROSS.EDU

ADMISSIONS

Very important factors considered include: Class rank, secondary school record, standardized test scores. *Important factors considered include:* Alumni/ae relation, character/personal qualities, essays, extracurricular activities, interview, recommendations. *Other factors considered include:* Geographical residence, minority status, talent/ability, volunteer work, work experience. SAT Reasoning and SAT Subject Tests or ACT required. TOEFL required of all international applicants. High school diploma is required, and GED is accepted. *Academic units recommended:* 4 English, 4 math, 4 science, 3 foreign language, 2 social studies, 2 history, 1 academic elective.

The Inside Word

The applicant pool at Holy Cross is strong; students are well advised to take the most challenging courses available to them in secondary school. Everyone faces fairly close scrutiny, but as is the case virtually everywhere, the College does have its particular interests. The admissions committee takes good care of candidates from the many Catholic high schools that are the source of dozens of solid applicants each year.

FINANCIAL AID

Students should submit: FAFSA, CSS/Financial Aid PROFILE, noncustodial (divorced/separated) parents' statement, business/farm supplement, parent and student federal tax returns. Regular filing deadline is 2/1. The Princeton Review suggests that all financial aid forms be submitted as soon as possible after 1/1. *Need-based scholarships/grants offered:* Pell, SEOG, state scholarships/grants, private scholarships, the school's own gift aid. *Loan aid offered:* FFEL Subsidized Stafford, FFEL Unsubsidized Stafford, FFEL PLUS, Federal Perkins, MDFA. Applicants will be notified of awards on or about 4/1.

FROM THE ADMISSIONS OFFICE

"When applying to Holy Cross, two areas deserve particular attention. First, the essay should be developed thoughtfully, with correct language and syntax in mind. That essay reflects for the Board of Admissions how you think and how you can express yourself. Second, activity beyond the classroom should be clearly defined. Since Holy Cross [only has] 2,800 students, the chance for involvement/participation is exceptional. The Board reviews many applications for academically qualified students. A key difference in being accepted is the extent to which a candidate participates in-depth beyond the classroom—don't be modest; define who you are.

"Beginning fall 2006, standardized test scores (i.e., SAT, SAT Subject Tests, and ACT) will be optional. Students may submit their scores if they believe the results paint a fuller picture of their achievements and potential, but those who don't submit scores will not be at a disadvantage in admissions decisions."

SELECTIVITY

Admissions Rating	**94**
# of applicants	4,969
% of applicants accepted	44
% of acceptees attending	32
# accepting a place on wait list	1,045
% admitted from wait list	9
# of early decision applicants	249
% accepted early decision	69

FRESHMAN PROFILE

Range SAT Verbal	580-670
Average SAT Verbal	631
Range SAT Math	580-680
Average SAT Math	629
**TPR Projected Range SAT Writing*	*620-680*
Minimum Paper TOEFL	550
Minimum Computer Based TOEFL	213
% graduated top 10% of class	60
% graduated top 25% of class	91
% graduated top 50% of class	99

DEADLINES

Early decision application deadline	12/15
Early decision notification	1/15
Regular application deadline	1/15
Regular notification	4/1
Nonfall registration?	yes

APPLICANTS ALSO LOOK AT AND OFTEN PREFER

Boston College
Brown University
Dartmouth College
Georgetown University
Tufts University
University of Notre Dame

AND SOMETIMES PREFER

Fairfield University
Loyola College in Maryland
Providence College
Villanova University

FINANCIAL FACTS

Financial Aid Rating	**93**
Annual tuition	$30,960
Room & Board	$9,220
Books and supplies	$700
Required fees	$484
% frosh rec. need-based scholarship or grant aid	41
% UG rec. need-based scholarship or grant aid	40
% frosh rec. need-based self-help aid	38
% UG rec. need-based self-help aid	39
% frosh rec. any financial aid	56
% UG rec. any financial aid	56
Avg. frosh grant	$16,424
Avg. frosh loan	$4,980
Independent 529 member?	No

THE COLLEGE OF NEW JERSEY

PO Box 7718, Ewing, NJ 08628-0718 • Admissions: 609-771-2131 • Fax: 609-637-5174

CAMPUS LIFE

Quality of Life Rating	**85**
Fire Safety Rating	**82**
Type of school	public
Environment	village

STUDENTS

Total undergrad enrollment	5,840
% male/female	41/59
% from out of state	5
% from public high school	85
% live on campus	65
% in (# of) fraternities	3 (8)
% in (# of) sororities	6 (7)
% African American	6
% Asian	5
% Caucasian	78
% Hispanic	7

SURVEY SAYS

Small classes
Lab facilities are great
Students are friendly
Campus feels safe
Students are happy
Lots of beer drinking

ACADEMICS

Academic Rating	**86**
Calendar	semester
Student/faculty ratio	13:1
Professors interesting rating	85
Professors accessible rating	86
% professors teaching UG courses	95
% classes taught by TAs	0
Most common lab size	20-29 students
Most common regular class size	10-19 students

MOST POPULAR MAJORS

Elementary education and teaching
English language and literature

STUDENTS SPEAK OUT

Academics

For "a price-is-right education with good professors, small class sizes, and extracurricular activities," many are turning to The College of New Jersey (TCN), a state liberal arts school "with a lot of potential" that "is just now really starting to expand." While still developing—one manifestation of which is the nonstop construction on campus—the school is already well on its way to "giving the typical college life that one has always dreamed about." All the key elements of a great education are here. Classes are "small enough for close attention by professors in class, large enough to constantly meet new people." The school offers "wonderful resources, if you are aware of them. For example, TCNJ has a lot of academic and job placement services that are there, just never utilized by the students." Most important, TCNJ is home to "a lot of smart students" and a faculty who, "on the whole, are available for guidance and help outside of class." Academics are demanding but satisfying here; as one student reported, "I have found that many of my classes have been a lot of work, but that I have come out of them with more knowledge than I would have expected." Students report that "the administration is surprisingly open-minded and constantly exploring new directions for the institution," but warn that day-to-day administrative tasks "often seem very unorganized. You may be sent to a few different departments for the answer to one question."

Life

While the weekend social scene at TCNJ has come a long way, the biggest party night here, surprisingly, is Tuesday, "because many people don't have any classes on Wednesday until late in the day (12:30–5:00 is reserved for club meetings, and also sometimes lecturers and things of that nature)." Not everyone is hungover on Wednesday morning, however. One student asserts, "plenty of people, myself included, don't drink, and there's plenty for us to do. A lot of people DO go home on weekends, but I have no idea why. It's not like there's anything better to do at home, besides take a shower without shower shoes." Sporting events occasionally mobilize the campus, with the annual football game against archrival Rowan the unquestioned highlight of the athletic schedule. "Tailgating for the Rowan game is a must for any fan of football or beer," reports one sports enthusiast. "I know it's not Penn State or anything like that, but it's still a great time." TCNJ's campus is "beautiful, except for the persistent construction." Hometown Ewing, on the other hand, is "lame. It requires some effort to find stuff to do off campus." One suggestion for spicing things up here: "TCNJ should also promote more interaction with other schools such as Rider, which is five miles away, yet I do not know one student from there."

Student Body

The undergrads of TCNJ are "very hardworking and dedicated to academics," but also know how to "maintain a balance between schoolwork and social life." They are an active bunch; explains one undergrad, "Most TCNJ students were involved in high school in something, often a high school sport. So, while the average TCNJ student had a good GPA and SAT score, she was also involved in extracurricular activities." Upon arriving at TCNJ, this student "becomes affiliated with some organization, whether a sorority or fraternity or a student group like government. This student likely wears Abercrombie & Fitch/American Eagle/Gap/Express clothing, [and] is Caucasian and Catholic with a middle- to upper-middle-class background and permanent residence in New Jersey." While the college is "trying to bring kids in from other states and add to the diversity," currently "diversity among the student population is not as great as I think the college would like to brag it is."

FINANCIAL AID: 609-771-2211 • E-MAIL: ADMISS@VM.TCNJ.EDU • WEBSITE: WWW.TCNJ.EDU

ADMISSIONS

Very important factors considered include: Character/personal qualities, class rank, secondary school record, standardized test scores, talent/ability. *Important factors considered include:* Essays, extracurricular activities, recommendations, volunteer work. *Other factors considered include:* Alumni/ae relation, geographical residence, interview, minority status, state residency, work experience. SAT Reasoning and SAT Subject Tests or ACT required. TOEFL required of all international applicants. High school diploma is required, and GED is accepted. *Academic units required:* 4 English, 2 math, 2 science (2 science lab), 2 foreign language, 2 social studies.

The Inside Word

New-found visibility has given a boost to the applicant pool at The College of New Jersey, but selectivity remains at about the level it has been for the past few years. Since the pool is somewhat better than in prior years, this still translates into a stronger entering class.

FINANCIAL AID

Students should submit: FAFSA. Regular filing deadline is 10/1. The Princeton Review suggests that all financial aid forms be submitted as soon as possible after 1/1. *Need-based scholarships/grants offered:* Pell, SEOG, state scholarships/grants, private scholarships, the school's own gift aid, Federal Nursing scholarships. *Loan aid offered:* Direct Subsidized Stafford, Direct Unsubsidized Stafford, Direct PLUS, FFEL Subsidized Stafford, FFEL Unsubsidized Stafford, FFEL PLUS, Federal Perkins, Federal Nursing, state loans. Applicants will be notified of awards on a rolling basis beginning on or about 7/15.

FROM THE ADMISSIONS OFFICE

"The College of New Jersey is one of the United States' great higher education success stories. With a long history as New Jersey's pre-eminent teacher of teachers, the college has grown in to a new role as educator of the state's best students in a wide range of fields. The College of New Jersey has created a culture of constant questioning—a place where knowledge is not merely received but reconfigured. In small classes, students and faculty members collaborate in a rewarding process: As they seek to understand fundamental principles, apply key concepts, reveal new problems, and pursue new lines of inquiry, students gain a fluency of thought in their disciplines. The college's 289-acre tree-lined campus is a union of vision, engineering, beauty, and functionality. Neoclassical Georgian Colonial architecture, meticulous landscaping, and thoughtful design merge in a dynamic system, constantly evolving to meet the needs of TCNJ students. About 50 percent of TCNJ's 2004 entering class will be academic scholars, with large numbers of National Merit finalists and semifinalists. More than 400 students in the class received awards from New Jersey's Outstanding Student Recruitment Program. The College of New Jersey is bringing together the best ideas from around the nation and building a new model for public undergraduate education on one campus . . . in New Jersey!

"The College of New Jersey will accept both the new and old SAT (administered prior to March 2005 and without a Writing component), as well as the ACT with or without the Writing component."

SELECTIVITY

Admissions Rating	**92**
# of applicants	6,485
% of applicants accepted	48
% of acceptees attending	40
# accepting a place on wait list	466
% admitted from wait list	17
# of early decision applicants	225
% accepted early decision	43

FRESHMAN PROFILE

Range SAT Verbal	575-670
Average SAT Verbal	622
Range SAT Math	595-690
Average SAT Math	639
**TPR Projected Range SAT Writing*	*620-680*
Minimum Paper TOEFL	550
Minimum Computer Based TOEFL	215
% graduated top 10% of class	64
% graduated top 25% of class	91
% graduated top 50% of class	100

DEADLINES

Early decision application deadline	11/15
Early decision notification	12/15
Regular application deadline	2/15
Regular notification	rolling
Nonfall registration?	yes

APPLICANTS ALSO LOOK AT AND OFTEN PREFER

Boston College, Boston U., N.Y.U., Penn State University Park, Rutgers U.—Rutgers College, Villanova U.

AND SOMETIMES PREFER

Bucknell U., Drexel U., Gettysburg College, Lafayette College, Lehigh U., Montclair State U., Rowan U., U. of Delaware, U. of Maryland—College Park

AND RARELY PREFER

College of William and Mary, Fordham U., Loyola College in Maryland, New Jersey Institute of Technology, SUNY at Binghamton, Syracuse U., U. of Richmond

FINANCIAL FACTS

Financial Aid Rating	**76**
Annual tuition	$14,059
Room & Board	$8,093
% frosh rec. need-based scholarship or grant aid	23
% UG rec. need-based scholarship or grant aid	21
% frosh rec. need-based self-help aid	29
% UG rec. need-based self-help aid	33
Avg. frosh grant	$3,500
Avg. frosh loan	$3,000
Independent 529 member?	No

College of the Ozarks

Office of Admissions, Point Lookout, MO 65726 • Admissions: 417-334-6411 • Fax: 417-335-2618

CAMPUS LIFE

Quality of Life Rating	**88**
Fire Safety Rating	**82**
Type of school	private
Affiliation	Presbyterian
Environment	rural

STUDENTS

Total undergrad enrollment	1,346
% male/female	45/55
% from out of state	33
% from public high school	85
% live on campus	84
% African American	1
% Asian	1
% Caucasian	94
% Hispanic	1
% Native American	1
% international	2
# of countries represented	16

SURVEY SAYS

Small classes
Students are friendly
Campus feels safe
Frats and sororities are unpopular or nonexistent
Very little drug use

ACADEMICS

Academic Rating	**81**
Calendar	semester
Student/faculty ratio	16:1
Professors interesting rating	82
Professors accessible rating	82
% professors teaching UG courses	100
% classes taught by TAs	0
Most common lab size	10-19 students
Most common regular class size	20-29 students

MOST POPULAR MAJORS

Agricultural business and management
business/managerial economics
communications, journalism, and related fields

STUDENTS SPEAK OUT

Academics

Offering a tuition-free education in exchange for weekly work-study hours, College of the Ozarks provides "an education for students who would not normally be able to afford it." A heavy emphasis on Christian values—both inside and outside of the academic halls—also makes this an ideal spot "for students who wish to earn their degree while growing closer to God." All of this adds up to a very personal education; "It's really like one big family," writes one undergraduate. Professors are praised for their willingness "to help the students in whatever way possible. They are very involved in the students' lives." In fact, at College of the Ozarks, the "administration and a few of the professors, live on campus, which allows us to go to them no matter what we may need," notes a freshman. Like the professors, the higher-ups in the administration are easily accessible. "They are not in their offices all day," a junior tells us. "They are out walking the campus and visiting with students." Even though they're talking to students, however, some undergrads wonder if they're listening. Responding to very strict campus regulations and having to live within a number of buildings (including dorms) that are in ill-repair, students complain that the "administration shows a complete lack of perspective on the students' needs, conditions, and desires."

Life

What did you expect? "Life is crazy busy at C of O." "We are required to work 15 hours a week on campus aside from our class hours," writes a sophomore. Students tell us that the work-for-tuition program "is a neat experience." They move up the job-rung hierarchy, starting in the cafeteria or bookstore, and progressively moving to sought-after positions in aviation or computers. Because students still need to cover the costs of books, room and board and other expenses, many find "off-campus work" to be a positive step toward a "debt-free" graduation. The campus offers a range of extracurricular activities, such as "bowling, movie night, dances, coffee houses, and things of that nature." In addition, a variety of "different Bible studies" pepper the campus, each drawing "high attendance on average." Things you won't find in Point Lookout include "parties or big dorm functions." In fact, due to the list of campus rules, life at C of O is rather tame. What exactly are those rules? A "zero tolerance policy for drugs and alcohol," restricted dorm visits by members of the opposite sex and "freshman cars are locked up on weekdays to keep us working instead of partying," to name a few. Also, as a sophomore explains, appearance codes are rigidly enforced: "We aren't really allowed to dress or look outrageous in any way. Guys aren't allowed piercings and girls are only allowed a few in their ears. Guys are required to cut their hair if it reaches their collar. No funky colored hair or hairstyles, either." Some students feel these rules send the message: "Don't express yourself unless you are told how." But most students have no problem with the rules, which they say "help build character."

Student Body

Your average College of the Ozarks undergrad is "someone who is a strong Christian" and "certainly more conservative" than many college students nationwide. It's also true that many of these students come from a "lower socioeconomic background," drawn to the college by the affordable educational opportunity. In general, there's a sense of conformity at C of O, not only in terms of background and religion, but also in terms of looks. "Everyone dresses the same and looks basically the same because of the strict dress and behavioral codes," writes a senior. But on the whole, "it doesn't matter what you look like or what you wear, we'll look at you for who you truly are inside, as a Christian should." And this is what defines a C of O undergrad: "Kind, happy, eager to help. Believe it or not, most of the campus is made up of just good people."

FINANCIAL AID: 417-334-6411 • E-MAIL: ADMISS4@COFO.EDU • WEBSITE: WWW.COFO.EDU

ADMISSIONS

Very important factors considered include: Character/personal qualities, class rank, interview, secondary school record. *Important factors considered include:* Extracurricular activities, recommendations, talent/ability, volunteer work. *Other factors considered include:* Alumni/ae relation, geographical residence, standardized test scores, state residency, work experience. ACT required. TOEFL required of all international applicants. High school diploma is required, and GED is accepted. *Academic units required:* 1 visual and peforming arts. *Academic units recommended:* 4 English, 3 math, 2 science (1 science lab), 2 foreign language, 3 social studies.

The Inside Word

The highly unusual nature of the College of the Ozarks translates directly into its admissions process. Because of the school's very purpose, providing educational opportunities to those with great financial need, one of the main qualifiers for admission is exactly that—demonstrated financial need. Despite not being a household word, Ozarks attracts enough interest to keep its admit rate consistently low from year to year. To be sure, the admissions process is competitive, but it's more important to be a good fit for the college philosophically and financially than it is to be an academic wizard. If you're a hard worker all around, you're just what they're looking for.

FINANCIAL AID

Students should submit: FAFSA. The Princeton Review suggests that all financial aid forms be submitted as soon as possible after 1/1. *Need-based scholarships/grants offered:* Pell, SEOG, state scholarships/grants, private scholarships, the school's own gift aid. Applicants will be notified of awards on or about 7/1. Federal Work-study Program available. Off-campus job opportunities are excellent.

FROM THE ADMISSIONS OFFICE

"College of the Ozarks is unique because of its no-tuition, work-study program, but also because it strives to educate the head, the heart, and the hands. At C of O, there are high expectations of students—the College stresses character development as well as study and work. An education from 'Hard Work U.' offers many opportunities, not the least of which is the chance to graduate debt-free. Life at C of O isn't all hard work and no play, however. There are many opportunities for fun. The nearby resort town of Branson, Missouri, offers ample opportunities for recreation and summer employment, and Table Rock Lake, only a few miles away, is a terrific spot to swim, sun, and relax. Numerous on-campus activities such as Mudfest, Luau Night, dances, and holiday parties give students lots of chances for fun without leaving the college. At 'Hard Work U.,' we work hard, but we know how to have fun, too.

"Applicants for fall 2006 are required to submit scores from the ACT or the new SAT. We will allow students to submit scores from the old (prior to March 2005) version of the SAT (or ACT) as well, and will use the student's best scores from either test. Writing scores are not required."

SELECTIVITY

Admissions Rating	**89**
# of applicants	2,393
% of applicants accepted	13
% of acceptees attending	89
# accepting a place on wait list	270

FRESHMAN PROFILE

Range ACT Composite	20-24
Average ACT Composite	22
Minimum Paper TOEFL	550
Minimum Computer Based TOEFL	213
Average HS GPA	3.6
% graduated top 10% of class	25
% graduated top 25% of class	53
% graduated top 50% of class	85

DEADLINES

Regular application deadline	8/20
Regular notification	rolling
Nonfall registration?	yes

APPLICANTS ALSO LOOK AT AND OFTEN PREFER

Southwest Missouri State University

AND SOMETIMES PREFER

Southwest Baptist University

FINANCIAL FACTS

Financial Aid Rating	**85**
Annual tuition	$0
Room & Board	$3,850
Books and supplies	$800
Required fees	$280
% frosh rec. need-based scholarship or grant aid	82
% UG rec. need-based scholarship or grant aid	89
% frosh rec. need-based self-help aid	73
% UG rec. need-based self-help aid	72
Avg. frosh grant	$12,467
Independent 529 member?	No

College of Saint Benedict/Saint John's University

PO Box 7155, Collegeville, MN 56321-7155 • Admissions: 320-363-2196 • Fax: 320-363-2750

CAMPUS LIFE

Quality of Life Rating	**89**
Fire Safety Rating	**80**
Type of school	private
Affiliation	Roman Catholic
Environment	village

STUDENTS

Total undergrad enrollment	3,828
% male/female	49/51
% from out of state	14
% from public high school	76
% live on campus	80
% African American	1
% Asian	2
% Caucasian	93
% Hispanic	1
% international	3
# of countries represented	39

SURVEY SAYS

Small classes
Great library
Students are friendly

ACADEMICS

Academic Rating	**86**
Calendar	semester
Student/faculty ratio	12:1
Professors interesting rating	86
Professors accessible rating	87
% professors teaching UG courses	100
% classes taught by TAs	0
Most common lab size	10-19 students
Most common regular class size	10-19 students

MOST POPULAR MAJORS

Business administration/management
speech and rhetorical studies

STUDENTS SPEAK OUT

Academics

Coeducation on single-sex campuses is what students get at all-women's College of Saint Benedict (CSB) and all-men's Saint John's University (SJU), two Benedictine schools whose partnership offers students two schools for the price of one. Undergraduates definitely see the benefits of the arrangement. One student explains, "The greatest strength of my school is the relationship between CSB and SJU. The men and women live on different campuses, but everything else is together. Also, we have two of almost everything: libraries, computer labs, eating places, music buildings, field houses, etc." Students enjoy the classic small school experience. They also feel lucky to have professors who "are always free outside the classroom and provide excellent guidance throughout college" and administrators who "are good at taking care of students on an individual basis." The personal touch only gets better as students approach graduation. Reports one student, "There are counselors and academic advisors all over the place, and the career resource center is constantly working to hook us up with alumni and other people through whom we can network. They really want to help you to figure out your future." As do many Catholic schools, CSB/SJU offers "numerous volunteer opportunities on and off campus. We also have many alternative spring break trips where students go and volunteer all across the country and in other countries. There are also a large number of people who study abroad."

Life

The setting of CSB/SJU is a mixed blessing. The school is located "in the middle of beautiful lake and forest country. We get beautiful falls and cold snowy winters. It's great for biking or hiking in the woods." On the downside, the rural setting can be boring to some students: "We are located in the middle of nowhere, so most of our social life revolves around trying to find new things to do while drinking." Although many students express this opinion, others are quick to point out that there are plenty of enjoyable activities, if you are willing to look for them. "There are groups on campus in charge of organizing fun events for you to do that help reduce drinking on campus. We have the Festival of Cultures, which is an event where all the internationals put on a show about their cultures; there is Pinestock, where professional bands come to play on campus; and there are lip-synching contests, which are very well attended." And then, of course, there's Saint John's football, which "gives everyone something to do on fall Saturday afternoons. It's huge." Intramural and club sports are also well supported. St. Cloud, "a decently large city," is only twenty minutes away for students who want to go "shopping, [to] movies, etc.," and Minneapolis is just an hour down the road.

Student Body

"The campus at CSB/SJU," students agree, "is like vanilla ice cream: all white. This really isn't the place to go to immerse yourself in cultural diversity; there simply isn't much." Explains one undergraduate, "We're a private school in central Minnesota; of course we aren't diverse. However, we are open to people from diverse backgrounds." Aside from the majority of "average Abercrombie-clad, middle- to upper-class white kids, the other big 'group' is the outdoorsy people, who like extreme sports and wear Patagonia and Chacos." There's also "a small chunk of the student body from Trinidad and the Bahamas that lend a little diversity." The student body "gets along well. Since classes are small, there is a chance to talk to your classmates, giving the students an opportunity to get to know each other well." One undergraduate says, "The greatest strength of this school is the amazing sense of community among all the students, faculty, staff, and administration." Many students are "concerned about religious and political issues" and are "very politically aware." According to our survey respondents, "students have generally conservative views."

COLLEGE OF SAINT BENEDICT/SAINT JOHN'S UNIVERSITY

FINANCIAL AID: 320-363-3664 • E-MAIL: ADMISSIONS@CSBSJU.EDU • WEBSITE: WWW.CSBSJU.EDU

ADMISSIONS

Very important factors considered include: Class rank, essays, recommendations, secondary school record, standardized test scores. *Important factors considered include:* Alumni/ae relation, character/personal qualities, extracurricular activities, geographical residence, minority status, state residency, talent/ability, volunteer work. *Other factors considered include:* Interview, work experience. SAT Reasoning or ACT required. TOEFL required of all international applicants. High school diploma is required, and GED is accepted. *Academic units recommended:* 4 English, 3 math, 2 science (2 science lab), 2 foreign language, 2 social studies, 4 academic electives.

The Inside Word

Though Saint John's University and the College of Saint Benedict have combined most of their efforts and operations on campus, admission remains distinct. Women must apply to the College of Saint Benedict and men to Saint John's. Since it is a joint admissions office, both are seeking exactly the same qualities in their students; in addition to solid academic records from high school, much attention is paid to the match a student makes with the schools. Candidates can expect their personal side to receive thorough evaluation within the admissions processes here.

FINANCIAL AID

Students should submit: FAFSA, institution's own financial aid form, federal tax and W-2 forms. The Princeton Review suggests that all financial aid forms be submitted as soon as possible after 1/1. *Need-based scholarships/grants offered:* Pell, SEOG, state scholarships/grants, the school's own gift aid. *Loan aid offered:* FFEL Subsidized Stafford, FFEL Unsubsidized Stafford, FFEL PLUS, Federal Perkins, state loans, various private loans. Applicants will be notified of awards on a rolling basis beginning on or about 3/15. Federal Work-study Program available. Institutional employment available. Off-campus job opportunities are good.

FROM THE ADMISSIONS OFFICE

"CSB/SJU believes that a student's hard work in high school deserves recognition—that's why renewable scholarships such as the Regents'/Trustees' (worth $38,000 over four years); the President's (worth from $22,000 to $32,000 over four years); and the Dean's (worth from $12,000 to $20,000 over four years) are awarded competitively based on the student's past academic achievement, college entrance test scores, and demonstrated leadership and service. Diversity Leadership Scholarships (worth up to $20,000 over four years) are awarded to students who have promoted diversity in their leadership and service work. Performing and Fine Arts Scholarships (worth up to $8,000 over four years) are awarded to students who have participated in and excelled in art, music, or theater in high school. Approximately 90 percent of the students currently attending the colleges receive financial assistance; many receive both scholarship and need-based assistance.

"Freshman applicants to CSB and SJU are required to submit scores from the old or new SAT. Students may also choose to submit scores from the ACT (with or without the Writing component) in lieu of the SAT."

SELECTIVITY

Admissions Rating	**84**
# of applicants	2,486
% of applicants accepted	85
% of acceptees attending	47

FRESHMAN PROFILE

Range SAT Verbal	520-640
Average SAT Verbal	584
Range SAT Math	550-660
Average SAT Math	608
**TPR Projected Range SAT Writing*	*570-660*
Range ACT Composite	23-28
Average ACT Composite	25
Minimum Paper TOEFL	500
Minimum Computer Based TOEFL	173
Average HS GPA	3.62
% graduated top 10% of class	29
% graduated top 25% of class	64
% graduated top 50% of class	93

DEADLINES

Regular notification	rolling
Nonfall registration?	yes

APPLICANTS ALSO LOOK AT AND SOMETIMES PREFER

Gustavus Adolphus College
Saint Olaf College
University of Saint Thomas (MN)

AND RARELY PREFER

Saint Cloud State University
University of Minnesota—Twin Cities

FINANCIAL FACTS

Financial Aid Rating	**91**
Annual tuition	$20,335
Room & Board	$5,789
Books and supplies	$700
Required fees	$350
% frosh rec. need-based scholarship or grant aid	66
% UG rec. need-based scholarship or grant aid	57
% frosh rec. need-based self-help aid	56
% UG rec. need-based self-help aid	55
% frosh rec. any financial aid	95
% UG rec. any financial aid	92
Avg. frosh grant	$12,820
Avg. frosh loan	$5,599
Independent 529 member?	No

COLLEGE OF WILLIAM AND MARY

PO BOX 8795, WILLIAMSBURG, VA 23187-8795 • ADMISSIONS: 757-221-4223 • FAX: 757-221-1242

CAMPUS LIFE

Quality of Life Rating	**84**
Fire Safety Rating	**60**
Type of school	public
Environment	village

STUDENTS

Total undergrad enrollment	5,582
% male/female	45/55
% from out of state	33
% live on campus	75
% in (# of) fraternities	33 (16)
% in (# of) sororities	34 (11)
% African American	6
% Asian	7
% Caucasian	67
% Hispanic	4
% Native American	1
% international	2
# of countries represented	50

SURVEY SAYS

No one cheats
Great library
Students are friendly
Campus feels safe
Students are happy

ACADEMICS

Academic Rating	**89**
Calendar	semester
Student/faculty ratio	11:1
Professors interesting rating	87
Professors accessible rating	84
% professors teaching UG courses	64
% classes taught by TAs	0
Most common regular class size	10-19 students

MOST POPULAR MAJORS

Biological and physical sciences
political science and government
psychology

STUDENTS SPEAK OUT

Academics

"Our history is an incredible strength," observes one William and Mary undergrad, pointing out that "it's pretty powerful to take classes in a building where Jefferson did, or to lounge on the Sunken Gardens where the British Army was once was encamped." More than 300 years after its founding, William and Mary is still "academically one of the best schools in the country, with an incredibly challenging curriculum and workload." Students see the challenge as a plus. "We're not just a degree factory," writes one. "The GPA you leave William and Mary with is one that you can really be proud of, because you earned it, and you had to work to earn it." This public institution "offers a wide selection of majors and courses in both the liberal and fine arts areas" and is "the ideal size.... It's big enough to provide students with plenty of opportunities both academically and socially, but small enough to make you feel like you're part of a community." Students also love that "for a non-research institution, there are a good number of opportunities to conduct research along with professors." They are not so excited, however, about state-mandated budget cuts that "have made it difficult to keep pace with private institutions. Some of our programs are diminishing, and it has really hurt us." Fortunately the cuts haven't yet impacted the fact that "each student here enjoys personal attention in smaller classes, and easily accessible professors in larger classes."

Life

"Traditions and history are the best thing about William and Mary," according to students. "Yule Log, Convocation, King and Queen Dance, and seniors ringing the bell on the Wren Tower are things all students here look forward to." The campus "is yet another strength. It's incredibly beautiful year-round, green and lush, with lots of shady spots for those unable to weather the Billsburg heat and humidity, and plenty of open space for games and a relaxing sunbathing/study session." Undergrads observe that "the Greek scene is huge" and that "the college is making strides to provide more late night entertainment and activities for the crowd that does not go to frat parties." The "level of student involvement is very high, with student-run organizations for everything and anything." Intercollegiate athletics "are good for a school of our size," and "musical groups are popular across campus. Even though the school isn't a conservatory, there is a great emphasis placed on a cappella groups and the choir." All these assets help offset the students' tumultuous relationship with their Williamsburg neighbors; reports one undergrad, "It seems as though the town really dislikes the student population. The town makes a lot of money on tourism, so most of the businesses cater to tourists, not students." In fact, recently passed housing laws and noise-disturbance laws seem "aimed primarily at restricting students' ability to live off-campus, but the Student Assembly is working on getting those repealed." In an effort to appease the town, "A newly-revised, extremely strict alcohol policy was put in place, which results in not much to do as far as parties on weekends."

Student Body

William and Mary undergrads "are all a little quirky and a little dorky in their own way, but because of that, we all fit in." Most students "were at the top of their high school class academically, athletically, and/or socially" and "are very involved in campus activities. There are over 200 clubs and organizations, so although students are involved in different types of clubs, they are all committed to activities outside of the classroom." Many originate from Northern Virginia and the DC area, a wealthy enclave where they grew up "friendly, but sheltered." They arrive ready for work; explains one student, "They're committed to their education: half of them do it for grades, and the other half are motivated because they've got big plans."

FINANCIAL AID: 757-221-2420 • E-MAIL: ADMISS@WM.EDU • WEBSITE: WWW.WM.EDU

ADMISSIONS

Very important factors considered include: Secondary school record, state residency. *Important factors considered include:* Class rank, essays, extracurricular activities, standardized test scores. *Other factors considered include:* Alumni/ae relation, character/personal qualities, geographical residence, minority status, recommendations, talent/ability, volunteer work, work experience. SAT Reasoning or ACT required. TOEFL required of all international applicants. High school diploma or equivalent is not required. *Academic units recommended:* 4 English, 4 math, 4 science (3 science lab), 4 foreign language, 4 social studies.

The Inside Word

The volume of applications at William and Mary is extremely high; thus admission is ultra-competitive. Only very strong students from out of state should apply. The large applicant pool necessitates a rapid-fire candidate evaluation process; each admissions officer reads roughly 100 application folders per day during the peak review season. But this is one admissions committee that moves fast without sacrificing a thorough review. There probably isn't a tougher public college admissions committee in the country.

FINANCIAL AID

Students should submit: FAFSA, CSS/Financial Aid PROFILE. CSS/Financial Aid PROFILE required of early decision applicants only. Regular filing deadline is 3/15. The Princeton Review suggests that all financial aid forms be submitted as soon as possible after 1/1. *Need-based scholarships/grants offered:* Pell, SEOG, state scholarships/grants, private scholarships, the school's own gift aid. *Loan aid offered:* FFEL Subsidized Stafford, FFEL Unsubsidized Stafford, FFEL PLUS, Federal Perkins. Applicants will be notified of awards on a rolling basis beginning on or about 3/10.

FROM THE ADMISSIONS OFFICE

"William and Mary is the second oldest institution of higher learning in the country. Yes, we have the lowest student/faculty ratio (12:1) of any public university. We're also know for what many have called the preeminent undergraduate business program in the U.S., a Model United Nations team that perennially vies for the world championship, and alumni who wrote everything from the revolutionary Declaration of Independence (Thomas Jefferson, Class of 1762) to the hilarious *Naked Pictures of Famous People* (Comedy Central's Jon Stewart, Class of 1984). In short, William and Mary offers a top-rated educational experience at a comparatively low cost and in the company of interesting people from a broad variety of backgrounds. So, if you are an academically strong, involved student looking for a challenge in a great campus community, William and Mary may well be the place for you.

"Applicants for fall 2006 may submit old or new SAT scores, and William and Mary will combine the best scores from all submitted tests. Students may choose to submit ACT scores; the best composite scores will be used provided it is a better score than the highest combined SAT."

SELECTIVITY

Admissions Rating	**97**
# of applicants	9,607
% of applicants accepted	35
% of acceptees attending	40
# accepting a place on wait list	1,265
% admitted from wait list	2

FRESHMAN PROFILE

Range SAT Verbal	630-730
Average SAT Verbal	674
Range SAT Math	620-710
Average SAT Math	661
**TPR Projected Range SAT Writing*	*650-720*
Range ACT Composite	28-31
Average ACT Composite	29
Minimum Paper TOEFL	600
Minimum Computer Based TOEFL	250
Average HS GPA	4
% graduated top 10% of class	80
% graduated top 25% of class	97
% graduated top 50% of class	100

DEADLINES

Early decision application deadline	11/1
Early decision notification	12/1
Regular application deadline	1/1
Regular notification	4/1
Nonfall registration?	yes

APPLICANTS ALSO LOOK AT AND OFTEN PREFER

Duke University
Georgetown University
University of Virginia

AND SOMETIMES PREFER

Brown University
Dartmouth College
Johns Hopkins University
Notre Dame de Namur University
University of North Carolina—Chapel Hill
Vanderbilt University
Washington and Lee University
Yale University

FINANCIAL FACTS

Financial Aid Rating	**72**
Annual in-state tuition	$6,430
Annual out-of-state tuition	$21,216
Room & Board	$5,794
Books and supplies	$825
% frosh rec. need-based scholarship or grant aid	23
% UG rec. need-based scholarship or grant aid	23
% frosh rec. need-based self-help aid	18
% UG rec. need-based self-help aid	21
Avg. frosh grant	$8,626
Avg. frosh loan	$3,202
Independent 529 member?	No

THE COLLEGE OF WOOSTER

847 COLLEGE AVENUE, WOOSTER, OH 44691 • ADMISSIONS: 330-263-2322 • FAX: 330-263-2621

CAMPUS LIFE

Quality of Life Rating	**79**
Fire Safety Rating	**76**
Type of school	private
Affiliation	Presbyterian
Environment	town

STUDENTS

Total undergrad enrollment	1,776
% male/female	47/53
% from out of state	45
% from public high school	78
% live on campus	99
% in (# of) fraternities	8 (4)
% in (# of) sororities	12 (6)
% African American	5
% Asian	1
% Caucasian	76
% Hispanic	1
% international	7
# of countries represented	37

SURVEY SAYS

Small classes
No one cheats
Lab facilities are great
Great library
Students are friendly
Low cost of living
Lots of beer drinking

ACADEMICS

Academic Rating	**87**
Calendar	semester
Student/faculty ratio	12:1
Professors interesting rating	88
Professors accessible rating	87
% professors teaching UG courses	100
% classes taught by TAs	0
Most common lab size	20-29 students
Most common regular class size	10-19 students

MOST POPULAR MAJORS

Communications studies/speech communication and rhetoric
English language and literature
history

STUDENTS SPEAK OUT

Academics

The College of Wooster offers undergraduates "the independence to explore and support to do so" through a demanding but satisfying academic program. Students hit the ground running with a mandatory freshman seminar that focuses on methods of critical inquiry. They don't let up until they finish their Senior Independent Study (IS) project, "a grueling process of writing an 80- to 100-page paper on the topic of one's choice within his [or her] major and working closely with a faculty member on the project." This capstone experience looms large throughout a student's tenure at the college. One student explains, "The IS process is a daunting, scary thing that hangs over your head essentially from the first day you arrive on campus. Yes, it does push you to your academic limit." The amount of independence the college provides requires a strong support network, and fortunately "professors are always available to help you not only with schoolwork, but [also] with personal problems. Most professors are very easy to approach and often befriend the students." It's also comforting to know that "the administration is very open at the school, and I can approach any administrator and discuss any concerns I may have." The school is small, which affords great opportunities to those who seek them. Reports one undergraduate, "I have had great experiences with all my professors! In fact I was able to get involved in research with the head of the department of my major the summer after my freshman year. It was an amazing experience!"

Life

The College of Wooster places heavy academic demands on its students. One student explains, "During the week, most people study hard-core (though a lot of times we'll take study breaks to Wal-Mart or events happening on campus). On the weekend, there is a lot of partying. For those of us who don't party, the college almost always has events planned." The party scene revolves around the Greek houses; students who want other options often go off campus. Writes one student, "At first it seems like Wooster is too small a town for any kind of activity to happen, but soon you learn where to find the fun stuff. You can head over to the corn maze, or the skating rink, or the movie theater, or the public library." On campus, "there's a pub/dance club, and we bring speakers and comedians to campus all the time." Intramurals and intercollegiate sports are a big deal—there is a sizable jock population—and "you'll often see students play Frisbee™ on the quad in the sunshine or go sliding in the mud on a rainy day." Summed up one undergrad, "I think that social life here is pretty typical of any college. Lots of people drink and party on weekends; lots of people don't. Either way, no one cares, and there are lots of other people in the same situation as you."

Student Body

Undergraduates agree that the college's admissions department does a good job of recruiting a "socially diverse" student body. Writes one, "We have many people from poorer or lower- middle-class families (such as myself), and there are individuals from wealthy and even famous families. For a student body of about 2,000, I think this diversity is unmatched." Another student adds, "[There is also] a huge international student population." Students manifest all attitudes and appearances; "there are the religious conservatives, the socialist liberals, the Greeks, the jocks, the preps, the geeks, the hippies . . . but it seems like most people are involved with too many things to fit any one of those labels. The college's academics revolve around independent study, and independence carries over to all aspects of life."

FINANCIAL AID: 800-877-3688 • E-MAIL: ADMISSIONS@WOOSTER.EDU • WEBSITE: WWW.WOOSTER.EDU

ADMISSIONS

Very important factors considered include: Class rank, secondary school record. *Important factors considered include:* Character/personal qualities, essays, recommendations, standardized test scores, talent/ability. *Other factors considered include:* Alumni/ae relation, extracurricular activities, geographical residence, interview, minority status, state residency, volunteer work, work experience. SAT Reasoning or ACT required. TOEFL required of all international applicants. High school diploma is required, and GED is accepted. *Academic units required:* 4 English, 3 math, 3 science, 2 foreign language, 3 social studies, 2 academic electives. *Academic units recommended:* 4 math, 4 science, 3 foreign language, 4 social studies.

The Inside Word

Wooster has a solid academic reputation and holds its own against formidable competition for students with many national-caliber liberal arts colleges. Applicants should not take the admissions process lightly because candidate evaluations are very thorough and personal.

FINANCIAL AID

Students should submit: FAFSA, institution's own financial aid form, CSS/Financial Aid PROFILE. Regular filing deadline is 2/15. The Princeton Review suggests that all financial aid forms be submitted as soon as possible after 1/1. *Need-based scholarships/grants offered:* Pell, SEOG, state scholarships/grants, private scholarships, the school's own gift aid. *Loan aid offered:* Direct Subsidized Stafford, Direct Unsubsidized Stafford, Direct PLUS, Federal Perkins, college/university loans from institutional funds. Applicants will be notified of awards on or about 4/1. Federal Work-study Program available. Off-campus job opportunities are good.

FROM THE ADMISSIONS OFFICE

"At The College of Wooster, our mission is to graduate educated, not merely trained, people; to produce responsible, independent thinkers, rather than specialists in any given field. Our commitment to independence is especially evident in IS, the college's distinctive program in which every senior works one-to-one with a faculty mentor to complete a project in the major. IS comes from 'independent study,' but, in reality, it is an intellectual collaboration of the highest order and permits every student the freedom to pursue something in which he or she is passionately interested. IS is the centerpiece of an innovative curriculum. More than just the project itself, the culture that sustains IS—and, in turn, is sustained by IS—is an extraordinary college culture. The same attitudes of student initiative, openness, flexibility, and individual support enrich every aspect of Wooster's vital residential college life.

"College of Wooster requires freshman applicants to submit scores from the old or new SAT. Students may also choose to submit scores from the ACT (with the Writing component) in lieu of the SAT."

SELECTIVITY

Admissions Rating	**87**
# of applicants	2,523
% of applicants accepted	72
% of acceptees attending	27
# accepting a place on wait list	140
% admitted from wait list	24
# of early decision applicants	54
% accepted early decision	87

FRESHMAN PROFILE

Range SAT Verbal	540-670
Average SAT Verbal	606
Range SAT Math	550-660
Average SAT Math	598
**TPR Projected Range SAT Writing*	*590-680*
Range ACT Composite	23-29
Average ACT Composite	26
Minimum Paper TOEFL	550
Minimum Computer Based TOEFL	213
Average HS GPA	3.55
% graduated top 10% of class	30
% graduated top 25% of class	63
% graduated top 50% of class	86

DEADLINES

Early decision application deadline	12/1
Early decision notification	12/15
Regular application deadline	2/15
Regular notification	4/1
Nonfall registration?	yes

APPLICANTS ALSO LOOK AT

AND OFTEN PREFER

Denison University, DePauw University, Saint Olaf College, Skidmore College

AND SOMETIMES PREFER

Beloit College, Kenyon College, Miami University

AND RARELY PREFER

Allegheny College, Dickinson College, Ohio University—Athens

FINANCIAL FACTS

Financial Aid Rating	**95**
Annual tuition	$28,005
Room & Board	$7,060
Books and supplies	$700
Required fees	$225
% frosh rec. need-based scholarship or grant aid	69
% UG rec. need-based scholarship or grant aid	63
% frosh rec. need-based self-help aid	54
% UG rec. need-based self-help aid	48
% frosh rec. any financial aid	97
% UG rec. any financial aid	96
Avg. frosh grant	$14,906
Avg. frosh loan	$4,245
Independent 529 member?	Yes

Colorado College

14 East Cache la Poudre Street, Colorado Springs, CO 80903 • Admissions: 719-389-6344 • Fax: 719-389-6816

CAMPUS LIFE

Quality of Life Rating	**77**
Fire Safety Rating	**60**
Type of school	private
Environment	metropolis

STUDENTS

Total undergrad enrollment	2,011
% male/female	47/53
% from out of state	71
% from public high school	58
% live on campus	86
% in (# of) fraternities	11 (3)
% in (# of) sororities	16 (3)
% African American	2
% Asian	4
% Caucasian	79
% Hispanic	7
% Native American	1
% international	2
# of countries represented	26

SURVEY SAYS

Small classes
Students are friendly
Students are happy
Intramural sports are popular
Lots of beer drinking
Hard liquor is popular

ACADEMICS

Academic Rating	**81**
Calendar	other
Student/faculty ratio	10:1
Professors interesting rating	90
Professors accessible rating	89
% professors teaching UG courses	100
% classes taught by TAs	0

MOST POPULAR MAJORS

Biology/biological sciences
economics
English language and literature

STUDENTS SPEAK OUT

Academics

The Block Plan stands as the hallmark of a Colorado College (CC) education. Students take just one course at a time in three-and-a-half-week blocks, allowing them to be "completely focused on one subject" to the point where many people are "living, breathing, and dreaming about their classes." The small class sizes facilitate discussion, and "if there's a raging debate going on, no one has another class they have to go to, so we can just continue." A content biology major writes, "The block plan allows classes to be as lab intensive as they want (a VERY good thing). I'm doing research now and can devote my time and energy to that without being distracted by tests, papers, and obligations from other courses." Instructors put as much into classes as students do. "Professors have a lot of time to spend with you if you have problems or need academic advice," report most undergrads. Students appreciate that "we call our professors by their first names and use their home phone numbers." From the mixed student comments on the administration, it's tough to discern if they are "extremely accessible and willing to listen to student interests" or "entirely separate from the student body." Most people agree, however, that the "new president, though a former politician, cuts through the bureaucratic red tape and administrative obstacles and is an incredibly cool guy."

Life

Aside from the academics, Colorado College's paradisiacal setting draws students primed to fill their nonclass hours with "mountain biking, rock climbing, skiing, hiking, and general outdoorsings (a term coined here at CC)." Though Colorado Springs sits more than two hours from the actual slopes, most students spend winter weekends and block breaks frolicking in fresh Rocky Mountain powder. When night falls, parkas are stashed and students earn their reputation for "partying hard any chance we get." Students have permission to "do pretty much whatever they want, whether that be starting an organization or drinking massive amounts of alcohol." The hockey and women's soccer teams, the only two Division I squads the school fields, enjoy an enthusiastic following, and students participate in a variety of community service activities and on-campus organizations. One student recounts, "One day I decided that I wanted to write for the student newspaper, and the next day they gave me two writing assignments. Where else does that happen?" With so much at their fingertips, CC students express contentment. The few gripes concern the leftist-beatnik–world music bent of student activities: "I wish they'd stop playing their stupid African drums outside my window all the time!"

Student Body

Some would tell you that Colorado College is home to a hefty population of "really smart, athletic hippies" who tend to be "left-wing, artistic social activists with a sense of humor." Others harbor less generous perceptions of their classmates: "Students at CC are generally either yuppies or neo-hippie trustafarians who pretend they aren't yuppies." Lest the population seem homogenous, surveys aver the existence of "a lot of atypical students, myself included, who only enhance the College." Though "very few minorities" attend CC, "people come from all different parts of the country and the world to form an amazing mixture of cultures, beliefs, and ideas." One student relates a heartwarming example: "I love being able to see a 'Goth' and a 'hippie' both play next to each other on an IM hockey team, and have the captain of the soccer team listen to some girl freestyle on her guitar." The school's "large lesbian and gay community" is reportedly "supported by the rest of the school." In the end, this eccentric crew falls under the collective umbrella of "intense people, people who want to do everything at full volume, from academics to sports to outdoor activities to political and social pursuits."

ADMISSIONS

Very important factors considered include: Class rank, essays, secondary school record, talent/ability. *Important factors considered include:* Character/personal qualities, extracurricular activities, recommendations, standardized test scores. *Other factors considered include:* Alumni/ae relation, interview, minority status, volunteer work, work experience. SAT Reasoning or ACT required. TOEFL required of all international applicants. High school diploma or equivalent is not required.

The Inside Word

Colorado College seeks thinkers with strong personalities. This makes for an admissions process that gives more credit to the match a candidate makes than simply to good numbers. As the volume of applications has swelled in recent years, CC has become increasingly selective.

FINANCIAL AID

Students should submit: FAFSA, CSS/Financial Aid PROFILE, noncustodial (divorced/separated) parents' statement. Regular filing deadline is 2/15. The Princeton Review suggests that all financial aid forms be submitted as soon as possible after 1/1. *Need-based scholarships/grants offered:* Pell, SEOG, state scholarships/grants, private scholarships, the school's own gift aid. *Loan aid offered:* FFEL Subsidized Stafford, FFEL Unsubsidized Stafford, FFEL PLUS, Federal Perkins. Applicants will be notified of awards on or about 3/20. Federal Work-study Program available. Institutional employment available. Off-campus job opportunities are good.

FROM THE ADMISSIONS OFFICE

"Students enter Colorado College for the opportunity to study intensely in small learning communities. Groups of students work closely with one another and faculty in discussion-based classes and hands-on labs. CC encourages a well-rounded education, combining the academic rigor of an honors college with rich programs in athletics, community service, student government, the arts, and more. The college encourages students to push themselves academically, and many continue their studies at the best graduate and professional schools in the nation. CC is a great choice for field study and for international study (CC ranks fourth nationally in the number of students studying abroad). CC also takes advantage of its location, using it's Baca campus in the San Luis Valley and the mountain cabin for a variety of classes. Its location at the base of the Rockies makes CC a great choice for students who enjoy backpacking, hiking, climbing, and skiing.

"Colorado College requires students to submit either the SAT or ACT. Scores are accepted for both with or without Writing component. CC uses the highest subscore on the SAT and the highest ACT composite. SAT Subject Tests are accepted for review, but are not required."

SELECTIVITY

Admissions Rating	**93**
# of applicants	4,172
% of applicants accepted	44
% of acceptees attending	32
# accepting a place on wait list	695

FRESHMAN PROFILE

Range SAT Verbal	600-690
Range SAT Math	610-690
**TPR Projected Range SAT Writing*	*630-690*
Range ACT Composite	25-30
Minimum Paper TOEFL	550
Minimum Computer Based TOEFL	213
% graduated top 10% of class	57
% graduated top 25% of class	77
% graduated top 50% of class	94

DEADLINES

Early decision application deadline	11/15
Early decision notification	12/15
Regular application deadline	1/15
Regular notification	4/1
Nonfall registration?	yes

APPLICANTS ALSO LOOK AT

AND OFTEN PREFER
Carleton College
Dartmouth College
Middlebury College
Pomona College
Stanford University

AND SOMETIMES PREFER
Colby College
Grinnell College
Macalester College

AND RARELY PREFER
Bates College
Kenyon College
Lewis & Clark College
University of Colorado—Boulder

FINANCIAL FACTS

Financial Aid Rating	**88**
Annual tuition	$30,048
Room & Board	$7,620
Books and supplies	$870
% frosh rec. need-based scholarship or grant aid	45
% UG rec. need-based scholarship or grant aid	40
% frosh rec. need-based self-help aid	39
% UG rec. need-based self-help aid	38
Avg. frosh grant	$17,550
Avg. frosh loan	$3,035
Independent 529 member?	Yes

COLORADO SCHOOL OF MINES

CSM STUDENT CENTER, 1600 MAPLE STREET, GOLDEN, CO 80401-1842 • ADMISSIONS: 303-273-3220 • FAX: 303-273-3509

CAMPUS LIFE

Quality of Life Rating	**62**
Fire Safety Rating	**60**
Type of school	public
Environment	village

STUDENTS

Total undergrad enrollment	2,667
% male/female	77/23
% from out of state	22
% from public high school	90
% live on campus	30
% in (# of) fraternities	20 (7)
% in (# of) sororities	20 (4)
% African American	1
% Asian	5
% Caucasian	77
% Hispanic	7
% Native American	1
% international	4
# of countries represented	62

SURVEY SAYS

Class discussions are rare
Small classes
Lab facilities are great
Great computer facilities
Lousy food on campus
Campus feels safe
Lots of beer drinking
Hard liquor is popular

ACADEMICS

Academic Rating	**76**
Calendar	semester
Student/faculty ratio	14:1
Professors interesting rating	67
Professors accessible rating	72
% professors teaching UG courses	86
% classes taught by TAs	0
Most common lab size	20-29 students
Most common regular class size	10-19 students

MOST POPULAR MAJORS

Chemical engineering
mathematics
mechanical engineering

STUDENTS SPEAK OUT

Academics

The Colorado School of Mines (CSM) focus on math, science, and engineering means that "you come here to be an engineer and make money. You don't come here to party or meet girls." By all accounts, it's a grueling process; as one undergrad put it, "Especially in the lower-level classes, professors make tests and homework as hard and time-consuming as they can." Students report that "CSM's professors are very knowledgeable in their fields," though they also cite problems with the administration's putting "a huge focus on research at the expense of teaching" and some old-school "teachers that have passed their expiration date." This leaves many undergrads with the impression that CSM "is a research facility with unachievable course work assignments." The administration as a whole receives mixed reviews, with complaints centering around "a lack of communication between different departments."

Life

Just how much of an extracurricular life a Mines student has depends largely on his time-management abilities. Some tell us that "between a full course load, doing homework, and taking an hour or so to mellow out, there is not very much time for anything else." Others tell us that it is possible to have fun here, although it's definitely a challenge. "There is usually a party on the weekends, either at fraternity houses or off-campus," and plenty here have figured out how to "make our own fun. Some examples include snow street luge, sledding on cafeteria trays, and pick-up games of ultimate Frisbee. Because of CSM's location, "Great skiing, backpacking, and mountaineering are in the backyard, not too far from here." Furthermore, "Denver's not too far, either, and it can take as little as 20 minutes to get to clubs." Although "there isn't a whole lot to do in Golden," CSM's hometown, the burg does boast one notable feature: the Coors Brewery, which the engineers here have endearingly dubbed "Coors Lab." Reports one student, "Coors Lab kicks ass! You can't go wrong with free beer!" Even when they're partying, class work is never far from these engineers' thoughts: "It is a rare thing when Mines students gather that some form of schoolwork is not discussed," writes one student.

Student Body

Quintessential Mines students are "very focused on school and obsessed with their grades and academic achievement." Notes one engineer here, "There are lots of valedictorians from high school who have to get a 4.0 or go crazy. No one smiles when walking down the sidewalk." While most are "really willing to work together to learn," they are otherwise "mostly introverts: friendly, but not outgoing." "There are a lot of international students that fit in pretty well" but "not very many ladies." Reports one student, "There is also a strong religious presence at Mines, more than I had expected."

FINANCIAL AID: 303-273-3301 • E-MAIL: ADMIT@MINES.EDU • WEBSITE: WWW.MINES.EDU

ADMISSIONS

Very important factors considered include: Class rank, secondary school record. *Important factors considered include:* Standardized test scores. *Other factors considered include:* Essays, extracurricular activities, interview, recommendations, talent/ability. SAT Reasoning or ACT required. TOEFL required of all international applicants. High school diploma is required, and GED is accepted. *Academic units required:* 4 English, 4 math, 3 science (3 science lab), 2 social studies, 3 academic electives. *Academic units recommended:* 2 foreign language, 2 history.

The Inside Word

Although the admissions process is rigorous and straightforward in its focus on academics, the admissions staff is more personable than at most technically oriented schools. Minorities and women are in demand.

FINANCIAL AID

Students should submit: FAFSA. The Princeton Review suggests that all financial aid forms be submitted as soon as possible after 1/1. *Need-based scholarships/grants offered:* Pell, SEOG, state scholarships/grants, private scholarships, the school's own gift aid. *Loan aid offered:* FFEL Subsidized Stafford, FFEL Unsubsidized Stafford, FFEL PLUS, Federal Perkins. Applicants will be notified of awards on or about 3/15. Federal Work-study Program available. Institutional employment available. Off-campus job opportunities are good.

FROM THE ADMISSIONS OFFICE

"CSM is a school focused on math, science, economics, and engineering. The academic environment is competitive but not cut-throat, and the social environment is informal and friendly. Campus facilities are excellent, with several new facilities having been constructed in the last several years and continued renovation and construction planned for the cafeteria, residence halls, and other Student Life areas in the next two years. The McBride Honors Program in the Humanities and the Study Abroad Program offer motivated students the chance to expand their experience at CSM, and career and graduate school opportunities for graduates have always been good. And of course, CSM's location in Golden, with all that Colorado has to offer, is an added bonus. All in all, CSM offers a combination of size, programs, facilities, and location that's hard to beat.

"Colorado School of Mines will accept—but will not require—scores submitted from the Writing portions of the new SAT or the ACT."

SELECTIVITY

Admissions Rating	**89**
# of applicants	3,049
% of applicants accepted	79
% of acceptees attending	29

FRESHMAN PROFILE

Range SAT Verbal	540-650
Average SAT Verbal	590
Range SAT Math	600-700
Average SAT Math	650
**TPR Projected Range SAT Writing*	*590-670*
Range ACT Composite	25-30
Average ACT Composite	28
Minimum Paper TOEFL	550
Average HS GPA	3.73
% graduated top 10% of class	47
% graduated top 25% of class	86
% graduated top 50% of class	100

DEADLINES

Regular application deadline	6/1
Regular notification	rolling
Nonfall registration?	yes

APPLICANTS ALSO LOOK AT AND OFTEN PREFER

California Institute of Technology
Massachusetts Institute of Technology
Stanford University
Texas A&M University—College Station
The University of Texas—Austin

AND SOMETIMES PREFER

Colorado State University
United States Air Force Academy
University of Colorado—Boulder

AND RARELY PREFER

Colorado College
University of Denver
University of Northern Colorado

FINANCIAL FACTS

Financial Aid Rating	**89**
Annual in-state tuition	$5,700
Annual out-of-state tuition	$19,030
Room & Board	$6,100
Books and supplies	$1,300
Required fees	$733
% frosh rec. need-based scholarship or grant aid	64
% UG rec. need-based scholarship or grant aid	63
% frosh rec. need-based self-help aid	70
% UG rec. need-based self-help aid	70
Avg. frosh grant	$4,500
Avg. frosh loan	$4,300
Independent 529 member?	No

COLORADO STATE UNIVERSITY

SPRUCE HALL, FORT COLLINS, CO 80523 • ADMISSIONS: 970-491-6909 • FAX: 970-491-7799

CAMPUS LIFE

Quality of Life Rating	**86**
Fire Safety Rating	**72**
Type of school	public
Environment	city

STUDENTS

Total undergrad enrollment	21,049
% male/female	49/51
% from out of state	18
% live on campus	23
% in (# of) fraternities	8 (20)
% in (# of) sororities	8 (15)
% African American	2
% Asian	3
% Caucasian	83
% Hispanic	6
% Native American	1
% international	1
# of countries represented	80

SURVEY SAYS

Great computer facilities
Great library
Athletic facilities are great
Students are friendly
Students love Fort Collins, CO
Great off-campus food
Student publications are popular
Lots of beer drinking

ACADEMICS

Academic Rating	**72**
Calendar	semester
Student/faculty ratio	18:1
Professors interesting rating	71
Professors accessible rating	73
% professors teaching UG courses	88
% classes taught by TAs	0
Most common lab size	20-29 students
Most common regular class size	20-29 students

MOST POPULAR MAJORS

Biology/biological sciences
kinesiology and exercise science
psychology

STUDENTS SPEAK OUT

Academics

Studies in engineering, biological and physical sciences, business, and especially veterinary medicine all receive enthusiastic thumbs-ups from the undergraduates of Colorado State University (CSU), a large public school that offers Colorado students myriad educational opportunities at very reasonable prices. Students here describe a typical large, research-oriented university atmosphere—large lecture classes, the occasional professor who clearly does not enjoy teaching undergraduates, TAs who don't speak English fluently—but also tell us that they feel well served by the university and are satisfied with their experiences here. Professors in the business school receive accolades for "the extensive amount of experience held by all." Students in the school's unique interior design program report that professors help guide them through a "prestigious program ending in a tough portfolio review." Students in the sciences laud their school's resources and reputation but warn that despite the 18:1 student/faculty ratio, some classes have "more than 200 students in them." The administration is widely praised; reports a typical undergrad, "For such a huge school, you'd never know it by the administration. They're always willing to work with you and help you out." Those eligible for the honors program should take note that "it's great. You get early registration and small class sizes, which are both big pluses on this campus. The work really is not much harder, and the best teachers teach the honors sections."

Life

Students tell us that "life at CSU is a pretty good collegiate experience. There is just enough partying and studying mixed with gorgeous surroundings to give anyone a taste of college life before having to [deal with] 'real life.'" Most students enjoy the outdoors; indeed, some here selected CSU because it is "located close to the mountains." During the summer, students go camping, whitewater rafting, "rock climbing, biking, kayaking, and fly fishing," and "during the winter we can go skiing." Many undergrads consider CSU a serious party school; reports one, "It is usually party time for the people around the school as soon as weekends start. Going to sleep early is never an option." The Greek community, host to many parties, "is the perfect size: large enough to have presence but small enough to be a tight-knit group. You don't have to be Greek to be cool, but if you're into that, it's a nice option." Students think Fort Collins is "a very safe town with little crime. There are lots of fun things to do here. There are around five clubs, tons of restaurants, outdoor activities, and many sporting events." And students point out, "Even if you can't find something to do here, we're close to Boulder and Denver" and "also within an hour of three other colleges, so you can stay close to old friends."

Student Body

"The students at CSU are generally friendly and courteous," writes one undergrad. "They (we) create an atmosphere that is inviting, energetic, and fun. That is the main reason I came to this university." A lot of kids "live in the surrounding area and go home frequently," and the student body is predominantly white; writes one student, "CSU is about 10 percent minority students [it's actually closer to 12 percent]. Coming from a town that is 48 percent Hispanic, this was very strange for me. I think the administrators are acutely aware of the lack of diversity on campus because they offered quite a few more financial aid packages to minority students." Many students feel that an increase in diversity would improve the CSU educational experience. CSU students, by their own account, are a friendly lot who include among their number "more than a few hippies, a couple of grunge students, and a few holy rollers." Most "actively enjoy outside activities." One undergrad adds, "I don't think it takes new students very long to fit in here."

FINANCIAL AID: 970-491-6321 • E-MAIL: ADMISSIONS@COLOSTATE.EDU • WEBSITE: WWW.COLOSTATE.EDU

ADMISSIONS

Very important factors considered include: Class rank, secondary school record, standardized test scores. *Important factors considered include:* Essays, recommendations. *Other factors considered include:* Alumni/ae relation, character/personal qualities, extracurricular activities, geographical residence, interview, minority status, state residency, talent/ability, volunteer work, work experience. SAT Reasoning or ACT required. TOEFL required of all international applicants. High school diploma is required, and GED is accepted. *Academic units required:* 4 English, 3 math, 2 science, 2 foreign language, 3 social studies. *Academic units recommended:* 4 math, 3 science (1 science lab).

The Inside Word

As with most large state schools, CSU employs a formula to determine a candidate's admission status. The school's Admissions Packet is available online or from the admissions office and can help pinpoint who gets in and who doesn't. The decision is based on GPA and standardized test scores.

FINANCIAL AID

Students should submit: FAFSA. The Princeton Review suggests that all financial aid forms be submitted as soon as possible after 1/1. *Need-based scholarships/grants offered:* Pell, SEOG, state scholarships/grants, private scholarships, the school's own gift aid. *Loan aid offered:* Direct Subsidized Stafford, Direct Unsubsidized Stafford, Direct PLUS, Federal Perkins, college/university loans from institutional funds, alternative loans. Applicants will be notified of awards on a rolling basis beginning on or about 3/1. Federal Work-study Program available. Institutional employment available. Off-campus job opportunities are good.

FROM THE ADMISSIONS OFFICE

"Colorado State University is recognized throughout the world for its excellence in academic programs from the baccalaureate to the post-graduate level. A student-centered research university, Colorado State offers more than 150 undergraduate programs of study within the university's eight colleges. More students come to Colorado State to earn their degrees in science, math, engineering, and technology than to any other school in Colorado. The university emphasizes active learning and provides a variety of opportunities for field experience, laboratory research, professional internships, and study abroad. Students come to Colorado State from all over the United States and 80 countries. The student/faculty ratio is 18:1; 99 percent of regular tenure-track faculty hold doctorate first professional, or other terminal degrees. A warm and welcoming place, the university values and promotes diversity and understands the importance of community in creating an excellent undergraduate learning experience.

"Freshman applicants for fall 2006 can submit ACT or SAT results. Admission and scholarship consideration is based upon the highest composite/combined score from any one test date. The ACT/SAT writing sections and SAT Subject Tests will not be used as part of the admission decision for fall 2006."

SELECTIVITY

Admissions Rating	**80**
# of applicants	11,653
% of applicants accepted	83
% of acceptees attending	42

FRESHMAN PROFILE

Range SAT Verbal	500-600
Average SAT Verbal	553
Range SAT Math	510-610
Average SAT Math	561
**TPR Projected Range SAT Writing*	*560-630*
Range ACT Composite	22-26
Average ACT Composite	24
Minimum Paper TOEFL	525
Minimum Computer Based TOEFL	197
Average HS GPA	3.54
% graduated top 10% of class	22
% graduated top 25% of class	52
% graduated top 50% of class	88

DEADLINES

Regular application deadline	7/1
Regular notification	within 1 to 2 weeks of completed application
Nonfall registration?	yes

APPLICANTS ALSO LOOK AT AND OFTEN PREFER

Arizona State University
Colorado School of Mines
Cornell University
Denver Career College—Colorado Springs
Texas A&M University—Galveston
University of California—Davis
University of Colorado—Colorado Springs

FINANCIAL FACTS

Financial Aid Rating	**81**
Annual in-state tuition	$2,940
Annual out-of-state tuition	$13,527
Room & Board	$5,766
Books and supplies	$900
Required fees	$850
% frosh rec. need-based scholarship or grant aid	28
% UG rec. need-based scholarship or grant aid	28
% frosh rec. need-based self-help aid	25
% UG rec. need-based self-help aid	33
% frosh rec. any financial aid	87
% UG rec. any financial aid	82
Avg. frosh grant	$4,060
Avg. frosh loan	$3,038
Independent 529 member?	No

COLUMBIA UNIVERSITY—COLUMBIA COLLEGE

212 HAMILTON HALL MC 2807, 1130 AMSTERDAM AVENUE, NY, NY 10027 • ADMISSIONS: 212-854-2521 • FAX: 212-894-1209

CAMPUS LIFE

Quality of Life Rating	**92**
Fire Safety Rating	**60**
Type of school	private
Environment	metropolis

STUDENTS

Total undergrad enrollment	4,115
% male/female	50/50
% from out of state	74
% from public high school	49
% live on campus	97
% African American	9
% Asian	12
% Caucasian	51
% Hispanic	8
% international	6
# of countries represented	54

SURVEY SAYS

Great computer facilities
Great library
Diverse student types on campus
Students love New York, NY
Great off-campus food
Campus feels safe
Students are happy

ACADEMICS

Academic Rating	**95**
Calendar	semester
Student/faculty ratio	6:1
Professors interesting rating	79
Professors accessible rating	74
% professors teaching UG courses	100
% classes taught by TAs	0
Most common regular class size	10-19 students

MOST POPULAR MAJORS

English language and literature
history
political science and government

STUDENTS SPEAK OUT

Academics

Columbia University's largest undergraduate school, Columbia College is an "academic powerhouse" that boasts offerings in a staggering array of disciplines, and one of the nation's few core curricula that students actually love. Even so, "how many schools can boast world-class education and location in the greatest city in the world? One: Columbia." Students here warn that "Columbia truly is hands-off. It's sink or swim, and you are the only person who can help yourself. Advising is minimal and the administration is a celebration of red tape." However, "for the independent-minded student, Columbia is the perfect environment." Central to the CU experience is the Core Curriculum, a sequence that immerses students in western philosophy, literature, and the fine arts. Many here will tell you that the Core "changed my life. It's a great feeling to read something junior year for another class and realize that I know where the ideas originated, and how they progressed." Profs here "are all extremely talented," and "accessible and knowledgeable," "but they also make sure that you understand that they are humans too, and not super people." Sums up one undergrad, "You will not have a laid-back, happy-go-lucky type of life at Columbia. Instead of spending your time on sculptured lawns with faculty mapping out the way to go, you will get on a crowded subway, push your way into. Some may think this kind of college experience is terrible. Columbia students are those who think it's the only way to go."

Life

Columbia's campus, a six-block-square urban oasis in the middle of New York's Morningside Heights neighborhood (Harlem is just to the north), includes 36 acres of open, grassy space for sunbathers and ultimate Frisbee™ fanatics. Few students linger long on campus when classes and studying are done, however; instead, they set off to explore the overstuffed metropolis that is their home. "One night on the weekends, you might go to a party with friends, a concert on campus, a Columbia-sponsored event; another night, you might go to a Broadway show, a club downtown, a Yankees game." The city provides access to "so many resources and opportunities off-campus. It's wonderful. I found a great internship this summer and since I am only a subway ride away, I can continue to work part-time during the school year." As one student put it, "In my New York City history class, we (150 students) take a bike ride through New York City, leaving campus at 11:00 P.M and returning at 7A.M. in the morning. In my art history class, we go to the Met; in my music class we go to Lincoln Center. Can you easily do this kind of thing at Yale or Harvard? No, you cannot. Yale has New Haven, Harvard has Boston, and Columbia has New York City. Make your choice."

Student Body

Columbia students are "stalwart NYC fans, and support hasn't flagged since 9/11. Students thrive on the city. They don't fear it." Some are from the Big Apple, while many others have merely adopted its mien; they are "very New York: they are not exceedingly polite, but can be; they mind their own business and don't butt into yours." These "extremely independent" students, according to one undergrad, "love being urbane, tortured intellectuals." Fortunately, "most students are like this and thus get along." Diversity is a bragging point for CU. Some here, however, caution that "in terms of a demographic breakdown, Columbia is diverse, but there is far less interaction than one might expect." Conservatives warn that CU "is downright über-liberal. 'Left-wing' is probably an understatement."

FINANCIAL AID: 212-854-3711 • WEBSITE: WWW.STUDENTAFFAIRS.COLUMBIA.EDU/ADMISSIONS/

ADMISSIONS

Very important factors considered include: Character/personal qualities, class rank, essays, recommendations, secondary school record, standardized test scores. *Important factors considered include:* Extracurricular activities, talent/ability. *Other factors considered include:* Alumni/ae relation, geographical residence, interview, minority status, volunteer work. SAT Reasoning and SAT Subject Tests or ACT required. TOEFL required of all international applicants. High school diploma is required, and GED is accepted. *Academic units recommended:* 4 English, 4 math, 4 science (4 science lab), 4 foreign language, 4 history, 4 academic electives.

The Inside Word

Columbia's application increases continue to outpace the rest of the Ivy League, and as a result the university keeps moving higher up in the Ivy pecking order. Crime is down in New York City, the football team wins (while still in baby-blue uniforms, no less!), and Columbia has become even more appealing. It's less selective than the absolute cream of the Ivy crop, but offers the advantage of being a bit more open and frank in discussing the admissions process with students, parents, and counselors—refreshing amid the typical shrouds of Ivy mystique.

FINANCIAL AID

Students should submit: FAFSA, institution's own financial aid form, CSS/Financial Aid PROFILE, noncustodial (divorced/separated) parents' statement, business/farm supplement, parent and student income tax returns. Regular filing deadline is 2/10. The Princeton Review suggests that all financial aid forms be submitted as soon as possible after 1/1. *Need-based scholarships/grants offered:* Pell, SEOG, state scholarships/grants, private scholarships, the school's own gift aid. *Loan aid offered:* FFEL Subsidized Stafford, FFEL Unsubsidized Stafford, FFEL PLUS, Federal Perkins, alternative loans. Applicants will be notified of awards on or about 4/1. Federal Work-study Program available. Institutional employment available. Off-campus job opportunities are good.

FROM THE ADMISSIONS OFFICE

"Columbia maintains an intimate college campus within one of the world's most vibrant cities. After a long day exploring the bustling streets of the Big Apple, the coziness of home waits within the Columbia gates. Nobel Prize-winning professors will challenge you in class discussions and sit down for a one-on-one afterward. The Core Curriculum attracts intensely free-minded students, eager to explore ideas. The discussions in the classrooms are only the beginning of your education. Like the music that wafts from our concert halls, ideas spill out from the classrooms, filling the lawns and electrifying the air. Friendships formed in the residence halls solidify during a game of Frisbee on South Lawn or over bagels on "The Steps," Columbia's urban beach. From your first day on campus, you will be part of our community.

"Columbia requires freshman applicants for fall 2006 to take the new version of the SAT. Two SAT Subject Tests are required; students are encouraged to take Subject Tests in fields in which they excel. Students may submit the results of the ACT (with the Writing section) in lieu of the SAT and SAT Subject Tests. (For the Fu Foundation School of Engineering and Applied Science, applicants must take any Mathematics test and either physics or chemistry)."

SELECTIVITY

Admissions Rating	**99**
# of applicants	15,006
% of applicants accepted	11
% of acceptees attending	62
# accepting a place on wait list	2,017
% admitted from wait list	2
# of early decision applicants	534
% accepted early decision	32

FRESHMAN PROFILE

Range SAT Verbal	660-760
Average SAT Verbal	706
Range SAT Math	660-760
Average SAT Math	703
**TPR Projected Range SAT Writing*	*670-740*
Range ACT Composite	27-32
Average ACT Composite	33
Minimum Paper TOEFL	600
Minimum Computer Based TOEFL	250
Average HS GPA	3.78
% graduated top 10% of class	85
% graduated top 25% of class	98
% graduated top 50% of class	100

DEADLINES

Early decision application deadline	11/1
Early decision notification	12/15
Regular application deadline	1/2
Regular notification	4/4
Nonfall registration?	no

APPLICANTS ALSO LOOK AT

AND OFTEN PREFER

Brown U., Harvard College, Massachusetts Institute of Technology, Princeton U., Stanford U., U. of Pennsylvania

AND SOMETIMES PREFER

Amherst College, Cornell U., Dartmouth College, Georgetown U.

AND RARELY PREFER

Barnard College, Emory U., Johns Hopkins U., Rice U.

FINANCIAL FACTS

Financial Aid Rating	**92**
Annual tuition	$30,260
Room & Board	$9,066
Required fees	$1,212
% frosh rec. need-based scholarship or grant aid	40
% UG rec. need-based scholarship or grant aid	40
% frosh rec. need-based self-help aid	40
% UG rec. need-based self-help aid	42
% frosh rec. any financial aid	42
% UG rec. any financial aid	41
Avg. frosh grant	$23,900
Avg. frosh loan	$3,282
Independent 529 member?	No

CONNECTICUT COLLEGE

270 MOHEGAN AVENUE, NEW LONDON, CT 06320 • ADMISSIONS: 860-439-2200 • FAX: 860-439-4301

CAMPUS LIFE

Quality of Life Rating	**72**
Fire Safety Rating	**60**
Type of school	private
Environment	town

STUDENTS

Total undergrad enrollment	1,796
% male/female	40/60
% from out of state	76
% from public high school	52
% live on campus	99
% African American	4
% Asian	4
% Caucasian	71
% Hispanic	4
% international	7
# of countries represented	39

SURVEY SAYS

Small classes
Students are friendly
Frats and sororities are unpopular or nonexistent
Lots of beer drinking
Hard liquor is popular

ACADEMICS

Academic Rating	**89**
Calendar	semester
Student/faculty ratio	11:1
Professors interesting rating	86
Professors accessible rating	86
% professors teaching UG courses	100
% classes taught by TAs	0
Most common lab size	10-19 students
Most common regular class size	10-19 students

MOST POPULAR MAJORS

English language and literature
political science and government
psychology

STUDENTS SPEAK OUT

Academics

Students at Connecticut College assert that their professors have "done cool things, and they bring those experiences to the classroom." Instructors are approachable and "truly are concerned with our education," and this dedication is complemented by the deans, "who are excellent, understanding people." The small academic setting affords undergraduates very personal attention. "In one class, the professor, one of the associate Deans of the college, scheduled a meeting with every student in our 100-plus person class to talk about the take home exam." Another student writes, "Some of my professors are now my personal confidants, and I can go to them for my academic or personal needs." This type of nurturing means that "even though I'm not an exceptional student, [I'm able] to do independent research during my freshman year." Top programs include dance, chemistry, biological sciences, religion, and psychology, and many students also laud the well-organized study abroad programs. The career center receives solid praise, particularly for the variety of "internships that focus on community action, international issues, and the environment."

Life

In general, students at "Conn" feel "pretty pampered" in their "playground for trust-fund babies." The weekend social scene centers largely on alcohol, and several students believe "sometimes it's hard to take part in college activities without being a part of the drinking scene." Those who do indulge "look forward to the huge campus-wide parties, like Festivus or Floralia, which are reason alone to come here—think Woodstock but less hippie." The school organizes Thursday Night Events (TNE's) that draw large numbers of freshmen and sophomores. And an organization called MOBROC (Musicians Organized for Band Rights On Campus), which sets up practice space and a performance venue for campus bands, provides another mainstay of nightlife. ("It's a big deal, but almost underground scene. No other East Coast school has an organization like it.") Alternatives to drinking include "playing out on Harkness Green," attending the "very popular a capella concerts," watching the "amazing student theater productions," "cheering for mediocre sports teams," or venturing in to New London, a town that "takes some time to learn to love."

Student Body

The stereotypical Conn student grew up "just outside Boston" (or somewhere else in New England, New Jersery, or New York) "helps to "keep J. Crew in business," "gets Tiffany's for Christmas," and "drives a Volkswagen with a ski rack on top." Even in this land of self-described WASPs, a few deviants manage to survive, including "our fair share of hippies, punks, straight edge, and D and D magic kids." Reportedly, these atypical students "flock together, just like the rest of the minorities on campus." Many students lament the lack of diversity at Conn, crying, "This is not the real world!" Surveys do point out however, that "a great deal is being done on administrative and student levels to deal with issues of diversity on campus." In the meantime, they content themselves with a "substantial international student population." Some people say the student body is "very supportive of students with differing sexual orientations," while others claim "gays and minorities are segregated." In the end, most students agree, "You basically know everyone on campus, at least by association, [which] makes for a very comfortable, caring environment."

FINANCIAL AID: 860-439-2200 • E-MAIL: ADMISSION@CONNCOLL.EDU • WEBSITE: WWW.CONNCOLL.EDU

ADMISSIONS

Very important factors considered include: Character/personal qualities, essays, extracurricular activities, minority status, recommendations, secondary school record. *Important factors considered include:* Alumni/ae relation, class rank, interview, standardized test scores, talent/ability, volunteer work, work experience. *Other factors considered include:* Geographical residence. SAT Subject Tests required. TOEFL required of all international applicants. High school diploma is required, and GED is accepted. *Academic units recommended:* 4 English, 4 math, 4 science (3 science lab), 2 foreign language, 2 social studies, 3 history, 3 academic electives.

The Inside Word

Late in 1994, Connecticut became the most recent college to drop the SAT I as a requirement for admission, citing the overemphasis that the test receives from the media and, in turn, students. The college is judicious about keeping their acceptance rate as low as possible. Candidates undergo a rigorous review of their credentials and should be strong students in order to be competitive. Still, the college's competition for students is formidable.

FINANCIAL AID

Students should submit: FAFSA, CSS/Financial Aid PROFILE, noncustodial (divorced/separated) parents' statement, business/farm supplement, federal tax returns; personal, partnership, federal W-2 forms. Regular filing deadline is 1/15. The Princeton Review suggests that all financial aid forms be submitted as soon as possible after 1/1. *Need-based scholarships/grants offered:* Pell, SEOG, state scholarships/grants, the school's own gift aid. *Loan aid offered:* FFEL Subsidized Stafford, FFEL Unsubsidized Stafford, FFEL PLUS, Federal Perkins, college/university loans from institutional funds. Applicants will be notified of awards on or about 4/1. Federal Work-study Program available. Institutional employment available. Off-campus job opportunities are good.

FROM THE ADMISSIONS OFFICE

"Distinguishing characteristics of the diverse student body at this small, highly selective college are honor and tolerance. Student leadership is pronounced in all aspects of the college's administration from exclusive jurisdiction of the honor code and dorm life to active representation on the president's academic and administrative cabinets. Differences of opinion are respected and celebrated as legitimate avenues to new understanding. Students come to Connecticut College seeking opportunities for independence and initiative and find them in abundance.

"Applicants must submit the results of either two SAT Subject Tests or the ACT. For candidates who choose to submit an ACT score, we will accept either the old or the new version, with or without the optional Writing component. Submission of SAT scores in addition to the required testing is optional."

SELECTIVITY

Admissions Rating	**94**
# of applicants	4,503
% of applicants accepted	34
% of acceptees attending	32
# accepting a place on wait list	973
% admitted from wait list	5
# of early decision applicants	199
% accepted early decision	60

FRESHMAN PROFILE

Range SAT Verbal	620-700
Average SAT Verbal	663
Range SAT Math	630-700
Average SAT Math	665
**TPR Projected Range SAT Writing*	*650-700*
Minimum Paper TOEFL	600
Minimum Computer Based TOEFL	250
% graduated top 10% of class	55
% graduated top 25% of class	79
% graduated top 50% of class	99

DEADLINES

Early decision application deadline	11/15
Early decision notification	12/15
Regular application deadline	1/1
Regular notification	4/1
Nonfall registration?	yes

APPLICANTS ALSO LOOK AT

AND OFTEN PREFER

Bates College
Boston College
Middlebury College
Vassar College
Wesleyan College

AND SOMETIMES PREFER

Bowdoin College
Colby College
Trinity University
Wesleyan University

AND RARELY PREFER

Skidmore College

FINANCIAL FACTS

Financial Aid Rating	**95**
Comprehensive fee	$41,975
Books and supplies	$800
% frosh rec. need-based scholarship or grant aid	38
% UG rec. need-based scholarship or grant aid	42
% frosh rec. need-based self-help aid	37
% UG rec. need-based self-help aid	40
% frosh rec. any financial aid	46
% UG rec. any financial aid	43
Avg. frosh grant	$24,009
Avg. frosh loan	$2,861
Independent 529 member?	No

Cooper Union

30 Cooper Square, New York, NY 10003 • Admissions: 212-353-4120 • Fax: 212-353-4342

CAMPUS LIFE

Quality of Life Rating	**73**
Fire Safety Rating	**60**
Type of school	private
Environment	metropolis

STUDENTS

Total undergrad enrollment	903
% male/female	65/35
% from out of state	41
% from public high school	65
% live on campus	20
% in (# of) fraternities	10 (2)
% in (# of) sororities	5 (1)
% African American	5
% Asian	25
% Caucasian	54
% Hispanic	8
% Native American	1
% international	9

SURVEY SAYS

Small classes
Athletic facilities need improving
Students are friendly
Diverse student types on campus
Students love New York, NY
Great off-campus food

ACADEMICS

Academic Rating	**87**
Calendar	semester
Student/faculty ratio	7:1
Professors interesting rating	62
Professors accessible rating	65
% professors teaching UG courses	100
% classes taught by TAs	0
Most common lab size	10-19 students
Most common regular class size	10-19 students

MOST POPULAR MAJORS

Architecture (BArch, BA/BS, MArch, MA/MS, PhD)
electrical, electronics, and communications engineering
fine arts and art studies

STUDENTS SPEAK OUT

Academics

You'll get a "free education" at Cooper Union—everyone receives a full-tuition scholarship for all four years—"but you have to pay it off with hard labor in the classroom." Cooper's "intense, engaging programs in engineering, art, and architecture" are the only options on the menu here; "while this seems narrow," explains one freshman, it "allows for more focus on those fields. As long as you're interested in one of the majors...you will receive one of the best educations in the country." The professors overall earn kudos for being "intelligent, accessible, [and] excellent," but a number of students complain that there are "too many adjunct professors," who are "underpaid" and teach "straight from the textbook." All professors expect a lot from students—"they can be quite sadistic toward the end of the semester, heaping more work on you than you could possibly handle," warns one electrical engineer—but "you never feel as if any of your effort is in vain." A number of students gripe about getting "mediocre grades" in exchange for "sweat" and "your immortal soul"—but just as many also point out that "you will leave knowing everything in your field about as well as it is possible to know it" and boast that Cooper students benefit from virtually "guaranteed job placement" after graduation. With "lots of work and little time," students learn to share the load: "We all work together to get projects done and to study for exams," explains one student. "I have spent the night before most of my major upper-level exams studying with about half, or more, of my classmates." That team spirit dissipates, though, come registration time, which "involves waiting on line on a cold New York City sidewalk from 2 A.M. to 9 A.M. just to get required classes, let alone electives." Some say that this "physical registration" is a consequence of Cooper's "free tuition," and gripe that "there's no money left" for such conveniences as mailing "bills or grades." That said, time after time we read that Cooper's greatest incentive "is that it's free." In that regard, "Cooper's strength is also its drawback."

Life

"The overall school experience is pretty much academic" at Cooper Union, as "there is not much time to have any fun." That said, "the experience is about who surrounds you in your classes," notes a senior. When students can make free time, they usually like to get away from Cooper. As one puts it, "I associate school with hard work." "The school consists of five buildings in the middle of the East Village," and the surrounding neighborhood is famous for its funky shops, cheap eateries, theaters, bars, and live music venues; conveniently located subways can whisk students just about anywhere in the five boroughs at any time of day. On campus, "The school organizes several events that may seem kind of ridiculous but often prove to be lots of fun, such as ice cream and karaoke night, study break (a lunch party during finals), and Peter Cooper's birthday celebration." Whether on or off campus, "there is always something happening at school where people can eat and interact."

Student Body

"Everyone at Cooper fits into one of three distinct groups: engineers, artists, or architects," undergrads here tell us. "We are very divided by major. For the most part, no one is left out of their respective group, but the groups don't mix well." Observes one student, "The engineering students tend to be the most strange and have all done very well in their high school careers and have very noticeable and unique talents. Art students tend to follow unique trends and are more creative and reclusive. Architecture students can be considered the link between engineering and art students." The average Cooper student is "a tad quirky with a nerdy sense of humor." "You'll find no cheerleader, jock, or regular, whimsical university students. Cooper students tend to all be extremely intelligent, ambitious, and studious individuals"—with an emphasis on individual.

FINANCIAL AID: 212-353-4130 • E-MAIL: ADMISSIONS@COOPER.EDU • WEBSITE: WWW.COOPER.EDU

ADMISSIONS

Very important factors considered include: Secondary school record, standardized test scores, talent/ability. *Important factors considered include:* Essays. *Other factors considered include:* Character/personal qualities, extracurricular activities, recommendations, volunteer work, work experience. SAT Reasoning or ACT required. TOEFL required of all international applicants. High school diploma is required, and GED is accepted. *Academic units required:* 4 English, 1 math, 1 science, 1 social studies, 1 history, 8 academic electives. *Academic units recommended:* 4 English, 4 math, 4 science, 2 foreign language, 4 social studies.

The Inside Word

It is ultra-tough to gain admission to Cooper Union, and will only get tougher. Loads of people apply here, and national publicity and the addition of dorms have brought even more candidates to the pool. Not only do students need to have top academic accomplishments but also they need to be a good fit for Cooper's offbeat milieu.

FINANCIAL AID

Students should submit: FAFSA, CSS/Financial Aid PROFILE, state aid form. Regular filing deadline is 4/15. The Princeton Review suggests that all financial aid forms be submitted as soon as possible after 1/1. *Need-based scholarships/grants offered:* Pell, SEOG, state scholarships/grants, private scholarships, the school's own gift aid. *Loan aid offered:* FFEL Subsidized Stafford, FFEL Unsubsidized Stafford, FFEL PLUS, Federal Perkins, college/university loans from institutional funds. Applicants will be notified of awards on or about 6/1. Federal Work-study Program available. Institutional employment available. Off-campus job opportunities are excellent.

FROM THE ADMISSIONS OFFICE

"Each of the three schools, architecture, art, and engineering, adheres strongly to preparation for its profession and is committed to a problem-solving philosophy of education in a unique, scholarship environment. A rigorous curriculum and group projects reinforce this unique atmosphere in higher education and contribute to a strong sense of community and identity in each school. With McSorley's Ale House and the Joseph Papp Public Theater nearby, Cooper Union remains at the heart of the city's tradition of free speech, enlightenment, and entertainment. Cooper's Great Hall has hosted national leaders, from Abraham Lincoln to Booker T. Washington, from Mark Twain to Samuel Gompers, from Susan B. Anthony to Betty Friedan, and more recently, President Bill Clinton.

"Applicants are permitted to submit the old or new version of the SAT I, but students are encouraged to take the new version. For the new SAT, the scores will be converted to a 1600 point scale by averaging the Reasoning and Writing scores and adding that to the Math score."

SELECTIVITY

Admissions Rating	**98**
# of applicants	2,414
% of applicants accepted	12
% of acceptees attending	70
# accepting a place on wait list	43
% admitted from wait list	23
# of early decision applicants	53
% accepted early decision	21

FRESHMAN PROFILE

Range SAT Verbal	620-700
Average SAT Verbal	680
Range SAT Math	630-750
Average SAT Math	710
**TPR Projected Range* SAT Writing*	*650-700*
Minimum Paper TOEFL	600
Minimum Computer Based TOEFL	250
Average HS GPA	3.6
% graduated top 10% of class	80
% graduated top 25% of class	100
% graduated top 50% of class	100

DEADLINES

Early decision application deadline	12/1
Early decision notification	12/23
Regular application deadline	1/1
Regular notification	4/1
Nonfall registration?	no

APPLICANTS ALSO LOOK AT AND OFTEN PREFER

Columbia University—Columbia College, Cornell University, Massachusetts Institute of Technology, New York University, University of California—Berkeley

AND SOMETIMES PREFER

Carnegie Mellon University, Georgia Institute of Technology, Harvey Mudd College, Rochester Institute of Technology

FINANCIAL FACTS

Financial Aid Rating	**93**
Annual tuition	$27,500
Room & Board	$13,000
Books and supplies	$1,800
Required fees	$1,400
% frosh rec. need-based scholarship or grant aid	32
% UG rec. need-based scholarship or grant aid	33
% frosh rec. need-based self-help aid	28
% UG rec. need-based self-help aid	31
% frosh rec. any financial aid	100
% UG rec. any financial aid	100
Avg. frosh grant	$27,500
Avg. frosh loan	$2,519
Independent 529 member?	No

CORNELL COLLEGE

600 FIRST STREET WEST, MOUNT VERNON, IA 52314-1098 • ADMISSIONS: 319-895-4477 • FAX: 319-895-4451

CAMPUS LIFE

Quality of Life Rating	**87**
Fire Safety Rating	**67**
Type of school	private
Affiliation	Methodist
Environment	rural

STUDENTS

Total undergrad enrollment	1,143
% male/female	43/57
% from out of state	67
% from public high school	92
% live on campus	88
% in (# of) fraternities	30 (7)
% in (# of) sororities	32 (7)
% African American	3
% Asian	1
% Caucasian	86
% Hispanic	3
% international	2
# of countries represented	15

SURVEY SAYS

Small classes
No one cheats
Lots of beer drinking

ACADEMICS

Academic Rating	**88**
Calendar	9 terms, 3.5 weeks long
Student/faculty ratio	11:1
Professors interesting rating	91
Professors accessible rating	97
% professors teaching UG courses	100
% classes taught by TAs	0
Most common regular class size	10-19 students

MOST POPULAR MAJORS

Economics
education
psychology

STUDENTS SPEAK OUT

Academics

Cornell College employs a unique block plan academic calendar called One-Course-At-A-Time (OCAAT), under which "you take one class, and only one class, for 18 days." Students love it, telling us that "If you're in a class you don't like, you only have to tough it out for 18 days. If you're in a class you really enjoy, you can devote all your time and energy to that one class for 18 days." OCAAT also makes it easy "to develop personal relationships with your professors, because there are no more than 25 students in a class and the professor of that class will only be teaching those 25 students during the 18 days of the course." and the intensive focus on a single subject provides for the close interaction with professors who "are more than willing to work individually with students on assignments and to answer questions. It is very obvious that all of the teachers care a lot about their students and genuinely want them to do well in their class. Therefore, they make themselves as available as possible to the students." Reports one student, "The professors make this school what it is. They come to teach, not to do research, although most of them are involved in exciting projects in which they often include students. Most don't hold scheduled office hours because they're there all the time, and they're always there for the students, whether it be to talk about last night's game or the upcoming test." Because Cornell "has been around so long, the college has good relations with the community, which means it's easy to find employment for after school or during the summer."

Life

Much of the fun on and around the Cornell campus is of the low-key variety, students tell us. Cornell's hometown of Mt. Vernon sets the pace; it's "an adorable little town, but without a lot of things to do for college students." There are a few choice destinations in town; writes one student, "The Lincoln Cafe is very popular, so it's sometimes hard to get a seat, but it's very good gourmet food. There is a place to grab an organic sandwich and coffee called Big Creek Market. They sell soups and sandwiches as well as organic groceries. There's also a nice little jewelry shop." On campus, "there are various different activities like sponsored movies, performances, and sledding." There are also "many organizations to support student interests." When students seek higher-energy entertainment, they get in their cars and travel to Iowa City or Cedar Rapids. Reports one student, "Iowa City is great for bars and food. The best sushi I've had is in Iowa City. There are also places like Riverside Theatre and movie theaters, too. There's a huge mall there for shopping and indoor ice skating. Cedar Rapids is good 'cause it's pretty close, and you can always find a decent place to eat." Iowa City is home to the University of Iowa; Cedar Rapids is home to Coe College and Mount Mercy College.

Student Body

"Everybody here at Cornell is very friendly," students report. "Just walking to or from class people will say 'hi' to you or smile at you. Everyone is more than willing to help you out or point you in the right direction." The typical undergrad "is middle-class, white" and from the Midwest; the school is not very diverse." Some here disagree with this conclusion, asserting that "Cornell is diverse, just not culturally. We do have diverse groups, like the jocks, the preps, the frat boys, the sorority girls, the science nerds, and the boarders, and all different types of groups that seem to easily join together, especially in the classroom environment."

FINANCIAL AID: 319-895-4216 • E-MAIL: ADMISSIONS@CORNELLCOLLEGE.EDU • WEBSITE: WWW.CORNELLCOLLEGE.EDU

ADMISSIONS

Very important factors considered include: Essays, recommendations, secondary school record. *Important factors considered include:* Character/personal qualities, class rank, extracurricular activities, standardized test scores, talent/ability, volunteer work. *Other factors considered include:* Alumni/ae relation, geographical residence, interview, minority status, religious affiliation/commitment, state residency, work experience. SAT Reasoning or ACT required. TOEFL required of all international applicants. High school diploma is required, and GED is accepted. *Academic units recommended:* 4 English, 4 math, 3 science (2 science lab), 3 foreign language, 1 social studies, 2 history, 1 academic elective.

The Inside Word

Given Cornell's relatively unique approach to study, it's no surprise that the admissions committee here focuses attention on both academic and personal strengths. Cornell's small, highly self-selected applicant pool is chock-full of students with solid self-awareness, motivation, and discipline. Pay particular attention to offering evidence of challenging academic course work and solid achievement on your high school record. Strong writers can do much for themselves under admissions circumstances such as these.

FINANCIAL AID

Students should submit: FAFSA, institution's own financial aid form, noncustodial (divorced/separated) parents' statement. Regular filing deadline is 3/1. The Princeton Review suggests that all financial aid forms be submitted as soon as possible after 1/1. *Need-based scholarships/grants offered:* Pell, SEOG, state scholarships/grants, private scholarships, the school's own gift aid. *Loan aid offered:* FFEL Subsidized Stafford, FFEL Unsubsidized Stafford, FFEL PLUS, Federal Perkins, college/university loans from institutional funds, McElroy Loan, Sherman Loan, United Methodist loan. Applicants will be notified of awards on a rolling basis beginning on or about 3/1. Federal Work-study Program available. Institutional employment available. Off-campus job opportunities are fair.

FROM THE ADMISSIONS OFFICE

"Very few colleges are truly distinctive like Cornell College. Founded in 1853, Cornell is recognized as one of the nation's finest colleges of the liberal arts and sciences. It is Cornell's combination of special features, however, that distinguishes it. An attractively diverse, caring residential college, Cornell places special emphasis on service and leadership. Foremost, it is a place where theory and practice are brought together in exciting ways through the college's One-Course-at-a-Time academic calendar. Here, students enjoy learning as they immerse themselves in a single subject for a three-and-a-half-week term. They and their professor devote all of their efforts to that course in an engagingly interactive learning environment. This academic system also offers wonderful enrichment experiences through field-based-study, travel abroad, student research, and meaningful internship opportunities. Nine terms are offered each year; 32 course credits are required for graduation with each course equal to four credit hours. Since all classes are on a standard schedule, students are able to pursue their extracurricular interests, whether in the performing arts, athletics, or interest groups, with the same passion with which they pursue their course work. Typically, each year applicants from all 50 states and more than 40 countries apply for admission. Cornell graduates are in demand, with more than two-thirds eventually earning advanced degrees. The college's beautiful hilltop campus is one of only two campuses nationwide listed on the National register of Historic Places. Located in the charming town of Mount Vernon, Cornell is also within commuting distance of Iowa City (home of the University of Iowa) and Cedar Rapids (the second largest city in the state).

"Freshman applicants for fall 2006 must take the new SAT (or the ACT with the Writing component). In addition, students may submit scores from the old (before March 2005) SAT (or ACT), and we will use their best scores from either test."

SELECTIVITY

Admissions Rating	**88**
# of applicants	1,716
% of applicants accepted	64
% of acceptees attending	27
# accepting a place on wait list	58
% admitted from wait list	26

FRESHMAN PROFILE

Range SAT Verbal	560-660
Average SAT Verbal	616
Range SAT Math	570-670
Average SAT Math	623
**TPR Projected Range SAT Writing*	*600-670*
Range ACT Composite	23-29
Average ACT Composite	26
Minimum Paper TOEFL	550
Minimum Computer Based TOEFL	213
Average HS GPA	3.51
% graduated top 10% of class	25
% graduated top 25% of class	60
% graduated top 50% of class	88

DEADLINES

Regular application deadline	3/1
Regular notification	4/1
Nonfall registration?	no

APPLICANTS ALSO LOOK AT

AND OFTEN PREFER
Carleton College
Grinnell College
Macalester College

AND SOMETIMES PREFER
Beloit College
Colorado College
Knox College

AND RARELY PREFER
Coe College
Lake Forest College
Ripon College

FINANCIAL FACTS

Financial Aid Rating	**89**
Annual tuition	$22,490
Room & Board	$6,240
Books and supplies	$920
Required fees	$160
% frosh rec. need-based scholarship or grant aid	81
% UG rec. need-based scholarship or grant aid	73
% frosh rec. need-based self-help aid	61
% UG rec. need-based self-help aid	63
% frosh rec. any financial aid	91
% UG rec. any financial aid	96
Avg. frosh grant	$15,445
Avg. frosh loan	$2,990
Independent 529 member?	No

Cornell University

Undergraduate Admissions, 410 Thurston Avenue, Ithaca, NY 14850 • Admissions: 607-255-5241 • Fax: 607-255-0659

CAMPUS LIFE

Quality of Life Rating	**83**
Fire Safety Rating	**70**
Type of school	private
Environment	town

STUDENTS

Total undergrad enrollment	13,577
% male/female	50/50
% from out of state	60
% live on campus	42
% in (# of) fraternities	27 (49)
% in (# of) sororities	24 (22)
% African American	5
% Asian	16
% Caucasian	58
% Hispanic	5
% international	7
# of countries represented	109

SURVEY SAYS

Great computer facilities
Great library
Great food on campus
Great off-campus food
Lots of beer drinking

ACADEMICS

Academic Rating	**89**
Calendar	semester
Student/faculty ratio	9:1
Professors interesting rating	75
Professors accessible rating	75
% professors teaching UG courses	100
% classes taught by TAs	0
Most common lab size	10-19 students
Most common regular class size	10-19 students

MOST POPULAR MAJORS

Agriculture
business/commerce
engineering

STUDENTS SPEAK OUT

Academics

With seven colleges and "a course catalog that is upwards of 680 pages long," Cornell University offers "unlimited resources and opportunities for undergraduates." Students say that "if you want to study it, you almost certainly can" at Cornell. Options include not only the expected arts, sciences, and engineering programs, but also standout offerings in hospitality administration, human ecology, industrial and labor relations, and agricultural science. All the choices create numerous opportunities for undergraduates; explains one student, "Cornell has so many academic facilities that it is very easy to get involved with research opportunities even as an undergraduate. I have been doing research in my major since the beginning of my sophomore year." (Research at Cornell, by the way, is abetted by "one of the [largest] most unified libraries in the world, with tons of workspace and tons of research materials.") Professors are very accommodating to undergraduates; explains one student, "I expected to find professors who were only concerned with their lab work and cared nothing about the students. And I am not going to lie: A few of the professors are like that. But the great majority [of them] really care about their students, offering help to whoever needs it and being generally concerned about their well-being." Although "the workload is very heavy, there is an unlimited amount of resources to help—profs, TAs, help centers, tutors, and fellow students." Undergraduates speak highly about their classmates, telling us that they "are pretty passionate about what they do, and there isn't a lack of intellectual or stimulating conversation. People aren't afraid to be smart here."

Life

Most Cornell students report a heavy workload that seriously eats into free time. Engineers report, "You go through the day expecting to spend some of the time in class (assuming you wake up in time and spend the thirty minutes walking to class in two feet of snow) and the rest in the library. When it's 2:00 A.M., then it's about time to go home, knowing you are one day closer to the weekend." Some students say, "The tough workweeks make Cornell a good party school on the weekends. Our weekends are short—just Friday and Saturday nights for the most part, unlike the Wednesday through Saturday weekends of some schools." The campus hosts numerous social sub-scenes, including a large Greek system (especially popular with underclassmen), a restaurant and bar scene (for upperclassmen), "the athletic crowd, [and] the theater crowd; there're about a million crowds, actually, each reflecting a million different interests." Being that Cornell is a large school, "there's really a lot to do on campus: There's a movie theater and a bowling alley on campus, and it seems like every weekend there [is an] a cappella concert or dance show going on." Students have mixed feelings about Ithaca but are unanimous in their praise of the campus, which they say "provides a glorious atmosphere."

Student Body

The allure of the Ivy League, the presence of lower-cost state-funded divisions, and generous financial aid packages contribute to a population that is "diverse beyond belief." One undergraduate adds, "I live on campus and have become friends with two students from Lebanon, one from Mexico City, and one from Jordan just in this last semester. There is a great variety of beliefs, political and otherwise, a great amount of tolerance and through that a great opportunity to learn about alternative cultures, beliefs, and ideas." While many students come from within New York State, "that doesn't lend itself to there being a 'typical' student because New York varies so greatly from one area to the next." Academically, "there are basically two types of students at Cornell: the social type and the studious type. The social type hits up the frat parties and typically joins a house as a freshman, then moves on to apartment parties and bars as they grow older. The studious type is only seen in class or the library. There isn't much in-between."

FINANCIAL AID: 607-255-5145 • E-MAIL: ADMISSIONS@CORNELL.EDU • WEBSITE: WWW.CORNELL.EDU

ADMISSIONS

Very important factors considered include: Essays, extracurricular activities, recommendations, secondary school record, standardized test scores, talent/ability. *Important factors considered include:* Class rank. *Other factors considered include:* Alumni/ae relation, character/personal qualities, geographical residence, interview, minority status, state residency, volunteer work, work experience. SAT Reasoning, SAT Subject Tests, or ACT required. TOEFL required of all international applicants. High school diploma or equivalent is not required. *Academic units required:* 4 English, 3 math. *Academic units recommended:* 3 science (3 science lab), 3 foreign language, 3 social studies, 3 history.

The Inside Word

Cornell is the largest of the Ivies, and its admissions operation is a reflection of the fairly grand scale of the institution: complex and somewhat intimidating. Candidates should not expect contact with admissions to reveal much in the way of helpful insights on the admissions process, as the university seems to prefer to keep things close to the vest. Only applicants with top accomplishments, academic or otherwise, will be viable candidates. The university is a very positive place for minorities, and the public status presents a value that's hard to beat.

FINANCIAL AID

Students should submit: FAFSA, institution's own financial aid form, CSS/Financial Aid PROFILE, noncustodial (divorced/separated) parents' statement, business/farm supplement, prior year tax forms. Regular filing deadline is 2/11. The Princeton Review suggests that all financial aid forms be submitted as soon as possible after 1/1. *Need-based scholarships/grants offered:* Pell, SEOG, state scholarships/grants, private scholarships, the school's own gift aid. *Loan aid offered:* Direct Subsidized Stafford, Direct Unsubsidized Stafford, Direct PLUS, FFEL Subsidized Stafford, FFEL Unsubsidized Stafford, FFEL PLUS, Federal Perkins, college/university loans from institutional funds, Key Bank alternative loan. Applicants will be notified of awards on or about 4/1. Federal Work-study Program available. Institutional employment available. Off-campus job opportunities are good.

FROM THE ADMISSIONS OFFICE

"Cornell University, an Ivy League school and land-grant college located in the scenic Finger Lakes region of central New York, provides an outstanding education to students in seven small to midsize undergraduate colleges: Agriculture & Life Sciences; Architecture, Art, & Planning; Arts & Sciences; Engineering; Hotel Administration; Human Ecology; and Industrial & Labor Relations. Cornellians come from all 50 states and more than 100 countries, and they pursue their academic goals in more than 100 departments. The College of Arts and Sciences, one of the smallest liberal arts schools in the Ivy League, offers more than forty majors, most of which rank near the top nationwide. Applied programs in the other six colleges also rank among the best in the world.

"Other special features of the university include a world-renowned faculty; 4,000 courses available to all students; an extensive undergraduate research program; superb research, teaching, and library facilities; a large, diverse study abroad program; and more than 600 student organizations and 36 varsity sports. Cornell's campus is one of the most beautiful in the country; students pass streams, rocky gorges, and waterfalls on their way to class. First-year students make their home on North Campus, a living-learning community that features a special advising center, faculty-in-residence, a fitness center, and traditional residence halls as well as theme-centered buildings such as Ecology House. Cornell University invites applications from all interested students and uses the Common Application exclusively with a short required Cornell Supplement.

"Students applying for admissions in the fall of 2006 will be permitted to submit scores from either the old or new SAT or ACT exams. We also require SAT Subject Tests. Subject Test requirements are college-specific, and will depend upon whether you are submitting the old or new version of the SAT or ACT exam."

SELECTIVITY

Admissions Rating	**97**
# of applicants	20,822
% of applicants accepted	29
% of acceptees attending	50
# accepting a place on wait list	2,411
% admitted from wait list	7
# of early decision applicants	1,120
% accepted early decision	44

FRESHMAN PROFILE

Range SAT Verbal	630-730
Range SAT Math	660-760
**TPR Projected Range SAT Writing*	*650-720*
Range ACT Composite	28-32
Minimum Paper TOEFL	550
Minimum Computer Based TOEFL	250
% graduated top 10% of class	85
% graduated top 25% of class	95
% graduated top 50% of class	99

DEADLINES

Early decision application deadline	11/1
Early decision notification	12/11
Regular application deadline	1/1
Regular notification	4/1
Nonfall registration?	no

APPLICANTS ALSO LOOK AT

AND OFTEN PREFER

Harvard College, Massachusetts Institute of Technology, Princeton University, Stanford University, Yale University

AND SOMETIMES PREFER

Columbia University—Columbia College, Duke University, University of California—Berkeley, University of Pennsylvania

AND RARELY PREFER

Boston University, Carnegie Mellon University, Johns Hopkins University, New York University

FINANCIAL FACTS

Financial Aid Rating	**94**
Annual tuition	$30,000
Room & Board	$9,882
Books and supplies	$660
Required fees	$167
% frosh rec. need-based scholarship or grant aid	46
% UG rec. need-based scholarship or grant aid	46
% frosh rec. need-based self-help aid	43
% UG rec. need-based self-help aid	47
% frosh rec. any financial aid	48
% UG rec. any financial aid	49
Avg. frosh grant	$21,257
Avg. frosh loan	$10,400
Independent 529 member?	No

Creighton University

2500 California Plaza, Omaha, NE 68178 • Admissions: 402-280-2703 • Fax: 402-280-2685

CAMPUS LIFE

Quality of Life Rating	**83**
Fire Safety Rating	**79**
Type of school	private
Affiliation	Roman Catholic
Environment	metropolis

STUDENTS

Total undergrad enrollment	3,888
% male/female	40/60
% from out of state	56
% from public high school	56
% live on campus	57
% in (# of) fraternities	21 (5)
% in (# of) sororities	28 (6)
% African American	3
% Asian	7
% Caucasian	83
% Hispanic	3
% Native American	1
% international	1
# of countries represented	43

SURVEY SAYS

Small classes
Lab facilities are great
Students are friendly
Intramural sports are popular

ACADEMICS

Academic Rating	**77**
Calendar	semester
Student/faculty ratio	13:1
Professors interesting rating	84
Professors accessible rating	83
% professors teaching UG courses	100
% classes taught by TAs	0
Most common lab size	10-19 students
Most common regular class size	20-29 students

MOST POPULAR MAJORS

Business administration/management
health/medical preparatory programs
psychology

STUDENTS SPEAK OUT

Academics

Creighton University, a small Jesuit-led school with big-school resources, "is one of the premiere premed factories of the Midwest," boasting "an outstanding science faculty that gears students up for the long road to and through medical school." With three undergraduate colleges and more than 50 available majors, Creighton offers a lot more than just great biology labs and killer organic chemistry classes; the school also excels in business, pre-law studies, nursing, and psychology. A core curriculum "allows students to take classes such as philosophy, religion, and foreign language" and ensures that "writing is a big part of the curriculum." Some here love the core, while others complain that it is "too time-consuming and leaves little time for students to pursue electives outside their major." About 45 Jesuits teach classes or work with students in various areas of the university; "they live on campus and are solely interested in the students' understanding of the material as well as their overall progress." Classes are small, "allowing for a lot of one-on-one attention," and "with five (professional and) graduate schools attached—all of them giving preference to Creighton undergraduates—the opportunities for undergraduate research are wonderful." Students' wish lists include an engineering program (there is none) and increased support for students in the arts.

Life

"A lot of people think, 'Oh, CU is all academics, no fun,' but that's far from the truth," writes one student. "If you're into the party scene, you can almost always find one on the weekends, and there are bars within long walking distance to campus in the Old Market. However, if you're into the quieter weekends, there are plenty of people like that as well. The residence halls and other organizations on campus have events all the time for students to participate in if the party scene is not you. And every weekend, there's groups of friends who just hang out and watch movies all night." Creighton's intercollegiate teams provide a popular rallying point for the student body; undergrads "are huge supporters of our teams and going to the games is a huge part of social life here." Observes one student, "We have awesome basketball and soccer teams, which is good because Omaha certainly isn't going to provide athletic team entertainment." What Omaha can provide—besides a good steak—is "a city that is surprisingly cultural and has a great musical and theatrical scene. Many students go to concerts on almost a weekly basis." Omaha also has "tons of fun things to do during the week and weekend. There are lots of restaurants and parks, bike trails, and camping, if you're the outdoors type," and if you're not, there's "enough of a nightlife for us. It's not a huge metropolis or anything, but it's a great city, and we live right in the heart of downtown."

Student Body

Creighton's "focused, ambitious" undergrads "are serious about getting a good education and spend quite a bit of time studying." They "usually had high high-school GPAs and test scores," "are involved in three or more activities per semester while juggling hard courses," and "share many of the same values, which makes it easy to have a large number of friends." Faith is among those values; while not everyone is Catholic, nearly everyone has a deep interest in religion, and "it is a common topic of dinner conversation." Conservative social and political views are also among those shared values; students say that the bounty of Midwesterners "have conservative mind frames," one undergrad writes. There are "a lot of athletic types, a good sign of both mental and physical health," and nearly everyone is friendly and fairly outgoing. Warns one transplanted Yankee, "As a person from the East Coast, I have had to change the way I act and dress to fit in here. Neither black clothing nor frowning will work here."

Creighton University

Financial Aid: 402-280-2731 • E-mail: admissions@creighton.edu • Website: www.admission.creighton.edu

ADMISSIONS

Very important factors considered include: Secondary school record. *Important factors considered include:* Recommendations, standardized test scores. *Other factors considered include:* Character/personal qualities, class rank, essays, extracurricular activities, minority status, talent/ability, volunteer work. SAT Reasoning or ACT required. TOEFL required of all international applicants. High school diploma is required, and GED is accepted. *Academic units required:* 4 English, 3 math, 2 science, 2 foreign language, 1 social studies, 1 history, 3 academic electives. *Academic units recommended:* 4 English, 3 math, 2 science, 2 foreign language, 1 social studies, 1 history, 3 academic electives.

The Inside Word

In this world of literal translation, even colleges and universities with admit rates that are higher than Creighton's refer to themselves as selective. While it should not be particularly difficult to get in, some applicants don't.

FINANCIAL AID

Students should submit: FAFSA, institution's own financial aid form. Regular filing deadline is 8/1. The Princeton Review suggests that all financial aid forms be submitted as soon as possible after 1/1. *Need-based scholarships/grants offered:* Pell, SEOG, state scholarships/grants, private scholarships, the school's own gift aid, Federal Nursing scholarships. *Loan aid offered:* FFEL Subsidized Stafford, FFEL Unsubsidized Stafford, FFEL PLUS, Federal Perkins, Federal Nursing, college/university loans from institutional funds. Applicants will be notified of awards on a rolling basis beginning on or about 3/15.

FROM THE ADMISSIONS OFFICE

"Students come to Creighton to become experts in their chosen fields . . . even if they haven't already chosen a field of study! About 45 percent of the graduating seniors from Creighton go immediately into medical, dentistry, pharmacy, law, and physical and occupational therapy professional graduate programs—this is the highest rate of any midwestern university. We also produce exceptional teachers, business professionals, scientists, journalists and writers, and community service advocates. Our size is ideal. With 3,700 undergraduates and, including professional school enrollment, a total of 6,537 attendees, our students feel they have the best of both worlds—first-rate academic programs and facilities but also a more intimate relationship with our faculty that often leads to involvement in research projects and internships. Creighton students tend to have a deeper focus on their careers and lifestyle choices. As students at a leading, national, Jesuit, liberal arts university our students are encouraged to examine the moral as well as factual dimension of issues. Most students also get involved in our leadership training programs and community service and/or campus ministry organizations. The campus has its own comfortable and safe sense of space, and the downtown corporate headquarters, restaurants, and music spots are just a five-minute walk away.

"Admissions and scholarship decisions are based on the traditional SAT/ACT scores. We use the best composite ACT score or the highest critical reading and highest Math SAT scores. The student's best scores from either test will be used."

SELECTIVITY

Admissions Rating	**88**
# of applicants	3,412
% of applicants accepted	86
% of acceptees attending	33
# accepting a place on wait list	85
% admitted from wait list	24

FRESHMAN PROFILE

Range SAT Verbal	550-650
Average SAT Verbal	600
Range SAT Math	560-650
Average SAT Math	605
**TPR Projected Range SAT Writing*	*600-670*
Range ACT Composite	24-28
Average ACT Composite	26
Minimum Paper TOEFL	550
Minimum Computer Based TOEFL	213
Average HS GPA	3.7
% graduated top 10% of class	39
% graduated top 25% of class	69
% graduated top 50% of class	92

DEADLINES

Regular application deadline	8/1
Regular notification	rolling
Nonfall registration?	yes

APPLICANTS ALSO LOOK AT AND OFTEN PREFER

Boston College
University of Notre Dame

AND SOMETIMES PREFER

Marquette University
Saint Louis University
Santa Clara University
Washington University in St. Louis

AND RARELY PREFER

Loyola University of Chicago
Regis University
University of Iowa
University of Nebraska—Lincoln

FINANCIAL FACTS

Financial Aid Rating	**88**
Annual tuition	$20,354
Room & Board	$7,200
Books and supplies	$1,000
Required fees	$764
% frosh rec. need-based scholarship or grant aid	59
% UG rec. need-based scholarship or grant aid	57
% frosh rec. need-based self-help aid	52
% UG rec. need-based self-help aid	51
% frosh rec. any financial aid	91
% UG rec. any financial aid	93
Avg. frosh grant	$20,270
Avg. frosh loan	$5,747
Independent 529 member?	Yes

DARTMOUTH COLLEGE

6016 McNutt Hall, Hanover, NH 03755 • Admissions: 603-646-2875 • Fax: 603-646-1216

CAMPUS LIFE

Quality of Life Rating	**97**
Fire Safety Rating	**60**
Type of school	private
Environment	village

STUDENTS

Total undergrad enrollment	3,998
% male/female	50/50
% from out of state	96
% from public high school	63
% live on campus	83
% in (# of) fraternities	39 (14)
% in (# of) sororities	34 (8)
% African American	7
% Asian	13
% Caucasian	58
% Hispanic	6
% Native American	4
% international	5

SURVEY SAYS

Great computer facilities
Great library
Campus feels safe
Frats and sororities dominate social scene
Lots of beer drinking

ACADEMICS

Academic Rating	**96**
Calendar	quarter
Student/faculty ratio	8:1
Professors interesting rating	87
Professors accessible rating	92
% professors teaching UG courses	100
% classes taught by TAs	0
Most common lab size	10-19 students
Most common regular class size	10-19 students

STUDENTS SPEAK OUT

Academics

Regarded as "the undergraduate school of the Ivies" because of the minimal and unobtrusive presence of graduate students, Dartmouth College seems to offer it all: "a beautiful campus, nurturing professors, a great library, world-class cultural performances and lectures, comfortable dorms, tasty food, and most importantly, bright, enthusiastic, and spirited peers with whom to share it all." Students praise the school's focus on undergraduates; one student says, "You get a lot of attention from professors, but still have the benefits of having graduate students around for class help sessions and as general resources." Professors at Dartmouth "are great scholars in their field. [And they] can actually teach instead of just being smart." If they couldn't teach, undergraduates assure us "they wouldn't be at Dartmouth." The school also offers "great opportunities to do research and internships, awesome lab facilities, [and] tremendously strong academics." And that's not all. "The factor most people tend to overlook is the strong alumni base. It's so easy to get internships while you're there, and after school the connections you make are invaluable."

Life

Undergraduates agree that "life is like summer camp" at Dartmouth. Students explain that "you're in a beautiful place, living with your best friends and having as much fun as you can. The only difference is going to class and studying, both things Dartmouth students take very seriously." Students are understandably happy to be at Dartmouth, and that helps generate "an incredible sense of community. As soon as you get here, you immediately feel like you're part of a group." Greek life adds to the community spirit. Students regard it as "an amazing compliment to the sometimes arduous demands of academia" and praise the Greek houses' "welcoming atmosphere and the 'come one, come all' attitude at their parties." That's good news for Independents, since "the Greek scene is pervasive and positive." Students note that "there's never any pressure to drink" and that there are a lot of things to do on campus. The Hop has shows and movies every night, the skating rink has open skate all winter long, and there are all kinds of lectures and discussions put on by the college and by groups on campus. Everyone goes to home games, especially hockey; intramural sports are big; there are several newspapers and literary publications; there are dance and a cappella groups, [and] the list goes on." Campus grounds include a golf course and ski way and excellent rock-climbing areas and hiking trails. In short, the school's outdoorsy reputation is well deserved.

Student Body

Dartmouth students look alike, for reasons that have nothing to do with their backgrounds. "The average Dartmouth student is usually too bundled up in warm clothes to distinguish them from everyone else," undergraduates clarify. However, "once you get past the ten layers of clothing that everyone wears, Dartmouth students are a bunch of extraordinarily bright, sexually charged, procrastinating, sensitive comedians who go out of their way to make you feel like the most important person in the world." They tend to be "outdoorsy people, but there are also those who aren't athletic at all, and everyone fits in fine." Dartmouth students "are either very liberal or very conservative." One student adds, "The campus is politically active. When talking to my friends at other schools, they are always amazed to hear how many people at Dartmouth are involved and aware of politics, both national and global." However, they never let political differences spoil the genial atmosphere. Students are "friendly, eloquent, and generally very happy."

FINANCIAL AID: 603-646-2451 • E-MAIL: ADMISSIONS.OFFICE@DARTMOUTH.EDU • WEBSITE: WWW.DARTMOUTH.EDU

ADMISSIONS

Very important factors considered include: Character/personal qualities, class rank, essays, extracurricular activities, recommendations, secondary school record, standardized test scores. *Important factors considered include:* Talent/ability, volunteer work. *Other factors considered include:* Alumni/ae relation, geographical residence, interview, minority status, work experience. SAT Reasoning and SAT Subject Tests or ACT required. TOEFL required of all international applicants. High school diploma or equivalent is not required. *Academic units recommended:* 4 English, 4 math, 4 science, 3 foreign language, 3 social studies.

The Inside Word

Applications for the class of 2007 were up 15 percent from the previous year's totals, making this small-town Ivy more selective in choosing who gets offered a coveted spot in the class. As is the case with those who apply to any of the Ivies or other highly selective colleges, candidates are up against (or benefit from) many institutional interests that go unmentioned in discussions of appropriate qualifications for admission. This makes an already stressful process even more so for most candidates.

FINANCIAL AID

Students should submit: FAFSA, CSS/Financial Aid PROFILE, noncustodial (divorced/separated) parents' statement, business/farm supplement, current W-2 forms or federal tax returns. Regular filing deadline is 2/1. The Princeton Review suggests that all financial aid forms be submitted as soon as possible after 1/1. *Need-based scholarships/grants offered:* Pell, SEOG, state scholarships/grants, the school's own gift aid. *Loan aid offered:* FFEL Subsidized Stafford, FFEL Unsubsidized Stafford, FFEL PLUS, Federal Perkins, college/university loans from institutional funds. Applicants will be notified of awards on or about 4/15. Federal Work-study Program available. Institutional employment available.

FROM THE ADMISSIONS OFFICE

"Dartmouth's mission is to endow students with the knowledge and wisdom needed to make creative and positive contributions to society. The college brings together a breadth of cultures, traditions, and ideas to create a campus that is alive with ongoing debate and exploration. The educational value of such discourse cannot be underestimated. From student-initiated round table discussions that attempt to make sense of world events to the late-night philosophizing in a dormitory lounge, Dartmouth students take advantage of their opportunities to learn from each other. The unique benefits of sharing in this interchange are accompanied by a great sense of responsibility. Each individual's commitment to the principles of community ensures the vitality of this learning environment.

"All applicants, including those who apply from foreign countries, are required to take the SAT (or ACT) and any two SAT Subject Tests. All testing must be completed by January of the senior year in high school. If standardized testing is repeated, the admissions committee only considers highest scores."

SELECTIVITY

Admissions Rating	**98**
# of applicants	11,734
% of applicants accepted	19
% of acceptees attending	50
# accepting a place on wait list	1,275
% admitted from wait list	2
# of early decision applicants	384
% accepted early decision	30

FRESHMAN PROFILE

Range SAT Verbal	670-770
Average SAT Verbal	713
Range SAT Math	690-780
Average SAT Math	719
**TPR Projected Range SAT Writing*	*680-740*
Average ACT Composite	30
Minimum Paper TOEFL	600
Minimum Computer Based TOEFL	250
Average HS GPA	3.73
% graduated top 10% of class	88
% graduated top 50% of class	100

DEADLINES

Early decision application deadline	11/1
Early decision notification	12/15
Regular application deadline	1/1
Regular notification	4/10
Nonfall registration?	no

APPLICANTS ALSO LOOK AT

AND OFTEN PREFER

Harvard College, Princeton University, Stanford University, Yale University

AND SOMETIMES PREFER

Amherst College, Brown University, Massachusetts Institute of Technology, Williams College

AND RARELY PREFER

Cornell University, Middlebury College, Northwestern University, University of Pennsylvania

FINANCIAL FACTS

Financial Aid Rating	**97**
Annual tuition	$30,279
Room & Board	$9,000
Books and supplies	$1,122
Required fees	$186
% frosh rec. need-based scholarship or grant aid	47
% UG rec. need-based scholarship or grant aid	47
% frosh rec. need-based self-help aid	45
% UG rec. need-based self-help aid	48
% frosh rec. any financial aid	48
% UG rec. any financial aid	50
Avg. frosh grant	$24,375
Avg. frosh loan	$3,759
Independent 529 member?	No

DAVIDSON COLLEGE

PO BOX 7156, DAVIDSON, NC 28035-7156 • ADMISSIONS: 704-894-2230 • FAX: 704-894-2016

CAMPUS LIFE

Quality of Life Rating	**97**
Fire Safety Rating	**60**
Type of school	private
Affiliation	Presbyterian
Environment	village

STUDENTS

Total undergrad enrollment	1,702
% male/female	50/50
% from out of state	81
% from public high school	52
% live on campus	91
% in (# of) fraternities	40 (8)
% African American	6
% Asian	2
% Caucasian	78
% Hispanic	4
% international	3
# of countries represented	34

SURVEY SAYS

Small classes
No one cheats
Lab facilities are great
Great computer facilities
School is well run
Students are friendly
Campus feels safe

ACADEMICS

Academic Rating	**97**
Calendar	semester
Student/faculty ratio	11:1
Professors interesting rating	99
Professors accessible rating	98
% professors teaching UG courses	100
% classes taught by TAs	0
Most common lab size	10-19 students
Most common regular class size	10-19 students

MOST POPULAR MAJORS

English language and literature
political science and government

STUDENTS SPEAK OUT

Academics

At Davidson the "boundaries between students and professors are set aside," affording undergraduates the respect due to "a person with a mind who is going to influence the world." Professors display a high level of sensitivity to student needs: "I wasn't even the one that brought up the fact that I needed help. My professor came to me, and I am so glad he did." Instructors make themselves easily available, even "coming in on weekends to give study sessions before tests or helping with personal problems." They keep students engaged by "stimulating class discussion and organizing curriculum-enriching events out of class." Unlike at most schools, Davidson students seem to approve of their required courses. "Because of our core curriculum, I have had to stretch myself in areas outside of my comfort zone, but that ultimately resulted in my current major." Many students single out the "strict honor code," which allows for self-scheduled and unproctored exams, as one of the best aspects of a Davidson education. "People don't come to Davidson unless they want to be part of an honor-bound community." Davidson's president "is probably one of the people we see the most around campus. Whether he's running, attending social events, or just hanging out with students, his vibrant personality and friendliness are representative of the entire school." On the small campus, "you know all the administration, and most of them know you," leading to an academic atmosphere where "the professors and administrative staff seem like family."

Life

Undergraduates at Davidson choose from a variety of social scenes, ranging from Patterson Court, where "there's always some sort of party going on," to religious groups that reflect the school's "strong connections to the Presbyterian church." Some students complain that "they need more things to do on the weekend that don't necessarily involve alcohol." Others point to additional events that round out the options, including "midnight movies, live bands, and theme events on Saturday nights." Overall, "Davidson goes to great lengths to make sure there is always some type of activity to go to no matter what your interests are." One student points out, "If there is ever something that you want to have on campus, it is easy enough to start it up yourself—with school funding." In Davidson's overachieving environment, students "focus on as many extracurriculars as they can cram into their schedule." A junior tells us, "Any one student can be involved in enough sports, activities, jobs, and volunteering that it is a miracle they finish their schoolwork and still have time to socialize and sleep." When campus life gets at all boring, "a little weekend trip to the beach or the mountains is in order." A short ride gets students to Charlotte, "a wellspring of culture, arts, clubs, bars, restaurants, [and] shopping."

Student Body

A Davidson student is "hardworking," sometimes "to the point of chronic fatigue." Other commonly used adjectives include "very bright," "type A," "studious," and "fairly religious." Several students agree, however, that the stereotypes of "conservative and always studying" don't convey the variety of the population. "Although Davidson has many students with a conservative viewpoint," writes one undergraduate, most "students are accepting and respectful of other opinions." Several people do point out a "definite line between the churchgoers and the people who sleep in on Sundays." One respondent, however, summarizes his view of the student body optimistically: "Though we disagree, though we argue, though we truly are different people, something amazing happens when we are all together."

FINANCIAL AID: 704-894-2232 • E-MAIL: ADMISSION@DAVIDSON.EDU • WEBSITE: WWW.DAVIDSON.EDU

ADMISSIONS

Very important factors considered include: Character/personal qualities, recommendations, secondary school record, volunteer work. *Important factors considered include:* Essays, extracurricular activities, talent/ability. *Other factors considered include:* Class rank, minority status, standardized test scores, work experience. SAT Reasoning or ACT required. SAT Subject Tests recommended. TOEFL required of all international applicants. High school diploma is required, and GED is not accepted. *Academic units required:* 4 English, 3 math, 2 science, 1 foreign language, 2 social studies and history. *Academic units recommended:* 4 math, 4 science, 4 foreign language, 4 social studies and history.

The Inside Word

Harbor no illusions regarding ease of admission here. Getting in is every bit as tough as staying in because an amazingly high percentage of those who are admitted choose to attend. Look for admission to become even more difficult as the college's name recognition increases.

FINANCIAL AID

Students should submit: FAFSA, CSS/Financial Aid PROFILE, noncustodial (divorced/separated) parents' statement, business/farm supplement, parent and student tax returns and W-2 forms, corporate tax returns if applicable. The Princeton Review suggests that all financial aid forms be submitted as soon as possible after 1/1. *Need-based scholarships/grants offered:* Pell, SEOG, state scholarships/grants, private scholarships, the school's own gift aid. *Loan aid offered:* FFEL Subsidized Stafford, FFEL Unsubsidized Stafford, FFEL PLUS, Federal Perkins, alternative loans. Applicants will be notified of awards on or about 4/1. Federal Work-study Program available. Institutional employment available. Off-campus job opportunities are excellent.

FROM THE ADMISSIONS OFFICE

"Davidson College is one of the nation's premier academic institutions, a college of the liberal arts and sciences respected for its intellectual vigor, the high quality of its faculty and students, and the achievements of its alumni. It is distinguished by its strong honor system, close interaction between professors and students, an environment that encourages both intellectual growth and community service, and a commitment to international education. Davidson places great value on student participation in extracurricular activities, intercollegiate athletics, and intramural sports. The college has a strong regional identity, which includes traditions of civility and mutual respect, and has historic ties to the Presbyterian Church.

"Applicants for the Class of 2010 are required to complete the SAT or the ACT Assessment. Recommended, are SAT Subject Tests (Mathematics and one of your choices) and the ACT Assessment plus Writing. Students are permitted to submit scores from the SAT I administered prior to March 2005. Davidson will utilize the scores that place the student in the greatest possible light."

SELECTIVITY

Admissions Rating	**97**
# of applicants	4,154
% of applicants accepted	27
% of acceptees attending	42
# of early decision applicants	188
% accepted early decision	45

FRESHMAN PROFILE

Range SAT Verbal	630-730
Average SAT Verbal	659
Range SAT Math	640-710
Average SAT Math	656
**TPR Projected Range SAT Writing*	*650-720*
Range ACT Composite	26-31
Average ACT Composite	28
Minimum Paper TOEFL	600
Minimum Computer Based TOEFL	250
% graduated top 10% of class	71
% graduated top 25% of class	94
% graduated top 50% of class	100

DEADLINES

Early decision application deadline	11/15
Early decision notification	12/15
Regular application deadline	1/2
Regular notification	4/1
Nonfall registration?	no

APPLICANTS ALSO LOOK AT AND OFTEN PREFER

Dartmouth College, Duke University, Princeton University, Stanford University, Swarthmore College, Williams College

AND SOMETIMES PREFER

University of North Carolina—Chapel Hill, University of Virginia, Vanderbilt University, Washington University in St. Louis

AND RARELY PREFER

Colgate University, Emory University, Furman University, University of Richmond, Wake Forest University

FINANCIAL FACTS

Financial Aid Rating	**97**
Annual tuition	$28,667
Room & Board	$8,158
% frosh rec. need-based scholarship or grant aid	33
% UG rec. need-based scholarship or grant aid	32
% frosh rec. need-based self-help aid	27
% UG rec. need-based self-help aid	29
Avg. frosh grant	$17,900
Avg. frosh loan	$2,671
Independent 529 member?	No

Deep Springs College

Applications Committee, HC 72 Box 45001, Dyer, NV 89010 • Admissions: 760-872-2000 • Fax: 760-872-4466

CAMPUS LIFE

Quality of Life Rating	**99**
Fire Safety Rating	**60**
Type of school	private
Environment	rural

STUDENTS

Total undergrad enrollment	26
% male/female	100/0
% from out of state	88
% live on campus	100

SURVEY SAYS

Small classes
No one cheats
Registration is a breeze
Great food on campus
Dorms are like palaces
Low cost of living
Intercollegiate sports are unpopular or nonexistent
Frats and sororities are unpopular or nonexistent
Student government is popular
Very little drug use

ACADEMICS

Academic Rating	**99**
Calendar	9
Student/faculty ratio	3:1
Professors interesting rating	83
Professors accessible rating	99
% professors teaching UG courses	100
% classes taught by TAs	0
Most common regular class size	fewer than 10 students

STUDENTS SPEAK OUT

Academics

Deep Springs is more than a college, it's a way of life, one that makes exceptional mental, physical, and ethical demands of the two-baker's-dozen men who attend. Undergraduates are responsible not only for demanding academic work but also for 20-plus hours per week of manual labor on the school ranch and the administration of the school. Yes, you read correctly: "For the most part at Deep Springs, the students are the administration," explains one student. "Eight-hour meetings to discuss the fate of a fellow student [are] never something someone looks forward to. But none of us would rather have it any other way." Adds another, "I can't complain [about anything here] without blaming myself. All the faculty is here because we hired them. If we wanted the president fired, it would take some convincing, but the trustees would listen to us if we had a just cause." The net result of the Deep Springs experience is a serious, tight community, one in which students "eat, study, work, and live together every single day, making you wish that for once you could sit in the reading room without falling into a three-hour conversation with a friend about the '80s, Isaac Newton, or what's for dinner tomorrow. You think by attending Deep Springs you'll never lack for a conversation topic again, until you go home for the first time." Students warn, "Ideally, we would have a larger selection of courses," but most agree that "nothing at Deep Springs could be improved without seriously changing the nature of the school."

Life

Life at Deep Springs, students agree, "is all about balancing its three pillars—labor, academics, and self-governance." The ultimate goal of which is to develop in students a deep sense of duty: "to train young men for lives of service to humanity." Most agree the experience is worth both the concomitant stress and the hard work. As one student recounts, "Being dairy boy these past two terms has taught me about responsibility, manure, and fatherhood. Walking out into the corral a few weeks ago to find a trembling baby Holstein being licked by one of our dairy cows changed my life forever." In their rare spare moments, students here must make their own fun; the ranch is in just about the middle of nowhere and offers no Greek life, no intercollegiate sports, and no drugs or alcohol (this policy is strictly enforced, all here assure us). Recreation includes "BB gun gentlemen's duels, air-guitar contests, hiking, swimming in the Upper Reservoir, sensory deprivation experiments, late-night cooking . . . you know, college stuff." Movies are popular; they're the only thing students here can watch on the school television, since "we have a TV and VCR, but no TV reception." Mostly, though, students amuse themselves with "late-night conversations in the library and the BH (Boarding House), mostly when we're trying to put off the paper(s) we have to write."

Student Body

The young men of Deep Springs are all "stubborn, smart, eccentric, and determined. Beyond those qualities, there are very few consistencies." The tiny population includes "artists, intellectuals, country bumpkins, Canadians, gay yogis, and snobs. Despite our small student body, there's a greater diversity of musical tastes here than in most HMVs." All students are extraordinary in some way. Notes one about his classmates, "They are more well traveled, well read, and well mannered than any people I have ever encountered in these numbers. It seems like between the 26 of us, we have been everywhere and seen everything." In their spare time, students "think about Martin Heidegger and Winona Ryder," but they rarely have spare time; as one undergrad cautioned, "We are an all-male college out in the middle of the desert whose students run the college and do a minimum of 20 hours of labor per week."

FINANCIAL AID: 760-872-2000 • E-MAIL: APCOM@DEEPSPRING.EDU • WEBSITE: WWW.DEEPSPRINGS.EDU

ADMISSIONS

Very important factors considered include: Character/personal qualities, essays, interview. *Important factors considered include:* Class rank, extracurricular activities, secondary school record, volunteer work, work experience. *Other factors considered include:* Minority status, recommendations, standardized test scores, talent/ability. SAT Reasoning or ACT required. High school diploma or equivalent is not required.

The Inside Word

The Application Committee comprises nine students, one faculty member, and one staff member. This is the body that evaluates candidates for admission. Finalists for admission write seven essays and travel to the valley for a several-day visit and a two-hour interview with the Applications Committee. There is likely to be no more rigorous, personal, or refreshing an admissions process to be found in U.S. higher education. This place requires serious commitment, and only the strong survive. Thorough self-assessment is a must before applying.

FINANCIAL AID

The Princeton Review suggests that all financial aid forms be submitted as soon as possible after 1/1. Applicants will be notified of awards on or about 4/15.

FROM THE ADMISSIONS OFFICE

"Founded in 1917, Deep Springs College lies isolated in a high desert valley of eastern California, 30 miles from the nearest town. Its enrollment is limited to 26 students, each of whom receives a full scholarship that covers tuition, room, and board and is valued at more than $50,000 per year. Students engage in rigorous academics, govern themselves, and participate in the operation of our cattle and alfalfa ranch. After two years, students generally transfer to other schools to complete their studies. Students regularly transfer to Harvard, the University of Chicago, and Brown, but also choose Cornell, Columbia, Stanford, Swarthmore, UC—Berkeley, and Yale.

"In 2002, Deep Springs students garnered four major national scholarship awards: three Truman Scholarships for public service careers—more than any other school in the country—and one Udall scholarship for careers in environmental studies and ecology.

"As of this book's publication, Deep Springs College did not have information available about their policy regarding the new SAT."

SELECTIVITY

Admissions Rating	**99**
# of applicants	161
% of applicants accepted	9
% of acceptees attending	100
# accepting a place on wait list	4
% admitted from wait list	100

FRESHMAN PROFILE

Range SAT Verbal	710-800
Average SAT Verbal	760
Range SAT Math	680-780
Average SAT Math	740
**TPR Projected Range SAT Writing*	*700-760*
Average HS GPA	3.89
% graduated top 10% of class	90
% graduated top 25% of class	90
% graduated top 50% of class	100

DEADLINES

Regular application deadline	11/15
Regular notification	4/7
Nonfall registration?	no

AND RARELY PREFER

Brown University
Columbia University—Columbia College
Cornell University
Harvard College
Stanford University
Swarthmore College
University of California—Berkeley
University of Chicago
Yale University

FINANCIAL FACTS

Financial Aid Rating	**99**
Annual tuition	$0
Books and supplies	$1,200
% frosh rec. any financial aid	100
% UG rec. any financial aid	100
Avg. frosh grant	$50,000
Independent 529 member?	No

DENISON UNIVERSITY

BOX H, GRANVILLE, OH 43023 • ADMISSIONS: 740-587-6276 • FAX: 740-587-6306

CAMPUS LIFE

Quality of Life Rating	**76**
Fire Safety Rating	**85**
Type of school	private
Environment	village

STUDENTS

Total undergrad enrollment	2,198
% male/female	44/56
% from out of state	58
% from public high school	69
% live on campus	98
% in (# of) fraternities	21 (8)
% in (# of) sororities	40 (6)
% African American	5
% Asian	3
% Caucasian	83
% Hispanic	3
% international	5
# of countries represented	31

SURVEY SAYS

Small classes
Lab facilities are great
Great computer facilities
Great library
Campus feels safe
Lots of beer drinking

ACADEMICS

Academic Rating	**89**
Calendar	semester
Student/faculty ratio	11:1
Professors interesting rating	86
Professors accessible rating	86
% professors teaching UG courses	100
% classes taught by TAs	0
Most common lab size	10-19 students
Most common regular class size	10-19 students

MOST POPULAR MAJORS

Communications and media studies
economics
English language and literature

STUDENTS SPEAK OUT

Academics

Students at this Ohioan liberal arts school agree that "the greatest strengths of Denison are the strong, rigorous curriculum and the easy access to [their] professors." The school's "intimate atmosphere" has "professors [who] are top-notch, [go] out of their way to be of assistance, and even make their home phone numbers accessible to students just in case a problem arises." At Denison, "students are pushed to reach their full potential. Many university professors are very open-minded when it comes to criticism and ideas that contradict their own." Our survey respondents praise the English, sociology, anthropology, psychology, and arts programs. Students report, "The science facilities are fabulous and getting even better because of the enormous new science center." The workload is often heavy, and students warn that "classes are tough at Denison mainly because of the very strict attendance and homework policies. Professors consider homework assignments and papers essential to the learning process and expect daily attendance. In short, if you snooze, you lose." However, there is plenty of help available to keep you from falling behind. One undergraduate adds, "There's free tutoring, which is great! And we have a writing center where they will look over your papers and things."

Life

Denison once had one of the nation's premier Greek scenes, but that was before the administration put the brakes on the Greeks and the party scene that accompanied them by requiring all undergraduate students to live on-campus. At the same time, the school "adopted a more aggressive approach to policing the Greeks." The Greeks are still here, claiming "about 33 percent of the campus, [and they] do a lot to make themselves visible," but the elimination of all off-campus housing—both apartments and Greek houses—"has resulted in an almost nonexistent social scene." Some students still drink, but they stick to small groups in dormitories, local bars, or Columbus (Columbus is a half hour's drive away). They don't hang much in hometown Granville, which "is not a very good college town. Everything closes very early (before nine)." Everything, that is, except "the two bars, The Granvilla ('Villa') and Brews. The bars are filled with us, and we love it because it is the party that we cannot have. Everyone is there having a crazy, fun time." Some students prefer the "comedians, bands, films, lectures, concerts, movies, etc., that come here and give a wide range of entertainment. There is also a great opportunity for fine arts entertainment with gallery openings, dance recitals, choir and orchestra concerts, student recitals, etc." Some students even see a windfall in the school's policy on student residence; one undergraduate writes, "The upside to strictly on-campus housing is that Denison has built four new apartment-style dorms. They truly are awesome. Each apartment has two bathrooms, four single rooms, a kitchen, and a living room."

Student Body

In the minds of many students, preppy fashion defines the Denison student body; one woman explains, "Be prepared to dress well. You will not attend class in your pajamas. Your hair will be done every day. You will wear makeup. You will tan in the winter. These words will become very familiar to you: Lord and Taylor, Easton Town Center, Abercrombie and Fitch, the Gap, Greek-only, Banana Republic." Not everyone fits the mold, although most students do. The rest form "a small counterculture hidden in many of the darker corners of campus, such as the coffeehouse and the cinema department." Some students believe that mandatory campus residence unintentionally makes the student body cliquish. Although the administration has made efforts to diversify demographics, the school still "needs more diversity."

FINANCIAL AID: 740-587-6279 • E-MAIL: ADMISSIONS@DENISON.EDU • WEBSITE: WWW.DENISON.EDU

ADMISSIONS

Very important factors considered include: Class rank, essays, recommendations, secondary school record, standardized test scores. *Important factors considered include:* Extracurricular activities, interview, talent/ability. *Other factors considered include:* Alumni/ae relation, character/personal qualities, geographical residence, minority status, religious affiliation/commitment, state residency, volunteer work, work experience. SAT Reasoning or ACT required. High school diploma is required, and GED is accepted. *Academic units required:* 4 English, 4 math, 4 science, 3 foreign language, 2 social studies, 1 history, 1 academic elective.

The Inside Word

Applicants who are statistically below Denison's freshman profile should proceed with caution. One of the simplest ways for a university to promote a reputation as an increasingly selective institution is to begin to cut off the bottom of the applicant pool. Only lack of success against heavy competition for students prevents Denison from being more aggressive in this regard.

FINANCIAL AID

Students should submit: FAFSA. The Princeton Review suggests that all financial aid forms be submitted as soon as possible after 1/1. *Need-based scholarships/grants offered:* Pell, SEOG, state scholarships/grants, private scholarships, the school's own gift aid. *Loan aid offered:* Direct Subsidized Stafford, Direct Unsubsidized Stafford, Direct PLUS, Federal Perkins, college/university loans from institutional funds. Applicants will be notified of awards on or about 4/1. Off-campus job opportunities are fair.

FROM THE ADMISSIONS OFFICE

"Denison is a college that can point with pride to its success in enrolling and retaining intellectually motivated, diverse, and well-balanced students who are being taught to become effective leaders in the twenty-first century. This year, over 50 percent of our first-year students were in the top 10 percent of their high school graduating class, their average SAT scores have risen above 1240—an increase of some 80 points over the last five years—18 percent of the class is multicultural, and 95 percent of our student body is receiving some type of financial assistance. Our First-Year Program focuses on helping students make a successful transition from high school to college, and the small classes and accessibility of faculty assure students the opportunity to interact closely with their professors and fellow students. We care about our students, and the loyalty of our 27,000 alumni proves that the Denison experience is one that lasts for a lifetime.

"Students applying for admission into the fall 2006 freshman class are required to take the new version of the SAT (or the ACT with the Writing section), but we will allow students to submit scores from the old (prior to March 2005) version of the SAT (or ACT) as well."

SELECTIVITY

Admissions Rating	**93**
# of applicants	4,947
% of applicants accepted	44
% of acceptees attending	28
# accepting a place on wait list	518
# of early decision applicants	122
% accepted early decision	87

FRESHMAN PROFILE

Range SAT Verbal	570-670
Average SAT Verbal	621
Range SAT Math	570-660
Average SAT Math	617
**TPR Projected Range SAT Writing*	*610-680*
Range ACT Composite	25-30
Average ACT Composite	27
Average HS GPA	3.6
% graduated top 10% of class	51
% graduated top 25% of class	78
% graduated top 50% of class	97

DEADLINES

Early decision application deadline	11/1
Early decision notification	2/1
Regular application deadline	1/15
Regular notification	4/1
Nonfall registration?	no

APPLICANTS ALSO LOOK AT

AND OFTEN PREFER

Bucknell University
University of Richmond
Vanderbilt University
Washington University in St. Louis

AND SOMETIMES PREFER

The College of Wooster
DePauw University
Kenyon College
Miami University

AND RARELY PREFER

Allegheny College
Hobart and William Smith Colleges
Ohio State University—Columbus

FINANCIAL FACTS

Financial Aid Rating	**91**
Annual tuition	$28,170
Room & Board	$8,120
Books and supplies	$1,800
Required fees	$750
% frosh rec. need-based scholarship or grant aid	49
% UG rec. need-based scholarship or grant aid	48
% frosh rec. need-based self-help aid	35
% UG rec. need-based self-help aid	37
% frosh rec. any financial aid	98
% UG rec. any financial aid	98
Avg. frosh grant	$17,921
Avg. frosh loan	$4,037
Independent 529 member?	Yes

DePaul University

1 East Jackson Boulevard, Chicago, IL 60604-2287 • Admissions: 312-362-8300 • Fax: 312-362-5749

CAMPUS LIFE

Quality of Life Rating	**92**
Fire Safety Rating	**78**
Type of school	private
Affiliation	Roman Catholic

STUDENTS

Total undergrad enrollment	14,239
% male/female	42/58
% from out of state	13
% from public high school	68
% live on campus	26
% African American	9
% Asian	8
% Caucasian	50
% Hispanic	11
% international	1
# of countries represented	85

SURVEY SAYS

Small classes
Athletic facilities are great
Diverse student types on campus
Students love Chicago, IL
Great off-campus food

ACADEMICS

Academic Rating	**78**
Calendar	quarter
Student/faculty ratio	18:1
Professors interesting rating	80
Professors accessible rating	80
% professors teaching UG courses	99
% classes taught by TAs	0
Most common lab size	fewer than 10 students
Most common regular class size	20-29 students

MOST POPULAR MAJORS

Accounting
Business administration/management
general studies

STUDENTS SPEAK OUT

Academics

Our survey says that DePaul students are among the nation's happiest, and why shouldn't they be? This Catholic school, which was founded by the Vincentians over a century ago, offers "excellent programs in business, music, and biology; [a] strong political science and public policy department; [and] one of the best communications departments in the country." The communications department is supported by "the student-run radio station WRDP and television station, which make learning about communications fun and more hands-on." The ancient Vincentian tradition meets the modern world through "up-to-date technology." One student adds, "DePaul is crazy about technology! Signing up for classes online and having assignments posted online (Blackboard) can be really helpful." Students happily tell us that "the faculty at DePaul and the organizations are very student-driven. You don't hear much about DePaul doing all kinds of big research in the news because the professors here are concerned with student success." That doesn't mean the school isn't at the forefront of educational developments; on the contrary, undergraduates praise the school's "cutting-edge fields of study. DePaul looks for what careers are opening up and gears classes to fulfill the needs of those careers." That suits this largely pre-professional student body perfectly; they also appreciate the "many great opportunities to get jobs and internships within the commercial district in Chicago." DePaul has two main campuses. One campus is in uptown Lincoln Park, [and] hosts liberal arts, music, education, and drama students; the other campus is in the downtown Loop, [and] is geared more toward business and computer science majors.

Life

DePaul students tell us that there's not much campus life at their school, in large part because of the large commuter population and Chicago's enticements. Undergraduates report, "Chicago is the base of DePaul life. Hopping on the El and walking around Michigan Avenue is almost a daily routine." A student adds, "[Activities include] art gallery openings, museums, dancing at clubs, restaurants, movies, shopping downtown, going to plays, going for walks around the neighborhoods, going to Cubs games, and just hanging out with my friends in apartments." Most students agree that when the sun goes down "DePaul is very much a 'bar school.' Parties in houses/apartments are very rare. If you aren't twenty-one [or] don't have a fake ID, you'll have to improvise." True to the school's Vincentian roots, community service also plays a major role in many students' lives: "My favorite part about DePaul is the huge emphasis on doing service work. Individuals from different religious backgrounds come together to do service work. There are clubs that do work once or twice a week together, and there are many opportunities for one-day service projects." Undergraduates praise DePaul's "amazing facilities, i.e., the gym, cafeteria, library, etc." and love that "the entire campus is roughly three blocks by three blocks. You can walk from one side of campus to the other in under fifteen minutes."

Student Body

Students report that "DePaul University is a very diverse campus" thanks to the school's demographic statistics. Undergraduates tell us that "everyone gets along with each other remarkably. There are open gay/lesbians, African Americans, Caucasians, Asians, and people of all different races who all accept each other for who they are." The university works hard to create this open atmosphere; it "strongly supports multiculturalism; we even have to take a class on it." The school also provides meeting space for Gay, Bisexual, Lesbian, Trans, Queer Alliance groups (despite the Church's doctrinal opposition to homosexuality). Politically, the student body divides along campus lines; kids at the Lincoln Park campus "tend to be liberal" and "like to study but also like to play and have fun," while students at the Loop campus tend to be "very conservative and quite stuffy—it's more professional in nature." Because there is not much available housing on campus, the student body is mostly local; however, the school's demographic "is starting to branch out to other states."

FINANCIAL AID: 312-362-8091 • E-MAIL: ADMITDPU@DEPAUL.EDU • WEBSITE: WWW.DEPAUL.EDU

ADMISSIONS

Very important factors considered include: Character/personal qualities, secondary school record. *Important factors considered include:* Class rank, essays, extracurricular activities, recommendations, standardized test scores, talent/ability, volunteer work, work experience. *Other factors considered include:* Alumni/ae relation, geographical residence, interview, minority status, religious affiliation/commitment, state residency. SAT Reasoning or ACT required. TOEFL required of all international applicants. High school diploma is required, and GED is accepted. *Academic units required:* 4 English, 2 math, 2 science (2 science lab), 2 social studies, 4 academic electives.

The Inside Word

Applicants to DePaul will find the admissions staff is genuinely committed to helping students. Candidates whose academic qualifications fall below normally acceptable levels are reviewed for other evidence of potential for success. The Latino student presence on campus has begun to increase significantly, due in large part to the university's major commitment to active involvement in the National Hispanic Institute, an organization that works with top Hispanic students from junior high through college.

FINANCIAL AID

Students should submit: FAFSA. Regular filing deadline is 5/1. The Princeton Review suggests that all financial aid forms be submitted as soon as possible after 1/1. *Need-based scholarships/grants offered:* Pell, SEOG, state scholarships/grants, private scholarships, the school's own gift aid. *Loan aid offered:* Direct Subsidized Stafford, Direct Unsubsidized Stafford, Direct PLUS, Federal Perkins. Applicants will be notified of awards on a rolling basis beginning on or about 2/15.

FROM THE ADMISSIONS OFFICE

"The nation's largest Catholic university, DePaul University is nationally recognized for its innovative academic programs that embrace a comprehensive 'learn by doing' approach. DePaul has two residential campuses and four commuter campuses in the suburbs. The Lincoln Park campus is located in one of Chicago's most exciting neighborhoods, filled with theaters, cafés, clubs, and shops. It is home to DePaul's College of Liberal Arts & Sciences, the School of Education, the Theater School, and the School of Music. New buildings on the 36-acre campus include residence halls, a science building, a student recreational facility, and the student center, which features a cyber café where students can surf the Web or gather with friends. The Loop campus, located in Chicago's downtown—a world-class center for business, government, law, and culture—is home to DePaul's College of Commerce; College of Law; School of Computer Science, Telecommunications, and Information Systems; School for New Learning; and School of Accountancy and Management Information Systems.

"Applicants for the fall 2006 freshman class are required to take either the ACT or the SAT. The Writing Test on the ACT and the Writing section on the SAT are not required for admission consideration; therefore, we will also accept results from tests taken prior to March 2005."

SELECTIVITY

Admissions Rating	**80**
# of applicants	10,087
% of applicants accepted	69
% of acceptees attending	33

FRESHMAN PROFILE

Range SAT Verbal	520-620
Average SAT Verbal	560
Range SAT Math	500-610
Average SAT Math	570
**TPR Projected Range SAT Writing*	*570-650*
Range ACT Composite	21-26
Average ACT Composite	24
Minimum Paper TOEFL	550
Minimum Computer Based TOEFL	213
Average HS GPA	3.3
% graduated top 10% of class	19
% graduated top 25% of class	43
% graduated top 50% of class	75

DEADLINES

Regular notification	rolling
Nonfall registration?	yes

APPLICANTS ALSO LOOK AT AND OFTEN PREFER

Loyola University of Chicago
Northwestern University
University of Chicago
University of Illinois at Urbana-Champaign
University of Notre Dame

AND SOMETIMES PREFER

Illinois State University
Indiana University—Bloomington
Marquette University
Northern Illinois University
University of Illinois—Chicago

FINANCIAL FACTS

Financial Aid Rating	**66**
Annual tuition	$19,700
Room & Board	$9,307
Books and supplies	$1,000
Required fees	$65
% frosh rec. need-based scholarship or grant aid	54
% UG rec. need-based scholarship or grant aid	52
% frosh rec. need-based self-help aid	56
% UG rec. need-based self-help aid	54
% frosh rec. any financial aid	65
% UG rec. any financial aid	68
Avg. frosh loan	$3,000
Independent 529 member?	No

DePauw University

101 E. Seminary, Greencastle, IN 46135 • Admissions: 765-658-4006 • Fax: 765-658-4007

CAMPUS LIFE

Quality of Life Rating	**78**
Fire Safety Rating	**76**
Type of school	private
Affiliation	Methodist
Environment	rural

STUDENTS

Total undergrad enrollment	2,350
% male/female	46/54
% from out of state	51
% from public high school	83
% live on campus	95
% in (# of) fraternities	75 (12)
% in (# of) sororities	74 (10)
% African American	5
% Asian	2
% Caucasian	86
% Hispanic	3
% international	2
# of countries represented	21

SURVEY SAYS

Small classes
Lab facilities are great
Frats and sororities dominate social scene
Lots of beer drinking

ACADEMICS

Academic Rating	**90**
Calendar	4-1-4
Student/faculty ratio	10:1
Professors interesting rating	91
Professors accessible rating	95
% professors teaching UG courses	100
% classes taught by TAs	0
Most common regular class size	10-19 students

MOST POPULAR MAJORS

Economics
English composition
mass communications/media studies

STUDENTS SPEAK OUT

Academics

DePauw University is the "the quintessential 'work hard, play hard' school." It offers students "value through a liberal arts experience firmly grounded in reality by generous opportunities to travel, study, and/or work abroad as a student." These opportunities include the highly praised Management Fellows Program, which "provides liberal arts students the business tools they need for the corporate world. It [also gives students] a phenomenal internship opportunity" that allows them to work from four to eight months and gain real work experience, earn money, and earn college credits. Another unique academic offering is the Winter Program, offered in January, which "allows a lot of students to study abroad for a few weeks." Undergraduates get to learn hands-on almost from the moment they arrive. Explains one student, "For the science students, it's all about the research experience. So many freshman are involved in research from their first semester on campus." All students at DePauw must complete "a strong liberal education with a challenging, heavy workload" administered by professors who enforce "an expectation of high academic standards." Students tell us that "classes are small and discussion based. You also get access to the best professors starting your freshman year." Undergraduates also appreciate how "DePauw really values technology. It seems that everything is done on the computer. We even have classes in computer laboratories where students can interact with their professor and take notes via a computer program."

Life

Few schools are as completely given over to frats and sororities as DePauw: "Life is dominated by the Greek system. Socially, everything rotates around the Greeks: informals, formals, parties, rush/recruitment, chapter meetings, philanthropies, everything." Even "some of the biggest service events of the year, such as Relay for Life, can only be participated in if you are on a sorority/fraternity team." Students know from the beginning that "the enormous Greek community shapes the personality of the campus," and most students choose the school because this is the college experience they seek. There are precious few other social options for students because "[hometown] Greencastle is a small town with not a lot of excitement to offer. It has a Super Wal-Mart, and that's about it." Those with cars note that "Indianapolis is close, so it's not at all that difficult to find alternatives to the frat scene once you leave campus." Although most students insist that "DePauw is a huge party school," they are equally adamant that the partying does not interfere with studies. An undergraduate adds, "We work super hard during the week. Sunday through Thursday nights are spent burning the midnight oil, but weekends are for blowing off steam. Most people party and pretend they are not workaholics." One student says, "I don't mind that the only things to do are study, drink beer, and watch football. If that's for you, then come to DePauw. If you need cultural events, good food, and erudite conversation, though, you're gonna be lonely."

Student Body

DePauw students are "typically white, upper-middle class, and very preppy;" they are fastidious about both their schoolwork ("We get good grades and take our classes seriously") and their appearance ("The typical DePauw student is well dressed and well put together. They take genuine care in their outward appearance"). Most are "incredibly involved in community service and athletics, whether a varsity sport, club sport, or intramural. And, of course, over 70 percent are involved in Greek organizations, which adds its own distinct flavor to the typical student." As this is a Midwestern, religiously affiliated school, "most people are conservative," although "liberal-minded students also have a strong union and are treated the same in and out of class." In recent years, we're told, "Diversity has increased, and with it the culture has been broadened. There is some ignorance in the areas of race and sexual orientation, though most students are fairly accepting."

Financial Aid: 765-658-4030 • E-mail: admission@depauw.edu • Website: www.depauw.edu

ADMISSIONS

Very important factors considered include: Class rank, secondary school record, standardized test scores. *Important factors considered include:* Essays, interview, recommendations. *Other factors considered include:* Alumni/ae relation, character/personal qualities, extracurricular activities, geographical residence, minority status, talent/ability, volunteer work, work experience. SAT Reasoning or ACT required. TOEFL required of all international applicants. High school diploma is required, and GED is accepted. *Academic units recommended:* 4 English, 4 math, 4 science (2 science lab), 4 foreign language, 4 social studies, 3 history, 10 academic electives.

The Inside Word

Students considering DePauw should not be deceived by the university's high acceptance rate. The impressive freshman profile indicates a high level of self-selection in the applicant pool.

FINANCIAL AID

Students should submit: FAFSA, institution's own financial aid form. Regular filing deadline is 2/15. The Princeton Review suggests that all financial aid forms be submitted as soon as possible after 1/1. *Need-based scholarships/grants offered:* Pell, SEOG, state scholarships/grants, private scholarships, the school's own gift aid. *Loan aid offered:* FFEL Subsidized Stafford, FFEL Unsubsidized Stafford, FFEL PLUS, Federal Perkins, college/university loans from institutional funds, alternative loans. Applicants will be notified of awards on or about 3/27. Federal Work-study Program available. Institutional employment available. Off-campus job opportunities are fair.

FROM THE ADMISSIONS OFFICE

"DePauw University is nationally recognized for intellectual and experiential challenge that links liberal arts education with life's work, preparing graduates for uncommon professional success, service to others, and personal fulfillment. DePauw graduates count among their ranks a Nobel laureate, a vice president and U.S. Congressman, Pulitzer Prize and Newbery Award authors, and a number of CEOs and humanitarian leaders. Our students demonstrate a love for learning, a willingness to serve others, the reason and judgment to lead, an interest in engaging worlds and cultures unknown to them, the courage to question their assumptions, and a strong commitment to community. Pre-professional and career exploration are encouraged through Winter Term, when more than 700 students pursue their own off-campus internships. This represents more students in experiential learning opportunities than at any other liberal arts college in the nation. Other innovative programs include Honor Scholars, Information Technology Associates Program, Management Fellows, Media Fellows, and Science Research Fellows, affording selected students additional seminar and internship opportunities.

"Freshman applicants for fall 2006 and thereafter are required to submit scores of the Writing section of the SAT or the ACT. Scores from previous SAT or ACT administrations will be considered, but a Writing score is required to complete an application for admission."

SELECTIVITY

Admissions Rating	**91**
# of applicants	3,485
% of applicants accepted	69
% of acceptees attending	27
# accepting a place on wait list	155
% admitted from wait list	10
# of early decision applicants	49
% accepted early decision	91

FRESHMAN PROFILE

Range SAT Verbal	550-660
Average SAT Verbal	605
Range SAT Math	570-660
Average SAT Math	610
**TPR Projected Range SAT Writing*	*600-670*
Range ACT Composite	23-29
Average ACT Composite	26
Minimum Paper TOEFL	560
Minimum Computer Based TOEFL	225
Average HS GPA	3.62
% graduated top 10% of class	53
% graduated top 25% of class	85
% graduated top 50% of class	97

DEADLINES

Early decision application deadline	11/1
Early decision notification	1/1
Regular application deadline	2/1
Regular notification	4/1
Nonfall registration?	yes

APPLICANTS ALSO LOOK AT

AND OFTEN PREFER
Indiana U.—Bloomington, Northwestern U., U. of Notre Dame, Vanderbilt U.

AND SOMETIMES PREFER
Denison U., Miami U., Purdue U.—West Lafayette, U. of Illinois at Urbana—Champaign

AND RARELY PREFER
Hanover College

FINANCIAL FACTS

Financial Aid Rating	**97**
Annual tuition	$26,100
Room & Board	$7,500
Books and supplies	$700
Required fees	$370
% frosh rec. need-based scholarship or grant aid	54
% UG rec. need-based scholarship or grant aid	50
% frosh rec. need-based self-help aid	40
% UG rec. need-based self-help aid	36
% frosh rec. any financial aid	98
% UG rec. any financial aid	99
Avg. frosh grant	$20,570
Avg. frosh loan	$3,550
Independent 529 member?	Yes

DICKINSON COLLEGE

PO BOX 1773, CARLISLE, PA 17013-2896 • ADMISSIONS: 717-245-1231 • FAX: 717-245-1442

CAMPUS LIFE

Quality of Life Rating	**79**
Fire Safety Rating	**86**
Type of school	private
Environment	city

STUDENTS

Total undergrad enrollment	2,280
% male/female	45/55
% from out of state	67
% from public high school	66
% live on campus	90
% in (# of) fraternities	17 (6)
% in (# of) sororities	26 (4)
% African American	4
% Asian	4
% Caucasian	86
% Hispanic	3
% international	3
# of countries represented	35

SURVEY SAYS

Small classes
Great computer facilities
Great library
Lots of beer drinking

ACADEMICS

Academic Rating	**89**
Calendar	semester
Student/faculty ratio	13:1
Professors interesting rating	87
Professors accessible rating	91
% professors teaching UG courses	100
% classes taught by TAs	0
Most common lab size	10-19 students
Most common regular class size	10-19 students

MOST POPULAR MAJORS

English language and literature
international business
political science and government

STUDENTS SPEAK OUT

Academics

Offering "an intense and global curriculum" driven by a study abroad program "unsurpassed by most institutions," Dickinson College pursues a mission of "preparing future leaders to become important movers and shapers in America and abroad." A focus on matters international is just one way in which Dickinson is "constantly defining itself as a revolutionary institution." The school also has "a strong tradition of encouraging students to go beyond the things that are familiar and comfortable, and to engage the world around them" through field work and participation in faculty research. The workload here can be tough; warns one undergraduate, "Academically, Dickinson can be a bit overwhelming, as much is demanded from each student; however, all the work will be worth it in the long run." Help is always available: "The classes tend to be pretty small, which creates a good learning environment. The professors are great [and] would love nothing more than to meet with every student in every one of their classes." Reviews of administrators are mixed, but most appreciate the personal touches, like the fact that "the president of the college has open hours at a café where students can just come in and talk to him." Despite a few complaints about the brass being "much more concerned with image than with students, something is working [since] we've jumped a lot in the rankings" in recent years. Add up all the plusses here and you'll understand why "Dickinson is getting harder and harder to get into. Suddenly, when I go home people recognize where I go to school."

Life

How you react to life at Dickinson depends largely on how you react to Carlisle, Dickinson's hometown. There are those who "love small towns like this one, which has tons of good restaurants. The biggest thing in the town is the 24-hour Super Wal-Mart, which sits atop a hill on the edge of town. For fun, there are a few things to do in the town, including dining, movies, and a bowling alley." Undergrads "who are 21 go out to the couple of bars and mix it up with the townies." Then there are those who insist adamantly that Carlisle "is not a college town" and "of campus there is virtually nothing to do." Most students fill their time by "getting involved in lots of different organizations, volunteer networks, and special housing activities," immersing themselves in Greek life, and hitting the party scene. Many students warn, however, that "the Dickinson Department of Public Safety is constantly on the prowl for underage drinking," and getting busted almost invariably results in a citation. But "if students don't like to be around [partying], there are always numerous things happening on campus that do not involve alcohol on the weekends and weeknights. There are always two or three evening lectures per week, as well as midnight movies, dry-dance parties, comedians, concerts—you name it, it has probably been done at Dickinson."

Student Body

Most students agree that at first glance, "Dickenson looks very preppy—the Louis Vuitton bags, popped collars, guys in pastels—but there is more to it than that. It took a bit of searching, but there are plenty of people here who run against the grain—and they all fit in fine. There may not be a ton of interaction between the sorority girls and the hippie kids, but there isn't any animosity." Since the late 1990's, Dickinson has aggressively recruited beyond its traditional core constituencies and has even established safe havens for targeted demographics: Arts Haüs, a residential community for "alternative punk kids," and Tree House, for environmentally conscious (i.e., hippie) students. Undergrads detect "a more politically active, alternative sub-culture 'within the limestone walls' that is rapidly emerging." The school is also home to "a large homosexual population, which is accepted by all students [and] many international students coming from numerous foreign countries." Sums up one junior, "The school is doing a great deal to make the campus more diverse. In my three years, I would say they have been successful in recruiting a more diverse student body, economically and ethnically."

DICKINSON COLLEGE

FINANCIAL AID: 717-245-1308 • E-MAIL: ADMIT@DICKINSON.EDU • WEBSITE: WWW.DICKINSON.EDU

ADMISSIONS

Very important factors considered include: Extracurricular activities, minority status, secondary school record, talent/ability, volunteer work. *Important factors considered include:* Alumni/ae relation, class rank, recommendations, standardized test scores, work experience. *Other factors considered include:* Character/personal qualities, essays, geographical residence, interview, state residency. SAT Reasoning or ACT recommended. TOEFL required of all international applicants. High school diploma is required, and GED is accepted. *Academic units required:* 4 English, 3 math, 3 science (2 science lab), 2 foreign language, 2 social studies, 2 academic electives. *Academic units recommended:* 3 foreign language.

The Inside Word

Dickinson's admissions process is typical of most small liberal arts colleges. The best candidates for such a place are those with solid grades and broad extracurricular involvement—the stereotypical "well-rounded student." Admissions selectivity is kept in check by a strong group of competitor colleges that fight tooth and nail for their cross-applicants.

FINANCIAL AID

Students should submit: FAFSA, CSS/Financial Aid PROFILE, state aid form, noncustodial (divorced/separated) parents' statement, business/farm supplement. Regular filing deadline is 2/1. The Princeton Review suggests that all financial aid forms be submitted as soon as possible after 1/1. *Need-based scholarships/grants offered:* Pell, SEOG, state scholarships/grants, private scholarships, the school's own gift aid. *Loan aid offered:* FFEL Subsidized Stafford, FFEL Unsubsidized Stafford, FFEL PLUS, Federal Perkins, college/university loans from institutional funds. Applicants will be notified of awards on or about 3/20. Federal Work-study Program available. Institutional employment available. Off-campus job opportunities are good.

FROM THE ADMISSIONS OFFICE

"College is more than a collection of courses. It is about crossing traditional boundaries, about seeing the interrelationships among different subjects, about learning a paradigm for solving problems, about developing critical thinking and communication skills, and about speaking out on issues that matter. Dickinson was founded to be different from the 15 colleges that existed in our nation before it: to provide a "useful" education, where students would learn by doing, through hands-on experiences and engagement with the community the region, the nation and the world. And this is truer today than ever, with workshop science courses replacing traditional lectures, fieldwork experiences in community studies where students take oral histories, and 12 study centers abroad in nontourist cities where students, under the guidance of a Dickinson faculty director, experience a true international culture. Almost 80 percent of the student body studies abroad, preparing them to compete and succeed in a complex global world.

"Applicants wishing to be considered for academic scholarships are required to submit scores from either the SAT or ACT, but Dickinson does not require results from either test for admission into the 2006 entering class."

SELECTIVITY

Admissions Rating	**92**
# of applicants	4,998
% of applicants accepted	49
% of acceptees attending	25
# accepting a place on wait list	270
% admitted from wait list	15
# of early decision applicants	292
% accepted early decision	69

FRESHMAN PROFILE

Range SAT Verbal	600-690
Average SAT Verbal	640
Range SAT Math	590-680
Average SAT Math	634
**TPR Projected Range SAT Writing*	*630-690*
Range ACT Composite	26-29
Average ACT Composite	28
Minimum Paper TOEFL	550
Minimum Computer Based TOEFL	250
% graduated top 10% of class	51
% graduated top 25% of class	82
% graduated top 50% of class	98

DEADLINES

Early decision application deadline	11/15
Early decision notification	12/15
Regular application deadline	2/1
Regular notification	3/31
Nonfall registration?	yes

APPLICANTS ALSO LOOK AT

AND OFTEN PREFER

Colgate University, Lafayette College

AND SOMETIMES PREFER

Bucknell University, Franklin & Marshall College, Gettysburg College, Kenyon College, Lehigh University

AND RARELY PREFER

Muhlenberg College, Penn State University Park, University of Delaware

FINANCIAL FACTS

Financial Aid Rating	**91**
Annual tuition	$31,800
Room & Board	$8,050
Books and supplies	$750
Required fees	$320
% frosh rec. need-based scholarship or grant aid	48
% UG rec. need-based scholarship or grant aid	49
% frosh rec. need-based self-help aid	44
% UG rec. need-based self-help aid	45
% frosh rec. any financial aid	56
% UG rec. any financial aid	58
Avg. frosh grant	$18,250
Avg. frosh loan	$3,466
Independent 529 member?	Yes

DREW UNIVERSITY

OFFICE OF COLLEGE ADMISSIONS, MADISON, NJ 07940-1493 • ADMISSIONS: 973-408-3739 • FAX: 973-408-3068

CAMPUS LIFE

Quality of Life Rating	**81**
Fire Safety Rating	**86**
Type of school	private
Affiliation	Methodist
Environment	village

STUDENTS

Total undergrad enrollment	1,578
% male/female	40/60
% from out of state	43
% from public high school	67
% live on campus	88
% African American	4
% Asian	6
% Caucasian	64
% Hispanic	6
% international	1
# of countries represented	14

SURVEY SAYS

Small classes
Frats and sororities are unpopular or nonexistent
Theater is popular
Student publications are popular

ACADEMICS

Academic Rating	**85**
Calendar	semester
Student/faculty ratio	12:1
Professors interesting rating	84
Professors accessible rating	85
% professors teaching UG courses	100
% classes taught by TAs	0
Most common lab size	10-19 students
Most common regular class size	10-19 students

MOST POPULAR MAJORS

English language and literature
political science and government
psychology

STUDENTS SPEAK OUT

Academics

Both as a small school with university resources and as a suburban school with easy access to big cities, Drew University successfully straddles divergent universes to fashion a unique undergraduate experience. With fewer than 2,000 undergrads, Drew can offer "perfect class sizes" that "really allow professors to teach their material well and students to get immediate feedback on questions they have." Explains one student, "Because of Drew's small size, professors and administrators are highly accessible. They go out of their way to make sure that you understand what you're being taught, that you feel like you're going in the right direction. They even e-mail you with clarifications at midnight about that day's lecture because they couldn't sleep, worried you might be confused." Despite the small-school vibe, Drew offers some big-school amenities, including "wonderful opportunities to study abroad, breadth requirements that cause students to take classes they might not think about taking, which can often open up doors for them, [and] strong job placement and internship programs." Some students warn, "Because Drew is so small, some upper-level classes are only offered every other year, which can make planning a major difficult. This is only true in the smaller departments, however, such as math and physics."

Life

"Drew has an extremely good balance between socializing and studying," students agree, pointing out that "we work hard during the week, but on any Thursday, Friday, or Saturday night, it is easy to find a party and drink, if that's what you want to do. It's just as easy, however, to stay in with friends and watch a movie or just hang out. The chill factor here is pretty high." Because "the alcohol policy is very lenient (it's basically 'If we don't see it, it's not happening'), alcohol is a popular pastime." Parties often occur in "The Suites," a residence for upperclassmen and are frequently hosted by male athletic teams. Some undergrads warn that these parties "are not always open to everyone," and "if you want to party and get drunk, it helps to be an athlete or friends with a large group of them." There is a lot more to life at Drew than drinking and working, though. The school boasts a very active theater department: "Theater is a very big part of Drew life. Students are more supportive of theatrical events than of most sporting events." Hometown Madison is "an art-oriented town, so there is a lot of opportunity for cultural activities," although be forewarned that "the town goes to sleep at 6:00." Fortunately, "New York City is close by, although it's harder to get there than the school would have you believe. Still, it's nice to be isolated in a safe suburb where you can be in NYC in an hour."

Student Body

"There are two main groups within the Drew student population," according to students: "the athletes and their friends" and the "artsy" crowd. The former congregate in such popular social science departments as political science, economics, and psychology; the latter dominate the theater department. Most students are active within the campus community, as "Drew is a predominantly student-run school. Students decide the activities, help work on policies, and generally run campus life. Drew is a campus of leaders, which is what makes it so exciting." Students are also active politically, with the balance tipped to the left; observes one student, "Drew can best be understood by viewing the movie *P.C.U.*—minus the Republicans." Drew's relatively high price tag, coupled with its proximity to northeastern wealth centers, means that "many students are loaded—sons and daughters of governors and ambassadors whose families have at least two houses somewhere around the world." The school "has a large gay population, and they tend to stick together but have no problems getting along with other students."

FINANCIAL AID: 973-408-3112 • E-MAIL: CADM@DREW.EDU • WEBSITE: WWW.DREW.EDU

ADMISSIONS

Very important factors considered include: Secondary school record. *Important factors considered include:* Class rank, standardized test scores. *Other factors considered include:* Alumni/ae relation, character/personal qualities, essays, extracurricular activities, interview, minority status, recommendations, talent/ability, volunteer work, work experience. SAT Reasoning or ACT required. TOEFL required of all international applicants. High school diploma or equivalent is not required. *Academic units recommended:* 4 English, 3 math, 2 science, 2 foreign language, 2 social studies, 2 history, 3 academic electives.

The Inside Word

Drew suffers greatly from the annual mass exodus of New Jersey's college-age residents and a lack of recognition by others. Application totals have significantly increased in recent years, but the university must begin to enroll more of its admitted students before any significant change in selectivity will occur. This makes Drew a great choice for solid students, and easier to get into than it should be given its quality.

FINANCIAL AID

Students should submit: FAFSA, CSS/Financial Aid PROFILE. Regular filing deadline is 2/15. The Princeton Review suggests that all financial aid forms be submitted as soon as possible after 1/1. *Need-based scholarships/grants offered:* Pell, SEOG, state scholarships/grants, private scholarships, the school's own gift aid. Non-need-based (college administered): State, academic, creative arts/performance. *Loan aid offered:* FFEL Subsidized Stafford, FFEL Unsubsidized Stafford, FFEL PLUS, Federal Perkins, state loans. Applicants will be notified of awards on or about 3/31. Federal Work-study Program available. Institutional employment available. Off-campus job opportunities are excellent.

FROM THE ADMISSIONS OFFICE

"At Drew, great teachers are transforming the undergraduate learning experience. With a commitment to teaching, Drew professors have made educating undergraduates their top priority. With a spirit of innovation, they have brought the most advanced technology and distinctive modes of experiential learning into the Drew classroom. The result is a stimulating and challenging education that connects the traditional liberal arts and sciences to the workplace and to the world.

"Drew University will require applicants for the 2006–2007 academic year to take either the new SAT or the ACT. The Selection Committee will consider the highest Verbal, Math, and Writing scores individually in its evaluation of candidates for admission."

SELECTIVITY

Admissions Rating	**85**
# of applicants	3,266
% of applicants accepted	70
% of acceptees attending	18
# accepting a place on wait list	329
% admitted from wait list	23
# of early decision applicants	78
% accepted early decision	89

FRESHMAN PROFILE

Range SAT Verbal	560-670
Average SAT Verbal	615
Range SAT Math	550-650
Average SAT Math	600
**TPR Projected Range SAT Writing*	*600-680*
Range ACT Composite	22-29
Average ACT Composite	25
Minimum Paper TOEFL	550
% graduated top 10% of class	37
% graduated top 25% of class	68
% graduated top 50% of class	92

DEADLINES

Early decision application deadline	12/1
Early decision notification	12/24
Regular application deadline	2/15
Regular notification	3/21
Nonfall registration?	yes

AND SOMETIMES PREFER

Connecticut College
Dickinson College
Franklin & Marshall College
Muhlenberg College
New York University
Rutgers University—Rutgers College
Skidmore College
Trinity College (CT)
Vassar College

FINANCIAL FACTS

Financial Aid Rating	**79**
Annual tuition	$29,000
Room & Board	$8,010
Books and supplies	$1,090
% frosh rec. need-based scholarship or grant aid	51
% UG rec. need-based scholarship or grant aid	50
% frosh rec. need-based self-help aid	38
% UG rec. need-based self-help aid	41
% frosh rec. any financial aid	85
% UG rec. any financial aid	79
Avg. frosh grant	$19,840
Avg. frosh loan	$14,490
Independent 529 member?	Yes

DREXEL UNIVERSITY

3141 CHESTNUT STREET, PHILADELPHIA, PA 19104 • ADMISSIONS: 215-895-2400 • FAX: 215-895-5939

CAMPUS LIFE

Quality of Life Rating	**63**
Fire Safety Rating	**60**
Type of school	private
Environment	metropolis

STUDENTS

Total undergrad enrollment	11,544
% male/female	60/40
% from out of state	42
% from public high school	70
% live on campus	38
% in (# of) fraternities	6 (11)
% in (# of) sororities	6 (5)
% African American	10
% Asian	12
% Caucasian	63
% Hispanic	3
% international	6
# of countries represented	105

SURVEY SAYS

Great computer facilities
Diverse student types on campus
Great off-campus food
Student publications are popular
Lots of beer drinking
Hard liquor is popular
(Almost) everyone smokes

ACADEMICS

Academic Rating	**73**
Calendar	quarter
Student/faculty ratio	10:1
Professors interesting rating	62
Professors accessible rating	61
% professors teaching UG courses	100
% classes taught by TAs	0
Most common lab size	20-29 students
Most common regular class size	10-19 students

MOST POPULAR MAJORS

Business administration/management
computer and information sciences
information science/studies

STUDENTS SPEAK OUT

Academics

"Learning in both the classroom and the workplace" is the focus of Drexel's co-op experience. Students alternate between academic quarters on campus and full-time jobs with university-approved employers. Co-op, which commences upon the completion of freshman year (exactly when it begins varies by program), is required of all majors in computer science, design arts, engineering, and information science and technology, as well as undergraduates selecting the co-op option in the Colleges of Arts and Sciences and Business. Students report, "The co-op program gives you a taste of what life will be like working at a full-time job, which can help you in deciding what you want to do when you graduate." They also appreciate "the money you make through co-op, since it helps with the cost of going to school." Drexel's strongest areas are in engineering, technology, and business disciplines. "This is definitely not a liberal arts school," students warn. According to undergraduates, Drexel professors are a mixed bag. The school "offers some of the greatest professors in the country. However, these professors are contrasted by some of the worst in the country." Many "are working professionals in their field, so they know exactly what they're talking about," but they are not always accessible and aren't all adept instructors. Students report, "Overall, the academic experience teaches you to deal with work on your own and not be 'hand-fed.' You can do well or terribly, depending on how you, the student, wish to do." Students are unanimous regarding their distaste for the administration, purveyors of the famous (or infamous) "Drexel shaft." Writes one student, "The offices and administrators: Who? What? They are entirely inaccessible."

Life

"Life at Drexel is different than at most schools due to co-op," which leaves "only half the student body on campus at any given time." With students coming and going from campus with such frequency, "there is little to no interest in student organizations;" "intramurals must fight the scheduling problems of a quarter system and students on co-op." The Greeks are stymied by a restrictive administration ("[the administration] does not allow fraternities to hold many functions"). Students would probably make a greater effort to drum up a campus life if Philadelphia and several other more active college campuses weren't so close to Drexel. Students tell us that "living in the city is great. If you get bored, you and your friends can just go wander around the city. You can go to the zoo, comedy clubs, art galleries, and museums." Philadelphia also has "four major sports teams that are great to watch" and "plenty of great bars." In addition, Drexel "is literally right next to University of Pennsylvania and the University of the Sciences in Philadelphia and about ten minutes from Temple, so there is always something to do with college-aged people." Aesthetes should be forewarned that Drexel's campus is made entirely of concrete. Students add, "The last nice piece of grass between buildings recently became a building."

Student Body

Although Drexel "isn't as diverse as some other schools, there are many minorities, and people seem to get along pretty well." Students say, "The majority of kids here are from Pennsylvania." Drexel's engineering focus means that "most of the student body is male and more conservative than many other schools." Undergraduates are rarely politically active. "Instead of worrying about politics and social causes as much, people are more concerned about their careers," students tell us. While some students are typically "book-worm-ish, somewhat intelligent, antisocial (keep door closed and/or play popular network computer games all day), there [are] also a good amount of cool, social people, too." The student body includes many legacies, as supported by a student who said that many students "have a parent or sibling who has attended the university."

FINANCIAL AID: 215-895-2535 • E-MAIL: ENROLL@DREXEL.EDU • WEBSITE: WWW.DREXEL.EDU

ADMISSIONS

Very important factors considered include: Class rank, essays, secondary school record, standardized test scores. *Important factors considered include:* Character/personal qualities, extracurricular activities, interview, recommendations, talent/ability. *Other factors considered include:* Alumni/ae relation, volunteer work, work experience. SAT Reasoning or ACT required. TOEFL required of all international applicants. High school diploma is required, and GED is accepted. *Academic units required:* 3 math, 1 science (1 science lab). *Academic units recommended:* 1 foreign language.

The Inside Word

Drexel's distinct nature creates a high level of self-selection in the applicant pool, and most decent students are admitted.

FINANCIAL AID

Students should submit: FAFSA. The Princeton Review suggests that all financial aid forms be submitted as soon as possible after 1/1. *Need-based scholarships/grants offered:* Pell, SEOG, state scholarships/grants, private scholarships, the school's own gift aid, United Negro College Fund. *Loan aid offered:* FFEL Subsidized Stafford, FFEL Unsubsidized Stafford, FFEL PLUS, Federal Perkins, Federal Nursing, college/university loans from institutional funds. Applicants will be notified of awards on a rolling basis beginning on or about 3/15.

FROM THE ADMISSIONS OFFICE

"Since its inception in 1891, Drexel University has gained national recognition among colleges and universities for its academic excellence, experiential education program (Drexel co-op), technological expertise, and curricular innovation. In 1998, Drexel began operating one of the Philadelphia region's premier medical and health sciences schools, MCP Hahnemann University. In April, Drexel's Board of Trustees unanimously voted to approve merging MCP Hahnemann into Drexel University.

"With the addition of the nation's largest private medical school, an outstanding college of nursing and health professions, and one of only two schools of public health in Pennsylvania, Drexel University now comprises 12 academic colleges and schools. By this summer, we will offer 175 degree programs to some 11,500 undergraduates and 4,200 graduate students. Alumni will number 90,000, and the size of the full-time faculty will exceed 1,000.

"The post-merger Drexel will join the fewer than 50 private universities classified by the Carnegie Foundation as Doctoral/Research Universities-Extensive, which include Carnegie Mellon, MIT, Caltech, and Penn. Drexel also joins the top 100 U.S. universities in federal research expenditures and market value of endowment. Another benefit of this merger is that qualified Drexel applicants can now pursue four new accelerated dual-degree programs in the health sciences: the bachelor's/MD in medicine; bachelor's/master's in nursing; bachelor's/doctor of physical therapy; and bachelor's/master's for physician assistants.

"By combining our expertise in advanced technology and cooperative education with academic programs in medicine and health-related fields, we can now offer our students a unique set of skills with which to succeed in today's ever-changing world.

"Students who plan to enter in fall 2006 will be the first class to take the new SAT for college admissions. Drexel is exploring ways in which the additional Writing component can be used in admissions or placement decisions."

SELECTIVITY	
Admissions Rating	**87**
# of applicants	12,157
% of applicants accepted	73
% of acceptees attending	24
# accepting a place on wait list	519
% admitted from wait list	44
FRESHMAN PROFILE	
Range SAT Verbal	540-640
Average SAT Verbal	590
Range SAT Math	560-670
Average SAT Math	620
**TPR Projected Range SAT Writing*	*590-660*
Minimum Paper TOEFL	550
Minimum Computer Based TOEFL	213
Average HS GPA	3.51
% graduated top 10% of class	34
% graduated top 25% of class	61
% graduated top 50% of class	91
DEADLINES	
Regular application deadline	3/1
Regular notification	rolling
Nonfall registration?	yes
FINANCIAL FACTS	
Financial Aid Rating	**63**
Annual tuition	$19,900
Room & Board	$8,600
% frosh rec. need-based scholarship or grant aid	25
% UG rec. need-based scholarship or grant aid	30
% frosh rec. need-based self-help aid	64
% UG rec. need-based self-help aid	64
Independent 529 member?	Yes

DUKE UNIVERSITY

2138 CAMPUS DRIVE, DURHAM, NC 27708 • ADMISSIONS: 919-684-3214 • FAX: 919-681-8941

CAMPUS LIFE

Quality of Life Rating	**67**
Fire Safety Rating	**60**
Type of school	private
Affiliation	Methodist
Environment	city

STUDENTS

Total undergrad enrollment	6,107
% male/female	52/48
% from out of state	85
% from public high school	59
% live on campus	82
% in (# of) fraternities	29 (21)
% in (# of) sororities	42 (14)
% African American	11
% Asian	13
% Caucasian	57
% Hispanic	7
% international	5
# of countries represented	89

SURVEY SAYS

Great computer facilities
Great library
Athletic facilities are great
Everyone loves the Blue Devils
Student publications are popular
Lots of beer drinking

ACADEMICS

Academic Rating	**93**
Calendar	semester
Student/faculty ratio	11:1
Professors interesting rating	77
Professors accessible rating	80
% professors teaching UG courses	96
% classes taught by TAs	4
Most common lab size	10-19 students
Most common regular class size	10-19 students

MOST POPULAR MAJORS

Economics
psychology
public policy analysis

STUDENTS SPEAK OUT

Academics

Duke University, "the fun younger brother of the aging Ivies," offers a "well-rounded atmosphere" that allows students to enjoy "top-ten academics, a beautiful campus, a wonderful climate, a fun social scene, and the toughest place for opposing teams to play basketball in the country." Biomedical engineering and premedical sciences are all strong here, taking advantage of Duke's position as a leading national medical research institute. In fact, academics are excellent across disciplines, although a junior advises that "small departments—like art history, history, literature—are run better and tend to have better teachers, while the more popular departments—such as political science and biology—are more bureaucratic and filled with tenured famous researchers who are not as interested in teaching." Duke expects a lot of work from students and "grading is very strict," but students "don't feel overly pressured." The school also operates under an honor code that "is taken very seriously. You see virtually no cheating." Students can single out particular strengths of their school when pressed, but they prefer to focus on the gestalt of the place; time and again they remind us that Duke is "a top-notch academic institution, unparalleled in the South, where emphasis is placed on both in-class academic experiences as well as cultivating sociable, friendly people who will be able to succeed in all future life situations."

Life

"Durham is far from a college town," Duke students agree, but fortunately "lots of activities occur at Duke," and Chapel Hill—a great college town—is only fifteen minutes down the road. Raleigh, with nightlife considerably more active than Durham's, is less than a half-hour away by car. Duke's campus hosts "many theater productions, dance shows, music concerts, guest speakers, and artists" as well as lectures and movies, many of which are free or greatly discounted. Duke students also love to sit around and shoot the breeze—"the benches on campus definitely help the social scene"—and point out that "conversations can range from a biology lab one minute to the current health-care debate the next, then eventually moving on to the difference between Protestants and Catholics and ending with a discussion of the next men's basketball game." Discussion often comes around to Duke basketball, which some claim "is what unites every single student at Duke. You can come to Duke not being a sports fan, but you will become a Blue Devil's fan. We are not only a highly recognized tier-one academic institution, but we also have one of the top basketball teams in the country." Undergrads also love that their "campus is absolutely gorgeous" and that "the weather in the South is beautiful," accommodating year-round outdoor activity. Duke has a party scene, or rather, several (centered on the Greek houses, dorms, and off-campus apartments) although this may be changing, as "strict alcohol policies are pushing a lot of weekend activity off campus."

Student Body

"A couple years ago, Duke may have been considered a school filled with rich white kids," students tell us, "but now, there's such a high number of minorities that that stereotype no longer applies. I think we have one of the highest African American student populations of any top-ranked university. The Asian population is considerable too." The numbers bear out these reports. Vestiges of the 'old Duke' remain, especially in the "Southern fraternity types" who "account for about 30 percent of the students." Cost limits economic diversity here somewhat, since many of the students pay full fare; "It is amazing to me how many students here are able to pay full price to attend the university without financial aid, given that it costs close to $40,000 per year," marvels one aid recipient. Students may not always form one big happy family—"self-segregation is evident everywhere"—but they all share a sincere love for the school. "I'd say 40 to 60 percent of the community is wearing some form of Duke gear at any given time," estimates one undergrad.

FINANCIAL AID: 919-684-6225 • E-MAIL: UNDERGRAD-ADMISSIONS@DUKE.EDU • WEBSITE: WWW.DUKE.EDU

ADMISSIONS

Very important factors considered include: Essays, extracurricular activities, recommendations, secondary school record, standardized test scores, talent/ability. *Important factors considered include:* Character/personal qualities, class rank. *Other factors considered include:* Alumni/ae relation, geographical residence, interview, minority status, state residency, volunteer work, work experience. SAT Reasoning and SAT Subject Tests or ACT required. High school diploma is required, and GED is not accepted. *Academic units recommended:* 4 English, 4 math, 4 science, 4 foreign language, 4 social studies.

The Inside Word

The way in which Duke discusses its candidate review process should be a basic model for all schools to use in their literature. Just about all highly selective admissions committees use rating systems similar to the one described above, but few are willing to publicly discuss them.

FINANCIAL AID

Students should submit: FAFSA, CSS/Financial Aid PROFILE, noncustodial (divorced/separated) parents' statement, business/farm supplement, parent and student income tax returns. Regular filing deadline is 2/1. The Princeton Review suggests that all financial aid forms be submitted as soon as possible after 1/1. *Need-based scholarships/grants offered:* Pell, SEOG, state scholarships/grants, private scholarships, the school's own gift aid, ROTC. *Loan aid offered:* FFEL Subsidized Stafford, FFEL Unsubsidized Stafford, FFEL PLUS, Federal Perkins, college/university loans from institutional funds, private loans. Applicants will be notified of awards on or about 4/1. Federal Work-study Program available. Institutional employment available. Off-campus job opportunities are good.

FROM THE ADMISSIONS OFFICE

"Duke University offers an interesting mix of tradition and innovation, undergraduate college and major research university, southern hospitality and international presence, and athletic prowess and academic excellence. Students come to Duke from all over the United States and the world and from a range of racial, ethnic, and socioeconomic backgrounds. They enjoy contact with a world-class faculty through small classes and independent study. More than 40 majors are available in the arts and sciences and engineering; arts and sciences students may also design their own curriculum through Program II. Certificate programs are available in a number of interdisciplinary areas. Special academic opportunities include FOCUS programs and seminars for first-year students, study abroad, study at the Duke Marine Laboratory and Duke Primate Center, the Duke in New York and Duke in Los Angeles arts programs, and several international exchange programs. While admission to Duke is highly selective, applications of U.S. citizens and permanent residents are evaluated without regard to financial need and the university pledges to meet 100 percent of the demonstrated need of all admitted U.S. students and permanent residents. A limited amount of financial aid is also available for foreign citizens, and the university will meet the full demonstrated need for those admitted students as well.

"Applicants for fall 2006, who are taking standardized tests on or after March 2005, must take either the ACT with the Writing exam or the new SAT plus two SAT Subject Tests (Mathematics required for applicants to the Pratt School of Engineering). Students may submit scores from the old SAT plus three SAT Subject Tests, but must include the SAT Subject Writing exam."

SELECTIVITY

Admissions Rating	**98**
# of applicants	16,749
% of applicants accepted	23
% of acceptees attending	43
# accepting a place on wait list	1,648
% admitted from wait list	6
# of early decision applicants	490
% accepted early decision	35

FRESHMAN PROFILE

Range SAT Verbal	660-750
Range SAT Math	670-780
**TPR Projected Range SAT Writing*	*670-730*
Range ACT Composite	29-34
Average ACT Composite	30
% graduated top 10% of class	90
% graduated top 25% of class	98
% graduated top 50% of class	100

DEADLINES

Early decision application deadline	11/1
Early decision notification	12/15
Regular application deadline	1/2
Regular notification	4/1
Nonfall registration?	no

APPLICANTS ALSO LOOK AT AND OFTEN PREFER

Harvard College
Princeton University
Stanford University
Yale University

AND SOMETIMES PREFER

Brown University
Columbia University—Columbia College
Cornell University
Dartmouth College
University of Pennsylvania

AND RARELY PREFER

Georgetown University
Northwestern University
University of North Carolina—Chapel Hill

FINANCIAL FACTS

Financial Aid Rating	**94**
Annual tuition	$31,420
Room & Board	$8,830
Books and supplies	$970
Required fees	$980
% frosh rec. need-based scholarship or grant aid	40
% UG rec. need-based scholarship or grant aid	39
% frosh rec. need-based self-help aid	37
% UG rec. need-based self-help aid	38
Avg. frosh grant	$7,400
Avg. frosh loan	$3,400
Independent 529 member?	No

Duquesne University

600 Forbes Avenue, Pittsburgh, PA 15282 • Admissions: 412-396-5000 • Fax: 412-396-5644

CAMPUS LIFE

Quality of Life Rating	**80**
Fire Safety Rating	**78**
Type of school	private
Affiliation	Roman Catholic
Environment	metropolis

STUDENTS

Total undergrad enrollment	5,549
% male/female	41/59
% from out of state	19
% from public high school	75
% live on campus	54
% in (# of) fraternities	16 (9)
% in (# of) sororities	14 (9)
% African American	4
% Asian	1
% Caucasian	82
% Hispanic	1
% international	2
# of countries represented	94

SURVEY SAYS

Small classes
Great off-campus food
Campus feels safe
Lots of beer drinking
(Almost) everyone smokes

ACADEMICS

Academic Rating	**75**
Calendar	semester
Student/faculty ratio	15:1
Professors interesting rating	74
Professors accessible rating	74
% professors teaching UG courses	70
% classes taught by TAs	5
Most common lab size	20-29 students
Most common regular class size	10-19 students

MOST POPULAR MAJORS

Communications studies/speech communication and rhetoric
marketing/marketing management
psychology

STUDENTS SPEAK OUT

Academics

Duquesne University offers a first-rate education at a relatively low cost. (The school's tuition is roughly two-thirds that charged by crosstown rival Carnegie Mellon University.) Undergraduates tout their school's commitment to "teaching Catholic values to accompany its excellent academic tradition." The excellent offerings in business and the health sciences are very popular. The professors who teach this program's courses "come from the professional world, and they bring years of business experience into the classroom." Professors in the health sciences "really make a point to get to know you personally and remember you years later. They are always open to meet with you, even when they're not currently your professor, and help in any way they can." Academics are generally difficult, although "the core classes are usually pretty easy and help boost your GPA." For the more challenging upper-level courses, "There are many people—students, tutors, and professors—who are willing to help." This support network helps to make this large university, which comprises ten schools, feel a little smaller and friendlier. An "amazing library and great research materials" also ease students' academic burdens.

Life

Duquesne is located in Pittsburgh's Central Business District, a site that provides easy access to all that the city offers. One student says, "The location of the school is one of its biggest strengths. It is located in one of the nicest parts of uptown Pittsburgh yet is just a short drive or walk to many exciting activities in the downtown area." The Southside "is right across the river, which works out really nicely for students. If you are old enough to drink, that is probably the best place to go." Another student adds, "The shopping is great at Station Square, and there are a ton of restaurants as well." Despite its urban setting, "Once you get on campus, you feel like you are in the suburbs. It's good, and everyone feels safe at school." Students love "the convenience of the campus buildings and things necessary for students. Although it has a small campus, Duquesne really makes the most of its space. There is beautiful landscaping, and the buildings are arranged nicely enough to leave students areas to just hang out and chill." While the party scene is pretty quiet—"we really have no frats on campus. The frats we go to are on Mount Washington and one that is closer to the Hill District, which isn't that convenient"—students can and do head over to University of Pittsburgh or Carnegie Mellon University, where parties are much more plentiful. About half the students live on campus, and "there is a fair amount of people who will go home almost every weekend."

Student Body

"Most students at Duquesne are white, middle- to upper-class private school kids who come from the eastern part of the United States, most from the general Pittsburgh area," students tell us. Some students "don't like the fact that there is very little diversity. Everyone seems so identical in their views. It is hard to have interesting class discussions with students who think so locally instead of globally." Although "the school can be a little cliquey," undergraduates are famously polite—"the strange thing is, here, everyone holds the door open for everyone! I have literally had to run to the door because someone was way up ahead holding it and waiting for me." Duquesne students "work hard but nothing too excessive. They like to party on the weekends and study on the weeknights." A large portion of the student population lives off campus; these students "have most interaction with other commuter students. The commuter council is a great organization for commuters to get involved in and helps the commuters to be more active on campus."

FINANCIAL AID: 412-396-6607 • E-MAIL: ADMISSIONS@DUQ.EDU • WEBSITE: WWW.DUQ.EDU

ADMISSIONS

Very important factors considered include: Essays, recommendations, secondary school record, standardized test scores. *Important factors considered include:* Character/personal qualities, class rank, extracurricular activities, interview, talent/ability, volunteer work. *Other factors considered include:* Alumni/ae relation, work experience. SAT Reasoning or ACT required. High school diploma is required, and GED is accepted. *Academic units required:* 4 English, 2 math, 2 science, 2 foreign language, 2 social studies, 4 academic electives.

The Inside Word

With such a high admit rate, the admissions process should create little anxiety in all but the weakest candidates.

FINANCIAL AID

Students should submit: FAFSA, institution's own financial aid form. Regular filing deadline is 5/1. The Princeton Review suggests that all financial aid forms be submitted as soon as possible after 1/1. *Need-based scholarships/grants offered:* Pell, SEOG, state scholarships/grants, private scholarships, the school's own gift aid, United Negro College Fund. *Loan aid offered:* FFEL Subsidized Stafford, FFEL Unsubsidized Stafford, FFEL PLUS, Federal Perkins, Federal Nursing, private alternative loans. Applicants will be notified of awards on a rolling basis beginning on or about 3/1.

FROM THE ADMISSIONS OFFICE

"Duquesne University was founded in 1878 by the Holy Ghost Fathers. Although it is a private, Roman Catholic institution, Duquesne is proud of its ecumenical reputation. The total University enrollment is 9,803. Duquesne University's attractive and secluded campus is set on a 48-acre hilltop ('the bluff') overlooking the large corporate metropolis of Pittsburgh's Golden Triangle. It offers a wide variety of educational opportunities, from the liberal arts to modern professional training. Duquesne is a medium-size university striving to offer personal attention to its students while having the versatility and opportunities of a true university. A deep sense of tradition is combined with innovation and flexibility to make the Duquesne experience both challenging and rewarding. The Palumbo Convocation/Recreation Complex features a 6,300-seat arena, home court to the university's Division I basketball teams; racquetball and handball courts, weight rooms, and saunas. Extracurricular activities are recognized as an essential part of college life, complementing academics in the process of total student development. Students are involved in nearly 100 university-sponsored activities, and Duquesne's location gives students the opportunity to enjoy sports and cultural events both on campus and citywide. There are six residence halls with the capacity to house 3,574 students.

"Although SAT Writing scores will not affect admissions decisions, all freshman applicants are required to take the new SAT (or the ACT with the Writing section). Applicants may choose to submit scores from the old (prior to March 2005) version of the SAT (or ACT) as well, and we will use the student's best scores from either test."

SELECTIVITY

Admissions Rating	**81**
# of applicants	3,221
% of applicants accepted	85
% of acceptees attending	44
# of early decision applicants	51
% accepted early decision	93

FRESHMAN PROFILE

Range SAT Verbal	510-600
Average SAT Verbal	557
Range SAT Math	510-610
Average SAT Math	562
**TPR Projected Range SAT Writing*	*570-630*
Range ACT Composite	21-26
Average ACT Composite	24
Average HS GPA	3.58
% graduated top 10% of class	27
% graduated top 25% of class	54
% graduated top 50% of class	84

DEADLINES

Early decision application deadline	11/1
Early decision notification	12/15
Regular application deadline	7/1
Regular notification	rolling
Nonfall registration?	yes

APPLICANTS ALSO LOOK AT

AND OFTEN PREFER

Penn State University Park
University of Pittsburgh—Pittsburgh Campus
Washington & Jefferson College

AND SOMETIMES PREFER

Allegheny College
Gannon University
Saint Vincent College
West Virginia University

AND RARELY PREFER

Marquette University
St. Bonaventure University

FINANCIAL FACTS

Financial Aid Rating	**79**
Annual tuition	$18,693
Room & Board	$7,820
Books and supplies	$600
Required fees	$1,667
% frosh rec. need-based scholarship or grant aid	71
% UG rec. need-based scholarship or grant aid	63
% frosh rec. need-based self-help aid	66
% UG rec. need-based self-help aid	61
% frosh rec. any financial aid	97
% UG rec. any financial aid	86
Avg. frosh grant	$10,226
Avg. frosh loan	$8,806
Independent 529 member?	No

EARLHAM COLLEGE

801 NATIONAL ROAD WEST, RICHMOND, IN 47374-4095 • ADMISSIONS: 765-983-1600 • FAX: 765-983-1560

CAMPUS LIFE

Quality of Life Rating	**73**
Fire Safety Rating	**74**
Type of school	private
Affiliation	Quaker
Environment	town

STUDENTS

Total undergrad enrollment	1,149
% male/female	42/58
% from out of state	72
% from public high school	68
% live on campus	88
% African American	7
% Asian	2
% Caucasian	76
% Hispanic	3
% international	6
# of countries represented	53

SURVEY SAYS

Small classes
Athletic facilities are great
Students are friendly
Campus feels safe
Low cost of living
Frats and sororities are unpopular or nonexistent
Political activism is popular

ACADEMICS

Academic Rating	**88**
Calendar	semester
Student/faculty ratio	12:1
Professors interesting rating	88
Professors accessible rating	95
% professors teaching UG courses	100
% classes taught by TAs	0
Most common lab size	20-29 students
Most common regular class size	10-19 students

MOST POPULAR MAJORS

Biology/biological sciences
English language and literature
psychology

STUDENTS SPEAK OUT

Academics

The undergraduates of Earlham College agree that "the underlying Quaker values are what make this school so great. It has nothing to do with religion and everything to do with community." Indeed, the "community [and] noncompetitive atmosphere" at Earlham are what students appreciate most. Nurturing this unique environment is "Earlham's principle of according equal respect to all people." This code means that "everyone, up to and including the school president, operates on a first-name basis, which really underscores the personal level of interaction." The result is a free flow of ideas and opinions; explains one undergraduate, "We are encouraged to discuss difficult issues, such as issues of diversity of religion, political views, cultural identities, etc., and people don't have to be afraid to disagree." Professors excel in the classroom. The profs here "have a lot of knowledge about and a huge passion for what they are teaching." Some students warn, "there are some problems with the administration, but they don't really affect the students." Also, because "classes are often only offered every other semester or once every two or four years, class conflicts often occur between two classes you deem necessary," cautioned one student, who proceeds to point out the benefits of attending a tiny school: "The small classes and closeness to professors allow for individual planning and independent study opportunities."

Life

Students agree that Earlham is "a place where you make your own fun," primarily because hometown Richmond doesn't have a whole lot to offer on the surface." For many, "The fun here comes from those late-night talks that last until the next morning. The intellectual part of this school never stops and is so cool that the fun in daily life is many times derived from being enlightened by one of your peers." Undergrads also report, "The events (speakers, poets, musicians) that are brought to campus are usually pretty good. The movies shown on campus are often worth checking out, too." Clubs and organizations claim a good portion of students' leisure time; writes one undergrad, "The thing that I like about extracurriculars here is that they aren't really 'extra' at all. Most students are involved in activities outside of class that are also somehow related to their academic interests." The party scene here is subdued; "You won't find big frat-like parties here (no frats). Every so often there's a rowdy party, but parties usually suck or are pretty mellow (the farm party and the Hash Run are usually pretty good). Just hanging out with a group of friends is usually your best bet for a 'party.'" Those seeking more excitement suggest road-tripping, noting that "Oxford [Ohio] (Miami University), Indianapolis, and Dayton are not far, so we can go hang out there."

Student Body

The typical Earlham student is "somewhat crunchy (but post-modern intellectual, too), politically left, could be barefoot, and is likely to [have] a piercing that is not in the ear." All the while any of them could be members or patrons of the college's "Hugging Club." Reports one student, "The best way to describe an Earlham student might be the absence of showering. It is probably that almighty funk that in its sticky, smelly way binds us together." Students are "politically and environmentally conscious," and "everyone seems to have practically the same views." One undergrad muses, "Most of the students are atypical—in fact, I'd say atypical is typical at Earlham." Adds one of the school's few social and political conservatives, "The school accepts everything that society apparently does not (homosexuals, alternative religions, drug use, alternative medicine, vegans)." Another adds that, "Overall, Earlham is a very tolerant place where students never have to be afraid to disagree." Several students noted that Earlham could benefit from a healthy dose of "non-liberals" to offer some balance.

EARLHAM COLLEGE

FINANCIAL AID: 765-983-1217 • E-MAIL: ADMISSION@EARLHAM.EDU • WEBSITE: WWW.EARLHAM.EDU

ADMISSIONS

Very important factors considered include: Character/personal qualities, essays, minority status, recommendations, secondary school record. *Important factors considered include:* Extracurricular activities, interview, standardized test scores, talent/ability, volunteer work. *Other factors considered include:* Alumni/ae relation, class rank, geographical residence, religious affiliation/commitment, state residency, work experience. SAT Reasoning or ACT required. TOEFL required of all international applicants. High school diploma is required, and GED is accepted. *Academic units required:* 4 English, 3 math, 2 science (2 science lab), 2 foreign language, 1 social studies, 1 history, 2 academic electives. *Academic units recommended:* 4 English, 4 math, 3 science (2 science lab), 3 foreign language, 1 social studies, 1 history, 8 academic electives.

The Inside Word

Like most colleges with a Religious Society of Friends affiliation, Earlham has a sincere interest in the person it admits. Essays and interviews carry virtually as much weight as the numbers. Quakers and minorities receive special consideration in the admissions process, but special consideration is what this place is really all about. In recent years, selectivity has increased along with the size of the applicant pool. Earlham deserves a much higher national public awareness level than it has.

FINANCIAL AID

Students should submit: FAFSA, institution's own financial aid form. Regular filing deadline is 3/1. The Princeton Review suggests that all financial aid forms be submitted as soon as possible after 1/1. *Need-based scholarships/grants offered:* Pell, SEOG, state scholarships/grants, private scholarships, the school's own gift aid. *Loan aid offered:* Direct Subsidized Stafford, Direct Unsubsidized Stafford, Direct PLUS, Federal Perkins, college/university loans from institutional funds. Applicants will be notified of awards on or about 3/30. Federal Work-study Program available. Off-campus job opportunities are good.

FROM THE ADMISSIONS OFFICE

"An Earlham education enhances intellectual growth and instills an enduring love of exploration and discovery. Students discover their interests and passions, travel to other parts of the world, encounter different people, reflect on their values, participate in community, and explore avenues for meaningful service. Well prepared to pursue additional education, more than 75 percent of Earlham alumni earn graduate degrees. Whatever their life choices, graduates join a proud tradition of Earlham alumni who are engaged in changing the world.

"Applicants for fall 2006 class are required to take the new version of the SAT (or the ACT with the Writing section). However, we will allow students to submit scores from the old version of the SAT or ACT (prior to March 2005) as well, using the student's best scores from either test."

SELECTIVITY

Admissions Rating	**88**
# of applicants	1,518
% of applicants accepted	72
% of acceptees attending	31
# accepting a place on wait list	85
# of early decision applicants	28
% accepted early decision	82

FRESHMAN PROFILE

Range SAT Verbal	580-690
Average SAT Verbal	640
Range SAT Math	530-650
Average SAT Math	600
**TPR Projected Range SAT Writing*	*620-690*
Range ACT Composite	24-29
Average ACT Composite	26
Minimum Paper TOEFL	550
Minimum Computer Based TOEFL	213
Average HS GPA	3.5
% graduated top 10% of class	30
% graduated top 25% of class	64
% graduated top 50% of class	90

DEADLINES

Early decision application deadline	12/1
Early decision notification	12/15
Regular application deadline	2/15
Regular notification	3/15
Nonfall registration?	yes

APPLICANTS ALSO LOOK AT

AND OFTEN PREFER
Macalester College
Oberlin College

AND SOMETIMES PREFER
Beloit College
The College of Wooster
Grinnell College

AND RARELY PREFER
Guilford College
Knox College

FINANCIAL FACTS

Financial Aid Rating	**82**
Annual tuition	$25,364
Room & Board	$5,740
Books and supplies	$850
Required fees	$678
% frosh rec. need-based scholarship or grant aid	62
% UG rec. need-based scholarship or grant aid	63
% frosh rec. need-based self-help aid	49
% UG rec. need-based self-help aid	55
% frosh rec. any financial aid	88
% UG rec. any financial aid	89
Avg. frosh grant	$14,391
Avg. frosh loan	$3,683
Independent 529 member?	Yes

ECKERD COLLEGE

4200 54TH AVENUE SOUTH, ST. PETERSBURG, FL 33711 • ADMISSIONS: 727-864-8331 • FAX: 727-866-2304

CAMPUS LIFE

Quality of Life Rating	**78**
Fire Safety Rating	**60**
Type of school	private
Affiliation	Presbyterian
Environment	city

STUDENTS

Total undergrad enrollment	1,662
% male/female	44/56
% from out of state	69
% from public high school	75
% live on campus	79
% African American	3
% Asian	2
% Caucasian	77
% Hispanic	4
% international	6
# of countries represented	44

SURVEY SAYS

Small classes
Frats and sororities are unpopular or nonexistent
Lots of beer drinking
Hard liquor is popular
(Almost) everyone smokes

ACADEMICS

Academic Rating	**80**
Calendar	4-1-4
Student/faculty ratio	13:1
Professors interesting rating	83
Professors accessible rating	82
% professors teaching UG courses	100
% classes taught by TAs	0
Most common lab size	fewer than 10 students
Most common regular class size	20-29 students

MOST POPULAR MAJORS

Business administration/management
international business
marine biology and biological oceanography

STUDENTS SPEAK OUT

Academics

Close, personalized touches from faculty and administrators are earmarks of the Eckerd (EC) undergraduate academic experience. One junior recounts "a professor that I had freshman year. Whenever I see him he still says hi to me and remembers my name. That's important to me; to be known as 'Megan,' rather than as '846134.'" Another student explains, "One night a semester, during exams, all the administration and some professors cook up a midnight breakfast free for all students." In addition to such a homey academic atmosphere, Eckerd's undergraduates are also able to participate in many facets of their education, thanks to "lots of hands-on experience in labs" and "lots of job/internship opportunities." Because the opportunities to get involved seem never ending, one senior calls the college "the school of second chances." Even if you stumble, you'll soon find an opportunity to get back on your feet. Considering the school's location on the waters of Florida's Boca Ciega Bay, it's not surprising that marine biology is one of the school's most popular majors; in fact, many opt to attend Eckerd over better known and more selective colleges and universities because of the impressive marine facilities and program. The school's study abroad and mentoring programs offer students terrific complements to the already strong educational opportunities at Eckerd. And if students ever find themselves dissatisfied with the academics at Eckerd—or anything else for that matter—they feel comfortable talking to the administration about their issues.

Life

"The school has water on three sides." And as you might expect, such a setting lends itself to water sports. The college's "waterfront program is spectacular," allowing students to "kayak, canoe, and sail free." Speaking of water, students tell us that this is a "wet campus," something that wouldn't have been said just a few years back when strict alcohol policies left much of the student body feeling socially hampered. Now that "the alcohol policy has changed, kids at EC drink like fish on the weekends and many weeknights." But you don't have to hit the bottle to have fun, promises one student: "If you want to find a good party, you can, but if you want to curl up with a nice book and stay in for the night, no one is going to hold it against you." Many students also keep busy by hitting the gym and exercising. "The gym is always full, and all of our fitness classes are busy," writes one undergraduate. Organized sports are also popular. The sailing team, for example, "routinely takes home big trophies," and basketball games always draw a healthy crowd. Another aspect of the Eckerd life that earns accolades is its "liberal pet policy," which "allows students to keep their animal friends with them." The one thing that students complain about is the campus itself, which includes many buildings that look like doctors' offices from the 1970s. But if the sight of campus gets to be too much to bear, escape is easy. "Tampa is 25 minutes away, St. Petersburg is five minutes, Sarasota is an hour, Miami three hours, and Orlando is an hour and a half."

Student Body

"Three of the most prominent groups on campus are hippies; rich, preppy kids; and foreign kids," says one undergrad. Another says, "There are three different types of people at our school: the hippies, the biology majors (very big at our school), and the athletes." Depending on who you talk to, you're likely to hear that there is plenty of patchouli in the air at Eckerd. Although the vast majority of students are white, this is a college that "celebrates diversity" by striving to attract "students from all socioeconomic and cultural backgrounds." On this note, a student asserts, "This is not a Florida school. I am a Kentucky girl with best friends from Connecticut, Washington State, Jamaica, Spain, and Venezuela."

Financial Aid: 727-864-8334 • E-mail: admissions@eckerd.edu • Website: www.eckerd.edu

ADMISSIONS

Very important factors considered include: Character/personal qualities, extracurricular activities, secondary school record. *Important factors considered include:* Essays, interview, recommendations, standardized test scores, talent/ability, volunteer work, work experience. *Other factors considered include:* Alumni/ae relation, class rank. SAT Reasoning or ACT required. TOEFL required of all international applicants. High school diploma is required, and GED is accepted. *Academic units required:* 4 English, 3 math, 3 science (2 science lab), 2 foreign language, 2 social studies, 1 history, 3 academic electives. *Academic units recommended:* 4 math, 4 science (3 science lab), 3 foreign language, 2 history, 3 academic electives.

The Inside Word

Budding marine biologists are by far the strongest students at Eckerd. They make up a significant percentage of the college's total applicant pool and do much to provide for a more impressive freshman profile. Applications totals have made significant strides over the past two years.

FINANCIAL AID

Students should submit: FAFSA. The Princeton Review suggests that all financial aid forms be submitted as soon as possible after 1/1. *Need-based scholarships/grants offered:* Pell, SEOG, state scholarships/grants, private scholarships, the school's own gift aid. *Loan aid offered:* FFEL Subsidized Stafford, FFEL Unsubsidized Stafford, FFEL PLUS, Federal Perkins. Applicants will be notified of awards on a rolling basis beginning on or about 2/1. Federal Work-study Program available. Institutional employment available. Off-campus job opportunities are excellent.

FROM THE ADMISSIONS OFFICE

"Eckerd's diverse student body comes from 49 states and 49 countries. In this international setting, the majors of international relations and international business are very popular. Close to 70 percent of our graduates spend at least one term studying abroad. The beautiful, waterfront campus is a perfect location for the study of marine science and environmental studies. We characterize Eckerd students as competent givers because of their extensive involvement in the life of the campus and their many volunteer service contributions to the local environment and the St. Petersburg community. The Academy of Senior Professionals draws to campus distinguished persons who have retired from fields our students aspire to enter. Academy members, such as the late novelist James Michener, Nobel Prize winner Elie Wiesel, and noted Black historian John Hope Franklin, enrich classes and offer valuable counsel for career and life planning.

"Students applying for admission into the fall 2006 freshman class are allowed to submit old or new SAT or ACT examination results, and Eckerd will use the best scores from either test. The Writing portion will not be considered when determining a student's admission or scholarship."

SELECTIVITY

Admissions Rating	**85**
# of applicants	2,284
% of applicants accepted	74
% of acceptees attending	28
# accepting a place on wait list	115
% admitted from wait list	31

FRESHMAN PROFILE

Range SAT Verbal	520-630
Average SAT Verbal	576
Range SAT Math	510-620
Average SAT Math	562
**TPR Projected Range SAT Writing*	*570-650*
Range ACT Composite	22-27
Average ACT Composite	24
Minimum Paper TOEFL	550
Minimum Computer Based TOEFL	215
Average HS GPA	3.3
% graduated top 10% of class	26
% graduated top 25% of class	54
% graduated top 50% of class	79

DEADLINES

Regular notification	rolling
Nonfall registration?	yes

APPLICANTS ALSO LOOK AT

AND OFTEN PREFER

College of Charleston
Rollins College
University of Central Florida

AND SOMETIMES PREFER

Stetson University
University of Miami
University of Tampa

AND RARELY PREFER

Florida Atlantic University
Florida Southern College
University of South Florida

FINANCIAL FACTS

Financial Aid Rating	**74**
Annual tuition	$25,804
Room & Board	$7,152
Books and supplies	$1,000
Required fees	$656
% frosh rec. need-based scholarship or grant aid	58
% UG rec. need-based scholarship or grant aid	56
% frosh rec. need-based self-help aid	58
% UG rec. need-based self-help aid	56
% frosh rec. any financial aid	95
% UG rec. any financial aid	95
Avg. frosh grant	$19,716
Avg. frosh loan	$4,383
Independent 529 member?	No

ELON UNIVERSITY

2700 CAMPUS BOX, ELON, NC 27244-2010 • ADMISSIONS: 336-278-3566 • FAX: 336-278-7699

CAMPUS LIFE

Quality of Life Rating	**88**
Fire Safety Rating	**77**
Type of school	private
Affiliation	United Church of Christ
Environment	town

STUDENTS

Total undergrad enrollment	4,622
% male/female	39/61
% from out of state	69
% from public high school	70
% live on campus	59
% in (# of) fraternities	25 (11)
% in (# of) sororities	44 (10)
% African American	7
% Asian	1
% Caucasian	86
% Hispanic	1
% international	1
# of countries represented	40

SURVEY SAYS

Small classes
Lab facilities are great
Great computer facilities
School is well run
Frats and sororities dominate social scene
Lots of beer drinking

ACADEMICS

Academic Rating	**87**
Calendar	4-1-4
Student/faculty ratio	15:1
Professors interesting rating	85
Professors accessible rating	90
% professors teaching UG courses	100
% classes taught by TAs	0
Most common lab size	20-29 students
Most common regular class size	10-19 students

MOST POPULAR MAJORS

Business administration/management
education
mass communications/media studies

STUDENTS SPEAK OUT

Academics

Situated in a region of the country noted for quality private and public higher education, Elon University toes a tough academic line. Because of its relatively small size, Elon can boast a learning environment in which professors "all give the students their phone numbers and e-mail addresses" and "are readily available outside of the classroom." "It's nice to know that your professors actually know your name," comments one student. Elon's professors tend to focus on hands-on and interactive learning, which means that "in the classroom, many professors do not lecture, but pose questions for the class to respond to." Students are balanced in their evaluation of these discussion-oriented profs: "I have had professors that have changed my life," writes one student, "and professors that really shouldn't be teaching at all." A unique feature of Elon academic offerings is a program in engineering it offers in conjunction with North Carolina State University, Georgia Tech, Virginia Tech, Columbia University, Washington University in St. Louis, and North Carolina A&T. Students completing the program receive degrees from both institutions. While Elon offers 48 majors from which students can choose, some find that "there are limitations on the classes offered, [especially when] compared to a larger school." "Despite the aspects of Elon that I would change," concludes one undergraduate, "I feel that it is a good school and would recommend it to anyone looking for a personal learning environment in a beautiful setting."

Life

Ever hear of former President George H. W. Bush? How about Queen Noor of Jordan, Nobel Peace Prize winner Desmond Tutu . . . did we mention broadcasting legend Walter Cronkite, Pulitzer Prize winner Anna Quindlen, or conservationist Jane Goodall? These are just a handful of the speakers who have appeared on campus recently. While students will admit that "there isn't a lot to do compared to a large school," they applaud the university for providing some impressive outlets—like these talks by headlining personalities. There are also "more than 150 student organizations," not to mention "events in The Zone, our student center, such as Monday night football or Midnight Meals every Thursday, which always include food and features anything from a movie to a comedian to 'The Art of Kissing.' " Students can also hit the Greek parties that dominate the late-night social scene in the "very small" town of Elon. If students want to escape campus for a few hours, they're able to find some appealing options in the vicinity. "We're an hour's drive from Raleigh [and Winston-Salem], 30 minutes from Durham and Greensboro." Nearby Burlington offers a little diversion in the form of bowling and restaurants. The university's emphasis on internships, volunteering, and studying abroad also encourages students to explore the world beyond campus. Overall, Elon students believe they live the good life in "a very country-club kind of place."

Student Body

"The Elon 'bubble' is a bit like *Beverly Hills: 90210*, only in North Carolina," jokes one student. "It's not uncommon to see kids driving around in BMWs and Lexuses" or donning wardrobes that leave some feeling that they are "living in an Abercrombie and Fitch" catalog. While "diversity may be lacking," there's a "feeling of camaraderie" at Elon that everyone notices "when they visit for the first time." "I guess it's just that good southern hospitality kicking in!" exclaims an undergrad. Much of Elon's student body hails from mid-atlantic and southern states, though some come from "as far away as Japan and Yugoslavia." Students describe their peers in a variety of ways, ranging from "very religious" to "liberally biased." "Most are also smart and come from good families," according to one student, while another adds, "courteous, intelligent, caring, and generous" to the list of appropriate adjectives describing his classmates. And, without question, the student population is "very Greek oriented."

ELON UNIVERSITY

FINANCIAL AID: 800-334-8448 • E-MAIL: ADMISSIONS@ELON.EDU • WEBSITE: WWW.ELON.EDU

ADMISSIONS

Very important factors considered include: Secondary school record, standardized test scores. *Important factors considered include:* Alumni/ae relation, essays, extracurricular activities, recommendations, talent/ability. *Other factors considered include:* Character/personal qualities, class rank, minority status, state residency, volunteer work, work experience. SAT Reasoning or ACT required. TOEFL required of all international applicants. High school diploma is required, and GED is accepted. *Academic units required:* 4 English, 3 math, 3 science (1 science lab), 2 foreign language, 1 social studies, 1 history, 1 academic elective. *Academic units recommended:* 4 math, 3 foreign language.

The Inside Word

Applicants with solid GPAs and test scores will have little trouble getting into Elon. To those who earn admission go the spoils! Elon has a standard liberal arts core curriculum, but goes above and beyond the call of duty in its commitment to provide each student with leadership training, internships, and study abroad opportunities. There are no flies on Elon kids.

FINANCIAL AID

Students should submit: FAFSA, institution's own financial aid form, CSS/Financial Aid PROFILE. The Princeton Review suggests that all financial aid forms be submitted as soon as possible after 1/1. *Need-based scholarships/grants offered:* Pell, SEOG, state scholarships/grants, private scholarships, the school's own gift aid. *Loan aid offered:* FFEL Subsidized Stafford, FFEL Unsubsidized Stafford, FFEL PLUS, Federal Perkins, state loans, college/university loans from institutional funds, privately funded alternative loans. Applicants will be notified of awards on a rolling basis beginning on or about 3/30. Federal Work-study Program available. Institutional employment available. Off-campus job opportunities are good.

FROM THE ADMISSIONS OFFICE

"With an enrollment of about 4,800, Elon is the ideal size and offers the comprehensive resources of a university in a close-knit community atmosphere. Academic offerings include 48 majors in the arts and sciences, business, communications, and education. Elon is recognized by the National Survey of Student Engagement as one of the nation's most effective universities in actively engaging students in hands-on learning experiences. Academic and cocurricular activities are seamlessly blended, especially in flagship programs known as the Elon Experiences: study abroad, internships, volunteer service, leadership, and undergraduate research. Participation is among the highest in the nation. Sixty-three percent of graduating seniors have studied abroad, 75 percent have done internships, and 88 percent have volunteered in the community. As one of the few schools in the nation with a 4-1-4 academic calendar, Elon allows students to devote January to travel abroad or to immerse themselves in innovative on-campus courses. Elon's historic and picturesque campus has been recognized as one of the most beautiful in the country. Recent additions include new residence halls, Carol Grotnes Belk Library, the Academic Village, and Belk Track and Rhodes Stadium, home of the NCAA Division I-AA Phoenix football team. The School of Communications building features the latest digital communications technologies and two television studios, and McMichael Science Center gives students access to a wide array of scientific instruments. A new building for political science opened in fall 2004 and groundbreaking for a new business center is planned for spring 2005.

"Freshman applicants for fall 2006 are required to take the new version of the SAT (or the ACT with the writing section), but we will allow students to submit scores from the old SAT or ACT (prior to March 2005) as well. The student's best scores from either test will be used."

SELECTIVITY

Admissions Rating	**90**
# of applicants	8,063
% of applicants accepted	41
% of acceptees attending	37
# accepting a place on wait list	2,877
% admitted from wait list	5
# of early decision applicants	310
% accepted early decision	68

FRESHMAN PROFILE

Range SAT Verbal	540-620
Average SAT Verbal	581
Range SAT Math	550-630
Average SAT Math	588
**TPR Projected Range SAT Writing*	*590-650*
Range ACT Composite	22-27
Average ACT Composite	26
Minimum Paper TOEFL	550
Minimum Computer Based TOEFL	213
Average HS GPA	3.63
% graduated top 10% of class	25
% graduated top 25% of class	59
% graduated top 50% of class	91

DEADLINES

Early decision application deadline	11/1
Early decision notification	12/1
Regular application deadline	1/10
Regular notification	12/1
Nonfall registration?	no

APPLICANTS ALSO LOOK AT AND OFTEN PREFER
James Madison University
University of North Carolina—Chapel Hill

AND SOMETIMES PREFER
North Carolina State University
Wake Forest University

AND RARELY PREFER
College of Charleston
Furman University

FINANCIAL FACTS

Financial Aid Rating	**81**
Annual tuition	$18,699
Room & Board	$6,422
Books and supplies	$900
Required fees	$250
% frosh rec. need-based scholarship or grant aid	34
% UG rec. need-based scholarship or grant aid	32
% frosh rec. need-based self-help aid	32
% UG rec. need-based self-help aid	31
% frosh rec. any financial aid	58
% UG rec. any financial aid	54
Avg. frosh grant	$5,882
Avg. frosh loan	$4,767
Independent 529 member?	No

EMERSON COLLEGE

120 BOYLSTON STREET, BOSTON, MA 02116-4624 • ADMISSIONS: 617-824-8600 • FAX: 617-824-8609

CAMPUS LIFE	
Quality of Life Rating	**84**
Fire Safety Rating	**95**
Type of school	private
Environment	metropolis

STUDENTS	
Total undergrad enrollment	3,076
% male/female	42/58
% from out of state	63
% from public high school	75
% live on campus	42
% in (# of) fraternities	3 (4)
% in (# of) sororities	3 (3)
% African American	2
% Asian	4
% Caucasian	76
% Hispanic	5
% international	3
# of countries represented	41

SURVEY SAYS

Small classes
Students love Boston, MA
College radio is popular
Theater is popular
(Almost) everyone smokes

ACADEMICS	
Academic Rating	**82**
Calendar	semester
Student/faculty ratio	15:1
Professors interesting rating	70
Professors accessible rating	78
% professors teaching UG courses	97
% classes taught by TAs	3
Most common lab size	10-19 students
Most common regular class size	10-19 students

MOST POPULAR MAJORS

Cinematography and film/video production
creative writing
visual and performing arts

STUDENTS SPEAK OUT

Academics

"It's about communications and performance arts" at Emerson College, a school that "is great for passionate, talented people because not only will they be accepted for who they are but they will also be celebrated and will get the connections they need to survive in the real world." Because of the school's singular focus, "the majority of the learning time at Emerson is not spent in the classroom, but in rehearsal, at a film shoot, or going to press with their headline story." Professors are usually professionals, "people who have been in the field and want to teach now for one reason or another." Professors bring real world experience to the classroom and empathize with their students. "Our professors understand what a tough field we might be getting ourselves into," writes one undergraduate, "especially those people who choose to go into the entertainment industry, and our professors take it as seriously as we do." Better still, "in many cases, they invite students to participate in their work outside of the college." Students get their hands dirty early, and as such, "Emerson tries to get freshmen using equipment (video and other media, not film) as soon as possible." Explains one undergraduate, "Most students finish all their general education requirements within their first year and a half (if not sooner) and get to spend the rest of their time at Emerson focusing on what they love." You may not write as many term papers as you would at another school, but that doesn't mean you won't work hard. One student explains, "While at larger schools you may write 20-page term papers at the end of every course, at Emerson you're more likely to do a video. They take as long, trust me."

Life

"Life at Emerson revolves around activities at the school," students report and add that "most people are usually working on a theater piece or a television show, or some other kind of art that relates to their education, but also counts as their fun activity." "There is always some student production or a comedy show to see [as well as] a giant movie theater on our campus grounds, which Emerson kids probably support solely." There are also "the campus television and radio station, which run 24 hours a day, so students are always there." And that's just within the confines of Emerson; step off school grounds (the term "campus" doesn't really apply), and you'll quickly discover that "Boston is an amazing place to live, [and it is] one of the best cities in the world for college students." The city offers "plenty to do, including concerts at the Hatch Shell, Red Sox Games, a movie theater next door, and everything in Boston only a few subway stops away." The only downside is that "things close pretty early because Boston is so conservative."

Student Body

"There is no typical student" at Emerson, undergraduates report. One student explains, "If you take your high school artsy kid, the band geek, the theater chic, and the overachieving student leader, you've got Emerson, but without the stereotypes and with more homosexuality." Many students confirm that Emerson's "rather large gay community is totally accepted" by the school's "population of creative people. People at Emerson are actors and actresses, advertising gurus, and entertainment reporters. I have met the coolest people who have exposed me to cultural scenes that I never knew existed." Students dream big: "Everyone thinks they are going to be the next big thing, and some people are a bit pretentious about it." Emerson students also lean far left politically, "enough that a Texas Democrat could feel like Jesse Helms." A high tuition and limited endowment means that "the student body is limited to mostly upper- middle-class and above students whose parents can afford to pay for the school. Were Emerson a public college with half the tuition, it would be a very diverse, very politically correct institution."

FINANCIAL AID: 617-824-8655 • E-MAIL: ADMISSION@EMERSON.EDU • WEBSITE: WWW.EMERSON.EDU

ADMISSIONS

Very important factors considered include: Secondary school record, standardized test scores. *Important factors considered include:* Character/personal qualities, essays, extracurricular activities, recommendations, talent/ability. *Other factors considered include:* Alumni/ae relation, class rank, interview, minority status, volunteer work, work experience. SAT Reasoning or ACT required. TOEFL required of all international applicants. High school diploma is required, and GED is accepted. *Academic units required:* 4 English, 3 math, 3 science, 3 foreign language, 3 social studies. *Academic units recommended:* 4 English, 3 math, 3 science, 3 foreign language, 3 social studies, 4 academic electives.

The Inside Word

Being in Boston does more for Emerson's selectivity than do rigorous admissions standards.

FINANCIAL AID

Students should submit: FAFSA, institution's own financial aid form, noncustodial (divorced/separated) parents' statement, business/farm supplement, tax returns. The Princeton Review suggests that all financial aid forms be submitted as soon as possible after 1/1. *Need-based scholarships/grants offered:* Pell, SEOG, state scholarships/grants, private scholarships, the school's own gift aid. *Loan aid offered:* FFEL Subsidized Stafford, FFEL Unsubsidized Stafford, FFEL PLUS, Federal Perkins, state loans. Applicants will be notified of awards on or about 4/1. Federal Work-study Program available. Institutional employment available. Off-campus job opportunities are excellent.

FROM THE ADMISSIONS OFFICE

"Founded in 1880, Emerson is one of the premier colleges in the United States for the study of communication and the performing arts. Students may choose from more than two dozen undergraduate and graduate programs supported by state-of-the-art facilities and a nationally renowned faculty. The campus is home to WERS-FM, the oldest noncommercial radio station in New England; the historic 1,200-seat Cutler Majestic Theatre; and *Ploughshares*, the award-winning literary journal for new writing. A new 11-story performance and production center houses expanded performance and rehearsal space, a theater design/technology center, makeup lab, and television studios with editing and control rooms.

"Located on Boston Common in the heart of the city's Theater District, the Emerson campus is walking distance from the Massachusetts State House, historic Freedom Trial, Newbury Street shops, financial district, and numerous restaurants and museums. Emerson's 2,800 undergraduate and 900 graduate students come from over 50 countries and 45 states and territories. There are more than 60 student organizations and performance groups, 13 NCAA Division III intercollegiate teams, student publications, and honor societies. The college also sponsors programs in Los Angeles, Kasteel Well (The Netherlands), summer film study in Prague, and course cross-registration with the six-member Boston ProArts Consortium.

"Students applying for admission into the fall 2006 entering class are required to take the new version of the SAT (or ACT with Writing section), but we will allow students to submit scores from the old version of the SAT or ACT (prior to March 2005) as well. SAT Subject Tests are optional."

SELECTIVITY

Admissions Rating	**91**
# of applicants	4,584
% of applicants accepted	48
% of acceptees attending	32
# accepting a place on wait list	900
% admitted from wait list	10

FRESHMAN PROFILE

Range SAT Verbal	580-670
Average SAT Verbal	628
Range SAT Math	540-640
Average SAT Math	591
**TPR Projected Range SAT Writing*	*620-680*
Range ACT Composite	24-28
Average ACT Composite	26
Minimum Paper TOEFL	550
Minimum Computer Based TOEFL	213
Average HS GPA	3.53
% graduated top 10% of class	32
% graduated top 25% of class	77
% graduated top 50% of class	99

DEADLINES

Regular application deadline	1/15
Regular notification	4/1
Nonfall registration?	yes

APPLICANTS ALSO LOOK AT

AND OFTEN PREFER
New York University

AND SOMETIMES PREFER
Ithaca College
University of Southern California

AND RARELY PREFER
Boston University
Syracuse University

FINANCIAL FACTS

Financial Aid Rating	**87**
Annual tuition	$22,976
Room & Board	$10,118
Books and supplies	$680
Required fees	$579
% frosh rec. need-based scholarship or grant aid	50
% UG rec. need-based scholarship or grant aid	42
% frosh rec. need-based self-help aid	57
% UG rec. need-based self-help aid	51
% frosh rec. any financial aid	78
% UG rec. any financial aid	68
Avg. frosh grant	$13,126
Avg. frosh loan	$3,062
Independent 529 member?	No

EMORY UNIVERSITY

BOISFEUILLET JONES CENTER, ATLANTA, GA 30322 • ADMISSIONS: 404-727-6036 • FAX: 404-727-4303

CAMPUS LIFE

Quality of Life Rating	**88**
Fire Safety Rating	**60**
Type of school	private
Affiliation	Methodist
Environment	metropolis

STUDENTS

Total undergrad enrollment	6,260
% male/female	43/57
% from out of state	83
% from public high school	66
% live on campus	70
% in (# of) fraternities	31 (12)
% in (# of) sororities	32 (12)
% African American	9
% Asian	16
% Caucasian	61
% Hispanic	3
% international	4
# of countries represented	50

SURVEY SAYS

Lab facilities are great
Great computer facilities
Great library
Students love Atlanta, GA
Great off-campus food
Campus feels safe
Lots of beer drinking

ACADEMICS

Academic Rating	**92**
Calendar	semester
Student/faculty ratio	7:1
Professors interesting rating	86
Professors accessible rating	84
% professors teaching UG courses	90
% classes taught by TAs	10
Most common lab size	10-19 students
Most common regular class size	10-19 students

MOST POPULAR MAJORS

Business administration/management
political science and government
psychology

STUDENTS SPEAK OUT

Academics

Emory University, a "great school for the intensely driven academic population," offers what many other great universities can't: a location that provides not only an enjoyable four-year undergraduate academic experience but also one that can be extremely practical. One student explains, "The external connections of the school are phenomenal, both in Atlanta in general and the culture it offers: the Center for Disease Control, the Carter Center, and the American Cancer Society." Another student agrees and adds, "This place is great for the summer job opportunities, and it's a great place to go to college. I've stayed here almost every summer, working at great internships that I could never do anywhere else." There are other colleges in Atlanta, of course, so why pick Emory? Most students choose it because they want to be pushed to their limits; it's a school where "academics are not a joke. Even if you coasted through high school, you will not do well if you slack off at Emory," especially if you pursue the school's blue chip pre-med and pre-business programs. Although Emory holds university status, students tell us that it has a real small school feel. Professors "are very willing to help, and that has been a catalyst for many students' success," while the administration "works hard to give the students what they want. Many facilities on campus have been built because students have asked for them." Students also love the fact that "the study abroad program is very strong here."

Life

Most students agree that the two foci of Emory social life are the Greek system and the nightlife of Buckhead (a section of town saturated with clubs and restaurants) and greater Atlanta. One student adds that "while Greek life is a dominant force on campus, there are many other things to do. Two-thirds of the campus is not in a fraternity or sorority." Many students that make up that two-thirds simply board the MARTA and "take off [to] go into Atlanta," which offers "bars, bars, clubs, and more clubs. Nightlife is definitely not lacking in Atlanta. Most students socialize off campus." While a few students "wish we had a stronger social life right on campus, so students wouldn't have to go into Atlanta to have something to do," most are happy with things just as they are. If they could change anything, they'd probably ask for an upgrade to Emory's intercollegiate sports programs. Writes one student, "School spirit is somewhat lacking, primarily because Emory offers only Division III athletics, and it has no football team." Another explains, "The school's philosophy is to be academically and culturally oriented, and they feel that a football team deters that. It's true, I can see their point, but school spirit is very lacking." However, some students add, "While intercollegiate sports have a very small fan turnout, we compensate for that with the popularity of intramural sports. Just about everyone plays for at least one or two teams."

Student Body

Emory's reputation as a bastion of "rich students from Long Island, mostly Jewish, who are interested in Gucci and Prada" has some basis in fact, but other students feel this is an overblown stereotype. In fact, students tell us that "this campus is very diverse, and Emory does a great job of maintaining and encouraging diversity and unique students." One student reports, "We represent a lot of different backgrounds, and our diversity is discussed frequently among us. We do, however, have our academic fervor in common." There are quite a few Yankees at the school, and some students detect "a split between Northerners and Southerners." There are also many wealthy kids—as there are at nearly all expensive private schools—but "many students, especially those on scholarships, do not come from as well-off families, but that makes no difference in interaction."

FINANCIAL AID: 800-727-6039 • E-MAIL: ADMISS@EMORY.EDU • WEBSITE: WWW.EMORY.EDU

ADMISSIONS

Very important factors considered include: Essays, recommendations, secondary school record, standardized test scores. *Important factors considered include:* Extracurricular activities. *Other factors considered include:* Alumni/ae relation, character/personal qualities, geographical residence, minority status, state residency, talent/ability, volunteer work, work experience. SAT Reasoning or ACT required. SAT Subject Tests recommended. High school diploma is required, and GED is not accepted. *Academic units required:* 4 English, 3 math, 2 science (2 science lab), 2 foreign language, 2 social studies, 2 history, 3 academic electives.

The Inside Word

Applications to Emory have doubled in the last six years. At the same time, the quality of the entering class has risen to record levels. As the South continues to increase its population and presence on the national scene, Emory will continue to increase its selectivity and prestige.

FINANCIAL AID

Students should submit: FAFSA, CSS/Financial Aid PROFILE, noncustodial (divorced/separated) parents' statement, families' W-2 forms. Regular filing deadline is 4/1. The Princeton Review suggests that all financial aid forms be submitted as soon as possible after 1/1. *Need-based scholarships/grants offered:* Pell, SEOG, state scholarships/grants, private scholarships, the school's own gift aid. *Loan aid offered:* FFEL Subsidized Stafford, FFEL Unsubsidized Stafford, FFEL PLUS, Federal Perkins, Federal Nursing, state loans, college/university loans from institutional funds. Applicants will be notified of awards on or about 4/15. Federal Work-study Program available. Off-campus job opportunities are excellent.

FROM THE ADMISSIONS OFFICE

"The combination Emory offers you is really a rarity in today's college marketplace. As an Emory student, you can still have the benefits of a small liberal arts college while enjoying the wider opportunities found in a major university. Emory College is the four-year undergraduate division of the university and provides a broad, rigorous liberal arts curriculum. At the same time, Emory University, with its nine major divisions, numerous centers for advanced study, and a host of prestigous affiliated institutions, provides the larger context, thus enriching your total college experience.

"All applicants are required to submit scores from the SAT or the ACT. For those students applying for the 2006–2007 school year, Emory will require one of the following: the old SAT (without Writing), the ACT (without Writing), the new SAT (which includes a Writing section), or the ACT with Writing."

SELECTIVITY

Admissions Rating	**98**
# of applicants	11,218
% of applicants accepted	39
% of acceptees attending	29
# accepting a place on wait list	800
% admitted from wait list	4
# of early decision applicants	514
% accepted early decision	60

FRESHMAN PROFILE

Range SAT Verbal	640-720
Average SAT Verbal	680
Range SAT Math	660-740
Average SAT Math	700
**TPR Projected Range SAT Writing*	*660-710*
Range ACT Composite	29-33
Average ACT Composite	31
Average HS GPA	3.8
% graduated top 10% of class	90
% graduated top 25% of class	99
% graduated top 50% of class	100

DEADLINES

Early decision application deadline	11/1
Early decision notification	12/15
Regular application deadline	1/15
Regular notification	4/1
Nonfall registration?	no

APPLICANTS ALSO LOOK AT AND OFTEN PREFER

Duke University
Northwestern University
Stanford University

AND SOMETIMES PREFER

Georgetown University
University of Pennsylvania
Washington University in St. Louis

AND RARELY PREFER

The George Washington University
Tufts University
Tulane University

FINANCIAL FACTS

Financial Aid Rating	**94**
Annual tuition	$30,384
Room & Board	$10,552
Books and supplies	$1,000
Required fees	$382
% frosh rec. need-based scholarship or grant aid	32
% UG rec. need-based scholarship or grant aid	35
% frosh rec. need-based self-help aid	28
% UG rec. need-based self-help aid	33
% frosh rec. any financial aid	57
% UG rec. any financial aid	59
Avg. frosh grant	$20,394
Avg. frosh loan	$3,129
Independent 529 member?	Yes

EUGENE LANG COLLEGE

65 West 11th Street, Office of Admission, New York, NY 10011 • Admissions: 212-229-5665 • Fax: 212-229-5166

CAMPUS LIFE

Quality of Life Rating	**83**
Fire Safety Rating	**60**
Type of school	private

STUDENTS

Total undergrad enrollment	887
% male/female	31/69
% from out of state	69
% from public high school	64
% live on campus	30
% African American	5
% Asian	3
% Caucasian	55
% Hispanic	6
% international	2
# of countries represented	15

SURVEY SAYS

Class discussions encouraged
Small classes
Students love New York, NY
Great off-campus food
Intercollegiate sports are unpopular or nonexistent
Frats and sororities are unpopular or nonexistent
Political activism is popular
(Almost) everyone smokes

ACADEMICS

Academic Rating	**87**
Calendar	semester
Student/faculty ratio	16:1
Professors interesting rating	83
Professors accessible rating	80
% professors teaching UG courses	100
% classes taught by TAs	25
Most common regular class size	10-19 students

MOST POPULAR MAJORS

Area, ethnic, cultural, and gender studies
creative writing
social sciences

STUDENTS SPEAK OUT

Academics

The Eugene Lang College "offers a space for various kinds of interdisciplinary learning, critical thinking, and nontraditional study, often placing the responsibility for a fine education on its independent students." Those who thrive here are individuals who "want to push themselves and truly challenge themselves academically. Professors say they teach at Lang because of the students, and there is a true sense of students' wanting to explore and learn for education's sake rather than to simply 'get ahead' in life." As "one of very few schools in the nation that has seminar-style learning" where "you're not just crammed into a lecture hall with 300 other students and talked at," Lang promotes "the ability to freely express yourself in all levels, whether individually, intellectually, or politically." Classes here "tend to have really long, poetic titles like, Hearing Art, Seeing Music, and the like," and "the material one learns at Lang is different then what would be core at another college, which is why the school attracts an interesting group of people and what makes for interesting conversations." Professors vary in teaching skills, but "the good professors who know a lot and know how to teach in 'the Lang style' (i.e., able to go off on tangents within the discussion and not lose focus of the bigger picture) are absolutely amazing." Because the school stresses independence, "you get out of Lang what you put into it. If you take advantage of what it has to offer, it can be one of the most rewarding and unique academic experiences in the country."

Life

"There is not much in the way of common space" in Eugene Lang's small facility, "so gatherings among students pretty much take to the streets." And they do take place: "We meet up with each other outside of the classroom and find that they have more in common than just a school. Often we are involved in the same music/art scene or political groups that exist outside of the school. The school just offers a starting point for relationships." Students spend most of their free time exploring New York City, where "there is always something to do that you've never done, or even heard of, before." The school is located on the northern end of Greenwich Village, the center of the city's youth social life. Public transportation makes the rest of Manhattan, and the other four boroughs of the city, easily accessible. Observes one undergrad, "Life in the city is incredible. Every possible opportunity is open to you. Living in the city allows me to apply the concepts I'm learning in the classroom to the world immediately around me through internships in politics, law, communications, etc." New York also "offers much more real interaction than the forced 'You like X college sports team? I love X college sports team,' interaction that so many colleges pride themselves on," students insist.

Student Body

Lang undergrads are "independent, analytical, passionate" and "more urban, academic, and aware than your average college student." Although "the 'typical' Lang student is often characterized as a pierced and tattooed hipster," Lang also "has students who listen to Britney Spears, were very popular in high school, and played multiple varsity sports but know what they want in education, so they came to Lang." Adds one undergrad, "You really can't be too weird or too normal for this place." Most Lang students "are extremely politically aware and very liberal." Lang boasts "an incredible amount of diversity in age, ethnicity, background, sexual identity, etc.," and students are cool with that.

Eugene Lang College

Financial Aid: 212-229-8930 • E-mail: Lang@newschool.edu • Website: www.lang.edu

ADMISSIONS

Very important factors considered include: Essays, recommendations, secondary school record. *Important factors considered include:* Character/personal qualities, interview, standardized test scores, talent/ability, volunteer work. *Other factors considered include:* Alumni/ae relation, class rank, extracurricular activities, geographical residence, minority status, work experience. SAT Reasoning or ACT required. TOEFL required of all international applicants. High school diploma is required, and GED is accepted. *Academic units required:* 4 English. *Academic units recommended:* 3 math, 3 science, 2 foreign language, 3 social studies, 2 history.

The Inside Word

The college draws a very self-selected and intellectually curious pool, and applications are up. Those who demonstrate little self-motivation will find themselves denied.

FINANCIAL AID

Students should submit: FAFSA, state aid form. The Princeton Review suggests that all financial aid forms be submitted as soon as possible after 1/1. *Need-based scholarships/grants offered:* Pell, SEOG, state scholarships/grants, private scholarships, the school's own gift aid. *Loan aid offered:* FFEL Subsidized Stafford, FFEL Unsubsidized Stafford, FFEL PLUS, Federal Perkins, college/university loans from institutional funds. Applicants will be notified of awards on a rolling basis beginning on or about 3/1. Federal Work-study Program available. Institutional employment available. Off-campus job opportunities are good.

FROM THE ADMISSIONS OFFICE

"Eugene Lang College offers students of diverse backgrounds an innovative and creative approach to a liberal arts education, combining stimulating classroom activity of a small, intimate college with rich resources of a dynamic, urban university—New School University. The curriculum at Lang College is challenging and flexible. Class size, limited to eighteen students, promotes energetic and thoughtful discussions and writing is an essential component of all classes. Students design their own program of study within one of thirteen interdisciplinary concentrations in the Social Sciences and Humanities. They also have the opportunity to pursue a five-year BA/BFA, BA/MA, or BA/MST at one of the university's six other divisions. Our Greenwich Village location means that all the cultural treasures of the city—museums, libraries, music, theater—are literally at your doorstep.

"As of this book's publication, Eugene Lang College did not have information available about their policy regarding the new SAT."

SELECTIVITY

Admissions Rating	**83**
# of applicants	854
% of applicants accepted	68
% of acceptees attending	40

FRESHMAN PROFILE

Range SAT Verbal	540-660
Average SAT Verbal	610
Range SAT Math	470-590
Average SAT Math	570
**TPR Projected Range SAT Writing*	*590-670*
Range ACT Composite	20-26
Average ACT Composite	27
Minimum Paper TOEFL	550
Average HS GPA	3.06
% graduated top 10% of class	13
% graduated top 25% of class	51
% graduated top 50% of class	90

DEADLINES

Early decision application deadline	11/15
Early decision notification	12/15
Regular application deadline	2/1
Regular notification	rolling
Nonfall registration?	yes

APPLICANTS ALSO LOOK AT

AND OFTEN PREFER
Bard College
New York University
Sarah Lawrence College

AND SOMETIMES PREFER
Hampshire College
Reed College

AND RARELY PREFER
Bennington College
St. John's College (MD)

FINANCIAL FACTS

Financial Aid Rating	**66**
Annual tuition	$24,920
Room & Board	$10,810
Books and supplies	$918
Required fees	$550
% frosh rec. need-based scholarship or grant aid	66
% UG rec. need-based scholarship or grant aid	63
% frosh rec. need-based self-help aid	60
% UG rec. need-based self-help aid	57
Avg. frosh grant	$10,906
Avg. frosh loan	$3,125
Independent 529 member?	No

THE EVERGREEN STATE COLLEGE

2700 Evergreen Pkwy. NW, Office of Admissions, Olympia, WA 98505 • Admissions: 360-867-6170 • Fax: 360-867-6576

CAMPUS LIFE

Quality of Life Rating	**81**
Fire Safety Rating	**60**
Type of school	public
Environment	town

STUDENTS

Total undergrad enrollment	3,907
% male/female	46/54
% from out of state	22
% live on campus	20
% African American	5
% Asian	5
% Caucasian	66
% Hispanic	5
% Native American	4

SURVEY SAYS

Small classes
Frats and sororities are unpopular or nonexistent
Political activism is popular

ACADEMICS

Academic Rating	**77**
Calendar	quarter
Student/faculty ratio	21:1
Professors interesting rating	90
Professors accessible rating	79
% professors teaching UG courses	100
% classes taught by TAs	0
Most common regular class size	20-29 students

STUDENTS SPEAK OUT

Academics

You want academic freedom? How much can you handle? If your answer to these questions is "How much have you got?" Evergreen State College (ESC) may be the school for you. With "no prerequisites to classes," "few tests given," and no letter grades assigned, ESC stresses education for its own sake, an ideal situation for the disciplined scholar who eschews competitive grade-grubbing. Most who choose ESC end up loving it; explains one student, "The freedom the school allows in choosing programs, classes, and 'majors' is a huge strength. Majors don't really exist at Evergreen, and there are no requirements to take. You take what interests you, and you develop your own education." Evaluation ("an in-depth evaluation written by the professor" rather than a letter grade) is done through "seminar, papers, and projects" rather than tests, "making learning less a 'memorization' thing and more real and important." The net result is that students are "constantly being challenged by their peers and faculty to look beyond the surface—we all expect to have an analytical dialogue regarding the material." In other words, "the atmosphere is casual and noncompetitive, but more intellectually demanding than any public institution this side of the Mississippi, perhaps in the entire [United States}." As you might expect at such a school, "Professors aren't your typical 'I talk, you listen' professors; they're regular people who really know what they're teaching and are willing to help you learn it if what they do in the classroom is not enough." Adds one student, "The good and bad thing about Evergreen is that you are solely responsible for your education."

Life

Life at Evergreen State is "relaxed" and "low-key," students agree. "Generally things are much slower here in Olympia," reports one student. "When you come from a larger city like Seattle, you should set your watch back two minutes and 'go with the flow.'" Many here "are perfectly content to just sit out in Red Square and meditate, play drums, or watch the clouds." Others relish the long discussions with other students, nature walks, and just plain hanging out. Parties "are chill, no big keggers;" as one student told us, they "are typically laid-back gatherings of friends." Unsurprisingly, the campus "is a politically charged environment, but not in an intimidating way." The more aesthetically inclined should be pleased to learn that the area is home to an active arts scene and that "there are always things going on downtown: plays, music, art openings, etc. There is a volunteer-run indie film theater and a great co-op. Because of the local independent music scene, there are a lot of shows to see for dirt cheap prices." Nature lovers extol the many virtues of the nearby Capitol Forest.

Student Body

"Trustafarian" is a term that came up often in Evergreen students' descriptions of one another. Some students describe the Evergreen students in terms of the typical "hippie:" "leftist, politically motivated (to the point of extreme, at times), environmentally aware, if not active [and] free-thinking." Most, however, stress the "atypical" nature of the student body: "There is no typical Evergreen student. Greeners are friendly, open-minded, and motivated." While students would like to see even more diversity on campus, they claim "everyone is pretty chill and easy to get along with." Most here immerse themselves in politics, art, community projects, and weed, not necessarily in that order. Undergrads happily report that "because this is a small school in a small but eccentric town, there is literally a little bit of everything that coexists in a happy academic environment."

FINANCIAL AID: 360-867-6205 • E-MAIL: ADMISSIONS@EVERGREEN.EDU • WEBSITE: WWW.EVERGREEN.EDU

ADMISSIONS

Very important factors considered include: Secondary school record, standardized test scores. *Important factors considered include:* Essays, state residency. *Other factors considered include:* Extracurricular activities, minority status, recommendations, talent/ability, volunteer work, work experience. SAT Reasoning or ACT required. TOEFL required of all international applicants. High school diploma is required, and GED is accepted. *Academic units required:* 4 English, 3 math, 2 science (1 science lab), 2 foreign language, 3 social studies, 1 visual and performing arts.

The Inside Word

Evergreen is one of the rare breed of "alternative" colleges—places where intellectual curiosity is a critical factor in the admissions process. Still, candidates must meet minimum academic standards to get a closer look from the admissions committee, and those with GPAs below 2.0 won't have a chance. A visit is a good idea for all candidates.

FINANCIAL AID

Students should submit: FAFSA, institution's own financial aid form. Regular filing deadline is 3/15. The Princeton Review suggests that all financial aid forms be submitted as soon as possible after 1/1. *Need-based scholarships/grants offered:* Pell, SEOG, state scholarships/grants, private scholarships, the school's own gift aid. *Loan aid offered:* FFEL Subsidized Stafford, FFEL Unsubsidized Stafford, FFEL PLUS, Federal Perkins, college/university loans from institutional funds. Applicants will be notified of awards on a rolling basis beginning on or about 4/15. Federal Work-study Program available. Institutional employment available. Off-campus job opportunities are good.

FROM THE ADMISSIONS OFFICE

"Evergreen, a public college of arts and sciences, is a national leader in developing full-time interdisciplinary studies programs. Students work closely with faculty (there are no teaching assistants) to study an issue or theme from the perspective of several academic disciplines. They apply what's learned to real world issues, complete projects in groups, and discuss concepts in seminars that typically involve a faculty member and 22 students. The emphasis on seminars, interdisciplinary problem-solving, and collaboration means students are well prepared for graduate school and the world of work. Our students tend to be politically active, environmentally savvy, and more concerned about social justice than competition and personal gain.

"Freshman applicants for fall 2006 are required to submit test scores from either the SAT or ACT tests. Scores submitted from the old (prior to March 2005) SAT will be accepted. The student's best composite score will be used in the admission process."

SELECTIVITY

Admissions Rating	**71**
# of applicants	1,534
% of applicants accepted	95
% of acceptees attending	33

FRESHMAN PROFILE

Range SAT Verbal	530-650
Average SAT Verbal	587
Range SAT Math	480-600
Average SAT Math	539
**TPR Projected Range SAT Writing*	*580-670*
Range ACT Composite	19-27
Average ACT Composite	23
Minimum Paper TOEFL	525
Minimum Computer Based TOEFL	197
Average HS GPA	3.12
% graduated top 10% of class	8
% graduated top 25% of class	23
% graduated top 50% of class	59

DEADLINES

Regular application deadline	3/1
Regular notification	rolling
Nonfall registration?	yes

APPLICANTS ALSO LOOK AT

AND OFTEN PREFER

Lewis & Clark College, University of California—Santa Cruz, University of Washington, Washington State University, Western Washington University

AND SOMETIMES PREFER

Eastern Washington University, Hampshire College, Portland State University, Reed College, University of Oregon

AND RARELY PREFER

Pacific Lutheran University, Seattle University, University of Montana—Missoula, University of Puget Sound, Warren Wilson College

FINANCIAL FACTS

Financial Aid Rating	**77**
Annual in-state tuition	$3,900
Annual out-of-state tuition	$14,514
Room & Board	$5,784
Books and supplies	$780
Required fees	$156
% frosh rec. need-based scholarship or grant aid	28
% UG rec. need-based scholarship or grant aid	45
% frosh rec. need-based self-help aid	34
% UG rec. need-based self-help aid	47
% frosh rec. any financial aid	43
% UG rec. any financial aid	51
Avg. frosh grant	$3,750
Avg. frosh loan	$3,065
Independent 529 member?	No

FAIRFIELD UNIVERSITY

1073 North Benson Road, Fairfield, CT 06824 • Admissions: 203-254-4100 • Fax: 203-254-4199

CAMPUS LIFE

Quality of Life Rating	**81**
Fire Safety Rating	**88**
Type of school	private
Affiliation	Roman Catholic-Jesuit
Environment	town

STUDENTS

Total undergrad enrollment	3,552
% male/female	43/57
% from out of state	75
% from public high school	50
% live on campus	80
% African American	2
% Asian	3
% Caucasian	81
% Hispanic	5
% international	1
# of countries represented	42

SURVEY SAYS

Small classes
Great library
Frats and sororities are unpopular or nonexistent
Lots of beer drinking
Hard liquor is popular

ACADEMICS

Academic Rating	**81**
Calendar	semester
Student/faculty ratio	13:1
Professors interesting rating	83
Professors accessible rating	80
% professors teaching UG courses	100
% classes taught by TAs	0
Most common lab size	10-19 students
Most common regular class size	20-29 students

MOST POPULAR MAJORS

Communications studies/speech communication and rhetoric
English language and literature
marketing/marketing management

STUDENTS SPEAK OUT

Academics

Fairfield University, "a small Jesuit University that provides so many opportunities because of its great resources and faculty," achieves the Jesuit ideal of "educating the whole person" through a "strong core curriculum" and extracurricular programs that "put the focus on finding balance in life." Through its four undergraduate divisions, Fairfield offers a wide range of choices to its relatively small student body, further accommodating students with "small class sizes" and "lots of class discussions, which is awesome because we get to see stuff from a different perspective." Students explain that "since we are a liberal arts school, we get a taste of everything, which is so much fun" and report that "we have really good nursing, business, and arts and science programs." One biology major writes, "I chose this school because it had an excellent science program. Now I get to study with a professor who worked on the Human Genome Project." Course work here "is tough and certainly requires studying," as professors "are understanding people but at the same time, take no crap. They are there to help us learn, and that is completely obvious. Overall, it is a challenging environment where a serious student can feel comfortable."

Life

Fairfield "is an extremely social school, both on and off campus. It's the antithesis of a suitcase school. Students tend to be very involved in a wide range of activities and the great social scene." Undergrads here enjoy a good party, whether it's at the beach, or the townhouses on campus. One student writes, "There are parties every night. You must be social in order to get the full experience at Fairfield." Many are apparently happy with only a partial experience; they skip the party scene, participating instead in "the many Fairfield University Student Association (FUSA)-sponsored events such as bowling, Broadway shows, Mega-Bingo, semi-formals, concerts, and comedians." Explains one student, "FUSA makes sure to plan things every single Thursday, Friday, and Saturday. There is always something to do." Campus ministry is also very active and very popular, as are such quiet diversions as "shopping in Westport or Greenwich or just hanging out with friends." The Stags, Fairfield's intercollegiate squads, compete in 19 men's and women's sports. Students here love that "it's easy enough to get to New York City," either by car or public transportation.

Student Body

The Fairfield stereotype is that "everyone falls into one of two basic categories: those who show up for class dressed like it's a Saturday night and they're going to a club, or those who get to class and look as though they need directions to the country club. If you don't fall into one of these categories in some sense, you are not Fairfield material." There is some debate here over the accuracy of Fairfield's nickname "J. Crew U"—while those who insist "there are many different kinds of people that go here," they'll point out that "the majority of the people here are white, though." Many of our respondents suggest that Fairfield needs to improve its lack of diversity: "Most of the kids on campus are white [though] the minorities are usually the most popular kids around." One sophomore's advice to "freshmen who come to me complaining of the social homogeny here: There are absolutely wonderful students who attend this school. Your challenge—and this is really not so hard—is to find them." Homogenous or not, Fairfield undergrads tend to be "smart, but not brainy" and often "have a strong interest in professional sports." Overall, "everyone is very friendly and get along well with one another."

FINANCIAL AID: 203-254-4125 • E-MAIL: ADMIS@MAIL.FAIRFIELD.EDU • WEBSITE: WWW.FAIRFIELD.EDU

ADMISSIONS

Very important factors considered include: Class rank, essays, recommendations, secondary school record, standardized test scores. *Important factors considered include:* Extracurricular activities. *Other factors considered include:* Alumni/ae relation, character/personal qualities, geographical residence, interview, minority status, talent/ability, volunteer work, work experience. SAT Reasoning or ACT required. TOEFL required of all international applicants. High school diploma is required, and GED is not accepted. *Academic units required:* 4 English, 3 math, 3 science (3 science lab), 2 foreign language, 3 social studies. *Academic units recommended:* 4 English, 4 math, 4 science (3 science lab), 4 foreign language, 4 social studies, 1 history. It is strongly recommended that music majors submit portfolios and theater majors submit resumes.

The Inside Word

Solid support from Catholic high schools goes a long way toward stocking the applicant pool. Important to note: Steady increases in the number of admission applications has nicely increased selectivity in recent years. Fairfield's campus and central location combined with improvements to the library, campus center, classrooms, athletic facilities, and campus residences, make this a campus worth seeing.

FINANCIAL AID

Students should submit: FAFSA, CSS/Financial Aid PROFILE, business/farm supplement. The Princeton Review suggests that all financial aid forms be submitted as soon as possible after 1/1. *Need-based scholarships/grants offered:* Pell, SEOG, state scholarships/grants, private scholarships, the school's own gift aid, United Negro College Fund. *Loan aid offered:* FFEL Subsidized Stafford, FFEL Unsubsidized Stafford, FFEL PLUS, Federal Perkins, Federal Nursing, state loans, private alternate loans. Applicants will be notified of awards on a rolling basis beginning on or about 4/1. Federal Work-study Program available. Institutional employment available. Off-campus job opportunities are good.

FROM THE ADMISSIONS OFFICE

"Fairfield University's primary objectives are to develop of the creative intellectual potential of its students and to foster in them ethical and religious values, and a sense of social responsibility. The Jesuit tradition inspires habits of heart and mind, and creates an educational experience which is both personal and powerful. Students learn in a supportive environment with faculty committed to individual development and personal enrichment. As the key to the lifelong process of learning, Fairfield has developed a core curriculum to introduce all students to the broad rand of liberal learning. Students choose from 32 majors and 19 interdisciplinary minors. They also have outstanding internships opportunities in Fairfield County and New York City. Fairfield grads wishing to continue their education are highly successful in gaining graduate and professional school admission, while others pursue extensive job opportunities throughout the region. Thirty three Fairfield students have been tapped as Fulbright scholars in the last ten years.

"Applicants to Fairfield University for the fall 2006 may submit the results from either the new version of the SAT or the old version. We will consider the student's best scores in the application process. Fairfield University does not require any SAT subject examinations."

SELECTIVITY

Admissions Rating	**89**
# of applicants	7,136
% of applicants accepted	64
% of acceptees attending	19
# accepting a place on wait list	1,715
% admitted from wait list	5
# of early decision applicants	140
% accepted early decision	72

FRESHMAN PROFILE

Range SAT Verbal	540-630
Average SAT Verbal	592
Range SAT Math	560-650
Average SAT Math	608
**TPR Projected Range SAT Writing*	*590-650*
Range ACT Composite	23-27
Average ACT Composite	26
Minimum Paper TOEFL	550
Minimum Computer Based TOEFL	213
Average HS GPA	3.0
% graduated top 10% of class	32
% graduated top 25% of class	73
% graduated top 50% of class	99

DEADLINES

Early decision application deadline	11/15
Early decision notification	12/15
Regular application deadline	1/15
Regular notification	4/1
Nonfall registration?	no

APPLICANTS ALSO LOOK AT

AND OFTEN PREFER
Georgetown University, University of Notre Dame

AND SOMETIMES PREFER
Boston College, College of the Holy Cross, Loyola College in Maryland, Providence College

AND RARELY PREFER
Boston University, Fordham University, University of Connecticut

FINANCIAL FACTS

Financial Aid Rating	**74**
Annual tuition	$27,450
Room & Board	$9,270
Books and supplies	$500
Required fees	$485
% frosh rec. need-based scholarship or grant aid	46
% UG rec. need-based scholarship or grant aid	44
% frosh rec. need-based self-help aid	42
% UG rec. need-based self-help aid	41
% frosh rec. any financial aid	80
% UG rec. any financial aid	78
Avg. frosh grant	$14,548
Avg. frosh loan	$3,435
Independent 529 member?	Yes

Fisk University

1000 Seventeenth Avenue North, Nashville, TN 37208-3051 • Admissions: 615-329-8665 • Fax: 615-329-8774

CAMPUS LIFE

Quality of Life Rating	**62**
Fire Safety Rating	**60**
Type of school	private
Environment	metropolis

STUDENTS

Total undergrad enrollment	812
% from out of state	71
% from public high school	85
% live on campus	65
% in (# of) fraternities	15 (4)
% in (# of) sororities	20 (4)
% African American	98
% international	2
# of countries represented	5

SURVEY SAYS

Small classes
Athletic facilities need improving
Students are friendly
Frats and sororities dominate social scene
Musical organizations are popular
Student government is popular
Very little drug use

ACADEMICS

Academic Rating	**69**
Calendar	semester
Student/faculty ratio	12:1
Professors interesting rating	73
Professors accessible rating	63
% professors teaching UG courses	100
% classes taught by TAs	0

STUDENTS SPEAK OUT

Academics

Fisk University is a historically African American school with a storied past that is evidenced by the many luminaries who have passed through its doors: W. E. B. Du Bois, James Weldon Johnson, and Nikki Giovanni are just a sampling of Fisk's impressive roster of graduates. Students say, "The historical value at Fisk is something that money can't buy." Today, the university "has many strong points. One would be the science department, another would be music, and yet another would be Black history." Business studies are enhanced because Fisk is "very well connected with the other surrounding universities and businesses." In all areas, the curriculum is demanding. One undergraduate agrees, "We study a lot here!" As at many small schools, Fisk has lately encountered fiscal problems (exacerbated by the lack of stability in the school's presidential office), forcing layoffs and a delay of facility upgrades. Students acknowledge these drawbacks but feel that the overall Fisk experience is still worthwhile. One student explains, "Fisk, first of all, is about offering the highest level of education possible. Second, it's about teaching African American students about their heritage, where they've come from, and where they're going. And third, they are preparing us to go out and be productive and competitive individuals in this world."

Life

Because of Fisk's demanding curriculum and small student body, campus life is "usually pretty boring, unless there's a party going on." Students spend much of their free time studying since "life at Fisk University is very education oriented. This is [neither] a party school nor a sports school." Otherwise, they're "kickin' it in the yard, which is where everyone goes to socialize, [or] getting involved in some kind of club, religious association, or Greek organization." The Greek houses, students inform us, are "a big thing on campus. Everyone wants to be Greek." When things get really boring, most students head off campus in search of entertainment. Fortunately, they're in Nashville, a growing city with much more to offer than country music. Because "the area of Nashville that we are located in is very gloomy, with housing projects right next to the school," students most often head to the neighboring campuses of Tennessee State or Vanderbilt. While both destinations are within walking distance, most students agree that "it is imperative to have transportation to get around the city. This is not a school for students looking to party unless they have a car."

Student Body

Students report, "Most of the students at Fisk are Black. You would think that because we are mostly Black, we are generally the same. This is not at all true." Diversity among the African American students exists in their places of origin, economic status, and interests. Explains one student, "There are people from islands, from Africa, from the North, South, East, and West, so we all bring our own cultures to the table and learn about different cultures, and we come to respect the social and regional differences in how we act." What students share in common is that most are "very knowledgeable, kind, attractive and have a great passion for their school's heritage and for their religious beliefs." They also like to look good. One student agrees, "We all dress in a classy style to keep ourselves prepared for the corporate world." The size of the student body has its benefits and drawbacks. One undergraduate reports, "There are times when I get tired of looking at the same people and knowing everyone on campus, but there are other times where knowing every face is comforting."

FINANCIAL AID: 615-329-8735 • E-MAIL: ADMISSIONS@FISK.EDU • WEBSITE: WWW.FISK.EDU

ADMISSIONS

Very important factors considered include: Character/personal qualities, class rank, essays, recommendations, secondary school record, standardized test scores, talent/ability. *Important factors considered include:* Alumni/ae relation, extracurricular activities, interview. *Other factors considered include:* Volunteer work. SAT Reasoning or ACT required. TOEFL required of all international applicants. High school diploma is required, and GED is accepted. *Academic units required:* 4 English, 3 math, 2 science (2 science lab), 1 foreign language, 1 history, 4 academic electives. *Academic units recommended:* 4 English, 3 math, 3 science (2 science lab), 2 foreign language, 1 social studies, 1 history, 4 academic electives.

The Inside Word

While a solid academic record is central to getting in, applicants to Fisk should not underestimate the personal side of admissions criteria. A high level of motivation and involvement in your school, church, and/or community goes a long way toward a successful candidacy.

FINANCIAL AID

Students should submit: FAFSA. Regular filing deadline is 2/15. The Princeton Review suggests that all financial aid forms be submitted as soon as possible after 1/1. *Need-based scholarships/grants offered:* Pell, SEOG, state scholarships/grants, private scholarships, the school's own gift aid, United Negro College Fund. *Loan aid offered:* Direct Subsidized Stafford, Direct Unsubsidized Stafford, Direct PLUS, Federal Perkins. Applicants will be notified of awards on or about 4/1. Federal Work-study Program available. Off-campus job opportunities are excellent.

FROM THE ADMISSIONS OFFICE

"Founded in 1866, the university is coeducational, private, and one of America's premier historically Black universities. The first Black college to be granted a chapter of Phi Beta Kappa Honor Society, Fisk serves a national student body, with an enrollment of 900 students. There are residence halls for men and women. The focal point of the 40-acre campus and architectural symbol of the university is Jubilee Hall, the first permanent building for the education of Blacks in the South, and named for the internationally renowned Fisk Jubilee Singers, who continue their tradition of singing the Negro spiritual. From its earliest days, Fisk has played a leadership role in the education of African Americans. Faculty and alumni have been among America's intellectual leaders. Among them include Fisk graduates Nikki Giovanni, poet/writer; John Hope Franklin, historian/scholar; David Lewis, professor/recipient of the prestigious Pulitzer Prize; Hazel O'Leary, U.S. Secretary of Energy; John Lewis, U.S. Representative—GA; and W. E. B. DuBois, the great social critic and cofounder of the NAACP. Former Fisk students whose distinguished careers bring color to American culture include Judith Jamison, director of the Alvin Ailey Dance Company, and Johnetta B. Cole, president of Spelman College. In proportion to its size, Fisk continues to contribute more alumni to the ranks of scholars pursuing doctoral degrees than any other institution in the United States.

"As of this book's publication, Fisk University did not have information available about their policy regarding the new SAT."

SELECTIVITY

Admissions Rating	**84**
# of applicants	1,146
% of applicants accepted	66
% of acceptees attending	29

FRESHMAN PROFILE

Range SAT Verbal	395-650
Average SAT Verbal	492
Range SAT Math	365-620
Average SAT Math	484
**TPR Projected Range SAT Writing*	*470-670*
Range ACT Composite	17-29
Average ACT Composite	19
Minimum Paper TOEFL	500
Minimum Computer Based TOEFL	250
Average HS GPA	3.0
% graduated top 10% of class	35
% graduated top 25% of class	48
% graduated top 50% of class	73

DEADLINES

Early decision application deadline	12/1
Regular application deadline	3/1
Regular notification	rolling
Nonfall registration?	yes

APPLICANTS ALSO LOOK AT AND SOMETIMES PREFER

Belmont University
Hampton University
Morehouse College
Spelman College

FINANCIAL FACTS

Financial Aid Rating	**80**
Annual tuition	$11,770
Room & Board	$6,230
Required fees	$680
% frosh rec. need-based scholarship or grant aid	58
% UG rec. need-based scholarship or grant aid	63
% frosh rec. need-based self-help aid	81
% UG rec. need-based self-help aid	85
Avg. frosh grant	$2,200
Avg. frosh loan	$6,700
Independent 529 member?	No

FLAGLER COLLEGE

74 KING STREET, PO BOX 1027, ST. AUGUSTINE, FL 32085-1027 • ADMISSIONS: 800-304-4208 • FAX: 904-826-0094

CAMPUS LIFE

Quality of Life Rating	**74**
Fire Safety Rating	**88**
Type of school	private
Environment	village

STUDENTS

Total undergrad enrollment	2,106
% male/female	39/61
% from out of state	32
% from public high school	84
% live on campus	35
% African American	2
% Asian	1
% Caucasian	90
% Hispanic	4
% international	1
# of countries represented	17

SURVEY SAYS

Small classes
Diversity lacking on campus
Frats and sororities are unpopular or nonexistent
Student publications are popular
Student government is popular

ACADEMICS

Academic Rating	**78**
Calendar	semester
Student/faculty ratio	21:1
Professors interesting rating	69
Professors accessible rating	77
% professors teaching UG courses	100
% classes taught by TAs	0
Most common regular class size	20-29 students

MOST POPULAR MAJORS

Business administration/management
elementary education and teaching

STUDENTS SPEAK OUT

Academics

In a setting where professors "wear floral shirts to class," Flagler students emphasize that the school's academics are "harder than they appear." Students regard their instructors as "extremely brilliant people who want to inspire rather than dictate what we should think and know." Another student confirms that opinion, commenting, "They foster and encourage your opinions, no matter how alike or different they are from their own." These "angels" are said to "really love their jobs and be totally accessible outside of the classroom." Flagler offers an innovative program in deaf education, "one of very few in the country," and classes in all areas are kept very small. Many respondents point out, "Both professors and members of the administration are actively involved in campus activities;" students can even "sit down with the president for an hour and talk." The administration, however, reportedly "plays parent too much," giving rise to the feeling that "it's Flagler's way or no way." Students also gripe about class attendance policies "reminiscent of ninth grade" and the school's "need to up admissions standards." But overall most students agree that "the tuition for a private school is relatively cheap," claiming the cost is "one-half of what it would be elsewhere." In summary, one senior remarks, "I have received a first-rate education through personal and nurturing means."

Life

Students commonly express the sentiment that life at Flagler "resembles high school, which can be a good or bad thing." While "community service projects to karaoke to bachelor bids" count among popular activities, surfing is by far the most widely enjoyed pastime. The beach and surrounding area also offer "parasailing, swimming, skydiving, and museum cruising." Regarding the prevalence of "studying at the beach," students challenge, "Beat that, Harvard, Yale, or Princeton!" Flagler's location in the "tourist trap" of St. Augustine, the oldest town in the U.S., means plenty of "cool shops and neat little pubs," though some students feel there's "not much to do here unless you're 80 years old or a tourist." On campus, rules prohibiting visitation between the male and female dorms are regarded as "unbearable" by most students, with one woman lamenting, "I have a lot of guy friends I can barely hang out with." Other students consider the policies "fair:" "This is just a conservative school, so if you don't like that, don't come." Though no boys are allowed, the girls adore their dorm, located in the former famous Ponce de Leon Hotel, where each room is different.

Students

The 1,900-student Flagler population, featuring a 3:2 female-male ratio, is made up of "exceptionally friendly and welcoming" people. Though the environment is "fairly conservative," students note that "even the more radical and liberal among us get along pretty well." One undergraduate tells us, "The majority of the students are of an upper-middle-class, white background, and that makes the student body a bit one-dimensional." A minority student writes, "As a Hispanic, I have felt deprived of my culture at this school." As far as the LGBT community, one woman reports, "I'm a lesbian, and my school seems to have the 'don't ask, don't tell' policy." Amid this largely homogenous group, where "the most diversity comes from foreign students," students claim, "Those of minority groups that we do have are not discriminated against, and most are actually very popular." The overall "close-knit atmosphere" is furthered by a collective willingness to "accept each others' differences."

FLAGLER COLLEGE

FINANCIAL AID: 904-819-6225 • E-MAIL: ADMISS@FLAGLER.EDU • WEBSITE: WWW.FLAGLER.EDU

ADMISSIONS

Very important factors considered include: Secondary school record, standardized test scores. *Important factors considered include:* Alumni/ae relation, character/personal qualities, essays, extracurricular activities, recommendations. *Other factors considered include:* Class rank, geographical residence, interview, state residency, talent/ability, volunteer work, work experience. SAT Reasoning or ACT required. TOEFL required of all international applicants. High school diploma is required, and GED is accepted. *Academic units required:* 4 English, 3 math, 2 science (1 science lab), 3 social studies, 1 history, 3 academic electives. *Academic units recommended:* 4 English, 4 math, 3 science (2 science lab), 2 foreign language, 4 social studies, 2 history, 3 academic electives.

The Inside Word

Flagler sets no bare minimums for most applicants but does require of its education candidates a minimum combined 1010 SAT I score or a composite 21 on the ACT. An on-campus interview is highly recommended. Use it as an excuse to visit St. Augustine in the winter; you'll be glad you did.

FINANCIAL AID

Students should submit: FAFSA, institution's own financial aid form, state aid form. The Princeton Review suggests that all financial aid forms be submitted as soon as possible after 1/1. *Need-based scholarships/grants offered:* Pell, SEOG, state scholarships/grants, private scholarships, the school's own gift aid. *Loan aid offered:* Direct Subsidized Stafford, Direct Unsubsidized Stafford, Direct PLUS, Federal Perkins. Applicants will be notified of awards on a rolling basis beginning on or about 4/1. Federal Work-study Program available.

FROM THE ADMISSIONS OFFICE

"Flagler College is an independent, four-year, coeducational, residential institution located in picturesque St. Augustine. A famous historic tourist center in northeast Florida, it is located to the south of Jacksonville and north of Daytona Beach. Flagler students have ample opportunity to explore the rich cultural heritage and international flavor of St. Augustine, and there's always time for a relaxing day at the beach, about four miles from campus. Flagler is one of the least expensive private colleges in the nation and is recognized in *MoneyGuide*, *U.S. News & World Report*, and *America's Best 100 Buys* as a top value in education at an affordable cost. The annual cost for tuition, room, and board at Flagler is about the same as state universities. The small student body helps to keep one from becoming 'just a number.' Flagler serves a predominately full-time student body and seeks to enroll students who can benefit from the type of educational experience the college offers. Because of the college's unique mission and distinctive characteristics, some students may benefit more from an educational experience at Flagler than others. The college's admission standards and procedures are designed to select from among the applicants those students most likely to succeed academically, to contribute significantly to the student life program at Flagler, and to become graduates of the college. Flagler College provides an exceptional opportunity for a private education at an extremely affordable cost.

"Freshman applicants for fall 2006 must take the new SAT (or the ACT with the Writing component). In addition, students may submit scores from the old (before March 2005) SAT (or ACT), and we will use their best scores from either test."

SELECTIVITY

Admissions Rating	**88**
# of applicants	2,313
% of applicants accepted	30
% of acceptees attending	71
# accepting a place on wait list	474
% admitted from wait list	10
# of early decision applicants	397
% accepted early decision	61

FRESHMAN PROFILE

Range SAT Verbal	540-620
Average SAT Verbal	568
Range SAT Math	520-600
Average SAT Math	560
**TPR Projected Range SAT Writing*	*590-650*
Range ACT Composite	22-26
Average ACT Composite	24
Minimum Paper TOEFL	550
Minimum Computer Based TOEFL	213
Average HS GPA	3.32
% graduated top 10% of class	16
% graduated top 25% of class	51
% graduated top 50% of class	99

DEADLINES

Early decision application deadline	12/1
Early decision notification	12/15
Regular application deadline	3/1
Regular notification	3/30
Nonfall registration?	yes

APPLICANTS ALSO LOOK AT AND OFTEN PREFER

Florida State U., U. of Central Florida, U. of Florida, U. of North Florida, U. of South Florida

AND SOMETIMES PREFER

Florida Atlantic U., Jacksonville U., Stetson U., U. of Miami, U. of Tampa

AND RARELY PREFER

Florida Gulf Coast U., Florida International U., Florida Southern College, Rollins College

FINANCIAL FACTS

Financial Aid Rating	**70**
Annual tuition	$8,600
Room & Board	$5,190
Books and supplies	$800
% frosh rec. need-based scholarship or grant aid	22
% UG rec. need-based scholarship or grant aid	22
% frosh rec. need-based self-help aid	36
% UG rec. need-based self-help aid	34
% frosh rec. any financial aid	70
% UG rec. any financial aid	85
Avg. frosh grant	$3,000
Avg. frosh loan	$2,625
Independent 529 member?	No

FLORIDA STATE UNIVERSITY

2500 UNIVERSITY CENTER, TALLAHASSEE, FL 32306-2400 • ADMISSIONS: 850-644-6200 • FAX: 850-644-0197

CAMPUS LIFE

Quality of Life Rating	**87**
Fire Safety Rating	**85**
Type of school	public
Environment	city

STUDENTS

Total undergrad enrollment	29,820
% male/female	43/57
% from out of state	15
% from public high school	89
% live on campus	14
% in (# of) fraternities	13 (27)
% in (# of) sororities	15 (23)
% African American	12
% Asian	3
% Caucasian	73
% Hispanic	10
% international	1
# of countries represented	134

SURVEY SAYS

Athletic facilities are great
Students are happy
Everyone loves the Seminoles
Frats and sororities dominate social scene
Lots of beer drinking

ACADEMICS

Academic Rating	**70**
Calendar	semester
Student/faculty ratio	22:1
Professors interesting rating	73
Professors accessible rating	71
% professors teaching UG courses	100
% classes taught by TAs	32
Most common regular class size	20-29 students

MOST POPULAR MAJORS

Criminal justice/safety studies
finance
psychology

STUDENTS SPEAK OUT

Academics

Florida State University's key selling points are that it has "a very strong school spirit that unites students of different backgrounds" and "the availability of everything you need, if you know where to look." This is a school where sunshine and football meet world-class research facilities and an impressive catalog of solid offerings. Undergraduates report great programs in engineering, music, business, and hospitality and add that "the biology sphere [is] undoubtedly the school's great strength." They also brag that "the various resources and facilities are by far one of FSU's strongest points. [The school has] 24-hour computer labs, eight libraries, and research opportunities in almost every field." On the downside, "there are too many grad students teaching classes. Many upper-level undergrad classes are also simultaneously grad classes but with a different name. So your classmate in one class could be your teacher in another!" Students also report that "it is sometimes difficult to get some alone time with your dean or professors, but that is expected because most of the professors teach more than one class and also participate in school organizations. Florida State is also a very large university, so the deans and administration are constantly busy dealing with students and their many problems." Students add that, while dealing with the university at large can be frustrating and time-consuming, "inside the individual colleges, everything is generally well organized."

Life

"It is all about having a good time while getting a great education" at FSU, and most students figure out how to juggle both tasks. Undergraduates report that Seminoles "are very focused on classes during the week. However, when the weekends roll around, it is all about football (in the fall) and partying! FSU students know how to have a good time, and there is always a party going on." Beer is the drink of choice, so it's no surprise that students say that, keg parties are popular for many people on the weekends, and "the bars are also extremely cheap. This makes for many distractions, especially for freshmen their first time away from home." There is also "tons to do around the town" that doesn't involve drinking: "shopping, helping within the community, concerts and entertainment around and on campus, intramural sports, and extreme sports, which are quite popular here (I went skydiving for the first time in Tallahassee)." Big events are seasonal. Football rules the fall ("from parties to tailgating to after-game celebrations, football season means fun, fun, fun!"), while "in the spring everyone goes to various spring break destinations and festivals (i.e., Panama City, Mardi Gras)." Students warn that getting onto and around campus can be a real hassle. "There are never any parking spaces unless you get to school an hour before the main parking garage opens," and "transportation on campus is difficult because buses run infrequently and are few in number." At least students enjoy great weather while they are waiting for the bus or looking for a parking space.

Student Body

"There is incredible diversity at Florida State," which mirrors the diversity of its home state's population. Students report, "You've got your standard issue of sports fanatics, plus an interesting pool of international students and minorities." Most students are "very involved in all aspects of campus life—in student organizations, Greek life, Senate, student unions, and major related organizations." They also show "lots of school spirit." Several clear dividing lines do separate students, however. One is Greek life, which is "huge, and people are always wearing their shirts and bags with their letters." The other is geographic. One student adds, "There are the North Florida types: very casual, wear jeans and collared shirts with hats; and then there are South Florida types: more trendy, often wear gel in their hair. Most students fit in with one of those two groups."

FINANCIAL AID: 850-644-5871 • E-MAIL: ADMISSIONS@ADMIN.FSU.EDU • WEBSITE: WWW.FSU.EDU

ADMISSIONS

Very important factors considered include: Secondary school record. *Important factors considered include:* Class rank, standardized test scores, state residency, talent/ability. *Other factors considered include:* Alumni/ae relation, character/personal qualities, essays, extracurricular activities, recommendations, volunteer work, work experience. SAT Reasoning or ACT required. TOEFL required of all international applicants. High school diploma is required, and GED is accepted. *Academic units required:* 4 English, 3 math, 3 science (2 science lab), 2 foreign language, 2 social studies, 1 history, 4 academic electives. *Academic units recommended:* 4 English, 4 math, 4 science (2 science lab), 2 foreign language, 2 social studies, 1 history, 4 academic electives.

The Inside Word

The high volume of applicants has everything to do with Florida State's selectivity, which continues to increase as budgets hold enrollment fairly level. Non-Floridians will find FSU's selection process to be a bit more welcoming than UF's, but just as impersonal. Performing arts auditions are quite competitive.

FINANCIAL AID

Students should submit: FAFSA. The Princeton Review suggests that all financial aid forms be submitted as soon as possible after 1/1. *Need-based scholarships/grants offered:* Pell, SEOG, state scholarships/grants, private scholarships, the school's own gift aid. *Loan aid offered:* FFEL Subsidized Stafford, FFEL Unsubsidized Stafford, FFEL PLUS, Federal Perkins. Applicants will be notified of awards on a rolling basis beginning on or about 3/15. Federal Work-study Program available. Institutional employment available. Off-campus job opportunities are good.

FROM THE ADMISSIONS OFFICE

"Established in 1851, Florida State University is seated on the oldest continuous site of higher education in Florida and holds the state's first chapter of Phi Beta Kappa. It enjoys an outstanding reputation for offering a wide range of innovative academic achievements, like our College of Medicine, the first in the nation in 20 years; conducting groundbreaking research; attracting renowned faculty; being one of the "most wired" universities in the U.S.; housing an exceptional Career Center; and producing successful graduates. Seventeen colleges and schools offer nearly 200 undergraduate majors, 198 graduate degrees, and professional degrees in law and medicine. A diverse student body has access to student services that include the University Honors Program, the Center for Academic Retention and Enhancement, Disabled Student Services, the International Center, the Center for Civic Education and Service, and the Undergraduate Academic Advising Center. FSU leads the way in global education with international programs in Costa Rica, the Czech Republic, England, France, Italy, Panama, Russia, Spain, Switzerland, Vietnam, and the West Indies.

"Students applying for the entering class of 2006 are required to submit the writing section of the new SAT and/or take the optional writing test of the ACT. Scores from the SAT taken before March 2005 are also acceptable. We will continue to use the highest sub scores on the ACT and SAT for admission purposes."

SELECTIVITY

Admissions Rating	**91**
# of applicants	22,127
% of applicants accepted	65
% of acceptees attending	44
# accepting a place on wait list	300

FRESHMAN PROFILE

Range SAT Verbal	530-630
Average SAT Verbal	580
Range SAT Math	540-630
Average SAT Math	584
**TPR Projected Range SAT Writing*	*580-650*
Range ACT Composite	22-27
Average ACT Composite	25
Minimum Paper TOEFL	550
Minimum Computer Based TOEFL	213
Average HS GPA	3.73
% graduated top 10% of class	55
% graduated top 25% of class	93
% graduated top 50% of class	100

DEADLINES

Regular application deadline	3/1
Regular notification	11/1, 12/15, 2/1, 3/1, 4/1
Nonfall registration?	yes

FINANCIAL FACTS

Financial Aid Rating	**80**
Annual in-state tuition	$2,290
Annual out-of-state tuition	$14,796
Room & Board	$6,488
Books and supplies	$800
Required fees	$748
% frosh rec. need-based scholarship or grant aid	29
% UG rec. need-based scholarship or grant aid	31
% frosh rec. need-based self-help aid	25
% UG rec. need-based self-help aid	32
% frosh rec. any financial aid	41
% UG rec. any financial aid	42
Avg. frosh grant	$6,884
Avg. frosh loan	$2,769
Independent 529 member?	No

FORDHAM UNIVERSITY

441 EAST FORDHAM ROAD, THEBAUD HALL, NEW YORK, NY 10458 • ADMISSIONS: 718-817-4000 • FAX: 718-367-9404

CAMPUS LIFE

Quality of Life Rating	**75**
Fire Safety Rating	**89**
Type of school	private
Affiliation	Roman Catholic
Environment	metropolis

STUDENTS

Total undergrad enrollment	7,391
% male/female	40/60
% from out of state	43
% from public high school	47
% live on campus	59
% African American	5
% Asian	6
% Caucasian	57
% Hispanic	11
% international	1
# of countries represented	50

SURVEY SAYS

Small classes
Great library
Great off-campus food
Campus feels safe
Frats and sororities are unpopular or nonexistent
Lots of beer drinking
Hard liquor is popular

ACADEMICS

Academic Rating	**84**
Calendar	semester
Student/faculty ratio	13:1
Professors interesting rating	77
Professors accessible rating	78
% classes taught by TAs	0
Most common regular class size	10-19 students

MOST POPULAR MAJORS

Business administration/management
communications and media studies
English language and literature

STUDENTS SPEAK OUT

Academics

Fordham University has campuses in the Bronx and Manhattan and "is all about the Jesuit tradition" of education. That tradition "places the total emphasis on working on a student-by-student basis, tailoring to each student's strengths and weaknesses" and "focuses on development of the whole person, not just on academics." Central to the Jesuit approach is Fordham's thorough core curriculum, which takes "almost two full years to complete." Some students describe it as "amazing because it introduces you to a wide variety of disciplines and topics," but others feel the core requirements are too onerous and too remote from their career goals. Comments one such student, "I understand that they want people to be thinkers, but all the core manages to do is make people feel as though their first two years are a meaningless waste of time." The Jesuit focus on individuals is facilitated by small class sizes. "When I first got here," writes one undergraduate, "I was amazed at how small classes were and how 'real' professors were teaching my classes. I've even been able to work on research projects with some of them and do an independent study—as a sophomore—with another." Close contact with influential professors and the school's urban setting translate into "great jobs and internships," something appreciated by the entire student body. Many warn that the school needs a major tech upgrade, telling us that "technology is far behind that of many schools" of lesser academic caliber and that "dorm Internet connections are slower than dialup."

Life

Fordham's Rose Hill campus in the Bronx, students tell us, is "the best location possible: It's close to the city, but far enough away for it not to be a distraction." It also boasts "the most gorgeous campus in New York City," which is "completely gated, and you need a school ID to get on to campus and into dorms after 6:00 P.M." Although the surrounding area "isn't the best neighborhood," it has lots to offer (above and beyond "teaching students street smarts"), including the New York Botanical Garden and the Bronx Zoo. Manhattan is a 15-minute subway ride away and provides "an unlimited source of entertainment." On campus, there's not much of a party scene "because the rules are very strict," so "many people go to local bars, to parties at off-campus apartments," or to Manhattan for fun. One student explains, "Life at school centers around a balance of classwork, activities in the city (Broadway plays, going out to eat, shopping, going to see other performing arts and concerts, Yankee games) and activities on campus (community service in local hospitals, watching our basketball and football games, and participating in the university band). Life can be as full as you choose to make it."

Student Body

The predominantly "upper-middle-class Irish or Italian Catholic" students at Fordham University "fall into one of two categories: resident students and commuters." Residents can be divided into "a few basic types of people: preppy, athletic, and/or trendy," while commuters "mostly hang out together, and they tend to be much more ethnically diverse than the resident students. Somehow, everyone manages to fit into a very multifaceted Fordham," in part because "students are very respectful and friendly to each other." Many are active outside the classroom; reports one undergraduate, "the typical student at Fordham not only goes to class, but [also] is involved in extracurricular activities both on and off campus, whether clubs on campus, or an internship, or working a part-time job." Adds another student, "Global Outreach is one of the most popular programs on campus. You travel to an impoverished area (national and foreign) and, with a group of other students, help out for a few days. What kind of student gives up his/her spring break to teach orphans in Romania or the poor in El Salvador? [A] Fordham student!"

FINANCIAL AID: 718-817-3800 • E-MAIL: ENROLL@FORDHAM.EDU • WEBSITE: WWW.FORDHAM.EDU

ADMISSIONS

Very important factors considered include: Class rank, secondary school record, standardized test scores. *Important factors considered include:* Character/personal qualities, essays, extracurricular activities, recommendations, talent/ability. *Other factors considered include:* Alumni/ae relation, geographical residence, interview, minority status, volunteer work, work experience. SAT Reasoning or ACT required. TOEFL required of all international applicants. High school diploma is required, and GED is accepted. *Academic units required:* 4 English, 3 math, 3 science, 2 foreign language, 2 social studies, 2 history, 6 academic electives. *Academic units recommended:* 4 English, 4 math, 4 science, 3 foreign language, 2 social studies, 2 history, 6 academic electives.

The Inside Word

Candidates are reviewed by a committee made up of admissions officers, faculty, administrators, and deans. Admission to Fordham is quite competitive and a solid flow of applicants from metropolitan area Catholic schools keeps their student profile sound.

FINANCIAL AID

Students should submit: FAFSA, CSS/Financial Aid PROFILE, noncustodial (divorced/separated) parents' statement, business/farm supplement. Regular filing deadline is 2/1. The Princeton Review suggests that all financial aid forms be submitted as soon as possible after 1/1. *Need-based scholarships/grants offered:* Pell, SEOG, state scholarships/grants, private scholarships, the school's own gift aid. *Loan aid offered:* FFEL Subsidized Stafford, FFEL Unsubsidized Stafford, FFEL PLUS, Federal Perkins. Applicants will be notified of awards on or about 4/1. Federal Work-study Program available. Institutional employment available. Off-campus job opportunities are excellent.

FROM THE ADMISSIONS OFFICE

"Fordham University offers a distinctive, values-centered educational experience that is rooted in the Jesuit tradition of intellectual rigor and personal attention. Located in New York City, Fordham offers to students the unparalleled educational, cultural and recreational advantages of one of the world's greatest cities. Fordham has three residential campuses in New York—the tree-lined, 85-acre Rose Hill in the Bronx, the cosmopolitan Lincoln Center campus in the heart of Manhattan's performing arts center, and the scenic Marymount campus located on the banks of the Hudson River in Tarrytown, New York. The university's state of the art facilities and buildings include one of the most technologically advanced libraries in the country. Fordham offers to its students a variety of majors, concentrations, and programs that can be combined with an extensive career planning and placement program. More than 2,600 organizations in the New York metropolitan area offer students internships that provide hands-on experience and valuable networking opportunities in fields such as business, communications, medicine, law, and education.

"Students applicants are required to take the new version of the SAT (or the ACT with or without the Writing section), but we will allow students to submit scores from the old (prior to March 2005) version of the SAT (or ACT) as well. We recommend that students provide score from only two SAT Subject Tests."

SELECTIVITY

Admissions Rating	**90**
# of applicants	14,261
% of applicants accepted	50
% of acceptees attending	24
# accepting a place on wait list	2,117
% admitted from wait list	20

FRESHMAN PROFILE

Range SAT Verbal	550-650
Average SAT Verbal	606
Range SAT Math	540-640
Average SAT Math	606
**TPR Projected Range SAT Writing*	*600-670*
Range ACT Composite	23-28
Average ACT Composite	27
Minimum Paper TOEFL	575
Minimum Computer Based TOEFL	231
Average HS GPA	3.64
% graduated top 10% of class	34
% graduated top 25% of class	72
% graduated top 50% of class	95

DEADLINES

Regular application deadline	1/15
Regular notification	4/1
Nonfall registration?	yes

APPLICANTS ALSO LOOK AT

AND OFTEN PREFER
Boston College, Columbia U.—Columbia College, Georgetown U., N.Y.U., U. of Notre Dame

AND SOMETIMES PREFER
Boston U., College of the Holy Cross, The George Washington U., Loyola College in Maryland, Northeastern U., Providence College, Villanova U.

AND RARELY PREFER
American U., Fairfield U., Hofstra U., Marist College, St. John's U.

FINANCIAL FACTS

Financial Aid Rating	**71**
Annual tuition	$26,200
Room & Board	$10,248
Books and supplies	$725
Required fees	$821
% frosh rec. need-based scholarship or grant aid	63
% UG rec. need-based scholarship or grant aid	62
% frosh rec. need-based self-help aid	55
% UG rec. need-based self-help aid	54
% frosh rec. any financial aid	67
% UG rec. any financial aid	62
Avg. frosh grant	$16,052
Avg. frosh loan	$2,792
Independent 529 member?	No

FRANKLIN & MARSHALL COLLEGE

PO Box 3003, Lancaster, PA 17604-3003 • Admissions: 717-291-3953 • Fax: 717-291-4381

CAMPUS LIFE

Quality of Life Rating	**71**
Fire Safety Rating	**88**
Type of school	private
Environment	town

STUDENTS

Total undergrad enrollment	1,931
% male/female	54/46
% from out of state	65
% from public high school	62
% live on campus	66
% African American	2
% Asian	4
% Caucasian	77
% Hispanic	3
% international	8
# of countries represented	63

SURVEY SAYS

Small classes
Great library
Lots of beer drinking
Hard liquor is popular

ACADEMICS

Academic Rating	**88**
Calendar	semester
Student/faculty ratio	11:1
Professors interesting rating	94
Professors accessible rating	92
% professors teaching UG courses	100
% classes taught by TAs	0
Most common lab size	10-19 students
Most common regular class size	20-29 students

MOST POPULAR MAJORS

Business administration/management
political science and government
psychology

STUDENTS SPEAK OUT

Academics

"The workload is tremendous" at Franklin & Marshall College, a small private college that produces "great acceptance rates into graduate and professional schools." The school's "great reputation for its premed program" as well as "its success in placing graduates in top law schools" are among the reasons students endure the "make-you-or-break-you academics" here; the fact that "the school is dedicated to helping students get interesting opportunities, such as internships, study-abroad programs, and independent research programs" is another attraction. And then there are the professors, identified by many as "the bright spot of the school. They are all very kind and helpful and enjoy teaching." Writes one student, "The professors enliven the classroom and their accessibility outside of the classroom makes the academic experience at F&M that much better." Good grades are hard to come by at F&M. Warns one undergrad, "F&M is known for its grade deflation. Professors do not inflate grades here. Students understand this and work hard." As one student puts it, "My parents must think I goof off sometimes when I come out with Bs, yet I work more than I ever have. Getting an A– here for me is like finding the Holy Grail." But after they've put in their long hours of study, "students realize how much they have truly learned, and how it was all worth it in the end. The results of the strong liberal arts education can be seen in F&M's extremely high number of acceptances to graduate, medical, and law schools."

Life

F&M has a long history of active Greek life on campus, despite the fact that the school "de-recognized" Greek organizations in 1988. In 2004, F&M brought the Greeks back into the fold, which should mean the popular system should grow even more popular in coming years. Even before the re-recognition, "frat parties were a huge part of campus life," in part due to a perceived lack of alternatives; many here feel that hometown Lancaster, PA, "is a pretty small city with not too much for a college student to do." Of course, F&M's famous academic workload pretty well takes care of students' weekdays. "Most students have no time for anything but work during the week, but party hardy when they get the chance on the weekend," undergrads agree. Come Friday afternoon, students "hang out and party at the off-campus frat houses or apartments," or they "enjoy events such as concerts, movies, comedy shows, lectures, and debates, which the college does a great job of setting up." A few adventurous undergrads venture into Lancaster, which we're told "has a few alternative venues, including the independent movie theater Zoetropolis, Chameleon Club, and Tally-Ho (a local gay club)." Lancaster also has "some excellent restaurants for when parents come up with the money to buy those kinds of dinners" and "great local shopping with a couple of big outlet malls." Many here "do volunteer work around the community," often in conjunction with their Greek organizations.

Student Body

"There are a significant number of your stereotypical Abercrombie frat boys and sorority girls" at F&M, "but there are also representatives of just about every other socio-demographic group you could think of," including "a very strong international population representing about 60 different countries." Notes one student, "My four best friends here are a Shia Muslim from Tanzania, a New York Catholic, a minister's daughter, and an extremely rural Baha'i." The sameness of much of the school's "conservative, preppy, middle-class majority" is further counterbalanced by "a lot of atypical students: gays, nerds, a few potheads, people with different religious beliefs. Most of them are considered very interesting to talk to and some of them are very popular on campus." Many who attend here "are not only capable academically but are also extremely talented in other areas such as sports, theater, and music."

FINANCIAL AID: 717-291-3991 • E-MAIL: ADMISSION@FANDM.EDU • WEBSITE: WWW.FANDM.EDU

ADMISSIONS

Very important factors considered include: Character/personal qualities, class rank, secondary school record. *Important factors considered include:* Essays, extracurricular activities, interview, minority status, recommendations, standardized test scores, talent/ability, volunteer work. *Other factors considered include:* Alumni/ae relation, geographical residence, work experience. SAT Reasoning or ACT required. TOEFL required of all international applicants. High school diploma is required, and GED is accepted. *Academic units required:* 4 English, 3 math, 2 science (2 science lab), 2 foreign language, 1 social studies, 2 history, 1 arts, music, and theater. *Academic units recommended:* 4 math, 3 science (3 science lab), 4 foreign language, 3 social studies, 3 history.

The Inside Word

Applicants who are serious about attending the college should definitely interview; it will also help to make it known that F&M is one of your top choices. The college loses a lot of its admits to competitor colleges and will take notice of a candidate who is likely to enroll.

FINANCIAL AID

Students should submit: FAFSA, institution's own financial aid form, CSS/Financial Aid PROFILE, noncustodial (divorced/separated) parents' statement, business/farm supplement. Regular filing deadline is 3/1. The Princeton Review suggests that all financial aid forms be submitted as soon as possible after 1/1. *Need-based scholarships/grants offered:* Pell, SEOG, state scholarships/grants, private scholarships, the school's own gift aid. *Loan aid offered:* FFEL Subsidized Stafford, FFEL Unsubsidized Stafford, FFEL PLUS, Federal Perkins, college/university loans from institutional funds. Applicants will be notified of awards on or about 3/15. Federal Work-study Program available. Off-campus job opportunities are good.

FROM THE ADMISSIONS OFFICE

"Franklin & Marshall students choose from a variety of fields of study, traditional and interdisciplinary, that typify liberal learning. Professors in all of these fields are committed to a common purpose, which is to teach students to think, speak, and write with clarity and confidence. Whether the course is in theater or in physics, the class will be small, engagement will be high, and discussion will dominate over lecture. Thus throughout their four years, beginning with the First Year Seminar, students at Franklin & Marshall are repeatedly invited to active participation in intellectual play at high levels. Our graduates consistently testify to the high quality of an F&M education as a mental preparation for life.

"Freshman applicants for fall 2006 who are submitting SAT scores may submit the new version of the SAT (since March 2005) or the older version of the SAT (prior to March 2005). Beginning with fall 2007, students should submit the new SAT."

SELECTIVITY

Admissions Rating	**91**
# of applicants	4,070
% of applicants accepted	49
% of acceptees attending	26
# of early decision applicants	245
% accepted early decision	72

FRESHMAN PROFILE

Range SAT Verbal	580-670
Average SAT Verbal	623
Range SAT Math	590-690
Average SAT Math	636
**TPR Projected Range SAT Writing*	*620-680*
Minimum Paper TOEFL	600
Minimum Computer Based TOEFL	250
% graduated top 10% of class	46
% graduated top 25% of class	77
% graduated top 50% of class	97

DEADLINES

Early decision application deadline	11/15
Early decision notification	12/15
Regular application deadline	2/1
Regular notification	4/1
Nonfall registration?	yes

APPLICANTS ALSO LOOK AT AND OFTEN PREFER

Cornell University
Hamilton College
Haverford College
University of Pennsylvania

AND SOMETIMES PREFER

Bucknell University
Colgate University
Dickinson College
Lafayette College
Lehigh University

FINANCIAL FACTS

Financial Aid Rating	**97**
Annual tuition	$30,390
Room & Board	$7,540
Books and supplies	$650
Required fees	$50
% frosh rec. need-based scholarship or grant aid	41
% UG rec. need-based scholarship or grant aid	37
% frosh rec. need-based self-help aid	41
% UG rec. need-based self-help aid	40
% frosh rec. any financial aid	66
% UG rec. any financial aid	62
Avg. frosh grant	$14,292
Avg. frosh loan	$3,625
Independent 529 member?	Yes

FRANKLIN W. OLIN COLLEGE OF ENGINEERING

OLIN WAY NEEDHAM, MA 02492-1245 • ADMISSIONS: 781-292-2222 • FAX: 781-292-2210

CAMPUS LIFE

Quality of Life Rating	**99**
Fire Safety Rating	**94**
Type of school	private
Environment	town

STUDENTS

Total undergrad enrollment	216
% male/female	55/45
% from out of state	90
% from public high school	76
% live on campus	100
% African American	3
% Asian	9
% Caucasian	64
% Hispanic	4
% international	1
# of countries represented	8

SURVEY SAYS

Small classes
No one cheats
Lab facilities are great
Great computer facilities
Students are friendly
Dorms are like palaces
Campus feels safe
Intercollegiate sports are unpopular or nonexistent
Frats and sororities are unpopular or nonexistent

ACADEMICS

Academic Rating	**98**
Calendar	semester
Student/faculty ratio	7:1
Professors interesting rating	99
Professors accessible rating	99
% professors teaching UG courses	100
% classes taught by TAs	0
Most common regular class size	20-29 students

MOST POPULAR MAJORS

Computer engineering
mechanical engineering

STUDENTS SPEAK OUT

Academics

For students at Franklin W. Olin College of Engineering, the best school to attend is the one they get to create. This young and "constantly evolving" technical institution hopes to receive accreditation in 2006, when the first graduating class earns their degrees. Now, students have the opportunity to "actively shape an innovative new school." At this nascent stage, "It's impossible for everything to run perfectly smooth," but students focus on "what a difference we're making for future students and how much we're learning about learning itself." Suggestions regarding curriculum and class structure are implemented swiftly. "Feedback is a huge and serious deal around here," resulting in hands-on projects, collaborative work, and creative problem solving. One student writes, "Freshmen get busy building miniature solar car racers during the first semester." A normal day could involve "software modeling, building parts in the machines shop, and programming." In the interest of training well-rounded individuals, AHS (arts, humanities, social sciences) classes are used to balance science/engineering and business/entrepreneurship courses in the "Olin Triangle." Students may also take courses through neighboring Brandeis, Babson, and Wellesley. Students regard their professors as "a team of superheroes who save us from the harshness of a typical engineering education with their passion for teaching." They interact on a personal, first-name basis in order to "establish a nurturing community for learning." It's all part of "participating in the greatest engineering teaching experiment of our time." These grand aspirations extend beyond school, to careers dedicated to "constantly striving to improve the world through innovation."

Life

With Olin's grinding workload, students know that balance is the key to survival. They need an outside pastime to turn to when the o-chem gets ugly. The school actively encourages "Passionate Pursuits" by offering nondegree credit and funds for pursuing an extracurricular interest. Envision this: A student shaves his head, a drunken rite of passage at many schools, but rather than pop a keg stand, everyone gathers 'round to discuss the friction coefficient of growing hair. Conversely, "it's not unusual to do physics until ten on Friday night and then go out." One student reports, "If parties are your thing, this is a great environment. It's very safe, supportive, and respectful." For the majority, social life means "watching a lot of movies together rather than getting completely plastered every night." Olin claims to breed "less stress than other tech schools," keeping things light with a well-timed practical joke or spontaneous sing-along. Recently, a school-wide game of capture the flag managed to drag most people away from the widespread hobby of "playing Halo on XBox." Rumors also persist that a bouncy castle materialized outside of a dormitory for a study break one weekend.

Student Body

Actually meeting the entire Olin student body would not take much longer than reading this paragraph. This tight group of 216 "awesome, awesome people" might just be "the most social bunch of nerds you'll ever find." One student says her peers walk the line between "socially adept geeks and brainy cool kids." Others also emphasize these future engineers of America "have good people skills and know how to have fun." These are engineering students who put down their protractors and "do everything from glass-blowing to swing dancing to professional theater." The only evident common denominator is that everyone "is passionate about something outside of school." Because they all get to know each other, "people here really understand and appreciate diversity and crazy and wild personalities." The group accommodates "variety in political beliefs, social lives, and ambition." Ultimately, a strong bond unites the Olin population since they share "a commitment to build [their] school together."

FRANKLIN W. OLIN COLLEGE OF ENGINEERING

FINANCIAL AID: 781-292-2364 • E-MAIL: INFO@OLIN.EDU • WEBSITE: WWW.OLIN.EDU

ADMISSIONS

Very important factors considered include: Character/personal qualities, essays, extracurricular activities, recommendations, secondary school record, talent/ability. *Important factors considered include:* Class rank, interview, minority status, standardized test scores, volunteer work. *Other factors considered include:* Geographical residence, state residency, work experience. SAT Reasoning and SAT Subject Tests or ACT required. High school diploma is required, and GED is accepted. *Academic units required:* 4 English, 4 math, 3 science (3 science lab), 2 foreign language, 2 social studies, 2 history.

The Inside Word

Although Franklin W. Olin College of Engineering is an extremely young institution—it first opened its doors to students in fall 2002—admissions is as tough as it gets. Students are judged not only on high school course work and standardized test scores but also on personal character. Students who exhibit creativity, passion, and an entrepreneurial spirit are favored over their less adventurous peers. Olin strives for gender balance; therefore, female applicants currently enjoy an admit rate about three times that of male applicants.

FINANCIAL AID

Students should submit: FAFSA. Regular filing deadline is 4/15. The Princeton Review suggests that all financial aid forms be submitted as soon as possible after 1/1. *Need-based scholarships/grants offered:* the school's own gift aid. Applicants will be notified of awards on a rolling basis beginning on or about 3/25. Off-campus job opportunities are good.

FROM THE ADMISSIONS OFFICE

"Every admitted student at Olin College receives a $130,000 four-year full-tuition scholarship. The endowment to support these scholarships, as well as the funds to build a brand new state-of-the-art campus, was provided by F. W. Olin Foundation. This commitment, in excess of $450 million, is among the largest grants in the history of U.S. higher education. It is the intention of the founders that this scholarship will be offered in perpetuity.

"The selection process at Olin College is unique to college admission. Each year a highly self-selecting pool of approximately 600 applications is reviewed on traditional selection criteria. Approximately 160 finalists are invited to one of two Candidates' Weekends in February and March. These candidates are grouped into five person teams for a weekend of design and build exercises, group discussions and interviews with Olin students, faculty, and staff. Written evaluations and recommendations for each candidate are prepared by all Olin participants and submitted to the faculty admission committee. The committee admits about 100 Candidates to yield a freshman class of 75. The result is that the freshman class is ultimately chosen on the strength of personal attributes such as leadership, cooperation, creativity, communication, and their enthusiasm for Olin College.

"A waiting list of approximately 20 is also established. Any wait list Candidate who is not offered a spot in the class may defer enrollment for one year—with the guarantee of the Olin Scholarship. Wait list students are strongly encouraged do something unusual, exciting, and productive during their sabbatical year.

"Students applying for admission into the fall 2006 freshman class are required to take the new version of the SAT (or the ACT with the writing section). Olin College also requires scores from three SAT Subject Tests: Math IC or IIC, a science of the student's choice, and any third SAT Subject Test of the student's choice."

SELECTIVITY

Admissions Rating	**99**
# of applicants	546
% of applicants accepted	23
% of acceptees attending	58
# accepting a place on wait list	20
% admitted from wait list	50

FRESHMAN PROFILE

Range SAT Verbal	710-770
Average SAT Verbal	740
Range SAT Math	710-800
Average SAT Math	750
**TPR Projected Range SAT Writing*	*700-740*
Range ACT Composite	31-34
Average ACT Composite	32

DEADLINES

Regular application deadline	1/6
Regular notification	3/21
Nonfall registration?	no

APPLICANTS ALSO LOOK AT

AND OFTEN PREFER

Duke University
Harvard College
Massachusetts Institute of Technology
Princeton University
University of California—Berkeley

AND SOMETIMES PREFER

California Institute of Technology
Carnegie Mellon University
Cornell University
Harvey Mudd College
Rensselaer Polytechnic Institute

AND RARELY PREFER

Brown University
Northwestern University
Rice University
Washington University in St. Louis
Worcester Polytechnic Institute

FINANCIAL FACTS

Financial Aid Rating	**99**
Annual tuition	$29,400
Room & Board	$10,720
Books and supplies	$750
Required fees	$100
% frosh rec. need-based scholarship or grant aid	20
% UG rec. need-based scholarship or grant aid	8
% frosh rec. any financial aid	100
% UG rec. any financial aid	100
Avg. frosh grant	$30,786
Independent 529 member?	No

FURMAN UNIVERSITY

3300 POINSETT HIGHWAY, GREENVILLE, SC 29613 • ADMISSIONS: 864-294-2034 • FAX: 864-294-3127

CAMPUS LIFE

Quality of Life Rating	**91**
Fire Safety Rating	**80**
Type of school	private
Environment	city

STUDENTS

Total undergrad enrollment	2,807
% male/female	44/56
% from out of state	72
% from public high school	63
% live on campus	90
% in (# of) fraternities	35 (8)
% in (# of) sororities	40 (8)
% African American	6
% Asian	2
% Caucasian	86
% Hispanic	1
% international	1
# of countries represented	26

SURVEY SAYS

Small classes
Students are friendly
Great off-campus food
Campus feels safe
Students are happy

ACADEMICS

Academic Rating	**84**
Calendar	3-2-3
Student/faculty ratio	12:1
Professors interesting rating	88
Professors accessible rating	85
% professors teaching UG courses	100
% classes taught by TAs	0
Most common lab size	fewer than 10 students
Most common regular class size	20-29 students

MOST POPULAR MAJORS

Business administration/management
history
political science and government

STUDENTS SPEAK OUT

Academics

Students report that "it's extremely hard to get an A" at Furman University. And this isn't a complaint. It's an affirmation of the "supportive and dynamic atmosphere" at Furman "that motivates students to constantly excel." Part of the process of excelling is overcoming difficulties. The academic experience of one sociology major "has sometimes felt like the aching, long-lasting pain of slowly removing a Band-Aid. In a word: stress!" Although professors range from "absolutely exceptional" to "terrible," they are very accessible. Students have plenty of chances to interact with them. One student explains, "A professor's purpose is teaching, not research or any other distractions like it." The programs that students specifically rave about include chemistry, psychology, and education. Undergraduates are also enthusiastic about the study abroad program. With nearly 20 programs or partnerships abroad, the university sends students to destinations such as the Galápagos Islands or the British Isles. Students roll their eyes at the administration, which a junior describes as "mainly concerned with replanting garden beds every week and maintaining an adequate amount of waterfowl for the Greenville community to feed by the lake." There is a sense that the administration and the student body exist on different planes. But nobody's saying the administration is full of bad folks. "The administration is very friendly and approachable," promises an undergraduate.

Life

Hometown Greenville, South Carolina, provides an ideal location for college life, according to most students. One student says of the actual campus, "Without a doubt [it is] one of the most beautiful campuses in the nation." While no one claims that Greenville is the most exciting place on earth, in it you'll find everything from "great little bars on Greenville's Main Street" to an array of shopping areas, restaurants, and movie theaters. With a larger-than-average religious population and a healthy legion of drinkers, students at Furman are either the sort who will "go out and get wasted or go to bed early so they can get up for church on Sunday. There is very little middle ground here." The students who enjoy going to parties lodge loud complaints against the university's dry campus policy. It's useful to know that "frat life is the biggest party scene at Furman." Many students get involved in organizing student activities or participate in student government. In total, there are more than 130 student organizations on campus. The very popular intramural sports events rope in nearly two-thirds of the student body, and the eight men's and nine women's NCAA Division I sports teams draw plenty of support. No matter who you are, you'll agree that "there's always something going on at Furman."

Student Body

One sophomore describes the two primary groups of students at Furman: "Bible bangers and alcoholics." Talk about a dichotomy. What connects all of these students, however, is that they're "all Type A high achievers." Everyone at Furman needs to be prepared for a decent amount of studying—even the drinkers. An undergraduate echoes fellow students, "The average student at Furman is white, drives an SUV, comes from a wealthy Southern family, is attractive, and does well both academically and in life in general." Adds another student, "Diversity is one of the few things Furman lacks." What it doesn't lack is friendliness. Your typical student is "always smiling."

FINANCIAL AID: 864-294-2204 • E-MAIL: ADMISSIONS@FURMAN.EDU • WEBSITE: WWW.FURMAN.EDU

ADMISSIONS

Very important factors considered include: Secondary school record. *Important factors considered include:* Character/personal qualities, class rank, essays, extracurricular activities, standardized test scores. *Other factors considered include:* Alumni/ae relation, minority status, recommendations, talent/ability, volunteer work, work experience. SAT Reasoning or ACT required. TOEFL required of all international applicants. High school diploma is required, and GED is accepted. *Academic units required:* 4 English, 3 math, 2 science (2 science lab), 2 foreign language, 3 social studies. *Academic units recommended:* 4 English, 4 math, 3 science (3 science lab), 3 foreign language, 4 social studies.

The Inside Word

While Furman is selective academically, there is a high level of self-selection on the part of its applicants. Good students who truly want to be here will encounter little resistance from the admissions committee.

FINANCIAL AID

Students should submit: FAFSA, institution's own financial aid form, state aid form. South Carolina residents must complete required state forms for South Carolina (when noted). Regular filing deadline is 1/15. The Princeton Review suggests that all financial aid forms be submitted as soon as possible after 1/1. *Need-based scholarships/grants offered:* Pell, SEOG, state scholarships/grants, private scholarships, the school's own gift aid. *Loan aid offered:* FFEL Subsidized Stafford, FFEL Unsubsidized Stafford, FFEL PLUS, Federal Perkins, state loans, donor sponsored loans for study abroad. Applicants will be notified of awards on or about 3/15. Federal Work-study Program available. Institutional employment available. Off-campus job opportunities are excellent.

FROM THE ADMISSIONS OFFICE

"From its position as a nationally-ranked independent, co-educational liberal arts college of 2,600 students, Furman takes great pride in its beautiful campus, its gifted student body, its distinguished and active faculty, and the many notable accomplishments of its alumni. Furman emphasizes engaged learning, a hands-on, problem-solving, and collaborative educational philosophy that encourages students to put into practice the theories and methods learned from texts and lectures. Using the latest in wired and wireless technology, students have multiple opportunities to become engaged in their academic pursuits through an array of internships, service-learning programs, faculty/student creative projects and significant undergraduate research. Furman offers an unusual combination of a top tier liberal arts college, 17 Division I men's and women's athletic teams, and a nationally competitive music program that features 26 performing ensembles. Students are involved in hundreds of organizations and clubs on campus ranging from professional organizations to fraternities and sororities. In sum, Furman is a diverse learning community, celebrating its differences, and committed to the development of the whole student.

"Students applying for admission for fall 2006 must submit scores from the new version of the SAT (or the ACT with the writing section). Math or Verbal scores submitted from the old SAT (before March 2005) or ACT will be used, if they are better than those from the new test."

SELECTIVITY

Admissions Rating	**94**
# of applicants	3,849
% of applicants accepted	58
% of acceptees attending	33
# accepting a place on wait list	749
# of early decision applicants	419
% accepted early decision	85

FRESHMAN PROFILE

Range SAT Verbal	580-690
Range SAT Math	590-680
**TPR Projected Range SAT Writing*	*620-690*
Range ACT Composite	25-30
Minimum Paper TOEFL	570
Minimum Computer Based TOEFL	230
Average HS GPA	3.8
% graduated top 10% of class	57
% graduated top 25% of class	84
% graduated top 50% of class	98

DEADLINES

Early decision application deadline	11/15
Early decision notification	12/15
Regular application deadline	1/15
Regular notification	3/15
Nonfall registration?	no

APPLICANTS ALSO LOOK AT

AND OFTEN PREFER

Duke University, University of North Carolina—Chapel Hill, Vanderbilt University, Wake Forest University, Washington and Lee University

AND SOMETIMES PREFER

Davidson College, Emory University, Georgia Institute of Technology, University of South Carolina—Columbia, Wofford College

AND RARELY PREFER

Auburn University, Clemson University

FINANCIAL FACTS

Financial Aid Rating	**82**
Annual tuition	$25,888
Room & Board	$6,912
Books and supplies	$750
Required fees	$464
% frosh rec. need-based scholarship or grant aid	43
% UG rec. need-based scholarship or grant aid	42
% frosh rec. need-based self-help aid	33
% UG rec. need-based self-help aid	27
% frosh rec. any financial aid	80
% UG rec. any financial aid	81
Avg. frosh grant	$17,100
Avg. frosh loan	$3,750
Independent 529 member?	Yes

George Mason University

4400 University Drive MSN 3A4, Fairfax, VA 22030-4444 • Admissions: 703-993-2400 • Fax: 703-993-2392

CAMPUS LIFE

Quality of Life Rating	**72**
Fire Safety Rating	**77**
Type of school	public
Environment	city

STUDENTS

Total undergrad enrollment	16,888
% male/female	46/54
% from out of state	7
% live on campus	24
% in (# of) fraternities	5 (9)
% in (# of) sororities	5 (8)
% African American	8
% Asian	16
% Caucasian	52
% Hispanic	7
% international	4

SURVEY SAYS

Great computer facilities
Great library
Diverse student types on campus
Great off-campus food
Lots of beer drinking
(Almost) everyone smokes

ACADEMICS

Academic Rating	**73**
Calendar	semester
Student/faculty ratio	15:1
Professors interesting rating	75
Professors accessible rating	68
% professors teaching UG courses	86
% classes taught by TAs	18
Most common lab size	10-19 students
Most common regular class size	20-29 students

MOST POPULAR MAJORS

International relations and affairs
political science and government
psychology

STUDENTS SPEAK OUT

Academics

George Mason University, a large public school with "an award-winning faculty," offers several options to students seeking a small-school environment. First is the Honors Program in General Education, which allows students to replace large, required intro classes with smaller, "more enlightening classes with names like reading cultural signs." Students love that the program "allows for more one-on-one interaction with professors and is a bit more challenging;" the most practical-minded undergrads here, however, question the applicability of honors courses to real life. The second option, New Century College, is even further afield from traditional undergraduate academics; it offers three integrative/self-designed degrees in a "seminar-style environment with collaborative faculty involvement." More conventional options are offered through seven of GMU's divisions; students report that the School of Management and the School of Public Policy are both excellent, benefiting from the fact that "the area attracts heaps of over-qualified people who wind up teaching here." GMU boasts "two Nobel Prize winners in its economics department and Washington, DC, insiders" in all government- and policy-related areas. Access to the DC area also allows for "a wonderful partnership with other DC universities, providing library links and also classes at Georgetown, Catholic, American, Marymount, Gallaudet, Maryland—College Park, and UDC (University of the District of Columbia)," as well as "great connections with potential employers in the Northern Virginia/DC area."

Life

Life at GMU is tempered by the fact that only one in five students live on campus, and a considerable number of them "seem to leave for the weekends." As a result, "the campus is deserted by Friday afternoon." Those who remain tell us either that "there is nothing to do" or, more frequently, "there are things to do, but you really have to look for them. We've got some campus activities like free movies at a movie theater in our student center, but they are often under-promoted and many students don't know what's going on." Weekends are generally spent "hanging out in the dorms on the weekends and watching movies" or, for those who are more adventurous and well-heeled, "taking the metro into DC to go to the museums, clubs, and restaurants. The only problem with that is it can be a bit expensive." There's more happening on campus during the week; the "college newspaper is top-notch," the basketball team "is fun to watch and highly supported because we don't have a football team," and "the athletic facilities are fantastic. We have a nice-sized weight room, a good quality training room, an indoor track, an outdoor track, plus many different various athletic fields. The coaching staff, trainers, and other personnel are very knowledgeable and helpful." Students belonging to fraternities and sororities assure us that "if you are in a Greek organization, there are always tons of things to do at GMU."

Student Body

"George Mason University is number one in the nation for the most diversity," students claim. One student reports, "On my freshman floor there were kids from seven nations other than America, which is quite diverse for a group of about thirty. We also have a huge population of returning students, so depending on which door you wait near, you're just as likely to see a stream of twentysomethings as you are a line of people who could be your parents." Student types run the gamut from "the frat types to the athletes, to sorority girls to the slackers, nerds, rich, poor, and average Joes. Everyone seems to interact pretty well." The predominant look on campus is "preppy lite;" as one student explains, "We don't flip up our collars like one expects from a Georgetown undergrad, but cashmere socks in the winter and Armani Exchange t-shirts in the summer aren't rare."

George Mason University

Financial Aid: 703-993-2353 • E-mail: admissions@gmu.edu • Website: www.gmu.edu

ADMISSIONS

Very important factors considered include: Secondary school record. *Important factors considered include:* Character/personal qualities, essays, recommendations, standardized test scores, talent/ability. *Other factors considered include:* Alumni/ae relation, class rank, extracurricular activities, geographical residence, interview, minority status, state residency, volunteer work, work experience. SAT Reasoning or ACT required. TOEFL required of all international applicants. High school diploma is required, and GED is accepted. *Academic units required:* 4 English, 3 math, 3 science (3 science lab), 2 foreign language, 3 social studies, 3 academic electives. *Academic units recommended:* 4 English, 4 math, 4 science (4 science lab), 3 foreign language, 4 social studies, 5 academic electives.

The Inside Word

George Mason is a popular destination for college for two key reasons: its proximity to Washington, DC, and the fact that it is not nearly as difficult to gain admission at Mason as it is at UVA or William and Mary, the two flagships of the Virginia state system. The university's quality faculty and impressive facilities make it worth taking a look if low-cost, solid programs in the DC area are high on your list.

FINANCIAL AID

Students should submit: FAFSA. The Princeton Review suggests that all financial aid forms be submitted as soon as possible after 1/1. *Need-based scholarships/grants offered:* Pell, SEOG, state scholarships/grants, private scholarships, the school's own gift aid. *Loan aid offered:* Direct Subsidized Stafford, Direct Unsubsidized Stafford, Direct PLUS, Federal Perkins, Federal Nursing. Applicants will be notified of awards on or about 4/1.

FROM THE ADMISSIONS OFFICE

"George Mason University enjoys the best location in the world. Our connections to the DC area result in faculty members who are engaged in the top research in their fields. We have professors who are regular contributors on all of the major news networks, and you can hardly listen to a program on National Public Radio without hearing from one of our scholars. This connectivity extends to our students, who take internships and get jobs at some of the best organizations and companies in the world. We have students at AOL/Time Warner, the National Institutes of Health, the Kennedy Center, the World Bank, the White House, and the National Zoo. We have all the advantages of the excitement of our nation's capital combined with the comfort and security of this beautiful suburban campus.

"At Mason, we pride ourselves on being among the most innovative universities in the world. Many of our degree programs are the first of their kind, including the first PhD program in Biodefense, the first DC-based undergraduate program in conflict resolution, the first integrated school of information technology and engineering based on computer related programs, and one of the most innovative performing arts management programs in the United States. As a result, George Mason University is at the forefront of the emerging field of biotechnology, is a natural leader in the performing arts, and holds a preeminent position in the fields of economics, electronic journalism, and history, just to name a few.

"George Mason University will accept the ACT, with or without the written portion, and either the old or new version of the SAT. Scores from the Writing section will not be considered in our admission decisions, as our faculty does not feel the Writing section reflects quality or methodology of our award winning writing across the curriculum program."

SELECTIVITY

Admissions Rating	**79**
# of applicants	10,103
% of applicants accepted	69
% of acceptees attending	33
# accepting a place on wait list	702
% admitted from wait list	16

FRESHMAN PROFILE

Range SAT Verbal	490-600
Average SAT Verbal	548
Range SAT Math	500-600
Average SAT Math	555
**TPR Projected Range SAT Writing*	*550-630*
Range ACT Composite	20-25
Minimum Paper TOEFL	570
Minimum Computer Based TOEFL	230
Average HS GPA	3.32
% graduated top 10% of class	15
% graduated top 25% of class	47
% graduated top 50% of class	91

DEADLINES

Regular application deadline	1/15
Regular notification	4/1
Nonfall registration?	yes

APPLICANTS ALSO LOOK AT AND OFTEN PREFER

James Madison University
University of Virginia
Virginia Tech

AND SOMETIMES PREFER

The George Washington University

FINANCIAL FACTS

Financial Aid Rating	**73**
Annual in-state tuition	$3,942
Annual out-of-state tuition	$14,310
Room & Board	$6,240
Books and supplies	$810
Required fees	$1,506
% frosh rec. need-based scholarship or grant aid	26
% UG rec. need-based scholarship or grant aid	28
% frosh rec. need-based self-help aid	27
% UG rec. need-based self-help aid	32
% frosh rec. any financial aid	26
% UG rec. any financial aid	44
Avg. frosh grant	$5,474
Avg. frosh loan	$2,593
Independent 529 member?	No

THE GEORGE WASHINGTON UNIVERSITY

2121 I STREET NW, SUITE 201, WASHINGTON, DC 20052 • ADMISSIONS: 202-994-6040 • FAX: 202-994-0325

CAMPUS LIFE

Quality of Life Rating	**76**
Fire Safety Rating	**60**
Type of school	private
Environment	metropolis

STUDENTS

Total undergrad enrollment	10,563
% male/female	44/56
% from out of state	98
% from public high school	70
% live on campus	67
% in (# of) fraternities	16 (12)
% in (# of) sororities	13 (9)
% African American	6
% Asian	10
% Caucasian	66
% Hispanic	5
% international	4
# of countries represented	101

SURVEY SAYS

Students love Washington, DC
Great off-campus food
Dorms are like palaces
Campus feels safe
Student publications are popular
Political activism is popular
Hard liquor is popular

ACADEMICS

Academic Rating	**82**
Calendar	semester
Student/faculty ratio	13:1
Professors interesting rating	70
Professors accessible rating	68
% professors teaching UG courses	67
% classes taught by TAs	3
Most common lab size	20-29 students
Most common regular class size	10-19 students

STUDENTS SPEAK OUT

Academics

"As advertised when you first visit [George Washington University (GW)], one of the [university's] greatest strengths lies in the fact that GW is located literally in the middle of Washington, DC. If you're political, this is the place to be." The university places a heavy emphasis on internships that land many of these politically oriented students in congressional offices on Capitol Hill or at lobbying firms on K Street. Students enjoy this "combination of practical and theoretical" learning and the great faculty. Not only are many faculty members well versed in both the professional and academic aspects of their disciplines but also "they wrote the textbook they use." "The school's amazing professors in the fields of economics, international affairs," and other globally relevant disciplines draw rave reviews from the student body. But some students grumble that the university could better its arts and science programs with more funding and a wider breadth of offerings. Many students opt for time away from GW's main campus (in the Foggy Bottom neighborhood of the District) to spend a year or more at the university's residential Mount Vernon campus, located just fifteen minutes away from the main campus. At Mount Vernon, students have full access to the courses and events of Foggy Bottom but can take advantage of a more traditional campus and smaller classes. The Mount Vernon campus recently initiated an honors program that mirrors the respected program already in place at Foggy Bottom. If students could change one thing about GW, it would probably be the administration. Grumbles one student, "GW, in classic Washington style, is a mountain of red tape."

Life

While GW's urban location does not offer students the sprawling acreage and groves of trees that you find on many rural college campuses, the university's grounds "in the heart of DC" provide a comfortable nesting ground for this student body. "I say with absolute certainty that our six city blocks feel like as much of a campus as 20 acres of grass would," asserts one undergraduate. Still, some students complain about the lack of a social scene and school spirit within those city blocks. "GW's not a big party school," due in part to the "strict laws of DC" and the tight campus regulations. But, as almost any student will tell you, the real fun happens in the city—and that's fine with them. "There are many shopping areas around GW, as well as bars, clubs, restaurants, jazz clubs, etc." "Whether playing Frisbee on the mall, looking at a Picasso at the Smithsonian, or shopping in Georgetown, there's something for everyone," says one satisfied student. And for those with a taste for the exotic, "one amazing aspect of DC is that you can indulge in a lot of different cuisines from around the world." If the world's finest museums, most popular public parks, and most recognizable monuments aren't appealing, students can just relax in their comfortable dorms. "In my freshman dorm," a student tells us, "I have a kitchen and a bathroom that is shared with three roommates."

Student Body

It's probably not surprising that many of the students who choose to attend school "three blocks west of the White House and three blocks north of the Vietnam War Memorial" are politically active. And taken as a whole, this student body leans heavily to the left. Within that left-leaning mass, you will find "all sorts of colors, sizes, religious and political affiliations, and sexual preferences represented." A student from the rural Midwest opines that the attitude on campus is "very tolerant," adding, "It's not atypical to see interracial couples, Jews and Arabs as friends, and two fraternity presidents dating each other." A satisfied first-year student says, "Maybe it's just that I have stars in my freshman eyes, but to me it seems like one big, happy family here."

The George Washington University

Financial Aid: 202-994-6620 • E-mail: gwadm@gwu.edu • Website: www.gwu.edu

ADMISSIONS

Very important factors considered include: Secondary school record. *Important factors considered include:* Class rank, essays, extracurricular activities, interview, recommendations, standardized test scores, talent/ability, volunteer work. *Other factors considered include:* Alumni/ae relation, character/personal qualities, geographical residence, minority status, work experience. SAT Reasoning or ACT required. TOEFL required of all international applicants. High school diploma is required, and GED is not accepted. *Academic units required:* 4 English, 2 math, 2 science (1 science lab), 2 foreign language, 2 social studies. *Academic units recommended:* 4 English, 4 math, 4 science, 4 foreign language, 4 social studies.

The Inside Word

The low percentage of admitted students who enroll at GW works to keep the admit rate relatively high. For strong students, this is definitely a low-stress admissions process. The university's location and access to faculty with impressive credentials are the main reasons for GW's sound freshman profile.

FINANCIAL AID

Students should submit: FAFSA, CSS/Financial Aid PROFILE. Regular filing deadline is 2/1. The Princeton Review suggests that all financial aid forms be submitted as soon as possible after 1/1. *Need-based scholarships/grants offered:* Pell, SEOG, state scholarships/grants, the school's own gift aid. *Loan aid offered:* FFEL Subsidized Stafford, FFEL Unsubsidized Stafford, FFEL PLUS, Federal Perkins. Applicants will be notified of awards on a rolling basis beginning on or about 3/24. Federal Work-study Program available. Institutional employment available. Off-campus job opportunities are excellent.

FROM THE ADMISSIONS OFFICE

"At GW, we welcome students who show a measure of impatience with the limitations of traditional education. At many universities, the edge of campus is the real world, but not at GW, where our campus and Washington, DC are seamless. We look for bold, bright students who are ambitious, energetic, and self-motivated. Here, where we are so close to the centers of thought and action in every field we offer, we easily integrate our outstanding academic tradition and faculty connections with the best internship and job opportunities of Washington, DC. A generous scholarship and financial assistance program attracts top students from all parts of the country and the world.

"Students applying for fall 2006 may send either an old or revised SAT score. Regardless of the version of the SAT submitted, we will use those scores that best work to the student's advantage. Applicants to the BA/MD, IEMP, and BA/JD programs are required to submit SAT Subject Tests. "

SELECTIVITY

Admissions Rating	**94**
# of applicants	20,159
% of applicants accepted	38
% of acceptees attending	35
# accepting a place on wait list	2,284
% admitted from wait list	8
# of early decision applicants	1,176
% accepted early decision	63

FRESHMAN PROFILE

Range SAT Verbal	590-690
Average SAT Verbal	620
Range SAT Math	590-680
Average SAT Math	620
**TPR Projected Range SAT Writing*	*620-690*
Range ACT Composite	25-30
Average ACT Composite	26
Minimum Paper TOEFL	550
Minimum Computer Based TOEFL	300
% graduated top 10% of class	59
% graduated top 25% of class	80
% graduated top 50% of class	99

DEADLINES

Early decision application deadline	12/1
Early decision notification	12/15
Regular application deadline	1/15
Regular notification	3/15
Nonfall registration?	yes

APPLICANTS ALSO LOOK AT AND OFTEN PREFER

Boston University
Emory University
Georgetown University
New York University
University of Virginia

AND SOMETIMES PREFER

American University
The Catholic University of America
Tufts University
University of Maryland—College Park
University of Vermont

FINANCIAL FACTS

Financial Aid Rating	**91**
Annual tuition	$34,000
Room & Board	$11,470
Books and supplies	$850
Required fees	$30
% frosh rec. need-based scholarship or grant aid	39
% UG rec. need-based scholarship or grant aid	38
% frosh rec. need-based self-help aid	35
% UG rec. need-based self-help aid	35
Avg. frosh grant	$11,800
Avg. frosh loan	$3,000
Independent 529 member?	Yes

GEORGETOWN UNIVERSITY

37TH AND P STREETS, NW, WASHINGTON, DC 20057 • ADMISSIONS: 202-687-3600 • FAX: 202-687-5084

CAMPUS LIFE

Quality of Life Rating	**85**
Fire Safety Rating	**89**
Type of school	private
Affiliation	Roman Catholic
Environment	metropolis

STUDENTS

Total undergrad enrollment	6,282
% male/female	46/54
% from out of state	98
% from public high school	45
% live on campus	78
% African American	7
% Asian	10
% Caucasian	69
% Hispanic	6
% international	4
# of countries represented	81

SURVEY SAYS

Students love Washington, DC
Great off-campus food
Students are happy
Frats and sororities are unpopular or nonexistent
Political activism is popular
Lots of beer drinking

ACADEMICS

Academic Rating	**93**
Calendar	semester
Student/faculty ratio	11:1
Professors interesting rating	82
Professors accessible rating	81
% professors teaching UG courses	100
% classes taught by TAs	8
Most common lab size	fewer than 10 students
Most common regular class size	10-19 students

MOST POPULAR MAJORS

Finance
international relations and affairs
political science and government

STUDENTS SPEAK OUT

Academics

It's impossible to separate the virtues of a Georgetown education with the opportunities afforded by the school's Washington, DC, location. The "out-of-this-world" internship opportunities include positions at "all kinds of businesses and law firms"; reports one seasoned senior, a considerable number of students "have a congressional internship during their time at Georgetown." Washington also provides a never-ending source of amazing faculty; boasts another senior, "I've had a 25-person class with Donna Brazile, a 50-person class with Madeleine Albright, and a 10-person class with Ron Faucheaux (editor of *Campaigns and Elections* magazine)." In the words of a first-year, "It is not uncommon after class to go back to your room, turn on CNN or MSNBC, and see your professor." With so many power brokers floating about, "Georgetown is easily the best school for finding a mentor: there are genius Jesuits, serving diplomats, authors, and other luminaries walking about campus every day, not only waiting to be approached, but approaching you." Assures one international political economy major, "even though they are busy, they are always available if you need help." Students point out that "Georgetown is also a great place to come if you want to study anything international or go abroad. Half of the junior class goes abroad, and the school offers or is affiliated with a lot of programs that support direct matriculation into a local university." While best known for its programs in the liberal arts, foreign affairs, language, and nursing, Georgetown, in the words of a senior, "embodies a unique combination of true academic commitment, social and political awareness, rich tradition, a diverse student body, and all the crazy fun of college."

Life

"Georgetown has a great social life," undergrads here agree; the school offers "tons of on- and off-campus parties as well as bars within walking distance." Extracurricular options include numerous "a cappella and theater groups on campus," and students can choose to attend any of the frequent on-campus lectures and readings. And, of course, there's always Hoyas basketball, which enjoys a fanatical following among the student body. Students like to spend free time in Washington, DC, which they hail as "an amazing place to live." The District "has a ton of free museums, exhibits, plays, and concerts." Reports one student, "I have been dancing for free at the Kennedy Center, seen concerts just a few minutes into Pennsylvania Avenue, visited museums (also free), eaten great food throughout DC, volunteered in after-school programs, and gone running along the canal and through the monuments at night. The public transportation in DC makes it easy to go anywhere without a car." Georgetown takes the edge off urban living with a campus that's "isolated by walls and gates…we've got all the fun of the city in a homier atmosphere." Prospective students should take note that "the cost of living in Georgetown as a whole is high, so you're definitely better off either having a job or learning to manage your money fast!"

Student Body

"You hear a lot about 'Joe and Jane Hoya,' the typical preppy types" at Georgetown—and while "there is definitely a strong presence of the rich boarding school students," there are "way more students from public schools of every stripe, from countries ranging from Romania to India to Spain, from all kinds of socioeconomic backgrounds, and with all kinds of interests." Although Georgetown is religiously affiliated, "this is not your typical Catholic university"; there is "lots of diversity across cultural, ethnic, and religious categories." A common thread among students is that they are all "very ambitious and driven. Also, most people tend to have either lived in another country, know more than two languages, or have traveled a lot. In general there's a big interest in learning about diverse cultures." Not surprisingly, most here "are highly political" and "conscious of international affairs." While students' views may differ, a sophomore promises, "There is a place for everyone on campus."

FINANCIAL AID: 202-687-4547 • WEBSITE: WWW.GEORGETOWN.EDU

ADMISSIONS

Very important factors considered include: Character/personal qualities, class rank, essays, recommendations, secondary school record, standardized test scores, talent/ability. *Important factors considered include:* Extracurricular activities, interview, volunteer work. *Other factors considered include:* Alumni/ae relation, geographical residence, minority status, state residency, work experience. SAT Reasoning or ACT required. SAT Subject Tests recommended. TOEFL required of all international applicants. High school diploma is required, and GED is accepted. *Academic units required:* 4 English, 2 math, 2 science, 2 foreign language, 2 social studies, 2 history. *Academic units recommended:* 4 English, 4 math, 4 science (1 science lab), 4 foreign language, 4 social studies.

The Inside Word

It was always tough to get admitted to Georgetown, but in the early 1980s Patrick Ewing and the Hoyas created a basketball sensation that catapulted the place into position as one of the most selective universities in the nation. There has been no turning back since. GU gets almost 10 applications for every space in the entering class, and the academic strength of the pool is impressive. Virtually 50 percent of the entire student body took AP courses in high school. Candidates who are wait-listed should hold little hope for an offer of admission; over the past several years Georgetown has taken very few off their lists.

FINANCIAL AID

Students should submit: FAFSA, CSS/Financial Aid PROFILE, noncustodial (divorced/separated) parents' statement, business/farm supplement, tax returns. Regular filing deadline is 2/1. The Princeton Review suggests that all financial aid forms be submitted as soon as possible after 1/1. *Need-based scholarships/grants offered:* Pell, SEOG, state scholarships/grants, private scholarships, the school's own gift aid. *Loan aid offered:* FFEL Subsidized Stafford, FFEL Unsubsidized Stafford, FFEL PLUS, Federal Perkins, Federal Nursing. Applicants will be notified of awards on or about 4/1.

FROM THE ADMISSIONS OFFICE

"Georgetown was founded in 1789 by John Carroll, who concurred with his contemporaries Benjamin Franklin and Thomas Jefferson in believing that the success of the young democracy depended upon an educated and virtuous citizenry. Carroll founded the school with the dynamic, Jesuit tradition of education, characterized by humanism and committed to the assumption of responsibility and action. Georgetown is a national and international university, enrolling students from all 50 states and over 100 foreign countries. Undergraduate students are enrolled in one of four undergraduate schools: the College of Arts and Sciences, School of Foreign Service, Georgetown School of Business, and Georgetown School of Nursing and Health Studies. All students share a common liberal arts core and have access to the entire university curriculum.

"Applicants that graduate from high school in 2006 have the option of submitting scores from either the new or existing version of the SAT. Only the Verbal and Math portions of the new SAT will be considered. The student's best composite score will be used in the admission process."

SELECTIVITY

Admissions Rating	**98**
# of applicants	14,855
% of applicants accepted	22
% of acceptees attending	47
# accepting a place on wait list	1,901
% admitted from wait list	1

FRESHMAN PROFILE

Range SAT Verbal	640-740
Range SAT Math	640-730
**TPR Projected Range SAT Writing*	*660-720*
Range ACT Composite	27-32
Minimum Paper TOEFL	200
% graduated top 10% of class	90
% graduated top 25% of class	98
% graduated top 50% of class	100

DEADLINES

Regular application deadline	1/10
Regular notification	4/1
Nonfall registration?	no

APPLICANTS ALSO LOOK AT

AND OFTEN PREFER

Duke University
Harvard College
University of Pennsylvania

AND SOMETIMES PREFER

Cornell University
University of Notre Dame
University of Virginia

AND RARELY PREFER

Boston College
The George Washington University
New York University
Northwestern University
Tufts University
University of California—Berkeley

FINANCIAL FACTS

Financial Aid Rating	**94**
Annual tuition	$29,808
Room & Board	$10,554
Books and supplies	$960
Required fees	$355
% frosh rec. need-based scholarship or grant aid	42
% UG rec. need-based scholarship or grant aid	37
% frosh rec. need-based self-help aid	37
% UG rec. need-based self-help aid	37
% frosh rec. any financial aid	44
% UG rec. any financial aid	43
Avg. frosh grant	$18,464
Avg. frosh loan	$2,010
Independent 529 member?	No

GEORGIA INSTITUTE OF TECHNOLOGY

219 UNCLE HEINE WAY, ATLANTA, GA 30332-0320 • ADMISSIONS: 404-894-4154 • FAX: 404-894-9511

CAMPUS LIFE

Quality of Life Rating	**63**
Fire Safety Rating	**88**
Type of school	public
Environment	metropolis

STUDENTS

Total undergrad enrollment	11,354
% male/female	72/28
% from out of state	31
% live on campus	53
% in (# of) fraternities	21 (31)
% in (# of) sororities	24 (12)
% African American	7
% Asian	15
% Caucasian	68
% Hispanic	3
% international	5
# of countries represented	121

SURVEY SAYS

Class discussions are rare
Great computer facilities
Athletic facilities are great
Diverse student types on campus
Students love Atlanta, GA
Great off-campus food
Everyone loves the Yellow Jackets
Lots of beer drinking

ACADEMICS

Academic Rating	**76**
Calendar	semester
Student/faculty ratio	14:1
Professors interesting rating	61
Professors accessible rating	62
% professors teaching UG courses	100
% classes taught by TAs	0
Most common lab size	10-19 students
Most common regular class size	10-19 students

MOST POPULAR MAJORS

Business administration/management
computer and information sciences
mechanical engineering

STUDENTS SPEAK OUT

Academics

Georgia Tech (GT) is not for the faint of heart. At this math, science, and engineering powerhouse, "professors use a savagely overwhelming number of assignments to weed out the weak." Those who can weather GT's challenges have phenomenal opportunities. As one go-getter tells us, "Academically this place is great. I've had an explosion of original ideas in physics and math since I've been here, and the professors have been nothing but encouraging [in] nurturing these pursuits. If you're not lazy, this place is the place to be." Agrees another student, "The overall academic experience, once you get comfortable, is accommodating. There are plenty of academic workshops with good tutors, an extensive library system connected with surrounding schools like Georgia State and Emory, a great co-op/internship program, and—my favorite—[scads] of undergrad research opportunities and funding." Students also brag that "the computers on-campus are extremely fast, and many professors put the readings for class online, so I love being at a technology school with super-fast access." As at most tech schools, "Profs are researchers first and teachers second," TAs "often do not speak English very well," and "classes do not slow down for anyone, even if no one is getting it."

Life

"Life at GT can be tough because school is so tough," students tell us. The demanding curriculum keeps students busy enough that "the majority of the social life falls on the weekend, as not much can be done during the week except studying." And "since many people are in state, lots of people leave campus on the weekends, which sometimes can give it an empty feeling." As a result, "fraternity parties are the only thing normally going on on-campus during the weekend." Fortunately, GT is located in the South's great city, Atlanta, so there are numerous options available to those who stick around after classes end—provided, of course, that they can spare the time away from their books. Students love Atlanta, telling us that "there are a lot of shows, movies, and festivals going on in the city at any given time." For fun and hooking up, students head to Buckhead, "the famous nightlife district of Atlanta." Atlanta is also conveniently located; observes one student, "The nice thing about Atlanta is it's in a very central location. It's only a few hours drive to either the beach or the mountains, and then, of course, with the international airport just a few minutes down the MARTA (Metropolitan Atlanta Rapid Transit Authority) line, you are connected with the rest of the world." Many never make it off campus, however: "Too many people are stuck playing computer games in their dorms" during their few leisure hours.

Student Body

Because of the heavy workload at Georgia Tech, most students are "overly stressed, worried about tomorrow's test, and driven by the desire for the degree. This student has only minimal time for social functions." Which is just as well, since "many lack basic social skills." They're the type of folks who "make fun of TV shows or movies that violate basic rules of physics. It's sort of dweeby, but in a good way." Observes one engineer, "There is a sizable population of people who are so weird that you can tell their major by the way they walk (e.g., CS [computer science] majors walk like they are uncoordinated)." Tech is home to "large populations of foreign students, especially from India and China." There is also a recognizable contingent of "'normal' white, fraternity, middle-class guys."

GEORGIA INSTITUTE OF TECHNOLOGY

FINANCIAL AID: 404-894-4160 • E-MAIL: ADMISSION@GATECH.EDU • WEBSITE: WWW.GATECH.EDU

ADMISSIONS

Very important factors considered include: Secondary school record. *Important factors considered include:* Character/personal qualities, essays, extracurricular activities, standardized test scores, talent/ability, volunteer work, work experience. *Other factors considered include:* Geographical residence, state residency. SAT Reasoning Test recommended. SAT Reasoning or ACT required. TOEFL required of all international applicants. High school diploma is required, and GED is accepted. *Academic units required:* 4 English, 4 math, 3 science (3 science lab), 2 foreign language, 3 social studies. *Academic units recommended:* 4 English, 4 math, 3 science (3 science lab), 2 foreign language, 3 social studies.

The Inside Word

Tech has made significant changes in its admissions requirements over the past six years, which by their nature have resulted in a somewhat more personal and well-rounded approach to selecting the entering class. Still, candidates must have solid grades and test scores in order to be competitive.

FINANCIAL AID

Students should submit: FAFSA, institution's own financial aid form. Regular filing deadline is 3/1. The Princeton Review suggests that all financial aid forms be submitted as soon as possible after 1/1. *Need-based scholarships/grants offered:* Pell, SEOG, state scholarships/grants, private scholarships, the school's own gift aid. *Loan aid offered:* FFEL Subsidized Stafford, FFEL Unsubsidized Stafford, FFEL PLUS, Federal Perkins, college/university loans from institutional funds, CitiAssist alternative loans. Applicants will be notified of awards on or about 4/1. Federal Work-study Program available. Institutional employment available. Off-campus job opportunities are excellent.

FROM THE ADMISSIONS OFFICE

"Georgia Tech consistently ranks among the nation's leaders in engineering, computing, management, architecture, and the sciences while remaining one of the best college buys in the country. The 330-acre campus of red brick buildings and green rolling hills is nestled in the heart of the fun, dynamic, and progressive city of Atlanta in the shadows of a majestic skyline dominated by the work of Georgia Tech-trained architects and designers. During the past decade, over $400 million invested in campus improvements has yielded new state-of-the-art academic and research buildings, apartment-style housing, enhanced social and recreational facilities, and the most extensive fiber-optic cable system on any college campus. Georgia Tech's combined commitment to technologically focused hands-on educational experiences, teamwork, great teaching, innovation, leadership development, and community service make it unique. Great things are happening at Georgia Tech. We hope you will join us, become a part of our community, and help us create the future.

"Freshman applicants for fall 2006 are required to submit scores from the Writing assessment portion of the SAT or ACT. Students may also submit scores from the old (prior to March 2005) SAT or ACT. Tech will use the highest combined scores regardless of test date."

SELECTIVITY

Admissions Rating	**94**
# of applicants	8,561
% of applicants accepted	70
% of acceptees attending	43

FRESHMAN PROFILE

Range SAT Verbal	600-690
Average SAT Verbal	644
Range SAT Math	650-740
Average SAT Math	690
**TPR Projected Range SAT Writing*	*630-690*
Range ACT Composite	25-32
Average ACT Composite	28
Minimum Paper TOEFL	600
Minimum Computer Based TOEFL	250
Average HS GPA	3.7
% graduated top 10% of class	66
% graduated top 25% of class	96
% graduated top 50% of class	99

DEADLINES

Regular application deadline	1/15
Regular notification	3/15
Nonfall registration?	yes

APPLICANTS ALSO LOOK AT AND OFTEN PREFER

Duke University, Massachusetts Institute of Technology, Stanford University, University of North Carolina—Chapel Hill, University of Virginia

AND SOMETIMES PREFER

Clemson University, Emory University, University of Georgia, University of Illinois at Urbana-Champaign

AND RARELY PREFER

North Carolina State University, University of Florida, Vanderbilt University, Virginia Tech

FINANCIAL FACTS

Financial Aid Rating	**70**
Annual in-state tuition	$3,638
Annual out-of-state tuition	$17,980
Room & Board	$6,458
Books and supplies	$1,000
Required fees	$1,010
% frosh rec. need-based scholarship or grant aid	17
% UG rec. need-based scholarship or grant aid	16
% frosh rec. need-based self-help aid	20
% UG rec. need-based self-help aid	20
% frosh rec. any financial aid	84
% UG rec. any financial aid	76
Avg. frosh grant	$5,994
Avg. frosh loan	$4,020
Independent 529 member?	No

Gettysburg College

Admissions Office, Eisenhower House, Gettysburg, PA 17325-1484 • Admissions: 717-337-6100 • Fax: 717-337-6145

CAMPUS LIFE

Quality of Life Rating	**87**
Fire Safety Rating	**60**
Type of school	private
Affiliation	Lutheran
Environment	village

STUDENTS

Total undergrad enrollment	2,453
% male/female	50/50
% from out of state	72
% from public high school	70
% live on campus	94
% in (# of) fraternities	40 (10)
% in (# of) sororities	26 (5)
% African American	4
% Asian	1
% Caucasian	92
% Hispanic	2
% international	2
# of countries represented	32

SURVEY SAYS

Small classes
Lab facilities are great
Great library
Frats and sororities dominate social scene
Lots of beer drinking

ACADEMICS

Academic Rating	**91**
Calendar	semester
Student/faculty ratio	11:1
Professors interesting rating	89
Professors accessible rating	91
% professors teaching UG courses	100
% classes taught by TAs	0
Most common regular class size	10-19 students

MOST POPULAR MAJORS

Business administration/management
political science and government
psychology

STUDENTS SPEAK OUT

Academics

"By far, the greatest strength of Gettysburg College is the small class size maintained in practically every subject and level," say students at this small southern Pennsylvania school. It's the small details that distinguish the Gettysburg experience for most undergraduates. One student says, "Class time isn't solely in the lecture hall. My classes have occurred at organic farms, state parks, and Chincoteague and Assateague Islands. They truly mean it when they challenge you to 'live outside the box' at Gettysburg." Students really appreciate "professors who make a habit out of responding to written papers in a personal way to highlight the strengths and weaknesses of the paper, with suggestions on how to develop the topic for further research. Because of the personalized attention received (largely due to the small classes and dedication of faculty), it is almost impossible for a student not to succeed here." Students also appreciate "the academic honor code [that] allows students the ability to take unproctored tests in the location of their choice and allows students the freedom to leave their laptops and other belongings alone in the library, college union building, dining hall, and dorm without having to worry about theft." Strong programs include the sciences, music, history, psychology, and business. Gettysburg "has a very popular abroad program that is easy to do, with programs in a wide variety of locations."

Life

"There is a lot to do on campus and off" at Gettysburg College, undergraduates report. One student reports, "You can take in a movie at the historic Majestic Theater or walk around the battlefields on the outskirts of campus. In the spring there are always tourists and reenactors walking the streets of town; it's like going to school in a living history museum, which I love." Underclassmen are most often drawn to the school's popular fraternity parties, which "are open to anyone on campus," although male underclassmen have a better chance of getting in if they arrive with one or more females. While many students love the Greek scene, others warn that "the parties get old quickly." To provide alternatives, the school "really tries to promote other activities on campus besides drinking on weekends. They show recent movies; have popular bands, such as Good Charlotte, come to campus; host popular comedians; [and] have dance parties in the on-campus nightclub." Many students participate in community service. One student says, "Community service is big, not surprising considering the great resources of the Center for Public Service. Students travel to places like Nicaragua, Native American reservations, Birmingham, Alabama, New York City, the Chesapeake Bay, and other places for community service-learning trips." Hometown Gettysburg, while small, offers many tourist attractions (outlet malls, miniature golf, battlefields) as well as "the most consistent display of beautiful sunsets year-round. You have never seen a sunset until you have witnessed one from the battlefields, which connect to campus."

Student Body

The "Gettysburg cliché" is the "J. Crew U. student: white, upper- or upper-middle class, who joins a sorority or a fraternity." According to students, there is some truth to the cliché. "I never expected to see so many Range Rovers and BMWs on a college campus," writes one nonplussed undergraduate, but adds, "Things have changed a bit in the past two years as they've raised the admissions standards." Now students "don't feel as overwhelmed by Abercrombie in the dining hall anymore." Most undergraduates "are involved on campus in the Greek life system, clubs, athletics, etc." There's a large jock group. Politically, students are very conservative. "Maybe this is selfish," writes one undergraduate, "but I think there should be more than just conservatives at the school. I think the school could improve with a little more diversity of thought and self-expression."

FINANCIAL AID: 717-337-6611 • E-MAIL: ADMISS@GETTYSBURG.EDU • WEBSITE: WWW.GETTYSBURG.EDU

ADMISSIONS

Very important factors considered include: Class rank, recommendations, secondary school record. *Important factors considered include:* Character/personal qualities, essays, extracurricular activities, interview, standardized test scores, talent/ability, volunteer work. *Other factors considered include:* Alumni/ae relation, geographical residence, minority status, work experience. SAT Reasoning or ACT required. TOEFL required of all international applicants. High school diploma is required, and GED is accepted. *Academic units required:* 4 English, 3 math, 3 science (3 science lab), 3 foreign language, 3 social studies, 3 history. *Academic units recommended:* 4 English, 4 math, 4 science (4 science lab), 4 foreign language, 4 social studies, 4 history.

The Inside Word

Gettysburg's small size definitely allows for a more personal approach to admission. The admissions committee puts a lot of energy into matchmaking, and last year it paid off with its largest freshman class in its history. Most Gettysburg types are good students and also match up well with competitor colleges, which makes this accomplishment even more laudable. Look for a somewhat more selective profile as a result.

FINANCIAL AID

Students should submit: FAFSA, CSS/Financial Aid PROFILE, noncustodial (divorced/separated) parents' statement, business/farm supplement. The Princeton Review suggests that all financial aid forms be submitted as soon as possible after 1/1. *Need-based scholarships/grants offered:* Pell, SEOG, state scholarships/grants, private scholarships, the school's own gift aid. *Loan aid offered:* FFEL Subsidized Stafford, FFEL Unsubsidized Stafford, FFEL PLUS, Federal Perkins, college/university loans from institutional funds. Applicants will be notified of awards on or about 3/30. Federal Work-study Program available. Institutional employment available. Off-campus job opportunities are good.

FROM THE ADMISSIONS OFFICE

"Four major goals of Gettysburg College to best prepare students to enter the twenty-first century, include: first, to accelerate the intellectual development of our first-year students by integrating them more quickly into the intellectual life of the campus; second, to use interdisciplinary courses combining the intellectual approaches of various fields; third, to encourage students to develop an international perspective through course work, study abroad, association with international faculty, and a variety of extracurricular activities; and fourth, to encourage students to develop (1) a capacity for independent study by ensuring that all students work closely with individual faculty members on an extensive project during their undergraduate years and (2) the ability to work with their peers by making the small group a central feature in college life.

"Gettysburg College requires that freshman applicants submit scores from the old or new SAT. Students may also choose to submit scores from the ACT (with or without the Writing component) in lieu of the SAT."

SELECTIVITY

Admissions Rating	**94**
# of applicants	4,839
% of applicants accepted	46
% of acceptees attending	32
# of early decision applicants	232
% accepted early decision	77

FRESHMAN PROFILE

Range SAT Verbal	600-670
Average SAT Verbal	630
Range SAT Math	600-670
Average SAT Math	630
**TPR Projected Range SAT Writing*	*630-680*
Average ACT Composite	28
Minimum Paper TOEFL	570
Minimum Computer Based TOEFL	290
% graduated top 10% of class	62
% graduated top 25% of class	84
% graduated top 50% of class	99

DEADLINES

Early decision application deadline	11/15
Early decision notification	12/15
Regular notification	4/1
Nonfall registration?	yes

APPLICANTS ALSO LOOK AT

AND OFTEN PREFER
Colgate University
AND SOMETIMES PREFER
Bucknell University
AND RARELY PREFER
Muhlenberg College

FINANCIAL FACTS

Financial Aid Rating	**98**
Annual tuition	$29,990
Room & Board	$7,906
Books and supplies	$500
Required fees	$250
% frosh rec. need-based scholarship or grant aid	57
% UG rec. need-based scholarship or grant aid	57
% frosh rec. need-based self-help aid	50
% UG rec. need-based self-help aid	50
% frosh rec. any financial aid	57
% UG rec. any financial aid	57
Avg. frosh grant	$23,640
Avg. frosh loan	$3,500
Independent 529 member?	Yes

Gonzaga University

502 E. Boone Avenue, Spokane, WA 99258 • Admissions: 509-323-6572 • Fax: 509-323-5780

CAMPUS LIFE

Quality of Life Rating	**80**
Fire Safety Rating	**83**
Type of school	private
Affiliation	Roman Catholic
Environment	city

STUDENTS

Total undergrad enrollment	4,007
% male/female	45/55
% from out of state	49
% from public high school	65
% live on campus	56
% African American	1
% Asian	6
% Caucasian	80
% Hispanic	3
% Native American	1
% international	1
# of countries represented	36

SURVEY SAYS

Small classes
Athletic facilities are great
Everyone loves the Bulldogs
Frats and sororities are unpopular or nonexistent

ACADEMICS

Academic Rating	**82**
Calendar	semester
Student/faculty ratio	11:1
Professors interesting rating	84
Professors accessible rating	85
% professors teaching UG courses	100
% classes taught by TAs	0
Most common lab size	10-19 students
Most common regular class size	20-29 students

MOST POPULAR MAJORS

Business/commerce
political science and government
psychology

STUDENTS SPEAK OUT

Academics

"From the professors to the groundskeepers, the people make Gonzaga what it is," students at this Jesuit university agree, citing "the very positive vibe to the whole university" as the school's greatest asset. Students credit the Jesuit approach to education, which focuses on "educating the whole person" as leading "the school to sponsor a lot of interesting lectures and classes," as well as "popular study-abroad programs (especially junior year in Florence)," and a "broad and far-reaching liberal-arts core curriculum [that] ensures that all students leave GU with a broader appreciation of the world." Of the core, undergrads observe that "many people arrive resenting the core requirements in philosophy and religion, but then they grow to love them." Throughout the curriculum, "Gonzaga has a wonderful reputation for holding academic ethics in high regard. The faculty makes it a priority to weave some discussion of ethics into every class offered at the university." The university's areas of strength include engineering, business, nursing, education, the sciences and "subjects loved dearly by Jesuits, such as history and philosophy. Gonzaga is a good 'thinking student's' school." With so many assets, it's no wonder Gonzaga is quickly building its national stature (its upstart basketball team has helped a little in this area, too). The accompanying increase in enrollment has not been trouble-free; reports one undergrad, "Gonzaga is starting to outgrow itself. More buildings are going to be built, but for now we have more students than our campus is used to accommodating."

Life

"School spirit is very high at Gonzaga due to the success of the basketball team," which has put up an impressive run of NCAA tournament appearances in recent years. "The spirit of the crowd at a home game is incredible" and has not been dampened at all by the team's move from its beloved old home (affectionately nicknamed 'the Kennel') to new, swankier digs. Otherwise, extracurricular life at GU is a mixed bag. Many students feel they "need more things to do on the weekend. Gonzaga's effort to provide events to go to and sponsoring of on-campus bands is commendable, but there are still many weekends where not much is going on." On the other hand, "Gonzaga's community service program is very good. The Knights (the closest thing Gonzaga has to a fraternity) is a group of male students who put on many community service events. The Knights' female counterpart, the Setons, do similar activities." The campus "strikes a good balance between beauty and utility. It's easily navigable and plush with vegetation nearly year-round, yet within walking distance of college are essentials like a grocery store, a laundromat, a video store, and plenty of fast food." Some complain that "the surrounding area is a bit sketchy; there've been too many vehicle break-ins and theft this year," but even they feel that "Spokane, on the whole, is a great town. It's fairly large, but people are friendly, and it often feels like a small town." Just about everyone agrees that the meal plan is "very bad," even by institutional standards.

Student Body

The student body "is a different breed. We don't have many of the tough, frat, 'I'm gonna beat up the next guy who looks at me' guys. Everything is more laid back. You can go up to anyone and talk to them and you at least won't get completely blown off, which is a refreshing change." Gonzaga is "a fairly conservative school, and compared to most colleges, most people are open-minded," although "students who are gay, while not ridiculed, won't find this environment especially nurturing" (although the school offers GLBT support and education). That's in part because GU is a Catholic school, with "a small but vocal contingent of very devout students" and many more that practice, but are only "somewhat religious." About half the students here are Catholic. There are a fair amount of "English as a second language students here, especially from Korea, Japan, and Mexico," and they provide most of the ethnic diversity on campus.

FINANCIAL AID: 800-793-1716 • E-MAIL: ADMISSIONS@GONZAGA.EDU • WEBSITE: WWW.GONZAGA.EDU

ADMISSIONS

Very important factors considered include: Character/personal qualities, secondary school record. *Important factors considered include:* Class rank, essays, extracurricular activities, recommendations, standardized test scores, talent/ability. *Other factors considered include:* Alumni/ae relation, interview, minority status, volunteer work, work experience. SAT Reasoning or ACT required. TOEFL required of all international applicants. High school diploma is required, and GED is not accepted. *Academic units required:* 4 English, 3 math, 3 science (3 science lab), 2 foreign language, 2 social studies, 2 history, 3 academic electives. *Academic units recommended:* 4 English, 4 math, 4 science (4 science lab), 4 foreign language, 3 social studies, 3 history, 3 academic electives.

The Inside Word

As with many religiously affiliated universities, getting into Gonzaga is largely a matter of making a good match philosophically. However, keep an eye on the steadily rising SAT/ACT requirements. As always, an above-average academic record is a given for admission.

FINANCIAL AID

Students should submit: FAFSA. Regular filing deadline is 2/1. The Princeton Review suggests that all financial aid forms be submitted as soon as possible after 1/1. *Need-based scholarships/grants offered:* Pell, SEOG, state scholarships/grants, private scholarships, the school's own gift aid, United Negro College Fund, Federal Nursing scholarships. *Loan aid offered:* FFEL Subsidized Stafford, FFEL Unsubsidized Stafford, FFEL PLUS, Federal Perkins, Federal Nursing, state loans, college/university loans from institutional funds. Applicants will be notified of awards on a rolling basis beginning on or about 3/1. Federal Work-study Program available. Institutional employment available. Off-campus job opportunities are good.

FROM THE ADMISSIONS OFFICE

"Education at Gonzaga is not comparable to an academic 'assembly line,' rather, it is person-to-person and face-to-face. This personal quality is also true of our admission and financial aid processes. Therefore, allow us to know you beyond the boundaries of your college application. Visit campus, phone us, e-mail us—let us see the person behind the data. Good luck with your college search and your applications. Go Zags!

"All sections of the new SAT will be accepted, but the new Written portion will not receive universal consideration until further studies are done which examine the success of under-represented college-bound groups. The Written score will be considered in cases where more information specific to writing ability would be helpful in decision making.

SELECTIVITY

Admissions Rating	**88**
# of applicants	3,867
% of applicants accepted	80
% of acceptees attending	31
# accepting a place on wait list	460
% admitted from wait list	37

FRESHMAN PROFILE

Range SAT Verbal	530-640
Average SAT Verbal	586
Range SAT Math	540-640
Average SAT Math	589
**TPR Projected Range SAT Writing*	*580-660*
Range ACT Composite	23-28
Average ACT Composite	26
Minimum Paper TOEFL	550
Minimum Computer Based TOEFL	213
Average HS GPA	3.63
% graduated top 10% of class	36
% graduated top 25% of class	71
% graduated top 50% of class	91

DEADLINES

Regular application deadline	2/1
Regular notification	3/15
Nonfall registration?	yes

APPLICANTS ALSO LOOK AT

AND OFTEN PREFER
University of Notre Dame

AND SOMETIMES PREFER
Loyola Marymount University
Santa Clara University
University of Washington

AND RARELY PREFER
University of San Francisco
Washington State University

FINANCIAL FACTS

Financial Aid Rating	**77**
Annual tuition	$21,730
Room & Board	$6,650
Books and supplies	$800
Required fees	$328
% frosh rec. need-based scholarship or grant aid	63
% UG rec. need-based scholarship or grant aid	58
% frosh rec. need-based self-help aid	45
% UG rec. need-based self-help aid	51
% frosh rec. any financial aid	86
% UG rec. any financial aid	78
Avg. frosh grant	$12,428
Avg. frosh loan	$4,633
Independent 529 member?	No

GOUCHER COLLEGE

1021 DULANEY VALLEY ROAD, BALTIMORE, MD 21204-2794 • ADMISSIONS: 410-337-6100 • FAX: 410-337-6354

CAMPUS LIFE

Quality of Life Rating	**86**
Fire Safety Rating	**60**
Type of school	private
Environment	city

STUDENTS

Total undergrad enrollment	1,345
% male/female	32/68
% from out of state	73
% from public high school	64
% live on campus	80
% African American	5
% Asian	3
% Caucasian	65
% Hispanic	3
% international	1

SURVEY SAYS

Small classes
Students are friendly
Frats and sororities are unpopular or nonexistent

ACADEMICS

Academic Rating	**86**
Calendar	semester
Student/faculty ratio	10:1
Professors interesting rating	87
Professors accessible rating	87
% professors teaching UG courses	100
% classes taught by TAs	0
Most common regular class size	10-19 students

MOST POPULAR MAJORS

Communications studies/speech communication and rhetoric
English language and literature
psychology

STUDENTS SPEAK OUT

Academics

"Despite its practically unknown name in the college world," Goucher College offers "rigorous but manageable academics" to its small, dedicated student body. Undergraduates at this Baltimore school extol its "balance of academics, clubs/activities, and social events. It's a great place to learn," in part because students can receive so much personal attention from their professors. "Leaders are nurtured at Goucher, and it's difficult to just slip by unnoticed. One has to work to be ignored," writes one student. Psychology and English are the most popular programs, collectively claiming about one-quarter of the student body. Pre-meds rate the biology department favorably, while performing artists give the dance program high grades. Students report that professors "are the best. They are easily accessible, knowledgeable, and willing to help you better yourself." Administrators "are extremely accessible, as well, and want to have direct contact with the students. How many college presidents have open hours so students can come in and chat?" Goucher is also proud of its study abroad program. The college "fosters an international/worldly view in students by requiring [them] to study abroad or [take] an internship." Students also love the Service Learning Program, which provides "so many opportunities to serve the community and make a difference in the world."

Life

"Everyone talks about the 'Goucher Bubble,'" students say, "and it's completely true that people just hang out on campus at the Gopher Hole (the campus coffeehouse) or hang out in the dorms. Although Goucher is very close to a big city and a 10-to-15-minute walk to town, people don't leave campus that much." Some students get "really involved on campus with many different clubs, organizations, and jobs," while others "tend to strive for social consciousness" by immersing themselves in political causes. Other students "just hang out with friends and play video games and poker." However, they don't party hard—at least not on campus. Students tell us that "if you are looking for a party school as seen on MTV and in the movies, this isn't it. If you want to go to a great school for learning and interesting people, Goucher is it." Fortunately, students can head to Towson University, a little over a mile down the road, when they seek a more party-oriented student body. They can also head into Towson itself, an upscale, northern enclave of Baltimore that "offers movie theaters, a four-story mall, restaurants, and other stores. It's a fun place to escape to." The Collegetown Shuttle bus connects Baltimore's major college campuses, giving students access to most areas of the city; even so, many students insist that a car is a necessity. One student cautions, "If you have a car, all of Baltimore is your playground. If you don't, I hope you like hanging out with your friends in your dorm room."

Student Body

Goucher students are "generally the kids who were 'outside the box' in high school, and they all fit together well at Goucher. The atypical students are the ones who would be perceived as 'typical' anywhere else." Undergraduates tend to break off into cliques defined either by major or by "type," for example, "punky kids, quirky kids, dancers, environmentalists, etc." One student says, "Different students have hardly any problems mixing together in social and academic situations," and overall students feel that "Goucher is amazing because it has such a strong community. Everyone knows everyone and loves it." Students tend to be "extremely liberal and want to be politically aware." One undergraduate observes, "We see ourselves as tolerant and open-minded, but when students express views that are not liberal, they are not always welcomed." Men constitute a minority at this former all women's college.

FINANCIAL AID: 410-337-6141 • E-MAIL: ADMISSION@GOUCHER.EDU • WEBSITE: WWW.GOUCHER.EDU

ADMISSIONS

Very important factors considered include: Recommendations, secondary school record. *Important factors considered include:* Essays, extracurricular activities, standardized test scores, talent/ability. *Other factors considered include:* Alumni/ae relation, character/personal qualities, class rank, interview, volunteer work, work experience. SAT Reasoning or ACT required. TOEFL required of all international applicants. High school diploma is required, and GED is accepted. *Academic units required:* 4 English, 3 math, 2 science (2 science lab), 2 foreign language, 2 social studies. *Academic units recommended:* 3 social studies.

The Inside Word

Goucher is in serious battle for the students to which it is best-suited and often fills the role of safety to some of the region's strongest colleges. Although the college is a solid choice in its own right, its admissions profile reflects modest competitiveness as a result of these circumstances.

FINANCIAL AID

Students should submit: FAFSA, CSS/Financial Aid PROFILE, noncustodial (divorced/separated) parents' statement, business/farm supplement. Regular filing deadline is 2/15. The Princeton Review suggests that all financial aid forms be submitted as soon as possible after 1/1. *Need-based scholarships/grants offered:* Pell, SEOG, state scholarships/grants, private scholarships, the school's own gift aid. *Loan aid offered:* Direct Subsidized Stafford, Direct Unsubsidized Stafford, Direct PLUS, Federal Perkins, college/university loans from institutional funds. Applicants will be notified of awards on or about 4/1.

FROM THE ADMISSIONS OFFICE

"A Goucher liberal arts education aims to prepare students for the real world. The college integrates thought and action, combining a strong liberal arts curriculum with hands-on learning in off-campus settings through internships, fieldwork, study abroad, and independent projects. Students can choose majors in 18 departments and four interdisciplinary areas, or they may design their own individualized program of study. Small classes taught by skilled faculty, strong international studies programs, and research with faculty are other key characteristics. Goucher has impressive resources in technology, including a campus fully wired for access to the Internet and the World Wide Web. Goucher's merit scholarship program is one of the top programs in the nation, offering strong students awards ranging from partial tuition to full tuition plus room and board.

"Freshman applicants to Goucher College are required to submit scores from either the new SAT or ACT (with the Writing component)."

SELECTIVITY

Admissions Rating	**88**
# of applicants	2,870
% of applicants accepted	68
% of acceptees attending	21
# accepting a place on wait list	355
% admitted from wait list	3

FRESHMAN PROFILE

Range SAT Verbal	560-660
Average SAT Verbal	607
Range SAT Math	530-630
Average SAT Math	581
**TPR Projected Range SAT Writing*	*600-670*
Range ACT Composite	23-27
Average ACT Composite	26
Minimum Paper TOEFL	550
Minimum Computer Based TOEFL	230
Average HS GPA	3.21
% graduated top 10% of class	28
% graduated top 25% of class	63
% graduated top 50% of class	91

DEADLINES

Regular application deadline	2/1
Regular notification	4/1
Nonfall registration?	yes

APPLICANTS ALSO LOOK AT

AND OFTEN PREFER
Boston University
Mount Holyoke College
New York University
Skidmore College

AND SOMETIMES PREFER
American University
Franklin & Marshall College
The George Washington University
Loyola College in Maryland
Trinity College (CT)

AND RARELY PREFER
Towson University
University of Mary Washington

FINANCIAL FACTS

Financial Aid Rating	**77**
Annual tuition	$27,100
Room & Board	$5,625
Books and supplies	$800
Required fees	$425
% frosh rec. need-based scholarship or grant aid	47
% UG rec. need-based scholarship or grant aid	53
% frosh rec. need-based self-help aid	41
% UG rec. need-based self-help aid	54
% frosh rec. any financial aid	83
% UG rec. any financial aid	92
Avg. frosh grant	$15,734
Avg. frosh loan	$3,895
Independent 529 member?	Yes

GRINNELL COLLEGE

GRINNELL, IA 50112-1690 • ADMISSIONS: 641-269-3600 • FAX: 641-269-4800

CAMPUS LIFE

Quality of Life Rating	**83**
Fire Safety Rating	**87**
Type of school	private
Environment	village

STUDENTS

Total undergrad enrollment	1,518
% male/female	46/54
% from out of state	75
% from public high school	75
% live on campus	88
% African American	4
% Asian	5
% Caucasian	69
% Hispanic	4
% Native American	1
% international	11
# of countries represented	59

SURVEY SAYS

Small classes
Campus feels safe
Low cost of living
Frats and sororities are unpopular or nonexistent
Political activism is popular

ACADEMICS

Academic Rating	**97**
Calendar	semester
Student/faculty ratio	9:1
Professors interesting rating	91
Professors accessible rating	96
% professors teaching UG courses	100
% classes taught by TAs	0
Most common lab size	10-19 students
Most common regular class size	10-19 students

MOST POPULAR MAJORS

Economics
English language and literature

STUDENTS SPEAK OUT

Academics

Rural Iowa's Grinnell College, true to its long-held reputation, remains "a rigorous liberal arts institution in a somewhat remote location, offering a total immersion in campus life and academia." Students here praise faculty, reporting that profs are "top-notch; the number of incredible teachers is staggering, and they are all readily available and in fact eager to assist students outside of class. They are all extremely intelligent and take an active interest in their students' lives." Students also caution that the workload is "intense." Recently, however, a mood of uneasiness has descended on students, caused by the direction in which they perceive Grinnell is headed. "The goal seems to be to [become] 'more competitive' with our 'peer institutions,' students say, which irks those who "choose Grinell because it was different." Students dislike the accompanying hassles (e.g., the attendant noise of building).

Life

Grinnell, students agree, is "in the middle of nowhere in Iowa. Which is good because everyone really wants to be at the school because they like it, not because they spent their entire time in high school daydreaming about the utopian lifestyle of a college in a small farm town in Iowa." The location naturally means that "we're sometimes short on things to go out and do" and that students must "make our own fun." Fortunately, the Grinnell campus is a fairly active one. "Throughout the week, the [administration] attempts to keep us entertained with music/theater events, movies, multicultural events, and colloquia," students report. When the weekend rolls around, there are "parties ranging from about four or five people in a dorm room to hundreds of people in a lounge or the Harris Center." There is no Greek system here, so "parties are almost always open to anyone who happens to walk by, and at such a small school that really helps build a sense of community." Students have mixed feelings about their hometown of Grinnell; some describe it as "small and cozy and a great place to 'escape to' within a ten-minute walk. There's a fabulous coffee shop downtown, Saint's Rest, as well as a one-screen movie theater and a bowling alley." Life here "is more enjoyable if you have a car," since "Iowa City and Des Moines are only 45 minutes to an hour away."

Student Body

"In one of the publications on campus, both prospective students and seniors were asked how popular they thought the average Grinnell student was in high school, on a scale of one to ten," reports one Grinnell undergrad. "Both agreed on the number [four]." Conclusion: "Most of the students at Grinnell are the people who did not fit into a single social group in high school." Nearly all feel they have found a comfortable home at Grinnell although more than a few admit to being somewhat cowed by their peers. Writes one, "One thing I will say about the students here is that almost everyone is brilliant. I was at the top of my class in high school and was quickly humbled when I arrived as a first-year." Most students lean well to the left politically; notes one, "Part of the appeal about Grinnell is its legendary social consciousness and sociopolitical activism." Grinnell students are not immune to self-segregation, however: "On the north side of [campus], students are sportily clad with some kind of personal touch. On the south side: hippie styling, dreads, and barefoot."

FINANCIAL AID: 641-269-3250 • E-MAIL: ASKGRIN@GRINNELL.EDU • WEBSITE: WWW.GRINNELL.EDU

ADMISSIONS

Very important factors considered include: Class rank, essays, extracurricular activities, recommendations, secondary school record, standardized test scores, talent/ability. *Important factors considered include:* Interview, minority status. *Other factors considered include:* Alumni/ae relation, character/personal qualities, geographical residence, state residency, volunteer work, work experience. SAT Reasoning or ACT required. TOEFL required of all international applicants. High school diploma is required, and GED is accepted. *Academic units recommended:* 4 English, 4 math, 4 science (3 science lab), 4 foreign language, 4 social studies.

The Inside Word

Grinnell has plenty of academically talented applicants. This enables the admissions committee to put a lot of energy into matchmaking, and gives candidates who have devoted time and energy to thought about themselves, their future, and Grinnell the opportunity to rise to the top. All applicants should consider interviewing; you're likely to leave with a positive impression.

FINANCIAL AID

Students should submit: FAFSA, institution's own financial aid form, noncustodial (divorced/separated) parents' statement. Regular filing deadline is 2/1. The Princeton Review suggests that all financial aid forms be submitted as soon as possible after 1/1. *Need-based scholarships/grants offered:* Pell, SEOG, state scholarships/grants, private scholarships, the school's own gift aid. *Loan aid offered:* FFEL Subsidized Stafford, FFEL Unsubsidized Stafford, FFEL PLUS, Federal Perkins, college/university loans from institutional funds. Applicants will be notified of awards on or about 4/1.

FROM THE ADMISSIONS OFFICE

"Grinnell students are committed to pursuing a liberal arts education in a challenging yet cooperative environment. Students are actively engaged in a myriad of community service, fine arts, athletics, and social and political organizations. Grinnellians are independent and exercise that independence through Grinnell's open curriculum and system of self governance. Grinnell hopes to produce individualism, social commitment, and intellectual self-awareness in its graduates.

"We require that applicants submit either the New SAT (taken prior to January of their senior year) or ACT scores. If students take both the New SAT I and ACT, we will consider the higher of the two scores. Unlike our SAT policy, we do not create a best composite score from multiple sittings of the ACT."

SELECTIVITY

Admissions Rating	**95**
# of applicants	2,970
% of applicants accepted	51
% of acceptees attending	29
# accepting a place on wait list	512
% admitted from wait list	6
# of early decision applicants	97
% accepted early decision	78

FRESHMAN PROFILE

Range SAT Verbal	640-760
Average SAT Verbal	684
Range SAT Math	650-730
Average SAT Math	683
**TPR Projected Range SAT Writing*	*660-740*
Range ACT Composite	28-32
Average ACT Composite	30
Minimum Paper TOEFL	550
Minimum Computer Based TOEFL	220
% graduated top 10% of class	67
% graduated top 25% of class	94
% graduated top 50% of class	100

DEADLINES

Early decision application deadline	11/20
Early decision notification	12/20
Regular application deadline	1/20
Regular notification	4/1
Nonfall registration?	no

AND SOMETIMES PREFER

Macalester College
Washington University in St. Louis

AND RARELY PREFER

Kenyon College
Lawrence University

FINANCIAL FACTS

Financial Aid Rating	**97**
Annual tuition	$27,504
Room & Board	$7,310
Books and supplies	$400
% frosh rec. need-based scholarship or grant aid	56
% UG rec. need-based scholarship or grant aid	49
% frosh rec. need-based self-help aid	43
% UG rec. need-based self-help aid	42
% frosh rec. any financial aid	91
% UG rec. any financial aid	89
Avg. frosh grant	$15,476
Avg. frosh loan	$4,483
Independent 529 member?	Yes

Grove City College

100 Campus Drive, Grove City, PA 16127-2104 • Admissions: 724-458-2100 • Fax: 724-458-3395

CAMPUS LIFE

Quality of Life Rating	**77**
Fire Safety Rating	**73**
Type of school	private
Affiliation	Presbyterian
Environment	rural

STUDENTS

Total undergrad enrollment	2,318
% male/female	51/49
% from out of state	48
% from public high school	85
% live on campus	90
% in (# of) fraternities	13 (8)
% in (# of) sororities	16 (8)
% Asian	2
% Caucasian	96
% international	1
# of countries represented	12

SURVEY SAYS

Small classes
Students are friendly
Diversity lacking on campus
Students are very religious
Campus feels safe
Low cost of living
Intramural sports are popular
Very little drug use

ACADEMICS

Academic Rating	**84**
Calendar	semester
Student/faculty ratio	16:1
Professors interesting rating	80
Professors accessible rating	88
% professors teaching UG courses	100
% classes taught by TAs	0
Most common lab size	20-29 students
Most common regular class size	20-29 students

MOST POPULAR MAJORS

Business administration/management
elementary education and teaching

STUDENTS SPEAK OUT

Academics

The Grove City College (GCC) environment allows students to be "continually challenged to learn more—more about my field of studies, more about the world around me, more about my faith, and more about myself." This "Ivy League school in disguise" runs according to a "Christian viewpoint that is refreshing and open-minded." Some students feel that the religious bent makes "almost every course become in some way, shape, or form a theology course." One respondent feels that the school's "pride in a 'rigorous curriculum' translates into standards that sometimes border on the ridiculous." Amid the challenging course work, students work with professors who are "inconceivably intelligent and brilliant in their fields" and "not afraid to stand up for liberty and truth." Undergraduates feel personally supported by the faculty, noting that instructors "go out of their way to help students understand material without robbing them of the learning experience." Students embrace their core curriculum, eager to "dabble in everything from physics to Spanish to philosophy, no matter what your major." Several students think "it seems that faculty and students mesh well, while the administration isolates itself." Reportedly, students and professors alike "voice their displeasure concerning administrative direction." On the one hand, a common sentiment goes, "Administration needs to get with the times and realize we're big boys and big girls and we can handle ourselves." On the other hand, one student writes, "Where else can you watch the president of the college team up with faculty members for a basketball game against students?" In the end, the school succeeds in "giving support to students in many ways, which lightens the academic load."

Life

A defining factor of Grove is the "definite focus on God." That means "Calvin and Luther are generally on the tip of the tongue here," and "we do have parties, just minus the alcohol." Employing a well-used double negative, one student writes "the party scene isn't nonexistent," but typically, students partake in "snowball fights, movie nights, Bible study, intermural bowling, ice cream socials, square dancing, lots of long conversations," and other activities that "don't involve breaking the law." Some students think that Greeks don't do much besides "wear matching sweatshirts," but others say, "Greek life gives variety, friendship, and fun that the campus does not offer." The anti-Greek faction goes so far as to say that fraternities and sororities are "the cause of all drinking and sex that goes on." "Intervisitation," that fated time when men and women are allowed to be in the same residences at the same time, means that "the freshmen dorms get loud and stay loud until 12:45." That early collegiate bedtime hints at the "atmosphere bordering on repressive at times." All told, certain students remark suggestively, "Don't let the Norman Rockwell facade fool you."

Student Body

Students offer three basic descriptions of TGs, or "typical Grovers." The first camp, "the home-schooled, very sheltered kids who go home every weekend and are engaged by sophomore year," give the campus its reputation, but many students will tell you that students are not as marriage-obsessed as outsiders believe. These kids are the ones "who would ask, 'What are hallucinogens?'" one student explains. Another group comprises "the normal, Nalgene bottle–carrying, Christian summer camp–working, service-oriented students." The leftovers are those who "slack off, drink, and get off campus." In general, most undergrads are "white, suburban, Christian Republicans." Many students point out, "We're diverse in our Christian denominations, but not our ethnicities," to the degree that "there are more amputees than minorities on this campus." In this "homogenous group," "there are a few gays/lesbians, and they probably don't fit in well." Reportedly, atypical students are "acknowledged as individuals and accepted for [whom] they are." The cumulative effect is "so many people who enjoy being around each other so much."

FINANCIAL AID: 724-458-2163 • E-MAIL: ADMISSIONS@GCC.EDU • WEBSITE: WWW.GCC.EDU

ADMISSIONS

Very important factors considered include: Character/personal qualities, essays, extracurricular activities, interview, religious affiliation/commitment, secondary school record, standardized test scores. *Important factors considered include:* Recommendations, talent/ability. *Other factors considered include:* Alumni/ae relation, class rank, geographical residence, minority status, state residency, volunteer work, work experience. SAT Reasoning or ACT required. TOEFL required of all international applicants. High school diploma is required, and GED is accepted. *Academic units recommended:* 4 English, 3 math, 3 science (2 science lab), 3 foreign language, 2 social studies, 2 history.

The Inside Word

If you're looking for a northeastern college with a Christian orientation, Grove City is a pretty good choice, but it's getting tougher to get in as we speak. Applications and standards are on the rise, and the college is fast becoming the newest addition to the lofty realm of the highly selective. Minorities are in short supply and will encounter a somewhat friendlier admissions process. All students should definitely follow the college's recommendation and interview.

FINANCIAL AID

Students should submit: Institution's own financial aid form, state aid form. Regular filing deadline is 4/15. The Princeton Review suggests that all financial aid forms be submitted as soon as possible after 1/1. *Need-based scholarships/grants offered:* State scholarships/grants, private scholarships, the school's own gift aid. *Loan aid offered:* Private, alternative loans. Applicants will be notified of awards on a rolling basis beginning on or about 3/15. Institutional employment available. Off-campus job opportunities are good.

FROM THE ADMISSIONS OFFICE

"A good college education doesn't have to cost a fortune. For decades, Grove City College has offered a quality education at costs among the lowest nationally. Since the 1990s, increased national academic acclaim has come to Grove City College. Grove City College is a place where professors teach. You will not see graduate assistants or teacher's aides in the classroom. Our professors are also active in the total life of the campus. More than 100 student organizations on campus afford opportunity for a wide variety of cocurricular activities. Outstanding scholars and leaders in education, science, and international affairs visit the campus each year. The environment at GCC is friendly, secure, and dedicated to high standards. Character-building is emphasized and traditional Christian values are supported.

"Applicants are asked to submit scores from the new SAT. Pending the results of further study into the virtues of the new Writing assessment section, GCC will use the combined Critical Reading and Math scores for admissions decisions. Students may also submit scores from the old SAT I for consideration."

SELECTIVITY

Admissions Rating	**95**
# of applicants	2,091
% of applicants accepted	47
% of acceptees attending	62
# accepting a place on wait list	938
% admitted from wait list	4
# of early decision applicants	303
% accepted early decision	47

FRESHMAN PROFILE

Range SAT Verbal	575-696
Average SAT Verbal	635
Range SAT Math	578-688
Average SAT Math	636
**TPR Projected Range SAT Writing*	*620-700*
Range ACT Composite	25-30
Average ACT Composite	28
Minimum Paper TOEFL	550
Minimum Computer Based TOEFL	213
Average HS GPA	3.73
% graduated top 10% of class	61
% graduated top 25% of class	89
% graduated top 50% of class	97

DEADLINES

Early decision application deadline	11/15
Early decision notification	12/15
Regular application deadline	2/1
Regular notification	3/15
Nonfall registration?	yes

APPLICANTS ALSO LOOK AT

AND OFTEN PREFER

Hillsdale College
Penn State University Park
Wheaton College (IL)

AND RARELY PREFER

Slippery Rock University of Pennsylvania
Thiel College

FINANCIAL FACTS

Financial Aid Rating	**62**
Annual tuition	$10,440
Room & Board	$5,344
Books and supplies	$900
% frosh rec. need-based scholarship or grant aid	42
% UG rec. need-based scholarship or grant aid	36
% frosh rec. need-based self-help aid	25
% UG rec. need-based self-help aid	25
Avg. frosh grant	$4,887
Avg. frosh loan	$6,055
Independent 529 member?	Yes

Guilford College

5800 West Friendly Avenue, Greensboro, NC 27410 • Admissions: 336-316-2100 • Fax: 336-316-2954

CAMPUS LIFE

Quality of Life Rating	**74**
Fire Safety Rating	**83**
Type of school	private
Affiliation	Quaker
Environment	city

STUDENTS

Total undergrad enrollment	2,511
% male/female	38/62
% from out of state	61
% from public high school	67
% live on campus	80
% African American	18
% Asian	1
% Caucasian	52
% Hispanic	1
% Native American	1
% international	1
# of countries represented	21

SURVEY SAYS

Small classes
Lab facilities are great
Great computer facilities
Frats and sororities are unpopular or nonexistent
(Almost) everyone smokes

ACADEMICS

Academic Rating	**85**
Calendar	semester
Student/faculty ratio	16:1
Professors interesting rating	85
Professors accessible rating	84
% professors teaching UG courses	100
% classes taught by TAs	0
Most common regular class size	10-19 students

MOST POPULAR MAJORS

Biological and biomedical sciences
Business administration/management
psychology

STUDENTS SPEAK OUT

Academics

Students at Guilford College laud their school's Quaker values of "friendliness, simplicity, and equality," telling us that the Quaker spirit makes Guilford "a great place to build one's confidence. Teachers and peers are supportive and friendly." Explains one undergrad, "Because the school was founded by the Society of Friends, Quakers, we believe in the equality of everyone. One way this manifests itself is that we refer to our professors by their first names rather than titles. This puts us all on much more equal footing, which I think enhances the learning process." Classes at Guilford "are primarily discussion-based; teachers want to learn from the students, as well as share what knowledge they have with them. Courses are also writing- and reading-intensive." Students here warn that "Guilford has some classes that will kick your butt in a good way. They get you thinking. You are forced to deal with things from outside the ordinary perspective." The profs, as at many small, teaching-oriented colleges, "are wonderful, and it's very refreshing to know that you have teachers that genuinely care about you and how you are doing. There is almost no way to slip through the cracks." Students especially appreciate how professors "will always help you until you understand the concept, and if you are not being challenged enough, they will make sure you get the challenges you need. It's also nice that at the end of the semester your professor has the class over for dinner at his house."

Life

Students love this "beautiful campus" in northwest Greensboro, one of three cities that constitute North Carolina's Triad (Winston-Salem and High Point are the other two). Students tell us that "Greensboro is a mecca for good underground music" and that the small city (population: 230,000) offers up some good eats as well as the expected array of movies, bars, and shopping. Chapel Hill, a quintessential college town an hour to the east, offers even more options. Many here are content to remain within the confines of the school, however, since "there is always something going on on campus: live music (tonight Holly Near is playing), concerts, movies, discussions (about peace in the Middle East, God and gender, art and social action, etc.), clubs, sports (ultimate Frisbee, rugby, etc.), special events put on by the Student Union (Mardi Gras ball, etc.), meditation groups, drum circle, art workshops, contra dancing, you name it." Campus theater productions "are always outstanding," while "the *Guilfordian* newspaper and Guilford radio station are [also] great." A number of students take advantage of the mild weather during the school year to enjoy "outdoor club trips, which have included skiing (in the mountains to the west), hiking/backpacking, and rafting." "Community service is popular" among many here as well. Small parties are the choice of most on the weekends despite the school's recent vigilance in enforcing its alcohol policies.

Student Body

"In high school there were always ways you could categorize people and pigeonhole them," notes one Guilford undergrad, continuing, "but there were always a few that didn't quite fit into these categories. Guilford is full of these kinds of people." Or, as another student here put it, "We're all unique . . . just like everyone else." Students tell us that "most of the campus is a very liberal, 'hippie' kind of place. There are the athletes, conservatives, and whatnot, although their numbers are small." Much of the student body leans hard left politically, actively demonstrating "a strong sense of social responsibility." Many report a clear divide between athletes and the rest of the student body, but report that otherwise students mostly get along.

GUILFORD COLLEGE

FINANCIAL AID: 336-316-2354 • E-MAIL: ADMISSION@GUILFORD.EDU • WEBSITE: WWW.GUILFORD.EDU

ADMISSIONS

Very important factors considered include: Secondary school record. *Important factors considered include:* Character/personal qualities, class rank, essays, recommendations, standardized test scores, volunteer work. *Other factors considered include:* Alumni/ae relation, extracurricular activities, geographical residence, interview, minority status, religious affiliation/commitment, state residency, talent/ability, work experience. SAT Reasoning or ACT required. TOEFL required of all international applicants. High school diploma is required, and GED is accepted. *Academic units required:* 4 English, 3 math, 2 science, 2 foreign language, 2 social studies, 1 history, 2 academic electives. *Academic units recommended:* 4 English, 3 math, 3 science, 2 foreign language, 1 social studies, 1 history, 2 academic electives.

The Inside Word

Guilford is indeed a sleeper and is likely to become more selective as it becomes better known. Its current acceptance rate is high mainly because the competition includes many of the best colleges and universities east of the Mississippi.

FINANCIAL AID

Students should submit: FAFSA, noncustodial (divorced/separated) parents' statement, business/farm supplement. The Princeton Review suggests that all financial aid forms be submitted as soon as possible after 1/1. *Need-based scholarships/grants offered:* Pell, SEOG, state scholarships/grants, private scholarships, the school's own gift aid. *Loan aid offered:* FFEL Subsidized Stafford, FFEL Unsubsidized Stafford, FFEL PLUS, Federal Perkins, college/university loans from institutional funds. Applicants will be notified of awards on a rolling basis beginning on or about 2/15.

FROM THE ADMISSIONS OFFICE

"We want you to know the following about Guilford:

1) Guilford is difficult. Not only will you have to adapt to the diversity at Guilford (we have students from 44 states and 21 countries) but also to the significant academic expectations. With an average class size of 18 students, our full-time professors (no graduate assistants) will see you often in class and expect daily contributions from you. Class participation is critical.

2) Our Quaker values of integrity, respect for difference, social justice, and responsibility are sure to challenge all students. You need to be a mature student to enroll at Guilford. No matter your background, academic preparation, values, thoughts, and beliefs, you will be challenged. We admit that our mission is idealistic; however, we expect our students to deal with very difficult issues. An education from Guilford prepares you for life in a rapidly changing world.

3) Community service and volunteerism is a hallmark of Guilford. Our Project Community (run by students) contributes more than 50,000 hours of community service to the Greensboro, North Carolina, community each year. Service is a true part of the daily experience at Guilford.

"For more information on Guilford, create your individualized online brochure at: www.guilford.edu/myguilford.

"Freshman applicants are required to submit scores from the new SAT (or ACT). However, students may choose to submit a portfolio in lieu of standardized tests. The content of the portfolio is limited only by the applicant's imagination; it must however, provide sufficient evaluative information to substitute for standardized test scores."

SELECTIVITY

Admissions Rating	**81**
# of applicants	2,407
% of applicants accepted	71
% of acceptees attending	26
# accepting a place on wait list	16
% admitted from wait list	6

FRESHMAN PROFILE

Range SAT Verbal	500-640
Average SAT Verbal	574
Range SAT Math	490-600
Average SAT Math	546
**TPR Projected Range SAT Writing*	*560-660*
Range ACT Composite	19-27
Average ACT Composite	24
Minimum Paper TOEFL	550
Minimum Computer Based TOEFL	213
Average HS GPA	3.1
% graduated top 10% of class	19
% graduated top 25% of class	42
% graduated top 50% of class	73

DEADLINES

Regular application deadline	2/15
Regular notification	rolling
Nonfall registration?	yes

APPLICANTS ALSO LOOK AT AND OFTEN PREFER

Oberlin College

AND SOMETIMES PREFER

Earlham College
Elon University
Goucher College
University of North Carolina—Chapel Hill

FINANCIAL FACTS

Financial Aid Rating	**76**
Annual tuition	$21,310
Room & Board	$6,530
Books and supplies	$800
Required fees	$330
% frosh rec. need-based scholarship or grant aid	60
% UG rec. need-based scholarship or grant aid	66
% frosh rec. need-based self-help aid	55
% UG rec. need-based self-help aid	61
% frosh rec. any financial aid	95
% UG rec. any financial aid	85
Avg. frosh grant	$14,250
Avg. frosh loan	$5,096
Independent 529 member?	Yes

GUSTAVUS ADOLPHUS COLLEGE

800 WEST COLLEGE AVENUE, SAINT PETER, MN 56082 • ADMISSIONS: 507-933-7676 • FAX: 507-933-7474

CAMPUS LIFE

Quality of Life Rating	**85**
Fire Safety Rating	**60**
Type of school	private
Affiliation	Lutheran
Environment	village

STUDENTS

Total undergrad enrollment	2,506
% male/female	43/57
% from out of state	21
% from public high school	92
% live on campus	87
% in (# of) fraternities	27 (7)
% in (# of) sororities	22 (5)
% African American	1
% Asian	4
% Caucasian	95
% Hispanic	1
% international	1
# of countries represented	20

SURVEY SAYS

Small classes
Great computer facilities
Students are friendly
Great food on campus
Campus feels safe
Low cost of living
Musical organizations are popular

ACADEMICS

Academic Rating	**86**
Calendar	4-1-4
Student/faculty ratio	13:1
Professors interesting rating	83
Professors accessible rating	87
% professors teaching UG courses	100
% classes taught by TAs	0
Most common lab size	10-19 students
Most common regular class size	10-19 students

MOST POPULAR MAJORS

Communications studies/speech communication and rhetoric
psychology

STUDENTS SPEAK OUT

Academics

At Gustavus Adophus College, a small Lutheran school in rural Minnesota, students enjoy "many opportunities to make the most out of [their] education through research, independent study, or simply the awesome, enthusiastic professors who care about what they teach." Reports one busy student, "As a sophomore, I am already involved with two research projects on campus and have come to know all three of the professors I am working with very well. The professors are really approachable and are passionate about what they teach." Business, biology, and music are among Gustavus' top departments; of the last, students crow that "the music program at Gustavus is phenomenal. Band, orchestra, or choir—the groups are just amazing, and the students are really talented. These groups perform nationally and internationally with excursions to Italy, China, and Spain." While "classes are challenging" and "professors often grade super-hard," students do not feel overburdened by their academic chores because "the school has a number of resources to help you out if you get overwhelmed," and profs "will bend over backward to help us learn." Despite the rigors of the curriculum, students find time to enjoy themselves. "The school stresses a balance between academics and extracurriculars," writes one student. Gustavus offers a short January term, during which "students try an entirely new subject for a month. It also provides a study-abroad opportunity for those that can't go abroad for an entire semester."

Life

Most students indicate a subdued but agreeable pace of life at Gustavus Adolphus: "As with all colleges, drinking is a social activity in which many students partake." Freshmen and sophomores often visit The Dive, "the on-campus dance club that has something going on every Friday and Saturday," while upperclassmen sometimes head for nearby bars. Those who abjure alcohol report that "the school does have a nice selection of on-campus, substance-free events, most of which are fun. These would include currently running movies, concerts, comedians, speakers, dancing, and other mingling events." Students also tell us that "community service organizations seem to involve a large majority of the students" and that "athletic events, both intercollegiate and intramural, are a favorite." Hometown Saint Peter is "friendly" and Mankato, home to Minnesota State University, is only 15 miles to the south. While many at this Lutheran school are religious, "religion here is what you make of it; those who want to be highly involved will find numerous opportunities to do so, but those who don't want to be involved are not hit over the head with it."

Student Body

The students of Gustavus are typically "Scandinavian, tall, blonde, attractive, intelligent, and especially nice," with "about half coming from large cities and the other half from farm areas." Most are midwestern and Lutheran, which helps explain their similarities in appearance. Despite their outward similitude, however, "there is a variety of different personality types at Gustavus," so "it is not too difficult for people to find a niche." The school also has "lots of international students that fit in with everyone." Music and athletics are the two most popular extracurricular activities. Athletes tend to live on the North Side of campus, near the athletic facilities. Reports one student, "The school has a North Side/South Side division, where the students on the North Side drink more and tend to be involved in sports, [and those] living on the South Side are more likely to be involved in the fine arts and are more serious about academics."

GUSTAVUS ADOLPHUS COLLEGE

FINANCIAL AID: 507-933-7527 • E-MAIL: ADMISSION@GUSTAVUS.EDU • WEBSITE: WWW.GUSTAVUS.EDU

ADMISSIONS

Very important factors considered include: Essays, secondary school record, standardized test scores. *Important factors considered include:* Character/personal qualities, class rank, extracurricular activities, interview, recommendations, religious affiliation/commitment, talent/ability. *Other factors considered include:* Alumni/ae relation, geographical residence, minority status, volunteer work, work experience. SAT Reasoning or ACT required. TOEFL required of all international applicants. High school diploma is required, and GED is accepted. *Academic units required:* 4 English, 3 math, 2 science (2 science lab), 2 foreign language, 2 social studies, 2 history. *Academic units recommended:* 4 English, 4 math, 3 science (3 science lab), 3 foreign language, 2 social studies, 2 history, 2 academic electives.

The Inside Word

While the college refers to itself as a national liberal arts college, the applicant pool is decidedly regional and mostly from Minnesota. The pool is also small and highly self-selected, which explains the high acceptance rate and solid freshman profile. Minorities and those who hail from far afield will find their applications met with enthusiasm by the admissions committee.

FINANCIAL AID

Students should submit: FAFSA, institution's own financial aid form, CSS/Financial Aid PROFILE, Students who want to receive an award by 3/1 must file the CSS/Financial Aid PROFILE. Regular filing deadline is 6/15. The Princeton Review suggests that all financial aid forms be submitted as soon as possible after 1/1. *Need-based scholarships/grants offered:* Pell, SEOG, state scholarships/grants, private scholarships, the school's own gift aid. *Loan aid offered:* Direct Subsidized Stafford, Direct Unsubsidized Stafford, Direct PLUS, Federal Perkins, state loans, college/university loans from institutional funds, alternative loans from private lenders. Applicants will be notified of awards on a rolling basis beginning on or about 3/1. Federal Work-study Program available. Institutional employment available. Off-campus job opportunities are good.

FROM THE ADMISSIONS OFFICE

"To better serve students and their families

"There is no application fee.

"Applications completed by November 1 will be notified of an admission decision by November 20. Applications completed after November 1 will be reviewed on a competitive rolling basis beginning December 20.

"Early financial aid awards will be available to admitted students who submit the CSS/Financial Aid PROFILE prior to February 15. Students who submit the FAFSA will continue to receive a financial aid award in a timely fashion.

"The college is committed to excellence, community, justice, service, and faith. These values are pervasive in the college community and can be seen throughout campus activities and events like Our Story workshop on African American culture, Nobel Conference, Building Bridges Diversity Conference, MAYDAY! Peace Conference, and NYSP summer sports camp. Campus facilities support student life and development. Recent projects include a 200-bed apartment and suite configuration residence hall (also houses an additional 200-bed youth hostel), cardiovascular exercise area, Nobel Hall of Science equipment additions of DNA sequencer, mass spectrometer microscope, cell growth culture labs, Old Main classroom renovation, International Center for residential living and international education, and Jackson Campus Center housing student services such as Diversity Center, Market Place cafeteria and Courtyard Café, Ticket Center, student activities offices and work space, Hillstrom Museum, bookstore, and much more.

"Gustavus Adolphus College requires freshman applicants to submit scores from the old or new SAT. Students may also choose to submit scores from the ACT (with or without the Writing component) in lieu of the SAT."

SELECTIVITY

Admissions Rating	**87**
# of applicants	2,648
% of applicants accepted	77
% of acceptees attending	32
# accepting a place on wait list	58
% admitted from wait list	3

FRESHMAN PROFILE

Range SAT Verbal	540-600
Average SAT Verbal	610
Range SAT Math	560-680
Average SAT Math	620
**TPR Projected Range SAT Writing*	*590-630*
Range ACT Composite	23-28
Average ACT Composite	26
Minimum Paper TOEFL	550
Minimum Computer Based TOEFL	213
Average HS GPA	3.64
% graduated top 10% of class	36
% graduated top 25% of class	69
% graduated top 50% of class	94

DEADLINES

Regular application deadline	4/1
Regular notification	rolling
Nonfall registration?	yes

APPLICANTS ALSO LOOK AT

AND OFTEN PREFER

Carleton College

University of Wisconsin—Madison

AND SOMETIMES PREFER

Saint Olaf College

University of Minnesota—Twin Cities

FINANCIAL FACTS

Financial Aid Rating	**85**
Annual tuition	$28,765
Room & Board	$5,810
Books and supplies	$700
% frosh rec. need-based scholarship or grant aid	65
% UG rec. need-based scholarship or grant aid	65
% frosh rec. need-based self-help aid	52
% UG rec. need-based self-help aid	54
% frosh rec. any financial aid	98
% UG rec. any financial aid	92
Avg. frosh grant	$7,958
Avg. frosh loan	$4,500
Independent 529 member?	Yes

HAMILTON COLLEGE

198 COLLEGE HILL ROAD, CLINTON, NY 13323 • ADMISSIONS: 315-859-4421 • FAX: 315-859-4457

CAMPUS LIFE

Quality of Life Rating	**74**
Fire Safety Rating	**60**
Type of school	private
Environment	town

STUDENTS

Total undergrad enrollment	1,762
% male/female	50/50
% from out of state	62
% from public high school	60
% live on campus	98
% in (# of) fraternities	34 (7)
% in (# of) sororities	20 (3)
% African American	4
% Asian	5
% Caucasian	77
% Hispanic	4
% Native American	1
% international	5
# of countries represented	40

SURVEY SAYS

Small classes
Great library
Lots of beer drinking
Hard liquor is popular

ACADEMICS

Academic Rating	**95**
Calendar	semester
Student/faculty ratio	9:1
Professors interesting rating	96
Professors accessible rating	91
% professors teaching UG courses	100
% classes taught by TAs	0
Most common lab size	10-19 students
Most common regular class size	10-19 students

MOST POPULAR MAJORS

Economics
political science and government
psychology

STUDENTS SPEAK OUT

Academics

According to a studious junior, Hamilton affords a "grueling but fulfilling education" in a "rigorous yet nurturing" environment. The college "really produces great writers and great thinkers," another student comments, and several respondents highlight the strength of the school's writing program, designed to ensure that graduates can wield the pen as effectively as the institution's namesake, Alexander Hamilton. The college's "very helpful and available" professors conduct classes in a "hands-on" manner and hold students to "very high standards." Luckily, instructors "really communicate the material well" and are always "there for you if you have a problem." The faculty has a reputation for being "eager to meet with students to help prepare for exams or write papers." They also develop camaraderie with their wards: "Only at Hamilton can you go to the pub and have a beer with your professor." Other students concur: "Your teacher is your best friend," and "professors are constantly having entire classes over for dinner." The small classes "concentrate on discussion," which means "you are expected to participate." A music major waxes, "I adore the fact that we call all the professors in our department by their first names." The administration is said to be "exceedingly accessible" as well as "concerned with student opinion and open to suggestions." Hamilton's president holds a weekly "open hour" to meet with students, and most "administrators know student names." In this supportive atmosphere, students aver that "if you have a vision, Hamilton will provide the funding and assistance to [help you] achieve your goals."

Life

For students sometimes it seems that life at Hamilton consists of "nothing but work and alcohol." Students attribute the drinking culture on campus to the fact that "it is always ass-cold winter" in central New York. Although "beer is readily available" and many students say they "drink for fun," a sophomore wants you to know that "drinking isn't compulsory, just common" in Clinton. While some students wish for "more things for people who don't drink to do," others point out "alternatives like movies, dance, theater, comedy, and other low-key activities." Fraternities and sororities are considered "integral" to Hamilton social life, and many students agree that things "would be better if the Greeks still had houses." Students also venture off campus in search of a colder beer. "Three words: The Village Tavern," a senior writes, referring to one of the two bars in town and the scene of many a Hamilton student's fond college memories. Students report that their adopted hometown of Clinton "is the textbook definition of boring," but nonetheless wish for improved town-gown relations. One student notes, "Being isolated on 'the Hill' can sometimes warp students' perception of the real world."

Student Body

A large number of respondents share the sentiment that "a small percentage of the students account for the Hamilton image of rich, white, and preppy." While the Greek population may be the most visible and "sometimes it seems like everyone is from old-money Greenwich," students emphasize that other types do coexist in Clinton. In general, "the majority of people are friendly, open-minded, and intelligent," and "most people smile, even if they don't know you," contributing to a "nice sense of community." Currently, students note the decidedly "homogeneous population" when it comes to race and ethnicity. One junior tells us, "I'm not sure that minorities feel welcome." But other students observe, "Hamilton's diversity is increasing. It has come a long way in a few years." According to a senior, "Even though Hamilton is sort of über-whitey land, it's clear that admissions and the administration are trying very hard to diversify the campus."

FINANCIAL AID: 800-859-4413 • E-MAIL: ADMISSION@HAMILTON.EDU • WEBSITE: WWW.HAMILTON.EDU

ADMISSIONS

Very important factors considered include: Class rank, recommendations, secondary school record. *Important factors considered include:* Character/personal qualities, essays, extracurricular activities, interview, minority status, standardized test scores. *Other factors considered include:* Alumni/ae relation, geographical residence, talent/ability, volunteer work, work experience. TOEFL required of all international applicants. High school diploma or equivalent is not required. *Academic units recommended:* 4 English, 3 math, 3 science, 3 foreign language, 3 social studies.

The Inside Word

Gaining admission to Hamilton is difficult and would be more so if the college didn't lose many of its shared applicants to competitor schools. The college's position as a popular safety for the top tier of northeastern colleges has always benefited the quality of its applicant pool, but it translates into a tough fight when it comes to getting admits to enroll. Although selectivity has risen significantly of late, Hamilton remains in the position of losing many of its best candidates to other, more prestigious schools. Students who view Hamilton as their first-choice college should definitely make it plain to the admissions committee—such news can often be influential, especially under circumstances like those mentioned here.

FINANCIAL AID

Students should submit: FAFSA, institution's own financial aid form, CSS/Financial Aid PROFILE, state aid form, noncustodial (divorced/separated) parents' statement, business/farm supplement. Regular filing deadline is 1/1. The Princeton Review suggests that all financial aid forms be submitted as soon as possible after 1/1. *Need-based scholarships/grants offered:* Pell, SEOG, state scholarships/grants, private scholarships, the school's own gift aid. *Loan aid offered:* FFEL Subsidized Stafford, FFEL Unsubsidized Stafford, FFEL PLUS, Federal Perkins, college/university loans from institutional funds. Applicants will be notified of awards on or about 4/1. Federal Work-study Program available. Institutional employment available.

FROM THE ADMISSIONS OFFICE

"One of Hamilton's most important characteristics is the exceptional interaction that takes place between students and faculty members. Whether in class or out, they work together, challenging one another to excel. Academic life at Hamilton is rigorous, and emerging from that rigor is a community spirit based on common commitment. It binds together student and teacher and stimulates self-motivation, thus making the learning process not only more productive but also more enjoyable and satisfying. Hamilton's Bristol Scholars program is merit-based, offering ten half-tuition scholarships. Both the Bristol and the need-based Schambach scholars program also offer special research opportunities with faculty on campus. National merit finalists also receive $2,000 a year.

"Applicants must complete one of three standardized test requirements: the SAT; the ACT Assessment Test; or three Subject Tests that include a quantitative test, a Verbal or written test, and a third of the student's choice. Visit the school's website for acceptable forms of each."

SELECTIVITY

Admissions Rating	**95**
# of applicants	4,445
% of applicants accepted	34
% of acceptees attending	30
# accepting a place on wait list	529
% admitted from wait list	14
# of early decision applicants	230
% accepted early decision	47

FRESHMAN PROFILE

Range SAT Verbal	620-710
Average SAT Verbal	661
Range SAT Math	640-710
Average SAT Math	668
**TPR Projected Range SAT Writing*	*650-700*
Minimum Paper TOEFL	600
Minimum Computer Based TOEFL	250
% graduated top 10% of class	68
% graduated top 25% of class	91
% graduated top 50% of class	99

DEADLINES

Early decision application deadline	11/15
Early decision notification	1/1
Regular application deadline	1/1
Regular notification	4/1
Nonfall registration?	yes

APPLICANTS ALSO LOOK AT

AND OFTEN PREFER

Amherst College
Middlebury College
Williams College

AND SOMETIMES PREFER

Bowdoin College
Colby College
Colgate University

AND RARELY PREFER

Dickinson College
Skidmore College
Union College (NY)

FINANCIAL FACTS

Financial Aid Rating	**95**
Annual tuition	$33,150
Room & Board	$8,310
Required fees	$200
% frosh rec. need-based scholarship or grant aid	50
% UG rec. need-based scholarship or grant aid	54
% frosh rec. need-based self-help aid	34
% UG rec. need-based self-help aid	39
Independent 529 member?	No

HAMPDEN-SYDNEY COLLEGE

PO BOX 667, HAMPDEN-SYDNEY, VA 23943 • ADMISSIONS: 434-223-6120 • FAX: 434-223-6346

CAMPUS LIFE

Quality of Life Rating	**82**
Fire Safety Rating	**81**
Type of school	private
Affiliation	Presbyterian
Environment	rural

STUDENTS

Total undergrad enrollment	1,082
% male/female	100/0
% from out of state	30
% from public high school	64
% live on campus	95
% in (# of) fraternities	34 (11)
% African American	2
% Asian	1
% Caucasian	64
% Hispanic	1
% international	1
# of countries represented	9

SURVEY SAYS

Small classes
No one cheats
Lots of beer drinking
Hard liquor is popular
(Almost) everyone smokes

ACADEMICS

Academic Rating	**86**
Calendar	semester
Student/faculty ratio	10:1
Professors interesting rating	98
Professors accessible rating	97
% professors teaching UG courses	100
% classes taught by TAs	0
Most common regular class size	10-19 students

MOST POPULAR MAJORS

Economics
history
political science and government

STUDENTS SPEAK OUT

Academics

"Hampden-Sydney is not for everybody," students at this traditional all-male college advise. "But if it is for you, one look will make your decision." What will that one look reveal? "The last true refuge for men who are looking to study hard and party hard with other true gentlemen who both dress and act with the highest level of class, and do not accept anything other than 100 percent manners, 100 percent class, 100 percent preppy, and 100 percent conservative all the time," students tell us. You'll also see a place where tradition is paramount; explains one undergrad, "Coming on 'The Hill' is like stepping back in time. Like those who have been here before us, we are not hesitant to walk around in madras and pink bow-ties." Other age-old traditions at this colonial-era institution include "the strongest Honor Code in the nation, one that tolerates no lying, cheating, or stealing," a mandatory Rhetoric program that "has made H-SC students famous for their writing," a solid core that creates "liberal arts Renaissance men who dabble in Plato's Republic, supply-side economics, the Federalist Papers, and Chaucer all in one day," and "a great network of graduates who work hard with Career Services to find other Hampden-Sydney graduates internships and future jobs." Students love that "opportunities are abundant for out-of-the-classroom experience (study abroad, May term abroad, internships)," and that "small class sizes allow you to know your teachers personally, and also hold you more accountable than a class with 200 kids."

Life

Hampden-Sydney's hometown of Farmville lives up to its name; it's "a very rural area, so there isn't much more than a Wal-Mart and a few fast food restaurants nearby." "If you are not comfortable just hanging out with a bunch of dudes, you will occasionally be bored," undergrads tell us, "but if you are pretty used to being in the middle of nowhere, this place can be a lot of fun." "Old traditions and strong Southern values are important" at Hampden-Sydney, and students expect their peers to embrace both. Tailgating, hunting, fishing, and perhaps most of all the Greek system are more than just diversions from schoolwork; they are a major source of its esprit de corps. Fraternities "drive the entire social scene of this school, and H-SC would be disastrously dull without them," most here agree, noting that the school's all-male status doesn't kill on-campus parties because "Girls from Longwood and Sweet Briar come often, and others come on big weekends. Hollins University, Randolph-Macon Women's College, Mary Baldwin College, University of Virginia, James Madison University and Virginia Tech are all within a reasonable distance." This well-unified campus grows even more united and spirited on game day; reports one undergrad, "Our teams (football, basketball, lacrosse) kick ass in the ODAC and usually finish the season in the NCAA tournaments."

Student Body

"There are a few atypical students" among the majority "white, heterosexual, Republican, middle- to upper-middle class students from the South, who tend to enjoy the outdoors more than most [and] who know the difference between casual, semi-formal, and formal dress." Other things a Hampden-Sydney gentleman knows that you may not? "We know how to treat women and alcohol. We party hard and work hard, as well." Those who don't fit the mold "keep to themselves, and most people don't like them and want them to leave." One student sums up the vibe here neatly: "We say grace, and we say 'ma'am,' and if you ain't into that, we don't give a damn." North Face and Polo "are a must in this haven from the average Joe," as is camouflage (during hunting season, anyway). Many here warn that Hampden-Sydney is not a hospitable environment for gay students.

HAMPDEN-SYDNEY COLLEGE

FINANCIAL AID: 804-223-6119 • E-MAIL: ADMISSIONS@HSC.EDU • WEBSITE: WWW.HSC.EDU

ADMISSIONS

Very important factors considered include: Character/personal qualities, essays, recommendations, secondary school record, standardized test scores. *Important factors considered include:* Class rank, extracurricular activities. *Other factors considered include:* Alumni/ae relation, interview, minority status, talent/ability, volunteer work, work experience. SAT Reasoning or ACT required. TOEFL required of all international applicants. High school diploma is required, and GED is accepted. *Academic units required:* 4 English, 3 math, 2 science (1 science lab), 2 foreign language, 1 social studies, 1 history, 3 academic electives. *Academic units recommended:* 4 math, 3 science, 3 foreign language.

The Inside Word

Hampden-Sydney is one of the last of its kind. Understandably, the applicant pool is heavily self-selected, and a fairly significant percentage of those who are admitted choose to enroll. This enables the admissions committee to be more selective, which in turn requires candidates to take the process more seriously than might otherwise be necessary. Students with consistently sound academic records should have little to worry about nonetheless.

FINANCIAL AID

Students should submit: FAFSA, CSS/Financial Aid PROFILE, state aid form. Regular filing deadline is 5/1. The Princeton Review suggests that all financial aid forms be submitted as soon as possible after 1/1. *Need-based scholarships/grants offered:* Pell, SEOG, state scholarships/grants, private scholarships, the school's own gift aid. *Loan aid offered:* FFEL Subsidized Stafford, FFEL Unsubsidized Stafford, FFEL PLUS, Federal Perkins, college/university loans from institutional funds, private loans. Applicants will be notified of awards on or about 3/15. Federal Work-study Program available. Institutional employment available. Off-campus job opportunities are good.

FROM THE ADMISSIONS OFFICE

"The spirit of Hampden-Sydney is its sense of community. As one of only 1,026 students, you will be in small classes and find it easy to get extra help or inspiration from professors when you want it. Many of our professors live on campus and enjoy being with students in the snack bar as well as in the classroom. They give you the best, most personal education as possible. A big bonus of small-college life is that everybody is invited to go out for everything, and you can be as much of a leader as you want to be. From athletics to debating to publications to fraternity life, this is part of the process that produces a well-rounded Hampden-Sydney graduate.

"Hampden-Sydney College requires either the SAT or ACT standardized test with essay. However, if a student has taken the old test and is satisfied with his scores, we will waive his taking the new test for 2006."

SELECTIVITY

Admissions Rating	**79**
# of applicants	1,207
% of applicants accepted	69
% of acceptees attending	38
# of early decision applicants	60
% accepted early decision	67

FRESHMAN PROFILE

Range SAT Verbal	520-620
Average SAT Verbal	571
Range SAT Math	520-630
Average SAT Math	573
**TPR Projected Range SAT Writing*	*570-650*
Range ACT Composite	21-28
Average ACT Composite	2
Minimum Paper TOEFL	570
Minimum Computer Based TOEFL	230
Average HS GPA	3.3
% graduated top 10% of class	13
% graduated top 25% of class	37
% graduated top 50% of class	80

DEADLINES

Early decision application deadline	11/15
Early decision notification	12/15
Regular application deadline	3/1
Regular notification	4/15
Nonfall registration?	yes

APPLICANTS ALSO LOOK AT AND OFTEN PREFER

University of Virginia, Virginia Tech

AND SOMETIMES PREFER

James Madison University, Sewanee—The University of the South, University of Georgia, University of Mississippi, University of North Carolina—Chapel Hill

AND RARELY PREFER

Randolph—Macon College

FINANCIAL FACTS

Financial Aid Rating	**81**
Annual tuition	$21,672
Room & Board	$7,370
Books and supplies	$900
Required fees	$910
% frosh rec. need-based scholarship or grant aid	54
% UG rec. need-based scholarship or grant aid	49
% frosh rec. need-based self-help aid	38
% UG rec. need-based self-help aid	39
% frosh rec. any financial aid	86
% UG rec. any financial aid	94
Avg. frosh grant	$17,936
Avg. frosh loan	$13,426
Independent 529 member?	Yes

HAMPSHIRE COLLEGE

ADMISSIONS OFFICE, 893 WEST STREET, AMHERST, MA 01002 • ADMISSIONS: 413-559-5471 • FAX: 413-559-5631

CAMPUS LIFE

Quality of Life Rating	**80**
Fire Safety Rating	**83**
Type of school	private
Environment	village

STUDENTS

Total undergrad enrollment	1,344
% male/female	43/57
% from out of state	84
% from public high school	70
% live on campus	93
% African American	3
% Asian	4
% Caucasian	72
% Hispanic	5
% international	3
# of countries represented	26

SURVEY SAYS

Small classes
No one cheats
Students aren't religious
Intercollegiate sports are unpopular or nonexistent
Frats and sororities are unpopular or nonexistent
Political activism is popular

ACADEMICS

Academic Rating	**88**
Calendar	4-1-4
Student/faculty ratio	12:1
Professors interesting rating	87
Professors accessible rating	84
% professors teaching UG courses	100
% classes taught by TAs	0
Most common lab size	fewer than 10 students
Most common regular class size	10-19 students

MOST POPULAR MAJORS

Liberal arts and sciences/liberal studies
social sciences
visual and performing arts

STUDENTS SPEAK OUT

Academics

Independent study and self-designed majors are the norm at Hampshire College, a small Pioneer Valley liberal arts school that "takes you up on your wager that all you need is academic freedom." Hampshire freshmen must complete the recently added First Year Program. ("Actual academic requirements for this year's freshman class have turned Hampshire mainstream," gripes one old-timer.) After that, students are pretty much on their own, although they must complete a concentration and an advanced study project. Most students meet the last two requirements through curricula of their own choosing. "Academically, Hampshire is a place where you can do whatever you want, as long as you are able to find a few professors who are willing to work with you on your self-constructed major," explains one student. Although the school is small, students' options are broadened considerably by Hampshire's participation in the Five-College Consortium, which allows students to cross-register at Amherst, Smith, University of Massachusetts, and Mount Holyoke. Some here warn that "Hampshire's academic structure is not for everyone. It's very well suited for people who have a strong idea of what they would like to study, but don't want to squeeze their interests into the confines of traditional majors. It's also good for people who want to explore several interests. However, if you're easily distracted and need someone to point you in a clear, well-defined direction, then Hampshire is probably not the place for you."

Life

"There's not much centralized activity" at Hampshire College, students here agree. As one student put it, "Everything is pretty laid-back and easygoing. People are really into the work they are doing, and they spend a lot of time thinking about that and talking to others about it." While campus is usually quiet, the other four area colleges and the towns of Amherst and Northampton offer all the action most students want. "If you're bored, it's your own fault," writes one undergrad. "The Pioneer Valley is a happening little place. Amherst and Northampton are both funky little college towns with lots to do in nice weather. There's excellent shopping at numerous vintage stores. The Pearl Street nightclub has cheap concerts every week. Ani DiFranco, Carrot Top, BB King, and Sonic Youth have been to Northampton at least once, to name a few." Furthermore, "if you want to escape, you can do that too. There are miles and miles of hiking trails within walking distance of campus, as well as biking trails. I knew that I wasn't going to have a car, so the free bus system was a humongous plus." Activity reaches its lowest ebb "during the long, hard winters." "That's when we start smoking marijuana," explains one student. Campus movies—"Indie, hip-hop, action, anime, classic low camp; we tend to like movies we can laugh with (or at least at)"—are also very popular.

Student Body

The "talented, artistic, quixotic, eccentric, and highly motivated" undergrads of Hampshire include a large group of "those kids in elementary school who were caught trying to dissect the pencil sharpener during math class. We're horrible at following rules." While students like to regard themselves as entirely unique, there is "definitely a stereotype of the pot-smoking, Phish-loving, hippie activist kid at Hampshire, and for the most part, I would say it's true." Critics might accuse these students of being self-absorbed; "I think that's true," agrees one undergrad. "We all spend a ridiculous amount of time thinking about ourselves and what we do, which makes us an incredibly self-aware (if sometimes egocentric) group of people." Politically, "Hampshire students are ultra-liberal. While many would claim that we are an open-minded community because all kinds of lifestyles and ethnic groups are accepted, just try bringing in a conservative speaker to campus, and students will be there quicker than the lifespan of a Hollywood marriage to protest, disrupt, and cause mayhem." Students are proud to report that Hampshire is extremely GLBT-friendly.

FINANCIAL AID: 413-559-5484 • E-MAIL: ADMISSIONS@HAMPSHIRE.EDU • WEBSITE: WWW.HAMPSHIRE.EDU

ADMISSIONS

Very important factors considered include: Essays, recommendations, secondary school record. *Important factors considered include:* Character/personal qualities, extracurricular activities, talent/ability. *Other factors considered include:* Alumni/ae relation, class rank, interview, minority status, standardized test scores, volunteer work, work experience. TOEFL required of all international applicants. High school diploma or equivalent is not required. *Academic units recommended:* 4 English, 4 math, 4 science (2 science lab), 3 foreign language, 2 social studies, 2 history.

The Inside Word

Don Quixote would be a fairly solid candidate for admission to Hampshire. The admissions committee (and it really is one, unlike at many colleges) looks to identify thinkers, dreamers, and the generally intellectually curious. It is important to have a solid record from high school, but high grades only go so far toward impressing the committee. Those who are denied usually lack self-awareness and are fairly poor communicators. Candidates should expect their essays to come under close scrutiny.

FINANCIAL AID

Students should submit: FAFSA, institution's own financial aid form, CSS/Financial Aid PROFILE, noncustodial (divorced/separated) parents' statement. Regular filing deadline is 2/1. The Princeton Review suggests that all financial aid forms be submitted as soon as possible after 1/1. *Need-based scholarships/grants offered:* Pell, SEOG, state scholarships/grants, private scholarships, the school's own gift aid. *Loan aid offered:* Direct Subsidized Stafford, Direct Unsubsidized Stafford, FFEL PLUS, Federal Perkins. Applicants will be notified of awards on or about 4/1. Off-campus job opportunities are good.

FROM THE ADMISSIONS OFFICE

"Students tell us they like our application. It is less derivative and more open-ended than most. Rather than assigning an essay topic, we ask to learn more about you as an individual and invite your ideas. Instead of just asking for lists of activities, we ask you how those activities (and academic or other endeavors) have shown some of the traits that lead to success at Hampshire (initiative, independence, persistence, for example). This approach parallels the work you will do at Hampshire, defining the questions you will ask and the courses and experiences that will help you to answer them, and integrating your interests.

"Hampshire College requires freshman applicants to submit scores from the old or new SAT. Students may also choose to submit scores from the ACT (with or without the Writing component) in lieu of the SAT."

SELECTIVITY

Admissions Rating	**87**
# of applicants	2,180
% of applicants accepted	59
% of acceptees attending	29
# accepting a place on wait list	436
% admitted from wait list	15
# of early decision applicants	38
% accepted early decision	62

FRESHMAN PROFILE

Range SAT Verbal	610-700
Average SAT Verbal	651
Range SAT Math	550-660
Average SAT Math	601
**TPR Projected Range SAT Writing*	*640-700*
Range ACT Composite	25-29
Average ACT Composite	27
Minimum Paper TOEFL	577
Minimum Computer Based TOEFL	233
Average HS GPA	3.28
% graduated top 10% of class	26
% graduated top 25% of class	33
% graduated top 50% of class	88

DEADLINES

Early decision application deadline	11/15
Early decision notification	12/15
Regular application deadline	1/15
Regular notification	4/1
Nonfall registration?	yes

APPLICANTS ALSO LOOK AT

AND OFTEN PREFER
Bard College
AND SOMETIMES PREFER
Sarah Lawrence College
AND RARELY PREFER
Skidmore College

FINANCIAL FACTS

Financial Aid Rating	**92**
Annual tuition	$31,939
Room & Board	$8,519
Books and supplies	$500
Required fees	$580
% frosh rec. need-based scholarship or grant aid	58
% UG rec. need-based scholarship or grant aid	56
% frosh rec. need-based self-help aid	58
% UG rec. need-based self-help aid	56
% frosh rec. any financial aid	70
% UG rec. any financial aid	61
Avg. frosh grant	$19,785
Avg. frosh loan	$2,625
Independent 529 member?	Yes

HAMPTON UNIVERSITY

OFFICE OF ADMISSIONS, HAMPTON UNIVERSITY, HAMPTON, VA 23668 • ADMISSIONS: 757-727-5328 • FAX: 757-727-5095

CAMPUS LIFE

Quality of Life Rating	**62**
Fire Safety Rating	**60**
Type of school	private
Environment	metropolis

STUDENTS

Total undergrad enrollment	5,200
% male/female	36/64
% from out of state	65
% from public high school	90
% live on campus	59
% in (# of) fraternities	5 (6)
% in (# of) sororities	4 (3)

SURVEY SAYS

Small classes
Great library
Everyone loves the Pirates
Frats and sororities dominate social scene
Musical organizations are popular
Student publications are popular
Student government is popular

ACADEMICS

Academic Rating	**73**
Calendar	semester
Student/faculty ratio	16:1
Professors interesting rating	65
Professors accessible rating	72
% professors teaching UG courses	100
% classes taught by TAs	0
Most common lab size	10-19 students
Most common regular class size	20-29 students

MOST POPULAR MAJORS

Business administration/ management
psychology

STUDENTS SPEAK OUT

Academics

"The spirit and pride of students is touching" at Hampton University (HU). Students at this historically Black school located on the gorgeous Virginia coastline enjoy a "strong business department" that draws about a quarter of its undergraduates. The school also boasts "a wonderful physics department with tons of research and scholarship opportunities" and an assortment of pre-medical sciences (one in ten grads go on to medical school thanks to a combination of these pre-medical courses). Communications and psychology are also very strong programs. Hampton takes "a very conservative approach" to academics; the school enforces a dress code and requires a rigorous, traditional curriculum. However, don't assume that the school doesn't keep pace with the times. Hampton is a highly connected university. Students say, "Technology on campus is a strong point. We have Web-based learning and registration, a large computer center in the library, T-3 connections, and great Ethernet access in dorm rooms, and the library." Additional perks include "lots of travel opportunities" and "a lot of opportunities for obtaining internships and doing research during the summer." Professors earn praise for being "down-to-earth and helpful." Students describe their professors as "good people and good teachers who really care about [them]." Students are less enthusiastic about the administration; students add, "[The administration] imposes way too many rules on the students. They have a tendency to treat us like children."

Life

Make no mistake about it, "HU has a lot of rules." Students must conform to a dress code that applies not only to academic time but also to most extracurricular activities. In addition, there is a dorm policy that makes male-female visitation hours "very scarce," and a code of conduct that some politically active students complain borders on repression of free speech. Hampton is "a drug-free campus and alcohol-free campus. People still drink and smoke weed on- and off-campus, but when they get caught, sometimes they get kicked out, and other times they receive severe punishments." It takes a lot of discipline to live in this type of strict environment. Students who can't adjust quickly grow to resent the restrictions, while students who can highly recommend Hampton life. One student says, "Hampton, also known as our 'home by the sea,' matches its challenging academic workload with its wonderful social atmosphere." Students tell us that "it's hard not to be active within the school. There are many different student organizations to join (fraternities, sororities, student government, and social, religious, political, and pre-alumni organizations)" and that there are many "poetry slams, spoken word events, talent shows, pageants, athletic events, and interesting on-campus seminars" to enjoy. The "beautiful waterfront campus always has an inspiring view and is kept immaculately clean." Virginia Beach and Norfolk are only a half-hour's drive off, so it's imperative "to either have a car or buddy up with someone with a car."

Student Body

Hampton is known in some circles as a stronghold of the wealthy and ostentatious. Some students say the image is justified. Explains one student, "Most—though definitely not all—Hampton students are privileged, upper-class, young Black people, and many do not recognize their privilege. Our bourgeois reputation is pretty accurate. You are likely to [see] designer clubbing attire and stiletto boots at 8:00 in the morning in January for no reason." A few students offer a somewhat different perspective. One student adds, "You see the Hampton stereotype, the stuck-up people, but that's not everyone. We're usually talking about them, and they usually don't have that many friends. The few they have are just like them, and they need to stick together." Hampton students are generally "hardworking, determined, fun loving, and very goal oriented," and they are appreciative of their school's HBCU (Historic Black Colleges and Universities) standing. "It's great to be surrounded by Black people who are trying to better themselves one way or another," sums up one undergraduate.

HAMPTON UNIVERSITY

FINANCIAL AID: 800-624-3341 • E-MAIL: ADMIT@HAMPTONU.EDU • WEBSITE: WWW.HAMPTONU.EDU

ADMISSIONS

Very important factors considered include: Character/personal qualities, essays, secondary school record, standardized test scores. *Important factors considered include:* Class rank, recommendations. *Other factors considered include:* Alumni/ae relation, extracurricular activities, talent/ability, volunteer work. SAT Reasoning or ACT required. TOEFL required of all international applicants. High school diploma is required, and GED is accepted. *Academic units required:* 4 English, 3 math, 2 science (2 science lab), 2 social studies, 6 academic electives. *Academic units recommended:* 2 foreign language.

The Inside Word

Hampton has less general visibility than such better-known historically Black colleges as Morehouse, Spelman, and Howard, but it has just as much of a tradition of academic quality. In recent years the university's profile has been boosted by hosting national workshops on counseling minority students in the college admissions process. Candidates can expect a personal and caring experience in the admissions process.

FINANCIAL AID

Students should submit: FAFSA, state aid form. The Princeton Review suggests that all financial aid forms be submitted as soon as possible after 1/1. *Need-based scholarships/grants offered:* Pell, SEOG, state scholarships/grants, private scholarships, the school's own gift aid, Federal Nursing scholarships. *Loan aid offered:* Direct Subsidized Stafford, Direct Unsubsidized Stafford, Direct PLUS, FFEL Subsidized Stafford, FFEL Unsubsidized Stafford, FFEL PLUS, Federal Perkins, alternative loans. Applicants will be notified of awards on a rolling basis beginning on or about 4/15. Federal Work-study Program available. Off-campus job opportunities are excellent.

FROM THE ADMISSIONS OFFICE

"Hampton attempts to provide the environment and structures most conducive to the intellectual, emotional, and aesthetic enlargement of the lives of its members. The university gives priority to effective teaching and scholarly research while placing the student at the center of its planning. Hampton will ask you to look inwardly at your own history and culture and examine your relationship to the aspirations and development of the world.

"As of this book's publication, Hampton University did not have information available about their policy regarding the new SAT."

SELECTIVITY

Admissions Rating	**83**
# of applicants	9,218
% of applicants accepted	57
% of acceptees attending	1

FRESHMAN PROFILE

Range SAT Verbal	470-560
Average SAT Verbal	526
Range SAT Math	460-550
Average SAT Math	516
**TPR Projected Range SAT Writing*	*530-600*
Range ACT Composite	17-21
Average ACT Composite	20
Minimum Paper TOEFL	550
Average HS GPA	3.0
% graduated top 10% of class	20
% graduated top 25% of class	45
% graduated top 50% of class	90

DEADLINES

Regular notification	rolling
Nonfall registration?	yes

APPLICANTS ALSO LOOK AT AND OFTEN PREFER

Florida A&M University
Spelman College
Tuskegee University

AND SOMETIMES PREFER

Howard University
University of Maryland—College Park
Virginia Tech

FINANCIAL FACTS

Financial Aid Rating	**74**
Annual tuition	$12,116
Room & Board	$6,424
Books and supplies	$770
Required fees	$1,390
% frosh rec. need-based scholarship or grant aid	15
% UG rec. need-based scholarship or grant aid	9
% frosh rec. need-based self-help aid	63
% UG rec. need-based self-help aid	57
Avg. frosh grant	$2,885
Avg. frosh loan	$2,254
Independent 529 member?	No

HANOVER COLLEGE

PO BOX 108, HANOVER, IN 47243-0108 • ADMISSIONS: 812-866-7021 • FAX: 812-866-7098

CAMPUS LIFE

Quality of Life Rating	**71**
Fire Safety Rating	**83**
Type of school	private
Affiliation	Presbyterian
Environment	rural

STUDENTS

Total undergrad enrollment	1,048
% male/female	46/54
% from out of state	30
% from public high school	85
% live on campus	96
% in (# of) fraternities	29 (5)
% in (# of) sororities	33 (4)
% African American	2
% Asian	3
% Caucasian	85
% Hispanic	1
% international	4
# of countries represented	17

SURVEY SAYS

Small classes
Lab facilities are great
Athletic facilities are great
Students are friendly
Low cost of living
Frats and sororities dominate social scene
Lots of beer drinking

ACADEMICS

Academic Rating	**87**
Calendar	4-4-1
Student/faculty ratio	11:1
Professors interesting rating	89
Professors accessible rating	89
% professors teaching UG courses	100
% classes taught by TAs	0
Most common regular class size	10-19 students

MOST POPULAR MAJORS

Business administration/management
chemistry
sociology

STUDENTS SPEAK OUT

Academics

Not far from the banks of the Ohio River in southeastern Indiana, Hanover College is the site of a beautiful campus where over 1,000 students pursue a liberal arts education. Hanover's small campus equals one large family. Most students speak glowingly about "professors who are accessible and extremely knowledgeable." In fact, students say that professors at Hanover are not only teachers but also "they're friends." A freshman says that "two married [professors] even included us in deciding whether to buy a big-screen TV." While it's tough to find a student at Hanover who'll complain about the professors, the jury's still out on the overall educational experience. Some undergraduates say that "every class offered challenges students to grow and develop skills of critical thinking," but others admit that they "could be pushed a little harder." One former high school valedictorian pleads, "More focus on academics! Less recruitment of football players!" A like-minded psychology major says that Hanover would make its academic offerings stronger if the college focused its "recruiting and catering" efforts on "top academic students." Fortunately, when students have grievances like these, they know that the administration is "very accessible and always willing to hear out students' opinions." One thing that the administration and students don't agree about is the campus-wide alcohol policy. A freshman explains, "The administration is currently banging heads with students over the drinking policy."

Life

Hanover is a small college located in a small, quiet Indiana town. "Because it's a small town, most activities are limited to campus," says a sophomore. A junior adds, "People often complain that there is nothing to do, but if you look at all Hanover offers, there are such a variety of organizations and programs that I have hardly any free time." Of the social opportunities offered on campus, "intramural sports and events through Greek life and Student Programming are the most popular things to do." While many of the on-campus events slow down on the weekends, fraternities and sororities spice up Hanover's nightlife. Although many students "go out to the fraternities for fun," some students want something more. One dissenting theater major says, "Students have no meaningful activities outside of class, and there is a void that the fraternities attempt to fill with booze." When students decide to seek fun in the surrounding community, they find that it "doesn't offer much more than Wal-Mart, fast-food restaurants, and movie theaters." On the flipside, this "small community" does provide a sense of security. One student says, "The fact that you can leave your backpack anywhere and the next day you will find it exactly where you left it" is very comforting. Just up the road from Hanover, the city of Madison provides a wider range of recreational outlets, renowned wineries, antique shops, fine dining, and historic architecture.

Student Body

Hanover's motto is "Powered by Thought," so it shouldn't be surprising to hear that one psychology major say of his classmates, "Some are very self-motivated." But he is quick to add, "While others are not." The major discrepancy within Hanover's student body is that some students are very academically minded, other students are decidedly not academically minded, and the rest fall somewhere in between. Aside from the varying academic goals, however, the "students are pretty much the same"—at least in terms of being largely "Christian, white, middle class/upper class, [and] Midwestern." Although students will readily concede that "Hanover is not incredibly diverse," they point out that "for its size and location, it does a good job of recruiting students from around the world." In fact, Hanover's 1,000 students represent 28 states and 17 countries. And with few exceptions, these students get along well. When asked what the greatest strengths of Hanover College are, a sophomore says, "The community."

FINANCIAL AID: 812-866-7030 • E-MAIL: ADMISSION@HANOVER.EDU • WEBSITE: WWW.HANOVER.EDU

ADMISSIONS

Very important factors considered include: Class rank, secondary school record. *Important factors considered include:* Essays, recommendations, standardized test scores, talent/ability. *Other factors considered include:* Alumni/ae relation, character/personal qualities, extracurricular activities, geographical residence, interview, minority status, state residency, volunteer work, work experience. SAT Reasoning or ACT required. TOEFL required of all international applicants. High school diploma is required, and GED is not accepted. *Academic units required:* 3 English, 3 math, 3 science (2 science lab), 2 foreign language, 2 social studies, 2 history, 2 academic electives. *Academic units recommended:* 4 English, 4 math, 4 science (3 science lab), 4 foreign language, 3 social studies, 3 history, 3 academic electives.

The Inside Word

Despite significant national publicity in recent years, Hanover still has a relatively small applicant pool. There is no doubt that these candidates are capable academically—few schools have as impressive a graduation rate or percentage of its alums going on to grad school. It pays to put some energy into the completion of the application process, especially given the sizable percentage of students awarded academic scholarships.

FINANCIAL AID

Students should submit: FAFSA. The Princeton Review suggests that all financial aid forms be submitted as soon as possible after 1/1. *Need-based scholarships/grants offered:* Pell, state scholarships/grants, private scholarships, the school's own gift aid. *Loan aid offered:* FFEL Subsidized Stafford, FFEL Unsubsidized Stafford, FFEL PLUS. Applicants will be notified of awards on or about 3/15. Institutional employment available. Off-campus job opportunities are fair.

FROM THE ADMISSIONS OFFICE

"Hanover College offers a unique community to all who live here. With 98 percent of our students residing on campus, the pursuit of academic excellence extends well beyond the confines of the classroom. This is enhanced by a caring faculty, 82 percent of whom hold earned doctoral degrees. The desire to meet academic challenges and the strong sense of community may be the two greatest contributors to the 88 percent retention rate of which Hanover is quite proud. These contributions are also apparent in that over the past five years more than 65 percent of our graduates have advanced their educational degrees. Hanover's total cost qualifies the college as one of the best values in the nation, and its sizable endowment, on a dollar-per-student ratio, places it in the top 10 percent nationally.

"Students applying for admission for the fall 2006 entering class are required to take the new version of the SAT (or the ACT with the writing section), but we will allow students to submit scores from the old (prior to March 2005) version of the SAT (or ACT) as well, and will use the students best scores from either test."

SELECTIVITY

Admissions Rating	**83**
# of applicants	1,659
% of applicants accepted	75
% of acceptees attending	31
# accepting a place on wait list	74
% admitted from wait list	38

FRESHMAN PROFILE

Range SAT Verbal	530-640
Average SAT Verbal	584
Range SAT Math	540-640
Average SAT Math	586
**TPR Projected Range SAT Writing*	*580-660*
Range ACT Composite	22-28
Average ACT Composite	25
Minimum Paper TOEFL	550
Minimum Computer Based TOEFL	213
% graduated top 10% of class	36
% graduated top 25% of class	71
% graduated top 50% of class	95

DEADLINES

Regular application deadline	3/1
Regular notification	rolling
Nonfall registration?	yes

APPLICANTS ALSO LOOK AT

AND OFTEN PREFER
Butler University
DePauw University

AND SOMETIMES PREFER
Centre College
Indiana University—Bloomington
Miami University
University of Evansville
Wabash College
Wittenberg University

AND RARELY PREFER
Earlham College
Kenyon College

FINANCIAL FACTS

Financial Aid Rating	**84**
Annual tuition	$21,150
Room & Board	$6,500
Books and supplies	$900
Required fees	$500
% frosh rec. need-based scholarship or grant aid	78
% UG rec. need-based scholarship or grant aid	66
% frosh rec. need-based self-help aid	46
% UG rec. need-based self-help aid	48
% frosh rec. any financial aid	96
% UG rec. any financial aid	93
Avg. frosh grant	$16,663
Avg. frosh loan	$2,783
Independent 529 member?	No

HARVARD COLLEGE

BYERLY HALL, 8 GARDEN STREET, CAMBRIDGE, MA 02138 • ADMISSIONS: 617-495-1551 • FAX: 617-495-8821

CAMPUS LIFE

Quality of Life Rating	**89**
Fire Safety Rating	**60**
Type of school	private
Environment	metropolis

STUDENTS

Total undergrad enrollment	6,649
% male/female	53/47
% from out of state	84
% from public high school	65
% live on campus	96
% African American	8
% Asian	18
% Caucasian	42
% Hispanic	8
% Native American	1
% international	7

SURVEY SAYS

Registration is a breeze
Great library
Students love Cambridge, MA
Student publications are popular

ACADEMICS

Academic Rating	**96**
Calendar	semester
Student/faculty ratio	8:1
Professors interesting rating	79
Professors accessible rating	71
% professors teaching UG courses	100
% classes taught by TAs	0
Most common lab size	fewer than 10 students
Most common regular class size	fewer than 10 students

MOST POPULAR MAJORS

Economics
political science and government
psychology

STUDENTS SPEAK OUT

Academics

"Harvard has distinguished faculty, an extremely accomplished and diverse student body, a million and one extracurriculars, and very generous alumni," a student at this ne plus ultra of American academia explains, adding "What more could you ask for from a school?" What more, indeed? With "unparalleled academics" and "a huge endowment that really allows Harvard to give its students every available resource," Harvard has it all for the aspiring intellectual. By throwing in Cambridge and Boston, have we discovered academic nirvana? Close, but not quite. Students complain that "Harvard would benefit from a more active advising system, because a substantial number of courses, including many options for fulfilling requirements under the core program, are offered only once every two years, and many students don't realize this." Even so, the pros far outweigh the cons here. Students especially love the "high number of tutorials and seminars, which are always taught by a professor to a small group of students. They are a great chance to find a mentor." They're also pretty psyched about "interacting with and learning from world experts in almost every subject" and their access to "the best university library in America." Four in five students admitted here attend; that figure pretty much says it all.

Life

"In terms of life in general, there is a lot of studying" at Harvard, "but letting it rule your life means you miss out on so many experiences. The happiest Harvard students are probably those who do their schoolwork but make sure that they have a life outside of it. Otherwise, you never meet people and you stress yourself out." Cambridge and Boston offer plenty of opportunities to get out, but "unfortunately, it's too easy to just get stuck on campus, especially since there's always something going on." Students report that "there is always a cultural show, musical concert, movie showing, information session, graduate-school talk, or colloquium to attend, and the hardest part is balancing all of the work with all the other interesting options on campus." Student clubs and organizations pull double duty, "serving a strong social function; for example, the board of the Gilbert and Sullivan Players has lots of meetings and produces shows, but then we throw about six parties a semester." Undergrads here tell us that "most people do one or two extracurriculars, often pretty intensely. There's not that frantic volunteering for everything that distinguishes the future Harvard student in high school. Once we get in, we skip the resume padders and only do the stuff we're actually into doing." Just about everyone here "lives on campus in the huge suites," and "since we are allowed to have parties with alcohol in our suites, that is a popular social activity."

Student Body

Harvard can handpick top candidates to create the degree of student diversity it wants, so it should come as no surprise that "there is no 'typical' student here. You get someone from West Philly who is the first person in his family to go to college; you have the daughter of a Saudi prince, who will be married to a 60-year-old oil baron after graduation; you get 'development cases' and legacies, with surnames like Kilroy and Lynch; and you get a range of students from blue- to white-collar backgrounds." Explains one student, "The admissions process goes to great lengths to find students that they feel will add to the community at Harvard. As a result, even a simple meal in the dining hall is always an entertaining part of the day, just laughing and goofing off with friends, or even debating about political issues." Undergrads here tend to be "multitalented, overextended, articulate," and "secure in their own fabulousness, so they really don't brag, and they'll totally be happy for you if you do something cool."

HARVARD COLLEGE

FINANCIAL AID: 617-495-1581 • E-MAIL: COLLEGE@FAS.HARVARD.EDU • WEBSITE: WWW.FAS.HARVARD.EDU

ADMISSIONS

Very important factors considered include: Character/personal qualities, extracurricular activities, recommendations, secondary school record, talent/ability. *Important factors considered include:* Class rank, essays, interview, standardized test scores. *Other factors considered include:* Alumni/ae relation, geographical residence, minority status, volunteer work, work experience. SAT Reasoning or ACT required. High school diploma or equivalent is not required. *Academic units recommended:* 4 English, 4 math, 4 science, 4 foreign language.

The Inside Word

It just doesn't get any tougher than this. Candidates to Harvard face dual obstacles—an awe-inspiring applicant pool and, as a result, admissions standards that defy explanation in quantifiable terms. Harvard denies admission to the vast majority, and virtually all of them are top students. It all boils down to splitting hairs, which is quite hard to explain and even harder for candidates to understand. Rather than being as detailed and direct as possible about the selection process and criteria, Harvard keeps things close to the vest—before, during, and after. They even refuse to admit that being from South Dakota is an advantage. Thus the admissions process does more to intimidate candidates than to empower them. Moving to a common application seemed to be a small step in the right direction, but with the current explosion of early decision applicants and a super-high yield of enrollees, things are not likely to change dramatically.

FINANCIAL AID

Students should submit: FAFSA, CSS/Financial Aid PROFILE, noncustodial (divorced/separated) parents' statement, business/farm supplement, tax returns. The Princeton Review suggests that all financial aid forms be submitted as soon as possible after 1/1. *Need-based scholarships/grants offered:* Pell, SEOG, state scholarships/grants, private scholarships, the school's own gift aid. *Loan aid offered:* Direct Subsidized Stafford, Direct Unsubsidized Stafford, Direct PLUS, Federal Perkins, state loans, college/university loans from institutional funds. Applicants will be notified of awards on or about 4/1. Federal Work-study Program available. Institutional employment available. Off-campus job opportunities are excellent.

FROM THE ADMISSIONS OFFICE

"The admissions committee looks for energy, ambition, and the capacity to make the most of opportunities. Academic ability and preparation are important, and so is intellectual curiosity—but many of the strongest applicants have significant nonacademic interests and accomplishments as well. There is no formula for admission, and applicants are considered carefully, with attention to future promise.

"Freshman applicants for fall 2006 may submit either the old SAT taken before March 2005, or the new SAT. The ACT with Writing component is also accepted. All students must also submit three SAT Subject Tests of their choosing."

SELECTIVITY

Admissions Rating	**99**
# of applicants	19,609
% of applicants accepted	11
% of acceptees attending	79

FRESHMAN PROFILE

Range SAT Verbal	700-800
Range SAT Math	700-790
**TPR Projected Range SAT Writing*	*700-760*
Range ACT Composite	30-34
% graduated top 10% of class	90
% graduated top 25% of class	98
% graduated top 50% of class	100

DEADLINES

Regular application deadline	1/1
Regular notification	4/1
Nonfall registration?	no

AND SOMETIMES PREFER

Princeton University
Stanford University
University of Pennsylvania
Yale University

AND RARELY PREFER

Amherst College
Georgetown University
Northwestern University
Williams College

FINANCIAL FACTS

Financial Aid Rating	**95**
Annual tuition	$26,066
Room & Board	$8,868
Books and supplies	$2,522
Required fees	$2,994
% frosh rec. need-based scholarship or grant aid	47
% UG rec. need-based scholarship or grant aid	48
% frosh rec. need-based self-help aid	34
% UG rec. need-based self-help aid	41
Avg. frosh grant	$23,750
Avg. frosh loan	$1,100
Independent 529 member?	No

HARVEY MUDD COLLEGE

301 EAST 12TH STREET, CLAREMONT, CA 91711-5990 • ADMISSIONS: 909-621-8011 • FAX: 909-621-8360

CAMPUS LIFE

Quality of Life Rating	**88**
Fire Safety Rating	**75**
Type of school	private
Environment	town

STUDENTS

Total undergrad enrollment	720
% male/female	70/30
% from out of state	15
% from public high school	80
% live on campus	95
% African American	1
% Asian	18
% Caucasian	49
% Hispanic	6
% international	4
# of countries represented	16

SURVEY SAYS

No one cheats
Lab facilities are great
Great computer facilities
Students are friendly
Low cost of living
Frats and sororities are unpopular or nonexistent

ACADEMICS

Academic Rating	**97**
Calendar	semester
Student/faculty ratio	8:1
Professors interesting rating	98
Professors accessible rating	99
% professors teaching UG courses	100
% classes taught by TAs	0
Most common lab size	20-29 students
Most common regular class size	10-19 students

MOST POPULAR MAJORS

Computer and information sciences
engineering
physics

STUDENTS SPEAK OUT

Academics

"Incredible math, science, and engineering programs," delivered in "a small school atmosphere, but with four other undergraduate schools [Claremont McKenna, Pomona, Pitzer, and Scripps Colleges] in walking distance," distinguish Harvey Mudd College, a tiny "powerhouse [where] every department is fantastic." Students love the "world-renowned" physics department and remind us that "every year we do extraordinarily well in math competitions." They also insist that "we have the best undergraduate chemistry department in the world and our engineering department is likewise top-notch." But what students love most is the professors who "choose to teach here because they want to focus on teaching, not on research; as a result, everything is organized around making the classes as good as possible, not around getting that next grant dollar." Whatever research is done here "provides opportunities for undergraduates to conduct original research with professors, usually over the summers (but sometimes during the semester)." The workload is massive and the grading system is brutal; "They really take their anti-grade inflation stance a bit too seriously," complains one student. Students shoulder their load in a "cooperative, accepting environment. At times it definitely feels like everyone sticks together because we're all going through a trial by fire." An "awesome honor code" sets the tone for the campus; there's "complete trust among all students and faculty. Most tests are self-administered take-home tests." A "broad range of requirements in both other sciences and humanities...ensure that students learn their field starting from a very strong and expansive background."

Life

"There is a lot of work to be done, and a lot of time is spent either doing homework or reading for class," Mudd students report, adding that "other than that, there are a great number of things people do for fun: sports, video/computer games, parties, movies," and "random acts of weirdness." Explains one student, "Every dorm has unusual traditions and pastimes. Mine has 'dorm togetherness activities,' which usually involve isopropanol and matches, and then food. Another dorm has competitions to see who can go to the most doughnut shops the fastest. Another has pick-up games of unicycle hockey." 'Pranking' is "a staple of campus culture, and one that the administration encourages." Pranks are "usually harmless, and everyone enjoys them. For example: Once people from Atwood, one of the dorms, snuck into another dorm, Sontag, to 'steal' the sofas and put them on Atwood's roof as a display of superiority." Students also entertain themselves by "leaving campus to see plays, visit museums, go to theme parks (Disneyland is only 30 minutes away), go to the beach, or explore Los Angeles." There are also four other Claremont campuses to enjoy. Mudd students brag that their campus "has the best parties of all the five Cs," but not the nicest campus; "Campus beauty is certainly lacking. The local decor is made up of squares of concrete we call warts: interesting, but not exactly inspiring."

Student Body

HMC students form "an incredible community" in which "everyone looks out for each other." Community is built into HMC's curriculum; one student explains, "Everyone takes Mudd's massive core that for the most part completely dictates the classes you will take as a freshman. As a result, the freshmen get to know each other really fast and quickly form many friendships. This sense of community is strengthened by the fact that dorms are not segregated by class year. By the end of the semester, there are countless friendships and relationships that extend across the class lines, which are close to nonexistent." Students grant that "a typical student at Mudd is probably a little more on the dorky side than your average American college student" because "Mudders all have an affinity for math and science, and some of us can get pretty obsessed with those subjects, [but] on the whole, Mudders aren't just a bunch of nerds. Almost everyone is friendly, most of us are pretty sociable and fun-loving, and some people are just plain partiers."

HARVEY MUDD COLLEGE

FINANCIAL AID: 909-621-8055 • E-MAIL: ADMISSION@HMC.EDU • WEBSITE: WWW.HMC.EDU

ADMISSIONS

Very important factors considered include: Character/personal qualities, class rank, essays, recommendations, secondary school record, standardized test scores. *Important factors considered include:* Alumni/ae relation, interview. *Other factors considered include:* Extracurricular activities, geographical residence, minority status, talent/ability, volunteer work, work experience. SAT Reasoning Test required. TOEFL required of all international applicants. High school diploma is required, and GED is accepted. *Academic units required:* 4 English, 4 math, 3 science (3 science lab). *Academic units recommended:* 2 foreign language, 1 social studies, 1 history.

The Inside Word

Harvey Mudd is a place for serious students, and its admissions process expects excellence from all candidates. Not to say that they don't have a sense of humor out there in Claremont. The college attracted national attention in the past by mailing recruitment literature that poked fun at the overly serious world of college admissions while at the same time showcasing the school's academic quality. Any admissions staff that contributes to the lessening of student stress in the college search and admissions process is to be commended.

FINANCIAL AID

Students should submit: FAFSA, CSS/Financial Aid PROFILE, state aid form, noncustodial (divorced/separated) parents' statement, business/farm supplement. Regular filing deadline is 2/1. The Princeton Review suggests that all financial aid forms be submitted as soon as possible after 1/1. *Need-based scholarships/grants offered:* Pell, SEOG, state scholarships/grants, private scholarships, the school's own gift aid. *Loan aid offered:* FFEL Subsidized Stafford, FFEL Unsubsidized Stafford, FFEL PLUS, Federal Perkins, college/university loans from institutional funds. Applicants will be notified of awards on or about 4/1. Federal Work-study Program available. Institutional employment available. Off-campus job opportunities are fair.

FROM THE ADMISSIONS OFFICE

"Students interested in HMC must have a talent and passion for science and mathematics. The college offers majors in mathematics, physics, engineering, chemistry, biology, and computer science. 'Mudders' have very diverse interests. Because nearly one-third of the course work at HMC is in the humanities and social sciences, HMC students also enjoy studying economics, psychology, philosophy, history, the fine arts, and literature.

"Freshman applicants for fall 2006 are required to submit test scores from the new SAT test. Scores submitted from the old (prior to March 2005) SAT will be accepted. The student's best composite score will be used in the admission process. SAT Subject Tests are required: Math Level II and one examination of choice. In addition, students submitting old SAT scores must also submit SAT Subject Test in Writing."

SELECTIVITY

Admissions Rating	**96**
# of applicants	1,904
% of applicants accepted	38
% of acceptees attending	27
# accepting a place on wait list	259
% admitted from wait list	13
# of early decision applicants	43
% accepted early decision	49

FRESHMAN PROFILE

Range SAT Verbal	610-730
Average SAT Verbal	700
Range SAT Math	710-800
Average SAT Math	750
**TPR Projected Range SAT Writing*	*640-720*
Minimum Paper TOEFL	600
Average HS GPA	3.8
% graduated top 10% of class	93
% graduated top 50% of class	100

DEADLINES

Early decision application deadline	11/15
Early decision notification	12/15
Regular application deadline	1/15
Regular notification	4/1
Nonfall registration?	no

APPLICANTS ALSO LOOK AT AND OFTEN PREFER

Massachusetts Institute of Technology
Stanford University

AND SOMETIMES PREFER

Cornell University
Rice University

AND RARELY PREFER

Virginia Tech
Worcester Polytechnic Institute

FINANCIAL FACTS

Financial Aid Rating	**95**
Annual tuition	$29,553
Room & Board	$9,485
Books and supplies	$800
Required fees	$684
% frosh rec. need-based scholarship or grant aid	58
% UG rec. need-based scholarship or grant aid	52
% frosh rec. need-based self-help aid	42
% UG rec. need-based self-help aid	47
% frosh rec. any financial aid	85
% UG rec. any financial aid	82
Avg. frosh grant	$16,439
Avg. frosh loan	$3,657
Independent 529 member?	Yes

HAVERFORD COLLEGE

370 W. LANCASTER AVENUE, HAVERFORD, PA 19041 • ADMISSIONS: 610-896-1350 • FAX: 610-896-1338

CAMPUS LIFE

Quality of Life Rating	**98**
Fire Safety Rating	**72**
Type of school	private
Environment	town

STUDENTS

Total undergrad enrollment	1,172
% male/female	47/53
% from out of state	81
% from public high school	57
% live on campus	99
% African American	6
% Asian	13
% Caucasian	71
% Hispanic	6
% Native American	1
% international	3
# of countries represented	38

SURVEY SAYS

Small classes
No one cheats
Lab facilities are great
Students are friendly
Campus feels safe
Students are happy
Frats and sororities are unpopular or nonexistent

ACADEMICS

Academic Rating	**98**
Calendar	semester
Student/faculty ratio	8:1
Professors interesting rating	95
Professors accessible rating	98
% professors teaching UG courses	100
% classes taught by TAs	0
Most common lab size	fewer than 10 students
Most common regular class size	10-19 students

MOST POPULAR MAJORS

Economics
English language and literature

STUDENTS SPEAK OUT

Academics

Haverford College "is the quintessence of the liberal arts experience: superb academics with an emphasis on teacher/student interaction." Originally a Quaker school, Haverford has "never forgotten its Quaker roots" and accordingly "is a community committed to the ideals of taking responsibility for your actions." This is a "high-pressure academic environment" but also "cooperative and nonthreatening." Students warn, "The sciences and math here are hard core; the humanities are somewhat less challenging," though "professors who are brilliant people and who truly care about their students" are there to ensure undergraduates' success. Haverford's Honor Code plays a prominent role in fostering a sense of unity; "the honor code here is amazing; it promotes a lot of trust and freedom in the community, which the students love," explains one undergrad. Students receive the red carpet treatment from the moment they arrive; "Haverford knows how to take care of freshmen," explains one undergrad. "When you come here, you get Customs People (like RAs, except cooler), Honor Code Orienteers, an Upper Class Advisor, Peer Awareness Facilitators, a faculty advisor, and a dean. So there are a million people whom you can go to for help and advisement." For those students with wanderlust, "Our study abroad office is excellent! I'm studying at the London School of Economics this year thanks to my accessible, helpful, and alarmingly organized study abroad dean." Students speak in similarly glowing terms about the rest of the administration, noting also the large degree of autonomy afforded them in running the school. Explains one student, "In terms of the administrators, Haverford is mostly run by the students. We start our own organizations. We allocate where the Student Council funds go."

Life

Haverford's rigorous curriculum means that "during the week, work pretty much dominates everything. Even if, by luck, you do not have work to do, all of your friends do, so you are pretty much bound to stay in the dorm." Students unwind on weekends, enjoying "a lot of activities, like dances, plays, concerts, and musicals. Last weekend, we had a play, a formal dance, a musical performance, and an improv group. It's pretty easy to find activities to keep you busy." While some here take advantage of nearby Philadelphia ("good history and culture, as well as a club scene and places like South Street to hang out at"), most tend to stick close to campus. And what a campus! "It's so beautiful that it's practically unbearable," gushes one undergrad. Parties here are generally low-key and usually involve alcohol and other substances; as with academics, the Honor Code applies. Reports one student, "I'm impressed by the leniency and respectfulness of security and the administration vis-à-vis drinking and substance use. They definitely trust students to be responsible for themselves and for one another, and I think that for the most part, that trust is well placed." Students report an active intramural sports program, lots of clubs and organizations (with ample opportunities to start your own), and a fair amount of political activity, most of which leans leftward.

Student Body

As befits an elite liberal arts school, Haverford is home to a student body "good at more things than you can count on your fingers and toes, and interested in just about everything." More than one student confided that "the typical student is a cool dork: someone with really funky interests and life experiences who loves sharing and learning, even if s/he's not amazing at performing or shmoozing a crowd." Most "probably own a pair of Birkenstocks but aren't quite as leftist as they make themselves out to be." Complains one conservative, "Haverford is accepting of anyone except for nonleft-wingers." While most feel that "there is a good amount of diversity here," especially for such a small, expensive school, many also report that the school needs to make an "effort to increase the diversity."

FINANCIAL AID: 610-896-1350 • E-MAIL: ADMITME@HAVERFORD.EDU • WEBSITE: WWW.HAVERFORD.EDU

ADMISSIONS

Very important factors considered include: Character/personal qualities, recommendations, secondary school record, standardized test scores. *Important factors considered include:* Class rank, essays, extracurricular activities, volunteer work. *Other factors considered include:* Alumni/ae relation, geographical residence, interview, minority status, talent/ability, work experience. TOEFL required of all international applicants. High school diploma is required, and GED is accepted. *Academic units required:* 4 English, 3 math, 1 science (1 science lab), 3 foreign language, 1 social studies. *Academic units recommended:* 4 math, 2 science.

The Inside Word

Candidate evaluation at Haverford is quite thorough, and the applicant pool is sizable and strong. Applicants who are successful through the initial academic review are then carefully considered for the match they make with the college. This part of the process is especially important at small schools like Haverford, and students should definitely spend some time assessing the reasons for their interest in attending before responding to essays and interviewing. Interviewing is a must.

FINANCIAL AID

Students should submit: FAFSA, CSS/Financial Aid PROFILE, state aid form, noncustodial (divorced/separated) parents' statement, business/farm supplement. Regular filing deadline is 1/31. The Princeton Review suggests that all financial aid forms be submitted as soon as possible after 1/1. *Need-based scholarships/grants offered:* Pell, SEOG, state scholarships/grants, private scholarships, the school's own gift aid. *Loan aid offered:* FFEL Subsidized Stafford, FFEL Unsubsidized Stafford, FFEL PLUS, Federal Perkins. Applicants will be notified of awards on or about 4/8. Federal Work-study Program available. Institutional employment available. Off-campus job opportunities are good.

FROM THE ADMISSIONS OFFICE

"Haverford strives to be a college in which integrity, honesty, and concern for others are dominant forces. The college does not have many formal rules; rather, it offers an opportunity for students to govern their affairs and conduct themselves with respect and concern for others. Each student is expected to adhere to the Honor Code as it is adopted each year by the Students' Association. Haverford's Quaker roots show most clearly in the relationship of faculty and students, in the emphasis on integrity, in the interaction of the individual and the community, and through the college's concern for the uses to which its students put their expanding knowledge. Haverford's 1,100 students represent a wide diversity of interests, backgrounds, and talents. They come from public, parochial, and independent schools across the United States, Puerto Rico, and twenty-eight foreign countries. Students of color are an important part of the Haverford community.

"Haverford College requires that all applicants submit the results of the new three-part SAT I exam or the ACT with the optional writing test. Two SAT Subject Tests are required."

SELECTIVITY

Admissions Rating	**97**
# of applicants	3,035
% of applicants accepted	29
% of acceptees attending	37
# accepting a place on wait list	831
# of early decision applicants	102
% accepted early decision	44

FRESHMAN PROFILE

Range SAT Verbal	640-740
Range SAT Math	640-720
**TPR Projected Range SAT Writing*	*660-720*
Minimum Paper TOEFL	600
Minimum Computer Based TOEFL	250
% graduated top 10% of class	79
% graduated top 25% of class	93
% graduated top 50% of class	100

DEADLINES

Early decision application deadline	11/15
Early decision notification	12/15
Regular application deadline	1/15
Regular notification	4/15
Nonfall registration?	no

APPLICANTS ALSO LOOK AT AND OFTEN PREFER

Brown University
Harvard College
Princeton University
Wellesley College
Yale University

AND SOMETIMES PREFER

Amherst College
Bryn Mawr College
Swarthmore College
University of Pennsylvania
Williams College

FINANCIAL FACTS

Financial Aid Rating	**80**
Annual tuition	$29,990
Room & Board	$9,420
Books and supplies	$1,028
Required fees	$280
% frosh rec. need-based scholarship or grant aid	40
% UG rec. need-based scholarship or grant aid	40
% frosh rec. need-based self-help aid	38
% UG rec. need-based self-help aid	38
% frosh rec. any financial aid	41
% UG rec. any financial aid	40
Avg. frosh grant	$21,762
Avg. frosh loan	$5,575
Independent 529 member?	No

HENDRIX COLLEGE

1600 WASHINGTON AVENUE, CONWAY, AR 72032 • ADMISSIONS: 501-450-1362 • FAX: 501-450-3843

CAMPUS LIFE

Quality of Life Rating	**86**
Fire Safety Rating	**75**
Type of school	private
Affiliation	Methodist
Environment	town

STUDENTS

Total undergrad enrollment	1,036
% male/female	43/57
% from out of state	42
% from public high school	80
% live on campus	85
% African American	4
% Asian	3
% Caucasian	70
% Hispanic	3
% Native American	2
% international	1
# of countries represented	10

SURVEY SAYS

Small classes
Lab facilities are great
Frats and sororities are unpopular or nonexistent

ACADEMICS

Academic Rating	**88**
Calendar	semester
Student/faculty ratio	11:1
Professors interesting rating	98
Professors accessible rating	96
% professors teaching UG courses	100
% classes taught by TAs	0
Most common lab size	10-19 students
Most common regular class size	10-19 students

MOST POPULAR MAJORS

Biology/biological sciences
history
psychology

STUDENTS SPEAK OUT

Academics

"The opportunities available are amazing" at Hendrix College, a small liberal arts school near Little Rock where students here benefit from "more than enough available money for research and special projects," especially in the school's well-respected science programs. For students in the sciences as well as the humanities, Hendrix offers a wide range of choices: "It doesn't matter what you're interested in academically, you will find faculty that will amaze you and that will open your mind to things you've never imagined," explains one junior. In all areas, "the academic environment feels collaborative." Hendrix is a place "where you are challenged daily in a rigorous academic setting"; as a result, students feel prepared to undertake "serious graduate work." Students describe professors as "truly exceptional," writing that they "are extremely accessible and go out of their way to help students." "This is not a school for people to fall into the cracks," notes a sophomore. The solid alumni network is hailed as "phenomenal." Writes one junior: "People who attend Hendrix really do stay connected for life." Students also praise the "very strong and plentiful financial aid packages." They worry, however, about course administrators that are plotting for the future. In the words of one international relations major, "There is a widely shared perception among students that the higher-ups have an agenda for Hendrix: to attract a wealthier, cleaner-cut brand of student to a pricier, cleaner-cut school... For high school graduates in a state with shocking rates of poverty and the most financially-strapped public schools in the nation, the increasing elitism of the state's premier liberal arts school cannot be a good thing."

Life

Most students agree that Hendrix is a largely self-contained community; undergrads don't spend a lot of time mixing in with either the residents of Conway or students at the town's two other schools, University of Central Arkansas and Central Baptist College. "It is not unusual not to leave campus for two or three days at a time," explains one student, and "this can lead to some serious cabin fever." Fortunately, Hendrix "always has something to offer pretty much every day of the week, from study break type events to lectures and concerts, drive-in movie nights, etc." There are "strong focuses in the campus on music and art," as well. "You name it, we've pretty much done it." "There is no Greek system," notes a junior; but students here still keep busy. Hendrix "even has Friday Afternoon Discussions on the most interesting topics, such as 'What do your dreams really mean?' or 'Women in modern religious movements.' Students are always engaged in conversations." "When the weather is nice, people often sit outside to study, chat, or toss around a Frisbee™." To get "good food" (and alcohol; Hendrix is in a "dry" county), "you have to make the 30-minute drive into Little Rock." Overall, writes one sophomore, "daily life is pretty laid back, and we like it that way."

Student Body

A number of students write that "at Hendrix, typical is atypical." Nevertheless, a few students supplied generalizations like the following: "most students are vegetarian, politically leftist, middle-class, interested in social justice issues, attentive, and incredibly involved... It doesn't feel too homogenous though. Some students are really rich or really poor; a few (a very few) vote Republican…and some of us are slackers. A few of us even eat meat." Undergrads pride themselves on their tolerance; explains one, "This is the most accepting and supportive crowd I've ever been around. Here, Bush-lovers (though they are a minority) and Bush-haters respectfully debate, devout Christians and atheists room together, and heterosexuals and homosexuals are best friends." Some here see a trend developing with each incoming class: "It does seem like the student body is tending more and more towards the athletic, ballcap-wearing, woo-hoo-Spring-Break-in-Cancun, business major folks," observes one undergrad. Although a number of students write that Hendrix "could definitely be more ethnically diverse," many still characterize the atmosphere as "accepting."

FINANCIAL AID: 501-450-1368 • E-MAIL: ADM@HENDRIX.EDU • WEBSITE: WWW.HENDRIX.EDU

ADMISSIONS

Very important factors considered include: Essays, secondary school record, standardized test scores. *Important factors considered include:* Character/personal qualities, class rank, extracurricular activities, interview, recommendations. *Other factors considered include:* Minority status, talent/ability, volunteer work. SAT Reasoning or ACT required. TOEFL required of all international applicants. High school diploma is required, and GED is accepted. *Academic units recommended:* 4 English, 3 math, 2 science, 2 foreign language, 3 social studies.

The Inside Word

Hendrix has a small but well-qualified applicant pool. The college is a sleeper, and is an especially good bet for students with strong grades who lack the test scores usually necessary for admission to colleges on a higher level of selectivity. Look for Hendrix to get tougher as they continue to garner attention from national publications. This place has been making the lists, and it is solid.

FINANCIAL AID

Students should submit: FAFSA, state aid form. The Princeton Review suggests that all financial aid forms be submitted as soon as possible after 1/1. *Need-based scholarships/grants offered:* Pell, SEOG, state scholarships/grants, private scholarships, the school's own gift aid. *Loan aid offered:* FFEL Subsidized Stafford, FFEL Unsubsidized Stafford, FFEL PLUS, Federal Perkins, Methodist loan. Applicants will be notified of awards on a rolling basis beginning on or about 3/1. Federal Work-study Program available. Institutional employment available. Off-campus job opportunities are excellent.

FROM THE ADMISSIONS OFFICE

"Hendrix students are participants, not spectators. They like to be involved and they like to know that what they do makes a difference. Hendrix students are voting members of almost every campus committee, which gives them an important voice in college governance. They are very hands-on about their education as well. Internships, study abroad, research projects, service projects, expressive arts projects and leadership development—these are all areas that Hendrix students find attractive. In fall 2005, Hendrix will introduce a new program that guarantees every Hendrix student will have at least three hands-on experiences selected from six categories. The program is called *Your Hendrix Odyssey: Engaging in Active Learning*. Students will receive transcript credit for their Odyssey projects. The benefits of this hands-on approach to learning are so obvious that we believe every Hendrix student should have the opportunity to participate. The college is raising money to provide grants and fellowships that will help remove the economic barriers to participation in out-of-class experiences. It is an exciting time to be a Hendrix student! The Hendrix curriculum is demanding, but the environment is one of support and cooperation—not competition. Hendrix students form a close-knit, inclusive community. They build lifetime connections and close friendships, the kind of relationships that grow in a residential college where learning is a 24/7 kind of thing. It doesn't hurt that the campus is beautifully maintained and that Hendrix graduates are admitted to top graduate schools and recruited for good jobs around the world.

"Hendrix College has no preference on which test (SAT/ACT) or version (old/new) is taken, but we strongly encourage all applicants to take one of the tests during their senior year. While the Writing scores will be considered, at this point weight will be given to the Critical Reading and Math of the SAT and the required sections of the ACT."

SELECTIVITY

Admissions Rating	**88**
# of applicants	1,027
% of applicants accepted	85
% of acceptees attending	34
# accepting a place on wait list	2

FRESHMAN PROFILE

Range SAT Verbal	590-700
Average SAT Verbal	642
Range SAT Math	560-670
Average SAT Math	609
**TPR Projected Range SAT Writing*	*620-700*
Range ACT Composite	24-30
Average ACT Composite	27
Minimum Paper TOEFL	550
Minimum Computer Based TOEFL	215
Average HS GPA	3.6
% graduated top 10% of class	38
% graduated top 25% of class	69
% graduated top 50% of class	91

DEADLINES

Regular application deadline	8/1
Regular notification	rolling
Nonfall registration?	yes

APPLICANTS ALSO LOOK AT

AND OFTEN PREFER

Rhodes College
University of Arkansas—Fayetteville
University of Central Arkansas

AND SOMETIMES PREFER

Southwestern University
The University of Texas—Austin
Trinity University

AND RARELY PREFER

Austin College
Lyon College

FINANCIAL FACTS

Financial Aid Rating	**84**
Annual tuition	$21,336
Room & Board	$6,010
Books and supplies	$900
Required fees	$300
% frosh rec. need-based scholarship or grant aid	60
% UG rec. need-based scholarship or grant aid	55
% frosh rec. need-based self-help aid	46
% UG rec. need-based self-help aid	45
% frosh rec. any financial aid	96
% UG rec. any financial aid	98
Avg. frosh grant	$10,315
Avg. frosh loan	$3,565
Independent 529 member?	Yes

Hillsdale College

33 East College Street, Hillsdale, MI 49242 • Admissions: 517-607-2327 • Fax: 517-607-2223

CAMPUS LIFE

Quality of Life Rating	**75**
Fire Safety Rating	**60**
Type of school	private
Environment	village

STUDENTS

Total undergrad enrollment	1,273
% male/female	48/52
% from out of state	56
% from public high school	60
% live on campus	85
% in (# of) fraternities	35 (3)
% in (# of) sororities	45 (3)
% international	2

SURVEY SAYS . . .

Small classes
No one cheats
Students are friendly
Low cost of living
Political activism is popular

ACADEMICS

Academic Rating	**92**
Calendar	semester
Student/faculty ratio	11:1
Profs interesting rating	98
Profs accessible rating	97
% profs teaching UG courses	100
% classes taught by TAs	0
Most common reg class size	less than 10 students

MOST POPULAR MAJORS

Biology/biological sciences
business administration and management
history

STUDENTS SPEAK OUT

Academics

"Hillsdale is built on a vision," students at this small school "steeped in the wisdom from classical Western history" tell us. That vision involves "imparting the wisdom of the past ages" through immersion in "Greco-Roman and Judeo-Christian classics" in order to "wrestle with the difficult questions facing the contemporary world." Everyone here agrees the school is conservative, although not everyone agrees on the term's exact meaning; some see the school exclusively as "a defender of free markets, limited government, and other conservative values," while others have a more nuanced view, telling us that "we're conservative in that we reach to the past to expand the number of interlocutors in class discussion, one incarnation of the 'Great Conversation.' That, I believe, defines Hillsdale and its true academic character." Coursework here is "challenging, with a strong emphasis on reading and writing." Required classes guarantee that "each student takes a class on the Constitution, Western Heritage, American Heritage, and the Great Books (The Odyssey, Dante's Inferno, Confessions of St. Augustine, etc)." History, classics, sciences, and business are all considered strong majors here; "If you want to go into politics or business, this is the place for you; there is a huge network of alums and donors waiting to give you jobs," writes one student. Sums up one student, "Hillsdale caters to students dissatisfied with 'modern' education and hungry for learning steeped in the wisdom from classical Western history. The emphasis is definitely on what is old and traditional, not what is new and trendy. Hillsdale is about grasping with the ideas, ideas that are fundamental to the human experience in history."

Life

"At Hillsdale, you have to be able to create your own fun," because the school is located in "a typical, small Midwestern town surrounded by cornfields, and it's not considered the most exciting place in the world." The student body, like the town, "is very small, and therefore no one is presenting you with 50 entertainment options every night." Campus life does offer some options; Greek life is very popular, and there's also "Swing Dancing on Friday nights; lessons and a band are available on campus and many people attend." Undergrads also "attend theatrical or musical performances, and the arts are well-supported here." There are parties, but a well-enforced dry campus policy means they must be found in off-campus houses. Hillsdale's sports program draws less interest, as it "is a significant weakness. We should not be a Division II school—we are far too small." As one student puts it, "May God have mercy on our football team, for our opponents have none." Popular road trip destinations include Jackson, Lansing, and Ann Arbor, the last of which "is only 50 minutes away. There countless coffee houses, book stores, restaurants, and night clubs can be found."

Student Body

"Typical students are smart and religious" at Hillsdale; they "go to church every Sunday and his/her religious beliefs come out in how he/she speaks and acts." Students guess that "about 11 percent are home schoolers," with many others arriving from religious prep schools. Although unified in their religious conservatism, students split on the issue of their right to party. An undergrad explains, "One group consists of overly-religious, holier-than-thou people who condemn the slightest bit of socialization. The second group are the ones standing on the speakers at a frat party with a beer in their hand. There is no middle ground, and everyone is a conservative white Christian." Just about everyone here has a passion for the world of ideas; as one student puts it, "Hillsdale is only really attractive to people who enjoy learning; people who want a degree that is more than just career preparation." Another adds, "Get ready for rich conversation, where invocations or allusions to Homer, Virgil, Augustine, Aquinas, Dante, Shakespeare, Descartes, Kant, Dickens, and T. S. Eliot are frequent, and the best students become part of a rich intellectual tradition."

FINANCIAL AID: 517-437-7341 • E-MAIL: ADMISSIONS@HILLSDALE.EDU/ADMISSIONS • WEBSITE: WWW.HILLSDALE.EDU

ADMISSIONS

Very important factors considered include: Character/personal qualities, secondary school record, standardized test scores. *Important factors considered include:* Class rank, essays, extracurricular activities, interview, recommendations, volunteer work, work experience. *Other factors considered include:* Alumni/ae relation, talent/ability. SAT Reasoning or ACT required; TOEFL required of all international applicants. High school diploma is required and GED is accepted. *Academic units recommended:* 4 English, 4 math, 3 science, (1 science lab), 2 foreign language, 1 social studies, 2 history.

Inside Word

Don't let Hillsdale's high acceptance rate fool you: at this point, the only folks who apply to this school are serious, solid candidates. As the school's national reputation grows, expect the number of applications to tick upward. While you don't have to be a political conservative to get in, a passionate and well-reasoned personal essay defending conservative values certainly can't hurt you.

FINANCIAL AID

Students should submit: FAFSA, institution's own financial aid form, noncustodial (divorced/separated) parent's statement, business/farm supplement, state aid form. The Princeton Review suggests that all financial aid forms be submitted as soon as possible after January 1. *Need-based scholarships/grants offered:* state scholarships/grants, private scholarships, the school's own gift aid,. *Loan aid offered:* College/university loans from institutional funds. Applicants will be notified of awards on a rolling basis beginning or about February 15. Institutional employment available. Off-campus job opportunities are good.

FROM THE ADMISSIONS OFFICE

"Personal attention is a hallmark at Hillsdale. Small classes are combined with teaching professors who make their students a priority. The academic environment at Hillsdale will actively engage you as a student. Extracurricular activities abound at Hillsdale with the over 50 clubs and organizations that offer excellent leadership opportunities. From athletics and the fine arts, to Greek life and community volunteer programs, you will find it difficult not to be involved in our thriving campus community. In addition, numerous study abroad programs, a conservation research venture in South Africa, a professional sales internship program with national placements and the Washington-Hillsdale Internship Program (WHIP) are just a few of the unique off-campus opportunities available to you at Hillsdale.

"Our strength as a college is found in our mission and in our curriculum. The core curriculum at Hillsdale contains the essence of the classical liberal arts education. Through it you are introduced to the history, the philosophical and theological ideas, the works of literature and the scientific discoveries that set Western Civilization apart. As explained in our mission statement, 'The college considers itself a trustee of modern man's intellectual and spiritual inheritance from the Judeo-Christian faith and Greco-Roman culture, a heritage finding its clearest expression in the American experiment of self-government under law.'

"We seek students who are ambitious, intellectually curious and who are ready to become leaders worthy of this heritage in their personal as well as professional lives.

"Applicants for fall of 2006 can meet admissions requirements by submitting the results of one of three tests: the new SAT, the old SAT (taken prior to March 2005), or the ACT (Writing section optional). We will use the student's best composite/combined score in the evaluation process. The SAT Subject Tests in Literature and U.S. History are recommended."

SELECTIVITY

Admissions Rating	**89**
# of applicants	1,060
% of applicants accepted	82
% of acceptees attending	43

FRESHMAN PROFILE

Range SAT Verbal	600-720
Average SAT Verbal	660
Range SAT Math	560-660
Average SAT Math	610
**TPR Projected Range SAT Writing*	*630-710*
Range ACT Composite	24-29
Average ACT Composite	27
Minimum Paper TOEFL	550
Minimum Computer Based TOEFL	200
Average HS GPA	3.6
% graduated top 10% of class	40
% graduated top 25% of class	78
% graduated top 50% of class	98

DEADLINES

Regular notification	rolling
Nonfall registration?	yes

FINANCIAL FACTS

Financial Aid Rating	**83**
Annual tuition	$17,000
Room & Board	$6,750
Books and supplies	$850
Required fees	$410
% frosh rec. need-based scholarship or grant aid	90
% UG rec. need-based scholarship or grant aid	86
% frosh rec. need-based self-help aid	90
% UG rec. need-based self-help aid	86
% frosh rec. any financial aid	83
% UG rec. any financial aid	86
Avg. frosh grant	$11,000
Avg. frosh loan	$3,500
Independent 529 member?	No

HIRAM COLLEGE

PO BOX 67, HIRAM, OH 44234 • ADMISSIONS: 800-362-5280 • FAX: 330-569-5944

CAMPUS LIFE

Quality of Life Rating	**71**
Fire Safety Rating	**70**
Type of school	private
Affiliation	Disciples of Christ
Environment	rural

STUDENTS

Total undergrad enrollment	1,087
% male/female	43/57
% from public high school	86
% live on campus	88
% African American	11
% Asian	1
% Caucasian	81
% Hispanic	1
% international	3
# of countries represented	17

SURVEY SAYS

Small classes
Great library
Students are friendly
Campus feels safe
Low cost of living
Lots of beer drinking

ACADEMICS

Academic Rating	**87**
Calendar	other
Student/faculty ratio	10:1
Professors interesting rating	87
Professors accessible rating	88
% professors teaching UG courses	100
% classes taught by TAs	0
Most common lab size	10-19 students
Most common regular class size	fewer than 10 students

MOST POPULAR MAJORS

Business/commerce
education

STUDENTS SPEAK OUT

Academics

One satisfied undergraduate tells us, "I believe that the education that most people get at Hiram is strong and often surpasses educations from larger institutions." Students at the college "want to suck the marrow out of their educational experience" and describe the course load as "challenging enough that it isn't a walk in the park, but it's not overwhelming by any means." Students feel legit calling most professors by their first names: "They want to get to know me as a person and not just another student in the classroom." Professors merit gold stars because "they are very willing to devote their time to help students or just to talk. This goes even for professors whose classes you might not be currently attending." Most instructors are "very understanding, down-to-earth people who encourage individual thought," and even grab lunch with students and send timely e-mail help over the weekends. The administration comes in a distant second in the popularity contest among the "grownups." Students cite "a lot of miscommunication" between departments. In all fairness, one student writes, "I know of very few other places where deans know many students' names." Other respondents call the staff "helpful," "attentive," and "available to explain their decisions."

Life

On certain desperate nights at Hiram, when "we'll be so bored that we'll just go and walk at night because that's the only thing to do," students have an eerie moment, and "the sudden realization that you are living in a cornfield begins to set in." Students quickly learn to accept the situation and make the best of it. Common weekend activities include "going from dorm to dorm drinking" and "driving to Taco Bell or Wal-Mart." Student organizations attempt to fill the activity void with events such as "toga parties, Springfest, Halloween, the Hiram version of Greek pledging, Homecoming, and athletic-related events." Students can hop the shuttle to Cleveland on Saturday nights, since "most programming is over by nine or so, and there's nothing else to do besides get into trouble." However, not everyone complains of tedium; in fact, there are "a lot of students who enjoy the peacefulness of Hiram," a place that manages to "teach you about the real world in a safe, almost surreal setting."

Student Body

Hiram is a school that "prides itself on being culturally diverse." Students report, "We have a very diverse group of students from all ethnic and economic groups" as well as people with "all sorts of backgrounds and belief structures." Even in this Hiram salad bowl, a few people notice that the population seems "almost segregated down racial lines sometimes." One student observes "tension between minority students or international students and white students." Nonetheless, respondents express a heartening enthusiasm regarding diversity: "It has been a great pleasure learning about so many cultures!" Reportedly, aside from being humanoid, "no two people are even remotely similar," but at the same time, "there is a group of people for everyone." These posses "tend to be a little on the exclusive side," limited to people with the same "interests, major, or residence hall," according to one respondent. Other common bonds include a past as "freaks in high school" and an interest in "discussing issues on a deeper level." One student summarizes the crew as "a friendly community who cares about what goes on around them and is accepting to new thoughts and ideas."

FINANCIAL AID: 330-569-5107 • E-MAIL: ADMISSION@HIRAM.EDU • WEBSITE: WWW.HIRAM.EDU

ADMISSIONS

Very important factors considered include: Secondary school record. *Important factors considered include:* Character/personal qualities, extracurricular activities, standardized test scores, talent/ability. *Other factors considered include:* Alumni/ae relation, class rank, essays, interview, minority status, recommendations, volunteer work, work experience. SAT Reasoning or ACT required. TOEFL required of all international applicants. High school diploma is required, and GED is accepted. *Academic units required:* 4 English, 3 math, 3 science (2 science lab), 2 foreign language, 3 social studies, 1 history, 2 academic electives. *Academic units recommended:* 3 foreign language.

The Inside Word

Students with consistent academic records will find little difficulty in gaining admission. The applicant pool is decidedly local; out-of-state candidates benefit from their scarcity.

FINANCIAL AID

The Princeton Review suggests that all financial aid forms be submitted as soon as possible after 1/1.

FROM THE ADMISSIONS OFFICE

"Hiram College offers several distinctive programs that set us apart from other small, private liberal arts colleges. Over half of Hiram's students participate in our nationally recognized study abroad program at some point during their four years here. In 2001–2002, Hiram faculty lead trips to England, France, Costa Rica, Pakistan, Greece, and Turkey; in 2002–2003, we visited Australia, Germany, Denmark, Zimbabwe, Israel, Guatemala, and Mexico. Because Hiram students receive credits for the courses taught by faculty on these trips, studying abroad will not impede progress in their majors or delay graduation. Another unique aspect of a Hiram education is our academic calendar, known as the Hiram Plan. Our semesters are divided into twelve-week and three-week periods. Students usually enroll in three courses during each twelve-week period, and one intensive course during the three-week periods. Many students spend the three-week periods on study abroad trips or taking unusual courses not typically offered during the twelve-week periods. In addition to numerous study abroad options and the Hiram Plan, our small classes (the average class size is fifteen) encourage interaction between students and their professors, both in and out of the classroom. Students can work with professors on original research projects, and often participate in musical groups and intramural sports teams alongside faculty members.

"For fall 2006 admission, Hiram College will accept either the new SAT or the old SAT, administered prior to March 2005 without a Writing component. The school will also accept the ACT with or without the Writing component."

SELECTIVITY

Admissions Rating	**82**
# of applicants	828
% of applicants accepted	86
% of acceptees attending	31

FRESHMAN PROFILE

Range SAT Verbal	510-640
Average SAT Verbal	573
Range SAT Math	490-600
Average SAT Math	566
**TPR Projected Range SAT Writing*	*570-660*
Range ACT Composite	21-26
Average ACT Composite	24
Minimum Paper TOEFL	550
Average HS GPA	3.39
% graduated top 10% of class	27
% graduated top 25% of class	55
% graduated top 50% of class	82

DEADLINES

Regular application deadline	4/15
Regular notification	rolling
Nonfall registration?	yes

APPLICANTS ALSO LOOK AT

AND OFTEN PREFER

Denison University
Kenyon College

AND SOMETIMES PREFER

The College of Wooster
John Carroll University

AND RARELY PREFER

Kent State University—Kent Campus
University of Akron

FINANCIAL FACTS

Financial Aid Rating	**60**
Annual tuition	$21,360
Room & Board	$7,103
Books and supplies	$600
Required fees	$500
Avg. frosh grant	$10,998
Avg. frosh loan	$5,176
Independent 529 member?	Yes

HOBART AND WILLIAM SMITH COLLEGES

629 SOUTH MAIN STREET, GENEVA, NY 14456 • ADMISSIONS: 315-781-3472 • FAX: 315-781-3471

CAMPUS LIFE

Quality of Life Rating	**74**
Fire Safety Rating	**96**
Type of school	private
Environment	village

STUDENTS

Total undergrad enrollment	1,825
% male/female	46/54
% from out of state	53
% from public high school	65
% live on campus	90
% in (# of) fraternities	15 (5)
% African American	4
% Asian	2
% Caucasian	87
% Hispanic	4
% international	2
# of countries represented	18

SURVEY SAYS

Small classes
Great computer facilities
Great library
Everyone loves the Statesmen
Lots of beer drinking
Hard liquor is popular

ACADEMICS

Academic Rating	**87**
Calendar	semester
Student/faculty ratio	11:1
Professors interesting rating	87
Professors accessible rating	85
% professors teaching UG courses	100
% classes taught by TAs	0
Most common regular class size	10-19 students

MOST POPULAR MAJORS

Economics
English language and literature
history

STUDENTS SPEAK OUT

Academics

"Immense study abroad opportunities, great internships, [and] an emphasis on interdisciplinary courses, majors, and minors" are among the chief attributes of Hobart and William Smith Colleges (HWS), a pair of associated single-sex colleges that share a campus, faculty, and administration. Students appreciate the "small, personal classes" that "require student involvement." This intimate setting helps to foster "a great sense of community." One student explains, "Everyone is friendly here—profs, students, and administration. Profs actually care about happiness of the students." Accordingly, instructors—who "provide both liberal and conservative viewpoints and encourage you to think outside of the box"—receive high grades from their students. Undergraduates especially praise their accessibility; one student says, "Teachers have met with me outside their office hours and been at school for extra help sessions as late as 10:00 P.M. because students still had questions," though it hasn't kept students from winning one Rhodes and five Goldwater scholarships over the past six years. As is the case with many small schools, "some programs are underfunded." Most students accept these limitations as the cost of close, caring instruction. One science student explains, "HWS is very supportive of work done off campus. I personally have done research at a different, larger university."

Life

Students report that the school is home to many different social scenes. Because "athletic programs are top notch," one scene revolves around sports; at least a few students say they're too busy studying and practicing to do much else. Another scene focuses on the "many organizations here that are easy to get involved with, and every organization is eager to have help." There's also the orbit of the "Student Life Office that coordinates many events on campus; FolkFest and HWS Day draw almost all of the student body out." The largest scene of all, however, is the party scene. HWS kids "have parties in their rooms or they go out together to the frats, which always have parties. The downtown bars are very popular, too." One student adds, "There is a large group of people that just think about Wednesday night, Friday night, and Saturday night parties and going to the bars." The campus "is absolutely beautiful, especially in the warm weather. When spring comes around, everyone comes together on the quad and you couldn't imagine being happy anywhere else." Hometown Geneva is "a small town with very few good restaurants and places to hang out. Many of us like to take weekend trips to Ithaca, Rochester, and Syracuse."

Student Body

Hobart and William Smith has a reputation as a stronghold of rich preppies, and while the stereotype has some basis in truth, it doesn't tell the whole story. One student says, "People like to characterize the typical 'Smithy'—the rich stuck-up girl—as the norm at our school. And there are a lot of people like this, probably more so than other schools. But there are also so many different people with unique personalities, and once you take your concentration away from the negative and become open to people, you realize that the majority of students are really nice." Another student points out, "upper-class students seem to stand out more. However, according to all the data they feed us, a large percentage of us are on financial aid!" One student describes the various ways everyone spends their time: "There are students here that go to class and do their work and chill at night. Then there are those students that get involved, set up new clubs, compete in athletics, and organize study groups. All students on this campus [can] find a group/club for them to get involved with and easily fit in."

HOBART AND WILLIAM SMITH COLLEGES

FINANCIAL AID: 315-781-3315 • E-MAIL: ADMISSIONS@HWS.EDU • WEBSITE: WWW.HWS.EDU

ADMISSIONS

Very important factors considered include: Essays, secondary school record. *Important factors considered include:* Character/personal qualities, class rank, extracurricular activities, recommendations, standardized test scores, volunteer work, work experience. *Other factors considered include:* Alumni/ae relation, geographical residence, interview, minority status, talent/ability. SAT Reasoning or ACT required. TOEFL required of all international applicants. High school diploma is required, and GED is accepted. *Academic units required:* 4 English, 3 math, 3 science (2 science lab), 2 foreign language, 2 social studies, 2 history, 2 academic electives. *Academic units recommended:* 3 foreign language, 4 academic electives.

The Inside Word

Hobart and William Smith lose a lot of students to their competitors, who are many and strong. This helps open up the gates a bit for more candidates. However, the schools' location, right on Seneca Lake, offers students a great place to study.

FINANCIAL AID

Students should submit: FAFSA, CSS/Financial Aid PROFILE, state aid form, noncustodial (divorced/separated) parents' statement, parents' and students' tax returns. Regular filing deadline is 2/1. The Princeton Review suggests that all financial aid forms be submitted as soon as possible after 1/1. *Need-based scholarships/grants offered:* Pell, SEOG, state scholarships/grants, private scholarships, the school's own gift aid. *Loan aid offered:* FFEL Subsidized Stafford, FFEL Unsubsidized Stafford, FFEL PLUS, Federal Perkins. Applicants will be notified of awards on or about 4/1. Federal Work-study Program available. Off-campus job opportunities are fair.

FROM THE ADMISSIONS OFFICE

"Hobart and William Smith Colleges seek students with a sense of adventure and a commitment to the life of the mind. Inside the classroom, students find the academic climate to be rigorous, with a faculty that is deeply involved in teaching and working with them. Outside, they discover a supportive community that helps to cultivate a balance and hopes to foster an integration among academics, extracurricular activities, and social life. Hobart and William Smith, as coordinate colleges, have an awareness of gender differences and equality and are committed to respect and a celebration of diversity.

"Freshman applicants for fall 2006 class are required to take either the ACT (old or new, with or without the optional Writing portion) or either version of the SAT. Their highest composite score will be used in admissions decisions. Students are encouraged to submit results of any SAT Subject Test they have taken."

SELECTIVITY

Admissions Rating	**87**
# of applicants	3,266
% of applicants accepted	63
% of acceptees attending	23
# accepting a place on wait list	338
% admitted from wait list	7
# of early decision applicants	106
% accepted early decision	79

FRESHMAN PROFILE

Range SAT Verbal	540-630
Average SAT Verbal	550
Range SAT Math	545-640
Average SAT Math	600
**TPR Projected Range SAT Writing*	*590-650*
Range ACT Composite	24-27
Minimum Paper TOEFL	550
Minimum Computer Based TOEFL	220
Average HS GPA	3.23
% graduated top 10% of class	31
% graduated top 25% of class	55
% graduated top 50% of class	95

DEADLINES

Early decision application deadline	11/15
Early decision notification	12/15
Regular application deadline	2/1
Regular notification	4/1
Nonfall registration?	no

APPLICANTS ALSO LOOK AT

AND OFTEN PREFER

Colgate University, Connecticut College, Trinity College (CT)

AND SOMETIMES PREFER

Dickinson College, Gettysburg College, Kenyon College, Skidmore College, St. Lawrence University

AND RARELY PREFER

Ithaca College, SUNY College at Geneseo, University of Rochester

FINANCIAL FACTS

Financial Aid Rating	**92**
Annual tuition	$30,076
Room & Board	$7,987
Books and supplies	$850
Required fees	$567
% frosh rec. need-based scholarship or grant aid	59
% UG rec. need-based scholarship or grant aid	61
% frosh rec. need-based self-help aid	48
% UG rec. need-based self-help aid	53
% frosh rec. any financial aid	74
% UG rec. any financial aid	64
Avg. frosh grant	$23,902
Avg. frosh loan	$2,356
Independent 529 member?	Yes

HOFSTRA UNIVERSITY

ADMISSIONS CENTER, BERNON HALL, HEMPSTEAD, NY 11549 • ADMISSIONS: 516-463-6700 • FAX: 516-463-5100

CAMPUS LIFE

Quality of Life Rating	**62**
Fire Safety Rating	**85**
Type of school	private
Environment	city

STUDENTS

Total undergrad enrollment	8,869
% male/female	47/53
% from out of state	27
% live on campus	44
% in (# of) fraternities	5 (18)
% in (# of) sororities	6 (10)
% African American	10
% Asian	4
% Caucasian	62
% Hispanic	8
% international	2
# of countries represented	61

SURVEY SAYS

Small classes
Great computer facilities
Great library
Lots of beer drinking
Hard liquor is popular
(Almost) everyone smokes

ACADEMICS

Academic Rating	**76**
Calendar	4-1-4
Student/faculty ratio	14:1
Professors interesting rating	68
Professors accessible rating	64
% professors teaching UG courses	79
% classes taught by TAs	0
Most common lab size	10-19 students
Most common regular class size	10-19 students

MOST POPULAR MAJORS

Accounting
marketing/marketing management
psychology

STUDENTS SPEAK OUT

Academics

For many who attend this up-and-coming university on Long Island, "Hofstra's growing academic reputation is its strength. It seems everywhere you turn, somebody tells you what a great school Hofstra is." Students are especially proud of the school's offerings in business, history, education, English, and communications. They also love that "the location is great for job opportunities" although some students complain that "the career center caters too much to business majors (and not enough [to] everyone else!)." You will find different types of professors at Hofstra. Students report, "Half of the professors are interested in teaching, and half of them could care less." Some people blame the spotty teaching on the student body; "professors are into the class if the students show a genuine interest." The administration receives a universal thumbs-down from undergraduates. One student adds, "You have better luck [of] getting something done [at] the DMV." However, in recent years, the school has taken note of this and have begun making universal improvements in student services.

Life

Much of Hofstra's active social scene revolves around Greek organizations and the bars surrounding the campus. "Time management is very important," writes one conscientious student. "Because we have so many bars close by, partying can take over one's life." Although "there are no Greek houses on campus, "fraternites and sororities sponsor many campus social events, most of which are well attended." Support for team sports, however, is not strong: "We have more winning teams than not amongst our intercollegiate teams, but nobody seems to care. Even for Homecoming, only half the stadium gets filled. That's just pathetic." Some students find the situation on and around campus stultifying; one student says, "The lack of campus life and activity is very depressing," a few students on the flip side, claim that "the greatest strength of the school is that everything is there for you—the clubs, sports, career services—you just have to go and seek them." Many students board the Long Island Railroad and trek into nearby New York City. While several students don't claim to be happy, a few stalwart Hofstra boosters claim, "there aren't really a lot of valid reasons for this unhappiness. The school has a lot to offer if students would just get off their asses and take advantage of it." Among other things, students can enjoy the "beautiful campus," complete with an arboretum.

Student Body

Students report that Hofstra has more than its fair share of status-conscious students. "Students always attend classes as if they are a fashion show, wearing Gucci and Armani and acting like they are in their late twenties," writes one student. Another student agrees, "It is common to see a Hofstra student with a cell phone in one hand and a cigarette in the other. And don't forget their Mercedes, BMW, or Expedition blasting the latest song." Most students hail "from Long Island, Boston, or New Jersey," and everyone here, we're told, "fits into one of four groups: Greek, commuter, jock, and 'other.'" Regarding the temperment of their peers, student opinion varies from "most are really friendly" to "they're New Yorkers, so they just seem unfriendly until you get to know them."

HOFSTRA UNIVERSITY

FINANCIAL AID: 516-463-6680 • E-MAIL: ADMITME@HOFSTRA.EDU • WEBSITE: WWW.HOFSTRA.EDU

ADMISSIONS

Very important factors considered include: Class rank, essays, recommendations, secondary school record, standardized test scores. *Important factors considered include:* Character/personal qualities, extracurricular activities, interview, talent/ability. *Other factors considered include:* Alumni/ae relation, geographical residence, minority status, volunteer work, work experience. SAT Subject Tests recommended. TOEFL required of all international applicants. High school diploma is required, and GED is accepted. *Academic units required:* 4 English, 3 math, 3 science (1 science lab), 2 foreign language, 3 social studies. *Academic units recommended:* 4 math, 4 science, 3 foreign language, 4 social studies.

The Inside Word

Hofstra wants to be national and has positioned itself very well with impressive facilities, appealing program offerings, solid athletic teams, and an effective national ad campaign. As a result, Hofstra's current student profile has increased dramatically. Presently, Hofstra is a solidly competitive regional university; it is a school to watch in the future.

FINANCIAL AID

Students should submit: FAFSA, state aid form. The Princeton Review suggests that all financial aid forms be submitted as soon as possible after 1/1. *Need-based scholarships/grants offered:* Pell, SEOG, state scholarships/grants, private scholarships, the school's own gift aid. *Loan aid offered:* FFEL Subsidized Stafford, FFEL Unsubsidized Stafford, FFEL PLUS, Federal Perkins. Applicants will be notified of awards on a rolling basis beginning on or about 3/15. Federal Work-study Program available. Institutional employment available. Off-campus job opportunities are excellent.

FROM THE ADMISSIONS OFFICE

"Hofstra University is a nationally-recognized university, which offers all the benefits of a traditional college experience, including challenging academic programs with small classes and faculty devoted to teaching, and a vibrant campus life. Hofstra enrolls students from almost every state and 59 foreign countries. Students choose from over 130 undergraduate programs in arts and sciences, business, communications, education and allied human services, and honors studies.

"A distinctive aspect of the Hofstra experience is our focus on teaching. All of our classes are taught by faculty, which includes recipients of top academic honors including National Endowment for the Humanities fellows, Guggenheim fellows, an Emmy Award winner, and major grant recipients. Thanks to a student/faculty ratio of 14:1 and average class size of 23, students work closely with their professors.

"Complementing the classroom experience is the incomparable resource of New York City, just 25 miles from campus. Our students make full use of the city for internships and as a social and cultural outlet.

"Hofstra's students have the resources they need, including a library with 1.2 million volumes and a wealth of technology resources for learning and research, including grid computing and wireless access. Students may study abroad on five continents and over 25 countries. Over 120 clubs and organizations provide students with the opportunity to become involved in a broad array of activities, as does Hofstra's 18 NCAA Division I athletic programs. There are 37 residence halls at Hofstra that offer a variety of living arrangements.

"Students applying for admission for fall 2006 may submit either the new SAT or the ACT for consideration. Students submitting the ACT will be required to complete the Writing component. Hofstra University will require a writing sample as part of its admission requirements for freshmen in 2006."

SELECTIVITY

Admissions Rating	**84**
# of applicants	11,503
% of applicants accepted	67
% of acceptees attending	23
# accepting a place on wait list	623
% admitted from wait list	59

FRESHMAN PROFILE

Range SAT Verbal	520-610
Average SAT Verbal	567
Range SAT Math	530-620
Average SAT Math	577
**TPR Projected Range SAT Writing*	*570-640*
Range ACT Composite	21-27
Average ACT Composite	24
Minimum Paper TOEFL	550
Minimum Computer Based TOEFL	213
Average HS GPA	3.22
% graduated top 10% of class	22
% graduated top 25% of class	54
% graduated top 50% of class	84

DEADLINES

Regular notification	rolling
Nonfall registration?	yes

APPLICANTS ALSO LOOK AT

AND OFTEN PREFER
Boston University
New York University

AND SOMETIMES PREFER
Fordham University
Penn State University Park
SUNY at Stony Brook
Syracuse University

AND RARELY PREFER
Adelphi University
Long Island University—C.W. Post

FINANCIAL FACTS

Financial Aid Rating	**67**
Annual tuition	$19,010
Room & Board	$9,000
Books and supplies	$900
Required fees	$1,002
% frosh rec. need-based scholarship or grant aid	61
% UG rec. need-based scholarship or grant aid	57
% frosh rec. need-based self-help aid	31
% UG rec. need-based self-help aid	31
% frosh rec. any financial aid	89
% UG rec. any financial aid	75
Avg. frosh grant	$9,569
Avg. frosh loan	$2,787
Independent 529 member?	No

HOLLINS UNIVERSITY

PO BOX 9707, ROANOKE, VA 24020-1707 • ADMISSIONS: 540-362-6401 • FAX: 540-362-6218

CAMPUS LIFE

Quality of Life Rating	**70**
Fire Safety Rating	**81**
Type of school	private
Environment	city

STUDENTS

Total undergrad enrollment	805
% male/female	0/100
% from out of state	49
% from public high school	74
% live on campus	79
% African American	9
% Asian	2
% Caucasian	85
% Hispanic	2
% Native American	1
% international	2
# of countries represented	9

SURVEY SAYS

Small classes
No one cheats
Great library
Frats and sororities are unpopular or nonexistent
(Almost) everyone smokes

ACADEMICS

Academic Rating	**86**
Calendar	4-1-4
Student/faculty ratio	9:1
Professors interesting rating	85
Professors accessible rating	88
% professors teaching UG courses	100
% classes taught by TAs	0
Most common lab size	fewer than 10 students
Most common regular class size	10-19 students

MOST POPULAR MAJORS

Creative writing
mass communications/media studies
psychology

STUDENTS SPEAK OUT

Academics

According to its students, the two greatest strengths of Hollins University are its small size and its all-girl demographic. The combination allows for a much more comfortable atmosphere because [you] don't have to impress guys, and it is much more intimate, so you know everyone and are comfortable talking to people and speaking up in class." This small western Virginia school boasts plenty of other assets as well, including "a strong and well-known internship program" used by over 80 percent of the student body. During the school's January term, the program places students in plum positions with the likes of The London Times, the Bronx Zoo, Amnesty International, the Centers for Disease Control, and the Metropolitan Museum of Art. The study abroad program, enjoyed by nearly 60 percent of all undergrads, is another winner; the school sponsors programs in Paris and London and accommodates student requests for learning opportunities in such varied locales as Seville; Osaka; Legon, Ghana; Havana; and Athens. Hollins "is mainly known for the arts," with strong departments in English, writing, art history, psychology, and mass communications. The sciences are reportedly excellent, too; writes one premed, "Small class sizes, small labs, and one-on-one instruction from professors are an advantage in the sciences, and we learn how to incorporate other aspects of life into medicine, psychology, chemistry, and biology. The resources are wonderful, and the department works to give each science major the resources she needs for research and learning."

Life

Hollins is justly famous for its equestrian team, which has placed among the nation's top ten for the past six years. The school competes in nine other varsity sports, with nearly one-quarter of the student body participating; many other students engage in club sports or take advantage of the Hollins Outdoor Program, which organizes white water rafting, hiking, caving and rock climbing excursions. The school is also famous for its many traditions, including a truly odd event known as Tinker Day, "some unknown day in October after the first frost. Before the actual day, seniors go through the residence hall banging on pots and pans (called 'Tinker Scares'). On the actual day, classes are cancelled, we eat Krispy Kreme donuts, and then we dress up in wacky costumes and hike Tinker Mountain. Up there we sing songs to our fellow classes and perform skits before having a yummy meal of fried chicken and chocolate Tinker Cake!" The Student Activities Board "offers a lot of fun things throughout each month, such as music groups, speakers, game nights, karaoke night, comedians" but otherwise "the campus is generally pretty quiet, although we have some good parties every now and then." Some tell us that "Hollins is generally considered a suitcase school," but others report that "While some underclassmen leave on weekends, many upperclassmen stay. There is a special bond between girls at Hollins that many students choose to embrace, and we enjoy spending time with one another." Many students travel to other schools, such as Virginia Tech, for weekend parties.

Student Body

"The majority of students are classified as either pearl girls or riders," Hollins women tell us. "Pearl girls are the girls who wear a strand of pearls and pearl earrings everyday to class, even if they are wearing their pj's. Riders are girls who horseback ride almost everyday, and many have their own horse on campus." But they're far from the only two groups on campus, students are quick to add. "The next most common stereotype would be the writers, those who want to write for a living. Then there are the NEFA (Near East Fine Arts) girls that are your bards and artists. And then there's everybody else, who just find their own little niche somewhere in between, or carve out their own place." Hollins hosts "a strong lesbian minority, and they are treated with respect." The typical student "is politically moderate to liberal, although there are a growing number of conservatives speaking out."

FINANCIAL AID: 540-362-6332 • E-MAIL: HUADM@HOLLINS.EDU • WEBSITE: WWW.HOLLINS.EDU

ADMISSIONS

Very important factors considered include: Secondary school record, standardized test scores. *Important factors considered include:* Essays, recommendations, talent/ability. *Other factors considered include:* Alumni/ae relation, character/personal qualities, class rank, extracurricular activities, interview, minority status, volunteer work, work experience. SAT Reasoning or ACT required. TOEFL required of all international applicants. High school diploma is required, and GED is accepted. *Academic units required:* 4 English, 3 math, 3 science, 3 foreign language, 3 social studies.

The Inside Word

Only candidates who overtly display their lack of compatibility with the Hollins milieu are likely to encounter difficulty in gaining admission. A high level of self-selection and its weak, but improving, freshman profile allow most candidates to relax.

FINANCIAL AID

Students should submit: FAFSA, state aid form. The Princeton Review suggests that all financial aid forms be submitted as soon as possible after 1/1. *Need-based scholarships/grants offered:* Pell, SEOG, state scholarships/grants, private scholarships, the school's own gift aid. *Loan aid offered:* Direct Subsidized Stafford, Direct Unsubsidized Stafford, Direct PLUS, Federal Perkins. Applicants will be notified of awards on a rolling basis beginning on or about 3/1. Federal Work-study Program available. Institutional employment available. Off-campus job opportunities are good.

FROM THE ADMISSIONS OFFICE

"Hollins University's slogan, 'Women who are going places start at Hollins,' endures because it captures what this independent liberal arts institution means to its students. Hollins has been a motivating force for women to go places creatively, intellectually, and geographically since it was founded over 160 years ago. As Hollins graduate and Pulitzer Prize winner Annie Dillard said, Hollins is a place "where friendships thrive, minds catch fire, careers begin, and hearts open to a world of possibility."

"Hollins offers majors in 29 fields. While perhaps best known for its creative writing discipline, the university features strong programs in the visual and performing arts and the social and physical sciences. Hollins also has an innovative general education program called Education Through Skills and Perspectives (ESP). In ESP, students acquire knowledge across the curriculum; the course helps each student find a rewarding field of study.

"One of the most sought-after programs at Hollins is the Batten Leadership Institute, a three-year comprehensive program designed to maximize each student's leadership style and potential, and teach them skills they will use both now and in the future. It is the only program of its kind in the nation.

"Hollins was among the first colleges in the nation to offer an international study abroad program. Today, more than half of Hollins' students—10 times the national average—study abroad.

"Internship opportunities are another of Hollins' distinctions. Thanks to an active, dedicated network of alumnae and friends of the university, one-third of Hollins students put their education to work with a diverse group of organizations.

"Hollins' slogan underscores the most important question each student is asked from the moment she arrives until the day she leaves, and it is asked by her professors, her peers, and especially by herself: 'Where do you want to go?'

"Presently, students applying for admission can submit scores from either the old or new version of the SAT, and Hollins will use the best scores from either test."

SELECTIVITY

Admissions Rating	**83**
# of applicants	729
% of applicants accepted	87
% of acceptees attending	29
# accepting a place on wait list	20
% admitted from wait list	15
# of early decision applicants	45
% accepted early decision	90

FRESHMAN PROFILE

Range SAT Verbal	550-670
Average SAT Verbal	607
Range SAT Math	500-610
Average SAT Math	552
**TPR Projected Range SAT Writing*	*600-680*
Range ACT Composite	22-28
Average ACT Composite	25
Minimum Paper TOEFL	550
Minimum Computer Based TOEFL	213
Average HS GPA	3.5
% graduated top 10% of class	29
% graduated top 25% of class	52
% graduated top 50% of class	90

DEADLINES

Early decision application deadline	12/1
Early decision notification	12/15
Regular application deadline	2/15
Regular notification	rolling
Nonfall registration?	yes

APPLICANTS ALSO LOOK AT AND OFTEN PREFER

James Madison University, Randolph—Macon Woman's College, Sweet Briar College, University of Mary Washington

AND SOMETIMES PREFER

Mary Baldwin College, Roanoke College, University of Virginia, Virginia Commonwealth University

FINANCIAL FACTS

Financial Aid Rating	**75**
Annual tuition	$22,470
Room & Board	$8,160
Books and supplies	$800
Required fees	$475
% frosh rec. need-based scholarship or grant aid	72
% UG rec. need-based scholarship or grant aid	70
% frosh rec. need-based self-help aid	60
% UG rec. need-based self-help aid	62
% frosh rec. any financial aid	96
% UG rec. any financial aid	92
Avg. frosh grant	$13,791
Avg. frosh loan	$4,108
Independent 529 member?	Yes

HOWARD UNIVERSITY

2400 SIXTH STREET, NW, WASHINGTON, DC 20059 • ADMISSIONS: 202-806-2700 • FAX: 202-806-4462

CAMPUS LIFE

Quality of Life Rating	**66**
Fire Safety Rating	**60**
Type of school	private

STUDENTS

Total undergrad enrollment	7,063
% male/female	33/67
% from out of state	90
% from public high school	80
% live on campus	59
% in (# of) fraternities	2 (10)
% in (# of) sororities	1 (8)
% African American	84
% international	7
# of countries represented	85

SURVEY SAYS

Small classes
Students are happy
Frats and sororities dominate social scene
Musical organizations are popular
Student publications are popular
Student government is popular
Political activism is popular

ACADEMICS

Academic Rating	**83**
Calendar	semester
Student/faculty ratio	8:1
Professors interesting rating	70
Professors accessible rating	67
% classes taught by TAs	0
Most common lab size	10-19 students
Most common regular class size	fewer than 10 students

MOST POPULAR MAJORS

Biology/biological sciences
journalism
radio and television

STUDENTS SPEAK OUT

Academics

A school with "a rich legacy" that "continues to produce successful leaders," Howard University is truly "one of the nation's most prestigious historically black universities." The history is worth noting; the parade of impressive Howard graduates includes Nobel-Prize winning author Toni Morrison and former UN ambassador and civil-rights activist Andrew Young. So too is the present; Howard is well-regarded for its "excellent biology program" and other premed majors, as well as for communications and business. With its outstanding reputation, Howard "attracts big companies that come looking for strong black students to employ, which makes it slightly easier for us as blacks to find jobs in today's market." Observes one undergrad, "We profit from an incredible amount of networking with large and prominent companies." Students also benefit from the school's location in DC, "a city where there are an unlimited number of resources open to students." Undergrads report that "academics at Howard are unparalleled; professors are masters of their skills, and the students are not here to play around, but to actually learn and earn their education." The school's famously bureaucratic administration remains true to its reputation; "Anything dealing with administration and student services tends to be long and unnecessarily tedious," students warn. They also caution that "the facilities definitely need upgrading."

Life

"During the week, most people's main priority is their classes" at Howard, "but weekends are a time to [take a] break." "There is always something to do in Washington DC," including "going to eat in exotic restaurants, watching movies, going to museums, and visiting other colleges and universities in the area." The school is "located literally in the middle of Washington, DC. It sits on top of a large hill (a rarity in the area), giving us a view of the city's landmarks." The surrounding neighborhood "was once considered the black Georgetown, the side of town for wealthy black intellectuals who were affiliated with Howard. They built large, fashionable row houses.... The area turned into a ghetto, though, when people began to move into the newer suburbs out of the city. Within the last few years, the neighborhood has been revitalized, and people are buying and fixing the abandoned mansions and row houses. It's still somewhat dangerous, especially at night, but it is coming around. It's wonderful to witness the growth of this neighborhood (with my school's help)." On campus there is "a wide array of student organizations available. There is something for everybody, and we have people from all types of cultural and socioeconomic backgrounds." Many involve community service, as "the students are aware of the struggles faced by minorities, and many study to make a difference in the lives of the disadvantaged. Many students take part in volunteer programs such as elementary tutoring." There's also "Greek life, parties, choirs, the arts, our great school newspaper, mock trials, student government, you name it." Homecoming, we're assured, "is a very big event every year, with lots of celebrities."

Student Body

The "outgoing, fashionable, confident" undergrads of Howard are "predominantly black," but "this doesn't mean we are all African American. Besides coming from all over the United States, we come from Africa, Trinidad, Jamaica, Haiti, and everywhere else." Americans contribute mightily to the geographic diversity, since "Black people are not all the same, in case you didn't know. Black students from New Orleans act completely differently than black students from New York, etc. Howard is one big melting pot of black culture, and I love that!" Most here "came from a high school where they were probably popular, were class presidents or held some sort of leadership role in some student activity, and think they can take over the world." Adds one student, "We are definitely leaders by nature. As different as we are, we all think that we can and will be the best at something. We all have a drive that cannot be taught, just developed."

FINANCIAL AID: 202-806-2800 • E-MAIL: ADMISSION@HOWARD.EDU • WEBSITE: WWW.HOWARD.EDU

ADMISSIONS

Very important factors considered include: Class rank, secondary school record, standardized test scores. *Important factors considered include:* Character/personal qualities, recommendations. *Other factors considered include:* Alumni/ae relation, essays, extracurricular activities, talent/ability, volunteer work, work experience. SAT Reasoning or ACT required. SAT Subject Tests recommended. TOEFL required of all international applicants. High school diploma is required, and GED is accepted. *Academic units required:* 4 English, 2 math, 2 science, 2 foreign language, 2 social studies, 2 history. *Academic units recommended:* 4 English, 3 math, 4 science (2 science lab), 2 foreign language, 2 social studies, 2 history, 4 academic electives.

The Inside Word

A large applicant pool and solid yield of acceptees who enroll is a combination that adds up to selectivity for Howard. Pay strict attention to the formula.

FINANCIAL AID

Students should submit: FAFSA. The Princeton Review suggests that all financial aid forms be submitted as soon as possible after 1/1. *Need-based scholarships/grants offered:* Pell, SEOG, state scholarships/grants, private scholarships, the school's own gift aid, Federal Nursing scholarships. *Loan aid offered:* Direct Subsidized Stafford, Direct PLUS, FFEL Subsidized Stafford, FFEL Unsubsidized Stafford, FFEL PLUS, Federal Perkins, Federal Nursing, state loans, college/university loans from institutional funds. Applicants will be notified of awards on a rolling basis beginning on or about 4/1. Federal Work-study Program available. Institutional employment available. Off-campus job opportunities are excellent.

FROM THE ADMISSIONS OFFICE

"Since its founding, Howard has stood among the few institutions of higher learning where African Americans and other minorities have participated freely in a truly comprehensive university experience. Thus, Howard has assumed a special responsibility to prepare its students to exercise leadership wherever their interest and commitments take them. Howard has issued approximately 99,318 degrees, diplomas, and certificates to men and women in the professions, the arts and sciences, and the humanities. The university has produced and continues to produce a high percentage of the nation's African American professionals in the fields of medicine, dentistry, pharmacy, engineering, nursing, architecture, religion, law, music, social work, education, and business. There are more than 8,906 students from across the nation and approximately 85 countries and territories attending the university. Their varied customs, cultures, ideas, and interests contribute to Howard's international character and vitality. More than 1,598 faculty members represent the largest concentration of African American scholars in any single institution of higher education.

"Beginning with the entering class of fall 2006 all applicants who have never been to college will be required to submit scores from either the new SAT or the ACT (with the Writing component)."

SELECTIVITY

Admissions Rating	**88**
# of applicants	8,860
% of applicants accepted	47
% of acceptees attending	35

FRESHMAN PROFILE

Range SAT Verbal	430-690
Average SAT Verbal	544
Range SAT Math	450-680
Average SAT Math	538
**TPR Projected Range SAT Writing*	*500-690*
Range ACT Composite	18-29
Average ACT Composite	22
Minimum Paper TOEFL	550
Minimum Computer Based TOEFL	213
Average HS GPA	3.2
% graduated top 10% of class	23
% graduated top 25% of class	49
% graduated top 50% of class	81

DEADLINES

Regular application deadline	2/15
Regular notification	rolling
Nonfall registration?	yes

APPLICANTS ALSO LOOK AT AND OFTEN PREFER

Hampton University
Morehouse College
Spelman College

AND SOMETIMES PREFER

Florida A&M University
The George Washington University
University of Maryland—College Park

AND RARELY PREFER

Morgan State University

FINANCIAL FACTS

Financial Aid Rating	**68**
Annual tuition	$10,840
Room & Board	$5,870
Books and supplies	$1,020
Required fees	$805
% frosh rec. need-based scholarship or grant aid	37
% UG rec. need-based scholarship or grant aid	29
% frosh rec. need-based self-help aid	49
% UG rec. need-based self-help aid	35
% frosh rec. any financial aid	67
% UG rec. any financial aid	51
Avg. frosh grant	$4,475
Avg. frosh loan	$9,457
Independent 529 member?	No

ILLINOIS INSTITUTE OF TECHNOLOGY

10 WEST 33RD STREET, CHICAGO, IL 60616 • ADMISSIONS: 312-567-3025 • FAX: 312-567-6939

CAMPUS LIFE

Quality of Life Rating	**64**
Fire Safety Rating	**71**
Type of school	private
Environment	metropolis

STUDENTS

Total undergrad enrollment	1,961
% male/female	75/25
% from out of state	30
% from public high school	74
% live on campus	56
% in (# of) fraternities	15 (7)
% in (# of) sororities	17 (3)
% African American	6
% Asian	14
% Caucasian	49
% Hispanic	7
% international	17
# of countries represented	90

SURVEY SAYS

Class discussions are rare
Small classes
Diverse student types on campus
Students love Chicago, IL
Great off-campus food
Very little drug use

ACADEMICS

Academic Rating	**64**
Calendar	semester
Student/faculty ratio	13:1
Professors interesting rating	61
Professors accessible rating	61
% professors teaching UG courses	65
% classes taught by TAs	0

MOST POPULAR MAJORS

Architecture (BArch, BA/BS, MArch, MA/MS, PhD)
computer and information sciences
electrical, electronics, and communications engineering

STUDENTS SPEAK OUT

Academics

The learning experience at the Illinois Institute of Technology (IIT) receives reviews from students ranging from hot to cold. On the hot side, students tell us that small class sizes—"almost all classes have 20 students or fewer"—ensure that "each student gets to interact directly with the professor." Sometimes interaction—or, more precisely, help—is what these students need. Explains one undergrad, "It's hard, hard, hard. It's tough, but it's tough with a point, and it makes you stronger every day." This is, of course, an institute of technology, so it is only fitting that the strongest departments lie in engineering and architecture. One satisfied architecture student boasts, "Professors in architecture are second to none. Most still practice and have a strong connection to the real world." This real world connection is reinforced through IPRO's, or Interprofessional Research Projects, which have outside sponsorship from companies, governmental agencies, and nonprofits and "are really beneficial to learning the trades." Within most majors, students receive a focused, professionally oriented education, which is evidenced by the fact that "all first-year students take a course called 'Introduction to the Profession.'" But this doesn't always go over well. "Requiring more literature and English classes would force students to learn better ways to express their thoughts." Others grumble about the number of instructors who lack "an adequate command of the English language." But the most vocal criticisms are aimed at the administration; top-shelf administrators "seem to be completely out of touch with reality." In defense of the administration, one student says that while management could use an overhaul, "their hearts and wishes for the school are in the right place."

Life

Illinois Institute of Technology's "architecturally famous campus" is just "a ten-minute train ride from downtown Chicago." Students love that "the El (Chicago's version of a subway) runs right through campus," which means that "all of the Windy City's attractions [are] within a close distance." While some students assure us that the campus itself is where "fun comes to fester and die," others declare that "there are approximately ten to fifteen events occurring per week," including "galas, formals, movies, entertainment nights, luncheons, student organization meetings, boat cruises, trips to malls, special cultural events, leaderships seminars, etc." A new cafeteria has improved the quality of food on campus, which was once described as "absolutely awful, even for dorm food."

Student Body

"There are many ethnic groups" represented on IIT's campus. Case in point: An American student says that his nights out often include "my three best friends, [who] are from the Czech Republic, Kenya, and Thailand." Students from India and of Indian descent are also reportedly well represented here. Though IIT attracts a large number of international students, it's less successful in its attempts to attract female students. "It gets really old fighting three other guys for one girl," complains one hapless male undergraduate. Male or female, national or international, these students will plainly admit that the "school is populated by nerds and nerds alone." When they say "nerds," students are referring to a population that is really smart and, though friendly when out in public, "would rather sit in their rooms and play computer games than talk to another human being."

FINANCIAL AID: 312-567-7219 • E-MAIL: ADMISSION@IIT.EDU • WEBSITE: WWW.IIT.EDU

ADMISSIONS

Very important factors considered include: Secondary school record, standardized test scores. *Important factors considered include:* Essays, recommendations. *Other factors considered include:* Character/personal qualities, class rank, extracurricular activities, interview, volunteer work, work experience. SAT Reasoning or ACT required. TOEFL required of all international applicants. High school diploma is required, and GED is not accepted. *Academic units required:* 4 English, 4 math, 3 science (2 science lab), 2 social studies, 2 history. *Academic units recommended:* 4 English, 4 math, 3 science (2 science lab), 2 social studies, 2 history.

The Inside Word

IIT's applicant pool is small and includes a strong element of self-selection. This means the majority get in, but not without solid academic preparation. While the committee evaluates other criteria, the bottom line is that candidates need fairly solid grades and better-than-average test scores in order to get admitted.

FINANCIAL AID

Students should submit: FAFSA. The Princeton Review suggests that all financial aid forms be submitted as soon as possible after 1/1. *Need-based scholarships/grants offered:* Pell, SEOG, state scholarships/grants, private scholarships, the school's own gift aid. *Loan aid offered:* FFEL Subsidized Stafford, FFEL Unsubsidized Stafford, FFEL PLUS, Federal Perkins, college/university loans from institutional funds. Applicants will be notified of awards on a rolling basis beginning on or about 3/1.

FROM THE ADMISSIONS OFFICE

"IIT is committed to providing students with the highest-caliber education through dedicated teachers, small class sizes, and undergraduate research opportunities. Classes are taught by senior faculty—not teaching assistants—who bring firsthand research experience into daily class discussion. The university's diverse student population mirrors the global work environment faced by all graduates. IIT promotes a unique interdisciplinary approach to learning. Students experience team-based, creative problem solving through two required Interprofessional Projects (IPROs). Our entrepreneurship program challenges students to develop start-up technology companies. The Leadership Academy teaches leadership skills that advance students in their personal and professional development. IIT's location in one of the nation's great cities affords many opportunities for internships and employment. The new, visually-enticing McCormick Tribune Campus Center and ultra-modern State Street Village residence halls provide exciting living and campus opportunities that are sure to create a positive student experience for years to come.

"Students applying for admission into the fall 2006 entering class are required to take the new version of the SAT (or the ACT with the writing section). Students will be allowed to submit scores from the old (prior to March 2005) version of the SAT (or ACT) as well, and we will use the student's best scores from either test."

SELECTIVITY

Admissions Rating	**90**
# of applicants	2,609
% of applicants accepted	61
% of acceptees attending	29

FRESHMAN PROFILE

Range SAT Verbal	570-670
Average SAT Verbal	620
Range SAT Math	630-710
Average SAT Math	675
**TPR Projected Range SAT Writing*	*610-680*
Range ACT Composite	26-30
Average ACT Composite	28
Minimum Paper TOEFL	550
Minimum Computer Based TOEFL	213
Average HS GPA	3.49
% graduated top 10% of class	37
% graduated top 25% of class	70
% graduated top 50% of class	92

DEADLINES

Regular notification	rolling
Nonfall registration?	yes

APPLICANTS ALSO LOOK AT AND OFTEN PREFER

Massachusetts Institute of Technology
Northwestern University
Purdue University—West Lafayette
University of Illinois at Urbana-Champaign

AND SOMETIMES PREFER

Case Western Reserve University
Georgia Institute of Technology
Marquette University
Milwaukee School of Engineering

FINANCIAL FACTS

Financial Aid Rating	**80**
Annual tuition	$22,218
Room & Board	$7,518
Books and supplies	$1,000
Required fees	$764
% frosh rec. need-based scholarship or grant aid	72
% UG rec. need-based scholarship or grant aid	57
% frosh rec. need-based self-help aid	50
% UG rec. need-based self-help aid	42
% frosh rec. any financial aid	100
% UG rec. any financial aid	91
Avg. frosh grant	$15,046
Avg. frosh loan	$8,316
Independent 529 member?	Yes

Illinois Wesleyan University

PO Box 2900, Bloomington, IL 61702-2900 • Admissions: 309-556-3031 • Fax: 309-556-3820

CAMPUS LIFE

Quality of Life Rating	**88**
Fire Safety Rating	**68**
Type of school	private
Environment	city

STUDENTS

Total undergrad enrollment	2,111
% male/female	44/56
% from out of state	13
% from public high school	80
% live on campus	81
% in (# of) fraternities	34 (6)
% in (# of) sororities	26 (4)
% African American	3
% Asian	2
% Caucasian	86
% Hispanic	3
% international	2
# of countries represented	17

SURVEY SAYS

Small classes
Lab facilities are great
Great computer facilities
Great library
Athletic facilities are great

ACADEMICS

Academic Rating	**87**
Calendar	4-4-1
Student/faculty ratio	12:1
Professors interesting rating	81
Professors accessible rating	84
% professors teaching UG courses	100
% classes taught by TAs	0
Most common lab size	10-19 students
Most common regular class size	10-19 students

MOST POPULAR MAJORS

Biology/biological sciences
Business administration/management
psychology

STUDENTS SPEAK OUT

Academics

"Students are the number one focus" at Illinois Wesleyan University (IWU), a "prestigious liberal arts university [that] offers a total all-around package" to Midwesterners who "don't want to go East to get a great education." Students love the biology and chemistry departments here; the political science, music, and theater programs are among the others that also garner accolades. Undergraduates appreciate IWU's "immense availability of resources—they're everywhere! We have so many computers and Ethernet connections that everyone I know has a computer or easy access to one at all hours of the day." But most of all, students cherish a faculty that "really cares about the students." Typical students "couldn't be more pleased with the educational experience [we] have had here at Illinois Wesleyan. The professors are fantastic. They make students want to attend class by making class interactive, fun, and often humorous." Students' only complaint is that the rest of the world still has not recognized their school's true worth. One undergraduate has a theory: "We might not get the reputation we deserve simply because the word 'Illinois' is in the name of the university—people unacquainted with us might mistakenly think we're a big state school." Those who choose IWU, though, soon learn that "academically, this school is much tougher than most 'rankings' place us. The pre-graduate programs are outstanding, but challenging. Students expecting to coast through this school usually leave within their first year. I've seen it happen to a number of friends and acquaintances."

Life

For a school of its size, IWU does a commendable job of keeping its campus abuzz with activity. "Whether it be various university-sponsored events or participation in the numerous extracurricular clubs and organizations, there is always something to do on campus when the students' noses aren't in their books." The new student center "has a lot of movies, comedians, and music groups to go see free. The university brings in tremendous speakers, such as the president of Bolivia, [and] everyone supports the sports teams, especially basketball." One student adds, "Games are always packed and the fraternities have their own sections where they get rowdy. It's a hostile environment for opponents." When Friday night rolls around, though, "Most students go to frat parties, where drinking is the main attraction. Some go to ISU (just down the road) on weekends, but our parties are better because you know everyone you are partying with, since there's only 2,100 of us here." Students agree that the party scene is lively but note that "although the bulk of people do go out to party to have fun, there really isn't any intense pressure to drink." Most social activity is confined to campus, since hometown Bloomington "is simply not a very exciting place, and even if there were a compelling reason to leave the campus, public transportation is nearly nonexistent." Nearby Normal is not much better; as one student put it, "The Bloomington/Normal community is rather small. It is like taking two Chicagoland suburbs and plopping them down in the middle of a cornfield."

Student Body

"There isn't too much animosity among the different groups" on IWU's campus, "whether they be Greeks or independents, females or males, minorities or majorities, gay or straight." Indeed, one student tells us, "Everyone is so friendly, even people I barely know say hi, and most people at least smile. Maybe it's the good old Midwest feeling that IWU radiates, but I think it's also because the students and faculty here are truly happy." Most students are "white and from the Chicago suburbs." Undergraduates report that "the school is attempting to incorporate more racial diversity, which is much needed." Politically, the student body skews toward the right; as one student explains, "The students on this campus are much more conservative than the faculty. It isn't unusual to have a Republican student on this campus support an argument with Bible verses and stories."

Illinois Wesleyan University

Financial Aid: 309-556-3096 • E-mail: iwuadmit@titan.iwu.edu • Website: www.iwu.edu

ADMISSIONS

Very important factors considered include: Interview, secondary school record. *Important factors considered include:* Character/personal qualities, class rank, essays, extracurricular activities, standardized test scores, talent/ability. *Other factors considered include:* Alumni/ae relation, geographical residence, minority status, recommendations, state residency, volunteer work, work experience. SAT Reasoning or ACT required. TOEFL required of all international applicants. High school diploma is required, and GED is accepted. *Academic units recommended:* 4 English, 3 math, 3 science (2 science lab), 3 foreign language, 2 social studies.

The Inside Word

Illinois Wesleyan is selective enough that serious candidates should exceed the suggested curriculum requirements to improve their chances for admission.

FINANCIAL AID

Students should submit: FAFSA, institution's own financial aid form. Regular filing deadline is 3/1. The Princeton Review suggests that all financial aid forms be submitted as soon as possible after 1/1. *Need-based scholarships/grants offered:* Pell, SEOG, state scholarships/grants, private scholarships, the school's own gift aid. *Loan aid offered:* FFEL Subsidized Stafford, FFEL Unsubsidized Stafford, FFEL PLUS, Federal Perkins, Federal Nursing, college/university loans from institutional funds. Applicants will be notified of awards on a rolling basis beginning on or about 2/1. Federal Work-study Program available. Institutional employment available. Off-campus job opportunities are good.

FROM THE ADMISSIONS OFFICE

"Illinois Wesleyan University attracts a wide variety of students who are interested in pursuing diverse fields such as vocal performance, biology, psychology, German, physics, or business administration. At IWU, students are not forced into either/or choices. Rather, they are encouraged to pursue multiple interests simultaneously—a philosophy that is in keeping with the spirit and value of a liberal arts education. The distinctive 4-4-1 calendar allows students to follow their interests each school year in two semesters followed by an optional month-long class in May. May term opportunities include classes on campus; research collaboration with faculty; travel and study in such places as Australia, China, South Africa, and Europe; as well as local, national, and international internships.

"The IWU mission statement reads in part: 'A liberal education at Illinois Wesleyan fosters creativity, critical thinking, effective communication, strength of character, and a spirit of inquiry; it deepens the specialized knowledge of a discipline with a comprehensive world view. It affords the greatest possibilities for realizing individual potential while preparing students for democratic citizenship and life in a global society. ... The university, through its policies, programs, and practices, is committed to diversity, social justice, and environmental sustainability. A tightly knit, supportive university community, together with a variety of opportunities for close interaction with excellent faculty, both challenges and supports students in their personal and intellectual development.

"Freshman applicants for fall 2006 may submit scores from either the old or new SAT exams. For the ACT, students may submit scores with or without the Writing section."

SELECTIVITY

Admissions Rating	**90**
# of applicants	2,932
% of applicants accepted	49
% of acceptees attending	38
# accepting a place on wait list	497
% admitted from wait list	11

FRESHMAN PROFILE

Range SAT Verbal	580-690
Average SAT Verbal	638
Range SAT Math	600-690
Average SAT Math	640
**TPR Projected Range SAT Writing*	*620-690*
Range ACT Composite	27-31
Average ACT Composite	29
Minimum Paper TOEFL	550
Minimum Computer Based TOEFL	213
% graduated top 10% of class	52
% graduated top 25% of class	83
% graduated top 50% of class	99

DEADLINES

Regular notification	rolling
Nonfall registration?	yes

APPLICANTS ALSO LOOK AT

AND OFTEN PREFER

Northwestern University
University of Notre Dame

AND SOMETIMES PREFER

University of Illinois at Urbana-Champaign
Washington University in St. Louis

AND RARELY PREFER

Augustana College (IL)
Marquette University

FINANCIAL FACTS

Financial Aid Rating	**85**
Annual tuition	$27,474
Room & Board	$6,426
Books and supplies	$650
Required fees	$150
% frosh rec. need-based scholarship or grant aid	60
% UG rec. need-based scholarship or grant aid	58
% frosh rec. need-based self-help aid	45
% UG rec. need-based self-help aid	47
% frosh rec. any financial aid	91
% UG rec. any financial aid	90
Avg. frosh grant	$13,680
Avg. frosh loan	$3,822
Independent 529 member?	No

INDIANA UNIVERSITY—BLOOMINGTON

300 North Jordan Avenue, Bloomington, IN 47405-1106 • Admissions: 812-855-0661 • Fax: 812-855-5102

CAMPUS LIFE

Quality of Life Rating	**91**
Fire Safety Rating	**60**
Type of school	public
Environment	town

STUDENTS

Total undergrad enrollment	29,062
% male/female	48/52
% from out of state	35
% live on campus	42
% in (# of) fraternities	16 (30)
% in (# of) sororities	18 (25)
% African American	4
% Asian	3
% Caucasian	85
% Hispanic	2
% international	4
# of countries represented	136

SURVEY SAYS

Great computer facilities
Great library
Athletic facilities are great
Students are happy
Everyone loves the Hoosiers
Student publications are popular
Lots of beer drinking
Hard liquor is popular

ACADEMICS

Academic Rating	**74**
Calendar	semester
Student/faculty ratio	18:1
Professors interesting rating	77
Professors accessible rating	79
% classes taught by TAs	0
Most common lab size	20-29 students
Most common regular class size	20-29 students

MOST POPULAR MAJORS

Business/commerce
communications technologies and support services
education

STUDENTS SPEAK OUT

Academics

"Perhaps our greatest strength, which some people tend to see as a weakness, is our size," writes an observant IU undergraduate who points to "the sheer magnitude of available majors and minors, organizations to join, and annual activities. It's mind-boggling. The benefit of a big school is that it can accommodate so many different interests, and can even accommodate changes in personal interest." Students caution that "since IU is such a big school, it's up to you to get as good or as bad an education as you would like. You can load up on BS classes like human sexuality (which everyone seems to take eventually) or take really hard classes that challenge you to think." A great education can certainly be found here, especially in the school's nationally renowned business and music programs; education, journalism, and the hard sciences are also reportedly strong, with the latter benefiting from "great opportunities to research with some world famous scientists." Undergrads across disciplines praise "smaller class sizes than you would expect," professors who "are easy to get along with and accessible," and an "extraordinary honors college." As is the case at many large universities, the administration gets mixed reviews. Some more forgiving students attribute bureaucratic headaches to the growing pains associated with the school recently going onto the PeopleSoft™ system, while other more splenetic types say simply that "Logic has no place in the IU administration."

Life

"Bloomington is a perfect college town, and it is absolutely beautiful," students agree, pointing out also that "the school interacts with the town as well as any campus in the country. Bloomington has to be one of the best college towns, and the town is based around the university, not the other way around like the big city schools (i.e., NYU, BU, BC, UCLA)." Add the "sheer beauty of the campus" and you begin to understand why students feel so at home in Bloomington. Then consider the other perks of life at IU: for instance, the "famed Hoosier basketball team," whose popularity "makes Indiana tickets the hardest to get in the country. They cannot keep up with the alumni and student season ticket requests, and therefore are unable to sell single-game tickets." Students want you to know that "support is also strong for soccer, swimming, volleyball, football, and baseball." Consider also the "wild party scene," which students generally love; explains one, "With 30-something thousand students going to IU, at least half of them are out partying on the weekend, so you can always find something wild, crazy, and drunken to do!" Best of all is the Little 500—"the greatest college weekend in the world," students claim—a bike race that "requires standing-room-only viewing from the thousands of students, faculty, and fans who come to watch the 30-plus teams compete. They train year round to win the event, riding thousands of miles just for the chance to win." The town of Bloomington itself offers "different types of entertainment in music, theater, and the arts" as well as a number of student-oriented eateries.

Student Body

"The thing about going to a big school is that there is a wide variety of kinds of people here," IU students enthusiastically explain. "We have frat and sorority snobs, pot-smoking hippies, library nerds, D-1 athletes, gays and lesbians, musicians, and so on. Basically, you will find a group to fit in with at IU." Undergrads arrive "from different states, different countries, and different social and economic backgrounds. Everyone seems to get along pretty well, despite their differences." Many here "are athletic and involved—working out is like a second major for some people—and extracurriculars are huge." While a lot of students "are very grade-focused and only want to learn enough to pass the test," there are also "a lot of serious students, too. They just don't stick out as much, or they look like the other kids and party as much as them, but take their work seriously as well."

ADMISSIONS

Very important factors considered include: Class rank, secondary school record. *Other factors considered include:* Alumni/ae relation, character/personal qualities, essays, extracurricular activities, geographical residence, interview, minority status, recommendations, standardized test scores, state residency, talent/ability, volunteer work, work experience. SAT Reasoning or ACT required. SAT Subject Tests recommended. High school diploma is required, and GED is accepted. *Academic units required:* 4 English, 3 math, 1 science (1 science lab), 2 social studies, 4 academic electives. *Academic units recommended:* 4 math, 3 science, 3 foreign language, 3 social studies.

The Inside Word

A high volume of applicants makes Indiana's individual admissions review process relatively selective for a university of its size. Candidates to the School of Music face a highly selective audition process.

FINANCIAL AID

Students should submit: FAFSA. Regular filing deadline is 3/1. The Princeton Review suggests that all financial aid forms be submitted as soon as possible after 1/1. *Need-based scholarships/grants offered:* Pell, SEOG, state scholarships/grants, private scholarships, the school's own gift aid. *Loan aid offered:* Direct Subsidized Stafford, Direct Unsubsidized Stafford, Direct PLUS, Federal Perkins, Federal Nursing, college/university loans from institutional funds. Applicants will be notified of awards on or about 3/10. Federal Work-study Program available. Institutional employment available. Off-campus job opportunities are excellent.

FROM THE ADMISSIONS OFFICE

"Indiana University—Bloomington, one of America's great teaching and research universities, extends learning and teaching beyond the walls of the traditional classroom. When visiting campus, students and parents typically describe IU as 'what a college should look and feel like.' Students bring their diverse experiences, beliefs, and backgrounds from all 50 states and 136 countries, which adds a richness and diversity to life at IU—a campus often cited as one of the most beautiful in the nation. Indiana University—Bloomington truly offers a quintessential college town, campus, and overall experience. Students enjoy all of the advantages, opportunities, and resources that a larger school can offer, while still receiving personal attention and support. For the third year in a row, *U.S. News & World Report* has recognized IU—Bloomington for the range of programs offered to help freshman succeed. Because of the variety of outstanding academic and cultural resources, students at IU have the best of both worlds.

"Indiana offers more than 5,000 courses and more than 100 undergraduate programs, with many known nationally and internationally. IU—Bloomington is known worldwide for outstanding programs in the arts, sciences, humanities, and social sciences as well as for highly rated schools of business, music, education, journalism, optometry, public and environmental affairs, and health, physical education, and recreation. Students can customize academic programs with double and individualized majors, internships, and research opportunities, while utilizing state-of-the-art technology at the nation's top wireless university, according to *Intel*. Representatives from more than 1,000 businesses, government agencies, and not-for-profit organizations come to campus each year to recruit IU students.

"IUB requires students applying for admission into the fall 2006 freshman class to take the new version of the SAT (or the ACT with the writing section). The university will use these writing sections in the way the SAT Subject Test Writing exam has been used: for possible credit, placement, or exemption from writing requirements."

SELECTIVITY

Admissions Rating	**75**
# of applicants	21,132
% of applicants accepted	83
% of acceptees attending	36

FRESHMAN PROFILE

Range SAT Verbal	490-600
Average SAT Verbal	544
Range SAT Math	500-620
Average SAT Math	560
**TPR Projected Range SAT Writing*	*550-630*
Range ACT Composite	22-27
Average ACT Composite	24
% graduated top 10% of class	23
% graduated top 25% of class	56
% graduated top 50% of class	95

DEADLINES

Nonfall registration?	yes

APPLICANTS ALSO LOOK AT

AND OFTEN PREFER

University of Illinois at Urbana-Champaign
University of Michigan—Ann Arbor
University of Notre Dame

AND SOMETIMES PREFER

Miami University
Purdue University—West Lafayette
University of Wisconsin—Madison

FINANCIAL FACTS

Financial Aid Rating	**64**
Annual in-state tuition	$4,946
Annual out-of-state tuition	$16,739
Room & Board	$6,006
Books and supplies	$740
Required fees	$791
% frosh rec. need-based scholarship or grant aid	27
% UG rec. need-based scholarship or grant aid	21
% frosh rec. need-based self-help aid	22
% UG rec. need-based self-help aid	16
% frosh rec. any financial aid	70
% UG rec. any financial aid	92
Avg. frosh grant	$4,530
Avg. frosh loan	$5,712
Independent 529 member?	No

INDIANA UNIVERSITY OF PENNSYLVANIA

216 PRATT HALL, INDIANA, PA 15705 • ADMISSIONS: 724-357-2230 • FAX: 724-357-6281

CAMPUS LIFE

Quality of Life Rating	**72**
Fire Safety Rating	**81**
Type of school	public
Environment	village

STUDENTS

Total undergrad enrollment	11,861
% male/female	44/56
% from out of state	3
% from public high school	95
% live on campus	32
% in (# of) fraternities	10 (19)
% in (# of) sororities	11 (14)
% African American	6
% Asian	1
% Caucasian	81
% Hispanic	1
% international	2
# of countries represented	74

SURVEY SAYS

Small classes
Frats and sororities dominate social scene
Student publications are popular
Lots of beer drinking
(Almost) everyone smokes

ACADEMICS

Academic Rating	**74**
Calendar	semester
Student/faculty ratio	17:1
Professors interesting rating	77
Professors accessible rating	77
% professors teaching UG courses	100
% classes taught by TAs	0
Most common regular class size students	20-29

MOST POPULAR MAJORS

Communications studies/speech communication and rhetoric
criminology
elementary education and teaching

STUDENTS SPEAK OUT

Academics

The Robert E. Cook Honors College is what distinguishes Indiana University of Pennsylvania (IUP) from your typical big-box state university. Reports one honors student, "The Honors College allows students to take interesting discussion-based classes instead of the standard liberal studies freshman classes. These honor classes are never lecture-based and have made me a much better writer and thinker." Students' only complaint about the honors program concerns its limited scope; as one student told us, "My academic experience has been pretty good; however, there needs to be more honors courses and an honors program in each academic college." Beyond the Honors College, "the rest of the university is pretty much only concerned with partying." While profs "are easily accessible and encouraging," they face "a huge obstacle: a student body with too much laziness." Since the Honors College covers only some of students' course work, all students must take at least some courses outside the college. Reports one student, "Required classes are large, freakishly easy, and completely made up of lecture time. My honors classes are absolutely excellent, with discussion 60 percent of the time." Even so, IUP offers plenty of challenges to those willing to step up to the plate. Sums up one undergrad, "IUP might not have ten sets of all the newest equipment, but it does train me in everything I need to know and gives me additional chances to learn outside of the school through its numerous internship and study abroad programs."

Life

Hometown Indiana, students at IUP tell us, "is not the place for city people who like a lot of excitement and nightclubs." The town "offers a myriad of bars but very little else." It is the birthplace of film legend Jimmy Stewart, and many feel "it could very well be named 'Jimmy Stewart–ville' for all the paraphernalia: the Jimmy Stewart Museum, the sign coming into town proclaiming that Indiana, Pennsylvania is the birthplace of Jimmy Stewart, and the showings of *It's a Wonderful Life* during the holidays at the local theater." Irreverent IUP undergrads occasionally "steal away in the middle of the night to put a dress and hat on the Jimmy Stewart statue, which proudly stands in front of the courthouse," giving you some idea of how little else there is to do here. Students tell us IUP was once a big party school, but that "life in general at IUP is changing. They have increased the police force in order to better enforce drug and alcohol laws." To fill the void, "IUP offers many student organizations and musical events from an anime club to equestrian team to dance squad to sororities and fraternities. If you have an interest, IUP is a good place to pursue it." Otherwise, students seek quiet entertainment of their own devising or, more often, pack up and go home when their last class ends. Pittsburgh is only an hour's drive away.

Student Body

With over 12,000 undergraduates, "there are students from all walks of life here at IUP. . . . The majority are related by the fact that they come from a middle-income family and are here to get the best education they can for their dollar." Many "are from within a 60-mile radius of the school," an area that is "very conservative Christian and not generally accepting of liberal viewpoints." IUP also has "a large population of African Americans and foreign students from all around the world, like Asia, Africa, and Europe." Students warn, however, "There is a visual segregation between the African American community and the rest of the campus," however, the school is working to be more embrasive of cultural/ethnic differences through student groups and initiatives. Most here "are more concerned with getting a job and money than being educated," according to their critics.

FINANCIAL AID: 724-357-2218 • E-MAIL: ADMISSIONS-INQUIRY@IUP.EDU • WEBSITE: WWW.IUP.EDU

ADMISSIONS

Very important factors considered include: Secondary school record. *Important factors considered include:* Class rank, standardized test scores, talent/ability. *Other factors considered include:* Alumni/ae relation, character/personal qualities, essays, extracurricular activities, interview, recommendations, volunteer work, work experience. SAT Reasoning or ACT required. TOEFL required of all international applicants. High school diploma is required, and GED is accepted. *Academic units recommended:* 4 English, 3 math, 3 science, 2 foreign language, 2 social studies, 1 history, 1 academic elective.

The Inside Word

IUP is impressive in many ways and should command more attention than it does. As a state school, it provides Pennsylvania residents with a great education at a rock-bottom price. Students applying to IUP with an average academic record will have little trouble getting admitted. Once on campus, students will find an unexpectedly diverse population who hail from many states and countries.

FINANCIAL AID

Students should submit: FAFSA. The Princeton Review suggests that all financial aid forms be submitted as soon as possible after 1/1. *Need-based scholarships/grants offered:* Pell, SEOG, state scholarships/grants, private scholarships, the school's own gift aid, United Negro College Fund. *Loan aid offered:* FFEL Subsidized Stafford, FFEL Unsubsidized Stafford, FFEL PLUS, Federal Perkins, private alternative loans. Applicants will be notified of awards on or about 3/15. Federal Work-study Program available. Institutional employment available. Off-campus job opportunities are good.

FROM THE ADMISSIONS OFFICE

"At IUP, we look at each applicant as an individual, not as a number. That means we'll review your application materials very carefully. When reviewing applications, the primary focus of the admissions committee is on the student's high school record and SAT scores. In addition, the committee often reviews the optional personal essay and letters of recommendations submitted by the student to help aid in the decision-making process. We're always happy to speak with prospective students. Call us toll free at 800-422-6830 or 724-357-2230 or email us at admissions-inquiry@iup.edu.

"Students applying for admission into the fall 2006 entering class are required to take the new version of the SAT (or the ACT with the writing section). Students will be allowed to submit scores from the old (prior to March 2005) version of the SAT (or ACT) as well, and we will use the student's best scores from either test."

SELECTIVITY

Admissions Rating	**79**
# of applicants	8,836
% of applicants accepted	55
% of acceptees attending	54

FRESHMAN PROFILE

Range SAT Verbal	480-570
Average SAT Verbal	543
Range SAT Math	470-560
Average SAT Math	534
Projected Range SAT Writing	540-610
Minimum Paper TOEFL	500
Minimum Computer Based TOEFL	300
Average HS GPA	3.36
% graduated top 10% of class	16
% graduated top 25% of class	35
% graduated top 50% of class	74

DEADLINES

Regular notification	rolling
Nonfall registration?	yes

APPLICANTS ALSO LOOK AT AND OFTEN PREFER

Clarion University of PA
Duquesne University
Millersville University of Pennsylvania
Penn State University Park
Shippensburg University of Pennsylvania
Westminster College

AND SOMETIMES PREFER

James Madison University
Kutztown University of Pennsylvania
Slippery Rock University of Pennsylvania
University of Delaware
West Virginia University

AND RARELY PREFER

Bloomsburg University of Pennsylvania
Lock Haven University of Pennsylvania
Mansfield University of Pennsylvania
Ohio University—Athens

FINANCIAL FACTS

Financial Aid Rating	**73**
Annual in-state tuition	$4,598
Annual out-of-state tuition	$11,496
Room & Board	$4,702
Books and supplies	$800
Required fees	$1,187
% frosh rec. need-based scholarship or grant aid	51
% UG rec. need-based scholarship or grant aid	50
% frosh rec. need-based self-help aid	63
% UG rec. need-based self-help aid	60
% frosh rec. any financial aid	81
% UG rec. any financial aid	77
Avg. frosh grant	$3,935
Avg. frosh loan	$2,896
Independent 529 member?	No

IOWA STATE UNIVERSITY

100 ALUMNI HALL, AMES, IA 50011-2011 • ADMISSIONS: 515-294-5836 • FAX: 515-294-2592

CAMPUS LIFE

Quality of Life Rating	**85**
Fire Safety Rating	**68**
Type of school	public
Environment	rural

STUDENTS

Total undergrad enrollment	20,993
% male/female	56/44
% from out of state	20
% from public high school	93
% live on campus	36
% in (# of) fraternities	12 (29)
% in (# of) sororities	12 (18)
% African American	3
% Asian	3
% Caucasian	84
% Hispanic	2
% international	3
# of countries represented	114

SURVEY SAYS

Great computer facilities
Great library
Athletic facilities are great
Campus feels safe
Everyone loves the Cyclones
Intramural sports are popular
Student publications are popular
Lots of beer drinking

ACADEMICS

Academic Rating	**72**
Calendar	semester
Student/faculty ratio	15:1
Professors interesting rating	63
Professors accessible rating	67
% professors teaching UG courses	70
% classes taught by TAs	20
Most common lab size	20-29 students
Most common regular class size	20-29 students

MOST POPULAR MAJORS

Management information systems
marketing/marketing management
mechanical engineering

STUDENTS SPEAK OUT

Academics

Undergraduates are drawn to Iowa State (ISU) by a number of standout programs (engineering, design, agriculture, and journalism, to name a few) and its low tuition, especially for native Iowans. Like many state schools, ISU is "trying to get by with huge budget cuts"; the school's efforts to address budget shortfalls have included substantial tuition increases. Despite the still-reasonable price of an ISU education, undergrads here are not happy about the situation. Gripes one, "Tuition has been spiraling out of control." Compounding students' financial frustration are large classes ("I have six classes this semester, and four of them have over 200 students in them, plus I have only one class that is under 50. That's just too big") and registration woes. Those who seek a hand-holding atmosphere, be forewarned: "Research is the purpose of Iowa State. There are a lot of excellent extension publications and extension specialists for your reference on most any subject. However, this also means that a lot of the professors don't seem to care about teaching. They are more interested in their research." While students grouse, they also understand that the university is doing the best it can in a bad financial situation; furthermore, they are not blind to the school's many assets. "Technical majors are very heavily recruited here, which makes it easier to get a job," writes one engineer. Another student points out that the Honors Program offers "smaller sections of most classes. The [honors] professors are accessible, helpful, and seem genuinely interested in teaching."

Life

The distinguishing trait of ISU campus life, students tell us, is "the strong sense of community. I've always been amazed at how close-knit the school manages to be with [23,000] undergraduates; it's the best of both worlds because we have the feel of a small college but the resources of a large university." Those resources mean that "there is something for everyone here. There are over 500 clubs and organizations." Undergrads love their "nationally recognized football, wrestling, hockey, and men's and women's basketball" teams, as well as "plenty of intramural opportunities [and] the largest broomball participation in the country." Campus bustles most noticeably "in the spring and fall, [when] most people hang around central campus or the yards by the dorms. In the winter, there are hockey and basketball games and stuff to do on campus sometimes. Winter is more boring than the warmer months." But when a Cyclone team isn't playing, "the big thing here is drinking." Students say, "There are plenty of bars with plenty of specials during the week." Alternatives for the under-21 set include "a dollar theatre at the mall for those students that don't mind seeing old movies," "ample places to eat, a nice mall, lots of places to run and road races to participate in, and many bike paths. Also, Des Moines is only 20 minutes away."

Student Body

How diverse is the Iowa State student body? It depends on which yardstick you use. "Iowa State does have a diverse student population by Iowa standards, but to someone outside of Iowa it might not seem so very diverse," explains one student. Most are "pretty small town–oriented, and Ames is a big town for them." They are "generally warm and friendly, appreciate the fact that they are at a great university, and respect other students." They also "don't spend a whole lot of time thinking about academics." ISU has "a large international student population who fit in well with the rest of the student body;" among these students is "a large population of East Asian students and, in the computer science department particularly, many people from India as well."

Iowa State University

Financial Aid: 515-294-2223 • E-mail: admissions@iastate.edu • Website: www.iastate.edu

ADMISSIONS

Very important factors considered include: Class rank, secondary school record, standardized test scores. *Other factors considered include:* Character/personal qualities, essays, extracurricular activities, geographical residence, interview, recommendations, state residency, talent/ability, volunteer work, work experience. SAT Reasoning or ACT required. TOEFL required of all international applicants. High school diploma is required, and GED is accepted. *Academic units required:* 4 English, 3 math, 3 science (2 science lab), 2 foreign language, 2 social studies. *Academic units recommended:* 4 math, 4 science (3 science lab), 4 foreign language, 4 social studies.

The Inside Word

With a decided lack of mystery in the admissions process and a super-high acceptance rate, Iowa State still attracts a solid student body. What we have here is living proof of the value of a good reputation and a little national press.

FINANCIAL AID

Students should submit: FAFSA. The Princeton Review suggests that all financial aid forms be submitted as soon as possible after 1/1. *Need-based scholarships/grants offered:* Pell, SEOG, state scholarships/grants, the school's own gift aid. *Loan aid offered:* Direct Subsidized Stafford, Direct Unsubsidized Stafford, Direct PLUS, Federal Perkins, state loans, college/university loans from institutional funds, private alternative loans. Applicants will be notified of awards on a rolling basis beginning on or about 4/1.

FROM THE ADMISSIONS OFFICE

"Iowa State University offers all the advantages of a major university along with the friendliness and warmth of a residential campus. There are more than 100 undergraduate programs of study in the Colleges of Agriculture, Business, Design, Education, Engineering, Family and Consumer Sciences, Liberal Arts and Sciences, and Veterinary Medicine. Our 1,700 faculty members include Rhodes Scholars, Fulbright Scholars, and National Academy of Sciences and National Academy of Engineering members. Recognized for its high quality of life, Iowa State has taken practical steps to make the university a place where students feel like they belong. Iowa State has been recognized for the high quality of campus life and the exemplary out-of-class experiences offered to its students. Along with a strong academic experience, students also have opportunities for further developing their leadership skills and interpersonal relationships through any of the more than 500 student organizations, 60 intramural sports, and a multitude of arts and recreational activities. All residence hall rooms are wired for Internet connections, and all students have the opportunity to create their own World Wide Web pages.

"For fall 2006 admission, Iowa State University will accept either the new SAT or the old SAT (administered prior to March 2005 and without a Writing component). The school will also accept the ACT with or without the Writing component."

SELECTIVITY

Admissions Rating	**81**
# of applicants	9,172
% of applicants accepted	90
% of acceptees attending	45

FRESHMAN PROFILE

Range SAT Verbal	530-650
Average SAT Verbal	590
Range SAT Math	550-690
Average SAT Math	620
**TPR Projected Range SAT Writing*	*580-670*
Range ACT Composite	22-27
Average ACT Composite	24
Minimum Paper TOEFL	500
Minimum Computer Based TOEFL	173
Average HS GPA	3.49
% graduated top 10% of class	24
% graduated top 25% of class	56
% graduated top 50% of class	92

DEADLINES

Regular application deadline	7/1
Regular notification	rolling
Nonfall registration?	yes

APPLICANTS ALSO LOOK AT

AND OFTEN PREFER

Purdue University—West Lafayette
University of Illinois at Urbana-Champaign
University of Minnesota—Twin Cities
University of Wisconsin—Madison

AND SOMETIMES PREFER

Drake University
Kansas State University
University of Nebraska—Lincoln
University of Northern Iowa

AND RARELY PREFER

Baylor University
Western Michigan University

FINANCIAL FACTS

Financial Aid Rating	**83**
Annual in-state tuition	$4,702
Annual out-of-state tuition	$14,404
Room & Board	$5,958
Books and supplies	$850
Required fees	$724
% frosh rec. need-based scholarship or grant aid	45
% UG rec. need-based scholarship or grant aid	43
% frosh rec. need-based self-help aid	42
% UG rec. need-based self-help aid	48
% frosh rec. any financial aid	87
% UG rec. any financial aid	77
Avg. frosh grant	$4,960
Avg. frosh loan	$7,721
Independent 529 member?	No

Ithaca College

100 Job Hall, Ithaca, NY 14850-7020 • Admissions: 607-274-3124 • Fax: 607-274-1900

CAMPUS LIFE

Quality of Life Rating	**77**
Fire Safety Rating	**74**
Type of school	private
Environment	village

STUDENTS

Total undergrad enrollment	6,005
% male/female	43/57
% from out of state	55
% from public high school	73
% live on campus	70
% in (# of) fraternities	1
% in (# of) sororities	1 (1)
% African American	2
% Asian	3
% Caucasian	87
% Hispanic	3
% international	3
# of countries represented	70

SURVEY SAYS

Great off-campus food
Frats and sororities are unpopular or nonexistent
Musical organizations are popular
College radio is popular
Theater is popular
Student publications are popular
Lots of beer drinking
Hard liquor is popular

ACADEMICS

Academic Rating	**81**
Calendar	semester
Student/faculty ratio	12:1
Professors interesting rating	80
Professors accessible rating	79
% professors teaching UG courses	99
% classes taught by TAs	1
Most common lab size	fewer than 10 students
Most common regular class size	10-19 students

MOST POPULAR MAJORS

Business administration/management
music/music and performing arts studies
radio and television

STUDENTS SPEAK OUT

Academics

With a "world-recognized music school," a stellar "communications department with amazing facilities," and "extremely strong programs in theater and physical therapy," Ithaca College stakes out a lot of high ground for a school of its size. Perhaps the school strives to achieve so much because of its formidable cross-town competition: Ithaca shares its namesake hometown with Cornell University. IC "offers a wide variety of majors [that] do a good job of opening your eyes to new ideas and the world." Business programs are popular, and many come for the "great programs in the entertainment industry. In the music school, the a cappella groups are so cool to go watch." The "fabulous" theater department "has a program in London for theater students and non-theater majors in theater. It's an amazing experience." The equally distinguished communications program is home to an active radio station and award-wining TV station. "Newswatch16, Ithaca College's own locally broadcasted news program won a College Emmy in the fall of 2003 for a spectacular broadcast." In all areas, professors "are very accessible and, because the class sizes are small, they actually know you." Teachers "love class discussions more than just lecturing, and there is always time for questions. Those who exert the extra effort to participate will generally excel more than those who sit in the shadows." At IC "you won't get lost in a sea of people, but it's large enough to offer diverse classes and lots of extracurriculars" as well as "a study abroad program that totally rocks!!!"

Life

"Everyone has fun on the weekends" at Ithaca College, "either through the college or through someone who is having a party. If not, you can travel two minutes to Cornell frats and party there, or go downtown and have tons of fun listening to music or eating out." There's "a lot of culture on and off campus—tons of music, theater, hippie stuff, political happenings." Variety reigns: "One day there's a sold-out football game; the next there's a gay pride rally or a drum circle on the quad." The weather dictates extracurricular life to some extent. "The first month or two of the fall semester, the weather is breathtaking and you get to experience all the beauty the Ithaca area has to offer. You can go hiking, cliff-jumping, camping, swimming, fishing, explore the head shops in the Commons, or just lay outside on one of the many grassy quads and relax in the sun—then the first snowstorm hits and everything changes. Your list of possible activities shortens drastically—unless you're a ski enthusiast, you're basically forced into hibernation until the last month or so of school, when the weather finally gets nice again." Intercollegiate athletics are "a big thing at IC. Even though we're only Division III, students get psyched for football games and such. Intramural and club sports are also big." But "even more people are into our musical and non-sporty exploits. If there was an NCAA thing for band and choir, we would be at the top of Division I."

Student Body

"Ithaca has several different types of 'typical students," undergrads here tell us. "As far as groups go, there seem to be the jocks, the preps, and the hippies. But even if you don't fit into these groups, you will fit in someplace else." Besides, at IC "jocks and hippies interact much more than they would at another school." While the "majority are white, come from privilege, don't have strong religious backgrounds, and are liberal and well-informed in politics," there are also plenty "who come from very religious backgrounds, and those who are conservative and/or Republican, those who are politically apathetic, a mixture of ethnic/minority students and foreign students, all of whom get along with the majority students, [and] a large gay community that seems to be generally accepted by the population. There is very little discrimination on this campus." Students see "an even spread of Protestant, Catholic, and Jewish faith students. There is even a strict 'Kosher Kitchen' in one of the campus dining halls."

FINANCIAL AID: 607-274-3131 • E-MAIL: ADMISSION@ITHACA.EDU • WEBSITE: WWW.ITHACA.EDU

ADMISSIONS

Very important factors considered include: Secondary school record, standardized test scores. *Important factors considered include:* Character/personal qualities, class rank, essays, extracurricular activities, interview, recommendations, talent/ability. *Other factors considered include:* Alumni/ae relation, volunteer work, work experience. SAT Reasoning or ACT required. TOEFL required of all international applicants. High school diploma is required, and GED is accepted. *Academic units required:* 4 English, 3 math, 3 science, 2 foreign language, 3 social studies, 1 academic elective.

The Inside Word

Ithaca has enjoyed a renaissance of interest from prospective students of late, and its moderately competitive admissions profile has been bolstered as a result. In addition to a thorough review of academic accomplishments, candidates are always given close consideration of their personal background, talents, and achievements. Programs requiring an audition or portfolio review are among the college's most demanding for admission; the arts have always been particularly strong.

FINANCIAL AID

Students should submit: FAFSA, CSS/Financial Aid PROFILE required of early decision applicants by 11/1. The Princeton Review suggests that all financial aid forms be submitted as soon as possible after 1/1. *Need-based scholarships/grants offered:* Pell, SEOG, state scholarships/grants, private scholarships, the school's own gift aid. *Loan aid offered:* FFEL Subsidized Stafford, FFEL Unsubsidized Stafford, FFEL PLUS, Federal Perkins, college/university loans from institutional funds. Applicants will be notified of awards on a rolling basis beginning on or about 2/15. Federal Work-study Program available. Off-campus job opportunities are good.

FROM THE ADMISSIONS OFFICE

"Ithaca College was founded in 1892 as a music conservatory, and it continues that commitment to performance and excellence. Its modern, residential 750-acre campus, equipped with state-of-the-art facilities, is home to the schools of Business, Communications, Health Sciences and Human Performance, Humanities and Sciences, and Music and our new Division of Interdisciplinary and International Studies. With more than 100 majors—from biochemistry to business administration, journalism to jazz, philosophy to physical therapy, and special programs in Washington, DC, Los Angeles, London, and Australia—students enjoy the curricular choices of a large campus in a personalized, smaller school environment. And Ithaca's students benefit from an education that emphasizes active learning, small classes, collaborative student-faculty research, and development of the whole student. Located in central New York's spectacular Finger Lakes region in what many consider the classic college town, the college has 25 highly competitive varsity teams, more than 130 campus clubs, two radio stations and a television station, as well as hundreds of concerts, recitals, and theater performances annually.

"Students applying for admission must have either SAT or ACT scores sent to Ithaca College by the testing agency. Students applying for fall 2006 admission may submit scores from the new SAT or the ACT with the Writing section. The college will also consider results of SAT Subject Tests, if submitted."

SELECTIVITY

Admissions Rating	**86**
# of applicants	10,401
% of applicants accepted	67
% of acceptees attending	21
# of early decision applicants	132
% accepted early decision	50

FRESHMAN PROFILE

Range SAT Verbal	540-640
Average SAT Verbal	594
Range SAT Math	550-640
Average SAT Math	596
**TPR Projected Range SAT Writing*	*590-660*
Minimum Paper TOEFL	550
Minimum Computer Based TOEFL	213
% graduated top 10% of class	33
% graduated top 25% of class	71
% graduated top 50% of class	97

DEADLINES

Early decision application deadline	11/1
Early decision notification	12/15
Regular application deadline	2/1
Regular notification	rolling
Nonfall registration?	yes

APPLICANTS ALSO LOOK AT

AND OFTEN PREFER

Boston University, Cornell University, New York University

AND SOMETIMES PREFER

Penn State University Park, Skidmore College, Syracuse University, Union College (NY), University of Rochester, University of Vermont

AND RARELY PREFER

SUNY at Binghamton, SUNY College at Geneseo, University of Delaware, University of Massachusetts—Amherst

FINANCIAL FACTS

Financial Aid Rating	**80**
Annual tuition	$25,194
Room & Board	$9,950
Books and supplies	$968
% frosh rec. need-based scholarship or grant aid	67
% UG rec. need-based scholarship or grant aid	66
% frosh rec. need-based self-help aid	63
% UG rec. need-based self-help aid	62
% frosh rec. any financial aid	88
% UG rec. any financial aid	86
Avg. frosh grant	$14,103
Avg. frosh loan	$5,007
Independent 529 member?	Yes

James Madison University

Sonner Hall, MSC 0101, Harrisonburg, VA 22807 • Admissions: 540-568-5681 • Fax: 540-568-3332

CAMPUS LIFE

Quality of Life Rating	**89**
Fire Safety Rating	**79**
Type of school	public
Environment	town

STUDENTS

Total undergrad enrollment	14,677
% male/female	40/60
% from out of state	29
% live on campus	39
% in (# of) fraternities	9 (15)
% in (# of) sororities	14 (8)
% African American	3
% Asian	5
% Caucasian	85
% Hispanic	2
% international	1
# of countries represented	53

SURVEY SAYS

Students are friendly
Great food on campus
Great off-campus food
Lots of beer drinking

ACADEMICS

Academic Rating	**80**
Calendar	semester
Student/faculty ratio	17:1
Professors interesting rating	85
Professors accessible rating	84
% professors teaching UG courses	100
% classes taught by TAs	1
Most common lab size	20-29 students
Most common regular class size	20-29 students

MOST POPULAR MAJORS

Communications studies/speech communication and rhetoric
marketing/marketing management
psychology

STUDENTS SPEAK OUT

Academics

Students at James Madison University, a state institution whose strengths include "a good business school" and solid health services programs, love their school's "welcoming environment, in which you feel comfortable within your surroundings, whether it is in class, one-on-one with a professor, out at a party, or sitting in your dorm room." "Almost all the students you meet are in love with this school," both for its "well-ranked academics" and for its capacity to deliver "more fun than you can have anywhere else." Undergrads here tout the school's technology-related disciplines, singling out the "unique integrated science and technology major" as an example of their school's eagerness to innovate. The physics department is also "exceptional," students report, "with professors who are friendly and willing to get to know you on a personal level" and a "small, research-oriented environment." In many other areas, students praise the faculty's "willingness to extend learning outside of the classroom if students have ideas for projects [and] research," and their "realistic method of teaching to prepare students for real-world job applications." Class sizes here vary widely by department; classes in disciplines with high enrollments are often overcrowded, especially at the introductory level, while students in less popular programs report that they "have very few classes with over 50 people in them."

Life

"Extracurricular activities are a definite strength" of JMU, where "there is something for everyone to get involved in. I don't know one person who is not involved with at least something or another on campus. This is not limited to fraternities or sororities, though Greek life is inviting and generally respected." Partying is big here; "We have made the top 25 party school list in Playboy," students brag, explaining that "it's not like we have those gigantic theme parties where half the school attends. Instead there are just so many apartment parties and each weekend. I'd say at least 50 on any Friday or Saturday. Thursday is also a big 'go out' day." Most here agree that "everyone is pretty balanced when it comes to work and play" and that "the attendance [at games] and strength of the athletic teams at JMU could stand to improve. No one is really interested in athletic events, nor do people really attend them, including the football games. Let's be serious: sports are a big part of the collegiate experience, and quite frankly we have one of the most pathetic sports programs of any school with 15,000 students." Undergrads here love to work out in their spare time; the University Recreation Center (UREC) "is always packed. It is an amazing facility with tons of options for an individual or group workout. UREC also hosts many of the intramural sports that JMU students are involved in."

Student Body

The "friendly and outgoing" student body of James Madison University evinces Southern courtesy; writes one Yankee transplant, "Everyone holds the door open for you, guys are nice and girls are too. Everyone is very trusting." "Republicans dominate" this Red State campus "and will aggressively defend their values." The school "has a fairly homogeneous population." Writes one student, "It isn't that people don't accept differences; it's that there just aren't any. I think people are even friendlier to those students who don't fit the mold as a way of saying, 'Hey, thank you for being different.' There is a kid in my dorm with blue hair. He is everyone's friend because they all want to be friends with the kid who has blue hair." Some point out that "each entering class appears to be more diverse." While "most students are from middle-class Virginia suburbs," the school attracts many others from "Washington DC, New York City, and Philadelphia."

James Madison University

Financial Aid: 540-568-7820 • E-mail: gotojmu@jmu.edu • Website: www.jmu.edu

ADMISSIONS

Very important factors considered include: Class rank, secondary school record, standardized test scores. *Other factors considered include:* Alumni/ae relation, character/personal qualities, essays, extracurricular activities, geographical residence, minority status, recommendations, state residency, talent/ability, volunteer work, work experience. SAT Reasoning or ACT required. TOEFL required of all international applicants. High school diploma is required, and GED is accepted. *Academic units required:* 4 English, 4 math, 3 science (3 science lab), 3 foreign language, 1 social studies, 3 history. *Academic units recommended:* 4 science.

The Inside Word

James Madison has prospered from the applications of students faced with severe competition for admission to UVA and William and Mary. Third place on the Virginia public university totem pole is not a bad spot to be, as JMU's admissions committee will attest. Pay attention when they stress that your high school schedule should be chock-full of challenging academic courses.

FINANCIAL AID

Students should submit: FAFSA. The Princeton Review suggests that all financial aid forms be submitted as soon as possible after 1/1. *Need-based scholarships/grants offered:* Pell, SEOG, state scholarships/grants, private scholarships, the school's own gift aid. *Loan aid offered:* FFEL Subsidized Stafford, FFEL Unsubsidized Stafford, FFEL PLUS, Federal Perkins. Applicants will be notified of awards on a rolling basis beginning on or about 4/1. Federal Work-study Program available. Institutional employment available. Off-campus job opportunities are good.

FROM THE ADMISSIONS OFFICE

"James Madison University's philosophy of inclusiveness—known as 'all together one'—means that students become a part of a real community that nurtures its own to learn, grow, and succeed. Our professors, many of whom have a wealth of real world experience, pride themselves on making teaching their top priority. We take seriously the responsibility to maintain an environment that fosters learning and encourages students to excel in and out of the classroom. Our rich variety of educational, social, and extracurricular activities include more than 100 innovative and traditional undergraduate majors and programs, a well-established study abroad program, a cutting-edge information security program, more than 280 student clubs and organizations, and a 147,000-square-foot, state-of-the-art recreation center. The university's picturesque, self-contained campus is located in the heart of the Shenandoah Valley, a four-season area that's easy to call home. Great food, fun times, exciting intercollegiate athletics, and rigorous academics all combine to create the unique James Madison experience. From the library to the residence halls and from our outstanding honors program to our highly successful career placement program, the university is committed to equipping our students with the tools they need to achieve their dreams.

"The new SAT will be used starting with the freshman applicants for fall 2006. High school students graduating in 2006 or 2007 will have the option of submitting scores from either the new or old versions of the SAT. The highest composite score will be used in admissions decisions."

SELECTIVITY

Admissions Rating	**89**
# of applicants	15,013
% of applicants accepted	63
% of acceptees attending	35
# accepting a place on wait list	1,614
% admitted from wait list	19
# of early decision applicants	2,141

FRESHMAN PROFILE

Range SAT Verbal	530-620
Average SAT Verbal	579
Range SAT Math	540-630
Average SAT Math	583
**TPR Projected Range SAT Writing*	*580-650*
Range ACT Composite	22-26
Minimum Paper TOEFL	570
Minimum Computer Based TOEFL	230
Average HS GPA	3.68
% graduated top 10% of class	31
% graduated top 25% of class	79
% graduated top 50% of class	99

DEADLINES

Regular application deadline	1/15
Regular notification	4/1
Nonfall registration?	no

APPLICANTS ALSO LOOK AT

AND OFTEN PREFER

College of William and Mary
University of Virginia

AND SOMETIMES PREFER

George Mason University
Penn State University Park
Rutgers University—Rutgers College
University of Delaware
University of Maryland—College Park
Villanova University
Virginia Tech

FINANCIAL FACTS

Financial Aid Rating	**61**
Annual in-state tuition	$5,476
Annual out-of-state tuition	$14,420
Room & Board	$3,880
% frosh rec. need-based scholarship or grant aid	16
% UG rec. need-based scholarship or grant aid	13
% frosh rec. need-based self-help aid	27
% UG rec. need-based self-help aid	23
% frosh rec. any financial aid	53
% UG rec. any financial aid	47
Avg. frosh grant	$4,673
Avg. frosh loan	$2,873
Independent 529 member?	No

JOHNS HOPKINS UNIVERSITY

3400 NORTH CHARLES STREET/140 GARLAND, BALTIMORE, MD 21218 • ADMISSIONS: 410-516-8171 • FAX: 410-516-6025

CAMPUS LIFE

Quality of Life Rating	**66**
Fire Safety Rating	**60**
Type of school	private
Environment	metropolis

STUDENTS

Total undergrad enrollment	4,201
% male/female	56/44
% from out of state	85
% from public high school	60
% live on campus	50
% in (# of) fraternities	22 (11)
% in (# of) sororities	20 (7)
% African American	5
% Asian	22
% Caucasian	62
% Hispanic	5
% international	5
# of countries represented	52

SURVEY SAYS

Lab facilities are great
Great computer facilities
Great library
Athletic facilities are great
Diverse student types on campus
Students are happy
Lots of beer drinking
Hard liquor is popular

ACADEMICS

Academic Rating	**86**
Calendar	semester
Student/faculty ratio	9:1
Professors interesting rating	63
Professors accessible rating	63
% professors teaching UG courses	96
% classes taught by TAs	0
Most common lab size	10-19 students
Most common regular class size	10-19 students

MOST POPULAR MAJORS

Biology/biological sciences
biomedical/medical engineering
international relations and affairs

STUDENTS SPEAK OUT

Academics

Johns Hopkins has earned a top reputation as an "excellent and challenging" university, with students who believe their school is "second to none." They value the "contacts you can make" with top professionals in a wide variety of fields. Professors, known to be "experts in their respective areas," take the time to "learn names, talk with students, and give them great advice," according to a student in the political science department, who adds, "Get to know them—it's worthwhile." Another student gushes, "I love the way instructors care about us," making themselves "generally available to offer help outside of class." One student in the "phenomenal" accelerated nursing program calls the course load "highly intense," which leaves "barely any time for social life." The most common complaint logged at Johns Hopkins concerns the perception that professors and administration alike prioritize research over teaching, leading some students to moan that professors think "undergraduates are peons who don't matter much." Students want to see more support for the arts at the school and say that professors in the humanities focus more on their role as teachers than their counterparts in the sciences. The administration, which "needs to be more helpful and understanding," in the words of a few respondents, "prioritizes engineering and medical research" over the needs of undergraduates. Current students remind prospective attendees that they will have to be "proactive to get the best education," but the rewards include the "immense amount of opportunity available for students with good ideas."

Life

In the "highly educational environment" of Johns Hopkins, it may seem that "there's not a lot to do besides fraternity parties and homework." Students report, "You have to find your own fun, but it isn't hard to do." Those who have a difficult time entertaining themselves can always fall back on the "instant social life that erupts when you join a fraternity." One undergrad writes, "We generally don't go out more than once or twice a week, but when we do, we live it up." A freshman majoring in international relations appreciates that "there's enough that you can find stuff to do but not so much that it is a distraction." Though one student whines that "Baltimore is a ghetto," many students head downtown when "there isn't much to do on campus." An upperclassman reassures students, "Once you are old enough for bars, it gets better," especially for those with wheels. Many surveys note the brand-spanking-new athletic center, which entices students to play sports and attend to their cardiovascular systems during study breaks. Some students say the school could improve in terms of "clubs and anything school supported," but others offer, "If you want to build a new social outlet, the money [from the school] is available."

Student Body

A typical student who chooses Johns Hopkins might be described as "overly ambitious," "introverted," and "hardworking." To some people, the assortment of "too many weirdos" that makes up the student body displays "little personality." On the one hand, a few students accuse their group of peers, in general, of being "ruled too much by their parents' wishes." On the other hand, one student tells us, "People surprise me (in a good way) every day." Even if "kids could be cooler," respondents agree that "most are good people" and "everyone tends to work together." Accusations of blandness aren't universal; some students boast that "everyone here has done interesting things." While many students say, "We all get along," the population seems to "lack of a sense of unified community," and at times "cultural barriers are very hard to break through."

JOHNS HOPKINS UNIVERSITY

FINANCIAL AID: 410-516-8028 • E-MAIL: GOTOJHU@JHU.EDU • WEBSITE: WWW.JHU.EDU

ADMISSIONS

Very important factors considered include: Character/personal qualities, essays, recommendations, secondary school record. *Important factors considered include:* Class rank, extracurricular activities, standardized test scores, talent/ability, volunteer work. *Other factors considered include:* Alumni/ae relation, geographical residence, interview, minority status, state residency, work experience. SAT Reasoning or ACT required. SAT Subject Tests recommended. TOEFL required of all international applicants. High school diploma is required, and GED is accepted. *Academic units recommended:* 4 English, 4 math, 3 science (2 science lab), 4 foreign language, 3 social studies, 3 history, 2 foreign language (for engineering majors).

The Inside Word

The admissions process at Hopkins demands to be taken seriously. Competition with the best colleges and universities in the country keeps the acceptance rate artificially high. Make certain that your personal credentials—essays, recommendations, and extracurricular activities—are impressive.

FINANCIAL AID

Students should submit: FAFSA, CSS/Financial Aid PROFILE, noncustodial (divorced/separated) parents' statement, business/farm supplement, prior and current year federal tax returns. Regular filing deadline is 2/15. The Princeton Review suggests that all financial aid forms be submitted as soon as possible after 1/1. *Need-based scholarships/grants offered:* Pell, SEOG, state scholarships/grants, private scholarships, the school's own gift aid. *Loan aid offered:* Direct Subsidized Stafford, Direct Unsubsidized Stafford, FFEL PLUS, Federal Perkins, college/university loans from institutional funds. Applicants will be notified of awards on or about 4/1.

FROM THE ADMISSIONS OFFICE

"The Hopkins tradition of preeminent academic excellence naturally attracts the very best students in the nation and from around the world. The Admissions Committee carefully examines each application for evidence of compelling intellectual interest and academic performance as well as strong personal recommendations and meaningful extracurricular contributions. Every applicant who matriculates to Johns Hopkins University was found qualified by the Admissions Committee through a 'whole person' assessment, and every applicant accepted for admission is fully expected to graduate. The Admissions Committee determines whom they believe will take full advantage of the exceptional opportunities offered at Hopkins, contribute the most to the educational process of the institution, and be the most successful in using what they have learned and experienced for the benefit of society.

"Freshman applicants for fall 2006 may take either the old SAT and three SAT Subject Tests (one must be Writing) or the ACT. Alternatively, students may take either the new SAT or the ACT with Writing component. For those submitting SAT scores, submitting scores from three SAT Subject Tests is recommended."

SELECTIVITY

Admissions Rating	**98**
# of applicants	11,102
% of applicants accepted	30
% of acceptees attending	32
# accepting a place on wait list	1,612
% admitted from wait list	8
# of early decision applicants	362
% accepted early decision	59

FRESHMAN PROFILE

Range SAT Verbal	640-730
Average SAT Verbal	680
Range SAT Math	660-760
Average SAT Math	706
**TPR Projected Range SAT Writing*	*660-720*
Range ACT Composite	27-32
Average ACT Composite	29
Minimum Paper TOEFL	600
Minimum Computer Based TOEFL	250
Average HS GPA	3.67
% graduated top 10% of class	80
% graduated top 25% of class	96
% graduated top 50% of class	99

DEADLINES

Early decision application deadline	11/15
Early decision notification	12/15
Regular application deadline	1/1
Regular notification	4/1
Nonfall registration?	no

APPLICANTS ALSO LOOK AT

AND OFTEN PREFER

Harvard College, Massachusetts Institute of Technology, Princeton U., U. of Pennsylvania, Yale U.

AND SOMETIMES PREFER

Brown U., Columbia U.—Columbia College, Cornell U., Duke U.

AND RARELY PREFER

Boston U., Carnegie Mellon U.

FINANCIAL FACTS

Financial Aid Rating	**89**
Annual tuition	$31,620
Room & Board	$9,924
Books and supplies	$850
Required fees	$500
% frosh rec. need-based scholarship or grant aid	39
% UG rec. need-based scholarship or grant aid	38
% frosh rec. need-based self-help aid	45
% UG rec. need-based self-help aid	41
% frosh rec. any financial aid	51
% UG rec. any financial aid	45
Avg. frosh grant	$22,893
Avg. frosh loan	$2,712
Independent 529 member?	No

JUNIATA COLLEGE

1700 MOORE STREET, HUNTINGDON, PA 16652 • ADMISSIONS: 814-641-3420 • FAX: 814-641-3100

CAMPUS LIFE

Quality of Life Rating	**85**
Fire Safety Rating	**84**
Type of school	private
Affiliation	Church of Brethren
Environment	village

STUDENTS

Total undergrad enrollment	1,378
% male/female	46/54
% from out of state	30
% from public high school	89
% live on campus	84
% African American	1
% Asian	1
% Caucasian	91
% Hispanic	1
% international	4
# of countries represented	26

SURVEY SAYS

Small classes
Lab facilities are great
Students are friendly
Campus feels safe
Low cost of living
Frats and sororities are unpopular or nonexistent

ACADEMICS

Academic Rating	**88**
Calendar	semester
Student/faculty ratio	13:1
Professors interesting rating	88
Professors accessible rating	91
% professors teaching UG courses	100
% classes taught by TAs	0
Most common lab size	10-19 students
Most common regular class size	10-19 students

MOST POPULAR MAJORS

Biology/biological sciences
Business administration/management
education

STUDENTS SPEAK OUT

Academics

"Science is definitely big" at Juniata College, a small, rural liberal arts college in central Pennsylvania, and the school clearly plans to keep it that way. Juniata recently opened a new science center with "state-of-the-art lab facilities and high tech gadgets [that] give students hands-on opportunities to really dive into research. There are great opportunities to prepare for graduate school." But "science isn't the only thing that we offer," students insist; many want you to know that "Juniata also has a much-overlooked yet highly competent education program" and that "you can't go wrong with English, communication, history, foreign languages, or philosophy," although a few warn that "certain departments are really small, and don't receive the support that the sciences have." Through a unique Program of Emphasis (POE) option, Juniata undergrads "can personalize their own program to get a better educational experience." One student writes, "Juniata's Program of Emphasis is a major strength. Students are able to have their major and involve other classes that they may be interested in. For an example, we have students who are computer science majors and also have an emphasis on acting. By allowing students to combine classes that may not be required, they can experience many different things." No matter what undergrads choose to study, "This school is about challenging yourself and your view on the world in preparation for becoming part of it."

Life

Because Juniata "is located in beautiful Huntingdon, PA," "there are a lot of things to do outdoors, such as hiking, camping, and biking [but] the town is predominantly residential, so with the exception of the bowling alley and movie theater, there is not much to do here." The college fills the void by "offering wonderful extracurricular activities, from the academic groups such as the Null Set (the mathematics club) and the Barristers Club (for pre-law students), to AWOL (our gay-straight alliance), to the Japanese Club and dozens of others." There's also "a very active campus ministry," as well as "concerts, speakers, shows, and screenings on campus all the time. It is impossible to do everything." Juniata's athletic teams "are another strength. Our men's and women's volleyball teams have both recently won NCAA championships…and our field hockey team is becoming one of the strongest in the nation." Furthermore, the JC calendar is peppered with "several unique traditions, such as Mountain Day, Mr. Juniata, Storming of the Arch, and Madrigal Tenting. These allow the entire Juniata community to get out and have fun with each other." When students seek larger crowds, they travel to Altoona or State College, each about a half-hour's drive away.

Student Body

The "self-driven" undergrads of Juniata "really love what they're studying, and it becomes their life. Once you've accepted that, the school really opens up to you. Everyone is equally interested in their own POE, so you find yourself in really interesting conversations about anything from science to politics to religion. It's great." A large proportion of "the kids who attend here play a varsity or club sport," so a "typical student at Juniata is an athlete." He or she is also "liberal, and proud of it. If you walked around here the day before Election Day 2004 and thought that this campus was a reflection of the rest of the country, you would think that there is no way in hell that George Bush would win the election." Most undergrads "are from Pennsylvania or the surrounding mid-Atlantic states," with a split of "half 'hicks,' half city kids." Although "this is mostly a middle- to upper-class, white, Christian campus…the new Office of Diversity has begun bringing in a promising increase in people of different ethnic and religious backgrounds, as well as different sexual orientations."

JUNIATA COLLEGE

FINANCIAL AID: 814-641-3142 • E-MAIL: INFO@JUNIATA.EDU • WEBSITE: WWW.JUNIATA.EDU

ADMISSIONS

Very important factors considered include: Character/personal qualities, essays, extracurricular activities, recommendations, secondary school record, standardized test scores. *Important factors considered include:* Alumni/ae relation, interview, minority status, talent/ability, volunteer work. *Other factors considered include:* Class rank. SAT Reasoning or ACT recommended. TOEFL required of all international applicants. High school diploma is required, and GED is accepted. *Academic units required:* 4 English, 3 math, 3 science (2 science lab), 2 foreign language, 1 social studies, 3 history. *Academic units recommended:* 4 English, 4 math, 4 science (2 science lab), 2 foreign language, 1 social studies, 3 history.

The Inside Word

Like at many traditional liberal arts schools, the admissions process at Juniata is a personal one. The school wants students who will decide to attend Juniata and stay for the next fours years. Among Juniata's bragging rights are that a staggering 40 percent of students graduate with a degree in science, 60 percent of undergrads design their own major, and 78 percent participate in internships.

FINANCIAL AID

Students should submit: FAFSA. Regular filing deadline is 3/1. The Princeton Review suggests that all financial aid forms be submitted as soon as possible after 1/1. *Need-based scholarships/grants offered:* Pell, SEOG, state scholarships/grants, private scholarships, the school's own gift aid. *Loan aid offered:* FFEL Subsidized Stafford, FFEL Unsubsidized Stafford, FFEL PLUS, Federal Perkins, college/university loans from institutional funds. Applicants will be notified of awards on a rolling basis beginning on or about 2/1. Federal Work-study Program available. Institutional employment available. Off-campus job opportunities are fair.

FROM THE ADMISSIONS OFFICE

"Juniata's unique approach to learning has a flexible, student-centered focus. With the help of two advisors, over half of Juniata's students design their own majors (called the "Program of Emphasis" or "POE"). Those who choose a more traditional academic journey still benefit from the assistance of two faculty advisors and interdisciplinary collaboration between multiple academic departments.

"In addition, all students benefit from the recent, significant investments in academic facilities that help students actively learn by doing. For example, the new Halbritter Performing Arts Center houses an innovative theatre program where theatre professionals work side by side with students; the Sill Business Incubator provides $5,000 in seed capital to students with a desire to start their own business; the LEEDS-certified Shuster Environmental Studies Field Station, located on nearby Raystown Lake, gives unparalleled hands-on study opportunities to students; and the von Liebig Center for Science provides opportunities for student/faculty research surpassing those available at even large universities.

"As the 2003 Middle States Accreditation Team noted, "Juniata is truly a student-centered college. There is a remarkable cohesiveness in this commitment—faculty, students, trustees, staff, and alumni, each from their own vantage point, describe a community in which the growth of the student is central." This cohesiveness creates a dynamic learning environment that enables students to think and grow intellectually, to evolve in their academic careers, and to graduate as active, successful participants in the global community.

"Freshman applicants for fall 2006 may submit either the new SAT (or the ACT with the Writing component) or the old (before March 2005) SAT (or ACT); we will use their best scores from either test. "

SELECTIVITY

Admissions Rating	**88**
# of applicants	1,761
% of applicants accepted	74
% of acceptees attending	30
# of early decision applicants	112
% accepted early decision	85

FRESHMAN PROFILE

Range SAT Verbal	530-630
Average SAT Verbal	580
Range SAT Math	540-630
Average SAT Math	582
**TPR Projected Range SAT Writing*	*580-650*
Minimum Paper TOEFL	550
Minimum Computer Based TOEFL	213
Average HS GPA	3.76
% graduated top 10% of class	38
% graduated top 25% of class	76
% graduated top 50% of class	99

DEADLINES

Early decision application deadline	11/15
Early decision notification	12/30
Regular application deadline	3/15
Regular notification	rolling
Nonfall registration?	yes

APPLICANTS ALSO LOOK AT AND OFTEN PREFER

Bucknell University

AND SOMETIMES PREFER

Dickinson College
Gettysburg College
Muhlenberg College
Ursinus College

AND RARELY PREFER

Allegheny College
Elizabethtown College
Lebanon Valley College
Susquehanna University
Washington & Jefferson College

FINANCIAL FACTS

Financial Aid Rating	**76**
Annual tuition	$25,260
Room & Board	$7,240
Books and supplies	$600
Required fees	$630
% frosh rec. need-based scholarship or grant aid	74
% UG rec. need-based scholarship or grant aid	75
% frosh rec. need-based self-help aid	57
% UG rec. need-based self-help aid	62
% frosh rec. any financial aid	99
% UG rec. any financial aid	96
Avg. frosh grant	$16,246
Avg. frosh loan	$3,195
Independent 529 member?	Yes

KALAMAZOO COLLEGE

1200 ACADEMY STREET, KALAMAZOO, MI 49006 • ADMISSIONS: 616-337-7166 • FAX: 269-337-7390

CAMPUS LIFE

Quality of Life Rating	**73**
Fire Safety Rating	**60**
Type of school	private
Environment	city

STUDENTS

Total undergrad enrollment	1,242
% male/female	44/56
% from out of state	26
% from public high school	85
% live on campus	75
% African American	3
% Asian	5
% Caucasian	82
% Hispanic	1

SURVEY SAYS

Small classes
No one cheats
Frats and sororities are unpopular or nonexistent

ACADEMICS

Academic Rating	**89**
Calendar	quarter
Student/faculty ratio	11:1
Professors interesting rating	90
Professors accessible rating	86
% professors teaching UG courses	100
% classes taught by TAs	0
Most common lab size	10-19 students
Most common regular class size	10-19 students

MOST POPULAR MAJORS

Economics
psychology

STUDENTS SPEAK OUT

Academics

Kalamazoo College (K-Zoo) has a plan for its students, called, appropriately enough, the K-Plan, which requires a liberal-arts-heavy curriculum and a Senior Individualized Project for students in all departments. "The dimensions of the K-Plan include lifelong learning, career readiness, intercultural understanding, social responsibility, and leadership," notes one student. Students love the optional components of the plan, reporting that "internships are highly encouraged, and students are assisted in every way to obtain an internship." Other students add that they "really have the best study-abroad program in the county. Almost all students go for at least three months, and as many as ten months." They are slightly less enthusiastic about the required aspects of the plan mostly because they entail an enormous amount of work. The curriculum is especially writing-intensive. Undergraduates report, "We write papers when we declare our majors, we write papers when we finish our majors, we write papers before we go abroad, we write papers before we come back from abroad, and we write masters-level theses before we graduate." A fast-moving quarterly academic calendar magnifies the academic intensity. Fortunately, the typical student is up to the challenge. One student sums up that mentality, "You don't find kids here that went to college 'because it's what you do.' Kids like that pick schools that are easier and cheaper. Most K-kids are pretty hardcore, and it's great because it keeps us all thinking about what we're really after in life and what we're going to do here to facilitate it."

Life

Thanks to the Liberal Arts Colloquium (LAC), the K-Plan figures not only into academic life, but also into Kalamazoo's extracurricular scene. The LAC consists of approximately 100 lectures and concerts annually. "Students must attend at least 25 LAC events before they graduate. I think this is a wonderful way to broaden the horizons of students," one undergraduate tells us. For many students, spare time is at a premium: "Students spend a lot of time studying, and a lot of time sitting around talking about how they need to study more," explains one student. Yet, some undergraduates still find the time to occasionally enjoy themselves. Kalamazoo has "no huge parties because we have no Greek life," but there are dorm get-togethers, bars in town, and parties at neighboring Western Michigan University. Undergraduates "go to school sporting events when they can, and if it's the weekend, there's usually a concert or movie or something that one can do." Also, "student organizations put on tons of events each quarter. We have Monte Carlo, [where] the professors are the dealers at all of the tables. There is a dance connected to it as well. In the spring we have Spring Fling where they bring big inflatable games, like sumo wrestling or boxing or obstacle courses for the students to play on all day." Otherwise, "fun consists of actually taking that once-a-day break from studies to listen to music, talk with friends, read a book, or just nap."

Student Body

"There are a lot of rich, yuppie kids" at Kalamazoo, as well as "a lot of quirky people." One student notes, "My friends and I joke that there's a check box on the school's application that says 'Are you weird? If so, please explain how.' And we mean that as a good thing!" The school draws heavily from both urban Detroit and the rural small towns of Michigan, creating "a strange mix of left-wing students and right-wing students—all very politically active—crammed together in a small school, pissing each other off and educating each other at the same time." The school is too small for folks to avoid one another, which students see as mostly a good thing. Undergrads agree that "there's one point that ties us all together, which is that each student is very passionate about something, be it a political, religious, or recreational topic, and they continue to do things to help the cause."

FINANCIAL AID: 269-337-7192 • E-MAIL: ADMISSION@KZOO.EDU • WEBSITE: WWW.KZOO.EDU

ADMISSIONS

Very important factors considered include: Extracurricular activities, secondary school record, standardized test scores, talent/ability. *Important factors considered include:* Character/personal qualities, class rank, essays, recommendations, volunteer work, work experience. *Other factors considered include:* Alumni/ae relation, geographical residence, interview, minority status, state residency. SAT Reasoning or ACT required. TOEFL required of all international applicants. High school diploma is required, and GED is accepted. *Academic units recommended:* 4 English, 3 math, 3 science, 3 foreign language, 2 social studies, 2 history.

The Inside Word

K-Zoo's applicant pool is small and self-selected academically, which leads to the unusual combination of a very high acceptance rate and an impressive freshman profile. The admissions committee expects candidates to show evidence of serious academic intent, suitability for the college, and a willingness to contribute to the life of the college. Candidates who underestimate the evaluation process risk denial.

FINANCIAL AID

Students should submit: FAFSA, institution's own financial aid form, noncustodial (divorced/separated) parents' statement. The Princeton Review suggests that all financial aid forms be submitted as soon as possible after 1/1. *Need-based scholarships/grants offered:* Pell, SEOG, state scholarships/grants, private scholarships, the school's own gift aid. *Loan aid offered:* Direct Subsidized Stafford, Direct Unsubsidized Stafford, Direct PLUS, Federal Perkins, state loans. Applicants will be notified of awards on or about 3/21. Federal Work-study Program available. Institutional employment available. Off-campus job opportunities are good.

FROM THE ADMISSIONS OFFICE

"Anyone can pursue any component of the K-Plan at any college, but it is rare to see the purposeful integration and high participation rate found at Kalamazoo. Over the last 40 years, 85 percent of our graduates have formally studied in another country while 80 percent have completed an internship or externship, and 100 percent complete a senior project. Our students often pursue international internships and senior project experiences, in addition to their planned study abroad terms. Also, Kalamazoo is one of the few selective liberal arts colleges to be found in a city—the Kalamazoo metro area has a population of approximately 225,000 with the advantage of being near a university of nearly 30,000 students. It is a diverse and vibrant community with wonderful access to the arts, athletics, service learning, and community service opportunities. We are a small and personal college with bigger opportunities.

"Kalamazoo College is one of 40 colleges selected to be in Loren Pope's popular book, *Colleges That Change Lives.* Loren selected Kalamazoo and the other 39 colleges based on reasonable cost, unique programs and curricula, and cocurricular activities that all contribute to dramatically changing the lives of those students who find us.

"As of this book's publication, Kalamazoo College did not have information available about their policy regarding the new SAT."

SELECTIVITY

Admissions Rating	**90**
# of applicants	1,603
% of applicants accepted	70
% of acceptees attending	34
# accepting a place on wait list	38
% admitted from wait list	21
# of early decision applicants	27
% accepted early decision	82

FRESHMAN PROFILE

Range SAT Verbal	620-720
Average SAT Verbal	657
Range SAT Math	610-700
Average SAT Math	643
**TPR Projected Range SAT Writing*	*650-710*
Range ACT Composite	26-30
Average ACT Composite	28
Minimum Paper TOEFL	550
Minimum Computer Based TOEFL	213
Average HS GPA	3.65
% graduated top 10% of class	48
% graduated top 25% of class	80
% graduated top 50% of class	97

DEADLINES

Early decision application deadline	11/15
Early decision notification	12/1
Regular application deadline	2/15
Regular notification	4/1
Nonfall registration?	no

APPLICANTS ALSO LOOK AT

AND OFTEN PREFER

Dartmouth College, Georgetown University, Northwestern University, University of Michigan—Ann Arbor

AND SOMETIMES PREFER

The College of Wooster, Denison University, Earlham College, Macalester College, Oberlin College, University of Notre Dame

AND RARELY PREFER

Albion College, Alma College, DePauw University, Hope College

FINANCIAL FACTS

Financial Aid Rating	**88**
Annual tuition	$24,351
Room & Board	$6,609
Books and supplies	$750
% frosh rec. need-based scholarship or grant aid	55
% UG rec. need-based scholarship or grant aid	51
% frosh rec. need-based self-help aid	48
% UG rec. need-based self-help aid	47
Avg. frosh grant	$12,510
Avg. frosh loan	$4,230
Independent 529 member?	Yes

KANSAS STATE UNIVERSITY

119 ANDERSON HALL, MANHATTAN, KS 66506 • ADMISSIONS: 785-532-6250 • FAX: 785-532-6393

CAMPUS LIFE

Quality of Life Rating	**87**
Fire Safety Rating	**60**
Type of school	public
Environment	village

STUDENTS

Total undergrad enrollment	18,893
% male/female	51/49
% from out of state	11
% from public high school	81
% live on campus	37
% in (# of) fraternities	20 (24)
% in (# of) sororities	20 (11)
% African American	3
% Asian	1
% Caucasian	88
% Hispanic	2
% international	1
# of countries represented	100

SURVEY SAYS

Great library
Athletic facilities are great
Students are friendly
Everyone loves the Wildcats
Student publications are popular
Lots of beer drinking

ACADEMICS

Academic Rating	**75**
Calendar	semester
Student/faculty ratio	21:1
Professors interesting rating	72
Professors accessible rating	74
% professors teaching UG courses	74
% classes taught by TAs	17
Most common regular class size	10-19 students

MOST POPULAR MAJORS

Animal sciences
journalism
mechanical engineering

STUDENTS SPEAK OUT

Academics

Kansas State University was founded under the Morrill Act, the 19th-century federal legislation designed to promote progress in agricultural science, engineering, and military tactics. Nearly 150 years after its founding, KSU still fulfills its original mission admirably; students here praise the school's offerings in pre-veterinary medicine, ecology, agronomy, biology, economics, engineering, and agriculture. "This is an ag school in the middle of farmland and the Bible Belt," students agree, noting that the liberal arts, while taught, definitely take a back seat to the more popular programs. Research opportunities abound here for ambitious undergrads, as "students turn out papers and projects and often are required to meet people in industry to practice solving industry problems." Experiential learning options are popular, too: "K-State does a great job helping students to get the experience they need while they are still taking classes," undergrads tell us. With nearly 20,000 fellow students, undergrads must be assertive to get the most of their educations here; points out one student, "All professors and administrators here are accessible, as long as the effort is made by the student." For those who seek it, support is available in many forms; "Success in the classroom is possible for anyone and the school makes sure to let you know what resources are available to do well, such as the library, tutoring, and assistance for the learning challenged." Still on the fence about K-State? Consider this: "We have the best ice cream on earth from our own cows. We sell meat from our own meat science department."

Life

Kansas State's hometown of Manhattan may not be the bustling metropolis that its name suggests, but it's big enough to suit most undergraduates. This "wonderful little town with tons of personality and good people" is home to Aggieville, "a mini-downtown across the street from the campus that has lots of bars as well as restaurants, bookstores, novelty shops, a laundromat, a pet shop, etc." Aggieville's bars are the center of social life for those older than 21; younger students congregate at house parties. Everyone, regardless of age, tailgates on game day, then "crams into the student section" to root on the Wildcats. "Student interaction at tailgating and sporting events is always a good time," undergrads agree, adding that there's "a lot of school spirit for the football team!" Women's basketball and track and field are other outstanding athletics programs; students tell us that "athletics at K-State are a major strength of the school. They are always a highlight of the week or month." There is smaller-scale diversion available here too; "every weekend, there are free activities and a movie at the student union, so there's always something to do if you don't have any money," and "during the week the Union is a great place to spend extra time. Usually, there are speakers in the plaza, booths lining the main corridor, and always people around." One student observes, "The number of activities in which to become involved is an important ingredient in the recipe for success here because it gives students an opportunity to meet people."

Student Body

"The highly friendly nature of the student body" is one of K-State's biggest assets, students tell us. "The friendliness makes incoming freshman feel welcome and safe. It's easy to make friends in your classes and in the dorms." Most undergrads here "come from small town backgrounds and they don't know a stranger." Writes one student, "The flair is definitely Midwestern. Walking to class, you'll pass your jocks in their workout attire, the cowboys in their wranglers, and the occasional prep." Most are "religious conservatives and they're going to stay that way." Explains one student, "Just about everyone is white, Republican, Christian, and from a smaller town with little experience with diversity. This doesn't mean they aren't nice or good people, they're just inexperienced."

KANSAS STATE UNIVERSITY

FINANCIAL AID: 785-532-6420 • E-MAIL: KSTATE@KSU.EDU • WEBSITE: WWW.CONSIDER.K-STATE.EDU

ADMISSIONS

Very important factors considered include: Class rank, secondary school record, standardized test scores. *Other factors considered include:* Recommendations, ACT required; SAT Reasoning or ACT required. SAT Subject Tests recommended. High school diploma is required, and GED is accepted. *Academic units recommended:* 4 English, 3 math, 3 science, 2 social studies, 1 history, 1 computer technology.

The Inside Word

As at most public universities, the admissions process is about as straightforward as it can get. Kansas high school grads are admitted with little trouble; out-of-state students are expected to be in the top third of their graduating class and to show evidence of academic potential via ACT scores. ACT is preferred, but SAT is acceptable. Don't be deceived by the seeming lack of rigor in admissions standards—K-State is chock full of strong students. Heightened national visibility for its athletic teams over the past few years will no doubt attract more applicants.

FINANCIAL AID

Students should submit: FAFSA. The Princeton Review suggests that all financial aid forms be submitted as soon as possible after 1/1. *Need-based scholarships/grants offered:* Pell, SEOG, state scholarships/grants, the school's own gift aid. *Loan aid offered:* FFEL Subsidized Stafford, FFEL Unsubsidized Stafford, FFEL PLUS, Federal Perkins, college/university loans from institutional funds. Applicants will be notified of awards on a rolling basis beginning on or about 3/15. Off-campus job opportunities are good.

FROM THE ADMISSIONS OFFICE

"Kansas State University offers strong academic programs, a lively intellectual atmosphere, a friendly campus community, and an environment where students achieve: K-State's total of Rhodes, Marshall, Truman, Goldwater, and Udall scholars since 1986 ranks first in the nation among state universities. In the Goldwater competition, only Princeton, Harvard and Duke have produced more winners. K-State's student government was named best in the nation in 1997 and 1995. The forensics squad finished seventh in the 2005. A K-State team finished in the top eight at the national debate tournement in 2003. Research facilities include the Konza Prairie, the world's largest tall grass prairie preserve, and the Macdonald Lab, the only university accelerator devoted primarily to atomic physics. Open House, held each spring, is a great way to explore K-State's more than 200 majors and options and 370 student organizations.

"Kansas State University requires ACT or SAT scores to complete a freshman applicant file. The SAT or ACT Writing score is not considered for admission to the university. Students may submit scores from any or all test dates. The best score from any one test date is used."

SELECTIVITY

Admissions Rating	**82**
# of applicants	10,066
% of applicants accepted	48
% of acceptees attending	72

FRESHMAN PROFILE

Range ACT Composite	21-26
Average ACT Composite	24
% graduated top 10% of class	32
% graduated top 25% of class	54
% graduated top 50% of class	80

DEADLINES

Regular notification	rolling
Nonfall registration?	yes

FINANCIAL FACTS

Financial Aid Rating	**73**
Annual in-state tuition	$4,110
Annual out-of-state tuition	$12,870
Room & Board	$5,738
Books and supplies	$1,030
Required fees	$555
% frosh rec. need-based scholarship or grant aid	34
% UG rec. need-based scholarship or grant aid	47
% frosh rec. need-based self-help aid	36
% UG rec. need-based self-help aid	42
% UG rec. any financial aid	53
Avg. frosh grant	$2,400
Avg. frosh loan	$1,317
Independent 529 member?	No

KENYON COLLEGE

ADMISSIONS OFFICE, RANSOM HALL, GAMBIER, OH 43022-9623 • ADMISSIONS: 740-427-5776 • FAX: 740-427-5770

CAMPUS LIFE

Quality of Life Rating	**90**
Fire Safety Rating	**66**
Type of school	private
Affiliation	Episcopal but nondenominational in practice
Environment	rural

STUDENTS

Total undergrad enrollment	1,605
% male/female	47/53
% from out of state	78
% from public high school	54
% live on campus	98
% in (# of) fraternities	27 (8)
% in (# of) sororities	10 (4)
% African American	3
% Asian	3
% Caucasian	83
% Hispanic	2
% international	3
# of countries represented	28

SURVEY SAYS

Small classes
No one cheats
Students are friendly
Campus feels safe
Students are happy
Lots of beer drinking

ACADEMICS

Academic Rating	**95**
Calendar	semester
Student/faculty ratio	10:1
Professors interesting rating	97
Professors accessible rating	96
% professors teaching UG courses	100
% classes taught by TAs	0
Most common regular class size	10-19 students

MOST POPULAR MAJORS

English language and literature
history
political science and government

STUDENTS SPEAK OUT

Academics

"'Learning in the company of friends' is the admissions office's slogan, and that's pretty close" to the way it is at Ohio's Kenyon College, students tell us. "We work hard but have fun." How hard? One freshman reports, "My intro classes are amazingly difficult. It is odd for me, as a 4.0+ high-school student, to hope for a C in my science classes." Fortunately, "The professors here honestly want you to do well in their classes. They make themselves readily available five days a week. You can go to their office hours or write them E-mails about anything you need help with." Other students have other resources to tap into for extra help; "There are people that get paid to help you in academics, as well as volunteers, so whenever you have trouble in a course, you are not alone in your plight." Students help each other out as well. "The academic atmosphere here is supportive rather than competitive," students tell us. "Rather than sabotaging each other's work, like the horror stories you hear about other schools, students will meet in groups to help each other understand the material." This support network helps students navigate the "small and very discussion-based classes [which] are focused on learning, with less emphasis on grades than on growth." The supportive, small-school vibe extends all the way to the top; as one student tells us, "'The administration is not the administration to Kenyon students, but rather Dean Martindell and Dean Omahan come to our coffeehouses, concerts, sports games, and seem to take an interest in how Kenyon students are doing with classes and with life in general."

Life

When students tell us that the environment at Kenyon is "chill," they're not just talking about the sharp Ohio winters. As one student explains, "Life at Kenyon is pretty laid-back. There's not a lot to do in town, so you have to make your own fun, but there is definitely a community atmosphere." Another undergraduate adds, "The best part about the Kenyon social scene is that everyone is invited everywhere, and no matter where you go, you will know someone! Frat parties are open to the whole campus." Undergraduates concede that "there's a lot of drinking here, [but] for the most part, it doesn't get out of hand." Also, "there are a lot of alternative activities: $1 movies in town, three-times-a-week movies (free!) at the auditorium, plenty of plays, concerts by coffeehouse-type artists, and random activities (e.g., an Indian Diwali [festival of lights] night, flag football, Polaroid scavenger hunt)." Many just hang in their rooms, shooting the breeze. "Small conversations can get intense here. A small conversation about yawning can become a ten-minute debate. It's not minutiae or boredom that inspires this; it's pure intellectual thought," reports one student. When they need to get away from the countryside, "people go into Columbus for the day to go shopping or to a nice restaurant. Mostly, though, people just stick around campus and hang out in residences."

Student Body

At Kenyon, the student body "is divided in half. On one hand, you get your J. Crew, and, on the other hand, you get the more 'crunchy' types. Or sometimes you get a bit of both: cashmere sweater with Birkenstocks." Most students are "liberal, left-leaning politically, and into the whole 'intellectual scene.'" They're also predominantly "smart, preppy Caucasians from stable upper-middle-class families, [but] Kenyon gives out a lot of scholarships, so there are kids here from every economic background." Students typically "tend to strike a good balance between studying, clubs, sports, partying, and just hanging out." Another student adds, "I also like the fact that almost everyone here is very excited about at least one thing they do." Undergraduates also appreciate the sense that "the campus, in fact the entire town, is permeated with genuine Ohio niceness."

FINANCIAL AID: 740-427-5430 • E-MAIL: ADMISSIONS@KENYON.EDU • WEBSITE: WWW.KENYON.EDU

ADMISSIONS

Very important factors considered include: Character/personal qualities, class rank, essays, recommendations, secondary school record. *Important factors considered include:* Extracurricular activities, interview, standardized test scores, talent/ability. *Other factors considered include:* Alumni/ae relation, geographical residence, minority status, state residency, volunteer work, work experience. SAT Reasoning or ACT required. TOEFL required of all international applicants. High school diploma is required, and GED is accepted. *Academic units required:* 4 English, 3 math, 3 science (3 science lab), 3 foreign language, 1 social studies, 1 history, 3 academic electives. *Academic units recommended:* 4 English, 4 math, 4 science (3 science lab), 4 foreign language, 2 social studies, 1 history, 4 academic electives, 1 fine arts.

The Inside Word

Kenyon pays close attention to matchmaking in the course of candidate selection; personal accomplishments are just as significant as academic ones. Applicants who rank the college high among their choices should definitely interview.

FINANCIAL AID

Students should submit: FAFSA, CSS/Financial Aid PROFILE, noncustodial (divorced/separated) parents' statement. Regular filing deadline is 2/15. The Princeton Review suggests that all financial aid forms be submitted as soon as possible after 1/1. *Need-based scholarships/grants offered:* Pell, SEOG, state scholarships/grants, private scholarships, the school's own gift aid. *Loan aid offered:* FFEL Subsidized Stafford, FFEL Unsubsidized Stafford, FFEL PLUS, Federal Perkins, college/university loans from institutional funds. Applicants will be notified of awards on or about 4/1. Federal Work-study Program available. Institutional employment available. Off-campus job opportunities are fair.

FROM THE ADMISSIONS OFFICE

"Students and alumni alike think of Kenyon as a place that fosters 'learning in the company of friends.' While faculty expectations are rigorous and the work challenging, the academic atmosphere is cooperative, not competitive. Indications of intellectual curiosity and passion for learning, more than just high grades and test scores, are what we look for in applications. Important as well are demonstrated interests in nonacademic pursuits, whether in athletics, the arts, writing, or another passion. Life in this small college community is fueled by the talents and enthusiasm of our students, so the admission staff seeks students who have a range of talents and interests.

"Students applying for admission into the fall 2006 class may take either/both the old or new SAT. Kenyon will consider the single best section scores from any and all SAT test results submitted. Standardized test scores are of secondary importance to the student's other application materials: high school transcript, recommendations, and the personal statement."

SELECTIVITY

Admissions Rating	**95**
# of applicants	3,808
% of applicants accepted	38
% of acceptees attending	32
# accepting a place on wait list	586
% admitted from wait list	3
# of early decision applicants	176
% accepted early decision	72

FRESHMAN PROFILE

Range SAT Verbal	620-730
Average SAT Verbal	674
Range SAT Math	610-690
Average SAT Math	649
**TPR Projected Range SAT Writing*	*650-720*
Range ACT Composite	27-31
Average ACT Composite	30
Minimum Paper TOEFL	570
Minimum Computer Based TOEFL	230
Average HS GPA	3.76
% graduated top 10% of class	50
% graduated top 25% of class	86
% graduated top 50% of class	98

DEADLINES

Early decision application deadline	12/1
Early decision notification	12/15
Regular application deadline	1/15
Regular notification	4/1
Nonfall registration?	no

APPLICANTS ALSO LOOK AT

AND OFTEN PREFER
Carleton College, Colby College, Middlebury College, Vassar College, Wesleyan U., Williams College

AND SOMETIMES PREFER
Bates College, Bowdoin College

AND RARELY PREFER
Beloit College, The College of Wooster, Denison U.

FINANCIAL FACTS

Financial Aid Rating	**88**
Annual tuition	$31,260
Room & Board	$5,270
Books and supplies	$950
Required fees	$910
% frosh rec. need-based scholarship or grant aid	40
% UG rec. need-based scholarship or grant aid	42
% frosh rec. need-based self-help aid	34
% UG rec. need-based self-help aid	38
% frosh rec. any financial aid	70
% UG rec. any financial aid	65
Avg. frosh grant	$18,958
Avg. frosh loan	$4,152
Independent 529 member?	Yes

KNOX COLLEGE

BOX K-148, GALESBURG, IL 61401 • ADMISSIONS: 309-341-7100 • FAX: 309-341-7070

CAMPUS LIFE

Quality of Life Rating	**83**
Fire Safety Rating	**72**
Type of school	private
Environment	town

STUDENTS

Total undergrad enrollment	1,167
% male/female	45/55
% from out of state	46
% from public high school	85
% live on campus	95
% in (# of) fraternities	28 (4)
% in (# of) sororities	17 (2)
% African American	5
% Asian	5
% Caucasian	72
% Hispanic	4
% international	8
# of countries represented	43

SURVEY SAYS

Small classes
Registration is a breeze
Great library
Students are happy

ACADEMICS

Academic Rating	**93**
Calendar	3-3 calendar
Student/faculty ratio	12:1
Professors interesting rating	98
Professors accessible rating	97
% professors teaching UG courses	100
% classes taught by TAs	0
Most common lab size	10-19 students
Most common regular class size	10-19 students

MOST POPULAR MAJORS

Anthropology
education
psychology

STUDENTS SPEAK OUT

Academics

"Freedom. Lots of freedom. Freedom to express, print, say, or do what you want." That's what small Knox College is all about, its students say, and that's why students praise this "extremely demanding" school. "If you're passionate and ambitious enough about something, you can make it happen at Knox," explains one undergrad. "New clubs are always starting, people get school money to fund trips to DC for protests, students direct their own plays, etc. The administration is supportive of just about anything." The student/faculty relationships here are "truly special, very relaxed, and very personal. Professors are more than educators. They dedicate their time to the students to ensure that everyone is getting out of the education what they put into it." The same holds true for student/administration relations; writes one student, "When I first visited Knox, I was greeted by Roger, who introduced himself as an alumnus. It wasn't until they introduced him in a speech that I knew he was the president of the college. But that's how it is at Knox: a very tight-knit community that works together." Knox is the kind of place that inspires long-term loyalty, which explains why "the amount of alumni that come back to speak to students is quite impressive." As one student summed up, "Rather than a school where one spends four years, Knox is a school that permeates your entire life."

Life

If you've never heard of Knox's hometown of Galesburg, you aren't alone. Students here concede that "Galesburg is . . well, Galesburg." Reported one undergrad, it "isn't exactly the center of the universe. Luckily for us, Knox is usually very conscious of this. They are very good about bringing in outside entertainment." Events include "student theatre, the choir, or sports, and while none of these events are sold out, they are fairly well attended. Outside speakers are sometimes scheduled, and their talks are often crammed full." Other options include "movie night in the Round Room, Jazz Night at Cherry Street, or a band playing in The Gizmo." Despite the availability of such varied activity, many here tell us that at Knox, "the weekends are weak, unless your friends consist of Keystone and Busch Light. Alcohol is a major factor at Knox. The Greek system is really strong." Despite the Greek presence, students tell us that the suite-style dorms, and not the Greek system, are the key to the school's social universe. "The suite system here is unique," explains one student. "Students usually live in a hall where all rooms open onto a common living area. This allows for interaction between everyone, not just the people that you live next to. In addition, you take a lot of classes together, so you can have a discussion on current issues or on an assignment for a class. It is very conducive to forming long-lasting friendships."

Student Body

Students are adamant that Knox College "has a pretty broad range of students" among its small population. "This campus is so diverse ethnically, and no one comes from the same background," writes one student. "Everyone has different interests, likes, and dislikes. We're here for a common purpose—to learn—but other than that, we're all different." Although the "majority of students here are white liberals," there is also "a crowd of more conservative and religious (mostly white American) population," and students report that relations among the various groups are remarkably stress-free. Knox's "high school jock frat boys who haven't really grown up yet, rich kids that want to be hippies, kids that actually are hippies, and geeks that are happy to be left alone and play computer games" share one more common trait: they were "probably all the kind of smart, kind of strange, but not-too-weird students in high school. We all kind of fit in but were never really popular."

FINANCIAL AID: 309-341-7149 • E-MAIL: ADMISSION@KNOX.EDU • WEBSITE: WWW.KNOX.EDU

ADMISSIONS

Very important factors considered include: Secondary school record. *Important factors considered include:* Class rank, essays, recommendations. *Other factors considered include:* Alumni/ae relation, character/personal qualities, extracurricular activities, interview, minority status, standardized test scores, talent/ability, volunteer work. SAT Reasoning or ACT required. TOEFL required of all international applicants. High school diploma is required, and GED is accepted. *Academic units recommended:* 4 English, 4 math, 3 science (2 science lab), 3 foreign language, 2 social studies, 2 history.

The Inside Word

A relatively small enrollment means a relatively small applicant pool, but he student body is nonetheless well qualified, and candidates should show solid academic accomplishment.

FINANCIAL AID

Students should submit: FAFSA, institution's own financial aid form. The Princeton Review suggests that all financial aid forms be submitted as soon as possible after 1/1. *Need-based scholarships/grants offered:* Pell, SEOG, state scholarships/grants, private scholarships, the school's own gift aid. *Loan aid offered:* Direct Subsidized Stafford, Direct Unsubsidized Stafford, Direct PLUS, Federal Perkins, college/university loans from institutional funds. Applicants will be notified of awards on a rolling basis beginning on or about 3/15. Federal Work-study Program available. Institutional employment available. Off-campus job opportunities are good.

FROM THE ADMISSIONS OFFICE

"Freedom to Flourish: The idea is simple. College should be a place where you discover yourself—where your talents are nourished and your aspirations become clear, a place that prepares you to turn your dreams into reality. But this is not the only reason college is important. By helping you learn to think clearly and independently, getting you ready to face the future with confidence, college should make you free. At Knox you are challenged to think for yourself and to explain your ideas. You learn how to analyze and to write clearly. Your mind and talents are stretched by exploring new areas of knowledge. You grow, too, in unexpected ways, through the rich opportunities and challenges of life in this creative, vital community. By graduation, you have received a sound, comprehensive education and are ready for the future. You will have the skills, background, and confidence to make the future your own.

"Knox College requires that freshman applicants for 2006 submit scores from either the new or old SAT. Students may opt to take the ACT (with or without Writing) in lieu of the SAT."

SELECTIVITY

Admissions Rating	**85**
# of applicants	1,868
% of applicants accepted	72
% of acceptees attending	27
# accepting a place on wait list	70
% admitted from wait list	11

FRESHMAN PROFILE

Range SAT Verbal	570-700
Average SAT Verbal	635
Range SAT Math	560-670
Average SAT Math	615
**TPR Projected Range SAT Writing*	*610-700*
Range ACT Composite	25-30
Average ACT Composite	27
Minimum Paper TOEFL	550
Minimum Computer Based TOEFL	213
% graduated top 10% of class	33
% graduated top 25% of class	64
% graduated top 50% of class	90

DEADLINES

Regular application deadline	2/1
Regular notification	3/31
Nonfall registration?	yes

APPLICANTS ALSO LOOK AT AND SOMETIMES PREFER

Cornell College
DePauw University
Illinois Wesleyan University

AND RARELY PREFER

Augustana College (IL)
Kalamazoo College
Loyola University of Chicago
Monmouth College (IL)

FINANCIAL FACTS

Financial Aid Rating	**89**
Annual tuition	$25,815
Room & Board	$6,285
Books and supplies	$900
Required fees	$285
% frosh rec. need-based scholarship or grant aid	66
% UG rec. need-based scholarship or grant aid	69
% frosh rec. need-based self-help aid	57
% UG rec. need-based self-help aid	62
% frosh rec. any financial aid	66
% UG rec. any financial aid	69
Avg. frosh grant	$16,434
Avg. frosh loan	$4,578
Independent 529 member?	Yes

LAFAYETTE COLLEGE

118 MARKLE HALL, EASTON, PA 18042 • ADMISSIONS: 610-330-5100 • FAX: 610-330-5355

CAMPUS LIFE

Quality of Life Rating	**70**
Fire Safety Rating	**60**
Type of school	private
Affiliation	Presbyterian
Environment	village

STUDENTS

Total undergrad enrollment	2,251
% male/female	53/47
% from out of state	70
% from public high school	68
% live on campus	96
% in (# of) fraternities	26 (7)
% in (# of) sororities	45 (6)
% African American	5
% Asian	2
% Caucasian	85
% Hispanic	3
% international	5
# of countries represented	46

SURVEY SAYS

Small classes
Lab facilities are great
Great computer facilities
Great library
Athletic facilities are great
Lots of beer drinking

ACADEMICS

Academic Rating	**89**
Calendar	semester
Student/faculty ratio	11:1
Professors interesting rating	78
Professors accessible rating	86
% professors teaching UG courses	100
% classes taught by TAs	0
Most common lab size	10-19 students
Most common regular class size	10-19 students

STUDENTS SPEAK OUT

Academics

"Lafayette's small size and exclusively undergraduate population create tight bonds between professors and students and open the door for research opportunities," students at this small-but-mighty liberal arts school tell us. That's true at many small schools; few others of this size can claim that "the small size does not prevent students from enjoying Division I sports, a nationally recognized engineering program, and great resources and facilities." Lafayette students can and do; they justifiably boast a "great math department, excellent programs in the sciences and engineering, [and] very good classes in the humanities and social sciences, which are under-noticed and underappreciated because of the well-known engineering programs." Students here benefit from a "strong emphasis on class discussion, individual attention from professors, [and] widely available internships and research opportunities with professors." Internships and externships are plentiful thanks in part to "a ton of alumni connections, people who have really stayed involved in the school after they graduated. They can provide resources, connections, ideas, opportunities and more. The sheer number of active alumni is amazing, and their willingness to interact with us is great." Lafayette also offers a number of "popular, widely used study-abroad programs," including six full-semester faculty-led opportunities (in Belgium, Greece, France, Germany, Spain, and Ghana).

Life

Lafayette "is located on a hill above downtown Easton, isolating most students on campus, or at least those without cars." Some here tell us that "there is not much to do on top of the hill except drink," which is why "weekends are spent partying." Not everyone feels that way, though. Some are glad to be secluded from Easton, which they describe as "a tad sketchy at night," and they're perfectly happy to remain on their "beautiful campus, with its amazing attention paid to planting and replanting color-coordinated flowers." Others tout the many alcohol-free options available; writes one student, "There is always something to do at Lafayette. There are movies, speakers, comedians, and singing groups available for students. Community service and sporting events are also popular." Because the school is so small, "there are endless opportunities to get involved. If there is an association you want to start, start it! If there is a play you want to write and/or produce, do it! If you have a great new business idea, go for it. Lafayette professors and administrators are very supportive of students' creativity." The campus and the region do a good job of pulling in top-flight entertainment; reports one undergrad, "The amount of performing arts we get at both the Williams Center for the Arts (which is the art and music and theater building) and at the State Theater for the Arts is immense. At Williams, you get a ton of great classical and jazz music. At the State Theater, you get comedians such as Jon Stewart, Jeff Foxworthy, Bill Engvall, Larry 'The Cable Guy', Ron White, Drew Carey, as well as plays such as *The Full Monty* and *The Graduate*."

Student Body

"The typical student at Lafayette is very concerned with academics"—you can't last here very long if you're not—"but able to go out and have fun at the same time." He or she also makes time for extracurriculars; observes one student, "The typical Lafayette student has a full plate. Not only is he or she a serious academic student but at the same time is involved in some sort of club or organization on campus, whether it be sports, volunteering, music, or academic-related." Students tell us that "Lafayette is not very diverse, but minorities do have organizations that hold events for the whole campus. The typical student is middle- to upper-class, white, and has generally not had to work for much in their lives, but the student body as a whole is very friendly and accepting." Undergrads tend to be "politically conservative and most are religiously affiliated."

FINANCIAL AID: 610-330-5055 • E-MAIL: ADMISSIONS@LAFAYETTE.EDU • WEBSITE: WWW.LAFAYETTE.EDU

ADMISSIONS

Very important factors considered include: Secondary school record. *Important factors considered include:* Alumni/ae relation, character/personal qualities, class rank, essays, extracurricular activities, minority status, recommendations, standardized test scores, talent/ability, volunteer work. *Other factors considered include:* Geographical residence, interview, work experience. SAT Reasoning or ACT required. TOEFL required of all international applicants. High school diploma or equivalent is not required. *Academic units recommended:* 4 English, 3 math, 2 science (2 science lab), 2 foreign language, 5 academic electives.

The Inside Word

Applications are reviewed three to five times and evaluated by as many as nine different committee members. In all cases, students who continually seek challenges and are willing to take risks academically win out over those who play it safe to maintain a high GPA.

FINANCIAL AID

Students should submit: FAFSA, CSS/Financial Aid PROFILE, noncustodial (divorced/separated) parents' statement, business/farm supplement. Regular filing deadline is 2/1. The Princeton Review suggests that all financial aid forms be submitted as soon as possible after 1/1. *Need-based scholarships/grants offered:* Pell, SEOG, state scholarships/grants, private scholarships. *Loan aid offered:* FFEL Subsidized Stafford, FFEL Unsubsidized Stafford, FFEL PLUS, Federal Perkins, state loans, college/university loans from institutional funds, HELP loans to parents. Applicants will be notified of awards on or about 4/1. Federal Work-study Program available. Institutional employment available. Off-campus job opportunities are good.

FROM THE ADMISSIONS OFFICE

"We choose students individually, one by one, and we hope that the ones we choose will approach their education the same way, as a highly individual enterprise. Our first-year seminars have enrollments limited to 15 or 16 students each in order to introduce the concept of learning not as passive receipt of information but as an active, participatory process. Our low average class size and 11:1 student/teacher ratio reflect that same philosophy. We also devote substantial resources to our Marquis Scholars Program, to one-on-one faculty-student mentoring relationships, and to other programs in engineering within a liberal arts context, giving Lafayette its distinctive character, articulated in our second-year seminars exploring values in science and technology. Lafayette provides an environment in which its students can discover their own personal capacity for learning, personal growth, and leadership.

"Freshman applicants for fall 2006 may submit the results from the current version of the SAT I, the current ACT, the new version of the SAT, or the results of the ACT with Writing component. The results of SAT Subject Tests are recommended but not required. Some academic departments will use scores for placement purposes."

SELECTIVITY

Admissions Rating	**95**
# of applicants	5,835
% of applicants accepted	36
% of acceptees attending	28
# accepting a place on wait list	1,697
% admitted from wait list	5
# of early decision applicants	244
% accepted early decision	66

FRESHMAN PROFILE

Range SAT Verbal	570-660
Average SAT Verbal	620
Range SAT Math	610-710
Average SAT Math	665
**TPR Projected Range SAT Writing*	*610-670*
Range ACT Composite	25-29
Average ACT Composite	28
Minimum Paper TOEFL	550
Average HS GPA	3.8
% graduated top 10% of class	59
% graduated top 25% of class	89
% graduated top 50% of class	100

DEADLINES

Early decision application deadline	2/15
Early decision notification	12/1
Regular application deadline	1/1
Regular notification	4/1
Nonfall registration?	yes

APPLICANTS ALSO LOOK AT

AND OFTEN PREFER

Boston College, Cornell University, Johns Hopkins University, Princeton University, Tufts University

AND SOMETIMES PREFER

Bucknell University, Colgate University, Lehigh University, Villanova University

AND RARELY PREFER

Franklin & Marshall College, Penn State University Park, Rensselaer Polytechnic Institute, Trinity College (CT)

FINANCIAL FACTS

Financial Aid Rating	**95**
Annual tuition	$27,178
Room & Board	$8,418
Books and supplies	$600
Required fees	$150
% frosh rec. need-based scholarship or grant aid	49
% UG rec. need-based scholarship or grant aid	51
% frosh rec. need-based self-help aid	33
% UG rec. need-based self-help aid	38
Avg. frosh grant	$20,552
Avg. frosh loan	$3,500
Independent 529 member?	No

LAKE FOREST COLLEGE

555 NORTH SHERIDAN ROAD, LAKE FOREST, IL 60045 • ADMISSIONS: 847-735-5000 • FAX: 847-735-6291

CAMPUS LIFE

Quality of Life Rating	**79**
Fire Safety Rating	**70**
Type of school	private
Affiliation	Presbyterian
Environment	village

STUDENTS

Total undergrad enrollment	1,361
% male/female	42/58
% from out of state	51
% from public high school	65
% live on campus	78
% in (# of) fraternities	19 (4)
% in (# of) sororities	15 (5)
% African American	4
% Asian	4
% Caucasian	78
% Hispanic	5
% international	9
# of countries represented	47

SURVEY SAYS

Small classes
Lots of beer drinking
Hard liquor is popular

ACADEMICS

Academic Rating	**86**
Calendar	semester
Student/faculty ratio	12:1
Professors interesting rating	94
Professors accessible rating	87
% professors teaching UG courses	100
% classes taught by TAs	0
Most common lab size	10-19 students
Most common regular class size	10-19 students

MOST POPULAR MAJORS

Business/commerce
communications studies/speech communication and rhetoric
psychology

STUDENTS SPEAK OUT

Academics

Lake Forest College is a small liberal arts school north of Chicago where "a whole lot of personal attention, a study abroad program that is cheap because of the great financial aid, [and] professors who really care about students and how they are doing both inside and outside the classroom," help make satisfied students. Strengths here include business, English, performing arts, communications, education, and psychology; students may sample courses in all these areas easily since "requirements are very loose, allowing you to take pretty much whatever courses you want." Undergrads here love the fact that "class sizes are so small that it's really hard to slack off. It feels really bad when your favorite professor writes 'I know you can do better' on the back of your paper." The small size of the school also means "you can have a great experience here, provided you make an effort to get to know your professors and administrators and get involved in the classroom." Outside the classroom there are "great leadership opportunities" available to go-getters. Other strengths include "great computer and science labs" and "a library that was just (massively) renovated."

Life

"Life at Lake Forest is generally laid back," with a pace set by the quiet, high-end suburb in which the school is located. Students complain that "the town is not very friendly and is very elitist and boring. Every place seems to close at 6 p.m." Fortunately, Chicago is only a commuter train ride away, a "great asset to the school, both for academics and entertainment. Many students travel into the city to go to shows, sporting events, or just to walk around." A few undergrads, however, complain that "it is not as easy to get into the city as they make it sound in the school brochure. It's an hour by train and it's tough to get off campus without a car. A lot of people get frustrated and start to feel claustrophobic with the campus and its location." While "the school tries to bring events on campus, not many people really show up." Undergrads prefer to hold small parties in their residences, find their way over to parties at Northwestern (about half as far away as downtown Chicago), or go home for the weekend. The campus is more active during the week, when "student involvement in organizations and student government is high. Also, there is great support for the athletic teams," as well as a high level of participation in sports; with 17 intercollegiate teams and fewer than 1,400 undergrads, there are "a lot of jocks here."

Student Body

Lake Forest has long had a reputation as a preppy haven, a reputation that still holds true; students tell us that a good number of students "are private-school kids from the suburbs. Lots of khaki and North Face jackets." While "there are some rich annoying people" here, "on the whole everyone is pretty nice and friendly, although cliques are created quickly and held onto quite tightly by much of the student body." Athletes are one of the biggest cliques; others include "the musical people who only hang with other musical people, the actors who only hang with other actors, etc. However, many students broaden their range of friends by participating in multiple activities." Undergrads report "a good amount of diversity for such a small school, although most of it comes from international kids" who, like most other groups, "hang out with each other most of the time."

Lake Forest College

Financial Aid: 847-735-5103 • E-mail: admissions@lakeforest.edu • Website: www.lakeforest.edu

ADMISSIONS

Very important factors considered include: Interview, recommendations, secondary school record. *Important factors considered include:* Character/personal qualities, essays, extracurricular activities, standardized test scores, talent/ability. *Other factors considered include:* Alumni/ae relation, class rank, geographical residence, state residency, volunteer work, work experience. SAT Reasoning or ACT required. TOEFL required of all international applicants. High school diploma is required, and GED is accepted. *Academic units required:* 4 English, 3 math, 3 science (2 science lab), 2 social studies, 2 history. *Academic units recommended:* 4 English, 4 math, 4 science (3 science lab), 4 foreign language, 3 social studies, 3 history, 2 academic electives.

The Inside Word

Candidates with a solid academic record will meet with little resistance on the road to acceptance. But remember that Lake Forest definitely has a prep-school-at-the-college-level feel. It pays to keep in mind the admissions committee's eagerness to assess the whole person when completing the application.

FINANCIAL AID

Students should submit: FAFSA, federal income tax return. Regular filing deadline is 5/1. The Princeton Review suggests that all financial aid forms be submitted as soon as possible after 1/1. *Need-based scholarships/grants offered:* Pell, SEOG, state scholarships/grants, private scholarships, the school's own gift aid. *Loan aid offered:* FFEL Subsidized Stafford, FFEL Unsubsidized Stafford, FFEL PLUS, Federal Perkins, college/university loans from institutional funds, alternative loans. Applicants will be notified of awards on a rolling basis beginning on or about 3/15. Federal Work-study Program available. Institutional employment available. Off-campus job opportunities are excellent.

FROM THE ADMISSIONS OFFICE

"Where you go to college can have everything to do with what you get out of college. As you think about the academic challenges and resources you seek—and the overall experience you desire—consider what Lake Forest College has to offer you.

"Lake Forest College is Chicago's national liberal arts college. Located 30 miles north of downtown Chicago, the College's proximity to the city provides Lake Forest students and faculty with unique academic, cultural, and employment resources. Through partnerships with a variety of cultural, educational, financial, research, and scientific institutions in Chicago and its environs, students are engaged in an active learning process that takes them beyond the traditional boundaries of the classroom, integrating the theoretical and the practical.

"The 1,380 students represent 47 countries and 47 states. Lake Forest College fosters interaction among a diverse community of students and faculty with a significant international and minority population. The faculty are dedicated teachers and accomplished scholars, with 98 percent holding a PhD or equivalent. The faculty do all the teaching; you will not find teaching assistants at Lake Forest. The College's Career Advancement Center (CAC) begins working with students during their first year on campus, and later provides mentoring opportunities with alumni from around the globe as well as internship assistance and job placement.

"College should be demanding, but not a relentless grind. With more than 80 student-run organizations and clubs, 17 varsity NCAA Division III teams, and a variety of intramural and club sports, students find many opportunities outside the classroom.

"Lake Forest College does not require the Writing component of the new SAT or ACT. We accept either the ACT or SAT scores and will use the student's best scores, as well as either the new or old (prior to March 2005) version."

SELECTIVITY

Admissions Rating	**87**
# of applicants	2,279
% of applicants accepted	63
% of acceptees attending	28
# accepting a place on wait list	122
% admitted from wait list	2
# of early decision applicants	31
% accepted early decision	67

FRESHMAN PROFILE

Range SAT Verbal	530-640
Average SAT Verbal	586
Range SAT Math	530-650
Average SAT Math	580
**TPR Projected Range SAT Writing*	*580-660*
Range ACT Composite	23-28
Average ACT Composite	25
Minimum Paper TOEFL	550
Minimum Computer Based TOEFL	220
Average HS GPA	3.4
% graduated top 10% of class	30
% graduated top 25% of class	57
% graduated top 50% of class	87

DEADLINES

Early decision application deadline	12/1
Early decision notification	12/20
Regular application deadline	2/15
Regular notification	3/15
Nonfall registration?	yes

APPLICANTS ALSO LOOK AT

AND OFTEN PREFER

Connecticut College, Kenyon College, Northwestern U.

AND SOMETIMES PREFER

Lewis & Clark College, U. of Denver, U. of Illinois at Urbana—Champaign, U. of Wisconsin—Madison

AND RARELY PREFER

DePaul U., Loyola U. of Chicago

FINANCIAL FACTS

Financial Aid Rating	**99**
Annual tuition	$27,000
Room & Board	$6,526
Books and supplies	$700
Required fees	$334
% frosh rec. need-based scholarship or grant aid	74
% UG rec. need-based scholarship or grant aid	71
% frosh rec. need-based self-help aid	50
% UG rec. need-based self-help aid	47
% frosh rec. any financial aid	90
% UG rec. any financial aid	90
Avg. frosh grant	$18,611
Avg. frosh loan	$4,097
Independent 529 member?	Yes

LAWRENCE UNIVERSITY

PO BOX 599, APPLETON, WI 54912-0599 • ADMISSIONS: 920-832-6500 • FAX: 920-832-6782

CAMPUS LIFE

Quality of Life Rating	**89**
Fire Safety Rating	**70**
Type of school	private
Environment	city

STUDENTS

Total undergrad enrollment	1,344
% male/female	46/54
% from out of state	58
% from public high school	84
% live on campus	98
% in (# of) fraternities	24 (5)
% in (# of) sororities	11 (3)
% African American	2
% Asian	3
% Caucasian	74
% Hispanic	3
% international	9
# of countries represented	53

SURVEY SAYS

Small classes
No one cheats
Lab facilities are great
Great library
Campus feels safe
Musical organizations are popular

ACADEMICS

Academic Rating	**89**
Calendar	trimester
Student/faculty ratio	11:1
Professors interesting rating	90
Professors accessible rating	97
% professors teaching UG courses	100
% classes taught by TAs	0
Most common regular class size	10-19 students

MOST POPULAR MAJORS

Biology/biological sciences
music performance
psychology

STUDENTS SPEAK OUT

Academics

"The conservatory is amazing, and so is the biology department" at Lawrence University, a small private Midwestern school between Oshkosh and Green Bay. But these high-profile programs aren't the only standouts here; on the contrary, "No major is a 'junk major' that one can fulfill without doing any work." "Lawrence is a very tough school academically. It is extremely rigorous when it comes to course work. There is time for athletics and fun, but know that you are coming here to study." Students warn that "there is no grade inflation. To do well here you cannot rest on your laurels. But by forcing you to work, Lawrence teaches you the skills to communicate effectively with the world." A trimester academic calendar further ratchets up the intensity; explains one student, "Everything moves very rapidly and you are stuck with major exams every three to five weeks for the most part." Lawrence professors "are amazing, and that's an understatement. Each is excited about his or her field in a way that inspires you to go above and beyond the class assignments. I took a physics class and wanted to be a physics major, then I took an intro-level religious studies course and wanted to take more religious studies courses." Students appreciate how "professors accept student input on textbooks, and some actively inquire as to the effectiveness of these texts. There's a sense at Lawrence that professors are constantly trying to improve the classroom experience." Pre-meds also love that "the percentage of Lawrentians who get into medical school is much higher than the national average."

Life

Hometown Appleton "isn't exactly a Mecca of culture," but Lawrence's "large music program and active theater community help compensate for what the town lacks." A few intrepid souls who aggressively explore Appleton report that it offers some surprise diversions; most here, however, never discover them. Rather, they stick near their "strictly residential campus, which keeps the student body really close-knit and aware of each other" but also "means we don't leave campus much, except to visit the bars and coffee shops on College Avenue." Many social events "take place in the frat quad," including "Jell-O Wrestling, The Foam Party, and Heaven and Hell Party," Students also have access to "casual fun, such as movies and guest speakers. National acts come to campus occasionally; we recently had Ben Folds here and also Lewis Black." Even so, many here feel that "The school needs to find better ways for students to relieve stress. The pressure here drives many students to intense stress levels. They need to find a way to balance the academic workload." Lawrence's campus is "beautiful, but tiny and hard pressed for space, so it gets more and more crowded with each new building."

Student Body

Lawrence attracts "bright, motivated, overachievers who are also creative and innovative." They are enthusiastic about learning, often self-admittedly to the point of geekiness. Writes one student, "The typical student at Lawrence was that dorky kid in your high school class who was reading Henry V for fun and writing grants to build Energy Gardens—and getting them." Adds another, "We are the band geeks, the drama nerds, the kids who went to French camp, the kids painting murals on the gym wall." While many here "are white and middle-class, we have a large number of international students from all over the world to accent our learning experience. Moreover, financial aid allows students from many demographic backgrounds to attend." Students agree that "discrimination here is almost a sin, with active campus groups for all races, sexual orientations, religious groups, you name it."

LAWRENCE UNIVERSITY

FINANCIAL AID: 920-832-6583 • E-MAIL: EXCEL@LAWRENCE.EDU • WEBSITE: WWW.LAWRENCE.EDU

ADMISSIONS

Very important factors considered include: Secondary school record. *Important factors considered include:* Alumni/ae relation, class rank, essays, minority status, recommendations, talent/ability. *Other factors considered include:* Character/personal qualities, extracurricular activities, interview, standardized test scores, volunteer work, work experience. TOEFL required of all international applicants. High school diploma is required, and GED is not accepted. *Academic units recommended:* 4 English, 3 math, 3 science, 2 foreign language, 3 social studies, 3 history.

The Inside Word

Although the admit rate is fairly high, getting into Lawrence demands an above-average academic record. Students who are serious about getting in to the university should stick with a very challenging high school courseload straight through senior year, put significant energy into their application essays, and definitely interview.

FINANCIAL AID

Students should submit: FAFSA, institution's own financial aid form. Regular filing deadline is 3/15. The Princeton Review suggests that all financial aid forms be submitted as soon as possible after 1/1. *Need-based scholarships/grants offered:* Pell, SEOG, state scholarships/grants, private scholarships, the school's own gift aid. *Loan aid offered:* Direct Subsidized Stafford, Direct Unsubsidized Stafford, Direct PLUS, FFEL PLUS, Federal Perkins. Applicants will be notified of awards on or about 4/15. Federal Work-study Program available. Off-campus job opportunities are good.

FROM THE ADMISSIONS OFFICE

"Lawrence students are characterized by their energy, commitment to community service, respect for each other, and desire to achieve their full potential. Campus activities are abundant, off-campus study programs are popular (more than half of the students take advantage of them), small classes are the norm (65 percent of the classes have 10 or fewer students in them), and, yes, winters can be "character-building." But the diversity of interests and experiences, the drive to excel, the wealth of cultural opportunities presented by the art, theater, and music departments, the quality of research students undertake alongside PhD faculty, and the general friendly attitude of everyone at the university contribute to a uniquely engaging living and learning environment.

"We seek students who are intellectual, imaginative, and innovative: qualities best quantified from a thorough review of each applicant's curriculum, academic performance, essay, activities, and recommendations. Accordingly, Lawrence considers—but does not require—the ACT and the SAT in its review of applications for admission and scholarship."

SELECTIVITY

Admissions Rating	**90**
# of applicants	1,970
% of applicants accepted	66
% of acceptees attending	27
# accepting a place on wait list	63
% admitted from wait list	14
# of early decision applicants	27
% accepted early decision	82

FRESHMAN PROFILE

Range SAT Verbal	560-690
Average SAT Verbal	625
Range SAT Math	570-690
Average SAT Math	625
**TPR Projected Range SAT Writing*	*600-690*
Range ACT Composite	25-30
Average ACT Composite	27
Minimum Paper TOEFL	575
Minimum Computer Based TOEFL	233
Average HS GPA	3.69
% graduated top 10% of class	36
% graduated top 25% of class	75
% graduated top 50% of class	96

DEADLINES

Early decision application deadline	11/15
Early decision notification	12/1
Regular application deadline	1/15
Regular notification	4/1
Nonfall registration?	no

APPLICANTS ALSO LOOK AT AND OFTEN PREFER

Carleton University
Northwestern University
University of Wisconsin—Madison

AND SOMETIMES PREFER

Beloit College
Grinnell College
Macalester College
Oberlin College

FINANCIAL FACTS

Financial Aid Rating	**99**
Annual tuition	$27,714
Room & Board	$6,438
Books and supplies	$600
Required fees	$210
% frosh rec. need-based scholarship or grant aid	56
% UG rec. need-based scholarship or grant aid	61
% frosh rec. need-based self-help aid	51
% UG rec. need-based self-help aid	57
% frosh rec. any financial aid	95
% UG rec. any financial aid	94
Avg. frosh grant	$15,260
Avg. frosh loan	$4,600
Independent 529 member?	Yes

LEHIGH UNIVERSITY

27 MEMORIAL DRIVE WEST, BETHLEHEM, PA 18015 • ADMISSIONS: 610-758-3100 • FAX: 610-758-4361

CAMPUS LIFE

Quality of Life Rating	**64**
Fire Safety Rating	**80**
Type of school	private
Environment	city

STUDENTS

Total undergrad enrollment	4,553
% male/female	59/41
% from out of state	71
% from public high school	64
% live on campus	67
% in (# of) fraternities	33 (23)
% in (# of) sororities	39 (9)
% African American	3
% Asian	6
% Caucasian	78
% Hispanic	2
% international	3
# of countries represented	43

SURVEY SAYS

Great computer facilities
Great library
Everyone loves the Mountain Hawks
Frats and sororities dominate social scene
Lots of beer drinking
Hard liquor is popular

ACADEMICS

Academic Rating	**77**
Calendar	semester
Student/faculty ratio	9:1
Professors interesting rating	77
Professors accessible rating	84
% professors teaching UG courses	100
% classes taught by TAs	0
Most common lab size	10-19 students
Most common regular class size	10-19 students

MOST POPULAR MAJORS

Finance
mechanical engineering
psychology

STUDENTS SPEAK OUT

Academics

Nearly half the students at prestigious Lehigh University study either engineering or business; a select few even combine the two through the "excellent and very selective integrated business and engineering honors program." These disciplines are undoubtedly the marquee attractions at this demanding midsize school, but other programs certainly stand out. Lehigh is "strong in architecture" and "has very competitive science programs," students tell us. The humanities, on the other hand, "could be expanded a bit more," although the school hopes to improve this with the new Arts Leigh initiative. In the most popular disciplines, "the work is extremely tough and you need to constantly keep on top of it all," with "some classes being mostly project-based, while others are mostly test-based." Grading can be a source of stress, as "your entire grade is based on a huge curve, especially in the science, math and engineering classes, so you never know how well you are doing until your grades are posted at the end of the semester." Fortunately, "the faculty here are generally extremely helpful, and any of the professors are more than willing to set up meeting times with students to discuss problems or to provide you with extra help." Undergrads also love that "Lehigh has amazing research facilities and brilliant professors with tons of real-world experience. As an example, one chemistry professor created a method to remove arsenic from wells in India and Bangladesh, and then helped incorporate that into the freshman engineering class." Such assets play well with area businesses, translating into "great opportunities for internships and great job placement rates for graduates."

Life

Lehigh, with its "heavy workload and active social life . . . embodies the 'work hard, play hard' mantra. We party here like there is no tomorrow," students tell us. Partying on 'The Hill,' "where all frat and sorority houses are situated, is the main attraction when we aren't studying, which is rare," but parties in non-Greek off-campus housing are also common, and "the two social groups don't really mix or interact." There are activities for non-drinkers—"There's swing dancing Saturday nights, and guest singers and poetry readings at Lamberton Hall" as well as "some good concerts and comedians on weekends"—but "even these events are mostly attended by people who drink, (before they) go to them, then go out and party afterwards." During the week "there is so much for the students to get involved with, which creates a lot of opportunities to partake in leadership roles and develop in many ways as a human being." College athletics are big, with the annual square-off against nearby Lafayette as the highlight of each season. Although hometown Bethlehem "has some wonderful places for students to go and is very affordable," many here prefer either to hang near campus or "take the bus to Philly for some real city entertainment. It's really convenient."

Student Body

Lehigh's "typically athletic" students "want to do well in class but also love to party." They all shop at the same places, procuring uniforms consisting of some combination of "khakis, Polos with popped collars, North Face fleece, Gucci, Prada, Coach, Dooney & Bourke, pointy boots, Ugg boots, and rainbow sandals. We are prepped out and name branded to the max; this is Lehigh." Some here observe that "the school is trying to diversify" and that "the freshman were more diverse in 2004–2005. Lots of freshman have 'fros, and you notice. You can identify the punk kids and the handful of goth kids; everyone knows who you are if you look different." Students tend to be apolitical; explains one undergrad, "Politics is not a big topic, and current events tend to not be known. You end up in the 'Lehigh Bubble' here." An added benefit of attending Lehigh is that the campus landscape guarantees a daily workout; most undergrads "have great legs from climbing our mountain day in and day out!"

FINANCIAL AID: 610-758-3181 • E-MAIL: ADMISSIONS@LEHIGH.EDU • WEBSITE: WWW.LEHIGH.EDU

ADMISSIONS

Very important factors considered include: Recommendations, secondary school record. *Important factors considered include:* Character/personal qualities, essays, extracurricular activities, standardized test scores, talent/ability, volunteer work. *Other factors considered include:* Alumni/ae relation, class rank, minority status, work experience. SAT Reasoning or ACT required. TOEFL required of all international applicants. High school diploma or equivalent is not required. *Academic units required:* 4 English, 3 math, 2 science (2 science lab), 2 foreign language, 2 social studies, 3 academic electives.

The Inside Word

Lots of work at bolstering Lehigh's public recognition for overall academic quality has paid off—liberal arts candidates will now find the admissions process to be highly selective. Students without solidly impressive academic credentials will have a rough time getting in regardless of their choice of programs, as will unenthusiastic but academically strong candidates who have clearly chosen Lehigh as a safety.

FINANCIAL AID

Students should submit: FAFSA, CSS/Financial Aid PROFILE, noncustodial (divorced/separated) parents' statement, business/farm supplement. Regular filing deadline is 2/1. The Princeton Review suggests that all financial aid forms be submitted as soon as possible after 1/1. *Need-based scholarships/grants offered:* Pell, SEOG, state scholarships/grants, private scholarships, the school's own gift aid, United Negro College Fund. *Loan aid offered:* FFEL Subsidized Stafford, FFEL Unsubsidized Stafford, FFEL PLUS, Federal Perkins, college/university loans from institutional funds, private educational alternative loans. Applicants will be notified of awards on or about 3/30. Off-campus job opportunities are excellent.

FROM THE ADMISSIONS OFFICE

"Lehigh University is located 50 miles north of Philadelphia and 75 miles southwest of New York City in Bethlehem, Pennsylvania, where a cultural renaissance has taken place with the opening of more than a dozen ethnic restaurants, the addition of several boutiques and galleries, and Lehigh's new Campus Square residential/retail complex. Lehigh combines learning opportunities of a large research university with the personal attention of a small, private college, by offering an education that integrates courses from four colleges and dozens of fields of study. Students customize their experience to their interests by tailoring majors and academic programs from more than 2,000 courses, changing majors, carrying a double major, or taking courses outside their college or major field of study. Lehigh offers unique learning opportunities through interdisciplinary programs such as music and engineering and computer science and business (www.lehigh.edu/specialprograms). The arts are essential to the learning experience and are integrated throughout the curriculum. Students develop their imagination and creativity while acquiring skills that will complement their professional development. Students have access to world-class faculty who offer their time and personal attention to help students learn and succeed. Students gain hands-on, real world experience and take part in activities that build confidence and help them develop as leaders. Lehigh's vibrant campus life offers many social and extracurricular activities. Choose from 140 clubs and social organizations or 25 intercollegiate sports teams or become one of the 3,500 students (75 percent) who participate in intramural and club programs.

"For the class entering fall 2006, Lehigh requires students to submit scores from either the old SAT or the new SAT (Reasoning Test) with the Writing component. Students may take the ACT with the Writing portion in lieu of the SAT. SAT Subject Tests (Formerly SATII) are recommended but not required."

SELECTIVITY

Admissions Rating	**96**
# of applicants	9,847
% of applicants accepted	38
% of acceptees attending	28
# accepting a place on wait list	1,270
% admitted from wait list	10
# of early decision applicants	403
% accepted early decision	56

FRESHMAN PROFILE

Range SAT Verbal	600-670
Average SAT Verbal	631
Range SAT Math	640-710
Average SAT Math	671
**TPR Projected Range SAT Writing*	*630-680*
Minimum Paper TOEFL	570
Minimum Computer Based TOEFL	230
% graduated top 10% of class	74
% graduated top 25% of class	98
% graduated top 50% of class	100

DEADLINES

Early decision application deadline	11/15
Early decision notification	12/15
Regular application deadline	1/1
Regular notification	4/1
Nonfall registration?	yes

APPLICANTS ALSO LOOK AT

AND OFTEN PREFER
Cornell University
University of Pennsylvania

AND SOMETIMES PREFER
Boston College
Bucknell University
Carnegie Mellon University
New York University

AND RARELY PREFER
Lafayette College
Penn State University Park
Rutgers University—Rutgers College

FINANCIAL FACTS

Financial Aid Rating	**88**
Annual tuition	$29,140
Room & Board	$8,230
Books and supplies	$800
Required fees	$200
% frosh rec. need-based scholarship or grant aid	48
% UG rec. need-based scholarship or grant aid	43
% frosh rec. need-based self-help aid	47
% UG rec. need-based self-help aid	44
% frosh rec. any financial aid	51
% UG rec. any financial aid	48
Avg. frosh grant	$19,980
Avg. frosh loan	$3,214
Independent 529 member?	No

LEWIS & CLARK COLLEGE

0615 SW Palatine Hill Road, Portland, OR 97219-7899 • Admissions: 503-768-7040 • Fax: 503-768-7055

CAMPUS LIFE

Quality of Life Rating	**91**
Fire Safety Rating	**89**
Type of school	private
Environment	city

STUDENTS

Total undergrad enrollment	1,845
% male/female	39/61
% from out of state	78
% from public high school	74
% live on campus	70
% African American	1
% Asian	5
% Caucasian	67
% Hispanic	4
% Native American	1
% international	4
# of countries represented	42

SURVEY SAYS

Small classes
Students love Portland, OR
Great off-campus food
Frats and sororities are unpopular or nonexistent
Political activism is popular

ACADEMICS

Academic Rating	**88**
Calendar	semester
Student/faculty ratio	12:1
Professors interesting rating	89
Professors accessible rating	90
% professors teaching UG courses	100
% classes taught by TAs	0
Most common lab size	20-29 students
Most common regular class size	10-19 students

MOST POPULAR MAJORS

English language and literature
international relations and affairs
psychology

STUDENTS SPEAK OUT

Academics

"The greatest strength of Lewis & Clark College is the strength of the community," students tell us, pointing out that "the majority of students and faculty are extremely personable. You become friends with everyone quickly." This "community, centered on academics, the outdoors, and a commitment to improving the world," boasts especially strong programs in psychology, premedical sciences, and international affairs; the last is bolstered by "very popular study abroad programs." One student writes, "Lewis & Clark's international perspective is especially appealing. There's an emphasis on a global world view with an effort to promote and influence change for the better in every situation. I know that attending this school will encourage me to grow and reach my full potential." Professors are "amazing people who really care about their students and how they are doing inside and outside of the classroom." They are "definitely available whenever you are having trouble or need to go over something from class. With a school like this, what you pay for is accessibility." Sums up one student, "The best thing about this school is that it is such a well-rounded package. It is in a wonderful area, has amazing professors, a beautiful campus, a great surrounding city, a healthy endowment, and motivated students."

Life

Lewis and Clark is in "an incredible location," abutting "a very pretty state park with a view of Mount Hood, right in the city of Portland." The setting is bucolic; "Even though it is 10 minutes away from downtown Portland, you wouldn't even know you are in a city," students tell us. The campus is so alluring that some rarely venture off; writes one student, "You can go three weeks or so without leaving campus, and Lewis and Clark has often been described as a bubble campus." For such homebodies, student organizations and the school "do a good job of creating things to do on campus. There are many concerts by local artists, open mic nights, poetry slams, lectures, forums, and free university classes." "There are always plenty of things to do on campus," reports one undergrad. Students anxious to explore the city happily note that "getting off campus is easy with the free shuttle the school provides. It drops you off right downtown in the heart of things." The city offers "excellent restaurants, music venues and coffee shops [but] seems to close down early, even on weekends." For those "not into the urban scene" or campus extracurriculars, "there are many outdoor activities available, if you have a car to get to them or are able to take advantage of the transportation provided by the college. "Rock climbing, camping, and backpacking are common activities."

Student Body

"There are many different types of Lewis & Clark students," including "academically minded individuals who attend the lectures and join clubs; athletes, who all seem to live and party together in one dorm; outdoorsy kids, who never seem to spend any time indoors; and students who do not fall neatly into any of these groups, such as international students or theater kids." The College has a reputation as a "pseudo-hippie" school, and there are certainly some students here who fit the bill; they "wear Birkenstocks and assorted clothing fitting the hippie stereotype, are usually unkempt, and smoke weed at least a few times during their college career." Republicans "are few and far between," among the "mainly liberal student body where everyone is doing their own thing."

FINANCIAL AID: 503-768-7090 • E-MAIL: ADMISSIONS@LCLARK.EDU • WEBSITE: WWW.LCLARK.EDU

ADMISSIONS

Very important factors considered include: Alumni/ae relation, minority status, secondary school record. *Important factors considered include:* Character/personal qualities, class rank, essays, extracurricular activities, interview, recommendations, standardized test scores, talent/ability, volunteer work. *Other factors considered include:* Geographical residence, state residency, work experience. TOEFL required of all international applicants. High school diploma is required, and GED is accepted. *Academic units recommended:* 4 English, 3 math, 3 science (2 science lab), 3 foreign language, 3 social studies, 1 fine arts.

The Inside Word

Admissions evaluations are thorough, and the Portfolio Path is an intriguing option that guarantees a purely personal evaluation. Few colleges of Lewis & Clark's quality are as accommodating to students.

FINANCIAL AID

Students should submit: FAFSA. The Princeton Review suggests that all financial aid forms be submitted as soon as possible after 1/1. *Need-based scholarships/grants offered:* Pell, SEOG, state scholarships/grants, private scholarships, the school's own gift aid. *Loan aid offered:* FFEL Subsidized Stafford, FFEL Unsubsidized Stafford, FFEL PLUS, Federal Perkins. Applicants will be notified of awards on a rolling basis beginning on or about 3/1.

FROM THE ADMISSIONS OFFICE

"The record number of applicants in recent years cited a variety of reasons they were drawn to Lewis & Clark. Many had to do with the multiple environments experienced by our students, including a small arts and sciences college with a 12:1 student/faculty ratio; a location only six miles from downtown Portland (metropolitan population 1.7 million); a setting in the heart of the Pacific Northwest, making more than 80 trips per year possible for our College Outdoors Program; and the rest of the world—almost 60 percent of our graduates included an overseas program in their curriculum. Since 1962, more than 8,600 students and 192 faculty members have participated in 512 programs in 66 countries on 6 continents. Our international curriculum has undergone a total review to better prepare graduates going into the twenty-first century.

"Lewis & Clark Colleges shows no preference for the old or new SAT (the old or new ACT). SAT Subject Test scores are not required."

SELECTIVITY

Admissions Rating	**91**
# of applicants	3,826
% of applicants accepted	65
% of acceptees attending	22
# accepting a place on wait list	382
% admitted from wait list	4

FRESHMAN PROFILE

Range SAT Verbal	610-690
Range SAT Math	590-670
**TPR Projected Range SAT Writing*	*640-690*
Range ACT Composite	26-30
Minimum Paper TOEFL	550
Minimum Computer Based TOEFL	213
Average HS GPA	3.6
% graduated top 10% of class	37
% graduated top 25% of class	77
% graduated top 50% of class	98

DEADLINES

Regular application deadline	2/1
Regular notification	4/1
Nonfall registration?	yes

APPLICANTS ALSO LOOK AT

AND OFTEN PREFER
Pomona College
University of California—Berkeley
Wesleyan University

AND SOMETIMES PREFER
Colorado College
University of Puget Sound
Whitman College
Willamette University

AND RARELY PREFER
Pitzer College
University of Colorado—Boulder
University of Oregon

FINANCIAL FACTS

Financial Aid Rating	**83**
Annual tuition	$26,154
Room & Board	$7,330
Books and supplies	$800
% frosh rec. need-based scholarship or grant aid	65
% UG rec. need-based scholarship or grant aid	60
% frosh rec. need-based self-help aid	48
% UG rec. need-based self-help aid	47
% frosh rec. any financial aid	81
% UG rec. any financial aid	66
Avg. frosh grant	$20,114
Avg. frosh loan	$18,654
Independent 529 member?	Yes

LOUISIANA STATE UNIVERSITY—BATON ROUGE

110 THOMAS BOYD HALL, BATON ROUGE, LA 70803 • ADMISSIONS: 225-578-1175 • FAX: 225-575-4433

CAMPUS LIFE

Quality of Life Rating	**83**
Fire Safety Rating	**79**
Type of school	public
Environment	metropolis

STUDENTS

Total undergrad enrollment	25,849
% male/female	48/52
% from out of state	18
% from public high school	53
% live on campus	23
% in (# of) fraternities	10 (19)
% in (# of) sororities	17 (15)
% African American	9
% Asian	3
% Caucasian	80
% Hispanic	2
% international	2
# of countries represented	124

SURVEY SAYS

Athletic facilities are great
Great off-campus food
Everyone loves the Tigers
Student publications are popular
Lots of beer drinking
Hard liquor is popular
(Almost) everyone smokes

ACADEMICS

Academic Rating	**70**
Calendar	semester
Student/faculty ratio	21:1
Professors interesting rating	70
Professors accessible rating	72
% professors teaching UG courses	82
% classes taught by TAs	10
Most common lab size	10-19 students
Most common regular class size	20-29 students

MOST POPULAR MAJORS

Biological and biomedical sciences
general studies
psychology

STUDENTS SPEAK OUT

Academics

In some ways, LSU is a victim of its own success. The school devotes considerable efforts and resources to its football team, with consistently excellent results; unfortunately, in the process the University has created the impression among many students that it is "a football school with an academic afterthought." That's a reputation LSU has been working to shed, and it's making headway. "As much fun as we like to have, we have an outstanding academic program that includes many nationally sponsored and world-renowned research projects," undergraduates brag. They also point out that their "history as both a Land Grant and a Sea Grant school gives [them] a strong interest in research and in local conservation." Research is abetted here by high-tech facilities. One student notes, "All the Internet connections are superfast. We have access to statistical programs and a willing professor to teach it in his off-time. Plus, Middleton Library is humongous." Adds another student, "I live in the IT College with a SmartLab on the first floor; the hardware in the SmartLab rivals the technology in my father's company's conference room." Professors run the gamut here, from devoted teachers to devoted researchers who resent teaching undergraduates. In general, "It is up to the student to succeed, and sometimes that means doing it on your own and teaching yourself." Some see the silver lining in this cloud. Writes one undergraduate, "I like it this way because there won't always be someone teaching you at work, so it's better that we learn now that we can't always depend on someone else to teach us how to do everything."

Life

Few student bodies devote more time to each game of the football season than do LSU undergraduates. Writes one student, "Tailgating before football games is as much as a sport as the game itself. RVs pack the campus starting on Thursday before the game and stay for a day after. If you go up to a random tailgater, smile, and say 'Geaux Tigers,' you can expect a beer, a burger, a side of jambalaya, and a new friend." So what do students do when football season is over? "Greek life is very big on campus. The typical student is frat-tastic," undergraduates tell us. And then there's Baton Rouge, a large city in its own right, yet also "a stereotypical college town, with most activities appealing to college-age students: bars, concerts." The city's "location between New Orleans and Lafayette" makes for fun road trips. Those who decide to stick around campus enjoy "one of the prettiest campuses anywhere, especially in the spring when the azaleas are in full bloom along with the stately oaks that are green all year long." LSU Lakes, "a gorgeous wealthy residential area through campus, makes good walking and running." The campus is also easy to navigate. One student writes, "It's a huge campus, but you can walk anywhere on it in 10 minutes or less."

Student Body

Undergraduates tell us "most students on the LSU campus look alike and are from similar backgrounds: white, upper-middle class, blond hair (girls), shaggy haircuts (boys), brand-name clothes, and generally conservative in their religious, political, and social values." They also note that "there are many students from around the world—from Asia, South America, Europe and Africa." Sore thumbs "are not a factor on a campus with [so many] people, because everyone can find someone with similar interests." Students "normally stay within their cliques. There are the Greek people who mainly associate with themselves, there are the alternative people who mainly associate with themselves, and there are the people in between who just go about their business." That all changes on game day; as one student puts it, "When it comes to football games, anyone in purple and gold is automatically your new best friend. It's really quite amazing how this school comes together during football games. LSU's school spirit is nothing short of amazing."

LOUISIANA STATE UNIVERSITY—BATON ROUGE

FINANCIAL AID: 225-578-3103 • E-MAIL: ADMISSIONS@LSU.EDU • WEBSITE: WWW.LSU.EDU

ADMISSIONS

Very important factors considered include: Secondary school record, standardized test scores. *Important factors considered include:* Class rank. *Other factors considered include:* Character/personal qualities, essays, extracurricular activities, interview, recommendations, talent/ability. SAT Reasoning or ACT required. SAT Subject Tests recommended. TOEFL required of all international applicants. High school diploma is required, and GED is accepted. *Academic units required:* 4 English, 3 math, 3 science, 2 foreign language, 3 social studies, 2 academic electives.

The Inside Word

The university is rare among formula-driven institutions in recognizing that some good students fall through the cracks in such systems. It is commendable that LSU's admissions committee is also willing to take a closer, more personal look if circumstances warrant.

FINANCIAL AID

Students should submit: FAFSA, institution's own financial aid form. The Princeton Review suggests that all financial aid forms be submitted as soon as possible after 1/1. *Need-based scholarships/grants offered:* Pell, SEOG, state scholarships/grants, private scholarships, the school's own gift aid, United Negro College Fund. *Loan aid offered:* FFEL Subsidized Stafford, FFEL Unsubsidized Stafford, FFEL PLUS, Federal Perkins. Applicants will be notified of awards on a rolling basis beginning on or about 3/1. Federal Work-study Program available. Institutional employment available. Off-campus job opportunities are excellent.

FROM THE ADMISSIONS OFFICE

"LSU holds a prominent position in U.S. higher education and is committed to meeting the challenge of pursuing intellectual development for its students, expanding the bounds of knowledge through research, and creating economic opportunities for Louisiana. LSU, one of only 25 universities nationwide designated as both a land-grant and sea-grant institution, also holds the Carnegie Foundation's doctoral research, extensive designation.

"LSU's instructional programs include 198 undergraduate and graduate/professional degrees. Outside of the classroom, residential colleges, service-learning opportunites, and over 300 registered student organizations contribute to an exciting and meaningful college experience.

"Louisiana State University offers the southern hospitality of a small community while providing the benefits of a large, technologically advanced institution.

"Freshman applicants for fall 2006 are required to take the new version of the SAT (or the ACT with the Writing component). LSU will accept scores from the old (prior to March 2005) version of the SAT (or ACT) and use the best scores from either test in making admission decisions."

SELECTIVITY

Admissions Rating	**82**
# of applicants	11,077
% of applicants accepted	78
% of acceptees attending	66

FRESHMAN PROFILE

Range SAT Verbal	520-630
Range SAT Math	530-640
**TPR Projected Range SAT Writing*	*570-650*
Range ACT Composite	22-36
Average ACT Composite	24
Minimum Paper TOEFL	550
Minimum Computer Based TOEFL	213
Average HS GPA	3.42
% graduated top 10% of class	23
% graduated top 25% of class	55
% graduated top 50% of class	80

DEADLINES

Regular application deadline	4/15
Regular notification	rolling
Nonfall registration?	yes

APPLICANTS ALSO LOOK AT

AND OFTEN PREFER

Harvard College
Massachusetts Institute of Technology
United States Air Force Academy

AND SOMETIMES PREFER

Arizona State University
University of Connecticut
The University of Texas—Austin

AND RARELY PREFER

Texas A&M University—College Station
University of Florida
University of Southern California

FINANCIAL FACTS

Financial Aid Rating	**72**
Annual in-state tuition	$2,855
Annual out-of-state tuition	$9,655
Room & Board	$5,882
Books and supplies	$1,000
Required fees	$1,371
% frosh rec. need-based scholarship or grant aid	43
% UG rec. need-based scholarship or grant aid	37
% frosh rec. need-based self-help aid	22
% UG rec. need-based self-help aid	28
% frosh rec. any financial aid	94
% UG rec. any financial aid	77
Avg. frosh grant	$4,200
Avg. frosh loan	$4,950
Independent 529 member?	No

LOYOLA COLLEGE IN MARYLAND

4501 NORTH CHARLES STREET, BALTIMORE, MD 21210 • ADMISSIONS: 410-617-5012 • FAX: 410-617-2176

CAMPUS LIFE

Quality of Life Rating	**89**
Fire Safety Rating	**85**
Type of school	private
Affiliation	Roman Catholic
Environment	village

STUDENTS

Total undergrad enrollment	3,414
% male/female	41/59
% from out of state	81
% from public high school	50
% live on campus	79
% African American	5
% Asian	2
% Caucasian	87
% Hispanic	2
% international	1
# of countries represented	22

SURVEY SAYS

Small classes
Athletic facilities are great
Dorms are like palaces
Frats and sororities are unpopular or nonexistent
Lots of beer drinking
Hard liquor is popular

ACADEMICS

Academic Rating	**83**
Calendar	semester
Student/faculty ratio	13:1
Professors interesting rating	84
Professors accessible rating	86
% professors teaching UG courses	72
% classes taught by TAs	0
Most common lab size	10-19 students
Most common regular class size	20-29 students

MOST POPULAR MAJORS

Business administration and management
communications studies/speech communication and rhetoric

STUDENTS SPEAK OUT

Academics

"Loyola is about the community experience, which can be seen in the way faculty and students are truly involved in the community," students at this small Jesuit liberal arts college in Baltimore report. Community service is just one of many ways in which a Loyola education embodies Jesuit ideals. The school also pursues the Jesuit raison d'être of educating the "whole person" through a thorough core curriculum that "pushes students to their full potential, requiring us to take classes that we would not necessarily choose to take" in such disciplines as writing, social science, philosophy, and theology. Professors here strive to create "an excellent environment for learning and discussion" in which "there is a general sense that everyone wants you to succeed. They let you know that they are willing to help you in whatever way they can, and they really mean it." This sense of community extends beyond the classroom; notes one undergraduate, "Professors do not just go home at the end of the day. They are present at school sporting events, concerts, plays and much more. They really make an effort to get to know all students." Students also appreciate the "unbeatable study abroad program" and the way "professors try to incorporate cultural aspects of Baltimore into their classes. There are often trips to see plays, museum visits, and community service events incorporated into the class." The school's location offers not only numerous cultural outlets, but also "many opportunities to network with high business executives and land great internships."

Life

Loyola students enjoy an "amazingly beautiful campus for such a great location. We're right in Baltimore, but away from the hustle and bustle of downtown in a suburban atmosphere." The campus hosts a wide range of activities, including "great annual events with huge turnouts, such as Loyolapalooza, the Fall Football Classic, and Crabfests," as well as "midnight breakfasts, basketball games, and other weekend activities [like] excellent school concerts with great bands and comedians," all of which help to fill up students' extracurricular calendars. Many undergraduates also cite Baltimore's "many museums, coffee shops, restaurants, the Inner Harbor and sporting events," as well as easy access to DC and Annapolis when joking that "there is almost too much to do here." Then there are those who love the area bars. Those who favor the bar scene—and there are quite a few of them—insist that "Loyola is a bar school. Everybody loves the Baltimore bars and everyone loves going to them. You can always be sure to find fellow Loyola students at any bar in Baltimore on any day of the week." Others temper their assessment, telling us, "A good amount of us do take advantage of the bar scene, but we are not out of control. There are plenty of activities to do aside from drinking." What students don't do is party in their "awesome dorms, [since] the college is looking to bust anyone and everyone for the slightest infringement on the rules."

Student Body

"Popped collars, Ugg boots, J. Crew, Abercrombie, American Eagle, flip-flops, and a North Face jacket" are all acceptable components of the unofficial Loyola uniform. Students also point out that "Although everyone may look the same, they really are different people. You can tell based on the variety of groups and clubs the campus offers." While many students here are admittedly materialistic—"There is the unspoken desire to outdo each other: Who has the most expensive car, who wears the better clothes, who has the best sunglasses"—they are "friendly and outgoing" and also have an altruistic side; "Volunteering is huge," many tell us. Although "the racial and social diversity at Loyola has increased greatly over the last few years," the student body remains "very homogeneous."

FINANCIAL AID: 410-617-2576 • WEBSITE: WWW.LOYOLA.EDU

ADMISSIONS

Very important factors considered include: Secondary school record. *Important factors considered include:* Standardized test scores. *Other factors considered include:* Alumni/ae relation, character/personal qualities, class rank, essays, extracurricular activities, minority status, recommendations, talent/ability, volunteer work, work experience. SAT Reasoning or ACT required. TOEFL required of all international applicants. High school diploma is required, and GED is accepted. *Academic units required:* 4 English, 3 math, 3 science, 2 history. *Academic units recommended:* 4 English, 4 math, 4 science, 3 history.

The Inside Word

Loyola is to be commended for notifying outstanding candidates of acceptance early in the applicant review cycle without demanding an early commitment in return. Traditional Early Decision plans are confusing, archaic, and unreasonable to students. A binding commitment is a huge price to pay to get a decision four months sooner. This is obviously one place that cares.

FINANCIAL AID

Students should submit: FAFSA, CSS/Financial Aid PROFILE, noncustodial (divorced/separated) parents' statement, business/farm supplement. Regular filing deadline is 2/15. The Princeton Review suggests that all financial aid forms be submitted as soon as possible after 1/1. *Need-based scholarships/grants offered:* Pell, SEOG, state scholarships/grants, private scholarships, the school's own gift aid. *Loan aid offered:* Direct Subsidized Stafford, Direct Unsubsidized Stafford, FFEL PLUS, Federal Perkins, college/university loans from institutional funds. Applicants will be notified of awards on or about 4/1. Federal Work-study Program available. Institutional employment available. Off-campus job opportunities are good.

FROM THE ADMISSIONS OFFICE

"To make a wise choice about your college plans, you will need to find out more. We extend to you these invitations. Question-and-answer periods with an admissions counselor are helpful to prospective students. An appointment should be made in advance. Admissions office hours are 9 A.M. to 5 P.M., Monday through Friday. College day programs and Saturday information programs are scheduled during the academic year. These programs include a video about Loyola, a general information session, a discussion of various majors, a campus tour, and lunch. Summer information programs can help high school juniors to get a head start on investigating colleges. These programs feature an introductory presentation about the college and a campus tour.

"Loyola College will continue to accept results of both the former SAT and ACT. In addition, Loyola will continue to combine the highest sub scores from multiple test administrations from both the old and new tests. Loyola will not explicitly require submission of results from the new SAT."

SELECTIVITY

Admissions Rating	**89**
# of applicants	6,979
% of applicants accepted	71
% of acceptees attending	19
# accepting a place on wait list	1,454
% admitted from wait list	33

FRESHMAN PROFILE

Range SAT Verbal	560-650
Average SAT Verbal	606
Range SAT Math	570-650
Average SAT Math	610
**TPR Projected Range SAT Writing*	*600-670*
Range ACT Composite	24-29
Average ACT Composite	26
Minimum Paper TOEFL	550
Minimum Computer Based TOEFL	213
Average HS GPA	3.0
% graduated top 10% of class	40
% graduated top 25% of class	77
% graduated top 50% of class	94

DEADLINES

Regular application deadline	1/15
Regular notification	4/1
Nonfall registration?	yes

APPLICANTS ALSO LOOK AT

AND OFTEN PREFER
Boston College
Georgetown University
University of Notre Dame

AND SOMETIMES PREFER
College of the Holy Cross
University of Richmond
Villanova University

AND RARELY PREFER
Fairfield University
Fordham University
Providence College

FINANCIAL FACTS

Financial Aid Rating	**93**
Annual tuition	$29,500
Room & Board	$7,560
Required fees	$1,310
% frosh rec. need-based scholarship or grant aid	38
% UG rec. need-based scholarship or grant aid	32
% frosh rec. need-based self-help aid	48
% UG rec. need-based self-help aid	41
% frosh rec. any financial aid	68
% UG rec. any financial aid	65
Avg. frosh grant	$13,370
Avg. frosh loan	$5,370
Independent 529 member?	Yes

LOYOLA MARYMOUNT UNIVERSITY

ONE LMU DRIVE, SUITE 100, LOS ANGELES, CA 90045 • ADMISSIONS: 310-338-2750 • FAX: 310-338-2797

CAMPUS LIFE

Quality of Life Rating	**96**
Fire Safety Rating	**60**
Type of school	private
Affiliation	Roman Catholic
Environment	village

STUDENTS

Total undergrad enrollment	5,655
% male/female	39/61
% from out of state	23
% live on campus	54
% in (# of) fraternities	8 (4)
% in (# of) sororities	12 (3)
% African American	7
% Asian	12
% Caucasian	53
% Hispanic	18
% Native American	1
% international	2
# of countries represented	71

SURVEY SAYS

Small classes
Athletic facilities are great
Students love Los Angeles, CA
Great off-campus food
Campus feels safe
Students are happy
Lots of beer drinking
Hard liquor is popular

ACADEMICS

Academic Rating	**83**
Calendar	semester
Student/faculty ratio	13:1
Professors interesting rating	84
Professors accessible rating	92
% professors teaching UG courses	100
% classes taught by TAs	0
Most common lab size	10-19 students
Most common regular class size	20-29 students

MOST POPULAR MAJORS

Business administration/management
communications, journalism, and related fields
psychology

STUDENTS SPEAK OUT

Academics

Jesuit Loyola Marymount University houses five undergraduate colleges, "each of which is very strong. We have business, communications and fine arts, film and television, science and engineering, and liberal arts. You really can't go wrong with a major," students assure us. All undergrads here must complete a thorough core curriculum "that ensures a great overall education," in which the core courses address "ethics, art, literature, social sciences, science, math, theology, philosophy, communication, and more. It is a strong education that makes us better people." Students also love the school's "philosophies of 'educating the whole person' and promoting social justice, which give us an attitude less focused on what we can do for ourselves and more focused on the greater good." With small classes (so small that attendance is taken and counted toward every grade), professors "are more like mentors: they all know your name, and they want to help students learn as much as possible. They come to teach at LMU knowing how personal the classroom environment is--no one is ever a number--and they do their best to help each student on a one-on-one basis." Explains one student, "All classes include discussion, participation, and projects that apply to the field being studied."

Life

LMU boasts "one of the most beautiful campuses ever, right on a bluff overlooking LA. With palm trees abounding, you definitely feel like you're in Southern California." Students also love that "the surrounding area is very safe, and many people, even females, say they feel safe walking around campus at night. Our school maintains strong security on campus." Undergrads here enjoy "a great sense of community" reinforced by "convo hour, which occurs every Tuesday and Thursday. It's an hour and a half when no one has classes, and a lot of the school socializes and participates in various activities and charity drives." A whopping "90-odd percent of students do some type of community service before graduating, whether it be a service organization, service trips to Mexico to build schools, giving campus tours, or Special Games—our version of the Special Olympics." In fact, "it seems everyone at LMU is involved in at least one organization, if not three or four." "All it takes is the motivation to use what LMU offers." The campus after-hours scene, however, faces "tough competition from LA," and "while the school is working on it, the social scene could still be better." It doesn't help that "a lot of people go home on weekends." Those who stick around bide their time by "going to parties and shopping" or "playing beer pong, clubbing, cruising down Sunset, or just hanging out and watching movies." Nothing is more popular than "going to the beach for fun to watch the sunset, have a bonfire, or just go for an early dive and hit the surf. It's great having it so close."

Student Body

"There is quite a bit of money at LMU," enough that "two students brought 49-inch plasma TVs to their freshman dorm this year." Perhaps they are friends with the "skinny rich-beyond-belief blonde girls whose version of 'scrubbing it' is wearing their Juicy Couture sweatshirts with their Manolo Blahniks." But "not everyone is rich. The school isn't overly snobby, and there is a niche for everyone." The "most visible" LMU archetype is "the vaguely wholesome, *Saved By the Bell: The College Years* jocky frat/sorority type," but there are also plenty of "serious student types who are always in the library and no one else ever really gets to know them" as well as "the artsy, theater/coffee-shop types who wear whatever expresses their feelings" as part of the "chill underground." Many in this last group "participate in the film department and the radio station and form their own close community." While "some students here are very LA, others are more focused politically and spiritually and are committed to social justice, service, and participation in student life." At LMU, it may be "easy to feel like you belong" but some say there still "needs to be a stronger sense of the differences in people, races, sexual orientations, and cultures."

LOYOLA MARYMOUNT UNIVERSITY

FINANCIAL AID: 310-338-2753 • E-MAIL: ADMISSIONS@LMU.EDU • WEBSITE: WWW.LMU.EDU

ADMISSIONS

Very important factors considered include: Secondary school record. *Important factors considered include:* Character/personal qualities, class rank, essays, standardized test scores, talent/ability. *Other factors considered include:* Alumni/ae relation, extracurricular activities, geographical residence, interview, recommendations, volunteer work, work experience. SAT Reasoning or ACT required. TOEFL required of all international applicants. High school diploma is required, and GED is accepted. *Academic units recommended:* 4 English, 3 math, 2 science (2 science lab), 3 foreign language, 3 social studies, 1 academic elective.

The Inside Word

Loyola Marymount's admissions committee is particular about candidate evaluation, but a large applicant pool has more to do with the university's moderate acceptance rate than does academic selectivity. Even so, underachievers will have difficulty getting in.

FINANCIAL AID

Students should submit: FAFSA, CSS/Financial Aid PROFILE. Regular filing deadline is 4/1. The Princeton Review suggests that all financial aid forms be submitted as soon as possible after 1/1. *Need-based scholarships/grants offered:* Pell, SEOG, state scholarships/grants, private scholarships, the school's own gift aid. *Loan aid offered:* FFEL Subsidized Stafford, FFEL Unsubsidized Stafford, FFEL PLUS, Federal Perkins, college/university loans from institutional funds. Applicants will be notified of awards on or about 5/1. Federal Work-study Program available. Institutional employment available. Off-campus job opportunities are excellent.

FROM THE ADMISSIONS OFFICE

"Loyola Marymount University is a dynamic, student-centered university. We are medium sized (5,000 undergraduates), and we are the only Jesuit University in the southwestern United States.

"Our campus is located in Westchester, a friendly, residential neighborhood that is removed from the hustle and bustle of Los Angeles yet offers easy access to all the richnesss of our most cosmopolitan environment. One mile from the ocean, our students enjoy ocean and mountain vistas as well as the moderate climate and crisp breezes characteristic of a coastal location.

"Loyola Marymount is committed to the ideals of Jesuit and Marymount education. We are a student-centered university, dedicated to the education of the whole person and to the preparation of our students for lives of service to their families, communities, and professions. Breadth and rigor are the hallmarks of the curriculum.

"Taken together, our academic program, our Jesuit and Marymount heritage, and our terrific campus environment afford our students unparalleled opportunity to prepare for life and leadership in the twenty-first century.

"Applicants into the fall 2006 entering class must submit results from either version of the SAT or ACT, but we expect most students will submit the new version of the SAT (or the ACT with the Writing section). We will use the student's best scores from either test."

SELECTIVITY

Admissions Rating	**90**
# of applicants	7,075
% of applicants accepted	60
% of acceptees attending	33

FRESHMAN PROFILE

Range SAT Verbal	530-620
Average SAT Verbal	573
Range SAT Math	540-630
Average SAT Math	583
**TPR Projected Range SAT Writing*	*580-650*
Minimum Paper TOEFL	550
Minimum Computer Based TOEFL	213
Average HS GPA	3.6
% graduated top 10% of class	30
% graduated top 25% of class	95
% graduated top 50% of class	99

DEADLINES

Regular notification	rolling
Nonfall registration?	yes

APPLICANTS ALSO LOOK AT

AND OFTEN PREFER

Stanford University
University of California—Los Angeles

AND SOMETIMES PREFER

University of California—Irvine
University of California—San Diego
University of California—Santa Barbara
University of Southern California

AND RARELY PREFER

Pepperdine University
Santa Clara University
University of California—Riverside

FINANCIAL FACTS

Financial Aid Rating	**73**
Annual tuition	$25,266
Room & Board	$7,966
Books and supplies	$820
Required fees	$430
% frosh rec. need-based scholarship or grant aid	44
% UG rec. need-based scholarship or grant aid	46
% frosh rec. need-based self-help aid	40
% UG rec. need-based self-help aid	43
Independent 529 member?	No

LOYOLA UNIVERSITY CHICAGO

820 NORTH MICHIGAN AVENUE, CHICAGO, IL 60611 • ADMISSIONS: 312-915-6500 • FAX: 312-915-7216

CAMPUS LIFE

Quality of Life Rating	**68**
Fire Safety Rating	**60**
Type of school	private
Affiliation	Roman Catholic-Jesuit
Environment	metropolis

STUDENTS

Total undergrad enrollment	7,841
% male/female	34/66
% from out of state	34
% from public high school	66
% live on campus	29
% in (# of) fraternities	7 (6)
% in (# of) sororities	5 (6)
% African American	7
% Asian	11
% Caucasian	62
% Hispanic	10
% international	2
# of countries represented	82

SURVEY SAYS

Small classes
Diverse student types on campus
Students love Chicago, IL
Great off-campus food
Lots of beer drinking
Hard liquor is popular
(Almost) everyone smokes

ACADEMICS

Academic Rating	**74**
Calendar	semester
Student/faculty ratio	13:1
Professors interesting rating	71
Professors accessible rating	68
% professors teaching UG courses	97
% classes taught by TAs	0
Most common lab size	fewer than 10 students
Most common regular class size	10-19 students

MOST POPULAR MAJORS

Biology/biological sciences
Business administration/management
psychology

STUDENTS SPEAK OUT

Academics

Students at Loyola University of Chicago "love the accessibility in curriculum, the richness of our core courses, and the availability for outreach to professors." And as far as the undergraduate student academic experience goes, it is that last element—the instructors—who receive the lion's share of praise from students. "The professors are great," writes one enthusiastic student. "They are always willing to go the extra mile to help you out with a paper or with something you don't understand. They also do a lot of research and writing in their own fields so it's exciting to see what they have accomplished." Standout programs include nursing and biology, both consistently receiving high marks from students. Undergraduates have had problems with the school's rapidly increasing enrollment in the past, but new facilities, including a residence hall and education and research center, have helped to quell the critics, like the one undergraduate that reminds us, "growth is not always a good thing." And where professors are very accessible, administrators are notoriously not. One student claims that it's "easier get a private audience with the Pope than to access the higher levels of our administration." Despite all the growing pains, it's still possible to study in a small class setting here, while taking advantage of the cultural and professional development opportunities offered by big-city setting of Chicago.

Life

Chicago defines the student life at Loyola, and the university's own L-stop makes the city very accessible. "Loyola's front yard is the 'L,' and the backyard is Lake Michigan," writes a sophomore, "so the location lends itself to going anywhere or just retreating." But don't come here for a jumping campus scene. "It's not your typical college experience. It's a city experience," writes one junior. Another undergraduate adds, "Campus events are few and far between and pathetic at best." In other words, "Fun revolves around Chicago, not Loyola." One senior gives a take on the campus's relation with Chicago: "People do not party on campus. We all live in Chicago, so we all disperse come the weekend." Luckily, "Chicago is a great playground for college students, [with plenty of] museums, bars, clubs, and sports." Students gripe bitterly about the university's strict on-campus rules, especially its rigid guest policy in the dorms. Residential life "is the worst part of the Loyola system," writes one sophomore—and its administrators are "disorganized, rude, and unreachable." Students would also like to see more school pride, which they think might be gained with "better and more athletic teams." Yet, the "high percentage of commuters discourages school spirit and community."

Student Body

The male-to-female ratio here is either the best thing about Loyola or the worst thing—depending, of course, on which side of the ratio you happen to find yourself. By the school's official count, two-thirds of students are females. "GET SOME MORE GUYS!" writes a female sophomore. Loyola's Jesuit Catholic affiliation also means that a majority of the students here are Catholic. While it may seem that every student here is a "Catholic student from a Catholic high school," a sizable minority, in fact, are not. "Individuality is the norm," writes one sophomore, "with students of all different backgrounds and beliefs interacting openly and freely." Another student claims that "students come from all socioeconomic backgrounds and cultures. Many different languages are spoken on campus." Other students do complain, however, that many of their peers here are "rich and incredibly spoiled." One sophomore agrees that there is polarization among the student body and writes, "The student population segregates itself."

Financial Aid: 773-508-3155 • E-mail: admission@luc.edu • Website: www.luc.edu

ADMISSIONS

Very important factors considered include: Secondary school record, standardized test scores. *Important factors considered include:* Character/personal qualities, essays, extracurricular activities, recommendations, volunteer work. *Other factors considered include:* Alumni/ae relation, class rank, geographical residence, interview, minority status, state residency, talent/ability, work experience. SAT Reasoning or ACT required. TOEFL required of all international applicants. High school diploma is required, and GED is accepted. *Academic units required:* 4 English, 2 math, 2 science, 2 social studies, 1 history. *Academic units recommended:* 4 English, 4 math, 3 science, 2 foreign language, 3 social studies, 2 history, 1 academic elective.

The Inside Word

The admissions process is fairly formulaic. Standards are attainable for most competitive candidates.

FINANCIAL AID

Students should submit: FAFSA. The Princeton Review suggests that all financial aid forms be submitted as soon as possible after 1/1. *Need-based scholarships/grants offered:* Pell, SEOG, state scholarships/grants, private scholarships, the school's own gift aid. *Loan aid offered:* FFEL Subsidized Stafford, FFEL Unsubsidized Stafford, FFEL PLUS, Federal Perkins, Federal Nursing. Applicants will be notified of awards on a rolling basis beginning on or about 2/15. Federal Work-study Program available. Institutional employment available. Off-campus job opportunities are excellent.

FROM THE ADMISSIONS OFFICE

"To accommodate recent record-breaking freshman classes, Loyola University Chicago will open newly constructed facilities in early 2005, including a state-of-the-art Life Sciences Education and Research Building and a modern residence hall. Loyola continues to enhance its undergraduate academic programs and add new majors in emerging fields. A new core curriculum, emphasizing learning outcomes, will debut in 2005. Nationally recognized researchers and scholars continue to teach freshman-level as well as advanced courses. These new developments build on Loyola's rich Jesuit tradition, which fosters academic excellence, instills service to others, and educates the whole person. Loyola's Lake Shore and Water Tower Campuses enable students to experience both traditional residential campus life and a vibrant urban environment. With more than 125 campus organizations offering numerous activities and events, as well as cultural, recreational, and internship opportunities throughout the world-class city of Chicago, undergraduate student education at Loyola extends well beyond the classroom. For more information about undergraduate academics, housing, student life, financial assistance and more, please visit: www.luc.edu/undergrad/.

"Pending further examination into the validity of the new Writing portions offered by the SAT and ACT, LUC will not require applicants to submit Writing scores from either test. All applicants are required to submit a writing sample with their application materials."

SELECTIVITY

Admissions Rating	**85**
# of applicants	11,732
% of applicants accepted	80
% of acceptees attending	19

FRESHMAN PROFILE

Range SAT Verbal	530-640
Average SAT Verbal	585
Range SAT Math	520-630
Average SAT Math	575
**TPR Projected Range SAT Writing*	*580-660*
Range ACT Composite	22-27
Average ACT Composite	25
Minimum Paper TOEFL	550
Minimum Computer Based TOEFL	213
Average HS GPA	3.66
% graduated top 10% of class	29
% graduated top 25% of class	64
% graduated top 50% of class	93

DEADLINES

Regular notification	rolling
Nonfall registration?	yes

APPLICANTS ALSO LOOK AT

AND OFTEN PREFER

DePaul University
Marquette University
Northwestern University
University of Illinois—Chicago
University of Illinois at Urbana-Champaign

AND SOMETIMES PREFER

Michigan State University
University of Michigan—Ann Arbor
University of Wisconsin—Madison
Washington University in St. Louis

AND RARELY PREFER

Illinois State University

FINANCIAL FACTS

Financial Aid Rating	**72**
Annual tuition	$23,900
Room & Board	$9,248
Books and supplies	$800
Required fees	$736
% frosh rec. need-based scholarship or grant aid	74
% UG rec. need-based scholarship or grant aid	73
% frosh rec. need-based self-help aid	63
% UG rec. need-based self-help aid	64
% frosh rec. any financial aid	74
% UG rec. any financial aid	75
Avg. frosh grant	$14,799
Avg. frosh loan	$2,751
Independent 529 member?	No

LOYOLA UNIVERSITY NEW ORLEANS

6363 ST. CHARLES AVENUE, BOX 18, NEW ORLEANS, LA 70118 • ADMISSIONS: 504-865-3240 • FAX: 504-865-3383

CAMPUS LIFE

Quality of Life Rating	**88**
Fire Safety Rating	**94**
Type of school	private
Affiliation	Roman Catholic
Environment	metropolis

STUDENTS

Total undergrad enrollment	3,618
% male/female	39/61
% from out of state	69
% from public high school	40
% live on campus	37
% in (# of) fraternities	19 (8)
% in (# of) sororities	20 (6)
% African American	10
% Asian	4
% Caucasian	65
% Hispanic	11
% Native American	1
% international	3
# of countries represented	56

SURVEY SAYS

Small classes
Great computer facilities
Great library
Students love New Orleans, LA
Great off-campus food
Lots of beer drinking
Hard liquor is popular
(Almost) everyone smokes

ACADEMICS

Academic Rating	**81**
Calendar	semester
Student/faculty ratio	13:1
Professors interesting rating	81
Professors accessible rating	80
% professors teaching UG courses	90
% classes taught by TAs	0
Most common lab size	10-19 students
Most common regular class size	10-19 students

MOST POPULAR MAJORS

Biology/biological sciences
communications studies/speech communication and rhetoric
psychology

STUDENTS SPEAK OUT

Academics

"It's about one-on-one contact with teachers" at Loyola University New Orleans, according to students at this "small, urban Jesuit school which for the most part upholds the Jesuit ideal of scholarship." Freshmen here brag that even the profs in intro classes are "very accessible, excellent in promoting class discussion, and most are experts in their fields. I appreciate that this is a rarity in introductory freshmen classes at other schools." Things only get better as students progress to upper-level course work; as one student in the business college told us, "I know almost all the professors and administrators. This is due to their availability to students and their genuine interest in helping out with what they can. Most professors transmit their passion and seem to have fun with their teaching experience." Administrators are also "highly accessible. Walking around campus, you can see the president of the school talking with students and all the teachers greeting their students by name." Students also appreciate the Jesuit focus "on educating a well-rounded person who is committed to giving back to the community." They also brag that Loyola is "a place of great diversity that allows students to gain knowledge in all areas of education as well as in matters of the world." Some worry about the school's recent growth spurt, complaining that currently "there are not enough professors to accommodate the increasing size of the university."

Life

Anyone who knows anything at all about New Orleans will understand why "pretty much everyone at Loyola is really happy with the school. It's hard not to be happy with living in New Orleans." New Orleans is a town that "always has something going on. There is a ton of ways to have fun: music (jazz and blues), bars and clubs to go out to, parks and places to go for the day, a cultural heritage to investigate further, etc." Because "on any given night of the week you can go out and have a great time with tons of people your own age," "it's easy to get involved in really shady situations, e.g., running into a classmate at 4 A.M. on a Tuesday on Bourbon Street." The university clearly isn't oblivious to its students' extracurricular activities. In fact, "the school even takes into account that we live in New Orleans when planning school holidays, which is nice. For example, we always get off for the days surrounding Mardi Gras." Students who stick close to campus will also find plenty to occupy their time, as "the Student Government Association and other organizations have been taking amazing steps over the past couple of years to do more on-campus programming, so there is pretty much always something going on at Loyola." And on the rare occasion when there's not, there's certainly something cooking at nearby universities. Given the irresistible pull of all these diversions, it's fortunate that "the workload isn't overwhelming."

Student Body

Undergrads at Loyola agree that their school "attracts all kinds of students, from Louisiana natives to out-of-state students, from preppy pre-law majors to music majors with alternative tastes." Students report approvingly of "a large number of minority students, something that is immediately apparent. There are people from different parts of the world, religions, appearances, political beliefs, schools of thought, etc. This makes being a part of Loyola very enriching." Some women complain that there are "a lot more females than males." The more eccentric students note that "it seems like many students here care more about their style of shoes than academics. But they are friendly people, and there are enough nonmainstream people here that one could find a group of people to hang out with."

Loyola University New Orleans

Financial Aid: 504-865-3231 • E-mail: admit@loyno.edu • Website: www.loyno.edu

ADMISSIONS

Very important factors considered include: Secondary school record, standardized test scores. *Important factors considered include:* Character/personal qualities, essays, extracurricular activities, interview, recommendations, talent/ability. *Other factors considered include:* Alumni/ae relation, class rank, volunteer work, work experience. SAT Reasoning or ACT required. TOEFL required of all international applicants. High school diploma is required, and GED is accepted. *Academic units required:* 4 English, 2 math, 2 science, 2 social studies. *Academic units recommended:* 4 English, 3 math, 3 science, 2 foreign language, 3 social studies.

The Inside Word

Students with a solid academic record can expect smooth sailing to admission at Loyola. The majority of the university's applicants are admitted. The admissions process is truly personal, and many of the weaker applicants benefit from Loyola's willingness to consider more than just numbers.

FINANCIAL AID

Students should submit: FAFSA. The Princeton Review suggests that all financial aid forms be submitted as soon as possible after 1/1. *Need-based scholarships/grants offered:* Pell, SEOG, private scholarships, the school's own gift aid. *Loan aid offered:* FFEL Subsidized Stafford, FFEL Unsubsidized Stafford, FFEL PLUS, Federal Perkins. Applicants will be notified of awards on a rolling basis beginning on or about 3/1. Federal Work-study Program available. Off-campus job opportunities are excellent.

FROM THE ADMISSIONS OFFICE

"Founded by the Jesuits in 1912, Loyola University New Orleans has had more than 35,000 graduates who have excelled in innumerable professions for more than 80 years. Loyola's rich Jesuit tradition, its commitment to academic excellence, and its ideal size set it apart from other academic institutions. The total enrollment is approximately 5,900 students, 3,800 of whom are undergraduates. Loyola has a student/faculty ratio of 13:1. Ninety-one percent of our faculty hold the highest degree in their field. Loyola offers more than 60 majors, the largest of which are communications, business, psychology, music, and pre-med. Our undergraduate students enjoy individual attention in a university that strives to educate the whole person, not only intellectually, but also spiritually, socially, and athletically. Students hail from all 50 states, Puerto Rico, the District of Columbia, and 56 foreign countries.

"Students applying for admission into the fall 2006 freshman class are required to take the new version of the SAT (or the ACT with the writing section), but we will allow students to submit scores from the old (prior to March 2005) version of the SAT (or ACT) as well. The highest composite score will be used in admissions decisions."

SELECTIVITY

Admissions Rating	**88**
# of applicants	3,713
% of applicants accepted	70
% of acceptees attending	31

FRESHMAN PROFILE

Range SAT Verbal	570-680
Average SAT Verbal	625
Range SAT Math	560-660
Average SAT Math	603
**TPR Projected Range SAT Writing*	*610-680*
Range ACT Composite	24-29
Average ACT Composite	27
Minimum Paper TOEFL	550
Minimum Computer Based TOEFL	213
Average HS GPA	3.7
% graduated top 10% of class	28
% graduated top 25% of class	60
% graduated top 50% of class	90

DEADLINES

Regular notification	rolling
Nonfall registration?	yes

APPLICANTS ALSO LOOK AT

AND OFTEN PREFER

Louisiana State University
Spring Hill College
Tulane University

AND SOMETIMES PREFER

Centenary College
Florida State University
Southern Methodist University
University of New Orleans
Xavier University of Louisiana

AND RARELY PREFER

Boston College
Vanderbilt University

FINANCIAL FACTS

Financial Aid Rating	**85**
Annual tuition	$24,410
Room & Board	$8,252
Books and supplies	$1,000
Required fees	$896
% frosh rec. need-based scholarship or grant aid	59
% UG rec. need-based scholarship or grant aid	52
% frosh rec. need-based self-help aid	46
% UG rec. need-based self-help aid	40
% frosh rec. any financial aid	84
% UG rec. any financial aid	87
Avg. frosh grant	$14,770
Avg. frosh loan	$4,730
Independent 529 member?	No

Lynchburg College

1501 Lakeside Drive, Lynchburg, VA 24501 • Admissions: 804-544-8300 • Fax: 804-544-8653

CAMPUS LIFE

Quality of Life Rating	**80**
Fire Safety Rating	**60**
Type of school	private
Affiliation	Disciples of Christ
Environment	city

STUDENTS

Total undergrad enrollment	1,933
% male/female	41/59
% from out of state	36
% from public high school	78
% live on campus	81
% in (# of) fraternities	8 (5)
% in (# of) sororities	10 (7)
% African American	8
% Asian	2
% Caucasian	81
% Hispanic	3
% Native American	1
% international	1
# of countries represented	12

SURVEY SAYS . . .

Small classes
Everyone loves the Hornets
Intramural sports are popular
Lots of beer drinking

ACADEMICS

Academic Rating	**78**
Calendar	semester
Student/faculty ratio	13:1
Profs interesting rating	81
Profs accessible rating	82
% profs teaching UG courses	100
% classes taught by TAs	0
Most common lab size	10-19 students
Most common reg class size	20-29 students

Academics

Students praise Lynchburg College for its ability to forge "connections with the professional world via internships and via its Senior Symposium class, which brings in a different lecturer each week, who is a renowned specialist in his/her given field." This focus on the "real world" is reflected in some of Lynchburg's areas of academic strength—political science, education, business, and environmental science. Lynchburg isn't just for pre-professionals, though. As one student explains, "Academically, LC is trying to diversify its programs, both undergraduate and graduate. It has fantastic theater, arts, and English departments." In all departments, students tell us, "The best part about LC is the class size. Your teacher knows you by name and is more than willing to help with anything. Some teachers even become your friends." Students see another benefit to the school's small size. One student reports, "I was able to participate in study-abroad trips, conferences, and panels that may not have been offered as much as they were at LC." Professors here are "a mixed bag," with "the lower caliber teachers in the general education courses" and "mostly good professors in the honors program."

Life

Lynchburg College was known as a party school, with most of the party scene located in senior off-campus houses. A confluence of reasons, such as neighbor complaints and poor maintenance of student housing chief among them, led Lynchburg to change its housing policy. Today, students may live only in on-campus housing or officially sanctioned apartments and townhouses, many a good distance from campus. "Since the college has cut down on off-campus living close to the school, the party life has really suffered," many students here tell us. Students still find ways to get a buzz, but it's not like it used to be. "The parties are normally on Thursdays and Saturdays, but they're usually pretty small now," one student explains. Not everyone is unhappy with the new arrangement, of course. In fact, many students welcome the change. Those who support the change would love to see the focus of extracurricular life shift to "speakers, sporting events, concerts, and comedians…movies, plays, meetings, community service, church," and "the great intramural program." Only time will tell if that shift will occur. In the meantime, students looking for wild fun usually head to Richmond or Charlottesville. They don't stick around Lynchburg, claim some, because "this is Jerry [Falwell]'s town, and it always will be."

Student Body

Lynchburg undergraduates are recognized as "achievers who like to have fun," who are "greatly involved in different organizations on campus" and "enjoy drinking and parties." Many take a pragmatic approach to their studies. Some students suggest that many are "struggling to do the absolute minimum necessary to be successful." At least that's how it's been in the past. The school is looking to shed its traditional image as an enclave of the preppy, and judging by the most recent freshman class, it may be succeeding. One undergraduate reports, "This year's freshman class is much more diverse than the classes of past years. Last year, a group supporting the gay and lesbian lifestyle started. It has been successful in educating the campus and has not received opposition from campus community."

FINANCIAL AID: (434) 544-8228 • E-MAIL: ADMISSIONS@LYNCHBURG.EDU • WEBSITE: WWW.LYNCHBURG.EDU

ADMISSIONS

Very important factors considered include: Secondary school record, standardized test scores. *Important factors considered include:* Class rank, interview. *Other factors considered include:* Essays, recommendations. SAT Reasoning or ACT required; TOEFL required of all international applicants. High school diploma is required and GED is accepted. *Academic units required:* 4 English, 3 math, 3 science, (2 science lab), 2 foreign language, 2 social studies, 2 history. *Academic units recommended:* 4 English, 4 math, 4 science, (3 science lab), 3 foreign language, 2 social studies, 2 history, 1 academic elective.

Inside Word

A slightly above average combination of high school grades and test scores should get most applicants in the door at Lynchburg. However, students who count on high test scores to compensate for below-average grades may be disappointed. Applicants who value a Christian affiliation and are from the region constitute a good match, although applicants from all faiths may apply.

FINANCIAL AID

Students should submit: FAFSA, state aid form. The Princeton Review suggests that all financial aid forms be submitted as soon as possible after January 1. *Need-based scholarships/grants offered:* Pell, SEOG, state scholarships/grants, the school's own gift aid. *Loan aid offered:* FFEL Subsidized Stafford, FFEL Unsubsidized Stafford, FFEL PLUS, Federal Perkins. Applicants will be notified of awards on or about March 5.

FROM THE ADMISSIONS OFFICE

"Lynchburg College is Virginia's most comprehensive private college, nationally recognized for going above and beyond in its commitment to student success. From the moment that prospective students step onto the spectacular campus, they are aware that LC is a place where they will have opportunities to grow intellectually, morally, and spiritually and that there are faculty, staff, and peer mentors waiting to support them in their quest to achieve their personal goals.

"The emphasis at Lynchburg College is on the development of the whole person, as evidenced by the low student-faculty ratio and an abundance of student organizations, athletic teams, intramural and club sports, and experiential learning opportunities, including service-learning, internships, study abroad, and faculty-student collaborative research.

"Lynchburg College seeks to enroll students who wish to take advantage of all that the school has to offer and who want to be part of a caring community. LC welcomes and encourages interested high school students to visit the campus to see for themselves why the college has received record numbers of applications and multiple national honors in recent years. The admissions office sponsors open houses and other events for prospective students throughout the year. For more information visit www.lynchburg.edu.

"We allow students to submit scores from either version of the SAT (or ACT) and will use the student's best scores from either test. Either test is acceptable. Pending further evaluation of Writing scores, the Critical Reading and Math scores of SAT will be the primary scores used for admission decisions."

SELECTIVITY	
Admissions Rating	**76**
# of applicants	3,700
% of applicants accepted	74
% of acceptees attending	21
FRESHMAN PROFILE	
Range SAT Verbal	460-560
Average SAT Verbal	516
Range SAT Math	460-550
Average SAT Math	516
**TPR Projected Range SAT Writing*	*530-600*
Range ACT Composite	19-23
Average ACT Composite	22
Minimum Paper TOEFL	525
Minimum Computer Based TOEFL	197
Average HS GPA	3.09
% graduated top 10% of class	13
% graduated top 25% of class	39
% graduated top 50% of class	74
DEADLINES	
Early decision application deadline	11/15
Early decision notification	12/15
Regular notification	rolling
Nonfall registration?	yes
FINANCIAL FACTS	
Financial Aid Rating	**75**
Annual tuition	$23,700
Room & Board	$5,600
Books and supplies	$600
Required fees	$245
% frosh rec. need-based scholarship or grant aid	66
% UG rec. need-based scholarship or grant aid	64
% frosh rec. need-based self-help aid	59
% UG rec. need-based self-help aid	58
% frosh rec. any financial aid	90
% UG rec. any financial aid	87
Avg. frosh grant	$14,334
Avg. frosh loan	$3,019
Independent 529 member?	No

MACALESTER COLLEGE

1600 GRAND AVENUE, ST. PAUL, MN 55105 • ADMISSIONS: 651-696-6357 • FAX: 651-696-6724

CAMPUS LIFE

Quality of Life Rating	**97**
Fire Safety Rating	**89**
Type of school	private
Affiliation	Presbyterian
Environment	metropolis

STUDENTS

Total undergrad enrollment	1,867
% male/female	44/56
% from out of state	75
% from public high school	66
% live on campus	68
% African American	3
% Asian	6
% Caucasian	73
% Hispanic	3
% Native American	1
% international	14
# of countries represented	86

SURVEY SAYS

Small classes
Frats and sororities are unpopular or nonexistent
Political activism is popular

ACADEMICS

Academic Rating	**94**
Calendar	semester
Student/faculty ratio	11:1
Professors interesting rating	87
Professors accessible rating	93
% professors teaching UG courses	100
% classes taught by TAs	0
Most common lab size	fewer than 10 students
Most common regular class size	10-19 students

MOST POPULAR MAJORS

Economics
English language and literature
political science and government

STUDENTS SPEAK OUT

Academics

Macalester College is "a small, personalized liberal arts college in the midst of a larger urban environment, which offers many resources and an extremely liberal environment." There's a "community feel" to Mac, where "students take academics seriously but without any cutthroat competition. There is an honest and genuine thirst for knowledge that doesn't turn vicious." The "fantastic working relationships between students and professors" further enhance the homey atmosphere, which undergrads love. They also appreciate Mac's "focus on internationalism," pointing out that "there are very few schools of our size ... [who] have an alum who is the secretary general of the UN (and Nobel Peace Prize Winner), a huge international student population, and presents forums, talks, and international roundtables that focus on pressing, intellectual, international matters." Mac is "academically demanding, sometimes to the point of insanity, but balancing it all is possible, [and] the professors are always there to help and support the students." In addition, "there is also a fantastic tutoring program called the MAX (Macalester Academic eXcellence), which all students go to for help in classes or to have papers peer edited." Administrators are described as generally helpful but "a little confused [because] they're cutting academic departments while surveying students about new athletic facilities."

Life

Mac students often cite the Twin Cities as one of their main reasons for choosing the College. The area, they agree, is "very cool, with lots of opportunities for culture." Mac is located in St. Paul, in "a great neighborhood for the bored college student, with lots of neat shops and restaurants, and when we get tired of Grand Avenue, we can explore the rest of the Twin Cities with their stellar music scene and great sporting events." Some here find that they explore the city less often than they had expected when they chose Mac, both because "typically Mac students don't have a lot of funds at their disposal" to pay for urban amenities and also because "between October and April it's winter here, and it's hard to motivate yourself to leave your nice, warm, dorm room." For the snowbound, there's "always something to do on campus, whether it's a movie, a conference, an 'American Idol' spoof, or a political protest," but "organized activities on campus tend to be under-attended, unfortunately." During the winter, "a lot of activity is centered on just chilling out in the dorms, partying a little and talking about life, and listening to music," which "is fun but can get old." Community service is popular—"the community service office has won numerous awards"—as is "studying abroad or getting off campus with internships and employment opportunities." Student organizations are also big, as "there seems to be a minority organization for every possible minority, political organizations, an active queer union, dance groups, international groups, [and] issue groups."

Student Body

"Walking from one end of campus to the other, it would not be uncommon to hear four or five different languages being spoken" at Macalester, where students representing over 80 different countries attended in 2004–2005. Mac undergrads tend to be very liberal; their visits to the Mall of America are as likely precipitated by an anti-sweatshop protest as by their desire to shop. The 'PC' atmosphere can be a bit stifling at times, students admit; "You end up debating whether 'white lie' is a racist term for hours on end. The costs of being overtly respectful sometimes borders on overwhelming PC-ness," explains one student. Mac students are typically quirky, nerdy, "intelligent, friendly, and grounded thrift store junkies [who] are likely to study abroad somewhere, probably in a third world country."

FINANCIAL AID: 651-696-6214 • E-MAIL: ADMISSIONS@MACALESTER.EDU • WEBSITE: WWW.MACALESTER.EDU

ADMISSIONS

Very important factors considered include: Secondary school record. *Important factors considered include:* Character/personal qualities, essays, extracurricular activities, recommendations, standardized test scores. *Other factors considered include:* Alumni/ae relation, class rank, interview, minority status, talent/ability, volunteer work, work experience. SAT Reasoning or ACT required. TOEFL required of all international applicants. High school diploma or equivalent is not required. *Academic units recommended:* 4 English, 3 math, 3 science (3 science lab), 3 foreign language, 3 social studies.

The Inside Word

Macalester is just a breath away from moving into the highest echelon of U.S. colleges; a gift of *Reader's Digest* stock several years ago has recently translated into over $500 million in endowment. As the college has reaped the benefits of this generous gift, the applicant pool has grown dramatically. Macalester is already among the 25 or so most selective colleges in the country. An interview is a good idea. Although interviews are offered across the country, we also encourage you to visit the campus.

FINANCIAL AID

Students should submit: FAFSA, CSS/Financial Aid PROFILE, noncustodial (divorced/separated) parents' statement, parent and student tax returns. Regular filing deadline is 2/8. The Princeton Review suggests that all financial aid forms be submitted as soon as possible after 1/1. *Need-based scholarships/grants offered:* Pell, SEOG, state scholarships/grants, private scholarships, the school's own gift aid. *Loan aid offered:* FFEL Subsidized Stafford, FFEL Unsubsidized Stafford, FFEL PLUS, Federal Perkins, state loans. Applicants will be notified of awards on or about 4/1. Federal Work-study Program available. Institutional employment available. Off-campus job opportunities are excellent.

FROM THE ADMISSIONS OFFICE

"Macalester students come from all 50 states and nearly 90 other countries. The campus is an international community, and the curriculum replete with global perspectives and the classroom abuzz with world views. Even the dining commons offers international options, giving the college high marks for food quality and variety. Most students study abroad for a semester or more, going to more than 50 countries in any given year. Internships relevant to academic and career goals are abundant and easily accessible. For over 30 years, Macalester's debate program has been ranked among the top 10 in the nation. A Macalester team has qualified for the International Collegiate Programming Contest in four of the past seven years, and recently tied with Stanford, Columbia, Carnegie-Mellon, and Harvard. The women's soccer team earned the highest cumulative GPA in the nation in 2003–2004 and has advanced to the national competition in eight of the past ten years. Each year Macalester students win an impressive number of post-graduate awards and fellowships. Recent graduates fare well in the job market and graduate programs. One reports the she was accepted into top med school choices: Mayo, Stanford, UCLS, and Minnesota, and another that he had a 'striking advantage over many other candidates' and is now enrolled in a PhD program in economics at Princeton University. Macalester continues to meet the full-financial need for all admitted students, as determined by standard methodology.

"Freshman applicants for fall 2006 may submit the results from either the old or the new version of the SAT, or the results of the ACT with Writing component. The admissions committee does not have a preference for one test over the other."

SELECTIVITY

Admissions Rating	**96**
# of applicants	4,405
% of applicants accepted	39
% of acceptees attending	28
# accepting a place on wait list	642
# of early decision applicants	132
% accepted early decision	48

FRESHMAN PROFILE

Range SAT Verbal	640-740
Average SAT Verbal	684
Range SAT Math	620-710
Average SAT Math	660
**TPR Projected Range SAT Writing*	*660-720*
Range ACT Composite	28-32
Average ACT Composite	30
Minimum Paper TOEFL	570
Minimum Computer Based TOEFL	230
% graduated top 10% of class	70
% graduated top 25% of class	96
% graduated top 50% of class	100

DEADLINES

Early decision application deadline	11/15
Early decision notification	12/15
Regular application deadline	1/15
Regular notification	3/30
Nonfall registration?	no

APPLICANTS ALSO LOOK AT

AND OFTEN PREFER
Brown University
University of Chicago
Vassar College

AND SOMETIMES PREFER
Grinnell College
Pomona College
Wesleyan College

AND RARELY PREFER
Colorado College
Kenyon College

FINANCIAL FACTS

Financial Aid Rating	**98**
Annual tuition	$28,474
Room & Board	$7,858
Books and supplies	$805
Required fees	$168
% frosh rec. need-based scholarship or grant aid	72
% UG rec. need-based scholarship or grant aid	69
% frosh rec. need-based self-help aid	72
% UG rec. need-based self-help aid	69
% frosh rec. any financial aid	76
% UG rec. any financial aid	73
Avg. frosh grant	$19,432
Avg. frosh loan	$2,394
Independent 529 member?	Yes

Manhattanville College

2900 Purchase Street, Admissions Office, Purchase, NY 10577 • Admissions: 914-323-5124 • Fax: 914-694-1732

CAMPUS LIFE

Quality of Life Rating	**80**
Fire Safety Rating	**60**
Type of school	private
Environment	village

STUDENTS

Total undergrad enrollment	1,533
% male/female	31/69
% from out of state	34
% live on campus	75
% African American	7
% Asian	3
% Caucasian	62
% Hispanic	17
% Native American	1
% international	9
# of countries represented	48

SURVEY SAYS

Small classes
Diverse student types on campus
Frats and sororities are unpopular or nonexistent
(Almost) everyone smokes

ACADEMICS

Academic Rating	**77**
Calendar	semester
Student/faculty ratio	11:1
Professors interesting rating	76
Professors accessible rating	73
% professors teaching UG courses	100
% classes taught by TAs	0
Most common regular class size	10-19 students

MOST POPULAR MAJORS

Business administration/management
psychology
sociology

STUDENTS SPEAK OUT

Academics

Ask students to describe the Manhattanville experience, and they'll likely use the word "family" time and again. "Manhattanville is a family. Professors' and administrators' doors are always open," writes a typical student. Giving rise to this homey atmosphere are "small and personal classrooms that contribute to a very engaging learning experience between yourself, your professor, and your classmates, all giving and taking equally and efficiently." The success of such an approach, of course, hinges on the quality of the faculty. Fortunately, "The professors are incredible, very down-to-earth. They greet you when they see you, and they give their home phone numbers so you can contact them at any time." Crowed one student, "My profs make me feel important so that I want to work harder for them." Upper-level administration is equally accessible. In fact, many students singled out President Berman as one of Manhattanville's greatest assets. "The president holds monthly dinners at his house, and many of us stay for hours to discuss various issues, both personal and school-related. He also attends most student events. How many other college students can say that they see and interact with the school's president at least once a week?" Students report that "The education department has made quite a name for itself and is helpful getting jobs for grad students," but add that the school is strong in many areas. Wrote one student, "Manhattanville offers a great liberal arts education, with strength in a variety of departments, from drama to computer science." A few warned that the small departments are very small; chemistry majors, for example, cross-register at SUNY at Purchase for a few of their classes.

Life

There's "not much to do on campus" at Manhattanville, students here agree, attributing the subdued social scene to several factors. Many report that "Security is ridiculously tight," and "there are no Greeks on campus, so there isn't even a place to have huge parties." The most compelling reason, perhaps, is that "most people go to New York City for fun. It is only 45 minutes by train" or on the free Valiant bus service provided by the school. Being "the most amazing cultural activity center in the world," students find no lack of things to do in the city. Campus fun consists of quiet activities; explains one undergrad, "There's pretty much always someone's room to go hang out in. Watching movies, playing video games, watching TV, playing guitar, drinking, playing Frisbee or lacrosse, and just talking are what people do—among a few other things—to have fun." Undergrads also tell us that "major sporting events and theater productions are lots of fun and are well attended." As one student summarizes, "Situated in a rich Westchester suburb, the campus is beautifully serene. Yet within 10 minutes of the campus is the center of Westchester County, offering plenty of great food, shopping, and night life."

Student Body

The "smart, sociable," "athletic, easygoing" undergrads of Manhattanville generally hail from New York and Connecticut, although there is also a sizeable international student population. Wrote one local, "The greatest strengths [of] my school are the extreme levels of diversity. There are students from Europe, [Asia], the Middle East, and the Caribbean. I have never known so many international people before!" A few complain, however, that "while there is diversity, students are segregated into their own groups." Others gripe that their classmates are "highly concerned with materialistic issues."

MANHATTANVILLE COLLEGE

FINANCIAL AID: 914-323-5357 • E-MAIL: ADMISSIONS@MVILLE.EDU • WEBSITE: WWW.MVILLE.EDU

ADMISSIONS

Very important factors considered include: Secondary school record, standardized test scores. *Important factors considered include:* Essays, extracurricular activities, interview, recommendations. *Other factors considered include:* Alumni/ae relation, character/personal qualities, geographical residence, talent/ability, volunteer work, work experience. SAT Reasoning or ACT required. TOEFL required of all international applicants. High school diploma is required, and GED is accepted. *Academic units required:* 4 English, 3 math, 2 science, 2 social studies, 5 academic electives.

The Inside Word

More than 30 years after going coed, this former women's college is still predominantly female and is still looking to boost its male population. The fact that the school accepts only half its male applicants speaks more to the quality of the applicant pool than to its selectiveness; if male and female candidates of equal qualifications are vying for the last seat in the freshman class, it will go to the male.

FINANCIAL AID

Students should submit: FAFSA, state aid form. The Princeton Review suggests that all financial aid forms be submitted as soon as possible after 1/1. *Need-based scholarships/grants offered:* Pell, SEOG, state scholarships/grants, private scholarships, the school's own gift aid. *Loan aid offered:* FFEL Subsidized Stafford, FFEL Unsubsidized Stafford, FFEL PLUS, Federal Perkins. Applicants will be notified of awards on a rolling basis beginning on or about 3/1. Federal Work-study Program available. Institutional employment available. Off-campus job opportunities are excellent.

FROM THE ADMISSIONS OFFICE

"Manhattanville's mission—to educate ethically and socially responsible leaders for the global community—is evident throughout the College, from academics to athletics to social and extracurricular activities. With 1,500 undergraduates from 53 nations and 37 states, our diversity spans geographic, cultural, ethnic, religious, socioeconomic, and academic backgrounds. Students are free to express their views in this tight-knit community, where we value the personal as well as the global. Any six students with similar interest can start a club, and most participate in a variety of campus-wide programs. Last year, students engaged in more than 19,000 hours of community service and social justice activity. Study abroad opportunities include not only the most desirable international locations, but also a semester-long immersion for living, studying, and working in New York City. In the true liberal arts tradition, students are encouraged to think for themselves and develop new skills—in music, the studio arts, on stage, in the sciences, or on the playing field. With more than 50 areas of study and a popular self-designed major, there is no limit to our academic scope. Our Westchester county location, just 35 miles north of New York City, gives students an edge for jobs and internships. Over the past few years, Manhattanville has been rated among the '100 Most Wired,' the '100 Most Undeservedly Under-Appreciated,' the '320 Hottest,' and in U.S. News & World Report's first tier. Last year, the men's and women's ice hockey teams were ranked #1 in the nation for Division III.

"As of this book's publication, Manhattanville College did not have information available about their policy regarding the new SAT."

SELECTIVITY

Admissions Rating	**83**
# of applicants	3,061
% of applicants accepted	57
% of acceptees attending	25
# accepting a place on wait list	100
# of early decision applicants	22
% accepted early decision	40

FRESHMAN PROFILE

Range SAT Verbal	480-610
Average SAT Verbal	560
Range SAT Math	470-600
Average SAT Math	550
**TPR Projected Range SAT Writing*	*540-640*
Range ACT Composite	20-24
Average ACT Composite	24
Minimum Paper TOEFL	550
Minimum Computer Based TOEFL	217
Average HS GPA	3.0
% graduated top 10% of class	21
% graduated top 25% of class	47
% graduated top 50% of class	77

DEADLINES

Early decision application deadline	12/1
Early decision notification	12/31
Regular application deadline	3/1
Regular notification	rolling
Nonfall registration?	yes

APPLICANTS ALSO LOOK AT

AND OFTEN PREFER
New York University

AND SOMETIMES PREFER
Fordham University

AND RARELY PREFER
College of Mount Saint Vincent

FINANCIAL FACTS

Financial Aid Rating	**75**
Annual tuition	$23,620
Room & Board	$10,130
Books and supplies	$800
Required fees	$950
% frosh rec. need-based scholarship or grant aid	57
% UG rec. need-based scholarship or grant aid	54
% frosh rec. need-based self-help aid	58
% UG rec. need-based self-help aid	55
% frosh rec. any financial aid	85
% UG rec. any financial aid	89
Avg. frosh grant	$15,500
Avg. frosh loan	$3,108
Independent 529 member?	No

MARIST COLLEGE

3399 NORTH ROAD, POUGHKEEPSIE, NY 12601-1387 • ADMISSIONS: 845-575-3226 • FAX: 845-575-3215

CAMPUS LIFE

Quality of Life Rating	**84**
Fire Safety Rating	**87**
Type of school	private
Environment	city

STUDENTS

Total undergrad enrollment	4,686
% male/female	43/57
% from out of state	40
% from public high school	75
% live on campus	56
% in (# of) fraternities	1 (3)
% in (# of) sororities	3 (5)
% African American	4
% Asian	2
% Caucasian	79
% Hispanic	6

SURVEY SAYS

Small classes
Great computer facilities
Great library
Campus feels safe
Students are happy
Lots of beer drinking

ACADEMICS

Academic Rating	**82**
Calendar	semester
Student/faculty ratio	15:1
Professors interesting rating	81
Professors accessible rating	84
% professors teaching UG courses	97
% classes taught by TAs	0
Most common lab size	20-29 students
Most common regular class size	20-29 students

MOST POPULAR MAJORS

Business administration/management
communications studies/speech communication and rhetoric
psychology

STUDENTS SPEAK OUT

Academics

Marist College's "simply spectacular" library, called "one of the nicest and most modern with a very high student-to-Internet connection ratio," stands as a testament to the college's commitment to academics. The professors count among "the most devoted I have ever met" and are "active participants in their field outside of class." One of the school's "greatest strengths is the interaction between professor and student," causing one student to point out, "Getting together to watch college hoops with your professor is not something you can do at every school." Most students save their criticism for the "mediocre assistant professors." Snipes one malcontent, "Adjunct professors in foundation courses are destroying the academic continuity of the college." "I rarely get into the classes I need for my major," is a common complaint, but most agree: "I go to classes because I enjoy them." The most popular and renowned programs include communications, business, education, fashion, IT, and the Public Praxis Program, "an exceptional blend of philosophy courses and community service." The Marist administration is composed of "consummate professionals" who also happen to be "very strict. They try to act like our parents." On the positive side, students share their residence halls with "mentors who help us with any problems we have, even if it's not related to academics." The school enjoys a "good reputation with surrounding businesses" and "many connections with large companies, especially IBM." The "great internship program" ensures that Marist undergrads are "well prepared for jobs after graduation."

Life

Many students characterize Marist as a "big bar school," as opposed to your run-of-the-mill "party school," and thus, an ID (of any degree of authenticity) is "crucial." Though the school hosts no on-campus sororities or fraternities, everybody apparently "knows how to have a good time while getting their work done." According to many, the surrounding town of Poughkeepsie is "very ghetto" and "economically challenged and in need of student involvement." Undergrads consider the school's strict guest policy, with its roots in Marist's Catholic past, "old-fashioned," making dorms "like a prison, especially for freshmen." Opines one, "We are college students, and having curfew for visiting other students is just inexplicable." A system based on "Priority Points," awarded for all types of campus involvement, dictates the on-campus housing lottery, and some students "think that this is a great thing." Others bitterly note, "This college needs to actually reward the students who spend a majority of their time going to class and studying." In terms of activities, many respondents praise the school-sponsored "bus trips to Broadway shows for only $25. You can't beat that!" The city looms only 90 minutes away, and closer to home, the "Hudson Valley has a large amount of history to explore."

Student Body

Among the population of 4,000, "there isn't a lot of diversity, culturally or socially." Many students are "white, middle-class Catholics," often from Long Island; one student notes, "Sometimes I look around campus and feel like I'm looking at a mirror." Students call for "more minority-oriented events" but still believe "the minority community mixes in very well with everyone, even though there are very few of us." "I know it's cheesy when you see kids of all different types playing Frisbee and laughing on the green outside in brochures," comments a student, "but it really does happen here." Perfect harmony is confronted by obstacles like "segregation between 'normal' students and athletes" and the perception that "commuters are generally not as valued as live-in students." Generally, however, friendliness abounds at Marist, where "everyone says 'hi' to everyone," which "makes you feel like a rock star."

FINANCIAL AID: 845-575-3230 • E-MAIL: ADMISSIONS@MARIST.EDU • WEBSITE: WWW.MARIST.EDU

ADMISSIONS

Very important factors considered include: Class rank, essays, recommendations, secondary school record, standardized test scores. *Important factors considered include:* Character/personal qualities, extracurricular activities, geographical residence, minority status, state residency, talent/ability, volunteer work, work experience. *Other factors considered include:* Alumni/ae relation. SAT Reasoning or ACT required. TOEFL required of all international applicants. High school diploma is required, and GED is accepted. *Academic units required:* 4 English, 3 math, 3 science (2 science lab), 2 social studies, 1 history, 2 academic electives. *Academic units recommended:* 4 math, 4 science (3 science lab), 2 foreign language.

The Inside Word

As the school's housing policy indicates, Marist places a strong emphasis on civic responsibility. Candidates who show a strong record of community service and leadership activities will have a definite leg up in the admissions process here.

FINANCIAL AID

Students should submit: FAFSA, institution's own financial aid form. Regular filing deadline is 5/1. The Princeton Review suggests that all financial aid forms be submitted as soon as possible after 1/1. *Need-based scholarships/grants offered:* Pell, SEOG, state scholarships/grants, private scholarships, the school's own gift aid. *Loan aid offered:* FFEL Subsidized Stafford, FFEL Unsubsidized Stafford, FFEL PLUS, Federal Perkins, alternative loans. Applicants will be notified of awards on or about 3/15. Federal Work-study Program available. Institutional employment available. Off-campus job opportunities are excellent.

FROM THE ADMISSIONS OFFICE

"Marist is a 'hot school' among prospective students. We are seeing a record number of applications each year. But the number of seats available for the freshman class remains the same, about 950. Therefore, becoming an accepted applicant is an increasingly competitive process. Our recommendations: Keep your grades up, score well on the SAT, participate in community service both in and out of school, and exercise leadership in the classroom, athletics, extracurricular activities, and your place of worship. We encourage a campus visit. When prospective students see Marist—our beautiful location on a scenic stretch of the Hudson River, the quality of our facilities, the interaction between students and faculty, and the fact that everyone really enjoys their time here—they want to become a part of the Marist College community. We'll help you in the transition from high school to college through an innovative first-year program that provides mentors for every student. You'll also learn how to use technology in whatever field you choose. We emphasize three aspects of a true Marist experience: excellence in education, service to others, and the pursuit of higher human values. At Marist, you will get a premium education, develop your skills, have fun and make lifelong friends, be given the opportunity to gain valuable experience through our internship and study abroad programs, and be ahead of the competition for graduate school or work.

"Marist will require the new SAT (or ACT with Writing component) for all freshmen entering in the fall of 2006. We recommend that all students take the test at least twice. Marist will use the best Verbal, Math and Writing scores from the SAT (or highest composite ACT score)."

SELECTIVITY

Admissions Rating	**89**
# of applicants	7,034
% of applicants accepted	49
% of acceptees attending	28
# accepting a place on wait list	985
% admitted from wait list	6

FRESHMAN PROFILE

Range SAT Verbal	550-620
Average SAT Verbal	580
Range SAT Math	550-630
Average SAT Math	589
**TPR Projected Range SAT Writing*	*600-650*
Range ACT Composite	23-27
Average ACT Composite	26
Minimum Paper TOEFL	550
Minimum Computer Based TOEFL	213
Average HS GPA	3.3
% graduated top 10% of class	24
% graduated top 25% of class	70
% graduated top 50% of class	94

DEADLINES

Regular application deadline	2/15
Regular notification	3/15
Nonfall registration?	yes

APPLICANTS ALSO LOOK AT

AND OFTEN PREFER
Boston College
College of the Holy Cross
SUNY at Binghamton
Villanova University

AND SOMETIMES PREFER
Fordham University
Loyola College in Maryland
Providence College
SUNY College at Geneseo

AND RARELY PREFER
Hofstra University
Iona College
Rider University

FINANCIAL FACTS

Financial Aid Rating	**71**
Annual tuition	$20,535
Room & Board	$9,218
Books and supplies	$1,150
Required fees	$480
% frosh rec. need-based scholarship or grant aid	63
% UG rec. need-based scholarship or grant aid	59
% frosh rec. need-based self-help aid	50
% UG rec. need-based self-help aid	53
% frosh rec. any financial aid	87
% UG rec. any financial aid	83
Avg. frosh grant	$8,712
Avg. frosh loan	$3,477
Independent 529 member?	No

MARLBORO COLLEGE

PO BOX A, SOUTH ROAD, MARLBORO, VT 05344-0300 • ADMISSIONS: 802-258-9236 • FAX: 802-451-7555

CAMPUS LIFE

Quality of Life Rating	**86**
Fire Safety Rating	**60**
Type of school	private
Environment	rural

STUDENTS

Total undergrad enrollment	357
% male/female	45/55
% from out of state	90
% from public high school	65
% live on campus	86
% African American	1
% Asian	1
% Caucasian	88
% Hispanic	1
% Native American	1
% international	1
# of countries represented	10

SURVEY SAYS

Small classes
No one cheats
Frats and sororities are unpopular or nonexistent
Student government is popular

ACADEMICS

Academic Rating	**99**
Calendar	semester
Student/faculty ratio	8:1
Professors interesting rating	99
Professors accessible rating	98
% professors teaching UG courses	100
% classes taught by TAs	0
Most common lab size	fewer than 10 students
Most common regular class size	fewer than 10 students

MOST POPULAR MAJORS

English language and literature
social sciences
visual and performing arts

STUDENTS SPEAK OUT

Academics

Finally, a school that offers, "a great undergrad program for students who would rather be in grad school." Tiny, remote Marlboro College "seeks to nurture critical thinking, effective writing, and engaged citizens" through a program that emphasizes closely supervised independent study and the ideal of self-government. The apex of Marlboro's nontraditional education is "the Plan," which requires students to design their own junior- and senior-year curricula, culminating in a senior research paper. Under the Plan, students "attend one-on-one tutorials with professors in which we spend the entire class asking all of the questions we want to ask and exploring the subjects we want to learn about." One undergrad writes, "The encouragement of critical thinking on both an academic and a social level is incredible here." Freshman and sophomore years are dedicated to more traditional classroom study; classes are "engaging and interesting, everyone is encouraged to speak, and every class is a lively discussion." Professors and administrators are not only mentors and facilitators of learning, but also serve as peers and friends, students tell us. Classes are small—the school has a student/faculty ratio of 8 to 1—a benefit that outweighs some of the drawbacks of the school's size, which "requires Marlboro to be very economical. While there are ways to make up for what the bigger universities have to offer, we must think realistically and be cost-conscious."

Life

Located "on a tiny hill in Vermont at least 20 minutes from the nearest town," Marlboro "really is in the middle of nowhere." Students learn to adapt to the low excitement level here. As one student explains, "I didn't realize that there was nothing to do here until my friend came to visit me. He was saying, 'Okay! Let's go do something!' and I realized that showing him the library and playing a round of ping-pong had already exhausted all of our options." One student warns, "It's a little boring. You are responsible for making your own entertainment. People try, but how many times can you go to see different mutations of the same band, and that annoying kid from next door reading his erotic beat poetry at the open mic?" Schoolwork keeps students busy a good part of the time, and many even appreciate how the lack of distraction facilitates academics. When it's time to unwind, "people hang out, watch movies, and play video games. Some people get completely plastered." An appreciation for the outdoors helps. Anyone who's willing can "take advantage of rock climbing, whitewater paddling, snowboarding, hiking, caving, mountain biking, cross-country skiing, and snowshoeing. None of it is more than 45 minutes away, and we have a great outdoor program (that loans equipment to students at no cost) which makes it easy for people to learn these things."

Students

"Atypical is typical, but not in an obnoxious way," Marlboro students report, pointing out that "we bathe; some girls even shave!" Notes one student, "Sometimes our nonconformity is manifest in our clothes, be it flashy hipness, dirty hippieness, caps with hoods, or just the standard drag-queen apparel." Students are fond of saying that everyone here "is really bright in some way or another." They "often come from alternative educational institutions—Waldorf schools, home schools, and special high schools of different kinds—so they sort of have that 'I'm not doing it the mainstream way' attitude about them." Most "are quite liberal in their thinking and are encouraged to share their views." Among their ranks are "many bisexual and gay students, but anyone can talk to anyone else. It's very open." Diversity here "is less focused on race than it is on sexuality and socioeconomics, where it truly is diverse. The geography and current demographic seems to be unappealing to some minority groups, which drives the administrators nuts." As one undergrad puts it, "The only segment of student demographics less represented than students of color are students of conformity."

MARLBORO COLLEGE

FINANCIAL AID: 800-343-0049 • E-MAIL: ADMISSIONS@MARLBORO.EDU • WEBSITE: WWW.MARLBORO.EDU

ADMISSIONS

Very important factors considered include: Character/personal qualities, essays, secondary school record. *Important factors considered include:* Class rank, extracurricular activities, interview, recommendations, standardized test scores, talent/ability, volunteer work, work experience. *Other factors considered include:* Alumni/ae relation, geographical residence, state residency. SAT Reasoning or ACT required. TOEFL required of all international applicants. High school diploma is required, and GED is accepted. *Academic units required:* 4 English, 3 math, 3 science, 3 social studies. *Academic units recommended:* 4 English, 3 math, 3 science (1 science lab), 3 foreign language, 3 social studies, 3 history, 3 academic electives.

The Inside Word

Don't be misled by Marlboro's high acceptance rate; the College's applicant pool consists mainly of candidates who are sincerely interested in a nontraditional path to their BA or BS. They also possess sincere intellectual curiosity, and students who don't should not bother applying. The admissions process here is driven by matchmaking and a search for those who truly want to learn. For the right kind of person, Marlboro can be a terrific college choice.

FINANCIAL AID

Students should submit: FAFSA, CSS/Financial Aid PROFILE, state aid form, noncustodial (divorced/separated) parents' statement. Regular filing deadline is 3/1. The Princeton Review suggests that all financial aid forms be submitted as soon as possible after 1/1. *Need-based scholarships/grants offered:* Pell, SEOG, state scholarships/grants, private scholarships, the school's own gift aid. *Loan aid offered:* FFEL Subsidized Stafford, FFEL Unsubsidized Stafford, FFEL PLUS, college/university loans from institutional funds. Applicants will be notified of awards on or about 4/1. Federal Work-study Program available. Institutional employment available. Off-campus job opportunities are fair.

FROM THE ADMISSIONS OFFICE

"Marlboro College is distinguished by its curriculum, praised in higher education circles as unique; it is known for its self-governing philosophy, in which each student, faculty, and staff has an equal vote on many issues affecting the community; and it is recognized for its 60-year history of offering a rigorous, exciting, self-designed course of study taught in very small classes and individualized study with faculty. Marlboro's size also distinguishes it from most other schools. With 300 students and a student/faculty ratio of 8 to 1, it is one of the nation's smallest liberal arts colleges. Few other schools offer a program where students have such close interaction with faculty, and where community life is inseparable from academic life. The result, the self-designed, self-directed Plan of Concentration, allows students to develop their own unique academic work by defining a problem, setting clear limits on an area of inquiry, and analyzing, evaluating, and reporting on the outcome of a significant project. A Marlboro education teaches you to think for yourself, articulate your thoughts, express your ideas, believe in yourself, and do it all with the clarity, confidence and self-reliance necessary for later success, no matter what postgraduate path you take.

" Freshman applicants graduating from high school in 2006 and beyond are required to submit scores from the SAT or ACT. Students who have taken either test prior to spring 2005 do not need to retake the test with the new Writing assessment components."

SELECTIVITY

Admissions Rating	**88**
# of applicants	367
% of applicants accepted	67
% of acceptees attending	45
# of early decision applicants	10
% accepted early decision	71

FRESHMAN PROFILE

Range SAT Verbal	590-690
Average SAT Verbal	660
Range SAT Math	510-650
Average SAT Math	590
**TPR Projected Range SAT Writing*	*620-690*
Range ACT Composite	26-32
Average ACT Composite	28
Minimum Paper TOEFL	550
Minimum Computer Based TOEFL	213
Average HS GPA	3.2
% graduated top 10% of class	42
% graduated top 25% of class	50
% graduated top 50% of class	85

DEADLINES

Early decision application deadline	11/15
Early decision notification	12/15
Regular application deadline	2/15
Regular notification	rolling
Nonfall registration?	yes

APPLICANTS ALSO LOOK AT

AND OFTEN PREFER

Bard College
Bennington College
Reed College

AND SOMETIMES PREFER

Antioch College
The Evergreen State College
Sarah Lawrence College

AND RARELY PREFER

College of the Atlantic
Hampshire College

FINANCIAL FACTS

Financial Aid Rating	**75**
Annual tuition	$26,940
Room & Board	$8,190
Books and supplies	$600
Required fees	$850
% frosh rec. need-based scholarship or grant aid	58
% UG rec. need-based scholarship or grant aid	62
% frosh rec. need-based self-help aid	54
% UG rec. need-based self-help aid	72
% frosh rec. any financial aid	67
% UG rec. any financial aid	82
Avg. frosh grant	$20,907
Avg. frosh loan	$2,483
Independent 529 member?	No

Marquette University

PO Box 1881, Milwaukee, WI 53201-1881 • Admissions: 414-288-7302 • Fax: 414-288-3764

CAMPUS LIFE

Quality of Life Rating	**80**
Fire Safety Rating	**70**
Type of school	public
Affiliation	Roman Catholic-Jesuit
Environment	metropolis

STUDENTS

Total undergrad enrollment	7,709
% male/female	45/55
% from out of state	58
% from public high school	56
% live on campus	51
% in (# of) fraternities	6 (9)
% in (# of) sororities	8 (9)
% African American	5
% Asian	4
% Caucasian	85
% Hispanic	4
% international	2
# of countries represented	80

SURVEY SAYS

Small classes
Great library
Students are friendly
Students are happy
Everyone loves the Golden Eagles
Student publications are popular
Lots of beer drinking
Hard liquor is popular

ACADEMICS

Academic Rating	**81**
Calendar	semester
Student/faculty ratio	15:1
Professors interesting rating	76
Professors accessible rating	83
% professors teaching UG courses	77
% classes taught by TAs	0
Most common lab size	10-19 students
Most common regular class size	10-19 students

MOST POPULAR MAJORS

Business administration/management
nursing/registered nurse training (RN, ASN, BSN, MSN)

STUDENTS SPEAK OUT

Academics

"There is really a lot more to Marquette than just the 'community service' opportunities and excellent basketball program that they advertise so much," notes one student at this solid, demanding Catholic school in Milwaukee. Undergrads here warn that "sometimes professors forget that we are college students and some of us work. The workloads can sometimes get out of hand." When students feel overwhelmed, however, they can take advantage of the "many opportunities to get help and ask questions." Marquette's faculty are "engaging, funny, and knowledgeable" and "encourage meeting outside of class and accessing them at all times, even at home. They have flexible office hours and truly try to get to know their students." Students single out for praise the "great chemistry department," the "extremely well-informed professors in the College of Engineering," and the b-school teachers "who have actual work experience." The core curriculum, required of all undergrads, earns students' approval. "While sometimes tedious, these classes provide a breadth of knowledge regardless of your major," notes one. Upperclassmen warn that "upper-division classes tend to have few sections and fill up quickly" and that "registration is done by a lottery, which prevents many upperclassmen from getting classes they need."

Life

Because academics are rigorous at Marquette, students' weekdays here are largely filled with classes, study sessions, and homework. Writes one student, "It is very typical to take heavy class loads, like at least 16 or 17 credits. I've had three 19-credit semesters, and because of that, many of us graduate on time or early. It is expected that you juggle lots of things. Otherwise it seems like you're 'lazy.'" Students know where to draw the line, however, and when the weekend comes, "the general population knows how to cut loose and have fun." How do they do that? "Marquette is a bar school. There are few house parties, and as a result of the lack of Greek life here, frat parties are also rarities. Bars are the most common form of weekend entertainment." Students also love the "major league baseball, shopping, theater, concerts, excellent nightlife downtown, Lake Michigan, etc." that Milwaukee offers and report that "the safety program here at Marquette is excellent. I feel safe living in the downtown area of Milwaukee, where the school is located." On campus, Marquette offers "a lot of activities every week," and of course "Division I intercollegiate sports. The men's B-ball team, in particular, rocks our world. We are the best fans and will do anything to support the Golden Eagles." As at many Jesuit schools, "most students are involved in community service. We live in an urban area, so it is quite easy to find volunteer work. A rescue mission is just one block from campus; many of us serve meals to the homeless."

Student Body

The "studious, religious, friendly, clean-cut" students of Marquette "are typically Catholic and from Wisconsin or Illinois." As one student relates, "You will not see many ethnic differences or hippie types around the campus." Economic backgrounds vary. Wrote one undergrad, "Looking at a student, you never know their story. Some have everything paid for. Others (like me) are working their tails off to pay their own way through college." Because Catholic prep schools feed Marquette heavily, the student body does have a large preppy contingent. Students "tend to be a bit on the conservative side" and are generally very polite. As one undergrad reported, "That's the one thing that impressed me most about Marquette: the way people hold the door for each other, the way eye contact is made with strangers, and the overall inviting atmosphere of campus."

ADMISSIONS

Very important factors considered include: Secondary school record. *Important factors considered include:* Class rank, recommendations, standardized test scores. *Other factors considered include:* Alumni/ae relation, character/personal qualities, essays, extracurricular activities, geographical residence, minority status, religious affiliation/commitment, state residency, talent/ability, volunteer work. SAT Reasoning or ACT required. High school diploma is required, and GED is accepted. *Academic units required:* 4 English, 2 math, 2 science (2 science lab), 2 foreign language, 2 social studies, 2 academic electives. *Academic units recommended:* 4 English, 4 math, 3 science (3 science lab), 2 foreign language, 3 social studies, 5 academic electives.

The Inside Word

Class rank may be an important requirement to the admissions office; but not to worry—in practice, less than one-tenth of Marquette's freshmen ranked in the bottom half of their graduating class, although the acceptance rate has declined in recent years. The university's low level of selectivity makes it a no-sweat proposition for most candidates.

FINANCIAL AID

Students should submit: FAFSA. Admission Application for merit scholarship. The Princeton Review suggests that all financial aid forms be submitted as soon as possible after 1/1. *Need-based scholarships/grants offered:* Pell, SEOG, state scholarships/grants, private scholarships, the school's own gift aid, Marquette merit-based scholarships. *Loan aid offered:* Direct Subsidized Stafford, Direct Unsubsidized Stafford, Direct PLUS, Federal Perkins, Federal Nursing, state loans, college/university loans from institutional funds, alternative and private loans. Applicants will be notified of awards on a rolling basis beginning on or about 3/21. Off-campus job opportunities are excellent.

FROM THE ADMISSIONS OFFICE

"Since 1881, Marquette has been noted for its commitment to educational excellence in the 450-year-old Jesuit, Catholic tradition. Marquette embraces the philosophy that true education should be more than an acquisition of knowledge. It should develop your intellect as well as your moral and spiritual character. This all-encompassing education will challenge you to develop the goals and values that will shape the rest of your life. Each of Marquette's 7,500 undergraduates are admitted as freshman to one of six colleges: Arts and Sciences, Business Administration, Communication, Engineering, Health Sciences, or Nursing. Many co-enroll in the School of Education. The faculty within these colleges are prolific writers and researchers, but more importantly, they all teach and advise students. Marquette is nestled in the financial center of Milwaukee, the nation's eighteenth largest city, allowing you to take full advantage of the city's cultural, professional, and governmental opportunities. Marquette's urban experience is unique; an 80-acre campus (with real grass and trees), an outdoor athletic complex, and an internationally diverse student body (90 percent of which live on or near campus) all make Marquette a close-knit community in which you can learn and live.

"Marquette applicants must submit scores from either the new version of the SAT or the ACT with Writing component. Higher composite scores from previous ACT or SAT examinations (without Writing) will be considered provided we have new scores on file. The highest composite score will be used in admissions decisions."

SELECTIVITY

Admissions Rating	**85**
# of applicants	10,206
% of applicants accepted	67
% of acceptees attending	26

FRESHMAN PROFILE

Range SAT Verbal	530-640
Average SAT Verbal	587
Range SAT Math	540-650
Average SAT Math	591
**TPR Projected Range SAT Writing*	*580-660*
Range ACT Composite	24-28
Average ACT Composite	26
Minimum Paper TOEFL	520
Minimum Computer Based TOEFL	190
% graduated top 10% of class	33
% graduated top 25% of class	64
% graduated top 50% of class	93

DEADLINES

Regular notification	1/15
Nonfall registration?	yes

APPLICANTS ALSO LOOK AT

AND OFTEN PREFER

Boston College
Case Western Reserve University
University of Michigan—Ann Arbor
University of Notre Dame

AND SOMETIMES PREFER

Augustana College (IL)
Loyola University of Chicago
Michigan State University
University of Wisconsin—Madison

AND RARELY PREFER

Carroll College (WI)
Milwaukee School of Engineering
St. Norbert College
University of Wisconsin—Milwaukee

FINANCIAL FACTS

Financial Aid Rating	**76**
Annual tuition	$22,950
Room & Board	$7,890
Books and supplies	$900
Required fees	$396
% frosh rec. need-based scholarship or grant aid	51
% UG rec. need-based scholarship or grant aid	53
% frosh rec. need-based self-help aid	49
% UG rec. need-based self-help aid	51
% frosh rec. any financial aid	88
% UG rec. any financial aid	85
Avg. frosh grant	$11,111
Avg. frosh loan	$4,349
Independent 529 member?	No

MASSACHUSETTS INSTITUTE OF TECHNOLOGY

MIT ADMISSIONS OFFICE, ROOM 3-108, 77 MASSACHUSETTS AVENUE, CAMBRIDGE, MA 02139 • ADMISSIONS: 617-253-4791

CAMPUS LIFE

Quality of Life Rating	**88**
Fire Safety Rating	**89**
Type of school	private
Environment	city

STUDENTS

Total undergrad enrollment	4,132
% male/female	57/43
% from out of state	91
% from public high school	71
% live on campus	93
% in (# of) fraternities	48 (27)
% in (# of) sororities	26 (5)
% African American	6
% Asian	28
% Caucasian	35
% Hispanic	12
% Native American	2
% international	7
# of countries represented	78

SURVEY SAYS

Lab facilities are great
Great computer facilities
Great library
Athletic facilities are great
Diverse student types on campus
Students love Cambridge, MA

ACADEMICS

Academic Rating	**96**
Calendar	4-1-4
Student/faculty ratio	7:1
Professors interesting rating	75
Professors accessible rating	76
% professors teaching UG courses	100
% classes taught by TAs	1
Most common lab size	10-19 students
Most common regular class size	fewer than 10 students

MOST POPULAR MAJORS

Business administration/management
electrical, electronics, and communications engineering
mechanical engineering

STUDENTS SPEAK OUT

Academics

Research heavyweight MIT "is the ultimate academic powerhouse," its students brag. MIT is the type of place where "almost everyone, including the teachers, loves to learn for the sake of learning, and you end up loving MIT for what it gives you while hating it for the work you have to do to succeed." Sure, "it's hard to get into and hard to stay in," but the rewards for all the difficult work include "professors who are just as eager to teach in their field as they are to research in it." The Undergraduate Research Opportunities Program puts students in the lab "doing cutting-edge work in almost any field. This can be invaluable, giving students a chance to get a real feel for what life is like in their chosen field, to learn a great deal, make good contacts with prestigious faculty members, and even earn a little cash." Not every professor here is entirely obliging. One student writes, "As is likely the case at most schools, professors range from excellent to terrible, but if you ask around, you can usually figure out which ones to avoid." The overarching spirit of MIT is one of cooperation. As one student puts it, "If you are willing to put in the work, there is always a way to get enough help to complete all assignments." Undergraduates appreciate how "The name 'MIT' opens many doors for internships and full-time jobs." They also love the freshman year grading system of pass/no record.

Life

MIT students have plenty of entertainment options available to them: Greek parties, lectures, clubs, on-campus performances and art shows, online gaming, and, of course, all that the city of Boston has to offer. The problem, however, "is that it's hard to enjoy yourself when you know that on Monday you have 54 hours of work that needs to be completed." Students do occasionally find time to close the books, though, and when they do, many head to the school's popular fraternities and sororities to unwind. Or they may undertake projects with the folks they live with. One student says, "Whether people live in the dorms, fraternities, sororities, or independent living groups, they almost always find an extremely close, tight-knit community there. Many MIT students end up managing budgets of tens, if not hundreds of thousands of dollars, in their living groups or other clubs. They build, fix, or maintain houses they live in or cabins in the woods. They plan shows and events that draw hundreds of people." Beyond campus are Cambridge and Boston. The latter "is an amazing city, although if you want to have time to take advantage of it more than once a month, go to Boston University. If you're not at a party Friday night, chances are you're in lab or studying in your dorm room," or shooting the breeze with a fellow student. "MIT is the only place where you will find yourself staying up until three in the morning debating the (hypothetical) chemical interactions of urine in a Brita filter based on various chemical models," explains one student.

Student Body

"There's a guy upstairs who unlocks his room with a thumbprint scanner," writes one MIT undergraduate, allowing us a peek into how many standard deviations from the norm some students fall into. While some students assert that "nearly all students at MIT are nerds," others take exception to this characterization. We're inclined to believe the student who tells us the following: "We have jocks/frat boys (who are really nerds inside), sorority girls (also nerds inside), theater people (nerds), artists (nerds), athletes (nerds), and even outright, full-on nerds." Undergraduates proudly report that "many MIT students will take a 'break' from work to help other people with their problem sets. This helpful nature combined with the ease of finding intelligent and interesting people to spend time with makes this institute worth attending." The diverse population includes "a very large number of people of Asian or Indian descent."

ADMISSIONS

Very important factors considered include: Character/personal qualities, secondary school record. *Important factors considered include:* Class rank, extracurricular activities, interview, recommendations, standardized test scores, talent/ability. *Other factors considered include:* Alumni/ae relation, essays, geographical residence, minority status, volunteer work, work experience. SAT Reasoning or ACT required. High school diploma or equivalent is not required. *Academic units recommended:* 4 English, 4 math, 4 science, 2 foreign language, 2 social studies.

The Inside Word

High academic achievement, lofty test scores, and the most rigorous high school courseload possible are prerequisites for a successful candidacy. Among the most selective institutions in the country, MIT's admissions operation is easily one of the most down-to-earth and accessible. Over the years they have shown both a sense of humor in admissions literature and an awareness that applying to such a prestigious and demanding place creates a high level of anxiety in students. Their relaxed and helpful approach does much to temper such stress.

FINANCIAL AID

Students should submit: FAFSA, CSS/Financial Aid PROFILE, noncustodial (divorced/separated) parents' statement, business/farm supplement, parents' complete federal income tax returns from prior year. Parent's W-2 forms from prior year. Regular filing deadline is 2/1. The Princeton Review suggests that all financial aid forms be submitted as soon as possible after 1/1. *Need-based scholarships/grants offered:* Pell, SEOG, state scholarships/grants, private scholarships, the school's own gift aid. *Loan aid offered:* Direct Subsidized Stafford, Direct Unsubsidized Stafford, Direct PLUS, Federal Perkins, college/university loans from institutional funds. Applicants will be notified of awards on or about 3/15. Federal Work-study Program available. Institutional employment available. Off-campus job opportunities are excellent.

FROM THE ADMISSIONS OFFICE

"The students who come to the Massachusetts Institute of Technology are some of America's—and the world's—best and most creative. As graduates, they leave here to make real contributions—in science, technology, business, education, politics, architecture, and the arts. From any class, many will go on to do work that is historically significant. These young men and women are leaders, achievers, producers. Helping such students make the most of their talents and dreams would challenge any educational institution. MIT gives them its best advantages: a world-class faculty, unparalleled facilities, remarkable opportunities. In turn, these students help to make the institute the vital place it is. They bring fresh viewpoints to faculty research: More than three-quarters participate in the Undergraduate Research Opportunities Program. They play on MIT's 41 intercollegiate teams as well as in its 15 musical ensembles. To their classes and to their out-of-class activities, they bring enthusiasm, energy, and individual style.

"For freshman admission fall 2006 MIT requires scores from either the SAT I (old/new) or the ACT (with or without the optional writing test). In addition, we require three SAT Subject Tests: one in Math (level IC or IIC), one in science (Physics, Chemistry, or Biology e/m), and the third in any area of your choosing."

SELECTIVITY

Admissions Rating	**99**
# of applicants	10,466
% of applicants accepted	16
% of acceptees attending	65
# accepting a place on wait list	604

FRESHMAN PROFILE

Range SAT Verbal	680-760
Average SAT Verbal	712
Range SAT Math	730-800
Average SAT Math	755
**TPR Projected Range SAT Writing*	*680-740*
Range ACT Composite	31-34
Average ACT Composite	32
Average HS GPA	4.1
% graduated top 10% of class	97
% graduated top 25% of class	99
% graduated top 50% of class	100

DEADLINES

Regular application deadline	1/1
Regular notification	3/25
Nonfall registration?	no

APPLICANTS ALSO LOOK AT

AND OFTEN PREFER
Harvard College
AND SOMETIMES PREFER
Yale University
AND RARELY PREFER
Carnegie Mellon University
Cornell University
Duke University
University of California—Berkeley
University of Pennsylvania

FINANCIAL FACTS

Financial Aid Rating	**96**
Annual tuition	$30,600
Room & Board	$9,100
Books and supplies	$1,050
Required fees	$200
% frosh rec. need-based scholarship or grant aid	63
% UG rec. need-based scholarship or grant aid	59
% frosh rec. need-based self-help aid	53
% UG rec. need-based self-help aid	54
% frosh rec. any financial aid	79
% UG rec. any financial aid	78
Avg. frosh grant	$23,645
Avg. frosh loan	$3,123
Independent 529 member?	Yes

McGill University

845 Sherbrooke Street West, Montreal, QC H3A 2T5, Canada • Admissions: 514-398-3910 • Fax: 514-398-3683

CAMPUS LIFE

Quality of Life Rating	**87**
Fire Safety Rating	**88**
Type of school	publicly funded private institution
Environment	metropolis

STUDENTS

Total undergrad enrollment	19,351
% male/female	39/61
% from out of state	29
% live on campus	7
% international	15
# of countries represented	138

SURVEY SAYS

Diverse student types on campus
Students love Montreal, QC
Great off-campus food
Student publications are popular
Lots of beer drinking

ACADEMICS

Academic Rating	**62**
Calendar	semester
Student/faculty ratio	14:1
Professors interesting rating	66
Professors accessible rating	64
% professors teaching UG courses	100
% classes taught by TAs	0
Most common lab size	10-19 students
Most common regular class size	10-19 students

MOST POPULAR MAJORS

English/language arts teacher education
political science and government
psychology

STUDENTS SPEAK OUT

Academics

McGill University has "an excellent reputation that is looked on favorably by graduate schools and employers." That reputation is built on "universally high academic standards, so there is no question that everyone here gets a good education" and also means that "an A at McGill means a lot, because it is very hard to get." Students tell us that "science and medicine, as well as music, are the noted strengths of McGill," and that any departments involved in research benefit from "the presence of groundbreaking work by teachers who are all masters of the material" as well as "a lot of funding, meaning that there are a lot of opportunities for students to get experiences that look great on your curriculum vitae." Success at McGill requires undergrads to be "very independent"—"sometimes it is impossible to navigate the bureaucracy," students warn, and "there is virtually no guidance; everything, even your class schedule, is done completely on your own, and if you mess up, it's your fault." Some undergrads see benefits in this; one points out, "This school churns out people with excellent time-management skills and pressure-coping mechanisms." First-year class sizes can be quite a shock—"All of my classes first year are prerequisites, and the class size is almost 600 in all my lectures," writes one science major—but "once you get to upper-level classes, you forget the lack of personality in the big lectures and fall into a more familiar pattern of small classes like in high school." Another positive: "Many of the larger science lectures are available online, so you can watch them again (slides and voice recording) to make sure your notes are complete."

Life

"Montreal is a perfect place to spend your university life," McGill students agree, and with "a beautiful campus where you can lie back on the lawn and take a nap in nice weather and forget you're in the middle of a huge metropolis," it's no wonder they feel that way. Montreal offers "great restaurants, fabulous arts, and plenty of things to do." "McGill's lucky to be located in such a great city," writes one undergrad. "There's less dependence on the school to keep students entertained. At the same time, I think it allows students to experience a wider variety of activities and cultures, and thus learn more about themselves." McGill's housing situation, which forces most students into off-campus housing after their first year, further integrates undergrads into the life of the city; "Living in your own apartment in a big city where the official language is French and where the University is smack dab in the middle of downtown, you learn some real life lessons here," explains one student. While some here report a "lack of campus life due to the fact that most students live off-campus," others tout the school's "clubs and services—we have so many of them and so many varieties!" One student advises, "It is important at a large university like McGill to join some clubs and organizations. If you don't, you end up feeling lost and alone."

Student Body

"The diversity of the student community at McGill never ceases to impress," as the university boasts a "multilingual student body and faculty. Working and studying with many kinds of people from all over the world makes studying here a great experience." Undergrads tell us that "It's hard to pinpoint the typical student. There are a number of 'types': well-dressed American and Torontonians with cell phones and Ugg boots, wealthy internationals, typical hippie/stoner/hacky-sacking folk, and last, but not least, the 'egghead,' who is rarely seen outside of the library." What they all have in common is that they are all bright; writes one undergrad, "It's humbling when you get here, because you are going to classes with really intelligent people. These are people who were also top students in their schools, people who also did lots of extracurricular activities and are overachievers; however, nobody seems to be bragging about these things."

FINANCIAL AID: 514-398-6013 • E-MAIL: ADMISSIONS@MCGILL.CA • WEBSITE: WWW.MCGILL.CA

ADMISSIONS

Very important factors considered include: Secondary school record, standardized test scores. *Important factors considered include:* Class rank. *Other factors considered include:* Recommendations. TOEFL required of all international applicants. High school diploma is required, and GED is not accepted.

The Inside Word

McGill is as tough as it comes in Canadian higher education. The university is provincially funded. As there are no geographic quotas, competition from applicants around the world is intense. The admissions process is thorough and demanding, and high SAT I and II scores just don't have the same clout across the border. Students who are serious about McGill should put extra energy into French classes. While English is the language of instruction, French is the language of Montreal, and those who speak it fare much better in everyday life than those who do not.

FINANCIAL AID

The Princeton Review suggests that all financial aid forms be submitted as soon as possible after 1/1.

FROM THE ADMISSIONS OFFICE

"McGill processes over 20,000 first-year and transfer applicants for the September session. Very few programs are available to non-Quebec students for January admission; consult the website for details.

"Applicants for fall 2006 may submit results from either version (old/new) of the SAT (plus at least three appropriate SAT Subject Tests). The ACT is accepted in lieu of the SAT and SAT Subject Test combination. Please note that certain programs can require specific SAT Subject Tests."

SELECTIVITY

Admissions Rating	**60**
# of applicants	21,718
% of applicants accepted	51
% of acceptees attending	48

FRESHMAN PROFILE

Minimum Paper TOEFL	577
Minimum Computer Based TOEFL	233
Average HS GPA	3.8

DEADLINES

Regular application deadline	1/15
Regular notification	3/1 to 7/29, thereafter on rolling basis
Nonfall registration?	yes

APPLICANTS ALSO LOOK AT AND OFTEN PREFER

Berkeley College
Harvard College
Princeton University
University of Michigan—Engineering

AND SOMETIMES PREFER

Queen's University
Universite de Montreal

FINANCIAL FACTS

Financial Aid Rating	**60**
In-province tuition	$1,366
Out-of-province tuition	$3,605
International tuition	$9,082-$10,033
Room & Board	$6,211
Books and supplies	$819
Required fees	$814
Avg. frosh grant	$3,000
Avg. frosh loan	$2,625
Independent 529 member?	No

MERCER UNIVERSITY—MACON

ADMISSIONS OFFICE, 1400 COLEMAN AVENUE, MACON, GA 31207-0001 • ADMISSIONS: 478-301-2650 • FAX: 478-301-2828

CAMPUS LIFE

Quality of Life Rating	**89**
Fire Safety Rating	**76**
Type of school	private
Affiliation	Baptist
Environment	city

STUDENTS

Total undergrad enrollment	4,561
% male/female	32/68
% from out of state	22
% live on campus	65
% in (# of) fraternities	26 (10)
% in (# of) sororities	27 (6)
% African American	29
% Asian	3
% Caucasian	60
% Hispanic	2
% international	2
# of countries represented	37

SURVEY SAYS

Small classes
Students are friendly
Great off-campus food
Frats and sororities dominate social scene
Student government is popular

ACADEMICS

Academic Rating	**84**
Calendar	semester
Student/faculty ratio	14:1
Professors interesting rating	86
Professors accessible rating	82
% classes taught by TAs	0
Most common lab size	20-29 students
Most common regular class size	10-19 students

MOST POPULAR MAJORS

Business administration/management
communications, journalism, and related fields
engineering

STUDENTS SPEAK OUT

Academics

If you're looking for a small school with "tough" academics that is equally devoted to scholastic development and spiritual growth, then read on. According to Mercer University's website, it's a Baptist-affiliated institution that's "guided by the historic principles of religious and intellectual freedom, while affirming religious and moral values that arise from the Judeo-Christian understanding of the world." Some students tell us that the whole Baptist thing is overdone, like this nontraditional student who describes herself as having "no religious preference" and choosing Mercer because of its location. Regarding instructors, the overriding opinion is that Mercer's "professors are smart as hell" and "care a great deal about their students." Whether or not students like the profs, they'd better be prepared to interact with them. "Real professors," as opposed to TAs, "teach the classes" at Mercer, and they "make it easy to come to talk to them if you have any problems." One student reports that his current schedule consists of "two classes in which there are only four students." But he's an upperclassman. Underclassmen can expect larger classes of less academic rigor. According to students, the old forest-for-the-trees axiom applies when speaking of Mercer's administration. Though the people in charge are "constantly trying to make Mercer better," they often fail to see how the students react to different policies. Students can at least count on honesty from management, however: "The administration speaks the truth," applauds an undergrad. "If there is a matter at the school that cannot be dealt with easily, they do not try to make light of the situation."

Life

Metaphorically, "Mercer is an island. Inside the walls, there's a feeling of protection and guidance." But when it comes to finding entertainment, many students choose to scale those walls. "For fun, people go to clubs, movies, bowling, community activities, the mall," and other places in the city of Macon, Georgia. With a population of about 125,000, Macon has attractions to suit a range of personalities. It's also the home of three other colleges and universities, each with some social options for interested students. Students with cars also take road trips to Atlanta (an hour north by car) or Athens, the home of the University of Georgia (an hour and a half northeast). The Mercer campus offers more than 100 student organizations, including the 16 Greek organizations that often take it upon themselves to serve up Mercer's local nightlife. "I love the Greek system," raves one student. When students take a break from their frat-hopping, they're often able to take advantage of the musical and theater performances that frequent campus. For instance, the university's Grand Opera House is a regular stop for nationally touring Broadway musicals. When all else fails, some students "choose the option of going home on the weekends."

Students

When you talk about diversity at Mercer, use music as your metaphor. Like this student, who estimates of his classmates, "They range from Christian rock to R&B to country." Music aside, most of Mercer's undergrads fit a similar mold: white, southern, financially comfortable, and Baptist. "If you would like a poorly done, southern version of *Beverly Hills 90210*, you'll love Mercer," cracks one student. Others use words like "snobs" and "cliques" when describing their peers. But these are the most critical voices. If you find your niche at Mercer, you'll discover "very friendly" students who "get along" in an "atmosphere of southern hospitality." If you spend a little time on campus, "it's not hard to find someone with compatible interests."

MERCER UNIVERSITY

FINANCIAL AID: 478-301-2670 • E-MAIL: ADMISSIONS@MERCER.EDU • WEBSITE: WWW.MERCER.EDU

ADMISSIONS

Very important factors considered include: Character/personal qualities, secondary school record, standardized test scores. *Important factors considered include:* Extracurricular activities, talent/ability, volunteer work. *Other factors considered include:* Interview, recommendations. SAT Reasoning or ACT required. TOEFL required of all international applicants. High school diploma is required, and GED is accepted. *Academic units required:* 4 English, 4 math, 3 science (2 science lab), 2 foreign language, 1 social studies, 2 history.

The Inside Word

Busy development and renovation on campus has Mercer on track to serve a larger and more diverse student body in the near future. Applicants with a commitment to academic achievement and recognition of their calling as Christians will likely thrive at Mercer.

FINANCIAL AID

Students should submit: FAFSA, institution's own financial aid form, state aid form. The Princeton Review suggests that all financial aid forms be submitted as soon as possible after 1/1. *Need-based scholarships/grants offered:* Pell, SEOG, state scholarships/grants, the school's own gift aid, Federal Nursing scholarships. *Loan aid offered:* Direct Subsidized Stafford, Direct Unsubsidized Stafford, Direct PLUS, Federal Perkins, Federal Nursing, college/university loans from institutional funds. Applicants will be notified of awards on a rolling basis beginning on or about 3/15. Federal Work-study Program available. Institutional employment available. Off-campus job opportunities are good.

FROM THE ADMISSIONS OFFICE

"The mission of the Mercer University Office of Admissions is to attract, admit, and enroll qualified and talented students who will ultimately become happy, successful alumni. We do this by becoming personally involved with each admitted student and family during the admissions process. Mercer admissions staff (98 percent of whom are Mercer graduates) takes time to know each admitted applicant on a personal level and are concerned about the family's questions regarding financial assistance, campus life, and academic affairs. High school and campus visits, regional receptions, and programs are all conducted by admissions staff who are knowledgeable about the high schools and two-year colleges in a particular region. This makes for a truly enjoyable and productive admissions experience for all involved.

"Freshman applicants for fall 2006 must take the new SAT, which includes a written essay, or the ACT with Writing component."

SELECTIVITY

Admissions Rating	**85**
# of applicants	2,711
% of applicants accepted	85
% of acceptees attending	25

FRESHMAN PROFILE

Range SAT Verbal	530-640
Average SAT Verbal	588
Range SAT Math	540-640
Average SAT Math	587
**TPR Projected Range SAT Writing*	*580-660*
Range ACT Composite	22-27
Average ACT Composite	25
Minimum Paper TOEFL	550
Minimum Computer Based TOEFL	213
Average HS GPA	3.5
% graduated top 10% of class	38
% graduated top 25% of class	65
% graduated top 50% of class	91

DEADLINES

Regular application deadline	7/1
Regular notification	rolling
Nonfall registration?	yes

APPLICANTS ALSO LOOK AT AND OFTEN PREFER

Emory University
Georgia Institute of Technology
Samford University
University of Georgia

AND SOMETIMES PREFER

Auburn University
Florida State University
Furman University
Stetson University
Vanderbilt University

AND RARELY PREFER

Clemson University
Georgia Southern University

FINANCIAL FACTS

Financial Aid Rating	**86**
Annual tuition	$22,050
Room & Board	$7,060
Books and supplies	$800
% frosh rec. need-based scholarship or grant aid	69
% UG rec. need-based scholarship or grant aid	66
% frosh rec. need-based self-help aid	43
% UG rec. need-based self-help aid	46
% frosh rec. any financial aid	97
% UG rec. any financial aid	96
Avg. frosh grant	$16,186
Avg. frosh loan	$7,183
Independent 529 member?	Yes

MIAMI UNIVERSITY

301 S. CAMPUS AVENUE, OXFORD, OH 45056 • ADMISSIONS: 513-529-2531 • FAX: 513-529-1550

CAMPUS LIFE

Quality of Life Rating	**84**
Fire Safety Rating	**76**
Type of school	public
Environment	village

STUDENTS

Total undergrad enrollment	15,011
% male/female	46/54
% from out of state	28
% live on campus	45
% in (# of) fraternities	22 (28)
% in (# of) sororities	27 (20)
% African American	3
% Asian	3
% Caucasian	87
% Hispanic	2
% Native American	1

SURVEY SAYS

Great computer facilities
Great library
Athletic facilities are great
Great food on campus
Great off-campus food
Frats and sororities dominate social scene
Lots of beer drinking

ACADEMICS

Academic Rating	**80**
Calendar	semester
Student/faculty ratio	17:1
Professors interesting rating	81
Professors accessible rating	79
% professors teaching UG courses	100
% classes taught by TAs	11
Most common lab size	20-29 students
Most common regular class size	20-29 students

MOST POPULAR MAJORS

Business administration/management
marketing/marketing management
zoology/animal biology

STUDENTS SPEAK OUT

Academics

Students at Miami University, a highly regarded public institution, brag that their school is "very devoted to its undergraduate program." "I have to admit that in my four years at the school, I only had one or two classes with 90 students," writes one undergrad. "Most of my classes were small (approximately 20 students) and were based around discussion." But this is no small liberal arts college; Miami is a full-scale university, with a wide variety of course offerings and myriad opportunities for students to distinguish themselves. "The best part of Miami is the opportunities," reports one student. "There are internships, clubs, classes, majors, minors, or traveling abroad." Adds another, "Through Miami, I've interned at the Democratic National Convention, studied a semester at our campus in Luxembourg, and attended our Washington, DC, Media Experience Program and got to talk with people like Sam Donaldson, Bob Dole, and Tim Russert." Be forewarned that Miami's curriculum is "challenging; you need to put serious time into your work." Fortunately, profs are "very approachable and always have convenient office hours. They love teaching and love their students." Students also tell us that "the alumni network is also amazing."

Life

Miami offers "a pretty good balance as a party/academic school. Most people stay in Sunday through Wednesday nights and study. However, the weekend definitely starts on Thursday, and partying can be pretty intense." Oxford's remote location contributes to the spirited party scene. Students explain that "being surrounded by cornfields means there's not a whole lot to do other than party on the weekends. So, yeah, there is a lot of drinking. But it's fun! There are a ton of bars uptown. There are plenty of house parties to go to." The Greek houses are also abuzz with activity, as "Greek life is definitely huge." "If partying isn't your thing, you will probably find college life to be pretty boring here," many warn. That's because "the town of Oxford has nothing to offer. There is a Wal-Mart and a grocery store. It is miniscule and at times very claustrophobic." Students praise the Miami campus, calling it a "beautiful, easy-leaning environment—lots of trees, pretty buildings, and red brick roads." They also tell us the school has a "great intramural program" that includes "broomball, a combination of hockey and soccer that is played on the ice. It is incredibly popular. It was the most fun I have ever had in a sport, and one of my most fond memories of my freshman year."

Student Body

Whether they agree or disagree with the stereotype, almost all students at Miami University concede that their school has a widespread reputation as '"J. Crew U." Writes one student, "If you were to take away the rich, white, Jetta/Audi-driving frat/sorority members, and the students who are more worried about their image than anything else, you would have a student body that could fill a small auditorium." Counters another, "Students joke about the Miami image more than they strive to conform to it. I have found most of the students to be friendly and open, and I have made many friends." Those who feel the stereotype is apt call their classmates "cliquish," "superficial," and "very unfriendly. The cement in front of them is more appealing than the person walking by. Saying 'Hi' to someone on the sidewalk seems to be a chore." Nearly everyone agrees that Miami students are "very driven," "socially conservative," and "white bread." The school is trying to recruit more minority students, but many here see it as an uphill battle. "It is somewhat difficult to attract minority students to a predominantly white, rural campus, regardless of how well the university markets itself," explains one student.

FINANCIAL AID: 513-529-8734 • E-MAIL: ADMISSION@MUOHIO.EDU • WEBSITE: WWW.MUOHIO.EDU

ADMISSIONS

Very important factors considered include: Character/personal qualities, class rank, essays, recommendations, secondary school record, standardized test scores, talent/ability. *Other factors considered include:* Alumni/ae relation, extracurricular activities, geographical residence, minority status, religious affiliation/commitment, state residency, volunteer work, work experience. SAT Reasoning or ACT required. TOEFL required of all international applicants. High school diploma is required, and GED is accepted. *Academic units recommended:* 4 English, 3 math, 3 science, 2 foreign language, 3 social studies, 1 fine arts.

The Inside Word

Miami is one of the few selective public universities with an admissions process similar to those at highly selective private colleges. The university takes into account a variety of institutional needs as well as the qualifications of individual candidates when making admissions decisions. Don't be deceived by a high acceptance rate; the academic requirements for admission are quite high.

FINANCIAL AID

Students should submit: FAFSA. The Princeton Review suggests that all financial aid forms be submitted as soon as possible after 1/1. *Need-based scholarships/grants offered:* Pell, SEOG, state scholarships/grants, private scholarships, the school's own gift aid. *Loan aid offered:* Direct Subsidized Stafford, Direct Unsubsidized Stafford, Direct PLUS, Federal Perkins, Federal Nursing, college/university loans from institutional funds, bank alternative loans. Applicants will be notified of awards on or about 3/31.

FROM THE ADMISSIONS OFFICE

"At Miami, you'll find a level of involvement—in your classes, in your research, in your extracurricular activities—that you won't find at other schools. What sets Miami apart and makes it a "Public Ivy" and a "Hidden Treasure" is the ability to give students a small-college experience within the excitement and opportunities of a large university, all at a public school cost. With more than 100 majors to choose from, and a liberal arts foundation that allows students to explore different areas of interest, finding the right career path is at the heart of what the MU experience is all about. Miami's reputation for producing outstanding graduates makes us a target school for top national firms. In fact, our Office of Career Services sponsors one of the largest career fairs in the country. For getting into the best possible graduate school, The Wall Street Journal ranks Miami at no. 22 among undergraduate colleges that feed into elite graduate programs. And our graduates' acceptance rate into law and medical school are far above the national average.

"Freshman applicants for fall 2006 must take the new SAT, which includes a written essay, or the ACT with Writing component. The Writing component of these tests, however, will not play a role in our decisions for fall 2006 admission. These scores will help simply help us collect important data that will be useful for future admission decisions."

SELECTIVITY

Admissions Rating	**89**
# of applicants	14,977
% of applicants accepted	71
% of acceptees attending	33
# accepting a place on wait list	1,522
% admitted from wait list	24
# of early decision applicants	576
% accepted early decision	78

FRESHMAN PROFILE

Range SAT Verbal	560-640
Average SAT Verbal	590
Range SAT Math	580-660
Average SAT Math	610
**TPR Projected Range SAT Writing*	*600-660*
Range ACT Composite	25-29
Average ACT Composite	26
Minimum Paper TOEFL	533
Minimum Computer Based TOEFL	200
Average HS GPA	3.7
% graduated top 10% of class	37
% graduated top 25% of class	75
% graduated top 50% of class	97

DEADLINES

Early decision application deadline	11/1
Early decision notification	12/15
Regular application deadline	1/31
Regular notification	3/15
Nonfall registration?	yes

APPLICANTS ALSO LOOK AT

AND OFTEN PREFER

Northwestern U., U. of Notre Dame, Vanderbilt U.

AND SOMETIMES PREFER

Boston College, Penn State University Park, U. of Illinois at Urbana—Champaign

AND RARELY PREFER

Denison U., Ohio State U.—Columbus, Ohio U.—Athens

FINANCIAL FACTS

Financial Aid Rating	**72**
Annual in-state tuition	\$8,353
Annual out-of-state tuition	\$18,103
Room & Board	\$6,680
Books and supplies	\$800
Required fees	\$1,334
% frosh rec. need-based scholarship or grant aid	15
% UG rec. need-based scholarship or grant aid	15
% frosh rec. need-based self-help aid	31
% UG rec. need-based self-help aid	29
% frosh rec. any financial aid	87
% UG rec. any financial aid	85
Independent 529 member?	No

MICHIGAN STATE UNIVERSITY

250 ADMINISTRATION BUILDING, EAST LANSING, MI 48824-1046 • ADMISSIONS: 517-355-8332 • FAX: 517-353-1647

CAMPUS LIFE

Quality of Life Rating	**78**
Fire Safety Rating	**60**
Type of school	public
Environment	town

STUDENTS

Total undergrad enrollment	35,107
% male/female	47/53
% from out of state	11
% live on campus	42
% African American	8
% Asian	5
% Caucasian	79
% Hispanic	3
% Native American	1
% international	3
# of countries represented	100

SURVEY SAYS

Great library
Everyone loves the Spartans
Student publications are popular
Lots of beer drinking
Hard liquor is popular

ACADEMICS

Academic Rating	**73**
Calendar	semester
Student/faculty ratio	18:1
Professors interesting rating	67
Professors accessible rating	70
% classes taught by TAs	0
Most common lab size	20-29 students
Most common regular class size	20-29 students

MOST POPULAR MAJORS

Accounting
education
psychology

STUDENTS SPEAK OUT

Academics

The fact that Michigan State (MSU) is such a "mega institution" has its ups and its downs. On the downside, "you do not get the advantage of having the professor's individual attention." In many cases, you don't get the advantage of having the professor, as some lower-level classes are enormous lectures taught by TAs. Another common complaint is that "many of the classes are taught by teachers that don't know a lick of English." An upside to MSU's size is the "plethora of academic resources" and the wide variety of "classes and majors available." And if you're really seeking a challenge, look into MSU's highly esteemed Honors College. To top students it offers "a small, personalized feel to a large campus," not to mention a streamlined registration process, access to certain graduate classes, and plenty of opportunities for independent studies, thesis work, and research projects. "James Madison College (JMC), the residential liberal arts school at Michigan State University," also draws praise. According to one JMC student, "It should be ranked in a different category from Michigan State University. It has great professors, none of the classes are taught by TAs, the faculty is always available, the classes are no more than 35 people, it's a competitive environment, and [it] is very challenging." Engineering, business, marketing, and various social sciences are among the most popular paths of study here, and we've also heard rave reviews for the writing, nursing, and veterinary programs.

Life

School spirit is alive and well in East Lansing, Michigan, which students describe as "the happiest place on earth." Students follow Big 10 sports religiously and tell us that Spartan games are "amazing and crazily fun to watch." During football season, thousands of students "get up at the butt-crack of dawn in order to get a good spot to tailgate" outside of Spartan Stadium. Greek life provides plenty of party opportunities for the underage revelers, while upperclassmen tend to make their way to off-campus parties or the "very popular" bar scene in East Lansing. Though few students will deny that MSU's "party school" reputation is deserved, they're quick to assert that drinking has been put under control of late. If MSU sounds appealing but drinking does not, "choosing a dorm with an alcohol-free option, a quiet floor, or an honors floor will make a HUGE difference in the types of people you meet." The university offers a multitude of "volunteering" opportunities and "school activities/groups" for students who want to exercise their hobbies and talents. MSU also plays host to "many famous speakers, entertainers, and scholars." Astoundingly, nearly half of the student population is involved in intramural sports. The city of East Lansing itself is a lively town, with "bars," "a good indie band scene," and "a multitude of diverse festivities such as the Native American Pow Wow of Love and the International Folk Festival and the East Lansing Arts Festival." One straight-shooting students says, "If you can't find something fun to do, you have some major social skills to work on."

Student Body

One thing's certain at Michigan State University: You're bound to run into a lot of students from Michigan. "It seems like 90 percent of our school is from Michigan," a student comments. Four-fifths of the student population is white, but there's still a mix of races and backgrounds. "However, the different racial groups do not really socialize with each other," notes an undergrad. "Whites stick with whites, blacks stick with blacks, etc." But don't misunderstand. Most MSU students are "friendly and welcoming." One student even goes so far as to say, "I am sure that nowhere else on the planet are there 40,000+ young people [that's undergrads and grads combined] that get along as well as those attending Michigan State University."

Michigan State University

Financial Aid: 517-353-5940 • E-mail: admis@msu.edu • Website: www.msu.edu

ADMISSIONS

Very important factors considered include: Secondary school record. *Important factors considered include:* Essays, standardized test scores. *Other factors considered include:* Class rank, extracurricular activities, geographical residence, minority status, recommendations, talent/ability, volunteer work, work experience. SAT Reasoning or ACT required. TOEFL required of all international applicants. High school diploma is required, and GED is accepted. *Academic units required:* 4 English, 3 math, 2 science, 2 foreign language, 3 social studies.

The Inside Word

Gaining admission to MSU is a matter of following the formulas. Grades, tests, and rank—numbers, numbers, numbers. Solid extracurricular involvement and recommendations may help borderline candidates.

FINANCIAL AID

Students should submit: FAFSA, institution's own financial aid form. Regular filing deadline is 6/30. The Princeton Review suggests that all financial aid forms be submitted as soon as possible after 1/1. *Need-based scholarships/grants offered:* Pell, SEOG, state scholarships/grants, private scholarships, the school's own gift aid, United Negro College Fund, Federal Nursing scholarships. *Loan aid offered:* FFEL Subsidized Stafford, FFEL Unsubsidized Stafford, FFEL PLUS, Federal Perkins, Federal Nursing, state loans, college/university loans from institutional funds. Applicants will be notified of awards on a rolling basis beginning on or about 3/15. Federal Work-study Program available. Institutional employment available. Off-campus job opportunities are excellent.

FROM THE ADMISSIONS OFFICE

"Although Michigan State University is a graduate and research institution of international stature and acclaim, your undergraduate education is a high priority. More than 2,600 instructional faculty members (90 percent of whom hold a terminal degree) are dedicated to providing academic instruction, guidance, and assistance to our undergraduate students. Our 35,000 undergraduate students are a select group of academically motivated men and women. The diversity of ethnic, racial, religious, and socioeconomic heritage makes the student body a microcosm of the state, national, and international community.

"Students applying for fall 2006 admission to Michigan State University are required to take the new version of the SAT or the ACT exam with the writing section. The writing assessment will be considered in the holistic review of the application for admission. SAT Subject Tests are not required."

SELECTIVITY

Admissions Rating	**83**
# of applicants	21,834
% of applicants accepted	79
% of acceptees attending	44

FRESHMAN PROFILE

Range SAT Verbal	490-620
Average SAT Verbal	556
Range SAT Math	515-650
Average SAT Math	579
**TPR Projected Range SAT Writing*	*550-650*
Range ACT Composite	22-27
Average ACT Composite	24
Minimum Paper TOEFL	550
Minimum Computer Based TOEFL	213
Average HS GPA	3.55
% graduated top 10% of class	24
% graduated top 25% of class	61
% graduated top 50% of class	93

DEADLINES

Regular notification	9/1
Nonfall registration?	yes

APPLICANTS ALSO LOOK AT

AND OFTEN PREFER

Central Michigan University
Eastern Michigan University
Kalamazoo College
University of Michigan—Ann Arbor
Western Michigan University

AND SOMETIMES PREFER

Indiana University—Bloomington
Oakland University
University of Illinois at Urbana-Champaign
University of Wisconsin—Madison

AND RARELY PREFER

Wayne State University

FINANCIAL FACTS

Financial Aid Rating	**72**
Annual in-state tuition	$6,893
Annual out-of-state tuition	$17,640
Room & Board	$5,458
Books and supplies	$826
Required fees	$812
% frosh rec. need-based scholarship or grant aid	25
% UG rec. need-based scholarship or grant aid	25
% frosh rec. need-based self-help aid	35
% UG rec. need-based self-help aid	31
% frosh rec. any financial aid	41
% UG rec. any financial aid	40
Avg. frosh grant	$3,895
Avg. frosh loan	$2,624
Independent 529 member?	No

Michigan Technological University

1400 Townsend Drive, Houghton, MI 49931 • Admissions: 906-487-2335 • Fax: 906-487-2125

CAMPUS LIFE

Quality of Life Rating	**80**
Fire Safety Rating	**91**
Type of school	public
Environment	village

STUDENTS

Total undergrad enrollment	5,586
% male/female	78/22
% from out of state	23
% live on campus	40
% in (# of) fraternities	8 (15)
% in (# of) sororities	13 (8)
% African American	2
% Asian	1
% Caucasian	86
% Hispanic	1
% Native American	1
% international	4
# of countries represented	53

SURVEY SAYS

Great computer facilities
Athletic facilities are great
Students are friendly
Campus feels safe
Frats and sororities dominate social scene
Lots of beer drinking

ACADEMICS

Academic Rating	**75**
Calendar	semester
Student/faculty ratio	11:1
Professors interesting rating	64
Professors accessible rating	75
% professors teaching UG courses	100
% classes taught by TAs	5
Most common lab size	10-19 students
Most common regular class size	10-19 students

MOST POPULAR MAJORS

Civil engineering
electrical, electronics, and communications engineering
mechanical engineering

STUDENTS SPEAK OUT

Academics

"Michigan Tech will definitely prepare you for your future," engineers at this small, tech powerhouse tell us, promising that "you will get a great education, and employers, especially in the Midwest, recognize Michigan Tech as a premier engineering school." More than half of MTU's undergraduates are enrolled in the College of Engineering. Among the other divisions, students tell us that "The School of Business and Economics is gaining a lot of ground" as the school attempts to diversify its appeal. Those efforts have produced mixed results, students report; while improvements to business and biology offerings are welcome, some here feel efforts to upgrade liberal arts offerings dilute MTU's strengths. "We're trying to be like the University of Michigan with great engineering and hundreds of other major programs, but we just don't have the money to do it all," writes one student. Like most tech schools, MTU "expects a lot of students," but as a result "you will graduate being very proficient in your field, and you'll have a competitive advantage over graduates from other universities." You may not even have to wait for graduation to benefit from that advantage, since "Michigan Tech has a great program for getting internships and co-ops." Professors "are involved in research and have professional commitments outside the classroom, but most are still there for the students. Have a problem? Schedule a time to meet with your professor and talk about it. Most will even find a time outside their scheduled office hours that works with [your] schedule to meet with you."

Life

Michigan Tech "is separated from the rest of the country. It's located in a small town in the very northern part of the UP (upper peninsula). Most students have an eight-plus hour drive home. This makes the community rather tight knit," which "helps when you get to the killer classes." The university combats its isolation by "providing entertainment for the students by way of comedians, musical acts, and plays." Students also enjoy "lots of Greek parties (the Greek scene is not exclusive, which is cool) [and] sporting events, like the very successful football and basketball programs. We also have an important ice hockey program." Do you like snow? We hope so because at MTU "it snows from October through April," which naturally has a huge impact on campus life. For fans of winter sports, MTU is a virtual paradise, with "several ski hills in close proximity to the campus. Snowmobiling, cross-country and downhill skiing, as well as ice skating are popular activities." Students also point out that hometown "Houghton is also beautiful in the summer, and is strategically located by large bodies of fresh water. When it's warm, we fish, hike, bike, rock-climb, and play the school golf course."

Student Body

One MTU student writes, "There doesn't seem to be a single typical student at Michigan Tech. There is a bipolar distribution with a lot of smart engineers that party little and study hard. There are also a lot of students that drink heavily and just barely get by in their classes. As with any school, there are many outliers that find their own niche here." Students tell us there are also quite a few "Indian, Chinese, and Middle Eastern" students; most other undergraduates are "white, Midwestern, from middle-class families [and] lean to the conservative side." Men far outnumber women here, which, one woman tells us, "You think would be great for women, but it's not. Once you take away the guys who won't even approach a girl, the ratio is more like two guys to every girl, and then out of all the guys who are single it is more like .5 guys to every girl. People think it is so easy to be a girl at Tech, but after a while you are just viewed as one of the guys, and then it is hard to get a date."

MICHIGAN TECHNOLOGICAL UNIVERSITY

FINANCIAL AID: 906-487-2622 • E-MAIL: MTU4U@MTU.EDU • WEBSITE: WWW.MTU.EDU

ADMISSIONS

Very important factors considered include: Class rank, secondary school record, standardized test scores. *Other factors considered include:* Alumni/ae relation, character/personal qualities, essays, extracurricular activities, interview, recommendations, talent/ability, volunteer work, work experience. SAT Reasoning or ACT required. TOEFL required of all international applicants. High school diploma is required, and GED is accepted. *Academic units required:* 3 English, 3 math, 2 science. *Academic units recommended:* 4 English, 4 math, 3 science, 1 foreign language, 1 social studies, 1 history, 1 academic elective.

The Inside Word

Michigan Tech has a pretty good reputation and a highly self-selected applicant pool. In light of this, students who are interested should not be deceived by the high admit rate and should spend a little time on self-assessment of their ability to handle an engineering curriculum. There's nothing gained by getting yourself into a program that you can't get out of successfully.

FINANCIAL AID

Students should submit: FAFSA. The Princeton Review suggests that all financial aid forms be submitted as soon as possible after 1/1. *Need-based scholarships/grants offered:* Pell, SEOG, state scholarships/grants, private scholarships, the school's own gift aid. *Loan aid offered:* Direct Subsidized Stafford, Direct Unsubsidized Stafford, Direct PLUS, Federal Perkins, state loans, college/university loans from institutional funds, external private loans. Applicants will be notified of awards on or about 5/1. Off-campus job opportunities are good.

FROM THE ADMISSIONS OFFICE

"Our students create the future at Michigan Tech. Our unique Enterprise program lets students work on real industry problems in wi-fi, video games, snowmobiles, homeland security, and nanotechnology. Students can choose from computing, environmental studies, engineering, the sciences, business, technology, and arts and human sciences as they begin their careers here. Outside of the classrooms and labs, students can enjoy our golf course, ski hill, trails and recreational forest, and great small-town atmosphere in beautiful Upper Michigan. In fact, the campus is located on Portage Waterway and is only minutes from Lake Superior.

"Although not required, it is recommend that students applying for admission into the fall 2006 entering class take the new SAT (or the ACT with the writing section). We will continue to allow students to submit scores from the old (prior to March 2005) version of the SAT (or ACT)."

SELECTIVITY

Admissions Rating	**82**
# of applicants	3,031
% of applicants accepted	94
% of acceptees attending	43

FRESHMAN PROFILE

Range SAT Verbal	530-650
Average SAT Verbal	588
Range SAT Math	570-670
Average SAT Math	619
**TPR Projected Range SAT Writing*	*580-670*
Range ACT Composite	23-28
Average ACT Composite	25
Minimum Paper TOEFL	500
Minimum Computer Based TOEFL	173
Average HS GPA	3.51
% graduated top 10% of class	28
% graduated top 25% of class	59
% graduated top 50% of class	87

DEADLINES

Regular notification	within 3 weeks of acceptance
Nonfall registration?	yes

AND SOMETIMES PREFER

Michigan State University
University of Michigan—Ann Arbor
University of Minnesota—Twin Cities
University of Wisconsin—Madison
Western Michigan University

AND RARELY PREFER

Grand Valley State University
Kettering University
Lawrence University
Milwaukee School of Engineering
Northern Michigan University

FINANCIAL FACTS

Financial Aid Rating	**76**
Annual in-state tuition	$7,446
Annual out-of-state tuition	$18,033
Room & Board	$6,792
Books and supplies	$1,044
Required fees	$63
% frosh rec. need-based scholarship or grant aid	52
% UG rec. need-based scholarship or grant aid	45
% frosh rec. need-based self-help aid	47
% UG rec. need-based self-help aid	47
% frosh rec. any financial aid	89
% UG rec. any financial aid	78
Avg. frosh grant	$3,408
Avg. frosh loan	$4,927
Independent 529 member?	No

MIDDLEBURY COLLEGE

THE EMMA WILLARD HOUSE, MIDDLEBURY, VT 05753-6002 • ADMISSIONS: 802-443-3000 • FAX: 802-443-2056

CAMPUS LIFE

Quality of Life Rating	**98**
Fire Safety Rating	**60**
Type of school	private
Environment	village

STUDENTS

Total undergrad enrollment	2,357
% male/female	48/52
% from out of state	93
% from public high school	52
% live on campus	97
% African American	3
% Asian	7
% Caucasian	70
% Hispanic	5
% international	8
# of countries represented	71

SURVEY SAYS

Small classes
Lab facilities are great
Athletic facilities are great
Campus feels safe

ACADEMICS

Academic Rating	**99**
Calendar	4-1-4
Student/faculty ratio	11:1
Professors interesting rating	99
Professors accessible rating	96
% professors teaching UG courses	100
% classes taught by TAs	0
Most common lab size	10-19 students
Most common regular class size	10-19 students

MOST POPULAR MAJORS

Economics
English language and literature
psychology

STUDENTS SPEAK OUT

Academics

Academically one of the most rigorous programs in the country, "top-rate" Middlebury College, tucked away in rural Vermont (about three and a half hours' drive to Boston, 45 minutes to Burlington, and two hours to Montreal) manages to offer the resources, facilities, and faculty excellence of a much larger school—while keeping enrollment for undergrads at around 2,300. Nationally recognized language, writing, and theater programs share the spotlight with a top-notch science curriculum—which has benefited in recent years from the construction of a new science center. One student is thrilled that "professors here actually teach. They manage classes, advising, and research demands seamlessly." Despite "tons of homework" and tough classes, students say there's little of the "cutthroat competition" that might characterize other schools of Middlebury's caliber. It might have something to do with the pristine location of "Club Midd," their "laid-back" atmosphere, and an excellent alumni network that makes finding a job after graduation a whole lot easier. Or it might be the result of a bit of grade inflation (some kids complain that "if you're smart, you can get A's and B's hardly doing any work"). But most likely, it's just Middlebury's special blend of a quality program, personal attention, and something a little more nebulous one student calls "attitude." In any case, Middlebury's got it. Sums up a senior, "Academically, I've been challenged, but also have had time to breathe and have fun."

Life

You'd think that at a place that gets "so cold your nostrils freeze together" folks would be spending most of their time inside. Not so at Club Midd! "We own our own ski mountain," notes a junior, one of the reasons why, come winter, most students head outside for fun. With skiing, hiking, rock climbing, mountain biking, kayaking, and fishing right in the college's backyard, you can see why "year round people are involved in outdoor activities." "Almost everyone is athletic one way or another," adds another senior. The school's facilities say as much—students can choose between a hockey rink, fitness center, pool, golf course, and "snow bowl" for fun. It's no surprise, then, that "sports are a major preoccupation here." The "work hard, play hard" ethos extends into socializing, too. A senior explains: "As opportunities for nightlife are virtually nonexistent, we drink. While fun, this does take its toll on one's health." And though there doesn't seem to be a shortage of school-sponsored activities and clubs (social houses and a "commons"-style dorm system provide social opportunities for underclassmen), some students complain that the Middlebury experience "varies between having amazing times to wanting to get the hell out of here." What's more, besides the professed lack of academic competition, "life can be very stressful," notes a junior; "everyone around is an overachiever, star athlete, talented musician, and very attractive."

Student Body

"Students here come from every corner of the world and every New England prep school," jokes a first-year on the subject of Middlebury's fairly homogenous student body (69 percent of its undergrads self-identify as "Caucasian"). A junior gives his take on the situation: "They're cool but the same. This is what I heard before I got here, and this is definitely true. [M]ost are rich and white" and from somewhere "just outside of Boston." Still, it's the people that most students say make the Middlebury experience what it is. Take it from this sophomore: "The main reason I fell in love with Midd was the students. At no other school did I see so many happy, outgoing students." Concludes a classmate, "The majority of the students are really smart and really cool, which makes a small school not feel that way."

FINANCIAL AID: 802-443-5158 • E-MAIL: ADMISSIONS@MIDDLEBURY.EDU • WEBSITE: WWW.MIDDLEBURY.EDU

ADMISSIONS

Very important factors considered include: Character/personal qualities, class rank, extracurricular activities, secondary school record, talent/ability. *Important factors considered include:* Essays, minority status, recommendations, standardized test scores. *Other factors considered include:* Alumni/ae relation, geographical residence, interview, volunteer work, work experience. SAT Reasoning Test and SAT Subject Tests or ACT required. High school diploma or equivalent is not required. *Academic units recommended:* 4 English, 4 math, 3 science (3 science lab), 4 foreign language, 3 social studies.

The Inside Word

While Middlebury benefits tremendously from its age-old position as an Ivy League safety, it is nonetheless a very strong and demanding place in its own right. Middlebury has a broad national applicant pool and sees more ACT scores than most eastern colleges, so submitting ACT scores to Middlebury is a more comfortable option than at most eastern schools.

FINANCIAL AID

Students should submit: CSS/Financial Aid PROFILE, state aid form, noncustodial (divorced/separated) parents' statement, business/farm supplement. Regular filing deadline is 12/31. The Princeton Review suggests that all financial aid forms be submitted as soon as possible after 1/1. *Need-based scholarships/grants offered:* Pell, SEOG, state scholarships/grants, private scholarships, the school's own gift aid. *Loan aid offered:* Direct Subsidized Stafford, Direct Unsubsidized Stafford, Direct PLUS, Federal Perkins, college/university loans from institutional funds. Applicants will be notified of awards on or about 4/1. Federal Work-study Program available. Institutional employment available. Off-campus job opportunities are good.

FROM THE ADMISSIONS OFFICE

"The successful Middlebury candidate excels in a variety of areas including academics, athletics, the arts, leadership, and service to others. These strengths and interests permit students to grow beyond their traditional 'comfort zones' and conventional limits. Our classrooms are as varied as the Green Mountains, the Metropolitan Museum of Art, or the great cities Russia and Japan. Outside the classroom, students informally interact with professors in activities such as intramural basketball games and community service. At Middlebury, students develop critical thinking skills, enduring bonds of friendship, and the ability to challenge themselves.

"Applicants must submit standardized test results in at least three different areas of study. This requirement may be met by any one of the following three options: the ACT (optional Writing Test recommended, but not required), the new SAT I, or three tests in different subject areas from the SAT Subject Tests, Advanced Placement, or International Baccalaureate exams."

SELECTIVITY

Admissions Rating	**98**
# of applicants	5,122
% of applicants accepted	26
% of acceptees attending	44
# accepting a place on wait list	1,266
% admitted from wait list	6
# of early decision applicants	283
% accepted early decision	38

FRESHMAN PROFILE

Range SAT Verbal	690-750
Average SAT Verbal	720
Range SAT Math	690-750
Average SAT Math	710
**TPR Projected Range SAT Writing*	*690-730*
Range ACT Composite	28-32
Average ACT Composite	30
% graduated top 10% of class	77
% graduated top 25% of class	96
% graduated top 50% of class	99

DEADLINES

Early decision application deadline	11/15
Early decision notification	12/15
Regular application deadline	1/1
Regular notification	4/1
Nonfall registration?	yes

APPLICANTS ALSO LOOK AT AND OFTEN PREFER

Amherst College
Dartmouth College
Harvard College
Princeton University
Williams College

AND SOMETIMES PREFER

Brown University
Yale University

AND RARELY PREFER

Bowdoin College
Hamilton College
Skidmore College
St. Lawrence University

FINANCIAL FACTS

Financial Aid Rating	**95**
Comprehensive fee	$40,400
Books and supplies	$750
% frosh rec. need-based scholarship or grant aid	37
% UG rec. need-based scholarship or grant aid	42
% frosh rec. need-based self-help aid	37
% UG rec. need-based self-help aid	42
% frosh rec. any financial aid	37
% UG rec. any financial aid	42
Avg. frosh grant	$20,161
Avg. frosh loan	$5,377
Independent 529 member?	Yes

MILLS COLLEGE

5000 MACARTHUR BOULEVARD, OAKLAND, CA 94613 • ADMISSIONS: 510-430-2135 • FAX: 510-430-3314

CAMPUS LIFE

Quality of Life Rating	**77**
Fire Safety Rating	**60**
Type of school	private
Environment	metropolis

STUDENTS

Total undergrad enrollment	762
% male/female	0/100
% from out of state	34
% from public high school	85
% live on campus	54
% African American	9
% Asian	9
% Caucasian	45
% Hispanic	9
% Native American	1
% international	5

SURVEY SAYS . . .

Lots of liberal students
Small classes
No one cheats
Great computer facilities
Students aren't religious
Great off-campus food
Frats and sororities are unpopular or nonexistent

ACADEMICS

Academic Rating	**72**
Calendar	semester
Student/faculty ratio	11:1
Profs interesting rating	82
Profs accessible rating	85
% profs teaching UG courses	100
% classes taught by TAs	0

STUDENTS SPEAK OUT

Academics

Like many liberal arts colleges, Mills College is "a small institution" where students "are able to get so much personal attention from all of our professors." In many cases, this close attention pays off: students report that professors make the classroom "hands-on and open to creativity." Some feel so inspired by in-class work that they'll "start their own discussion groups outside of the classroom." But the dissenters claim that just because "the teachers care about what they're teaching," it doesn't mean that they're teaching it well. The students at Mills have their pick of 34 majors, and while this isn't a shabby number, undergrads admit that the academic "selection seems a bit limited at times." Self-designed majors are possible, though, and if a student really wants to get a new major tacked onto the list, she can at least wander over to the administrative offices and have a chat with a higher-up. Though the administration can appear "out to get you" at times, it's generally open to discussion and suggestions. One student boasts, "The president tries to get to know all of the [student] population."

Life

When the women at Mills College aren't thinking "about how evil men and corporations are," they like to let loose and have some fun. First-year students are indoctrinated with "parties where practically the whole freshwoman class shows up, and everyone enjoys themselves like crazy." There are also spontaneous gatherings at which "everyone will just sit and talk and listen to music and dance." Organized events are sponsored by the 30 or so on-campus groups, including Mouthing Off, the campus' "queer alliance" which runs "very successful dances." But students tell us that the true fun begins a few steps away from campus. Situated in Oakland, California, Mills is in close proximity to many other college campuses—particularly UC Berkeley—as well as the whole San Francisco Bay area. For the big-school party scene, "most of the students do go to Berkeley." And students take BART, the mass transit system that webs through the Bay area, when they're in the mood for attending "poetry readings or slams, trying new restaurants, going to plays or museums, hiking in the woods nearby, or shopping." Some students grumble, however, that more of these sorts of events should be brought to the Mills campus: "The school could stand to try to incorporate the outside world into our community more so that we don't feel so secluded." Fortunately, the college has a residential system that requires students to interact and bond with their dorm mates. "Life can and does evolve in the dorm," explains a student. It's also worth mentioning that Mills' "dorms are beautiful and historic buildings" that are adorned with "courtyards and gardens and sunrooms."

Student Body

"The students here are rad," reports one happy student, adding that her classmates are also "different, creative, and intelligent." But they do have their similarities. Particularly, every single one of them is female. "A group of ethnically, sexually, religiously diverse women," adds one Mills undergrad. But not diverse in mindset, suggests another student. "There seems to be a large percentage of men-haters here, as well as people who don't like to accept religious opinions [held] by students." Also, if you aren't a leftist-socialist-Nader voter or at least one of leftist leanings," some students say that your opinions will not be taken seriously. Whether they call themselves "progressive" or "narrow-minded," most students are proud to be members of the Mills community. A student nods, "Our pride is our greatest strength."

FINANCIAL AID: 510-430-2000 • E-MAIL: ADMISSION@MILLS.EDU • WEBSITE: WWW.MILLS.EDU

ADMISSIONS

Very important factors considered include: Secondary school record. *Important factors considered include:* Character/personal qualities, class rank, essays, extracurricular activities, recommendations, standardized test scores. *Other factors considered include:* Alumni/ae relation, interview, minority status, talent/ability, volunteer work, work experience. SAT Reasoning Test required; SAT Subject Tests recommended. TOEFL required of all international applicants. High school diploma is required and GED is accepted. *Academic units recommended:* 4 English, 3 math, 3 science, (3 science lab), 3 foreign language, 3 social studies, 3 history.

Inside Word

Mills' 13-page application is a solid indicator of just how closely the school considers its candidates. Grades, test scores, recommendations, an essay, and extracurricular interests and activities all come into play here. Candidates who are deficient in one area have ample opportunity to make up for shortfalls in other areas.

FINANCIAL AID

Students should submit: FAFSA, institution's own financial aid form, state aid form, noncustodial (divorced/separated) parent's statement. Regular filing deadline is February 15. The Princeton Review suggests that all financial aid forms be submitted as soon as possible after January 1. *Need-based scholarships/grants offered:* Pell, SEOG, state scholarships/grants, private scholarships, the school's own gift aid. *Loan aid offered:* FFEL Subsidized Stafford, FFEL Unsubsidized Stafford, FFEL PLUS, Federal Perkins, college/university loans from institutional funds. Applicants will be notified of awards on a rolling basis beginning or about March 1. Federal Work-Study Program available. Off-campus job opportunities are excellent.

FROM THE ADMISSIONS OFFICE

"Nestled in the foothills of Oakland, California on the east shore of the San Francisco Bay, Mills College is home to one of the most dynamic liberal arts educations available to women today. Consistently ranked one of the top 75 liberal arts colleges in the nation, Mills offers a renowned education for students who are seeking an intimate, collaborative college experience. It's the perfect choice for women who want to be part of an intellectual community that truly celebrates the active pursuit of knowledge.

"You'll learn from distinguished professors who are truly dedicated to teaching. They will not only know your name, they'll use it as they explore and discuss ideas with you. You'll interact with dynamic women of different backgrounds, ethnicities, cultures, ages, and mindsets, making your learning rich and inspiring. As part of the Mills community, you will find yourself an active, engaged participant in your own learning, working closely with professors and fellow students in a challenging environment that encourages self-expression.

"With more than 35 different majors to choose from—including a self-designed program—you'll have lots of educational options. The classroom debate will be your intellectual catalyst, but you'll find plenty of opportunities to express yourself, both in and out of the classroom.

"Mills students also enjoy the green rolling hills and century-old eucalyptus trees of the 135-acre park-like campus they call home. From the moment students set foot on the campus, they know that Mills is a different kind of college.

"First-year applicants are required to submit college entrance examination scores. Mills College accepts either The College Board's SAT Reasoning Test or the ACT Assessment. A student's overall candidacy may be enhanced by the submission of SAT Subject Tests."

SELECTIVITY

Admissions Rating	**85**
# of applicants	463
% of applicants accepted	83
% of acceptees attending	35

FRESHMAN PROFILE

Range SAT Verbal	540-670
Average SAT Verbal	602
Range SAT Math	490-610
Average SAT Math	549
**TPR Projected Range SAT Writing*	*590-680*
Range ACT Composite	19-27
Average ACT Composite	25
Minimum Paper TOEFL	550
Minimum Computer Based TOEFL	220
Average HS GPA	3.52
% graduated top 10% of class	35
% graduated top 25% of class	64
% graduated top 50% of class	96

DEADLINES

Regular notification	rolling
Nonfall registration?	yes

FINANCIAL FACTS

Financial Aid Rating	**79**
Annual tuition	$25,250
Room & Board	$9,400
Books and supplies	$930
Required fees	$1,835
% frosh rec. need-based scholarship or grant aid	76
% UG rec. need-based scholarship or grant aid	76
% frosh rec. need-based self-help aid	77
% UG rec. need-based self-help aid	76
% frosh rec. any financial aid	95
% UG rec. any financial aid	97
Avg. frosh grant	$20,108
Avg. frosh loan	$3,885
Independent 529 member?	Yes

MILLSAPS COLLEGE

1701 NORTH STATE STREET, JACKSON, MS 39210-0001 • ADMISSIONS: 601-974-1050 • FAX: 601-974-1059

CAMPUS LIFE

Quality of Life Rating	**85**
Fire Safety Rating	**60**
Type of school	private
Affiliation	Methodist
Environment	metropolis

STUDENTS

Total undergrad enrollment	1,068
% male/female	48/52
% from out of state	47
% from public high school	64
% live on campus	82
% in (# of) fraternities	54 (6)
% in (# of) sororities	56 (6)
% African American	11
% Asian	3
% Caucasian	81
% Hispanic	1

SURVEY SAYS

Small classes
Students are friendly
Frats and sororities dominate social scene
Lots of beer drinking
Hard liquor is popular

ACADEMICS

Academic Rating	**88**
Calendar	semester
Student/faculty ratio	12:1
Professors interesting rating	95
Professors accessible rating	91
% professors teaching UG courses	100
% classes taught by TAs	0
Most common lab size	20-29 students
Most common regular class size	10-19 students

MOST POPULAR MAJORS

Business administration and management
English language and literature
psychology

STUDENTS SPEAK OUT

Academics

"You'll write more than you've ever written before" at Millsaps College. About one-third of a student's tenure is spent fulfilling core requirements, nearly all of which include a substantial writing component. All of this writing forces students to learn to express themselves and "really think outside the box. I've enjoyed learning and enjoyed the difficulties; it's made me a better student and a better person." Agrees one undergrad, "Millsaps College is about thinking for yourself, finding out what you are passionate about, and then using that vocation to make a positive difference in your community and society as a whole." Students here enjoy a solid support network; the "knowledgeable, enthusiastic, and down-to-earth professors truly care about the students and want us to succeed" and are "always eager to help the students outside of class." Administrators are equally accessible; notes one student, "About once a month, we have a lunch with the deans in the cafeteria, and students can come to them with suggestions and comments or just to hang out." Adds another, "I feel that the school really listens to the student voice and takes the student opinion into account when making decisions."

Life

Millsaps is a rock-solid Greek school. "Greek life is huge," explains one undergrad. But Greeks and independents "get along well. The school is just too small to be petty over a few letters." Recent administrative policy changes, however, have curtailed the once-wild parties that typified Millsaps campus life; currently, all parties must be registered with the school, Thursday parties are forbidden, and alcohol regulations are more strictly enforced. The results have a lot of upperclassmen, who remember wilder days gone by, complaining that the "new dry rush rule is horrible." Non-Greek options, many complain, are few. The Jackson neighborhood in which Millsaps is located "isn't exactly one you'd want to walk through, so you have to drive a ways to go anywhere safe." Many here find greater Jackson equally forbidding, resulting in "the 'Millsaps Bubble;' once you are here, you are stuck in this bubble and oblivious to the world around you." Yet there are still several that say the area's "relatively good music scene [and] many social opportunities" are fulfilling. Dorm regulations are strictly enforced; one undergraduate warns, "Any social activity in the dorm is really discouraged. I was once asked to 'Stop making so much noise!' at 4 o'clock on a Friday afternoon. My door was open, and my TV was on." Students also complain that "Millsaps could use more school spirit in supporting our intercollegiate teams." Students often road-trip to New Orleans when they want to blow off steam.

Student Body

Millsaps undergrads tell us that their school is "fairly diverse as far as the students go, for being such a small school." The typical student is an "upper-middle-class, intelligent, achieving person from a southern family, either from Louisiana, Mississippi, Alabama, or Tennessee. However, at Millsaps there is no real 'norm' for student types. Students are more associated with what organization they are a part of, be that an athletic team, a sorority or fraternity, or a philanthropic organization." Undergrads "are particularly politically aware and are often very involved with political campaigns." They are also "pretty intellectual and there is always good conversation." Many agree that "the small student body definitely gives the campus a comfortable vibe." A few warn, however, that the tiny population means that "people will know who you shacked with, when you left, what you were wearing, and what type of toothpaste you used when you got home before you enter the 'caf' for lunch. Everyone knows everyone. You learn to deal with it."

MILLSAPS COLLEGE

FINANCIAL AID: 601-974-1220 • E-MAIL: ADMISSIONS@MILLSAPS.EDU • WEBSITE: WWW.GO.MILLSAPS.EDU

ADMISSIONS

Very important factors considered include: Character/personal qualities, secondary school record, standardized test scores. *Important factors considered include:* Class rank, essays, extracurricular activities, interview, recommendations, talent/ability, volunteer work. *Other factors considered include:* Work experience. SAT Reasoning or ACT required. TOEFL required of all international applicants. High school diploma is required, and GED is accepted. *Academic units required:* 4 English, 3 math, 3 science (1 science lab), 2 social studies, 2 history. *Academic units recommended:* 4 English, 4 math, 4 science (1 science lab), 2 social studies, 2 history, 2 academic electives.

The Inside Word

Despite the college's seemingly deep-probing evaluation process, candidates with a solid track record in high school encounter little resistance in gaining admission. In reality, there is little room for extensive matchmaking by the admissions staff. The high percentage of acceptees who choose to enroll, comparatively, makes getting in less than definite for candidates with weak academic credentials.

FINANCIAL AID

Students should submit: FAFSA, institution's own financial aid form. The Princeton Review suggests that all financial aid forms be submitted as soon as possible after 1/1. *Need-based scholarships/grants offered:* Pell, SEOG, state scholarships/grants, private scholarships, the school's own gift aid. *Loan aid offered:* FFEL Subsidized Stafford, FFEL Unsubsidized Stafford, FFEL PLUS, Federal Perkins, college/university loans from institutional funds. Applicants will be notified of awards on a rolling basis beginning on or about 3/15. Federal Work-study Program available. Institutional employment available. Off-campus job opportunities are good.

FROM THE ADMISSIONS OFFICE

"Millsaps offers outstanding value in nationally ranked liberal arts education. Your academic journey begins with introduction to liberal arts studies, a comprehensive freshman experience that develops reasoning, communication, quantitative thinking, historical consciousness, aesthetic judgment, global, and multicultural awareness, and valuing and decision-making. Throughout your Millsaps years you'll be encouraged to think differently; learn critical, analytical skills; embrace independence of thought; and prepare for study in your chosen major. We offer unique opportunities such as study abroad and in the field at our Yucatan Program; an exploration of your personal and professional future in relation to issues of ethics, values, faith, and the common good through our Faith & Work Initiative; highly respected pre-professional programs in law, medicine, and social work; and a five-year business track leading to an MBA or master's in accountancy with a liberal arts perspective that is accredited by the Association to Advance Collegiate Schools of Business. Our student body included Mississippi's 2003–2004 Rhodes scholar and the faculty included the Carnegie Foundation's 2003 Mississippi Professor of the Year. Our courses are taught without graduate assistants and our intimate student-faculty-community relationship is a hallmark of a Millsaps education. The emerging cultural climate in Jackson, Mississippi's capital city, provides unique artistic, athletic, and social opportunities in the modern South. We encourage you to look at Millsaps College. You'll appreciate the quality of our educational experience in comparison to the costs you'll discover at other national liberal arts institutions. Millsaps College: where minds matter.

"Although it is not required, Millsaps College highly recommends that students take the ACT Writing test for fall 2006 admission."

SELECTIVITY

Admissions Rating	**86**
# of applicants	1,007
% of applicants accepted	85
% of acceptees attending	32

FRESHMAN PROFILE

Range SAT Verbal	520-660
Average SAT Verbal	593
Range SAT Math	540-640
Average SAT Math	590
**TPR Projected Range SAT Writing*	*570-670*
Range ACT Composite	23-29
Average ACT Composite	26
Minimum Paper TOEFL	550
Minimum Computer Based TOEFL	220
Average HS GPA	3.52
% graduated top 10% of class	35
% graduated top 25% of class	69
% graduated top 50% of class	92

DEADLINES

Regular notification	rolling
Nonfall registration?	yes

APPLICANTS ALSO LOOK AT

AND OFTEN PREFER

Rhodes College
Sewanee—The University of the South
Vanderbilt University
Washington University in St. Louis

AND SOMETIMES PREFER

Birmingham—Southern College
Furman University
Trinity University
Tulane University

AND RARELY PREFER

Centenary College of Louisiana
Hendrix College
Loyola University New Orleans
Samford University
Spring Hill College

FINANCIAL FACTS

Financial Aid Rating	**77**
Annual tuition	$19,490
Room & Board	$7,566
Books and supplies	$1,000
Required fees	$1,200
% frosh rec. need-based scholarship or grant aid	65
% UG rec. need-based scholarship or grant aid	55
% frosh rec. need-based self-help aid	46
% UG rec. need-based self-help aid	44
% frosh rec. any financial aid	98
% UG rec. any financial aid	94
Avg. frosh grant	$14,820
Avg. frosh loan	$3,728
Independent 529 member?	No

MONMOUTH UNIVERSITY (NJ)

MONMOUTH U., 400 CEDAR AVENUE, WEST LONG BRANCH, NJ 07764-1898 • ADMISSIONS: 732-571-3456 • FAX: 732-263-5166

CAMPUS LIFE

Quality of Life Rating	**73**
Fire Safety Rating	**60**
Type of school	private
Environment	village

STUDENTS

Total undergrad enrollment	4,448
% male/female	41/59
% from out of state	8
% from public high school	82
% live on campus	43
% in (# of) fraternities	8 (7)
% in (# of) sororities	9 (6)
% African American	5
% Asian	2
% Caucasian	78
% Hispanic	4

SURVEY SAYS . . .

Small classes
Lots of beer drinking
Hard liquor is popular
(Almost) everyone smokes

ACADEMICS

Academic Rating	**75**
Calendar	semester
Student/faculty ratio	14:1
Profs interesting rating	75
Profs accessible rating	78
% profs teaching UG courses	85
% classes taught by TAs	0
Most common lab size	
Most common reg class size	10-19 students

STUDENTS SPEAK OUT

Academics

West Long Branch, New Jersey's Monmouth University "is a comfortably-sized school (not too big, not too small) with helpful faculty and staff members and many opportunities for real-world experience." Most students find professors to be "fair, knowledgeable, and most importantly, willing to compromise," though some note that "the quality of professors varies from class to class." Overall, students agree that "the quality of instruction at Monmouth is good." The school's new president, Paul Gaffney, "is very interested in student affairs and can be seen regularly at campus events. He has even helped incoming freshmen move into their dorms," says one student, adding, "The lower-level administrators aren't as impressive, but do treat students as human beings, which is always nice." Communications is a popular major at Monmouth; many students were lured to the school by its impressive $13 million Jules L. Plangere Jr. Center for Communication and Instructional Technology, a "state-of-the-art facility" that features a "brand-new $5 million television and radio production studio." MU students have wrestled with in-person class registration hassles in the past, but students report that "we have online registration now (thank God!), so no more waiting in line, although sometimes the servers are slow on the first day of registration."

Life

"Monmouth is in perfect proximity to the beach or the city," undergrads tell us. "A person can hop on the train and be in New York City in 45 minutes, or drive two minutes up the road and be at the beach." Students seeking other means of entertainment "go to bars, clubs, an athletic event, Greek house, or hang out in their room or apartment." There are "great local clubs like The Stone Pony and the Groove Lounge, and there are also coffee houses like Starbucks and The Ink Well." Students also frequent the local mall, which is ten minutes away. In addition, the University sponsors "a lot of events on campus, from concerts to guest speakers." Monmouth is somewhat of a suitcase school; "a lot of people go home on the weekend because they live so close." Students feel confident in the campus security at Monmouth. Writes one, "Security is always around. I can walk from my car at 1:00 A.M. and feel safe. I also feel safe when walking from my night classes."

Students

Monmouth undergrads are split down the middle when it comes to describing the student body. On one side, the words "rich, preppy, cliquey, Gucci, [and] Armani" routinely pop up in descriptions. On the flipside, undergrads describe their fellow students as "friendly, involved, outgoing, [and] fun." Students of both opinions, however, agree that most MU undergrads hail from a "white, upper-middle class" background. As one student explains, "There are a lot of upper-class students who come from wealth. The people I've met are generally all nice and friendly. But I've heard stories that say otherwise. I think it depends on who you meet. There are intelligent, hardworking students, and others who aren't. It's a mix of many different people." Another student adds, that "Monmouth is a lot like high school" in that "There are lots of different groups of kids on campus and all types of people fit in. You just have to find your group."

Monmouth University (NJ)

Financial Aid: 732-571-3463 • E-mail: admission@monmouth.edu • Website: www.monmouth.edu

ADMISSIONS

Very important factors considered include: Secondary school record, standardized test scores. *Other factors considered include:* Alumni/ae relation, character/personal qualities, class rank, essays, extracurricular activities, interview, recommendations, volunteer work, work experience. SAT Reasoning or ACT required; TOEFL required of all international applicants. High school diploma is required and GED is accepted. *Academic units required:* 4 English, 3 math, 2 science, (1 science lab), 2 history, 5 academic electives. *Academic units recommended:* 2 foreign language, 2 social studies.

Inside Word

B students with average standardized test scores should have little trouble getting into Monmouth University, whose admissions standards are fairly generous. However, a rapidly decreasing acceptance rate following the elimination of a popular admissions program means that entry is by no means a sure thing.

FINANCIAL AID

Students should submit: FAFSA. The Princeton Review suggests that all financial aid forms be submitted as soon as possible after January 1. *Need-based scholarships/grants offered:* Pell, SEOG, state scholarships/grants, private scholarships, the school's own gift aid. *Loan aid offered:* Direct Subsidized Stafford, Direct Unsubsidized Stafford, Direct PLUS, Federal Perkins, state loans, college/university loans from institutional funds. Applicants will be notified of awards on a rolling basis beginning or about February 4. Federal Work-Study Program available. Institutional employment available. Off-campus job opportunities are excellent.

FROM THE ADMISSIONS OFFICE

"Monmouth University offers a well-rounded but bold academic environment with plenty of opportunities—personal, professional, and social. Monmouth graduates are poised for success and prepared to assume leadership roles in their chosen professions because the university invests in students beyond the classroom.

"Monmouth emphasizes hands-on learning, while providing exceptional undergraduate and graduate degree programs. There are programs for medical scholars, honors students, marine scientists, software engineers, teachers, musicians, broadcast producers, and more. Faculty members are lively participants in the education of their students. These teacher/scholars, dedicated to excellence, are often recognized experts in their fields. Students may be in a class with no more than 35 students (half of Monmouth's classes have fewer than 21 students) learning from qualified professors who know each student by name.

"Monmouth recognizes its students are the energy of its campus. The Monmouth community celebrates itself with cultural events, festivals, active student clubs, and organizations that reflect its school spirit. Athletics play a big part in campus life. A well-established member of the NCAA Division I, Monmouth Athletics is a rising tide supported by some of the best fans in the Northeast.

"The president of Monmouth University, Paul G. Gaffney II, believes the reputation of the university starts with the achievements and successes of its students. At Monmouth, students find the support and guidance needed to make their mark in the world.

"Monmouth University…where leaders look forward.

"Students applying for admission for fall 2006 are encouraged to take the new SAT (or the ACT with the Writing section), but we will allow students to submit scores from the old (prior to March 2005) version of the SAT (or ACT) as well, and will use the student's best scores from either test."

SELECTIVITY	
Admissions Rating	**75**
# of applicants	5,279
% of applicants accepted	66
% of acceptees attending	27
# accepting a place on wait list	548
% admitted from wait list	2
# of early decision applicants	128
% accepted early decision	83

FRESHMAN PROFILE	
Range SAT Verbal	480-560
Average SAT Verbal	525
Range SAT Math	490-570
Average SAT Math	534
**TPR Projected Range SAT Writing*	*540-600*
Range ACT Composite	21-24
Average ACT Composite	23
Minimum Paper TOEFL	525
Minimum Computer Based TOEFL	197
Average HS GPA	3.0
% graduated top 10% of class	9
% graduated top 25% of class	30
% graduated top 50% of class	60

DEADLINES	
Early decision application deadline	12/1
Early decision notification	1/1
Regular application deadline	3/1
Regular notification	prior to 4/1
Nonfall registration?	yes

FINANCIAL FACTS	
Financial Aid Rating	**70**
Annual tuition	$19,108
Room & Board	$7,911
Books and supplies	$900
Required fees	$596
% frosh rec. need-based scholarship or grant aid	27
% UG rec. need-based scholarship or grant aid	28
% frosh rec. need-based self-help aid	50
% UG rec. need-based self-help aid	52
% frosh rec. any financial aid	95
% UG rec. any financial aid	88
Avg. frosh grant	$8,277
Avg. frosh loan	$10,461
Independent 529 member?	No

MONTANA TECH OF THE UNIVERSITY OF MONTANA

1300 WEST PARK STREET, BUTTE, MT 59701 • ADMISSIONS: 406-496-4178 • FAX: 406-496-4710

CAMPUS LIFE

Quality of Life Rating	**73**
Fire Safety Rating	**60**
Type of school	public
Environment	village

STUDENTS

Total undergrad enrollment	1,913
% male/female	56/44
% from out of state	10
% live on campus	15
% Caucasian	71
% Hispanic	1
% Native American	1
% international	1
# of countries represented	16

SURVEY SAYS

Small classes
Great computer facilities
Frats and sororities are unpopular or nonexistent
Lots of beer drinking

ACADEMICS

Academic Rating	**77**
Calendar	semester
Student/faculty ratio	16:1
Professors interesting rating	76
Professors accessible rating	79
% professors teaching UG courses	100
% classes taught by TAs	0
Most common lab size	10-19 students
Most common regular class size	fewer than 10 students

MOST POPULAR MAJORS

Business administration/management
engineering
petroleum engineering

STUDENTS SPEAK OUT

Academics

Montana Tech students know exactly what they want from their college: a reputable degree that translates quickly into a plum job. According to the students here, that's exactly what the school delivers. As a surprising number of students in our survey remind us, Tech has a fantastic job placement rate in its areas of strength, which include petroleum, environmental, metallurgical, geological, geophysical, and mining engineering ("Anything that deals with the oil and gas industries" is how one helpful engineer summarizes it), nursing, mathematics, and computer science. Explains one student, "We have a great reputation with employers as very good students [who are] willing to work." Like most tech schools, "Tech is very difficult. The first couple of years are spent by professors trying to weed out the slackers, but once you get through all that and get to know your professors, they are actually really friendly and very helpful." Professors also "have industry experience, which is vital to producing good professionals." Small classes promote "a feeling of community. At Tech it is strange for a professor not to know what your name and major are if you are in his class." Students also appreciate that "Tech gives aid to tons of students in every field. Even if you don't qualify for much need-based aid, you can still get scholarships in your field of study."

Life

"Most people are academically focused, but still like to have fun" at Tech. Unfortunately, however, "Life here isn't all that exciting. Since it is so small, it's hard to get anything going on campus." The main outlets for extracurricular activity are sporting events—football and men's basketball "both get a lot of support from the students"—parties and the bar scene, quiet fun (hanging out with friends, going to movies, bowling, playing billiards), and outdoor activities. Many students here "take part in the excellent hiking, camping, fishing, kayaking, and rock climbing" spots nearby. And there's plenty of excellent skiing within driving distance of the campus. Be forewarned, "The weather puts a damper on what there is to do for fun. It's already snowed at least three times," reported one student in October, adding that "the weather is in the low 40s to high 30s most of the time," at least during academic semesters. As one undergrad advises, "If you don't like winter, don't come here." Hometown Butte is "a rough and rowdy mining town" with "not much to offer, so a lot of people end up drinking for fun." Although the town has a few champions among the student body, most prefer Missoula, "for the shopping and nightlife." Bear in mind that Missoula is 120 miles away, but in Montana terms, that's spitting distance.

Student Body

"Most Tech students are from rural Montana and are familiar with an agricultural lifestyle," students tell us, noting that the occasional city kid who finds his way here usually finds the experience a little disorienting. It's the kind of place where "the dorms have gun racks in them for the hunters," and few would have it any other way. Like the population of their home state, Montana Tech students are "typically Caucasian and conservative." Those from outside the state generally come from Canada or overseas; "There is a large contingency of well-to-do Arab students from oil producing countries in the Middle East, and they have a good relationship with the rest of the student body,"

MONTANA TECH OF THE UNIVERSITY OF MONTANA

FINANCIAL AID: 406-496-4212 • E-MAIL: ADMISSIONS@MTECH.EDU • WEBSITE: WWW.MTECH.EDU

ADMISSIONS

Important factors considered include: Class rank, secondary school record, standardized test scores, SAT Reasoning and SAT Subject Tests or ACT required. TOEFL required of all international applicants. High school diploma is required, and GED is accepted. *Academic units required:* 4 English, 3 math, 2 science, 3 social studies, 2 years of foreign language, visual and performing arts, computer science, or vocational education units. *Academic units recommended:* 4 English, 4 math, 4 science (2 science lab), 2 foreign language.

The Inside Word

Underrecognized schools like Montana Tech can be a godsend for students who are strong academically but not likely to be offered admission to nationally renowned technical institutes. In fact, because of its small size and relatively remote location, Montana Tech is a good choice for anyone leaning toward a technical career. You'd be hard-pressed to find many other places that are as low-key and personal in this realm of academe.

FINANCIAL AID

Students should submit: FAFSA. The Princeton Review suggests that all financial aid forms be submitted as soon as possible after 1/1. *Need-based scholarships/grants offered:* Pell, SEOG, state scholarships/grants, private scholarships, the school's own gift aid. *Loan aid offered:* FFEL Subsidized Stafford, FFEL Unsubsidized Stafford, FFEL PLUS, Federal Perkins, college/university loans from institutional funds. Applicants will be notified of awards on or about 4/1.

FROM THE ADMISSIONS OFFICE

"Characterize Montana Tech by listening to what employers say. They tell us Tech graduates stand out with an incredible work ethic and top-notch technical skills. Last year, 130 employers came to our small campus competing for our students and graduates. The benefactors? The students! Montana Tech has had a ten-year placement rate of over 95 percent. Learning takes place in a personalized environment, in first-class academic facilities, and in the heart of the Rocky Mountains. Student at Tech work hard and play hard. Outdoor recreation provides a great balance to the rigors of the course work at Montana Tech. It's is not a large, multifaceted university with lots of frills, but our students get a terrific education, and in the end, great jobs!

"The new version of the SAT (or the ACT with the writing section) is recommended for students applying for admission into the fall 2006 class. Students who do not take the tests with the Writing component may be required to take an additional English Placement test from the college before they enroll."

SELECTIVITY

Admissions Rating	**73**
# of applicants	413
% of applicants accepted	99
% of acceptees attending	72

FRESHMAN PROFILE

Range SAT Verbal	460-580
Average SAT Verbal	530
Range SAT Math	510-620
Average SAT Math	539
**TPR Projected Range SAT Writing*	*530-620*
Range ACT Composite	21-27
Average ACT Composite	22
Minimum Paper TOEFL	525
Minimum Computer Based TOEFL	195
Average HS GPA	3.2
% graduated top 10% of class	11
% graduated top 25% of class	44
% graduated top 50% of class	67

DEADLINES

Regular notification	rolling
Nonfall registration?	yes

APPLICANTS ALSO LOOK AT

AND OFTEN PREFER
Michigan Technological University

AND SOMETIMES PREFER
Colorado School of Mines
Montana State University—Bozeman
University of Montana—Missoula
University of Washington
Western Montana College

AND RARELY PREFER
Carroll College (MT)

FINANCIAL FACTS

Financial Aid Rating	**77**
Annual in-state tuition	$3,350
Annual out-of-state tuition	$8,060
Room & Board	$4,980
Books and supplies	$800
Required fees	$1,000
% frosh rec. need-based scholarship or grant aid	58
% UG rec. need-based scholarship or grant aid	62
% frosh rec. need-based self-help aid	57
% UG rec. need-based self-help aid	50
Avg. frosh grant	$1,000
Avg. frosh loan	$2,000
Independent 529 member?	No

Moravian College

1200 Main Street, Bethlehem, PA 18018 • Admissions: 610-861-1320 • Fax: 610-625-7930

CAMPUS LIFE

Quality of Life Rating	**85**
Fire Safety Rating	**86**
Type of school	private
Affiliation	Moravian
Environment	city

STUDENTS

Total undergrad enrollment	1,828
% male/female	39/61
% from out of state	39
% from public high school	77
% live on campus	69
% in (# of) fraternities	14 (3)
% in (# of) sororities	22 (4)
% African American	2
% Asian	2
% Caucasian	81
% Hispanic	3
% international	1
# of countries represented	14

SURVEY SAYS

Small classes
Great computer facilities
Great library
Students are friendly
Low cost of living

ACADEMICS

Academic Rating	**84**
Calendar	semester
Student/faculty ratio	12:1
Professors interesting rating	83
Professors accessible rating	86
% professors teaching UG courses	100
% classes taught by TAs	0
Most common lab size	10-19 students
Most common regular class size	10-19 students

MOST POPULAR MAJORS

Business administration/management
psychology
sociology

STUDENTS SPEAK OUT

Academics

The sixth-oldest undergraduate institution in the United States (founded in 1742), there's no arguing that Moravian College is "a historic institution." But this small eastern Pennsylvanian liberal arts school also knows how to keep up with the times; through its Learning in Common general education curriculum, Moravian exposes all undergraduates to a broad range of skills taught within a multidisciplinary framework, preparing them, in theory, to adapt to rapid and dramatic changes in the world, no matter what fields they choose to pursue. Undergraduates appreciate the approach, telling us that there are "few, if any, colleges that rival our curriculum." Students also give high marks to the business, education, nursing, art, and music departments (the last two of which are housed separately, on the school's Priscilla Payne Hard Campus). Professors here "are mostly all amazing. These teachers get to know their students and make sure that they are available to the students, and our classes are small, allowing engaging, open, free discussion." While the school is small—"If you went to a small high school, Moravian isn't going to be a big shift for you"—academic options are unusually broad thanks to the school's participation in the Lehigh Valley Association of Independent Colleges, which allows students to take classes and use the libraries at Lafayette College, Lehigh University, Muhlenberg College, DeSales University, and Cedar Crest College. The school works hard to offer "an infinite number of opportunities for students, such as on-campus jobs, internships, [and] study abroad programs."

Life

"The greatest strength of Moravian is combining the emphasis on academics with enjoying college life," undergraduates tell us, observing that "everyone here realizes that students don't want to study 100 percent of the time, so the workload is reasonable, sports are very important, and there are many on-campus activities." Those activities include "plenty of concerts, plays, and speakers, as well as movies and athletic events." Student clubs and organizations are popular, with a number of students involved in numerous extracurricular endeavors. Fraternities and sororities figure into the mix. While "there's always a party" somewhere, "there's always another option, too, [so] there's no excuse for anyone being bored and not making friends" here. Those on a budget appreciate that "most of the activities are free of charge, or there's a student discount" and that "a lot of the fun around here comes from just hanging out with friends whenever you can, and there is almost always time for that." All these activities dovetail into a renewed sense of campus vitality. "While Moravian was once considered to be a 'suitcase' college, these days more and more students stay on campus. They feel they miss out on too much leaving for the weekend." Students are also fond of Bethlehem, describing its downtown as "a lovely, scenic area that is good for light shopping and browsing. Our school provides trips to the mall and grocery store, which are always fun breaks to take with friends."

Student Body

Many Moravian students see themselves in the context of their closest neighbors; writes one undergrad, "Moravian is surrounded by Lehigh, Lafayette and Muhlenberg, which are known as more prissy schools, where the students are a lot more stuck up. There isn't a lot of priss at Moravian." Here, "the typical student comes from the Mid-Atlantic region, grew up in suburbia, and is often of a middle-class background." Most are "very friendly; they smile and say 'hi' to one another." Observers detect a clear difference between students on the Main Campus and their counterparts on the Priscilla Payne Hard Campus, who are relatively "more artsy, more open-minded, dress different, and are more city-smart."

FINANCIAL AID: 610-861-1330 • E-MAIL: ADMISSIONS@MORAVIAN.EDU • WEBSITE: WWW.MORAVIAN.EDU

ADMISSIONS

Very important factors considered include: Character/personal qualities, class rank, secondary school record. *Important factors considered include:* Essays, extracurricular activities, interview, recommendations, standardized test scores, volunteer work. *Other factors considered include:* Alumni/ae relation, geographical residence, talent/ability, work experience. SAT Reasoning or ACT required. TOEFL required of all international applicants. High school diploma is required, and GED is accepted. *Academic units required:* 4 English, 3 math, 2 science (2 science lab), 2 foreign language, 4 social studies. *Academic units recommended:* 4 math, 3 foreign language.

The Inside Word

Moravian is a small liberal arts school with all the bells and whistles. Applicants will find a pretty straightforward admissions process—solid grades and test scores are required. Counselors will look closely to find the extras—community service, extracurricular activities—that make students stand out from the crowd. Moravian has many programs that should not be overlooked, including music, education, and the sciences.

FINANCIAL AID

Students should submit: FAFSA, CSS/Financial Aid PROFILE, noncustodial (divorced/separated) parents' statement, business/farm supplement, copies of parent and student W-2 and 1040 forms. Regular filing deadline is 3/15. The Princeton Review suggests that all financial aid forms be submitted as soon as possible after 1/1. *Need-based scholarships/grants offered:* Pell, SEOG, state scholarships/grants, private scholarships, the school's own gift aid. *Loan aid offered:* FFEL Subsidized Stafford, FFEL Unsubsidized Stafford, FFEL PLUS, Federal Perkins. Applicants will be notified of awards on a rolling basis beginning on or about 4/1. Federal Work-study Program available. Institutional employment available. Off-campus job opportunities are good.

FROM THE ADMISSIONS OFFICE

"Founded in 1742, Moravian is proud of its history as one of America's oldest and most respected liberal arts colleges. The low student/faculty ratio allows for an immediate and unusually close bond. The Moravian family, comprising current students and faculty, as well as alumni and emeritus professors, praises the college as a supportive environment for learning, personal exploration, and character development. The overarching emphasis of our curriculum is on scholarship enriched by self-discovery. In the last five years, Moravian has produced four Fulbright scholars, a Goldwater scholar, a Rhodes finalist, a Truman Scholar finalist, and three NCAA Postgraduate Scholars. Its robust varsity athletic program has produced All-American student athletes, Academic All-Americans, national champions, a national Player of the Year, and several Olympic hopefuls. In the fall of 2005, the college will dedicate Rocco Calvo Field, a state of the art synthetic multi-sport field and the eight lane Timothy Breidegam Olympic track. At the heart of the campus is a new $20 million academic building. It houses 15 new classrooms, four faculty departments, laboratories, research facilities, and "smart" classrooms for easy technological interface. In 2004, the college established a unique Leadership Center, the goal of which is to engage the campus community is discussion, discovery, and dialogue about the many aspects of leadership as applied to the academic disciplines, professions, the community, and campus organizations. The college welcomes inquiries from students eager to participate in an environment of self-directed, life-long learning.

"Applicants fall 2006 must submit scores from either the new SAT or the ACT with Writing. Writing scores will establish a base-line for later years and will generally not be used for admission or scholarship consideration. Scores from previously administered SAT's will also be considered if submitted by fall 2006 applicants."

SELECTIVITY

Admissions Rating	**81**
# of applicants	1,954
% of applicants accepted	63
% of acceptees attending	31
# accepting a place on wait list	187
% admitted from wait list	12
# of early decision applicants	103
% accepted early decision	71

FRESHMAN PROFILE

Range SAT Verbal	510-600
Average SAT Verbal	563
Range SAT Math	510-610
Average SAT Math	569
**TPR Projected Range SAT Writing*	*570-630*
Minimum Paper TOEFL	550
Minimum Computer Based TOEFL	213
% graduated top 10% of class	27
% graduated top 25% of class	57
% graduated top 50% of class	93

DEADLINES

Early decision application deadline	1/15
Early decision notification	12/15
Regular application deadline	3/1
Regular notification	3/15
Nonfall registration?	yes

APPLICANTS ALSO LOOK AT

AND OFTEN PREFER
Bucknell University
Franklin & Marshall College
Ursinus College

AND SOMETIMES PREFER
Juniata College
Muhlenberg College
Susquehanna University

AND RARELY PREFER
Albright College
Lebanon Valley College
Wilkes University

FINANCIAL FACTS

Financial Aid Rating	**75**
Annual tuition	$24,813
Room & Board	$7,530
Books and supplies	$760
Required fees	$450
% frosh rec. need-based scholarship or grant aid	79
% UG rec. need-based scholarship or grant aid	75
% frosh rec. need-based self-help aid	69
% UG rec. need-based self-help aid	67
% frosh rec. any financial aid	95
% UG rec. any financial aid	92
Avg. frosh grant	$12,467
Avg. frosh loan	$3,445
Independent 529 member?	Yes

Mount Holyoke College

Office of Admissions, Newhall Center, South Hadley, MA 01075 • Admissions: 413-538-2023 • Fax: 413-538-2409

CAMPUS LIFE

Quality of Life Rating	**90**
Fire Safety Rating	**60**
Type of school	private
Environment	village

STUDENTS

Total undergrad enrollment	2,095
% male/female	0/100
% from out of state	74
% from public high school	65
% live on campus	93
% African American	4
% Asian	11
% Caucasian	52
% Hispanic	5
% Native American	1
% international	14
# of countries represented	69

SURVEY SAYS

Small classes
Lab facilities are great
Great library
Diverse student types on campus
Campus feels safe
Frats and sororities are unpopular or nonexistent

ACADEMICS

Academic Rating	**95**
Calendar	semester
Student/faculty ratio	9:1
Professors interesting rating	96
Professors accessible rating	90
% professors teaching UG courses	100
% classes taught by TAs	0
Most common lab size	10-19 students
Most common regular class size	10-19 students

MOST POPULAR MAJORS

Biology/biological sciences
English language and literature
psychology

STUDENTS SPEAK OUT

Academics

"Empowering" is a word the women of Mount Holyoke often use when describing their school. Holyoke's "nurturing environment" means that "no matter who you are, what your interests, background, ethnicity, or religion, you are treated as an intelligent woman who has the right to be listened to. No place could be more supportive," one student says. The school is nurturing, but not mollycoddling; students warn that "academically, Mount Holyoke College is challenging. You cannot get behind and expect to catch up." Not that students mind; they tell us that "Mount Holyoke's academic reputation, and the fact that it lives up to that reputation, is commendable," and that its trial by fire makes its students "stronger writers, thinkers, friends, students, daughters, sisters, but most of all, better people." Holyoke's offerings are augmented by its participation in the Five College Consortium, "which allows students to take classes at any of the other four institutions (Smith, Amherst, Hampshire, UMass) around the Pioneer Valley. I love having that kind of freedom, and like being able to vary my classroom environments," writes one student. Another education-broadening experience is the school's popular study abroad program. Still, other opportunities present themselves in the many independent study options available. One student reports, "Professors are sincerely interested in developing student research projects and helping students find and partake in projects that sincerely interest them."

Life

The Mount Holyoke campus is quiet—not dead, mind you, just quiet—a situation most students appreciate. As one undergraduate puts it, "One of the greatest strengths of this school is that you are able to study without any distraction, but if you choose to party you are able to." Hometown South Hadley is similarly quiet, although students are less enthusiastic about its lack of activity. "South Hadley is about as sad as you get for a college town," students tell us, although rarely without also pointing out that "Amherst and Northampton, two towns with plenty of shopping and other things of interest, are close by and easily reached by the PVTA (our bus system)." The campus may not always be bustling, but it is always beautiful. Students lovingly describe "greens surrounded only by classic brick buildings, covered in ivy." One rapturous undergraduate writes, "In the fall, the colors welcome students. In the winter, the skating rink is within walking distance of many sledding hills and cross-country skiing trails. In the spring, the lakes are home to baby geese and the campus is covered in flowers." Holyoke is also home to the "best golf course and equestrian center ever, dorms like palaces, [which have] dining rooms right downstairs [serving] food that's better than any other school I've been to, with a wide variety of choices and special attention paid to vegetarians and vegans," writes one enthusiastic student. Beyond campus, "There's plenty to do in the Pioneer Valley: hiking, climbing, and camping. And Boston is only an hour and a half away."

Student Body

Mount Holyoke women "fall into all sorts of categories, whether it be because of their style in clothing, what they like to do outside of the classroom, or sexual orientation." Students feel that a "large international population also provides for a very diverse atmosphere," as does the sizable lesbian contingent. If there is common ground among all students, it is that they are "outgoing super-achievers who spend far more time in the library than they do at parties." Undergraduates "are generally serious about their work, interested in their world, and politically left." Students pride themselves on their tolerance, although campus conservatives complain that it's selective. One undergraduate tells us, "A word to the wise, unless you agree with the vast majority on campus—or at least the vocal majority—keep your mouth shut or wear flame-retardant clothing."

FINANCIAL AID: 413-538-2291 • E-MAIL: ADMISSION@MTHOLYOKE.EDU • WEBSITE: WWW.MTHOLYOKE.EDU

ADMISSIONS

Very important factors considered include: Class rank, essays, recommendations, secondary school record. *Important factors considered include:* Character/personal qualities, extracurricular activities, interview, talent/ability, volunteer work, work experience. *Other factors considered include:* Alumni/ae relation, geographical residence, minority status, standardized test scores. TOEFL required of all international applicants. High school diploma is required, and GED is accepted. *Academic units recommended:* 4 English, 3 math, 3 science (3 science lab), 3 foreign language, 3 history, 1 academic elective.

The Inside Word

Mount Holyoke has benefited well from the renaissance of interest in women's colleges; selectivity and academic quality are on the rise. Considering that the college was already fairly selective, candidates are well advised to take the admissions process seriously. Matchmaking is a significant factor here; strong academic performance, well-written essays, and an understanding of and appreciation for "the Mount Holyoke experience" will usually carry the day.

FINANCIAL AID

Students should submit: FAFSA, CSS/Financial Aid PROFILE, noncustodial (divorced/separated) parents' statement, business/farm supplement. Regular filing deadline is 2/1. The Princeton Review suggests that all financial aid forms be submitted as soon as possible after 1/1. *Need-based scholarships/grants offered:* Pell, SEOG, state scholarships/grants, private scholarships, the school's own gift aid. *Loan aid offered:* Direct Subsidized Stafford, Direct Unsubsidized Stafford, Direct PLUS, Federal Perkins, college/university loans from institutional funds. Applicants will be notified of awards on or about 4/1. Federal Work-study Program available. Institutional employment available. Off-campus job opportunities are good.

FROM THE ADMISSIONS OFFICE

"Did you know that the majority of students who choose Mount Holyoke do so simply because it is an outstanding liberal arts college? After a semester or two, they start to appreciate the fact that Mount Holyoke is a women's college, even though most Mount Holyoke students never thought they'd go to a women's college when they started their college search. Students talk of having 'space' to really figure out who they are. They speak about feeling empowered to excel in traditionally male subjects such as science and technology. They talk about the remarkable array of opportunities—for academic achievement, career exploration, and leadership—and the impressive, creative accomplishments of their peers. If you're looking for a college that will challenge you to be your best, most powerful self and to fulfill potential, Mount Holyoke should be at the top of your list.

"Submission of standardized test scores is optional for most applicants to Mount Holyoke College. However, the TOEFL is required of students for whom English is not their primary language, and the SAT Subject Tests are required for home-schooled students."

SELECTIVITY

Admissions Rating	**93**
# of applicants	2,912
% of applicants accepted	56
% of acceptees attending	35
# accepting a place on wait list	264
% admitted from wait list	20
# of early decision applicants	158
% accepted early decision	61

FRESHMAN PROFILE

Range SAT Verbal	610-700
Average SAT Verbal	648
Range SAT Math	580-680
Average SAT Math	625
**TPR Projected Range SAT Writing*	*640-700*
Range ACT Composite	26-30
Average ACT Composite	28
Minimum Paper TOEFL	600
Minimum Computer Based TOEFL	250
Average HS GPA	3.59
% graduated top 10% of class	54
% graduated top 25% of class	79
% graduated top 50% of class	98

DEADLINES

Early decision application deadline	11/15
Early decision notification	1/1
Regular application deadline	1/15
Regular notification	4/1
Nonfall registration?	yes

APPLICANTS ALSO LOOK AT

AND OFTEN PREFER

Brown University, Wellesley College

AND SOMETIMES PREFER

Cornell University, Smith College, Vassar College

AND RARELY PREFER

Connecticut College, New York University, Skidmore College

FINANCIAL FACTS

Financial Aid Rating	**98**
Annual tuition	$32,430
Room & Board	$9,550
Books and supplies	$750
Required fees	$168
% frosh rec. need-based scholarship or grant aid	61
% UG rec. need-based scholarship or grant aid	62
% frosh rec. need-based self-help aid	58
% UG rec. need-based self-help aid	62
% frosh rec. any financial aid	62
% UG rec. any financial aid	65
Avg. frosh grant	$22,357
Avg. frosh loan	$3,321
Independent 529 member?	Yes

MUHLENBERG COLLEGE

2400 WEST CHEW STREET, ALLENTOWN, PA 18104-5596 • ADMISSIONS: 484-664-3200 • FAX: 484-664-3234

CAMPUS LIFE

Quality of Life Rating	**75**
Fire Safety Rating	**91**
Type of school	private
Affiliation	Lutheran
Environment	city

STUDENTS

Total undergrad enrollment	2,378
% male/female	42/58
% from out of state	69
% from public high school	77
% live on campus	91
% in (# of) fraternities	19 (4)
% in (# of) sororities	20 (4)
% African American	2
% Asian	2
% Caucasian	91
% Hispanic	4
% international	1

SURVEY SAYS

Small classes
Students are friendly
Theater is popular
Lots of beer drinking
(Almost) everyone smokes

ACADEMICS

Academic Rating	**86**
Calendar	semester
Student/faculty ratio	12:1
Professors interesting rating	82
Professors accessible rating	84
% professors teaching UG courses	100
% classes taught by TAs	0
Most common lab size	10-19 students
Most common regular class size	10-19 students

MOST POPULAR MAJORS

Business administration/management
communications studies/speech communication and rhetoric
psychology

STUDENTS SPEAK OUT

Academics

Students praise the "amazing" theater and science departments at Muhlenberg College. Notes one undergrad, "The single greatest strength [of this school] is the reputation of the science departments. The rigor I have faced here as a biology major, although at times extremely tough, has been also very rewarding." Muhlenberg also boasts "excellent" departments of English and history; the business and philosophy departments here "aren't too shabby either." Indeed, Muhlenberg has a lot to offer for an institution with less than 3,000 students. Undergrads appreciate how "the small student body allows the professors to tailor the education for each student." As one student told us, "The best part about my school is its smallness—something I thought I would hate about Muhlenberg turned out to be what makes it so great." Another benefit of the school's small size: "Since we don't have a graduate school, we don't have any graduate students, so undergrads have opportunities to do research." Prospective students are forewarned that "this is a tough school to get into and to stay in, due to a heavy workload." While profs pile on the work, they are also "extremely approachable and welcome you to speak with them about anything, not just class work. They can help you succeed in school if you take the initiative to get to know them." Sums up one student here: "Muhlenberg is what you make of it; if you're ambitious, the school will be good to you; if you're not, most likely you'll get swept along for the ride."

Life

The "beautiful and safe" Muhlenberg campus provides a serene setting to counteract students' hectic academic schedules. "Life is very busy," notes one student. "The best days are the ones where you have a spare hour or two to sit out on the lawn and read or study with some friends when the weather is nice. The front lawn is great; it always gets crowded with kids just hanging out in the spring and fall or playing in the snow in the winter." An active social scene, however, is not part of what clutters most kids' calendars. There are school-sponsored activities offered, but "most are lame," and as far as the Greek scene goes, the frats "are now either kicked off campus or on probation, so now we are becoming a bar and house party school." Hometown Allentown offers little. Explains one undergrad, "Allentown is technically a city, but don't expect it to be like Manhattan. The college is located in the middle of the suburbs, and most people don't go downtown." Adds another, "I wish they would just pick up the whole damn school and move it out of Allentown." Students enjoy "a few sporting events, mainly men's soccer and women's rugby." Even so, most who can do so seek entertainment elsewhere, often in Philadelphia or New York City. Unfortunately, "freshmen are not allowed to have cars on campus due to major lack of parking space and the rule is pretty strictly enforced," which is why they "tend to flock to the fraternities or hang out in their dorm rooms."

Student Body

Muhlenberg's student body is predominantly white and affluent, students here agree. Detractors describe their peers as people "who have never worked in their lives, drive BMWs and have exorbitant allowances." They "tend to be conservative" and cliquish; reports one, "I don't think anyone really goes out of their way to make new friends once they have found their clique. That's not to say people aren't friendly, though. Overall, the students all get along with each other." Theater majors tend to be the major exception to the preppy, conservative stereotype; their ranks include a disproportionate number of iconoclasts as well as gay students. Despite its Lutheran affiliation, "most kids here are Roman Catholic or Jewish."

FINANCIAL AID: 484-664-3175 • E-MAIL: ADMISSION@MUHLENBERG.EDU • WEBSITE: WWW.MUHLENBERG.EDU

ADMISSIONS

Very important factors considered include: Character/personal qualities, secondary school record, talent/ability. *Important factors considered include:* Class rank, essays, extracurricular activities, interview, recommendations, standardized test scores, volunteer work. *Other factors considered include:* Alumni/ae relation, geographical residence, minority status, work experience. TOEFL required of all international applicants. High school diploma is required, and GED is accepted. *Academic units required:* 4 English, 3 math, 2 science (2 science lab), 2 foreign language, 2 history, 1 academic elective. *Academic units recommended:* 4 math, 3 science, 4 foreign language, 2 social studies.

The Inside Word

Muhlenberg's inquiries and applications continue to increase, which serves to reinforce its selectivity. Competition for students among small Pennsylvania liberal arts colleges is quite heated, and the college is among the more competitive of the lot.

FINANCIAL AID

Students should submit: FAFSA, institution's own financial aid form, CSS/Financial Aid PROFILE, noncustodial (divorced/separated) parents' statement. Regular filing deadline is 2/15. The Princeton Review suggests that all financial aid forms be submitted as soon as possible after 1/1. *Need-based scholarships/grants offered:* Pell, SEOG, state scholarships/grants, private scholarships, the school's own gift aid. *Loan aid offered:* FFEL Subsidized Stafford, FFEL Unsubsidized Stafford, FFEL PLUS, Federal Perkins, private. Applicants will be notified of awards on or about 4/1.

FROM THE ADMISSIONS OFFICE

"Listening to our own students, we've learned that most picked Muhlenberg mainly because it has a long-standing reputation for being academically demanding on one hand, but personally supportive on the other. We expect a lot from our students, but we also expect a lot from ourselves in providing the challenge and support they need to stretch, grow, and succeed. It's not unusual for professors to put their home phone numbers on the course syllabus and encourage students to call them at home with questions. Upperclassmen are helpful to underclassmen. 'We really know about collegiality here,' says an alumna who now works at Muhlenberg. 'It's that kind of place.' The supportive atmosphere and strong work ethic produce lots of successes. The pre-med and pre-law programs are very strong, as are programs in theater arts, English, psychology, the sciences, business, and accounting. 'When I was a student here,' recalls Dr. Walter Loy, now a professor emeritus of physics, 'we were encouraged to live life to its fullest, to do our best, to be honest, to deal openly with others, and to treat everyone as an individual. Those are important things, and they haven't changed at Muhlenberg.'

"Students have the option of submitting SAT or ACT scores (including the Writing sections on each), or submitting a graded paper with teacher's comments and grade on it from junior or senior year and interviewing with a member of the admissions staff. Muhlenberg will accept old or new SAT scores and will use the student's best scores from either test."

SELECTIVITY

Admissions Rating	**93**
# of applicants	4,040
% of applicants accepted	45
% of acceptees attending	31
# accepting a place on wait list	1,306
% admitted from wait list	1
# of early decision applicants	263
% accepted early decision	71

FRESHMAN PROFILE

Range SAT Verbal	560-660
Average SAT Verbal	608
Range SAT Math	560-660
Average SAT Math	612
**TPR Projected Range SAT Writing*	*600-670*
Minimum Paper TOEFL	550
Minimum Computer Based TOEFL	213
Average HS GPA	3.52
% graduated top 10% of class	43
% graduated top 25% of class	76
% graduated top 50% of class	97

DEADLINES

Early decision application deadline	1/15
Early decision notification	2/1
Regular application deadline	2/15
Regular notification	3/15
Nonfall registration?	yes

APPLICANTS ALSO LOOK AT

AND OFTEN PREFER

Bucknell U., Lafayette College, Lehigh U., Villanova U.

AND SOMETIMES PREFER

Dickinson College, Franklin & Marshall College, Gettysburg College, U. of Delaware

AND RARELY PREFER

Drew U., Penn State University Park, Rutgers U.—Rutgers College, Susquehanna U.

FINANCIAL FACTS

Financial Aid Rating	**94**
Annual tuition	$26,570
Room & Board	$7,025
Books and supplies	$1,000
Required fees	$230
% frosh rec. need-based scholarship or grant aid	46
% UG rec. need-based scholarship or grant aid	43
% frosh rec. need-based self-help aid	32
% UG rec. need-based self-help aid	30
% frosh rec. any financial aid	75
% UG rec. any financial aid	78
Avg. frosh grant	$12,827
Avg. frosh loan	$3,138
Independent 529 member?	Yes

NEW COLLEGE OF FLORIDA

5700 NORTH TAMIAMI TRAIL, SARASOTA, FL 34243-2197 • ADMISSIONS: 941-359-4269 • FAX: 941-359-4435

CAMPUS LIFE

Quality of Life Rating	**94**
Fire Safety Rating	**74**
Type of school	public
Environment	town

STUDENTS

Total undergrad enrollment	692
% male/female	38/62
% from out of state	19
% from public high school	83
% live on campus	68
% African American	2
% Asian	3
% Caucasian	82
% Hispanic	9
% international	2
# of countries represented	27

SURVEY SAYS

Small classes
Campus feels safe
Intercollegiate sports are unpopular or nonexistent
Frats and sororities are unpopular or nonexistent

ACADEMICS

Academic Rating	**93**
Calendar	4-1-4
Student/faculty ratio	10:1
Professors interesting rating	97
Professors accessible rating	94
% professors teaching UG courses	100
% classes taught by TAs	0
Most common regular class size	10-19 students

MOST POPULAR MAJORS

Anthropology
psychology
sociology

STUDENTS SPEAK OUT

Academics

Students enjoy "the freedom to study whatever you're interested in to make things happen and take action" at the New College of Florida, an innovative state school where "taking responsibility for yourself academically and socially, and learning how to function in a community that truly cares about each person" define the undergraduate experience. In consultation with a faculty advisor, students design their own curricula, meeting at the beginning of each semester to plot out a course of study (which include classes, tutorials, research projects, and study abroad), define academic objectives, and sign a contract outlining the semester's goals. Instead of grades, students receive written narrative evaluations of their work. All students must complete three independent study projects (completed during January interterm) and a senior thesis, which must be defended before a committee of three faculty members. It takes a special student to flourish here; explains one who has, "If you are self-motivated, New College provides a great opportunity to work closely with professors to provide an intellectually stimulating and challenging educational experience. Self-motivation, however, is the key; without it you will receive a second-rate education and probably not be any better for it in the end." Undergraduates warn that "You can't take the lack of grades as joke—you still need to focus and do your work [because] your professors expect a lot from you, as if they were your parents. Because they trust the students to do their work—and they do—students are able to have the freedom of designing their own education." For those with the self-discipline and academic drive required by this unique program, "The academic experience is unparalleled because you are given so many opportunities to advance in your area of interest."

Life

"There is always something social happening on campus" at New College, although it's "not so much planned, organized events, as it is hangouts with welcoming groups of students watching a movie, cooking dinner, playing music or just sitting around talking." There are also regular school-sponsored parties, which many students take advantage of, and "tons of free food all the time." One student sums up weekend life here thusly: "Scene: a Friday night. If you're in a square court filled with palm trees and there aren't 20 people drunk and discussing Hegel, planning a bike ride to a local beach for a nude swim, or dancing to Outkast and Violent Femmes, then you aren't at New College." (Oh, and just so you'll be in-the-know, parties aren't called "parties" at this school where students are proud to be cranks. They're called "walls.") Other benefits of a New College education include "amazing dorms" that "not only provide a good place for study and relaxation, but also somehow facilitate the need for privacy (private entrances) and social interaction (court yard design)." And then there are the school's environs, which include "St. Armand's Circle and Lido Beach, less then 10 minutes from campus." Sarasota "is a beautiful, artsy community, but not much of a college town," although "the downtown isn't too bad. We usually get discounts for shows at Van Wezel, which is halfway to the beach. Dinner out is always a treat; there are lots of tasty places to go around here. And the dollar theater is awesome!"

Student Body

Reports one New College undergrad, "Whenever I pass somebody on campus, they're always talking about French politics or particle physics or weird linguistic connections from the Indus Valley...I love it." Another agrees, "You will never want for intellectual conversation during your undergraduate experience if New College is your undergraduate choice. Everyone can learn something from everyone here." The typical student here is "outspoken, intellectual, non-mainstream liberal, warm, open, curious, driven [and] would be atypical anywhere else." Above all, they are "interested in nothing besides the demolition of boredom on all fronts."

New College of Florida

Financial Aid: 941-359-4255 • E-mail: admissions@ncf.edu • Website: www.ncf.edu

ADMISSIONS

Very important factors considered include: Essays, secondary school record. *Important factors considered include:* Character/personal qualities, recommendations, standardized test scores. *Other factors considered include:* Alumni/ae relation, class rank, extracurricular activities, geographical residence, interview, state residency, talent/ability, volunteer work, work experience. SAT Reasoning or ACT required. TOEFL required of all international applicants. High school diploma is required, and GED is accepted. *Academic units required:* 4 English, 3 math, 3 science (2 science lab), 2 foreign language, 3 social studies, 3 academic electives. *Academic units recommended:* 4 English, 3 math, 3 science (2 science lab), 2 foreign language, 3 social studies, 5 academic electives.

The Inside Word

Applications keep rolling in to New College like the evening tide on Sarasota Bay. Increases in the academic quality of entering students are virtually perpetual, as is recognition by the media. Perhaps the biggest drawback is a high attrition rate for a college of this caliber—just as the admissions committee strives to choose wisely, so should prospective students. Don't apply simply because it's a great buy; make sure that it's what you're seeking. In order to be successful, candidates must demonstrate a high level of intellectual curiosity, self-awareness, and maturity. It also helps to be a strong writer, given that the application an optional process requires candidates to submit, and graded paper from school. Did we forget to mention high grades and test scores? They'll help, too, but if you're someone with lots of "potential" as opposed to "credentials," the admissions committee might still vote you in provided you've put together some very convincing evidence that you make a match and deserve a shot.

FINANCIAL AID

Students should submit: FAFSA. The Princeton Review suggests that all financial aid forms be submitted as soon as possible after 1/1. *Need-based scholarships/grants offered:* Pell, state scholarships/grants, private scholarships, the school's own gift aid. *Loan aid offered:* FFEL Subsidized Stafford, FFEL Unsubsidized Stafford, FFEL PLUS. Applicants will be notified of awards on or about 3/15.

FROM THE ADMISSIONS OFFICE

"New College provides the opportunity to obtain a very high-quality education for the very affordable cost of attending a public college. Students work in close consultation with faculty to develop individualized programs of seminars, tutorials, independent research, and off-campus experiences. The student who will do best at New College is one who is independent, broad-minded, self-confident, and capable of rigorous academic work. The very nature of New College requires one to be dedicated to education and the pursuit of individual growth.

"Students applying for fall 2006 must submit scores from the SAT (or ACT scores). It is not required that they take the new version of the SAT (or the ACT with the writing section). We will allow students to submit scores from either version of the SAT (or ACT) and will use the student's best scores from either test."

SELECTIVITY

Admissions Rating	**93**
# of applicants	716
% of applicants accepted	53
% of acceptees attending	49
# accepting a place on wait list	32
% admitted from wait list	47

FRESHMAN PROFILE

Range SAT Verbal	630-720
Average SAT Verbal	676
Range SAT Math	590-670
Average SAT Math	639
**TPR Projected Range SAT Writing*	*650-710*
Range ACT Composite	26-30
Average ACT Composite	27
Minimum Paper TOEFL	560
Minimum Computer Based TOEFL	220
Average HS GPA	3.95
% graduated top 10% of class	52
% graduated top 25% of class	81
% graduated top 50% of class	95

DEADLINES

Regular application deadline	5/1
Regular notification	rolling
Nonfall registration?	yes

APPLICANTS ALSO LOOK AT

AND OFTEN PREFER
University of Florida

AND SOMETIMES PREFER
Grinnell College
Hampshire College
University of Miami
University of South Florida

AND RARELY PREFER
Eckerd College
Reed College
Sarah Lawrence College

FINANCIAL FACTS

Financial Aid Rating	**90**
Annual in-state tuition	$3,452
Annual out-of-state tuition	$18,460
Room & Board	$6,006
Books and supplies	$800
% frosh rec. need-based scholarship or grant aid	34
% UG rec. need-based scholarship or grant aid	38
% frosh rec. need-based self-help aid	23
% UG rec. need-based self-help aid	31
% frosh rec. any financial aid	34
% UG rec. any financial aid	39
Avg. frosh grant	$10,983
Avg. frosh loan	$2,417
Independent 529 member?	No

NEW JERSEY INSTITUTE OF TECHNOLOGY

UNIVERSITY HEIGHTS, NEWARK, NJ 07102 • ADMISSIONS: 973-596-3300 • FAX: 973-596-3461

CAMPUS LIFE

Quality of Life Rating	**61**
Fire Safety Rating	**60**
Type of school	public
Environment	metropolis

STUDENTS

Total undergrad enrollment	4,944
% male/female	81/19
% from out of state	9
% from public high school	80
% live on campus	28
% in (# of) fraternities	7 (19)
% in (# of) sororities	5 (8)
% African American	10
% Asian	22
% Caucasian	35
% Hispanic	13
% international	6
# of countries represented	98

SURVEY SAYS

Small classes
Great computer facilities
Diverse student types on campus
Campus feels safe

ACADEMICS

Academic Rating	**70**
Calendar	semester
Student/faculty ratio	13:1
Professors interesting rating	61
Professors accessible rating	61
% professors teaching UG courses	70
% classes taught by TAs	0
Most common regular class size	10-19 students

MOST POPULAR MAJORS

Architecture (BArch, BA/BS, MArch, MA/MS, PhD)
computer and information sciences
information technology

STUDENTS SPEAK OUT

Academics

Mathematics, science, technology, and architecture offerings all shine at New Jersey Institute of Technology, a "leader in the field of technology in the tri-state area" whose public-school pricing allows students to "graduate without the bank owning our first-borns, which is a definite plus." As at many prestigious tech-oriented schools, "The professors are generally hired for research rather than teaching ability, [so] there are some who cannot teach, and they aren't that great at grading assignments or handing back papers, either." Students hasten to add that "There are also plenty of great professors who work hard for the students" and "a handful are wonderful teachers" as well as "good people. Many are tied to industry, which really helps in the long run." In the short run, too, since those connections help provide "so many opportunities in research and internships." The demanding undergraduate curriculum means "You have to be serious about studies if you are choosing NJIT. There is no time for fun and games." Students groan about the demands made on them but also recognize the benefits; "NJIT is an intense academic university that allows students to be prepared for the working world," explains one architect. Another plus of studying at NJIT is "how well the students interact, especially during exam time. Seniors help juniors, who help sophomores, who help freshman. It's helpful when someone who has taken the courses you're taking at the moment can put things into perspective, and give you hints about what may be on the test."

Life

NJIT is "not the best school socially, but few engineering schools are," students here concede. Since "a lot of classes give amazing amounts of homework, it is hard to have a normal social life. Most nights are spent doing homework late, then getting a few hours of fun before passing out." Extracurricular life has improved recently with the addition of new recreation facilities; one student notes, "The game room has been improved, with pool tables, bowling, and arcades, and a much-needed pub on campus." The Institute also boasts "a pretty good gym to work out in, and a brand new soccer field." Undergrads note optimistically that "Our team sports are all performing better, and the students are starting to feel a sense of competition building. There are plenty of parties on Thursday nights on campus, organized by frats or clubs." And, of course, "Possibilities are endless because New York City is minutes away" by affordable public transportation, opening the door to "major league sports, world-class museums, and theater." Hometown Newark, although much maligned by students and locals, offers "great food and restaurants less than half a mile away from campus, in the Ironbound section." Students also appreciate how the "small classes and campus make a 'small-town' atmosphere during the semester," even though they also acknowledge that "the campus is ugly; there's not a lot of green space here."

Student Body

"There are two types of students at NJIT," writes one student, elaborating: "The first are the ones who are involved with athletics, clubs, organizations, and other things. The others are the antisocial ones. These people stay in their dorms and play computer games all day." How many of each category populate this campus? One student offers some pertinent data: "Class attendance dropped 32 percent the day Halo 2 came out." Like the region surrounding it, "NJIT is a total melting pot; the mix of ethnic backgrounds of students is diverse." While many say the various groups interact well, just as many others describe the student body as "clusters of ethnic groups isolated from each other." Because of curricular demands, "Everyone is pretty smart. But you also have the very smart people." When asked in what ways his school could stand to improve, one succinct information technologist wrote "GIRLS!" reflecting a sentiment running through much of the student body. The male to female ratio is about 4:1.

NEW JERSEY INSTITUTE OF TECHNOLOGY

FINANCIAL AID: 973-596-3480 • E-MAIL: ADMISSIONS@NJIT.EDU • WEBSITE: WWW.NJIT.EDU

ADMISSIONS

Very important factors considered include: Class rank, secondary school record, standardized test scores. *Other factors considered include:* Alumni/ae relation, character/personal qualities, essays, extracurricular activities, geographical residence, interview, minority status, recommendations, religious affiliation/commitment, state residency, talent/ability, volunteer work, work experience. SAT Reasoning or ACT required. TOEFL required of all international applicants. High school diploma is required, and GED is accepted. *Academic units required:* 4 English, 4 math, 2 science (2 science lab), 4. *Academic units recommended:* 2 foreign language, 1 social studies, 1 history, 2 academic electives.

The Inside Word

NJIT is a great choice for students who aspire to technical careers but don't meet the requirements for better known and more selective universities. To top it off, it's a pretty good buy.

FINANCIAL AID

Students should submit: FAFSA. Regular filing deadline is 5/15. The Princeton Review suggests that all financial aid forms be submitted as soon as possible after 1/1. *Need-based scholarships/grants offered:* Pell, SEOG, state scholarships/grants, private scholarships, the school's own gift aid. *Loan aid offered:* Direct Subsidized Stafford, Direct Unsubsidized Stafford, Direct PLUS, FFEL Subsidized Stafford, FFEL Unsubsidized Stafford, FFEL PLUS, Federal Perkins, state loans, college/university loans from institutional funds. Federal Work-study Program available. Off-campus job opportunities are good.

FROM THE ADMISSIONS OFFICE

"Talented high school graduates from across the nation come to NJIT to prepare for leadership roles in architecture, business, engineering, medical, legal, science, and technological fields. Students experience a public research university conducting more than $75 million in research that maintains a small-college atmosphere at a modest cost. Our attractive 45-acre campus is just minutes from New York City and less than an hour from the Jersey shore. Students find an outstanding faculty and a safe, diverse, caring learning and residential community. All dormitory rooms have sprinklers. NJIT's academic environment challenges and prepares students for rewarding careers and full-time advanced study after graduation. The campus is computing-intensive. For five consecutive years, *Yahoo! Internet Life* ranked NJIT among America's Most Wired Universities.

"Students applying for admission to NJIT for fall 2006 may provide scores from either version of the SAT, or the ACT. The new writing sample scores will be collected but will not be used for admission purposes for 2006. SAT Subject Test scores are not required for any major."

SELECTIVITY

Admissions Rating	**80**
# of applicants	2,538
% of applicants accepted	58
% of acceptees attending	46
# accepting a place on wait list	25
% admitted from wait list	44

FRESHMAN PROFILE

Range SAT Verbal	490-600
Average SAT Verbal	544
Range SAT Math	560-660
Average SAT Math	608
**TPR Projected Range SAT Writing*	*550-630*
Minimum Paper TOEFL	550
Minimum Computer Based TOEFL	213
% graduated top 10% of class	24
% graduated top 25% of class	57
% graduated top 50% of class	86

DEADLINES

Regular application deadline	4/1
Regular notification	rolling
Nonfall registration?	yes

APPLICANTS ALSO LOOK AT AND OFTEN PREFER

The College of New Jersey
Drexel University
Rensselaer Polytechnic Institute
Rutgers University—Rutgers College

AND SOMETIMES PREFER

Penn State University Park
Virginia Tech
Worcester Polytechnic Institute

FINANCIAL FACTS

Financial Aid Rating	**78**
Annual in-state tuition	$7,918
Annual out-of-state tuition	$13,716
Room & Board	$8,242
Books and supplies	$1,200
Required fees	$1,262
% frosh rec. need-based scholarship or grant aid	55
% UG rec. need-based scholarship or grant aid	43
% frosh rec. need-based self-help aid	47
% UG rec. need-based self-help aid	29
Avg. frosh grant	$4,400
Avg. frosh loan	$2,500
Independent 529 member?	No

New Mexico Institute of Mining & Technology

Campus Station, 801 Leroy Place, Socorro, NM 87801 • Admissions: 505-835-5424 • Fax: 505-835-5989

CAMPUS LIFE

Quality of Life Rating	**63**
Fire Safety Rating	**60**
Type of school	public
Environment	rural

STUDENTS

Total undergrad enrollment	1,148
% male/female	75/25
% from out of state	15
% from public high school	80
% live on campus	59
% African American	1
% Asian	3
% Caucasian	71
% Hispanic	19
% Native American	3
% international	3
# of countries represented	30

SURVEY SAYS

Class discussions are rare
Small classes
Frats and sororities are unpopular or nonexistent
(Almost) everyone smokes

ACADEMICS

Academic Rating	**79**
Calendar	semester
Student/faculty ratio	12:1
Professors interesting rating	74
Professors accessible rating	67
% professors teaching UG courses	85
% classes taught by TAs	0
Most common lab size	10-19 students
Most common regular class size	fewer than 10 students

MOST POPULAR MAJORS

Computer and information sciences
electrical, electronics, and communications engineering
physics

STUDENTS SPEAK OUT

Academics

New Mexico Institute of Mining and Technology—known simply as "Tech" to insiders—is a school geared toward students interested in geological science, engineering, or computers. Like most such "science-oriented" schools, students at Tech ("Techies") are no strangers to hard work. "At Tech, you must be prepared to be a serious student because professors expect a lot from their students." Tech's atmosphere doesn't suffer, perhaps because "it's a small school where you can get to know personally the people in the financial aid office, student accounts, the registrar, etc." A few praise the financial aid packages, and many commend the professors for being researchers as well as teachers: "It is an incredible feeling to listen to a lecture by someone who actually does research in that field and enjoys teaching." And to top it all off, "The research opportunities are incredible. We have an explosives field for the materials engineering department, and our computer science department does Department of Defense cryptography. The physics department has done experiments on NASA's Vomit Comet (which simulates zero gravity)." While students sometimes grumble that "Tech is very difficult," they appreciate how "most departments have help sessions almost every day for most of the day; just drop by with a problem and you'll have an upper-level student or grad student helping you understand." And they also realize that the hard work "means that you are going to learn the material and be an expert by the time you graduate."

Life

With its rural location, Tech doesn't offer much in the way of urban fun. Outdoor activities such as rock climbing and mountain biking are popular. In addition, "there are events like movies, barbeques, dancing, or theatrical events every week. You can also use the athletic facilities or play with dry ice for fun." Otherwise, though, Tech's surroundings don't offer a whole lot; Socorro, according to its harshest critics, is "a depressed town that flaunts the failure of the American Dream." Tech's distance from an urban center is particularly appreciable for the handful of students who grumble about the food. Culinary discontentment aside, there is fun to be had at Tech—even for those who don't enjoy outdoor activities. Popular indoor activities include "dances, movies, and computer games." Students tell us that "large, crazy parties are fairly infrequent, but they exist. Small social gatherings are more common and often involve something nerdy, whether it be video games or mixing volatile chemicals." Once each semester "there are weekend school-wide celebrations, known as 'Forty-niners' and 'Spring Fling,' which have plenty of alcohol." Writes one sophomore: "Techies have to make their own fun and we do—after we finish our homework."

Student Body

The "friendly oddballs" of Tech "are mostly nerds...no, actually, we're all nerds." It's the kind of place where "half the students on campus built their own computers" and, in the words of one junior, some students seem "surgically attached to their computers." While Techies assert that they know how to party, they "also take pride in knowing the chemical formula of the substances they consume." Students characterize their peers by major, writing that "the science people tend to spend a lot of time outside; the engineers tend to be in the library; and the computer science people tend to be in their rooms." A physics major writes that "all the students are incredibly interested in their fields." There aren't many women at Tech (a member of this minority notes that "the guy-to-girl ratio at Tech is rather ridiculous"); one male student observes, "to find an attractive girl who has no boyfriend is like finding Brigadoon." That said, a good portion of the student body consists of "people with senses of humor who make the best out of the town and life on campus."

NEW MEXICO INSTITUTE OF MINING & TECHNOLOGY

FINANCIAL AID: 505-835-5333 • E-MAIL: ADMISSION@ADMIN.NMT.EDU • WEBSITE: WWW.NMT.EDU

ADMISSIONS

Very important factors considered include: Secondary school record, standardized test scores. *Other factors considered include:* Class rank, extracurricular activities, talent/ability. SAT Reasoning and SAT Subject Tests or ACT required. TOEFL required of all international applicants. High school diploma is required, and GED is accepted. *Academic units required:* 4 English, 3 math, 2 science (2 science lab), 2 social studies, 1 history, 3 academic electives. *Academic units recommended:* 4 English, 4 math, 4 science (3 science lab), 2 foreign language, 3 social studies, 1 history.

The Inside Word

A 2.5 GPA and a 21 ACT score is far from stringent. This is one of those situations that call for serious self-examination. Are you really ready to take on the demands of a fairly solid technical institute? If you aren't sure, you should probably pass, even if you're admissible.

FINANCIAL AID

Students should submit: FAFSA, institution's own financial aid form. Regular filing deadline is 6/1. The Princeton Review suggests that all financial aid forms be submitted as soon as possible after 1/1. *Need-based scholarships/grants offered:* Pell, SEOG, state scholarships/grants, private scholarships, the school's own gift aid. *Loan aid offered:* FFEL Subsidized Stafford, FFEL Unsubsidized Stafford, FFEL PLUS, Federal Perkins, state loans. Applicants will be notified of awards on a rolling basis beginning on or about 4/1. Federal Work-study Program available. Institutional employment available. Off-campus job opportunities are fair.

FROM THE ADMISSIONS OFFICE

"More than a century old, New Mexico Tech has research programs at the cutting edge of today's technology. This is exciting for students because many of them get jobs working for professors or for one of our many research divisions, learning skills they will use in graduate schools or high-tech careers. Pulsars, thunderstorms, volcanoes, lightning, quasars, earthquakes, energetic materials, and caves are just a few of the areas we study. We also teach and work in areas of computer and information security, business management, and several fields of engineering. Many of our research divisions are known worldwide in their fields, including Magdalena Ridge Observatory, the Energetic Materials Research and Testing Center, and Langmuir Laboratory for Atmospheric Research. Recent graduates with engineering degrees received starting salaries averaging $51,755, those with computer science degrees averaged $55,583, and those with degrees in both computer science and electrical engineering started at $63,333.

"As of this book's publication, New Mexico Institute of Mining & Technology did not have information available about their policy regarding the new SAT."

SELECTIVITY

Admissions Rating	**83**
# of applicants	363
% of applicants accepted	98
% of acceptees attending	80

FRESHMAN PROFILE

Range SAT Verbal	570-670
Average SAT Verbal	596
Range SAT Math	580-680
Average SAT Math	612
**TPR Projected Range SAT Writing*	*610-680*
Range ACT Composite	23-29
Average ACT Composite	26
Minimum Paper TOEFL	540
Minimum Computer Based TOEFL	207
Average HS GPA	3.6
% graduated top 10% of class	37
% graduated top 25% of class	59
% graduated top 50% of class	88

DEADLINES

Regular application deadline	8/1
Regular notification	rolling
Nonfall registration?	yes

APPLICANTS ALSO LOOK AT

AND OFTEN PREFER
California Institute of Technology
Massachusetts Institute of Technology

AND SOMETIMES PREFER
Colorado School of Mines
University of New Mexico

AND RARELY PREFER
Arizona State University
New Mexico State University

FINANCIAL FACTS

Financial Aid Rating	**88**
Annual in-state tuition	$3,280
Annual out-of-state tuition	$9,911
Room & Board	$4,470
Books and supplies	$800
% frosh rec. need-based scholarship or grant aid	21
% UG rec. need-based scholarship or grant aid	29
% frosh rec. need-based self-help aid	25
% UG rec. need-based self-help aid	31
Avg. frosh grant	$4,600
Avg. frosh loan	$2,412
Independent 529 member?	No

NEW YORK UNIVERSITY

22 WASHINGTON SQUARE NORTH, NEW YORK, NY 10011 • ADMISSIONS: 212-998-4500 • FAX: 212-995-4902

CAMPUS LIFE

Quality of Life Rating	**81**
Fire Safety Rating	**64**
Type of school	private
Environment	metropolis

STUDENTS

Total undergrad enrollment	19,826
% male/female	39/61
% from out of state	65
% from public high school	69
% live on campus	54
% in (# of) fraternities	5 (14)
% in (# of) sororities	3 (13)
% African American	5
% Asian	14
% Caucasian	43
% Hispanic	7
% international	4
# of countries represented	143

SURVEY SAYS

Great library
Diverse student types on campus
Students love New York, NY
Great off-campus food
Hard liquor is popular
(Almost) everyone smokes

ACADEMICS

Academic Rating	**85**
Calendar	semester
Student/faculty ratio	12:1
Professors interesting rating	74
Professors accessible rating	67
% classes taught by TAs	0
Most common lab size	20-29 students
Most common regular class size	10-19 students

MOST POPULAR MAJORS

Drama and dramatics/theater arts
finance
liberal arts and sciences/liberal studies

STUDENTS SPEAK OUT

Academics

When people rave about the strong academics at New York University (NYU), they are often referring to one of the many colleges under the university's umbrella. The Tisch School of the Arts and The Stern School of Business have established themselves as frontrunners in their respective fields, but undergraduates urge us not to forget about the other schools: The College of Arts and Science, the Gallatin School of Individualized Study, The Steinhardt School of Education, The Ehrenkranz School of Social Work, The College of Nursing, and The School of Continuing and Professional Studies. Furthermore, each school has its own feel. So what do all students enjoy regardless of their undergraduate school? The university's enviable location in Lower Manhattan, and its long history of academic excellence attracts, across the board, some the world's most accomplished scholars. While some of the faculty can be difficult to find outside of class, "many professors are wonderful teachers and easily accessible." Another undergraduate adds, "I like the professors here because they have passion." Yet, because NYU is a large school in America's biggest city, the students who get the most out of their academic experiences are the ones who are able to take the reins. As one student explains, "It is a school and environment where the chances of success are dependent solely on the student's ability to avoid distractions, [maintain] motivation to achieve his/her goals, and [use] his/her creative ability to map the different roads that can lead to [those] goals, as in the real world." Even the go-getters who thrive at NYU have trouble cutting through the red tape that has become a symbol of the university's administration. As one student puts it, trying to get in touch with the proper people in the administration to get something done "is like trying to get attention from inanimate objects."

Life

Student life at New York University boils down to an equation: "NYU = NYC." As one student further explains, "NYU students use the city as their playground." In Greenwich Village, where the heart of the campus is located, "the possibilities for any kind of social life are endless." And that's not counting the rest of the city. "For fun, what don't we do?" poses an eager undergraduate. "There are dance clubs, [a countless number] of bars, museums, tons of great restaurants, shopping (if you have money), Broadway, off-Broadway, off-off-Broadway, sports (Yankees, Mets, Knicks, Giants, and so on), Central Park, random ethnic festivals and street fairs, all sorts of cool neighborhoods, fabulous people-watching, and even just walking down the street is completely fascinating." However, the amenities of city life do come at a cost. "Campus life plays a minimal role in student life," explains one student. Because the university buildings and the student residences are quite spread out, there is not a strong sense of community at NYU. "If you're looking for a school with a football team and cheerleaders and people who wave flags and paint faces to show their pride," says one undergraduate, "NYU is not the place for you." That said, "Joining a club or simply making an effort to say hi will easily get you friends," promises another student.

Student Body

"There is no typical student at NYU," students explain. "NYU has everything: the Ivy League go-getting types, the vegan protestors, the hard working recent immigrants, a big vibrant Jewish community, a vocal African American community, a huge LGBT community, an Arab community—everything, really." In general, it is fair to say that the NYU community "does tilt to the left," though "the typical 'Sternie' business student is politically conservative and comes from a wealthy family." It is important to remember that the student body at each school will take a slightly different shape. "The one thing that almost all NYU students have in common is that they love New York City." One great benefit of all of this diversity, as one student puts it, is that after a little while at NYU, "the concept of discrimination seems ultimately foreign."

FINANCIAL AID: 212-998-4444 • E-MAIL: ADMISSIONS@NYU.EDU • WEBSITE: WWW.NYU.EDU

ADMISSIONS

Very important factors considered include: Secondary school record, standardized test scores. *Important factors considered include:* Character/personal qualities, class rank, essays, extracurricular activities, recommendations, talent/ability. *Other factors considered include:* Alumni/ae relation, minority status, volunteer work, work experience. SAT Reasoning or ACT required. SAT Subject Tests recommended. TOEFL required of all international applicants. High school diploma is required, and GED is accepted. *Academic units required:* 4 English, 3 math, 3 science (2 science lab), 2 foreign language, 4 history. *Academic units recommended:* 4 math, 3 science lab.

The Inside Word

NYU is more selective than most large private universities but, except for a few particularly choosy programs, no more personal in its evaluation of candidates. A solid GPA and test scores go further toward getting in than anything else. Still, the university is very serious about projecting a highly selective image, and it's dangerous to take your application too lightly. Since the completion of several major dormitories in the late 1980s, NYU has turned its attention to increasing the national profile of its student body. Applications have increased by more than half over the past five years.

FINANCIAL AID

Students should submit: FAFSA, state aid form, early decision applicants may submit an institutuional form for an estimated award. Regular filing deadline is 2/15. The Princeton Review suggests that all financial aid forms be submitted as soon as possible after 1/1. *Need-based scholarships/grants offered:* Pell, SEOG, state scholarships/grants, private scholarships, the school's own gift aid. *Loan aid offered:* FFEL Subsidized Stafford, FFEL Unsubsidized Stafford, FFEL PLUS, Federal Perkins, Federal Nursing. Applicants will be notified of awards on a rolling basis beginning on or about 4/1. Federal Work-study Program available. Off-campus job opportunities are excellent.

FROM THE ADMISSIONS OFFICE

"NYU is distinctive both in the quality of education we provide and in the exhilarating atmosphere in which our students study and learn. As an undergraduate in one of our eight small- to medium-size colleges, you will enjoy a small faculty/student ratio and a dynamic, challenging learning environment that encourages lively interaction between students and professors. At the same time, you will have available to you all the resources of a distinguished university dedicated to research and scholarship at the highest levels, including a curriculum that offers over 2,500 courses and 160 programs of study and a faculty that includes some of the most highly regarded scholars, scientists, and artists in the country. New York University is a vital, vibrant community. There is an aura of energy and excitement here, a sense that possibilities and opportunities are limited only by the number of hours in a day. The educational experience at NYU is intense, but varied and richly satisfying. You will be actively engaged in your own education, both in the classroom and beyond.

"Applicants for freshman admission fall 2006 must take the new version of the SAT (or the ACT with the writing section). However, students may submit scores from the old (prior to March 2005) version of the SAT (or ACT) as well; we will use the student's best scores from either test. Two SAT Subject Tests are recommended."

SELECTIVITY

Admissions Rating	**95**
# of applicants	34,457
% of applicants accepted	35
% of acceptees attending	38
# accepting a place on wait list	2,078
% admitted from wait list	8
# of early decision applicants	1,210
% accepted early decision	42

FRESHMAN PROFILE

Range SAT Verbal	610-700
Average SAT Verbal	658
Range SAT Math	610-710
Average SAT Math	660
**TPR Projected Range SAT Writing*	*640-700*
Range ACT Composite	27-31
Average ACT Composite	29
Minimum Paper TOEFL	600
Minimum Computer Based TOEFL	250
Average HS GPA	3.6
% graduated top 10% of class	63
% graduated top 25% of class	91
% graduated top 50% of class	99

DEADLINES

Early decision application deadline	11/1
Early decision notification	12/15
Regular application deadline	1/15
Regular notification	4/1
Nonfall registration?	yes

FINANCIAL FACTS

Financial Aid Rating	**75**
Annual tuition	$28,328
Room & Board	$11,210
Books and supplies	$700
Required fees	$1,766
% frosh rec. need-based scholarship or grant aid	54
% UG rec. need-based scholarship or grant aid	53
% frosh rec. need-based self-help aid	52
% UG rec. need-based self-help aid	50
% frosh rec. any financial aid	62
% UG rec. any financial aid	64
Avg. frosh grant	$13,629
Avg. frosh loan	$4,351
Independent 529 member?	No

North Carolina State University

Box 7103, Raleigh, NC 27695 • Admissions: 919-515-2434 • Fax: 919-515-5039

CAMPUS LIFE

Quality of Life Rating	**82**
Fire Safety Rating	**77**
Type of school	public
Environment	metropolis

STUDENTS

Total undergrad enrollment	20,302
% male/female	58/42
% from out of state	7
% from public high school	90
% live on campus	33
% in (# of) fraternities	8 (25)
% in (# of) sororities	10 (15)
% African American	10
% Asian	5
% Caucasian	81
% Hispanic	2
% Native American	1
% international	1
# of countries represented	103

SURVEY SAYS

Great computer facilities
Great library
Athletic facilities are great
Students love Raleigh, NC
Everyone loves the Wolfpack
Intramural sports are popular
Lots of beer drinking

ACADEMICS

Academic Rating	**79**
Calendar	semester
Student/faculty ratio	16:1
Professors interesting rating	77
Professors accessible rating	68
% professors teaching UG courses	100
% classes taught by TAs	6
Most common lab size	10-19 students
Most common regular class size	20-29 students

MOST POPULAR MAJORS

Business administration/management
computer engineering
electrical, electronics, and communications engineering

STUDENTS SPEAK OUT

Academics

North Carolina State University (NC State or NCSU), "a traditional engineering and agricultural school," located in the state's burgeoning capital, serves up a broad range of outstanding academics. Academic offerings are bolstered by cutting-edge technology and exceptional, school-spirit-lifting athletic teams, resulting in a satisfied student body. As one student puts it, "I've loved everything about NC State. Coming here was the best decision of my life. Raleigh is an awesome town, and NC State is a rising school not only in academics, but also in athletics." Engineering, mathematics, design, and textiles are among the best-known disciplines. Business administration is popular, and students also praise NCSU's oft-overlooked humanities and social sciences, telling us that the school "has an excellent liberal arts college and is rarely given credit for it." As at many tech-oriented schools, "course loads can be tough, and instructors can be overwhelming, but the one thing they all try to impress [on you] is getting you ready for the real world." The school attempts to ease the transition from high school to college with its "first-year course-repeat policy," allowing students a second go at courses that overwhelmed them the first time around. As at most large schools, "It is easy to get lost in the system. Once you choose a college that you like within the university, there is not as much of a problem."

Life

At NC State, "Athletics are very important, particularly football, [and] are a common topic of conversation," explains one student. "No one is 'sort of' a fan, and the Student Wolfpack Club, an organization sponsoring NCSU Athletics, is the most popular and largest organization here." Another student writes, "In the early fall, students generally focus on football, which involves tailgating and a lot of camaraderie. As the semester progresses, basketball and football are both quite popular, and basketball fever carries on into the spring." Wolfpack boosters love to participate in sports as much as they love to watch them. "Once the weather has warmed up enough, the students generally move outdoors to play some kind of sport," such as volleyball, soccer, ultimate Frisbee, or football. The university's gym "doesn't always have the most regular hours, but the facilities there are first class." There is a lot to do beyond sports, too. As one student puts it, "If you like to be social, this is the place to be, especially if you live on campus. There is always something to do around campus in your downtime. [There are] a ton of clubs and organizations that are always looking for new members, [including] many large Christian groups." Another student adds that there are also "tons of service and volunteer activities going on in which the university takes part." The campus, students concede, "is defiantly not the world's most beautiful campus. If you like brick, this is the place to be."

Student Body

NC State draws a varied student body, predominantly from inside the Tar Heel state. Within those parameters there's plenty of diversity because "students come from all kinds of families and all different environments," ranging from the state's small mountain towns to its major cities to the rural stretches down east to the vast Atlantic coast. The typical student is "very smart and technically minded" and generally "extremely friendly." One Yankee writes, "Coming from the Northeast, I was not used to the friendliness down here. It is one of the big factors that drew me to NC State." Undergraduates share "a very strong sense of community," especially during football season, when Wolfpack pride runs strongest. Of course, at a school this large "there are so many different types of people that everyone pretty much fits in." As one student puts it, "NC State prides itself on diversity. A walk through campus would prove this."

NORTH CAROLINA STATE UNIVERSITY

FINANCIAL AID: 919-515-2421 • E-MAIL: UNDERGRAD_ADMISSIONS@NCSU.EDU • WEBSITE: WWW.NCSU.EDU

ADMISSIONS

Very important factors considered include: Class rank, secondary school record, standardized test scores. *Other factors considered include:* Alumni/ae relation, character/personal qualities, essays, extracurricular activities, geographical residence, minority status, recommendations, state residency, talent/ability, volunteer work, work experience. SAT Reasoning or ACT required. TOEFL required of all international applicants. High school diploma is required, and GED is not accepted. *Academic units required:* 4 English, 3 math, 3 science (1 science lab), 2 foreign language, 1 social studies, 1 history, 1 academic elective. *Academic units recommended:* 4 English, 4 math, 4 science (1 science lab), 2 foreign language, 1 social studies, 1 history, 4 academic electives.

The Inside Word

Prospective students should be certain to investigate additional requirements for the college they wish to enter; universities that admit students to specific programs often vary standards significantly. Nonresidents will find it dramatically easier to get into NC State than to UNC, but application totals have gone up at state and eventually selectivity will follow.

FINANCIAL AID

Students should submit: FAFSA, institution's own financial aid form. The Princeton Review suggests that all financial aid forms be submitted as soon as possible after 1/1. *Need-based scholarships/grants offered:* Pell, SEOG, state scholarships/grants, private scholarships, the school's own gift aid. *Loan aid offered:* FFEL Subsidized Stafford, FFEL Unsubsidized Stafford, FFEL PLUS, Federal Perkins, state loans, college/university loans from institutional funds. Applicants will be notified of awards on a rolling basis beginning on or about 3/1.

FROM THE ADMISSIONS OFFICE

"NC State is arguably the most popular university in the state, with more NC students seeking admission than at any other college or university. Over 12,000 students from across the nation seek one of the 3,600 available freshman spaces. Students choose NC State for its strong and varied academic programs (approximately 90), national reputation for excellence, low cost, location in Raleigh and the Research Triangle Park area, and very friendly atmosphere. Our students like the excitement of a large campus and the many opportunities it offers, such as Cooperative Education, Study Abroad, extensive honors programming, and theme residence halls. Each year, hundreds of NC State graduates are accepted into medical or law schools or other areas of advanced professional study. More corporate and government entities recruit graduates from NC State than from any other university in the United States. In 1999, IBM hired more graduates from NC State than from any other university in the United States.

"Freshman applicants for fall 2006 must take either the new SAT, which includes a written essay, or the ACT with the Writing component. Students may also submit scores from either the old SAT (taken before March 2005) or the ACT, but the new Writing score is still required."

SELECTIVITY

Admissions Rating	**91**
# of applicants	13,947
% of applicants accepted	59
% of acceptees attending	47
# accepting a place on wait list	500
% admitted from wait list	20

FRESHMAN PROFILE

Range SAT Verbal	530-630
Average SAT Verbal	580
Range SAT Math	570-660
Average SAT Math	613
**TPR Projected Range SAT Writing*	*580-650*
Range ACT Composite	22-27
Average ACT Composite	25
Minimum Paper TOEFL	550
Minimum Computer Based TOEFL	213
Average HS GPA	4.09
% graduated top 10% of class	43
% graduated top 25% of class	83
% graduated top 50% of class	98

DEADLINES

Regular application deadline	2/1
Regular notification	rolling
Nonfall registration?	yes

APPLICANTS ALSO LOOK AT

AND OFTEN PREFER
University of North Carolina—Chapel Hill

AND SOMETIMES PREFER
University of North Carolina—Charlotte
Wake Forest University

AND RARELY PREFER
Auburn University
Clemson University
Georgia Institute of Technology
University of South Carolina—Columbia

FINANCIAL FACTS

Financial Aid Rating	**79**
Annual in-state tuition	$3,205
Annual out-of-state tuition	$15,403
Room & Board	$6,851
Books and supplies	$800
Required fees	$1,162
% frosh rec. need-based scholarship or grant aid	41
% UG rec. need-based scholarship or grant aid	38
% frosh rec. need-based self-help aid	33
% UG rec. need-based self-help aid	32
% frosh rec. any financial aid	67
% UG rec. any financial aid	53
Avg. frosh grant	$5,794
Avg. frosh loan	$3,617
Independent 529 member?	No

NORTHEASTERN UNIVERSITY

360 HUNTINGTON AVENUE, 150 RICHARDS HALL, BOSTON, MA 02115 • ADMISSIONS: 617-373-2200 • FAX: 617-373-8780

CAMPUS LIFE

Quality of Life Rating	**82**
Fire Safety Rating	**83**
Type of school	private
Environment	metropolis

STUDENTS

Total undergrad enrollment	14,618
% male/female	49/51
% from out of state	65
% in (# of) fraternities	4 (11)
% in (# of) sororities	4 (7)
% African American	6
% Asian	7
% Caucasian	67
% Hispanic	5
% international	5
# of countries represented	123

SURVEY SAYS

Great computer facilities
Great library
Athletic facilities are great
Students love Boston, MA
Great off-campus food
Lots of beer drinking
Hard liquor is popular

ACADEMICS

Academic Rating	**79**
Calendar	semester
Student/faculty ratio	16:1
Professors interesting rating	64
Professors accessible rating	65
% professors teaching UG courses	100
% classes taught by TAs	0
Most common regular class size	10-19 students

MOST POPULAR MAJORS

Business/commerce
engineering
health services/allied health

STUDENTS SPEAK OUT

Academics

For "incorporating classroom learning with real world application in the middle of a great city," Northeastern University is hard to beat. That's because of the school's celebrated cooperative education (co-op) program, which "gives students a chance to try out jobs in the 'real world' and adjust their career paths accordingly. Co-op gives you the chance to meet new friends, both students and professionals, make some money, and build your resume." "Co-op is the reason many people are at this school," students agree, pointing out that "Through the co-op program students are able to bring more to the table than the average college student. Many of the upperclassman have had experience working within their major beyond serving coffee and copying files for the higher-ups." They warn, however, that "co-ops are not just handed to you, and you must not assume that you will be guaranteed a co-op just by being a NU student. Many friends of mine have suffered through a semester working at the mall on 'no-op.'" A large school, NU excels in a number of areas; students report that health science, business, engineering, and criminal justice are all solid here. As at many large schools, the bureaucracy can be overwhelming; many students reference "the NU shuffle," explaining that "no one is ever willing to help you with a problem. All they're trained to do is send you to someone else." Advisors are in unfortunately short supply, as "each advisor has hundreds of students. Getting a meeting with them is like pulling teeth. Once you get closer to graduation and advisors become more important to you, you get little help, if any."

Life

"Campus life is very small at NU," students tell us explaining, "We have a city to play in. Why waste time on campus where there's not much to do?" NU, located in the heart of Boston, is "in a great area in terms of proximity to places to eat and places to have fun. We are just a few minutes' walk away from Fenway Park and the surrounding bars, as well as Newberry Street, the Prudential Center, and Copley Square." The city is "a lot of fun during the day, with shopping and museums and other tourist attractions," and it's just as fun at night, especially if you're over 21. "Life at Northeastern is all about bars," confides one student. When the weekend rolls around, "many students go out to parties, which can be found ongoing every night," or they "go to basketball and hockey games." They also "take weekend road trips to Cape Cod or just bike and rollerblade around the city, weather permitting, see a lot of movies, [or] just explore the city and goof around." Although "the majority of the school parties," students who are "not into drinking" will "definitely find a niche, and it won't be hard."

Student Body

Undergraduates report that "the vast majority of the school is comprised of people very concerned with their appearance and club life." At a school this size though, those outside the "vast majority" constitute a sizeable population, so "you can hang out with a bunch of different people from different groups, and you all get along well." There are students from all socioeconomic, ethnic, and racial backgrounds contentedly "all mixed together." Atypical students "have many resources and clubs available that cater to their ethnicity, sexual orientation, etc."

Financial Aid: 617-373-3190 • E-mail: admissions@neu.edu • Website: www.northeastern.edu

ADMISSIONS

Very important factors considered include: Secondary school record. *Important factors considered include:* Character/personal qualities, class rank, essays, extracurricular activities, recommendations, standardized test scores, talent/ability. *Other factors considered include:* Alumni/ae relation, geographical residence, minority status, volunteer work, work experience. SAT Reasoning or SAT Subject Tests required. TOEFL required of all international applicants. High school diploma is required, and GED is accepted. *Academic units required:* 4 English, 3 math, 3 science (2 science lab), 2 foreign language, 3 social studies, 2 history. *Academic units recommended:* 4 math, 4 science (4 science lab), 4 foreign language.

The Inside Word

Northeastern is one of the Boston area's most selective schools which makes it a desirable school for students who want a college experience in an urban environment. Northeastern has a large applicant pool and a low acceptance rate. Northeastern's admissions process relies on a comprehensive review process where personal qualities and interests are as important as academic achievement.

FINANCIAL AID

Students should submit: FAFSA, CSS/Financial Aid PROFILE. The Princeton Review suggests that all financial aid forms be submitted as soon as possible after 1/1. *Need-based scholarships/grants offered:* Pell, SEOG, state scholarships/grants, private scholarships, the school's own gift aid, Federal Nursing scholarships. *Loan aid offered:* FFEL Subsidized Stafford, FFEL Unsubsidized Stafford, FFEL PLUS, Federal Perkins, Federal Nursing, state loans, MEFA, TERI, Signature, Mass. No Interest Loan (NIL), CitiAssist. Applicants will be notified of awards on a rolling basis beginning on or about 2/15. Federal Work-study Program available. Institutional employment available. Off-campus job opportunities are excellent.

FROM THE ADMISSIONS OFFICE

"Northeastern students take charge of their education in a way you'll find nowhere else because a Northeastern education is like no other. We integrate challenging liberal arts and professional studies with the world's largest cooperative education program, where undergraduates alternate semesters of full-time study with semesters of paid work in fields relevant to their professional interests and major, giving them nearly two years of professional experience upon graduation. Northeastern's dynamic of academic excellence and workplace experience means that our students are better prepared to succeed in the lives they choose. On top of that, they experience all of this on a beautifully landscaped, 67-acre campus in the heart of Boston, where culture, commerce, civic pride, and college students from around the globe are all a part of the mix.

"Freshman applicants for fall 2006 must take the new SAT (which includes a written essay) or the ACT with Writing component."

SELECTIVITY

Admissions Rating	**92**
# of applicants	24,436
% of applicants accepted	42
% of acceptees attending	27
# accepting a place on wait list	1,045
% admitted from wait list	49

FRESHMAN PROFILE

Range SAT Verbal	550-650
Average SAT Verbal	596
Range SAT Math	570-660
Average SAT Math	615
**TPR Projected Range SAT Writing*	*600-670*
Range ACT Composite	24-28
Average ACT Composite	26
Minimum Paper TOEFL	550
Minimum Computer Based TOEFL	213
Average HS GPA	3.52
% graduated top 10% of class	36
% graduated top 25% of class	67
% graduated top 50% of class	93

DEADLINES

Regular application deadline	2/1
Regular notification	3/15 and 4/1
Nonfall registration?	yes

APPLICANTS ALSO LOOK AT

AND OFTEN PREFER

Boston College, Boston U., The George Washington U., N.Y.U., Tufts U., U. of Massachusetts—Amherst

AND SOMETIMES PREFER

Bentley College, Providence College, Quinnipiac U., Syracuse U., U. of Maryland—College Park, Worcester Polytechnic Institute

AND RARELY PREFER

American U., Penn State University Park, U. of Connecticut

FINANCIAL FACTS

Financial Aid Rating	**65**
Annual tuition	$26,750
Room & Board	$10,180
Books and supplies	$900
Required fees	$330
% frosh rec. need-based scholarship or grant aid	67
% UG rec. need-based scholarship or grant aid	60
% frosh rec. need-based self-help aid	60
% UG rec. need-based self-help aid	57
% frosh rec. any financial aid	87
% UG rec. any financial aid	72
Avg. frosh grant	$13,965
Avg. frosh loan	$3,588
Independent 529 member?	No

NORTHWESTERN UNIVERSITY

PO Box 3060, 1801 Hinman Avenue, Evanston, IL 60208-3060 • Admissions: 847-491-7271

CAMPUS LIFE

Quality of Life Rating	**75**
Fire Safety Rating	**60**
Type of school	private
Environment	town

STUDENTS

Total undergrad enrollment	7,988
% male/female	47/53
% from out of state	74
% from public high school	73
% live on campus	65
% in (# of) fraternities	30 (22)
% in (# of) sororities	39 (19)
% African American	5
% Asian	17
% Caucasian	60
% Hispanic	5
% international	5
# of countries represented	51

SURVEY SAYS

Great library
Athletic facilities are great
Great off-campus food
Frats and sororities dominate social scene
Theater is popular
Student publications are popular

ACADEMICS

Academic Rating	**77**
Calendar	quarter
Student/faculty ratio	7:1
Professors interesting rating	74
Professors accessible rating	74
% professors teaching UG courses	100
% classes taught by TAs	2
Most common lab size	10-19 students
Most common regular class size	fewer than 10 students

MOST POPULAR MAJORS

Economics
engineering
journalism

STUDENTS SPEAK OUT

Academics

Students at prestigious Northwestern University love that their school is "one of the most academically rigorous in the country, but without the pompousness and cutthroat competitiveness of all those East Coast institutions." Northwestern certainly has a lot to offer; the school has "practically every program possible, from journalism to communications to engineering to theater; [professors who] are generally very accessible if you seek them out; [a] writing arts center that brings in great authors to teach classes; a quarterly academic calendar that creates a very intense curriculum but also allows a student to take a variety of classes;" and, a homey Midwestern vibe. Students warn that freshman and sophomore years—during which students slog through distribution requirements and large intro lecture classes—can be a rough go, "but once you get into upper-level classes, they are much more discussion-based, and are smaller." Furthermore, "the administration of the general College of the Arts and Sciences (which deals with most underclassman issues) does little to help you choose a major or answer questions. The administrations in the specialized schools, such as the journalism and engineering schools, are much better attuned to their students." Northwestern's specialized schools are its crown jewels. The theater programs "allow a full liberal-arts experience with conservatory-level training," the school of communication "has a great, very intimate administration, with professors who are very knowledgeable and interested in teaching," and the school of engineering "is very intense, even though everyone takes only four classes."

Life

Life at Northwestern can be grueling "because with the quarter system, classes are easy to fall behind in, and it's not as if there's a shortage of work." Schoolwork gives most kids a pretty full plate, but that does not stop them from piling more on. Most succumb to "the demand to be involved heavily in extracurricular activities of all varieties: newspaper, Greek system, philanthropy, student government, and sports." As another student reports, "What is amazing to see is the number of student-run organizations on campus that produce plays, organize rallies for women's/racial rights, put on orchestra performances, and undertake a whole spectrum of things which I can hardly begin to explain." On the social side, another student says, "There is a lot of Greek life, but not as much in the stereotypical way, more in a social-club-type way." There's also Chicago, the city that "makes life at this school great. Chicago offers anything you can dream of: concerts, theater, restaurants, shopping, sports, and on and on." When they stay close to home, undergraduates enjoy a "beautiful campus, with lots of heavily wooded green space. You can't beat living by Lake Michigan, which is gorgeous," says one student. The only drawback is the weather. Another student reports, "It is currently minus three with a wind chill of –20! Winters here are lousy, and it really puts a damper on winter socials."

Student Body

"It is difficult to create a profile of a typical Northwestern student," undergraduates tell us, "because the school draws from such a wide group of people. There are students from Dubai and students from Chicago. It really runs the gamut." There are, however, a few common threads running through the student body. Undergraduates are typically "nerdy but fun, and very passionate, which makes for lots of interesting people." They're also ambitious, "gonna-be-somebody-someday people" whose ranks include "a lot of theater and artsy types as well as science buffs and aspiring journalists." Most take schoolwork very seriously. "One-third of the kids never leave their dorm rooms, one-third of the kids only leave their dorms to do extracurricular stuff like plays or journalism, and the last one-third are depressed because they wish they had gone to a state school with their friends where there's actually a party scene," writes one undergraduate. Reportedly there are large Asian and Jewish populations. Students tell us, "There's a good amount of racial and religious minorities, but less economic diversity."

FINANCIAL AID: 847-491-7400 • E-MAIL: UG-ADMISSION@NORTHWESTERN.EDU • WEBSITE: WWW.NORTHWESTERN.EDU

ADMISSIONS

Very important factors considered include: Class rank, essays, secondary school record, standardized test scores. *Important factors considered include:* Character/personal qualities, extracurricular activities, recommendations, talent/ability. *Other factors considered include:* Alumni/ae relation, interview, minority status, volunteer work, work experience. SAT Reasoning or ACT required. TOEFL required of all international applicants. High school diploma or equivalent is not required. *Academic units recommended:* 4 English, 3 math, 2 science (2 science lab), 2 foreign language, 2 social studies, 1 academic elective.

The Inside Word

Northwestern's applicant pool is easily among the best in the country. Candidates face both a rigorous evaluation by the admissions committee and serious competition from within the pool. The best approach (besides top grades and a strong personal background) is to take the committee up on their recommendations to visit the campus or interview with an alumnus/a and submit SAT Subject Test scores. The effort it takes to get in is well worth it.

FINANCIAL AID

Students should submit: FAFSA, CSS/Financial Aid PROFILE, noncustodial (divorced/separated) parents' statement, business/farm supplement, parent and student federal tax returns. Regular filing deadline is 2/1. The Princeton Review suggests that all financial aid forms be submitted as soon as possible after 1/1. *Need-based scholarships/grants offered:* Pell, SEOG, state scholarships/grants, private scholarships, the school's own gift aid, United Negro College Fund. *Loan aid offered:* FFEL Subsidized Stafford, FFEL Unsubsidized Stafford, FFEL PLUS, Federal Perkins, college/university loans from institutional funds. Applicants will be notified of awards on or about 4/15. Federal Work-study Program available. Institutional employment available. Off-campus job opportunities are excellent.

FROM THE ADMISSIONS OFFICE

"Consistent with its dedication to excellence, Northwestern provides both an educational and an extracurricular environment that enable its undergraduate students to become accomplished individuals and informed and responsible citizens. To the students in all its undergraduate schools, Northwestern offers liberal learning and professional education to help them gain the depth of knowledge that will empower them to become leaders in their professions and communities. Furthermore, Northwestern fosters in its students a broad understanding of the world in which we live as well as excellence in the competencies that transcend any particular field of study: writing and oral communication, analytical and creative thinking and expression, quantitative and qualitative methods of thinking.

"Applicants for fall 2006 are required to take the new SAT or the ACT with the Writing section. Northwestern will allow students to submit scores from the old (prior to March 2005) SAT (or ACT) as well, and will use the student's best scores from either test. However, Writing scores will be required."

SELECTIVITY

Admissions Rating	**97**
# of applicants	15,637
% of applicants accepted	30
% of acceptees attending	41
# accepting a place on wait list	1,199
% admitted from wait list	13
# of early decision applicants	552
% accepted early decision	50

FRESHMAN PROFILE

Range SAT Verbal	650-740
Average SAT Verbal	687
Range SAT Math	670-760
Average SAT Math	702
**TPR Projected Range SAT Writing*	*670-720*
Range ACT Composite	29-33
Average ACT Composite	30
Minimum Paper TOEFL	600
Minimum Computer Based TOEFL	250
% graduated top 10% of class	82
% graduated top 25% of class	96
% graduated top 50% of class	100

DEADLINES

Early decision application deadline	11/1
Early decision notification	12/15
Regular application deadline	1/1
Regular notification	4/15
Nonfall registration?	yes

APPLICANTS ALSO LOOK AT

AND OFTEN PREFER
Harvard College, Yale University

AND SOMETIMES PREFER
Columbia University—Columbia College, Princeton University, Stanford University, University of Chicago

AND RARELY PREFER
DePaul University, Marquette University

FINANCIAL FACTS

Financial Aid Rating	**95**
Annual tuition	$31,644
Room & Board	$9,873
Books and supplies	$1,419
Required fees	$145
% frosh rec. need-based scholarship or grant aid	42
% UG rec. need-based scholarship or grant aid	41
% frosh rec. need-based self-help aid	43
% UG rec. need-based self-help aid	41
% frosh rec. any financial aid	60
% UG rec. any financial aid	60
Avg. frosh grant	$19,926
Avg. frosh loan	$2,252
Independent 529 member?	No

OBERLIN COLLEGE

101 NORTH PROFESSOR STREET, OBERLIN, OH 44074 • ADMISSIONS: 440-775-8411 • FAX: 440-775-6905

CAMPUS LIFE

Quality of Life Rating	**82**
Fire Safety Rating	**60**
Type of school	private
Environment	rural

STUDENTS

Total undergrad enrollment	2,807
% male/female	45/55
% from out of state	90
% from public high school	66
% live on campus	73
% African American	6
% Asian	8
% Caucasian	74
% Hispanic	5
% Native American	1
% international	6

SURVEY SAYS

Small classes
Great library
Frats and sororities are unpopular or nonexistent
Musical organizations are popular
Political activism is popular

ACADEMICS

Academic Rating	**95**
Calendar	4-1-4
Student/faculty ratio	10:1
Professors interesting rating	92
Professors accessible rating	88
% professors teaching UG courses	100
% classes taught by TAs	0
Most common lab size	10-19 students
Most common regular class size	10-19 students

MOST POPULAR MAJORS

English language and literature
history

STUDENTS SPEAK OUT

Academics

"Oberlin provides the personal attention and small classes of a liberal arts college," students at this tiny northern Ohio school brag, "combined with facilities that rival many top universities. [With] one of the best music conservatories in the country [and] great programs in the sciences, economics, and art," Oberlin offers a rigorous curriculum in "an extremely challenging environment that does not pit student against student. Obies are competitive in the sense that they want to achieve and succeed, but not in a way that takes away from group work and the overall class environment." The school uses "interactive discussions, passionate teachers, and stimulating material" in its efforts to "turn students' minds into filters, so they learn to criticize the world." The process begins as soon as undergraduates arrive via the recently instituted freshman seminar program. Students also report favorably on the school's Winter Term— "a great opportunity to get an internship, take on a personal project, or get involved in the community"—and the Experimental College, "which allows you to get credit for a wide variety of student-taught subjects, ranging from karate to Korean." The school's willingness to undertake progressive programs enhances its generally left-liberal approach to education, which students see as both a strength and an occasional weakness. While some praise the curriculum's ability to "help us see through the filter of commercialism," others complain about "too many trendy PC identity classes dealing with gender, sexuality, and race.

Life

Life at Oberlin, students tell us, "is very community oriented. Despite being near Cleveland, we don't all pour out of campus every weekend. We bring the entertainment to us or create our own. There is so much talent here, especially with a conservatory!" As one undergraduate puts it, "There's so much to do here every week that you can only hope to do a fraction of it. Plays, concerts, lectures, and ad hoc adventures abound. People are always starting clubs—there are probably more extracurriculars per student here than anywhere else. Aside from that, people spend a lot of time talking, hanging out, pulling pranks, making art, climbing trees, reading, or whatever." No wonder some kids tell us "there is a very real Oberlin bubble; the isolation and unnatural quality of this environment make us all go a little crazy once the semester gets under way." The town surrounding the college is "small, very small. Parties off campus generally consist of cops watching streams of kids flock to one house, waiting an appropriate amount of time, and then breaking it up." While some students tell us the town "leaves much to be desired," others contend that their community "has everything you need: a grocery store, Chinese food, bakeries, movie theater, great music and arts, and about four or five dry cleaners." Because Oberlin profs pile on the work, "by the middle of the semester there really ceases to be much social life, as people lock themselves in their rooms to study."

Student Body

The student body of Oberlin "is made up of kids who really have the urge to speak out and contribute, whether it is directly through environmental or volunteer work or indirectly through the arts or humanities. [These] well-intentioned, genuinely nice, out-of-the-box-smart, tree-hugging vegans who are out to save the world from corporate corruption, industrial pollution, world hunger, and Republicans" describe themselves as "intense, irreverent, intellectual, and a little zany. It keeps things interesting and exciting, both in and out of class." Obies tell us, "It's a wonderful school for queer people." Some feel that "if Oberlin could attract more conventional students as well as ultra-hippy kids, there would be greater diversity on the campus."

Oberlin College

Financial Aid: 440-775-8142 • E-mail: college.admissions@oberlin.edu • Website: www.oberlin.edu

ADMISSIONS

Very important factors considered include: Alumni/ae relation, class rank, secondary school record, standardized test scores. *Important factors considered include:* Character/personal qualities, essays, extracurricular activities, recommendations, talent/ability. *Other factors considered include:* Geographical residence, interview, minority status, state residency, volunteer work, work experience. SAT Reasoning or ACT required. TOEFL required of all international applicants. High school diploma is required, and GED is accepted. *Academic units required:* 4 English, 4 math, 3 science, 3 foreign language, 3 social studies.

The Inside Word

The admissions process at Oberlin is especially demanding for candidates to the Conservatory of Music, which seeks only the best-prepared musicians for its excellent program. All applicants to the college face a thorough and rigorous review of their credentials by the admissions committee regardless of their choice of major. Take our advice—visit the campus to interview, and put extra effort into admissions essays.

FINANCIAL AID

Students should submit: FAFSA, CSS/Financial Aid PROFILE, noncustodial (divorced/separated) parents' statement, business/farm supplement. Regular filing deadline is 2/15. The Princeton Review suggests that all financial aid forms be submitted as soon as possible after 1/1. *Need-based scholarships/grants offered:* Pell, SEOG, state scholarships/grants, private scholarships, the school's own gift aid. *Loan aid offered:* Direct Subsidized Stafford, Direct Unsubsidized Stafford, Direct PLUS, Federal Perkins, college/university loans from institutional funds. Applicants will be notified of awards on or about 4/1.

FROM THE ADMISSIONS OFFICE

"Oberlin College is an independent, coeducational, liberal arts college. It comprises two divisions, the College of Arts and Sciences, with roughly 2,300 students enrolled, and the Conservatory of Music, with about 600 students. Students in both divisions share one campus; they also share residence and dining halls as part of one academic community. Many students take courses in both divisions. Oberlin awards the Bachelor of Arts and the Bachelor of Music degrees; a five-year program leads to both degrees. Selected master's degrees are offered in the Conservatory. Oberlin is located 35 miles southwest of Cleveland. Founded in 1833, Oberlin College is highly selective and dedicated to recruiting students from diverse backgrounds. Oberlin was the first coeducational college in the United States, as well as a historic leader in educating black students. Oberlin's 440-acre campus provides outstanding facilities, modern scientific laboratories, a large computing center, a library unexcelled by other college libraries for the depth and range of its resources, and the Allen Memorial Art Museum.

"Freshman applicants for fall 2006 must take the new SAT (which includes a written essay), or the ACT with Writing component."

SELECTIVITY

Admissions Rating	**96**
# of applicants	5,824
% of applicants accepted	40
% of acceptees attending	32
# accepting a place on wait list	791
% admitted from wait list	8
# of early decision applicants	176
% accepted early decision	63

FRESHMAN PROFILE

Range SAT Verbal	634-730
Average SAT Verbal	683
Range SAT Math	610-710
Average SAT Math	656
***TPR Projected Range SAT Writing**	*650-720*
Range ACT Composite	26-31
Average ACT Composite	30
Minimum Paper TOEFL	600
Minimum Computer Based TOEFL	200
Average HS GPA	3.55
% graduated top 10% of class	67
% graduated top 25% of class	85
% graduated top 50% of class	96

DEADLINES

Early decision application deadline	11/15
Early decision notification	12/20
Regular application deadline	1/15
Regular notification	4/1
Nonfall registration?	no

APPLICANTS ALSO LOOK AT

AND OFTEN PREFER
Brown University, Stanford University, Swarthmore College, Wesleyan University, Yale University

AND SOMETIMES PREFER
Carleton College, Grinnell College, Macalester College

AND RARELY PREFER
Connecticut College

FINANCIAL FACTS

Financial Aid Rating	**78**
Annual tuition	$30,925
Room & Board	$7,643
Books and supplies	$734
Required fees	$188
% frosh rec. need-based scholarship or grant aid	54
% UG rec. need-based scholarship or grant aid	54
% frosh rec. need-based self-help aid	56
% UG rec. need-based self-help aid	55
% frosh rec. any financial aid	61
% UG rec. any financial aid	60
Avg. frosh grant	$23,500
Avg. frosh loan	$4,000
Independent 529 member?	Yes

OGLETHORPE UNIVERSITY

4484 PEACHTREE ROAD, NE, ATLANTA, GA 30319 • ADMISSIONS: 404-364-8307 • FAX: 404-364-8491

CAMPUS LIFE

Quality of Life Rating	**87**
Fire Safety Rating	**60**
Type of school	private
Environment	metropolis

STUDENTS

Total undergrad enrollment	900
% male/female	35/65
% from out of state	37
% from public high school	77
% live on campus	54
% in (# of) fraternities	33 (4)
% in (# of) sororities	25 (3)
% African American	20
% Asian	3
% Caucasian	65
% Hispanic	3
% international	3
# of countries represented	26

SURVEY SAYS

Small classes
Students love Atlanta, GA
Great off-campus food

ACADEMICS

Academic Rating	**88**
Calendar	semester
Student/faculty ratio	11:1
Professors interesting rating	97
Professors accessible rating	93
% professors teaching UG courses	100
% classes taught by TAs	0
Most common regular class size	10-19 students

MOST POPULAR MAJORS

Business administration/management
English language and literature

STUDENTS SPEAK OUT

Academics

How well students fit into the Oglethorpe approach to education depends on how enthusiastically they embrace the school's core curriculum, a set of nine interdisciplinary courses focusing on such themes as "Narratives of the Self" and "Human Nature and the Social Order." Nearly all student respondents to our survey love the core because it "allows students to learn about the thinkers that have shaped Western civilization, which reduces cultural illiteracy." Students appreciate the interdisciplinary approach; writes one, "Classes at Oglethorpe challenge us to think and introduce us to new concepts. Thanks to our core program, these concepts often build upon one another, so that I feel like my education is really coming together." What makes the core so effective are "the small class sizes and the availability of professors to easily voice concerns." As one student puts it, "The size [of the student body] allows students more opportunities to fine-tune their education by working with professors on a personal level. Instead of getting lost in the shuffle of huge classes and being just another name on a list of advisees, most students develop personal relationships with their advisors, professors, and staff of the school." Best of all, Oglethorpe "is set in a big city. Not only do you get an intimate education, but you also have endless resources in a city like Atlanta." Oglethorpe's professors, students agree, "are our greatest strength. It is hard to find a full-time professor who has not completed their doctorate degree or not been published. And you never find a professor on this campus that relies on an assistant to teach his or her classes. Every teacher takes pride in teaching their subject to every class."

Life

"Social life is pretty low key" at Oglethorpe, due in equal measures to the small student body and the heavy workload for most majors. Greek parties "are generally open to all students, and on weekends that's where at lot of people end up for lack of anything else better to do, but there's no pressure to be involved in that scene." There's an active theater department here that mounts frequent productions, but otherwise "life here is sometimes boring with little activity on campus." Fortunately, "with the city at your fingertips, there are a lot of things one can do, like shopping, coffee shops, museums, and concerts." Atlanta also has "lots of clubs, both your typical ones and the indie ones, and there are lots of other things to do (provided you have the money)." Oglethorpe is located well to the north of Atlanta's bustling downtown, meaning "the bothersome noises of traffic and the like don't reach the students' ears." The school isn't too secluded, though; it's "only five minutes from grocery stores, restaurants, movie theaters, malls, and pretty much everything you need." Undergraduates love the "gorgeous campus" that "looks like a castle." Writes one, "The neo-gothic architecture of the buildings has more character than [that of] most collegiate buildings."

Student Body

Oglethorpe's core curriculum presupposes a value to learning beyond its immediate professional applications, so it should come as no surprise that "most students here are intelligent and want to learn. Their objective is often not 'career prep,' but more of becoming a learned person." They're the kind of kids "who were oddballs at their high schools. Of course, there are lots of different kinds of oddball, so we have a strange blend of people that all match because they're all so different. While the typical student is smart and creative, there's lots of variety, from anime nerds to soccer-playing sorority girls." The school is home to "a lot of 'alternative people,' but also a large number of the typical everyday type. Also, there are a significant number of gay students who are quite outspoken." "The gender ratio is heavily skewed towards females, though this has been improving." Politically, there "are about as many liberals as conservatives."

FINANCIAL AID: 404-364-8356 • E-MAIL: ADMISSION@OGLETHORPE.EDU • WEBSITE: WWW.OGLETHORPE.EDU

ADMISSIONS

Very important factors considered include: Essays, interview, secondary school record. *Important factors considered include:* Standardized test scores. *Other factors considered include:* Alumni/ae relation, character/personal qualities, class rank, extracurricular activities, recommendations, talent/ability, volunteer work, work experience. SAT Reasoning or ACT required. TOEFL required of all international applicants. High school diploma is required, and GED is accepted. *Academic units required:* 4 English, 3 math, 2 science, 3 social studies. *Academic units recommended:* 2 foreign language.

The Inside Word

With rising national interest in the South, it won't be long before the academic strength found at Oglethorpe attracts wider attention and more applicants. At present, it's much easier to gain admission here than at many universities of similar quality. Go to Atlanta for a campus interview—you'll leave impressed.

FINANCIAL AID

Students should submit: FAFSA, institution's own financial aid form, state aid form. Regular filing deadline is 9/1. The Princeton Review suggests that all financial aid forms be submitted as soon as possible after 1/1. *Need-based scholarships/grants offered:* Pell, SEOG, state scholarships/grants, private scholarships, the school's own gift aid, United Negro College Fund. *Loan aid offered:* Direct Subsidized Stafford, Direct Unsubsidized Stafford, Direct PLUS, FFEL Subsidized Stafford, FFEL Unsubsidized Stafford, FFEL PLUS, Federal Perkins. Applicants will be notified of awards on or about 3/1. Federal Work-study Program available. Institutional employment available. Off-campus job opportunities are excellent.

FROM THE ADMISSIONS OFFICE

"Promising students and outstanding teachers come together at Oglethorpe University in an acclaimed program of liberal arts and sciences. Here you'll find an active intellectual community on a beautiful English Gothic campus just 10 miles from the center of Atlanta, capital of the Southeast, site of the 1996 Summer Olympics, and home to 4 million people. If you want challenging academics, the opportunity to work closely with your professors, and the stimulation of a great metropolitan area, consider Oglethorpe, a national liberal arts college in a world-class city.

"Applicants for fall 2006 are required to take the new SAT (or the ACT with the Writing section). Students may also submit scores from the old (prior to March 2005) SAT (or ACT), and we will use the student's best scores from either test. It is recommended that students submit scores from two SAT Subject Tests."

SELECTIVITY

Admissions Rating	**89**
# of applicants	746
% of applicants accepted	66
% of acceptees attending	35

FRESHMAN PROFILE

Range SAT Verbal	540-660
Average SAT Verbal	617
Range SAT Math	530-640
Average SAT Math	603
**TPR Projected Range SAT Writing*	*590-670*
Range ACT Composite	21-28
Average ACT Composite	26
Minimum Paper TOEFL	550
Average HS GPA	3.7
% graduated top 10% of class	43
% graduated top 25% of class	66
% graduated top 50% of class	90

DEADLINES

Nonfall registration?	yes

APPLICANTS ALSO LOOK AT

AND OFTEN PREFER

Emory University
Florida State University

AND SOMETIMES PREFER

Furman University
Georgia Institute of Technology
Sewanee—The University of the South
University of Georgia
Vanderbilt University

AND RARELY PREFER

Berry College
Mercer University—Macon

FINANCIAL FACTS

Financial Aid Rating	**83**
Annual tuition	$20,900
Room & Board	$7,100
Books and supplies	$600
% frosh rec. need-based scholarship or grant aid	69
% UG rec. need-based scholarship or grant aid	58
% frosh rec. need-based self-help aid	59
% UG rec. need-based self-help aid	58
Avg. frosh grant	$11,018
Avg. frosh loan	$2,934
Independent 529 member?	Yes

Ohio Northern University

525 South Main Street, Ada, OH 45810 • Admissions: 419-772-2260 • Fax: 419-772-2313

CAMPUS LIFE

Quality of Life Rating	**76**
Fire Safety Rating	**60**
Type of school	private
Affiliation	Methodist
Environment	village

STUDENTS

Total undergrad enrollment	2,065
% male/female	54/46
% from out of state	13
% live on campus	64
% in (# of) fraternities	17 (7)
% in (# of) sororities	14 (4)
% African American	1
% Asian	1
% Caucasian	97
% Hispanic	1
% international	1
# of countries represented	15

SURVEY SAYS

Small classes
Great library
Students are friendly
Campus feels safe
Low cost of living

ACADEMICS

Academic Rating	**80**
Calendar	quarter
Student/faculty ratio	13:1
Professors interesting rating	78
Professors accessible rating	84
% professors teaching UG courses	100
% classes taught by TAs	0
Most common regular class size	20-29 students

MOST POPULAR MAJORS

Management science
mechanical engineering

STUDENTS SPEAK OUT

Academics

"Most students are in some sort of science" at Ohio Northern University, "whether it is engineering, pharmacy, biology, chemistry, math, or physics," and most agree that "the science programs are amazing" here. The College of Pharmacy is the star of the show at ONU, students concur. Writes one, "Within the state, I feel this school boasts the best known and respected six-year program. I feel very confident that upon leaving here I will know more information than will be necessary to do well on my boards and on rotations." Students in all science and tech majors report that "we have so many research opportunities, publications, and presentations as a result of being at this university." Elaborates one undergrad, "I have been on trips with my professors and been given the option to present my research findings at major conferences. A bigger school would not have allowed me to accomplish so much." ONU's small-school setting "provides a challenging but nurturing environment" with "professors who are very student-oriented and educated in their fields. This place is perfect for fostering growth and development in each of its students." Business administration is among ONU's other strong suits; the program provides "lots of chances for internships and practical experiences," students tell us.

Life

Ohio Northern is located in Ada, a town that "has more corn than people." Asks one student, "Ever heard of Ada? Neither has anyone else. I interviewed students for scholarships, and they asked, 'So what do you do for fun?' and no joke, I had to mention Wal-Mart. There is so little to do here that going to Wal-Mart is as exciting as a road trip. There is one bar, one restaurant, three stop lights, and a Hardee's. People generally go to Lima for entertainment; that's how small it is." Fortunately, "the school does its very best to lay out an array of cool activities that keep students happy. For example, there are free athletic classes available in the evenings (yoga, pilates, kickboxing), a small bowling alley on campus, movies shown regularly on campus, and numerous active extracurricular groups with which to associate." The Greek system "is responsible for much of the students' social life," with "parties to be found every Tuesday, Friday, and Saturday, if you look hard enough." Students also find creative ways to amuse themselves, "holding a Mud Volleyball tournament at the beginning of the year, and around Halloween, there are many haunted cornfields. In the winter, we go ice skating, and the popular Polar Bowl is a large football tournament in the snow." As at many small, remote schools, "a lot of people enjoy drinking because there is not much else to do. But there's not pressure that you have to drink." Students warn that there's not much time for fun here anyway, at least for those in demanding majors. "We are on the quarter system, and I almost never have any real relaxation time," explains one pharmacy major.

Student Body

"There are a lot of bookworms and a lot of partiers, and not much in between" at ONU, say students, reckoning about "a 60/40 split" between the two groups. High admissions standards means "the typical student is very smart," while the school's religious affiliation means there are "many ultra-conservative Christians, with faith permeating many aspects of life, even organizations that have no apparent connection to religion." There are also those who feel that "sometimes the religious kids can be a bit much for the rest of the student population." Diversity is not the school's strong suit; explains one undergrad, "Ohio Northern is trying its darndest to get a collection of different students to come to this university. I think I could count on my hands the number of African American students here, although they are welcomed with open arms and not treated differently. If anything, we're glad to see different people come because they are different. Everyone here is white, WASP, and Republican, and many are from small Ohio towns."

FINANCIAL AID: 419-772-2272 • E-MAIL: ADMISSIONS-UG@ONU.EDU • WEBSITE: WWW.ONU.EDU

ADMISSIONS

Very important factors considered include: Secondary school record, standardized test scores. *Important factors considered include:* Class rank, extracurricular activities, interview. *Other factors considered include:* Character/personal qualities, essays, recommendations, talent/ability, volunteer work, work experience. SAT Reasoning or ACT required. TOEFL required of all international applicants. High school diploma is required, and GED is accepted. *Academic units required:* 4 English, 2 math, 2 science (2 science lab), 2 social studies, 2 history, 4 academic electives. *Academic units recommended:* 4 English, 4 math, 3 science (2 science lab), 2 foreign language, 3 social studies, 2 history, 4 academic electives.

The Inside Word

Solid grades from high school are a pretty sure ticket for admission to Ohio Northern. Students who are above average academically are in good positions to take advantage of a very large number of no-need scholarships.

FINANCIAL AID

Students should submit: FAFSA, institution's own financial aid form. Regular filing deadline is 6/1. The Princeton Review suggests that all financial aid forms be submitted as soon as possible after 1/1. *Need-based scholarships/grants offered:* Pell, SEOG, state scholarships/grants, private scholarships, the school's own gift aid, external scholarships. *Loan aid offered:* FFEL Subsidized Stafford, FFEL Unsubsidized Stafford, FFEL PLUS, Federal Perkins, college/university loans from institutional funds, alternative loans, Federal Health Professions Loan. Applicants will be notified of awards on a rolling basis beginning on or about 2/15. Federal Work-study Program available. Institutional employment available. Off-campus job opportunities are good.

FROM THE ADMISSIONS OFFICE

"Ohio Northern's purpose is to help students develop into self-reliant, mature men and women capable of clear and logical thinking and sensitive to the higher values of truth, beauty, and goodness. ONU selects its student body from among those students possessing characteristics congruent with the institution's objectives. Generally, a student must be prepared to use the resources of the institution to achieve personal and educational goals.

"Students applying for admission for fall 2006 are urged to take the new SAT (or the ACT with the writing section), but we will allow students to submit scores from the old (prior to March 2005) SAT (or ACT) as well. The student's best composite scores will be used for scholarship purposes."

SELECTIVITY	
Admissions Rating	**87**
# of applicants	2,841
% of applicants accepted	80
% of acceptees attending	33

FRESHMAN PROFILE	
Range SAT Verbal	520-630
Average SAT Verbal	570
Range SAT Math	540-650
Average SAT Math	600
**TPR Projected Range SAT Writing*	*570-650*
Range ACT Composite	23-28
Average ACT Composite	25
Minimum Paper TOEFL	550
Minimum Computer Based TOEFL	213
Average HS GPA	3.57
% graduated top 10% of class	40
% graduated top 25% of class	70
% graduated top 50% of class	91

DEADLINES	
Regular application deadline	8/15
Regular notification	rolling
Nonfall registration?	yes

AND SOMETIMES PREFER

Bowling Green State University
Miami University
Ohio State University—Columbus
University of Toledo
Wittenberg University

FINANCIAL FACTS	
Financial Aid Rating	**82**
Annual tuition	$24,435
Room & Board	$6,030
Books and supplies	$900
Required fees	$210
% frosh rec. need-based scholarship or grant aid	86
% UG rec. need-based scholarship or grant aid	83
% frosh rec. need-based self-help aid	86
% UG rec. need-based self-help aid	83
Independent 529 member?	No

Ohio State University—Columbus

110 Enarson Hall, 54 West 12th Avenue, Columbus, OH 43210 • Admissions: 614-292-3980 • Fax: 614-292-4818

CAMPUS LIFE

Quality of Life Rating	**79**
Fire Safety Rating	**82**
Type of school	public
Environment	metropolis

STUDENTS

Total undergrad enrollment	36,097
% male/female	53/47
% from out of state	9
% from public high school	88
% live on campus	25
% in (# of) fraternities	6 (39)
% in (# of) sororities	7 (21)
% African American	8
% Asian	5
% Caucasian	79
% Hispanic	2
% international	3
# of countries represented	85

SURVEY SAYS

Great library
Diverse student types on campus
Great off-campus food
Everyone loves the Buckeyes
Student publications are popular
Lots of beer drinking

ACADEMICS

Academic Rating	**72**
Calendar	quarter
Student/faculty ratio	14:1
Professors interesting rating	65
Professors accessible rating	68
% classes taught by TAs	0
Most common lab size	20-29 students
Most common regular class size	20-29 students

MOST POPULAR MAJORS

Biology/biological sciences
English language and literature
psychology

STUDENTS SPEAK OUT

Academics

"In terms of resources, Ohio State University is a wonderful school," a place where you can access "just about any class you want, tons of knowledgeable professors, a huge library, and thousands of opportunities for research, study abroad, cultural events, etc." Undergraduates here appreciate that "the school is a huge research facility, which is a big plus because it means the education in the research areas is premium." Points out one student, "The research opportunities mean that we can attract some of the best professors and students. This makes Ohio State a well-known institution in the job market worldwide. It also means that there's always someone around to help if you just can't seem to get something." Business studies are popular, as are engineering and the social sciences, but no matter what your interest, you're likely to find it here, as "OSU offers over 170 majors as well as the opportunity to create your own program of study. Academic diversity is a major strong point." Students tell us that "there are a lot of professors who are here just for research, and teaching is something that they have to do," but that "there are also teachers who love what they do and really connect with students." Course availability is also a problem; "Our scheduling system makes it difficult for non-honors students to get into every class they need in a given quarter," warns one undergrad. Students in the honors program have no such difficulties; they enjoy "priority scheduling" and "classes taught by professors, not TAs." Concludes one student, "The Honors College is the way to go. Priority scheduling is a godsend."

Life

"With one of the largest schools in the country and the fifteenth-largest city in the country, you will find something to do every single day" at OSU, and "whether that is studying or partying, you will have fun doing it." Favored activities change with the seasons; "autumn quarter brings football Saturdays and is always pretty rowdy. Winter quarter is cold and fairly quiet. Come spring quarter, the weather gets nice and parties are happening everywhere." There are parties for anyone who wants one, but "there are also so many other alternatives to parties on campus. Every mall, theater, store, etc., is within walking distance or on a bus route with easy access." Because "OSU is kind of like a miniature city where most of the population is in the same walk of life, and in some cases, it's actually bigger than the towns its students are from," the school can draw big-name entertainment "like Chris Rock, Ludacris, and 311, as well as movie sneak previews, carnivals, and lectures, and the student activities board budget is big enough so that these events are often free." The school's relationship with hometown Columbus yields "discounted tickets to soccer games, symphony concerts, and other fun activities. And in Columbus there is always something going on. Hockey games, arena football, concerts, etc." In short, "you basically are nuts if you are bored on this campus."

Student Body

"You'd be hard pressed to find a student body with more school spirit and a genuine desire to get involved, including community service activities," than the students at OSU, at least by their own reckoning. These "friendly, down-to-earth, and focused" undergrads "have typically loved the Buckeyes since they were young," and "evidence of Buckeye pride is apparent everywhere on campus." That's the common link here; otherwise, "there is no typical student at OSU. There are lots of African Americans, Asians, Indians, etc. We're probably about 50/50 Democrat/Republican. There are a lot of gay/lesbian people, also. Everyone seems pretty open to people of different ethnicities/lifestyles." As at most large schools, "the population is divided along program lines. For example, all of the art and art ed students hang out together, while the business students are all going to business dinners constantly, and the engineering students are the ones partying together every Thursday night."

FINANCIAL AID: 614-292-0300 • E-MAIL: ASKABUCKEYE@OSU.EDU (FRESHMEN AND TRANSFER)• WEBSITE: WWW.OSU.EDU

ADMISSIONS

Very important factors considered include: Class rank, secondary school record, standardized test scores. *Important factors considered include:* Essays, extracurricular activities, minority status, talent/ability, volunteer work, work experience. *Other factors considered include:* Character/personal qualities, geographical residence, recommendations, state residency. SAT Reasoning or ACT required. TOEFL required of all international applicants. High school diploma is required, and GED is accepted. *Academic units required:* 4 English, 3 math, 2 science (2 science lab), 2 foreign language, 2 social studies, 1 academic elective, 1 visual and performing arts. *Academic units recommended:* 4 English, 4 math, 3 science (3 science lab), 3 foreign language, 3 social studies, 1 academic elective, 1 visual and performing arts.

The Inside Word

Although admissions officers consider extracurriculars and other personal characteristics of candidates, there is a heavy emphasis on numbers—grades, rank, and test scores. Although admissions standards have become increasingly competitive in recent years, OSU is still worth a shot for the average student. The university's great reputation and affordable cost make it a good choice for anyone looking at large schools.

FINANCIAL AID

Students should submit: FAFSA. The Princeton Review suggests that all financial aid forms be submitted as soon as possible after 1/1. *Need-based scholarships/grants offered:* Pell, SEOG, state scholarships/grants, private scholarships, the school's own gift aid. *Loan aid offered:* Direct Subsidized Stafford, Direct Unsubsidized Stafford, Direct PLUS, Federal Perkins, Federal Nursing, college/university loans from institutional funds. Applicants will be notified of awards on or about 4/5. Federal Work-study Program available. Institutional employment available. Off-campus job opportunities are fair.

FROM THE ADMISSIONS OFFICE

"Few universities have changed as much as The Ohio State University has in the last decade. Ohio State has undergone a physical transformation, attracted undergraduates of exceptional scholarly talent, and seen its reputation for academic excellence thrive.

"Despite remarkable rankings in most academic programs, the true strength of Ohio State's academic experience is the dialogue between faculty and students that is rarely found among large, research universities.

"With each incoming class, a new academic standard is set as the quality of its students reaches new heights. One of the nation's richest First Year Experience programs helps students transition from talented freshmen to distinguished graduates.

"Ohio State is undergoing unprecedented physical change. The Fisher College of Business complex has been joined by a unique World Media and Culture Center, the $30 million Knowlton School of Architecture, two state-of-the-art recreation centers, and even a university-dedicated highway exit. The university's commitment to both tradition and technology make Ohio State an historic and modern atmosphere in which to learn.

"Although Ohio State is a university of change, it still has phenomenal faculty, incredible programs, competitive tuition, supportive environments, and distinctive tradition. Students never lack for something to do or fail to find a unique place. Whether participating in one of 650 student organizations, attending a lecture by a renowned author or politician, or simply sitting on the Oval, students find their niche at Ohio State, and become part of its living history.

"Students applying for admission are required to submit one Writing score (new SAT or the ACT with Writing) in order for their applications to be complete. The Writing score will not be used to determine admissibility for students entering in 2006. It will be used for research purposes only."

SELECTIVITY

Admissions Rating	**81**
# of applicants	16,954
% of applicants accepted	76
% of acceptees attending	47
# accepting a place on wait list	288
% admitted from wait list	1

FRESHMAN PROFILE

Range SAT Verbal	520-630
Average SAT Verbal	581
Range SAT Math	550-660
Average SAT Math	604
**TPR Projected Range SAT Writing*	*570-650*
Range ACT Composite	23-28
Average ACT Composite	2
Minimum Paper TOEFL	527
Minimum Computer Based TOEFL	197
% graduated top 10% of class	34
% graduated top 25% of class	71
% graduated top 50% of class	96

DEADLINES

Regular application deadline	2/1
Regular notification	rolling
Nonfall registration?	yes

APPLICANTS ALSO LOOK AT AND OFTEN PREFER

Bowling Green State University
Case Western Reserve University
Miami University
Ohio University—Athens
Purdue University—West Lafayette
University of Cincinnati

AND RARELY PREFER

Bellarmine University

FINANCIAL FACTS

Financial Aid Rating	**70**
Annual in-state tuition	$7,383
Annual out-of-state tuition	$17,970
Room & Board	$6,909
Books and supplies	$1,044
Required fees	$63
% frosh rec. need-based scholarship or grant aid	52
% UG rec. need-based scholarship or grant aid	45
% frosh rec. need-based self-help aid	47
% UG rec. need-based self-help aid	47
% frosh rec. any financial aid	54
% UG rec. any financial aid	49
Independent 529 member?	No

OHIO UNIVERSITY—ATHENS

120 CHUBB HALL, ATHENS, OH 45701 • ADMISSIONS: 740-593-4100 • FAX: 740-593-0560

CAMPUS LIFE

Quality of Life Rating	**87**
Fire Safety Rating	**60**
Type of school	public
Environment	rural

STUDENTS

Total undergrad enrollment	16,937
% male/female	47/53
% from out of state	8
% from public high school	86
% live on campus	43
% in (# of) fraternities	12 (20)
% in (# of) sororities	13 (13)
% African American	3
% Asian	1
% Caucasian	92
% Hispanic	1
% international	2
# of countries represented	109

SURVEY SAYS

Great computer facilities
Great library
Athletic facilities are great
Students are friendly
Students are happy
Lots of beer drinking
Hard liquor is popular
(Almost) everyone smokes

ACADEMICS

Academic Rating	**75**
Calendar	quarter
Student/faculty ratio	19:1
Professors interesting rating	78
Professors accessible rating	78
% professors teaching UG courses	100
% classes taught by TAs	17
Most common lab size	10-19 students
Most common regular class size	10-19 students

MOST POPULAR MAJORS

Human development and family studies
journalism
kinesiology and exercise science

STUDENTS SPEAK OUT

Academics

Ohio University caters to the career-minded Ohioan looking for the greatest "bang for the buck" in education. With solid programs in education, telecommunications, and journalism, OU is the springboard to many real world success stories. Undergraduates enjoy many of the accoutrements normally associated with private liberal arts schools, including "small classes," professors who are "approachable and love when students stop by during office hours, [and] wonderful tutoring hours and great tutors. Ohio University makes it very difficult for someone to fail." Large lectures are rare and usually not all that bad. One student tells us, "Ohio University has only one 400-person classroom on campus, and although that can be a very scary experience to take a class there, they are always excellent, and the professors are the best in their [respective] fields. I had three classes in this room through my three years here at OU, and they rank up there as three of my favorite overall." OU more closely resembles its large-state-school peers in its administration. Students tell us, "It's very difficult to get into the classes you need" and that the school is "highly bureaucratic, none of the offices can work smoothly together. You always have to visit five different people to get something done and always wind up having to actually deal with the first person you saw." Ohio University runs on a quarterly academic schedule, making it "extremely easy to fall behind," says one student. "If I don't keep up with my readings for class, pretty soon I'm in a deep hole. It's not long after you begin a class that you are taking midterms again. Then a few more weeks and it's finals time! It's definitely stressful."

Life

"Ohio University is the perfect mixture of business with pleasure," students tell us, adding, "We get the work done on the weekdays so we can party hard on the weekends." Most agree that OU is "a rip-roaring good-time party school." Much of OU social life involves the "19 bars along a two-block stretch of the main drag in town. Each bar has its own personality, and people can always be found at their favorite, so it is easy to meet up with acquaintances because they will probably always be at the same bar." Of course, you have to be 21 to get into a bar, so "for the first two years you're here, house parties rule." The exceptions are the Homecoming and Halloween events, both of which are huge, well-loved celebrations. Students also love their campus, which "is beautiful year-round." Their recreation center, called the Ping, features "a cardio room that overlooks the foothills of the Appalachian Mountains and makes workouts fun." Even freshman dorms are "great, almost like apartments." Students' wish lists include hopes for "a better sports program. It sucks not caring about your own football team."

Student Body

The University's "very laid-back and friendly" undergrads can "usually be found in sweats and flip-flops generally all year round. We have a very casual atmosphere." There are, however, "quite a few students that dress up for class, so don't worry about looking overdressed." While there is "a majority of white, middle- to upper-class students, students not meeting this profile seem to fit in just as well." The diversity seems to not bother anyone as there are "many different groups of people here—musicians, athletes, hippies, frat boys, quiet people—but we all get along." There are also "a lot of international students, who fit in very well but rarely socialize with the American students." Students also tell us, "OU is LGBT-friendly."

FINANCIAL AID: 740-593-4141 • E-MAIL: ADMISSIONS.FRESHMEN@OHIOU.EDU • WEBSITE: WWW.OHIOU.EDU

ADMISSIONS

Very important factors considered include: Secondary school record. *Important factors considered include:* Class rank, standardized test scores. *Other factors considered include:* Alumni/ae relation, character/personal qualities, essays, extracurricular activities, minority status, recommendations, talent/ability, volunteer work, work experience. SAT Reasoning and SAT Subject Tests or ACT required. High school diploma is required, and GED is accepted. *Academic units required:* 4 English, 3 math, 3 science, 2 foreign language, 3 social studies, 1 visual and performing arts.

The Inside Word

There's little mystery in applying to Ohio. The admissions process follows the formula approach to some extent, and those whose numbers plug in well will get good news.

FINANCIAL AID

Students should submit: FAFSA. The Princeton Review suggests that all financial aid forms be submitted as soon as possible after 1/1. *Need-based scholarships/grants offered:* Pell, SEOG, state scholarships/grants, private scholarships, the school's own gift aid. *Loan aid offered:* Direct Subsidized Stafford, Direct Unsubsidized Stafford, Direct PLUS, Federal Perkins. Institutional short term loans are repaid in 30 to 60 days.

FROM THE ADMISSIONS OFFICE

"Chartered in 1804, Ohio University symbolizes America's early commitment to higher education. Its historic campus provides a setting matched by only a handful of other universities in the country. Students choose Ohio University mainly because of its academic strength, but the beautiful setting and college-town atmosphere are also factors in their decision. Ohio University is the central focus of Athens, Ohio, located approximately 75 miles southeast of Columbus. We encourage prospective students to come for a visit and experience the beauty and academic excellence of Ohio University.

"Ohio University—Athens: Freshman applicants for fall 2006 are required to take either the new version of the SAT or the ACT (with Writing). However, we will allow students to submit scores from the old version of the SAT (prior to March 2005) or ACT as well, and will use the student's best scores from either test."

SELECTIVITY

Admissions Rating	**77**
# of applicants	12,417
% of applicants accepted	86
% of acceptees attending	36
# accepting a place on wait list	296
% admitted from wait list	100

FRESHMAN PROFILE

Range SAT Verbal	490-600
Average SAT Verbal	550
Range SAT Math	490-600
Average SAT Math	550
**TPR Projected Range SAT Writing*	*550-630*
Range ACT Composite	20-25
Average ACT Composite	23
Average HS GPA	3.44
% graduated top 10% of class	17
% graduated top 25% of class	47
% graduated top 50% of class	86

DEADLINES

Regular application deadline	2/1
Regular notification	rolling
Nonfall registration?	yes

APPLICANTS ALSO LOOK AT AND OFTEN PREFER

Bowling Green State University
Kent State University—Kent Campus
Miami University
Ohio State University—Columbus

AND SOMETIMES PREFER

Oberlin College
University of Cincinnati
University of Dayton
Wittenberg University

FINANCIAL FACTS

Financial Aid Rating	**63**
Annual in-state tuition	$7,404
Annual out-of-state tuition	$15,396
Room & Board	$7,539
Books and supplies	$840
% frosh rec. need-based scholarship or grant aid	23
% UG rec. need-based scholarship or grant aid	23
% frosh rec. need-based self-help aid	44
% UG rec. need-based self-help aid	43
Avg. frosh grant	$4,606
Independent 529 member?	No

OHIO WESLEYAN UNIVERSITY

ADMISSIONS OFFICE, 61 SOUTH SANDUSKY STREET, DELAWARE, OH 43015 • ADMISSIONS: 740-368-3020 • FAX: 740-368-3314

CAMPUS LIFE

Quality of Life Rating	**77**
Fire Safety Rating	**60**
Type of school	private
Affiliation	Methodist
Environment	town

STUDENTS

Total undergrad enrollment	1,917
% male/female	47/53
% from out of state	41
% from public high school	75
% live on campus	84
% in (# of) fraternities	40 (11)
% in (# of) sororities	28 (6)
% African American	4
% Asian	2
% Caucasian	82
% Hispanic	1
% international	9
# of countries represented	47

SURVEY SAYS

Small classes
Lab facilities are great
Students are friendly
Students are happy
Lots of beer drinking

ACADEMICS

Academic Rating	**82**
Calendar	semester
Student/faculty ratio	13:1
Professors interesting rating	81
Professors accessible rating	82
% professors teaching UG courses	100
% classes taught by TAs	0
Most common lab size	10-19 students
Most common regular class size	10-19 students

MOST POPULAR MAJORS

Business/managerial economics
psychology
zoology/animal biology

STUDENTS SPEAK OUT

Academics

Students love the academic approach at Ohio Wesleyan University (OWU), where their curriculum leads them to discover "how various disciplines can be integrated to form a greater whole, how to question what we know, and how to critically analyze the world around us." As one student put it, "The overall experience at OWU is one of practicum," a constant focus on practical application of advanced theory. Students also brag of the "countless opportunities and experiences in a variety of fields waiting for students" at OWU. "If there's something you want," explained one student, "all you have to do is ask and someone will help you get it." Undergrads warn that "while classes can be tough, professors really want you to succeed and truly learn the material." Instructors are truly mentors. "Their real reason for being here is to teach," students agree. "They may also do research, but that is secondary, and they always use us (undergrad students) to assist with any research (which looks great on our resumes)." Noted one student, "It's incredible to walk around campus and have both faculty and administrators call you by your first name. I've been able to develop great relationships with professors, which has allowed me to learn so much more on a personal level." Students also praise the "great new science center" and note that "by next semester, we are supposed to be optically connected, which should [make] our Internet run much [more smoothly]."

Life

OWU students "want to have a good time, but are very studious when it comes to class work. Students have their priorities straight at OWU." Once they've fulfilled their academic obligations, though, undergrads feel free to cut loose. Most agree that "Ohio Wesleyan always has a variety of things going on. If you really like the party scene, you can find that, but if you are not looking for that, there are many things that you can do instead." While "Greek life is popular, the Student Activities Board provides an enormous amount of fun options" away from Frat Row, as the board is "very in tune with students' wishes. They provide free movies once a month at the local movie theater and get bands to play at our Springfest concert." Undergrads also have "tons of clubs to choose from." Reports one, "There are clubs that are religious in nature: Tauheed (Islamic), Hillel (Jewish), Methodist Student Movement and many others. I think these groups enrich life on campus far beyond any other aspect." Students here are "very community-service oriented. There are many opportunities for students to be engaged in serving the community in Delaware, Columbus, and pretty much anywhere in the world (every Spring Break Mission Week allows that)." Hometown Delaware gets poor marks, but OWU's proximity to OSU and Columbus eases the pain.

Student Body

OWU is home to a "diverse group of students, especially for a school with" less than 2,000 undergraduates. "The student body prides itself on its diversity. Because of this, we enjoy a gamut of ethnic clubs and social events. It creates an atmosphere in which you can learn, not only about the richness of other cultures, but more about yourself as well." The student body includes "a large international student population, which fits in wonderfully on our campus: a lot of brilliantly smart Pakistani and Indian kids," as well as "Ohio kids and a surprisingly large population from Connecticut." One thing students here share in common: they are "involved, involved, involved in many student clubs, community service organizations, and other groups."

OHIO WESLEYAN UNIVERSITY

FINANCIAL AID: 740-368-3050 • E-MAIL: OWUADMIT@OWU.EDU • WEBSITE: WWW.OWU.EDU

ADMISSIONS

Very important factors considered include: Character/personal qualities, essays, interview, recommendations, secondary school record. *Important factors considered include:* Alumni/ae relation, class rank, extracurricular activities, geographical residence, minority status, standardized test scores, talent/ability, volunteer work. *Other factors considered include:* Work experience. SAT Reasoning or ACT required. SAT Subject Tests recommended. TOEFL required of all international applicants. High school diploma is required, and GED is accepted. *Academic units required:* 4 English, 3 math, 3 science, 3 foreign language, 3 social studies. *Academic units recommended:* 4 math, 4 science, 4 foreign language, 4 social studies.

The Inside Word

OWU's competitive admit rate results in a strong candidate pool. The university received a record number of applications last year. Students need to put some thought into the completion of their applications. OWU's thorough admissions process definitely focuses on the personal side of all candidates; everyone who applies gets the attention they deserve.

FINANCIAL AID

Students should submit: FAFSA, institution's own financial aid form. Regular filing deadline is 5/1. The Princeton Review suggests that all financial aid forms be submitted as soon as possible after 1/1. *Need-based scholarships/grants offered:* Pell, SEOG, state scholarships/grants, private scholarships, the school's own gift aid. *Loan aid offered:* FFEL Subsidized Stafford, FFEL Unsubsidized Stafford, FFEL PLUS, Federal Perkins, state loans, college/university loans from institutional funds. Applicants will be notified of awards on a rolling basis beginning on or about 2/15. Federal Work-study Program available. Institutional employment available. Off-campus job opportunities are excellent.

FROM THE ADMISSIONS OFFICE

"Balance describes Ohio Wesleyan. Males make up 47 percent of the student body, while females make up 54 percent. There are 40 percent of all students who are members of Greek life. Twelve percent of all students are international and 8 percent of them are U.S. minorities. Exceptional teaching and academics are hallmarks of an OWU education, and features such as the Woltemade Center for Economics, Business and Entrepreneurship, and the Arneson Institute for Practical Politics set us apart from other institutions of our kind. OWU houses a newly renovated $34 million science center and newly renovated fine art facilities. Our mission places a premium on community service learning and practical experience with more than 85 percent of students participating in community service activities before graduation. Our annual Sagan National Colloquium is a semester-long program that brings leaders in academics, business, science, and the arts to campus for lectures, panel discussions, readings exhibits, and performances related to a selected topic of importance to the community and the world. Ohio Wesleyan University is a competitive member of NCAA Division III and the North Coast Athletic Conference, with three National Championships in soccer in the last six years.

"Ohio Wesleyan is located in a small town setting and is near Columbus, the state capital and the sixteenth largest city in the United States.

"Applicants for fall 2006 may submit the old SAT (taken before March 2005), the new SAT, or both. Best scores from either test will be considered in the application review. Additionally, students may submit the ACT in lieu of the SAT."

SELECTIVITY

Admissions Rating	**85**
# of applicants	2,803
% of applicants accepted	74
% of acceptees attending	27
# accepting a place on wait list	37
% admitted from wait list	51
# of early decision applicants	43
% accepted early decision	86

FRESHMAN PROFILE

Range SAT Verbal	550-660
Average SAT Verbal	606
Range SAT Math	560-660
Average SAT Math	605
**TPR Projected Range SAT Writing*	*600-670*
Range ACT Composite	24-28
Average ACT Composite	27
Minimum Paper TOEFL	550
Minimum Computer Based TOEFL	213
Average HS GPA	3.4
% graduated top 10% of class	28
% graduated top 25% of class	54
% graduated top 50% of class	79

DEADLINES

Early decision application deadline	12/1
Early decision notification	12/30
Regular notification	rolling
Nonfall registration?	yes

APPLICANTS ALSO LOOK AT

AND OFTEN PREFER

American University, Cornell University, Harvard College

AND SOMETIMES PREFER

Gettysburg College, Wheaton College (MA)

AND RARELY PREFER

The College of Wooster, Denison University, Kenyon College, Miami University

FINANCIAL FACTS

Financial Aid Rating	**81**
Annual tuition	$26,460
Room & Board	$7,330
Books and supplies	$2,050
Required fees	$360
% frosh rec. need-based scholarship or grant aid	60
% UG rec. need-based scholarship or grant aid	57
% frosh rec. need-based self-help aid	50
% UG rec. need-based self-help aid	47
% frosh rec. any financial aid	96
% UG rec. any financial aid	96
Avg. frosh grant	$13,338
Avg. frosh loan	$4,606
Independent 529 member?	Yes

PENNSYLVANIA STATE UNIVERSITY—UNIVERSITY PARK

201 SHIELDS BUILDING, BOX 3000, UNIVERSITY PARK, PA 16802-3000 • ADMISSIONS: 814-865-5471 • FAX: 814-863-7590

CAMPUS LIFE

Quality of Life Rating	**83**
Fire Safety Rating	**60**
Type of school	public
Environment	village

STUDENTS

Total undergrad enrollment	33,958
% male/female	53/47
% from out of state	23
% live on campus	38
% in (# of) fraternities	13 (55)
% in (# of) sororities	10 (25)
% African American	4
% Asian	6
% Caucasian	84
% Hispanic	3
% international	2

SURVEY SAYS

Great library
Athletic facilities are great
Everyone loves the Nittany Lions
Intramural sports are popular
Frats and sororities dominate social scene
Student publications are popular
Lots of beer drinking
Hard liquor is popular

ACADEMICS

Academic Rating	**75**
Calendar	semester
Student/faculty ratio	17:1
Professors interesting rating	65
Professors accessible rating	66
% classes taught by TAs	0
Most common lab size	20-29 students
Most common regular class size	20-29 students

STUDENTS SPEAK OUT

Academics

State universities are typically gigantic institutions, and they fall into two broad categories: the type that students grumblingly trundle through, and the type that students absolutely love. Penn State is of the latter variety. It is one of those gargantuan schools that somehow instills a profound pride of place in its undergraduates. Students brag of "top-notch facilities and academics, superior sports programs, an excellent social scene, and the beautiful campus and friendly college town atmosphere. All these make PSU second-to-none in the U.S. for overall undergraduate experience." Even the common complaints about large schools are soft-pedaled by students. One tells us, "People say that 'you are only a number at Penn State.' I would like to clarify this and say that 'you are only a number if you choose to be a number.'" Another student agrees with this sentiment: "Penn State is stereotyped as a school with little access to faculty, but that is farthest from the truth. Faculty and such go out of their way to help with your needs." Perhaps the greatest source of student satisfaction, however, is the "incredible alumni network. We have the number one dues-paying alumni network in the world, with over 146,000 members." No wonder "Penn State is known as Happy Valley, and nothing describes this place better."

Life

"With 35,000 students, there's never a dull moment" at Penn State, where there are "opportunities to get involved with anything you can ever imagine. Even though it's a large school, if you get involved, it does not seem big at all." Topping students' lists of favorite activities is "Penn State football, which definitely takes over the campus during the fall semester. Sports in Happy Valley are huge!" Partying is a close second. Undergraduates report that "every night revolves around which fraternities are hosting parties, and which other organizations are invited that night. Independents get to drink for free, and there are no cover charges." The University offers a nonalcoholic option (called Late Night Penn State), "but that usually involves cotton candy and the pathetic theater clubs singing songs from their latest shows. It's more fun to sit in your room and watch TV." On-campus concerts are a better alternative, since "world-class artists such as Aerosmith, Garth Brooks, Cher, and the Red Hot Chili Peppers can be seen at the Bryce Jordan Center, number one among ticket sales for a college venue in the world." Of course, it's not all fun and games; students have to study, too. "The workload is a lot, but there's enough time to get it done before it's time to go out and party," students cheerfully report. Is there anything about PSU they don't love? "The weather sucks at University Park! It snows from October through April and rains any other time," offers one undergraduate.

Student Body

There are many towns in the United States with populations smaller than the undergraduate count at PSU, so it's not surprising that "you will find almost every type of student you can imagine here." While "the majority are white and middle class, there are also thousands of international students here from countries such as China, India, and Japan, and a large African American population as well." The diversity leads one student to conclude, "If a student complains about not having any friends at Penn State, they are just antisocial." While undergraduates come in all shapes, shades, and sizes, the archetypal Nittany Lion is "white, in good shape, into the party scene, preppy or a jock, and pretty all-American." Most students agree that "students of different races don't interact often. It's not because they don't want to or are rude to one another, they just don't tend to mix all that much."

FINANCIAL AID: 814-865-6301 • E-MAIL: ADMISSIONS@PSU.EDU • WEBSITE: WWW.PSU.EDU

ADMISSIONS

Very important factors considered include: Secondary school record, standardized test scores. *Other factors considered include:* Alumni/ae relation, character/personal qualities, class rank, essays, extracurricular activities, recommendations, talent/ability, volunteer work, work experience. SAT Reasoning or ACT required. TOEFL required of all international applicants. High school diploma is required, and GED is accepted. *Academic units required:* 4 English, 3 math, 3 science, 2 foreign language, 3 social studies.

The Inside Word

Penn State is deluged with applicants (they claim to receive more SAT score reports than any other college in the country), which makes it especially important for candidates to have better-than-average grades and test scores. Although a personal essay and information on extracurricular activities are requested, the university's formula focuses on the numbers. At schools this large it's hard for the admissions process to be more individualized.

FINANCIAL AID

Students should submit: FAFSA. The Princeton Review suggests that all financial aid forms be submitted as soon as possible after 1/1. *Need-based scholarships/grants offered:* Pell, SEOG, state scholarships/grants, private scholarships, the school's own gift aid. *Loan aid offered:* FFEL Subsidized Stafford, FFEL Unsubsidized Stafford, FFEL PLUS, Federal Perkins, college/university loans from institutional funds, private loans. Applicants will be notified of awards on a rolling basis beginning on or about 2/15. Federal Work-study Program available. Off-campus job opportunities are good.

FROM THE ADMISSIONS OFFICE

"Unique among large public universities, Penn State combines the nearly 35,000-student setting of its University Park campus with 20 academically and administratively integrated undergraduate locations—small-college settings ranging in size from 600 to 3,400 students. Each year, more than 60 percent of incoming freshmen begin their studies at these residential and commuter campuses, while nearly 40 percent begin at the University Park Campus. The smaller locations focus on the needs of new students by offering the first two years of most Penn State baccalaureate degrees in settings that stress close interaction with faculty. Depending on the major selected, students may choose to complete their degree at University Park or one of the smaller locations. Your application to Penn State qualifies you for review for any of our campuses. Your two choices of location are reviewed in the order given. Entrance difficulty is based, in part, on the demand. Due to its popularity, the University Park campus is the most competitive for admission.

"Freshman applicants for fall 2006 may submit the results from the current version of the SAT, the current ACT, the new version of the SAT, or the results of the new ACT with Writing Test. The Writing portions of these tests will not necessarily be factored into admission decisions."

SELECTIVITY

Admissions Rating	**90**
# of applicants	30,122
% of applicants accepted	58
% of acceptees attending	34

FRESHMAN PROFILE

Range SAT Verbal	530-630
Average SAT Verbal	593
Range SAT Math	560-660
Average SAT Math	617
**TPR Projected Range SAT Writing*	*580-650*
Minimum Paper TOEFL	550
Average HS GPA	3.56
% graduated top 10% of class	41
% graduated top 25% of class	80
% graduated top 50% of class	98

DEADLINES

Regular notification	rolling
Nonfall registration?	yes

APPLICANTS ALSO LOOK AT AND OFTEN PREFER

Carnegie Mellon University
Cornell University
Lehigh University
University of Maryland—College Park
University of Michigan—Ann Arbor

AND SOMETIMES PREFER

Emory University
Georgetown University
Harvard College
Johns Hopkins University
University of Virginia

FINANCIAL FACTS

Financial Aid Rating	**64**
Annual in-state tuition	$9,374
Annual out-of-state tuition	$19,286
Room & Board	$6,230
Books and supplies	$992
Required fees	$448
% frosh rec. need-based scholarship or grant aid	27
% UG rec. need-based scholarship or grant aid	30
% frosh rec. need-based self-help aid	40
% UG rec. need-based self-help aid	43
Avg. frosh grant	$2,800
Avg. frosh loan	$3,193
Independent 529 member?	No

PEPPERDINE UNIVERSITY

24255 PACIFIC COAST HIGHWAY, MALIBU, CA 90263-4392 • ADMISSIONS: 310-456-4861 • FAX: 310-506-4861

CAMPUS LIFE

Quality of Life Rating	**96**
Fire Safety Rating	**60**
Type of school	private
Affiliation	Church of Christ
Environment	village

STUDENTS

Total undergrad enrollment	3,115
% male/female	44/56
% from out of state	48
% live on campus	49
% in (# of) fraternities	15 (6)
% in (# of) sororities	15 (8)
% African American	7
% Asian	10
% Caucasian	55
% Hispanic	11
% Native American	1
% international	6

SURVEY SAYS

Lab facilities are great
Dorms are like palaces
Campus feels safe
Students are happy

ACADEMICS

Academic Rating	**89**
Calendar	semester
Student/faculty ratio	12:1
Professors interesting rating	92
Professors accessible rating	89
% professors teaching UG courses	100
% classes taught by TAs	0
Most common lab size	20-29 students
Most common regular class size	10-19 students

MOST POPULAR MAJORS

Business administration/management
organizational communication
psychology

STUDENTS SPEAK OUT

Academics

"Combining great academic integrity and a sublime location with Christian morals and school spirit," Pepperdine University "integrates faith and learning and develops leaders with high goals and high regard for humanity," students at this Church of Christ school tell us. With its posh Malibu setting and its reputation for wealthy students, Pepp is regarded as "Club Med with church and professors" by a number of its students. The school differs from Club Med, though, in at least one significant way; everyone who comes here is expected to work, and work hard, throughout his or her four-year tenure. Pepp's "challenging curriculum" includes required classes in the classics; reports one student, "No class has influenced my life as much as the Great Books classes. They consistently challenged my beliefs and made me intellectually sounder. It's a lot of work, but for an even bigger payoff." Undergrads love the study abroad program, which "the school has perfected. If you are on the fence about coming to Pepperdine, talk to any student who has been overseas." Writes one student, "My two semesters in Buenos Aires was a great learning, as well as life, experience." Students here happily report that "an overwhelming majority of professors are wonderful in every way; they are not only amazingly smart, but also good, nice people," and that "the school's administration is deeply concerned for the students, and their dedication is evident through their attitudes and willingness to help students."

Life

Pepperdine is located in Malibu, "a wonderful place to take a vacation, or to live if you're really rich." It's not such a great college setting, although it's not without its assets. Writes one student, "Even though it's a pain to drive into LA all the time, it's nice to retreat back to Pepperdine. When visiting UCLA or USC, there is so much noise and so many people. It's refreshing to call serene Pepperdine home." Also, "It is fun seeing celebrities at Blockbuster or in their pajamas at the drug store, and you couldn't ask for a more beautiful place to have a university," especially given the ocean view from many dorm rooms. Still, "there is nothing to do in Malibu except eat at expensive restaurants and go to the beach, and the town virtually shuts down at 10 P.M.," so "you have to head into LA to do anything that would be considered nightlife." On campus, "The quality of life is unmatched. There are spacious dorms with private bathrooms and working gas fireplaces. The sprinklers keep the grass green. People unfamiliar with campus often mistake it for a country club." Religious students happily report that "worship and religion opportunities are offered daily. Also, campus ministries provide a lot of opportunities for spiritual growth and fellowship with God, but the spiritual atmosphere isn't suffocating. It's there, but it isn't forced upon the students." Aesthetes add that "there's also a lot going on with fine arts, whether it's the museum or the theater."

Student Body

Conspicuous displays of wealth are not uncommon at Pepperdine, where "the latest must-have item is always in abundance and often precedes the national trend. There are plenty of Louis Vuitton purses, Ugg boots and Chanel sunglasses. Even the guys here wear Seven jeans." Explains one undergrad, many of the students "come from wealthy families and arrive on campus in Mercedes and are wearing the latest clothes they picked up on Rodeo Drive," seem bewildered by some of the obnoxious, flowing displays of wealth." Rich or poor, most students here are "very much Republicans and not afraid to defend their political stances." Some here tell us that "the biggest dividing line on campus is probably religion. Pepperdine draws many conservative Christians, but also attracts those without faith, and often these students feel out of place [during] required convocations, where prayer and worship songs are included."

PEPPERDINE UNIVERSITY

FINANCIAL AID: 310-506-4301 • E-MAIL: ADMISSION-SEAVER@PEPPERDINE.EDU • WEBSITE: WWW.PEPPERDINE.EDU

ADMISSIONS

Very important factors considered include: Character/personal qualities, essays, extracurricular activities, recommendations, religious affiliation/commitment, secondary school record, standardized test scores. *Important factors considered include:* Talent/ability, volunteer work. *Other factors considered include:* Alumni/ae relation, interview, minority status, work experience. SAT Reasoning or ACT required. TOEFL required of all international applicants. High school diploma is required, and GED is accepted. *Academic units recommended:* 4 English, 4 math, 4 science, 3 foreign language, 3 social studies, 3 history, 2 academic electives.

The Inside Word

A stunning physical location enables the admissions office to produce beautiful catalogs and viewbooks, which, when combined with the university's reputation for academic quality, help to attract a large applicant pool. In addition to solid grades and test scores, successful applicants typically have well-rounded extracurricular backgrounds. Involvement in school, church, and community is an overused cliché in the world of college admissions, but at Pepperdine it's definitely one of the ingredients in successful applications.

FINANCIAL AID

Students should submit: FAFSA, institution's own financial aid form. Regular filing deadline is 2/15. The Princeton Review suggests that all financial aid forms be submitted as soon as possible after 1/1. *Need-based scholarships/grants offered:* Pell, SEOG, state scholarships/grants, private scholarships, the school's own gift aid. *Loan aid offered:* FFEL Subsidized Stafford, FFEL Unsubsidized Stafford, FFEL PLUS, Federal Perkins, state loans, college/university loans from institutional funds. Applicants will be notified of awards on or about 4/1. Federal Work-study Program available. Institutional employment available. Off-campus job opportunities are excellent.

FROM THE ADMISSIONS OFFICE

"As a selective university, Pepperdine seeks students who show promise of academic achievement at the collegiate level. However, we also seek students who are committed to serving the university community, as well as others with whom they come into contact. We look for community service activities, volunteer efforts, and strong leadership qualities, as well as a demonstrated commitment to academic studies and an interest in the liberal arts.

"The school has not yet determined how its testing policy will be affected by the new Writing section of the SAT."

SELECTIVITY

Admissions Rating	**95**
# of applicants	5,503
% of applicants accepted	37
% of acceptees attending	39
# accepting a place on wait list	719
% admitted from wait list	1

FRESHMAN PROFILE

Range SAT Verbal	550-660
Average SAT Verbal	612
Range SAT Math	580-680
Average SAT Math	628
**TPR Projected Range SAT Writing*	*600-670*
Range ACT Composite	24-29
Average ACT Composite	26
Minimum Paper TOEFL	550
Minimum Computer Based TOEFL	220
Average HS GPA	3.61
% graduated top 10% of class	72
% graduated top 25% of class	95
% graduated top 50% of class	99

DEADLINES

Regular notification	4/1
Nonfall registration?	yes

APPLICANTS ALSO LOOK AT

AND OFTEN PREFER

Stanford University, University of California—Los Angeles, University of California—Santa Barbara, University of Pennsylvania, University of San Diego, University of Southern California

AND SOMETIMES PREFER

New York University, Santa Clara University, University of California—Berkeley, University of California—Irvine, University of California—San Diego, Vanderbilt University

AND RARELY PREFER

Biola University, Chapman University, Gonzaga University

FINANCIAL FACTS

Financial Aid Rating	**79**
Annual tuition	$26,280
Room & Board	$7,930
Books and supplies	$500
Required fees	$90
% frosh rec. need-based scholarship or grant aid	54
% UG rec. need-based scholarship or grant aid	51
% frosh rec. need-based self-help aid	45
% UG rec. need-based self-help aid	43
Avg. frosh grant	$30,548
Avg. frosh loan	$5,554
Independent 529 member?	Yes

Pitzer College

1050 North Mills Avenue, Claremont, CA 91711-6101 • Admissions: 909-621-8129 • Fax: 909-621-8770

CAMPUS LIFE

Quality of Life Rating	**88**
Fire Safety Rating	**60**
Type of school	private
Environment	village

STUDENTS

Total undergrad enrollment	927
% male/female	41/59
% from out of state	43
% live on campus	73
% African American	6
% Asian	10
% Caucasian	44
% Hispanic	13
% Native American	1
% international	2
# of countries represented	9

SURVEY SAYS

Small classes
Great library
Students are friendly
Students are happy
Frats and sororities are unpopular or nonexistent
Political activism is popular

ACADEMICS

Academic Rating	**94**
Calendar	semester
Student/faculty ratio	11:1
Professors interesting rating	97
Professors accessible rating	88
% professors teaching UG courses	100
% classes taught by TAs	0
Most common regular class size	10-19 students

MOST POPULAR MAJORS

Fine arts and art studies
psychology
sociology

STUDENTS SPEAK OUT

Academics

Pitzer College is the lovably quirky member of the Claremont College system, a repository of individualism and unconventional education in this otherwise traditional consortium. Notes one satisfied undergrad, "No one tells you what to do or how much to read; everyone just does it because they want to, because they enjoy the material, and because they want to learn." Those who adapt to the system love how "It is very easy to design your own course work, curriculum, and major. You have to take the initiative to control your education here, and that is one of the aspects of Pitzer that truly enables students to grow and mature as individuals." You won't be going it totally alone, though. Pitzer's professors "make it a point to be available for students by keeping regular office hours, making appointments outside of those hours if necessary [and] inviting students to their homes for end of the semester gatherings." This inclusive spirit extends to the school's administration as well; undergrads are "involved with decisions made by the board of trustees! The President invites students to sit on committees to make important decisions like facilitating the college's master plan, building new dorms, redesigning the dining halls, or reviewing professors." Sums up one undergrad, "Pitzer is about constantly questioning the status quo and the mainstream, constantly thinking about better alternatives or creative solutions, and constantly reevaluating the way you see yourself, your community, and the world around you."

Life

Between the Five Cs (i.e. the Claremont College Consortium) and Los Angeles, Pitzer students enjoy a wealth of entertainment and enrichment options. Partiers report that "You can count on a major party on one of the campuses every night except Sunday. Nights generally start with friends just hanging out or 'pre-gaming' in dorms and then heading out to one of the on campus parties. Since there is no frat scene, the parties are open to all students. Room parties are also popular." Those looking for something a little more intellectually stimulating "watch movies, take in a guest lecture, hang at the coffee shop, or sit around and play board games." Los Angeles is a popular destination "for music and sporting events, and the LA beaches (Laguna Beach is closest) are only 45 minutes away. They're popular for surfing and sun-bathing all year long." Students generally don't hang around the surrounding community of Claremont, "a cute town, but one that's not there to quench your rebellion, so you can't rely on it for dancing or partying. If you'd like to look at antiques or shop for the newest herbal teas, Claremont Village is the place to be." Students caution that "our dorms are getting old and look even older than they really are. But they're comfortable, fairly spacious, and economical for the school."

Student Body

The typical Pitzer undergrad tends to be "passionate, creative, dynamic, and socially involved. Even the so-called 'jock' sub-group volunteers to mentor young people in the surrounding area and are capable of passionately debating some issue of importance." Almost everyone here "is aware of what's going on in the world and in politics, and is likely to be left wing politically." Pitzer has long had the reputation of a 'hippie' school, and while "there are still remnants of hippies around, walking around with no shoes, no shaving (for guys or girls), caring about the environment, these days there are more preppy people wearing Abercrombie and sipping chai tea." No matter what demographic they fit, "Pitzer students tend to be really laid back (not judgmental or snobby). You don't have to spend ridiculous amounts of money buying 'fashionable' clothing if you don't want to, because stuff like that doesn't impress people here. It's nice to leave all the horrible things about high school in high school and just relax for a few years."

FINANCIAL AID: 909-621-8208 • E-MAIL: ADMISSION@PITZER.EDU • WEBSITE: WWW.PITZER.EDU

ADMISSIONS

Very important factors considered include: Class rank, essays, recommendations, secondary school record. *Important factors considered include:* Character/personal qualities, extracurricular activities, minority status, talent/ability, volunteer work. *Other factors considered include:* Alumni/ae relation, geographical residence, interview, standardized test scores, state residency, work experience. TOEFL required of all international applicants. High school diploma is required, and GED is accepted. *Academic units recommended:* 4 English, 3 math, 3 science (3 science lab), 3 foreign language, 2 social studies, 1 history.

The Inside Word

This is a place where applicants can feel confident in letting their thoughts flow freely on admissions essays. Not only does the committee read them (a circumstance more rare in college admissions than one is led to believe), but also they've set up the process to emphasize them! Thus, what you have to say for yourself will go much further than numbers in determining your suitability for Pitzer. Paying greater attention to essays also helps Pitzer create a dynamic and engaging freshman class each year.

FINANCIAL AID

Students should submit: FAFSA, CSS/Financial Aid PROFILE, state aid form, noncustodial (divorced/separated) parents' statement, business/farm supplement. Regular filing deadline is 2/1. The Princeton Review suggests that all financial aid forms be submitted as soon as possible after 1/1. *Need-based scholarships/grants offered:* Pell, SEOG, state scholarships/grants, private scholarships, the school's own gift aid. *Loan aid offered:* FFEL Subsidized Stafford, FFEL Unsubsidized Stafford, FFEL PLUS, Federal Perkins, college/university loans from institutional funds. Applicants will be notified of awards on or about 4/1. Federal Work-study Program available. Institutional employment available. Off-campus job opportunities are fair.

FROM THE ADMISSIONS OFFICE

"Pitzer is about opportunities. It's about possibilities. The students who come here are looking for something different from the usual 'take two courses from column A, two courses from column B, and two courses from column C.' That kind of arbitrary selection doesn't make a satisfying education at Pitzer. So we look for students who want to have an impact on their own education, who want the chief responsibility—with help from their faculty advisors—in designing their own futures.

"Pitzer College allows applicants to choose from a variety of required admission credentials, including standardized tests (i.e. ACT and SAT). We will accept the old SAT, the new SAT, the ACT, and the ACT with the Writing component from students applying for fall 2006 who choose to use this option."

SELECTIVITY

Admissions Rating	**92**
# of applicants	2,670
% of applicants accepted	47
% of acceptees attending	17
# accepting a place on wait list	195
% admitted from wait list	8

FRESHMAN PROFILE

Range SAT Verbal	580-680
Range SAT Math	570-650
**TPR Projected Range SAT Writing*	*620-680*
Minimum Paper TOEFL	587
Minimum Computer Based TOEFL	240
Average HS GPA	3.58
% graduated top 10% of class	45
% graduated top 25% of class	75
% graduated top 50% of class	92

DEADLINES

Regular application deadline	1/15
Regular notification	4/1
Nonfall registration?	no

APPLICANTS ALSO LOOK AT AND OFTEN PREFER

Claremont McKenna College
Occidental College
Pomona College
Scripps College
University of California—Berkeley
University of California—Los Angeles
University of Southern California

AND SOMETIMES PREFER

Boston University
Colorado College
Lewis & Clark College
New York University,
Whitman College

FINANCIAL FACTS

Financial Aid Rating	**98**
Annual tuition	$28,112
Room & Board	$8,222
Books and supplies	$900
% frosh rec. need-based scholarship or grant aid	27
% UG rec. need-based scholarship or grant aid	39
% frosh rec. need-based self-help aid	26
% UG rec. need-based self-help aid	38
% frosh rec. any financial aid	28
% UG rec. any financial aid	38
Avg. frosh grant	$24,458
Avg. frosh loan	$4,913
Independent 529 member?	Yes

Pomona College

333 North College Way, Claremont, CA 91711-6312 • Admissions: 909-621-8134 • Fax: 909-621-8952

CAMPUS LIFE

Quality of Life Rating	**95**
Fire Safety Rating	**60**
Type of school	private
Environment	village

STUDENTS

Total undergrad enrollment	1,540
% male/female	50/50
% from out of state	65
% from public high school	60
% live on campus	97
% in (# of) fraternities	3 (4)
% African American	6
% Asian	13
% Caucasian	56
% Hispanic	9
% international	2
# of countries represented	16

SURVEY SAYS

Small classes
No one cheats
Lab facilities are great
Great library
Students are friendly
Dorms are like palaces

ACADEMICS

Academic Rating	**97**
Calendar	semester
Student/faculty ratio	8:1
Professors interesting rating	89
Professors accessible rating	85
% professors teaching UG courses	100
% classes taught by TAs	0
Most common lab size	10-19 students
Most common regular class size	10-19 students

MOST POPULAR MAJORS

Biology/biological sciences
economics
English language and literature

STUDENTS SPEAK OUT

Academics

In the words of its students, Pomona offers "the best atmosphere available to college students in the United States." This pint-sized school has that "small college atmosphere"—but because it's part of a five-college consortium and allows cross-registration at all the other colleges (Claremont McKenna, Harvey Mudd, Pitzer, Scripps), students benefit from the "perfect combination" of a "small liberal arts education with the resources of a larger university." Students happily report that professors "devote their time almost exclusively to undergraduate education" and get to know their students on a personal level—"even outside of office hours." "I routinely get a page or two of feedback on my essays," reports a content student. This kind of attention seems to be the rule, not the exception. One double major tells us, "I know eight deans and associate deans on a first-name basis, and my experience is by no means unusual for PC students." How tightly are administrators involved in students' lives? Pretty tightly: "Some even live in the dorms!" "When I hear about my friends' experiences at large universities, I sometimes wonder how they can live the way they do," writes one senior. While a friendly, discussion-based atmosphere is the norm in most classrooms, students assure us that the academics are rigorous; simply put, "Pomona makes you think way too hard." Keep in mind, however, that a lot of that hard thinking "is done in bathing suits in the courtyards." There may be some sweating before exams, but the college strives to maintain "a collaborative environment rather than a competitive one"—and this keeps students productive and content.

Life

"Life is very chill" at Pomona College, where the average student "wears flip-flops year-round" and boasts impressive Frisbee skills. Social bonding begins in the first year through the popular "sponsor groups"—10 to 18 freshmen "sponsored" by two sophomores who help the newbies adjust to college life—a program which, students believe, is "one of our great strengths." The party scene is "focused around the five colleges, which provide a sufficient social scene for students most nights of the week. The college funds parties on weekends, so organizations can easily sponsor parties and get a hold of kegs. For fun, people will socialize at such parties, hang out with friends, and sometimes go explore the bigger LA scene." But while "alcohol is definitely a factor at Pomona…we have the option of substance-free housing, which is very popular, as well as sub-free events." "The mountains, the beach," and other "natural locales" are also equally accessible. No matter what students choose to do with their down time, however, they all have their priorities straight; writes one typical student, "People here seem to almost always be very responsible in terms of work before play."

Student Body

"That Southern California vibe" is alive and well at Pomona College. Students proudly report that Pomona undergrads "are all really friendly, helpful, polite, and take a liking to making new friends." But not everyone thinks Pomona students are as chill as they claim to be. "Don't believe the BS about students being laid-back at Pomona," writes a senior. "They are definitely intense and competitive." Whether edgy or easygoing, almost every student at Pomona has one thing in common: politically liberal leanings. "Lots of liberal superheroes out to change the world" is how one sophomore describes her schoolmates. The widespread liberalism makes it tough for "those who differ in political views," because they "can sometimes be made to feel uncomfortable." Liberal, conservative, or somewhere in between, however, Pomona undergraduates rate themselves as among "the happiest students in the country"—mostly because they know how to strike a healthy balance between work and play. Among all the things they love about their school, undergrads agree that "the students are the single best thing about Pomona College."

FINANCIAL AID: 909-621-8205 • E-MAIL: ADMISSIONS@POMONA.EDU • WEBSITE: WWW.POMONA.EDU

ADMISSIONS

Very important factors considered include: Character/personal qualities, class rank, essays, extracurricular activities, interview, recommendations, secondary school record, standardized test scores, talent/ability. *Other factors considered include:* Alumni/ae relation, geographical residence, minority status, volunteer work, work experience. SAT Reasoning and SAT Subject Tests or ACT required. TOEFL required of all international applicants. High school diploma or equivalent is not required. *Academic units required:* 4 English, 3 math, 3 science (2 science lab), 3 foreign language, 2 social studies. *Academic units recommended:* 4 English, 4 math, 3 science (2 science lab), 4 foreign language, 2 social studies.

The Inside Word

Even though it is tough to get admitted to Pomona, students will find the admissions staff to be accessible and engaging. An applicant pool full of such well-qualified students as those who typically apply, in combination with the college's small size, necessitates that candidates undergo as personal an admissions evaluation as possible. This is how solid matches are made and how Pomona does a commendable job of keeping an edge on the competition.

FINANCIAL AID

Students should submit: FAFSA, CSS/Financial Aid PROFILE, state aid form, noncustodial (divorced/separated) parents' statement, business/farm supplement, tax returns for both the student and parents. Regular filing deadline is 2/1. The Princeton Review suggests that all financial aid forms be submitted as soon as possible after 1/1. *Need-based scholarships/grants offered:* Pell, SEOG, state scholarships/grants, private scholarships, the school's own gift aid. *Loan aid offered:* FFEL Subsidized Stafford, FFEL Unsubsidized Stafford, FFEL PLUS, Federal Perkins, college/university loans from institutional funds. Applicants will be notified of awards on or about 4/10. Federal Work-study Program available. Institutional employment available. Off-campus job opportunities are fair.

FROM THE ADMISSIONS OFFICE

"Perhaps the most important thing to know about Pomona College is that we are what we say we are. There is enormous integrity between the statements of mission and philosophy governing the college and the reality that students, faculty, and administrators experience. The balance in the curriculum is unusual. Sciences, social sciences, humanities, and the arts receive equal attention, support, and emphasis. Most importantly, the commitment to undergraduate education is absolute. Teaching awards remain the highest honor the trustees can bestow upon faculty. The typical method of instruction is the seminar and the average class size of 14 offers students the opportunity to become full partners in the learning process. Our location in the Los Angeles basin and in Claremont, with five other colleges, provides a remarkable community.

"Pomona College requires either the new SAT plus two SAT Subject Tests (in different fields) OR the ACT. Scores from the old SAT (pre-March 2005) and the ACT are acceptable. For the old SAT, scores must be submitted with the results of three SAT Subject Tests, one of which must be the writing test."

SELECTIVITY

Admissions Rating	**99**
# of applicants	4,927
% of applicants accepted	20
% of acceptees attending	41
# of early decision applicants	123
% accepted early decision	31

FRESHMAN PROFILE

Range SAT Verbal	690-770
Average SAT Verbal	730
Range SAT Math	680-760
Average SAT Math	730
**TPR Projected Range SAT Writing*	*690-740*
Range ACT Composite	30-34
Average ACT Composite	32
Minimum Paper TOEFL	600
Minimum Computer Based TOEFL	250
Average HS GPA	3.9
% graduated top 10% of class	86
% graduated top 25% of class	99
% graduated top 50% of class	100

DEADLINES

Early decision application deadline	11/15
Early decision notification	12/15
Regular application deadline	1/2
Regular notification	4/10
Nonfall registration?	no

APPLICANTS ALSO LOOK AT AND OFTEN PREFER

Harvard College
Princeton University
Stanford University
University of California—Berkeley
Yale University

AND SOMETIMES PREFER

Claremont McKenna College
Dartmouth College
University of California—Los Angeles
Wesleyan University
Williams College

AND RARELY PREFER

Pitzer College
University of California—Davis

FINANCIAL FACTS

Financial Aid Rating	**99**
Annual tuition	$28,100
Room & Board	$10,380
Books and supplies	$850
% frosh rec. need-based scholarship or grant aid	52
% frosh rec. need-based self-help aid	52
% frosh rec. any financial aid	56
% UG rec. any financial aid	54
Avg. frosh grant	$23,500
Avg. frosh loan	$2,000
Independent 529 member?	Yes

PRINCETON UNIVERSITY

PO Box 430, Admission Office, Princeton, NJ 08544-0430 • Admissions: 609-258-3060 • Fax: 609-258-6743

CAMPUS LIFE

Quality of Life Rating	**98**
Fire Safety Rating	**88**
Type of school	private
Environment	village

STUDENTS

Total undergrad enrollment	4,678
% male/female	53/47
% from out of state	85
% from public high school	55
% live on campus	98
% African American	8
% Asian	13
% Caucasian	63
% Hispanic	7
% Native American	1
% international	8

SURVEY SAYS

No one cheats
Lab facilities are great
Great computer facilities
Great library
Athletic facilities are great
School is well run
Campus feels safe
Students are happy
Lots of beer drinking

ACADEMICS

Academic Rating	**88**
Calendar	semester
Student/faculty ratio	5:1
Professors interesting rating	85
Professors accessible rating	95
% professors teaching UG courses	56
% classes taught by TAs	0

MOST POPULAR MAJORS

English language and literature
history
political science and government

STUDENTS SPEAK OUT

Academics

Princeton undergrads are adamant that their school is the "best place to get an undergraduate education," boasting as it does "a combination of comprehensive resources, exceptional faculty, and brilliant students." Unlike many other prestigious universities, "the focus is all on undergraduate education" at Princeton, which has no business, law, or medical schools. There are fewer than 2,000 graduate students (all master's), enabling Princeton to ensure undergraduates access to "Nobel laureates who teach you and give you appointments" as well as "a wealth of academic, monetary, and social resources that students benefit from during and after their studies on campus." With fewer grads to elbow them out of the way, undergrads tell us that "the professors treat us like colleagues. They make themselves available and are intensely interested in the ideas of undergraduates." There is "an emphasis on independent undergraduate research, and funding is ample," as are resources at the library, which "has an amazing number and variety of books and other resources." The administration "truly runs like butter. From the application process to enrolling to being enrolled.... If you made an error in one of these processes, to my experience, it's sometimes corrected for you!" No wonder one Princeton undergrad sums up the experience here this way: "They spoil you with amazing resources, world-class professors, beautiful architecture, great people, fun social life, and the inability of the school to say no to anything that you want."

Life

Eating clubs, a phenomenon unique to Princeton, "are the center of social life" at this "country-club like school." One student explains how they work: "During day time, the club houses serve as a place for upperclassmen to dine. (You don't have to join one because they are a bit costly.) Clubs range from those permanently soaked in beer and alcohol to some that are the most pretentious things one may lay an eye on, with gold lined and embossed plates, cutlery and serviettes, and waiters to serve food to the students." All 11 eating clubs are located on Prospect Avenue, known to students simply as "the Street," and they function not only as dining halls but also as bars and party sites. Many hail the clubs "as great places to party because there is always somewhere to fit in. Because everyone parties on one street it is impossible to go out and not see someone you know." Others dismiss the clubs as "pretentious and pompous," especially the selective "bicker" clubs "in which current members choose new members," much as a Greek house screens pledges. Campus life tends to stay contained within the campus, as the surrounding town "closes up at 10 P.M.," but students are content with the situation. "Since everyone lives on campus and 'the Street' is so close, there is virtually no reason to need a car," explains one student. Adds another, "The best part is that even though Princeton is a small town, there is a train station on campus that takes you to Philly or New York in 45 minutes. Students use the 'dinky,' as the train's called, all the time."

Student Body

"Sure, Princeton's a bit East Coast preppy," undergrads here admit, "but everyone is unique and has her own style, which is totally welcomed and accepted. Princeton is a very kind, low-key, and charming place." It's also a place full of extremely accomplished people. Writes one student, "I have friends who are Presidential Scholars, stayed with the UN Secretary General in Paris over fall break, produced hip hop CDs, or represented different countries at the Olympics. Back home, I would have thought it amazing if I could meet just one of these people. If I stopped thinking of my friends as friends and thought of what they have accomplished, it's mind boggling, and a little humbling." Thanks to "a generous financial aid system," "not everyone is a spoiled rotten, BMW-driving, snooty rich kid. We have students from very diverse backgrounds."

FINANCIAL AID: 609-258-3330 • WEBSITE: WWW.PRINCETON.EDU

ADMISSIONS

Very important factors considered include: Character/personal qualities, class rank, essays, extracurricular activities, recommendations, secondary school record, standardized test scores, talent/ability. *Important factors considered include:* Alumni/ae relation, geographical residence, volunteer work, work experience. *Other factors considered include:* Interview, minority status. SAT Reasoning and SAT Subject Tests or ACT required. High school diploma or equivalent is not required. *Academic units recommended:* 4 English, 4 math, 3 science, 4 foreign language, 2 social studies, 2 history.

The Inside Word

Princeton is much more open about the admissions process than the rest of their Ivy compatriots. The admissions staff evaluates candidates' credentials using a 1–5 rating scale, common among highly selective colleges. Princeton's recommendation to interview should be considered a requirement, given the ultra-competitive nature of the applicant pool. In addition, three SAT Subject Tests are required; no joke, indeed.

FINANCIAL AID

Students should submit: FAFSA, institution's own financial aid form, noncustodial (divorced/separated) parents' statement. Regular filing deadline is 2/1. The Princeton Review suggests that all financial aid forms be submitted as soon as possible after 1/1. *Need-based scholarships/grants offered:* Pell, SEOG, state scholarships/grants, private scholarships, the school's own gift aid. *Loan aid offered:* FFEL Subsidized Stafford, FFEL Unsubsidized Stafford, FFEL PLUS, Federal Perkins, college/university loans from institutional funds. Applicants will be notified of awards on or about 4/1.

FROM THE ADMISSIONS OFFICE

"Methods of instruction [at Princeton] vary widely, but common to all areas is a strong emphasis on individual responsibility and the free interchange of ideas. This is displayed most notably in the wide use of preceptorials and seminars, in the provision of independent study for all upperclass students and qualified underclass students, and in the availability of a series of special programs to meet a range of individual interests. The undergraduate college encourages the student to be an independent seeker of information and to assume responsibility for gaining both knowledge and judgment that will strengthen later contributions to society.

"All applicants must submit results of either the new or old SAT, as well as SAT Subject Tests in three different subject areas. Students applying for the Class of 2010 and beyond will be required to submit results from the new version of the SAT."

SELECTIVITY

Admissions Rating	**99**
# of applicants	13,695
% of applicants accepted	13
% of acceptees attending	68
# accepting a place on wait list	1,045
% admitted from wait list	8
# of early decision applicants	581
% accepted early decision	32

FRESHMAN PROFILE

Range SAT Verbal	680-770
Range SAT Math	690-790
**TPR Projected Range SAT Writing*	*680-740*
Average HS GPA	3.83
% graduated top 10% of class	94
% graduated top 25% of class	99
% graduated top 50% of class	100

DEADLINES

Early decision application deadline	11/1
Early decision notification	12/15
Regular application deadline	11/1
Regular notification	4/4
Nonfall registration?	no

APPLICANTS ALSO LOOK AT AND SOMETIMES PREFER

Harvard College
Massachusetts Institute of Technology
Stanford University
Yale University

FINANCIAL FACTS

Financial Aid Rating	**99**
Annual tuition	$31,450
Room & Board	$8,763
Books and supplies	$990
% frosh rec. need-based scholarship or grant aid	52
% UG rec. need-based scholarship or grant aid	49
% frosh rec. need-based self-help aid	52
% UG rec. need-based self-help aid	49
% frosh rec. any financial aid	52
% UG rec. any financial aid	50
Avg. frosh grant	$26,500
Independent 529 member?	Yes

PROVIDENCE COLLEGE

RIVER AVENUE AND EATON STREET, PROVIDENCE, RI 02918 • ADMISSIONS: 401-865-2535 • FAX: 401-865-2826

CAMPUS LIFE

Quality of Life Rating	**72**
Fire Safety Rating	**96**
Type of school	private
Affiliation	Roman Catholic
Environment	city

STUDENTS

Total undergrad enrollment	4,125
% male/female	43/57
% from out of state	81
% from public high school	57
% live on campus	75
% African American	2
% Asian	2
% Caucasian	82
% Hispanic	2
% international	1
# of countries represented	18

SURVEY SAYS

Small classes
Diversity lacking on campus
Students are happy
Everyone loves the Friars
Intramural sports are popular
Frats and sororities are unpopular or nonexistent
Lots of beer drinking
Hard liquor is popular

ACADEMICS

Academic Rating	**83**
Calendar	semester
Student/faculty ratio	12:1
Professors interesting rating	79
Professors accessible rating	80
% professors teaching UG courses	100
% classes taught by TAs	0
Most common lab size	10-19 students
Most common regular class size	10-19 students

MOST POPULAR MAJORS

Business administration/management
marketing/marketing management
special education

STUDENTS SPEAK OUT

Academics

Providence College (PC), a small, Catholic, liberal arts school run by the Dominicans, is two schools in one. For the majority of students, it is a proving ground, an academic boot camp where success translates into "the ability to find work in their specialized fields very soon after graduation because of the school's reputation with employers." For a smaller group of students, it's the locus of intellectual fulfillment for its own sake. One student tells us, "Once I discovered the 10 percent of the students who are actually intellectually stimulating it became great." Nowhere is this divide more apparent than in students' attitude toward the Development of Western Civilization, a demanding two-year sequence of survey courses covering the canon of "great books" as well as the history of the arts. Many here dismiss the sequence as a waste of time. Others however, praise this centerpiece of the curriculum, telling us that it "is taught in such a way that makes me want to learn more and apply what I learn to my own life. I feel like I am not only growing as a student, but as a person." As an added bonus, students tell us, "The traditional CIV scream at midnight in the quad the night before the CIV final can make it worth the work. Fireworks, streaking, water-balloon fights, you get the picture." Those considering PC should know that this is a serious Catholic school, as one student explains, "This school has a very Catholic influence. In CIV, for example, philosophy is studied as how it can be applied to the Catholic belief. Plus, the core requirements are very Catholic-centered."

Life

Students laughingly and lovingly refer to PC as "Party College," telling us "the school definitely lives up to its nickname." Most students, "whether of age or not, go to local bars to hang out any given night of the week or clubbing, [so] a fake ID is as necessary as oxygen." Second on students' extracurricular to-do list is hanging out in downtown Providence, which is "fantastic. The downtown area of Providence is a good time with a large selection of excellent restaurants, good shopping, and fun bars and clubs. We often go to Providence Place Mall or the ever popular Thayer Street to mix with the Brown and RISD crowd on weekends." Undergraduates also love that Providence is "an hour from the beach, Boston is an hour and NYC is only three hours away, so if for some reason you need to get away, it is possible." Intercollegiate athletics are popular. One student writes, "Having a sports program that is nationally recognized is also cool. Going to the hockey and basketball games gives students something to do that's entertaining and provides a lot of school spirit."

Student Body

At PC, "The student body has a strong community and familial vibe. We get along great." And why wouldn't they, most students ask. "We're all the same." Nearly all of our survey respondents agree that, "PC is overwhelmingly white. Students tend to be Catholics from New England." They also look as though they "stepped right off the pages of an Abercrombie and Fitch catalog. It would be shocking to see someone who didn't look practically just like everyone else. They are typically athletic, involved partiers, but very much your average preppy college student." Cliquishness is common. "Although most students here are friendly, there is not very much interaction between social groups beyond the friendly conversations. Basically, everyone finds a group of friends and sticks with them, morning through night, for the next four years," notes one student. As for religion, "Masses are quite well attended, although this doesn't always translate into moral behavior during the other six days of the week."

PROVIDENCE COLLEGE

FINANCIAL AID: 401-865-2286 • E-MAIL: PCADMISS@PROVIDENCE.EDU • WEBSITE: WWW.PROVIDENCE.EDU

ADMISSIONS

Very important factors considered include: Secondary school record. *Important factors considered include:* Character/personal qualities, essays, extracurricular activities, recommendations, standardized test scores, volunteer work, work experience. *Other factors considered include:* Alumni/ae relation, class rank, geographical residence, minority status, religious affiliation/commitment, state residency, talent/ability. SAT Reasoning or ACT required. TOEFL required of all international applicants. High school diploma is required, and GED is not accepted. *Academic units required:* 4 English, 4 math, 3 science (2 science lab), 3 foreign language, 2 social studies, 2 history. *Academic units recommended:* 4 English, 4 math, 4 science (3 science lab), 3 foreign language, 1 social studies, 2 history.

The Inside Word

Providence's reputation for quality is solidly in place among above-average graduates of northeastern Catholic high schools, who account for almost a quarter of the applicant pool. The strength of these candidates is one of the primary factors that allow the college to be choosy about who gets in. Successful candidates usually project a well-rounded, conservative image.

FINANCIAL AID

Students should submit: FAFSA, CSS/Financial Aid PROFILE. Regular filing deadline is 2/1. The Princeton Review suggests that all financial aid forms be submitted as soon as possible after 1/1. *Need-based scholarships/grants offered:* Pell, SEOG, state scholarships/grants, private scholarships, the school's own gift aid. *Loan aid offered:* Direct Subsidized Stafford, Direct Unsubsidized Stafford, Direct PLUS, FFEL Subsidized Stafford, FFEL Unsubsidized Stafford, FFEL PLUS, Federal Perkins. Applicants will be notified of awards on or about 4/1. Off-campus job opportunities are excellent.

FROM THE ADMISSIONS OFFICE

"Infused with the history, tradition, and learning of a 700-year-old Catholic teaching order, the Dominican Friars, Providence College offers a value-affirming environment where students are enriched through spiritual, social, physical, and cultural growth as well as through intellectual development. Providence College offers over 35 programs of study leading to baccalaureate degrees in business, education, the sciences, arts, and humanities. Our faculty is noted for a strong commitment to teaching. A close student/faculty relationship allows for in-depth classwork, independent research projects, and detailed career exploration. While noted for the physical facilities and academic opportunities associated with larger universities, Providence also fosters personal growth through a small, spirited, family-like atmosphere that encourages involvement in student activities and athletics.

"Applicants for fall 2006 class are required to take the new version of the SAT (or the ACT with the writing section). Providence College will not accept scores from the old (prior to March 2005) version of the SAT (or ACT). SAT Subject Tests are not required for admission."

SELECTIVITY

Admissions Rating	**92**
# of applicants	7,827
% of applicants accepted	54
% of acceptees attending	25
# accepting a place on wait list	1,526
% admitted from wait list	14

FRESHMAN PROFILE

Range SAT Verbal	550-640
Average SAT Verbal	597
Range SAT Math	560-650
Average SAT Math	604
**TPR Projected Range SAT Writing*	*600-660*
Range ACT Composite	23-27
Average ACT Composite	25
Minimum Paper TOEFL	550
Minimum Computer Based TOEFL	213
Average HS GPA	3.42
% graduated top 10% of class	42
% graduated top 25% of class	82
% graduated top 50% of class	98

DEADLINES

Regular application deadline	1/15
Regular notification	4/1
Nonfall registration?	yes

APPLICANTS ALSO LOOK AT

AND OFTEN PREFER

Boston College, College of the Holy Cross, Georgetown U., Tufts U., U. of Notre Dame, U. of Richmond

AND SOMETIMES PREFER

Boston U., Loyola College in Maryland, Northeastern U., Villanova U.

AND RARELY PREFER

Fairfield U., Fordham U., Saint Anselm College, Stonehill College, U. of Connecticut, U. of Massachusetts—Amherst, The U. of Scranton

FINANCIAL FACTS

Financial Aid Rating	**73**
Annual tuition	$24,800
Room & Board	$9,270
Books and supplies	$750
Required fees	$510
% frosh rec. need-based scholarship or grant aid	51
% UG rec. need-based scholarship or grant aid	55
% frosh rec. need-based self-help aid	54
% UG rec. need-based self-help aid	62
% frosh rec. any financial aid	78
% UG rec. any financial aid	75
Avg. frosh grant	$11,000
Avg. frosh loan	$4,625
Independent 529 member?	No

Purdue University—West Lafayette

1080 Schleman Hall, West Lafayette, IN 47907 • Admissions: 765-494-1776 • Fax: 765-494-0544

CAMPUS LIFE

Quality of Life Rating	**73**
Fire Safety Rating	**60**
Type of school	public
Environment	town

STUDENTS

Total undergrad enrollment	30,391
% male/female	59/41
% from out of state	26
% live on campus	30
% in (# of) fraternities	18 (50)
% in (# of) sororities	17 (28)
% African American	3
% Asian	5
% Caucasian	83
% Hispanic	2
% international	6
# of countries represented	128

SURVEY SAYS

Great computer facilities
Athletic facilities are great
Everyone loves the Boilermakers
Frats and sororities dominate social scene
Lots of beer drinking
Hard liquor is popular

ACADEMICS

Academic Rating	**70**
Calendar	semester
Student/faculty ratio	15:1
Professors interesting rating	63
Professors accessible rating	64
% classes taught by TAs	0
Most common lab size	10-19 students
Most common regular class size	20-29 students

MOST POPULAR MAJORS

Business administration and management
mechanical engineering
psychology

STUDENTS SPEAK OUT

Academics

There is a perception, both on campus and off, that Purdue's main campus in West Lafayette is "mostly an engineer's college with a bunch of science-type majors and a few liberal arts degrees thrown in together," and with one in four students here pursuing an engineering degree, it's easy to understand why. But Purdue has a lot more to offer than a well-regarded engineering degree; the university's programs in pharmacy, nursing, business, hotel management, agriculture, and veterinary science all enjoy solid, well-earned reputations. Students in these competitive programs warn that "just about all of the classes you take in the first couple of years are 'weed-out' classes" and that "far too many courses are taught by TAs and grad students," a disconcerting number of whom "don't speak English very well." Engineers point out that "while all the classes are hard, there are always places to go to get assistance. There are always extra-help sessions, study groups, tutors available, etc., if I ever need help." Upper-level classes "are smaller in size and are very much hands on. The professors and class sizes make learning information easier." Many here cite "the limited opportunity to take liberal arts electives" as a drawback. Gripes one film major, "The film program is a joke. If you want to be an engineer, Purdue is great. If you want to study art or film, go somewhere else."

Life

With more than 30,000 undergraduates, Purdue can offer "something for everyone. If you want to join a church group, there are plenty of them. If you want to be in a fraternity, there are a lot of them. Ski club, psychology club, people who like The Princeton Review club... we've probably got it." Agrees one undergrad, "There are so many opportunities to get involved. No matter what you are interested in, you are bound to find others that are interested in the same area." Students here "love Big Ten football" and especially enjoy Breakfast Club, a home-game-day tradition in which students dress in costumes and pre-game in local bars, which open at 7:00 A.M. for the occasion. "It's like Halloween every home football game," explains one student. Students like to party even when they're dressed in civvies, the sun is down, and the football team is nowhere in sight; they tell us that "During the week most people hit the books hard, but on thirsty Thursday and during the weekends, fun here is getting drunk at parties or, if you're 21, in the bars." Purdue's Greek scene "is incredible, and you don't get a lot of the Greeks vs. non-Greeks like at other schools. Everyone parties together and has a good time!" Students here love the fact that "there are tons of kids around all the time. A few people go home on the weekends, but I'd say that 95 percent stay at school on the weekends." Indianapolis and Chicago are both within easy road-trip distance when urban life beckons.

Student Body

"Purdue is very representative of a typical small, rural Midwestern town," as "most of the non-engineers are local Hoosiers. The engineers are a far more diverse group and are generally more academic." The engineering program draws a lot of international students; reports one engineer, "I have friends from at least 20 countries and most of the 50 states. Everyone mixes together and works together to get through these crazy engineering classes!" A "decent number of the students here are members of the Greek system," and "are generally preppy types who wear a lot of Abercrombie." Like their home state, Purdue students "are pretty conservative, and liberal activism is very low. What there is usually is countered by the College Republicans."

Financial Aid: 765-494-5050 • E-mail: admissions@purdue.edu • Website: www.purdue.edu

ADMISSIONS

Very important factors considered include: Class rank, secondary school record, standardized test scores. *Other factors considered include:* Alumni/ae relation, geographical residence, recommendations, state residency, work experience. SAT Reasoning or ACT required. TOEFL required of all international applicants. High school diploma is required, and GED is accepted. *Academic units required:* 4 English, 3 math, 2 science (2 science lab), 2 foreign language. *Academic units recommended:* 4 English, 3 math, 3 science (3 science lab), 2 foreign language.

The Inside Word

The fact that Purdue holds class rank as one of its most important considerations in the admission of candidates is troublesome. There are far too many inconsistencies in ranking policies and class size among the 25,000-plus high schools in the U.S. to place so much weight on an essentially incomparable number. The university's high admit rate thankfully renders the issue relatively moot, even though applications have increased.

FINANCIAL AID

Students should submit: FAFSA. The Princeton Review suggests that all financial aid forms be submitted as soon as possible after 1/1. *Need-based scholarships/grants offered:* Pell, SEOG, state scholarships/grants, private scholarships, the school's own gift aid. *Loan aid offered:* FFEL Subsidized Stafford, FFEL Unsubsidized Stafford, FFEL PLUS, Federal Perkins, college/university loans from institutional funds. Applicants will be notified of awards on or about 4/15. Federal Work-study Program available. Institutional employment available. Off-campus job opportunities are good.

FROM THE ADMISSIONS OFFICE

"Although it is one of America's largest universities, Purdue does not 'feel' big to its students. The main campus in West Lafayette was built around a master plan that keeps walking time between classes to a maximum of 12 minutes. Purdue is a comprehensive university with an international reputation in a wide range of academic fields. A strong work ethic prevails at Purdue. As a member of the Big 10, Purdue has a strong and diverse athletic program. Purdue offers over 700 clubs and organizations. The residence halls and Greek community offer many participatory activities for students. Numerous convocations and lectures are presented each year. Purdue is all about people, and allowing students to grow academically as well as socially, preparing them for the real world.

"Applicants seeking admission into the fall 2006 entering class are required to submit scores from the new Writing component of the SAT (or ACT)."

SELECTIVITY

Admissions Rating	**83**
# of applicants	24,003
% of applicants accepted	80
% of acceptees attending	35

FRESHMAN PROFILE

Range SAT Verbal	500-610
Average SAT Verbal	558
Range SAT Math	530-650
Average SAT Math	591
**TPR Projected Range SAT Writing*	*560-640*
Range ACT Composite	22-28
Average ACT Composite	25
Minimum Paper TOEFL	550
Minimum Computer Based TOEFL	213
Average HS GPA	3.4
% graduated top 10% of class	27
% graduated top 25% of class	60
% graduated top 50% of class	92

DEADLINES

Regular notification	rolling
Nonfall registration?	yes

APPLICANTS ALSO LOOK AT AND OFTEN PREFER AND SOMETIMES PREFER

Indiana University—Bloomington
Rose—Hulman Institute of Technology
University of Illinois at Urbana-Champaign
Valparaiso University

FINANCIAL FACTS

Financial Aid Rating	**76**
Annual in-state tuition	$6,092
Annual out-of-state tuition	$18,700
Room & Board	$7,020
Books and supplies	$940
% frosh rec. need-based scholarship or grant aid	15
% UG rec. need-based scholarship or grant aid	13
% frosh rec. need-based self-help aid	36
% UG rec. need-based self-help aid	36
% frosh rec. any financial aid	73
% UG rec. any financial aid	77
Avg. frosh grant	$5,432
Avg. frosh loan	$4,404
Independent 529 member?	No

QUINNIPIAC UNIVERSITY

275 MOUNT CARMEL AVENUE, HAMDEN, CT 06518 • ADMISSIONS: 203-582-8600 • FAX: 203-582-8906

CAMPUS LIFE

Quality of Life Rating	**77**
Fire Safety Rating	**60**
Type of school	private
Environment	town

STUDENTS

Total undergrad enrollment	5,329
% male/female	39/61
% from out of state	70
% from public high school	80
% live on campus	70
% in (# of) fraternities	6 (2)
% in (# of) sororities	8 (3)
% African American	2
% Asian	2
% Caucasian	77
% Hispanic	4
% international	1
# of countries represented	20

SURVEY SAYS

Small classes
Great computer facilities
Great library
Campus feels safe
Lots of beer drinking
Hard liquor is popular
(Almost) everyone smokes

ACADEMICS

Academic Rating	**81**
Calendar	semester
Student/faculty ratio	15:1
Professors interesting rating	80
Professors accessible rating	79
% professors teaching UG courses	88
% classes taught by TAs	0
Most common lab size	10-19 students
Most common regular class size	10-19 students

MOST POPULAR MAJORS

Communications technologies and support services
physical therapy/therapist
psychology

STUDENTS SPEAK OUT

Academics

Students looking for a medium-sized university with career-focused programs and a liberal arts foundation should consider Quinnipiac University (QU). Though the school's undergraduate population is a substantial 5,000, Quinnipiac offers the academic support and personal attention typical of small colleges. Students report that "class sizes are usually under 20" and "the professors make an effort to learn not only your name, but who you really are." Undergrads say that QU professors "are there to teach you, help you, and get to know you, not to fail you or know you by a number." In fact, it is through many channels that the school displays its dedication to helping students succeed, and many note that the school's Learning Center "has tutors, who have been an essential component to hard science classes" and can be a "big help" if you are struggling with academics. Some students, however, feel that the classes at Quinnipiac could stand to be more competitive. In the words of one: "I have been satisfied but not challenged at Quinnipiac." Additionally, many debate the school's use of numerous adjunct professors. While some students claim "the part-time teachers are not devoted to your studies," others insist "the adjuncts here are incredible. They bring their real world experience to the classroom." Regarding majors, "physical therapy, communications, and pre-med here are all very strong and hard to get into." Though administrators are "friendly and personable" when you get them one-on-one, the overall structure is plagued by a "lack of communication between the different departments in the school."

Life

Students say that "one of QU's greatest strengths is its location: 10 minutes away from Connecticut's cultural center and geographically right between New York and Boston." In addition, there is a "state park directly across from the campus," "the beautiful Sleeping Giant Mountain, which provides a beautiful backdrop for campus every season." Students say they like to take advantage of "concerts, plays, coffeehouses, lectures, restaurants, shopping" in nearby New Haven, as well as the town's "Thirsty Thursdays," which "are almost always happening." For recreation, students say, "it's really relaxing to climb Sleeping Giant or to sit out on the quad and drink a milkshake." In addition, "there are so many different organizations to be involved in, and that creates more opportunity to meet new people and form great friendships." Though students advise that "there is very little academic or intellectual conversation outside the classroom," they also note that "studying is pretty important to most people here." One undergrad summarizes life: "During the week the library is usually full. However, come the start of the weekend (usually Thursday nights) many students choose to drink." On that note, students tell us that, "beer pong, partying, and cigarette smoking are favorite pastimes."

Student Body

"Many of the students at Quinnipiac are alike: well-dressed, upper-middle-class people," according to one undergrad. "Everyone's personality is very similar," adds another. Considering these observations, it's no surprise that students also report that "there is very little diversity" at QU. Not everyone's complaining, however. Opines one undergrad: "I like my classmates because so many of them are just like me. Sometimes I wish it were more diverse, but then at the same time I think the reason everyone gets along so well is because we're all so much alike." Characterization of the student body runs from "shallow and materialistic" to "warm" and "friendly," but many agree, "Like everywhere else there are certain groups, but they are always interacting with each other, and it's easy to make friends with them all."

QUINNIPIAC UNIVERSITY

FINANCIAL AID: 203-582-8750 • E-MAIL: ADMISSIONS@QUINNIPIAC.EDU • WEBSITE: WWW.QUINNIPIAC.EDU

ADMISSIONS

Very important factors considered include: Secondary school record. *Important factors considered include:* Class rank, essays, recommendations, standardized test scores. *Other factors considered include:* Alumni/ae relation, extracurricular activities, interview, minority status, volunteer work, work experience. SAT Reasoning or ACT required. TOEFL required of all international applicants. High school diploma is required, and GED is accepted. *Academic units required:* 4 English, 3 math, 3 science (2 science lab), 2 social studies, 3 academic electives, 4 science and math (in PT, OT, or PA). *Academic units recommended:* 2 foreign language.

The Inside Word

Quinnipiac boasts a wide range of opportunities for study and social pursuits in a geographic locale equidistant from multiple cultural centers, not to mention a very responsive faculty.

FINANCIAL AID

Students should submit: FAFSA. The Princeton Review suggests that all financial aid forms be submitted as soon as possible after 1/1. *Need-based scholarships/grants offered:* Pell, SEOG, state scholarships/grants, private scholarships, the school's own gift aid, Federal Nursing scholarships. *Loan aid offered:* FFEL Subsidized Stafford, FFEL Unsubsidized Stafford, FFEL PLUS, Federal Perkins, Federal Nursing, state loans. Applicants will be notified of awards on a rolling basis beginning on or about 2/15. Federal Work-study Program available. Institutional employment available. Off-campus job opportunities are good.

FROM THE ADMISSIONS OFFICE

"The appeal of Quinnipiac University continues to grow each year. Our students come from a variety of states and backgrounds. Seventy-five percent of the freshman class is from out-of-state. Students come from 25 states and 18 countries. Nearly 30 percent of current undergraduates plan to stay at Quinnipiac to complete their graduate degree.

"As admission becomes more competitive and our enrollment remains stable, the university continues to focus on its mission: to provide outstanding academic programs in a student-oriented environment on a campus with a strong sense of community. The development of an honors program, a highly-regarded emerging leaders student life program, and a 'writing across the curriculum' initiative in academic affairs, form the foundation for excellence in business, communications, health sciences, education, liberal arts and law.

"The University is state of the art in technology—with a fully digital high-definition production studio in the School of Communications; the Terry Goodwin '67 Financial Technology Center which provides a high-tech simulated trading floor in the School of Business; a critical care lab for our nursing and physician assistant majors, and a computer program that requires all incoming students to purchase a university recommended laptop with wireless capabilities supported by a campus-wide network."

"More than 70 student organizations, 21 Division I teams (The 'Bobcats'), recreation and intramurals in a newly expanded recreation/fitness center, community service, student publications, and a strong student government offer a variety of outside of class experiences to the student body. Clubs such as the International Student Club, Hillel, Community Action Project, Habitat for Humanity, Christian Fellowship, and others get students involved in campus life. Multicultural awareness is supported through the Black Student Union, Asian/Pacific Islander Association, Latino Cultural Society, and GLASS.

"An active alumni association reflects the strong connection Quinnipiac has with its graduates, and they give the faculty high marks for career preparation.

"An outstanding location and campus atmosphere make Quinnipiac a great choice.

"Freshman applicants for fall 2006 must take the new SAT (or the ACT with the Writing component). In addition, students may submit scores from the old (before March 2005) SAT (or ACT), and we will use their best scores from either test. We do not require any SAT Subject Tests."

SELECTIVITY

Admissions Rating	**87**
# of applicants	10,624
% of applicants accepted	55
% of acceptees attending	23
# accepting a place on wait list	1,020
% admitted from wait list	15

FRESHMAN PROFILE

Range SAT Verbal	520-580
Average SAT Verbal	555
Range SAT Math	540-600
Average SAT Math	560
**TPR Projected Range SAT Writing*	*570-620*
Range ACT Composite	22-27
Average ACT Composite	24
Minimum Paper TOEFL	550
Minimum Computer Based TOEFL	213
Average HS GPA	3.4
% graduated top 10% of class	21
% graduated top 25% of class	55
% graduated top 50% of class	89

DEADLINES

Regular notification	rolling
Nonfall registration?	yes

APPLICANTS ALSO LOOK AT

AND OFTEN PREFER
Boston University
University of Connecticut
Villanova University

AND SOMETIMES PREFER
Fairfield University
Fordham University
Providence College
Syracuse University

AND RARELY PREFER
Assumption College
Hofstra University,
Sacred Heart University

FINANCIAL FACTS

Financial Aid Rating	**65**
Annual tuition	$23,360
Room & Board	$10,300
Books and supplies	$800
Required fees	$980
% frosh rec. need-based scholarship or grant aid	60
% UG rec. need-based scholarship or grant aid	57
% frosh rec. need-based self-help aid	53
% UG rec. need-based self-help aid	52
% frosh rec. any financial aid	70
% UG rec. any financial aid	68
Avg. frosh grant	$13,019
Avg. frosh loan	$2,625
Independent 529 member?	No

RANDOLPH-MACON COLLEGE

PO Box 5005, Ashland, VA 23005 • Admissions: 804-752-7305 • Fax: 804-752-4707

CAMPUS LIFE

Quality of Life Rating	**71**
Fire Safety Rating	**98**
Type of school	private
Affiliation	Methodist
Environment	village

STUDENTS

Total undergrad enrollment	1,102
% male/female	47/53
% from out of state	33
% from public high school	65
% live on campus	84
% in (# of) fraternities	40 (6)
% in (# of) sororities	40 (4)
% African American	6
% Asian	1
% Caucasian	90
% Hispanic	1
% international	1
# of countries represented	18

SURVEY SAYS

Small classes
Athletic facilities are great
Frats and sororities dominate social scene
Lots of beer drinking
Hard liquor is popular
(Almost) everyone smokes

ACADEMICS

Academic Rating	**83**
Calendar	4-1-4
Student/faculty ratio	11:1
Professors interesting rating	92
Professors accessible rating	89
% professors teaching UG courses	100
% classes taught by TAs	0
Most common regular class size	10-19 students

MOST POPULAR MAJORS

Business/managerial economics
psychology
sociology

STUDENTS SPEAK OUT

Academics

If what you seek is a "great education to prepare you for the real world while still having a great, fun social life," then Randolph-Macon College (R-MC) just might be the undergraduate institution for you. The curriculum provides a solid liberal arts education to the pragmatic student body. Undergrads here are accomplished—one in four proceeds immediately to grad school upon graduation. As one student tells it, "Word is that R-MC is easy to get into but hard to stay [in], and I believe that's completely true; you really have to work to get what you want out of your experience." Support comes primarily from a dedicated faculty; explained one student, "Our slogan says it best: 'Believe in the Moment of Connection.' Our professors are very close to us. The administration tries to be." More than one undergraduate thinks "the greatest strength of my school has to be its size and the many benefits that come with that. We are only a little over 1,100 students, so classes are never over 25 students." Many students complain that the administration is inconsistent, and "their goals are not really the goals of the students."

Life

"Greek life is a major part of campus life at our school," observes one R-MC student. Surprisingly few students here complain about the divisive effect Greek organizations often present, however, probably because "they provide so many student activities, even for those students who are not members." Notes one student approvingly, "Everyone gets along no matter what the differences may be (e.g., Greeks and non-Greeks are all friends). People look out for each other here. There is a real sense of community." This unity is obvious at every Yellow Jackets' home game; "sporting events such as men's basketball and football are popular, and they have a pretty big turnout for their games," writes one student. Outdoor enthusiasts speak highly of Macon Outdoors, a campus organization "dedicated to exploring the outdoors" through "rafting, skiing, hiking, kayaking, mountain biking, canoeing, and rock climbing" trips. Complains one student, "I have trouble finding things to do on the weekends because I don't drink." Some students commit to clubs, organizations, and public service. Those who don't usually frequent the Greek houses or "entertain themselves in downtown Richmond," just a half-hour to the south.

Student Body

Randolph-Macon is "slowly becoming more diverse;" even so, the vast majority of undergraduates "come from a mid- to upper-socioeconomic-level background and tend to be Republican." The typical student is "from Virginia, Maryland, or Pennsylvania and New Jersey" and mostly "concerns him- or herself with the ongoing social aspects of campus, with little to no regard for what is going on in the outside world," writes one undergrad. Students here are sociable and easygoing about their academic commitments: "People go out and party and still get their work done." Undergraduates are often "involved in many different aspects of college life. [They are] active in sports (either competitive or intramural) and most likely also have a job somewhere on campus or in the nearby community."

RANDOLPH-MACON COLLEGE

FINANCIAL AID: 804-752-7259 • E-MAIL: ADMISSIONS@RMC.EDU • WEBSITE: WWW.RMC.EDU

ADMISSIONS

Very important factors considered include: Secondary school record. *Important factors considered include:* Class rank, essays, recommendations, standardized test scores. *Other factors considered include:* Alumni/ae relation, character/personal qualities, extracurricular activities, interview, minority status, talent/ability, volunteer work, work experience. SAT Reasoning or ACT required. TOEFL required of all international applicants. High school diploma is required, and GED is accepted. *Academic units required:* 4 English, 3 math, 3 science (2 science lab), 2 foreign language, 1 social studies, 2 history, 1 academic elective. *Academic units recommended:* 4 English, 4 math, 4 science (4 science lab), 4 foreign language, 4 social studies, 2 history.

The Inside Word

Candidates who are excellent students and good testers are very likely to receive scholarships at Randolph-Macon. The college has an average yield of admits who enroll, and every strong student who signs on gives the freshman academic profile a boost. If the competition among Virginia colleges weren't so strong, admission to Randolph-Macon would be much tougher.

FINANCIAL AID

Students should submit: FAFSA, state aid form, R-MC entitlement eligibility form, college prepaid education program form. Regular filing deadline is 3/1. The Princeton Review suggests that all financial aid forms be submitted as soon as possible after 1/1. *Need-based scholarships/grants offered:* Pell, SEOG, state scholarships/grants, private scholarships, the school's own gift aid. *Loan aid offered:* FFEL Subsidized Stafford, FFEL Unsubsidized Stafford, FFEL PLUS, Federal Perkins, college/university loans from institutional funds. Applicants will be notified of awards on or about 3/15. Federal Work-study Program available. Institutional employment available. Off-campus job opportunities are excellent.

FROM THE ADMISSIONS OFFICE

"Randolph-Macon College, located in historic Ashland, just north of Richmond, is a coeducational, liberal arts and sciences college with a mission fulfilled through a combination of personal interaction and academic rigor. The student/faculty ratio is 11:1 and the average class size is 16 students. Enrollment is kept at approximately 1,150 to maintain this intimate atmosphere. Randolph-Macon College has an outstanding national reputation for its internships, study abroad, and undergraduate research. Founded in 1830, Randolph-Macon College is the oldest United Methodist Church–affiliated college in the nation, is a Phi Beta Kappa college, and is ranked as a Baccalaureate I college by the Carnegie Foundation. It offers the broadest liberal arts core curriculum of any college in Virginia.

"The college prepares students for any future, including success in securing a job or in gaining acceptance to graduate or professional school. The college offers a wide variety of social and recreational opportunities through more than 100 campus organizations. Forty percent of the students participate in one or more community service activities; 70 percent play intramural sports; 40 percent join a fraternity or sorority; and everyone has a voice in student government. A $9.5 million sports and recreation center is very popular with students, and a new performing arts center offers a wealth of cultural arts programs. In addition, freshmen residence halls were recently renovated 'Peaks of Excellence' center is now open to assist students with internships, study abroad, and undergraduate research.

"Freshman applicants for fall 2006 must take the new SAT, which includes a written essay, or the ACT with Writing component."

SELECTIVITY

Admissions Rating	**80**
# of applicants	1,720
% of applicants accepted	77
% of acceptees attending	24
# accepting a place on wait list	53
% admitted from wait list	9
# of early decision applicants	39
% accepted early decision	81

FRESHMAN PROFILE

Range SAT Verbal	520-600
Average SAT Verbal	561
Range SAT Math	500-610
Average SAT Math	553
**TPR Projected Range SAT Writing*	*570-630*
Range ACT Composite	19-24
Minimum Paper TOEFL	550
Minimum Computer Based TOEFL	213
Average HS GPA	3.33
% graduated top 10% of class	22
% graduated top 25% of class	48
% graduated top 50% of class	81

DEADLINES

Early decision application deadline	11/15
Early decision notification	12/1
Regular application deadline	3/1
Regular notification	4/1
Nonfall registration?	yes

APPLICANTS ALSO LOOK AT

AND OFTEN PREFER

University of Virginia

AND SOMETIMES PREFER

Hampden—Sydney College, James Madison University, Roanoke College, University of Mary Washington, Virginia Tech

AND RARELY PREFER

Sweet Briar College, University of Richmond

FINANCIAL FACTS

Financial Aid Rating	**77**
Annual tuition	$21,990
Room & Board	$6,510
Books and supplies	$1,000
Required fees	$635
% frosh rec. need-based scholarship or grant aid	63
% UG rec. need-based scholarship or grant aid	58
% frosh rec. need-based self-help aid	50
% UG rec. need-based self-help aid	50
% frosh rec. any financial aid	98
% UG rec. any financial aid	95
Avg. frosh grant	$13,130
Avg. frosh loan	$4,300
Independent 529 member?	No

RANDOLPH-MACON WOMAN'S COLLEGE

2500 RIVERMONT AVENUE, LYNCHBURG, VA 24503-1526 • ADMISSIONS: 434-947-8100 • FAX: 434-947-8996

CAMPUS LIFE

Quality of Life Rating	**85**
Fire Safety Rating	**77**
Type of school	private
Affiliation	Methodist
Environment	city

STUDENTS

Total undergrad enrollment	705
% male/female	0/100
% from out of state	55
% from public high school	80
% live on campus	89
% African American	9
% Asian	3
% Caucasian	73
% Hispanic	4
% international	8
# of countries represented	46

SURVEY SAYS

Small classes
No one cheats
Diverse student types on campus
Dorms are like palaces
Low cost of living
Frats and sororities are unpopular or nonexistent

ACADEMICS

Academic Rating	**89**
Calendar	semester
Student/faculty ratio	9:1
Professors interesting rating	93
Professors accessible rating	94
% professors teaching UG courses	100
% classes taught by TAs	0
Most common lab size	10-19 students
Most common regular class size	fewer than 10 students

MOST POPULAR MAJORS

English language and literature
psychology

STUDENTS SPEAK OUT

Academics

Students at Randolph-Macon Woman's College (R-MWC) love the small-school charm that imbues their academic experience. "This is NOT a finishing school," undergrads here say time and again. It's the kind of place where "many professors seem to take it upon themselves as a personal mission to not award high grades," and course work is "difficult. It is not too bad to get along if you took a few AP courses in high school, but if you just skated through easier classes, you may have trouble." Professors, the women here agree, are "without a doubt the best thing about R-MWC. They care about the students and actually interact with them." Students also love R-MWC's honor code, which they describe as "amazing. Self-scheduled exams, freedom in leaving belongings in public areas, and a general feeling of cooperation are wonderful things to have in a college environment." These assets help make up for Macon's shortcomings, which include "a student body so small that it leaves only a few options in terms of classes."

Life

Tradition is central to R-MWC extracurricular life. These traditions include the Even-Odd rivalry ("women that graduate in even years are even and women that graduate in odd years are odd; it helps create a bond based on graduation year"); Ring Week ("where juniors and [freshmen] are paired up to exchange little gifts and the first year decorates the junior's door and gives the junior her ring"); and Pumpkin Parade ("similar to Ring Week, but with sophomores and seniors, pumpkin carving and a candlelight parade"). Students love these distinguishing touches, but wish the school could supplement them with a more active social calendar. Explained one student, "We are completely restricted by the school's visitation and alcohol policies. The school seems to still be stuck in an era when most schools in the area were single-sex, and there was more incentive for men to come here." As a result, "many students feel they must go off-campus for fun," and so they do, road-tripping to "Charlottesville, home of UVA, which attracts a lot of live music," and Roanoke, which "has a decent nightlife, with three nightclubs and an all-night coffee shop." They rarely hang around hometown Lynchburg, which "is not a college town, despite having over 12,000 college students (combining our school, Liberty University, Lynchburg College, and Sweet Briar College)." As they do every time we survey them, the women of R-MWC brag that "we have the best dining service! They cook us real food (and I'm talking real chicken parmesan, steak, fried cod, shrimp) and if you can't find anything to eat (which is next to impossible), just go find Jeff, our head chef. He'll make you whatever you want!"

Student Body

"There is definitely a range" of women at R-MWC, "from the super-traditional girly girls who spend many a weekend at Hampden-Sydney or VMI looking for their future husbands to very liberal feminists who never look for guys; from girls who party and drink nearly every weekend to girls [who] think that a good time is a hot cup of tea and a Jane Austen novel." Students tell us that "everyone gets along pretty well. Of course, on an all-female campus, there's always someone PMS-ing, but that's life." Many speak of a sense of sisterhood; as one student explained, "With so few students, all of them women, and nearly all living on campus, it is understandable that we would be a bit closer than many other colleges." Another benefit of attending an all-women's college: "It really decreases the emphasis on fashion, makeup, and the like."

RANDOLPH-MACON WOMAN'S COLLEGE

FINANCIAL AID: 434-947-8128 • E-MAIL: ADMISSIONS@RMWC.EDU • WEBSITE: WWW.RMWC.EDU

ADMISSIONS

Very important factors considered include: Character/personal qualities, secondary school record. *Important factors considered include:* Class rank, essays, extracurricular activities, recommendations, standardized test scores, talent/ability. *Other factors considered include:* Alumni/ae relation, interview, minority status, volunteer work, work experience. SAT Reasoning or ACT required. TOEFL required of all international applicants. High school diploma is required, and GED is accepted. *Academic units required:* 4 English, 3 math, 2 science (2 science lab), 3 foreign language, 2 history, 2 academic electives.

The Inside Word

The admissions process at Randolph-Macon Woman's College works pretty much as it does at most small liberal arts colleges, with one worthwhile exception: Each candidate is assigned to an admissions staff member who functions as an advocate for the student throughout the process. It's nice to have somewhat regular contact with someone in the admissions office over the course of the cycle. This saves time restating problems, questions, and circumstances every time you call or write. It also helps the college make a strong positive impression on applicants.

FINANCIAL AID

Students should submit: FAFSA, state aid form. The Princeton Review suggests that all financial aid forms be submitted as soon as possible after 1/1. *Need-based scholarships/grants offered:* Pell, SEOG, state scholarships/grants, private scholarships, the school's own gift aid. *Loan aid offered:* FFEL Subsidized Stafford, FFEL Unsubsidized Stafford, FFEL PLUS, Federal Perkins, college/university loans from institutional funds, private. Applicants will be notified of awards on a rolling basis beginning on or about 3/1. Federal Work-study Program available. Institutional employment available. Off-campus job opportunities are good.

FROM THE ADMISSIONS OFFICE

"Randolph-Macon Woman's College students appreciate the college's personalized approach to their educational program. Their individualized Macon Plan, which includes study abroad, internships, career guidance, leadership development, and one-on-one faculty advising, allows the student superior opportunities and direction in achieving their goals and dreams. The college has recently inaugurated a four-year global leadership program. The Honor System is a vital part of life at R-MWC, providing students with a living and learning environment based on integrity, trust, and mutual respect. A diverse student population from 43 states and 40 countries offers exceptional opportunities to learn about different cultures and perspectives. The college's solid academic reputation coupled with an impressive array of alumnae who are leaders in nearly every career field imaginable positions R-MWC as one of the finest liberal arts colleges in the nation.

"If you are bright, ambitious, and motivated, Randolph-Macon Woman's College is the place for you!

"First-year applicants for fall 2006 must submit either the SAT or ACT. At this time, the Writing component scores for both the new SAT and the new ACT will be recommended but not required, and Randolph-Macon Woman's College will accept the scores from either the new or old versions of both tests."

SELECTIVITY

Admissions Rating	**86**
# of applicants	792
% of applicants accepted	88
% of acceptees attending	30
# of early decision applicants	21
% accepted early decision	91

FRESHMAN PROFILE

Range SAT Verbal	540-660
Average SAT Verbal	603
Range SAT Math	510-613
Average SAT Math	564
**TPR Projected Range SAT Writing*	*590-670*
Range ACT Composite	21-29
Average ACT Composite	24
Minimum Paper TOEFL	550
Minimum Computer Based TOEFL	213
Average HS GPA	3.4
% graduated top 10% of class	36
% graduated top 25% of class	71
% graduated top 50% of class	92

DEADLINES

Early decision application deadline	11/15
Early decision notification	12/15
Regular application deadline	3/1
Regular notification	rolling
Nonfall registration?	yes

APPLICANTS ALSO LOOK AT AND OFTEN PREFER

Duke University
Smith College
Wellesley College

AND SOMETIMES PREFER

College of William and Mary
Mount Holyoke College
Sweet Briar College
University of Virginia

AND RARELY PREFER

Hollins University
James Madison University

FINANCIAL FACTS

Financial Aid Rating	**84**
Annual tuition	$22,550
Room & Board	$8,610
Required fees	$480
% frosh rec. need-based scholarship or grant aid	72
% UG rec. need-based scholarship or grant aid	70
% frosh rec. need-based self-help aid	59
% UG rec. need-based self-help aid	59
% frosh rec. any financial aid	99
% UG rec. any financial aid	96
Avg. frosh grant	$16,800
Avg. frosh loan	$2,454
Independent 529 member?	Yes

REED COLLEGE

3203 SE WOODSTOCK BOULEVARD, PORTLAND, OR 97202-8199 • ADMISSIONS: 503-777-7511 • FAX: 503-777-7553

CAMPUS LIFE

Quality of Life Rating	**93**
Fire Safety Rating	**60**
Type of school	private
Environment	village

STUDENTS

Total undergrad enrollment	1,273
% male/female	45/55
% from out of state	86
% from public high school	66
% live on campus	57
% African American	2
% Asian	6
% Caucasian	62
% Hispanic	5
% Native American	1
% international	4
# of countries represented	38

SURVEY SAYS

Great computer facilities
Campus feels safe
Frats and sororities are unpopular or nonexistent

ACADEMICS

Academic Rating	**99**
Calendar	semester
Student/faculty ratio	10:1
Professors interesting rating	99
Professors accessible rating	96
% professors teaching UG courses	100
% classes taught by TAs	0
Most common lab size	10-19 students
Most common regular class size	10-19 students

MOST POPULAR MAJORS

English language and literature
psychology

STUDENTS SPEAK OUT

Academics

Reed College is the epitome of an American educational paradigm, the small teaching-oriented college where students pursue education for its own sake, not for the financial rewards the education may bring. "Reed is about serious, no-nonsense academics in an irreverent community of like-minded scholars," explains one Reedie. "People looking to come here should be aware that they will be in for one heck of a ride and should be prepared to be challenged like they've never been before," warns one student. Undergraduates must come to class prepared and ready to be engaged, as the school relies primarily on the discussion-oriented conference setting for instruction. "The conference-style classes are great," offers one student, "because with such a small class, a great discussion can be had every day." Another student notes, " If you're quiet, you'll learn to talk! In classes of fewer than 10 people, it's impossible to hide in the corner." Critical to this style of teaching is a talented, devoted faculty; fortunately, "Reed professors are here to teach. They are hired for their teaching ability, promoted for their teaching ability, and granted tenure based on their teaching ability. Professors work as hard as students do to prepare and teach their classes." Sounds perfect? It's not, of course, but fortunately, "when there are problems or issues, it is really easy to complain to the right people without a tremendous amount of runaround. It's pretty amazing, the amount of access we have to the administration and our professors."

Life

Because of the near-endless stream of academic assignments, many Reedies "spend too much time being too stressed out. Although Reedies work very hard, they also spend far too much time worrying about their work and not being able to relax." Even so, undergraduates do find time to enjoy a vital, engaging extracurricular scene. One undergrad writes, "There are many random funky events, like the 40-person samba band that we bring to campus sometimes, or the naked passion dance, or Renn Fayre, a huge, wild, weekend-long party at the end of the school year." Another adds, "We fund lots of cool artistic and musical stuff all the time, and people really know how to have a good time. The school brings shows and performers to campus, and subsidizes tickets for some off-campus events." Supplementing all the campus activity is the city of Portland, which "is wonderful. There are lots of hip thrift shops, cool diners and restaurants (that accommodate vegans like me). Good music is always around, coffee/ tea shops are abundant, and public transportation is great." For a more elaborate getaway, students can "go to Mt. Hood and spend a night at Reed's ski cabin, where you can play in the snow and make a communal dinner and not think about academics for 24 hours." Because Reedies pride themselves on their iconoclasm, "sports are frowned upon by many, as are typical male/female activities like makeup and showering."

Student Body

Does the Reed student body live up to its age-old image? Some say no, some say sort of. "Freaky, drugged-out hippy stereotypes are a load of bunk. Anyone like that would flunk out after a semester," asserts one undergrad. "Reed does have an enormous number of trustafarians, but then we also have just as many goths, poor kids who dress rich, middle-of-the-road kids, and even a growing number of preppies," counters another. Nearly everyone agrees that "we are geeks, every last one of us [and] the only thing about the typical Reedie is that they would not fit in anywhere else." However, many add, "A lot of Reedies are determined to be different from the 'norm,' but they often wind up being different in exactly the same way." We also heard numerous warnings that "at times the political liberalism of the student body is undoubtedly stifling to fundamentalist Christians and Republicans, which is slightly ironic given the 'open-mindedness' that Reedies claim to pride themselves on."

FINANCIAL AID: 800-547-4750 • E-MAIL: ADMISSION@REED.EDU • WEBSITE: WWW.REED.EDU

ADMISSIONS

Very important factors considered include: Essays, secondary school record. *Important factors considered include:* Class rank, interview, recommendations, standardized test scores. *Other factors considered include:* Alumni/ae relation, character/personal qualities, extracurricular activities, minority status, talent/ability, volunteer work, work experience. SAT Reasoning or SAT Subject Tests required. TOEFL required of all international applicants. High school diploma is required, and GED is accepted. *Academic units recommended:* 4 English, 4 math, 4 science (3 science lab), 4 foreign language, 1 social studies, 3 history.

The Inside Word

Despite the progressive nature of the educational attitudes and student body at Reed, the college zealously avoids such labeling in admissions literature, preferring to portray itself in a much more traditional fashion. While a social conscience is definitely an asset, applicants should devote particular attention to discussing their intellectual curiosity and academic interests in essays and/or interviews.

FINANCIAL AID

Students should submit: FAFSA, institution's own financial aid form, CSS/Financial Aid PROFILE, noncustodial (divorced/separated) parents' statement. Regular filing deadline is 1/15. The Princeton Review suggests that all financial aid forms be submitted as soon as possible after 1/1. *Need-based scholarships/grants offered:* Pell, SEOG, state scholarships/grants, private scholarships, the school's own gift aid. *Loan aid offered:* FFEL Subsidized Stafford, FFEL Unsubsidized Stafford, FFEL PLUS, Federal Perkins, state loans. Applicants will be notified of awards on or about 4/1. Federal Work-study Program available. Institutional employment available. Off-campus job opportunities are good.

FROM THE ADMISSIONS OFFICE

"Dedication to the highest standards of academic scholarship is central to a Reed education. A well-structured curriculum and small classes with motivated students and dedicated faculty provide the environment in which a student's quest for learning can be given broad rein. Students most likely to derive maximum benefit from a Reed education are individuals who possess a high degree of self-discipline and a genuine enthusiasm for academic work.

"Prospective students may correspond with current Reed students at writeareedie@reed.edu. Campus visits may be useful while classes are in session; however, interviews and tours are available throughout most of the year.

"Reed will accept either version of the SAT. Until we are convinced that the new SAT offers us significant information that we do not already factor into the admission matrix, Reed will not change its approach to standardized tests. Writing sections are recommended, though not required."

SELECTIVITY

Admissions Rating	**95**
# of applicants	2,485
% of applicants accepted	47
% of acceptees attending	29
# accepting a place on wait list	733
% admitted from wait list	3
# of early decision applicants	108
% accepted early decision	60

FRESHMAN PROFILE

Range SAT Verbal	660-750
Average SAT Verbal	698
Range SAT Math	610-710
Average SAT Math	661
**TPR Projected Range SAT Writing*	*670-730*
Range ACT Composite	28-31
Average ACT Composite	30
Minimum Paper TOEFL	610
Minimum Computer Based TOEFL	259
Average HS GPA	3.8
% graduated top 10% of class	59
% graduated top 25% of class	87
% graduated top 50% of class	98

DEADLINES

Early decision application deadline	11/15
Early decision notification	12/15
Regular application deadline	1/15
Regular notification	4/1
Nonfall registration?	no

APPLICANTS ALSO LOOK AT

AND OFTEN PREFER
Stanford University

AND SOMETIMES PREFER
Oberlin College
University of Chicago

AND RARELY PREFER
St. John's College (MD)

FINANCIAL FACTS

Financial Aid Rating	**76**
Annual tuition	$30,670
Room & Board	$8,070
Books and supplies	$950
Required fees	$230
% frosh rec. need-based scholarship or grant aid	42
% UG rec. need-based scholarship or grant aid	50
% frosh rec. need-based self-help aid	43
% UG rec. need-based self-help aid	49
Avg. frosh grant	$23,086
Avg. frosh loan	$2,584
Independent 529 member?	Yes

RENSSELAER POLYTECHNIC INSTITUTE

110 EIGHTH STREET, TROY, NY 12180-3590 • ADMISSIONS: 518-276-6216 • FAX: 518-276-4072

CAMPUS LIFE

Quality of Life Rating	**61**
Fire Safety Rating	**92**
Type of school	private
Environment	city

STUDENTS

Total undergrad enrollment	4,888
% male/female	75/25
% from out of state	49
% from public high school	79
% live on campus	56
% in (# of) fraternities	39 (31)
% in (# of) sororities	18 (4)
% African American	4
% Asian	12
% Caucasian	70
% Hispanic	5
% international	4
# of countries represented	70

SURVEY SAYS

Registration is a breeze
Lab facilities are great
Great computer facilities
Frats and sororities dominate social scene
Lots of beer drinking
Hard liquor is popular

ACADEMICS

Academic Rating	**76**
Calendar	semester
Student/faculty ratio	14:1
Professors interesting rating	61
Professors accessible rating	66
% professors teaching UG courses	100
% classes taught by TAs	0
Most common lab size	20-29 students
Most common regular class size	20-29 students

MOST POPULAR MAJORS

Business, management, marketing, and related support services
computer and information sciences
electrical, electronics, and communications engineering

STUDENTS SPEAK OUT

Academics

In recent years Rensselaer Polytechnic Institute, the venerable math/science/engineering heavyweight of the Hudson Valley, has made "strong efforts to diversify the school into a university, rather than [being satisfied with its stature as] a technical institute. Arts programs, both electronic and conventional, are now receiving funding, along with new biotechnology programs." The goal—to "transform RPI to Rensselaer, a one-word synonym for an Ivy League-quality school"—has both champions and critics among the student body, who either praise "new programs that will help us provide the world with graduates very driven to do great things" or assert that "RPI is not and never could or should be a more liberal school. RPI is engineering and it should stay that way." While attempting to broaden the curriculum, Rensselaer remains "a very technology-oriented school that deals with cutting-edge innovations in science and engineering" and "emphasizes diversity, integrity, and above all, leadership in the context of a world-class research university." The workload here is tremendous and the concepts taught difficult to master, but students are protected by an institutional safety net; one engineer explains, "The learning assistance center has an early detection system that warns students who are below average and offers assistance. If they notice the slightest drop in performance, they will contact you in regards to what's up." For many here, "RPI's greatest strengths are its variety of options for students to gain experience in their field. We have an excellent career development center, a study abroad program, undergraduate research programs, internships and co-ops, which are very popular." Placement services are excellent thanks to "many corporate connections; alumni are always coming back and recruiting and many large and small companies love to recruit here."

Life

"Fraternity life is huge on campus," report RPI students, who note that the school is home to over 30 Greek organizations. "If you're a girl you're associated with at least one. If you're a guy who isn't associated with one, you don't have much of a social life." Explains one student, "Everyone either goes to frat parties on the weekend or stays in and plays video games." Not that there aren't other options; as one undergraduate points out, "If you want to do something on campus and be involved, it's incredibly easy to do so. The people who say otherwise are just apathetic. Between movie nights on campus, union sponsored events, fraternity and sorority events, and downtown, there are tons of things to do." Everyone agrees that "hockey is king here; everyone goes and it is amazing to watch." The team competes in NCAA Division I; RPI's 22 other varsity teams play in Division III and are not as enthusiastically supported. When regarding hometown Troy, students are mixed. While some claim that "the city is devoid of all life and fun," others assert that "downtown Troy, although not the best place to hang out at night, is pretty cool. There are some beautiful buildings and some neat shops and small eateries." An even-handed student avers, "While the city of Troy is improving, it has a long way to go before it becomes a suitable location for Rensselaer."

Student Body

"The former stereotype for RPI, as everyone knows, was that we tend to be kind of nerdy bookworms, and that we are not very involved in campus activities." Students also tell us "that is no longer true. Students are now much more involved in things all over campus, from our excellent football and hockey teams, to our 150plus clubs and activities, to new programs popping up all over campus." The school hasn't switched over entirely, of course; as one student explains, "Fifty percent of us are computer nerds who play video games and have their own social networks. The other 50 percent are normal college students who like to party and have a fun time." While the male-female ratio is quite unbalanced here, "It's not as big of a problem as it is made out to be, due to the closeness of other colleges, especially Russell Sage, an all-girls school.

RENSSELAER POLYTECHNIC INSTITUTE

FINANCIAL AID: 518-276-6813 • E-MAIL: ADMISSIONS@RPI.EDU • WEBSITE: WWW.RPI.EDU

ADMISSIONS

Very important factors considered include: Secondary school record. *Important factors considered include:* Character/personal qualities, class rank, extracurricular activities, standardized test scores. *Other factors considered include:* Alumni/ae relation, essays, geographical residence, minority status, recommendations, talent/ability, volunteer work, work experience. SAT Reasoning or ACT required. TOEFL required of all international applicants. High school diploma is required, and GED is accepted. *Academic units required:* 4 English, 4 math, 3 science, 2 social studies. *Academic units recommended:* 4 science, 3 social studies.

The Inside Word

Although scores and numbers may not be the only consideration of the admissions committee at RPI, it is important to remember that you have to have high ones in order to stay in the running for admission. Here in Troy and at many other highly selective colleges and universities, the first review weeds out those who are academically weak and without any special considerations. Underrepresented minorities and women are high on the list of desirables in the applicant pool here, and go through the admissions process without any hitches if reasonably well qualified.

FINANCIAL AID

Students should submit: FAFSA. The Princeton Review suggests that all financial aid forms be submitted as soon as possible after 1/1. *Need-based scholarships/grants offered:* Pell, SEOG, state scholarships/grants, private scholarships, the school's own gift aid, Gates Millennium Scholarship. *Loan aid offered:* FFEL Subsidized Stafford, FFEL Unsubsidized Stafford, FFEL PLUS, Federal Perkins, college/university loans from institutional funds. Applicants will be notified of awards on or about 3/25. Federal Work-study Program available. Institutional employment available. Off-campus job opportunities are good.

FROM THE ADMISSIONS OFFICE

"The oldest degree-granting technological research university in North America, Rensselaer was founded in 1824 to instruct students to apply 'science to the common purposes of life.' Rensselaer offers more than 100 programs and 1,000 courses leading to bachelor's, master's, and doctoral degrees. Undergraduates pursue studies in architecture, engineering, humanities and social sciences, management and technology, science, and information technology (IT). A pioneer in interactive learning, Rensselaer provides real-world, hands-on educational opportunities that cut across academic disciplines. Students have ready access to laboratories and attend classes involving lively discussion, problem solving, and faculty mentoring.

"New programs and facilities are enriching the student experience. The Office of First-Year Experience provides programs for students and their primary support persons that begin even before students arrive on campus. The new $80-million Biotechnology and Interdisciplinary Studies Center offers space for scientific research and discovery, while newly renovated residence halls, wireless computing network, and studio classrooms create a fertile environment for study and learning. The $100 million Experimental Media and Performing Arts Center opening in 2008 will encourage students to explore and create at the intersection of engineering and the arts.

"Rensselaer offers recreational and fitness facilities plus numerous student-run organizations and activities, including fraternities and sororities, a newspaper, a radio station, drama and musical groups, and more than 130 clubs. In addition to intramural sports, NCAA varsity sports include a Division I men's ice hockey team and 22 Division III men's and women's teams in 13 sports. Women's ice hockey is being elevated to Division I.

"Applicants for fall 2006 may submit scores from either version of the SAT. Their combined best scores will be used in admissions decisions. The ACT may be substituted for the SAT. Applicants to the accelerated program must either take the ACT or submit Math and Science scores from SAT Subject Tests."

SELECTIVITY

Admissions Rating	**91**
# of applicants	5,406
% of applicants accepted	75
% of acceptees attending	27
# accepting a place on wait list	266
% admitted from wait list	26
# of early decision applicants	152
% accepted early decision	84

FRESHMAN PROFILE

Range SAT Verbal	580-690
Average SAT Verbal	633
Range SAT Math	640-730
Average SAT Math	687
**TPR Projected Range SAT Writing*	*620-690*
Range ACT Composite	24-28
Average ACT Composite	26
Minimum Paper TOEFL	570
Minimum Computer Based TOEFL	230
% graduated top 10% of class	63
% graduated top 25% of class	94
% graduated top 50% of class	99

DEADLINES

Early decision application deadline	11/15
Early decision notification	12/31
Regular application deadline	1/1
Regular notification	3/31
Nonfall registration?	yes

APPLICANTS ALSO LOOK AT AND OFTEN PREFER

Cornell University, Massachusetts Institute of Technology

AND SOMETIMES PREFER

Boston University, Carnegie Mellon University, University of Rochester

AND RARELY PREFER

Clarkson University, Rochester Institute of Technology, SUNY at Binghamton, Syracuse University

FINANCIAL FACTS

Financial Aid Rating	**89**
Annual tuition	$31,000
Room & Board	$9,506
Books and supplies	$1,722
Required fees	$857
% frosh rec. need-based scholarship or grant aid	72
% UG rec. need-based scholarship or grant aid	72
% frosh rec. need-based self-help aid	47
% UG rec. need-based self-help aid	47
% frosh rec. any financial aid	94
% UG rec. any financial aid	87
Avg. frosh grant	$20,299
Avg. frosh loan	$5,959
Independent 529 member?	No

Rhodes College

Office of Admissions, 2000 North Parkway, Memphis, TN 38112 • Admissions: 901-843-3700 • Fax: 901-843-3631

CAMPUS LIFE

Quality of Life Rating	**99**
Fire Safety Rating	**60**
Type of school	private
Affiliation	Presbyterian
Environment	metropolis

STUDENTS

Total undergrad enrollment	1,601
% male/female	42/58
% from out of state	72
% live on campus	76
% in (# of) fraternities	49 (6)
% in (# of) sororities	53 (6)
% African American	4
% Asian	3
% Caucasian	86
% Hispanic	1
% international	1
# of countries represented	7

SURVEY SAYS

Small classes
No one cheats
Athletic facilities are great
Students are happy

ACADEMICS

Academic Rating	**94**
Calendar	semester
Student/faculty ratio	11:1
Professors interesting rating	94
Professors accessible rating	97
% professors teaching UG courses	100
% classes taught by TAs	0
Most common lab size	10-19 students
Most common regular class size	10-19 students

MOST POPULAR MAJORS

Biology/biological sciences
Business administration/management
English language and literature

STUDENTS SPEAK OUT

Academics

Students who choose small schools usually do so seeking up-close-and-personal relationships with caring, adept professors. Those who choose to come to Rhodes College for this reason are not disappointed. They tell us, "The faculty is quite possibly the best part of our college. They are real people who are more than qualified for their positions and who actively seek to get to know their students and care about the school as a whole." In return for all this help and attention, Rhodes expects results from students. The school "puts much emphasis on preparing students for graduate school. Therefore, papers that are heavily graded and commented upon by professors at Rhodes are a major part of classes." As one student puts it, "Rhodes students are very prepared for graduate school and know how to write extremely well, thanks to the numerous papers assigned." The results tell the story. Approximately one in three Rhodes graduates proceeds to graduate school soon after graduating. Of course, these results come at a price. "The workload at Rhodes is very heavy, often causing sleep deprivation," students warn.

Life

Rhodes places serious academic demands on students' time, but undergraduates still find time to have some fun. "Life at Rhodes is definitely high quality, despite the numerous hours put into academic studies," observes one. Extracurricular life "is centered around the organizations you belong to." Greek organizations "are very popular at Rhodes, but most would agree that their popularity is a good thing. Plus, most parties are open, so anyone can go. And there are also many things to do outside of Greek life." One student reports, "There isn't something that doesn't have a club or organization here. And if you find something that doesn't and a few people who want to do it with you, go to the administration, and it happens." In addition, "For fun on-campus, Rhodes Activities Board organizes all kinds of events. Plus, the McCoy Theater hosts several plays a year as well as Rhodes's hilarious late-night improv troupe, Contents Under Pressure." Beyond campus is Memphis, "an awesome city. The social possibilities are endless. [The city] has great culture, so we see the sights on the weekends. For nightlife, there's downtown, with Beale Street, Peabody Place (where movies are $5 with a student ID), the Flying Saucer (famous among Rhodents for Monday night Pint Night), plus tons of fabulous restaurants, like the Rendevous and Huey's. Also, the Cooper-Young district has cute artsy stores and yummy food." With so much to do, it's no wonder that "students tend to become over involved in activities, which creates the common look of dark circles under students' eyes."

Student Body

Rhodes has a long-standing reputation in its region as a school for wealthy whites (many people refer to it simply as "the country club"), and this reputation has hampered recent efforts to diversify the population. "One of the problems is that we have such a small minority population that many minorities do not want to apply because they will be just that, the minority," explains one student. Despite the hurdles their school faces, students agree that "the school has been trying to increase the diversity, and it is getting better." Undergraduates "are usually the high achievers that were involved in everything during high school," but they're also "genuinely friendly and accepting. The students are genuinely kind and supportive toward each other. [They] tend to identify themselves as religious but actually rarely go to services. Politically the student body is almost a 50-50 split between conservatives and liberals." Despite the school's reputation, not everyone is fabulously wealthy. One student comments, "I would say that most students are middle class or better, but not everyone is rich. In fact, a majority of people have some sort of scholarship coming into Rhodes."

FINANCIAL AID: 901-843-3810 • E-MAIL: ADMINFO@RHODES.EDU • WEBSITE: WWW.RHODES.EDU

ADMISSIONS

Very important factors considered include: Class rank, secondary school record, standardized test scores. *Important factors considered include:* Alumni/ae relation, character/personal qualities, essays, extracurricular activities, interview, minority status, recommendations, talent/ability. *Other factors considered include:* Geographical residence, state residency, volunteer work, work experience. SAT Reasoning or ACT required. TOEFL required of all international applicants. High school diploma is required, and GED is accepted. *Academic units required:* 4 English, 3 math, 2 science (2 science lab), 2 foreign language, 2 social studies, 2 history, 3 academic electives. *Academic units recommended:* 4 math.

The Inside Word

Rhodes is one of the best-kept secrets in higher education, familiar mainly to those in the Southeast but beginning to develop more national recognition. Its student body is very impressive academically. Only the college's upper-echelon competition—the best universities in the South—prevents the admissions committee from being even more selective. Even so, candidates should be prepared for a thorough review of their academic qualifications and the match they make with Rhodes.

FINANCIAL AID

Students should submit: FAFSA, CSS/Financial Aid PROFILE. The Princeton Review suggests that all financial aid forms be submitted as soon as possible after 1/1. *Need-based scholarships/grants offered:* Pell, SEOG, state scholarships/grants, private scholarships, the school's own gift aid. *Loan aid offered:* FFEL Subsidized Stafford, FFEL Unsubsidized Stafford, FFEL PLUS, Federal Perkins. Applicants will be notified of awards on or about 4/10.

FROM THE ADMISSIONS OFFICE

"It's not just one characteristic that makes Rhodes different from other colleges, it's a special blend of features that sets us apart. We are a selective liberal arts college, yet without a cutthroat atmosphere; we are a small community, yet located in a major city; we are in a metropolitan area, yet offer one of the most beautiful and serene campuses in the nation. Our students are serious about learning and yet know how to have fun in an atmosphere of trust and respect brought about by adherence to the honor code. And they know that learning at Rhodes doesn't mean sitting in a lecture hall and memorizing the professor's lecture. It means interaction, discussion, and a process of teacher and student discovering knowledge together. Community service is an integral part of the culture at Rhodes. Our students are keenly aware of their social responsibility, and over 80 percent are involved as volunteers throughout their college years. Rhodes is a place that welcomes new people and new ideas. It's a place of energy and light, not of apathy and complacency. Everyone who is a part of the Rhodes community is striving to be the best at what she/he does.

"Applicants for fall 2006 are required to take the new SAT or the ACT with or without the Writing section. Students may also submit scores from the old SAT, and their best scores from either test will be used. Home school students must submit two SAT Subject Tests from areas other than English and Math."

SELECTIVITY

Admissions Rating	**94**
# of applicants	3,429
% of applicants accepted	54
% of acceptees attending	25
# accepting a place on wait list	472
% admitted from wait list	12
# of early decision applicants	62
% accepted early decision	73

FRESHMAN PROFILE

Range SAT Verbal	600-690
Average SAT Verbal	646
Range SAT Math	590-680
Average SAT Math	636
**TPR Projected Range SAT Writing*	*630-690*
Range ACT Composite	25-30
Average ACT Composite	28
Minimum Paper TOEFL	550
Minimum Computer Based TOEFL	213
Average HS GPA	3.66
% graduated top 10% of class	51
% graduated top 25% of class	82
% graduated top 50% of class	99

DEADLINES

Early decision application deadline	11/1
Early decision notification	12/1
Regular application deadline	2/1
Regular notification	4/1
Nonfall registration?	yes

APPLICANTS ALSO LOOK AT

AND OFTEN PREFER

Davidson College, Vanderbilt University, Washington State University

AND SOMETIMES PREFER

Furman University, Trinity University, University of Richmond

AND RARELY PREFER

Emory University, Sewanee—The University of the South, Southern Methodist University

FINANCIAL FACTS

Financial Aid Rating	**77**
Annual tuition	$25,646
Room & Board	$6,904
Books and supplies	$870
Required fees	$310
% frosh rec. need-based scholarship or grant aid	44
% UG rec. need-based scholarship or grant aid	39
% frosh rec. need-based self-help aid	31
% UG rec. need-based self-help aid	28
Avg. frosh grant	$11,891
Avg. frosh loan	$3,386
Independent 529 member?	Yes

RICE UNIVERSITY

MS 17 PO BOX 1892, HOUSTON, TX 77251-1892 • ADMISSIONS: 713-348-7423 • FAX: 713-348-5952

CAMPUS LIFE

Quality of Life Rating	**99**
Fire Safety Rating	**89**
Type of school	private
Environment	metropolis

STUDENTS

Total undergrad enrollment	2,933
% male/female	51/49
% from out of state	47
% from public high school	71
% live on campus	71
% African American	7
% Asian	15
% Caucasian	55
% Hispanic	11
% Native American	1
% international	3
# of countries represented	29

SURVEY SAYS

No one cheats
Great off-campus food
Frats and sororities are unpopular or nonexistent

ACADEMICS

Academic Rating	**96**
Calendar	semester
Student/faculty ratio	5:1
Professors interesting rating	89
Professors accessible rating	88
% professors teaching UG courses	92
% classes taught by TAs	6
Most common regular class size	10-19 students

MOST POPULAR MAJORS

Biology/biological sciences
economics
English language and literature

STUDENTS SPEAK OUT

Academics

Rice University is "a small school with the scientific research capacities of a large university" whose "reputation is strong in a diverse number of areas: our Jones School of Business, our School of Architecture, our Engineering and Music schools are all huge strengths." The humanities, although less heralded, are also solid at this top-tier institution. The school's greatest strength, though, may be its ability to draw an extremely bright and intellectually curious student body. As one student explains, "If you were made in high school to feel ashamed of your true enjoyment of reading and learning, apply here. You won't be alone, as most Rice students are, first and foremost, budding scholars." Students and professors form a strong academic community at Rice. Writes one student: "Professors become intellectual bridge-builders, and they take a real interest in the development of individual minds." This air of mutual respect is exemplified and reinforced by the school's honor code, which "is taken very seriously, and no one cheats because that would be dismissing what the school stands for and decreasing the integrity of the degree earned. Take-home tests are common; cheating is unheard of." Coursework here is extremely demanding —"If you take a science or engineering class at Rice and you get an A, you will have learned. There are no easy A's, and actually, there aren't many easy B's either"—but as a result, "students get a great education, which is what we came here for."

Life

"Hands down, the residential colleges system, and lack of Greek life, make Rice an incomparably tight-knit, unique, spirited school," students here report. The colleges "dominate the social scene, holding parties almost weekly, usually with various themes such as its two largest: Night of Decadence (NOD) (synonymous with 'campus-wide undergarment party') and Bacchanalia complete with togas. Other parties include '80s or Pimps and Hos. Each week a different college sponsors 'Pub Night' with free drinks and pizza. Parties are well attended and dancing is very popular." The college system's proponents, who are many, tell us that "it unites a variety of people who might not otherwise spend any time together, and provides the same spirit of unity and crazy enthusiasm that a frat would." Students here want you to know that "despite the amount of work we always have to do, we have a great time. Rice is a really fun place." The campus is active: "The Shepherd School puts on fabulous concerts, there are always plays going on, and there are loads of clubs to join. If that's not enough there's usually a sporting event of some sort and those are all free." Then there's Houston; reports one student, "the location of the campus couldn't be better. We're in one of the truly well-heeled areas of Houston, graced by long-boughed oaks—'a tree for every student', boasts the admissions rhetoric—and home to many cultural institutions, such as the better museums, restaurants, and pubs of the greater Houston area."

Student Body

"No matter who you are or what you're into, you will find friends who are intelligent, approachable, and often wickedly funny" at Rice. Undergrads here "are passionate about what they are learning and can converse wildly on a number of subjects. People complain sometimes about how hard Rice is, but they are happy to be here." They're also happy that their classmates "are not pretentious. No one cares what car you drive or even if you have a car. No one will exclude you if you are on financial aid." While "everyone is so different that you couldn't even begin to generalize," a few generalizations do in fact hold true. One is that "there are tons of engineering majors here, and they're always building things or writing code." The other is that science and engineering students are convinced they work harder than anyone else on campus, and humanities students "get sick and tired of hearing about it."

FINANCIAL AID: 713-348-4958 • E-MAIL: ADMISSION@RICE.EDU • WEBSITE: WWW.RICE.EDU

ADMISSIONS

Very important factors considered include: Character/personal qualities, class rank, essays, extracurricular activities, recommendations, secondary school record, standardized test scores, talent/ability. *Other factors considered include:* Alumni/ae relation, geographical residence, interview, minority status, state residency, volunteer work, work experience. SAT Reasoning or ACT required. TOEFL required of all international applicants. High school diploma or equivalent is not required. *Academic units required:* 4 English, 3 math, 2 science (2 science lab), 2 foreign language, 2 social studies, 3 academic electives. *Academic units recommended:* 4 English, 4 math, 4 science (3 science lab), 4 foreign language, 2 social studies, 2 academic electives.

The Inside Word

Rice has gotten loads of positive publicity over the past few years. As a result, what was already an extremely selective university is even more so. Candidates with less than the most impressive applications are not likely to last long in the admissions process.

FINANCIAL AID

Students should submit: FAFSA, CSS/Financial Aid PROFILE, noncustodial (divorced/separated) parents' statement, business/farm supplement. The Princeton Review suggests that all financial aid forms be submitted as soon as possible after 1/1. *Need-based scholarships/grants offered:* Pell, SEOG, state scholarships/grants, private scholarships, the school's own gift aid. *Loan aid offered:* FFEL Subsidized Stafford, FFEL Unsubsidized Stafford, FFEL PLUS, Federal Perkins, college/university loans from institutional funds. Applicants will be notified of awards on or about 4/15. Federal Work-study Program available. Institutional employment available. Off-campus job opportunities are excellent.

FROM THE ADMISSIONS OFFICE

"We seek students of keen intellect and diverse backgrounds who show potential to succeed at Rice and will also contribute to the educational environment of those around them.

"Student applications are reviewed within the context of the division to which they apply. Admission committee decisions are based not only on high school grades and test scores but also on such qualities as leadership, participation in extracurricular activities, and personal creativity. Admission is extremely competitive; Rice attempts to seek out and identify those students who have demonstrated exceptional ability and the potential for personal and intellectual growth.

"Our individualized, holistic evaluation process employs many different means to identify these qualities in applicants.

"Freshman applicants for fall 2006 may take the old SAT (or ACT), in addition to three SAT Subject Tests, one in Writing and two others in fields related to the candidate's proposed area of study. Students may also take the new SAT (or ACT with Writing component) and two SAT Subject Tests in proposed fields of study."

SELECTIVITY

Admissions Rating	**98**
# of applicants	8,106
% of applicants accepted	22
% of acceptees attending	40
# of early decision applicants	168
% accepted early decision	30

FRESHMAN PROFILE

Range SAT Verbal	660-760
Range SAT Math	670-780
**TPR Projected Range SAT Writing*	*670-740*
Range ACT Composite	30-34
Minimum Paper TOEFL	600
Minimum Computer Based TOEFL	250
% graduated top 10% of class	86
% graduated top 25% of class	95
% graduated top 50% of class	99

DEADLINES

Early decision application deadline	11/1
Early decision notification	12/15
Regular application deadline	1/10
Regular notification	4/1
Nonfall registration?	no

APPLICANTS ALSO LOOK AT AND OFTEN PREFER

Harvard College
Stanford University
Yale University

AND SOMETIMES PREFER

Berkeley College
Cornell University
Duke University

AND RARELY PREFER

Carnegie Mellon University
The University of Texas—Austin
Washington University in St. Louis

FINANCIAL FACTS

Financial Aid Rating	**99**
Annual tuition	$23,310
Room & Board	$8,980
Books and supplies	$800
Required fees	$436
% frosh rec. need-based scholarship or grant aid	32
% UG rec. need-based scholarship or grant aid	33
% frosh rec. need-based self-help aid	22
% UG rec. need-based self-help aid	31
% frosh rec. any financial aid	66
% UG rec. any financial aid	64
Avg. frosh grant	$17,262
Avg. frosh loan	$2,532
Independent 529 member?	Yes

RIDER UNIVERSITY

2083 LAWRENCEVILLE ROAD, LAWRENCEVILLE, NJ 08648 • ADMISSIONS: 609-896-5042 • FAX: 609-895-6645

CAMPUS LIFE

Quality of Life Rating	**71**
Fire Safety Rating	**85**
Type of school	private
Environment	village

STUDENTS

Total undergrad enrollment	4,038
% male/female	40/60
% from out of state	24
% from public high school	80
% live on campus	56
% in (# of) fraternities	12 (8)
% in (# of) sororities	12 (7)
% African American	8
% Asian	3
% Caucasian	75
% Hispanic	5
% international	1
# of countries represented	12

SURVEY SAYS

Small classes
Frats and sororities dominate social scene
Student government is popular
Lots of beer drinking
(Almost) everyone smokes

ACADEMICS

Academic Rating	**78**
Calendar	semester
Student/faculty ratio	13:1
Professors interesting rating	79
Professors accessible rating	81
% professors teaching UG courses	95
% classes taught by TAs	0
Most common lab size	10-19 students
Most common regular class size	10-19 students

MOST POPULAR MAJORS

Business administration/management
elementary education and teaching
finance

STUDENTS SPEAK OUT

Academics

Rider University, its undergrads tell us, "is about teaching you the necessary knowledge for your intended major while really focusing on making and sharpening the skills that make you stand out as a leader." For one in three students here, that major is business-related, an area in which Rider excels. Students praise the College of Business Administration, singling out DAARSTOC—"an executive skill-building organization that has prepared me more for the business world than any other organization possibly could have"—for its unique contribution to their education. Business undergrads also appreciate "the opportunities to get involved" through internships and volunteer work, telling us that they "foster your leadership development and prepare you for the real world by teaching you and allowing you to practice the 'soft skills' that are essential to success in any career." The School of Education, part of the College of Liberal Arts, Education, & Sciences, offers an excellent program in elementary education, while the science departments, which "provide so many opportunities to do work-study lab work" are also among the most popular with students. Throughout the university, Rider emphasizes a cross-curricular approach to instruction. Students recognize the benefits; writes one, "Every class basically coexists with [all of the] others, and when you're a senior, you see how all your courses come full circle to give you a better understanding of your major." Professors here "truly care and will do anything to help you succeed, whether it's helping you outside of the classroom with certain material, or helping you to get an internship or full-time job."

Life

Rider is "centrally located between NYC and Philly," giving students plenty of reasons to flee campus in search of fun, and when the weekends arrive many—although certainly not all—do just that. A number of students return home on weekends, giving Rider its "suitcase college" reputation. An increasing number are sticking around, though, and that number is bound to increase further in coming years when new residence halls "with apartment and suite-style rooms [and the] multimillion dollar student recreation center currently under construction" open. On and around campus, "Our student entertainment council is allocated a lot of money and uses it wisely. Between movies, concerts, comedians, and themed Bronc Buffets, there is so much to do you can't possibly make all the events." Parties are frequent and well-attended; notes one undergrad, "Fraternities have parties on the weekend, but Rider does its best to offer the student body options on the weekends. Don't you worry, we do our fair share of partying, but that's just not all we're about." Hometown Lawrenceville "is not much of a town, everything is a drive away. There is nowhere to walk to."

Student Body

Rider undergrads tend to be "rich kids from New Jersey with nice cars," although "great financial aid packages" bring in talented students from other economic strata. Most here take a pragmatic approach to education; they will put in exactly the amount of work required to get good grades, but rarely more. "Not too many are particularly studious, except when mid-terms and finals roll around; then, everyone is a Rhodes Scholar," explains one undergrad. Without an impending academic deadline, the majority here would "prefer to party, hang out with friends, and have a good time four or five nights a week." A substantial minority bucks the trend, though; writes one from among their ranks, "The typical student at Rider unfortunately overshadows how amazing the top 30 percent of Rider students are. The majority are uninformed and really don't take ownership in their University. But the top 30 percent are so amazing that I feel they could beat the top 30 percent in leadership ability and performance in jobs anywhere, because they are all so driven, passionate, and prepared."

FINANCIAL AID: 609-896-5360 • E-MAIL: ADMISSIONS@RIDER.EDU • WEBSITE: WWW.RIDER.EDU

ADMISSIONS

Very important factors considered include: Class rank, secondary school record, standardized test scores. *Important factors considered include:* Essays, recommendations. *Other factors considered include:* Alumni/ae relation, character/personal qualities, extracurricular activities, interview, talent/ability, volunteer work, work experience. SAT Reasoning or ACT required. TOEFL required of all international applicants. High school diploma is required, and GED is accepted. *Academic units required:* 4 English, 2 math. *Academic units recommended:* 3 math, 3 science, 3 foreign language, 2 social studies, 2 history.

The Inside Word

In the admissions world there are two all-important mandates: recruit the college's home state, and recruit JERSEY! As a school in the Garden State, Rider deserves some special attention for the diverse group of students it brings in each year. Students who wish to attend need to have a solid academic record and good test scores. A few bumps in your academic past, however, shouldn't pose too much of a threat.

FINANCIAL AID

Students should submit: FAFSA. Regular filing deadline is 6/1. The Princeton Review suggests that all financial aid forms be submitted as soon as possible after 1/1. *Need-based scholarships/grants offered:* Pell, SEOG, state scholarships/grants, private scholarships, the school's own gift aid. *Loan aid offered:* FFEL Subsidized Stafford, FFEL Unsubsidized Stafford, FFEL PLUS, Federal Perkins, state loans, college/university loans from institutional funds, alternative loans. Applicants will be notified of awards on a rolling basis beginning on or about 4/15. Federal Work-study Program available. Institutional employment available. Off-campus job opportunities are good.

FROM THE ADMISSIONS OFFICE

"Freshman applicants for fall 2006 are required to take either the SAT or ACT exams. Writing components from either exam are recommended optional but not required. Students may submit scores from the old (prior to March 2005) SAT or ACT, and we will use the highest scores from either test."

SELECTIVITY	
Admissions Rating	**74**
# of applicants	4,197
% of applicants accepted	85
% of acceptees attending	25
FRESHMAN PROFILE	
Range SAT Verbal	470-570
Average SAT Verbal	530
Range SAT Math	470-580
Average SAT Math	529
**TPR Projected Range SAT Writing*	*530-610*
Minimum Paper TOEFL	550
Minimum Computer Based TOEFL	213
Average HS GPA	3.12
% graduated top 10% of class	13
% graduated top 25% of class	36
% graduated top 50% of class	70
DEADLINES	
Regular notification	within 3 to 4 weeks of receipt of application
Nonfall registration?	yes
FINANCIAL FACTS	
Financial Aid Rating	**72**
Annual tuition	$22,910
Room & Board	$8,840
Books and supplies	$1,000
Required fees	$560
% frosh rec. need-based scholarship or grant aid	71
% UG rec. need-based scholarship or grant aid	67
% frosh rec. need-based self-help aid	60
% UG rec. need-based self-help aid	53
% frosh rec. any financial aid	72
% UG rec. any financial aid	69
Avg. frosh grant	$11,949
Avg. frosh loan	$3,535
Independent 529 member?	Yes

RIPON COLLEGE

300 SEWARD STREET, PO BOX 248, RIPON, WI 54971 • ADMISSIONS: 920-748-8337 • FAX: 920-748-8335

CAMPUS LIFE

Quality of Life Rating	**73**
Fire Safety Rating	**62**
Type of school	private
Environment	village

STUDENTS

Total undergrad enrollment	885
% male/female	48/52
% from out of state	28
% from public high school	75
% live on campus	83
% in (# of) fraternities	30 (5)
% in (# of) sororities	20 (3)
% African American	2
% Asian	2
% Caucasian	86
% Hispanic	3
% Native American	1
% international	1
# of countries represented	13

SURVEY SAYS

Small classes
Students are friendly
Low cost of living
Intramural sports are popular
Lots of beer drinking
Hard liquor is popular

ACADEMICS

Academic Rating	**84**
Calendar	semester
Student/faculty ratio	14:1
Professors interesting rating	88
Professors accessible rating	87
% professors teaching UG courses	100
% classes taught by TAs	0
Most common lab size	10-19 students
Most common regular class size	10-19 students

MOST POPULAR MAJORS

Business administration/management
education

STUDENTS SPEAK OUT

Academics

Most students here are glad they chose Ripon. As one undergrad told us, "I'm glad I went to a small school where I get lots of personalized help and everyone—professors, administrators, town people—is so friendly because it's so small." Student satisfaction with their experiences here is impressive, and the school has responded to past complaints of shortened library hours and delayed improvements to the school with action. The profs, undergrads agree, "love to teach" and offer an educational experience that is "very personalized. The faculty and staff do their best at providing a wealth of knowledge through individual interaction. Classes tend to have many discussions, and the student's opinion is the basis for learning." Agrees another student, "From the president to professors, everyone goes out of their way to cater to the students' needs. It's an open-door policy at all levels." Several students singled out the mathematics and economics departments, deeming them "superb." If you're seeking "a nice, little hometown college in the middle of Farmland, Wisconsin, with a friendly, laid-back atmosphere." Ripon College might just be the place for you.

Life

Because the town of Ripon "doesn't have a lot more to offer socially than bars, and the larger towns are all a half-hour to [an] hour away," life at Ripon College revolves around "the big social scene in the dorms (nearly all students live on-campus)" as well as the school's robust Greek community. Students describe an active campus, complete with an arts scene ("Virtually every play is sold out each season, and there are several art and photo shows"), sporting events ("We try to support our sports teams as much as possible, especially football and basketball. It's easy because you are friends with the people playing. A lot of people are involved in intercollegiate and intramural sports. We are a sports-oriented campus"), student organizations ("There are about 30 clubs on campus, and the student senate and campus political groups are very active"), and, of course, partying ("For about half of the weekends, there is usually a lounge party sponsored by a fraternity. When these occur, independents, Greeks, and freshmen all seem to come together for a night of fun"). Comedians and speakers visit this remote campus with surprising frequency; reported one student, "Groups like College Republicans bring in high-profile speakers like Ben Stein and Alan Keyes during weeknights." And while the town of Ripon itself is dead, larger towns are not too far afield. Oshkosh and Fond du Lac are about a half-hour's drive off; Milwaukee and Madison offer a wider variety of options for those up for a 90-minute trek.

Student Body

"I think there are two types of typical students" at Ripon, reported one student. "One is friendly, outgoing, majoring in at least two subjects, and involved in lots of activities. The other does nothing except varsity sports and is majoring in exercise science, but is moderately good-looking." Diversity is minimal here, since "we are a small campus in the middle of nowhere Wisconsin. The typical student is white and middle-class, usually from the Midwest." However, "there is quite a sizable minority from other places," especially from overseas. Notes one freshman, "I am from Nevada, and there are two Russians and three natives of Hong Kong on my floor alone." The majority fit the Abercrombie and Fitch mold, while "atypical students look like the remnants of a bad Nickelodeon show, all trying their hardest to be the most different."

FINANCIAL AID: 920-748-8101 • E-MAIL: ADMINFO@RIPON.EDU • WEBSITE: WWW.RIPON.EDU

ADMISSIONS

Very important factors considered include: Interview, secondary school record. *Important factors considered include:* Character/personal qualities, class rank, extracurricular activities, recommendations, standardized test scores. *Other factors considered include:* Alumni/ae relation, essays, talent/ability, volunteer work. SAT Reasoning or ACT required. TOEFL required of all international applicants. High school diploma is required, and GED is accepted. *Academic units required:* 4 English, 2 math, 2 science, 2 social studies. *Academic units recommended:* 4 math, 4 science, 2 foreign language, 4 social studies.

The Inside Word

Candidates for admission to Ripon should prepare their applications with the knowledge that they will be subjected to a very thorough and demanding review. Even though the college faces formidable competition from other top midwestern liberal arts colleges and highly selective universities, the admissions staff succeeds at enrolling a very impressive freshman class each year. That doesn't happen without careful matchmaking and a lot of personal attention.

FINANCIAL AID

Students should submit: FAFSA. The Princeton Review suggests that all financial aid forms be submitted as soon as possible after 1/1. *Need-based scholarships/grants offered:* Pell, SEOG, state scholarships/grants, private scholarships, the school's own gift aid. *Loan aid offered:* FFEL Subsidized Stafford, FFEL Unsubsidized Stafford, FFEL PLUS, Federal Perkins. Applicants will be notified of awards on a rolling basis beginning on or about 3/1. Federal Work-study Program available. Institutional employment available. Off-campus job opportunities are good.

FROM THE ADMISSIONS OFFICE

"Since its founding in 1851, Ripon College has adhered to the philosophy that the liberal arts offer the richest foundation for intellectual, cultural, social, and spiritual growth. Academic strength is a 150-year tradition at Ripon. We attract excellent professors who are dedicated to their disciplines; they in turn attract bright, committed students from 36 states and 19 countries. Ripon has a national reputation for academic excellence—evidenced by a 2002 Rhodes scholar, the college's third, and a 2003 Fulbright scholar—as well as a friendly, relaxed atmosphere, small class size, and the availability of outstanding facilities. Ripon is also a community. Not only do you see your professor in the classroom, but you can relate to them in a variety of other social situations. Ripon offers a rigorous curriculum in 30 major areas, including unique pre-professional programs. There is also ample opportunity for cocurricular involvement.

"Applicants for the fall 2006 entering must submit scores from either the ACT (writing section not required) or the SAT. We will allow students to submit scores from the old (prior to March 2005) version of either test and will use their best scores for admissions decisions."

SELECTIVITY

Admissions Rating	**80**
# of applicants	959
% of applicants accepted	82
% of acceptees attending	26

FRESHMAN PROFILE

Range SAT Verbal	500-590
Average SAT Verbal	550
Range SAT Math	490-610
Average SAT Math	535
**TPR Projected Range SAT Writing*	*560-620*
Range ACT Composite	20-27
Average ACT Composite	23
Minimum Paper TOEFL	550
Minimum Computer Based TOEFL	220
Average HS GPA	3.43
% graduated top 10% of class	22
% graduated top 25% of class	57
% graduated top 50% of class	87

DEADLINES

Regular notification	rolling
Nonfall registration?	yes

APPLICANTS ALSO LOOK AT

AND OFTEN PREFER
Lawrence University
Marquette University
University of Wisconsin—Madison

AND SOMETIMES PREFER
Grinnell College
Illinois Wesleyan University

AND RARELY PREFER
Beloit College
Cornell College
Lake Forest College
Saint Olaf College

FINANCIAL FACTS

Financial Aid Rating	**88**
Annual tuition	$20,490
Room & Board	$5,360
Books and supplies	$1,000
Required fees	$240
% frosh rec. need-based scholarship or grant aid	80
% UG rec. need-based scholarship or grant aid	80
% frosh rec. need-based self-help aid	67
% UG rec. need-based self-help aid	63
% frosh rec. any financial aid	99
% UG rec. any financial aid	97
Avg. frosh grant	$13,825
Avg. frosh loan	$3,744
Independent 529 member?	Yes

ROCHESTER INSTITUTE OF TECHNOLOGY

60 LOMB MEMORIAL DRIVE, ROCHESTER, NY 14623-5604 • ADMISSIONS: 585-475-6631 • FAX: 585-475-7424

CAMPUS LIFE

Quality of Life Rating	**68**
Fire Safety Rating	**99**
Type of school	private
Environment	city

STUDENTS

Total undergrad enrollment	11,750
% male/female	71/29
% from out of state	45
% from public high school	85
% live on campus	60
% in (# of) fraternities	5 (19)
% in (# of) sororities	5 (10)
% African American	5
% Asian	7
% Caucasian	71
% Hispanic	3
% international	4
# of countries represented	90

SURVEY SAYS

Small classes
Lab facilities are great
Great computer facilities
Great library
Athletic facilities are great
Great off-campus food

ACADEMICS

Academic Rating	**79**
Calendar	quarter
Student/faculty ratio	14:1
Professors interesting rating	65
Professors accessible rating	63
% professors teaching UG courses	95
% classes taught by TAs	0
Most common lab size	10-19 students
Most common regular class size	10-19 students

MOST POPULAR MAJORS

Computer and information sciences
information technology
photography

STUDENTS SPEAK OUT

Academics

Come to the Rochester Institute of Technology (RIT) for what students call "a great technical education with a side of liberal arts and almost anything else that you desire." The school "utilizes the newest and most advanced technologies," thanks to sponsorships and partnerships with "corporate giants like Xerox, Kodak, and Bausch and Lomb." Not only do engineers and scientists reap the benefits of this techno-paradise, but art students also prosper. One writes, "Some programs really feel rewarding and involving here, like the film and animation program, and other arts programs give creative bohemians some experience with twenty-first-century technology." The result of all this high-tech training is that "RIT is well known in the business world; and 90 percent of grads are hired within six months. That's only the graduates, of course. Not everyone makes it through," since "the academic environment is strenuous and it is very easy to get behind," thanks in large part to the quarterly academic calendar. Fortunately, most professors "are readily available outside of the classroom, and are very friendly." The administration, in contrast, is seen as aloof, less concerned about addressing current students' complaints than about raising money and planning for the school's long-term future. That future, by the way, could be very different from the present. One undergraduate explains, "The college of engineering and the college of science want the university to become a research institution, while the college of liberal arts, imaging arts, and the school for the deaf fear that growth in graduate programs would negatively affect the quality of undergraduate education."

Life

"Most RIT students study, study, study," undergraduates tell us. "Art students are running around working on projects, and engineers spend late nights in the labs." Students' desire to succeed and the quarter system combine to create an "incredibly stressful" atmosphere, "especially toward the end of the quarter." Some try to relieve stress with alcohol, and most succeed despite the school's "many restrictions on alcohol." Undergrads evade the restrictions by heading off campus to student apartments for parties. Once an extracurricular sinkhole, RIT is currently "making some ground on the social elements. They've recently added a number of social venues, including a popular coffee shop, and a recently opened field house which has helped bring concerts and other events to campus. Some students have even developed affection for their wintry hometown. One student writes, "When I first came to Rochester, I was disheartened by the industrial 'rust belt' look of it. But the longer I live here, the more I love it. It's a place I could see myself settling down in for the first few years after college." Another undergraduate shares this sentiment: "Nightlife in Rochester is pretty good. I usually go to independent film theaters and ethnic restaurants off campus." College hockey is "popular, and draws substantial, rowdy crowds on weekends," and is likely to become even bigger as the men's team enters the NCAA Division I in 2005.

Student Body

Despite its reputation as a "geek" school, "RIT has an interesting mix of scientists, engineers, business students, arts students, and liberal arts students." The heavy science and engineering presence, however, means "RIT attracts a disproportionately high number of, for lack of a better word, dorks. However, there are a fair share of balanced individuals." Among other interesting facts about the school's student body, RIT's partnership with the National Technical Institute for the Deaf "translates into about 10 to 15 percent of the students being hearing impaired." One student tells us that "there are so many diverse cultures, and that really amazed me when I got here." Unfortunately, "this is not a very social campus," and students tend to stick within small groups defined by major, ethnicity, hearing status, and/or sexual preference.

Rochester Institute of Technology

Financial Aid: 585-475-2186 • E-mail: admissions@rit.edu • Website: www.rit.edu

ADMISSIONS

Very important factors considered include: Secondary school record. *Important factors considered include:* Class rank, standardized test scores. *Other factors considered include:* Alumni/ae relation, character/personal qualities, essays, extracurricular activities, geographical residence, interview, minority status, recommendations, talent/ability, volunteer work, work experience. SAT Reasoning or ACT required. TOEFL required of all international applicants. High school diploma is required, and GED is accepted. *Academic units required:* 4 English, 2 math, 2 science (1 science lab), 4 social studies, 10 academic electives. *Academic units recommended:* 4 English, 3 math, 3 science (2 science lab), 3 foreign language, 4 social studies, 5 academic electives.

The Inside Word

RIT is not as competitive as the top tier of technical schools, but its location and contacts with major research corporations make it a top choice for many students. The acceptance rate is deceptively high when considered in conjunction with the student academic profile and the high yield of admitted students who enroll. There is a strong element of self-selection at work in the applicant pool; the successful candidate is one who is solid academically and ready to hit the ground running.

FINANCIAL AID

Students should submit: FAFSA, state aid form. Regular filing deadline is 3/15. The Princeton Review suggests that all financial aid forms be submitted as soon as possible after 1/1. *Need-based scholarships/grants offered:* Pell, SEOG, state scholarships/grants, private scholarships, the school's own gift aid. *Loan aid offered:* Direct Subsidized Stafford, Direct Unsubsidized Stafford, Direct PLUS, Federal Perkins, private bank loans. Applicants will be notified of awards on a rolling basis beginning on or about 3/15. Federal Work-study Program available. Institutional employment available. Off-campus job opportunities are excellent.

FROM THE ADMISSIONS OFFICE

"A nationally respected leader in professional and career-oriented education, RIT has been described as one of America's most imitated institutions and has been recognized as one of the nation's leading universities. RIT has also been rated the number one comprehensive university in the East for its scientific and technology programs. RIT's strength lies in its dedication to providing superior career preparation for today's students. This has attracted excellent faculty to RIT and has led to the development of academic programs that combine small classes and an emphasis on undergraduate teaching, modern classroom facilities, and work experience gained through the university's cooperative education program. Few universities provide RIT's variety of career-oriented programs. Our eight colleges offer outstanding programs in business, engineering, art and design, science and mathematics, liberal arts, photography, hotel management, computer science, and other areas. RIT's National Technical Institute for the Deaf (NTID) is the world's largest mainstreamed college program for the deaf and hearing impaired.

"Students applying for freshman admission to RIT for fall 2006 must submit test scores from either the new SAT (with Writing section) or the ACT. Students who complete the ACT may submit scores with or without the optional Writing section, but the Writing section is recommended."

SELECTIVITY

Admissions Rating	**88**
# of applicants	9,108
% of applicants accepted	67
% of acceptees attending	37
# accepting a place on wait list	150
% admitted from wait list	17
# of early decision applicants	713
% accepted early decision	76

FRESHMAN PROFILE

Range SAT Verbal	540-640
Range SAT Math	570-670
**TPR Projected Range* SAT Writing	*590-660*
Range ACT Composite	23-28
Minimum Paper TOEFL	550
Minimum Computer Based TOEFL	215
Average HS GPA	3.7
% graduated top 10% of class	31
% graduated top 25% of class	66
% graduated top 50% of class	92

DEADLINES

Early decision application deadline	12/1
Early decision notification	1/15
Regular application deadline	2/1
Regular notification	rolling
Nonfall registration?	yes

APPLICANTS ALSO LOOK AT

AND OFTEN PREFER

Carnegie Mellon University
Cornell University
Massachusetts Institute of Technology

AND SOMETIMES PREFER

Rensselaer Polytechnic Institute
Syracuse University
University of Rochester

AND RARELY PREFER

Clarkson College
Drexel University

FINANCIAL FACTS

Financial Aid Rating	**91**
Annual tuition	$21,447
Room & Board	$8,136
Books and supplies	$600
Required fees	$357
% frosh rec. need-based scholarship or grant aid	67
% UG rec. need-based scholarship or grant aid	67
% frosh rec. need-based self-help aid	63
% UG rec. need-based self-help aid	63
% frosh rec. any financial aid	81
% UG rec. any financial aid	75
Avg. frosh grant	$10,300
Avg. frosh loan	$4,400
Independent 529 member?	Yes

ROLLINS COLLEGE

CAMPUS BOX 2720, WINTER PARK, FL 32789-4499 • ADMISSIONS: 407-646-2161 • FAX: 407-646-1502

CAMPUS LIFE

Quality of Life Rating	**76**
Fire Safety Rating	**79**
Type of school	private
Environment	town

STUDENTS

Total undergrad enrollment	1,759
% male/female	40/60
% from out of state	51
% from public high school	58
% live on campus	66
% in (# of) fraternities	38 (5)
% in (# of) sororities	40 (5)
% African American	5
% Asian	4
% Caucasian	74
% Hispanic	8
% Native American	1
% international	3
# of countries represented	43

SURVEY SAYS

Small classes
Athletic facilities are great
Students love Winter Park, FL
Great off-campus food
Students are happy
Lots of beer drinking
Hard liquor is popular

ACADEMICS

Academic Rating	**85**
Calendar	semester
Student/faculty ratio	11:1
Professors interesting rating	77
Professors accessible rating	74
% professors teaching UG courses	100
% classes taught by TAs	0
Most common regular class size	10-19 students

MOST POPULAR MAJORS

Economics
international business
psychology

STUDENTS SPEAK OUT

Academics

Students at small, exclusive Rollins College in Winter Park, Florida (just six miles north of Orlando), praise their school for its devoted faculty, attentive administration, and "solid reputation for academics, which has job recruiters impressed." Professors here earn high marks because they "genuinely care about their students and are always willing to help in or outside of class about any issue. Every teacher I have had has proved to be excellent at keeping lectures interesting and getting students involved." Also, "due to small class sizes, it is very easy to find a time to meet, and you aren't jockeying with 100 other students for five minutes of the professor's time." In such an environment, "you get a lot of personal attention," leading to a student body extremely satisfied with its academic experience. The school gets bonus points for "numerous study abroad programs that are easy to become involved in" and "an appeals committee that meets every week and actually pays attention to students' problems. The small school atmosphere minimizes the bureaucratic bull."

Life

"Don't be surprised to see a group of frat guys lying by the pool in their plaid and checkered bathing suits and discussing the hot spots of the Caribbean," as one student describes a typical day on the Rollins campus, adding, "Let's put it this way: we have shirts that say 'Rollins College Country Club.'" In keeping with the country club vibe, the Rollins campus has a "laid-back atmosphere. If you are someone who wants to spend a few extra years just relaxing, Rollins is definitely the place." The campus is "beautiful, in the Spanish style." Undergrads also appreciate how "the small campus means no walk to class is more than five minutes, and everything is very accessible." Academics are demanding here, but even so, "partying is not just reserved for the weekends!" During the week, students try to finish their studies early enough to "go clubbing in downtown Orlando." Notes one student, "The local music scene in Orlando is pretty strong, and it's always worthwhile to check out the bands." On weekends, "everyone heads to their condos at the nearby beaches." The allure of the beach means that "the campus really empties out on the weekends." Students also pack up and head for the shore on Fox Day, "when the school president puts a big fox statue on the school lawn. It means that all classes are canceled. Everyone goes to the beach." Students agree that Orlando is great for shopping, restaurants, and fun.

Student Body

The students of Rollins College are rich. How rich are they? As one undergrad put it, "Trust funds. Lots of Prada and Gucci. It's not uncommon to see students driving BMWs, Mercedes, and other fancy and expensive cars. The girls never wear the same clothes twice, and they brush their hair during class." Many students wish for more diversity on campus but say that "minority students who choose not to distance themselves from the other students on campus are usually accepted." Writes one student, "I think there are definitely some snobs here, but they are still nice people. A lot of kids here went to boarding schools, so sometimes you'll find kids that think the world should revolve around them because they have money. I'm from a public school, though, and I have no trouble getting along with them." Many also warn that "Rollins is small. It's high school all over again. 'So and so is dating so and so and oh-my-gosh, did you hear about her?' A lot of the cattiness and snobbishness that people talk about is not just rumor."

FINANCIAL AID: 407-646-2395 • E-MAIL: ADMISSION@ROLLINS.EDU • WEBSITE: WWW.ROLLINS.EDU

ADMISSIONS

Very important factors considered include: Secondary school record. *Important factors considered include:* Essays, extracurricular activities, recommendations, standardized test scores, talent/ability. *Other factors considered include:* Alumni/ae relation, character/personal qualities, class rank, interview, minority status, volunteer work, work experience. SAT Reasoning or ACT required. SAT Subject Tests recommended. TOEFL required of all international applicants. High school diploma is required, and GED is accepted. *Academic units required:* 4 English, 3 math, 2 science, 2 foreign language, 2 social studies, 2 history, 2 academic electives. *Academic units recommended:* 4 English, 4 math, 4 science, 3 foreign language, 3 social studies, 3 history, 3 academic electives.

The Inside Word

It's fairly important to put together a well-rounded candidacy when applying to Rollins. Grades and test scores are significant, but the admissions committee puts a great deal of emphasis on the whole package when evaluating candidates. Despite this thorough personal approach, solid numbers will still be enough on their own to get you admitted, provided you don't take the process too lightly.

FINANCIAL AID

Students should submit: FAFSA, institution's own financial aid form. Regular filing deadline is 3/1. The Princeton Review suggests that all financial aid forms be submitted as soon as possible after 1/1. *Need-based scholarships/grants offered:* Pell, SEOG, state scholarships/grants, private scholarships, the school's own gift aid. *Loan aid offered:* Direct Subsidized Stafford, Direct Unsubsidized Stafford, Direct PLUS, Federal Perkins, college/university loans from institutional funds. Applicants will be notified of awards on a rolling basis beginning on or about 3/1. Federal Work-study Program available. Off-campus job opportunities are excellent.

FROM THE ADMISSIONS OFFICE

"As you begin the college selection process, remember that you are in control of your destiny. Your academic record—course load, grades earned, test scores—are the most important part of your application credentials. But Rollins also pays close attention to your personal dimension—interests, strengths, values, and potential to contribute to college life. Don't sell yourself short in the application process. Be proud of what you've accomplished and who you are, and be honest when you describe yourself. Finally, the Admission Committee always likes to see candidates who express interest in the college. If we're your first choice, apply Early Decision. Each year we admit approximately one-third of the entering class through the Early Decision process. Are you unsure about your choice? If you can, schedule some visits, meet with an admission counselor, tour campus, and spend time in a class so you can see for yourself what Rollins and other colleges are all about. Take control of your destiny, and enjoy the process along the way.

"First-year applicants for fall 2006 may submit either SAT or ACT scores for admission consideration. Candidates are strongly encouraged to complete the new Writing components, but results without Writing will be considered. Each candidate's best score combination will be used in the selection process."

SELECTIVITY

Admissions Rating	**89**
# of applicants	2,598
% of applicants accepted	59
% of acceptees attending	31
# accepting a place on wait list	200
% admitted from wait list	15
# of early decision applicants	192
% accepted early decision	70

FRESHMAN PROFILE

Range SAT Verbal	540-640
Average SAT Verbal	592
Range SAT Math	540-640
Average SAT Math	592
**TPR Projected Range SAT Writing*	*590-660*
Minimum Paper TOEFL	550
Minimum Computer Based TOEFL	213
Average HS GPA	3.4
% graduated top 10% of class	39
% graduated top 25% of class	68
% graduated top 50% of class	91

DEADLINES

Early decision application deadline	11/15
Early decision notification	12/15
Regular application deadline	2/15
Regular notification	4/1
Nonfall registration?	yes

APPLICANTS ALSO LOOK AT

AND OFTEN PREFER
Vanderbilt University

AND SOMETIMES PREFER
Emory University
Furman University
Tulane University
University of Florida
University of Miami

AND RARELY PREFER
Eckerd College
Stetson University

FINANCIAL FACTS

Financial Aid Rating	**88**
Annual tuition	$26,910
Room & Board	$8,570
Books and supplies	$550
Required fees	$790
% frosh rec. need-based scholarship or grant aid	40
% UG rec. need-based scholarship or grant aid	40
% frosh rec. need-based self-help aid	38
% UG rec. need-based self-help aid	38
% frosh rec. any financial aid	67
% UG rec. any financial aid	71
Avg. frosh grant	$17,291
Avg. frosh loan	$3,948
Independent 529 member?	Yes

ROSE-HULMAN INSTITUTE OF TECHNOLOGY

5500 WABASH AVENUE-CM 1, TERRE HAUTE, IN 47803-3999 • ADMISSIONS: 812-877-8213 • FAX: 812-877-8941

CAMPUS LIFE

Quality of Life Rating	**84**
Fire Safety Rating	**73**
Type of school	private
Environment	town

STUDENTS

Total undergrad enrollment	1,760
% male/female	81/19
% from out of state	53
% from public high school	80
% live on campus	59
% in (# of) fraternities	37 (8)
% in (# of) sororities	43 (2)
% African American	3
% Asian	3
% Caucasian	91
% Hispanic	2
% international	1
# of countries represented	16

SURVEY SAYS

Small classes
Lab facilities are great
Great computer facilities
Athletic facilities are great
School is well run
Students are friendly
Campus feels safe
Very little drug use

ACADEMICS

Academic Rating	**87**
Calendar	quarter
Student/faculty ratio	13:1
Professors interesting rating	88
Professors accessible rating	90
% professors teaching UG courses	100
% classes taught by TAs	0
Most common lab size	20-29 students
Most common regular class size	20-29 students

MOST POPULAR MAJORS

Chemical engineering
electrical, electronics, and communications engineering
mechanical engineering

STUDENTS SPEAK OUT

Academics

The engineering school with a heart: that could be the slogan for the Rose-Hulman Institute of Technology, according to students here. "Everyone here is very personable and accessible," writes one undergrad. "There aren't too many schools where the president will routinely sit down and eat lunch with the students." Agrees another, "The relationships are very personal. I've had teachers invite us to their house and even come in late at night to hold a study session. When I see a professor around town, it's so cool to talk to them. They know who you are." The "small class size and individual attention to students' needs" at Rose "ensure that a rigorous engineering curriculum is understood by all students." Rigorous indeed—as one engineer put it, "Rose is a great school if you have no problem with devoting your life to studying for four years." The workload requires "110 percent effort," and the material can be downright soporific; explains one student, "The Rose-Hulman professors' ability to send their students into a zombie-like state from the amount of homework and studying is matched only by the excitement they show during classes while teaching stuff they love." As you might expect, profs here "all have quirks ranging from being an anglophile to being a hippie to climbing Mt. Kilimanjaro." In this way, they match the students; explains one, "The professors are all really unique; you know you have the right major when they remind you of you." One such idiosyncratic student thinks—and writes—like a pirate. Quoth the scholar-brigand of his instructors: "Argh, the profs, they be good, matey. I be gettin' a good book-learnin'."

Life

As at most engineering schools, "Life at Rose is spent mostly studying and always worrying if we haven't. Everyone is excited about the good salaries they will earn after college, or the stuff they'll be equipped to do." Reports one student, "Everything revolves around homework. Last year after two guys in the sophomore engineering curriculum disagreed about an equation, one hog-tied the other and scribbled his version all over his body. This is our idea of a joke." When books are closed and computers shut down, Rose is a "very Greek-oriented" school; "For the most part, if you're an upperclassman and aren't Greek, you've got nothing to do," complains one sophomore engineer. Some here make their own entertainment ("We have hall sports. This includes shooting frozen oranges at cardboard boxes with slingshots. And lubricating the floor and sliding in your socks," reports one resourceful undergrad), while many others simply "spend a lot of time in their rooms on their computers. We like to tool it up and play LAN games on our kick-ass network. Yeah!" Intramural sports are also popular. Terre Haute, unfortunately, doesn't offer much in the way of off-campus diversion. Now, you are no doubt wondering: "What do the pirates at Rose-Hulman do for fun?" Answer: "Thar she blows! We enjoy math, cars, sports, and women."

Student Body

Rose's "religious, conservative" students "have glasses [and] pasty white skin" and are mostly "hard working, small-town kids that learn well hands-on. There are a lot of incredibly technically gifted students here. It is a techie's paradise!" The majority "are male and have problems communicating with members of the opposite sex (welcome to an engineering school!)." These self-described "tools" like to "play video games constantly or computer games," although a sizable subpopulation is into athletics. "We're very diverse socially," notes one wry student. "We have everyone from computer nerds to computer jocks." The few women here note, kind of optimistically, that "the odds are good, but the goods are odd." Pirates at this school are apparently homophobes; wrote one, "Shiver me timbers, they hate gay people and love naked wenches."

FINANCIAL AID: 812-877-8259 • E-MAIL: ADMIS.OFC@ROSE-HULMAN.EDU • WEBSITE: WWW.ROSE-HULMAN.EDU

ADMISSIONS

Very important factors considered include: Class rank, secondary school record, standardized test scores. *Important factors considered include:* Character/personal qualities, minority status, recommendations. *Other factors considered include:* Alumni/ae relation, extracurricular activities, interview, talent/ability, volunteer work, work experience. SAT Reasoning or ACT required. TOEFL required of all international applicants. High school diploma is required, and GED is not accepted. *Academic units required:* 4 English, 4 math, 2 science (2 science lab), 2 social studies, 4 academic electives. *Academic units recommended:* 5 math, 3 science.

The Inside Word

Nine years ago, after 100 years as an all-male institution, Rose-Hulman opened its doors to women. The results have been largely successful—each of the last two freshman classes were 20 percent women. The Institute expects to continue at this pace as it builds up the female presence on its campus; thus, for adventurous, ambitious, and technologically-minded women, Rose-Hulman will be a relatively easy admit for the foreseeable future. "Relatively" is the key word here; academic standards are high and so are the expectations of the admissions committee.

FINANCIAL AID

Students should submit: FAFSA. The Princeton Review suggests that all financial aid forms be submitted as soon as possible after 1/1. *Need-based scholarships/grants offered:* Pell, SEOG, state scholarships/grants, the school's own gift aid. *Loan aid offered:* Direct Subsidized Stafford, Direct Unsubsidized Stafford, Direct PLUS, Federal Perkins. Applicants will be notified of awards on or about 3/10. Federal Work-study Program available.

FROM THE ADMISSIONS OFFICE

"Rose-Hulman is generally considered one of the premier undergraduate colleges of engineering and science. We are nationally known as an institution that puts teaching above research and graduate programs. At Rose-Hulman, professors (not graduate students) teach the courses and conduct their own labs. Department chairmen teach freshmen. To enhance the teaching at Rose-Hulman, computers have become a prominent addition to not only our labs but also in our classrooms and residence halls. Additionally, all students are now required to purchase laptop computers. Ninety million dollars in new facilities have been added in the last six years.

"Students applying for admission into the fall 2006 class may submit either the SAT or ACT, and the student's best scores from either test will be considered. Both new and old SAT test scores are acceptable. The Writing portion of either test will not be required for admission to the freshman class of 2006."

SELECTIVITY

Admissions Rating	**92**
# of applicants	3,088
% of applicants accepted	70
% of acceptees attending	22

FRESHMAN PROFILE

Range SAT Verbal	570-680
Average SAT Verbal	620
Range SAT Math	640-730
Average SAT Math	680
**TPR Projected Range SAT Writing*	*610-680*
Range ACT Composite	27-32
Average ACT Composite	29
Minimum Paper TOEFL	550
Minimum Computer Based TOEFL	210
% graduated top 10% of class	62
% graduated top 25% of class	96
% graduated top 50% of class	100

DEADLINES

Regular application deadline	3/1
Regular notification	rolling
Nonfall registration?	no

APPLICANTS ALSO LOOK AT

AND OFTEN PREFER

Carnegie Mellon University
Case Western Reserve University
Purdue University—West Lafayette
University of Illinois at Urbana-Champaign

AND SOMETIMES PREFER

Georgia Institute of Technology
Massachusetts Institute of Technology
Northwestern University
Washington University in St. Louis

AND RARELY PREFER

Ohio State University—Columbus
University of Michigan—Ann Arbor

FINANCIAL FACTS

Financial Aid Rating	**71**
Annual tuition	$25,686
Room & Board	$7,065
Books and supplies	$1,200
Required fees	$450
% frosh rec. need-based scholarship or grant aid	72
% UG rec. need-based scholarship or grant aid	69
% frosh rec. need-based self-help aid	65
% UG rec. need-based self-help aid	64
% frosh rec. any financial aid	99
% UG rec. any financial aid	99
Avg. frosh grant	$7,969
Avg. frosh loan	$7,243
Independent 529 member?	Yes

RUTGERS UNIVERSITY—NEW BRUNSWICK

65 DAVIDSON ROAD, PISCATAWAY, NJ 08854-8097 • ADMISSIONS: 732-932-4636 • FAX: 732-445-0237

CAMPUS LIFE

Quality of Life Rating	**64**
Fire Safety Rating	**84**
Type of school	public
Environment	town

STUDENTS

Total undergrad enrollment	26,366
% male/female	48/52
% from out of state	8
% live on campus	47
% African American	9
% Asian	22
% Caucasian	55
% Hispanic	8
% international	2

SURVEY SAYS

Great computer facilities
Great library
Athletic facilities are great
Diverse student types on campus
Student publications are popular
Lots of beer drinking
Hard liquor is popular
(Almost) everyone smokes

ACADEMICS

Academic Rating	**72**
Calendar	semester
Student/faculty ratio	14:1
Professors interesting rating	61
Professors accessible rating	62
% professors teaching UG courses	70
% classes taught by TAs	20
Most common lab size	20-29 students
Most common regular class size	10-19 students

STUDENTS SPEAK OUT

Academics

What to expect from this large state school? Quality education at an "incredibly affordable price," students say. The New Brunswick campus alone encompasses twelve separate colleges, each with its own focus. Among them are historic Rutgers' College, the environmentally focused Cook College,the all-women's Douglass College, the well-regarded School of Engineering, plus schools in nursing, pharmacy, public policy, communication, and business. With so much to choose from, it takes a real self-starter to make the most of a Rutgers experience. "The school has a lot to offer if you can find it," writes a sophomore. "The professors are some of the best in their fields," adds another student. It's not surprising, then, that students want more face time with professors—and less with their TAs. But some programs give you more individual attention than others. One senior writes, "Since I am a physics major, most of my classes are around ten people and my professors are available almost all the time." For students in majors with higher enrollments, however, "good luck getting the classes you want." This brings us to the so-called "RU Screw," which has come to symbolize all the ways individual students feel ignored or overlooked by the school's administration—everything from slow bus service among campuses to rude front office staff. One student, takes a more levelheaded approach: "Although many people complain about the 'RU Screw,' there's bound to be some frustration when an administration has to handle over 20,000 undergraduates." The recent creation of the Office of the Ombudsperson seeks to help students resolve their campus difficulties, and is a step in the right direction.

Life

One clever senior describes this place as a "small community with a large population." According to another student there is no shortage of opportunity for extracurricular activities. "There are a thousand and one different activities to join, so there's no excuse for not getting involved in something. At the beginning of every fall semester, there's a huge involvement fair on College Avenue where all the organizations set up tables to attract people." One student has discovered that New Brunswick "is very suburban, but it's like a mini city. There are clubs and lounges downtown, but dorming is probably the quickest way to meet people and have friends for life." A sophomore adds, "Hanging out in the dorms can be fun. It is not always necessary to go off campus. Since there is more than one campus, you can always find something to do or somewhere to go." At Rutgers, "partying is prominent," and students have the option to join a number of fraternities and sororities. Aside from partying, though, students have football games, the annual Rutgers and Spring Fests, free movie nights, and guest comedians to keep them entertained. Still, for some students that is not enough to make up for sleepy New Brunswick. They are left to mourn the "dead social life on weekends." One thing most students lament together is the overcrowded and painfully slow inter-campus bus system. "Transportation definitely needs to improve," one freshman warns.

Student Body

Students differ across the various New Brunswick colleges, whose populations tend to be self-selecting. In the engineering school, for example, you'll find a more scientific crowd. In the Douglass College, you'll find only women. One student puts it this way: "There are academically oriented students, socially-oriented students, and students that fall in the middle." With such a large student population, the campus itself is ethnically and socioeconomically diverse. But getting all those groups to mix is not always easy. "Different races hardly associate with each other!" complains one junior. Nevertheless, says another student, there are "limitless chances to meet a variety of different people—everyone can find their niche."

FINANCIAL AID: 732-932-7057 • WEBSITE: WWW.RUTGERS.EDU

ADMISSIONS

Very important factors considered include: Class rank, secondary school record, standardized test scores. *Other factors considered include:* Essays, extracurricular activities, geographical residence, interview, minority status, recommendations, state residency, talent/ability, volunteer work, work experience. SAT Reasoning or ACT required. TOEFL required of all international applicants. High school diploma is required, and GED is accepted. *Academic units required:* 4 English, 3 math, 2 science, 2 foreign language, 5 academic electives. *Academic units recommended:* 4 math, 2 foreign language.

The Inside Word

New Jersey residents are finally acknowledging that the flagship of their state university system is among the finest public universities in the nation. As a result, getting in keeps getting tougher every year as more and more New Jersey residents elect to stay home for college.

FINANCIAL AID

Students should submit: FAFSA. The Princeton Review suggests that all financial aid forms be submitted as soon as possible after 1/1. *Need-based scholarships/grants offered:* Pell, SEOG, state scholarships/grants, private scholarships, the school's own gift aid, Outside scholarships. *Loan aid offered:* Direct Subsidized Stafford, Direct Unsubsidized Stafford, Direct PLUS, Federal Perkins, state loans, college/university loans from institutional funds educational loans. Applicants will be notified of awards on a rolling basis beginning on or about 2/1. Federal Work-study Program available. Institutional employment available. Off-campus job opportunities are good.

FROM THE ADMISSIONS OFFICE

"Rutgers, The State University of New Jersey, one of only 61 members of the Association of American Universities, is a research university, which attracts students from across the nation and around the world. What does it take to be accepted for admission to Rutgers University? There's no single answer to that question. Our primary emphasis is on your past academic performance as indicated by your high school grades (particularly in required academic subjects), your class rank, the strength of your academic program, your standardized test scores on the SAT or ACT, any special talents you may have, and your participation in school and community activities. We seek students with a broad diversity of talents, interests, and backgrounds. Above all else, we're looking for students who will get the most out of a Rutgers education—students with the intellect, initiative, and motivation to make full use of the opportunities we have to offer.

"In order to complete the application by our December 1 priority date, fall 2006 first-year applicants should take the new SAT Reasoning Test or ACT including the Writing component no later than November of their senior year of high school. Students who graduated more than two years ago or who have completed more than 12 credits since high school are not required to submit test scores."

SELECTIVITY

Admissions Rating	**87**
# of applicants	24,434
% of applicants accepted	61
% of acceptees attending	32

FRESHMAN PROFILE

Range SAT Verbal	540-640
Range SAT Math	570-670
**TPR Projected Range SAT Writing*	*590-660*
Minimum Paper TOEFL	550
% graduated top 10% of class	39
% graduated top 25% of class	80
% graduated top 50% of class	99

DEADLINES

Regular notification	2/28
Nonfall registration?	yes

APPLICANTS ALSO LOOK AT

AND OFTEN PREFER

Cornell University
University of Pennsylvania
University of Virginia

AND SOMETIMES PREFER

Boston College
Montclair State University
New Jersey Institute of Technology
Penn State University Park

AND RARELY PREFER

The George Washington University
Seton Hall University

FINANCIAL FACTS

Financial Aid Rating	**75**
Annual in-state tuition	$6,793
Annual out-of-state tuition	$13,828
Room & Board	$8,357
Books and supplies	$800
Required fees	$1,771
% frosh rec. need-based scholarship or grant aid	35
% UG rec. need-based scholarship or grant aid	34
% frosh rec. need-based self-help aid	46
% UG rec. need-based self-help aid	44
% frosh rec. any financial aid	54
% UG rec. any financial aid	51
Avg. frosh grant	$7,585
Avg. frosh loan	$2,881
Independent 529 member?	No

Saint Anselm College

100 Saint Anselm Drive, Manchester, NH 03102-1310 • Admissions: 603-641-7500 • Fax: 603-641-7550

CAMPUS LIFE

Quality of Life Rating	**75**
Fire Safety Rating	**60**
Type of school	private
Affiliation	Roman Catholic
Environment	village

STUDENTS

Total undergrad enrollment	1,960
% male/female	42/58
% from out of state	77
% from public high school	65
% live on campus	86
% African American	1
% Asian	1
% Caucasian	78
% Hispanic	1
% international	1
# of countries represented	15

SURVEY SAYS

Great library
Diversity lacking on campus
Great food on campus
Lots of beer drinking

ACADEMICS

Academic Rating	**85**
Calendar	semester
Student/faculty ratio	14:1
Professors interesting rating	85
Professors accessible rating	85
% professors teaching UG courses	100
% classes taught by TAs	0
Most common lab size	10-19 students
Most common regular class size	10-19 students

MOST POPULAR MAJORS

Business administration/management
nursing
psychology

STUDENTS SPEAK OUT

Academics

"There is a really strong sense of community among students, faculty, and the monastic community" at Saint Anselm College, a small, Benedictine, liberal arts school in frosty New England. Students love "the one-on-one support of professors and the mentorship they provide," telling us, "if you are looking toward graduate study, you will stand out among other candidates due to the freedom you have to get involved with professors' work here." Notes one undergrad, "When people here say their doors are always open, they really mean it. Countless times I have been able to walk right into the offices of the Dean, the Dean of Students, any professor, and even the President. Their commitment to the students is absolutely unquestionable." Most here love "the very strong humanities program," a required two-year sequence that "teaches you to think about what is important in life. The overarching theme of the program is 'portraits of human greatness.' It provides discussion on things many normally would not think about." Required philosophy and theology classes as well as an intermediate-level language requirement all "help you become a more well-rounded person." Saint A's is notoriously tough academically; "I have never had to work so hard in my life for a good grade, but I have also never enjoyed learning as much as I am enjoying it here," writes one student. Observes another, "Saint A's is nicknamed 'Saint C's.' It is extremely difficult to receive an 'A' here, which makes the students work harder to be the few who do receive them."

Life

Saint Anselm "is a beautiful, small, and homey school" where "you are truly welcomed when you get here." After that, it's time to get to work. "You cannot have too much of a social life here at St. Anselm because the course requirements are so challenging," students warn, but "that's not to say you can't have fun." Students report that "from Monday to Thursday there isn't a whole lot that goes on unless you join a club or sport." Weekends are more active, as there's "always something entertaining to do, from open mic nights, to trips into Boston/NYC, to gingerbread house-building contests. These are always student-run and student-funded." You'll also "find a party if you're on a mission to find one, but it will most likely be off-campus [because] the rules on campus are so strict that it feels like you're in ninth grade again." Students often make the trip into Manchester, which "has a lot going on, from our semi-pro hockey team, the Manchester Monarchs (only $11 a ticket), to bars and clubs that hold college nights specifically targeting Saint A's students," as well as "a mall, places to eat, go bowling, and see movies." There's a lot of good skiing in the area, too, and Boston isn't too far down the road. Community service is big; in fact, "about 80 percent of students and faculty are involved to some degree." One student sums up life this way: "Our school is infamous for strict inter-visitation hours, an arduous humanities program, hours of reading, severe grade deflation, and monks around the campus."

Student Body

The "mostly white, Irish Catholic" undergrads of Saint Anselm "are more than likely to talk with a Boston accent," as "most kids are from Boston or from small towns in New England." Prep-school grads are strongly represented, but so are public-school students. Explains one undergrad, "There are mainly two groups of students: the ones who received excellent aid packages and the ones whose parents are very well-off. The wealth of some students can be a put-off to others" and there are a few reports of rudeness between the two groups. Most here "are hard-working, friendly, and love being involved. By involved, I do not just mean in volunteer work (though we have a large amount of that on campus), but involved in intramural sports, clubs, and other activities." While "there aren't many atypical students…those who are here are welcomed."

SAINT ANSELM COLLEGE

FINANCIAL AID: 603-641-7110 • E-MAIL: ADMISSION@ANSELM.EDU • WEBSITE: WWW.ANSELM.EDU

ADMISSIONS

Very important factors considered include: Character/personal qualities, secondary school record. *Important factors considered include:* Class rank, essays, recommendations, standardized test scores, talent/ability. *Other factors considered include:* Alumni/ae relation, extracurricular activities, geographical residence, interview, minority status, volunteer work, work experience. SAT Reasoning or ACT required. TOEFL required of all international applicants. High school diploma is required, and GED is accepted. *Academic units required:* 4 English, 3 math, 3 science (3 science lab), 2 foreign language, 2 social studies, 1 history, 3 academic electives. *Academic units recommended:* 4 math, 4 science, 4 foreign language, 2 history.

The Inside Word

St. Anselm gets a predominately regional applicant pool, and Massachusetts is one of its biggest suppliers of students. An above average-academic record should be more than adequate to gain admission.

FINANCIAL AID

Students should submit: FAFSA, CSS/Financial Aid PROFILE. Regular filing deadline is 3/15. The Princeton Review suggests that all financial aid forms be submitted as soon as possible after 1/1. *Need-based scholarships/grants offered:* Pell, SEOG, state scholarships/grants, private scholarships, the school's own gift aid. *Loan aid offered:* FFEL Subsidized Stafford, FFEL Unsubsidized Stafford, FFEL PLUS, Federal Perkins, GATE student loans. Applicants will be notified of awards on or about 3/15. Federal Work-study Program available. Institutional employment available. Off-campus job opportunities are excellent.

FROM THE ADMISSIONS OFFICE

"Why St. Anselm? The answer lies with our graduates. Not only do our alumni go on to successful careers in medicine, law, human services, and other areas, but they also make connections on campus that last a lifetime. With small classes, professors are accessible and approachable. The Benedictine monks serve not only as founders of the college, but as teachers, mentors, and spiritual leaders.

"St. Anselm is rich in history, but certainly not stuck in a bygone era. In fact, the college has launched a $50 million fundraising campaign, which will significantly increase funding for financial aid, academic programs, and technology. New initiatives include the New Hampshire Institute of Politics, where the guest list includes every major candidate from the 2000 presidential race, as well as other political movers and shakers. Not a political junkie? No problem. The NHIOP is a diverse undertaking that also involves elements of psychology, history, theology, ethics, and statistics.

"St. Anselm encourages students to challenge themselves academically and to lead lives that are both creative and generous. On that note, more than 40 percent of our students participate in community service locally and globally. Each year, about 150 students take part in Spring Break Alternative to help those less fortunate across the United States and Latin America. High expectations and lofty goals are hallmarks of a St. Anselm College education, and each student is encouraged to achieve his/her full potential here. Why St. Anselm? Accept the challenge and soon you will discover your own answers.

"Freshman applicants for fall 2006 must take the SAT or the ACT. Students may submit scores from the old or new SAT. The best scores from either test will be used in admissions decisions."

SELECTIVITY

Admissions Rating	**85**
# of applicants	3,214
% of applicants accepted	66
% of acceptees attending	25
# accepting a place on wait list	425
% admitted from wait list	31
# of early decision applicants	66
% accepted early decision	81

FRESHMAN PROFILE

Range SAT Verbal	520-600
Average SAT Verbal	551
Range SAT Math	510-600
Average SAT Math	556
**TPR Projected Range SAT Writing*	*570-630*
Range ACT Composite	22-26
Average ACT Composite	23
Minimum Paper TOEFL	550
Minimum Computer Based TOEFL	213
Average HS GPA	3.14
% graduated top 10% of class	18
% graduated top 25% of class	56
% graduated top 50% of class	88

DEADLINES

Early decision application deadline	11/15
Early decision notification	12/1
Regular notification	rolling
Nonfall registration?	yes

APPLICANTS ALSO LOOK AT

AND OFTEN PREFER

Boston College, College of the Holy Cross, Fairfield University, Providence College, Stonehill College

AND SOMETIMES PREFER

Saint Michael's College, University of Massachusetts—Amherst, University of New Hampshire

AND RARELY PREFER

Assumption College, Merrimack College

FINANCIAL FACTS

Financial Aid Rating	**74**
Annual tuition	$22,700
Room & Board	$8,580
Books and supplies	$750
Required fees	$750
% frosh rec. need-based scholarship or grant aid	74
% UG rec. need-based scholarship or grant aid	71
% frosh rec. need-based self-help aid	68
% UG rec. need-based self-help aid	67
Avg. frosh grant	$7,696
Avg. frosh loan	$2,427
Independent 529 member?	No

SAINT LOUIS UNIVERSITY

221 NORTH GRAND BOULEVARD, SAINT LOUIS, MO 63103 • ADMISSIONS: 314-977-2500 • FAX: 314-977-7136

CAMPUS LIFE

Quality of Life Rating	**67**
Fire Safety Rating	**60**
Type of school	private
Affiliation	Roman Catholic
Environment	metropolis

STUDENTS

Total undergrad enrollment	6,928
% male/female	44/56
% from out of state	51
% live on campus	52
% in (# of) fraternities	23 (13)
% in (# of) sororities	16 (5)
% African American	8
% Asian	5
% Caucasian	71
% Hispanic	2
% international	2
# of countries represented	76

SURVEY SAYS

Great library
Students are friendly
Students are happy
Lots of beer drinking
Hard liquor is popular
(Almost) everyone smokes

ACADEMICS

Academic Rating	**79**
Calendar	semester
Student/faculty ratio	12:1
Professors interesting rating	66
Professors accessible rating	71
% professors teaching UG courses	81
% classes taught by TAs	0
Most common lab size	20-29 students
Most common regular class size	10-19 students

MOST POPULAR MAJORS

Nursing/registered nurse training (RN, ASN, BSN, MSN)
psychology

STUDENTS SPEAK OUT

Academics

Students praise Saint Louis University (SLU), a big-city Jesuit school, as "a small, private institution that really cares for its students. Due to its small size, you aren't just a 'face in the crowd' here." A renowned physical therapy/occupational therapy program, the "nationally ranked aviation school," the premed program, and the "recently expanded Cook School of Business" receive the highest praise here, but students report that, in all areas, "the classes are really small, and teachers are really accessible, once you get past your introductory classes." Students in the most prestigious programs report that "there is a heavy workload, and everybody is pretty serious about studying during the week and even on the weekends." Others tell us that "academics are what you want them to be here. If you want a challenge, you can find those classes easily. If you want the easy way out, ask around for names of those professors" that offer them. Profs at SLU "really make an effort to reach out to the students and make us think. Also, they are available outside class and genuinely help out anyone in need." Undergrads also appreciate the way that "SLU tries to give every student the opportunity to grow and learn by offering many ways to get involved. The academic [curriculum] works together with the residence hall system, and all support the experience gained from participating in student organizations and extracurricular activities."

Life

Like most students in big cities, undergrads at Saint Louis University report that their extracurricular fun usually takes place beyond the campus gates. "The great thing about SLU is that it is located in a very urban environment with tons of cultural and entertaining things to do," explains one student. "There's never a dull moment. We have easy access to museums, zoos, the Fox Theatre, and downtown sporting events." Adds another, "There's Forest Park to visit on nice days, the Arch, the Science Center, a fabulous zoo, ice skating, movie theaters, and lots of great malls." The campus is connected to most city hot spots by MetroLink, St. Louis' light rail system; some here wish the school would offer shuttle bus service, but most seem to handle the public transportation experience without much trouble. Those who choose not to venture out can enjoy "a beautiful campus, with tons of fountains, statues, and flowers." The Greeks exert a major influence on campus social life, and "there is a strong separation between Greeks and non-Greeks. Since there aren't houses—just a Greek dorm—there aren't any open parties. Greek functions tend to be exclusive."

Student Body

Drawing heavily from private Catholic schools in the Midwest, Saint Louis University is home to "many students who are preppy, snobby, rich kids." However, "since SLU gives out good scholarships, the economic classes here vary a little bit." Diversity is enhanced by the fact that "there [are] a great deal of international students, since we have our own campus in Madrid." Minority representation is considerable, too, although most here agree that "all the different races and ethnic groups are segregated." Some feel the school could do better in this area; as one put it, "I also wish there was more diversity; not only ethnically, but different kinds of personalities. It seems that while most people here are down-to-earth, everyone is preppy. I wish we had more hippie types, and musicians, and the like: something different." Many here consider themselves "smart, caring, and into volunteering/helping out the community."

SAINT LOUIS UNIVERSITY

FINANCIAL AID: 314-977-2350 • E-MAIL: ADMITME@SLU.EDU • WEBSITE: WWW.SLU.EDU

ADMISSIONS

Very important factors considered include: Secondary school record, standardized test scores. *Important factors considered include:* Essays, extracurricular activities. *Other factors considered include:* Alumni/ae relation, character/personal qualities, class rank, interview, recommendations, talent/ability, volunteer work. SAT Reasoning or ACT required. TOEFL required of all international applicants. High school diploma is required, and GED is accepted. *Academic units required:* 4 English, 4 math, 3 science, 2 foreign language, 3 social studies, 3 academic electives. *Academic units recommended:* 4 English, 4 math, 3 science, 2 foreign language, 3 social studies, 3 academic electives.

The Inside Word

Students who are ranked in the top half of their graduating class will have a fairly easy path to admission at Saint Louis. Those who are not can find success in the admissions process by presenting strong supporting documents such as recommendation letters, essays, etc.

FINANCIAL AID

Students should submit: FAFSA. The Princeton Review suggests that all financial aid forms be submitted as soon as possible after 1/1. *Need-based scholarships/grants offered:* Pell, SEOG, state scholarships/grants, private scholarships, the school's own gift aid, Federal Nursing scholarships. *Loan aid offered:* FFEL Subsidized Stafford, FFEL Unsubsidized Stafford, FFEL PLUS, Federal Perkins, Federal Nursing. Applicants will be notified of awards on a rolling basis beginning on or about 3/1.

FROM THE ADMISSIONS OFFICE

"A hot midwestern university with a growing national and international reputation, Saint Louis University gives students the knowledge, skills, and values to build a successful career and make a difference in the lives of those around them.

"Students live and learn in a safe and attractive campus environment. The beautiful urban, residential campus offers loads of internship, outreach, and recreational opportunities. Ranked as one of the best educational values in the country, the university welcomes students from all 50 states and 80 foreign countries who pursue rigorous majors that invite individualization. Accessible faculty, study abroad opportunities, and many small, interactive classes make SLU a great place to learn.

"A leading Jesuit, Catholic university, SLU's goal is to graduate men and women of competence and conscience—individuals who are not only capable of making wise decisions, but who also understand why they made them. Since 1818, Saint Louis University has been dedicated to academic excellence, service to others, and preparing students to be leaders in society. Saint Louis University truly is the place *where knowledge touches lives.*

"For fall 2006 admission, Saint Louis University will accept either the new SAT or the old SAT (administered prior to March 2005 and without a Writing component). The school will also accept the ACT with or without the Writing component."

SELECTIVITY

Admissions Rating	**87**
# of applicants	6,692
% of applicants accepted	80
% of acceptees attending	27

FRESHMAN PROFILE

Range SAT Verbal	540-645
Range SAT Math	550-660
**TPR Projected Range SAT Writing*	*590-670*
Range ACT Composite	23-29
Average ACT Composite	26
Minimum Paper TOEFL	525
Minimum Computer Based TOEFL	194
Average HS GPA	3.63
% graduated top 10% of class	30
% graduated top 25% of class	64
% graduated top 50% of class	87

DEADLINES

Regular notification	rolling
Nonfall registration?	yes

APPLICANTS ALSO LOOK AT

AND OFTEN PREFER

University of Notre Dame
Washington University in St. Louis

AND SOMETIMES PREFER

Loyola University of Chicago
Marquette University
Truman State University
University of Missouri—Columbia

AND RARELY PREFER

Rockhurst University
University of Missouri—Saint Louis

FINANCIAL FACTS

Financial Aid Rating	**67**
Annual tuition	$23,360
Room & Board	$7,780
Books and supplies	$1,040
Required fees	$198
% frosh rec. need-based scholarship or grant aid	72
% UG rec. need-based scholarship or grant aid	67
% frosh rec. need-based self-help aid	61
% UG rec. need-based self-help aid	58
% frosh rec. any financial aid	97
% UG rec. any financial aid	94
Avg. frosh grant	$12,453
Avg. frosh loan	$7,823
Independent 529 member?	Yes

SAINT MARY'S COLLEGE OF CALIFORNIA

PO BOX 4800, MORAGA, CA 94575-4800 • ADMISSIONS: 925-631-4224 • FAX: 925-376-7193

CAMPUS LIFE

Quality of Life Rating	**70**
Fire Safety Rating	**78**
Type of school	private
Affiliation	Roman Catholic
Environment	village

STUDENTS

Total undergrad enrollment	3,330
% male/female	38/62
% from out of state	17
% from public high school	64
% live on campus	64
% African American	5
% Asian	7
% Caucasian	40
% Hispanic	14
% Native American	1
% international	2
# of countries represented	29

SURVEY SAYS

Small classes
Lab facilities are great
Frats and sororities are unpopular or nonexistent
Lots of beer drinking
Hard liquor is popular

ACADEMICS

Academic Rating	**73**
Calendar	4-1-4
Student/faculty ratio	12:1
Professors interesting rating	81
Professors accessible rating	82
% professors teaching UG courses	100
% classes taught by TAs	0
Most common regular class size	10-19 students

MOST POPULAR MAJORS

Business administration/management
communications studies/speech communication and rhetoric
liberal arts and sciences/liberal studies

STUDENTS SPEAK OUT

Academics

A private college with a beautiful San Francisco Bay area campus, Saint Mary's offers its students a well-rounded education while remaining loyal to the Lasallian traditions upon which the school was founded. At the "core of the core curriculum," as the college puts it, is the Collegiate Seminar Program, which requires students to take a total of four seminars—two their freshman year—focusing on texts that have influenced Western thought. The clear dedication of the faculty encourages students to step up to the academic challenges of the College. "Professors are incredible," a junior beams, "totally committed and accessible, and [they] want to help students to succeed." The fact that students are able to meet these professors in small classroom environments enhances the learning experience. "I feel comfortable participating in all of my classes because of the small size," comments an international business major. It is because of this consistent and intimate interaction that one student is able to promise that "during your four years, you will meet a handful of professors that will change your life both academically and emotionally." Some undergraduates do feel, however, that the personal attention feels too much like hand-holding. "The college experience at Saint Mary's is like high school number two," says one such student. One thing that most high schools do not offer, however, is study abroad—an opportunity that these students can take advantage of. Each year the College sends students to programs in Africa, Asia, Europe, and Latin America. Students who qualify can travel abroad during the monthlong January term, a special facet of the Saint Mary's academic experience that allows students to pursue nontraditional subjects, internships, or travel that will complement their on-campus studies.

Life

With San Francisco just miles away, Saint Mary's College's location makes it tough to sympathize with those who complain that "life is rather boring." A junior reports that "people complain about having nothing to do in the immediate area—which is true—but San Francisco is 20 minutes away, [and] Walnut Creek is 20 minutes away. If you have access to a car, there's stuff to do." And even without a car, the intrigues of the metropolis are just a quick BART (Bay Area Rapid Transit) ride away. Some students prefer to go the other way, though, toward the great outdoors, that is. Hiking, biking, fishing, climbing—all are easily accessible from Saint Mary's beautiful campus. Whether students are heading for the hills or the nightclubs, campus tends to grow quiet on the weekends. Many people simply "go home every weekend," groans a junior. Those who stick around on the weekends can tell you that "people like to party." But this isn't always easy, due to strictly enforced alcohol rules that lead one student to gripe, "The school treats us like children, and Public Safety has real power/control issues." A sophomore adds that parties always "get broken up by 12:00 A.M." On the bright side, when the party is broken up, there's one of the country's most vibrant cities a short car ride away.

Student Body

While you'll find "lots of white, upper-class people with nice cars and fancy clothes" who come from private schools somewhere in California, students tell us that a closer look at the student body will turn up a wide range of backgrounds and interests. "You will find many people with your common interests, making it easy to have fun and make friends," guarantees an undergraduate. Though the students at the college are often thought of as religious and conservative, a biology major reminds us that things can change; he knows some "nonreligious or somewhat religious," students, as well as a few "socially liberal" folks. But whether you bump into one of the old-school conservatives or new-school liberals, you can rest assured that you will find a friendly face. Undergraduates gush about classmates who "are unbelievably cordial and inclusive."

SAINT MARY'S COLLEGE OF CALIFORNIA

FINANCIAL AID: 925-631-4370 • E-MAIL: SMCADMIT@STMARYS-CA.EDU • WEBSITE: WWW.STMARYS-CA.EDU

ADMISSIONS

Very important factors considered include: Secondary school record, standardized test scores. *Important factors considered include:* Essays, recommendations. *Other factors considered include:* Alumni/ae relation, character/personal qualities, class rank, extracurricular activities, geographical residence, interview, minority status, religious affiliation/commitment, talent/ability, volunteer work, work experience. SAT Reasoning or ACT required. TOEFL required of all international applicants. High school diploma is required, and GED is accepted. *Academic units required:* 4 English, 3 math, 2 science (1 science lab), 2 foreign language, 1 social studies, 1 history, 3 academic electives. *Academic units recommended:* 4 English, 4 math, 3 science (1 science lab), 3 foreign language, 1 social studies, 1 history, 2 academic electives.

The Inside Word

The typical Saint Mary's admit is a better-than-average student who has attending a Catholic college very high on his or her list of preferences. The applicant pool is full of such candidates. Candidates should give serious attention to the application process, as they are guaranteed close scrutiny despite the college's high admit rate.

FINANCIAL AID

Students should submit: FAFSA, state aid form. Regular filing deadline is 3/2. The Princeton Review suggests that all financial aid forms be submitted as soon as possible after 1/1. *Need-based scholarships/grants offered:* Pell, SEOG, state scholarships/grants, private scholarships, the school's own gift aid. *Loan aid offered:* FFEL Subsidized Stafford, FFEL Unsubsidized Stafford, FFEL PLUS, Federal Perkins. Applicants will be notified of awards on or about 3/15. Federal Work-study Program available. Institutional employment available. Off-campus job opportunities are excellent.

FROM THE ADMISSIONS OFFICE

"Today, Saint Mary's College continues to offer a value-oriented education by providing a classical liberal arts background second to none. The emphasis here is on teaching an individual how to think independently and responsibly, how to analyze information in all situations, and how to make choices based on logical thinking and rational examination. Such a program develops students' ability to ask the right questions and to formulate meaningful answers, not only within their professional careers but also for the rest of their lives. Saint Mary's College is committed to preparing young men and women for the challenge of an ever-changing world, while remaining faithful to an enduring academic and spiritual heritage. We believe the purpose of a college experience is to prepare men and women for an unlimited number of opportunities. We believe this is best accomplished by educating the whole person, both intellectually and ethically. We strive to recruit, admit, enroll, and graduate students who are generous, faith-filled, and human, and we believe this is reaffirmed in our community of brothers, in our faculty, and in our personal concern for each student.

"For freshman applicants fall 2006, we will accept either version of the SAT. The ACT is also accepted. The ACT Writing assessment is optional. The highest verbal and the highest math scores attained on the SAT will be used. SAT Subject Tests are not required."

SELECTIVITY

Admissions Rating	**70**
# of applicants	3,354
% of applicants accepted	83
% of acceptees attending	22
# accepting a place on wait list	196
% admitted from wait list	30

FRESHMAN PROFILE

Range SAT Verbal	500-590
Average SAT Verbal	544
Range SAT Math	490-600
Average SAT Math	551
**TPR Projected Range SAT Writing*	*560-620*
Minimum Paper TOEFL	525
Minimum Computer Based TOEFL	197
Average HS GPA	3.34

DEADLINES

Regular application deadline	2/1
Regular notification	rolling
Nonfall registration?	yes

APPLICANTS ALSO LOOK AT

AND OFTEN PREFER

Stanford University
University of California—Berkeley
University of Notre Dame

AND SOMETIMES PREFER

Loyola Marymount University
Santa Clara University
University of California—Davis
University of California—San Diego

AND RARELY PREFER

Gonzaga University
University of California—Santa Barbara
University of California—Santa Cruz
University of the Pacific

FINANCIAL FACTS

Financial Aid Rating	**71**
Annual tuition	$25,000
Room & Board	$9,530
Books and supplies	$1,048
Required fees	$150
% frosh rec. need-based scholarship or grant aid	62
% UG rec. need-based scholarship or grant aid	55
% frosh rec. need-based self-help aid	64
% UG rec. need-based self-help aid	59
% frosh rec. any financial aid	74
% UG rec. any financial aid	76
Avg. frosh grant	$16,175
Avg. frosh loan	$3,256
Independent 529 member?	Yes

SAINT MARY'S COLLEGE OF MARYLAND

ADMISSIONS OFFICE, 18952 E. FISHER ROAD, ST. MARYS CITY, MD 20686-3001 • ADMISSIONS: 240-895-5000 • FAX: 240-895-5001

CAMPUS LIFE

Quality of Life Rating	**91**
Fire Safety Rating	**70**
Type of school	public
Environment	rural

STUDENTS

Total undergrad enrollment	1,858
% male/female	42/58
% from out of state	18
% from public high school	79
% live on campus	81
% African American	7
% Asian	4
% Caucasian	80
% Hispanic	3
% international	1
# of countries represented	29

SURVEY SAYS

Small classes
Students are friendly
Campus feels safe
Low cost of living
Students are happy
Frats and sororities are unpopular or nonexistent

ACADEMICS

Academic Rating	**86**
Calendar	semester
Student/faculty ratio	13:1
Professors interesting rating	89
Professors accessible rating	93
% professors teaching UG courses	100
% classes taught by TAs	0
Most common lab size	10-19 students
Most common regular class size	10-19 students

MOST POPULAR MAJORS

Economics
English language and literature
psychology

STUDENTS SPEAK OUT

Academics

As the state's public honors college (it's "not a Catholic college," clarifies one junior), St. Mary's College of Maryland offers its 2,000 undergrads the work-heavy, personalized education of a private school at public-school prices—a fact that regularly places the college among the "best buys" in higher education. Students describe the professors as "really awesome people" who are "passionate about their area of focus," and extol their "willingness to help or even just talk with students outside class time." "You're almost always on a first-name basis with them and have their home phone numbers and email addresses," boasts one double major. While "not every professor is going to be absolutely fantastic," we see many variations of the refrain: "The professors rock!" While SMCM's administration receives an array of kudos, it also takes a few knocks. A diplomatic junior writes that though administration members "do their best" to maintain dialog with students, they're often "too removed from the concerns of the students." Because of an enrollment increase a couple of years ago, students occasionally grumble about "understaffed" departments, "temporary professors," or "a shortage of classes and housing." Construction, most likely a result of such growth, grates on many students' nerves—but such are the (temporary) growing pains of small colleges trying to bulk up. Overall, students seem content, describing their education as "challenging but stimulating" and their workload as "heavy." One sophomore writes, "I have learned, laughed, and worked like crazy...but it's all been worth it." A final piece of advice for prospective students: "Take a lot of AP classes and do well on the AP exams...this will help you place out of a number of general education requirements that are not nearly as strong as many other classes."

Life

Because the "beautiful" SMCM campus lies along the St. Mary's River in the heart of Maryland's Chesapeake Bay region, water sports and other outdoor recreational activities are inescapable here. "You can take out boats, kayaks, etc. just by giving them your student ID," boasts a junior. "Calvert Cliffs is just down the road, too, which is a pretty awesome place to hike." The campus location clearly has its benefits. But "we live in the boonies," admits a sophomore. SMCM is "not located near any big cities or areas that have a lot of off-campus activities" (historic St. Mary's City adjoins the campus; and Washington, DC, is a two-hour drive)—so students rely on campus life to keep them busy. There's "a lot of political activism," "widespread environmental interest," a "wealth of clubs and recreational opportunities," popular athletic programs on the intramural, club, and varsity levels, and, of course, classes to keep these undergrads well occupied. Although some say they drink on weekends, they're quick to add that there are "a lot of students" who don't "party/drink" and that there is "little or no pressure to drink if you're not into it." Overall, the students "lead pretty balanced lives." "Everyone here is all about having fun," says a junior, "but [they] are really serious about getting their work done too."

Student Body

Students describe their classmates as "open," "down-to-earth," "laid back," and write that the only attribute "typical" of a Seahawk is uniqueness. In the cafeteria, "you can witness a girl wearing Abercrombie & Fitch sitting with a farm girl, a goth, a hippie, and they are all hysterically laughing." Another thing you'll notice in the cafeteria: SMCM has a "large vegan/vegetarian population." Students are "on the whole more likely to be liberal"; and at SMCM, "closed minded behavior is usually not taken well by most students." Students are so trusting of each other that "no one locks any doors on campus... Knocking is just not a St. Mary's thing to do!" If undergrads could shake a magic wand, they'd like to see SMCM become more "ethnically diverse." "The school is made up of mostly white, higher-income level kids," says a senior. That said, everyone is "accepted and accepting."

St. Mary's College of Maryland

Financial Aid: 240-895-3000 • E-mail: admissions@smcm.edu • Website: www.smcm.edu

ADMISSIONS

Very important factors considered include: Essays, secondary school record, standardized test scores. *Important factors considered include:* Extracurricular activities, recommendations, talent/ability. *Other factors considered include:* Alumni/ae relation, character/personal qualities, class rank, geographical residence, interview, minority status, state residency, volunteer work, work experience. SAT Reasoning or ACT required. TOEFL required of all international applicants. High school diploma is required, and GED is accepted. *Academic units required:* 4 English, 3 math, 3 science (2 science lab), 1 social studies, 2 history, 7 academic electives. *Academic units recommended:* 4 English, 4 math, 4 science (3 science lab), 4 foreign language, 1 history, 8 academic electives.

The Inside Word

There are few better choices than St. Mary's for better-than-average students who are not likely to get admitted to one of the top 50 or so colleges in the country. It is likely that if funding for public colleges is able to stabilize, or even grow, that this place will soon be joining the ranks of the best. Now is the time to take advantage, before the academic expectations of the admissions committee start to soar.

FINANCIAL AID

Students should submit: FAFSA. Regular filing deadline is 3/1. The Princeton Review suggests that all financial aid forms be submitted as soon as possible after 1/1. *Need-based scholarships/grants offered:* Pell, SEOG, state scholarships/grants, private scholarships, the school's own gift aid. *Loan aid offered:* FFEL Subsidized Stafford, FFEL Unsubsidized Stafford, FFEL PLUS, Federal Perkins. Applicants will be notified of awards on or about 4/1. Federal Work-study Program available. Institutional employment available. Off-campus job opportunities are good.

FROM THE ADMISSIONS OFFICE

"St. Mary's College of Maryland occupies a distinctive niche and represents a real value in American higher education. It is a public college, dedicated to the ideal of affordable, accessible education but committed to quality teaching and excellent programs for undergraduate students. The result is that St. Mary's offers the small college experience of the same high caliber usually found at prestigious private colleges, but at public college prices. Designated by the state of Maryland as 'a public honors college,' one of only two public colleges in the nation to hold that distinction, St. Mary's has become increasingly attractive to high school students. Admission is very selective.

"For freshman fall 2006, applicants must take the new version of the SAT, but students may submit scores from the old (prior to March 2005) SAT, and admissions will use the student's best scores from either test. The ACT with the Writing section is also accepted."

SELECTIVITY

Admissions Rating	**89**
# of applicants	2,321
% of applicants accepted	57
% of acceptees attending	32
# accepting a place on wait list	340
% admitted from wait list	5
# of early decision applicants	176
% accepted early decision	69

FRESHMAN PROFILE

Range SAT Verbal	580-690
Average SAT Verbal	631
Range SAT Math	570-660
Average SAT Math	616
**TPR Projected Range SAT Writing*	*620-690*
Minimum Paper TOEFL	550
Minimum Computer Based TOEFL	260
Average HS GPA	3.45
% graduated top 10% of class	39
% graduated top 25% of class	70
% graduated top 50% of class	90

DEADLINES

Early decision application deadline	12/1
Early decision notification	1/1
Regular application deadline	1/15
Regular notification	4/1
Nonfall registration?	yes

APPLICANTS ALSO LOOK AT AND SOMETIMES PREFER

College of William and Mary
Guilford College
Kenyon College

FINANCIAL FACTS

Financial Aid Rating	**82**
Annual in-state tuition	$9,063
Annual out-of-state tuition	$17,940
Room & Board	$7,980
Books and supplies	$1,000
Required fees	$1,833
% frosh rec. need-based scholarship or grant aid	19
% UG rec. need-based scholarship or grant aid	19
% frosh rec. need-based self-help aid	19
% UG rec. need-based self-help aid	19
% frosh rec. any financial aid	59
% UG rec. any financial aid	62
Avg. frosh grant	$6,495
Avg. frosh loan	$2,625
Independent 529 member?	No

Saint Michael's College

One Winooski Park, Colchester, VT 05439 • Admissions: 802-654-3000 • Fax: 802-654-2906

CAMPUS LIFE

Quality of Life Rating	**95**
Fire Safety Rating	**69**
Type of school	private
Affiliation	Roman Catholic
Environment	town

STUDENTS

Total undergrad enrollment	1,930
% male/female	45/55
% from out of state	77
% from public high school	68
% live on campus	92
% African American	1
% Asian	1
% Caucasian	94
% Hispanic	1
% international	2
# of countries represented	18

SURVEY SAYS . . .

Small classes
Frats and sororities are unpopular or nonexistent

ACADEMICS

Academic Rating	**87**
Calendar	semester
Student/faculty ratio	12:1
Profs interesting rating	94
Profs accessible rating	88
% profs teaching UG courses	100
% classes taught by TAs	0
Most common lab size	10-19 students
Most common reg class size	10-19 students

MOST POPULAR MAJORS

Business administration/management
English language and literature
psychology

Academics

The inclusive atmosphere at Saint Michael's college is "all about creating a comfortable, caring place for students, professors, visitors, and neighboring people." First-year students quickly find themselves in seminars, and "lecture-based classes always leave room for questions." An English major appreciates that professors "aren't afraid to teach passionately." They keep in touch "even while I was abroad or home for the summer. They would e-mail me articles I might enjoy or just say hello," says a junior in sociology. Students expected conservative teachers at a Catholic school but found "90 percent liberals" instead. The broad-minded approach encourages students "to challenge yourself, your peers, professors, and leaders around the world." The faculty spans "geniuses who deserve to be at a better school and charlatans who somehow got tenure." SMC isn't considered a school for science majors—its emphasis is on study abroad and international programming—subsequently a physics major finds him/herself in "classes of one and four people;" however, program numbers are climbing. The college's main strength lies in the mandated religion courses "are more like ethical discussions than anything else." Students report that they can easily find help from their classmates. "The student-staffed tutoring program and writing center are both well run and provide a comfortable environment for improving one's academics." As an institution "devoted to social justice and community service," much of the learning "happens outside of the classroom." The college prioritizes "a high level of awareness regarding world events" among its students.

Life

Burlington, Vermont, considered "the best location imaginable," wins Saint Mike's students over with its charming waterfront and blooming music scene. "Church Street is so interesting and quaint with tons of cool stores and interesting side shops." When May finals roll around, "Everyone loves to go down to North Beach and sunbathe. Some daring ones even go in Lake Champlain." Students survive the winters by employing a two-pronged attack of winter sports and drinking. The school-subsidized $25 season passes to Smuggler's Notch ski resort helps students save money for the bars. The under-21 crowd gets drunk before and after the alcohol-free dances or makes the trek to Montreal. Of the "40 groups with substantial budgets on campus," MOVE attracts the most students, putting more than 85 percent to work in community service at some point during their SMC career. Many students sign up for "correctional volleyball," where they play with local inmates. The popular Wilderness Program leads hiking and climbing outings, even a kayaking trip to Maine. An upperclassman asserts, "There is no way you could ever be bored on this campus."

Student Body

Students find that their school "lives up to all the hype about having a friendly and supportive community." For example, "everyone hugs at Saint Mike's. Whenever you see anyone you know, you are a greeted by a big hug." SUV-driving, Lacoste-sporting "hockey jocks," and Birkenstock-wearing, jam-band-listening hippies can be found embracing each other. Even a Republican Yankees fan from Vermont claims to get along with the majority "Democrat Red Sox fans from Massachusetts." Among the 2,000 students, we find common ground in a shared enthusiasm for winter sports, marijuana, and (mostly left-wing) political action. A senior offers the general template: "Most students do volunteer work, enjoy low-key partying, and care about grades but more about experiences."

FINANCIAL AID: 802-654-3243 • E-MAIL: ADMISSION@SMCVT.EDU • WEBSITE: WWW.SMCVT.EDU

ADMISSIONS

Very important factors considered include: Class rank, secondary school record. *Important factors considered include:* Character/personal qualities, essays, extracurricular activities, recommendations, standardized test scores, talent/ability. *Other factors considered include:* Alumni/ae relation, geographical residence, interview, minority status, volunteer work, work experience. SAT Reasoning or ACT required; TOEFL required of all international applicants. High school diploma is required and GED is accepted. *Academic units required:* 4 English, 3 math, 3 science, (2 science lab), 3 foreign language, 3 social studies. *Academic units recommended:* 4 English, 4 math, 4 science, (3 science lab), 4 foreign language, 4 social studies.

Inside Word

The school is as selective as it is because it trusts students to live up to its Catholic and academic standards without a lot of handholding after admittance. The noninterventionist attitude on campus spills over into nearby Burlington, but keep in mind that Vermont as a whole is strict about underage drinking.

FINANCIAL AID

Students should submit: FAFSA, Parent and Student Federal Tax forms and W-2's. Regular filing deadline is March 15. The Princeton Review suggests that all financial aid forms be submitted as soon as possible after January 1. *Need-based scholarships/grants offered:* Pell, SEOG, state scholarships/grants, private scholarships, the school's own gift aid. *Loan aid offered:* FFEL Subsidized Stafford, FFEL Unsubsidized Stafford, FFEL PLUS, Federal Perkins. Applicants will be notified of awards on a rolling basis beginning or about April 1. Federal Work-Study Program available. Institutional employment available. Off-campus job opportunities are excellent.

FROM THE ADMISSIONS OFFICE

"Saint Michael's is a residential, Catholic, liberal arts college for students who want to make the world a better place. As one of only 20 Catholic colleges nationwide allowed to host a prestigious Phi Beta Kappa chapter on campus, it is clear why U.S. News & World Report has ranked Saint Michael's as one of the 15 finest master's universities in the North for 15 consecutive years.

"A Saint Michael's education will prepare you for life, as each of our 29 majors is grounded in our liberal studies core. Our superb faculty are committed first and foremost to teaching, and are known for really caring about their students while simultaneously challenging them to reach higher than they ever thought possible. Because of our holistic approach, Saint Michael's graduates are prepared for their entire careers, not just their first job out of college.

"With nearly 90 percent of students living on campus, our "24/7" living and learning environment means exceptional teaching goes beyond the classroom. The remarkable sense of community encourages students to get involved, take risks and think differently. A unique passion for social justice issues on campus reflects the heritage of the Edmundite priests who founded Saint Michael's in 1904.

"Saint Michael's is situated just outside of Burlington—Vermont's largest city and a true college town. Students take advantage of some of the best skiing in the East through an agreement with Smugglers' Notch ski resort—an all-access season pass is provided to any Saint Michael's student in good academic standing.

"We require applicants to submit the new SAT or the ACT taken with Writing component. Pending faculty assessment on the test's virtues, the Writing section will not play a large role in admissions decision making."

SELECTIVITY

Admissions Rating	**85**
# of applicants	2,755
% of applicants accepted	70
% of acceptees attending	27
# accepting a place on wait list	271
% admitted from wait list	3

FRESHMAN PROFILE

Range SAT Verbal	520-610
Average SAT Verbal	563
Range SAT Math	520-610
Average SAT Math	561
**TPR Projected Range SAT Writing*	*570-640*
Range ACT Composite	21-25
Minimum Paper TOEFL	550
Minimum Computer Based TOEFL	213
Average HS GPA	3.46
% graduated top 10% of class	19
% graduated top 25% of class	55
% graduated top 50% of class	88

DEADLINES

Regular application deadline	2/1
Regular notification	4/1
Nonfall registration?	yes

APPLICANTS ALSO LOOK AT

AND OFTEN PREFER
Boston College
College of the Holy Cross

AND SOMETIMES PREFER
Fairfield University
Stonehill College
University of Vermont

AND RARELY PREFER
Quinnipiac University
Saint Anselm College
University of Massachusetts-Amherst
University of New Hampshire

FINANCIAL FACTS

Financial Aid Rating	**79**
Annual tuition	$26,550
Room & Board	$6,560
Books and supplies	$1,200
Required fees	$220
% frosh rec. need-based scholarship or grant aid	64
% UG rec. need-based scholarship or grant aid	63
% frosh rec. need-based self-help aid	59
% UG rec. need-based self-help aid	60
% frosh rec. any financial aid	81
% UG rec. any financial aid	86
Avg. frosh grant	$13,255
Avg. frosh loan	$4,175
Independent 529 member?	Yes

Saint Olaf College

1520 Saint Olaf Avenue, Northfield, MN 55057 • Admissions: 507-646-3025 • Fax: 507-646-3832

CAMPUS LIFE

Quality of Life Rating	**99**
Fire Safety Rating	**60**
Type of school	private
Affiliation	Lutheran
Environment	village

STUDENTS

Total undergrad enrollment	2,976
% male/female	42/58
% from out of state	45
% from public high school	86
% live on campus	96
% African American	1
% Asian	4
% Caucasian	85
% Hispanic	2
% international	1
# of countries represented	18

SURVEY SAYS

Great library
Athletic facilities are great
Students are friendly
Great food on campus
Frats and sororities are unpopular or nonexistent
Musical organizations are popular

ACADEMICS

Academic Rating	**91**
Calendar	4-1-4
Student/faculty ratio	13:1
Professors interesting rating	91
Professors accessible rating	88
% professors teaching UG courses	100
% classes taught by TAs	0
Most common lab size	10-19 students
Most common regular class size	20-29 students

MOST POPULAR MAJORS

Biology/biological sciences
economics
English language and literature

STUDENTS SPEAK OUT

Academics

St. Olaf College is well known for its music programs, but there's much more to this school than its ensembles and soloists. According to undergrads, St. Olaf is "very strong from a liberal arts perspective," and a top institution for "fine arts, math, [and] sciences." It's this thorough slate of offerings that attracts top students of all talents, including, of course, musicians; writes one, "This was the only place where I could get a conservatory-level music education, take classes from internationally-known composers, get a great liberal arts background, and play on good athletic teams. People here are really well rounded." Students also love the school's "amazing study abroad opportunities; most of the student body travels abroad at some point. Having a short January term makes it easy even for people with busy academic or sporting schedules." Most of all, Oles cherish the hominess of their campus, rhapsodizing about professors "who invite a 90-piece orchestra over to their house for dinner" and similar communal touchstone experiences. Notes one student, "I think that everyone here feels a special connection with the campus, whether it's from the beautiful limestone buildings, the autumn colors that blanket the campus, or the oh-so-tasty chocolate-chip-cookie-smell that wafts over from the local Malt-o-Meal factory. I look around during various seasons and think, 'How am I so lucky to get to experience this?' It truly is magnificent, except, of course, during that inevitable two-week period in January when the wind chill stays constant at an average of about –20 and it's too cold even to snow."

Life

"Campus life is centered on campus, not in the town of Northfield," students say, because "while Northfield is an extremely nice town, we just don't get off campus much. Being on a hill creates what we call the St. Olaf Bubble—it's not the real world." It's also not a dull world. The school "has plenty of stuff going on. The student government brings in many activities—concerts, free movies, speakers—and it's not too hard to find something to do or someone to hang out with." Students here "tend to be active in some kind of organization. Many are in music groups (so many that my non-musical friend has officially designated herself 'audience member'), and there are also many political groups/special interest groups (Oles for Dean, Amnesty International, Habitat for Humanity, etc.). The presence of Christianity is also widely felt; there are several groups like FCA and Intervarsity, weekly Bible studies, and daily chapel." Students explain that "because most of the student body lives on campus all four years, we have a very close student body. This makes it a lot of fun to go to the bars in town, or just to the room next door to hang out." As you might expect, "Music is huge here. For example, Christmas Festival: Five hundred students, one month, two hours of music on the program, and thousands of people competing for tickets. It's awesome."

Student Body

Oles are "hard-working and intelligent, very social and helpful, [and] a little sick of all the people talking about how blond, Norwegian, etc. we are. It is just not that true. Yes, we are mostly white, and maybe for people from other areas of the country, it seems very blond. But that is just Minnesota for you. Minnesotans are blonder and more Norwegian than in other states." Many here "are extremely political, and although the college leans towards the left, we have an extremely vocal right side as well." Regardless of politics, undergraduates are socially conscious; the school "has a great volunteer network on campus, in the local community, and worldwide." Oles are serious about their school work and have a genuine curiosity about intellectual subjects; they "have critical minds and never hesitate to contribute to a discussion or a critique." Most "are working toward graduate school, medical school, law school, or business school."

SAINT OLAF COLLEGE

FINANCIAL AID: 507-646-3019 • E-MAIL: ADMISSIONS@STOLAF.EDU • WEBSITE: WWW.STOLAF.EDU

ADMISSIONS

Very important factors considered include: Essays, secondary school record. *Important factors considered include:* Character/personal qualities, extracurricular activities, recommendations, standardized test scores, talent/ability, volunteer work, work experience. *Other factors considered include:* Alumni/ae relation, class rank, geographical residence, interview, minority status, religious affiliation/commitment, state residency. SAT Reasoning or ACT required. TOEFL required of all international applicants. High school diploma is required, and GED is accepted. *Academic units required:* 4 English, 2 math, 2 science (1 science lab), 2 foreign language, 1 social studies, 1 history, 2 academic electives. *Academic units recommended:* 4 English, 4 math, 4 science (2 science lab), 4 foreign language, 2 social studies, 2 history, 4 academic electives.

The Inside Word

St. Olaf truly deserves a more national reputation; the place is a bastion of excellence and has always crossed applications with the best schools in the Midwest. Despite its lack of widespread recognition, it is a great choice. Candidates benefit from the relative anonymity of the college through an admissions process, which, while demanding, isn't as tough as other colleges of St. Olaf's caliber.

FINANCIAL AID

Students should submit: FAFSA, CSS/Financial Aid PROFILE, noncustodial (divorced/separated) parents' statement. The Princeton Review suggests that all financial aid forms be submitted as soon as possible after 1/1. *Need-based scholarships/grants offered:* Pell, SEOG, state scholarships/grants, private scholarships, the school's own gift aid. *Loan aid offered:* FFEL Subsidized Stafford, FFEL Unsubsidized Stafford, FFEL PLUS, Federal Perkins, Federal Nursing, state loans, college/university loans from institutional funds. Applicants will be notified of awards on a rolling basis beginning on or about 3/1. Federal Work-study Program available. Off-campus job opportunities are fair.

FROM THE ADMISSIONS OFFICE

"With 3,000 students, St. Olaf College, a residential campus in Northfield, Minnesota, combines a leading liberal arts experience with the dynamic energy of a small university. Forty-four academic majors, 27 intercollegiate sports, a world-renowned music program and a nationally recognized commitment to international study help this college of the Lutheran church fulfill its mission to develop mind, body, and spirit. St. Olaf leads the nation in the number of graduates who have earned a PhD in theology/religion and in mathematics. Its rigorous academic program has produced three Rhodes scholars and over 50 Fulbright scholars in the past decade.

"As of this book's publication, Saint Olaf College did not have information available about their policy regarding the new SAT."

SELECTIVITY

Admissions Rating	**92**
# of applicants	3,144
% of applicants accepted	64
% of acceptees attending	38
# accepting a place on wait list	104
% admitted from wait list	8
# of early decision applicants	107
% accepted early decision	82

FRESHMAN PROFILE

Range SAT Verbal	600-710
Average SAT Verbal	650
Range SAT Math	590-700
Average SAT Math	640
**TPR Projected Range SAT Writing*	*630-700*
Range ACT Composite	25-30
Average ACT Composite	27
Minimum Paper TOEFL	550
Minimum Computer Based TOEFL	213
Average HS GPA	3.65
% graduated top 10% of class	48
% graduated top 25% of class	79
% graduated top 50% of class	98

DEADLINES

Early decision application deadline	11/15
Early decision notification	12/6
Regular notification	3/1
Nonfall registration?	no

APPLICANTS ALSO LOOK AT AND SOMETIMES PREFER

Carleton College
Gustavus Adolphus College
Luther College
University of Minnesota—Twin Cities
University of Wisconsin—Madison

FINANCIAL FACTS

Financial Aid Rating	**98**
Annual tuition	$26,500
Room & Board	$6,300
Books and supplies	$950
% frosh rec. need-based scholarship or grant aid	62
% UG rec. need-based scholarship or grant aid	62
% frosh rec. need-based self-help aid	62
% UG rec. need-based self-help aid	62
% frosh rec. any financial aid	81
% UG rec. any financial aid	80
Avg. frosh grant	$15,540
Avg. frosh loan	$5,020
Independent 529 member?	Yes

Salisbury University

Admissions Office, 1101 Camden Avenue, Salisbury, MD 21801 • Admissions: 410-543-6161 • Fax: 410-546-6016

CAMPUS LIFE

Quality of Life Rating	**81**
Fire Safety Rating	**77**
Type of school	public
Environment	town

STUDENTS

Total undergrad enrollment	6,022
% male/female	44/56
% from out of state	14
% from public high school	85
% live on campus	46
% in (# of) fraternities	5 (6)
% in (# of) sororities	6 (5)
% African American	8
% Asian	3
% Caucasian	80
% Hispanic	2
% international	1
# of countries represented	27

SURVEY SAYS

Small classes
Lab facilities are great
Great computer facilities
Students are happy
Lots of beer drinking

ACADEMICS

Academic Rating	**76**
Calendar	4-1-4
Student/faculty ratio	16:1
Professors interesting rating	77
Professors accessible rating	78
% professors teaching UG courses	100
% classes taught by TAs	2
Most common lab size	20-29 students
Most common regular class size	20-29 students

MOST POPULAR MAJORS

Business administration/management
communications studies/speech communication and rhetoric
elementary education and teaching

STUDENTS SPEAK OUT

Academics

"Small, personable, and beautiful" Salisbury University, a state school on Maryland's Eastern Shore, is "large enough to be diverse, yet small enough to walk anywhere you need to go." Students here love that "teachers get to know you as students rather than a number, and they are able to help you at a more personable level." Salisbury is probably best known for its Perdue School of Business, the most popular program among undergraduates. Students report that "the school is about teaching students how to become more professional and giving them the skills to be successful in the real world of business." Also noteworthy is the Henson School of Science, which recently received a boost via a new facility "with incredible resources and great technology that provide a flood of information." And don't forget education, Salisbury's longest-running program; "Salisbury was originally a teacher's school before it opened its doors to other majors," undergrads remind us. Students across programs laud the "great internship opportunities, excellent study-abroad programs, and professors who are dedicated and open minded." As at all smaller schools and nearly all state-funded schools, not all aspects of academic life are first-rate. Arts and music students complain that "the school constantly underfunds us," and everyone agrees that "the library is ancient and small, only two floors with mostly old reference books no one uses." An honors program offers top students "small, almost entirely discussion-based classes."

Life

"Salisbury is a big party school," many students tell us, and apparently locals agree: The "farmer's town" of Salisbury recently passed restrictions on off-campus housing intended to curtail the party scene. As you might guess, town-gown relations aren't the best. One student reports, "The locals hate us; we do not get along whatsoever. They are not willing to accept the fact that we are here and we are not leaving." The school and students are trying to address the problem by scheduling more appealing on-campus events and providing services such as SafeRide, a "student-run drunk bus that gets the kids home safe, for free, and without getting written up." But there's more going on at Salisbury besides the parties. Students can dabble in "over 100 active student organizations" including "a student-run program called SOAP that schedules movies, comedians and other interesting stuff" as well as "school-sponsored trips, activities, and on-campus festivals." Athletics are solid, as "Salisbury is among the top teams in Division III in almost every sport." When the weather is nice, students frequently take the half-hour drive to Ocean City and other beach resort areas. Annapolis, Baltimore, and DC are the nearest large cities, but most here agree that "they are a bit far" for regular visits.

Student Body

Students tell us that at Salisbury, "everyone fits in somewhere." That includes "those who want to party and drink all the time, those who like to study all the time, those who study all week and party and drink on the weekends, and those who just like to chill out and have fun." One junior tells us her motto is: "Study hard so you can party harder." Most students are "very laid back and dress comfortably," like those who enjoying coming to "class in his or her pajamas, yet who still manages to finish the work that is supposed to be done." Salisbury's students, generally speaking, are "active in either a social group, fraternity, or club…study for about two hours a day outside of class," and "come from Maryland, Delaware, or New Jersey." While there are "a lot of white, middle-class preppy types" here, they mix in with "students from all over the world, so it's very diverse and interesting." Out of all of this come "a lot of unique or atypical students, especially in the art, anthropology, biology, philosophy, and music departments." Some students detect a divide between the minority (on-campus residents) and the majority (commuters), pointing out that "people who live on campus have a lot more time to interact with one another."

FINANCIAL AID: 410-543-6165 • E-MAIL: ADMISSIONS@SALISBURY.EDU • WEBSITE: WWW.SALISBURY.EDU

ADMISSIONS

Very important factors considered include: Secondary school record, state residency. *Important factors considered include:* Alumni/ae relation, class rank, extracurricular activities, geographical residence, standardized test scores, talent/ability. *Other factors considered include:* Character/personal qualities, essays, interview, minority status, recommendations, volunteer work, work experience. SAT Reasoning or ACT required. TOEFL required of all international applicants. High school diploma is required, and GED is accepted. *Academic units required:* 4 English, 3 math, 3 science (2 science lab), 2 foreign language, 3 social studies. *Academic units recommended:* 4 English, 4 math, 4 science (3 science lab), 3 foreign language, 3 social studies, 3 academic electives.

The Inside Word

As a part of the new wave of public institutions of higher learning focusing their energies on undergraduate research, Salisbury has seen its admissions standards and the quality of its freshman class steadily improve over the past few years. As a result, candidate review is also more personalized than the formula-driven approaches of most public colleges. The admissions committee will pay close attention to the match you make with the university, evaluating your entire background instead of simply your numbers—though most students are strong academically to begin with.

FINANCIAL AID

Students should submit: FAFSA. The Princeton Review suggests that all financial aid forms be submitted as soon as possible after 1/1. *Need-based scholarships/grants offered:* Pell, SEOG, state scholarships/grants, the school's own gift aid. *Loan aid offered:* Direct Subsidized Stafford, Direct Unsubsidized Stafford, Direct PLUS, Federal Perkins. Applicants will be notified of awards on a rolling basis beginning on or about 4/1. Federal Work-study Program available. Institutional employment available. Off-campus job opportunities are good.

FROM THE ADMISSIONS OFFICE

"Friendly, convenient, safe, and beautiful are just a few of the words used to describe the campus of Salisbury University. The campus is a compact, self-contained community that offers the full range of student services. Beautiful, traditional-style architecture and impeccably landscaped grounds combine to create an atmosphere that inspires learning and fosters student pride. Located just 30 minutes from the beaches of Ocean City, Maryland, SU students enjoy a year-round resort social life as well as an inside track on summer jobs. Situated less than two hours from the urban excitement of Baltimore and Washington, DC, greater Salisbury makes up for its lack of size—its population is about 80,000—by being strategically located. Within easy driving distance of a number of other major cities, including New York City, Philadelphia, and Norfolk, Salisbury is the hub of the Delmarva Peninsula, a mostly rural region flavored by the salty air of the Chesapeake Bay and Atlantic Ocean.

"Applicants for fall 2006 are required to take the new SAT or the ACT with the Writing section, but we will allow students to submit scores from the old version of the SAT (prior to March 2005) as well. The highest composite score will be used in admissions decisions."

SELECTIVITY

Admissions Rating	**83**
# of applicants	5,067
% of applicants accepted	61
% of acceptees attending	32

FRESHMAN PROFILE

Range SAT Verbal	510-590
Average SAT Verbal	553
Range SAT Math	530-610
Average SAT Math	568
**TPR Projected Range SAT Writing*	*570-620*
Minimum Paper TOEFL	550
Minimum Computer Based TOEFL	213
Average HS GPA	3.45
% graduated top 10% of class	18
% graduated top 25% of class	50
% graduated top 50% of class	87

DEADLINES

Regular notification	3/15
Nonfall registration?	yes

APPLICANTS ALSO LOOK AT AND AND SOMETIMES PREFER

St. Mary's College of Maryland
Towson University
University of Maryland—Baltimore County

AND RARELY PREFER

University of Maryland—College Park

FINANCIAL FACTS

Financial Aid Rating	**66**
Annual in-state tuition	$4,546
Annual out-of-state tuition	$12,124
Room & Board	$7,050
Books and supplies	$900
Required fees	$1,430
% frosh rec. need-based scholarship or grant aid	26
% UG rec. need-based scholarship or grant aid	18
% frosh rec. need-based self-help aid	28
% UG rec. need-based self-help aid	34
% frosh rec. any financial aid	70
% UG rec. any financial aid	82
Avg. frosh grant	$4,589
Avg. frosh loan	$3,543
Independent 529 member?	No

SAMFORD UNIVERSITY

800 LAKESHORE DRIVE, BIRMINGHAM, AL 35229 • ADMISSIONS: 205-726-3673 • FAX: 205-726-2171

CAMPUS LIFE

Quality of Life Rating	**94**
Fire Safety Rating	**74**
Type of school	private
Affiliation	Baptist
Environment	town

STUDENTS

Total undergrad enrollment	2,811
% male/female	35/65
% from out of state	54
% from public high school	65
% live on campus	65
% in (# of) fraternities	29 (7)
% in (# of) sororities	34 (7)
% African American	6
% Asian	1
% Caucasian	89
% Hispanic	1

SURVEY SAYS

Small classes
Lab facilities are great
Great computer facilities
Students love Birmingham, AL
Great off-campus food

ACADEMICS

Academic Rating	**84**
Calendar	4-1-4
Student/faculty ratio	12:1
Professors interesting rating	89
Professors accessible rating	87
% professors teaching UG courses	72
% classes taught by TAs	0
Most common lab size	fewer than 10 students
Most common regular class size	10-19 students

MOST POPULAR MAJORS

Business administration/management
journalism
nursing/registered nurse training (RN, ASN, BSN, MSN)

STUDENTS SPEAK OUT

Academics

"Samford University is definitely not your average college stereotype," students tell us, pointing out that "you either love it or you hate it. However, if it is your type of school, it's heaven on earth." Those who fit in best are conservative, Southern, and either Baptist or very comfortable with Baptist values. The "focus on Christian heritage" is strong here, as is the imperative to "use the knowledge obtained to bring glory and honor to God." Some students temper this assertion somewhat, pointing out that "although SU is a Southern Baptist college with a very strong religious background, no one is bombarded with Christianity. Everyone has the right to choose what they believe in here." During class, efforts are made in getting "to know each and every one of the students. Classes are small, which encourages a climate of discussion and deliberation." Professors here are "excellent teachers/facilitators who are more than willing to collaborate with students, be confronted, entertain varying opinions, maintain an open mind, and help willing students to succeed both academically and in other aspects of their field of study, such as internships, conferences, graduate school recommendations, etc." A "very good pharmacy program," solid nursing and business programs, diverse offerings in journalism and communication, and the visual and performing arts are among the most popular programs. Sums up one student, "The overall academic experience here is a very challenging and rewarding one."

Life

Samford's hometown of Birmingham is "a great medium-size city with tons of activities and things to do," students here tell us. The city "is starting to develop as a creative core. It's got amazing parks. It is slowly becoming the culinary capital of the South, with an amazing variety of ethnic restaurants. There are plenty of coffee shops, theaters, and art galleries to attend. Birmingham may not have several of everything, but it has one of everything, which, for its size, is enough." The city has a decent club scene, too—some here indulge, but many do not. On campus, "there is a huge variety of events offered" including "concerts, games, theatrical performances, and bonfires." There's also "an abundance of root-beer keggers and dance parties at frat houses, as well as late night coffee and pancake runs." (One student divulges that while "fraternities and sororities do not encourage drinking, a lot of them do it. Call them 'closet drinkers' if you will.") Despite the campus activity and the city's many attractions, "everyone who lives close by leaves on the weekend. It's maddening to stay on campus—unless you have a car, because there's lots to do in Birmingham." Campus rules are predictably strict at this conservative Christian school. "The dorms are all single-sex, which is fine, but all the university buildings close down by 10 P.M. (on weekends). That means there is no on-campus place for mixed-gender groups of larger-than-clique size to meet or socialize." Welcome to "life in a calm, quiet, Christian bubble."

Student Body

"You have well-mannered, educated, tactful, Southern gentleman and belles" at Samford, and, according to some, not much else. "Life is great!" says one senior. "Everyone dresses nice, is polite, and is constantly smiling." But another students laments: "I think we need improvement in diversity, and not just in ethnic diversity. Students need exposure to others in order to realize that you aren't going to hell if you aren't Southern Baptist, if you drink, or if you skip church. The school seems to nurture this type of student a lot." One sophomore explains, "If you're gay, you're literally breaking a school policy." "More students from the Northeast and West Coast" would help, some here believe. For now, the Samford archetype is "a very conservative, cookie-cutter sorority girl" (there are "many more women than men" here) who, according to a stereotype accepted by many, is "here to get her MRS [degree]." Some say Samford is where "tomorrow's businessmen, right-wing pastors, and housewives" come to "learn, fall in love, and prepare to live in the suburbs." Undergrads are "very conservative," "very preppy, and always dress up for class. You will get condescending looks if you wear a tee-shirt and jeans."

ADMISSIONS

Very important factors considered include: Character/personal qualities, essays, recommendations, religious affiliation/commitment, secondary school record, standardized test scores. *Important factors considered include:* Alumni/ae relation, class rank, extracurricular activities, interview. *Other factors considered include:* Geographical residence, minority status, state residency, talent/ability, volunteer work, work experience. SAT Reasoning or ACT required. TOEFL required of all international applicants. High school diploma is required, and GED is accepted. *Academic units required:* 4 English, 3 math, 3 science (2 science lab), 2 social studies, 2 history. *Academic units recommended:* 2 foreign language.

The Inside Word

Samford's use of admission credentials in scholarship considerations is something that is quite common at colleges across the country. Students should always complete their applications as if such is the case. Even for universities where you are clearly admissible academically, giving some additional attention to essays and visiting for an interview can make the difference between being a scholarship winner and taking on an additional summer job.

FINANCIAL AID

Students should submit: FAFSA. The Princeton Review suggests that all financial aid forms be submitted as soon as possible after 1/1. *Need-based scholarships/grants offered:* Pell, SEOG, state scholarships/grants, private scholarships, the school's own gift aid. *Loan aid offered:* FFEL Subsidized Stafford, FFEL Unsubsidized Stafford, FFEL PLUS, Federal Perkins, college/university loans from institutional funds. Applicants will be notified of awards on a rolling basis beginning on or about 5/1. Federal Work-study Program available. Institutional employment available. Off-campus job opportunities are excellent.

FROM THE ADMISSION OFFICE

"Students who are drawn to Samford are well-rounded individuals who not only expect to be challenged, but are excited by the prospect. It is the critical and creative way you think, it is the articulate way you write and speak, it is the joy of learning that stays with you throughout your life, and it is the clarity of decision-making guided by Christian principles.

"As of this book's publication, Samford University did not have information available about their policy regarding the new SAT."

SELECTIVITY

Admissions Rating	**85**
# of applicants	1,952
% of applicants accepted	88
% of acceptees attending	39

FRESHMAN PROFILE

Range SAT Verbal	500-620
Average SAT Verbal	578
Range SAT Math	510-610
Average SAT Math	572
**TPR Projected Range SAT Writing*	*560-650*
Range ACT Composite	22-28
Average ACT Composite	25
Minimum Paper TOEFL	550
Minimum Computer Based TOEFL	213
Average HS GPA	3.62
% graduated top 10% of class	33
% graduated top 25% of class	63
% graduated top 50% of class	88

DEADLINES

Regular notification	rolling
Nonfall registration?	yes

APPLICANTS ALSO LOOK AT AND SOMETIMES PREFER

Auburn University
Baylor University
Florida State University
University of Georgia

FINANCIAL FACTS

Financial Aid Rating	**72**
Annual tuition	$13,944
Room & Board	$5,768
Books and supplies	$400
% frosh rec. need-based scholarship or grant aid	41
% UG rec. need-based scholarship or grant aid	37
% frosh rec. need-based self-help aid	36
% UG rec. need-based self-help aid	37
% frosh rec. any financial aid	80
% UG rec. any financial aid	95
Avg. frosh grant	$2,360
Avg. frosh loan	$6,948
Independent 529 member?	Yes

SANTA CLARA UNIVERSITY

500 El Camino Real, Santa Clara, CA 95053 • Admissions: 408-554-4700 • Fax: 408-554-5255

CAMPUS LIFE

Quality of Life Rating	**87**
Fire Safety Rating	**86**
Type of school	private
Affiliation	Roman Catholic
Environment	city

STUDENTS

Total undergrad enrollment	4,391
% male/female	45/55
% from out of state	32
% from public high school	45
% live on campus	44
% African American	3
% Asian	19
% Caucasian	56
% Hispanic	13
% Native American	1
% international	4
# of countries represented	34

SURVEY SAYS

Small classes
Great computer facilities
Athletic facilities are great
Campus feels safe
Students are happy
Lots of beer drinking

ACADEMICS

Academic Rating	**86**
Calendar	quarter
Student/faculty ratio	12:1
Professors interesting rating	89
Professors accessible rating	89
% professors teaching UG courses	82
% classes taught by TAs	0
Most common lab size	10-19 students
Most common regular class size	20-29 students

MOST POPULAR MAJORS

Communications and media studies
finance
psychology

STUDENTS SPEAK OUT

Academics

Students at Santa Clara University consider it the "best Catholic school in the West." The "excessive and insane" workload stands as a hallmark of the SCU education. A sophomore warns, "It is a hard school, I won't lie." Some students even believe they do more than their counterparts up the highway at Stanford, without the recognition. The civil engineering, physics, and business departments score big points with students, and "the math department is too awesome for words." Communications draws many undergraduates, too, thanks to exciting concentrations like video production. Even core classes manage to "provoke curiosity in the subject." Several students talk about instructors who transcend typical class expectations to create meaningful experiences. According to a junior, SCU "Professors are brilliant, fascinating, humane people who have been nothing short of an inspiration to my friends and me." A physics major found his philosophy professor to be "one of the most passionate people I've known, and his class helped to change my outlook on the world." The faculty also strives to make students feel comfortable. "There is a program where gay-friendly professors have a sticker on their door saying 'Safe space,' and I have never seen an office without a sticker." The Jesuit factor stresses "the importance of social justice and activism" within the academic environment. A senior biology major writes, "I like the balance they create by trying to cultivate you morally and spiritually without infringing on your own beliefs." Between faculty, administrators, and classmates, "There is always someone to give advice and always so many resources to build you up."

Life

Though Santa Clarans may be working harder than other students, they're not partying harder. "If you find a party at Santa Clara, it's guaranteed that by 10:00 P.M. either the police will try to shut it down or the beer will run out." Cops dwell in their station across the street from campus, which routinely encourages students to head to "San Jose State or Stanford for a livelier party scene." A sophomore explains, "The once-flourishing Greek system of the 1980s and 1990s is still here," just autonomous from the university. Some students maintain their "party like it's your job" attitude even in the face of these obstacles and declare Wednesday an official party night. For casual fun, people hang out on campus at The Bronco for pool and big-screen TVs. With no football team, sports fans transfer their fervor to soccer. The "very active music, dance, visual, and theater arts departments" keep the campus cultured. "There are a lot of performances and galleries and opportunities to be seen by the community." Students love the local climate and routinely hop the Cal train up to San Francisco; those with cars or connections can hit the beach or the slopes. Even at the start of a busy week in Silicon Valley, "We have a great turnout for mass on Sunday nights at 10:00 P.M.."

Student Body

Santa Clara lies closer to Santa Barbara than Santa Cruz on the spectrum of California style. Californians will likely get this, but for out-of-state students, this means that students are more LA trendy than San Francisco bohemian—more elective surgery, fewer body piercings. The country club surroundings and well-manicured students "look like they came out of Beverly Hills." Though women outnumber men, one out-of-state student has "noticed a lot of California surfer dudes." Channeling the university's recruiting material, a sophomore writes, "There technically is diversity, and that is one of the things the school is trying to stress." Interaction between groups lags behind these efforts. "Most students won't go to the Boat Dance because it is sponsored by the multicultural club. If you aren't 'multicultural' then you just don't do it." What sets these students apart from any old popular kids from private Catholic high schools is their "faith-based motivation to work for social justice and human rights." Several respondents note an "emphasis on being very ethical, doing the right thing, and helping out in the community."

FINANCIAL AID: 408-554-4505 • WEBSITE: WWW.SCU.EDU

ADMISSIONS

Very important factors considered include: Secondary school record. *Important factors considered include:* Character/personal qualities, essays, recommendations, standardized test scores, talent/ability, volunteer work. *Other factors considered include:* Alumni/ae relation, class rank, extracurricular activities, geographical residence, minority status, work experience. SAT Reasoning or ACT required. TOEFL required of all international applicants. High school diploma is required, and GED is not accepted. *Academic units required:* 4 English, 4 math, 3 science (2 science lab), 3 foreign language, 1 social studies, 1 history, 2 academic electives. *Academic units recommended:* 4 English, 4 math, 4 science (2 science lab), 4 foreign language, 2 social studies, 1 history, 2 academic electives, 1 fine arts.

The Inside Word

Santa Clara deserves recognition as a rising star that still manages to be highly personal and accessible. It's always better when an admissions staff regards you as a person, not an enrollment target. Unfortunately, such is not always the case. It would be hard to find a place that is more receptive to minority students. There is a very significant minority presence here because Santa Clara works hard and earnestly to make everyone feel at home. The university's popularity is increasing across the board, which proves that nice guys sometimes finish first.

FINANCIAL AID

Students should submit: FAFSA, CSS/Financial Aid PROFILE. The Princeton Review suggests that all financial aid forms be submitted as soon as possible after 1/1. *Need-based scholarships/grants offered:* Pell, SEOG, state scholarships/grants, private scholarships, the school's own gift aid. *Loan aid offered:* Direct Subsidized Stafford, Direct Unsubsidized Stafford, Direct PLUS, Federal Perkins, private alternative loans. Applicants will be notified of awards on a rolling basis beginning on or about 4/1.

FROM THE ADMISSIONS OFFICE

"Santa Clara University, located one hour south of San Francisco, offers its undergraduates an opportunity to be educated within a challenging, dynamic, and caring community. The university blends a sense of tradition and history (as the oldest college in California) with a vision that values innovation and a deep commitment to social justice. Santa Clara's faculty members are talented scholars who are demanding, supportive, and accessible. The students are serious about academics, are ethnically diverse, and enjoy a full range of athletic, social, community service, religious, and cultural activities—both on campus and through the many options presented by our northern California location. The undergraduate program includes three divisions: the College of Arts and Sciences, the School of Business, and the School of Engineering.

"For fall 2006, Santa Clara University will accept either the new SAT or the old SAT. The ACT may be taken in lieu of, or in addition to, the SAT. The ACT Writing component is optional. The highest verbal and the highest math scores attained on the SAT will be used."

SELECTIVITY

Admissions Rating	**90**
# of applicants	7,649
% of applicants accepted	57
% of acceptees attending	27
# accepting a place on wait list	1,382
% admitted from wait list	11

FRESHMAN PROFILE

Range SAT Verbal	550-640
Average SAT Verbal	592
Range SAT Math	560-660
Average SAT Math	613
**TPR Projected Range SAT Writing*	*600-660*
Range ACT Composite	24-28
Average ACT Composite	26
Minimum Paper TOEFL	550
Minimum Computer Based TOEFL	213
Average HS GPA	3.6
% graduated top 10% of class	37
% graduated top 25% of class	72
% graduated top 50% of class	100

DEADLINES

Regular application deadline	1/15
Regular notification	4/1
Nonfall registration?	yes

APPLICANTS ALSO LOOK AT AND OFTEN PREFER

Loyola Marymount U., U. of California—Berkeley, U. of California—Davis, U. of California—Los Angeles, U. of Southern California

AND SOMETIMES PREFER

Boston College, Pepperdine U., U. of California—Santa Barbara, U. of Notre Dame, U. of San Diego

AND RARELY PREFER

Creighton U., Gonzaga U., Saint Mary's College of California, U. of California—Santa Cruz, U. of San Francisco

FINANCIAL FACTS

Financial Aid Rating	**79**
Annual tuition	$28,899
Room & Board	$10,032
% frosh rec. need-based scholarship or grant aid	38
% UG rec. need-based scholarship or grant aid	39
% frosh rec. need-based self-help aid	17
% UG rec. need-based self-help aid	26
% frosh rec. any financial aid	83
% UG rec. any financial aid	69
Avg. frosh grant	$12,320
Avg. frosh loan	$5,034
Independent 529 member?	No

SARAH LAWRENCE COLLEGE

ONE MEAD WAY, BRONXVILLE, NY 10708-5999 • ADMISSIONS: 914-395-2510 • FAX: 914-395-2676

CAMPUS LIFE

Quality of Life Rating	**68**
Fire Safety Rating	**91**
Type of school	private
Environment	metropolis

STUDENTS

Total undergrad enrollment	1,185
% male/female	27/73
% from out of state	82
% from public high school	65
% live on campus	86
% African American	5
% Asian	4
% Caucasian	77
% Hispanic	3
% Native American	1
% international	2
# of countries represented	32

SURVEY SAYS

Class discussions encouraged
Small classes
No one cheats
Frats and sororities are unpopular or nonexistent
Theater is popular
Political activism is popular
(Almost) everyone smokes

ACADEMICS

Academic Rating	**96**
Calendar	semester
Student/faculty ratio	6:1
Professors interesting rating	98
Professors accessible rating	94
% professors teaching UG courses	100
% classes taught by TAs	0
Most common regular class size	10-19 students

STUDENTS SPEAK OUT

Academics

Sarah Lawrence gives students "the ability to choose: choose your classes, choose your don (advisor), choose to do everything, or choose to do one specific thing. It's all about having the freedom to design your own academic plan, to make your own choices about your own life." With no core curriculum and no formal majors, SLC students are limited in their class selections here only by catalog listings and their own areas of interests. SLC undergrads take three classes per semester. There are few exams; rather, students write lots of short papers for class plus "15- to 35-page semester-long papers" based on their work in conferences, "semi-weekly one-on-one meetings with professors." Undergrads can request to see their grades, but many bypass that option and choose to focus on the thorough written evaluations they receive for each course. Most here love the freedom, although a few warn that "you can create a very unfocused academic program and screw yourself over on transferring to another school" if you aren't careful. Also, "no grades for some students tends to translate into 'I don't have to do anything if I don't want to,'" a problem especially for those who have trouble self-motivating. For those amenable to the system—particularly those interested in theater, dancing, studio arts, writing, philosophy, and education, the school's strongest areas—SLC can be the perfect place, a school that "deeply encourages a personal creativity and fosters accomplishment. While you're here, you can really do anything academically or creatively. It is this freedom that truly allows you to bloom into a creative and intelligent adult."

Life

Undergrads at SLC tend to congregate in small groups, often to enjoy a quiet evening discussing school, cooking dinner, and watching movies. New York City is close by, so "going to the city for concerts, shopping, and museum-hopping" is regularly added to many students' day planners. On campus, "there's always something of interest going on, whether it be a classical music performance, a theater show, an ice cream social, or Ultimate Frisbee™." Political activism is also big. Parties, however, are infrequent; "Large, open parties have to be registered with the college, which makes the social situation a little weird," students tell us. So, too, does the lopsided female to male ratio—which, coupled with the small student body, is seen as a severe limitation to social life by quite a few students. SLC's campus "is beautiful and cozy, with lots of trees, grass, boulders, and pathways. Most of the dorms are also beautiful," although some complain that "the older buildings are falling apart on the inside. They need to be refurbished." Town–gown relations with Bronxville and nearby Yonkers could be better; writes one student, "We could try to create more to do in the town of Bronxville, as relations are somewhat strained. In reality, there's not much of a relationship at all."

Student Body

"With the school motto being 'You are different; so are we,' the atypical student is the typical student" at Sarah Lawrence. Adds another, "Sarah Lawrence is made up of the kids who didn't have anywhere to sit at lunch in high school, and we all get along famously, even the people who don't fit into that category." Undergrads are "for the most part highly intelligent and are able to bring up conversations that not only are thought-provoking, but also a lot of fun to participate in." They "are creatively inclined and politically aware. Students usually have an academic area of interest along with an artistic passion." Some feel that "the school could stand to be a little more politically diverse. A few more Republicans wouldn't hurt things." The student body includes "a large number of students who are either gay, lesbian, bisexual, or queer. There are a good number of straight students too, however, and there is little discrimination over sexual orientation, whatever that orientation may be." Some women complain of "an overdose of estrogen here. The hetero males who do go to SLC are spoiled by the abundance of female students."

SARAH LAWRENCE COLLEGE

FINANCIAL AID: 914-395-2570 • E-MAIL: SLCADMIT@SLC.EDU • WEBSITE: WWW.SARAHLAWRENCE.EDU

ADMISSIONS

Very important factors considered include: Character/personal qualities, essays, recommendations, secondary school record. *Important factors considered include:* Extracurricular activities, talent/ability, volunteer work, work experience. *Other factors considered include:* Alumni/ae relation, class rank, geographical residence, interview, minority status. TOEFL required of all international applicants. High school diploma or equivalent is not required. *Academic units required:* 4 English, 2 math, 2 science, 2 foreign language, 2 history. *Academic units recommended:* 4 English, 4 math, 4 science, 4 foreign language, 4 social studies, 4 history.

The Inside Word

The public generally views Sarah Lawrence as an artsy "alternative" college. The college itself avoids this image, preferring instead to evoke an impression that aligns them with more traditional and prestigious northeastern colleges such as the Ivies, Little Ivies, and former Seven Sisters. Both the total number of applicants and the selectivity of the admissions process have increased over the past few years.

FINANCIAL AID

Students should submit: FAFSA, CSS/Financial Aid PROFILE, noncustodial (divorced/separated) parents' statement. Regular filing deadline is 2/1. The Princeton Review suggests that all financial aid forms be submitted as soon as possible after 1/1. *Need-based scholarships/grants offered:* Pell, SEOG, state scholarships/grants, private scholarships, the school's own gift aid. *Loan aid offered:* FFEL Subsidized Stafford, FFEL Unsubsidized Stafford, FFEL PLUS, Federal Perkins. Applicants will be notified of awards on or about 4/1.

FROM THE ADMISSIONS OFFICE

"Students who come to Sarah Lawrence are curious about the world, and they have an ardent desire to satisfy that curiosity. Sarah Lawrence offers such students two innovative academic structures: the seminar/conference system and the arts components. Courses in the humanities, social sciences, natural sciences, and mathematics are taught in the seminar/conference style. The seminars enroll an average of 11 students and consist of lecture, discussion, readings, and assigned papers. For each seminar, students also have private tutorials, called conferences, where they conceive of individualized projects and shape them under the direction of professors. Arts components let students combine history and theory with practice. Painters, printmakers, photographers, sculptors and filmmakers, composers, musicians, choreographers, dancers, actors, and directors work in readily available studios, editing facilities, and darkrooms, guided by accomplished professionals. The secure, wooded campus is 30 minutes from New York City, and the diversity of people and ideas at Sarah Lawrence make it an extraordinary educational environment.

"Sarah Lawrence College no longer uses standardized test scores in the admissions process. This decision reflects our conviction that overemphasis on test preparation can distort results and make the application process inordinately stressful, and that academic success is better predicted by the student's course rigor, their grades, recommendations, and writing ability."

SELECTIVITY

Admissions Rating	**93**
# of applicants	2,558
% of applicants accepted	44
% of acceptees attending	29
# accepting a place on wait list	539
# of early decision applicants	89
% accepted early decision	44

FRESHMAN PROFILE

Range SAT Verbal	620-710
Range SAT Math	550-640
**TPR Projected Range SAT Writing*	*650-700*
Range ACT Composite	25-30
Minimum Paper TOEFL	600
Minimum Computer Based TOEFL	250
Average HS GPA	3.6
% graduated top 10% of class	39
% graduated top 25% of class	75
% graduated top 50% of class	95

DEADLINES

Early decision application deadline	11/15
Early decision notification	12/15
Regular application deadline	1/1
Regular notification	4/1
Nonfall registration?	no

APPLICANTS ALSO LOOK AT

AND OFTEN PREFER
Barnard College
New York University
Vassar College

AND SOMETIMES PREFER
Bard College
Oberlin College
Smith College

AND RARELY PREFER
Goucher College
Hampshire College
Mount Holyoke College

FINANCIAL FACTS

Financial Aid Rating	**87**
Annual tuition	$30,120
Room & Board	$10,394
Books and supplies	$600
Required fees	$704
% frosh rec. need-based scholarship or grant aid	44
% UG rec. need-based scholarship or grant aid	46
% frosh rec. need-based self-help aid	45
% UG rec. need-based self-help aid	45
% frosh rec. any financial aid	49
% UG rec. any financial aid	48
Avg. frosh grant	$20,874
Avg. frosh loan	$2,438
Independent 529 member?	No

Scripps College

1030 Columbia Avenue, Mailbox #1265, Claremont, CA 91711 • Admissions: 909-621-8149 • Fax: 909-607-7508

CAMPUS LIFE

Quality of Life Rating	**93**
Fire Safety Rating	**74**
Type of school	private
Environment	town

STUDENTS

Total undergrad enrollment	815
% male/female	0/100
% from out of state	56
% from public high school	64
% live on campus	97
% African American	3
% Asian	13
% Caucasian	60
% Hispanic	6
% international	1
# of countries represented	21

SURVEY SAYS

Small classes
Great library
Great food on campus
Dorms are like palaces
Campus feels safe
Frats and sororities are unpopular or nonexistent

ACADEMICS

Academic Rating	**96**
Calendar	semester
Student/faculty ratio	11:1
Professors interesting rating	91
Professors accessible rating	89
% professors teaching UG courses	100
% classes taught by TAs	0
Most common regular class size	10-19 students

MOST POPULAR MAJORS

Fine/studio arts
political science and government
psychology

STUDENTS SPEAK OUT

Academics

The young women at Scripps College encounter "very involved and politically aware" professors who are "excited to hear what you think about." Students enjoy plenty of out-of-class contact with instructors: "A lot of teachers eat in the dining hall, and on any given day there are probably eight faculty members eating lunch in Malott Commons." The core curriculum is "hell to get through, but it's kind of a bonding experience for all the first-years to complain about, and it sticks with you forever." Discussion plays a large part in Scripps's small classes; as one state-school transfer puts it, "I feel like I've died [and] gone to heaven." Most students agree, "Although the workload is very high and demanding, it is worth [it]," but several survey respondents lament, "students here are very competitive when it comes to grades." As one of the Claremont Colleges, Scripps encourages students to take classes at any of the four other schools, which, according to one undergrad, "allows me so many options for courses." Some people encounter difficulty in registering for classes, "but professors are flexible about letting you into a class if there is room." Complaints are logged regarding the "rather stuffy" administration, which has a reputation for being "unresponsive to our needs and desires." Others believe that those in charge "treat the school as a corporation for profit rather than an institution of learning." Personal interaction with higher-ups is available, whether it's "petting President Bekavac's dogs" or chatting with the load advisor "for a half-hour about how I am adjusting to life here." In any case, by the time students graduate, they have been "taught to think differently, to think for [themselves]."

Life

The Scripps campus itself "doesn't really have parties. The dorms are like hotels, which is nice, but not exactly conducive to socializing and fun." But the other Claremont campuses, such as Harvey Mudd, where "the blended drinks flow like water," are "more party and drinking-friendly." The result is that "between the five colleges, there are parties six nights a week." As much as students appreciate the options and "estrogen-balancing effect" provided by the other campuses, they also like "coming back to Scripps to sleep and relax in peace." Aside from campus parties, students strike out for Los Angeles, which is an hour away, or drive to local movie theaters and shopping centers. The campus café, the Motley, draws a loyal crowd for blackberry mochas, musical events, and art exhibits. When students aren't "organizing around social justice issues," they might be found "painting pet rocks for each other" or "creating elaborate sock puppet plays." The fitness facility is called "a pretty busy place," though "not a lot of Scripps students participate in sports," besides ever-popular Frisbee.

Student Body

"Scrippsies" could be described as "pretty liberal, artsy, and philosophical" women who "know their own opinions and aren't ashamed of them." Hailing mostly from the West Coast, the population includes "wealthy, pretty party girls; lesbians; heterosexual feminists; political activists; and quiet, studious types." Though there is an "outspoken queer population," some students feel the outside world gets the "mistaken impression that we are all lesbians." Several respondents note that the campus displays "some ethnic diversity, but it's still overwhelmingly white." One student tells us the population includes "some Asian students, fewer Hispanic students, and even fewer black students." Certain people attest to a "marginalization of women of color," but a 52-year-old Latina reports that she feels "well received in all my classes," despite being married and living off campus. Overall, this lively, contentious, and intelligent community "somehow strangely mixes together and makes one really interesting group."

FINANCIAL AID: 909-621-8275 • E-MAIL: ADMISSION@SCRIPPSCOLLEGE.EDU • WEBSITE: WWW.SCRIPPSCOLLEGE.EDU

ADMISSIONS

Very important factors considered include: Alumni/ae relation, character/personal qualities, essays, extracurricular activities, interview, minority status, recommendations, secondary school record, talent/ability, volunteer work, work experience. *Important factors considered include:* Class rank, geographical residence, standardized test scores. SAT Reasoning or ACT required. TOEFL required of all international applicants. High school diploma is required, and GED is accepted. *Academic units recommended:* 4 English, 4 math, 4 science, 4 foreign language, 4 social studies and history.

The Inside Word

With a graded paper required in addition to application essays, it is safe to say that Scripps is going to take a long, hard look at the writing ability of its candidates. Colleges that require such papers often use them to temper the unnatural aura that sometimes envelops the application essay-writing process; a school paper will usually reflect a student's work under more normal circumstances. Here's a classic case where you should pay little heed to the high admit rate; academic standards are formidable and admissions committee expectations high.

FINANCIAL AID

Students should submit: FAFSA, CSS/Financial Aid PROFILE, noncustodial (divorced/separated) parents' statement, business/farm supplement, verification worksheet, parent and student federal tax returns. The Princeton Review suggests that all financial aid forms be submitted as soon as possible after 1/1. *Need-based scholarships/grants offered:* Pell, SEOG, state scholarships/grants, private scholarships, the school's own gift aid, federal work-study. *Loan aid offered:* FFEL Subsidized Stafford, FFEL Unsubsidized Stafford, FFEL PLUS, Federal Perkins, college/university loans from institutional funds. Applicants will be notified of awards on or about 4/1.

FROM THE ADMISSIONS OFFICE

"At Scripps we believe that learning involves much more than amassing information. The truly educated person is one who can think analytically, communicate effectively, and make confident, responsible choices. Scripps classes are small (the average class size is 15) so that they foster an atmosphere where students feel comfortable participating, testing old assumptions, and exploring new ideas. Our curriculum is based on the traditional components of a liberal arts education: a set of general requirements in a wide variety of disciplines including foreign language, natural science, and writing; a multicultural requirement; a major that asks students to study one particular field in depth; and a variety of electives that allows considerable flexibility. What distinguishes Scripps from other liberal arts colleges is an emphasis on interdisciplinary courses.

"First year applicants for fall 2006 must submit results of the new SAT or the ACT. Additionally, students may submit scores from the old SAT (taken before March 2005), and best scores from either test administration will be evaluated. SAT Subject Tests are not required."

SELECTIVITY

Admissions Rating	**95**
# of applicants	1,721
% of applicants accepted	49
% of acceptees attending	24
# accepting a place on wait list	404
% admitted from wait list	8
# of early decision applicants	29
% accepted early decision	40

FRESHMAN PROFILE

Range SAT Verbal	630-740
Average SAT Verbal	681
Range SAT Math	610-700
Average SAT Math	653
**TPR Projected Range SAT Writing*	*650-720*
Range ACT Composite	26-31
Minimum Paper TOEFL	600
Minimum Computer Based TOEFL	250
Average HS GPA	4.05
% graduated top 10% of class	67
% graduated top 25% of class	93
% graduated top 50% of class	99

DEADLINES

Early decision application deadline	11/1
Early decision notification	12/15
Regular application deadline	1/15
Regular notification	4/1
Nonfall registration?	yes

APPLICANTS ALSO LOOK AT

AND OFTEN PREFER

Occidental College, Smith College, University of California—Berkeley, University of California—San Diego, Wellesley College

AND SOMETIMES PREFER

Bryn Mawr College, Claremont McKenna College, Mount Holyoke College, Pomona College, University of California—Los Angeles

FINANCIAL FACTS

Financial Aid Rating	**95**
Annual tuition	$31,332
Room & Board	$9,500
Books and supplies	$800
Required fees	$168
% frosh rec. need-based scholarship or grant aid	40
% UG rec. need-based scholarship or grant aid	46
% frosh rec. need-based self-help aid	35
% UG rec. need-based self-help aid	43
% frosh rec. any financial aid	58
% UG rec. any financial aid	63
Avg. frosh grant	$22,251
Avg. frosh loan	$3,166
Independent 529 member?	No

SEATTLE UNIVERSITY

ADMISSIONS OFFICE, 900 BROADWAY, SEATTLE, WA 98122-4340 • ADMISSIONS: 206-296-2000 • FAX: 206-296-5656

CAMPUS LIFE

Quality of Life Rating	**98**
Fire Safety Rating	**60**
Type of school	private
Affiliation	Roman Catholic-Jesuit

STUDENTS

Total undergrad enrollment	3,739
% male/female	38/62
% from out of state	41
% live on campus	38
% African American	5
% Asian	21
% Caucasian	50
% Hispanic	7
% Native American	1
% international	10
# of countries represented	76

SURVEY SAYS

Small classes
No one cheats
Students are friendly
Diverse student types on campus
Students love Seattle, WA
Campus feels safe
Students are happy
Frats and sororities are unpopular or nonexistent

ACADEMICS

Academic Rating	**88**
Calendar	quarter
Student/faculty ratio	14:1
Professors interesting rating	96
Professors accessible rating	92
% professors teaching UG courses	73
% classes taught by TAs	0
Most common lab size	20-29 students
Most common regular class size	10-19 students

MOST POPULAR MAJORS

Finance
marketing/marketing management
nursing/registered nurse training (RN, ASN, BSN, MSN)

STUDENTS SPEAK OUT

Academics

When students say that their "professors tend to rival gods" and think they're "like manna from heaven—smart, sweet, sharp, challenging," one might suspect exaggeration. But students at Seattle University (SU) will tell you that their high opinions of the professors are right on the money. Sure, there are "a few nutty professors, and a few horrible ones," but most students appreciate the "very interactive" educations they receive in the small, personal classrooms and under accessible profs. Many undergrads will tell you that the pervasive Jesuit focus on social service is one the university's crowning attributes. "SU does a good job teaching about the importance of serving others and being a part of the world we live in. I think I am a far more open-minded person now than when I was a freshman." To promote diversity of thought, the university requires that students "take two religion classes and three philosophy classes."

Student Life

The campus is only one part of Seattle University. "The city is the other part of the school." And students generally agree that "life off campus and in the city is awesome." SU is "within walking distance" of "a plethora of quirky and inexpensive coffee shops, vintage stores, movie theaters, performance theaters, dance clubs, open markets, and parks." "Have you ever heard of Broadway in Seattle? Or Capitol Hill?" asks one student. Broadway and Capitol Hill comprise this lively area immediately surrounding campus, and "it is a crazy place to venture." "From drag queens to homeless people, it epitomizes urban life." If students want to escape city living, this too is quite easy. "You can drive for an hour and hit the slopes," says an outdoor enthusiast. "We've got excellent winter and summer outdoor fun." Even with all of this activity swirling outside the campus walls, students and administration try to provide plenty of on-campus social options. Although "the school has no Greek system," it's certainly not an atmosphere starved of parties. "There are drugs and alcohol here," and some of the big bashes are even school sponsored. After these fêtes students sober up and realize that the day is full of other options, such as "speakers, roundtable discussions, luncheons, and conferences." At night, students settle into their dorm rooms, which some claim are inadequate. Others say that the dorms are safe and nurturing environments, with "priests living on every floor, plus two RAs, and tons of support groups." With the many perks at SU, there remains one challenge for students who haven't grown up in the Pacific Northwest: "You need to get used to the rain."

Students

"The only way to describe students" at Seattle University "is with the word community." "Yeah, people have their groups of friends, but it's not like you can't hang out with anyone and everyone" here. SU undergraduates "are very diverse in preferences, from ravers to religious to athletic." It's true that "many are [from the] upper class," but even these students "don't have a classist mentality." One undergrad reports, "As for diversity, there have been times when I've looked around while in a crowd of students and realized I was the only straight, white person there." "The ethnic mix is healthy" at this university in the Pacific Northwest, and "even though most students are Christian, they lean to the left politically." The biggest lesson you can learn about Seattle University is that its student body is a conglomerate of many individuals. "Everyone does his or her own thing," sums up one student.

FINANCIAL AID: 206-296-2000 • E-MAIL: ADMISSIONS@SEATTLEU.EDU • WEBSITE: WWW.SEATTLEU.EDU

ADMISSIONS

Very important factors considered include: Recommendations, secondary school record, standardized test scores, volunteer work. *Important factors considered include:* Character/personal qualities, class rank, essays, extracurricular activities, talent/ability. *Other factors considered include:* Alumni/ae relation, geographical residence, interview, minority status, state residency, work experience. SAT Reasoning or ACT required. TOEFL required of all international applicants. High school diploma is required, and GED is accepted. *Academic units required:* 4 English, 3 math, 2 science (2 science lab), 2 foreign language, 3 social studies, 2 academic electives. *Academic units recommended:* 3 science (3 science lab), 2 foreign language.

The Inside Word

Like most Catholic universities, Seattle places a heavy premium on community service. Candidates with a record demonstrating commitment to helping others have a definite leg up at this competitive school.

FINANCIAL AID

Students should submit: FAFSA. The Princeton Review suggests that all financial aid forms be submitted as soon as possible after 1/1. *Need-based scholarships/grants offered:* Pell, SEOG, state scholarships/grants, private scholarships, the school's own gift aid. *Loan aid offered:* Direct Subsidized Stafford, Direct Unsubsidized Stafford, Direct PLUS, Federal Perkins, Federal Nursing. Applicants will be notified of awards on a rolling basis beginning on or about 4/1. Federal Work-study Program available. Institutional employment available. Off-campus job opportunities are excellent.

FROM THE ADMISSIONS OFFICE

"Seattle University provides an ideal environment for motivated students interested in self-reliance, awareness of different cultures, social justice, and the fulfillment that comes from making a difference. Our location in the center of one of the nation's most diverse and progressive cities enables us to attract a student body, faculty, and staff rich in diversity. Our urban setting promotes the development of leadership skills and independence as well as providing a variety of opportunities for students to apply what they learn through internships, clinical experiences, and volunteer work. It is an environment that allows us to 'connect the mind to what matters.'

"Our academic offerings are designed to provide leadership opportunities as well as to develop global awareness and enable graduates to serve society through a demanding liberal arts and sciences foundation. In the Jesuit tradition, we teach our students how to think, not what to think. Professional undergraduate offerings include highly respected schools of business, nursing, and science and engineering, as well as career-oriented liberal arts programs such as creative writing, journalism, communications, and criminal justice.

"While located in the center of the city, Seattle University is a true residential campus, including students from 48 states and territories and 76 different nations. Washington State has designated the campus as an 'official backyard sanctuary' for its striking landscaping and environmentally conscious practices—several buildings enjoy official 'green' designations, and the student-run recycling program continually receives national recognition. Additionally, Seattle University is proud of its distinction as the most ethnically diverse institution in the Northwest—all students are valued and respected for their individual strengths, experiences, and worth.

"Pending the results of an examination into the validity of the Writing portion of the new SAT, Seattle University will continue to accept the old SAT and will use the sub scores from Critical Reading and Math sections to determine placement. In lieu of the SAT, students may also take the ACT (with the Writing component)."

SELECTIVITY

Admissions Rating	**86**
# of applicants	2,985
% of applicants accepted	78
% of acceptees attending	29

FRESHMAN PROFILE

Range SAT Verbal	510-620
Average SAT Verbal	568
Range SAT Math	510-620
Average SAT Math	564
**TPR Projected Range SAT Writing*	*570-650*
Range ACT Composite	21-27
Average ACT Composite	24
Minimum Paper TOEFL	520
Minimum Computer Based TOEFL	190
Average HS GPA	3.52
% graduated top 10% of class	33
% graduated top 25% of class	63
% graduated top 50% of class	89

DEADLINES

Regular application deadline	2/1
Regular notification	rolling
Nonfall registration?	yes

APPLICANTS ALSO LOOK AT

AND OFTEN PREFER
Santa Clara University
University of Puget Sound

AND SOMETIMES PREFER
Gonzaga University
University of Portland
University of Washington

AND RARELY PREFER
Pacific Lutheran University
Western Washington University

FINANCIAL FACTS

Financial Aid Rating	**88**
Annual tuition	$20,070
Room & Board	$6,858
Books and supplies	$1,125
% frosh rec. need-based scholarship or grant aid	68
% UG rec. need-based scholarship or grant aid	58
% frosh rec. need-based self-help aid	59
% UG rec. need-based self-help aid	55
Independent 529 member?	No

SETON HALL UNIVERSITY

ENROLLMENT SERVICES, 400 SOUTH ORANGE AVENUE, SOUTH ORANGE, NJ 07079 • ADMISSIONS: 973-761-9332 • FAX: 973-275-2040

CAMPUS LIFE

Quality of Life Rating	**62**
Fire Safety Rating	**60**
Type of school	private
Affiliation	Roman Catholic
Environment	village

STUDENTS

Total undergrad enrollment	5,009
% male/female	48/52
% from out of state	25
% from public high school	70
% live on campus	42
% in (# of) fraternities	13 (11)
% in (# of) sororities	8 (12)
% African American	11
% Asian	8
% Caucasian	53
% Hispanic	9
% international	2
# of countries represented	49

SURVEY SAYS

Small classes
Great computer facilities
Diverse student types on campus
College radio is popular
Lots of beer drinking
Hard liquor is popular
(Almost) everyone smokes

ACADEMICS

Academic Rating	**74**
Calendar	semester
Student/faculty ratio	15:1
Professors interesting rating	64
Professors accessible rating	66
% professors teaching UG courses	65
% classes taught by TAs	1
Most common lab size	10-19 students
Most common regular class size	10-19 students

MOST POPULAR MAJORS

Communications studies/speech communication and rhetoric
criminal justice/safety studies
nursing/registered nurse training (RN, ASN, BSN, MSN)

STUDENTS SPEAK OUT

Academics

Students at Seton Hall praise their school's pre-professional and career-specific programs. The education department, for example, "has a wonderful staff who are readily available and very resourceful," writes one future teacher. A nursing student reported having "an overall good experience with my professors." And a business student bragged that everyone in the b-school is "helpful, nice, and accessible." Students generally praise the deans as "very personable," and report that priests "are very nice too." There's general approbation of the full-time professors, who "work hard to help the students" and who, "because of our wireless campus and email system, are very accessible day or night!" Despite all these assets, Seton Hall also receives some very loud complaints from its undergraduates. "Registration and the money aspect are horrible," most here agree. They also warn that "advisors are the worst part of the entire process. They either don't know what they're doing or they just don't care." Others grouse that "the instructors for the core classes haven't been the best quality" and that "a lot of adjunct professors arrive here after a long day's work at their other job and don't teach us anything." Summing up both the good and bad here, one student writes, "At Seton Hall you can find small class sizes, professors who care, students who are willing to help each other and a feeling like you belong to a really big family. Seton Hall has its problems with parking for commuters, living spaces for residents, long lines at the financial aid office, and even longer lines at the bookstore to buy high-priced books."

Life

"A lot of parties go on at Seton Hall" even though the university "has worked really hard to prevent students from doing the typical party scene." Notes one student, "At the beginning of last year, Seton Hall started putting pressure on the South Orange Police. The parties are at Greek houses, which are off campus, and now most parties get broken up by the cops." The university crackdown is the result of frequent complaints from the school's neighbors; notes one student bluntly, "The town of South Orange hates college students." As a result, students either hit the frat parties or "travel away from campus, and usually away from South Orange if they plan to do most things." The net result is that many students feel that "Seton Hall University has absolutely no social life for a student who cares naught for alcohol." A good portion of the student body goes home after classes; as one student put it, "On the weekends the place is so deserted." Many who stick around "just take the train to New York City, which isn't that expensive or hard to get to. It's only a 20-minute ride, so it's what most of us do for fun here. We head for a bar or club in the city." About the only time the campus truly comes together is to watch the Pirates shoot hoops.

Student Body

Seton Hall is "a very ethnically and culturally diverse school," but by nearly all accounts, students separate themselves into ethnic and racial enclaves. Students typically "are from New York or New Jersey. They are Catholic and either white or Hispanic. On the weekends, everyone goes home, so the campus is deserted except for out-of-state and international students." Mr. Blackwell would probably side with those who complained that their classmates "wear way too much makeup and try to be J. Lo or Ja Rule. It's sick." Added another critic, "Black pants, tight shirts, and the 'Jersey' look, which is trendy, set the tone. There's Coach, Fendi, Gucci, and Tiffany's everywhere. These people think they're upper class." Undergrads tend to be "uninterested in politics at the local, state, and national levels." Most are "involved in at least one extracurricular activity, have a part-time job, and know when to have fun and when to buckle down to do their work."

FINANCIAL AID: 973-761-9332 • E-MAIL: THEHALL@SHU.EDU • WEBSITE: WWW.SHU.EDU

ADMISSIONS

Very important factors considered include: Essays, recommendations, secondary school record, standardized test scores. *Important factors considered include:* Extracurricular activities, volunteer work, work experience. *Other factors considered include:* Character/personal qualities, class rank, interview, talent/ability. SAT Reasoning or ACT required. TOEFL required of all international applicants. High school diploma is required, and GED is accepted. *Academic units required:* 4 English, 3 math, 1 science, 2 foreign language, 2 social studies, 4 academic electives.

The Inside Word

Getting into Seton Hall shouldn't be too stressful for most average students who have taken a full college-prep curriculum in high school. In the New York metropolitan area there are a lot of schools with similar characteristics, and collectively they take away the large proportion of Seton Hall's admits. Above average students who are serious about the university should be able to parlay their interest into some scholarship dollars, over 300 full scholarships this year.

FINANCIAL AID

Students should submit: FAFSA. The Princeton Review suggests that all financial aid forms be submitted as soon as possible after 1/1. *Need-based scholarships/grants offered:* Pell, SEOG, state scholarships/grants, private scholarships, the school's own gift aid. *Loan aid offered:* FFEL Subsidized Stafford, FFEL Unsubsidized Stafford, FFEL PLUS, Federal Perkins, state loans. Applicants will be notified of awards on a rolling basis beginning on or about 3/1. Federal Work-study Program available. Institutional employment available. Off-campus job opportunities are excellent.

FROM THE ADMISSIONS OFFICE

"As the oldest and largest diocesan university in the United States, Seton Hall University is committed to providing its students with a diverse environment focusing on academic excellence and ethical development. Outstanding faculty, a technologically advanced campus, and a values-centered curriculum challenge Seton Hall students. Through these things and the personal attention students receive, they are prepared to be leaders in their professional and community lives in a global society. Seton Hall's campus offers students up-to-date facilities, including an award-winning library facility opened in 1994 and the state-of-the art Kozlowski Hall, which opened in 1997. The university has invested more than $25 million in the past five years to provide its students and faculty with leading edge information technology. The Mobile Computing Program is widely recognized as one of the nation's best. In 1999 and 2000, Seton Hall was ranked as one of the nation's Most Wired universities by *Yahoo! Internet Life* magazine. Recent additions to Seton Hall's academic offerings include the School of Diplomacy and International Relations and a number of dual-degree health sciences programs, including physical therapy, physician assistant, and occupational therapy.

"Starting with all freshmen who enter Seton Hall University in fall 2006, the Writing component on either the SAT or ACT assessments will be required. However, this Writing test will be used for a correlation study only and will not be used for admission or scholarship decisions."

SELECTIVITY

Admissions Rating	**80**
# of applicants	5,750
% of applicants accepted	82
% of acceptees attending	27
# accepting a place on wait list	960
% admitted from wait list	62

FRESHMAN PROFILE

Range SAT Verbal	490-600
Average SAT Verbal	549
Range SAT Math	500-610
Average SAT Math	553
**TPR Projected Range SAT Writing*	*550-630*
Minimum Paper TOEFL	550
Minimum Computer Based TOEFL	213
Average HS GPA	3.3
% graduated top 10% of class	26
% graduated top 25% of class	54
% graduated top 50% of class	85

DEADLINES

Regular notification	rolling
Nonfall registration?	yes

APPLICANTS ALSO LOOK AT

AND OFTEN PREFER

New York University
Rutgers, The State University of New Jersey—New Brunswick/Piscataway Campus
Villanova University

AND SOMETIMES PREFER

Fairfield University
Fordham University
University of Connecticut

AND RARELY PREFER

Hofstra University
St. Bonaventure University

FINANCIAL FACTS

Financial Aid Rating	**66**
Annual tuition	$19,530
Room & Board	$8,550
Books and supplies	$1,200
Required fees	$2,050
% frosh rec. need-based scholarship or grant aid	35
% UG rec. need-based scholarship or grant aid	34
% frosh rec. need-based self-help aid	52
% UG rec. need-based self-help aid	48
% frosh rec. any financial aid	88
% UG rec. any financial aid	77
Independent 529 member?	No

SEWANEE—UNIVERSITY OF THE SOUTH

735 UNIVERSITY AVENUE, SEWANEE, TN 37383-1000 • ADMISSIONS: 931-598-1238 • FAX: 931-538-3248

CAMPUS LIFE

Quality of Life Rating	**89**
Fire Safety Rating	**60**
Type of school	private
Affiliation	Episcopal
Environment	rural

STUDENTS

Total undergrad enrollment	1,359
% male/female	48/52
% from out of state	78
% from public high school	52
% live on campus	92
% in (# of) fraternities	70 (11)
% in (# of) sororities	68 (6)
% African American	4
% Asian	2
% Caucasian	97
% Hispanic	2
% international	2
# of countries represented	25

SURVEY SAYS

Small classes
No one cheats
Athletic facilities are great
Students are friendly
Campus feels safe
Students are happy
Frats and sororities dominate social scene
Lots of beer drinking
Hard liquor is popular

ACADEMICS

Academic Rating	**91**
Calendar	semester
Student/faculty ratio	10:1
Professors interesting rating	99
Professors accessible rating	97
% professors teaching UG courses	100
% classes taught by TAs	0
Most common lab size	10-19 students
Most common regular class size	10-19 students

STUDENTS SPEAK OUT

Academics

Among the "storied traditions" at Sewanee—The University of the South—the most prominent is the Order of Gownsmen, a student honor society whose members wear gowns to class "to recognize Sewanee's ties with the English universities of Oxford and Cambridge [and] keep our reputation high and our school a comfortable place," students tell us. As at many southern schools, tradition is the cement that holds the community together. The bricks and mortar are the academics, "by far the greatest strength of Sewanee. Classes are challenging and stimulating at all colleges, but at Sewanee, learning is alive. You don't just take a course; you develop relationships with a preeminent member in the field: your professors." The "emphasis on active learning and incredible student-faculty interaction is probably Sewanee's greatest, and most often overlooked, strength," students tell us. The heavy workload here is "focused on producing excellent communicators. No matter the major or area of discipline, all professors demand that their students be able to write well when communicating their ideas." One student observes, "Professors are amazing: engaging students outside of the classroom by arranging field trips, outdoor activities, and dinners at their houses. They are tireless in devoting attention to willing students and know us very well. Therefore, they expect much out of us and push us to excel, by encouraging study abroad, writing recommendations for summer internships, and supporting research." Grading here can be tough; "A C+ at Sewanee would be an A anywhere else," many concur.

Life

"Sewanee is beautiful," students agree, telling us that "there are caves, streams, and mountains on campus, and on top of it all are beautifully ornate academic buildings that are modeled after Oxford's. The campus is 10,000 acres in all, giving you tons of places to explore." Sewanee's massive grounds serve as a magnet for outdoorsy types, and the school does its best to accommodate them. One student writes, "We have an awesome outdoor program that organizes and sponsors hiking, caving, climbing, bicycling, canoeing, skydiving, and snowshoeing trips." While "there are so many things to do here on campus for fun, both dry and with alcohol," most students drink recreationally on a regular basis. "Considering there is no cable and cell phones are practically forbidden (not like they would work on the mountain anyway), everyone turns to alcohol," explains one student. Undergrads point out that "people do a lot of work during the week—I practically live in the library during the week, as do many students here—but starting Thursday night, the students do a complete turnaround. The party scene is alive and thriving here at Sewanee." Frat parties are the center of the action; "Our Greek system is different from most schools," students explain. "We do not live in the houses and all parties are open."

Student Body

Sewanee is "largely Episcopalian, and the overwhelming majority of students are Christian. This is, of course, to be expected considering the religious affiliation of the school." Most here "love the outdoors, love to have a good time, and know when to study." Undergrads report, "Although Sewanee is taking steps to attract a more diverse student body, the majority of students here are white Southerners." Preppy is still the predominant look on campus; "You will never see as many popped collars, polo insignias, pearl necklaces, seersucker suits, or bowties as you will see at around campus at The University of the South," observes one student. Not everyone here is happy about the school's "slow, but detectable" progress toward diversity; some worry that Sewanee's beloved traditions will disappear as its core demographic loses preeminence. Their worries seem premature, at least for the immediate future.

SEWANEE—UNIVERSITY OF THE SOUTH

FINANCIAL AID: 931-598-1312 • E-MAIL: COLLEGEADMISSION@SEWANEE.EDU • WEBSITE: WWW.SEWANEE.EDU

ADMISSIONS

Very important factors considered include: Recommendations, secondary school record. *Important factors considered include:* Character/personal qualities, essays, extracurricular activities, standardized test scores, volunteer work, work experience. *Other factors considered include:* Alumni/ae relation, class rank, geographical residence, interview, minority status, talent/ability. SAT Reasoning or ACT required. TOEFL required of all international applicants. High school diploma is required, and GED is not accepted. *Academic units required:* 4 English, 3 math, 2 science (2 science lab), 2 foreign language, 1 social studies, 1 history. *Academic units recommended:* 4 English, 4 math, 4 science (3 science lab), 4 foreign language, 2 social studies, 2 history.

The Inside Word

The admissions office at Sewanee is very personable and accessible to students. Its staff includes some of the most well-respected admissions professionals in the South, and it shows in the way they work with students. Despite a fairly high acceptance rate, candidates who take the admissions process here lightly may find themselves disappointed. Applicant evaluation is too personal for a lackadaisical approach to succeed.

FINANCIAL AID

Students should submit: FAFSA, institution's own financial aid form. The Princeton Review suggests that all financial aid forms be submitted as soon as possible after 1/1. *Need-based scholarships/grants offered:* Pell, SEOG, state scholarships/grants, private scholarships, the school's own gift aid. *Loan aid offered:* FFEL Subsidized Stafford, FFEL Unsubsidized Stafford, FFEL PLUS, Federal Perkins, state loans, college/university loans from institutional funds, private alternative loans. Applicants will be notified of awards on or about 4/1. Federal Work-study Program available. Institutional employment available. Off-campus job opportunities are fair.

FROM THE ADMISSIONS OFFICE

"Sewanee, is consistently ranked among the top tier of national liberal arts universities. Sewanee is committed to an academic curriculum that focuses on the liberal arts as the most enlightening and valuable form of undergraduate education. Founded by leaders of the Episcopal church in 1857, Sewanee continues to be owned by 28 Episcopal dioceses in 12 states. The university is located on a 10,000-acre campus atop Tennessee's Cumberland Plateau between Chattanooga and Nashville. The university has an impressive record of academic achievement—24 Rhodes scholars and 24 NCAA post-graduate scholarship recipients have graduated from Sewanee.

"Sewanee will require all applicants for fall 2006 to take the new SAT or the ACT with the Writing Test. We will consider previous scores in Math and Critical Reading from previous administrations of the SAT to be considered when calculating a student's highest composite score, but students are required to take the new SAT."

SELECTIVITY

Admissions Rating	**90**
# of applicants	2,070
% of applicants accepted	64
% of acceptees attending	30
# accepting a place on wait list	133
% admitted from wait list	23
# of early decision applicants	115
% accepted early decision	77

FRESHMAN PROFILE

Range SAT Verbal	580-660
Range SAT Math	570-660
**TPR Projected Range SAT Writing*	*620-670*
Range ACT Composite	24-29
Minimum Paper TOEFL	550
Minimum Computer Based TOEFL	220
Average HS GPA	3.45
% graduated top 10% of class	40
% graduated top 25% of class	67
% graduated top 50% of class	92

DEADLINES

Early decision application deadline	11/15
Early decision notification	12/15
Regular application deadline	2/1
Regular notification	4/1
Nonfall registration?	no

APPLICANTS ALSO LOOK AT

AND OFTEN PREFER

University of North Carolina—Chapel Hill
Washington and Lee University

AND SOMETIMES PREFER

Davidson College
Vanderbilt University
Wake Forest University

AND RARELY PREFER

Rhodes College
University of Georgia
University of Tennessee—Knoxville

FINANCIAL FACTS

Financial Aid Rating	**98**
Annual tuition	$25,374
Room & Board	$7,120
Books and supplies	$600
Required fees	$206
% frosh rec. need-based scholarship or grant aid	35
% UG rec. need-based scholarship or grant aid	45
% frosh rec. need-based self-help aid	29
% UG rec. need-based self-help aid	37
Independent 529 member?	Yes

Siena College

515 Loudon Road, Loudonville, NY 12211 • Admissions: 518-783-2423 • Fax: 518-783-2436

CAMPUS LIFE

Quality of Life Rating	**76**
Fire Safety Rating	**98**
Type of school	private
Affiliation	Roman Catholic
Environment	town

STUDENTS

Total undergrad enrollment	3,213
% male/female	43/57
% from out of state	12
% live on campus	70
% African American	2
% Asian	3
% Caucasian	88
% Hispanic	3

SURVEY SAYS

Small classes
Frats and sororities are unpopular or nonexistent
College radio is popular
Lots of beer drinking
Hard liquor is popular

ACADEMICS

Academic Rating	**76**
Calendar	semester
Student/faculty ratio	14:1
Professors interesting rating	71
Professors accessible rating	80
% professors teaching UG courses	100
% classes taught by TAs	0
Most common lab size	10-19 students
Most common regular class size	20-29 students

MOST POPULAR MAJORS

Biology/biological sciences
marketing/marketing management
psychology

STUDENTS SPEAK OUT

Academics

According to its students, a Siena education is an experience with plenty of benefits and drawbacks. On the one hand, "most of the professors are very good people and easy to talk to and get along with." Like the professors, the friars (this college has Franciscan roots) "often take time out of their own schedules to interact [with], empathize [with], and lead Siena students." Nonetheless, many students feel that their classroom experiences are limited. One student says that she has "noticed many professors [who] are not enthusiastic about teaching," and many of the adjunct faculty members "are not worth your time and effort." Of course, we hear different reports from the three schools within the college: the School of Liberal Arts, the School of Business, and the School of Science. Overall, students tell us that liberal arts professors are especially knowledgeable, a degree in business carries substantial regional weight, and delving into a science major provides very rewarding challenges as well as a lot of work. Each student's college career begins with the two-semester Foundations Sequence—a thorough examination of a number of classic and contemporary texts. Core courses at other colleges often draw complaints, but not here. What does draw the most complaints at Siena is the administration. One student explains, "Time after time, since I've arrived here, decisions have been made regarding student life or academics with minimal to no consultation of students." If you end up at Siena, you might want to follow the advice of this student: "If you do not treat the administration as the enemy from day one, they will listen to you and respect you."

Life

Siena College has a quiet campus in Loudonville, a small town in upstate New York. Albany is just a couple miles up the road, so students looking for nightlife off campus will often pile into cabs and head to the capital city for the clubs and bars. But if a good party is what students are after—and, more often than not, it is—there's no need to leave campus. "Siena is a party school," one student assures us, "don't let anybody tell you otherwise." The real on-campus action takes place at "the many townhouse parties," where the upperclassmen live. The student body appreciates athletics and makes sure that the campus gym facilities are well used. A range of other on-campus activities are available for students, though they receive mixed reviews. A less-than-enthusiastic student comments, "It would seem that the target age group for most campus-sponsored activities is 12-16." Others, however, are excited about the fact that "there are a lot of activities for students to get involved in or attend." The more popular events include the annual Winter Weekend and Sienafest. When exactly is Winter Weekend held? Well, "there are only two seasons in Loudonville: September and winter," as one student wryly puts it. In other words, Winter Weekend is not in September.

Student Body

When a student tells us that "it seems that most everyone is the same at Siena," what she means is that Siena's student body is an overwhelmingly Caucasian and Catholic crowd with conservative views and roots in New York State. "Conformity is the name of the game here at good ol' S-I-E-N-A," an undergraduate remarks. Some students believe that the college is heavy on cliques, but a classmate qualifies that argument, claiming that "there are no cliques at Siena because everyone is the same!" Along these lines, a student offers this stylistic breakdown of the student body: "Basically, there are three types of students at Siena," she says, "Abercrombie, Gap, and Banana Republic." Though students do not deny having superficial streaks, they quickly point out that "most everyone is friendly," and that one beneficial result of so much homogeneity is that disputes between student groups are rare.

SIENA COLLEGE

FINANCIAL AID: 518-783-2427 • E-MAIL: ADMIT@SIENA.EDU • WEBSITE: WWW.SIENA.EDU

ADMISSIONS

Very important factors considered include: Secondary school record. *Important factors considered include:* Extracurricular activities, standardized test scores, talent/ability. *Other factors considered include:* Alumni/ae relation, character/personal qualities, class rank, essays, geographical residence, interview, minority status, recommendations, state residency, volunteer work, work experience. SAT Reasoning or ACT required. TOEFL required of all international applicants. High school diploma is required, and GED is accepted. *Academic units required:* 4 English, 3 math, 3 science (3 science lab), 1 social studies, 3 history. *Academic units recommended:* 4 English, 4 math, 4 science (3 science lab), 3 foreign language, 1 social studies, 3 history.

The Inside Word

Students who have consistently solid grades should have no trouble getting admitted. There is hot competition for students between colleges in New York State; Siena has to admit the large majority of its applicants in order to meet freshman class enrollment targets.

FINANCIAL AID

Students should submit: FAFSA, state aid form. The Princeton Review suggests that all financial aid forms be submitted as soon as possible after 1/1. *Need-based scholarships/grants offered:* Pell, SEOG, state scholarships/grants, private scholarships, the school's own gift aid. *Loan aid offered:* FFEL Subsidized Stafford, FFEL Unsubsidized Stafford, FFEL PLUS, Federal Perkins. Applicants will be notified of awards on or about 4/1. Off-campus job opportunities are good.

FROM THE ADMISSIONS OFFICE

"Siena is a coeducational, independent liberal arts college with a Franciscan tradition. It is a community where the intellectual, personal, and social growth of all students is paramount. Siena's faculty calls forth the best Siena students have to give—and the students do the same for them. Students are competitive, but not at each other's expense. Siena's curriculum includes 23 majors in three schools—liberal arts, science, and business. In addition, there are over a dozen pre-professional and special academic programs. With a student/faculty ratio of 14:1, class size ranges between 15 and 35 students. Siena's 152-acre campus is located in Loudonville, a suburban community within two miles of the New York State seat of government in Albany. With 15 colleges in the area, there is a wide variety of activities on weekends. Regional theater, performances by major concert artists, and professional sports events compete with the activities on the campus. Within 50 miles are the Adirondacks, the Berkshires, and the Catskills, providing outdoor recreation throughout the year. Because the capital region's easy, friendly lifestyle is so appealing, many Siena graduates try to find their first jobs in upstate New York.

"Freshman applicants must submit the SAT or ACT with the Writing component."

SELECTIVITY

Admissions Rating	**84**
# of applicants	4,145
% of applicants accepted	60
% of acceptees attending	29
# accepting a place on wait list	494
% admitted from wait list	11
# of early decision applicants	48
% accepted early decision	59

FRESHMAN PROFILE

Range SAT Verbal	510-590
Average SAT Verbal	554
Range SAT Math	520-610
Average SAT Math	569
**TPR Projected Range SAT Writing*	*570-620*
Range ACT Composite	23-26
Average ACT Composite	25
Minimum Paper TOEFL	550
Minimum Computer Based TOEFL	213
Average HS GPA	3.6
% graduated top 10% of class	10
% graduated top 25% of class	61
% graduated top 50% of class	94

DEADLINES

Early decision application deadline	12/1
Early decision notification	12/15
Regular application deadline	3/1
Regular notification	3/15
Nonfall registration?	yes

APPLICANTS ALSO LOOK AT

AND OFTEN PREFER

Providence College, Villanova U.

AND SOMETIMES PREFER

Fairfield U., Fordham U., Loyola College in Maryland, Marist College, The U. of Scranton

AND RARELY PREFER

Le Moyne College, Sacred Heart U., SUNY at Albany

FINANCIAL FACTS

Financial Aid Rating	**72**
Annual tuition	$20,100
Room & Board	$7,985
Books and supplies	$875
Required fees	$175
% frosh rec. need-based scholarship or grant aid	72
% UG rec. need-based scholarship or grant aid	70
% frosh rec. need-based self-help aid	55
% UG rec. need-based self-help aid	56
% frosh rec. any financial aid	84
% UG rec. any financial aid	84
Avg. frosh grant	$11,000
Avg. frosh loan	$2,800
Independent 529 member?	No

SIMMONS COLLEGE

300 THE FENWAY, BOSTON, MA 02115 • ADMISSIONS: 617-521-2051 • FAX: 617-521-3190

CAMPUS LIFE

Quality of Life Rating	**86**
Fire Safety Rating	**60**
Type of school	private
Environment	city

STUDENTS

Total undergrad enrollment	1,294
% male/female	0/100
% from out of state	43
% from public high school	81
% live on campus	75
% African American	6
% Asian	6
% Caucasian	68
% Hispanic	3
% international	4
# of countries represented	26

SURVEY SAYS

Small classes
Students love Boston, MA
Great off-campus food
Frats and sororities are unpopular or nonexistent

ACADEMICS

Academic Rating	**85**
Calendar	semester
Student/faculty ratio	12:1
Professors interesting rating	84
Professors accessible rating	83
% professors teaching UG courses	100
% classes taught by TAs	0
Most common regular class size	10-19 students

MOST POPULAR MAJORS

Communications studies/speech communication and rhetoric
nursing/registered nurse training (RN, ASN, BSN, MSN)

STUDENTS SPEAK OUT

Academics

At Simmons College, its all-female, grade-conscious setting demonstrates that "the girls are here to learn." A senior admits, "It might sound cheesy, but the school is really about helping students find their voice." Professors facilitate this process by "treating everyone with respect, dignity, and compassion." Students feel their teachers are "actually on our side, ready to help with almost anything." Extensive office hours and prompt e-mail responses indicate professors' high level of accessibility. "When you find an amazing professor, you can be sure that s/he is available to you in a big way," writes a senior. The political science, international relations, and communications departments rank high with students, while the nursing and physical therapy programs benefit from proximity to some of the nation's top hospitals. "When I look out my window, I see Beth Israel Deaconess Medical Center, and one block down are the rest of the great hospitals in the Longwood Medical Area." This practical training bridges academic work and professional preparation. "All of my professors in the nursing program have wanted me to succeed and have advised me in my career choices." A few departments, such as music and psychology, could use a few more faculty members to cover class demand. Complaints surface regarding Culture Matters (officially the "Multidisciplinary Core Course"), a class required of all first year students. But in most classes, students notice a payoff. "I've seen an amazing improvement in my writing, class participation, and overall attention to detail in my reading." The school places "a high premium on making sure everyone feels comfortable," so that education can be a personal experience. "By the time we graduate, we're far more self-confident."

Life

Be warned: "This is a learning environment, not a place to party or make out with the newest meat from MIT." It's true that on-campus life can feel like "a bizarre combination of a nunnery and Sesame Street." Entertainment veers towards that sleepover-party image of single-sex institutions, complete with "pajamas, movies, and drinks." If Simmons were located in the boonies, the regimen of knitting, Ms. Pac-Man, political rallies, and field hockey could get old. But it's in the middle of Boston, a "huge college-oriented city" that beckons with Newbury Street shopping, hip coffee shops, Red Sox games, and the male-female ratio of the real world. "The school buys bulk discounted tickets to plays and musicals and even the ballet." Participation in the Colleges of Fenway Consortium links the school to its neighbors, though some students seem to have thought before they enrolled that Simmons would host more coed events. Students like coming home to Simmons as much as they like getting away. "It always feels like a safe and secure place to study after a long weekend out." A fair number of entering students seem to experience a rough adjustment period but grow to love the school after getting accustomed and involved.

Student Body

Simmons women see themselves as open-minded, overachieving feminists who are "just as engaging at a party as in the classroom." Students routinely take on crazy class-hours, club leadership positions, and multiple majors. Recently, the vibe of the school has started to shift "from being all about grades to being more about community." The small, liberal student body accepts lesbianism readily—"You become very accustomed to same-sex relationships"—but "Republicans or Yankees fans might want to tread carefully." Many student activists organize around political issues of gender, race, and class. They note a divide between students "on a first-name basis with every financial aid officer and those whose parents can afford a small island in the Pacific." They are also sensitive to the fact that "there are more cleaning people than students of color." However, a junior points out, "With each incoming class, Simmons becomes more and more diverse." Ultimately, students cultivate "solidarity around being a woman," whether that woman is moneyed Cape Cod stock or a gender-bending punk.

FINANCIAL AID: 617-521-2001 • E-MAIL: UGADM@SIMMONS.EDU • WEBSITE: WWW.SIMMONS.EDU

ADMISSIONS

Very important factors considered include: Secondary school record. *Important factors considered include:* Character/personal qualities, class rank, essays, recommendations, standardized test scores. *Other factors considered include:* Extracurricular activities, interview, talent/ability, volunteer work, work experience. SAT Reasoning or ACT required. TOEFL required of all international applicants. High school diploma or equivalent is not required. *Academic units required:* 4 English, 3 math, 3 science, 3 foreign language, 3 social studies, 3 history. *Academic units recommended:* 4 English, 4 math, 3 science, 4 foreign language, 4 social studies, 3 history.

The Inside Word

Most of the best women's colleges in the country are in the Northeast, including those Seven Sister schools (roughly the female equivalent of the formerly all-male Ivies) that remain women's colleges. The competition for students is intense, and although Simmons is a strong attraction for many women, there are at least a half-dozen competitors who draw the better students away. For the majority of applicants there is little need for anxiety while awaiting a decision. Its solid academics, Boston location, and bountiful scholarship program make Simmons well worth considering for any student opting for a women's college.

FINANCIAL AID

Students should submit: FAFSA, noncustodial (divorced/separated) parents' statement, business/farm supplement, parents' income tax returns. The Princeton Review suggests that all financial aid forms be submitted as soon as possible after 1/1. *Need-based scholarships/grants offered:* Pell, SEOG, state scholarships/grants, private scholarships, the school's own gift aid. *Loan aid offered:* FFEL Subsidized Stafford, FFEL Unsubsidized Stafford, FFEL PLUS, Federal Perkins, state loans, college/university loans from institutional funds. Applicants will be notified of awards on or about 3/15. Federal Work-study Program available. Institutional employment available. Off-campus job opportunities are good.

FROM THE ADMISSIONS OFFICE

"Simmons believes passionately in an 'educational contract' that places students first and helps them build successful careers, lead meaningful lives, and realize a powerful return on their investment.

"Simmons is truly a 100-year-old university in Boston, with a tradition of providing women with a collaborative environment that stimulates dialogue, enhances listening, catalyzes action, and spurs personal and professional growth.

"Simmons honors this contract by delivering a quality education and measurable success through our singular approach to professional preparation, intellectual exploration, and community orientation.

"As of this book's publication, Simmons College did not have information available about their policy regarding the new SAT."

SELECTIVITY

Admissions Rating	**84**
# of applicants	2,041
% of applicants accepted	67
% of acceptees attending	30
# accepting a place on wait list	46
% admitted from wait list	4

FRESHMAN PROFILE

Range SAT Verbal	510-610
Average SAT Verbal	558
Range SAT Math	500-590
Average SAT Math	539
**TPR Projected Range SAT Writing*	*570-640*
Average ACT Composite	24
Minimum Paper TOEFL	560
Minimum Computer Based TOEFL	220
Average HS GPA	3.16
% graduated top 10% of class	20
% graduated top 25% of class	56
% graduated top 50% of class	89

DEADLINES

Regular application deadline	2/1
Regular notification	4/15
Nonfall registration?	yes

APPLICANTS ALSO LOOK AT

AND OFTEN PREFER
Boston University
Smith College

AND SOMETIMES PREFER
Clark University
Mount Holyoke College
Northeastern University
University of New Hampshire
University of Vermont

AND RARELY PREFER
Emmanuel College
Suffolk University
University of Connecticut
University of Massachusetts—Amherst

FINANCIAL FACTS

Financial Aid Rating	**77**
Annual tuition	$24,680
Room & Board	$10,200
Books and supplies	$800
Required fees	$760
% frosh rec. need-based scholarship or grant aid	83
% UG rec. need-based scholarship or grant aid	78
% frosh rec. need-based self-help aid	70
% UG rec. need-based self-help aid	71
% frosh rec. any financial aid	83
% UG rec. any financial aid	78
Avg. frosh grant	$9,177
Avg. frosh loan	$3,127
Independent 529 member?	No

SIMON'S ROCK COLLEGE OF BARD

84 ALFORD ROAD, GREAT BARRINGTON, MA 01230 • ADMISSIONS: 413-528-7312 • FAX: 413-528-7334

CAMPUS LIFE

Quality of Life Rating	**70**
Fire Safety Rating	**86**
Type of school	private
Environment	village

STUDENTS

Total undergrad enrollment	370
% male/female	42/58
% from out of state	80
% live on campus	85
% African American	2
% Asian	4
% Caucasian	48
% Hispanic	2
% Native American	1
% international	1

SURVEY SAYS

Small classes
Athletic facilities are great
Students aren't religious
Campus feels safe
Frats and sororities are unpopular or nonexistent
(Almost) everyone smokes

ACADEMICS

Academic Rating	**77**
Calendar	semester
Student/faculty ratio	8:1
Professors interesting rating	91
Professors accessible rating	87
% professors teaching UG courses	100
% classes taught by TAs	0
Most common lab size	fewer than 10 students
Most common regular class size	10-19 students

MOST POPULAR MAJORS

Cell/cellular biology and histology
creative writing
psychology

STUDENTS SPEAK OUT

Academics

Tiny Simon's Rock College of Bard, which admits exceptional high school sophomores and juniors to its college-level program, "is a fantastic opportunity for students who were either bored in high school (the overachievers) or the really smart kids who never did a damn thing, but want to now. Hating high school isn't enough, though; you really have to work hard here." With barely 400 enrollees, "there are usually only about eight people in a class. You can take the class wherever you want it to go. And if you can't, you can stay after and talk it over with the teacher one-on-one." The school offers students the freedom "to do independent study or take a 300-level course as a freshman or do practically anything else. All you have to do is ask." Notes one student, "This school is really one giant test of one's own motivation and determination." Although "there isn't a huge variety of majors and classes available," students tell us that "every semester when the course catalog comes out, it's never a question of finding interesting courses to take; it's always a matter of working them into a workable schedule." They also explain that "because of the interdisciplinary nature of academics here, the limited number of majors isn't a huge problem." Furthermore, "if something you want to study isn't being covered, it's remarkably easy to set up a tutorial dedicated to that subject because professors are extraordinarily available and receptive."

Life

"Life at Simon's Rock can be very boring since it's located in a small town," undergrads at this tiny college concede, "but you can find happiness with your friends and student life staff." Diversion comes primarily in the form of "a peculiar form of 'hanging out'—Simon's Rock should really be a verb rather than a noun. This sort of hanging out involves either being outside smoking or inside watching the *Fight Club* DVD a lot and having conversations that range from the emotionally charged to goofy to intellectual." Go-getters note that "the schools is always really helpful to students. Since many of the students are younger, some too young to drive, they offer town trips every day, and on weekends they often take groups to go ice-skating, bowling, roller skating, miniature golfing, or just to the movies. They also have mall trips, and student groups often go to other colleges to meet other students and to get ideas as to how to incorporate Simon's Rock into the larger college community." Many, however, don't take advantage of these opportunities, instead resorting to immersion in computer games, pot-smoking, or pure tedium. Location and the size of the school are major roadblocks to a more active social scene. "It would be nice if there were stronger campus organizations, but it's difficult for that to happen given the small size of the school and the demanding nature of the classes," explains one student. Notes another, "The location of the school doesn't help one bit." It's so secluded that "there's no television reception, and cell phones are useless, too."

Student Body

Traditionally regarded as a lefty-weirdo haven, Simon's Rock "seems to be getting more conservative and preppy with each entering class." The transition is a slow one, however. According to one student, "the average Simon's Rock student probably smokes both cigarettes and marijuana, is interested in arts and humanities, considers him- or herself to be politically active, and is probably vegetarian or vegan." And oddballs still predominate; as one student put it, "We all come from something abnormal, due to the fact that we are entering college a year or two early. And these abnormalities, although strikingly different, form a common bond." Adds another, "The townies call us 'the freaks on the hill.' My mom calls us 'the patients.'" Because it's a school of 400 students, "everyone knows everybody."

FINANCIAL AID: 413-528-7297 • E-MAIL: ADMIT@SIMONS-ROCK.EDU • WEBSITE: WWW.SIMONS-ROCK.EDU

ADMISSIONS

Very important factors considered include: Character/personal qualities, essays, interview, recommendations, talent/ability. *Important factors considered include:* Extracurricular activities, secondary school record, standardized test scores, volunteer work. *Other factors considered include:* Alumni/ae relation, minority status, work experience. SAT Reasoning or ACT required. TOEFL required of all international applicants. High school diploma or equivalent is not required. *Academic units recommended:* 2 English, 2 math, 2 science (1 science lab), 2 foreign language, 2 social studies, 2 history, 2 academic electives.

The Inside Word

There is no other college like Simon's Rock in the country, and no other similar admissions process. Applying to college doesn't get any more personal, and thus any more demanding, than it does here. If you're not ready to tap your potential as a thinker in college beginning with completion of the application, avoid Simon's Rock. Simply hating high school isn't going to get you in. Self-awareness, intellectual curiosity, and a desire for more formidable academic challenges than those typically found in high school will.

FINANCIAL AID

Students should submit: FAFSA, CSS/Financial Aid PROFILE, noncustodial (divorced/separated) parents' statement, business/farm supplement, parent and student federal tax forms, federal verification worksheet. The Princeton Review suggests that all financial aid forms be submitted as soon as possible after 1/1. *Need-based scholarships/grants offered:* Pell, SEOG, state scholarships/grants, the school's own gift aid. *Loan aid offered:* FFEL Subsidized Stafford, FFEL Unsubsidized Stafford, FFEL PLUS, Federal Perkins, state loans, alternative eductional loans. Applicants will be notified of awards on a rolling basis beginning on or about 2/15. Federal Work-study Program available. Institutional employment available. Off-campus job opportunities are good.

FROM THE ADMISSIONS OFFICE

"Simon's Rock is dedicated to one thing: to allow bright, highly motivated students the opportunity to pursue college work leading to the AA and BA degrees at an age earlier than our national norm.

"Simon's Rock College of Bard will accept either the new SAT or the old SAT (administered prior to March 2005 and without a Writing component), as well as the ACT with or without the Writing component."

SELECTIVITY	
Admissions Rating	**60**
# of applicants	247
% of applicants accepted	79
% of acceptees attending	72
FRESHMAN PROFILE	
Range SAT Verbal	600-700
Average SAT Verbal	650
Range SAT Math	570-660
Average SAT Math	615
**TPR Projected Range SAT Writing*	*630-700*
Range ACT Composite	24-30
Average ACT Composite	27
Minimum Paper TOEFL	550
Minimum Computer Based TOEFL	200
DEADLINES	
Regular application deadline	7/1
Nonfall registration?	yes
FINANCIAL FACTS	
Financial Aid Rating	**70**
Annual tuition	$30,687
Room & Board	$8,088
Books and supplies	$2,000
Required fees	$500
% frosh rec. need-based scholarship or grant aid	55
% UG rec. need-based scholarship or grant aid	48
% frosh rec. need-based self-help aid	46
% UG rec. need-based self-help aid	41
% frosh rec. any financial aid	78
% UG rec. any financial aid	71
Avg. frosh grant	$19,644
Avg. frosh loan	$2,625
Independent 529 member?	No

SKIDMORE COLLEGE

815 NORTH BROADWAY, SARATOGA SPRINGS, NY 12866-1632 • ADMISSIONS: 518-580-5570 • FAX: 518-580-5584

CAMPUS LIFE

Quality of Life Rating	**85**
Fire Safety Rating	**60**
Type of school	private
Environment	town

STUDENTS

Total undergrad enrollment	2,609
% male/female	41/59
% from out of state	70
% from public high school	60
% live on campus	76
% African American	3
% Asian	5
% Caucasian	73
% Hispanic	4
% international	1
# of countries represented	28

SURVEY SAYS

Small classes
Great off-campus food
Frats and sororities are unpopular or nonexistent
Lots of beer drinking

ACADEMICS

Academic Rating	**89**
Calendar	semester
Student/faculty ratio	9:1
Professors interesting rating	84
Professors accessible rating	87
% professors teaching UG courses	100
% classes taught by TAs	0
Most common lab size	10-19 students
Most common regular class size	10-19 students

MOST POPULAR MAJORS

Business administration/management
English language and literature
psychology

STUDENTS SPEAK OUT

Academics

Skidmore College puts the emphasis on the "arts" in "liberal arts college." Nearly one in five undergraduates major in the visual or performing arts. The school also does a fine job developing future arts patrons through its popular business major. Undergraduates speak favorably of both the yin and yang of their school's academic offerings. Business "is a great program jumpstarted through real-life case studies and interactions among executives," while the arts departments benefit from "the high quantity of artists, which fuels the place and gives it this energy for invention and enthusiasm for exploration." Small classes—"the largest 'lecture' class is about 25 to 30 students"—foster strong student-teacher bonds, which in turn allow for "endless opportunities, although they require student initiative." Many students tell us that "Skidmore is a very challenging school academically." A vocal minority, however, complain and "wish that the academics were more challenging and that professors had less tolerance for average work." An undergraduate concludes, "Skidmore provides an academically rigorous environment, but only for those students who choose to challenge and dedicate themselves to their studies."

Life

Weather permitting, the Skidmore campus is a beehive of activity. As one student explains, "We have athletic events, movies, theatrical performances, art galleries, restaurants, political rallies, famous speakers, and interesting people to talk to. I have never had so many unique and exciting things to do in my life." Those seeking a party will find it. Those who want to avoid the party scene are able to. One undergraduate writes, "There are a lot of hard-core party people, a lot of chill, easygoing party people, and a lot of sober party people. Everyone is looking to have a good time on weekends, but that could mean getting trashed or it could mean watching movies with friends." Whatever your preference, "because of Skidmore's small size, a student can really be anything he or she wants to be. If you've always wanted to be in a band, you can do that here. If you want to start your own publication, you can do that, too. It just takes some motivation." Furthermore, if you just want to relax and do nothing, you can enjoy the "gorgeous campus, [dormitories] known for their big room size," or the town of Saratoga Springs, which is "only a short walk away." The town has "great shopping and fabulous restaurants," students report. Outdoorsy types appreciate their "access to endless amounts of Adirondack and Green Mountain hiking. In the winter, the skiing is awesome." Because of the harsh winters, social life is "really dependent on weather. Wintertime, which is most of the school year, is kinda gloomy, but when it's nice out everyone gets really happy, and there's a lot of stuff to do."

Student Body

The Skidmore student body has "a huge mix of kids, from WASPs to JAPs to athletes to stoners." The school is geographically diverse. "Many people are from New York State (and NYC) or the Boston area, but there are many people from the Midwest, Mid-Atlantic, New England, and the West Coast as well," students tell us. Artists and business majors are the two most prominent archetypes. One undergraduate explains, "If you're a business major, you are probably wealthy, white, drink a lot, probably Republican, and probably play sports. If you're an art major, you are wealthy, white, probably gay, from New York City, a pot-smoker, and don't like to be categorized." Another student notes that "there are plenty of students who fit neither stereotypes and still mix in well with the school's atmosphere." The business students are about the only Republicans. The rest of the student body leans pretty far to the left politically.

Skidmore College

Financial Aid: 518-580-5750 • E-mail: admissions@skidmore.edu • Website: www.skidmore.edu

ADMISSIONS

Very important factors considered include: Recommendations, secondary school record. *Important factors considered include:* Character/personal qualities, class rank, essays, extracurricular activities, standardized test scores, talent/ability, volunteer work, work experience. *Other factors considered include:* Alumni/ae relation, geographical residence, interview, minority status. SAT Reasoning or ACT required. TOEFL required of all international applicants. High school diploma is required, and GED is accepted. *Academic units recommended:* 4 English, 4 math, 4 science (3 science lab), 4 foreign language, 4 social studies.

The Inside Word

Although Skidmore overlaps applicants with some of the best colleges and universities in the Northeast, it's mainly viewed as a safety. Still, this makes for a strong applicant pool, and those students who do enroll give the college a better-than-average freshman academic profile. The entire admissions operation at Skidmore is impressive and efficient, proof that number two does indeed try harder.

FINANCIAL AID

Students should submit: FAFSA, CSS/Financial Aid PROFILE. Regular filing deadline is 1/15. The Princeton Review suggests that all financial aid forms be submitted as soon as possible after 1/1. *Need-based scholarships/grants offered:* Pell, SEOG, state scholarships/grants, the school's own gift aid. *Loan aid offered:* FFEL Subsidized Stafford, FFEL Unsubsidized Stafford, FFEL PLUS, Federal Perkins. Applicants will be notified of awards on or about 4/1. Federal Work-study Program available. Institutional employment available. Off-campus job opportunities are fair.

FROM THE ADMISSIONS OFFICE

"New for 2005 is Skidmore's First Year Experience (FYE), a year-long curricular, residential, and programmatic initiative that immediately engages each first-year student with a faculty mentor-advisor, with 14 other students in an innovative Scribner Seminar, and with the entire College via a thematically-linked series of artistic, cultural, and social events. FYE's centerpiece, 40 distinctive Scribner Seminars—ranging from African cinema, to the ethics of tobacco and alcohol advertising, to the biotech revolution—encourage each student to actively and creatively participate in his or her own learning. Individual seminar instructors will also function as faculty mentor-advisors for those 15 students, and will provide both a curricular and co-curricular perspective not only on the specific seminar topic but the liberal arts in general. In most cases, students will live in residence halls in close proximity to other students in their seminar.

"Even prior to arrival on campus, first-year students will have been in telephone contact with summer advisors, selected their preferred Scribner Seminar, explored summer reading intended to provide a thematic umbrella for all students, and gotten to know—at least virtually—their seminar classmates.

"The First-Year Experience is just the beginning of the expectation that students will creatively craft an experience leading to intensive work in a major field of study. It is also a singular manifestation of Skidmore's commitment to the belief that Creative Thought Matters—that every life, career, and endeavor is made more profound with creative ability at its core.

"Applicants for fall 2006 are required to take the new version of the SAT (or the ACT with the Writing section). However, we will allow students to submit scores from the old (prior to March 2005) version of the SAT, and will use the student's best scores from either test. We recommend that students provide scores for two SAT Subject Test examinations."

SELECTIVITY

Admissions Rating	**93**
# of applicants	6,032
% of applicants accepted	48
% of acceptees attending	24
# accepting a place on wait list	996
# of early decision applicants	246
% accepted early decision	60

FRESHMAN PROFILE

Range SAT Verbal	580-670
Average SAT Verbal	626
Range SAT Math	580-670
Average SAT Math	624
**TPR Projected Range SAT Writing*	*620-680*
Range ACT Composite	26-29
Average ACT Composite	27
Minimum Paper TOEFL	580
Minimum Computer Based TOEFL	243
Average HS GPA	3.32
% graduated top 10% of class	49
% graduated top 25% of class	81
% graduated top 50% of class	97

DEADLINES

Early decision application deadline	11/15
Early decision notification	12/15
Regular application deadline	1/15
Regular notification	4/1
Nonfall registration?	yes

APPLICANTS ALSO LOOK AT

AND OFTEN PREFER

Boston College, Colby College, Wesleyan University

AND SOMETIMES PREFER

Connecticut College, New York University, Syracuse University

AND RARELY PREFER

Ithaca College, University of Vermont, Wheaton College (MA)

FINANCIAL FACTS

Financial Aid Rating	**93**
Annual tuition	$30,800
Room & Board	$8,710
Books and supplies	$750
Required fees	$308
% frosh rec. need-based scholarship or grant aid	40
% UG rec. need-based scholarship or grant aid	43
% frosh rec. need-based self-help aid	40
% UG rec. need-based self-help aid	43
% frosh rec. any financial aid	40
% UG rec. any financial aid	43
Avg. frosh grant	$21,445
Avg. frosh loan	$2,724
Independent 529 member?	Yes

Smith College

7 College Lane, Northampton, MA 01063 • Admissions: 413-585-2500 • Fax: 413-585-2527

CAMPUS LIFE

Quality of Life Rating	**95**
Fire Safety Rating	**73**
Type of school	private
Environment	town

STUDENTS

Total undergrad enrollment	2,692
% male/female	0/100
% from out of state	72
% from public high school	74
% live on campus	87
% African American	6
% Asian	10
% Caucasian	54
% Hispanic	6
% Native American	1
% international	7
# of countries represented	65

SURVEY SAYS

Small classes
Great library
Great off-campus food
Dorms are like palaces
Frats and sororities are unpopular or nonexistent

ACADEMICS

Academic Rating	**94**
Calendar	semester
Student/faculty ratio	9:1
Professors interesting rating	94
Professors accessible rating	88
% professors teaching UG courses	100
% classes taught by TAs	0
Most common lab size	10-19 students
Most common regular class size	10-19 students

MOST POPULAR MAJORS

Political science and government
psychology
visual and performing arts

STUDENTS SPEAK OUT

Academics

"Fantastic academics" that demand "insane amounts of studying and work" have always been the signature feature of a Smith education, and the women who attend this elite Northeastern school wouldn't have it any other way. One student explains, "Classes are so incredibly challenging, you work your ass off to succeed, but you do it because the professors are so great and because the work is interesting." With no core requirements to fulfill, Smithies "can spend much more time taking classes they are interested in. It makes you feel like you are getting more out of your college education." So too do professors who "really care and are willing to explain, discuss, re-explain and work with you until you have a solid grasp of the material." An "amazing library" is among Smith's many resources; what students can't find here in the library or course catalog, they can easily seek out at one of the other member schools in the Five College Consortium (Amherst, Mount Holyoke, Hampshire, and UMass); shuttle buses carry students among the different campuses. As one student sums up, Smith is "unabashedly a women's college, devoted to providing incredible education and opportunities to women from around the globe."

Life

Smith undergrads adore the school's unique housing system, under which "students live in a beautiful 19th-century house with 40 of their closest friends." Almost all of the "amazing" dorms "have hardwood floors and big windows" and typically include "dining rooms with kitchen staffs." The system not only allows students to manage their stressful academics in comfort, but also provides them with a ready support network of peers. The houses are just one of many traditions that unite the Smith community; Friday afternoon tea is another. Reports one student, "The kitchen staff bakes cookies and all sorts of pastries and it's a nice time to unwind after the week. We also have candlelight dinner every Thursday night and dinner is served family style as opposed to buffet." Extracurricular life at Smith tends to be on the quiet side, and students approve; writes one, "Being at Smith you get the best of all worlds. Parties here tend to be smaller, lower-key events, but having the Five College connection you get your choice of any party you'd want. Go to UMass for frats and big dance parties. Go to Hampshire for a more chill, laid-back vibe. Go to Amherst for something a little more formal." The campus also hosts regular "dances, poetry readings, movies, lectures, cultural events, you name it." Hometown Northampton, "just a five-minute walk from campus," also shoulders some of the burden. The town "is full of extremely unique stores, boutiques, indie movie theatres, concert venues, bars, coffee houses, and restaurants."

Student Body

If people who "use the word 'hegemony' in everyday conversation" and who cherish "freedom from the oppressive hetero-normative patriarchy "—or even know what that means—sound like your kind of folks, you may be a Smith woman. Smithies are "typically politically active, love to learn, and champion about four different causes. They are quirky and dorky but love to go out and have a good time. And they want to save the world." The crusading can occasionally be overbearing—"Smith students can be vicious when defending their own beliefs and ideas and attacking those who disagree with them," warns one woman, but overall students regard one another as "caring" and "supportive." Like hometown Northampton, "Smith is a very gay-friendly environment"—students report that there are "a lot of lesbians" on campus, and "quite a few 'boys.'" Straight undergrads think "it's important to stress how easy it is to meet guys. Many hetero women are scared to come here because they believe the stereotype about Smith being solely a haven for man-hating lesbians. It really is not true."

FINANCIAL AID: 413-585-2530 • E-MAIL: ADMISSION@SMITH.EDU • WEBSITE: WWW.SMITH.EDU

ADMISSIONS

Very important factors considered include: Character/personal qualities, recommendations, secondary school record. *Important factors considered include:* Class rank, essays, extracurricular activities, interview, standardized test scores, talent/ability. *Other factors considered include:* Alumni/ae relation, minority status, volunteer work, work experience. SAT Reasoning or ACT required. TOEFL required of all international applicants. High school diploma or equivalent is not required. *Academic units recommended:* 4 English, 3 math, 3 science (3 science lab), 3 foreign language, 2 history.

The Inside Word

Don't be fooled by the relatively high acceptance rate at Smith (or at other top women's colleges). The applicant pool is small and highly self-selected, and it's fairly tough to get admitted. Only women who have taken the most challenging course loads in high school and achieved at a superior level will be competitive.

FINANCIAL AID

Students should submit: FAFSA, CSS/Financial Aid PROFILE, noncustodial (divorced/separated) parents' statement, business/farm supplement. Regular filing deadline is 2/1. The Princeton Review suggests that all financial aid forms be submitted as soon as possible after 1/1. *Need-based scholarships/grants offered:* Pell, SEOG, state scholarships/grants, private scholarships, the school's own gift aid. *Loan aid offered:* Direct Subsidized Stafford, Direct Unsubsidized Stafford, FFEL PLUS, Federal Perkins, state loans, college/university loans from institutional funds. Applicants will be notified of awards on or about 4/1. Federal Work-study Program available. Institutional employment available. Off-campus job opportunities are good.

FROM THE ADMISSIONS OFFICE

"Smith students choose from 1,000 courses in more than 50 areas of study. There are no specific course requirements outside the major; students meet individually with faculty advisers to plan a balanced curriculum. Smith programs offer unique opportunities, including the chance to study abroad, or at another college in the United States, and to learn firsthand about the federal government. The Ada Comstock Scholars Program encourages women beyond the traditional age to return to college and complete their undergraduate studies. Smith is located in the scenic Connecticut River valley of western Massachusetts near a number of other outstanding educational institutions. Through the Five College Consortium, Smith, Amherst, Hampshire, and Mount Holyoke colleges and the University of Massachusetts enrich their academic, social, and cultural offerings by means of joint faculty appointments, joint courses, student and faculty exchanges, shared facilities, and other cooperative arrangements. Smith is the only women's college to offer a major in engineering; it's also the only college in the country that offers a guaranteed paid internship program ("Praxis").

"Smith requires either the new SAT plus two SAT Subject Tests or the ACT. Scores from older versions of the SAT (pre-March 2005 version) and the ACT are acceptable. For the old SAT, scores must be submitted with the results of three SAT Subject Tests, one of which should be the writing test."

SELECTIVITY

Admissions Rating	**94**
# of applicants	2,993
% of applicants accepted	57
% of acceptees attending	41
# accepting a place on wait list	255
# of early decision applicants	156
% accepted early decision	81

FRESHMAN PROFILE

Range SAT Verbal	590-700
Average SAT Verbal	640
Range SAT Math	570-670
Average SAT Math	620
**TPR Projected Range SAT Writing*	*620-700*
Range ACT Composite	25-30
Average ACT Composite	27
Minimum Paper TOEFL	600
Minimum Computer Based TOEFL	250
Average HS GPA	3.8
% graduated top 10% of class	59
% graduated top 25% of class	90
% graduated top 50% of class	99

DEADLINES

Early decision application deadline	11/15
Early decision notification	12/15
Regular application deadline	1/15
Regular notification	4/1
Nonfall registration?	no

APPLICANTS ALSO LOOK AT

AND OFTEN PREFER
Brown University

AND SOMETIMES PREFER
Wellesley College

AND RARELY PREFER
Mount Holyoke College

FINANCIAL FACTS

Financial Aid Rating	**96**
Annual tuition	$27,330
Room & Board	$9,490
Books and supplies	$1,500
Required fees	$214
% frosh rec. need-based scholarship or grant aid	61
% UG rec. need-based scholarship or grant aid	60
% frosh rec. need-based self-help aid	61
% UG rec. need-based self-help aid	60
% frosh rec. any financial aid	63
% UG rec. any financial aid	74
Avg. frosh grant	$22,721
Avg. frosh loan	$2,109
Independent 529 member?	Yes

SONOMA STATE UNIVERSITY

1801 EAST COTATI AVENUE, ROHNERT PARK, CA 94928 • ADMISSIONS: 707-664-2778 • FAX: 707-664-2060

CAMPUS LIFE

Quality of Life Rating	**75**
Fire Safety Rating	**60**
Type of school	public
Environment	town

STUDENTS

Total undergrad enrollment	6,677
% male/female	37/63
% from out of state	1
% from public high school	87
% live on campus	35
% in (# of) fraternities	6 (4)
% in (# of) sororities	5 (4)
% African American	2
% Asian	5
% Caucasian	68
% Hispanic	11
% Native American	1
% international	1

SURVEY SAYS

Small classes
Great computer facilities
Great library
Students are friendly
Dorms are like palaces
Campus feels safe
Students are happy

ACADEMICS

Academic Rating	**64**
Calendar	semester
Student/faculty ratio	25:1
Professors interesting rating	79
Professors accessible rating	75
% professors teaching UG courses	98
% classes taught by TAs	1
Most common lab size	20-29 students
Most common regular class size	20-29 students

MOST POPULAR MAJORS

Business administration/management
liberal arts and sciences studies and humanities
psychology

STUDENTS SPEAK OUT

Academics

Like most state schools, lately Sonoma State University (SSU) is struggling to cope with reduced government funding. While students here still brag about "personalized classroom experiences" and "good, easily available advising," an increasing number express concerns over cutbacks. "Not enough teachers are hired full-time," writes one student, "and because of this, many teachers teach at more than one campus. These teachers are not as accessible and less familiar with how the subject is taught across the campus." Still, many students praise Sonoma's full-time faculty ("Professors have been very thorough and helpful in teaching subjects, and they seem genuinely pleased to be sharing their knowledge with each class") and its marquee programs in music, business, environmental studies, and liberal studies. They warn that introductory general education (GE) classes are really "very easy." "The GE professors seem to only be going through the motions, like because it is a GE class, it doesn't really matter. Upper-division teaching, however, is excellent, with superior professors directly connected to current job fields."

Life

"The atmosphere is laid-back" at Sonoma State University. A little too laid-back for many; students tell us that "everyone complains about there being nothing to do" here. One problem lies with Sonoma's hometown of Rohnert Park, which has "no college-town atmosphere." Students describe it as "a family kind of place. It's a very small town with only a few bars." The other is the proximity of more enticing destinations: Chico ("On the weekends the school is fairly quiet, as most students make the trek to Chico State for some fun," writes one student), Santa Rosa ("lots of bars and malls"), and, of course, San Francisco, which is less than an hour's drive from campus. With so many students heading elsewhere for fun, "the campus pretty much closes down on weekends, so there's not much to do at school then." Students report that "the university is really good about attaining entertainment like movie nights, comedians, local bands playing in the quad, and field trips off campus," but also tell us that such events are not always well attended. "Collegiate and intramural sports are popular among a wide variety of students," but not enough to keep the majority of students on campus once classes end, although the recent addition of a state-of-the-art recreation center has helped improve matters. On a positive note, students brag that "the coast and redwoods are nearby and are a great place for a drive or a walk," that the "residential communities are amazing. We live in phat-ass apartments. It's way nicer than any other schools' dorms I have ever seen," and that "great local wine is consumed in copious amounts here."

Student Body

Many SSU undergrads concede that "there is little diversity" on this "mostly white, mostly female, middle- to upper-class campus." Students feel that SSU has a good diversity of personality types, however. "Since SSU is strong in liberal arts, media, sciences, and business, there are all types here, and good students represent all shapes, colors, and political opinions across the spectrum." Notes one undergrad, "Some of us study very hard, others hardly at all; some spend years messing around, some get in and out very quickly; some are courteous and helpful, others are deterrents to learning." Another observes that "there is a big gay population, but they're not ostentatious. There are large Jewish and Christian populations. Everyone is pretty much accepted at face value, whether you play lacrosse or major in computer science."

Sonoma State University

Financial Aid: 707-664-2389 • E-mail: admitme.@sonoma.edu • Website: www.sonoma.edu

ADMISSIONS

Very important factors considered include: Secondary school record, standardized test scores. *Important factors considered include:* Geographical residence, minority status, state residency. SAT Reasoning or ACT required. TOEFL required of all international applicants. High school diploma is required, and GED is accepted. *Academic units required:* 4 English, 3 math, 2 science (1 science lab), 2 foreign language, 1 history, 3 academic electives, 1 visual and performing arts.

The Inside Word

Admission by formula is the rule at Sonoma State, consistent with its role in the Cal State system. Plug in to the formula, and sign up for class—there's no mystery to candidate selection here. Solid courses, grades, and test scores lead the way into the freshman class.

FINANCIAL AID

Students should submit: FAFSA. The Princeton Review suggests that all financial aid forms be submitted as soon as possible after 1/1. *Need-based scholarships/grants offered:* Pell, SEOG, state scholarships/grants, private scholarships, the school's own gift aid. *Loan aid offered:* Direct Subsidized Stafford, Direct Unsubsidized Stafford, Direct PLUS, Federal Perkins. Applicants will be notified of awards on a rolling basis beginning on or about 3/15. Federal Work-study Program available. Institutional employment available. Off-campus job opportunities are good.

FROM THE ADMISSIONS OFFICE

"Sonoma State University occupies 275 acres in the beautiful wine country of Sonoma County, in northern California. Located at the foot of the Sonoma hills, the campus is an hour's drive north of San Francisco and centrally located between the Pacific Ocean to the west and the wine country to the north and east. SSU is deeply committed to the teaching of the liberal arts and sciences. The campus has earned a national reputation as a leader in integrating the use of technology into its curriculum. Within its 32 academic departments, SSU awards bachelor's degrees in 41 areas of specialization and master's degrees in 14 areas. In addition, the university offers a joint master's degree in mathematics with San Francisco State University. The campus ushered in the 21st century with the opening of a new library and technology center, the Jean and Charles Schulz Information Center.

"All freshmen applicants are required to provide SAT or ACT scores. Fall 2006 applicants are encouraged to take the new SAT or the ACT. In addition, students may submit scores from the old (before March 2005) SAT, and we will use their best scores from either test."

SELECTIVITY

Admissions Rating	**60**
# of applicants	8,392
% of applicants accepted	70
% of acceptees attending	19

FRESHMAN PROFILE

Range SAT Verbal	470-570
Average SAT Verbal	519
Range SAT Math	470-570
Average SAT Math	524
**TPR Projected Range SAT Writing*	*530-610*
Range ACT Composite	19-24
Average ACT Composite	22
Minimum Paper TOEFL	500
Minimum Computer Based TOEFL	173
Average HS GPA	3.23

DEADLINES

Regular application deadline	1/31
Regular notification	rolling
Nonfall registration?	yes

FINANCIAL FACTS

Financial Aid Rating	**84**
Annual in-state tuition	$0
Annual out-of-state tuition	$8,136
Books and supplies	$1,260
Required fees	$3,408
% frosh rec. need-based scholarship or grant aid	15
% UG rec. need-based scholarship or grant aid	24
% frosh rec. need-based self-help aid	23
% UG rec. need-based self-help aid	33
% frosh rec. any financial aid	26
% UG rec. any financial aid	37
Avg. frosh grant	$6,055
Avg. frosh loan	$2,574
Independent 529 member?	No

SOUTHERN METHODIST UNIVERSITY

PO BOX 750181, DALLAS, TX 75275-0181 • ADMISSIONS: 214-768-0103 • FAX: 214-768-2507

CAMPUS LIFE

Quality of Life Rating	**94**
Fire Safety Rating	**85**
Type of school	private
Affiliation	Methodist
Environment	town

STUDENTS

Total undergrad enrollment	6,090
% male/female	46/54
% from out of state	31
% from public high school	61
% live on campus	40
% in (# of) fraternities	29 (14)
% in (# of) sororities	35 (13)
% African American	5
% Asian	6
% Caucasian	75
% Hispanic	9
% Native American	1
% international	4
# of countries represented	90

SURVEY SAYS

Great computer facilities
Great library
Students love Dallas, TX
Great off-campus food
Students are happy
Frats and sororities dominate social scene

ACADEMICS

Academic Rating	**85**
Calendar	semester
Student/faculty ratio	12:1
Professors interesting rating	87
Professors accessible rating	86
% professors teaching UG courses	92
% classes taught by TAs	0
Most common lab size	10-19 students
Most common regular class size	10-19 students

MOST POPULAR MAJORS

Advertising
finance
psychology

STUDENTS SPEAK OUT

Academics

At Southern Methodist University (SMU), first-year students are welcomed into the academic community with "a very strong orientation program, allowing incoming freshmen to find their niche before classes even begin." A student writes, "Every freshman gets to meet with their professor for one-on-one attention." Those ties can develop over the years, resulting in what one student describes as "personal relationships with almost all of my professors." Instructors "genuinely want to be in the classroom," according to undergraduates, and their focus is "teaching, not research." Students say their professors are knowledgeable and available people who make an effort to give "individual attention, even in a large class." While some students joke that "this school is about drinking, hot people, fun parties, and oh yeah, class," others would have the world know that comments like that one is why the school is chronically "academically underrated." One undergraduate tells us she was pleasantly surprised by the University's academic rigor: "You don't realize it is so good until you compare [experiences with] other students at other schools once you're here." Students generally feel "challenged, but not overwhelmed with academic difficulty." A degree from SMU comes with substantial networking value. One junior mentioned, "It's about getting a good education while making connections to help you succeed later in life." Overall, this "student-centered university [offers] an atmosphere for kids to learn about a profession and about themselves, so they will succeed in the real world."

Life

Just because SMU students have to study does not mean they can't dress well and have fun while they are at it. Hallways turn to runways, as "students would never show up to class in anything less than what would be expected to be worn out on a Friday night anywhere else." The social life on this "hard-core Greek" campus centers on "all the glory of Frat Row," where one will find "sweaty frat boys, cheap Keystone beer, and girls looking like a million bucks." One enthusiast explains, "If you're not a big drinker, you're going to feel like a wimp." Football games present more opportunity for preening and partying. On campus, "there is always something going on," except for the "totally dead" time on Saturday and Sunday mornings when everyone is recovering from the previous night's revelry. Beyond the pristine grounds, Dallas beckons, with the "highest per capita percentage of restaurants in the nation." The medium-sized school is "small enough to see friends every day on campus but large enough to meet new people every day," resulting in an "incredible mix of educational and social experiences."

Student Body

The stereotype of an SMU student features "Louis Vuitton bags adorned with sorority pins, Daddy's credit card, [and] bronzed tans year-round." These kids are "just plain rich," with their BMWs and high-cost coifs. Reportedly, the emphasis on fashion has spread from the famously beautiful female population to a "new class of metrosexuals," or straight guys who know how to dress with sophistication. Yet, some students speak out against this upper-crust label, claiming they "are not a bunch of clones." One student diplomatically describes her peers as "socially, fashionably, politically, and academically conscious." Other people say the "beautiful student body" perception is too much belabored. A student gives what she thinks is a more accurate characterization of the SMU poster child: "White, upper middle class, wears Greek T-shirts and flip-flops to class, drives an old SUV." Nearly everyone is Southern, "friendly, [and] very conservative," which explains why "you can meet people [easily and quickly]." As for atypical students, they can be "found in the art and drama departments."

Southern Methodist University

Financial Aid: 214-768-2058 • E-mail: ugadmission@smu.edu • Website: www.smu.edu/admission

ADMISSIONS

Very important factors considered include: Class rank, essays, recommendations, secondary school record, standardized test scores. *Important factors considered include:* Character/personal qualities, extracurricular activities, talent/ability, volunteer work, work experience. *Other factors considered include:* Alumni/ae relation, interview. SAT Reasoning or ACT required. TOEFL required of all international applicants. High school diploma is required, and GED is not accepted. *Academic units required:* 4 English, 3 math, 3 science (2 science lab), 2 foreign language, 1 social studies, 2 history. *Academic units recommended:* 4 English, 4 math, 4 science (3 science lab), 3 foreign language, 2 social studies, 3 history.

The Inside Word

SMU's School of the Arts is one of the best in the country, and applicants face a very competitive admissions process. The university in general is not quite as selective, but the expectations are high enough so that average students with academic inconsistencies or weak test scores can expect to encounter a rocky road to admission.

FINANCIAL AID

Students should submit: FAFSA, CSS/Financial Aid PROFILE, noncustodial (divorced/separated) parents' statement, business/farm supplement. The Princeton Review suggests that all financial aid forms be submitted as soon as possible after 1/1. *Need-based scholarships/grants offered:* Pell, SEOG, state scholarships/grants, private scholarships, the school's own gift aid. *Loan aid offered:* FFEL Subsidized Stafford, FFEL Unsubsidized Stafford, FFEL PLUS, Federal Perkins, state loans, college/university loans from institutional funds. Applicants will be notified of awards on a rolling basis beginning on or about 3/15. Federal Work-study Program available. Institutional employment available. Off-campus job opportunities are excellent.

FROM THE ADMISSIONS OFFICE

"SMU students balance challenging academic programs with a total campus experience that enables them to choose their own path of achievement. Small classes ensure that students receive personal attention. Classes are taught by professors who are dedicated to teaching undergraduates while producing new knowledge enriching the classroom. Students also have access to visiting dignitaries ranging from former presidents to Nobel laureates. Reflecting its student-centered focus, SMU is one of the few universities to have a voting student member on its Board of Trustees. Internships, community service, student research opportunities, and study abroad programs abound. SMU also offers a thriving Honors Program and one of the top merit scholarship programs in the nation. More than 400 arts events each year add a special vitality to campus life, and nearly 200 student organizations provide opportunities for leadership. SMU welcomes a diverse student body from every state and 90 countries; 72% of students receive some form of financial aid. Graduates attend some of the best graduate and professional schools in the nation. They find promising career opportunities through SMU's close ties with Dallas, a center of commerce and culture and gateway to the global community.

"SMU requires either the ACT or SAT. Assessment of written communication skills remains an important component of the SMU application review process. To that end, it is recommended that applicants use every opportunity, including the ACT or SAT, to display their writing skills in the application process."

SELECTIVITY

Admissions Rating	**88**
# of applicants	6,434
% of applicants accepted	64
% of acceptees attending	32
# accepting a place on wait list	682
% admitted from wait list	14

FRESHMAN PROFILE

Range SAT Verbal	540-640
Range SAT Math	560-660
**TPR Projected Range SAT Writing*	*590-660*
Range ACT Composite	24-28
Minimum Paper TOEFL	550
Minimum Computer Based TOEFL	213
Average HS GPA	3.46
% graduated top 10% of class	36
% graduated top 25% of class	67
% graduated top 50% of class	91

DEADLINES

Regular application deadline	3/15
Regular notification	rolling
Nonfall registration?	yes

APPLICANTS ALSO LOOK AT

AND OFTEN PREFER

University of Southern California
Vanderbilt University

AND SOMETIMES PREFER

The University of Texas—Austin
Trinity University
Tulane University
University of Miami

AND RARELY PREFER

Baylor University
Texas Christian University
University of Arizona
University of Colorado—Boulder

FINANCIAL FACTS

Financial Aid Rating	**83**
Annual tuition	$23,846
Room & Board	$9,208
Books and supplies	$600
Required fees	$3,034
% frosh rec. need-based scholarship or grant aid	29
% UG rec. need-based scholarship or grant aid	33
% frosh rec. need-based self-help aid	27
% UG rec. need-based self-help aid	31
% frosh rec. any financial aid	76
% UG rec. any financial aid	58
Avg. frosh grant	$7,093
Avg. frosh loan	$4,032
Independent 529 member?	Yes

SOUTHWESTERN UNIVERSITY

ADMISSIONS OFFICE, PO BOX 770, GEORGETOWN, TX 78627-0770 • ADMISSIONS: 512-863-1200 • FAX: 512-863-9601

CAMPUS LIFE

Quality of Life Rating	**87**
Fire Safety Rating	**60**
Type of school	private
Affiliation	Methodist
Environment	town

STUDENTS

Total undergrad enrollment	1,276
% male/female	41/59
% from out of state	9
% from public high school	84
% live on campus	83
% in (# of) fraternities	30 (4)
% in (# of) sororities	30 (4)
% African American	4
% Asian	4
% Caucasian	76
% Hispanic	13
% Native American	1
% international	1
# of countries represented	9

SURVEY SAYS

Small classes
No one cheats
Great computer facilities
Great library
Students are friendly
Campus feels safe

ACADEMICS

Academic Rating	**89**
Calendar	semester
Student/faculty ratio	10:1
Professors interesting rating	94
Professors accessible rating	93
% professors teaching UG courses	100
% classes taught by TAs	0
Most common lab size	10-19 students
Most common regular class size	fewer than 10 students

MOST POPULAR MAJORS

Business administration/management
communications studies/speech communication and rhetoric
psychology

STUDENTS SPEAK OUT

Academics

At this liberal arts university of nearly 1,300 undergrads, students extol the accessibility of Southwestern's professors and administrators. "The teachers and administrators are so easy to get in touch with it's silly," writes a freshman. Boasts another first-year: "I love how approachable everyone is. I've had lunch with the president twice." The flip side to having professors who "give out their home phone numbers" and "take the time to get to know you" is increased accountability: professors also "require attendance" at their classes. A political science major describes the academic experience as "rigorous but rewarding." Southwestern challenges its students "academically, intellectually, and personally—inside and outside of the classroom," writes a junior. As a result, students benefit from "a lot of intellectual conversation"—but also feel the burden of "lots of homework." While students may grumble a little about the hours they log in the library, they assure us that "graduate schools and employers know that Southwestern produces good graduates, so the hard work is well worth it." They boast that undergrads have the opportunity "to participate in scholarship and actual research." Some students mention that they'd like to see "more options for class offerings" and "online registration," (complaining that "in-person registration" is "an ordeal"). These gripes aside, students are overall quite content; in the words of a senior: "Southwestern has been an overwhelmingly positive experience."

Life

Georgetown, "a sleepy Texas town north of Austin," is the home of Southwestern University. "Small and historical," Georgetown feels to some undergrads like a "retirement community," with "little to offer college students after 10 P.M." The town of Round Rock, just "a few miles away," brings a bit more excitement, but the real action takes place in Austin. "Austin's only about 30 minutes away," and this is where students go to find "urban-related activities" such as "shows, readings, concerts, or food." On campus, nightlife is "non-existent"—with the notable exception of fraternity parties, which take place on weekends and on Wednesday nights (at "Study Break" events). The students who aren't involved in Greek life like to "hang out at someone's apartment, go into Austin, [or] drive home for the weekend." Outdoor activities are also popular at Southwestern; if you're looking to play Ultimate Frisbee™, "there is generally a game…going on 24/7." Another popular pastime is hitting up The Cove, an on-campus student facility "which has pool tables, food, BYOB on some nights, foosball, shuffle puck, a fireplace, comfy chairs, and tables where students can hang out." Still, students groan that they "need more things to do on campus." "There are a lot of different organizations and events," but "there is very low participation usually." Boredom drives many of these students to "leave town on the weekends"—but those who do stick around know there's one place they can always go: "It is normal for the library to have students studying on Friday and Saturday nights."

Student Body

Southwestern prides itself on being a "friendly" place, and as such, "people all get along extremely well" and "respect" "others' views." The undergrad population here is "very politically active," including vocal extremes ranging from "white republican Christians" to "liberal tree huggers," as one sophomore puts it. Many observe that Southwestern has a number of students of "upper-middle-class backgrounds" who hail from Texas. One common thread among all students, in the words of a freshman, is that "everybody here is 'the geek'… meaning 'smart kid compared to the rest of the posse.' We have the gorgeous preppy geeks, athletic jock geeks, philosophical genius geeks, writer geeks, math geeks, everything." What the school lacks, students say, is "racial diversity." "There are very few minority students on campus," laments a senior. And with a clear majority of women on campus, female students sigh that "at times," they "feel a little boy-starved." Overall, students feel "comfortable" here; writes one freshman: "I personally am an atypical student, and I fit in fine."

FINANCIAL AID: 512-863-1259 • E-MAIL: ADMISSION@SOUTHWESTERN.EDU • WEBSITE: WWW.SOUTHWESTERN.EDU

ADMISSIONS

Very important factors considered include: Class rank, essays, recommendations, secondary school record, standardized test scores. *Important factors considered include:* Character/personal qualities, extracurricular activities, interview, talent/ability. *Other factors considered include:* Alumni/ae relation, geographical residence, minority status, volunteer work, work experience. SAT Reasoning or ACT required. TOEFL required of all international applicants. High school diploma is required, and GED is accepted. *Academic units required:* 4 English, 4 math, 3 science (2 science lab), 2 foreign language, 3 social studies, 3 history.

The Inside Word

Southwestern is one of the best "sleepers" in the nation. Admissions standards are high, but they would be even more so if more people knew of this place. Academic excellence abounds, the administration is earnest and helpful, and the school has attracted national recognition. If you could thrive in a small-town, close-knit environment, Southwestern definitely deserves a look.

FINANCIAL AID

Students should submit: FAFSA. Regular filing deadline is 3/1. The Princeton Review suggests that all financial aid forms be submitted as soon as possible after 1/1. *Need-based scholarships/grants offered:* Pell, SEOG, state scholarships/grants, private scholarships, the school's own gift aid. *Loan aid offered:* FFEL Subsidized Stafford, FFEL Unsubsidized Stafford, FFEL PLUS, Federal Perkins, state loans, college/university loans from institutional funds. Applicants will be notified of awards on or about 5/1.

FROM THE ADMISSIONS OFFICE

"On the outskirts of Texas's vibrant capital city of Austin is Southwestern University, the state's first institution of higher learning. Southwestern is committed to helping students achieve personal and professional success as well as a passion for life-long learning. The Paideia Program, funded in 2002 by an $8.5 million grant, is a distinctive new option for select students beginning the sophomore year that provides opportunities to compare, contrast, and integrate knowledge and skills gained in various areas of study. In addition to their regular studies, students work with the same Paideia Professor over a three-year period in seminar groups of ten. They work to discover the powerful connections between Southwestern's rigorous academic experience and the dynamic programs available outside the classroom—through leadership, service, intercultural learning, and collaborative research or creative works. All Southwestern students discover that a premiere liberal arts education leads to high acceptance rates into prestigious graduate and professional programs and careers right out of college. Southwestern is today what it has always been: a highly personal liberal arts experience that equips students with the strengths they need to develop fulfilling lives.

"Southwestern University will accept both the old and new SAT score formats. The Writing component of the new SAT will be considered in a comprehensive manner, along with overall academic record, application essay, extra-curricular activities, recommendations, and a personal interview."

SELECTIVITY

Admissions Rating	**88**
# of applicants	1,888
% of applicants accepted	66
% of acceptees attending	30
# accepting a place on wait list	131
% admitted from wait list	6
# of early decision applicants	77
% accepted early decision	75

FRESHMAN PROFILE

Range SAT Verbal	580-690
Average SAT Verbal	634
Range SAT Math	570-670
Average SAT Math	624
**TPR Projected Range SAT Writing*	*620-690*
Range ACT Composite	24-29
Average ACT Composite	27
Minimum Paper TOEFL	570
Minimum Computer Based TOEFL	230
% graduated top 10% of class	47
% graduated top 25% of class	83
% graduated top 50% of class	95

DEADLINES

Early decision application deadline	11/1
Early decision notification	12/1
Regular application deadline	2/15
Regular notification	4/1
Nonfall registration?	yes

APPLICANTS ALSO LOOK AT AND OFTEN PREFER

Rice University, Vanderbilt University

AND SOMETIMES PREFER

Rhodes College, Texas A&M University—College Station, Trinity University, Tulane University, The University of Texas—Austin

AND RARELY PREFER

Austin College, Baylor University, Southern Methodist University, Texas Christian University

FINANCIAL FACTS

Financial Aid Rating	**86**
Annual tuition	$21,900
Room & Board	$7,640
Books and supplies	$700
% frosh rec. need-based scholarship or grant aid	46
% UG rec. need-based scholarship or grant aid	50
% frosh rec. need-based self-help aid	30
% UG rec. need-based self-help aid	37
Avg. frosh grant	$8,285
Avg. frosh loan	$17,612
Independent 529 member?	Yes

SPELMAN COLLEGE

350 SPELMAN LANE, SOUTH WEST, ATLANTA, GA 30314 • ADMISSIONS: 404-270-5193 • FAX: 404-270-5201

CAMPUS LIFE

Quality of Life Rating	**70**
Fire Safety Rating	**60**
Type of school	private
Environment	metropolis

STUDENTS

Total undergrad enrollment	2,063
% male/female	0/100
% from out of state	68
% from public high school	84
% live on campus	59
% in (# of) sororities	1 (4)
% African American	95
% international	2
# of countries represented	18

SURVEY SAYS

Small classes
Lab facilities are great
Campus feels safe
Frats and sororities dominate social scene
Student government is popular
Very little drug use

ACADEMICS

Academic Rating	**64**
Calendar	semester
Student/faculty ratio	11:1
Professors interesting rating	69
Professors accessible rating	63
% professors teaching UG courses	100
% classes taught by TAs	0
Most common lab size	10-19 students
Most common regular class size	10-19 students

MOST POPULAR MAJORS

Political science and government
psychology

STUDENTS SPEAK OUT

Academics

Dr. Beverly Tatum promised Spelman College students "nothing less than the best" when she became president of the school in 2002, and according to undergrads here, she's delivered on that promise. The women who attend this historically black college report that the school succeeds in "instilling in the minds of young black women that anything is possible" through a "superb and rigorous academic experience" and a "focus on empowering the total self. As a black woman at a black school, you never feel intimidated or like an outcast." The curriculum reinforces black identity—"classes like 'African Diaspora and the world' change not only how you think, but who you are as a person," students report—alongside traditional academic disciplines. Academically, Spelman excels in many areas. Premed sciences are among the school's strong suits; writes one undergrad, "If you want a stronghold for women interested in the sciences, come to Spelman. It seems like everyone I talk to is a science major (although we do have a good amount of women's studies, political science, and economics majors)." For programs not offered on campus, students can take advantage of Spelman's membership in the Atlanta University Center, "the largest consortium of black colleges in the nation," in order to take classes and utilize resources at four other schools nearby. An added benefit of the consortium is that "during the day, Spelman almost looks like a coed college due to cross-registration," allowing students the benefit of both single-sex education and coeducation.

Life

"Spelman is a place that fulfills all of your academic and social needs," students tell us, observing that "even while going to class and the library, you are sure to [see] someone you know to help ease the stress of studying. The campus also provides great social events. Every Friday, for example, Spelman has Market Friday, where off-campus vendors and student groups set up booths." Students also "hang out on the Strip, the area between our neighbors Morehouse and Clark Atlanta, where you will find a lot of people at any given time." Mostly, though, students like to spend their free time enjoying Atlanta, "a great city to go to school in. Museums, theater, and sports are probably the most popular major events in the area. Many music artists and other celebrities flock to Atlanta for concerts and special events as well." A "trusty-dusty, if rarely on-time, AUC shuttle takes students to clubs and other places of interest. There's also the local transit system (MARTA) which you can take to the mall, clubs, theatres, restaurants, Underground Atlanta, and anywhere else in the Atlanta and Metro area." Students tell us that the Spelman campus is "small but absolutely beautiful." Facilities, however, need an upgrade. Writes one undergrad, "There is no air conditioning in over half of the dorms. There are just some basic things that must improve."

Student Body

The black women who attend Spelman "are from everywhere: the West, Midwest, East Coast, South, and 19 other countries. We do have a few students of other ethnic groups as well, and it's not like they fade into the woodwork; everyone is friendly to them, and they participate in class and play sports and do everything that the 'typical' version of a Spelman student would do." Many here "are from an upper-income household, and many came from predominantly white communities looking to experience an HBCU [historically black college or university]." Students can be "very opinionated and enjoy expressing those opinions," as evidenced in 2004 by a high-profile controversy over a planned campus visit by rap artist Nelly; observes one student, "As a whole Spelman women are politically and socially aware and are active people who make it their business to cause change. We are politically active, and we do a lot of community service here, go into the community to tutor students, build homes—everything."

FINANCIAL AID: 404-270-5212 • E-MAIL: ADMISS@SPELMAN.EDU • WEBSITE: WWW.SPELMAN.EDU

ADMISSIONS

Very important factors considered include: Class rank, essays, recommendations, secondary school record, standardized test scores. *Other factors considered include:* Alumni/ae relation, character/personal qualities, extracurricular activities, talent/ability, volunteer work, work experience. SAT Reasoning or ACT required. TOEFL required of all international applicants. High school diploma is required, and GED is accepted. *Academic units required:* 4 English, 2 math, 2 science, 2 foreign language, 2 social studies, 2 academic electives. *Academic units recommended:* 3 math, 3 science, 3 foreign language.

The Inside Word

No historically Black college in the country has a batter graduation rate or a more competitive admissions process than Spelman, and on top of this, application totals were up 25 percent last season. Successful candidates show strong academic records with challenging course loads and solid grades. Applicant evaluation is very personal; it is quite important to show depth of character and social consciousness.

FINANCIAL AID

Students should submit: FAFSA, state aid form. The Princeton Review suggests that all financial aid forms be submitted as soon as possible after 1/1. *Need-based scholarships/grants offered:* Pell, SEOG, state scholarships/grants, private scholarships, the school's own gift aid, United Negro College Fund. *Loan aid offered:* FFEL Subsidized Stafford, FFEL Unsubsidized Stafford, FFEL PLUS, Federal Perkins. Applicants will be notified of awards on a rolling basis beginning on or about 2/1. Federal Work-study Program available. Institutional employment available. Off-campus job opportunities are fair.

FROM THE ADMISSIONS OFFICE

"As an outstanding historically Black college for women, Spelman strives for academic excellence in liberal arts education. This predominantly residential private college provides students with an academic climate conducive to the full development of their intellectual and leadership potential. The college is a member of the Atlanta University Center consortium, and Spelman students enjoy the benefits of a small college while having access to the resources of the other four participating institutions. The purpose extends beyond intellectual development and professional career preparation of students. It seeks to develop the total person. The college provides an academic and social environment that strengthens those qualities that enable women to be self-confident as well as culturally and spiritually enriched. This environment attempts to instill in students both an appreciation for the multicultural communities of the world and a sense of responsibility for bringing about positive change in those communities.

"Applicants for fall 2006 are required to submit standardized test scores from an appropriate venue (i.e. ACT, TOEFL, SAT). The highest composite score will be used in admissions decisions. Writing scores from either the SAT or ACT will not be taken into consideration in the admission process."

SELECTIVITY

Admissions Rating	**60**
# of applicants	4,345
% of applicants accepted	39
% of acceptees attending	29

FRESHMAN PROFILE

Range SAT Verbal	500-580
Average SAT Verbal	547
Range SAT Math	490-580
Average SAT Math	536
**TPR Projected Range SAT Writing*	*560-620*
Range ACT Composite	20-24
Average ACT Composite	22
Minimum Paper TOEFL	500
Minimum Computer Based TOEFL	250
Average HS GPA	3.4

DEADLINES

Regular application deadline	2/1
Regular notification	4/1
Nonfall registration?	yes

APPLICANTS ALSO LOOK AT

AND OFTEN PREFER

Georgia Institute of Technology

AND SOMETIMES PREFER

Clark Atlanta University
Florida A&M University
Hampton University
Howard University
Tuskegee University

AND RARELY PREFER

Emory University
University of Georgia
University of Maryland—College Park

FINANCIAL FACTS

Financial Aid Rating	**62**
Annual tuition	$12,700
Room & Board	$8,040
Required fees	$2,240
% frosh rec. need-based scholarship or grant aid	83
% UG rec. need-based scholarship or grant aid	90
% frosh rec. need-based self-help aid	64
% UG rec. need-based self-help aid	83
% frosh rec. any financial aid	87
% UG rec. any financial aid	87
Avg. frosh grant	$3,500
Avg. frosh loan	$2,625
Independent 529 member?	Yes

St. Bonaventure University

PO Box D, St. Bonaventure, NY 14778 • Admissions: 716-375-2400 • Fax: 716-375-4005

CAMPUS LIFE

Quality of Life Rating	**69**
Fire Safety Rating	**60**
Type of school	private
Affiliation	Roman Catholic
Environment	rural

STUDENTS

Total undergrad enrollment	2,170
% male/female	50/50
% from out of state	24
% from public high school	70
% live on campus	79
% African American	2
% Asian	1
% Caucasian	54
% Hispanic	1
% international	2
# of countries represented	22

SURVEY SAYS

Small classes
Students are friendly
Everyone loves the Bonnies
Frats and sororities are unpopular or nonexistent
College radio is popular
Lots of beer drinking
Hard liquor is popular

ACADEMICS

Academic Rating	**77**
Calendar	semester
Student/faculty ratio	15:1
Professors interesting rating	83
Professors accessible rating	83
% professors teaching UG courses	100
% classes taught by TAs	0
Most common lab size	10-19 students
Most common regular class size	10-19 students

MOST POPULAR MAJORS

Business administration/management
elementary education and teaching
journalism

STUDENTS SPEAK OUT

Academics

One rough translation of the Italian buona ventura is "the good journey," and this has become the operant metaphor for an education at Saint Bonaventure University, a small Franciscan university in upstate New York. Reports one undergraduate here, "Since I've begun 'the good journey,' I've found that every professor I've ever encountered is the most down-to-earth person who would do anything in order for you to earn the grade you desire." Indeed, students here agree that "the professors are really caring and are here because they love their jobs and they love the students." Undergrads are especially excited about the journalism program, pointing out that "a lot of the mass communications faculty have years of experience in the job place, which is helpful." Historically, they've been generally less enthusiastic about Clare College, the university division through which Bona administers its challenging and catholic core curriculum. Notes a typical student, "Clare College is a little too demanding for the 100-level courses and required courses it offers, but overall it is something that the school prides itself on, and I feel privileged to have gone through it." Part of the problem with Clare is the disconnect between its admirable goal of broad intellectual inquiry and most students' desire to focus on career-related subjects; observes one student, "Sometimes the atmosphere on campus reflects a lack of concern over educational studies, and it feels as though people often forget that they are at a liberal arts school." Those who 'get it' praise Bona's efforts to "provide a broad education about the world while also providing that very precise education about your major and learning values at the same time."

Life

Bona is "in the middle of nowhere, and it's freezing outside for about 70 percent of the school year," so students "do the same thing anyone else would do under the circumstances; we drink with friends." Students agree that Bona is "definitely a party school. While on campus parties are tough to pull off, there is a party off campus every night. Almost anyone can get into the local bars and there are many houses off campus that have triple keggers nightly." Some here even express incredulity that Bona fell off our list of the nation's biggest party schools; "Don't worry, we will be back on it next year," students assure us. We'll see. Bona undergrads also tell us that "besides partying, our school offers many programs and clubs that you can participate in. Many students go up to Mt. Irenaeus for a relaxing and spiritual weekend. There are always floor programs going on and there is a club for each major which take field trips." The radio station is very popular; college sports are big too. Bona has "tons of intramural sports that are fun to participate in. Every semester there are a few tournaments of various sports where you can arrange to have you and friends on a team together. It is fun just to be social."

Student Body

"Most students are white, Catholic, and come from middle-class families" at Bona, and while "there are not many atypical students, those who are fit in fine, thanks to our Franciscan values." Many "live within two hours of campus" and have bonded with the school—usually through its sports teams—long before attending the school. Writes one student, "If you go anywhere off campus wearing your Bona gear, someone is likely to yell 'Go Bonas' at you. It's an instant bond." Most here "have both party animal and Catholic tendencies," although there are some who lean more toward the former." Most everyone here "is interested in, and usually active in, some sort of sport."

St. Bonaventure University

Financial Aid: 716-375-2528 • E-mail: admissions@sbu.edu • Website: www.sbu.edu

ADMISSIONS

Very important factors considered include: Character/personal qualities, interview, recommendations, secondary school record. *Important factors considered include:* Essays, extracurricular activities, standardized test scores, talent/ability, volunteer work. *Other factors considered include:* Alumni/ae relation, class rank, work experience. SAT Reasoning or ACT required. TOEFL required of all international applicants. High school diploma is required, and GED is accepted. *Academic units required:* 4 English, 3 math, 3 science, 2 foreign language, 4 social studies. *Academic units recommended:* 4 English, 3 math, 3 science (3 science lab), 2 foreign language, 4 social studies.

The Inside Word

Saint Bonaventure is a safety for many students applying to more selective Catholic universities, but it does a good job of enrolling a sizable percentage of its admits. Most solid students needn't worry about admission; even so, candidates who rank St. Bonnie as a top choice should still submit essays and interview.

FINANCIAL AID

Students should submit: FAFSA, institution's own financial aid form, state aid form. The Princeton Review suggests that all financial aid forms be submitted as soon as possible after 1/1. *Need-based scholarships/grants offered:* Pell, SEOG, state scholarships/grants, private scholarships, the school's own gift aid. *Loan aid offered:* FFEL Subsidized Stafford, FFEL Unsubsidized Stafford, FFEL PLUS, Federal Perkins, college/university loans from institutional funds. Applicants will be notified of awards on a rolling basis beginning on or about 4/1. Federal Work-study Program available. Institutional employment available. Off-campus job opportunities are excellent.

FROM THE ADMISSIONS OFFICE

"The Saint Bonaventure University family has been imparting the Franciscan tradition to men and women of a rich diversity of backgrounds for more than 130 years. This tradition encourages all who become a part of it to face the world confidently, respect the earthly environment, and work for productive change in the world. The charm of our campus and the inspirational beauty of the surrounding hills provide a special place where growth in learning and living is abundantly realized. The Richter Student Fitness Center, scheduled to be completed in 2004, will provide all students with state-of-the-art facilities for athletics and wellness. Academics at Saint Bonaventure are challenging. Small classes and personalized attention encourage individual growth and development for students. Saint Bonaventure's nationally known Schools of Arts and Sciences, Business Administration, Journalism/Mass Communication, and Education offer majors in 31 disciplines. The School of Graduate Studies also offers several programs leading to the master's degree.

"Applicants for fall 2006 can submit scores from either the old or new SAT, as well as the ACT. For students who have taken both versions, the best composite score from either the old or new SAT will be used. The Biology Subject Test is required only for students applying to one of our Dual Admission medical programs."

SELECTIVITY

Admissions Rating	**74**
# of applicants	1,834
% of applicants accepted	85
% of acceptees attending	37

FRESHMAN PROFILE

Range SAT Verbal	480-580
Average SAT Verbal	524
Range SAT Math	490-590
Average SAT Math	535
**TPR Projected Range SAT Writing*	*540-620*
Range ACT Composite	19-24
Average ACT Composite	22
Minimum Paper TOEFL	550
Minimum Computer Based TOEFL	213
Average HS GPA	3.1
% graduated top 10% of class	11
% graduated top 25% of class	36
% graduated top 50% of class	71

DEADLINES

Regular application deadline	4/15
Regular notification	rolling
Nonfall registration?	yes

APPLICANTS ALSO LOOK AT

AND OFTEN PREFER
Providence College
SUNY College at Geneseo
Villanova University

AND SOMETIMES PREFER
Ithaca College
Le Moyne College
Niagara University
Siena College
SUNY at Buffalo

AND RARELY PREFER
Syracuse University

FINANCIAL FACTS

Financial Aid Rating	**78**
Annual tuition	$18,650
Room & Board	$6,910
Books and supplies	$600
Required fees	$835
% frosh rec. need-based scholarship or grant aid	75
% UG rec. need-based scholarship or grant aid	71
% frosh rec. need-based self-help aid	64
% UG rec. need-based self-help aid	60
Avg. frosh grant	$10,928
Avg. frosh loan	$3,410
Independent 529 member?	No

ST. JOHN'S COLLEGE (MD)

PO BOX 2800, ANNAPOLIS, MD 21404 • ADMISSIONS: 410-626-2522 • FAX: 410-269-7916

CAMPUS LIFE

Quality of Life Rating	**93**
Fire Safety Rating	**87**
Type of school	private
Environment	town

STUDENTS

Total undergrad enrollment	473
% male/female	55/45
% from out of state	85
% from public high school	58
% live on campus	73
% African American	1
% Asian	2
% Caucasian	89
% Hispanic	3
% Native American	1
% international	1
# of countries represented	12

SURVEY SAYS

Class discussions encouraged
No one cheats
Registration is a breeze
Frats and sororities are unpopular or nonexistent
(Almost) everyone smokes

ACADEMICS

Academic Rating	**98**
Calendar	semester
Student/faculty ratio	9:1
Professors interesting rating	97
Professors accessible rating	94
% professors teaching UG courses	100
% classes taught by TAs	0
Most common regular class size	10-19 students

MOST POPULAR MAJORS

Liberal arts and sciences studies and humanities

STUDENTS SPEAK OUT

Academics

"The only elective at St. John's College is your choice to attend," explains one student. "From there on out, the program will teach you everything you thought you knew." That's because the entire curriculum at SJC is required, a four-year survey of intellectual history that "starts at the beginning (ancient Greece) and works its way through the years to modern times. Starting from Euclidian geometry, we end up at relativity. Starting at Aristotelian biology, we end up at quantum mechanics and genetics. The school teaches you that you can only learn where you are by understanding where you have been." Classes here "are all discussion-based; there are no lectures, and classes are never larger than 20 students." Faculty members are referred to as "tutors" rather than professors; they must teach every subject in the curriculum and primarily "serve as guides to learning and add to the discussion. They are, as Socrates says, midwives to ideas." Tutors "come from a wide variety of deeply academic backgrounds, but their specializations have little to do with our curriculum. In the classroom, they are glorified students, as puzzled as the rest of us." The result is "an unbelievable academic community" in which "philosophy is not a game, but rather a crucial guide for living." St. John's is the perfect student for those "ready to confront history's original thinkers directly" and those who want to "teach themselves how to think, how to read and digest information, and how to appreciate the beauty of the written word."

Life

"Class discussions often spill into out-of-class venues" at St. John's, where "on a beautiful sunny day you'll be struck by the vast numbers of people reading outside on the lawns, benches, chairs and steps of the quad, front and back campus." There's a rhythm to life on this campus; "Monday and Thursday nights are largely taken up by seminar (All students have seminar 8–10 P.M.), and though there is often drinking, hanging out on the quad, and animated discussion afterwards, there isn't much in the way of organized activity." However, "every other Saturday night from 10:30 P.M. until 2 A.M. there are waltz parties, which consist mostly of swing dancing, though waltz, polka, and tango are also played." Also, "the college Film Society shows movies almost every Saturday night." A student group called Reality "organizes occasional non-waltz parties such as Oktoberfest, a Halloween Party, and a weekend of debauchery at the end of the year." Student organizations include a theater group, a chorus, an orchestra, a society called Melee that "battles with swords made of plastic piping wrapped in foam," a group called Mabel the Swimming Wonder Monkey that "watches bad movies and mocks them," and a sizeable Christian Fellowship. The highlight of the year, according to most, is the fall croquet match against the Naval Academy. Some here tell us they never leave campus; others report that "trips to Baltimore and Washington are frequent, as well as small groups of students going to concerts."

Student Body

St. John's students report "a definite feeling among students that we've all been Johnnies all our lives, but just didn't have a name for it before." The community here is tight, both because it "is fairly self-selecting, so that most students who come here are invested in their education and self-improvement," and also because "we have a common ground that unites us in the shared curriculum. We're not fragmented by major." An "egalitarian intramural sports program that does not exclude any students and the lack of fraternities and politically partisan groups" also helps. This eclectic group includes "students who graduated at the top of their class in high school, some at the bottom, and some who left high school to come to college."

FINANCIAL AID: 410-626-2502 • E-MAIL: ADMISSIONS@SJCA.EDU • WEBSITE: WWW.SJCA.EDU

ADMISSIONS

Very important factors considered include: Essays. *Important factors considered include:* Alumni/ae relation, character/personal qualities, interview, recommendations, secondary school record. *Other factors considered include:* Class rank, extracurricular activities, minority status, standardized test scores, talent/ability, volunteer work, work experience. TOEFL required of all international applicants. High school diploma is required, and GED is accepted. *Academic units required:* 3 math, 2 foreign language. *Academic units recommended:* 4 English, 4 math, 3 science (3 science lab), 4 foreign language, 2 social studies, 2 history.

The Inside Word

St. John's has one of the most personal admissions processes in the country. The applicant pool is highly self-selected and extremely bright, so don't be fooled by the high acceptance rate—every student who is offered admission deserves to be here. Candidates who don't give serious thought to the kind of match they make with the college and devote serious energy to their essays are not likely to be successful.

FINANCIAL AID

Students should submit: FAFSA, CSS/Financial Aid PROFILE, noncustodial (divorced/separated) parents' statement, business/farm supplement. The Princeton Review suggests that all financial aid forms be submitted as soon as possible after 1/1. *Need-based scholarships/grants offered:* Pell, SEOG, state scholarships/grants, the school's own gift aid. *Loan aid offered:* FFEL Subsidized Stafford, FFEL Unsubsidized Stafford, FFEL PLUS, Federal Perkins, college/university loans from institutional funds. Applicants will be notified of awards on a rolling basis beginning on or about 11/1. Federal Work-study Program available. Institutional employment available. Off-campus job opportunities are excellent.

FROM THE ADMISSIONS OFFICE

"The purpose of the admission process is to determine whether an applicant has the necessary preparation and ability to complete the St. John's program satisfactorily. The essays are designed to enable applicants to give a full account of themselves. They can tell the committee much more than statistical records reveal. Previous academic records show whether an applicant has the habits of study necessary at St. John's. Letters of reference, particularly those of teachers, are carefully read for indications that the applicant has the maturity, self-discipline, ability, energy, and initiative to succeed in the St. John's program. St. John's attaches little importance to 'objective' test scores, and no applicant is accepted or rejected because of such scores.

"St. John's College does not require the results of standardized tests, except in the case of international students, home schooled students, and those who will not receive a high school diploma. Results of the ACT or SAT are sufficient for these students."

SELECTIVITY

Admissions Rating	**90**
# of applicants	535
% of applicants accepted	67
% of acceptees attending	38

FRESHMAN PROFILE

Range SAT Verbal	660-760
Range SAT Math	600-690
**TPR Projected Range SAT Writing*	*670-740*
Minimum Paper TOEFL	600
Minimum Computer Based TOEFL	250
% graduated top 10% of class	47
% graduated top 25% of class	74
% graduated top 50% of class	93

DEADLINES

Regular notification	2 weeks after receipt of completed application
Nonfall registration?	yes

APPLICANTS ALSO LOOK AT AND OFTEN PREFER

Swarthmore College
University of Chicago
University of Virginia

AND SOMETIMES PREFER

Kenyon College
Oberlin College
Reed College
Smith College

AND RARELY PREFER

Bard College

FINANCIAL FACTS

Financial Aid Rating	**76**
Annual tuition	$30,570
Room & Board	$7,610
Books and supplies	$275
Required fees	$200
% frosh rec. need-based scholarship or grant aid	44
% UG rec. need-based scholarship or grant aid	50
% frosh rec. need-based self-help aid	59
% UG rec. need-based self-help aid	54
% frosh rec. any financial aid	60
% UG rec. any financial aid	60
Avg. frosh grant	$16,498
Avg. frosh loan	$3,125
Independent 529 member?	No

St. John's College (NM)

1160 Camino Cruz Blanca, Santa Fe, NM 87505 • Admissions: 505-984-6060 • Fax: 505-984-6162

CAMPUS LIFE

Quality of Life Rating	**97**
Fire Safety Rating	**60**
Type of school	private
Environment	city

STUDENTS

Total undergrad enrollment	435
% male/female	56/44
% from out of state	90
% from public high school	71
% live on campus	75
% African American	1
% Asian	2
% Caucasian	81
% Hispanic	7
% Native American	1
% international	2
# of countries represented	10

SURVEY SAYS

Class discussions encouraged
Small classes
No one cheats
Registration is a breeze
Students are happy
Intercollegiate sports are unpopular or nonexistent
Frats and sororities are unpopular or nonexistent

ACADEMICS

Academic Rating	**99**
Calendar	semester
Student/faculty ratio	8:1
Professors interesting rating	99
Professors accessible rating	99
% professors teaching UG courses	100
% classes taught by TAs	0
Most common regular class size	10-19 students

STUDENTS SPEAK OUT

Academics

To have any sort of serious discussion about the academic experience of students at St. John's College, one must begin with an understanding of "the Program," which, in a nutshell, is a guided tour through the high points of Western thought. Students actually read the books other people consider doorstops and grapple with primary texts straight from the big thinkers of history. "I thought I knew what a number was, but then I began to study Euclid. I thought I knew what freedom was, but then I read Herodotus," writes one typical undergrad. At St. John's, it is more important to learn "how we arrived at the facts" than the facts themselves. This is radical intellectualism for students who've always dreamed of "a double major in Philosophy and Math with a triple minor in History of Science, History of Music, and History of Language." The professors, called tutors, are considered "more experienced learners" rather than fonts of knowledge, and they serve to focus all of the paradigm deconstruction, world-view disruption, and interdisciplinary connection. Tutors routinely teach outside of their field of expertise, "so they learn with us." Students recognize the luxury of having such "brilliant, dedicated, understanding, and inspiring" guides to "aggressively critique our arguments." For this experiment in erudition to work, however, students "have to show a great deal of integrity." Everyone arrives at class with scribbles in the margins and an open mind. Slackers are shunned for "harming the class dynamic and cooperative learning process." Above all, students want to learn to think and communicate lucidly. The rigorous subject matter hands them the heaviest weights for all the cerebral workouts necessary to achieving such a goal. At a place where "education is an end and not a means," the right kind of minds—quick, receptive and reflective—may experience true "transformation."

Life

A first-year "Johnnie" assures prospective applicants, "There are things to do other than the Program." Typically those include "reading lighter material [or] simply making each other laugh." Students value the idea of balance in their lives and take frequent breaks to practice Brazilian jiu-jitsu, drum up a game of Go, throw some pottery, dust off the cello, or learn to tango. Hiking the nearby trails or gazing at the stars gives students the chance to ponder beauty and the cosmos directly and revive their brains with some fresh air. One freshman likes to "walk out [the] back door to the top of a mountain with friends and watch the sunset." The small population limits the number of community-organized activities, but "people still pursue their interests on their own." An upperclassman writes, "I've been able to direct or codirect at least one play every year since I started here, including freshman year." Students resist the incomplete image of St. John's as "either as a geek preserve or drug haven. We're neither." Though "the average Johnnie likes jazz, beer, and hedonism" almost as much as books, all drunken conversation ultimately relates back to the pursuit of truth.

Student Body

A senior emphasizes, "It is important to understand what a tiny, tiny campus we have. You will have your boyfriend in class, your ex in class, your ex's new girlfriend in class, and you need to be able to separate out your emotional involvement, or someone's going to call you on it." Outsiders have "exaggerated the bizarre, cult-like qualities" in the past; students are quick to clarify, "It's an open, loving, dysfunctional family and not a closed, bitter one." Also, not all of these misfits fit the bleary-eyed, borderline-insane reputation surrounding the school. "There are very grounded people with regular schedules of sleeping, eating and thinking non-philosophical things." Despite the liberal political leanings of the student body, "This isn't really a good place for wandering hippie types who subscribe to a pluralist philosophy of absolute tolerance." People either "like to learn, like to think, like to work very hard, or some combination of those."

ST. JOHN'S COLLEGE (NM)

FINANCIAL AID: 505-984-6058 • E-MAIL: ADMISSIONS@MAIL.SJCSF.EDU • WEBSITE: WWW.SJCSF.EDU

ADMISSIONS

Very important factors considered include: Character/personal qualities, essays, interview, talent/ability. *Important factors considered include:* Extracurricular activities, recommendations, secondary school record. *Other factors considered include:* Class rank, standardized test scores, volunteer work, work experience. TOEFL required of all international applicants. High school diploma or equivalent is not required. *Academic units required:* 3 math, 2 foreign language. *Academic units recommended:* 4 math, 3 science (3 science lab), 4 foreign language, 2 social studies, 2 history.

The Inside Word

Self-selection drives this admissions process—over one-half of the entire applicant pool each year indicates that St. John's is their first choice, and half of those admitted send in tuition deposits. Even so, no one in admissions takes things for granted, and neither should any student considering an application. The admissions process is highly personal on both sides of the coin. Only the intellectually curious and highly motivated need apply.

FINANCIAL AID

Students should submit: FAFSA, CSS/Financial Aid PROFILE, noncustodial (divorced/separated) parents' statement, business/farm supplement. The Princeton Review suggests that all financial aid forms be submitted as soon as possible after 1/1. *Need-based scholarships/grants offered:* Pell, SEOG, state scholarships/grants, private scholarships, the school's own gift aid. *Loan aid offered:* FFEL Subsidized Stafford, FFEL Unsubsidized Stafford, FFEL PLUS, Federal Perkins, college/university loans from institutional funds. Applicants will be notified of awards on a rolling basis beginning on or about 12/1. Federal Work-study Program available. Institutional employment available. Off-campus job opportunities are excellent.

FROM THE ADMISSIONS OFFICE

"St. John's appeals to students who value good books, love to read, and are passionate about discourse and debate. There are no lectures and virtually no tests or electives. Instead, classes of 16–20 students occur around conference tables where professors are as likely to be asked to defend their points of view as are students. Great books provide the direction, context, and stimulus for conversation. The entire student body adheres to the same, all-required arts and science curriculum. Someone once said 'A classic is a house we still live in,' and at St. John's, students and professors alike approach each reading on the list as if the ideas it holds were being expressed for the first time—questioning the logic behind a geometrical proof, challenging the premise of a scientific development, or dissecting the progression of modern political theory as it unfolds.

"As of this book's publication, St. John's College (NM) did not have information available about their policy regarding the new SAT."

SELECTIVITY

Admissions Rating	**85**
# of applicants	339
% of applicants accepted	82
% of acceptees attending	43
# accepting a place on wait list	25
% admitted from wait list	80

FRESHMAN PROFILE

Range SAT Verbal	630-740
Average SAT Verbal	700
Range SAT Math	560-660
Average SAT Math	610
**TPR Projected Range SAT Writing*	*650-720*
Range ACT Composite	25-31
Average ACT Composite	28
Minimum Paper TOEFL	550
Minimum Computer Based TOEFL	213
% graduated top 10% of class	38
% graduated top 25% of class	54
% graduated top 50% of class	86

DEADLINES

Regular notification	rolling
Nonfall registration?	yes

APPLICANTS ALSO LOOK AT

AND OFTEN PREFER
Deep Springs College
Stanford University

AND SOMETIMES PREFER
Bard College
Claremont McKenna College
Rice University
University of Chicago

AND RARELY PREFER
Grinnell College
Oberlin College
Whitman College

FINANCIAL FACTS

Financial Aid Rating	**95**
Annual tuition	$32,374
Room & Board	$7,876
Books and supplies	$275
Required fees	$200
% frosh rec. need-based scholarship or grant aid	67
% UG rec. need-based scholarship or grant aid	64
% frosh rec. need-based self-help aid	68
% UG rec. need-based self-help aid	64
Avg. frosh grant	$14,500
Avg. frosh loan	$3,285
Independent 529 member?	No

St. John's University

8000 Utopia Parkway, Queens, NY 11439 • Admissions: 718-990-2000 • Fax: 718-990-5728

CAMPUS LIFE

Quality of Life Rating	**66**
Fire Safety Rating	**80**
Type of school	private
Affiliation	Roman Catholic
Environment	metropolis

STUDENTS

Total undergrad enrollment	12,302
% male/female	42/58
% from out of state	10
% live on campus	17
% in (# of) fraternities	8 (23)
% in (# of) sororities	7 (23)
% African American	17
% Asian	15
% Caucasian	41
% Hispanic	15
% international	3
# of countries represented	130

SURVEY SAYS

Small classes
Diverse student types on campus
Everyone loves the Red Storm
(Almost) everyone smokes

ACADEMICS

Academic Rating	**70**
Calendar	semester
Student/faculty ratio	18:1
Professors interesting rating	61
Professors accessible rating	62
% professors teaching UG courses	91
% classes taught by TAs	0
Most common lab size	20-29 students
Most common regular class size	20-29 students

MOST POPULAR MAJORS

Criminal justice/law enforcement administration
finance
pharmacy (PharMD, BS/BPharM)

STUDENTS SPEAK OUT

Academics

St. John's attracts high-caliber students thanks in part to the challenging academic programs and "strong alumni base and emphasis on ethics in the Catholic tradition." Once on campus, students find professors who are "very knowledgeable and, above all, very personable." With a student-faculty ratio of 18:1, small class sizes ensure "a lot of attention from my professor;" this personal approach extends to student advisors, as "there's plenty of academic advisement for anyone who needs it." The computer science, government and politics, and pharmacy departments receive high marks from undergraduates. This academic rigor doesn't lead to "the fierce, cutthroat competition between students you see at other schools." Students laud the generous financial aid offered by the school and also praise the "attentive" and "helpful" administration. Throw in "superior computer facilities" and a well-run freshman center, and students start gushing, "My academic experience has been a triumphant one thus far."

Life

"I'm involved in a lot of volunteer groups at school, and most of the people I know are too," writes an altruistic student. "St. John's really encourages giving back to the community." Other students spend their time at "comedy shows, talent shows, fashion shows," or other free activities sponsored by the student life committee. Sports are another common obsession: "If you want to play basketball, well then, you've found your haven." The location in New York City is also commonly cited as a huge plus: "What isn't there to do in NYC?" Sometimes students lament the strong commuter component of campus life, and even among the 2,500 residents, many go home every weekend: "It's still a commuter school no matter how many dorms there are." Most agree, however, that "overall the campus vibe is good here." Those who do live at St. John's tell us that Jamaica Estates offers "off-campus restaurants, pizza joints, delis, cafes, bars, shops, diners. There is a lot of nightlife in Queens and even more in Manhattan."

Student Body

Many students share the sentiment, "I love how diverse this school is!" Apparently, St. John's admits "students from almost every single background" who still manage to "get along really well." Maybe this is because "Queens is the most ethnically diverse county in the country," reflecting the student body from "many different nations." Yet onn the other hand, certain students paint a less harmonious picture with comments like, "My sexual orientation has left me ostracized" and "I just wish that people were more open-minded about certain topics here."

ST. JOHN'S UNIVERSITY

FINANCIAL AID: 1-888-9-STJOHNS • E-MAIL: ADMISSIONS@STJOHNS.EDU • WEBSITE: WWW.STJOHNS.EDU

ADMISSIONS

Very important factors considered include: Secondary school record. *Important factors considered include:* Class rank, essays, recommendations, standardized test scores. *Other factors considered include:* Character/personal qualities, extracurricular activities, interview, talent/ability, work experience. SAT Reasoning or ACT required. TOEFL required of all international applicants. High school diploma is required, and GED is accepted. *Academic units required:* 4 English.

The Inside Word

St. John's should receive strong consideration from anyone looking for a large institution with good facilities and resources, as well as a good connection to the community, even amidst the sometimes maddening spread of New York City. Socioeconomic and ethnic diversity ensure a place for you within the student body.

FINANCIAL AID

Students should submit: FAFSA, state aid form. The Princeton Review suggests that all financial aid forms be submitted as soon as possible after 1/1. *Need-based scholarships/grants offered:* Pell, SEOG, state scholarships/grants, private scholarships, the school's own gift aid. *Loan aid offered:* FFEL Subsidized Stafford, FFEL Unsubsidized Stafford, FFEL PLUS, Federal Perkins. Applicants will be notified of awards on a rolling basis beginning on or about 3/15. Off-campus job opportunities are excellent.

FROM THE ADMISSIONS OFFICE

"Why not have it all? Students at St. John's University enjoy the very best of college life: world-class academics, lively campus community, high-tech resources, and the know-how to succeed.

"Founded by the Vincentian Fathers in 1870, St. John's offers a residential college experience in dynamic New York City. Hailing from 38 states and 148 countries, students pursue nearly 100 majors in pharmacy and allied health, the arts, the natural and applied sciences, business, and education. Our professors are leading scholars, 90 percent of whom hold a PhD or other comparable degree.

"St. John's blends classroom learning, confidence-building skills, and real-world experience:

- With a WiFi network and laptops for new students, St. John's is the only New York university in Intel's top ten "Most Unwired Colleges."
- Through our Discover New York course, students see plays, tour museums, and visit ethnic neighborhoods to experience the arts, business, and history in action.
- Across the New York area and around the globe, our students gain experience through supervised service activities in Academic Service Learning.
- Guided by professors with global connections, students earn course credit in Europe, Africa, and Asia through our Study Abroad Program.
- And our Big East, Division I men's and women's athletic teams keep students cheering.

"St. John's has three residential New York campuses: our 105-acre campus in Queens, New York; our picturesque Staten Island campus; and our Manhattan campus, in the heart of the Financial District. There are also graduate centers in Oakdale, New York, and Rome, Italy.

"Applicants for fall 2006 must submit a Writing section score from either the new SAT or the ACT. While no minimum score on this portion of either exam is required, the admission committee may review and evaluate student essays within the context of the admission process or for assessment purposes."

SELECTIVITY

Admissions Rating	**82**
# of applicants	17,632
% of applicants accepted	62
% of acceptees attending	27

FRESHMAN PROFILE

Range SAT Verbal	460-570
Average SAT Verbal	516
Range SAT Math	470-590
Average SAT Math	535
**TPR Projected Range SAT Writing*	*530-610*
Minimum Paper TOEFL	500
Minimum Computer Based TOEFL	173
Average HS GPA	3.5
% graduated top 10% of class	23
% graduated top 25% of class	51
% graduated top 50% of class	80

DEADLINES

Nonfall registration?	yes

APPLICANTS ALSO LOOK AT

AND OFTEN PREFER
Fordham University
SUNY at Stony Brook

AND SOMETIMES PREFER
New York University
SUNY at Binghamton

AND RARELY PREFER
LaSalle University
LeMoyne—Owen College

FINANCIAL FACTS

Financial Aid Rating	**72**
Annual tuition	$22,800
Room & Board	$11,000
Books and supplies	$1,000
Required fees	$480
% frosh rec. need-based scholarship or grant aid	75
% UG rec. need-based scholarship or grant aid	72
% frosh rec. need-based self-help aid	80
% UG rec. need-based self-help aid	79
% frosh rec. any financial aid	96
% UG rec. any financial aid	91
Avg. frosh grant	$11,852
Avg. frosh loan	$4,081
Independent 529 member?	No

ST. LAWRENCE UNIVERSITY

PAYSON HALL, CANTON, NY 13617 • ADMISSIONS: 315-229-5261 • FAX: 315-229-5818

CAMPUS LIFE

Quality of Life Rating	**76**
Fire Safety Rating	**67**
Type of school	private
Environment	village

STUDENTS

Total undergrad enrollment	2,102
% male/female	48/52
% from out of state	50
% from public high school	68
% live on campus	95
% in (# of) fraternities	12 (3)
% in (# of) sororities	21 (4)
% African American	2
% Asian	1
% Caucasian	69
% Hispanic	3
% international	4
# of countries represented	24

SURVEY SAYS

Small classes
Great library
Athletic facilities are great
Students are happy
Everyone loves the Saints
Lots of beer drinking

ACADEMICS

Academic Rating	**88**
Calendar	semester
Student/faculty ratio	11:1
Professors interesting rating	87
Professors accessible rating	88
% professors teaching UG courses	98
% classes taught by TAs	0
Most common lab size	10-19 students
Most common regular class size	10-19 students

MOST POPULAR MAJORS

English language and literature
political science and government
psychology

STUDENTS SPEAK OUT

Academics

St. Lawrence students love the "really comfortable, home-like atmosphere" engendered by "the size of the student body and the relative isolation of our campus from any real cities." Small class sizes are the norm at this small liberal arts college in the "north country" of New York State, meaning that "classes are discussion seminars rather than lectures. This allows students to make a more personal connection—not only with their fellow students, but also with their fellow professors." Professors "are all passionate about their subjects, easy to talk to, have good senses of humor, and available outside of class. If you can't make it to their office hours, they are willing to schedule a meeting time." Add "great research, independent projects, internships, and study abroad opportunities in 14 countries" as well as "a great diversity of classes offered here that makes it is almost impossible to not become enriched," and you'll understand why students here feel so favorably about SLU academics. But wait; there's more! Students also tell us that "the alumni connections are amazing and a great thing to have later on after college, especially for internships or actual jobs."

Life

"At St. Lawrence, there isn't much to do for fun except make your own fun." Some students here immerse themselves in campus life; writes one, "It's most important to be extremely active and try to enjoy what the campus has to offer to the fullest. From intramurals to the student government, there is always something to interest everyone." Students enthusiastically support their Division I hockey teams, which "add interest on an otherwise dull campus in the dead of winter," and enjoy special events like Peak Weekend ("It's for those who hike, I mean really hike, and those who just like to own hiking stuff. The Outing Club, the second oldest after Dartmouth, attempts to get college students on all 36 high peaks in the Adirondacks") and Snowbowl ("lots of sledding and beer"). Most students eventually find their way to SLU's lively party scene. "We do drink a lot," confesses one student. "The school tries to hide it, but St. Lawrence students can handle their booze almost any night of the week and still keep pace with the demanding academic program." For many, "the social scene at St. Lawrence gets a little monotonous. The area doesn't have much to offer, and the main weekend activities revolve around drinking with friends." Many warn that winters are long and exceedingly cold. Road trips to Canada, especially to Ottawa or Montreal, are popular diversions.

Student Body

St. Lawrence has long had a reputation as a preppy haven. Students here tell us that about half the student body fits that stereotype; writes one, the typical "Larry" likes "wearing his polo shirt with the collar turned up, [wearing] a North Face fleece, and carrying a Nalgene bottle. A Muffy, the female Larry, can be spotted with her Vera Bradley bags, Tiffany's heart bracelet, and an inordinate number of shoes." Admits one majority student, "St. Lawrence plays into the hands of the classic prep, so many of us seem to come from New England boarding schools, while the remainder are from upscale areas. We look and act like we stepped right out of the pages of The Official Preppy Handbook, and most of us seem proud of it." However, "there are also environmentalists, hippies, the outdoors people, and everyone else" at SLU, although "there aren't many punks and skaters, and people of these types tend to find themselves the token 'oddball' of the dorm." Everyone seems to agree that "we are quite a 'white' school and are lacking a bit in diversity." Many here are "involved in everything. I can't think of anyone who doesn't have extracurriculars. There is an organization for anything you can imagine." Many are active in community service.

St. Lawrence University

Financial Aid: 315-229-5265 • E-mail: admissions@stlawu.edu • Website: www.stlawu.edu

ADMISSIONS

Very important factors considered include: Character/personal qualities, recommendations, secondary school record. *Important factors considered include:* Class rank, essays, extracurricular activities, interview, minority status. *Other factors considered include:* Alumni/ae relation, geographical residence, standardized test scores, talent/ability, volunteer work, work experience. TOEFL required of all international applicants. High school diploma is required, and GED is accepted. *Academic units recommended:* 4 English, 4 math, 4 science, 4 foreign language, 2 social studies, 2 history.

The Inside Word

St. Lawrence has a rough time convincing students to commit to spending four years in relative isolation. Serious competition from many fine northeastern colleges also causes admissions standards to be less selective than the university would like. This makes St. Lawrence an especially good choice for academically sound but average students who are seeking an excellent small college experience and/or an outdoorsy setting.

FINANCIAL AID

Students should submit: FAFSA, institution's own financial aid form, noncustodial (divorced/separated) parents' statement, income tax returns and W-2 forms. Regular filing deadline is 2/15. The Princeton Review suggests that all financial aid forms be submitted as soon as possible after 1/1. *Need-based scholarships/grants offered:* Pell, SEOG, state scholarships/grants, the school's own gift aid. *Loan aid offered:* Direct Subsidized Stafford, Direct Unsubsidized Stafford, FFEL Subsidized Stafford, FFEL Unsubsidized Stafford, FFEL PLUS, Federal Perkins, college/university loans from institutional funds, Gate Student Loan Program. Applicants will be notified of awards on or about 3/30. Federal Work-study Program available. Institutional employment available. Off-campus job opportunities are poor.

FROM THE ADMISSIONS OFFICE

"St. Lawrence is an independent, nondenominational, liberal arts and sciences university located in northern New York. The student body of 2,000 men and women choose from among more than 30 majors and minors; classes are small, with an emphasis on experiential learning, interdisciplinary study, and independent research. St. Lawrence is a residential college where living and learning are combined through the First-Year Program, theme cottages, and international study. St. Lawrence students are well rounded and involved, with many drawn to the 1,000-acre campus for the opportunity it provides for outdoor recreation. The campus, located in the town of Canton, is halfway between the Adirondack Park and the city of Ottawa. Students are active in various organizations centered on the arts, politics, community service, and athletics, with 32 intercollegiate teams offered. St. Lawrence alumni are loyal and active, providing internships for undergraduates and demonstrating their commitment through giving generously of their time and resources.

"Beginning with applications for entry in fall 2006, the submission of standardized test scores (SAT or ACT) is optional. Students must indicate on the St. Lawrence Common Application supplement which scores, if any, they wish to have considered in the application process. "

SELECTIVITY

Admissions Rating	**89**
# of applicants	2,985
% of applicants accepted	61
% of acceptees attending	31
# accepting a place on wait list	312
% admitted from wait list	8
# of early decision applicants	122
% accepted early decision	75

FRESHMAN PROFILE

Range SAT Verbal	530-630
Average SAT Verbal	583
Range SAT Math	540-620
Average SAT Math	580
**TPR Projected Range SAT Writing*	*580-650*
Range ACT Composite	23-27
Average ACT Composite	25
Minimum Paper TOEFL	600
Minimum Computer Based TOEFL	250
Average HS GPA	3.43
% graduated top 10% of class	37
% graduated top 25% of class	73
% graduated top 50% of class	95

DEADLINES

Early decision application deadline	11/15
Early decision notification	12/15
Regular application deadline	2/15
Regular notification	3/30
Nonfall registration?	yes

APPLICANTS ALSO LOOK AT

AND OFTEN PREFER
Dartmouth College, Middlebury College, Williams College

AND SOMETIMES PREFER
Bowdoin College, Colby College, Colgate University

AND RARELY PREFER
Denison University, Gettysburg College

FINANCIAL FACTS

Financial Aid Rating	**86**
Annual tuition	$30,270
Room & Board	$7,755
Books and supplies	$650
Required fees	$210
% frosh rec. need-based scholarship or grant aid	66
% UG rec. need-based scholarship or grant aid	67
% frosh rec. need-based self-help aid	61
% UG rec. need-based self-help aid	62
% frosh rec. any financial aid	84
% UG rec. any financial aid	83
Avg. frosh grant	$18,835
Avg. frosh loan	$4,448
Independent 529 member?	No

STANFORD UNIVERSITY

UNDERGRADUATE ADMISSION, OLD UNION 232, STANFORD, CA 94305-3005 • ADMISSIONS: 650-723-2091 • FAX: 650-723-6050

CAMPUS LIFE

Quality of Life Rating	**91**
Fire Safety Rating	**70**
Type of school	public
Environment	rural

STUDENTS

Total undergrad enrollment	1,858
% male/female	42/58
% from out of state	18
% from public high school	79
% live on campus	81
% African American	7
% Asian	4
% Caucasian	80
% Hispanic	3
% international	1
# of countries represented	29

SURVEY SAYS

Small classes
Students are friendly
Campus feels safe
Low cost of living
Students are happy
Frats and sororities are unpopular or nonexistent

ACADEMICS

Academic Rating	**86**
Calendar	semester
Student/faculty ratio	13:1
Professors interesting rating	89
Professors accessible rating	93
% professors teaching UG courses	100
% classes taught by TAs	0
Most common lab size	10-19 students
Most common regular class size	10-19 students

MOST POPULAR MAJORS

Economics
English language and literature
psychology

STUDENTS SPEAK OUT

Academics

Considered by many as the West Coast's one-man answer to the Ivy League, Stanford offers "a mix of incredible academics and a laid-back atmosphere" that many exceptional applicants choose over the likes of Harvard, Princeton, and Yale. And that "laid-back" thing is significant. "Despite the fact that Stanford is academically rigorous and demanding, Stanford students very rarely get depressed," undergrads agree. "Sure, it gets stressful at times, but you learn to deal." The "downright fabulous" members of the student body and "the great weather" might provide some potent coping mechanisms, but the faculty really helps to make "Stanford a very well-balanced university." Professors are "interested in getting to know students personally," so much so that they "literally beg students to attend office hours." Of course, this is a very prestigious, research-driven university with a wide range of departments and faculty, which means that not every professor is going to hold a student's hand. Academics in the larger departments can be "very impersonal for a private school." Outgoing or aloof, Stanford's professors are lauded as "the foremost minds in their fields. You take classes from people who write the textbooks that everyone else uses." Along these lines, a sophomore tells us, "My freshman year I was able to take classes from a former Secretary of Defense, the Chairman of the Joint Chiefs, a Pulitzer Prize-winning author, and a Nobel Prize-winning physicist." The in-class opportunities are supplemented by frequent visits to campus by "leaders in the fields of literature, music, science, and statesmanship."

Life

It's true that Stanford students "work hard," but they "play hard too." At Stanford, playing hard comes in various forms. One prominent form, of course, is partying. On any given Friday (or Saturday) night, "you can find most students heading out to one of the many parties that are held around campus." Others choose to hit "local bars/clubs, and on occasion [ride] into San Francisco" for the city's nightlife. Given the "perfect" weather, it's hardly surprising that undergrads also like to take it outdoors for a good time. "Running, swimming, and sunbathing are some of the more common outdoor activities," but "hiking, biking, surfing, and road tripping in the beautiful California scenery" have their share of enthusiasts, too. As you're probably starting to realize, this is an athletic student body. And because "almost all Stanford sports teams are nationally ranked," sports events of all sorts—even "the less popular sports"—draw plenty of fans to the bleachers. If all of this isn't enough, the university's undergrads have literally hundreds of organizations to choose from, ranging from the Arabesque Middle Eastern Dance Club to the Quiz Bowl Club. "Most students are used to being leaders in some regard," explains a junior. "This lends itself to a very active student body, but often there are more new clubs and activities than there are people to fill them." Though students tend to be "very busy," the overriding feeling, again, is "laid back."

Student Body

"If there is any one thing that typifies a Stanford student, it is that they all fit the 'duck' analogy. That is, calm on top, but *busy, busy* underneath." Considering its achievements, there's a certain "modesty" that runs through this student body. Nobody toots their own horn. Nobody acts like they're overwhelmed. Nobody lets on that they're trying really, really hard to clean up in their classes. But these students are "very driven, even if they don't say so and pretend it's not true." The truth is that these undergrads are a "multifaceted, multitalented [group who] are always stressed about academics." Many different backgrounds and experiences are represented at Stanford. "You would never know that he or she spoke fluent German, wrote a novel, or went to the Olympics," a student says of his classmates. "Despite all their accomplishments, they are really down to earth and very chill." A senior sums it up best: "We have it all: academics, athletics, myriad activities, gorgeous California weather, and chill California personalities."

FINANCIAL AID: 650-723-3058 • E-MAIL: ADMISSIONS@STANFORD.EDU • WEBSITE: WWW.STANFORD.EDU

ADMISSIONS

Very important factors considered include: Essays, secondary school record, standardized test scores. *Important factors considered include:* Extracurricular activities, recommendations, talent/ability. *Other factors considered include:* Alumni/ae relation, character/personal qualities, class rank, geographical residence, interview, minority status, state residency, volunteer work, work experience. SAT Reasoning or ACT required. TOEFL required of all international applicants. High school diploma is required, and GED is accepted. *Academic units required:* 4 English, 3 math, 3 science (2 science lab), 1 social studies, 2 history, 7 academic electives. *Academic units recommended:* 4 English, 4 math, 4 science (3 science lab), 4 foreign language, 1 history, 8 academic electives.

The Inside Word

Not only is Stanford a pinnacle of academic excellence, but among the nation's ultra-selective universities it is one of the most compassionate toward students, both those who attend and those who aspire to attend. It isn't easy for an admissions staff to be warm and caring when your reputation is based in part on how many candidates you say no to. In our opinion, Stanford is the best of the best in this regard. Students who haven't devoted themselves to excellence in the same fashion that Stanford itself has are not likely to meet with success in gaining admission.

FINANCIAL AID

Students should submit: FAFSA. Regular filing deadline is 3/1. The Princeton Review suggests that all financial aid forms be submitted as soon as possible after 1/1. *Need-based scholarships/grants offered:* Pell, SEOG, state scholarships/grants, private scholarships, the school's own gift aid. *Loan aid offered:* FFEL Subsidized Stafford, FFEL Unsubsidized Stafford, FFEL PLUS, Federal Perkins. Applicants will be notified of awards on or about 4/1. Federal Work-study Program available. Institutional employment available. Off-campus job opportunities are good.

FROM THE ADMISSIONS OFFICE

"We look for distinctive students who exhibit energy, curiosity, and a love of learning in their classes and lives. The most compelling applicants are those who derive pleasure from learning from its own sake. We offer such students renowned yet approachable faculty members, extraordinary academic resources, and a living and learning environment that rewards those who seek excellence in everything they do. From their first days on campus, Stanford students can explore virtually unlimited opportunities that will fuel their intellectual passions and help them fulfill their academic and personal promise.

"For fall 2006, we will accept a student's highest individual Verbal score and Math score from a combination of both the old and new SAT. We also accept the ACT. We also strongly recommend two SAT Subject Tests, including Math Level II."

SELECTIVITY

Admissions Rating	**89**
# of applicants	2,321
% of applicants accepted	57
% of acceptees attending	32
# accepting a place on wait list	340
% admitted from wait list	5
# of early decision applicants	176
% accepted early decision	69

FRESHMAN PROFILE

Range SAT Verbal	580-690
Average SAT Verbal	631
Range SAT Math	570-660
Average SAT Math	616
**TPR Projected Range SAT Writing*	*620-690*
Minimum Paper TOEFL	550
Minimum Computer Based TOEFL	260
Average HS GPA	3.45
% graduated top 10% of class	39
% graduated top 25% of class	70
% graduated top 50% of class	90

DEADLINES

Early decision application deadline	12/1
Early decision notification	1/1
Regular application deadline	1/15
Regular notification	4/1
Nonfall registration?	yes

APPLICANTS ALSO LOOK AT AND SOMETIMES PREFER

College of William and Mary
Guilford College
Kenyon College

FINANCIAL FACTS

Financial Aid Rating	**82**
Annual in-state tuition	$9,063
Annual out-of-state tuition	$17,940
Room & Board	$7,980
Books and supplies	$1,000
Required fees	$1,833
% frosh rec. need-based scholarship or grant aid	19
% UG rec. need-based scholarship or grant aid	19
% frosh rec. need-based self-help aid	19
% UG rec. need-based self-help aid	19
% frosh rec. any financial aid	59
% UG rec. any financial aid	62
Avg. frosh grant	$6,495
Avg. frosh loan	$2,625
Independent 529 member?	No

STATE UNIVERSITY OF NEW YORK AT ALBANY

OFFICE OF UNDERGRAD ADMISSIONS, 1400 WASHINGTON AVE., ALBANY, NY 12222 • ADMISSIONS: 518-442-5435 • FAX: 518-442-5383

CAMPUS LIFE

Quality of Life Rating	**61**
Fire Safety Rating	**81**
Type of school	public
Environment	city

STUDENTS

Total undergrad enrollment	10,968
% male/female	50/50
% from out of state	5
% live on campus	58
% in (# of) fraternities	2 (19)
% in (# of) sororities	5 (15)
% African American	8
% Asian	6
% Caucasian	62
% Hispanic	7
% international	2
# of countries represented	87

SURVEY SAYS

Great library
Diverse student types on campus
Lots of beer drinking
Hard liquor is popular
(Almost) everyone smokes

ACADEMICS

Academic Rating	**65**
Calendar	semester
Student/faculty ratio	19:1
Professors interesting rating	61
Professors accessible rating	61
% professors teaching UG courses	93
% classes taught by TAs	13
Most common lab size	10-19 students
Most common regular class size	20-29 students

MOST POPULAR MAJORS

Business administration/management
English language and literature
psychology

STUDENTS SPEAK OUT

Academics

SUNY—Albany is an excellent example of a typical large state university. Its assets include broad course offerings in a wide range of departments and world-class research, "especially in the fields of science and nanotechnology." One student agrees, "There is so much to take and learn about." The school's location in New York's capital also "offers a lot of opportunities for political science and business majors." Reports one business undergraduate, "Major firms come up here to recruit, making it easy to obtain an internship and eventually a job." The downside of Albany is that many feel that "you are a number here. Unless you make a point to let your professors know your name, they don't care." Warns one student, "Albany puts a lot of responsibility on the student; there is no hand-holding. Professors are available, resources are accessible, and involvement is possible, but it is entirely on the student to sink or swim." Most professors "do their best to try to help you if you have a problem; however, they are very busy and have many students." Some professors, unfortunately, seem to be "here to do research, not to teach." Students advise that "the study groups on campus are very helpful, and not all students take advantage of them." Weighing the good and bad, most students would probably agree that Albany offers "a quality education with a reasonable price tag."

Life

Students at Albany overwhelmingly agree that "campus life is pretty boring around these parts." Nearly everyone tells us that the bars are the place to be, even for underclassmen, especially since "the bars rarely check ID." The location is so crucial to social life that, by junior year, many students "move downtown by the bars." Many students warn that "Albany is a good school, but the partying can take over your normal good student. You have to be mature to learn to balance both." Teetotalers have few options; writes one, "If you don't drink, then you basically don't have a social life. I don't drink, so I don't have a life." The harsh winters don't help social situations. "The snowstorms and coldness make Albany a very tough place to live, and sometimes students are very depressed," explains one student. Some students find refuge in "political groups such as NYPIRG [New York Public Interest Research Group], and minority groups such as ASIA [Albany State Indian Alliance], which are very popular on campus." Others seek out the city's nonalcoholic offerings, which include "great restaurants. Many people go to them if they have the money." An upgrade to the school's athletic program, many students believe, might offer an attractive alternative to the bar scene; but for now, "students get in free to our football games, and still no one goes. The school definitely has no school spirit, especially with the athletics."

Student Body

With only 7.8 percent of students coming from outside of the state, the key to understanding the student body of SUNY—Albany is an understanding of the body politic of New York State. It is plain to most undergraduates that despite its upstate location, the student population at SUNY—Albany more closely reflects the demographics of New York City and Long Island, as "there is a very strong Jewish population on this campus," as well as "a lot of African American and Hispanic" students. Undergraduates also tell us that "since the school is so [large], it allows for everyone to fit into their own clique." However, some students detect "a little bit of tension between Long Islanders, [students from] New York City (any of the five boroughs), and Upstaters."

State University of New York at Albany

Financial Aid: 518-442-5757 • E-mail: ugadmissions@albany.edu • Website: www.albany.edu

ADMISSIONS

Very important factors considered include: Character/personal qualities, class rank, secondary school record, standardized test scores. *Important factors considered include:* Essays, recommendations. *Other factors considered include:* Alumni/ae relation, extracurricular activities, geographical residence, minority status, talent/ability, volunteer work, work experience. SAT Reasoning or ACT required. TOEFL required of all international applicants. High school diploma is required, and GED is accepted. *Academic units required:* 4 English, 2 math, 2 science (2 science lab), 1 foreign language, 3 social studies, 2 history, 5 academic electives. *Academic units recommended:* 4 math, 3 science (3 science lab), 3 foreign language.

The Inside Word

While the SUNY system's budgetary woes have abated to a degree, funding uncertainties continue to be a problem. Applications and standards are on the rise. Albany is the third most selective SUNY campus. Perhaps the university's status as the training camp site for the New York Giants will bring both revenue and facilities to aid a turnaround. Without increased private funding, Albany is likely to remain a relatively easy path into a SUNY university center.

FINANCIAL AID

Students should submit: FAFSA, NY State residents should apply for TAP online at www.hesc.com. Regular filing deadline is 4/15. The Princeton Review suggests that all financial aid forms be submitted as soon as possible after 1/1. *Need-based scholarships/grants offered:* Pell, SEOG, state scholarships/grants. *Loan aid offered:* FFEL Subsidized Stafford, FFEL Unsubsidized Stafford, FFEL PLUS, Federal Perkins. Applicants will be notified of awards on a rolling basis beginning on or about 3/15. Federal Work-study Program available. Institutional employment available. Off-campus job opportunities are excellent.

FROM THE ADMISSIONS OFFICE

"Increasing numbers of well-prepared students are discovering the benefits of study in SUNY Albany's nationally ranked programs and are taking advantage of outstanding internship and employment opportunities in Upstate New York's "Tech Valley." The already strong undergraduate program will be enhanced, beginning with the expansion of the journalism program, while accelerated degree options enable ambitious students to earn a combined bachelor's/master's in one of 30 fields. Nine schools and colleges, including the nation's first College of Nanoscale Science and Engineering, offer bachelor's, master's, and doctoral programs on three different campuses, to more than 11,000 undergraduates and 5,000 graduate students. An award-winning advisement program helps students take advantage of all these options by customizing the undergraduate experiences. More than two-thirds of Albany graduates go on for advanced degrees, and acceptance to law and medical school is above the national average. Student life on campus includes 150 clubs, honors societies, and other groups, and 19 Division I varsity teams. With 13 other colleges in the Region, Albany is a great college town, adjacent to spectacular natural and recreational centers of New York and New England.

"Freshman applicants for fall 2006 must take the new SAT (or the ACT with Writing component)."

SELECTIVITY

Admissions Rating	**85**
# of applicants	17,171
% of applicants accepted	56
% of acceptees attending	21

FRESHMAN PROFILE

Range SAT Verbal	510-600
Range SAT Math	530-620
**TPR Projected Range SAT Writing*	*570-630*
Minimum Paper TOEFL	550
Minimum Computer Based TOEFL	213
Average HS GPA	3.37
% graduated top 10% of class	20
% graduated top 25% of class	57
% graduated top 50% of class	95

DEADLINES

Regular application deadline	3/1
Regular notification	rolling
Nonfall registration?	yes

FINANCIAL FACTS

Financial Aid Rating	**71**
Annual in-state tuition	$4,350
Annual out-of-state tuition	$10,610
Room & Board	$7,540
Books and supplies	$800
Required fees	$1,460
% frosh rec. need-based scholarship or grant aid	50
% UG rec. need-based scholarship or grant aid	50
% frosh rec. need-based self-help aid	45
% UG rec. need-based self-help aid	46
% frosh rec. any financial aid	63
% UG rec. any financial aid	60
Avg. frosh grant	$5,312
Avg. frosh loan	$3,334
Independent 529 member?	No

STATE UNIVERSITY OF NEW YORK AT BINGHAMTON

PO BOX 6000, BINGHAMTON, NY 13902-6001 • ADMISSIONS: 607-777-2171 • FAX: 607-777-4445

CAMPUS LIFE

Quality of Life Rating	**62**
Fire Safety Rating	**63**
Type of school	public
Environment	town

STUDENTS

Total undergrad enrollment	10,898
% male/female	51/49
% from out of state	6
% from public high school	87
% live on campus	58
% in (# of) fraternities	8 (20)
% in (# of) sororities	7 (15)
% African American	5
% Asian	17
% Caucasian	52
% Hispanic	6
% international	4
# of countries represented	87

SURVEY SAYS

Great computer facilities
Great library
Diverse student types on campus
Campus feels safe
Lots of beer drinking
Hard liquor is popular
(Almost) everyone smokes

ACADEMICS

Academic Rating	**75**
Calendar	semester
Student/faculty ratio	22:1
Professors interesting rating	63
Professors accessible rating	62
% professors teaching UG courses	90
% classes taught by TAs	9
Most common lab size	20-29 students
Most common regular class size	20-29 students

MOST POPULAR MAJORS

Business administration/management
English language and literature
psychology

STUDENTS SPEAK OUT

Academics

Branded as Binghamton University, SUNY at Binghamton is "a top-rate school that's way more competitive than most private schools in the northeast, and you get it at a state school price," students here report. Undergrads tell us that "Your quality of education really depends on what school you will be in," adding that BU boasts "a good management program," a "strong science department, especially in biology, psychology, and the premed programs," a "very strong political science program offering a popular major called politics, philosophy, and law that yields high law school acceptance rates," and "engineering and nursing programs that give the students what they need." Workloads also vary by school, from "killer math and science classes" and "very hard classes in the special schools (engineering, management, and nursing)," to "everything else, which is okay though still competitive." Similarly, professors can range from good to bad, from the requisite "science profs so caught up in their own research they seem to see teaching as an annoying obligation" and "math TAs who do not speak English" to "social science teachers who really care" and "management profs who demand the best and in return pass along their industry connections." For most students, the administration is either a whipping boy or an afterthought; writes one student, "Academics appear to run themselves. I don't see the administration worrying about them at all; they are too preoccupied with admissions, housing, and their precious up-and-coming basketball team!"

Life

Just about everyone at BU agrees that "Binghamton is not the most exciting city in the world. Many would argue that the only reason the town is still around after almost all of the big employers packed up and left is the university." How this affects student life varies; some look at the town and conclude that "there are not many places that students can go. There are bars, frats, and movies, and these places get old quick." Others discover "some little gems in Binghamton, such as galleries on Washington Street, the Art Mission, and the Lost Dog Cafe for local music and a nice break from the bars." It's the same story on campus; while some complain that "there isn't much to do but drink," others counter that "there is so much to do on campus, but most people are too lazy to explore the different clubs and activities. I feel bad for the students who are missing out on the wide array of on-campus activities, because I know so many of them waste their time drinking either in their dorm rooms or at frat parties." Students "who wish to remain sober have Late Nite Binghamton, which offers free music, movies, drinks, and others games and/or crafts every night on the weekends." Things may perk up here in the future; school spirit is on the rise because "we've recently moved up to Division I in the NCAA."

Student Body

As you might expect at a school with more than 10,000 undergrads, "there is a wide array of students at Binghamton University." Their ranks include "many students from down in Long Island, New York City, and the suburbs," as well as "students from upstate New York." Upstate students tell us "it is very easy to feel a little alienated because upstate is regarded as heinously uncool by the downstaters and also because a lot of students arrive with a whole network of friends already in place." While geographic diversity is limited mostly to the different regions of New York State, "there is plenty of ethnic diversity here. The Black and Latino Student Unions are both very active groups on campus. The Hillel is also very active as there is a large Jewish population. Asian students make up a large minority. Different groups do not necessarily interact, but there is no tension among groups, either."

STATE UNIVERSITY OF NEW YORK AT BINGHAMTON

FINANCIAL AID: 607-777-2428 • E-MAIL: ADMIT@BINGHAMTON.EDU • WEBSITE: WWW.BINGHAMTON.EDU

ADMISSIONS

Very important factors considered include: Secondary school record, standardized test scores. *Important factors considered include:* Class rank, essays, extracurricular activities, recommendations, volunteer work. *Other factors considered include:* Alumni/ae relation, character/personal qualities, geographical residence, minority status, state residency, talent/ability, work experience. SAT Reasoning or ACT required. TOEFL required of all international applicants. High school diploma is required, and GED is accepted. *Academic units required:* 4 English, 3 math, 2 science, 3 foreign language, 2 social studies. *Academic units recommended:* 4 math, 3 science, 3 foreign language, 3 history.

The Inside Word

Binghamton's admissions process is highly selective, but fairly simple. Candidates go through a process that considers an applicant's grades, course selections, and SAT or ACT results. Out-of-state enrollment is small for a public university of Binghamton's reputation, but the University's enrollment management strategy includes enhancing efforts to recruit students from further afield.

FINANCIAL AID

Students should submit: FAFSA, state aid form. The Princeton Review suggests that all financial aid forms be submitted as soon as possible after 1/1. *Need-based scholarships/grants offered:* Pell, SEOG, state scholarships/grants, private scholarships, the school's own gift aid. *Loan aid offered:* Direct Subsidized Stafford, Direct Unsubsidized Stafford, Direct PLUS, Federal Perkins, Federal Nursing, college/university loans from institutional funds. Applicants will be notified of awards on a rolling basis beginning on or about 3/15.

FROM THE ADMISSIONS OFFICE

"SUNY—Binghamton University has established itself as the premier public university in the northeast, because of our outstanding undergraduate programs, vibrant campus culture and committed faculty. Students are academically motivated, but there is a great deal of mutual help as they compete against the standard of a class rather than each other. Faculty and students work side by side in research labs or on artistic pursuits. Achievement, exploration and leadership are hallmarks of a Binghamton education. Add to that a campuswide commitment to internationalization that includes a robust study abroad program, cultural offerings, languages and international studies, and you have a place where graduates leave prepared for success.

"Students applying for freshman admission for fall 2006 are required to take the new version of the SAT (or the ACT with the Writing section). SAT Subject Test scores are not required for admission."

SELECTIVITY

Admissions Rating	**92**
# of applicants	20,116
% of applicants accepted	44
% of acceptees attending	24
# accepting a place on wait list	622
% admitted from wait list	34

FRESHMAN PROFILE

Range SAT Verbal	570-650
Average SAT Verbal	607
Range SAT Math	600-690
Average SAT Math	643
**TPR Projected Range SAT Writing*	*610-670*
Range ACT Composite	24-28
Average ACT Composite	26
Minimum Paper TOEFL	550
Minimum Computer Based TOEFL	213
Average HS GPA	3.6
% graduated top 10% of class	40
% graduated top 25% of class	83
% graduated top 50% of class	99

DEADLINES

Regular notification	rolling
Nonfall registration?	yes

APPLICANTS ALSO LOOK AT

AND OFTEN PREFER
Columbia University—Columbia College, Cornell University, University of Pennsylvania

AND SOMETIMES PREFER
New York University, Penn State University Park, Rensselaer Polytechnic Institute, University of Maryland—College Park, University of Michigan—Ann Arbor

AND RARELY PREFER
Fordham University, Rutgers University—Rutgers College, SUNY at Stony Brook

FINANCIAL FACTS

Financial Aid Rating	**83**
Annual in-state tuition	$4,350
Annual out-of-state tuition	$10,610
Room & Board	$7,710
Books and supplies	$800
Required fees	$1,406
% frosh rec. need-based scholarship or grant aid	41
% UG rec. need-based scholarship or grant aid	44
% frosh rec. need-based self-help aid	43
% UG rec. need-based self-help aid	46
% frosh rec. any financial aid	81
% UG rec. any financial aid	72
Avg. frosh grant	$4,415
Avg. frosh loan	$3,291
Independent 529 member?	No

State University of New York at Buffalo

15 Capen Hall, Buffalo, NY 14260-1660 • Admissions: 716-645-6900 • Fax: 716-645-6411

CAMPUS LIFE

Quality of Life Rating	**70**
Fire Safety Rating	**70**
Type of school	public
Environment	metropolis

STUDENTS

Total undergrad enrollment	17,509
% male/female	54/46
% from out of state	2
% live on campus	38
% in (# of) fraternities	2 (19)
% in (# of) sororities	4 (14)
% African American	7
% Asian	9
% Caucasian	65
% Hispanic	4
% international	6
# of countries represented	113

SURVEY SAYS

Great computer facilities
Great library
Diverse student types on campus
Student publications are popular
Lots of beer drinking
Hard liquor is popular
(Almost) everyone smokes

ACADEMICS

Academic Rating	**70**
Calendar	semester
Student/faculty ratio	15:1
Professors interesting rating	62
Professors accessible rating	62
% professors teaching UG courses	73
% classes taught by TAs	12
Most common lab size	20-29 students
Most common regular class size	20-29 students

MOST POPULAR MAJORS

Business administration/management
mechanical engineering
psychology

STUDENTS SPEAK OUT

Academics

"It is so easy to make connections that will help you later in life" at SUNY at Buffalo (aka University at Buffalo, or UB), a "flagship SUNY school" that students feel offers "the equivalent of a private school education for the price of a public school." One student tells us, "Academically, UB is something to be respected. The engineering and business programs are worthwhile, and the school takes pride in upholding their excellence." Students in our survey also offer rave reviews of the biology department (and other science programs), the architecture program, and offerings in communication. UB provides "a noncompetitive learning environment (good thing) that prepares you well for life beyond the university, whether that be grad school [or] work." The school also offers "a lot of freedom to make your own choices academically" and "great access to internship opportunities." The curriculum is demanding but, in most areas, not grueling. One student adds, "If you study and do your homework, you should have no problem getting through here." While most students find that professors are "not very approachable," outgoing students report otherwise. Writes one, "Professors here are surprisingly accessible if you are willing to do a little work."

Life

The university's two campuses—the urban South Campus, home to students in the medical and architectural sciences, and the suburban North Campus, home to most other undergraduates—have distinct cultures. Most students agree that South is the place to be. It's where "all the good partying is," plus "Main Street on the South Campus has tons of bars and pizzerias to visit." North Campus, by contrast, "is a cement wasteland situated within the cultural void that is Amherst, New York." Students who live on North Campus (many complain that school buses connecting the campuses don't run often enough) "have little opportunity to escape suburbia's death grip, so they never realize how very wrong their perceptions of Buffalo as a boring, uncool city are." Students who have cars (or the tenacity to wait in the cold for the bus) reap the benefits of Buffalo's "coffeehouses, art galleries, museums, unparalleled architecture, nightlife (includes bars that stay open until 4:00 A.M.), fantastic restaurants, concerts, shopping, and the like." Campus comes alive for special events. Students report that "the Student Association tries to play a large part in daily life. And with a budget of about $2.2 million, they bring huge acts to school (like No Doubt, Dave Matthews, Ja Rule, LL Cool J, Jimmy Fallon, [and] Dave Chapelle)." Intercollegiate athletics are not that popular. Explains one student, "We do have a large division of athletics, but our football team is terrible, and, despite the unparalleled efforts of our administration, nobody really cares about sports."

Student Body

The student body at UB is extremely diverse. Writes one, "There are so many different people here and not just race-wise or concerning sexual orientation or religion. People here are so different than [who] I knew in high school—there are hippies, computer obsessives, musicians, Republicans, card players, and artists." Adds another, "You have every kind of student here. You have lazy ones who just want to get drunk and high. You have the hardworking kids who are going to Harvard for grad school. You have upper-middle-class kids, and you have kids who are dirt poor. With ethnicity you have a model UN when it comes to UB." Students observe that "although many people tend to congregate into groups based on ethnicity, they do not intentionally exclude others. I feel welcome in any group of people regardless of race, and I think many of my fellow students would agree."

State University of New York at Buffalo

Financial Aid: 866-838-7257 • E-mail: ub-admissions@buffalo.edu • Website: www.buffalo.edu

ADMISSIONS

Very important factors considered include: Class rank, secondary school record, standardized test scores. *Other factors considered include:* Character/personal qualities, essays, extracurricular activities, geographical residence, minority status, recommendations, talent/ability, volunteer work, work experience. SAT Reasoning or ACT required. TOEFL required of all international applicants. High school diploma is required, and GED is accepted. *Academic units recommended:* 4 English, 3 math, 3 science, 3 foreign language, 4 social studies.

The Inside Word

Buffalo was formerly a private university and was absorbed into the SUNY system. Its admissions process reflects this private heritage to the extent possible (applications are centrally processed for the entire system in Albany). It's one of the few SUNY schools with a freshman academic profile higher than its published admissions standards. Although Binghamton is academically the most selective of the SUNY University Centers, Buffalo is in many ways closer to what other states refer to as the flagship of the state system.

FINANCIAL AID

Students should submit: FAFSA. The Princeton Review suggests that all financial aid forms be submitted as soon as possible after 1/1. *Need-based scholarships/grants offered:* Pell, SEOG, state scholarships/grants, private scholarships, the school's own gift aid, Federal Nursing scholarships. *Loan aid offered:* Direct Subsidized Stafford, Direct Unsubsidized Stafford, Direct PLUS, Federal Perkins, Federal Nursing, college/university loans from institutional funds. Applicants will be notified of awards on a rolling basis beginning on or about 2/1.

FROM THE ADMISSIONS OFFICE

"The University at Buffalo (UB) is among the nation's finest public research universities—a learning community where you'll work side by side with world-renowned faculty, including Nobel, Pulitzer, National Medal of Science, and other award winners. As the largest, most comprehensive university center in the State University of New York (SUNY) system, UB offers more undergraduate majors than any public university in New York or New England. With opportunities for joint degrees and combined five-year bachelor's and master's degrees, you'll be free to chart an academic course that meets your individual goals—you can even design your own major. Our unique University Honors and University at Buffalo Scholars scholarship programs offer an enhanced academic experience, including opportunities for independent study, advanced research, and specialized advisement. The university is committed to providing the latest information technology—and is widely considered to be one of the most wired universities in the country. UB also places a high priority on offering an exciting campus environment. With nonstop festivals, Division I sporting events, concerts, and visiting lecturers, you'll have plenty to do outside of the classroom. We encourage you and your family to visit campus to see UB up close and in person. Our Visit UB campus tours and presentations are offered year-round.

"Freshman applicants for fall 2006 must take the new SAT (or the ACT with Writing component)."

SELECTIVITY	
Admissions Rating	**86**
# of applicants	18,207
% of applicants accepted	56
% of acceptees attending	31
# accepting a place on wait list	1,000
% admitted from wait list	10
# of early decision applicants	406
% accepted early decision	74

FRESHMAN PROFILE	
Range SAT Verbal	520-610
Average SAT Verbal	556
Range SAT Math	550-640
Average SAT Math	584
**TPR Projected Range SAT Writing*	*570-640*
Range ACT Composite	24-28
Average ACT Composite	24
Minimum Paper TOEFL	550
Minimum Computer Based TOEFL	213
Average HS GPA	3.1
% graduated top 10% of class	24
% graduated top 25% of class	62
% graduated top 50% of class	94

DEADLINES	
Early decision application deadline	11/1
Early decision notification	12/15
Regular notification	rolling
Nonfall registration?	yes

FINANCIAL FACTS	
Financial Aid Rating	**78**
Annual in-state tuition	$4,350
Annual out-of-state tuition	$10,610
Room & Board	$8,086
Books and supplies	$795
Required fees	$1,616
% frosh rec. need-based scholarship or grant aid	35
% UG rec. need-based scholarship or grant aid	33
% frosh rec. need-based self-help aid	52
% UG rec. need-based self-help aid	50
% frosh rec. any financial aid	67
% UG rec. any financial aid	75
Avg. frosh grant	$3,282
Avg. frosh loan	$3,414
Independent 529 member?	No

STATE UNIVERSITY OF NEW YORK AT STONY BROOK

OFFICE OF ADMISSIONS, STONY BROOK, NY 11794-1901 • ADMISSIONS: 631-632-6868 • FAX: 631-632-9898

CAMPUS LIFE

Quality of Life Rating	**62**
Fire Safety Rating	**60**
Type of school	public
Environment	town

STUDENTS

Total undergrad enrollment	13,694
% male/female	51/49
% from out of state	4
% from public high school	90
% live on campus	59
% in (# of) fraternities	1 (16)
% in (# of) sororities	1 (16)
% African American	10
% Asian	23
% Caucasian	36
% Hispanic	8
% international	5
# of countries represented	90

SURVEY SAYS

Great computer facilities
Great library
Diverse student types on campus
Lots of beer drinking
(Almost) everyone smokes

ACADEMICS

Academic Rating	**73**
Calendar	semester
Student/faculty ratio	14:1
Professors interesting rating	61
Professors accessible rating	61
% professors teaching UG courses	88
% classes taught by TAs	0
Most common lab size	20-29 students
Most common regular class size	10-19 students

MOST POPULAR MAJORS

Biology/biological sciences
health professions and related sciences
psychology

STUDENTS SPEAK OUT

Academics

With its solid reputation in the sciences, mathematics, and engineering, Stony Brook University has developed into one of the best known schools in New York's State university system. Students tell us that this reputation is well deserved; writes one, "They put a lot of money into science programs, so you get a decent science- or engineering-related education. The professors are brilliant, too. Not all of them are good teachers, but still it's an honor to be taught by them, and usually, all you have to do is glance through the textbook to clarify something you didn't understand." Students also love that "it is very easy for students to get involved in research." The school's assets help soften the blow of its deficiencies, which include teacher assistants "from other countries, so it is often very difficult to understand or talk to them;" the school's large size; and an administration that sometimes seems "equivalent to chaos. There is no communication between departments who should be working together." The most prestigious programs are also the most rigorous. Students say, "We have a variety of curriculums with different degrees of 'challengingness,' depending on the prerequisites and concepts covered."

Life

The charms of extracurricular life at Stony Brook are apparently lost on many of its students. One student explains, "There are so many things to do on campus, [that] it's crazy; but many students don't take advantage of them." Agrees a junior, "It took me two years to realize how much the campus has to offer. There are many clubs and organizations to participate in, [as well as] choirs and theater; and if you are into parties, there is an array of parties on and off campus." Adds another student, "Student Activities has something planned every Wednesday afternoon: advising sessions, career opportunities, homecoming kickoffs, barbecues, [and] DJs. The athletic programs at Stony Brook are excellent, especially the facilities. The recently completed stadium and the relatively new athletic arena are in excellent condition. Our beloved Seawolves collegiate sports and intramurals keep most athletic people busy." Beyond campus, "Port Jefferson is a great place for fun; and for the students [who are twenty-one or older], there are pubs and great restaurants. There is also a mall and many other stores. It's a busy town." Kids still gripe about life on campus primarily because close to "half the students are commuters, and a large portion of the students who actually live on campus are from the city, and the train station is right on campus. So, the campus is mostly dead on weekends because almost everyone goes home."

Student Body

"There is really no typical student" at Stony Brook, students tell us, "yet there are common groups of students. For example, there are the strongly academic-oriented students, always studying, spending little time at social events; there are the students who mix studying with pleasure; and then there are those students who party more than they study. Everyone somehow finds their place at Stony Brook." Many students who fall into the first group make up the school's powerhouse science and math departments. Students tell us that a surprising number of them are international students. The large international population means that "everyone on campus is so different; there is an overwhelming number of ethnic backgrounds and religions on campus." Also, about half of the students "are commuters who have lived in the area their entire lives."

State University of New York at Stony Brook

Financial Aid: 631-632-6840 • E-mail: enroll@stonybrook.edu • Website: www.stonybrook.edu

ADMISSIONS

Very important factors considered include: Secondary school record, standardized test scores. *Important factors considered include:* Class rank. *Other factors considered include:* Alumni/ae relation, character/personal qualities, essays, extracurricular activities, interview, recommendations, talent/ability, volunteer work, work experience. SAT Reasoning or ACT required. TOEFL required of all international applicants. High school diploma is required, and GED is accepted. *Academic units required:* 4 English, 3 math, 3 science, 2 foreign language, 4 history. *Academic units recommended:* 4 English, 4 math, 4 science, 3 foreign language, 4 history.

The Inside Word

Graduate programs continue to receive national accolades, and the New York State legislature has been somewhat kinder to SUNY of late. Stony Brook's athletic programs have moved to NCAA Division I, America East Conference, in hopes of generating greater visibility and increases in applications. For the near future, admission will remain relatively easy for solid students.

FINANCIAL AID

Students should submit: FAFSA. The Princeton Review suggests that all financial aid forms be submitted as soon as possible after 1/1. *Need-based scholarships/grants offered:* Pell, SEOG, state scholarships/grants, the school's own gift aid. *Loan aid offered:* FFEL Subsidized Stafford, FFEL Unsubsidized Stafford, FFEL PLUS, Federal Perkins. Applicants will be notified of awards on a rolling basis beginning on or about 3/1. Federal Work-study Program available. Off-campus job opportunities are good.

FROM THE ADMISSIONS OFFICE

"Stony Brook is ranked among the 50 best universities in North America and one of the 150 best universities worldwide in the London Times Higher Education Supplement—placing Stony Brook in the top two percent of all universities in the world. In addition, Kiplinger's Personal Finance has ranked Stony Brook one of the "100 Best Values" among public universities.

"The Wall Street Journal has ranked us eighth in the nation among public institutions placing students in the elite graduate schools in medicine, law, and business. Our graduates include the leader of the Imaging Team for the Cassini mission to Saturn, the President of Stanford University, a Pulitzer Prize winning investigative journalist for the Washington Post, and a Grammy award-winning performer with the Metropolitan Opera Company, and more than 100,000 others.

"Situated amidst 1,100 lush, wooded acres on the North Shore of Long Island, life at Stony Brook is as rewarding outside the classroom as it is inside. Our students benefit from both the resources of a major research university and the close-knit communities of innovative undergraduate colleges, with a student-faculty ratio of 14:1. Guaranteed campus housing for all four years, students enjoy outstanding recreational facilities that include a new stadium, modern student activities center, and indoor sports complex. In addition, the Staller Center for the Arts offers spectacular theatrical and musical performances throughout the year.

"We invite students who possess both intellectual curiosity and academic ability to explore the countless exciting opportunities available at Stony Brook.

"Freshmen applying for admission to the university for fall 2006 are required to take the new version of the SAT (or the ACT with the Writing section). SAT Subject Test scores in Math and one other area of the student's choice are recommended, but not required."

SELECTIVITY

Admissions Rating	**89**
# of applicants	17,701
% of applicants accepted	49
% of acceptees attending	25

FRESHMAN PROFILE

Range SAT Verbal	510-620
Average SAT Verbal	565
Range SAT Math	560-660
Average SAT Math	611
**TPR Projected Range SAT Writing*	*570-650*
Minimum Paper TOEFL	550
Minimum Computer Based TOEFL	213
Average HS GPA	3.6
% graduated top 10% of class	33
% graduated top 25% of class	69
% graduated top 50% of class	97

DEADLINES

Regular notification	2/1
Nonfall registration?	yes

APPLICANTS ALSO LOOK AT AND OFTEN PREFER

Boston University
New York University
SUNY at Binghamton

AND SOMETIMES PREFER

Cornell University
Penn State University Park
SUNY at Albany
SUNY at Buffalo

AND RARELY PREFER

University of Maryland—College Park
University of Michigan—Ann Arbor

FINANCIAL FACTS

Financial Aid Rating	**67**
Annual in-state tuition	$4,350
Annual out-of-state tuition	$10,610
Room & Board	$7,730
Books and supplies	$900
Required fees	$1,039
% frosh rec. need-based scholarship or grant aid	53
% UG rec. need-based scholarship or grant aid	53
% frosh rec. need-based self-help aid	44
% UG rec. need-based self-help aid	47
% frosh rec. any financial aid	76
% UG rec. any financial aid	72
Avg. frosh grant	$5,548
Avg. frosh loan	$2,905
Independent 529 member?	No

STATE UNIVERSITY OF NEW YORK COLLEGE AT GENESEO

1 COLLEGE CIRCLE, GENESEO, NY 14454-1401 • ADMISSIONS: 716-245-5571 • FAX: 716-245-5550

CAMPUS LIFE

Quality of Life Rating	**72**
Fire Safety Rating	**65**
Type of school	public
Environment	rural

STUDENTS

Total undergrad enrollment	5,375
% male/female	39/61
% from out of state	1
% from public high school	80
% live on campus	55
% in (# of) fraternities	10 (8)
% in (# of) sororities	12 (11)
% African American	2
% Asian	5
% Caucasian	83
% Hispanic	3
% international	2
# of countries represented	34

SURVEY SAYS

Small classes
Students are friendly
Campus feels safe
Low cost of living
Students are happy
Lots of beer drinking
Hard liquor is popular

ACADEMICS

Academic Rating	**78**
Calendar	semester
Student/faculty ratio	19:1
Professors interesting rating	73
Professors accessible rating	73
% professors teaching UG courses	100
% classes taught by TAs	0
Most common regular class size	20-29 students

MOST POPULAR MAJORS

Biology/biological sciences
Business administration/management
education

STUDENTS SPEAK OUT

Academics

Forget every preconception you have about state schools or the SUNY system. SUNY Geneseo bucks nearly every expectation; a small teaching-oriented school on a beautiful campus, "Geneseo is the epitome of college life. The people, the classes, the area, and the campus life are ideal for students coming from every different background, just as long as they are looking to grow as a person and a student." One undergrad gushes, "This is a great school with many opportunities and 'extras' for a great price. Many of the private schools I looked at didn't have half the programs or clubs that Geneseo offers." Although small, Geneseo is big enough to "offer many different majors and is strong in those majors," especially when it comes to the sciences. Professors here "are extremely dedicated to undergraduate learning and are always willing to help (with a few exceptions, of course)." Most have impressive credentials, too. One student writes, "My first year here, one of my professors had worked as a United Nations Advisor, and another had previously run for Congress. Geneseo is a place where you can learn from people who have had real-life experience in their fields." To "stimulate the students' interests," most professors "require a lot of group work and class discussion. They are very accessible and do their best to notify students about due dates, study tips, and resources (which they provide an ample supply of) outside of class through E-mails, office hours, or review sessions." Students note that "TAs don't teach lecture classes. Sometimes they teach labs, but even then they're closely monitored by professors."

Life

"Geneseo is in the middle of nowhere, so we make our own fun," students tell us, adding that "while there are many jokes about cow tipping, you'll have a hard time finding someone who's actually done it." To keep students engaged, "the clubs and organizations on campus are constantly putting on events. It is very easy to get involved because there is a club for everyone. Geneseo often hosts guest lecturers, and has interesting scholarly events." There are also "some awesome shows put on by the theater and music departments. And all of the events on campus are either free or very low cost." Intramural sports are popular, too, with "broomball being a favorite for everyone," and intercollegiate hockey games that "are well-attended and can be a lot of fun." There's a lively party scene here, but there is also "a large number of students who don't drink at all [and] a new program called 'Late Knight' which provides alcohol-free entertainment on weekend nights." When all else fails, Geneseo's hills draw plenty of thrill-seekers. "You see a lot of students sledding in the winter or mud sliding in the spring." Another draw is the great outdoors at Letchworth State Park, which "is just a few minutes away by car, and is a great place to hike, picnic, or camp. Many students also bring bikes and ride around the campus and surrounding countryside on weekends." And, why not? The surrounding Genesee Valley "is really nice and the sunsets are amazing." When big-city distraction is a necessity, Rochester is not too far away.

Student Body

"Students at Geneseo work really hard; the library is always packed, [but] we also like to have fun and get involved. Everyone I know is part of at least one student organization." Most here "come from Rochester, Buffalo, New York City, or Long Island," and their ranks include "preppy people, people who study, people who are religious, gays, minorities, everything. What's amazing is how people get along so well." Even if the gender scale has a bit of a tilt to it: nearly two out of three students are female. "Boys, obviously, do exist at Geneseo," writes one woman, "but the lack of males is sort of a running joke among the students." "Minority students are few and far between," but the school does have "a very active Asian population, with an Asian theater group among the cultural organizations."

State University of New York College at Geneseo

Financial Aid: 585-245-5731 • E-mail: admissions@geneseo.edu • Website: www.geneseo.edu

ADMISSIONS

Very important factors considered include: Class rank, secondary school record, standardized test scores. *Important factors considered include:* Essays, extracurricular activities, minority status, recommendations, talent/ability. *Other factors considered include:* Character/personal qualities, volunteer work. SAT Reasoning or ACT required. TOEFL required of all international applicants. High school diploma is required, and GED is accepted. *Academic units recommended:* 4 English, 4 math, 4 science, 4 foreign language, 4 social studies.

The Inside Word

Geneseo is the most selective of SUNY's 13 undergraduate colleges and more selective than three of SUNY's university centers. No formula approach is used here. Expect a thorough review of both your academic accomplishments (virtually everyone here graduated in the top half of their high school classes) and your extracurricular/personal side. Admissions standards are tempered only by a somewhat low yield of admits who enroll; this keeps the admit rate higher than it might otherwise be.

FINANCIAL AID

Students should submit: FAFSA, state aid form. Regular filing deadline is 2/15. The Princeton Review suggests that all financial aid forms be submitted as soon as possible after 1/1. *Need-based scholarships/grants offered:* Pell, SEOG, state scholarships/grants, private scholarships, the school's own gift aid. *Loan aid offered:* FFEL Subsidized Stafford, FFEL Unsubsidized Stafford, FFEL PLUS, Federal Perkins, state loans, alternative loans. Applicants will be notified of awards on a rolling basis beginning on or about 3/15. Federal Work-study Program available. Institutional employment available. Off-campus job opportunities are fair.

FROM THE ADMISSIONS OFFICE

"Geneseo has carved a distinctive niche among the nation's premier public liberal arts colleges. Founded in 1871, the college occupies a 220-acre hillside campus in the historic Village of Geneseo, overlooking the scenic Genesee Valley. As a residential campus—with nearly two-thirds of the students living in college residence halls—it provides a rich and varied program of social, cultural, recreational, and scholarly activities. Geneseo is noted for its distinctive core curriculum and the extraordinary opportunities it offers undergraduates to pursue independent study and research with faculty who value close working relationships with talented students. Equally impressive is the remarkable success of its graduates, nearly one-third of whom study at leading graduate and professional schools immediately following graduation.

"For fall 2006, SUNY Genesco will accept any SAT or ACT score submitted by an applicant."

SELECTIVITY

Admissions Rating	**93**
# of applicants	8,661
% of applicants accepted	44
% of acceptees attending	27
# accepting a place on wait list	1,314
% admitted from wait list	2
# of early decision applicants	107
% accepted early decision	58

FRESHMAN PROFILE

Range SAT Verbal	600-670
Average SAT Verbal	621
Range SAT Math	600-670
Average SAT Math	631
**TPR Projected Range SAT Writing*	*630-680*
Range ACT Composite	26-28
Average ACT Composite	27
Minimum Paper TOEFL	525
Minimum Computer Based TOEFL	197
Average HS GPA	3.7
% graduated top 10% of class	50
% graduated top 25% of class	86
% graduated top 50% of class	99

DEADLINES

Early decision application deadline	11/15
Early decision notification	12/15
Regular application deadline	1/15
Regular notification	rolling
Nonfall registration?	yes

APPLICANTS ALSO LOOK AT AND OFTEN PREFER

Boston College, Colgate U., Cornell U.

AND SOMETIMES PREFER

Skidmore College, SUNY at Binghamton, U. of Rochester

AND RARELY PREFER

Nazareth College of Rochester, SUNY at Stony Brook, Syracuse U.

FINANCIAL FACTS

Financial Aid Rating	**60**
Annual in-state tuition	$4,350
Annual out-of-state tuition	$10,610
Room & Board	$6,820
Books and supplies	$700
Required fees	$1,085
% frosh rec. need-based scholarship or grant aid	40
% UG rec. need-based scholarship or grant aid	47
% frosh rec. need-based self-help aid	40
% UG rec. need-based self-help aid	47
% frosh rec. any financial aid	65
% UG rec. any financial aid	76
Avg. frosh grant	$1,900
Avg. frosh loan	$3,200
Independent 529 member?	No

State University of New York—Purchase College

Admissions Office, 735 Anderson Hill Road, Purchase, NY 10577 • Admissions: 914-251-6300 • Fax: 914-251-6314

CAMPUS LIFE

Quality of Life Rating	**62**
Fire Safety Rating	**60**
Type of school	public
Environment	town

STUDENTS

Total undergrad enrollment	3,344
% male/female	45/55
% from out of state	17
% live on campus	65
% African American	8
% Asian	4
% Caucasian	62
% Hispanic	10
% international	2
# of countries represented	33

SURVEY SAYS

Small classes
Frats and sororities are unpopular or nonexistent
Musical organizations are popular
Theater is popular
Student publications are popular
Political activism is popular
(Almost) everyone smokes

ACADEMICS

Academic Rating	**79**
Calendar	semester
Student/faculty ratio	14:1
Professors interesting rating	80
Professors accessible rating	67
% professors teaching UG courses	100
% classes taught by TAs	1
Most common lab size	10-19 students
Most common regular class size	10-19 students

MOST POPULAR MAJORS

Liberal arts and sciences/liberal studies
psychology
visual and performing arts

STUDENTS SPEAK OUT

Academics

Conservatory programs in dance, music, theater arts, film, and professional training in art and design are the main attractions at SUNY—Purchase College, a small state school nestled in the affluent suburbs of New York City. These "world-class conservatory programs at state university prices" mean that "there is a lot of art on campus." But there is more to Purchase than just the arts. One student, who was not admitted to the music conservatory but entered the school of liberal arts and sciences instead, explains, "I wasn't expecting much from the science end because this is an art/music school, but I was surprised. The teachers are really knowledgeable in the fields they teach." Students also note that "the academic support on campus is excellent, although a lot of students do not take advantage of this. The resource staff at the library is phenomenal and will help you find what you need even if it's not in the library." Although many students have complained about a lack of organization in the administration and large amounts of red tape, the school has responded by establishing a student advising center, streamlining the student affairs office and building a new academic services facility that will centralize all student services.

Life

Purchase is home to a vibrant arts scene. One student says, "We have one of the best performing arts centers in the United States, as well as plenty of art shows, dance shows, theater shows, and opera recitals. We have a nationally recognized museum on campus, as well as good discussions by some very influential people." There are also "a lot of on-campus bands, many 'zines written by students, and student art showings." In short, Purchase is the kind of place where "there is practically no one at basketball games, but the ballet is packed." Political and arts organizations are popular, students tell us, but there's not much of a party scene. When students want that type of fun, they generally hop a bus or train and head for New York City. Many students also take advantage of the athletic facility and the wide array of athletic programs. "Aesthetes" that they are, students have plenty of complaints about campus design. "Everything is brown brick. It's very gloomy and depressing, with few flowers and shrubs, just trees. Landscaping and some paint could go a long way here," observes one critic. Students also report that many facilities are in need of a serious upgrade.

Student Body

Purchase students pride themselves on their dedication, their iconoclasm, and their idiosyncrasies. One undergraduate says, "The typical conservatory student here is a bleary-eyed, sleep-deprived, stressed-out workaholic completely in love with their chosen career path. The typical nonconservatory student perceives him/herself as an artist, a rebel, a revolutionary, a unique individual, and an independent thinker." More often than not, the student "has at least one of the following: a clashing/weird, funky fashion sense; piercings; tattoos; five different colors in their hair; a unique hairstyle; paint splattered all over them." Nearly all respondents expressed admiration for and a sense of belonging in the student body as a whole. Purchase "is very diverse, with a large number of homosexual students, politically and socially liberal students, politically and socially conservative students, art students, academics, dancers, actors, etc. Everyone fits in because there are no two people alike."

State University of New York College at Purchase

Financial Aid: 914-251-6350 • E-mail: admissn@purchase.edu • Website: www.purchase.edu

ADMISSIONS

Very important factors considered include: Essays, secondary school record, standardized test scores. *Important factors considered include:* Recommendations. *Other factors considered include:* Extracurricular activities, interview, talent/ability. SAT Reasoning Test required. TOEFL required of all international applicants. High school diploma is required, and GED is accepted.

The Inside Word

The overall admit rate at Purchase College is low, athough admissions requirements vary greatly depending on the academic program. Almost all applicants wishing to major in the visual or performing arts must audition or submit a portfolio. Admission is less competitive for candidates wishing to major in the liberal arts or sciences.

FINANCIAL AID

Students should submit: FAFSA, state aid form. The Princeton Review suggests that all financial aid forms be submitted as soon as possible after 1/1. *Need-based scholarships/grants offered:* Pell, SEOG, state scholarships/grants, private scholarships, the school's own gift aid. *Loan aid offered:* FFEL Subsidized Stafford, FFEL Unsubsidized Stafford, FFEL PLUS, Federal Perkins. Applicants will be notified of awards on a rolling basis beginning on or about 3/1. Federal Work-study Program available. Institutional employment available. Off-campus job opportunities are excellent.

FROM THE ADMISSIONS OFFICE

"A highly selective college, Purchase College provides a total educational experience, that mirrors the supportive environment of a private college at public college prices. Purchase is the only public 4-year college that fuses the educational goals and traditions of the liberal arts with arts conservatories in music, dance, theater, film, design technology, and a school of art and design. Conservatory programs stress professional training, close cohort–based education providing apprenticeships with professionals and opportunities in the New York arts scene.

"At Purchase you will find a unique arts atmosphere for liberal arts students as well as conservatory students. Attend student performances, or go to the five-theater Performing Arts Center and The Neuberger Museum of Art (the country's eighth largest campus art museum) for the arts and entertainment. Involve yourself in distinctive curricular and cocurricular experiences, have access to the latest in technology, obtain internships, and avail yourself of the services of career development. You can choose from a wide array of majorsin the humanities, sciences and social sciences or disciplinary fields as journalism, creative writing, environmental science or new media. And there are pre-professional programs in law, medicine, and education.

"If you want to study abroad you can participate in summer programs in Italy, France, or Spain. Live and learn with your friends by joining a residential Learning Community or a Freshman Interest Group. As a high achieving student, you could be eligible for a Presidential or Merit scholarship. Purchase College is situated on 500 acres in suburban Westchester County. Come visit us!

"Admissions requirements vary with each program in the college and can include auditions, portfolio reviews, essays, writing samples, and interviews.

"Pending further evaluation, Purchase College strongly urges students planning to apply for fall 2006 to take the new SAT (or the ACT with the Writing section)."

SELECTIVITY

Admissions Rating	**85**
# of applicants	6,899
% of applicants accepted	29
% of acceptees attending	32
# of early decision applicants	6
% accepted early decision	75

FRESHMAN PROFILE

Range SAT Verbal	520-620
Average SAT Verbal	576
Range SAT Math	490-590
Average SAT Math	543
**TPR Projected Range SAT Writing*	*570-650*
Minimum Paper TOEFL	550
Minimum Computer Based TOEFL	213
Average HS GPA	3.04
% graduated top 10% of class	9
% graduated top 25% of class	40
% graduated top 50% of class	74

DEADLINES

Early decision application deadline	11/1
Early decision notification	12/5
Regular notification	5/1
Nonfall registration?	yes

APPLICANTS ALSO LOOK AT

AND OFTEN PREFER

The Juilliard School
New York University

AND SOMETIMES PREFER

Brandeis University
Carnegie Mellon University
SUNY at Stony Brook

AND RARELY PREFER

Emerson College
Hofstra University

FINANCIAL FACTS

Financial Aid Rating	**66**
Annual in-state tuition	$4,350
Annual out-of-state tuition	$10,610
Room & Board	$7,540
Books and supplies	$1,100
Required fees	$1,092
% frosh rec. need-based scholarship or grant aid	40
% UG rec. need-based scholarship or grant aid	38
% frosh rec. need-based self-help aid	52
% UG rec. need-based self-help aid	50
% frosh rec. any financial aid	80
% UG rec. any financial aid	66
Avg. frosh grant	$5,285
Avg. frosh loan	$3,305
Independent 529 member?	No

Stephens College

1200 East Broadway, Box 2121, Columbia, MO 65215 • Admissions: 800-876-7207 • Fax: 573-876-7237

CAMPUS LIFE

Quality of Life Rating	**95**
Fire Safety Rating	**60**
Type of school	private
Environment	city

STUDENTS

Total undergrad enrollment	633
% male/female	4/96
% from out of state	55
% from public high school	75
% live on campus	70
% in (# of) sororities	8 (2)
% African American	9
% Asian	2
% Caucasian	85
% Hispanic	3

SURVEY SAYS

Small classes
Registration is a breeze
Students are friendly
Great off-campus food
Campus feels safe
Students are happy
Theater is popular

ACADEMICS

Academic Rating	**88**
Calendar	semester
Student/faculty ratio	10:1
Professors interesting rating	88
Professors accessible rating	90
% professors teaching UG courses	100
% classes taught by TAs	0
Most common lab size	fewer than 10 students
Most common regular class size	10-19 students

MOST POPULAR MAJORS

Drama and dramatics/theater arts
education
fashion/apparel design

STUDENTS SPEAK OUT

Academics

"It's all about theater, dance, fashion design, and marketing" at Stephens College, a small all-women's school (almost, that is; the school admits a few men to its theater department) "with an emphasis in almost every class on women's history and women's issues." Stephens is "a strict school academically, which really prepares you for the real world. Small classes and teachers who really care can be a great blessing for your education." The school's very existence and success, students say, empower them. "Stephens is about providing confidence and the ability to back that confidence up, for women, in a predominantly male world," explains one undergrad. Profs receive high marks for their "amazing real world experience in their fields. The theater professors have actually acted and directed in the business, the dance professors are from New York, and the broadcasting teacher spent many years on TV." Better still, they know how to share their expertise with undergrads; as one student told us, "You really have an opportunity to bond with [profs] and make them your friend once you're done with their class. They're always willing to listen to what you have to say and how you feel about what they're teaching." On the downside, students feel that the "nonarts departments need more attention" and that "the facilities here are outdated, and the library is weak and in need of updates."

Life

Stephens students love Columbia, "a three-college town where there's always something to do." The city has a lot to offer these aesthetically inclined undergrads; explains one student, "The largest majors on campus are theater, fashion, and dance, so most of our student body is very creative. Even those not in one of these majors have an appreciation for art, and there are a lot of opportunities in downtown Columbia for us to see independent films, a poetry readings, local musicians, or the work of local artists." Because "Mizzou is two blocks away, girls have all the chances in the world to meet guys" and "go hang out at frat parties." Students here tell us that "the majority of our student body aren't hard partiers, and those who are tend to live off-campus where they can drink and party to their own satisfaction." Most here are too busy and too deeply involved in their studies to devote much time to partying. Wrote one theater major, "As far as theater is concerned, most of us are completely consumed by the department, which is a good thing. Like Annie Potts said of her experience here, you really do 'eat, breathe, live theater.' Most of us seem to love being so busy, but others don't like the idea of rehearsing or working on a crew a good deal of the afternoon and evening and then having to do homework way into the wee hours of the morning." Just about everyone here agrees that "the food is really bad and greasy."

Student Body

"There is no 'typical Stephens woman,'" many Stephens women insist. "We are all unique: short, tall, fat, thin, black, white, Asian, Hispanic, brainiac, or sorority lover . . . we all find our niche here." Others tell us that "Stephens is mostly white students, but everyone here observes diversity and at least respects it" and report that "most students are middle class and from Missouri, or from a surrounding state. Most are in the arts (theater, dance, fashion)." Students outside the most popular majors "are respected by professors, but don't always get treated the same by students." Notes one undergrad, "While there are definite social cliques—the fashion majors, dancers, theater people, etc.—we all get along." As at many unaffiliated women's schools, "sexual orientation isn't an issue here. There is a good mixture of heterosexual and gay/bisexual people. It may seem like there are quite a few lesbians and bisexuals, but in reality, it's just that they feel more open here."

STEPHENS COLLEGE

FINANCIAL AID: 573-876-7106 • E-MAIL: APPLY@WC.STEPHENS.EDU • WEBSITE: WWW.STEPHENS.EDU

ADMISSIONS

Very important factors considered include: Character/personal qualities, essays, recommendations, secondary school record, standardized test scores. *Important factors considered include:* Extracurricular activities, talent/ability. *Other factors considered include:* Class rank, interview, volunteer work, work experience. SAT Reasoning or ACT required. TOEFL required of all international applicants. High school diploma is required, and GED is accepted. *Academic units recommended:* 4 English, 2 math, 2 science, 2 foreign language, 2 social studies.

The Inside Word

Each candidate's application is read by three members of the admissions committee, and essays carry much more significance than test scores. You'll get a lot of personal attention from the admissions staff here; with the kind of competition Stephens faces for students, they have to work pretty hard here to bring in the freshman class. Their success is a testament to the quality of the college.

FINANCIAL AID

Students should submit: FAFSA. The Princeton Review suggests that all financial aid forms be submitted as soon as possible after 1/1. *Need-based scholarships/grants offered:* Pell, SEOG, state scholarships/grants, private scholarships, the school's own gift aid. *Loan aid offered:* FFEL Subsidized Stafford, FFEL Unsubsidized Stafford, FFEL PLUS, Federal Perkins. Applicants will be notified of awards on a rolling basis beginning on or about 2/1. Federal Work-study Program available. Institutional employment available. Off-campus job opportunities are excellent.

FROM THE ADMISSIONS OFFICE

"Historically committed to meeting the changing needs of women, Stephens College engages students in an innovative educational experience that focuses on pre-professional fields and the performing arts and grounded in the liberal arts. Graduates of Stephens are career-ready women of distinction who are connected through a supportive network of alumnae across the world, confident in themselves, and inspired by our tradition of the ten ideals as core values that enrich women's lives.

"The women's college setting offers to its students stimulating classroom discussion and close interaction with professors and peers. Bridging theory and application, students engage in hands-on learning opportunities (education majors in our on-campus children's laboratory school and theater in Iowa, for example) as well as internship experiences in their first year of study. The Stephens campus is within walking distance of a thriving downtown, shared by more than 26,000 students at area colleges and universities.

"As of this book's publication, Stephens College did not have information available about their policy regarding the new SAT."

SELECTIVITY

Admissions Rating	**82**
# of applicants	408
% of applicants accepted	79
% of acceptees attending	48

FRESHMAN PROFILE

Range SAT Verbal	540-610
Average SAT Verbal	574
Range SAT Math	480-580
Average SAT Math	525
**TPR Projected Range SAT Writing*	*590-640*
Range ACT Composite	21-26
Average ACT Composite	24
Minimum Paper TOEFL	550
Minimum Computer Based TOEFL	213
Average HS GPA	3.5
% graduated top 10% of class	17
% graduated top 25% of class	56
% graduated top 50% of class	85

DEADLINES

Regular notification	rolling
Nonfall registration?	yes

APPLICANTS ALSO LOOK AT AND SOMETIMES PREFER

University of Missouri—Columbia

AND RARELY PREFER

Butler University

FINANCIAL FACTS

Financial Aid Rating	**79**
Annual tuition	$18,230
Room & Board	$7,180
Books and supplies	$750
% frosh rec. need-based scholarship or grant aid	54
% UG rec. need-based scholarship or grant aid	65
% frosh rec. need-based self-help aid	63
% UG rec. need-based self-help aid	75
% frosh rec. any financial aid	97
% UG rec. any financial aid	75
Avg. frosh grant	$12,062
Avg. frosh loan	$3,329
Independent 529 member?	Yes

STEVENS INSTITUTE OF TECHNOLOGY

CASTLE POINT ON HUDSON, HOBOKEN, NJ 07030 • ADMISSIONS: 201-216-5194 • FAX: 201-216-8348

CAMPUS LIFE

Quality of Life Rating	**75**
Fire Safety Rating	**98**
Type of school	private
Environment	village

STUDENTS

Total undergrad enrollment	1,726
% male/female	76/24
% from out of state	35
% from public high school	80
% live on campus	75
% in (# of) fraternities	34 (10)
% in (# of) sororities	31 (3)
% African American	4
% Asian	16
% Caucasian	53
% Hispanic	9
% international	7
# of countries represented	52

SURVEY SAYS

Small classes
Diverse student types on campus
Students love Hoboken, NJ
Great off-campus food
Campus feels safe
Frats and sororities dominate social scene
Lots of beer drinking

ACADEMICS

Academic Rating	**72**
Calendar	semester
Student/faculty ratio	9:1
Professors interesting rating	61
Professors accessible rating	61
% professors teaching UG courses	100
% classes taught by TAs	0
Most common lab size	10-19 students
Most common regular class size	10-19 students

MOST POPULAR MAJORS

Computer and information sciences
computer engineering
mechanical engineering

STUDENTS SPEAK OUT

Academics

"Academic expectations are high" at Stevens Institute of Technology, a New Jersey engineering, science, and mathematics stronghold. According to undergraduates, "engineering students are required to take more credits than at nearly any other school." Anyone who "manages to graduate from Stevens with an engineering or science degree," students tell us, "can handle anything. The stress level that students experience here is extremely high." Another engineering student adds, "Many students actually feel relieved by the time they graduate because they know that they won't be working as hard in the 'real world.'" Students endure this academic rigor, so they can have access to "great internships and co-op jobs," enjoy the "high level of name recognition in the engineering world," and have access to the "very strong opportunities to make good money after graduation." As at most science and tech schools, professors are probably brilliant; we say "probably" because many students don't understand them well enough to say for sure. That's because "most of them don't speak English too well or just can't communicate properly with the class." Although "some professors are not very helpful—they are intimidating to approach, succinct with any answers, not understanding the question perhaps—others are so amazingly generous with their time that it actually makes you feel good that someone would sit down for you and only you (not several students) for an hour of their time to help you with your assignment."

Life

The school's location, students agree, is "perfect. It is close to New York City without actually being in New York City (no dealing with traffic and noise), and it's right on the Hudson River, overlooking the city. Hoboken is a fun place to be, too." One student explains, "Anything you need to wind down is available. We have the river and pier for scenery, New York City for the city, and Hoboken for great food and charm." Of course, there are also campus goings-on, which include "the outdoor club and gym for physical activities, artistic outlets with the theater, choir, so many sports, so many cultural clubs, tutoring, and reviews." Therefore, "student life at Stevens is all in the hands of the student." Students say "Greek life is very active and plays a huge role in the social activity on campus." The campus also hosts numerous shows. Undergraduates tell us that "there has been huge growth in the number of campus activities since the creation of the Entertainment Committee, which works to make sure students get big-name professional entertainment right on campus, as well as movies and carnivals." The only thing that is scarce is spare time and someone to enjoy it with. Many male students feel there is "no time to spend on girls" because of the school and its demanding curriculum; that's okay though, as there are "no girls to spend time on."

Student Body

Many Stevens students remind us that it "is an engineering and computer science school. As such, you get the geeks and the dorks and the nerds. Everyone here is a bit shy of mainstream in some way, shape, or form, and it works wonderfully." Other students argue that "while there may be a few dorks on campus, they are the exception, not the norm. Many students are on varsity athletic teams and are involved with many extracurricular activities." There is probably a little bit of both student types. One student says, "The student body at Stevens can be generalized into two groups. The first half sits in their rooms with Star Wars figurines playing Dungeons and Dragons. The other half [is made up of] fun, outgoing people who get their work done, but know how to let loose and have a good time." Stevens is ethnically and geographically diverse, but male students say that its male-female ratio is "horrible."

STEVENS INSTITUTE OF TECHNOLOGY

FINANCIAL AID: 201-216-5194 • E-MAIL: ADMISSIONS@STEVENS.EDU • WEBSITE: WWW.STEVENS.EDU

ADMISSIONS

Very important factors considered include: Character/personal qualities, essays, interview, recommendations, secondary school record. *Important factors considered include:* Class rank, extracurricular activities, standardized test scores, talent/ability, volunteer work, work experience. *Other factors considered include:* Alumni/ae relation. SAT Reasoning or ACT required. TOEFL required of all international applicants. High school diploma is required, and GED is not accepted. *Academic units required:* 4 English, 4 math, 3 science (3 science lab), 2 history. *Academic units recommended:* 4 English, 4 math, 4 science (4 science lab), 2 foreign language, 2 social studies, 2 history, 4 academic electives.

The Inside Word

Stevens is indeed impressive and legitimately near the top of the "second tier" of technical schools. Above-average students who would run into difficulty trying to gain admission to the MITs and Caltechs of the world will find a much more receptive admissions process here. Given its solid reputation and metropolitan New York location, it's an excellent choice for techies who want to establish their careers in the area.

FINANCIAL AID

Students should submit: FAFSA. The Princeton Review suggests that all financial aid forms be submitted as soon as possible after 1/1. *Need-based scholarships/grants offered:* Pell, SEOG, state scholarships/grants, private scholarships, the school's own gift aid. *Loan aid offered:* Direct Subsidized Stafford, Direct Unsubsidized Stafford, Direct PLUS, Federal Perkins, state loans, Signature Loans, TERI Loans, NJ CLASS, CitiAssist. Applicants will be notified of awards on a rolling basis beginning on or about 3/30. Federal Work-study Program available. Off-campus job opportunities are excellent.

FROM THE ADMISSIONS OFFICE

"The quality and achievements of our graduates are the greatest hallmarks of a Stevens education. Almost all of our students have had technical, pre-professional experience outside the classroom during their undergraduate years. Among other benefits, this enables them to be the finest candidates for prestigious graduate schools or positions of employment in industry. The most striking indication of this is that most of our graduates receive a job offer prior to graduation, and Stevens has been ranked eleventh among the Top 550 institutions that produce presidents, vice presidents, and directors of U.S. companies. In 2003, Stevens was ranked as the number one 'Most Connected Campus' in the nation by The Princeton Review, and again in 2004 as one of the "Nation's Most Entrepreneurial Campuses." Stevens was also recognized by the Sloan Consortium for 'Excellence in Institution-Wide Online Teaching and Learning Programming." However, outstanding academics need to be balanced with an outstanding campus life, and at Stevens students will find more than 70 student organizations and 22 NCAA Division III athletics teams. Plus, with our Hoboken location overlooking the Hudson River and New York City skyline, Stevens offers a campus environment like no other.

"Students applying for admission into the fall 2006 class may submit either the new or the old SAT. Stevens will take their best score from each section of the test. At this time, the new written portion of the SAT will not be given as much weight in the admissions process."

SELECTIVITY

Admissions Rating	**89**
# of applicants	2,195
% of applicants accepted	53
% of acceptees attending	38
# accepting a place on wait list	220
% admitted from wait list	5
# of early decision applicants	87
% accepted early decision	83

FRESHMAN PROFILE

Range SAT Verbal	560-670
Range SAT Math	630-720
**TPR Projected Range SAT Writing*	*600-680*
Range ACT Composite	25-30
Minimum Paper TOEFL	550
Minimum Computer Based TOEFL	213
Average HS GPA	3.8
% graduated top 10% of class	52
% graduated top 25% of class	32
% graduated top 50% of class	98

DEADLINES

Early decision application deadline	11/15
Early decision notification	12/15
Regular application deadline	2/15
Regular notification	3/15
Nonfall registration?	no

APPLICANTS ALSO LOOK AT

AND OFTEN PREFER
Carnegie Mellon University, Cornell University, Massachusetts Institute of Technology, Princeton University

AND SOMETIMES PREFER
Johns Hopkins University, Lehigh University, New York University

AND RARELY PREFER
Drexel University, New Jersey Institute of Technology, Rensselaer Polytechnic Institute

FINANCIAL FACTS

Financial Aid Rating	**71**
Annual tuition	$27,300
Room & Board	$8,930
Books and supplies	$900
Required fees	$250
% frosh rec. need-based scholarship or grant aid	56
% UG rec. need-based scholarship or grant aid	54
% frosh rec. need-based self-help aid	58
% UG rec. need-based self-help aid	60
% frosh rec. any financial aid	83
% UG rec. any financial aid	76
Avg. frosh grant	$24,523
Avg. frosh loan	$3,748
Independent 529 member?	Yes

SUFFOLK UNIVERSITY

8 ASHBURTON PLACE, BOSTON, MA 02108 • ADMISSIONS: 617-573-8460 • FAX: 617-742-4291

CAMPUS LIFE

Quality of Life Rating	**91**
Fire Safety Rating	**98**
Type of school	private
Environment	metropolis

STUDENTS

Total undergrad enrollment	4,244
% male/female	42/58
% from out of state	18
% from public high school	66
% live on campus	18
% African American	3
% Asian	7
% Caucasian	61
% Hispanic	5
% international	10
# of countries represented	100

SURVEY SAYS

Small classes
Diverse student types on campus
Students love Boston, MA
Great off-campus food

ACADEMICS

Academic Rating	**73**
Calendar	semester
Student/faculty ratio	12:1
Professors interesting rating	81
Professors accessible rating	76
% professors teaching UG courses	90
% classes taught by TAs	1
Most common lab size	10-19 students
Most common regular class size	20-29 students

MOST POPULAR MAJORS

Business administration/management
communications studies/speech communication and rhetoric
sociology

STUDENTS SPEAK OUT

Academics

"Suffolk University is about diversity and a solid education in an ideal location," agree students at this comprehensive university in downtown Boston. A large international population—enhanced by Suffolk's permanent campuses in Madrid, Spain, and Dakar, Senegal—accounts for much of the diversity. Nontraditional students also add to the mix ("This school is all about second chances," explains one undergrad who returned to school after a long layoff). All here appreciate how "the school is very dedicated to its students," offering small classes and going the extra mile to line up co-op and internship opportunities. Students in management- and government-related areas especially benefit from the school's downtown location and its strong ties to city businesses and government. Suffolk undergrads, however, save their highest praise for the faculty whom they describe as "a fantastic resource, always willing to help anyone who asks for it. They also do their best to challenge students in classes without setting them up for failure." Brags one student, "Many [adjunct faculty] teach at schools such as Harvard or Boston College. I definitely feel like I'm getting the same education as I would at Ivy League schools but in much smaller classes." Not to mention that they're getting it at a much lower price. Students also appreciate how "the administration is easily accessible and open to student feedback."

Life

Suffolk does not have a traditional, enclosed campus; rather, the school consists of a collection of buildings scattered across Boston's Beacon Hill neighborhood, not far from the Government Center and the famous Boston Commons. Few people mind, however, because the city of Boston itself offers undergraduates a rich bounty of experiences. Students tell us that "there is so much to do here, from theater to dining to Red Sox games to movies. Boston is such a cultural city!" Beantown is also home to numerous other colleges and universities (Boston University, Boston College, Harvard, MIT, and Emerson, to name just a few), making it "a giant college campus with endless possibilities!" A new dorm opened in fall 2003 that will double the school's residential capacity. Students hope that the increase in residents will result in a more cohesive, active student body.

Student Body

"Suffolk's greatest strength is the diversity" of its student body. "Everyday I seem to meet someone from another country. Just the other day I met someone from Bolivia," writes one student. Internationals are a significant percentage of the population here and "seem to fit in quite well." Suffolk is also home to "a fairly large constituency of adult professionals who have returned to school (often attending night classes intermixed with 'traditional' students)," as well as "a large gay population." Most students come from the New England/New York area" and are of the down-to-earth variety; "there's not a lot of blue-blood here," explains one student. "But that's a good thing, I think. Understand that blue-bloods aren't discouraged or ostracized, just not the norm." Students are generally practical and goal-oriented, the type of people who "get the job done and still make time to spend with friends."

FINANCIAL AID: 617-573-8470 • E-MAIL: ADMISSION@SUFFOLK.EDU • WEBSITE: WWW.SUFFOLK.EDU

ADMISSIONS

Very important factors considered include: Secondary school record. *Important factors considered include:* Character/personal qualities, class rank, essays, extracurricular activities, recommendations, standardized test scores, volunteer work, work experience. *Other factors considered include:* Alumni/ae relation, geographical residence, interview, state residency. SAT Reasoning or ACT required. TOEFL required of all international applicants. High school diploma is required, and GED is accepted. *Academic units required:* 4 English, 3 math, 2 science (1 science lab), 2 foreign language, 1 history, 4 academic electives. *Academic units recommended:* 4 English, 4 math, 3 science (2 science lab), 3 foreign language, 1 social studies, 2 history, 4 academic electives.

The Inside Word

Graduating senior Paul Fisette says, "They tell me the real world is a terrible place we will be magically transported to on May 23 after receiving our diploma. Before you get too disheartened, I offer a glimmer of hope! We aren't graduating from a secluded 1,000 acre university; we are graduating from Suffolk and what people often do not realize is that we have been kicking the real world square in the teeth since the moment we arrived here. While our friends at other schools complained about the cafeteria food, we were working to pay for school, take night classes, while balancing this with a semblance of a social life. No complaints! I belong to a school where things haven't been handed to people on a silver platter, where we learned as much through living in Boston as we did sitting in a classroom. So as for the real world, I say bring it on. We're ready!"

FINANCIAL AID

Students should submit: FAFSA, institution's own financial aid form. Regular filing deadline is 4/1. The Princeton Review suggests that all financial aid forms be submitted as soon as possible after 1/1. *Need-based scholarships/grants offered:* Pell, SEOG, state scholarships/grants, private scholarships, the school's own gift aid. *Loan aid offered:* Direct Subsidized Stafford, Direct Unsubsidized Stafford, Direct PLUS, Federal Perkins. Applicants will be notified of awards on a rolling basis beginning on or about 3/1. Federal Work-study Program available. Off-campus job opportunities are good.

FROM THE ADMISSIONS OFFICE

"Ask any student, and they'll tell you: the best thing about Suffolk is the professors. They go the extra mile to help students to succeed. Suffolk faculty members are noted scholars and experienced professionals, but first and foremost, they are teachers and mentors. Suffolk's faculty is of the highest caliber. Ninety-four percent of the faculty hold PhDs. Suffolk maintains a 12:1 student/faculty ratio with an average class size of 19.

"The university was selected as one of the "Best 201" colleges by the Best 201 Colleges for the Real World (2001/2002) and one of *Barron's Best Buys in College Education*. Career preparation is a high priority at Suffolk. Many students work during the school year in paid internships, co-op jobs, or work-study positions. Suffolk has an excellent job placement record. More than 94 percent of recent graduates are either employed or enrolled in graduate school at the time of graduation.

"The university's academic programs emphasize quality teaching, small class size, and real-world career applications, and an international experience. There are more than 30 study abroad sites available to students. The undergraduate academic program offers more than 70 majors and 1,000 courses.

"We require applicants to submit the new SAT or the ACT taken with the Writing component. Pending faculty assessment on the test's virtues, the Writing sections will not play a large role in admissions decisions."

SELECTIVITY	
Admissions Rating	**70**
# of applicants	5,006
% of applicants accepted	85
% of acceptees attending	24
# accepting a place on wait list	60
% admitted from wait list	13
FRESHMAN PROFILE	
Range SAT Verbal	450-550
Average SAT Verbal	506
Range SAT Math	450-550
Average SAT Math	497
**TPR Projected Range SAT Writing*	*520-600*
Range ACT Composite	17-22
Minimum Paper TOEFL	525
Minimum Computer Based TOEFL	197
Average HS GPA	2.92
% graduated top 10% of class	5
% graduated top 25% of class	25
% graduated top 50% of class	63
DEADLINES	
Regular notification	rolling
Nonfall registration?	yes
FINANCIAL FACTS	
Financial Aid Rating	**66**
Annual tuition	$21,140
Room & Board	$10,020
Books and supplies	$1,000
Required fees	$80
% frosh rec. need-based scholarship or grant aid	51
% UG rec. need-based scholarship or grant aid	47
% frosh rec. need-based self-help aid	57
% UG rec. need-based self-help aid	53
% frosh rec. any financial aid	77
% UG rec. any financial aid	70
Avg. frosh grant	$6,175
Avg. frosh loan	$3,615
Independent 529 member?	No

SUSQUEHANNA UNIVERSITY

514 UNIVERSITY AVENUE, SELINSGROVE, PA 17870 • ADMISSIONS: 570-372-4260 • FAX: 570-372-2722

CAMPUS LIFE

Quality of Life Rating	**79**
Fire Safety Rating	**70**
Type of school	private
Affiliation	Lutheran
Environment	village

STUDENTS

Total undergrad enrollment	1,972
% male/female	44/56
% from out of state	40
% from public high school	85
% live on campus	77
% in (# of) fraternities	21 (5)
% in (# of) sororities	24 (4)
% African American	2
% Asian	2
% Caucasian	93
% Hispanic	2
% international	1
# of countries represented	9

SURVEY SAYS

Small classes
Great computer facilities
Great library
Athletic facilities are great
Students are friendly
Lots of beer drinking

ACADEMICS

Academic Rating	**81**
Calendar	semester
Student/faculty ratio	14:1
Professors interesting rating	83
Professors accessible rating	87
% professors teaching UG courses	100
% classes taught by TAs	0
Most common lab size	10-19 students
Most common regular class size	20-29 students

MOST POPULAR MAJORS

Biology/biological sciences
Business administration/management
communications studies/speech communication and rhetoric

STUDENTS SPEAK OUT

Academics

Susquehanna University, a Lutheran affiliated institution situated in central Pennsylvania, boasts "a great teacher-to-student ratio and a close-knit community that comes from having only 2,000 students on campus." The size of the school, students here tell us, "allows you to try many new and different things that you would miss out on at a bigger university" and "makes us a little community where you know so many people. You get to know your professors very well, feel extremely comfortable going to see them outside of class, and get the attention and help that you need." Students report that SU's business program "is wonderful and challenging." The music, writing, and arts programs here also earn students' praise, while natural science programs benefit from "lots of opportunities for undergraduate research." Students also appreciate the school's "amazing dedication in finding us internships and jobs" and how SU "encourages us to study abroad and in different specialty programs to learn as much as we can in different environments." The school is "looking to the future with building initiatives. The music and arts building was finished two years ago and new athletic fields were created last year. The campus center (and cafeteria) are being renovated over summer 2005." Additionally, a new residence hall is scheduled to open in fall 2006 and the science department is reportedly "working on plans for a second science building." Observes one student, "The university is continually improving, in both aesthetics and in the quality of education."

Life

"Extracurricular activities are very strong" at SU. Students tell us that "there is a great network of volunteer organizations that work on campus and throughout the local area, from on-campus recycling to mentoring at the middle school. Club sports are also strong," as are the school's Division III intercollegiate athletics. Greek life is also big, with approximately one in four students pledging. Campus organizations "offer a variety of events like movies, spring weekend parties, and different social events." And because the school is small, "you can be involved with a lot of different activities at the same time." The high level of campus activity is necessary, because hometown Selinsgrove "is a nice small town, but it has nothing in the way of entertainment and girls, and the mall sucks—so stock up before you get here." Many students address the boredom of rural seclusion by partying hard, a situation the administration has tried to address recently with predictable results: Plenty of students complain that "we expected a college and instead we got a babysitting service." Undergrads here also gripe that the school is currently overcrowded, with a lot of 'forced triples' in freshman dorms. They report that those renovations are coming along "slowly, so we'll see what it will look like next year."

Student Body

"Susquehanna, located in rural central Pennsylvania, undoubtedly lacks diversity," students write. "The average student is of one of two varieties: white, middle-class, Pennsylvania farm children or white, upper-middle-class kids from in or around New York City." Those from the area "often leave on weekends, especially during freshman year, which is annoying because it makes it hard to get to know them." SU undergrads know how to "strike the balance between academics with extracurricular activities. We are involved in athletics, community service, religious groups and Greek life." Undergrads note "the presence of certain cliques here; for instance, music and drama production, sorority girls, sports teams, frats, etc. However, these groups are not set in stone and many people have many different friends in numerous cliques." Most students here "dress preppy and carry cell phones," but "there is always someone dressed in sweats or pajama, too. There are also some atypical students who wear goth or bohemian-style clothing, but that doesn't usually seem to affect how they fit in."

FINANCIAL AID: 570-372-4450 • E-MAIL: SUADMISS@SUSQU.EDU • WEBSITE: WWW.SUSQU.EDU

ADMISSIONS

Very important factors considered include: Class rank, secondary school record, standardized test scores. *Important factors considered include:* Character/personal qualities, essays, extracurricular activities, interview, minority status, recommendations, talent/ability, volunteer work. *Other factors considered include:* Alumni/ae relation, geographical residence, religious affiliation/commitment, state residency, work experience. TOEFL required of all international applicants. High school diploma is required, and GED is accepted. *Academic units required:* 4 English, 3 math, 3 science (2 science lab), 2 foreign language, 1 social studies, 1 history, 2 academic electives. *Academic units recommended:* 4 English, 4 math, 4 science (3 science lab), 3 foreign language, 3 social studies, 2 history, 3 academic electives.

The Inside Word

Susquehanna is about as low profile as universities come in the age of MTV. Getting in is made easier by the serious competition the university faces from numerous like institutions in the region, some with significantly better reputations.

FINANCIAL AID

Students should submit: FAFSA, CSS/Financial Aid PROFILE, business/farm supplement, parent and student federal tax documents. Regular filing deadline is 5/1. The Princeton Review suggests that all financial aid forms be submitted as soon as possible after 1/1. *Need-based scholarships/grants offered:* Pell, SEOG, state scholarships/grants, private scholarships, the school's own gift aid. *Loan aid offered:* FFEL Subsidized Stafford, FFEL Unsubsidized Stafford, FFEL PLUS, Federal Perkins, college/university loans from institutional funds. Applicants will be notified of awards on a rolling basis beginning on or about 2/15. Federal Work-study Program available. Institutional employment available. Off-campus job opportunities are good.

FROM THE ADMISSIONS OFFICE

"Students tell us they are getting both a first-rate education and practical experience to help them be competitive upon graduation. Faculty, especially in psychology, marketing, and the sciences, regularly encourage students in their research. Students also do internships at such sites as the White House, Continental Insurance, Estee Lauder, State Street Global Advisors, and Cable News Network. About 90 percent of our graduates go on for advanced degrees or get jobs in their chosen field within six months of graduation. Keeping up with the latest in information technology is easy for our students now that all residence hall rooms have connections to the computer network. Even though the university has six micro-computing laboratories, including one open 24 hours a day, many students find it convenient to use their own PCs to 'surf the 'Net' from their rooms. Small classes, the opportunity to work closely with professors, and the sense of campus community all contribute to the educational experience here. More than 100 student organizations provide lots of opportunity for leadership and involvement in campus life.

"Susquehanna will consider a student's top standardized test score (old or new, SAT or ACT) when evaluating their application. Students are also encouraged to consider SU's alternative to standardized tests, The Write Option. Under The Write Option, a student may submit graded writing samples instead of SAT or ACT scores."

SELECTIVITY

Admissions Rating	**84**
# of applicants	2,464
% of applicants accepted	70
% of acceptees attending	31
# accepting a place on wait list	305
% admitted from wait list	2
# of early decision applicants	150
% accepted early decision	85

FRESHMAN PROFILE

Range SAT Verbal	530-620
Range SAT Math	540-630
**TPR Projected Range SAT Writing*	*580-650*
Minimum Paper TOEFL	550
Minimum Computer Based TOEFL	213
% graduated top 10% of class	35
% graduated top 25% of class	69
% graduated top 50% of class	95

DEADLINES

Early decision application deadline	11/15
Early decision notification	12/15
Regular application deadline	3/1
Regular notification	rolling
Nonfall registration?	yes

APPLICANTS ALSO LOOK AT

AND OFTEN PREFER

Bucknell University
Franklin & Marshall College
Lafayette College
Villanova University

AND SOMETIMES PREFER

Dickinson State University
Gettysburg College
Muhlenberg College
Penn State University Park

AND RARELY PREFER

Elizabethtown College
Lebanon Valley College
Lycoming College

FINANCIAL FACTS

Financial Aid Rating	**77**
Annual tuition	$24,810
Room & Board	$6,840
Books and supplies	$700
Required fees	$315
% frosh rec. need-based scholarship or grant aid	63
% UG rec. need-based scholarship or grant aid	63
% frosh rec. need-based self-help aid	53
% UG rec. need-based self-help aid	53
% frosh rec. any financial aid	92
% UG rec. any financial aid	92
Avg. frosh grant	$14,380
Avg. frosh loan	$3,140
Independent 529 member?	No

Swarthmore College

500 College Avenue, Swarthmore, PA 19081 • Admissions: 610-328-8300 • Fax: 610-328-8580

CAMPUS LIFE

Quality of Life Rating	**87**
Fire Safety Rating	**78**
Type of school	private
Environment	metropolis

STUDENTS

Total undergrad enrollment	1,459
% male/female	48/52
% from out of state	85
% from public high school	57
% live on campus	94
% in (# of) fraternities	7 (2)
% African American	6
% Asian	16
% Caucasian	50
% Hispanic	9
% Native American	1
% international	6
# of countries represented	46

SURVEY SAYS

Small classes
Great library
Campus feels safe
Low cost of living
Political activism is popular

ACADEMICS

Academic Rating	**99**
Calendar	semester
Student/faculty ratio	8:1
Professors interesting rating	96
Professors accessible rating	95
% professors teaching UG courses	100
% classes taught by TAs	0
Most common lab size	fewer than 10 students
Most common regular class size	10-19 students

MOST POPULAR MAJORS

Biology/biological sciences
economics
political science and government

STUDENTS SPEAK OUT

Academics

"A Swarthmore day is a 28-hour day," notes one student, reflecting on the notoriously heavy workload at this elite liberal arts school. Don't let the reputation scare you off, though; as one student explained, "Academics at Swat are hard; everyone knows that coming in. But that doesn't mean they aren't enjoyable." Furthermore, "Swarthmore has a tremendous support network anchored by the professors and administration (as well as other students). When help is needed, there is always someone to turn to." The support is essential, since "the overall stress level here is high from balancing classes, activities, and social life." What do students get in return for their fretting and sweating? Academic freedom, for one; "students at Swarthmore manage to study anything and everything that interests them and may do so [to] whatever depth they choose." They also get "campus resources, including many public computers, electronics in the classroom, and free transportation to nearby campuses and Philadelphia to name a few." And let's not forget professors who "love to really get to know their students. They email you back within an hour, invite you to their homes for dinner, ask you to baby-sit for their kids, and always schedule appointments out of their office hours." Finally, students here enjoy an environment in which "learning is the goal, not the means." One thing they don't get, though, is an easy A; "As one of our T-shirts says: 'Anywhere else it would have been an A.'"

Life

Life at Swarthmore, most here agree, is "intense. Between the challenging classes, extracurricular commitments, and small community, people here tend to stress a lot and complain frequently. However, just about everybody who makes it through to graduation looks back on their four (or five or six) years as the most incredible time in their life." On top of their mountain of schoolwork, students "tend to be very involved in campus life and in a wide range of activities. People can be in student government and active in a minority organization and in a play, all at the same time." Accordingly, students have to get their fun on the run and learn to enjoy little pleasures. "Swatties love to have discussions," writes one student. "They will talk about a subject, everything from the gender politics of *Wuthering Heights* to the imagery of *Lord of the Rings*, for hours on end." They also "love walking around the gorgeous campus and taking walks in the acres of [the] well-kept arboretum around us." When it's time to party, Swatties do it for free: all on-campus activities are paid for out of the student activity fund. Notes one student, "It's quite possible to go months without spending money on things to do." Others, however, warn that "campus events are enjoyable for the first two years, but after that get a little old." That's when students head off campus, not to surrounding Swarthmore, which is "a pretty small suburb," but to Philadelphia. There's a train stop "at the foot of campus" that runs kids straight downtown.

Student Body

The "brilliant, creative, engaging, and always ready for a discussion on anything and everything" students of Swarthmore maintain "a very high level of intellectual and social idealism." This social idealism manifests itself in a pervasive political leftism; "almost everyone is so far left politically/ideologically that the Democratic party seems right-wing," explains one undergrad. Many here are "over-involved. A typical Swattie is involved in a ludicrous number of extracurriculars: clubs, sports, volunteering, committees (besides all the work for class!)." Also, "whether a jock or a partygoer, a published writer or world traveler, everyone at Swarthmore has a little bit of dork deep down inside of them, and it's the common bond between us all." As one student put it, "People are unconcerned with matters of fashion, pop culture, and sometimes hygiene." Most Swatties "come from an upper-middle-class background."

FINANCIAL AID: 610-328-8358 • E-MAIL: ADMISSIONS@SWARTHMORE.EDU • WEBSITE: WWW.SWARTHMORE.EDU

ADMISSIONS

Very important factors considered include: Character/personal qualities, class rank, essays, recommendations, secondary school record, standardized test scores. *Important factors considered include:* Extracurricular activities. *Other factors considered include:* Alumni/ae relation, geographical residence, interview, minority status, talent/ability, volunteer work, work experience. SAT Reasoning and SAT Subject Tests or ACT required. High school diploma or equivalent is not required.

The Inside Word

Swarthmore is as good as they come; among liberal arts colleges there is none better. Candidates face an admissions process that is appropriately demanding and thorough. Even the best qualified of students need to complete their applications with a meticulous approach—during candidate evaluation, serious competition is just another file away. Those who are fortunate enough to be offered admission usually have shown the committee that they have a high level of intellectual curiosity, self-confidence, and motivation.

FINANCIAL AID

Students should submit: FAFSA, institution's own financial aid form, CSS/Financial Aid PROFILE, state aid form, noncustodial (divorced/separated) parents' statement, business/farm supplement, federal tax return, W-2 forms, year-end paycheck stub. Regular filing deadline is 2/15. The Princeton Review suggests that all financial aid forms be submitted as soon as possible after 1/1. *Need-based scholarships/grants offered:* Pell, SEOG, state scholarships/grants, private scholarships, the school's own gift aid. *Loan aid offered:* FFEL Subsidized Stafford, FFEL Unsubsidized Stafford, FFEL PLUS, Federal Perkins, state loans, college/university loans from institutional funds. Applicants will be notified of awards on or about 4/1. Federal Work-study Program available. Institutional employment available. Off-campus job opportunities are good.

FROM THE ADMISSIONS OFFICE

"Swarthmore is a highly selective college of liberal arts and engineering, located 11 miles southwest of Philadelphia. Founded as a coeducational institution in 1864, it is nonsectarian but reflects many traditions and values of its Quaker founders and attracts students who are engaged in the community as well as the classroom. Swarthmore's Honors Program provides an option to study in small seminars during the junior and senior years. A small school by deliberate policy, Swarthmore has an enrollment of about 1,450, with a student/faculty ratio of 8:1. It attracts students from 50 states and 46 countries.

"Applicants must submit either the new SAT plus two SAT Subject Tests or the ACT with Writing component. Scores from older versions of the SAT (pre-March 2005 version) and the ACT are acceptable. For the old SAT, scores must be submitted with the results of three SAT Subject Tests, one of which must be the Writing test."

SELECTIVITY

Admissions Rating	**98**
# of applicants	3,680
% of applicants accepted	38
% of acceptees attending	26
# of early decision applicants	141
% accepted early decision	45

FRESHMAN PROFILE

Range SAT Verbal	680-770
Average SAT Verbal	719
Range SAT Math	670-760
Average SAT Math	711
**TPR Projected Range SAT Writing*	*680-740*
% graduated top 10% of class	89
% graduated top 25% of class	97
% graduated top 50% of class	100

DEADLINES

Early decision application deadline	11/15
Early decision notification	12/15
Regular application deadline	1/1
Regular notification	4/1
Nonfall registration?	no

FINANCIAL FACTS

Financial Aid Rating	**97**
Annual tuition	$29,782
Room & Board	$9,314
Books and supplies	$982
Required fees	$312
% frosh rec. need-based scholarship or grant aid	53
% UG rec. need-based scholarship or grant aid	48
% frosh rec. need-based self-help aid	52
% UG rec. need-based self-help aid	46
% frosh rec. any financial aid	53
% UG rec. any financial aid	51
Avg. frosh grant	$24,421
Avg. frosh loan	$2,047
Independent 529 member?	No

SWEET BRIAR COLLEGE

PO BOX B, SWEET BRIAR, VA 24595 • ADMISSIONS: 434-381-6142 • FAX: 434-381-6152

CAMPUS LIFE

Quality of Life Rating	**89**
Fire Safety Rating	**60**
Type of school	private
Environment	rural

STUDENTS

Total undergrad enrollment	542
% male/female	0/100
% from out of state	59
% from public high school	62
% live on campus	90
% African American	2
% Asian	2
% Caucasian	85
% Hispanic	2
% international	3
# of countries represented	14

SURVEY SAYS

Small classes
No one cheats
Lab facilities are great
Great computer facilities
Great library
Students are friendly
Dorms are like palaces
Students are happy
Frats and sororities are unpopular or nonexistent
Student government is popular

ACADEMICS

Academic Rating	**94**
Calendar	semester
Student/faculty ratio	7:1
Professors interesting rating	97
Professors accessible rating	98
% professors teaching UG courses	100
% classes taught by TAs	0
Most common regular class size	fewer than 10 students

MOST POPULAR MAJORS

Biology/biological sciences
international relations and affairs
psychology

STUDENTS SPEAK OUT

Academics

Students at this small, all-women's liberal arts school tell us that "Sweet Briar is about doing it all: playing a varsity sport, holding a leadership position in ten different clubs, having a boyfriend, having three campus jobs, and earning an amazing GPA, all while wearing pearls and a pink bow in your hair." With a few more than 700 undergraduates, Sweet Briar can afford to lavish individual attention on each student and to provide leadership and research opportunities to practically everyone who wants them. Students boast that "professors should really be called 'mentors.' With their real world experience and knowledge, that's what they are." They also tell us that guaranteed small class sizes mean "there is no not doing your homework. It keeps you on your toes and encourages you to become more disciplined." A deep and broad-ranging set of general education requirements means all students receive a solid grounding in literature, philosophy, social science, mathematics, ethics, foreign language, and physical education; nearly all majors conclude with a capstone senior seminar. Undergraduates love the school's honor code, which "really works. By pledging your work, you are afforded so much more flexibility than having to take proctored exams." They also speak approvingly of the school's study abroad program, the "connections with alumnae to obtain awesome internships," and the fact that "being [in an] all-women [school] allows us to focus more on our studies."

Life

Tradition plays a central role in the life of Sweet Briar College, where "every month there is a school-wide activity involving some sort of tradition." Women at Sweet Briar have enjoyed step singing, a lantern bearing ceremony, Founders' Day, the 'Hitching Post Fight' (a mock battle between first- and second-year students), and 'Tap Clubs' (Sweet Briar's version of sororities) for many years. Students tell us that "the more involved you are in campus events and leadership positions, the more fun you will have here at Sweet Briar." The college "gets fantastic speakers such as Sally Ride, Jane Goodall, and Salman Rushdie," as well as "bands about twice a month, comedians, game nights, movies, and other events on campus." One student observes, "Sweet Briar's strength is its flexibility. Any student from anywhere can find something they love about this place. If you're an outdoors person, you'll be in heaven. If you are more of a city girl, there is all manner of shopping and clubbing within thirty minutes of driving. Everyone can find a niche at SBC." Most campus activity takes place during the week, since "for fun, we party off-campus on weekends. Often we go to our brother school, Hampden-Sydney, or to University of Virginia. Sometimes we go to Washington and Lee or Virginia Tech. But on weekends no one stays on campus, and few people go into Lynchburg for serious fun." The college's campus "is beautiful and quickly feels like home rather than a school." The dorms "are gorgeous as well."

Student Body

"Sweet Briar is often portrayed as the perfect Southern all-women's school, where all the students are here after 'finishing school' to find a husband," but that's not an entirely accurate portrait. It's true that many students "arrive looking as if they could have come out of the 'Preppy Handbook,' but Sweet Briar changes them." One undergraduate explains, "Freshman year most women are cookie-cutter: from a wealthy family, have a 'preppy' look, get up for class an hour in advance to put makeup on and get involved in the same things. But with each semester the individual becomes more celebrated, and women find that they [can] go their own way and still be part of a group." The school is working on increasing diversity; reports one student, "Right now the student body consists mainly of middle-class, Christian, Caucasian women, but that is changing. The president's initiative to make Sweet Briar more diverse is embraced by the entire community."

FINANCIAL AID: 434-381-6156 • E-MAIL: ADMISSIONS@SBC.EDU • WEBSITE: WWW.SBC.EDU

ADMISSIONS

Very important factors considered include: Secondary school record. *Important factors considered include:* Class rank, essays, interview, recommendations, standardized test scores. *Other factors considered include:* Alumni/ae relation, character/personal qualities, extracurricular activities, minority status, talent/ability, volunteer work, work experience. SAT Reasoning or ACT required. TOEFL required of all international applicants. High school diploma is required, and GED is accepted. *Academic units required:* 4 English, 3 math, 2 science (3 science lab), 2 foreign language, 3 social studies. *Academic units recommended:* 4 English, 4 math, 4 science (3 science lab), 4 foreign language, 4 social studies.

The Inside Word

A small applicant pool tempers selectivity greatly but also allows the admissions committee to take a longer look at most candidates than is typical in college admission. Despite the small applicant pool, candidates are usually well-qualified academically.

FINANCIAL AID

Students should submit: FAFSA, noncustodial (divorced/separated) parents' statement, business/farm supplement. Regular filing deadline is 3/1. The Princeton Review suggests that all financial aid forms be submitted as soon as possible after 1/1. *Need-based scholarships/grants offered:* Pell, SEOG, state scholarships/grants, private scholarships, the school's own gift aid. *Loan aid offered:* Direct Subsidized Stafford, Direct Unsubsidized Stafford, Direct PLUS, Federal Perkins, college/university loans from institutional funds. Applicants will be notified of awards on a rolling basis beginning on or about 3/1. Federal Work-study Program available. Institutional employment available. Off-campus job opportunities are good.

FROM THE ADMISSIONS OFFICE

"The woman who applies to Sweet Briar is mature and far-sighted enough to know what she wants from her college experience. She is intellectually adventuresome, more willing to explore new fields, and more open to challenging her boundaries. Sweet Briar attracts the ambitious, confident woman who enjoys being immersed not only in a first-rate academic program, but in a variety of meaningful activities outside the classroom. Our students take charge and revel in their accomplishments. This attitude follows graduates, enabling them to compete confidently in the corporate world and in graduate school.

"Applicants for fall 2006 are encouraged but not required to take the new SAT or the ACT with Writing component. Beginning with applicants for the 2007–2008 academic year, Sweet Briar will require either the new SAT or the ACT with the Writing component."

SELECTIVITY

Admissions Rating	**83**
# of applicants	495
% of applicants accepted	79
% of acceptees attending	43
# of early decision applicants	56
% accepted early decision	97

FRESHMAN PROFILE

Range SAT Verbal	530-645
Average SAT Verbal	586
Range SAT Math	500-610
Average SAT Math	548
**TPR Projected Range SAT Writing*	*580-670*
Range ACT Composite	22-26
Average ACT Composite	23
Minimum Paper TOEFL	550
Minimum Computer Based TOEFL	213
Average HS GPA	3.4
% graduated top 10% of class	24
% graduated top 25% of class	47
% graduated top 50% of class	90

DEADLINES

Early decision application deadline	12/1
Early decision notification	12/15
Regular application deadline	2/1
Regular notification	3/1
Nonfall registration?	yes

APPLICANTS ALSO LOOK AT AND OFTEN PREFER

College of William and Mary
Mount Holyoke College
Randolph—Macon Woman's College

AND SOMETIMES PREFER

Hollins University
University of Richmond
Vanderbilt University

FINANCIAL FACTS

Financial Aid Rating	**93**
Annual tuition	$22,230
Room & Board	$9,030
Books and supplies	$600
Required fees	$200
% frosh rec. need-based scholarship or grant aid	54
% UG rec. need-based scholarship or grant aid	51
% frosh rec. need-based self-help aid	50
% UG rec. need-based self-help aid	48
% frosh rec. any financial aid	72
% UG rec. any financial aid	65
Avg. frosh grant	$13,154
Avg. frosh loan	$3,675
Independent 529 member?	Yes

SYRACUSE UNIVERSITY

201 TOLLEY, ADMINISTRATION BUILDING, SYRACUSE, NY 13244 • ADMISSIONS: 315-443-3611 • FAX: 315-443-4226

CAMPUS LIFE

Quality of Life Rating	**64**
Fire Safety Rating	**97**
Type of school	private
Environment	city

STUDENTS

Total undergrad enrollment	10,750
% male/female	44/56
% from out of state	55
% from public high school	80
% live on campus	73
% in (# of) fraternities	12 (22)
% in (# of) sororities	16 (19)
% African American	6
% Asian	6
% Caucasian	71
% Hispanic	4
% international	3
# of countries represented	65

SURVEY SAYS

Great library
Everyone loves the Orange
Frats and sororities dominate social scene
Student publications are popular
Lots of beer drinking
Hard liquor is popular

ACADEMICS

Academic Rating	**83**
Calendar	semester
Student/faculty ratio	12:1
Professors interesting rating	71
Professors accessible rating	74
% professors teaching UG courses	95
% classes taught by TAs	6
Most common lab size	20-29 students
Most common regular class size	fewer than 10 students

MOST POPULAR MAJORS

Marketing/marketing management
political science and government
psychology

STUDENTS SPEAK OUT

Academics

At Syracuse University (SU), the spotlight shines on internal schools with uncontestable national reputations. The Newhouse School of Communications and The Maxwell School of Citizenship & Public Affairs are two such places. Students enrolled in other top departments, such as religion, information studies, bioengineering, and architecture, beg to make their voice heard and direct our attention to "a number of specialized areas that many people overlook." A student in the "extremely prestigious" art program tells us, "Work is very independent, and attention is focused on technical improvement and process." Consistently, no matter a student's school allegiance, professors are hailed for their dedication, accessibility, and plain old teaching savvy. The university demonstrates "dedication and attention to all undergraduates," and students enrolled in the honors program enjoy access to top faculty, smaller classes, and early registration. Many students report "strong connections with faculty, in class, outside of class, and working together on projects." Complaints arise surrounding certain "student teachers," but for the most part teacher assistants have reputations for being "very devoted to helping [students] understand the material." Students rely on "word-of-mouth to find the best classes." Popular opinion says the environment "is not big on intellectualism," but most students feel stimulated during their time at Syracuse and graduate as "independent thinkers."

Life

Let it snow—Syracuse students don't care! Yes, much of that cold manna from the heavens falls on Syracuse town, but as one student puts it, "there's always a ton of stuff going on around campus: concerts, movies, speakers, etc." For those who do like to play outside, "Skiing is popular." Otherwise, "people stick to indoor activities—like partying." At Syracuse "the Greek scene is hot," while hordes of students descend upon the Marshall Street bar and restaurant scene. This, along with athletics, galvanizes student experiences. Orangemen basketball—the 2003 national champions—draws rowdy crowds, as do football and lacrosse games. When the weather gets them down, students fortify their spirits with "bowling, hiking, shopping downtown, and taking day trips to local lakes." One student pithily notes, "there really is everything available to you here; transportation is as easy as pie, policies flexible, and friends of plenty." Crouse Hill attracts a late-night sledding crowd. "Quilting groups" and service fraternities offer more wholesome activities. Students participate in the "thriving visual and performing arts community" or the Daily Orange, the popular student newspaper thought by many people to be "the best institution on campus." "A great social life is available here to any student, no matter what he or she is interested in." The university's combination of solid academics and opportunities for amusement results in "the true college experience."

Student Body

Undergraduates have many different opinions about what the typical student at Syracuse is like. Many students say that the most visible group "comes from a lot of money and enjoys partying." Others note a seemingly disproportionate number of Long Islanders and "Soprano country" kids. But the numbers don't lie; Syracuse has strong diversity numbers, both ethnic and geographic. Although inherent diversity exists, students note that, "no one communicates outside their own group." The university tries to facilitate interaction, however, with "good programs for sexual orientation, gender, and racial equality." A senior comments, "There seems to be a high level of openness and no real pressure to conform to any popular standard." One student says, "I lived on a floor with hippies, frat guys, and architecture students, and it was still calm." Another student adds, "We're a melting pot of aspiring youth stuck in winter. We're like, 'Why not just all accept each other?'"

FINANCIAL AID: 315-443-1513 • E-MAIL: ORANGE@SYR.EDU • WEBSITE: WWW.SYRACUSE.EDU

ADMISSIONS

Very important factors considered include: Character/personal qualities, class rank, essays, interview, recommendations, secondary school record, standardized test scores, talent/ability. *Important factors considered include:* Extracurricular activities. *Other factors considered include:* Minority status, volunteer work, work experience. SAT Reasoning or ACT required. TOEFL required of all international applicants. High school diploma is required, and GED is accepted. *Academic units required:* 4 English, 3 math, 3 science (3 science lab), 2 foreign language, 3 social studies, 5 academic electives. *Academic units recommended:* 4 English, 3 math, 3 science (3 science lab), 3 foreign language, 3 social studies, 5 academic electives.

The Inside Word

Syracuse is a nationally recognized university which draws a large applicant pool. At the same time, it has reduced the size of the freshman class, so the university has gotten more selective over the past few years. Most above-average students should still be strong candidates; although many weaker students are also able to benefit from Syracuse's individualized admissions process, they must show true promise in order to have a shot. Candidates for the Newhouse School will encounter even greater competition for admission.

FINANCIAL AID

Students should submit: FAFSA, CSS/Financial Aid PROFILE, noncustodial (divorced/separated) parents' statement, business/farm supplement. Regular filing deadline is 2/1. The Princeton Review suggests that all financial aid forms be submitted as soon as possible after 1/1. *Need-based scholarships/grants offered:* Pell, SEOG, state scholarships/grants, the school's own gift aid. *Loan aid offered:* FFEL Subsidized Stafford, FFEL Unsubsidized Stafford, FFEL PLUS, Federal Perkins. Applicants will be notified of awards on or about 4/1.

FROM THE ADMISSIONS OFFICE

"Syracuse University is set on a beautiful residential campus that encompasses more than 200 acres and 170 buildings. Situated on a hill, overlooking downtown Syracuse, the school gives students the opportunity to enjoy the traditional college environment while realizing the social and recreational opportunities of a medium-size city.

"Syracuse University is committed to priorities that place its students first and foremost in importance. Small classes, intensive advising, emphasis on transition to college in the first year, and active learning characterize a systematic approach to assuring a productive teaching and learning environment. Improved classroom opportunities through smaller classes provide students with close attention from faculty.

"In virtually every aspect of students' lives at Syracuse, choices abound. The range of courses available, opportunities for study abroad and internships, the scope of residential living possibilities, the array of co-curricular and extracurricular clubs and organizations (there are nearly 300), and the opportunity to participate in the Honors Program makes SU an exciting place to attend. Students at Syracuse University have the choice of more than 200 undergraduate majors and nearly 70 undergraduate minors. Syracuse combines the best characteristics of a research institution with a traditional focus on the highest quality teaching, advising, and mentoring. It is a student-centered research university and is committed to giving students the very best educational experiences available.

"Freshman applicants for fall 2006 will be required to take the new SAT (or ACT with the Writing component). The new SAT Verbal and Math sections will be used in the admissions decisions, since they differ from the old version. There will not be considerable weight given to the Writing section."

SELECTIVITY

Admissions Rating	**91**
# of applicants	16,019
% of applicants accepted	59
% of acceptees attending	28
# accepting a place on wait list	883
% admitted from wait list	18
# of early decision applicants	477
% accepted early decision	63

FRESHMAN PROFILE

Range SAT Verbal	570-650
Range SAT Math	580-670
**TPR Projected Range SAT Writing*	*610-670*
Minimum Paper TOEFL	550
Minimum Computer Based TOEFL	213
Average HS GPA	3.6
% graduated top 10% of class	44
% graduated top 25% of class	80
% graduated top 50% of class	98

DEADLINES

Early decision application deadline	11/15
Early decision notification	12/31
Regular application deadline	1/1
Regular notification	3/15
Nonfall registration?	yes

APPLICANTS ALSO LOOK AT AND SOMETIMES PREFER

Boston University
Cornell University
New York University
Penn State University Park
University of Maryland—College Park

FINANCIAL FACTS

Financial Aid Rating	**86**
Annual tuition	$25,720
Room & Board	$9,970
Books and supplies	$1,190
Required fees	$1,112
% frosh rec. need-based scholarship or grant aid	54
% UG rec. need-based scholarship or grant aid	52
% frosh rec. need-based self-help aid	51
% UG rec. need-based self-help aid	51
% frosh rec. any financial aid	75
% UG rec. any financial aid	75
Avg. frosh grant	$14,588
Avg. frosh loan	$4,100
Independent 529 member?	Yes

TCU

Office of Admissions, TCU Box 297013, Fort Worth, TX 76129 • Admissions: 817-257-7490 • Fax: 817-257-7268

CAMPUS LIFE

Quality of Life Rating	**87**
Fire Safety Rating	**89**
Type of school	private
Affiliation	Disciples of Christ
Environment	metropolis

STUDENTS

Total undergrad enrollment	7,024
% male/female	40/60
% from out of state	20
% from public high school	95
% live on campus	44
% in (# of) fraternities	34 (13)
% in (# of) sororities	36 (16)
% African American	5
% Asian	2
% Caucasian	79
% Hispanic	6
% Native American	1
% international	4
# of countries represented	75

SURVEY SAYS

Small classes
Great computer facilities
Athletic facilities are great
Students love Fort Worth, TX
Great off-campus food
Frats and sororities dominate social scene
Lots of beer drinking

ACADEMICS

Academic Rating	**80**
Calendar	semester
Student/faculty ratio	15:1
Professors interesting rating	83
Professors accessible rating	83
% professors teaching UG courses	97
% classes taught by TAs	2
Most common lab size	20-29 students
Most common regular class size	10-19 students

MOST POPULAR MAJORS

Advertising
Business administration/management
communications studies/speech communication and rhetoric

STUDENTS SPEAK OUT

Academics

TCU, students tell us, "is a medium-size school that lets everyone feel like they're in a community college environment." It's a university large enough to provide students with excellent research opportunities, yet small enough that most professors and administrators have open-door policies. Reports one student, "Most of the professors here treat us more like equals than students; it's nice to have professors who don't look down on you because you're young." Similarly, administrators "almost always have open doors, so students can go in and chat with them." TCU is not without its big-school problems, however; several students here complain that "the advisors are not totally sure what they are doing, and I hear a lot of students are not sure what classes to take, and are misinformed about some curriculum courses." For serious students, however, TCU's only major drawback is the student body; writes one disappointed undergrad, "Most people are not thinking much at all except about the next test. There is not a strong forum for exchanging ideas, and it's not cultivated outside the classroom." Adds another ambitious scholar, "TCU is a party school. The majority of the students could care less about learning. [They] are mostly concerned about what party they are going to on Friday night." Opportunities for the highly motivated exist in the honors program ("pushed me to new levels of studying and learning") and the study abroad program ("Studying abroad was perhaps one of the most eye-opening and amazing experiences I [had] in my years at TCU. I went to Australia and learned so much about myself just by taking myself out of the 'TCU Bubble'").

Life

"TCU is all about Greek Life," students here agree; the school "has an overwhelming Greek population that permeates and sadly sometimes overshadows the actual education aspect of the school." As one student put it, "If you are interested in Greek life, then TCU is definitely the place for you. Even though statistics show that only 35 to 40 percent of students are Greek, the reality is that it feels as if 90 to 95 percent are. They always have mixers, fundraisers, and many other functions that make them very visible on campus." Be forewarned that "there is huge pressure to be a part of Greek recruitment as a freshman. [Those] who don't join any organizations often feel really isolated. It's all about social connections here." Because "Greek housing is located in a completely separate area of campus and is far away from the other residence halls," the Greeks tend to socialize only with each other. Fortunately, there's Fort Worth, which is "great for going out and exploring. There are great places to eat and shop and even some great places to go and enjoy the culture. We love the stockyards and Billy Bob's." There's also an active bar scene right across the street from campus; also nearby "you can find the zoo, botanical gardens, or a nearby strip of shops where students can go and hang out." A little further down the road is Dallas. Of course, there's always TCU sports and the home team Horned Frogs; notes one student, "Being in Texas, everyone rallies around the football team. Games are a big deal, and lots of people go."

Student Body

"Everyone here is good-looking and never seems to go to class." The typical student is "rich, white, and Greek;" "conservative, but friendly;" and "very marriage-oriented; we joke about obtaining a 'Mrs.' degree." Alternative students, "the ones who wear dreads or skater clothes or have funky-dyed hair, all band together. All ten of them." Diversity at TCU arrives primarily in the form of international students, who "mostly associate among themselves." Most students are devout Christians who manage to reconcile their beliefs with the school's vigorous party scene.

FINANCIAL AID: 817-257-7858 • E-MAIL: FROGMAIL@TCU.EDU • WEBSITE: WWW.TCU.EDU

ADMISSIONS

Very important factors considered include: Character/personal qualities, class rank, essays, recommendations, secondary school record, standardized test scores. *Important factors considered include:* Extracurricular activities, geographical residence, minority status, religious affiliation/commitment, talent/ability, volunteer work, work experience. *Other factors considered include:* Alumni/ae relation, interview. SAT Reasoning or ACT required. TOEFL required of all international applicants. High school diploma is required, and GED is not accepted. *Academic units required:* 4 English, 3 math, 3 science, 2 foreign language, 3 social studies, 2 academic electives. *Academic units recommended:* 4 English, 4 math, 4 science, 4 foreign language, 4 social studies, 4 academic electives.

The Inside Word

The most important element of the admissions process at TCU is finding academically, well-rounded students. Most applicants are admitted, notwithstanding TCU's challenging academic standards and increasing selectivity.

FINANCIAL AID

Students should submit: FAFSA, institution's own financial aid form. Regular filing deadline is 5/1. The Princeton Review suggests that all financial aid forms be submitted as soon as possible after 1/1. *Need-based scholarships/grants offered:* Pell, SEOG, state scholarships/grants, private scholarships, the school's own gift aid. *Loan aid offered:* FFEL Subsidized Stafford, FFEL Unsubsidized Stafford, FFEL PLUS, Federal Perkins, Federal Nursing, state loans. Applicants will be notified of awards on a rolling basis beginning on or about 3/1. Federal Work-study Program available. Institutional employment available. Off-campus job opportunities are excellent.

FROM THE ADMISSIONS OFFICE

"TCU is a major teaching and research university with the feel of a small college. The friendly campus community welcomes new students before classes begin, at Frog Camp, where students find three days of fun meeting new friends, learning campus traditions, and serving the community. The TCU experience continues with opportunities like freshman seminars that are small classes with top faculty; cutting-edge technology and equipment such as Internet access in every residence hall room and major classroom and lab upgrades; a liberal arts and sciences core curriculum; and real-life application through faculty-directed research, group projects, and internships. While TCU faculty members are recognized for research, their main focus is on teaching and mentoring students. The historic relationship to the Christian Church (Disciples of Christ) means that instead of imposing a particular viewpoint, TCU encourages students to consider and follow their own beliefs. The university's mission—to educate individuals to think and act as ethical leaders and responsible citizens in the global community—influences everything from course work to study abroad to the way Horned Frogs act and interact. From National Merit Scholars to those just now realizing their academic potential, TCU attracts and serves students who are learning to change the world.

"TCU will accept either the old or new SAT (or the ACT with or without Writing component in lieu of both) in admission and scholarship processes. Students who submit results from the older exam will not be required to submit a new SAT. The Writing sections will be considered alongside the TCU essay."

SELECTIVITY

Admissions Rating	**84**
# of applicants	8,061
% of applicants accepted	64
% of acceptees attending	31
# accepting a place on wait list	748
% admitted from wait list	19

FRESHMAN PROFILE

Range SAT Verbal	530-630
Range SAT Math	550-640
**TPR Projected Range SAT Writing*	*580-650*
Range ACT Composite	23-28
Minimum Paper TOEFL	550
Minimum Computer Based TOEFL	213
% graduated top 10% of class	32
% graduated top 25% of class	68
% graduated top 50% of class	95

DEADLINES

Regular application deadline	2/15
Regular notification	4/1
Nonfall registration?	yes

FINANCIAL FACTS

Financial Aid Rating	**75**
Annual tuition	$21,280
Room & Board	$6,980
Books and supplies	$810
Required fees	$40
% frosh rec. need-based scholarship or grant aid	40
% UG rec. need-based scholarship or grant aid	38
% frosh rec. need-based self-help aid	32
% UG rec. need-based self-help aid	35
% frosh rec. any financial aid	78
% UG rec. any financial aid	72
Avg. frosh grant	$10,277
Avg. frosh loan	$13,460
Independent 529 member?	Yes

TEMPLE UNIVERSITY

1801 NORTH BROAD STREET, PHILADELPHIA, PA 19122-6096 • ADMISSIONS: 215-204-7200 • FAX: 215-204-5694

CAMPUS LIFE

Quality of Life Rating	**83**
Fire Safety Rating	**60**
Type of school	public
Environment	metropolis

STUDENTS

Total undergrad enrollment	22,780
% male/female	43/57
% from out of state	23
% from public high school	79
% live on campus	22
% in (# of) fraternities	1 (13)
% in (# of) sororities	1 (12)
% African American	20
% Asian	8
% Caucasian	57
% Hispanic	3
% international	3
# of countries represented	124

SURVEY SAYS

Great computer facilities
Great library
Athletic facilities are great
Diverse student types on campus
Great off-campus food
Campus feels safe
Lots of beer drinking
(Almost) everyone smokes

ACADEMICS

Academic Rating	**78**
Calendar	semester
Student/faculty ratio	17:1
Professors interesting rating	72
Professors accessible rating	73
% classes taught by TAs	0
Most common lab size	20-29 students
Most common regular class size	10-19 students

MOST POPULAR MAJORS

Elementary education and teaching
journalism
psychology

STUDENTS SPEAK OUT

Academics

Temple students love their school for its ability to integrate "a good education with significant life experiences." The school has earned a "great scholastic reputation" while prioritizing "real-life, hands-on experience with internships, co-ops, and experiential learning that prepare you for life beyond college." Many students agree that Temple helps students "develop thinking skills, ask questions, and wake up to see what the reality is." Professors are praised for "incorporating things from outside of the classroom into the lectures and discussions." Instructors both "know their material" and find "effective ways to relate it to the students." The University's heterogeneous student body is reflected in the faculty, "a diverse, intelligent group" that "finds delight in sharing their knowledge with us." In particular, students gush about the professors and classes in the honors program. Honors classes "tend to be smaller, more interesting, and contain people who seem to actually enjoy learning." These courses provide "an atmosphere where discussions create more learning than a lecture would." The "extremely supportive" professors involved in the program "go out of their way to keep in contact with the students." For those not enrolled in the honors program, "course selection and advising can be difficult." One student values that Temple "can also be very interesting and experimental with its class offerings." As far as logistics go, one respondent writes, " I have had no problem contacting [the] administration when I need help with a problem." Though a few students say "The bureaucracy sucks," most agree that "the education can be magic," not to mention affordable.

Life

Temple's urban location largely defines the campus' feel. Though the school organizes "free good food, movies, guest speakers, parties, festivals, and cultural bus trips," most students choose to make their own fun in surrounding Philadelphia, "which is easy because we are directly connected to public transportation." Undergraduates agree, "From theater and museums to shops, clubs, and cafés, Philly has a lot to do." Students just have to "be able to take care of themselves in the city" since the surrounding area is described as "dodgy." One respondent articulates both sides of the issue: "Temple's main strength is the fact that it is in Philadelphia, but this takes away much of the close-knit campus feel." Certain issues do bring people together: "Political activism has become more popular recently, especially concerns over the government and foreign affairs." Fraternities pitch in on the weekend social scene, throwing parties attended mainly by underclassmen and those who live on campus. Commuters claim to have a "completely different life" than their resident counterparts, marked mainly by parking headaches.

Student Body

One student sums it up when she writes, "We call it Diversity University." Repeatedly, surveys emphasize that the undergraduate population includes students from every imaginable racial, ethnic, religious, and class background. A few unifying factors do emerge: "A typical student is a fairly hardworking, goal-oriented, middle-class American looking to carve out a future for his or herself." But as soon as you think you have a beat on it, someone says, "It is impossible to define a typical student because Temple is full of every different type of person." Students appreciate the diversity, claiming that the mix of "various backgrounds challenges opinions and feeds into active class discussions." In this "huge melting pot," respondents claim, "everyone's differences become their connection to other people." Certain students shatter the utopian image by telling us, "Most people seem to stick to their own groups, dictated by either major, race, [or] economic status." Other people call the campus "annoyingly anonymous" because it is "very much a commuter school." Despite these minor grumbles, Temple students predominantly "look past the stereotypes" and accept their peers "for whom they are and what they are trying to achieve."

Temple University

Financial Aid: 215-204-8760 • E-mail: tuadm@mail.temple.edu • Website: www.temple.edu

ADMISSIONS

Very important factors considered include: Class rank, secondary school record. *Important factors considered include:* Standardized test scores. *Other factors considered include:* Alumni/ae relation, character/personal qualities, essays, extracurricular activities, recommendations, talent/ability, volunteer work, work experience. SAT Reasoning or ACT required. TOEFL required of all international applicants. High school diploma is required, and GED is accepted. *Academic units required:* 4 English, 3 math, 2 science (1 science lab), 2 foreign language, 2 social studies, 1 history, 1 academic elective. *Academic units recommended:* 4 English, 4 math, 3 science (2 science lab), 2 foreign language, 2 social studies, 2 history, 3 academic electives.

The Inside Word

Nearly 50 percent of Temple's applicants are from outside Pennsylvania, 25 percent are from the Philadelphia area, and 25 percent from elsewhere in Pennsylvania. Admissions standards are moderately selective in general (60 percent acceptance rate), but candidates for the College of Music, in particular, face a rigorous review.

FINANCIAL AID

Students should submit: FAFSA. The Princeton Review suggests that all financial aid forms be submitted as soon as possible after 1/1. *Need-based scholarships/grants offered:* Pell, SEOG, state scholarships/grants, private scholarships, the school's own gift aid, Federal Nursing scholarships. *Loan aid offered:* FFEL Subsidized Stafford, FFEL Unsubsidized Stafford, FFEL PLUS, Federal Perkins, Federal Nursing, college/university loans from institutional funds. Applicants will be notified of awards on a rolling basis beginning on or about 2/15. Federal Work-study Program available. Institutional employment available. Off-campus job opportunities are excellent.

FROM THE ADMISSIONS OFFICE

"Temple combines the academic resources and intellectual stimulation of a large research university with the intimacy of a small college. The university experienced record growth in attracting new students from all 50 states and over 125 countries: up 60 percent in three years. Students choose from 130 undergraduate majors. Special academic programs include honors, learning communities for first-year undergraduates, co-op education, and study abroad. Temple has seven regional campuses, including Main Campus and the Health Sciences Center in historic Philadelphia, suburban Temple University, Ambler, and overseas campuses in Tokyo and Rome. Main Campus is home to the Tuttleman Learning Center, with 1,000 computer stations linked to Paley Library. The Center is a hub for emerging learning technologies and is designed for the high-tech students of today and tomorrow. The Liacouras Center is a state-of-the-art entertainment, recreation, and sports complex that hosts concerts, plays, trade shows, and college and professional athletics. It also includes the Independence Blue Cross Student Recreation Center, a major fitness facility for students now and in the future. Students can also take advantage of the new Student Fieldhouse. The university has constructed two new dorms, built to meet an unprecedented demand for main campus housing.

"Applicants for fall 2006 are required to take the new version of the SAT (or the ACT with writing), but students may submit scores from the old SAT as well. The best Verbal and Math scores from either test will be considered."

SELECTIVITY

Admissions Rating	**82**
# of applicants	16,681
% of applicants accepted	63
% of acceptees attending	36

FRESHMAN PROFILE

Range SAT Verbal	490-590
Range SAT Math	500-600
**TPR Projected Range SAT Writing*	*550-620*
Range ACT Composite	19-24
Minimum Paper TOEFL	525
Minimum Computer Based TOEFL	195
Average HS GPA	3.24
% graduated top 10% of class	17
% graduated top 25% of class	50
% graduated top 50% of class	90

DEADLINES

Regular application deadline	4/1
Regular notification	rolling
Nonfall registration?	yes

APPLICANTS ALSO LOOK AT

AND OFTEN PREFER

Lehigh University, Penn State University Park, University of Pennsylvania, University of Pittsburgh—Pittsburgh Campus

AND SOMETIMES PREFER

Drexel University, New York University, , Rutgers, The State University of New Jersey—New Brunswick/Piscataway Campus, Saint Joseph's University (PA), Villanova University

AND RARELY PREFER

Gettysburg College, LaSalle University, West Chester University of Pennsylvania, Widener University

FINANCIAL FACTS

Financial Aid Rating	**78**
Annual in-state tuition	$8,622
Annual out-of-state tuition	$15,788
Room & Board	$7,522
Books and supplies	$800
Required fees	$480
% frosh rec. need-based scholarship or grant aid	70
% UG rec. need-based scholarship or grant aid	67
% frosh rec. need-based self-help aid	60
% UG rec. need-based self-help aid	58
% frosh rec. any financial aid	86
% UG rec. any financial aid	89
Avg. frosh grant	$5,010
Avg. frosh loan	$2,778
Independent 529 member?	No

Texas A&M University—College Station

Admissions Counseling, College Station, TX 77843-1265 • Admissions: 979-845-3741 • Fax: 979-847-8737

CAMPUS LIFE

Quality of Life Rating	**94**
Fire Safety Rating	**77**
Type of school	public
Environment	town

STUDENTS

Total undergrad enrollment	35,605
% male/female	51/49
% from out of state	3
% live on campus	25
% in (# of) fraternities	3 (33)
% in (# of) sororities	6 (23)
% African American	2
% Asian	3
% Caucasian	82
% Hispanic	10
% Native American	1
% international	1
# of countries represented	128

SURVEY SAYS

Great computer facilities
Great library
Athletic facilities are great
Students are friendly
Everyone loves the Aggies
Lots of beer drinking

ACADEMICS

Academic Rating	**73**
Calendar	semester
Student/faculty ratio	20:1
Professors interesting rating	69
Professors accessible rating	71
% professors teaching UG courses	75
% classes taught by TAs	25
Most common lab size	10-19 students
Most common regular class size	20-29 students

MOST POPULAR MAJORS

Biological and physical sciences
multi/interdisciplinary studies
operations management and supervision

STUDENTS SPEAK OUT

Academics

For most students who attend this icon of the Lone Star State, Texas A&M (TAMU) is more than a school. It's a way of life. Sure, students seek out and receive a solid education and a respected degree, but students choose this school because they know and love the many deep-rooted traditions that make up A&M culture. They're given to pronouncements like "Texas A&M is all about fidelity, faith, family, and learning," and if they have any sense of irony about their devotion to alma mater, they sure don't reveal it in surveys. Student pride extends to academic offerings as well. One student explains, "We have some of the premier undergraduate and graduate programs in engineering, business, and the sciences. It is pretty well known that an A&M degree counts for something." The curriculum challenges students. One undergraduate warns, "Don't expect to whiz through just because it is a public university. It's easy to fall behind." Students also point out that "help is always readily available. You just have to take advantage of it." Because A&M is a research institution, "the administration is focused entirely on research initiatives and budget constraints. And the faculty is largely committed to research and considers teaching an imposition." However, there are plenty of professors dedicated to teaching. One student tells us, "I have often had professors with classes of hundreds go the extra mile to get into contact with students. They freely give out their phone numbers, telling us to call anytime we have a problem."

Life

The numerous traditions at A&M include Aggie football, saying "howdy," Midnight Yell, Replant, Aggie baseball, dorm unity, and Big Event. If you're not already familiar with most of these, perhaps A&M is not the school for you. There is a minority of students who find these traditions "stupid and annoying," and they admit they "have a hard time fitting in." Thursday night kicks off the A&M weekend, during which "most everyone goes out to bars and clubs to drink and [to have] a good time." The schedule is slightly amended during the fall to accommodate Aggie football. One student explains, "The whole fall semester is encompassed by the football schedule. Friday nights are devoted to Midnight Yell [and] Saturdays for the games. People travel to games at other schools." Campus life also offers "lots of concerts and lots of clubs," but that's about it. One student says, "College Station is notorious for having a university nearly the size of the University of Texas in Austin, yet a city that seems to lack 'things to do.'" Students don't seem to mind: "It seems that people at A&M are almost always visibly happy, except on exam days."

Student Body

"Most everyone at TAMU—College Station is Caucasian, has strong Texas pride, goes to country bars on Thursday nights, and has a fair amount of ambition in school." Although there is "a large Indian/Pakistani and Asian population in engineering and architecture, as well as other majors," among the more than 44,000 students, most of the student body is made up of Texan, white, Christian, and conservative people. And we do mean very conservative. One of the campus's few liberals writes, "Texas A&M's major weakness is the 'George W. Bush is God' mentality. To say this school leans to the right is a drastic understatement." It takes a special type of student to fit in—just as it takes a special and different type of student to fit in at the University of Texas at Austin, for example. For the right student, "Aggieland" is a little slice of heaven. One student says, "Just by taking a brief walk through campus and having a total stranger say 'howdy' to you, you can feel the welcoming spirit and pride in tradition that we Aggies hold so near and dear to our hearts and uphold every single day."

Texas A&M University—College Station

Financial Aid: 979-845-3236 • E-mail: admissions@tamu.edu • Website: www.tamu.edu

ADMISSIONS

Very important factors considered include: Class rank, extracurricular activities, secondary school record, standardized test scores, state residency, talent/ability. *Important factors considered include:* Essays, volunteer work, work experience. *Other factors considered include:* Alumni/ae relation, character/personal qualities, geographical residence, recommendations. SAT Reasoning or ACT required. TOEFL required of all international applicants. High school diploma is required, and GED is accepted. *Academic units required:* 4 English, 3 math, 3 science (2 science lab), 2 foreign language, 2 social studies, 1 history. *Academic units recommended:* 4 English, 3 math, 3 science (2 science lab), 2 foreign language, 2 social studies, 1 history, 1 computer course.

The Inside Word

Texas A&M has a very impressive record of enrolling strong students. A super-high percentage of these admits enroll, which, when combined with the university's impressive graduation rate, is probably the best testament to A&M's reputation. Don't be deceived by the fairly high admit rate, however—for it to be significantly lower, there would have to be a huge increase in the size of the already enormous applicant pool. African American and Hispanic applicants may find it somewhat easier going, as applications from those groups declined last season. Affirmative action issues in Texas ultimately cloud the picture for out-of-state minority applicants, at least until it becomes more clear what steps will or will not be taken in the admissions processes at Texas schools. The current approach guarantees admission for those Texas students graduating in the top 10 percent of their high school class.

FINANCIAL AID

Students should submit: FAFSA, institution's own financial aid form (for transfer students). The Princeton Review suggests that all financial aid forms be submitted as soon as possible after 1/1. *Need-based scholarships/grants offered:* Pell, SEOG, state scholarships/grants, private scholarships, the school's own gift aid. *Loan aid offered:* FFEL Subsidized Stafford, FFEL Unsubsidized Stafford, FFEL PLUS, Federal Perkins, state loans, college/university loans from institutional funds. Applicants will be notified of awards on a rolling basis beginning on or about 4/15.

FROM THE ADMISSIONS OFFICE

"Established in 1876 as the first public college in the state, Texas A&M University has become a world leader in teaching, research, and public service. Located in College Station in the heart of Texas, it is centrally situated among three of the country's 10 largest cities: Dallas, Houston, and San Antonio. Texas A&M is ranked nationally in these four areas: enrollment (seventh in enrollment, 44,813 for fall 2003); enrollment of top students (sixth in number of new National Merit Scholars for fall 2001); value of research (sixteenth with $407 million in 2001); and endowment ($3.4 billion as of 2003).

"Freshman applicants for fall 2006 are required to take the new SAT or the ACT. We will not accept scores from the old SAT. We will use the applicant's best single testing date score in decision-making."

SELECTIVITY

Admissions Rating	**86**
# of applicants	17,324
% of applicants accepted	72
% of acceptees attending	57
# accepting a place on wait list	1,778
% admitted from wait list	42

FRESHMAN PROFILE

Range SAT Verbal	520-640
Average SAT Verbal	578
Range SAT Math	550-660
Average SAT Math	605
**TPR Projected Range SAT Writing*	*570-660*
Range ACT Composite	23-28
Average ACT Composite	25
Minimum Paper TOEFL	550
% graduated top 10% of class	49
% graduated top 25% of class	78
% graduated top 50% of class	92

DEADLINES

Regular application deadline	2/15
Regular notification	rolling
Nonfall registration?	yes

APPLICANTS ALSO LOOK AT

AND OFTEN PREFER

Rice University

AND SOMETIMES PREFER

Baylor University
Louisiana State University
Texas Tech University
The University of Texas—Austin

AND RARELY PREFER

Southern Methodist University
Stephen F. Austin State University

FINANCIAL FACTS

Financial Aid Rating	**82**
Annual in-state tuition	$3,675
Annual out-of-state tuition	$11,415
Room & Board	$6,887
Books and supplies	$1,186
Required fees	$2,280
% frosh rec. need-based scholarship or grant aid	38
% UG rec. need-based scholarship or grant aid	35
% frosh rec. need-based self-help aid	22
% UG rec. need-based self-help aid	26
Avg. frosh grant	$3,280
Avg. frosh loan	$4,350
Independent 529 member?	No

Transylvania University

300 North Broadway, Lexington, KY 40508-1797 • Admissions: 859-233-8242 • Fax: 859-233-8797

CAMPUS LIFE

Quality of Life Rating	**91**
Fire Safety Rating	**87**
Type of school	private
Affiliation	Disciples of Christ
Environment	city

STUDENTS

Total undergrad enrollment	1,109
% male/female	41/59
% from out of state	22
% from public high school	85
% live on campus	80
% in (# of) fraternities	55 (4)
% in (# of) sororities	55 (4)
% African American	2
% Asian	2
% Caucasian	88
% Hispanic	1

SURVEY SAYS . . .

Small classes
Athletic facilities are great
Frats and sororities dominate social scene
Lots of beer drinking

ACADEMICS

Academic Rating	**88**
Calendar	semester/4-4-1
Student/faculty ratio	13:1
Profs interesting rating	94
Profs accessible rating	93
% profs teaching UG courses	100
% classes taught by TAs	0
Most common reg class size	10-19 students

MOST POPULAR MAJORS

Business/commerce
psychology

STUDENTS SPEAK OUT

Academics

Transylvania University "prides itself in its rich history, academic excellence, personable campus, and friendly environment." Students rave about the school's strong sense of community; as one student notes, "Professors, administration, and the students are always including each other in activities." Another student adds, "The professors are always available and I never feel badly about going and asking them questions. They seem to like seeing students all the time." Undergrads report that "Academics are tough, and studying is definitely a must. But classes are fun and small, allowing for you to have lots of individual attention." The school also offers resources such as a writing center and a number of tutoring programs, which students describe as "very helpful." The university also has an "excellent premedical program" with "an awesome acceptance rate into medical school." Students also say that the "education department is fantastic," and also rave about the "great science program." The administration is "highly aware of student opinions and genuinely cares about and reacts to student needs and wants." In case any administrators are reading, several undergrads suggested that "the dorms could all use a face lift."

Life

"Work hard, play hard" is the credo by which most Transylvania students abide. As one undergrad explains, "Student life at Transylvania is almost as busy as the course work. There is always something going on, from Greek functions to cafeteria themes to concerts and movie nights." Campus is located in downtown Lexington, KY, "a great city that's not too big or small." In the city, students have access to "tons of restaurants, bars, and a nice mall. There is a Starbucks down the street. A favorite hangout is the Atomic Cafe, a cool restaurant and bar with yummy food." On campus, Transylvania "has awesome facilities where we can work out or play games (such as the William T. Young Campus Center and the Clive M. Beck Athletic and Recreational Center), and the school is always willing to listen to our suggestions." The Student Activities Board "normally has something happening every month, such as on-campus concerts, carnivals, or movie nights." Greek life is also alive and well at Transylvania. As one student explains, "Greeks do not have 'houses.' We are a wet campus. Most of the partying goes on right here in the halls on campus. People who take things to extremes get in trouble."

Student Body

Transylvania students are "highly motivated, serious about school, friendly, [and] very involved in campus activities." More than half of the students go Greek, but "the campus and student body are both small enough that Greeks hang out with non-Greeks often." As one undergrad notes, "Students should not feel obligated to join a fraternity or sorority just to fit in." The Transylvania student body is "not very diverse," but students "are accepting of differences, especially race, gender, and sexual orientation." Undergrads report that the student body as a whole "promotes and encourages diversity." The school's small size creates a very close-knit environment. "At Transylvania, you want to see the plays because you know people in them," one undergrad explains. "You want to go to sporting events because you can support your friends. Walking to class, tons of people say 'hi' to you because they actually know you!"

FINANCIAL AID: 859-233-8239 • E-MAIL: ADMISSIONS@TRANSY.EDU • WEBSITE: WWW.TRANSY.EDU

ADMISSIONS

Very important factors considered include: Secondary school record, standardized test scores. *Important factors considered include:* Class rank, essays, extracurricular activities, recommendations. *Other factors considered include:* Alumni/ae relation, character/personal qualities, geographical residence, interview, talent/ability, volunteer work, work experience. SAT Reasoning or ACT required; TOEFL required of all international applicants. High school diploma is required and GED is accepted. *Academic units required:* 4 English, 3 math, 3 science, 2 social studies. *Academic units recommended:* 4 English, 3 math, 3 science, 2 foreign language, 2 social studies, 1 history, 1 academic elective.

Inside Word

Applicants who become successful students at TU have the wherewithal to rise to challenging academic demands and the discipline to do so in an ethical fashion. If you're looking for a place to disappear into an ocean of faces, try the University of Kentucky down the road.

FINANCIAL AID

Students should submit: FAFSA, Regular filing deadline is March 1. The Princeton Review suggests that all financial aid forms be submitted as soon as possible after January 1. *Need-based scholarships/grants offered:* Pell, SEOG, state scholarships/grants, private scholarships, the school's own gift aid. *Loan aid offered:* FFEL Subsidized Stafford, FFEL Unsubsidized Stafford, FFEL PLUS, Federal Perkins, college/university loans from institutional funds. Applicants will be notified of awards on a rolling basis beginning or about March 15. Federal Work-Study Program available. Off-campus job opportunities are excellent.

FROM THE ADMISSIONS OFFICE

"Bright, highly motivated students come to Transylvania for our personal approach to learning and our record of success in preparing them for rewarding careers and fulfilling lives. They attend small classes (many have fewer than 10 students) with highly qualified professors (no teaching assistants) and tackle faculty-directed student research projects in intriguing subjects like neurotransmitters and receptors, computer animation, and local Hispanic culture. Graduate and professional schools value this kind of experience—Transylvania graduates have won prestigious scholarships and distinguished themselves at highly selective graduate, law, and medical schools at the nation's elite universities, including Harvard, Stanford, Duke, Princeton, and Vanderbilt.

"Transylvania students consider the world their classroom. They enjoy May term travel courses to study the ancient polis in Greece, language and culture in France, and tropical ecology in Hawaii. Study abroad takes them to Germany, England, Japan, Mexico, and many other destinations, for a summer, a semester, or a year.

"You'll find Transylvania, a small college, nestled in a beautiful neighborhood of a big city. Transylvania students soak up the advantages of Lexington, Kentucky, with its 260,000 population, numerous internship and job opportunities, and lots of entertainment. On campus, we have more than 50 co-curricular activities and 16 varsity teams competing in NCAA Division III.

"We've been here a long time—Transylvania celebrates its 225th anniversary in 2005 as the oldest college west of the Allegheny Mountains and the 16th in the nation. The college offers an excellent modern liberal arts education with a rare historic character.

"Applicants for fall 2006 are not required to submit Writing scores from the new SAT or the ACT. We will allow students to submit scores from either the old version of the SAT or ACT, and will use the student's best scores from either test."

SELECTIVITY	
Admissions Rating	**87**
# of applicants	1,134
% of applicants accepted	88
% of acceptees attending	32
FRESHMAN PROFILE	
Range SAT Verbal	540-650
Average SAT Verbal	590
Range SAT Math	535-645
Average SAT Math	590
**TPR Projected Range SAT Writing*	*590-670*
Range ACT Composite	23-28
Average ACT Composite	26
Minimum Paper TOEFL	550
Minimum Computer Based TOEFL	213
Average HS GPA	3.5
% graduated top 10% of class	44
% graduated top 25% of class	77
% graduated top 50% of class	95
DEADLINES	
Regular application deadline	2/1
Regular notification	rolling
Nonfall registration?	yes
FINANCIAL FACTS	
Financial Aid Rating	**80**
Annual tuition	$17,880
Room & Board	$6,340
Books and supplies	$750
Required fees	$710
% frosh rec. need-based scholarship or grant aid	60
% UG rec. need-based scholarship or grant aid	48
% frosh rec. need-based self-help aid	49
% UG rec. need-based self-help aid	46
% frosh rec. any financial aid	99
% UG rec. any financial aid	98
Avg. frosh grant	$11,639
Avg. frosh loan	$2,448
Independent 529 member?	Yes

Trinity College (CT)

300 Summit Street, Hartford, CT 06016 • Admissions: 860-297-2180 • Fax: 860-297-2287

CAMPUS LIFE

Quality of Life Rating	**63**
Fire Safety Rating	**60**
Type of school	private
Environment	metropolis

STUDENTS

Total undergrad enrollment	2,145
% male/female	49/51
% from out of state	78
% from public high school	43
% live on campus	92
% in (# of) fraternities	20 (7)
% in (# of) sororities	16 (7)
% African American	5
% Asian	6
% Caucasian	66
% Hispanic	5
% international	2
# of countries represented	28

SURVEY SAYS

Small classes
Great computer facilities
Great library
Lots of beer drinking
Hard liquor is popular

ACADEMICS

Academic Rating	**89**
Calendar	semester
Student/faculty ratio	10:1
Professors interesting rating	80
Professors accessible rating	83
% professors teaching UG courses	100
% classes taught by TAs	0
Most common lab size	20-29 students
Most common regular class size	10-19 students

MOST POPULAR MAJORS

Economics
history
political science and government

STUDENTS SPEAK OUT

Academics

Because of a flurry of recent administrative changes (the school has had four presidents in four years), Connecticut's Trinity College appears to be a school in constant flux. Students paint a different picture; they describe an upbeat institution that is progressing toward a more rigorous academic program without losing sight of what has made the school popular (small class sizes, caring professors, and solid liberal arts and sciences). Students tell us, "Trinity fosters interpersonal growth by allowing for the formation of close relationships with faculty and peers in a small-school environment. There is a more pronounced academic atmosphere than there has been in the past because the college is admitting a different type of student: one that is more focused, ambitious, and goal-oriented." One student describes professors as "extremely demanding with an exception or two," and adds, "But they are also the most accessible and engaging I have ever had, which fosters great professor/student interaction." Undergraduates also praise Trinity's curricular innovations. One student writes, "For freshmen seminars, the best are the 'reacting to the past' seminars, where students reenact historically important controversial events, such as the French Revolution. These seminars are very popular with students and project all sides of past political events in a way that allows students to learn much more and become more interested and involved in class." Another student reports, "[The school] offers great major flexibility. I'm designing my own major in human rights."

Life

Students agree that Trinity was a huge party school in the not-so-distant past. Many students still swear that "Trinity is a party school. It is hard to find other people who do not drink." An increasing number of students, however, counter that "Trinity may have once been a party school, but it is far from being true now. The days of 'raging 24/7' are over because the amount of work the professors assign is too much if [you] would like to graduate with 'good' grades." For the most part, students still agree that there's not much more to do except to party "[because of] the size of the school and the fact that it is in such a bad neighborhood that you really don't want to venture outside." Brave students who do venture off campus tell us that "Hartford offers many opportunities for fun" and many opportunities to engage in community service. Hartford's "central location in the Northeast puts us about an hour-and-a-half away from Boston and New York." On campus, there's Cinestudio, "an awesome movie theater that shows great independent and second-run movies" and "a great emphasis on sports, both intercollegiate and intramural."

Student Body

Trinity has long been known as a holding pen for "rich, snobby prep school kids." These "pink Polo with popped collar" kids may be the most instantly recognizable group on campus, but they are hardly the only ones who attend the school. In recent years, Trinity has stepped up efforts to diversify the student body, with noticeable results. Writes one senior, "In my time at Trinity, I have seen a transformation in the type of student. In the beginning, they were all rich, lazy prep school kids with exceptions, now there are not as many lazy, rich prep school kids. I see many more minorities, many, many more students in the library at all times, and an overcohesiveness among the student body." There can't be that many slackers; nearly one in five students proceed directly to grad school upon matriculating. Perhaps this is why one student says, "Most students at Trinity are engaged and interesting. Everyone has something in particular in which they are the best at, whether it be acting, writing, science, or even our five-time national champion squash team!"

TRINITY COLLEGE (CT)

FINANCIAL AID: 860-297-2046 • E-MAIL: ADMISSIONS.OFFICE@TRINCOLL.EDU • WEBSITE: WWW.TRINCOLL.EDU

ADMISSIONS

Very important factors considered include: Secondary school record. *Important factors considered include:* Character/personal qualities, class rank, essays, extracurricular activities, interview, minority status, recommendations, standardized test scores, talent/ability. *Other factors considered include:* Alumni/ae relation, geographical residence, volunteer work, work experience. TOEFL required of all international applicants. High school diploma is required, and GED is accepted. *Academic units required:* 4 English, 3 math, 2 science (2 science lab), 2 foreign language, 2 history.

The Inside Word

Trinity's Ivy safety status and well-deserved reputation for academic quality enables it to enroll a fairly impressive student body, but many of its best applicants go elsewhere. The price tag is high, and the college's competitors include a large portion of the best schools in the country. Minority candidates with sound academic backgrounds will encounter a most accommodating admissions committee.

FINANCIAL AID

Students should submit: FAFSA, CSS/Financial Aid PROFILE, noncustodial (divorced/separated) parents' statement, federal income tax returns. Regular filing deadline is 2/1. The Princeton Review suggests that all financial aid forms be submitted as soon as possible after 1/1. *Need-based scholarships/grants offered:* Pell, SEOG, state scholarships/grants, private scholarships, the school's own gift aid. *Loan aid offered:* Direct Subsidized Stafford, Direct Unsubsidized Stafford, Direct PLUS, FFEL Subsidized Stafford, FFEL Unsubsidized Stafford, FFEL PLUS, Federal Perkins, college/university loans from institutional funds. Applicants will be notified of awards on or about 4/1. Federal Work-study Program available. Institutional employment available. Off-campus job opportunities are good.

FROM THE ADMISSIONS OFFICE

"An array of distinctive curricular options—including an interdisciplinary neuroscience major and a professionally accredited engineering degree program, a unique Human Rights Program, a tutorial college for selected sophomores, a Health Fellows Program, and interdisciplinary programs such as the Cities Program, Interdisciplinary Science Program, and InterArts—is one reason record numbers of students are applying to Trinity. In fact, applications are up 80 percent over the past five years. In addition, the college has been recognized for its commitment to diversity; students of color have represented approximately 20 percent of the freshman class for the past four years, setting Trinity apart from many of its peers. Trinity's capital city location offers students unparalleled 'real world' learning experiences to complement classroom learning. Students take advantage of extensive opportunities for internships for academic credit and community service, and these opportunities extend to Trinity's global learning sites in cities around the world. Trinity's faculty is a devoted and accomplished group of exceptional teacher-scholars; our 100-acre campus is beautiful; Hartford is an educational asset that differentiates Trinity from other liberal arts colleges; our global connections and foreign study opportunities prepare students to be good citizens of the world; and our graduates go on to excel in virtually every field. We invite you to learn more about why Trinity might be the best choice for you.

"Students applying for admission for the entering class of fall 2006 may submit the following testing options: the new the SAT, old SAT with the SAT Subject Test in Writing, the ACT with the Writing section, or three SAT Subject Tests."

SELECTIVITY

Admissions Rating	**94**
# of applicants	5,510
% of applicants accepted	36
% of acceptees attending	28
# accepting a place on wait list	1,377
% admitted from wait list	1
# of early decision applicants	271
% accepted early decision	60

FRESHMAN PROFILE

Range SAT Verbal	590-700
Average SAT Verbal	650
Range SAT Math	620-710
Average SAT Math	660
**TPR Projected Range SAT Writing*	*620-700*
Range ACT Composite	25-29
Average ACT Composite	27
Minimum Paper TOEFL	550
Minimum Computer Based TOEFL	210
% graduated top 10% of class	51
% graduated top 25% of class	81
% graduated top 50% of class	95

DEADLINES

Early decision application deadline	11/15
Early decision notification	12/15
Regular application deadline	1/15
Regular notification	4/1
Nonfall registration?	no

APPLICANTS ALSO LOOK AT AND OFTEN PREFER

Amherst College, Harvard College, Tufts University, University of Pennsylvania, Yale University

AND SOMETIMES PREFER

Middlebury College, Wesleyan University

AND RARELY PREFER

Boston University, Colgate University, Connecticut College, Fairfield University

FINANCIAL FACTS

Financial Aid Rating	**94**
Annual tuition	$28,740
Room & Board	$7,810
Books and supplies	$850
Required fees	$1,490
% frosh rec. need-based scholarship or grant aid	43
% UG rec. need-based scholarship or grant aid	45
% frosh rec. need-based self-help aid	37
% UG rec. need-based self-help aid	38
Avg. frosh grant	$25,000
Avg. frosh loan	$3,521
Independent 529 member?	No

Trinity University

One Trinity Place, San Antonio, TX 78212 • Admissions: 210-999-7207 • Fax: 210-999-8164

CAMPUS LIFE

Quality of Life Rating	**93**
Fire Safety Rating	**60**
Type of school	private
Environment	metropolis

STUDENTS

Total undergrad enrollment	2,406
% male/female	48/52
% from out of state	35
% from public high school	67
% live on campus	78
% in (# of) fraternities	30 (8)
% in (# of) sororities	28 (6)
% African American	2
% Asian	6
% Caucasian	70
% Hispanic	11
% international	5
# of countries represented	30

SURVEY SAYS

Small classes
Great computer facilities
Great library
Great off-campus food
Dorms are like palaces

ACADEMICS

Academic Rating	**88**
Calendar	semester
Student/faculty ratio	10:1
Professors interesting rating	92
Professors accessible rating	93
% professors teaching UG courses	100
% classes taught by TAs	0
Most common lab size	10-19 students
Most common regular class size	10-19 students

MOST POPULAR MAJORS

Business administration/management
communications and media studies
foreign languages/modern languages

STUDENTS SPEAK OUT

Academics

"The academics are very strong no matter the major you choose" at Trinity University, a tiny powerhouse of a university located deep in the heart of Texas. The school's "very rigorous undergraduate programs" all include a wide-ranging common curriculum requiring students to master writing, mathematical, computer, and foreign language skills. All students must also fulfill requirements in six areas of knowledge (called Fundamental Understandings in the course catalog). Students tell us that "the broad requirements of the curriculum make for a great base. You can still complete your area of study, all the while learning things you never thought you would, taking classes in subjects you are interested in, but don't necessarily coincide with classes in your major." Those who come here should arrive prepared to log serious hours in the library; writes one student, "No matter what major you decide to pursue, you better believe that there will be work involved." Professors help students meet the challenge; they're "always available, largely brilliant, and willing to discuss damn near anything with a student one-on-one." Undergrads also appreciate that their professors "are open to letting students help with their research projects." Other assets include "an absolutely amazing study-abroad program" and an endowed lecture series that is "known for bringing in very influential people as guest speakers. In the past few years we have had John Glen, Rudy Giuliani, Queen Noor, and Brit Hume." Another student reports, "Tonight they had this woman from the Iraqi Governing Council in an auditorium that sat maybe 250. I can't tell you how many world leaders I've asked questions to."

Life

"The greatest strength of Trinity," students tell us, "is that it is wonderfully located in the middle of San Antonio, yet it feels like you're in the Hill Country." Here it is easy "to study and concentrate on work," but the school also "has a strong sense of community," one reinforced by the "collective cursing of students hiking up Cardiac Hill to get to class from the dorms." Trinity's otherwise "beautiful campus with great architecture" is encircled by "a great city, where there's always something to do, from going to the movies to great restaurants to the Riverwalk to local rodeos...pretty much anything you could want to do is available here." Many choose to stick around campus. Trinity requires on-campus residence for the first three years, which many students like, citing again that "sense of community that most other campuses don't have." Extracurricular opportunities "are huge, especially intramural sports and student organizations." The Greek scene "is also big, but going Greek is not necessary to be considered 'cool' and not necessary to have good social life." Parties are frequent, but "Trinity's campus is dry, so parties are held off campus." The "terrific Division III athletic teams" here "struggle for support," with the exception of the men's soccer team, "which was number one in the nation in 2003."

Student Body

"You know that kid who makes the rather intelligent off-hand comments in your government and English classes?" queries one Trinity undergrad. "Well, they all go to Trinity. That isn't to say we're all loudmouths, but we're all pretty academic minded." Indeed, "Everyone was one of the 'smart kids' in high school. Even the football players at Trinity are smart, and even the 'cool people' here are just a little nerdy. Everyone studies." While "most here are from a Southern, somewhat-elite background, not all students are like that, and you can definitely find students of all types." One student writes, "While Trinity isn't all rich white kids, there are a few of them, and while they don't exhibit any elitism or anything, they just view the world in a different way and sometimes their cultural ignorance can get kind of old." Trinity's minority population "consists largely of persons with Hispanic and Asian ethnicity. There are a fair number of these students, but African Americans are largely unaccounted for on campus."

FINANCIAL AID: 210-999-8315 • E-MAIL: ADMISSIONS@TRINITY.EDU • WEBSITE: WWW.TRINITY.EDU

ADMISSIONS

Very important factors considered include: Character/personal qualities, class rank, secondary school record, standardized test scores. *Important factors considered include:* Essays, extracurricular activities, recommendations, talent/ability. *Other factors considered include:* Alumni/ae relation, geographical residence, interview, state residency, volunteer work, work experience. SAT Reasoning or ACT required. TOEFL required of all international applicants. High school diploma is required, and GED is accepted. *Academic units required:* 4 English, 3 math, 3 science (2 science lab), 2 foreign language, 3 social studies, 1 academic elective. *Academic units recommended:* 4 English, 4 math, 3 science (3 science lab), 3 foreign language, 3 social studies.

The Inside Word

There is no disputing that Trinity has bought academic excellence in its student body. For this reason alone, above-average students who need significant financial assistance in order to attend college should definitely consider applying. There is no question that it's an extremely capable student body and that there are significant benefits to be derived from attending.

FINANCIAL AID

Students should submit: FAFSA. Regular filing deadline is 4/1. The Princeton Review suggests that all financial aid forms be submitted as soon as possible after 1/1. *Need-based scholarships/grants offered:* Pell, SEOG, state scholarships/grants, private scholarships, the school's own gift aid. *Loan aid offered:* FFEL Subsidized Stafford, FFEL Unsubsidized Stafford, FFEL PLUS, Federal Perkins, state loans, college/university loans from institutional funds. Applicants will be notified of awards on or about 4/1. Federal Work-study Program available. Institutional employment available. Off-campus job opportunities are good.

FROM THE ADMISSIONS OFFICE

"Three qualities separate Trinity University from other selective, academically challenging institutions around the country. First, Trinity is unusual in the quality and quantity of resources devoted almost exclusively to its undergraduate students. Those resources give rise to a second distinctive aspect of Trinity—its emphasis on undergraduate research. Our students prefer being involved over observing. With superior laboratory facilities and strong, dedicated faculty, our undergraduates fill many of the roles formerly reserved for graduate students. With no graduate assistants, our professors often go to their undergraduates for help with their research. Finally, Trinity stands apart for the attitude of its students. In an atmosphere of academic camaraderie and fellowship, our students work together to stretch their minds and broaden their horizons. For quality of resources, for dedication to undergraduate research, and for the disposition of its student body, Trinity University holds a unique position in American higher education.

"Students applying for admission must submit either the ACT or the SAT (both the new and the old version are acceptable). The highest composite test scores from one or multiple dates are evaluated. The SAT Writing section and ACT Writing component are not required, but may be reviewed if submitted."

SELECTIVITY

Admissions Rating	**92**
# of applicants	4,000
% of applicants accepted	60
% of acceptees attending	30
# accepting a place on wait list	159
# of early decision applicants	58
% accepted early decision	65

FRESHMAN PROFILE

Range SAT Verbal	600-690
Average SAT Verbal	643
Range SAT Math	620-690
Average SAT Math	653
**TPR Projected Range SAT Writing*	*630-690*
Range ACT Composite	27-31
Average ACT Composite	29
Minimum Paper TOEFL	600
Minimum Computer Based TOEFL	250
Average HS GPA	3.5
% graduated top 10% of class	51
% graduated top 25% of class	81
% graduated top 50% of class	97

DEADLINES

Early decision application deadline	11/1
Early decision notification	12/15
Regular notification	4/1
Nonfall registration?	yes

APPLICANTS ALSO LOOK AT

AND OFTEN PREFER
Rice University
The University of Texas—Austin

AND SOMETIMES PREFER
Southern Methodist University
Texas A&M University—College Station
Texas Christian University
Tulane University

AND RARELY PREFER
Rhodes College

FINANCIAL FACTS

Financial Aid Rating	**87**
Annual tuition	$19,806
Room & Board	$7,805
Books and supplies	$620
Required fees	$774
% frosh rec. need-based scholarship or grant aid	41
% UG rec. need-based scholarship or grant aid	39
% frosh rec. need-based self-help aid	31
% UG rec. need-based self-help aid	33
% frosh rec. any financial aid	26
% UG rec. any financial aid	74
Avg. frosh grant	$11,539
Avg. frosh loan	$2,625
Independent 529 member?	Yes

TRUMAN STATE UNIVERSITY

McCLAIN HALL 205, 100 EAST NORMAL, KIRKSVILLE, MO 63501 • ADMISSIONS: 660-785-4114 • FAX: 660-785-7456

CAMPUS LIFE

Quality of Life Rating	**78**
Fire Safety Rating	**66**
Type of school	public
Environment	village

STUDENTS

Total undergrad enrollment	5,482
% male/female	42/58
% from out of state	26
% from public high school	80
% live on campus	48
% in (# of) fraternities	31 (19)
% in (# of) sororities	22 (10)
% African American	4
% Asian	2
% Caucasian	86
% Hispanic	2
% international	4
# of countries represented	51

SURVEY SAYS

Small classes
Great computer facilities
Great library
Athletic facilities are great
Students are friendly
Campus feels safe
Students are happy
Lots of beer drinking

ACADEMICS

Academic Rating	**85**
Calendar	semester
Student/faculty ratio	15:1
Professors interesting rating	85
Professors accessible rating	87
% professors teaching UG courses	98
% classes taught by TAs	1
Most common lab size	20-29 students
Most common regular class size	20-29 students

MOST POPULAR MAJORS

Biology/biological sciences
Business administration/management
English language and literature

STUDENTS SPEAK OUT

Academics

Truman State University, a "highly selective school that strives to provide a quality education at an affordable price," offers "students willing to be pushed academically" a demanding but worthwhile undergraduate experience. "Truman is known for its rigorous classes and is not for the faint at heart," cautions one undergrad. Others temper their warnings, reporting that "the academics can be challenging, but not overwhelming. There are some tough classes, but those only serve to teach me more." Students agree that a Truman degree is worth the hard work because "the school has a great reputation. Job recruiters know that Truman graduates are high quality." Excellent professors soften the impact of the heavy workload; "the teachers are incredibly student-oriented, and they are always available for assistance," explains one undergrad. Observes another, "I think people who are willing to move to Kirksville to teach are here . . . because they like what they do." The administration makes every effort to keep class sizes small, a fact students appreciate. "The size of Truman is really one of its greatest strengths. Truman provides a very 'at home' kind of feeling," notes one student. "The classes are small, and you get to know the people in your major throughout your years, so there is always great networking after college," adds another.

Life

The workload is heavy at Truman State, so "people at this school tend to study hard during the week and leave the weekends for partying." The weekend party scene is fairly active: "Weekend nights are usually spent at house parties or the bars, which tend to be popular hangouts for local students," one student reports, even though "alcohol rules are extremely strict. There is a bit of tension between the community and campus in the area of parties and enforcement of alcohol laws." Many here remain happily outside the party scene, telling us that they remain busy by "hiking or boating at Thousand Hills State Park; seeing a play, movie, musical, or performance on campus; participating in discussion groups; watching movies with friends; and enjoying any number of other activities." Others note that "many students join organizations to meet others with like interests." The Student Activities Board "is always bringing movies, comedians, and music acts to campus for free or a small fee," and the Greek community is also active here. All of these options help make up for the fact that Kirksville "is the smallest town ever. There is not a lot to do in town on a Friday or Saturday night." Some see an upside to Kirksville's size and remote location: "Even though Kirksville is small, it is very quaint, and the people are very friendly. It really grows on you," writes one student.

Student Body

If you want to envision the Truman State student body, you should "think midwestern. Think conservative living. Think very smart. Truman is not a place to come if any of these things freak you out." Truman "does not have a lot of diversity." In fact, most here agree that "Truman needs to work on recruiting a more diverse student body. There's a big need to avoid just enrolling white, straight midwesterners." Students brag, "Being a highly selective university, Truman draws some of the best and brightest in the area," but also see a downside: "Unfortunately, the typical student is pretty dorky. Many of our students care so much about academics that they care very little about their appearance." A substantial number of Truman undergrads are religious; "we have a large Catholic population from the St. Louis area." Most "have pretty conservative views; however, they are also incredibly down-to-earth and friendly." The school has a "high female-to-male ratio."

FINANCIAL AID: 660-785-4130 • E-MAIL: ADMISSIONS@TRUMAN.EDU • WEBSITE: WWW.TRUMAN.EDU

ADMISSIONS

Very important factors considered include: Class rank, secondary school record, standardized test scores. *Important factors considered include:* Essays. *Other factors considered include:* Alumni/ae relation, character/personal qualities, extracurricular activities, geographical residence, minority status, state residency, talent/ability, volunteer work, work experience. SAT Reasoning or ACT required. TOEFL required of all international applicants. High school diploma is required, and GED is accepted. *Academic units required:* 4 English, 3 math, 3 science (2 science lab), 2 foreign language, 3 social studies, 1 fine arts. *Academic units recommended:* 4 English, 4 math, 3 science (2 science lab), 2 foreign language, 3 social studies, 1 fine arts.

The Inside Word

Truman is among the next-in-line among public universities joining the ranks of the highly selective. It's tough to get admitted, and application totals increased last year. Serious students with conservative attitudes make the best match.

FINANCIAL AID

Students should submit: FAFSA, institution's own financial aid form. The Princeton Review suggests that all financial aid forms be submitted as soon as possible after 1/1. *Need-based scholarships/grants offered:* Pell, SEOG, state scholarships/grants, private scholarships, the school's own gift aid. *Loan aid offered:* FFEL Subsidized Stafford, FFEL Unsubsidized Stafford, FFEL PLUS, Federal Perkins, Federal Nursing, state loans, college/university loans from institutional funds. Applicants will be notified of awards on a rolling basis beginning on or about 3/1. Federal Work-study Program available. Off-campus job opportunities are good.

FROM THE ADMISSIONS OFFICE

"Truman's talented student body enjoys small classes where undergraduate research and personal interaction with professors are the norm. Truman's commitment to providing an exemplary liberal arts and sciences education with nearly 200 student organizations and outstanding internship and study abroad opportunities allows students to compete in top graduate schools and the job market.

"Students applying for fall 2006 admission to Truman State University can submit scores from both versions of the SAT, as well as the ACT. The best scores from either test will be considered. The Writing section is not currently required for admission to Truman."

SELECTIVITY

Admissions Rating	**89**
# of applicants	4,567
% of applicants accepted	84
% of acceptees attending	39

FRESHMAN PROFILE

Range SAT Verbal	570-670
Average SAT Verbal	622
Range SAT Math	570-670
Average SAT Math	620
**TPR Projected Range SAT Writing*	*610-680*
Range ACT Composite	25-30
Average ACT Composite	27
Minimum Paper TOEFL	550
Minimum Computer Based TOEFL	213
Average HS GPA	3.76
% graduated top 10% of class	45
% graduated top 25% of class	81
% graduated top 50% of class	99

DEADLINES

Regular application deadline	3/1
Regular notification	rolling
Nonfall registration?	yes

APPLICANTS ALSO LOOK AT

AND OFTEN PREFER

Saint Louis University
University of Missouri—Columbia
Washington University in St. Louis

AND SOMETIMES PREFER

Southwest Missouri State University
University of Illinois at Urbana-Champaign

AND RARELY PREFER

Illinois State University
Illinois Wesleyan University
University of Iowa

FINANCIAL FACTS

Financial Aid Rating	**89**
Annual in-state tuition	$5,740
Annual out-of-state tuition	$9,920
Room & Board	$5,380
Books and supplies	$900
Required fees	$122
% frosh rec. need-based scholarship or grant aid	15
% UG rec. need-based scholarship or grant aid	16
% frosh rec. need-based self-help aid	30
% UG rec. need-based self-help aid	30
% frosh rec. any financial aid	96
% UG rec. any financial aid	93
Avg. frosh grant	$5,392
Avg. frosh loan	$4,267
Independent 529 member?	No

TUFTS UNIVERSITY

BENDETSON HALL, MEDFORD, MA 02155 • ADMISSIONS: 617-627-3170 • FAX: 617-627-3860

CAMPUS LIFE

Quality of Life Rating	**90**
Fire Safety Rating	**97**
Type of school	private
Environment	town

STUDENTS

Total undergrad enrollment	4,888
% male/female	47/53
% from out of state	74
% from public high school	60
% live on campus	75
% in (# of) fraternities	15 (11)
% in (# of) sororities	4 (3)
% African American	7
% Asian	13
% Caucasian	56
% Hispanic	8
% international	6
# of countries represented	65

SURVEY SAYS

Great computer facilities
Great library
Great food on campus
Great off-campus food
Campus feels safe
Students are happy
Student publications are popular
Lots of beer drinking

ACADEMICS

Academic Rating	**89**
Calendar	semester
Student/faculty ratio	10:1
Professors interesting rating	87
Professors accessible rating	84
% professors teaching UG courses	100
% classes taught by TAs	1
Most common lab size	10-19 students
Most common regular class size	10-19 students

MOST POPULAR MAJORS

Economics
English language and literature
international relations and affairs

STUDENTS SPEAK OUT

Academics

The boilerplate description of Tufts University—that it's the school for kids who couldn't get into one of the Ivies—may be accurate; however, this description places too much emphasis on Tufts's silver medal standing and downplays that Tufts is everyone's second choice precisely because its offerings are competitive with those of the Ivies. Tufts has a renowned faculty. One student agrees, "I can't say how often I hear their names on NPR or read in magazines that one has discovered or written something or other." The school is especially highly regarded in the field of international relations. Students say, "The presence of the Fletcher School of Law and Diplomacy on campus means that not only are classes available to advanced students but [also] important people in the international relations field often come for lectures." Pre-medical studies, engineering, and the liberal arts are also strong at Tufts. Unlike many Ivies, Tufts focuses on its undergraduates; "TAs only teach labs and study groups, while professors teach the actual classes." One undergraduate reports, "You could be the only freshman in a classroom filled with sophomores and juniors and your professor would still ask you your opinion, know your name, and treat you [as] a friend when he or she sees you in the dining hall." This "small-college" vibe extends right up to the top; the school's president "makes it a priority to be personally involved with students. Living right on campus, he is an advisor to undergraduates, has kids at his house for dinner or to go running, and is always available for appointments." Students also praise the career services at Tufts.

Life

The Tufts curriculum places heavy demands on students. Undergraduates report that "life at school revolves around classes. In general, most Tufts students take their grades very seriously." Students still manage to find some time during their busy weeks to blow off steam. One undergraduate says, "I love Tufts because I love being around intelligent people and being able to have an intellectual discussion, to go to a class and then spend a couple hours talking about the subjects, whether philosophy or international relations, with my friends. I'm just as happy staying in as going out." Other students enjoy the "absolutely gorgeous" campus in their spare time, while others run off to "well-publicized, interesting guest lectures, a cappella concerts," student-produced plays and art exhibits, and "large-scale, free campus events, such as Tuftonia's Day Fireworks, the Naked Quad Run, and Spring Fling." Freshmen also flock to "incredibly crowded frat parties," although as students grow older the allure of these shindigs wanes. Boston is only a few minutes away, so "on weekends, a good part of the student population takes the T into the city. Boston is a great resource for fun and entertainment." Students appreciate that they can enjoy a night in the big city, then retreat to the "safe suburban environment" of Medford.

Student Body

Students concede that "with a private school in the 'burbs of Boston, you're going to have your Prada shoes and Gucci bags," but quickly add that they are "impressed with how much diversity there actually is within the student body." They also note that "underrepresented minorities on campus seem to be comfortable and have a strong presence," but that different populations are "very self-segregated, which is frustrating." In all, just about everyone "can find a place here." One student adds, "What makes Tufts unique is that there are frats that attract a certain type of student as well as places like Oxfam Cafe, which serves vegetarian/vegan cuisine, where a different crowd of students hang out." Undergraduates also report that "there is a lot of political activism on campus."

FINANCIAL AID: 617-627-2000 • E-MAIL: ADMISSIONS.INQUIRY@ASE.TUFTS.EDU • WEBSITE: WWW.TUFTS.EDU

ADMISSIONS

Very important factors considered include: Secondary school record. *Important factors considered include:* Character/personal qualities, class rank, essays, extracurricular activities, minority status, recommendations, standardized test scores, talent/ability, volunteer work, work experience. *Other factors considered include:* Alumni/ae relation, geographical residence, interview. SAT Reasoning and SAT Subject Tests or ACT required. TOEFL required of all international applicants. High school diploma is required, and GED is accepted. *Academic units recommended:* 4 English, 3 math, 2 science, 3 foreign language, 2 history.

The Inside Word

Tufts has little visibility outside the Northeast and little personality either. Still it manages to attract and keep an excellent student body, mostly from right inside its own backyard. In order to be successful, candidates must have significant academic accomplishments and submit a thoroughly well-prepared application—the review is rigorous, and the standards are high.

FINANCIAL AID

Students should submit: FAFSA, CSS/Financial Aid PROFILE, noncustodial (divorced/separated) parents' statement, business/farm supplement, parent and student federal income tax returns. Regular filing deadline is 2/15. The Princeton Review suggests that all financial aid forms be submitted as soon as possible after 1/1. *Need-based scholarships/grants offered:* Pell, SEOG, state scholarships/grants, private scholarships, the school's own gift aid. *Loan aid offered:* FFEL Subsidized Stafford, FFEL Unsubsidized Stafford, FFEL PLUS, Federal Perkins, state loans, college/university loans from institutional funds. Applicants will be notified of awards on or about 4/1. Federal Work-study Program available. Institutional employment available. Off-campus job opportunities are good.

FROM THE ADMISSIONS OFFICE

"Tufts University, on the boundary between Medford and Somerville, sits on a hill overlooking Boston, five miles northwest of the city. The campus is a tranquil New England setting within easy access by subway and bus to the cultural, social, and entertainment resources of Boston and Cambridge. Since its founding in 1852 by members of the Universalist church, Tufts has grown from a small liberal arts college into a nonsectarian university of over 7,000 students. By 1900 the college had added a medical school, a dental school, and graduate studies. The University now also includes the Fletcher School of Law and Diplomacy, the Graduate School of Arts and Sciences, the School of Veterinary Medicine, the School of Nutrition, the Sackler School of Graduate Biomedical Sciences, and the Gordon Institute of Engineering Management.

"Applicants for fall 2006 are required to submit scores (including the Writing assessment) from either the SAT or ACT. Also required are two SAT Subject Tests (candidates for the School of Engineering are encouraged to submit Math 2C and either Chemistry or Physics)."

SELECTIVITY	
Admissions Rating	**97**
# of applicants	14,728
% of applicants accepted	27
% of acceptees attending	32
# of early decision applicants	551
% accepted early decision	45

FRESHMAN PROFILE	
Range SAT Verbal	640-730
Range SAT Math	650-740
**TPR Projected Range SAT Writing*	*660-720*
Range ACT Composite	27-32
Minimum Paper TOEFL	200
Minimum Computer Based TOEFL	300
% graduated top 10% of class	74
% graduated top 25% of class	94
% graduated top 50% of class	99

DEADLINES	
Early decision application deadline	11/15
Early decision notification	12/15
Regular application deadline	1/1
Regular notification	4/1
Nonfall registration?	no

FINANCIAL FACTS	
Financial Aid Rating	**94**
Annual tuition	$28,859
Room & Board	$8,640
Books and supplies	$800
Required fees	$734
% frosh rec. need-based scholarship or grant aid	36
% UG rec. need-based scholarship or grant aid	37
% frosh rec. need-based self-help aid	34
% UG rec. need-based self-help aid	37
% frosh rec. any financial aid	39
% UG rec. any financial aid	40
Avg. frosh grant	$20,049
Avg. frosh loan	$2,911
Independent 529 member?	No

TULANE UNIVERSITY

6823 ST. CHARLES AVENUE, NEW ORLEANS, LA 70118 • ADMISSIONS: 504-865-5731 • FAX: 504-862-8715

CAMPUS LIFE

Quality of Life Rating	**86**
Fire Safety Rating	**78**
Type of school	private
Environment	city

STUDENTS

Total undergrad enrollment	7,952
% male/female	47/53
% from out of state	70
% live on campus	65
% in (# of) fraternities	33 (14)
% in (# of) sororities	35 (9)
% African American	8
% Asian	3
% Caucasian	56
% Hispanic	3
% international	2
# of countries represented	100

SURVEY SAYS

Athletic facilities are great
Students love New Orleans, LA
Great off-campus food
Students are happy
Lots of beer drinking
Hard liquor is popular

ACADEMICS

Academic Rating	**85**
Calendar	semester
Professors interesting rating	76
Professors accessible rating	80
% classes taught by TAs	0
Most common lab size	10-19 students
Most common regular class size	10-19 students

MOST POPULAR MAJORS

Business/commerce
engineering
social sciences

STUDENTS SPEAK OUT

Academics

"Tulane offers some of the best academics in the country." The school is true to the spirit of its hometown of New Orleans; therefore: exposing students to "a more relaxed atmosphere with some of the most talented and fascinating people you will ever meet." The famous nightlife of New Orleans makes it difficult for some students to remain focused solely on academics; however, students who "have the amazing ability to party hard and study harder know what it takes to succeed, and they do it while having fun." Undergraduates agree that "the school's academics are fantastic. The professors are great, and the educational resources outstanding." They also appreciate that "classes are usually pretty small, even the introductory ones" and that "very few, if any, profs care more about research than they do about us." The workload in most areas is "tough but not overwhelming," with assistance readily available to students who fall behind. One student adds, "I was having trouble at the beginning of the semester. All of my professors sat with me one-on-one and worked with me until I understood the material." Administrators, from the top down, earn similar praise. Students report that the university's president "has done an amazing job of balancing much needed university construction and improvements, while staying [with]in budget, still offering amazing scholarships, and keeping student morale at a high level. As if this wasn't enough, he even teaches leadership classes."

Life

"The combination of Tulane University and New Orleans really does offer students the opportunity to make whatever they want of their college experience," undergraduates say. They also agree that "there is no better college town than New Orleans. There is absolutely something to do at all hours every day, year-round. The music is fantastic and so is the food. The night life absolutely cannot be beat." According to some students, drinking age laws are rarely enforced. One student reports, "Mardi Gras is year-round." Of course, New Orleans is more than a nonstop party; the city also offers "plays and art things downtown, with great shopping on Magazine Street, [and] amazing food." On campus, "there are so many clubs and organizations that it can cater to nearly everyone's needs. There is a strong emphasis on community work at Tulane, and on weekends, students tutor children in the community, restore and paint local houses, and mentor at-risk youth." The school also has "excellent sports teams, but very few students attend the games. While students have a great deal of school pride that they attend Tulane, they are unwilling to go to sporting events to show their school spirit."

Student Body

"Rarely will you find people from Louisiana here," some undergraduates say, which explains "why Tulane is mostly a northern school, just placed in the heart of New Orleans." The school is more geographically diverse than it is economically diverse. Undergraduates tell us that the "vast majority of students are rich, and they love to show it off, which gets really old, really fast." A generous financial aid office, however, ensures that not everyone fits this mold. Tulane kids "actually act like college students. You won't find 'high school drama' here." Students also say that "concerning sexual orientation and gender issues, the Tulane community is pretty liberal and doesn't really make much of a statement on these issues. People really don't care one way or the other, and New Orleans definitely has an open-minded policy, too." One undergraduate reports that students can be vain and adds, "I have found only a few students who don't care about their appearance more than their future."

FINANCIAL AID: 504-865-5723 • E-MAIL: UNDERGRAD.ADMISSION@TULANE.EDU • WEBSITE: WWW.TULANE.EDU

ADMISSIONS

Very important factors considered include: Class rank, secondary school record, standardized test scores. *Important factors considered include:* Character/personal qualities, essays, recommendations. *Other factors considered include:* Alumni/ae relation, extracurricular activities, interview, talent/ability, volunteer work, work experience. SAT Reasoning or ACT required. TOEFL required of all international applicants. High school diploma is required, and GED is accepted. *Academic units required:* 4 English, 3 math, 3 science (3 science lab), 2 foreign language, 3 social studies. *Academic units recommended:* 4 English, 4 math, 4 science (3 science lab), 3 foreign language, 3 social studies, 3 academic electives.

The Inside Word

Tulane's applicant pool is highly national in origin and very sound academically. The university's competitors include many of the best universities in the country, which tempers its selectivity significantly due to the loss of admitted students. Nonetheless, Tulane is an excellent choice for just about anyone looking for a quality institution that is on the move. Prestige and the value of a Tulane degree stand to increase as the South continues to grow in population and political influence.

FINANCIAL AID

Students should submit: FAFSA, CSS/Financial Aid PROFILE, noncustodial (divorced/separated) parents' statement, business/farm supplement. Regular filing deadline is 2/1. The Princeton Review suggests that all financial aid forms be submitted as soon as possible after 1/1. *Need-based scholarships/grants offered:* Pell, SEOG, state scholarships/grants, private scholarships, the school's own gift aid. *Loan aid offered:* FFEL Subsidized Stafford, FFEL Unsubsidized Stafford, FFEL PLUS, Federal Perkins. Applicants will be notified of awards on a rolling basis beginning on or about 2/1. Federal Work-study Program available. Institutional employment available. Off-campus job opportunities are good.

FROM THE ADMISSIONS OFFICE

"With 5,000 full-time undergraduate students in five divisions, Tulane University offers the personal attention and teaching excellence traditionally associated with liberal arts colleges together with the facilities and interdisciplinary resources found only at major research universities—with both complemented by the exciting, historic setting of New Orleans, America's most interesting city. Senior faculty regularly teach introductory and lower-level courses, and 74 percent of the classes have 25 or fewer students. The close student-teacher relationship pays off. Tulane graduates are among the country's most likely to be selected for several prestigious fellowships that support graduate study abroad. Founded in 1834 and reorganized as Tulane University in 1884, Tulane is one of the major private research universities in the South. The Tulane campus offers a traditional collegiate setting in an attractive residential neighborhood.

"Tulane University will accept the new SAT or the old SAT (administered prior to March 2005 and without a Writing component). For students submitting an ACT score, the ACT with the Writing component is required."

SELECTIVITY

Admissions Rating	**94**
# of applicants	17,572
% of applicants accepted	45
% of acceptees attending	21
# accepting a place on wait list	2,337
# of early decision applicants	81
% accepted early decision	39

FRESHMAN PROFILE

Range SAT Verbal	628-725
Average SAT Verbal	667
Range SAT Math	603-700
Average SAT Math	653
**TPR Projected Range SAT Writing*	*650-720*
Range ACT Composite	28-32
Average ACT Composite	30
Minimum Paper TOEFL	550
Minimum Computer Based TOEFL	213
Average HS GPA	3.6
% graduated top 10% of class	59
% graduated top 25% of class	75
% graduated top 50% of class	100

DEADLINES

Early decision application deadline	11/1
Early decision notification	12/15
Regular application deadline	1/15
Regular notification	4/15
Nonfall registration?	no

APPLICANTS ALSO LOOK AT

AND OFTEN PREFER

Duke U., Emory U., Vanderbilt U.

AND SOMETIMES PREFER

Florida State U., Northwestern U., The U. of Texas—Austin, Washington U. in St. Louis

AND RARELY PREFER

Rollins College, Skidmore College, Southern Methodist U., U. of Richmond

FINANCIAL FACTS

Financial Aid Rating	**89**
Annual tuition	$28,900
Room & Board	$7,925
Books and supplies	$800
Required fees	$2,310
% frosh rec. need-based scholarship or grant aid	47
% UG rec. need-based scholarship or grant aid	39
% frosh rec. need-based self-help aid	29
% UG rec. need-based self-help aid	29
% frosh rec. any financial aid	92
% UG rec. any financial aid	91
Avg. frosh grant	$17,674
Avg. frosh loan	$4,783
Independent 529 member?	Yes

UNION COLLEGE (NY)

GRANT HALL, SCHENECTADY, NY 12308 • ADMISSIONS: 518-388-6112 • FAX: 518-388-6986

CAMPUS LIFE

Quality of Life Rating	**70**
Fire Safety Rating	**86**
Type of school	private
Environment	town

STUDENTS

Total undergrad enrollment	2,144
% male/female	55/45
% from out of state	56
% from public high school	70
% live on campus	88
% in (# of) fraternities	29 (9)
% in (# of) sororities	27 (3)
% African American	3
% Asian	6
% Caucasian	84
% Hispanic	4
% international	2
# of countries represented	18

SURVEY SAYS

Small classes
Great library
Frats and sororities dominate social scene
Lots of beer drinking
Hard liquor is popular

ACADEMICS

Academic Rating	**90**
Calendar	trimester
Student/faculty ratio	11:1
Professors interesting rating	88
Professors accessible rating	92
% professors teaching UG courses	100
% classes taught by TAs	0
Most common lab size	10-19 students
Most common regular class size	10-19 students

MOST POPULAR MAJORS

Economics
political science and government
psychology

STUDENTS SPEAK OUT

Academics

A renowned engineering program and widely available opportunities for study abroad are the marquee features at Union College, a small liberal arts school in upstate New York. It is almost impossible to slack off and get by at Union: "You need to do your work, and professors notice if you're not in class. Attendance is key," warns one student. Another adds, "There are a lot of classes that require writing papers and research reports." Even so, students know how good they have it. "There is a great deal of communication and cooperation between the administration and the students," writes one undergraduate. "The sense of community is something I didn't feel at any other school I visited." Another student agrees, "Union does a good job of making sure everything runs smoothly and overall [does] a good job of making [itself] 'student (and parent)-friendly.'" Union profs earn high marks from students, who tell us, "The professors are what makes Union such an excellent institution. The overall academic experience is highly positive [because professors] go beyond the duty of holding required office hours. They usually invite students over to their homes for dinner." Add in the "great resources [and] a study abroad program that something like 75 percent of the students take advantage of," and the Union College picture is certainly complete.

Life

Everyone agrees that Union College is "a big school for frat parties on the weekend. Social life is based around fraternities, football games, and our men's ice hockey team." While almost everyone acknowledges that weekends are pretty wild, most also point out that "at Union, there is a partylike atmosphere at certain times that make the school seem like a party school, but during the week most people are in tune to their school work." Beyond the frats, "there are lots of other possibilities," although reportedly very few students take advantage of them. They include "movies that play every weekend, comedians who come, and bands. There are countless clubs, ranging from community service to ballroom dancing, and plenty of opportunities for free meals. There are also places to ski/snowboard nearby. Albany is pretty close, as well, and there are many things to do there." Some dismiss hometown Schenectady as "too dangerous," but others disagree. One such dissenter writes, "People who visit think that the town of Schenectady looks like it's dying. But they're wrong—it isn't the biggest or the best college town, but there's a lot to do: restaurants, a museum, a library, shopping, even one of the oldest theaters in the country, Proctor's Theater, which gets Broadway shows." One student finds another positive about Union; "The campus is beautiful. Whether it is fall, winter, or spring, the campus looks amazing."

Student Body

The preppier the school, the more students' descriptions of one another focus on their wardrobes. At Union, nearly every respondent categorized classmates by what was in their closets. "Girls wear a lot of Lilly Pulitzer and bows in their hair, and the boys are all Abercrombie models with their faded jeans. Everyone looks alike," writes one student. "It's all Polo collars turned up, Vera Bradley bags, name-brand everything," offers another. Once they finish their fashion reviews, students also note, "Almost no one here is from anywhere other than New York, New Jersey, Connecticut, or greater Boston," and that their classmates are "friendly, intelligent, at class on time, always ready for class discussions and lectures, and after class partying with friends." Union College students perceive their classmates as having major ambitions for their post-college years.

FINANCIAL AID: 518-388-6123 • E-MAIL: ADMISSIONS@UNION.EDU • WEBSITE: WWW.UNION.EDU

ADMISSIONS

Very important factors considered include: Class rank, secondary school record. *Important factors considered include:* Character/personal qualities, extracurricular activities, recommendations, standardized test scores. *Other factors considered include:* Alumni/ae relation, essays, geographical residence, interview, minority status, state residency, talent/ability, volunteer work, work experience. SAT Reasoning or ACT required. TOEFL required of all international applicants. High school diploma is required, and GED is not accepted. *Academic units required:* 4 English, 3 math, 2 science (2 science lab), 2 foreign language, 1 social studies, 1 history. *Academic units recommended:* 4 English, 4 math, 4 science (4 science lab), 4 foreign language, 2 social studies, 2 history.

The Inside Word

In this age of MTV-type admissions videos and ultra-glossy promotional literature, Union is decidedly more low-key than most colleges. The college is a bastion of tradition and conservatism and sticks to what it knows best when it comes to recruitment and admission. Students who are thinking about Union need to be prepared with as challenging a high school curriculum as possible and solid grades across the board.

FINANCIAL AID

Students should submit: FAFSA, CSS/Financial Aid PROFILE, state aid form, noncustodial (divorced/separated) parents' statement, business/farm supplement. Regular filing deadline is 2/1. The Princeton Review suggests that all financial aid forms be submitted as soon as possible after 1/1. *Need-based scholarships/grants offered:* Pell, SEOG, state scholarships/grants, private scholarships, the school's own gift aid. *Loan aid offered:* FFEL Subsidized Stafford, FFEL Unsubsidized Stafford, FFEL PLUS, Federal Perkins, college/university loans from institutional funds. Applicants will be notified of awards on or about 4/1. Federal Work-study Program available. Off-campus job opportunities are good.

FROM THE ADMISSIONS OFFICE

"'Breadth' and 'flexibility' characterize the Union academic program. Whether the subject is the poetry of ancient Greece or the possibilities of developing fields such as nanotechnology, Union students can choose among nearly 1,000 courses—a range that is unusual among America's highly selective colleges. Students can major in a single field, combine work in two or more departments, or even create their own organizing theme major. Undergraduate research is strongly encouraged, and more than half of Union's students take advantage of the college's extensive international study program.

"Students applying to enter Union in the fall of 2006 must submit the SAT (new or old version), or the ACT (with or without the Writing section), or two SAT Subject Tests. In our evaluation, we will use the best scores for each test."

SELECTIVITY

Admissions Rating	**94**
# of applicants	4,060
% of applicants accepted	49
% of acceptees attending	28
# accepting a place on wait list	681
% admitted from wait list	15
# of early decision applicants	165
% accepted early decision	68

FRESHMAN PROFILE

Range SAT Verbal	570-660
Average SAT Verbal	610
Range SAT Math	590-680
Average SAT Math	640
**TPR Projected Range SAT Writing*	*610-670*
Average ACT Composite	27
Minimum Paper TOEFL	600
Minimum Computer Based TOEFL	250
Average HS GPA	3.48
% graduated top 10% of class	59
% graduated top 25% of class	83
% graduated top 50% of class	98

DEADLINES

Early decision application deadline	11/15
Early decision notification	12/15
Regular application deadline	1/15
Regular notification	4/1
Nonfall registration?	no

APPLICANTS ALSO LOOK AT

AND OFTEN PREFER
Colby College
Colgate University

AND SOMETIMES PREFER
Hamilton College
Lafayette College
Skidmore College

AND RARELY PREFER
Rensselaer Polytechnic Institute
University of Rochester

FINANCIAL FACTS

Financial Aid Rating	**96**
Comprehensive fee	$38,703
Books and supplies	$450
% frosh rec. need-based scholarship or grant aid	48
% UG rec. need-based scholarship or grant aid	48
% frosh rec. need-based self-help aid	40
% UG rec. need-based self-help aid	45
% frosh rec. any financial aid	58
% UG rec. any financial aid	53
Avg. frosh grant	$18,404
Avg. frosh loan	$2,848
Independent 529 member?	No

UNITED STATES AIR FORCE ACADEMY

2304 CADET DRIVE, SUITE 200, USAF ACADEMY, CO 80840-5025 • ADMISSIONS: 719-333-2520 • FAX: 719-333-3012

CAMPUS LIFE

Quality of Life Rating	**89**
Fire Safety Rating	**60**
Type of school	public
Environment	metropolis

STUDENTS

Total undergrad enrollment	4,157
% male/female	83/17
% from out of state	95
% live on campus	100
% African American	5
% Asian	6
% Caucasian	81
% Hispanic	7
% Native American	1
% international	1
# of countries represented	22

SURVEY SAYS

Small classes
Lab facilities are great
Great computer facilities
Great library
Campus feels safe
Everyone loves the Falcons
Intramural sports are popular
Frats and sororities are unpopular or nonexistent
Very little drug use

ACADEMICS

Academic Rating	**98**
Calendar	semester
Student/faculty ratio	9:1
Professors interesting rating	95
Professors accessible rating	99
% professors teaching UG courses	100
% classes taught by TAs	0
Most common lab size	10-19 students
Most common regular class size	10-19 students

MOST POPULAR MAJORS

Business administration/management
engineering
social sciences

STUDENTS SPEAK OUT

Academics

Cadets speak glowingly of the United States Air Force Academy—training ground for tomorrow's elite Air Force officers. Writes a typical student, "I am convinced that USAFA is the best education available. [It's] one giant fraternity, where all cadets endure the challenge of academics, athletics, and military instruction. This place produces the best leaders and prepares its cadets for anything they will encounter." The workload here, by all accounts, is tremendous; as one student put it, "They purposely place 25 hours of tasks in every 24-hour day. It's tough, but if you work as a team and put forth all your effort every day, this place won't be too bad." Fortunately, professors "do not go home after they leave class. They stay for a full day, giving extra instruction whenever needed." Students appreciate the fact that "the funding for all aspects of education (not just academics, [but also] athletics, leadership, and character) is essentially unlimited, so the absolute best is not an exception: it is a rule." The "large core here" ensures cadets "some unique undergrad experiences like working with electron microscopes, nuclear magnetic resonance, and real cadavers." The curriculum also includes "classes in honor, character development, human relations, and leadership. During the summer we have other programs [such as] Jump (skydiving) and Soaring (flying gliders)." Even those overwhelmed by the school's demands admit that though "it's about the last place on Earth you would want to attend, it's the first place on Earth you would want to be from."

Life

Life at USAFA is rigorous, to put it mildly. "It's hard; there's so much to do with 23 credit hours, athletics, military stuff, religion, and community service," writes one cadet. "Overall it's a good experience; we learn time management very quickly." Freshman year—fourth class cadet status, technically speaking—is "quite harsh," filled with a back-breaking academic schedule, training evaluations conducted by upperclassmen (sentimentally referred to as "beat-downs"), mandatory athletics, and frequent training sessions. Weekends "are a welcome relief," writes one fourth class cadet, "except for one weekend a month when inspections, parades, and training sessions happen all Friday evening and into Saturday afternoon." Things improve somewhat in subsequent years, although "you can't go out during the school week until your senior year, and even then it's very limited, so our occasional free weekends are the times when we all let loose." In fact, until senior year, students' lives "are very structured, time allotted to do everything." During their rare sojourns off campus, students find that "the location is great because it affords students the opportunity to ski, hike, fish, shop, and just about anything else you could want to do." Notes one student, "There are two big cities (Denver and Colorado Springs) within driving distance and they both have active night scenes."

Student Body

The "straightforward, open-minded, goal-oriented individuals" who populate the USAFA "are teammates. We'd help each other out of trouble in a second. We're that close." Explains one student, "Due to the military stresses placed on them in the first year, they make great friends much quicker than I would imagine civilian students would in their freshman year." This closeness continues throughout their educations; explains one, "Without my fellow classmates there would be no way for me to make it through USAFA. Everyone here is extremely competitive, but we all help each other out as much as possible because we are in this institution together. You will NEVER understand the awesome level of friendship here." Cadets "get along really well, for the most part. We also have our share of geeks, athletes, and power-hungry tightwads who make the place less than amiable, but for the most part they even out and we all get along." Many cadets reported that "attitudes here have become more serious since September 11. There is a sense of purpose and drive, and a clear goal" shared by all.

UNITED STATES AIR FORCE ACADEMY

E-MAIL: RR_WEBMAIL@USAFA.AF.MIL • WEBSITE: WWW.ACADEMYADMISSIONS.COM

ADMISSIONS

Very important factors considered include: Character/personal qualities, interview, secondary school record, standardized test scores. *Important factors considered include:* Class rank, essays, extracurricular activities, talent/ability, volunteer work, work experience. *Other factors considered include:* Alumni/ae relation, minority status, recommendations. SAT Reasoning or ACT required. High school diploma is required, and GED is not accepted. *Academic units recommended:* 4 English, 4 math, 4 science (4 science lab), 2 foreign language, 3 social studies, 3 history, 1 academic elective.

The Inside Word

Candidates to the service academies face some of America's most challenging admissions standards. Air Force is no exception in this regard. In addition to a very rigorous academic review, students must first win a nomination from their congressman and pass a demanding physical fitness exam. If you make it through, it's worth the hard work and effort—few students turn down an offer of admission and the chance to join the fold of an elite student body. Admit rates are among the nation's lowest annually.

FINANCIAL AID

The Princeton Review suggests that all financial aid forms be submitted as soon as possible after 1/1. Off-campus job opportunities are poor.

FROM THE ADMISSIONS OFFICE

"Applicants for fall 2006 are required to take the new SAT (or the ACT with the Writing section), but students may submit scores from the old SAT or ACT as well, and will use the student's best scores from either test. "

SELECTIVITY

Admissions Rating	**97**
# of applicants	13,068
% of applicants accepted	15
% of acceptees attending	67

FRESHMAN PROFILE

Range SAT Verbal	590-670
Average SAT Verbal	629
Range SAT Math	620-700
Average SAT Math	663
**TPR Projected Range SAT Writing*	*620-680*
Average ACT Composite	29
Average HS GPA	3.8
% graduated top 10% of class	57
% graduated top 25% of class	85
% graduated top 50% of class	99

DEADLINES

Regular application deadline	1/31
Regular notification	rolling
Nonfall registration?	no

APPLICANTS ALSO LOOK AT AND SOMETIMES PREFER

United States Coast Guard Academy
United States Merchant Marine Academy
United States Military Academy
United States Naval Academy

FINANCIAL FACTS

Financial Aid Rating	**99**
Annual tuition	$0
Independent 529 member?	No

UNITED STATES COAST GUARD ACADEMY

31 MOHEGAN AVENUE, NEW LONDON, CT 06320-8103 • ADMISSIONS: 800-883-8724 • FAX: 860-701-6700

CAMPUS LIFE

Quality of Life Rating	**63**
Fire Safety Rating	**83**
Type of school	public
Environment	town

STUDENTS

Total undergrad enrollment	994
% male/female	71/29
% from out of state	94
% from public high school	77
% live on campus	100
% African American	3
% Asian	4
% Caucasian	85
% Hispanic	5
% Native American	1
% international	1
# of countries represented	15

SURVEY SAYS

Small classes
No one cheats
Campus feels safe
Everyone loves the Bears
Intramural sports are popular
Frats and sororities are unpopular or nonexistent
Political activism is unpopular or nonexistent
Very little drug use

ACADEMICS

Academic Rating	**87**
Calendar	semester
Student/faculty ratio	9:1
Professors interesting rating	70
Professors accessible rating	90
% professors teaching UG courses	100
% classes taught by TAs	0
Most common lab size	fewer than 10 students
Most common regular class size	10-19 students

MOST POPULAR MAJORS

Business administration and management
engineering
political science and government

STUDENTS SPEAK OUT

Academics

The United States Coast Guard Academy "brings together a diverse group of people dedicated to a common goal and teaches them how to live and work together to become leaders and to truly function as a team. We all live in the same building, eat the same meals, and go through the same training." If learning "personal discipline and how to balance a lot of responsibility with a heavy class load" sounds appealing to you—and you like the sea—then the CGA may be the right fit for you. Benefits include a free education ("although you put in enough mandatory extracurricular work to work your way though a normal college"), a "guaranteed job for five years after you graduate," and "incredible summer training programs that include all-expenses-paid trips (on Coast Guard ships) to places like Hawaii, Alaska, and Bermuda." Students can choose from only eight majors (the majority of which have the word 'engineering' in them somewhere), and much of the coursework here is required; "Every cadet has to take mandatory classes of calculus I & II, chemistry I & II, physics I & II, morals and ethics, world & American government, criminal justice, health, static engineering design, basic naval architecture, English and literature, introduction to electrical engineering, and macroeconomics, before and while we are taking our major-area classes. We all leave here very well-rounded." While professors "are tough and push us hard," students enjoy "an incredible support network of teachers, students, mentors, coaches and staff that take an integral role in helping us to achieve our personal and professional goals in and out of the Coast Guard."

Life

"Life is very regimented" at CGA, as students "all live in the same building, wake up at the same time, attend formations, and eat together." The experience "is a mix of military training, academics, and other activities. The first year is all about indoctrination. You will carry about 20+ credit hours, military work (duty and always having your uniform and room ready for inspection), and required activity credits." Even after first year, "We are not given many of the freedoms that most college students have. We aren't allowed to go out on weeknights and the rest of our liberty is restricted." As a result, cadets report, "When we are given the opportunity to go out or go on vacation, we go hard." The strict regulations work for some students, but others "become cynical by the time they have become seniors. Sometimes I regret not experiencing the kind of life that normal college students get to have." Stress relievers include club sports, which "are incredible considering the size of the school." Days out enjoying "the picturesque New England setting" and trips to New York City and Boston also help.

Student Body

"Because of the uniform, there is no discrimination like the petty discrimination of cliques in high school" at CGA. "We are shipmates, no matter where you were from or what you were like in your previous life as a civilian." One student explains, "Since we know we'll be working together for the rest of our military careers, people treat others with the utmost respect. There is no cheating, no stealing, no lying. If someone says they'll do something, they will." Most students are "A-type personalities" who "come from backgrounds in which [they] have always excelled academically, socially, and athletically. A-typical students are those who miss one or more of those traits." One cadet warns, "Atypical students quickly become typical students. We make sure of that!" Those who cannot fit the mold "do not perform well or are discharged."

United States Coast Guard Academy

E-MAIL: ADMISSIONS@CGA.USCG.MIL • WEBSITE: WWW.CGA.EDU

ADMISSIONS

Very important factors considered include: Character/personal qualities, class rank, extracurricular activities, secondary school record, standardized test scores. *Important factors considered include:* Essays, recommendations, talent/ability. *Other factors considered include:* Alumni/ae relation, interview, volunteer work, work experience. SAT Reasoning or ACT required. TOEFL required of all international applicants. High school diploma is required, and GED is accepted. *Academic units required:* 4 English, 4 math, 3 science (3 science lab).

The Inside Word

The Coast Guard is the smallest service academy, regarded by many as a well-kept secret. Just like the other military service academies, admission is highly selective. Candidates must go through a rigorous admissions process that includes a medical exam and physical fitness evaluation. Those who pass muster join a very proud service. If you're a woman and thinking about a service academy, be aware that the Corps of Cadets at the Coast Guard Academy is 30 percent women!

FINANCIAL AID

The Princeton Review suggests that all financial aid forms be submitted as soon as possible after 1/1.

FROM THE ADMISSIONS OFFICE

"Founded in 1876, the United State Coast Guard Academy has a proud tradition as one of the finest colleges in the country. When you've earned your four-year bachelor of science degree and a commission as an Ensign, you're prepared professionally, physically, and mentally as a leader and lifelong learner. You'll build friendships to last a lifetime, study with inspiring teachers in small classes, and train during the summer aboard America's Tall Ship EAGLE and the service's newest, most sophisticated ships and aircraft. Top performers spend their senior summer traveling on exciting internships. No Congressional nominations, appointments are awarded competitively on a nationwide basis. Graduates must serve for five years and have unmatched opportunities to attend flight training and graduate school, all funded by the Coast Guard. Your leadership potential and desire to serve your fellow Americans are what counts. Our student body reflects the best America has to offer—with all its potential and diversity!

"Applicants for fall 2006 are required to take the new SAT (or the ACT with the Writing section), but students may submit scores from the old SAT or ACT as well, and will use the student's best scores from either test."

SELECTIVITY

Admissions Rating	**96**
# of applicants	1,848
% of applicants accepted	22
% of acceptees attending	78

FRESHMAN PROFILE

Range SAT Verbal	580-670
Average SAT Verbal	621
Range SAT Math	620-680
Average SAT Math	649
**TPR Projected Range SAT Writing*	*620-680*
Range ACT Composite	25-30
Average ACT Composite	27
Minimum Paper TOEFL	560
Minimum Computer Based TOEFL	220
Average HS GPA	3.64
% graduated top 10% of class	56
% graduated top 25% of class	90
% graduated top 50% of class	100

DEADLINES

Regular application deadline	1/31
Regular notification	rolling
Nonfall registration?	no

FINANCIAL FACTS

Financial Aid Rating	**99**
Annual tuition	$0
Independent 529 member?	No

UNITED STATES MERCHANT MARINE ACADEMY

OFFICE OF ADMISSIONS, KINGS POINT, NY 11024-1699 • ADMISSIONS: 516-773-5391 • FAX: 516-773-5390

CAMPUS LIFE

Quality of Life Rating	**66**
Fire Safety Rating	**60**
Type of school	public
Environment	village

STUDENTS

Total undergrad enrollment	1,007
% male/female	86/14
% from out of state	87
% from public high school	70
% live on campus	100
% international	2
# of countries represented	3

SURVEY SAYS

Small classes
Everyone loves the Mariners
Frats and sororities are unpopular or nonexistent
Political activism is unpopular or nonexistent
Lots of beer drinking
Very little drug use

ACADEMICS

Academic Rating	**81**
Calendar	trimester
Student/faculty ratio	11:1
Professors interesting rating	61
Professors accessible rating	76
% classes taught by TAs	0
Most common lab size	10-19 students
Most common regular class size	10-19 students

MOST POPULAR MAJORS

Engineering
naval architecture and marine engineering
transportation and materials moving services

STUDENTS SPEAK OUT

Academics

Mention sailors and most people think of swearing, drinking, and port-of-call carousing, and while this image applies on rare occasions to students at the United States Merchant Marine Academy (USMMA), the focus here is decidedly on academics. At the beginning of the second semester of freshman year, midshipmen select a major—one of six available: "deck or engine, [meaning Marine Transportation or Marine Engineering] with a few subcategories in each." From that point forward, they have their course schedule laid out by the Academy. "I get one elective in four years," one midshipman notes. The academic program receives high praise, specifically because classroom learning is complemented by "one of four years of actual working experience." That experience comes during Sea Year, and students say, "Sea Year Courses, which are done while training on various merchant ships throughout the world, are the most difficult of the academy's courses." Professors are characterized as "dedicated," some to the point of being "slave drivers." The small classes, lack of TAs, and mandatory class attendance policy ensure that students get the attention they need to manage the "very heavy course load" and regimental requirements. Even deans pitch in and "tutor students when they can." Students submit mixed opinions when it comes to the administration, though the superintendent is widely respected. Some midshipmen perceive an "open door" attitude from administrators, but others claim that the "administration thinks we are whiny brats." Most students look forward to the high-paying careers available to them after graduation and appreciate the "excellent leadership training" they receive at the Academy.

Life

"This school is a country club if you disregard the marching," one USMMA student observes. Marching and other regimental activities constitute much of life in Kings Point, prompting some students to feel at times like "inmates" on campus. Some report "sleeping two to four hours a night" to accommodate the intense academic and regimental schedule. Basically, "freshmen don't have lives," but even first-years point out, "We are here to train." As they progress, midshipmen begin to enjoy more "individual freedoms [and] privileges, which are granted based upon seniority and individual performance." To blow off steam, "most people work out nearly every day or play sports." When the weekend rolls around, "it's all about New York City," which is only 20 to 30 minutes away by train. One student writes, "I typically utilize some of our perks, such as free admission to Mets games, the U.S. Open, Yankees games, and David Letterman." Though rumors suggest "a few people have actually gone into museums" during these outings to the Big Apple, students mainly hit the bars, "on the prowl due to the lack of women at school." Other people choose to "sail all over Long Island on the weekends." A common sentiment goes something like, "Life at school is very busy, and there are not many times to just 'chill,' as my regular college friends call it."

Students

The typical USMMA student is reported to be a "white male between the ages of 18 and 22;" only about 100 women attend the Academy. Also, the population includes "very few students that are of a different ethnicity," but one minority student writes frankly, "I have not found this to be a problem." This might be partly due to the pervasive notion that "having people from many different areas of the country and world makes for an increased awareness of life in general and how people act." Respondents agree that "most students have similar political views," which translates to "no hippies." "Everyone becomes 'typical' by necessity because of the regimentation of the school." Strong bonds form during an "indoctrination period" that each incoming class undergoes, the "evident esprit de corps" solidified by the "cramped quarters" and "repressive regime" in which they exist. These solid connections endure after graduates set sail: "The merchant marine community is so small that there is also the advantage of an excellent network of contacts."

United States Merchant Marine Academy

Financial Aid: 516-773-5295 • E-mail: admissions@usmma.edu • Website: www.usmma.edu

ADMISSIONS

Very important factors considered include: Character/personal qualities, secondary school record, standardized test scores. *Important factors considered include:* Class rank, essays, extracurricular activities, geographical residence, recommendations, talent/ability. *Other factors considered include:* Interview, minority status, state residency, volunteer work, work experience. SAT Reasoning or ACT required. TOEFL required of all international applicants. High school diploma is required, and GED is not accepted. *Academic units required:* 4 English, 3 math, 3 science (1 science lab), 8 academic electives. *Academic units recommended:* 4 English, 4 math, 4 science (2 science lab), 2 foreign language, 4 social studies.

The Inside Word

Academic criteria are only part of the admissions game here; you must also meet the Academy's physical requirements. The school catalog has three pages of requirements concerning vision, hearing, weight and body fat percent, skin condition, and respiratory health. You also need to know how to swim.

FINANCIAL AID

Students should submit: FAFSA, institution's own financial aid form. Regular filing deadline is 5/1. The Princeton Review suggests that all financial aid forms be submitted as soon as possible after 1/1. *Need-based scholarships/grants offered:* Pell, private scholarships. *Loan aid offered:* FFEL Subsidized Stafford, FFEL Unsubsidized Stafford, FFEL PLUS. Applicants will be notified of awards on a rolling basis beginning on or about 1/31. Off-campus job opportunities are poor.

FROM THE ADMISSIONS OFFICE

"What makes the U.S. Merchant Marine Academy different from the other federal service academies? The difference can be summarized in two phrases that appear in our publications. The first: 'The World Is Your Campus.' You will spend a year at sea—a third of your sophomore year and two-thirds of your junior year—teamed with a classmate aboard a U.S. merchant ship. You will visit an average of 18 foreign nations while you work and learn in a mariner's true environment. You will graduate with seafaring experience and as a citizen of the world. The second phrase is 'Options and Opportunities.' Unlike students at the other federal academies, who are required to enter the service connected to their academy, you have the option of working in the seagoing merchant marine and transportation industry or applying for active duty in the Navy, Coast Guard, Marine Corps, Air Force, or Army. Nearly 29 percent of our most recent graduating class entered various branches of the Armed Forces with an officer rank. As a graduate of the U.S. Merchant Marine Academy, you will receive a Bachelor of Science degree, a government-issued merchant marine officer's license, and a Naval Reserve commission (unless you have been accepted for active military duty). No other service academy offers so attractive a package.

"Freshman applicants for fall 2006 must take the new SAT (or the ACT with the Writing component). Students may additionally submit scores from the old SAT or ACT. For home schooled students, we recommend scores from SAT Subject Tests in Chemistry and Physics. Writing scores will be used in academic placement."

SELECTIVITY

Admissions Rating	**94**
# of applicants	1,797
% of applicants accepted	21
% of acceptees attending	77
# accepting a place on wait list	283
% admitted from wait list	1

FRESHMAN PROFILE

Range SAT Verbal	570-690
Average SAT Verbal	630
Range SAT Math	590-670
Average SAT Math	625
**TPR Projected Range SAT Writing*	*610-690*
Range ACT Composite	25-31
Average ACT Composite	28
Minimum Paper TOEFL	550
Minimum Computer Based TOEFL	213
Average HS GPA	3.6
% graduated top 10% of class	26
% graduated top 25% of class	64
% graduated top 50% of class	96

DEADLINES

Early decision application deadline	11/1
Early decision notification	12/31
Regular application deadline	3/1
Regular notification	rolling
Nonfall registration?	no

APPLICANTS ALSO LOOK AT AND OFTEN PREFER

United States Naval Academy

AND SOMETIMES PREFER

United States Air Force Academy
United States Coast Guard Academy
United States Military Academy

AND RARELY PREFER

Maine Maritime Academy
Massachusetts Maritime Academy
SUNY Maritime College

FINANCIAL FACTS

Financial Aid Rating	**98**
Annual tuition	$0
Required fees	$3,500
% frosh rec. need-based scholarship or grant aid	18
% UG rec. need-based scholarship or grant aid	6
% frosh rec. need-based self-help aid	23
% UG rec. need-based self-help aid	8
Avg. frosh grant	$2,229
Avg. frosh loan	$2,625
Independent 529 member?	No

United States Military Academy

600 Thayer Road, West Point, NY 10996-1797 • Admissions: 845-938-4041 • Fax: 845-938-3021

CAMPUS LIFE

Quality of Life Rating	**65**
Fire Safety Rating	**60**
Type of school	public
Environment	village

STUDENTS

Total undergrad enrollment	4,175
% male/female	85/15
% from out of state	92
% from public high school	86
% live on campus	100
% African American	7
% Asian	7
% Caucasian	77
% Hispanic	6
% Native American	1
% international	1
# of countries represented	16

SURVEY SAYS

Small classes
No one cheats
Great computer facilities
Great library
Campus feels safe
Intramural sports are popular
Frats and sororities are unpopular or nonexistent
Very little drug use

ACADEMICS

Academic Rating	**97**
Calendar	semester
Student/faculty ratio	7:1
Professors interesting rating	88
Professors accessible rating	98
% professors teaching UG courses	100
% classes taught by TAs	0
Most common lab size	10-19 students
Most common regular class size	10-19 students

STUDENTS SPEAK OUT

Academics

At West Point, students tell us, "We forge leaders. Not build, not make, not teach; forge. Forging involves heat, pressure, and time." How? For starters, you will pretty much combine a full day's study with another full day's drills and exercise every day, especially during freshman and sophomore years. As one student explains, "The days normally start at 0600 and end at 2400 for most people. Our free time is filled by 'developmental' activities intended to help us become officers. We have no lives until we are in our third year." Not only are underclassmen's daily schedules fully prescribed, but so is their course of study; all classes during the first two years are required general education classes that are "very broad. It is hard to retain information because of the volume of material we have to learn each semester." To make the experience even more challenging, West Point employs the "Thayer method of teaching," in which students "teach themselves the material the night before [as homework], and the teacher explains it if we have any questions" in class. Fortunately, "Instructors are great, and they will make time to provide additional instruction outside the classroom." Still, it is just about as tough a row to hoe as there is. What's the payoff? Only an "awesome campus, free education, awesome academic and military opportunities for all cadets, free room and board, plus a small paycheck each month." Plus, things do ease up a little during the third and fourth years. As one student sums up, "You get a lot done in one day, and at the end of it, you're very proud of everything you're able to accomplish."

Life

Many agree that life at West Point is "far stricter than anyone could imagine." For plebes (freshmen) and yearlings (sophomores), "There is essentially no free time during the day. There's mandatory drill (practice marching for parades), mandatory intramurals, chain of command duties, mandatory lectures/meetings, and academia." One plebe notes, "As freshmen, we are only allowed one weekend per semester to get out of here on our own. It gets quite depressing. For a wild Friday or Saturday night, we generally throw in a DVD on our computers and fall asleep around 10:00 P.M." No wonder underclassmen "try to leave on trip sections with different organizations as much as possible to get out of here." It does not stay that way. "Things are a little better your last two years; still, you'll be more than ready to break out at graduation," notes one undergraduate. When upperclassmen have free time, "most people go to a place on campus [where] they are allowed to drink. But they have to be 21, of course. [Others] get involved with the clubs, hang out with friends, [and] have pickup games of football or basketball during the warmer months." Or, understandably enough, they sleep.

Student Body

It takes an exceptional student to get into West Point, and an even more exceptional student to survive its grind. The typical student "is the All-American kid; he played sports and was in all sorts of stuff in high school. Most are religious. All want to be the best, but without screwing other people over." To make it at West Point, you have to "fit into a very small category: physically fit, intelligent, and willing to live a regimented lifestyle." The fitness part is critical. "If you are not physically fit, don't come here," students warn. They are also extremely goal-oriented; they have to be to "handle the suck" that is life for an underclassman. Otherwise, students have little to say about each other's distinguishing traits and for good reason. "A lot of students are the same because we are molded to think similarly." As one wry student puts it, "The typical students at my school all wear the same clothes, have weapons in their rooms, and get graded on how well they beat up their classmates."

FINANCIAL AID: 845-938-3516 • E-MAIL: ADMISSIONS@USMA.EDU • WEBSITE: WWW.USMA.EDU

ADMISSIONS

Very important factors considered include: Character/personal qualities, class rank, essays, extracurricular activities, recommendations, secondary school record, standardized test scores. *Important factors considered include:* Interview, minority status, talent/ability, volunteer work. *Other factors considered include:* Geographical residence, work experience. SAT Reasoning or ACT required. High school diploma is required, and GED is accepted. *Academic units recommended:* 4 English, 4 math, 2 science (2 science lab), 2 foreign language, 3 social studies, 1 history, 3 academic electives.

The Inside Word

Students considering a candidacy at West Point need to hit the ground running in the second half of their junior year. Don't delay initiating the application and nomination processes; together they constitute a long, hard road that includes not one but several highly competitive elements. Successful candidates must demonstrate strength both academically and physically, be solid citizens and contributors to society, and show true fortitude and potential for leadership. Admissions processes at other top schools can seem like a cakewalk compared to this, but those who get a nomination and pass the physical part of the process have made it through the hardest part.

FINANCIAL AID

The Princeton Review suggests that all financial aid forms be submitted as soon as possible after 1/1. *Need-based scholarships/grants offered:* All cadets are on active duty as members of the United States Army and receive an annual salary of approximately $8,880.20. Room and board, medical and dental care is provided by the army. A one-time deposit of $2,400 is required upon admission (if needed, loans for the deposit are available for $100 to $2,400) to help pay for the initial issue of uniforms, books, supplies, equipment, and fees. A cadet's salary pays for uniforms, activities, services, books, sundries, and other personal effects throughout the four-year experience. Upon graduation, cadets are awarded a bachelor of science degree and are commissioned in the army as second lieutenants with a five-year active duty service obligation. Off-campus job opportunities are poor.

FROM THE ADMISSIONS OFFICE

"Applicants for summer 2006 are required to take the new SAT (or the ACT with the Writing component). Students may also submit scores from the old SAT or ACT, and their best scores will be used regardless of test date."

SELECTIVITY

Admissions Rating	**96**
# of applicants	10,843
% of applicants accepted	13
% of acceptees attending	84
# accepting a place on wait list	684
% admitted from wait list	53

FRESHMAN PROFILE

Range SAT Verbal	570-660
Average SAT Verbal	627
Range SAT Math	600-690
Average SAT Math	641
**TPR Projected Range SAT Writing*	*610-670*
Range ACT Composite	26-30
Average ACT Composite	28
Average HS GPA	3.67
% graduated top 10% of class	50
% graduated top 25% of class	81
% graduated top 50% of class	97

DEADLINES

Regular application deadline	2/28
Regular notification	rolling
Nonfall registration?	no

APPLICANTS ALSO LOOK AT

AND OFTEN PREFER
University of Rochester

AND SOMETIMES PREFER
Tulane University
United States Naval Academy
University of Notre Dame
University of Oklahoma
Villanova University

AND RARELY PREFER
Carnegie Mellon University
University of Florida

FINANCIAL FACTS

Financial Aid Rating	**99**
Annual tuition	$0
Books and supplies	$664
Independent 529 member?	No

UNITED STATES NAVAL ACADEMY

117 Decatur Road, Annapolis, MD 21402 • Admissions: 410-293-4361 • Fax: 410-295-1815

CAMPUS LIFE

Quality of Life Rating	**90**
Fire Safety Rating	**86**
Type of school	public
Environment	village

STUDENTS

Total undergrad enrollment	4,349
% male/female	83/17
% from out of state	94
% from public high school	60
% live on campus	100
% African American	7
% Asian	5
% Caucasian	77
% Hispanic	9
% Native American	2
% international	1
# of countries represented	21

SURVEY SAYS

Small classes
No one cheats
Lab facilities are great
Great computer facilities
Campus feels safe
Everyone loves the navy
Intramural sports are popular
Frats and sororities are unpopular or nonexistent
Very little drug use

ACADEMICS

Academic Rating	**92**
Calendar	semester
Student/faculty ratio	7:1
Professors interesting rating	82
Professors accessible rating	99
% professors teaching UG courses	100
% classes taught by TAs	0
Most common regular class size	20-29 students

MOST POPULAR MAJORS

Economics
political science and government
systems engineering

STUDENTS SPEAK OUT

Academics

The United States Naval Academy "produces leaders, not just people with book knowledge" through a grueling academic and physical ordeal that forges graduates who are "strong morally, mentally, and physically, able to cope in any place that they are put, and able to overcome any obstacle that lies in their way." This "nonstop competition from start to finish [instills] discipline, time management, and dedication," as well as "great moral and ethical values" in midshipmen. All students receive a full scholarship, but no one here would tell you she or he is getting a free ride; "It is a an expensive education shoved up your rear a nickel at a time," wryly notes one student. "Academics are extremely hard" because, in large part, "there is very little time to do your work, with the military aspect taking up a great deal of time." The USNA offers a "solid curriculum" reinforced by small classes ("even freshmen-level courses never exceed 21 students per class"), tremendous resources ("we have the money to access all kinds of amazing things"), and a solid faculty ("I take classes from a former Chairman of the Joint Chiefs of Staff and other respected professionals"). Sums up one student, "This school sets and maintains a standard unimaginable at other colleges and universities, and the feeling of accomplishment at the end of the day is hard to beat."

Life

"Every midshipman may complain at one time or another about many aspects of life at the Naval Academy, but overall I believe it is what we want," notes one student at the USNA. "We did not come here for an easy experience. We came here to be the best. And the administration, officers, and professors expect exactly that from us." Be forewarned, that "your first year will be extremely hard here," as "plebe year is something that you'll have to experience in order to believe." For plebes, "life is as restricted as it gets, short of prison. No music and movies, and you can only go out on Saturdays. We have mandatory drill, training, and physical exercise, along with student and military chains of command that restrict weekend liberty and what clothes we can wear, among other things." Throughout all four years, students "do an enormous amount of professional training, from summer training cruises to character development and leadership classes," and they "work out all the time." Campus recreation includes extracurricular activities "of every size and description;" when they get liberty ("you get more each year"), students head to Annapolis or to other nearby campuses. "For fun, there are about 10 bars within walking distance, for those of age." Students agree: it's a rough life, but "even the people who say they hate it rarely ever leave. There's nothing like being in King Hall (our dining hall) with 4,000 other midshipmen banging crab mallets on the table during the annual fall Crab Feast, or walking into Memorial Hall late at night and reading the names of graduates that have died in combat and remembering that 'they have set the course.'"

Student Body

"Contrary to what one might expect, there is a tremendous variety of students," at the United States Naval Academy. "They come from all over the country and many different socioeconomic classes and walks of life. No one can tell what kind of financial background you have; we all wear the same uniform, get the same pay, and get in effect full scholarship and free room and board." Many "were high-school athletes who lettered in two or more varsity sports while having a 3.9 GPA in classes," the type of people who "excelled at almost everything they tried their hand at in high school and continue to excel at USNA." Despite the diversity of backgrounds, "there are almost [no] students who are atypical, because this is not an environment hospitable to them."

United States Naval Academy

E-mail: webmail@gwmail.usna.com • Website: www.usna.edu

ADMISSIONS

Very important factors considered include: Character/personal qualities, class rank, essays, extracurricular activities, interview, recommendations, secondary school record, standardized test scores. *Important factors considered include:* Talent/ability. *Other factors considered include:* Alumni/ae relation, geographical residence, minority status, state residency, volunteer work, work experience. SAT Reasoning or ACT required. TOEFL required of all international applicants. High school diploma or equivalent is not required. *Academic units recommended:* 4 English, 4 math, 2 science (1 science lab), 2 foreign language, 2 history, 1 introductory computer and typing course.

The Inside Word

It doesn't take a genius to recognize that getting admitted to Annapolis requires true strength of character; simply completing the arduous admissions process is an accomplishment worthy of remembrance. Those who have successful candidacies are strong, motivated students, and leaders in both school and community. Perseverance is an important character trait for anyone considering the life of a midshipman—the application process is only the beginning of a truly challenging and demanding experience.

FINANCIAL AID

The Princeton Review suggests that all financial aid forms be submitted as soon as possible after 1/1.

FROM THE ADMISSIONS OFFICE

"The Naval Academy offers you a unique opportunity to associate with a broad cross-section of the country's finest young men and women. You will have the opportunity to pursue a four-year program that develops you mentally, morally, and physically as no civilian college can. As you might expect, this program is demanding, but the opportunities are limitless and more than worth the effort. To receive an appointment to the academy, you need four years of high school preparation to develop the strong academic, athletic, and extracurricular background required to compete successfully for admission. You should begin preparing in your freshman year and apply for admission at the end of your junior year. Selection for appointment to the academy comes as a result of a complete evaluation of your admissions package and completion of the nomination process. Complete admissions guidance may be found at www.usna.edu.

"SAT results from tests prior to March 2005 and ACT results from tests prior to February 2005 will be used by the Naval Academy, and no conversion of scores is necessary due to compatibility of old and new scoring systems."

SELECTIVITY

Admissions Rating	**96**
# of applicants	14,423
% of applicants accepted	10
% of acceptees attending	84

FRESHMAN PROFILE

Range SAT Verbal	580-680
Average SAT Verbal	648
Range SAT Math	610-710
Average SAT Math	670
**TPR Projected Range SAT Writing*	*620-680*
Minimum Paper TOEFL	200
% graduated top 10% of class	54
% graduated top 25% of class	81
% graduated top 50% of class	96

DEADLINES

Regular application deadline	1/31
Regular notification	rolling
Nonfall registration?	no

APPLICANTS ALSO LOOK AT

AND OFTEN PREFER

Duke University
Harvard College
United States Air Force Academy
University of Virginia

AND SOMETIMES PREFER

Georgia Institute of Technology
Massachusetts Institute of Technology
Penn State University Park
United States Military Academy

AND RARELY PREFER

Boston University
Purdue University—West Lafayette
St. John's College (MD)

FINANCIAL FACTS

Financial Aid Rating	**99**
Annual tuition	$0
Independent 529 member?	No

THE UNIVERSITY OF ALABAMA—TUSCALOOSA

BOX 870132, TUSCALOOSA, AL 35487-0132 • ADMISSIONS: 205-348-5666 • FAX: 205-348-9046

CAMPUS LIFE

Quality of Life Rating	**83**
Fire Safety Rating	**76**
Type of school	public
Environment	city

STUDENTS

Total undergrad enrollment	16,202
% male/female	47/53
% from out of state	20
% from public high school	90
% live on campus	24
% in (# of) fraternities	20 (27)
% in (# of) sororities	26 (19)
% African American	13
% Asian	1
% Caucasian	84
% Hispanic	1
% Native American	1
% international	1
# of countries represented	83

SURVEY SAYS

Great library
Athletic facilities are great
Students are happy
Everyone loves the Crimson Tide
Frats and sororities dominate social scene
Lots of beer drinking

ACADEMICS

Academic Rating	**74**
Calendar	semester
Student/faculty ratio	20:1
Professors interesting rating	75
Professors accessible rating	80
% professors teaching UG courses	68
% classes taught by TAs	12
Most common lab size	20-29 students
Most common regular class size	20-29 students

MOST POPULAR MAJORS

Business administration/management
finance
marketing/marketing management

STUDENTS SPEAK OUT

Academics

Students at The University of Alabama (UA), a gargantuan southern state university, believe that several factors help to mitigate the impersonality typical of other mega-universities. "Because Alabama is in the South, there is an overall friendliness between professors and students, as long as you show up for class not hung-over, as many students do," explains one student. "As a freshman, I have already developed strong bonds with two of my professors. Out of all my introductory classes, only one is a large lecture class. I love it here!" This big school is also made to feel a little smaller by "great student advisors. You can walk in anytime and get one to talk to you about your grades, progress, or problems. If you slip up and have a bad semester, they're there for you." As at most big schools, "it is the luck of the draw in getting a good teacher or professor," and "the administration is okay at best. They are fairly helpful during registration, and the records office usually runs pretty smoothly. However, the financial aid office and Student Receivables (bursar's office) are ridiculous." Undergrads choose from nine educational divisions: commerce and business administration, education, communication, engineering, arts and sciences, nursing, social work, human environmental sciences, and New College—a unique, independent study program. They observe that "while the bigger colleges have nicer facilities and equipment, the smaller colleges have more faculty and support for each student."

Life

Students report that "Alabama is a great place if you are looking for a good time, from going to the bars, to sitting on the porch with friends, to a huge victory party (after football games). We have anything you would want to do on any night of the week." More than a few students, it should be noted, mentioned with pride that 'Bama received a "#2 Party School" ranking in a previous edition of this book. Those not into partying often agree that "life at Alabama is fairly monotonous. There is 'The Strip,' the main street through the campus with bars and restaurants and other little shops, and that's about it. There are no clubs here, just several bars, and that's pretty much the only entertainment on weekends." There's also a large, powerful, and, by many accounts, elitist Greek scene; writes one student, "The thing at Alabama is to be Greek. If you aren't, there are a lot of things unavailable to you." Students adore their Crimson Tide teams; reports one student, "People really love sports here, especially football. It's a really athletic school with great recreational facilities."

Student Body

The "overwhelmingly conservative" students of 'Bama admit to a wide, well-defined divide running between the Greek and independent communities. Writes one GDI, "The Greeks can be nice individually, but as a group they can be somewhat snobbish." Independents especially resent the sense that "the Greek system here at the university, referred to by many simply as 'The Machine,' basically runs the school. They control the SGA and nearly every campus group. For non-Greek students, it's hard to escape from under their umbrella." Students report that "there's a lot of ethnic diversity here at UA; however, the groups almost never mix. I wouldn't say there's any animosity. The groups just don't have anything in common with each other." Some go further; groused one Jewish student, "Make no mistake about it, there is more racism here than I have ever experienced in my life. Even in the campus dining area, there is a clear line of the 'white side' and the 'black side.'"

FINANCIAL AID: 205-348-6756 • E-MAIL: ADMISSIONS@UA.EDU • WEBSITE: WWW.UA.EDU

ADMISSIONS

Very important factors considered include: Secondary school record, standardized test scores. *Important factors considered include:* Class rank. *Other factors considered include:* Alumni/ae relation, character/personal qualities, essays, extracurricular activities, interview, recommendations, talent/ability, volunteer work, work experience. SAT Reasoning or ACT required. TOEFL required of all international applicants. High school diploma is required, and GED is accepted. *Academic units required:* 4 English, 3 math, 3 science (2 science lab), 1 foreign language, 3 social studies, 1 history, 5 academic electives. *Academic units recommended:* 4 English, 3 math, 3 science (2 science lab), 1 foreign language, 3 social studies, 1 history, 5 academic electives.

The Inside Word

There's no mystery in Alabama's formula-driven approach to admission; any solid "B" student is likely to meet with success. What selectivity there is in the process exists mainly because of the volume of applications. Recommendations are not likely to play a significant role in the admission of applicants unless they are borderline candidates.

FINANCIAL AID

Students should submit: FAFSA. The Princeton Review suggests that all financial aid forms be submitted as soon as possible after 1/1. *Need-based scholarships/grants offered:* Pell, SEOG, state scholarships/grants, private scholarships, the school's own gift aid, Federal Nursing scholarships. *Loan aid offered:* Direct Subsidized Stafford, Direct Unsubsidized Stafford, Direct PLUS, Federal Perkins, college/university loans from institutional funds. Applicants will be notified of awards on a rolling basis beginning on or about 4/1.

FROM THE ADMISSIONS OFFICE

"Since its founding in 1831 as the first public university in the state, The University of Alabama has been committed to providing the best, most complete education possible for its students. Our commitment to that goal means that as times change, we sharpen our focus and methods to keep our graduates competitive in their fields. By offering outstanding teaching in a solid core curriculum enhanced by multimedia classrooms and campus-wide computer labs, The University of Alabama keeps its focus on the future while maintaining a traditional college atmosphere. Extensive international study opportunities, internship programs, and co-operative education placements help our students prepare for successful futures. Consisting of 11 colleges and schools offering 220 degrees in more than 100 fields of study, the university gives its students a wide range of choices and offers courses of study at the bachelor's, master's, specialist, and doctoral levels. The university emphasizes quality and breadth of academic opportunities and challenging programs for well-prepared students through its Honors College (including the University Honors Program, International Honors Program, and Computer-Based Honors Programs and Blount Undergraduate Initiative [liberal arts program]. One-third of undergraduates are from out-of-state providing an enriching social and cultural environment.

"Applicants for the 2006 freshmen class will be may submit either the new SAT or the old SAT (administered before March 2005). For those students electing to take the ACT test, the Writing component is not required for admission to the University of Alabama."

SELECTIVITY

Admissions Rating	**79**
# of applicants	9,106
% of applicants accepted	77
% of acceptees attending	48

FRESHMAN PROFILE

Range SAT Verbal	490-620
Average SAT Verbal	553
Range SAT Math	500-610
Average SAT Math	561
**TPR Projected Range SAT Writing*	*550-650*
Range ACT Composite	21-26
Average ACT Composite	24
Minimum Paper TOEFL	500
Minimum Computer Based TOEFL	173
Average HS GPA	3.36
% graduated top 10% of class	22
% graduated top 25% of class	45
% graduated top 50% of class	76

DEADLINES

Regular application deadline	8/1
Regular notification	rolling
Nonfall registration?	yes

APPLICANTS ALSO LOOK AT AND OFTEN PREFER

Birmingham—Southern College
Florida State University
University of Georgia
University of Tennessee—Knoxville
Vanderbilt University

AND SOMETIMES PREFER

Auburn University
Loyola University New Orleans
Mississippi State University
Oglethorpe University
Samford University

FINANCIAL FACTS

Financial Aid Rating	**77**
Annual in-state tuition	$4,630
Annual out-of-state tuition	$12,664
Room & Board	$4,734
Books and supplies	$800
% frosh rec. need-based scholarship or grant aid	20
% UG rec. need-based scholarship or grant aid	24
% frosh rec. need-based self-help aid	24
% UG rec. need-based self-help aid	33
% frosh rec. any financial aid	68
% UG rec. any financial aid	74
Avg. frosh grant	$3,662
Avg. frosh loan	$3,220
Independent 529 member?	No

UNIVERSITY OF ARIZONA

PO Box 210040, Tucson, AZ 85721-0040 • Admissions: 520-621-3237 • Fax: 520-621-9799

CAMPUS LIFE

Quality of Life Rating	**74**
Fire Safety Rating	**60**
Type of school	public
Environment	metropolis

STUDENTS

Total undergrad enrollment	27,853
% male/female	47/53
% from out of state	27
% from public high school	90
% live on campus	18
% in (# of) fraternities	7 (25)
% in (# of) sororities	11 (20)
% African American	3
% Asian	6
% Caucasian	66
% Hispanic	15
% Native American	2
% international	3
# of countries represented	124

SURVEY SAYS

Great computer facilities
Great library
Athletic facilities are great
Everyone loves the Wildcats
Frats and sororities dominate social scene
Student publications are popular
Lots of beer drinking
Hard liquor is popular

ACADEMICS

Academic Rating	**61**
Calendar	semester
Student/faculty ratio	19:1
Professors interesting rating	68
Professors accessible rating	77
% professors teaching UG courses	78
% classes taught by TAs	22
Most common lab size	20-29 students
Most common regular class size	20-29 students

MOST POPULAR MAJORS

Elementary education and teaching
political science and government
psychology

STUDENTS SPEAK OUT

Academics

Students at the University of Arizona (U of A) enjoy that sought-after combination of reasonable tuition and solid reputation, and they know it. "I can't believe the diversity of academic opportunities and relatively low cost of education and living," gushes a junior. The academic rigor surprises some admitted students, who report, "It's definitely harder than I expected it to be." Overall, "A majority of the students take school very seriously." Even at a large state school, professors "try very hard to make learning fun and interesting." Another student concurs, "The professors are very knowledgeable and seem to genuinely care about teaching." Undergraduates find their instructors "very understanding [and] highly skilled in their fields." Teaching assistants "who work with classes are almost always really passionate, energetic, and ambitious." Noteworthy programs include nutrition and the "extremely well-known dance department." Unfortunately, some students moan about the administration "canceling classes and important programs while pouring more money into weight rooms for their athletes." Bigger is not always better to some in Tucson. One undergraduate writes, "I just wish classes were smaller, so it would be easier to learn." For one student "graduating in four years is almost impossible." While the administration is typically "ready with answers to your questions, you sort of have to stumble your way through" early on.

Life

Any description of the University of Arizona would not be complete without tribute to the "constant party" that animates the campus. Pretty much "Monday through Sunday you can find a place to drink and go wild." Active Greek chapters generate a steady flow of "great parties and date dashes." Off campus, the action centers on Fourth Avenue, "where the bars are," along with restaurants and movie theaters. Historically, local Tucson residents have complained about house parties thrown by U of A students, and the communities are working together to address the conflict. Everyone, town and gown, unites around Wildcat basketball. "The team is always awesome," notes one student. School spirit also shines at volleyball and softball games. When it's sunny, it's time to bask in "the near-perfect weather most of the year." When it's snowy, "some people go up to Mt. Lemon and go skiing or snowboarding." Students also take advantage of other "outdoor recreation opportunities, like hiking and mountain biking," but some feel constrained without a car. Other options include "going to the mall and playing sports." In a great fusion of academic and social life, many students take to "sunbathing and people-watching outside while they study to pass exams."

Student Body

When you break it down, the U of A population sorts into "all types: athletes, nerds, Greeks, hippies, [and] preppies." Students can choose a "sun-bleached, name-brand, party" crowd or the "laid-back, more academically-minded" scene. A typical student "loves sports, loves our teams, and loves to party." Anomalous students do persist, but they are usually "too busy demonstrating against wars and stuff" to muddle the dominant image. The school also hosts a visible "population of out-of-staters." The student body includes "students of all backgrounds, religions, ethnicities, and incomes" who coexist in a "very open, accepting, and friendly environment." One undergraduate says of his colleagues, "While some are well-rounded, passionate, intelligent individuals, the vast majority, socially speaking, seem to be stuck somewhere between middle school and high school." Whatever one's taste in friends, with nearly 30,000 other undergraduates, "you can't not find someone like you."

University of Arizona

Financial Aid: 520-621-1858 • E-mail: appinfo@arizona.edu • Website: www.arizona.edu

ADMISSIONS

Very important factors considered include: Secondary school record. *Important factors considered include:* Class rank, standardized test scores. *Other factors considered include:* Character/personal qualities, essays, extracurricular activities, geographical residence, interview, minority status, recommendations, state residency, talent/ability, volunteer work, work experience. SAT Reasoning or ACT required. High school diploma is required, and GED is accepted. *Academic units required:* 4 English, 4 math, 3 science (3 science lab), 2 foreign language, 1 social studies, 1 history, 1 fine arts. *Academic units recommended:* 4 English, 4 math, 3 science (3 science lab), 2 foreign language, 1 social studies, 1 history, 1 fine arts.

The Inside Word

The University of Arizona uses formulas and cutoffs in the admissions process; however, the admissions office prides itself on reading every application. Volume processing means that very little time is spent on individual applicants: You either have what is required, or you don't.

FINANCIAL AID

Students should submit: FAFSA. The Princeton Review suggests that all financial aid forms be submitted as soon as possible after 1/1. *Need-based scholarships/grants offered:* Pell, SEOG, state scholarships/grants, private scholarships, the school's own gift aid, Federal Nursing scholarships. *Loan aid offered:* FFEL Subsidized Stafford, FFEL Unsubsidized Stafford, FFEL PLUS, Federal Perkins, Federal Nursing, college/university loans from institutional funds. Applicants will be notified of awards on a rolling basis beginning on or about 4/1. Federal Work-study Program available. Institutional employment available. Off-campus job opportunities are good.

FROM THE ADMISSIONS OFFICE

"Surrounded by mountains and the dramatic beauty of the Sonoran Desert, the University of Arizona offers a top-drawer education in a resort-like setting. Some of the nation's highest ranked departments make their homes at this oasis of learning in the desert. In addition to producing cloudless sunshine 350 days per year, the clear Arizona skies provide an ideal setting for one of the country's best astronomy programs. Other nationally rated programs include nursing, sociology, management information systems, anthropology, creative writing, and computer and aerospace engineering. The university balances a strong research component with an emphasis on teaching—faculty rolls include Nobel and Pulitzer Prize winners. Famous Chinese astrophysicist and political dissident Fang Lizhi continues his landmark studies here; he now teaches physics to undergraduates. The wealth of academic choices—the university offers 118 majors—is supplemented by an active, progressive campus atmosphere; conference-winning basketball, softball, and football teams; and myriad recreational opportunities.

"As of this book's publication, the University of Arizona did not have information available about their policy regarding the new SAT."

SELECTIVITY

Admissions Rating	**60**
# of applicants	23,725
% of applicants accepted	83
% of acceptees attending	29

FRESHMAN PROFILE

Range SAT Verbal	490-610
Average SAT Verbal	552
Range SAT Math	500-620
Average SAT Math	563
**TPR Projected Range SAT Writing*	*550-640*
Range ACT Composite	21-26
Average ACT Composite	23

DEADLINES

Regular application deadline	4/1
Regular notification	rolling
Nonfall registration?	yes

APPLICANTS ALSO LOOK AT

AND OFTEN PREFER
University of California—Irvine
University of Washington

AND SOMETIMES PREFER
Ohio University—Athens
University of California—Los Angeles
University of California—Santa Barbara
University of Colorado—Boulder
University of Wisconsin—Madison

AND RARELY PREFER
Arizona State University
Baylor University
Northern Arizona University

FINANCIAL FACTS

Financial Aid Rating	**60**
Annual in-state tuition	$3,998
Annual out-of-state tuition	$12,978
Room & Board	$7,108
Books and supplies	$762
Required fees	$95
% frosh rec. need-based scholarship or grant aid	31
% UG rec. need-based scholarship or grant aid	33
% frosh rec. need-based self-help aid	18
% UG rec. need-based self-help aid	27
Independent 529 member?	No

University of Arkansas—Fayetteville

232 Silas Hunt Hall, Fayetteville, AR 72701 • Admissions: 479-575-5346 • Fax: 479-575-7515

CAMPUS LIFE

Quality of Life Rating	**76**
Fire Safety Rating	**76**
Type of school	public
Environment	town

STUDENTS

Total undergrad enrollment	13,124
% male/female	51/49
% from out of state	14
% from public high school	95
% live on campus	31
% in (# of) fraternities	9 (16)
% in (# of) sororities	11 (10)
% African American	5
% Asian	3
% Caucasian	84
% Hispanic	2
% Native American	2
% international	2
# of countries represented	103

SURVEY SAYS

Great library
Athletic facilities are great
Students love Fayetteville, AR
Great off-campus food
Everyone loves the Razorbacks
Frats and sororities dominate social scene
Lots of beer drinking

ACADEMICS

Academic Rating	**72**
Calendar	semester
Student/faculty ratio	17:1
Professors interesting rating	67
Professors accessible rating	67
% professors teaching UG courses	96
% classes taught by TAs	27
Most common lab size	20-29 students
Most common regular class size	20-29 students

MOST POPULAR MAJORS

Elementary education and teaching
finance
marketing/marketing management

STUDENTS SPEAK OUT

Academics

Like the Wal-Mart chain headquartered in its home city, the University of Arkansas (UA) offers just about anything anyone could want at a reasonable cost. And many students bring a Wal-Mart shopper's attitude to their academic duties; they want to get in, get what they need with as little hassle as possible, and get out as quickly and easily as possible. That's not to say there aren't hard workers and serious students here. Rather, it's that the vast majority simply want career-advancing degrees and good football tickets, and not necessarily in that order. As one bookworm glumly noted, "Most classes that are offered as discussion-based evolve into lectures, but this is as much the fault of poor student preparation as anything else." As at many large state universities, "With professors, you win some, and you lose some. Too many of the professors and grad students are here for their research and not to share their knowledge." The administration, students tell us, "is just like any other bureaucracy." Reported one undergrad, "I have no idea who my academic dean is, and anytime there is a problem with my transcript, it seems as if I have to run in circles to take care of it." Despite these drawbacks, UA still has plenty to offer: a "good learning opportunity, if you know how to take advantage of it" at a fraction of the cost charged by smaller, upscale/boutique schools.

Life

At UA, "people seem to really focus on their studies when they have to, but when the weekend comes around, everyone does something besides study." During football season, that "something" is cheering on the Razorbacks, who "are a huge part of this school." Reports one student, "On game days, off-campus students have virtually no access to campus, and I think even on campus students have to find another place to park their cars." Students also flock to Dickson Street, "the major street in town, located just down the hill from the school. Within the past ten years, it's turned into a solid three blocks of bars, liquor stores, and restaurants." Consequently, "there's a lot of partying. There are quite a few clubs in town for people who like to dance and some nice bars and restaurants for the quieter ones." The Greek scene here, most agree, is pretty big. There's more to UA than just football and keggers, however; the Walton Arts Center and Dickson Street Theater help nurture a "strong arts scene. Many of the local coffee shops display local work. There is also a very strong indie music scene." Also, "Fayetteville is surrounded by great natural beauty, so things like fishing, hiking, camping, climbing, spelunking, and other outdoor stuff is easily accessible."

Student Body

Most UA undergrads concede that "the largest group on campus consists of white kids from all over the state who arrive at the university more excited about the social aspects than the academic aspects." Even though this seems the norm, one can find "many students who are quite intense about their education; the honors students especially" tend to be "scholarly." As at many southern schools, students have a propensity for religion and conservatism. "We are in the Bible Belt, so Christianity is a big deal, and white, southern look-alikes are [the norm]," explains one student, "but there are many foreign students, and people still come from all over the country." One international notes that "the university does a wonderful job at bringing [foreign students] into the community through the International Students' Office. For instance, I was part of a Conversation Group during my freshman year that met once a week to help us become comfortable with speaking English."

University of Arkansas—Fayetteville

Financial Aid: 479-575-3806 • E-mail: uofa@uark.edu • Website: www.uark.edu/admissions

ADMISSIONS

Very important factors considered include: Class rank, secondary school record, standardized test scores. *Other factors considered include:* Alumni/ae relation, character/personal qualities, essays, extracurricular activities, geographical residence, minority status, state residency, talent/ability, volunteer work, work experience. SAT Reasoning or ACT required. TOEFL required of all international applicants. High school diploma is required, and GED is accepted. *Academic units required:* 4 English, 4 math, 3 science (2 science lab), 3 social studies, 2 academic electives. *Academic units recommended:* 2 foreign language.

The Inside Word

Admission is very straightforward here at Arkansas' flagship university campus. Average college prep students (with a 2.75 or better GPA) will encounter a clear path into the freshman class. The university will also consider those with lower grades for possible conditional admission.

FINANCIAL AID

Students should submit: FAFSA. The Princeton Review suggests that all financial aid forms be submitted as soon as possible after 1/1. *Need-based scholarships/grants offered:* Pell, SEOG, state scholarships/grants, private scholarships, the school's own gift aid. *Loan aid offered:* FFEL Subsidized Stafford, FFEL Unsubsidized Stafford, FFEL PLUS, Federal Perkins, college/university loans from institutional funds. Applicants will be notified of awards on a rolling basis beginning on or about 4/1. Federal Work-study Program available. Institutional employment available. Off-campus job opportunities are excellent.

FROM THE ADMISSIONS OFFICE

"The University of Arkansas aims to become one of the top 50 public research universities, fueled by a historic $300 million gift received entirely in cash in March 2003 from the Walton Family Charitable Support Foundation. The largest gift ever to a public university, it established and endowed an undergraduate honors college and provides financial support to nearly 2,000 students. In 2004, the U of A provided more than $250,000 to support undergraduate research and more than $350,000 for study abroad. The U of A's growing academic stature is exemplified by student accomplishment. Since 1990 U of A undergraduates have won 27 Goldwater Scholarships; 12 have been recognized by the USA Today All-USA College Academic Team; 16 have received National Science Foundations graduate fellowships; 10 have received Fulbright scholarships; six have received British Marshall scholarships; six have received Truman scholarships; four have received Udall scholarships; three have received Madison scholarships; three have received Tylenol scholarships; and one has received a Rhodes scholarship. All students who attend the U of A benefit from a range of choice in 208 academic programs; and yet, as research universities go, U of A is on the small side. The student/faculty ratio is 17:1, which allows students to receive individual attention from faculty. The university is located in Fayetteville, a small city on the beautiful Ozark Plateau. It's friendly, safe, diverse, and offers awesome recreational opportunities, a robust economy, vibrant cultural life, and a moderate climate. In 2004, a Washington, DC nonprofit group named it one of the most livable communities in the United States.

"The University of Arkansas—Fayetteville will accept either the new SAT or the old SAT (administered prior to March 2005 and without a Writing component), as well as the ACT with or without the Writing component."

SELECTIVITY

Admissions Rating	**86**
# of applicants	5,819
% of applicants accepted	78
% of acceptees attending	55

FRESHMAN PROFILE

Range SAT Verbal	510-650
Average SAT Verbal	580
Range SAT Math	510-650
Average SAT Math	580
**TPR Projected Range SAT Writing*	*570-670*
Range ACT Composite	22-28
Average ACT Composite	25
Minimum Paper TOEFL	550
Minimum Computer Based TOEFL	213
Average HS GPA	3.6
% graduated top 10% of class	36
% graduated top 25% of class	64
% graduated top 50% of class	90

DEADLINES

Regular application deadline	8/15
Regular notification	rolling
Nonfall registration?	yes

APPLICANTS ALSO LOOK AT

AND OFTEN PREFER
University of Central Arkansas
AND SOMETIMES PREFER
Arkansas State University
AND RARELY PREFER
Oklahoma State University

FINANCIAL FACTS

Financial Aid Rating	**72**
Annual in-state tuition	$4,115
Annual out-of-state tuition	$11,405
Room & Board	$5,927
Books and supplies	$851
Required fees	$1,020
% frosh rec. need-based scholarship or grant aid	23
% UG rec. need-based scholarship or grant aid	23
% frosh rec. need-based self-help aid	20
% UG rec. need-based self-help aid	25
% frosh rec. any financial aid	71
% UG rec. any financial aid	67
Avg. frosh grant	$4,003
Avg. frosh loan	$2,592
Independent 529 member?	No

UNIVERSITY OF CALIFORNIA—BERKELEY

110 SPROUL HALL #5800, BERKELEY, CA 94720-5800 • ADMISSIONS: 510-642-3175 • FAX: 510-642-7333

CAMPUS LIFE

Quality of Life Rating	**78**
Fire Safety Rating	**76**
Type of school	public
Environment	metropolis

STUDENTS

Total undergrad enrollment	22,880
% male/female	46/54
% from out of state	11
% from public high school	85
% live on campus	35
% in (# of) fraternities	10 (38)
% in (# of) sororities	10 (19)
% African American	4
% Asian	41
% Caucasian	31
% Hispanic	11
% Native American	1
% international	3

SURVEY SAYS

Great computer facilities
Great library
Diverse student types on campus
Great off-campus food
Student publications are popular
Political activism is popular

ACADEMICS

Academic Rating	**89**
Calendar	semester
Student/faculty ratio	15:1
Professors interesting rating	76
Professors accessible rating	71
% professors teaching UG courses	100
% classes taught by TAs	0
Most common regular class size	fewer than 10 students

MOST POPULAR MAJORS

Computer engineering
English language and literature
political science and government

STUDENTS SPEAK OUT

Academics

"Prestige" and "opportunity" often popped up in students' descriptions of University of California—Berkeley, a school universally acknowledged as one of the top research institutions in the nation. Incoming undergrads here know they've been admitted to an academic Mecca, home to "many Nobel laureates" and "an extremely challenging, top-notch educational experience." Students say that the faculty here, "even the lecturers, are simply amazing. Faculty members are renowned researchers with world-class recognitions and awards. The lecturers are major executives and/or experts in the relevant industries; they truly enrich the Berkeley education by bringing into light the life applications of the disciplines they teach." Opportunities for undergraduate research "are abundant, and with some effort, just about anyone who's actively looking for a job (research or not) on campus can find one." Students warn that nothing comes easy here; "Be prepared to fight every inch of the way, because this is not a school where a professor will take you by the hand and lead you to the promise-land," writes one student. Another observes, "Academically, Berkeley is harder than it looks…[professors] do not inflate grades, so if you score the mean, you will get a B-/C+ in the class." A huge school, Berkeley allows students access to "an amazing number and variety of courses" and "teaches them to fend for themselves," but also means that "you have to learn things the hard way, which isn't always nice."

Life

"Life's tough at Berkeley" because "classes are generally very unforgiving, so students don't find much time to do anything other than study." When students can break free of the books, a world of options awaits them, both on campus and off. Undergrads tell us that "most of us start our day walking through Sproul Plaza getting news from every other group on campus, whether it be a movie playing in Wheeler, or a general meeting or someone coming to speak." Students participate in "hundreds of student organizations" and "really show their school spirit with regards to athletics; our football games are always packed with rowdy fans." For those seeking one, there's a lively party scene; one student reports, "On every Tuesday, Thursday, Friday, and Saturday night, you can bet there will be a host of different fraternity and sorority parties, in addition to co-op and house parties. Many of the Greek parties take place at clubs or bars in the city, and the location is always rented out exclusively for the students. On any other night of the week, there are local bars and clubs that are always fun." Then there's Berkeley with its "amazing variety of restaurants" and trips to San Francisco. Yet despite the many social opportunities, many students tell us they don't feel especially connected to the Berkeley social scene. Explains one undergrad, "Students live up to hours away via car or BART, since high rent prices in the city of Berkeley force many out of the city's limits. If kids don't find a niche in some group or activity, they end up completely lost for a social life."

Student Body

"There is no typical student" at this school of 23,000 undergraduates, Berkeley students insist. "If you walk into a lecture hall and you had to group people into what 'crowd' they were in high school, it would be near impossible," explains one student. "Not only are there the jocks, the sorority girls, the band geeks, and the drama nerds, there are also the 'save the tree frog, legalize marijuana business people' and the 'squirrel fishing, classical music club committee, soccer fanatics.' The only one thing that most of these kids have in common is that they are all ridiculously smart." The school has a large minority population, but "African Americans are under-represented, as are Latinos. Diversity seems to be defined as a lack of whites, but you can hardly call a student population wherein 40 percent of its members are Asian 'diverse.'" Because "nobody at UC—Berkeley is going to take your hand to help you find your own path," Berkeley students "must forge their own road by critically analyzing and thinking independently," and therefore "grow intellectually at an alarming rate."

FINANCIAL AID: 510-642-6442 • E-MAIL: OUARS@UCLINK.BERKELEY.EDU • WEBSITE: WWW.BERKELEY.EDU

ADMISSIONS

Very important factors considered include: Essays, secondary school record, state residency. *Important factors considered include:* Character/personal qualities, extracurricular activities, standardized test scores, talent/ability, volunteer work, work experience. *Other factors considered include:* Geographical residence. SAT Reasoning or ACT required. TOEFL required of all international applicants. High school diploma is required, and GED is accepted. *Academic units required:* 4 English, 3 math, 2 science (2 science lab), 2 foreign language, 2 social studies, 2 history, 1 academic elective, 1 visual and performing arts. *Academic units recommended:* 4 English, 4 math, 3 science (3 science lab), 3 foreign language, 2 social studies, 2 history, 1 academic elective, 1 visual and performing arts.

The Inside Word

Berkeley is the most selective campus of the UC system. There is little room for deviation in any applicant's academic profile and out-of-state students find the going even tougher, with available spaces few and far between.

FINANCIAL AID

Students should submit: FAFSA, state aid form. Regular filing deadline is 3/2. The Princeton Review suggests that all financial aid forms be submitted as soon as possible after 1/1. *Need-based scholarships/grants offered:* Pell, SEOG, state scholarships/grants, private scholarships, the school's own gift aid. *Loan aid offered:* Direct Subsidized Stafford, Direct Unsubsidized Stafford, Direct PLUS, Federal Perkins, college/university loans from institutional funds. Applicants will be notified of awards on or about 4/15. Federal Work-study Program available. Institutional employment available. Off-campus job opportunities are excellent.

FROM THE ADMISSIONS OFFICE

"One of the top public universities in the nation and the world, the University of California, Berkeley offers a vast range of courses and a full menu of extracurricular activities. Berkeley's academic programs are internationally recognized for their excellence. Undergraduates can choose one of 100 majors. Thirty-five departments are top-ranked, more than any other college or university in the country. Access to one of the foremost university libraries enriches studies. There are 23 specialized libraries on campus and distinguished museums of anthropology, paleontology, and science.

"All applicants must take the ACT Assessment plus the new ACT Writing Test or the new SAT Reasoning Test. In addition, all applicants must take two SAT Subject Tests in two different subject areas. (If a Math SAT Subject Test is chosen by the applicant, he/she must take the Math Level 2 exam.)"

SELECTIVITY

Admissions Rating	**98**
# of applicants	36,580
% of applicants accepted	25
% of acceptees attending	41

FRESHMAN PROFILE

Range SAT Verbal	580-710
Average SAT Verbal	629
Range SAT Math	620-740
Average SAT Math	671
**TPR Projected Range SAT Writing*	*620-700*
Minimum Paper TOEFL	550
Minimum Computer Based TOEFL	213
Average HS GPA	3.93
% graduated top 10% of class	98
% graduated top 25% of class	100
% graduated top 50% of class	100

DEADLINES

Regular application deadline	11/30
Regular notification	Decisions available on website by 3/31
Nonfall registration?	yes

APPLICANTS ALSO LOOK AT

AND OFTEN PREFER
Stanford University

AND SOMETIMES PREFER
University of California—Los Angeles

AND RARELY PREFER
University of California—Davis
University of California—San Diego
University of California—Santa Barbara
University of California—Santa Cruz

FINANCIAL FACTS

Financial Aid Rating	**85**
Annual in-state tuition	$0
Annual out-of-state tuition	$23,686
Room & Board	$11,630
Books and supplies	$1,240
Required fees	$5,956
% frosh rec. need-based scholarship or grant aid	50
% UG rec. need-based scholarship or grant aid	49
% frosh rec. need-based self-help aid	39
% UG rec. need-based self-help aid	38
Independent 529 member?	No

UNIVERSITY OF CALIFORNIA—DAVIS

178 MARK HALL, DAVIS, CA 95616 • ADMISSIONS: 530-752-2971 • FAX: 530-752-1280

CAMPUS LIFE

Quality of Life Rating	**84**
Fire Safety Rating	**76**
Type of school	public
Environment	town

STUDENTS

Total undergrad enrollment	23,018
% male/female	44/56
% from public high school	85
% African American	3
% Asian	39
% Caucasian	39
% Hispanic	11
% Native American	1
% international	2
# of countries represented	118

SURVEY SAYS

Great library
Athletic facilities are great
Student publications are popular

ACADEMICS

Academic Rating	**81**
Calendar	quarter
Student/faculty ratio	19:1
Professors interesting rating	72
Professors accessible rating	73
% classes taught by TAs	0
Most common lab size	20-29 students
Most common regular class size	20-29 students

MOST POPULAR MAJORS

Biology/biological sciences
economics
psychology

STUDENTS SPEAK OUT

Academics

UC—Davis may be best-known for its "tremendous life sciences division." Writes one student, "This campus claims to have more biology majors than any other campus in the U.S. and I believe it." Students tout "the undergraduate research opportunities" as "perhaps the greatest in the nation," but they are quick to point out that there's more to UC—Davis than just the hard sciences. "It's not all just biology and chemistry courses," writes a human development major. "Because I branched out a little, I was able to experience far more than the average biology major. Everything I'm learning is interconnecting in ways I didn't think about before." Students find their professors to be "friendly" and "interesting." "While every once in a while you get a bad egg," a senior writes, "the majority [of faculty] are very good." Undergrads agree that while "most of the professors are very accessible, you need to make the first move." As at most schools, the upper-level courses highlight the academic experience. Advancing to upper classes also opens up "opportunities to get involved in internships here and abroad." At all levels, "UC—Davis offers a challenging curriculum that effectively prepares us for advanced degrees, while also teaching us the importance of arranging our schedule to accommodate our demanding school work."

Life

"Many of the students are very environment-friendly" at UC—Davis, and they love to take advantage of "all the outdoor activities you can sign up for, like hiking, backpacking, camping, and ski trips. Going for walks along the arboretum or picnics at Putah Creek are nice, especially during the spring, when there are ducks everywhere. Seriously, they're all over campus." Students also appreciate the "mass recycling programs for every kind of waste—including food waste—and the use of reusable containers and cups that is encouraged in all dining facilities." Hometown Davis "is a small town that closes down around 9:00 or 10:00 P.M., even on weekends. If you want a nice small town with friendly people, then this is the place for you. But if you are looking for nightlife, then maybe a more urban environment would be better." It's good to note that the student body is large enough to sustain a fairly active campus, with regular movies, a hopping intramural sports program, and "lots of performances at the top-notch Mondavi Performing Arts Center, [varying] from operas and ballets, to gospel singers and nude dance troops." College sports promise to become more popular in the future, as "we're moving up to Division I, which is super-promising."

Student Body

UC—Davis is home to over 20,000 undergraduates, so "no matter where you go on campus, you're bound to find someone you can totally relate to in the same room, and someone else who's the complete opposite." Demanding academics and the Northern California setting mean that "we're a school of dedicated students who are relatively mellow and not too rowdy. It is a good environment for going to college." The typical undergrad here is "either white or Asian in ethnicity, at least a little religious, [and] initially wanted to go to another school (Davis was their second choice)."

UNIVERSITY OF CALIFORNIA—DAVIS

FINANCIAL AID: 530-752-2390 • E-MAIL: FRESHMANADMISSIONS@UCDAVIS.EDU • WEBSITE: WWW.UCDAVIS.EDU

ADMISSIONS

Very important factors considered include: Essays, secondary school record, standardized test scores. *Important factors considered include:* Character/personal qualities, class rank, extracurricular activities, state residency, talent/ability, volunteer work. *Other factors considered include:* Geographical residence, work experience. SAT Reasoning and SAT Subject Tests or ACT required. TOEFL required of all international applicants. High school diploma is required, and GED is accepted. *Academic units required:* 4 English, 3 math, 2 science (2 science lab), 2 foreign language, 2 social studies, 1 academic elective, 1 visual and performing arts. *Academic units recommended:* 4 English, 4 math, 3 science (3 science lab), 3 foreign language, 2 social studies, 1 academic elective, 1 visual and performing arts.

The Inside Word

California's discontinuation of affirmative action in the UC admission process has created much uncertainty regarding the future of candidate selection in the system. A higher percentage of students are admitted to Davis than to Berkeley or UCLA, but don't forget that the UC system in general is geared toward the best and brightest of California's high school students.

FINANCIAL AID

Students should submit: FAFSA. The Princeton Review suggests that all financial aid forms be submitted as soon as possible after 1/1. Federal Work-study Program available. Institutional employment available. Off-campus job opportunities are good.

FROM THE ADMISSIONS OFFICE

"UC—Davis prides itself on its academic rigor and its vibrant college-town atmosphere. In a recent survey that included undergraduate students from eight of the UC campuses, UC—Davis students were second most likely to recommend their school to prospective applicants. UC—Davis has programs that are ranked among the best in the nation as well as more than 100 majors. The most satisfied students at UC—Davis are those who take advantage of the myriad opportunities, including social and recreational events, research and internship positions, and programs such as UC—Davis Washington Center or Bodega Marine Laboratory.

"All applicants must take the ACT Assessment plus the new ACT Writing Test or the new SAT Reasoning Test. In addition, all applicants must take two SAT Subject Tests in two different subject areas. (If a Math SAT Subject Test is chosen by the applicant, he/she must take the Math Level II exam.)"

SELECTIVITY

Admissions Rating	**96**
# of applicants	31,527
% of applicants accepted	55
% of acceptees attending	25

FRESHMAN PROFILE

Range SAT Verbal	550-630
Average SAT Verbal	562
Range SAT Math	560-670
Average SAT Math	608
**TPR Projected Range SAT Writing*	*600-650*
Range ACT Composite	21-27
Average ACT Composite	24
Minimum Paper TOEFL	550
Minimum Computer Based TOEFL	213
Average HS GPA	3.74
% graduated top 10% of class	95
% graduated top 25% of class	100
% graduated top 50% of class	100

DEADLINES

Regular application deadline	11/30
Regular notification	rolling
Nonfall registration?	no

APPLICANTS ALSO LOOK AT

AND OFTEN PREFER

University of California—Berkeley
University of California—Los Angeles

AND SOMETIMES PREFER

California Polytechnic State University—San Luis Obispo
University of California—Santa Barbara
University of California—Santa Cruz

AND RARELY PREFER

University of California—Irvine
University of California—Riverside
University of California—San Diego

FINANCIAL FACTS

Financial Aid Rating	**76**
Annual in-state tuition	$5,853
Annual out-of-state tuition	$24,777
Books and supplies	$1,415
Required fees	$7,557
% frosh rec. need-based scholarship or grant aid	37
% UG rec. need-based scholarship or grant aid	41
% frosh rec. need-based self-help aid	41
% UG rec. need-based self-help aid	45
Avg. frosh grant	$6,500
Avg. frosh loan	$3,300
Independent 529 member?	No

University of California—Los Angeles

405 Hilgard Avenue, Box 951436, Los Angeles, CA 90095-1436 • Admissions: 310-825-3101 • Fax: 310-206-1206

CAMPUS LIFE

Quality of Life Rating	**86**
Fire Safety Rating	**60**
Type of school	public
Environment	metropolis

STUDENTS

Total undergrad enrollment	24,946
% male/female	43/57
% from out of state	5
% from public high school	80
% live on campus	35
% in (# of) fraternities	14 (27)
% in (# of) sororities	11 (18)
% African American	3
% Asian	37
% Caucasian	33
% Hispanic	15
% international	4
# of countries represented	132

SURVEY SAYS

Great computer facilities
Great library
Athletic facilities are great
Students love Los Angeles, CA
Great off-campus food
Student publications are popular

ACADEMICS

Academic Rating	**75**
Calendar	quarter
Student/faculty ratio	18:1
Professors interesting rating	62
Professors accessible rating	61
% professors teaching UG courses	100
% classes taught by TAs	0
Most common lab size	20-29 students
Most common regular class size	10-19 students

MOST POPULAR MAJORS

Economics
political science and government
psychology

STUDENTS SPEAK OUT

Academics

"UCLA is about discovering what direction you want to go in life and then taking the initiative, and the wealth of opportunities, to go out and do it," students at this large, prestigious state school tell us. The benefits of size and tremendous resources mean that "there's just so much to do for everyone" here. Explains one student, "I'm an engineering student, but I wanted to go to a school where I could get a great engineering education while also having opportunities to take part in other programs. Here I can take engineering classes and also explore ancient Greece, biology of cancer, and several other fascinating classes through the general education requirements." For those in the sciences, "there are many chances to do research here. Being a research university, the professors and administration often stress the importance and the benefits of research. The benefits include recognition and scholar awards as well as grants and an edge over other students when applying for graduate school." The academic experience at UCLA "can be highly independent. Professors are not always the best teachers. They're mostly concerned with their research, and many treat teaching as a second priority. That's not to say that there aren't amazing professors who inspire you to learn; there are plenty. And although classes (especially science classes) are large, there are plenty of services for helping students with studies." Students have help sorting professorial gems from duds through "the professor review website, which is absolutely amazing. I pick classes based on what it says because it is pretty accurate." Students warn that UCLA "is really competitive because the school is full of overachievers" and that "the quarter schedule strangles the syllabus for time."

Life

"UCLA is a great place to have free time," students report, because "there are endless possibilities as to what to do; no one can ever get bored. Out of all of the schools in California, you would be hard-pressed to find a better combination of social life, academics, and food in one place. Not to mention [the fact that] you're bordered by Bel Air, Beverly Hills, Santa Monica, and Westwood. It's pretty hard to top that." Westwood is a student favorite, an area "filled with lots of good restaurants that are generally affordable for college students. There are a huge amount of theaters, movie theaters, and stand-up joints in the local area, and it is easy to get free tickets on campus to many shows." Westwood is also "the main place where people go and party, pre-party, or after-party. People are focused on school but are also ready to party." Greater Los Angeles offers the beach, "lots of free sneaks of upcoming films and talks by actors and directors about their work," and numerous other diversions. On campus "there are tons of ways to get involved. The campus newspaper and musical theater program are both amazing and very professional. Frat and apartment parties are also very popular on campus." Sums up one student, "If someone is not happy at UCLA, then they are not happy with their own life. It's not the school."

Student Body

"There are around 35,000 students at UCLA, so it is hard to describe the 'average' student," as the school is home to "top athletes, non-stop partiers, bookworms—any type of person you could imagine." Most are "well-prepared and serious about success at UCLA. It's hard to get into this school, so students' high-school prep was indeed rigorous and weeded out any people less serious." Most respondents agree that while the student body can "be very cliquish," UCLA is diverse—"and not just ethically diverse; it is also religiously and socially diverse." Some complain that "African Americans are underrepresented" but otherwise laud the school for its ability to draw students of all backgrounds.

University of California—Los Angeles

Financial Aid: 310-206-0400 • E-mail: ugadm@saonet.ucla.edu • Website: www.ucla.edu

ADMISSIONS

Very important factors considered include: Essays, secondary school record, standardized test scores, talent/ability. *Important factors considered include:* Extracurricular activities, state residency, volunteer work, work experience. *Other factors considered include:* Character/personal qualities. SAT Reasoning and SAT Subject Tests or ACT required. TOEFL required of all international applicants. High school diploma is required, and GED is accepted. *Academic units required:* 4 English, 3 math, 2 science (2 science lab), 2 foreign language, 2 history, 1 academic elective, 1 visual and performing arts. *Academic units recommended:* 4 math, 3 science (3 science lab), 3 foreign language.

The Inside Word

Since California's voters acted to discontinue affirmative action in the UC admission process, there was much uncertainty regarding the future of candidate selection in the system. Through innovative policies UCLA still attracts and admits respectable numbers of African American and Hispanic students. UCLA is the second most selective university in the UC system.

FINANCIAL AID

Students should submit: FAFSA. The Princeton Review suggests that all financial aid forms be submitted as soon as possible after 1/1. *Need-based scholarships/grants offered:* Pell, SEOG, state scholarships/grants, private scholarships, the school's own gift aid, United Negro College Fund, Federal Nursing scholarships, National Merit. *Loan aid offered:* FFEL Subsidized Stafford, FFEL Unsubsidized Stafford, FFEL PLUS, Federal Perkins, Federal Nursing, state loans, college/university loans from institutional funds. Applicants will be notified of awards on or about 3/15. Off-campus job opportunities are good.

FROM THE ADMISSIONS OFFICE

"Undergraduates arrive at UCLA from throughout California and around the world with exceptional levels of academic preparation. They are attracted by our acclaimed degree programs, distinguished faculty, and the beauty of a park-like campus set amid the dynamism of the nation's second largest city. UCLA's highly ranked undergraduate programs incorporate cutting-edge technology and teaching techniques that hone the critical-thinking skills and the global perspectives necessary for success in our rapidly changing world. The diversity of these programs draws strength from a student body that mirrors the cultural and ethnic vibrancy of Los Angeles. Generally ranked among the nation's top half-dozen universities, UCLA is at once distinguished and dynamic, academically rigorous and responsive.

"All applicants must take the ACT Assessment plus the new ACT Writing Test or the new SAT Reasoning Test. In addition, all applicants must take two SAT Subject Tests in two different subject areas. (If a Math SAT Subject Test is chosen by the applicant, he/she must take the Math Level II exam.)"

SELECTIVITY

Admissions Rating	**98**
# of applicants	43,199
% of applicants accepted	23
% of acceptees attending	37

FRESHMAN PROFILE

Range SAT Verbal	570-690
Average SAT Verbal	629
Range SAT Math	610-720
Average SAT Math	660
**TPR Projected Range SAT Writing*	*610-690*
Range ACT Composite	24-30
Average ACT Composite	27
Minimum Paper TOEFL	550
Minimum Computer Based TOEFL	220
Average HS GPA	4.12
% graduated top 10% of class	97
% graduated top 25% of class	100
% graduated top 50% of class	100

DEADLINES

Regular application deadline	11/30
Regular notification	rolling
Nonfall registration?	no

FINANCIAL FACTS

Financial Aid Rating	**85**
Annual in-state tuition	$0
Annual out-of-state tuition	$17,304
Room & Board	$11,928
Books and supplies	$1,485
Required fees in-state	$6,484
Required fees out-of state	$7,001
% frosh rec. need-based scholarship or grant aid	48
% UG rec. need-based scholarship or grant aid	51
% frosh rec. need-based self-help aid	34
% UG rec. need-based self-help aid	41
Independent 529 member?	No

University of California—Riverside

1138 Hinderaker Hall, Riverside, CA 92521 • Admissions: 951-827-3411 • Fax: 951-827-6344

CAMPUS LIFE

Quality of Life Rating	**63**
Fire Safety Rating	**85**
Type of school	public
Environment	city

STUDENTS

Total undergrad enrollment	15,089
% male/female	46/54
% from out of state	1
% from public high school	86
% live on campus	28
% in (# of) fraternities	3 (20)
% in (# of) sororities	3 (22)
% African American	7
% Asian	42
% Caucasian	20
% Hispanic	24
% international	2
# of countries represented	33

SURVEY SAYS

Great library
Athletic facilities are great
Students are friendly
Diverse student types on campus
Lots of beer drinking
(Almost) everyone smokes

ACADEMICS

Academic Rating	**74**
Calendar	quarter
Student/faculty ratio	18:1
Professors interesting rating	62
Professors accessible rating	62
% professors teaching UG courses	100
% classes taught by TAs	0
Most common lab size	20-29 students
Most common regular class size	20-29 students

MOST POPULAR MAJORS

Business administration/management
social sciences

STUDENTS SPEAK OUT

Academics

Students at the University of California (UC)—Riverside call their school an "excellent learning environment" with "instructors who actually care about the students and teach for the love of teaching." One student writes, "People used to think that UC Riverside was the bastard child of the UC system. It's not." In fact, a junior business major proclaims that he actually chose Riverside over heavy hitters UC Berkeley and UCLA, crowing that "the academic element [at Riverside] is unbeatable." Many undergraduates are drawn by the "great computer science program," others by the "generous financial aid." Students praise professors for being "very understanding and easily accessible." One respondent tells us, "Upper-division classes are very personal and a great chance to get to know professors." Certain students complain, however, that "high-level courses should not be taught by graduate students," which a few seem to be. A senior psychology major whines that, as at many large state universities, "some professors are more interested in their research than talking to undergraduates." Another student feels that "some of my classes are watered down," while others ask for "more lab sections." Riverside is experiencing some "growing pains" as the enrollment increases somewhat dramatically, and this may be the cause of some of the glitches students perceive in the administrative processes. One senior reports, "Administrators hide in their offices and pray you don't come to see them," and several surveys claim that the administration spends too much time interfering with the Greek system. Another undergrad counters these assertions, though, declaring that he chose Riverside because it "caters to each student's needs." Overall, the school is set up so that students have "a great opportunity to interact with staff, faculty, and administrators."

Life

Day-to-day existence at Riverside is defined by the "great campus and community environment." A high percentage of respondents commented on the school's physical beauty ("I like the fact that it is so green"), with only minor complaints regarding the ongoing construction. Students agree that the campus "could always use more programming," but many undergraduates stay involved with extracurricular activities. A savvy business major notes, for instance, that "our clubs and organizations have many professional ties." Most people think a football team is in order to improve school spirit. In the meantime, it's the fraternities and sororities that bring the campus together. "Without the Greek system, UC—Riverside would be boring." People also perceive a need for more "events where the different cliques come together." Since the surrounding area is "not very exciting," most people "leave Riverside to have fun," which requires wheels. Still, some civic-minded students think locally: "We need to help out the surrounding community, especially East Riverside, right down the street."

Student Body

The Riverside population is "small but not too small" (at least by UC standards), just the right size so that students "start to recognize a lot of faces," making the whole place feel "very comfortable and homey." One student comments, "You get to know a lot of people from the dorms in your first year." Most students count the campus' marked diversity as one of the school's greatest strengths: "I never thought I would meet so many people who are so different from me with whom I have so much in common." Amid this heterogeneous group, everyone seems "easy to get along with" and "pretty chill." Certain people report that their peers are "generally quiet and not voluntarily social," while others feel the student body is largely "friendly and sociable." Either way, students appreciate the environment where "everyone is always willing to help anyone."

University of California—Riverside

Financial Aid: 951-827-3878 • E-mail: ugadmiss@pop.ucr.edu • Website: www.ucr.edu

ADMISSIONS

Very important factors considered include: Essays, secondary school record, standardized test scores. *Other factors considered include:* Extracurricular activities, talent/ability, volunteer work, work experience. SAT Reasoning and SAT Subject Tests or ACT required. TOEFL required of all international applicants. High school diploma is required, and GED is accepted. *Academic units required:* 4 English, 3 math, 2 science (2 science lab), 2 foreign language, 2 history, 1 academic elective, 1 visual and performing arts. *Academic units recommended:* 4 math, 3 science (3 science lab), 3 foreign language.

The Inside Word

The state of California's ban on affirmative action in the UC admission process has created much uncertainty regarding the future of candidate selection in the system. Though African American and Hispanic admissions have dropped system-wide, UC Riverside stands out in its ability to fight this decline—it's one of only two UC schools where minority admissions have grown. Riverside's admit rate is sufficiently high to mean smooth sailing for those who fit into the formulas well.

FINANCIAL AID

Students should submit: FAFSA, state aid form. Regular filing deadline is 3/2. The Princeton Review suggests that all financial aid forms be submitted as soon as possible after 1/1. *Need-based scholarships/grants offered:* Pell, SEOG, state scholarships/grants, private scholarships, the school's own gift aid. *Loan aid offered:* Direct Subsidized Stafford, Direct Unsubsidized Stafford, Direct PLUS, Federal Perkins. Applicants will be notified of awards on a rolling basis beginning on or about 3/1. Federal Work-study Program available. Institutional employment available. Off-campus job opportunities are excellent.

FROM THE ADMISSIONS OFFICE

"The University of California—Riverside offers the quality, rigor, and facilities of a major research institution, while assuring its undergraduates personal attention and a sense of community. Academic programs, teaching, advising, and student services all reflect the supportive attitude that characterizes the campus. Among the exceptional opportunities are the UC Riverside/UCLA Thomas Haider Program in Biomedical Sciences, which provides an exclusive path to UCLA's Geffen School of Medicine; the University Honors Program; an extensive undergraduate research program; UC's largest undergraduate degree program in business administration in Southern California; and UC's only bachelor's degree in creative writing. More than 200 student clubs and organizations and a variety of athletic and arts events give students a myriad of ways to get involved and have fun.

"All applicants must take the ACT Assessment plus the new ACT Writing Test or the new SAT Reasoning Test. In addition, all applicants must take two SAT Subject Tests in two different subject areas. (If a Math SAT Subject Test is chosen by the applicant, he/she must take the Math Level II exam.)"

SELECTIVITY	
Admissions Rating	**92**
# of applicants	18,425
% of applicants accepted	79
% of acceptees attending	24
FRESHMAN PROFILE	
Range SAT Verbal	460-570
Average SAT Verbal	514
Range SAT Math	500-630
Average SAT Math	560
**TPR Projected Range SAT Writing*	*530-610*
Range ACT Composite	18-24
Average ACT Composite	21
Minimum Paper TOEFL	550
Minimum Computer Based TOEFL	213
Average HS GPA	3.42
% graduated top 10% of class	94
% graduated top 25% of class	100
% graduated top 50% of class	100
DEADLINES	
Regular application deadline	11/30
Regular notification	rolling
Nonfall registration?	no
FINANCIAL FACTS	
Financial Aid Rating	**79**
Annual in-state tuition	$0
Annual out-of-state tuition	$16,476
Room & Board	$9,800
Books and supplies	$1,600
Required fees	$6,685
% frosh rec. need-based scholarship or grant aid	48
% UG rec. need-based scholarship or grant aid	53
% frosh rec. need-based self-help aid	46
% UG rec. need-based self-help aid	49
% frosh rec. any financial aid	75
% UG rec. any financial aid	72
Avg. frosh grant	$9,615
Avg. frosh loan	$6,764
Independent 529 member?	No

UNIVERSITY OF CALIFORNIA—SAN DIEGO

9500 GILMAN DRIVE, 0021, LA JOLLA, CA 92093-0021 • ADMISSIONS: 858-534-4831 • FAX: 858-534-5723

CAMPUS LIFE

Quality of Life Rating	**74**
Fire Safety Rating	**60**
Type of school	public
Environment	village

STUDENTS

Total undergrad enrollment	20,339
% male/female	48/52
% from out of state	2
% live on campus	33
% in (# of) fraternities	10 (19)
% in (# of) sororities	10 (14)
% African American	1
% Asian	38
% Caucasian	34
% Hispanic	10
% international	3
# of countries represented	70

SURVEY SAYS

Class discussions are rare
Registration is a breeze
Great computer facilities
Great library
Athletic facilities are great
Great off-campus food
Campus feels safe

ACADEMICS

Academic Rating	**81**
Calendar	quarter
Student/faculty ratio	19:1
Professors interesting rating	63
Professors accessible rating	65
% classes taught by TAs	10
Most common lab size	20-29 students
Most common regular class size	10-19 students

STUDENTS SPEAK OUT

Academics

University of California—San Diego (UCSD), most students agree, "is dedicated to math and the sciences," the departments in which it has built its reputation as a statewide powerhouse. Pre-meds and engineers agree that it's Valhalla (that is, if your idea of Valhalla involves dawn-to-midnight studying); others temper their enthusiasm, telling us that "academically, it varies. I always hear how fabulous this place is for science majors, but nonscience majors get the shaft." Which is too bad, since there are other solid departments here; they simply take a back seat to the star attractions. Like most prestigious math and science schools, "UCSD does not focus its energy on the undergraduate experience. It works to maintain the happiness of its faculty and the administration, often at the cost of student happiness." Because many classes involve lectures by profs and discussion sections led by TAs, "how much you get out of a class is really determined by how good your TA is, not the professor." While some TAs are excellent, others "do not know the class material thoroughly and tend to confuse us." No wonder one engineer told us that "when you get into college, you have to learn to be proactive. You literally teach yourself in a lot of the classes." Students are much more bullish on UCSD's administration, thanks largely to the six-college system, which divides the large university into smaller schools. "What is great about UCSD is its college system. It is really like six small liberal arts colleges all located next to each other," writes one student. Many here warn that the quarterly academic calendar really ratchets up the pressure; "once third week hits, you have papers/midterms every week until finals."

Life

Students at UCSD agree that theirs is not the typical college experience. "The university definitely suffers from a lack of social life," most here agree, the combined result of a hardworking student body and inhospitable surroundings. It's the kind of place where "for fun, a lot of people are glued to their computers playing computer games or talking on AIM™." Hometown La Jolla offers no help; explains one student, "La Jolla is extremely snobby. They won't let fast food restaurants or new movie theaters be built. In general, without a car at UCSD, you aren't going to get to do anything." There is a Greek system here, but "La Jolla banned a Greek Row and won't allow for them to own houses." Adds one student, "The major problem is that rent is so high in this area that there is no concentrated student population other than on campus." Because of the lack of any sense of community at UCSD, "there is no school spirit." On the bright side, "we live in paradise because the beaches are so close. Surfing is very popular. So are intramural sports." Those fortunate enough to have cars report "a great indie movie, art, theater, and music scene in San Diego," but add that "the best concerts are mostly 21+, so too bad for 18-year-olds." But frosh still manage to get their kicks. As one freshman put it, "The border is half an hour away, and clubs in Tijuana offer drinking and dancing for the 18- to 20-year-olds. What do you think we do?"

Student Body

Because of UCSD's prominent premed and engineering programs, "most students here are goal-oriented nerds who like to study all the time." Notes one undergrad, "The typical student is an Asian or Caucasian biology or engineering student that spends 60 hours a week studying, .0002 hours a week socializing with other people, .003 hours a week bathing, and the rest of the time is spent playing Counter-Strike™." The school is also home to "lots of stoners, and most of them are chill," as well as "a strong religious community." The school is large enough for each subpopulation to create its own cozy community.

UNIVERSITY OF CALIFORNIA—SAN DIEGO

FINANCIAL AID: 858-534-4480 • E-MAIL: ADMISSIONSINFO@UCSD.EDU • WEBSITE: WWW.UCSD.EDU

ADMISSIONS

Very important factors considered include: Character/personal qualities, essays, secondary school record, standardized test scores, state residency, talent/ability, volunteer work. *Important factors considered include:* Extracurricular activities. *Other factors considered include:* Work experience. SAT Reasoning or ACT required. TOEFL required of all international applicants. High school diploma is required, and GED is accepted. *Academic units required:* 4 English, 3 math, 2 science lab, 2 foreign language, 2 history, 1 academic elective, 1 visual and performing arts. *Academic units recommended:* 4 English, 4 math, 3 science lab, 3 foreign language, 2 history, 1 academic elective, 1 visual and performing arts.

The Inside Word

The state of California's discontinuance of affirmative action in the UC admission process created much uncertainty regarding the future of candidate selection in the system, and admissions of African American and Hispanic students have fallen significantly system-wide. Increased national awareness and its reputation for excellence in the sciences is making UCSD more and more popular with high school seniors. Even greater selectivity cannot be far behind.

FINANCIAL AID

Students should submit: FAFSA, state aid form. Regular filing deadline is 6/1. The Princeton Review suggests that all financial aid forms be submitted as soon as possible after 1/1. *Need-based scholarships/grants offered:* Pell, SEOG, state scholarships/grants, private scholarships, the school's own gift aid. *Loan aid offered:* FFEL Subsidized Stafford, FFEL Unsubsidized Stafford, FFEL PLUS, Federal Perkins, college/university loans from institutional funds, alternative loans. Applicants will be notified of awards on a rolling basis beginning on or about 3/15. Federal Work-study Program available. Institutional employment available. Off-campus job opportunities are excellent.

FROM THE ADMISSIONS OFFICE

"UCSD is recognized for the exceptional quality of its academic programs: a recent Johns Hopkins study rated UCSD faculty first nationally among public institutions in science; *U.S. News & World Report* rates UCSD seventh in the nation among state-supported colleges and universities; Kiplinger's '100 Best Values in Public Colleges' ranks UCSD tenth in the nation. UCSD ranks fifth in the nation and first in the University of California system for the amount of federal research dollars spent on research and development; and the university ranks tenth in the nation in the excellence of its graduate programs and the quality of its faculty, according to the most recent National Research Council college rankings.

"All applicants must take the ACT Assessment plus the new ACT Writing Test or the new SAT Reasoning Test. In addition, all applicants must take two SAT Subject Tests in two different subject areas. (If a Math SAT Subject Test is chosen by the applicant, he/she must take the Math Level II exam.)"

SELECTIVITY

Admissions Rating	**96**
# of applicants	41,330
% of applicants accepted	42
% of acceptees attending	22

FRESHMAN PROFILE

Range SAT Verbal	540-660
Average SAT Verbal	593
Range SAT Math	590-700
Average SAT Math	646
**TPR Projected Range SAT Writing*	*590-670*
Range ACT Composite	23-29
Average ACT Composite	25
Minimum Paper TOEFL	550
Average HS GPA	3.98
% graduated top 10% of class	99
% graduated top 25% of class	100
% graduated top 50% of class	100

DEADLINES

Regular application deadline	11/30
Regular notification	rolling
Nonfall registration?	yes

APPLICANTS ALSO LOOK AT AND OFTEN PREFER

University of California—Berkeley
University of California—Los Angeles

AND SOMETIMES PREFER

California Polytechnic State University—San Luis Obispo
Stanford University
University of California—Davis

AND RARELY PREFER

San Diego State University

FINANCIAL FACTS

Financial Aid Rating	**78**
Annual in-state tuition	$4,629
Annual out-of-state tuition	$18,109
Room & Board	$8,622
Books and supplies	$1,275
Required fees	$521
% frosh rec. need-based scholarship or grant aid	47
% UG rec. need-based scholarship or grant aid	41
% frosh rec. need-based self-help aid	41
% UG rec. need-based self-help aid	38
Avg. frosh grant	$5,014
Avg. frosh loan	$4,668
Independent 529 member?	No

UNIVERSITY OF CALIFORNIA—SANTA BARBARA

OFFICE OF ADMISSIONS, 1210 CHEADLE HALL, SANTA BARBARA, CA 93106-2014 • ADMISSIONS: 805-893-2881 • FAX: 805-893-2676

CAMPUS LIFE

Quality of Life Rating	**89**
Fire Safety Rating	**92**
Type of school	public
Environment	city

STUDENTS

Total undergrad enrollment	18,114
% male/female	45/55
% from out of state	5
% from public high school	85
% live on campus	26
% in (# of) fraternities	8 (18)
% in (# of) sororities	10 (19)
% African American	3
% Asian	16
% Caucasian	52
% Hispanic	17
% Native American	1
% international	1
# of countries represented	112

SURVEY SAYS

Great library
Students love Santa Barbara, CA
Students are happy
Student publications are popular
Lots of beer drinking
Hard liquor is popular

ACADEMICS

Academic Rating	**79**
Calendar	quarter
Student/faculty ratio	17:1
Professors interesting rating	74
Professors accessible rating	75
% classes taught by TAs	0
Most common lab size	20-29 students
Most common regular class size	20-29 students

MOST POPULAR MAJORS

Economics
psychology

STUDENTS SPEAK OUT

Academics

"People are happy" at the University of California—Santa Barbara (UCSB), and why shouldn't they be? Or, to frame the question as one student does, "What better place to explore one's world and mind than in a place of sunshine and beauty?" Especially when "the classes, professors, and facilities are all top-notch." Undergraduates appreciate a "well-balanced" college experience, telling us, "We have some great athletic programs, an awesome environment, intelligent students, and a fun community." And some fine academic departments as well. Students say, "The physics department is amazing, engineering professors are great, [and] the psychology department is outstanding." Throughout the curriculum, "UCSB offers tremendous classes and the right professors to teach them." The school's university status means that "the school focuses much of its attention on research. Undergraduates are encouraged to pursue their own research interests, guided by our world-renowned faculty." It also means "there are tons of majors" to choose from, as well as fantastic facilities. "Our library has eight stories of books, magazines, periodicals, copiers, printers, computers, the works! This is a great place to do research," gushes one student. Prepare to be challenged at UCSB, but "not in a high school manner, i.e., excessive workload, but rather to be challenged intellectually."

Life

"The essential aspect of UCSB is location," students agree, pointing out, "the campus offers vistas of both the Pacific Ocean and the mountains to the north." The location also contributes "wonderful weather, which makes for a very active campus. The majority of people can be seen outside playing Frisbee or softball in the park, running, surfing, bike riding (there are bike paths everywhere, and everyone bikes) and also skateboarding." Surrounding campus are Isla Vista— "a small college town where [many] students live [that is] home to insane parties"—and Santa Barbara, a city with "a lively downtown area for recreation of all types: shopping, clubs, and many good restaurants." All in all, UCSB's idyllic setting results in "a relaxed atmosphere, an ideal place in which to learn and enjoy life." Enjoyment comes in many forms. Undergraduates tell us, "At night, one has many options. There is always the Isla Vista party scene. For the more subdued, there is the school theater and other special performances/guest lectures, night walks along the beach, and the ever-enchanting downtown Santa Barbara, where music (from classical to jazz to club) and great food mingle to produce a truly lovely evening." There are also "phenomenal athletic programs" to enjoy, as "every team seems to win and every student takes an active role in supporting" them. The campus knows its SoCal customers. In the cafeteria, "vegetarian fare is always on the menu, with a surprisingly wide range of choices. Food from all over the globe is represented and variation is always present."

Student Body

The typical UCSB student "comes from an affluent or upper-middle-class family. Roughly two-thirds are from southern California and one-third are from northern California." Although "the majority of students are white, Latino/Chicano students are well represented on campus, as are Asians." Only a small minority of students come from out of state. One such student writes, "Everyone is from California and cannot understand people who are not. When I tell students that I am from New Jersey, most of them do not even know where it is on a map—no joke." Students exude California style and attitude. They are "very relaxed [and] know how to enjoy themselves. The typical male student has shaggy blond hair, a nice tan, skinny, and a surfboard or skateboard attached to him. The typical girl has her belly button pierced, halter tops and miniskirts on when it's 50 degrees outside, and shoes to match her sunglasses." Students tell us, "For the people who don't fit into this mold, it's no big deal. Everyone is pretty accepting of everyone else."

UNIVERSITY OF CALIFORNIA—SANTA BARBARA

FINANCIAL AID: 805-893-2432 • E-MAIL: APPINFO@SA.UCSB.EDU • WEBSITE: WWW.UCSB.EDU

ADMISSIONS

Very important factors considered include: Essays, secondary school record. *Important factors considered include:* Character/personal qualities, class rank, extracurricular activities, standardized test scores, talent/ability. *Other factors considered include:* Volunteer work, work experience. SAT Reasoning or SAT Subject Tests required. TOEFL required of all international applicants. High school diploma is required, and GED is accepted. *Academic units required:* 4 English, 3 math, 2 science (2 science lab), 2 foreign language, 2 social studies, 2 history, 2 academic electives. *Academic units recommended:* 4 math, 3 science (3 science lab), 3 foreign language.

The Inside Word

Although applications from members of underrepresented minority groups dipped following the 1997 state ban on the use of affirmative action in admissions, the picture has changed dramatically in the past few years. As a result of UC—Santa Barbara's vigorous outreach and recruiting efforts, applications from members of underrepresented minority groups have climbed steadily, as have acceptances. For the fall 2001 entering freshman class, the number of applicants accepted who are members of underrepresented minority groups has returned to pre-1997 levels.

FINANCIAL AID

Students should submit: FAFSA. Regular filing deadline is 5/31. The Princeton Review suggests that all financial aid forms be submitted as soon as possible after 1/1. *Need-based scholarships/grants offered:* Pell, SEOG, state scholarships/grants, the school's own gift aid. Work-study is also available as need-based aid. *Loan aid offered:* Direct PLUS, Federal Perkins. Applicants will be notified of awards on a rolling basis beginning on or about 3/15. Federal Work-study Program available. Institutional employment available. Off-campus job opportunities are excellent.

FROM THE ADMISSIONS OFFICE

"The University of California—Santa Barbara is a major research institution offering undergraduate and graduate education in the arts, humanities, sciences and technology, and social sciences. Large enough to have excellent facilities for study, research, and other creative activities, the campus is also small enough to foster close relationships among faculty and students. The faculty numbers more than 900. A member of the most distinguished system of public higher education in the nation, UC Santa Barbara is committed equally to excellence in scholarship and instruction. Through the general education program, students acquire good grounding in the skills, perceptions, and methods of a variety of disciplines. In addition, because they study with a research faculty, they not only acquire basic skills and broad knowledge but also are exposed to the imagination, inventiveness, and intense concentration that scholars bring to their work. UCSB is one of 62 members of the prestigous Association of American Universities.

"All applicants must take the ACT Assessment plus the new ACT Writing Test or the new SAT Reasoning Test. In addition, all applicants must take two SAT Subject Tests in two different subject areas. (If a Math SAT Subject Test is chosen by the applicant, he/she must take the Math Level II exam.)"

SELECTIVITY

Admissions Rating	**94**
# of applicants	36,963
% of applicants accepted	53
% of acceptees attending	20

FRESHMAN PROFILE

Range SAT Verbal	520-640
Average SAT Verbal	579
Range SAT Math	550-660
Average SAT Math	603
**TPR Projected Range SAT Writing*	*310-660*
Range ACT Composite	21-28
Average ACT Composite	25
Minimum Paper TOEFL	550
Minimum Computer Based TOEFL	213
Average HS GPA	3.76
% graduated top 10% of class	95
% graduated top 25% of class	100
% graduated top 50% of class	100

DEADLINES

Regular application deadline	11/30
Regular notification	3/15
Nonfall registration?	yes

APPLICANTS ALSO LOOK AT

AND OFTEN PREFER

University of California—Berkeley
University of California—Los Angeles
University of California—San Diego

AND SOMETIMES PREFER

University of California—Davis

AND RARELY PREFER

California Polytechnic State University—San Luis Obispo
University of California—Santa Cruz

FINANCIAL FACTS

Financial Aid Rating	**75**
Annual out-of-state tuition	$16,956
Room & Board	$9,897
Books and supplies	$1,406
Required fees	$480
% frosh rec. need-based scholarship or grant aid	45
% UG rec. need-based scholarship or grant aid	43
% frosh rec. need-based self-help aid	34
% UG rec. need-based self-help aid	37
% frosh rec. any financial aid	64
% UG rec. any financial aid	58
Avg. frosh grant	$8,706
Avg. frosh loan	$9,998
Independent 529 member?	No

UNIVERSITY OF CALIFORNIA—SANTA CRUZ

ADMISSIONS, COOK HOUSE, 1156 HIGH STREET, SANTA CRUZ, CA 95064 • ADMISSIONS: 831-459-4008 • FAX: 831-459-4452

CAMPUS LIFE

Quality of Life Rating	**82**
Fire Safety Rating	**83**
Type of school	public
Environment	town

STUDENTS

Total undergrad enrollment	13,647
% male/female	46/54
% from out of state	5
% from public high school	96
% live on campus	42
% in (# of) fraternities	1 (9)
% in (# of) sororities	1 (7)
% African American	3
% Asian	18
% Caucasian	52
% Hispanic	14
% Native American	1
% international	2

SURVEY SAYS

Great computer facilities
Great library
Students are friendly
Campus feels safe
Political activism is popular

ACADEMICS

Academic Rating	**80**
Calendar	quarter
Student/faculty ratio	19:1
Professors interesting rating	77
Professors accessible rating	76
% professors teaching UG courses	100
% classes taught by TAs	0
Most common lab size	20-29 students
Most common regular class size	20-29 students

MOST POPULAR MAJORS

English language and literature
psychology

STUDENTS SPEAK OUT

Academics

Historically, the University of California—Santa Cruz (UCSC) has offered one of the University of California system's closest approximations of the small-school experience. Despite a large student body and a faculty full of research studs, UCSC has traditionally fostered a "culture of teaching." Things have changed somewhat in recent years. Due in part to its increasing popularity, "the school has gradually been mainstreaming itself, trying to make itself into a little UCLA in the forest, and, in the process, it has calcified some of the academic flexibility that makes UCSC a unique institution." Even so, undergraduates report that "this culture of teaching is still a definitive feature of UCSC, although it's not as radical as it used to be. Professors are expected to be accessible on a higher level than at most large public universities, the bureaucracy is considerably less noticeable than at huge institutions like Berkeley, and there is an unusually high level of collaboration between undergraduates and professors on research." The university also alleviates the anonymity of big-school life through its residential colleges, "where you can become close to a smaller group of students to feel like you 'belong.'" Students tell us that the hard sciences, such as biology, are fast becoming the most prominent departments at UCSC.

Life

"Santa Cruz is a pretty laid-back place to just hang out and relax," students tell us, adding, "at the same time, there are some good clubs and fun places to go out as well." Fun can be as simple as taking in the natural surroundings; the campus is "in the middle of the forest, and the beach is only three minutes away. It's the most awesome campus overall." The school is home to many beach fanatics who enjoy surfing, scuba diving, sailing, and swimming. The area is also welcoming to hikers, campers, and bicyclists. The town of Santa Cruz provides "great shops, restaurants, movie theaters, [and] a great art scene. There is always a show you can go to, from gallery exhibits to multicultural activities and tons of musical acts." It also has a "huge bar scene" for those old enough to drink legally; "IDs are strictly enforced, so if you're under 21, forget about getting in. Fakes don't fool the bouncers cause they go to UCSC, too." While the school has shed some of its hippie image in recent years, UCSC has not entirely outpaced its past. Reportedly, "every Fall Quarter, when the first rain of the year starts to hit the ground, students start streaming toward Porter College and doffing their clothes. Over the next few hours, herds of students stampede through every residential college on campus, wearing nothing but sneakers, hiking boots, or flip-flops."

Student Body

Once a legendary bastion of "vegetarian hippies and surfers," UCSC has been broadening its student population in recent years to include "not only hippies but also nerds, jocks, druggies, preps, partygoers, ravers. You name it, we have it." Most maintain an open attitude toward their fellow students. "No one looks twice no matter how weird or different you may look or be here. There is a significant [number of] gay/lesbian students who are pretty well accepted." Some tell us there is an unusually wide variety among the quality of students. One undergraduate explains, "UC—Santa Cruz seems to have a two-caste society. On the one hand, there are the students clinging to the UC system by their fingernails, Santa Cruz being their last hope before being banished. On the other hand, there is a large number of gifted students who recognize the potential for undergraduate excellence. The two groups make for an odd couple, but each has things to learn from the other, and it all works out in the end."

University of California—Santa Cruz

Financial Aid: 831-459-2963 • E-mail: admissions@ucsc.edu • Website: www.admissions.ucsc.edu

ADMISSIONS

Very important factors considered include: Class rank, essays, secondary school record, standardized test scores, state residency. *Important factors considered include:* Character/personal qualities, extracurricular activities, geographical residence, talent/ability. *Other factors considered include:* Volunteer work, work experience. SAT Reasoning and SAT Subject Tests or ACT required. TOEFL required of all international applicants. High school diploma is required, and GED is accepted. *Academic units required:* 4 English, 3 math, 2 science (2 science lab), 2 foreign language, 1 social studies, 1 history, 1 academic elective. *Academic units recommended:* 4 English, 4 math, 3 science (3 science lab), 3 foreign language, 1 social studies, 1 history, 1 academic elective.

The Inside Word

Don't be deceived by the high acceptance rate at Santa Cruz; there are lots of engaging, intellectually motivated students here, and only active learners need apply. The state of California's ban on affirmative action in the UC admission process has created much uncertainty regarding the future of candidate selection in the system, but Santa Cruz is one of only two UC units that have been able to keep minority admission rates from declining precipitously.

FINANCIAL AID

Students should submit: FAFSA, state aid form. Regular filing deadline is 5/1. The Princeton Review suggests that all financial aid forms be submitted as soon as possible after 1/1. *Need-based scholarships/grants offered:* Pell, SEOG, state scholarships/grants, private scholarships, the school's own gift aid. *Loan aid offered:* Direct Subsidized Stafford, Direct Unsubsidized Stafford, Direct PLUS, Federal Perkins, college/university loans from institutional funds. Applicants will be notified of awards on a rolling basis beginning on or about 4/1. Off-campus job opportunities are good.

FROM THE ADMISSIONS OFFICE

"Since its founding in 1965, UC Santa Cruz has earned a national reputation as a campus devoted to excellence in undergraduate teaching, graduate study and research, and professional education. Its academic plan and physical design combine the advantages of a small-college setting with the intensive research and academic strengths traditional to the University of California. At UC Santa Cruz, undergraduate courses are taught by the same faculty who conduct cutting-edge research. In a national survey of more than 60 elite research universities by the Association of American Universities, UC Santa Cruz ranked fifteenth for students in all disciplines whose bachelor's degrees led to doctorates. The campus is growing selectively and is investing half a billion dollars in new and improved infrastructure.

"All applicants must take the ACT Assessment plus the new ACT Writing Test or the new SAT Reasoning Test. In addition, all applicants must take two SAT Subject Tests in two different subject areas. (If a Math SAT Subject Test is chosen by the applicant, he/she must take the Math Level II exam.)"

SELECTIVITY

Admissions Rating	**93**
# of applicants	23,308
% of applicants accepted	70
% of acceptees attending	19

FRESHMAN PROFILE

Range SAT Verbal	520-640
Average SAT Verbal	564
Range SAT Math	530-640
Average SAT Math	573
**TPR Projected Range SAT Writing*	*570-660*
Range ACT Composite	21-27
Average ACT Composite	23
Minimum Paper TOEFL	550
Minimum Computer Based TOEFL	220
Average HS GPA	3.46
% graduated top 10% of class	90
% graduated top 25% of class	100
% graduated top 50% of class	100

DEADLINES

Regular application deadline	11/30
Regular notification	rolling
Nonfall registration?	no

APPLICANTS ALSO LOOK AT AND OFTEN PREFER

Stanford University
University of California—Berkeley
University of California—Los Angeles

AND SOMETIMES PREFER

University of California—Davis
University of California—San Diego
University of California—Santa Barbara

AND RARELY PREFER

San Francisco State University
San Jose State University
University of California—Riverside

FINANCIAL FACTS

Financial Aid Rating	**85**
Annual in-state tuition	$0
Annual out-of-state tuition	$16,956
Room & Board	$10,947
Books and supplies	$1,302
Required fees	$7,023
% frosh rec. need-based scholarship or grant aid	43
% UG rec. need-based scholarship or grant aid	43
% frosh rec. need-based self-help aid	42
% UG rec. need-based self-help aid	40
Independent 529 member?	No

UNIVERSITY OF CENTRAL FLORIDA

P.O. BOX 160111, ORLANDO, FL 32816-0111 • ADMISSIONS: 407-823-3000 • FAX: 407-823-5625

CAMPUS LIFE

Quality of Life Rating	**92**
Fire Safety Rating	**76**
Type of school	public
Environment	city

STUDENTS

Total undergrad enrollment	34,940
% male/female	45/55
% from out of state	3
% live on campus	20
% in (# of) fraternities	13 (24)
% in (# of) sororities	12 (17)
% African American	8
% Asian	5
% Caucasian	69
% Hispanic	12
% Native American	1
% international	1
# of countries represented	145

SURVEY SAYS . . .

Great computer facilities
Athletic facilities are great
Students love Orlando, FL
Great off-campus food
Campus feels safe
Frats and sororities dominate social scene

ACADEMICS

Academic Rating	**74**
Calendar	semester
Student/faculty ratio	19:1
Profs interesting rating	71
Profs accessible rating	71
% profs teaching UG courses	100
% classes taught by TAs	6
Most common lab size	20-29 students
Most common reg class size	20-29 students

MOST POPULAR MAJORS

Management information systems
marketing/marketing management
psychology

Academics

With its "great engineering and computer science departments, through which many undergraduates can get hands-on experience in their field via research," the University of Central Florida is a school "so career-oriented that non-declared majors are practically corralled into 'Career Exploration' camps." And yet this is hardly a cut-throat, high-pressure school; on the contrary, students extol UCF's "laid-back attitude. We may not be as highly regarded as an Ivy League school, but there are amazing things going on here that don't require enormous amounts of pressure. You'll do well because you want to, not because your school's reputation mandates it." Those "amazing things" occur not only in the aforementioned wonk disciplines, but also in hospitality management, mass communications, education, and business. The liberal and fine arts, on the other hand, "need to have more money allocated to them" and suffer in comparison to their more career-driven academic counterparts. To mitigate the drawbacks of big-school impersonality, UCF offers a number of personalizing services. "Every large lecture class has a 'SI' (Supplemental Instruction) where there is a student who previously passed the class with an A, who also provides free tutoring." In addition, "There is a large Student Academic Resource Center where students can go for free tutoring in any subject." UCF undergrads also benefit from "awesome technology on campus and in the classroom. The whole campus is wired with wireless internet. There is a strong emphasis on technology, and when a department is funded, well it is extremely well funded. Corporate partnerships are big here."

Life

Even though "UCF is really large," you "don't have to feel like you're lost in the mix" here because "there's a place for everyone, and the school, student government, and campus activities board make it easy to find it." Undergrads boast that "there is something to do almost every night of the week on campus. There is almost every imaginable intramural sport, and there is quite a bit to do off campus as well." The area surrounding the school features "lots of restaurants and places to shop. Students can go to movie theaters, bowling alleys, parks, and even campus-organized events" in their free time. Then there's downtown Orlando, "which is great, and the UCF SGA is adept at exploiting the local resources (e.g., Universal Studios and the rest of International Drive)." The city has a decent nightlife, with "a large segment of young/professional/hip people living in Orlando and populating the bars and clubs." Ask students how life here could improve and most will mention the football team, which went 0-11 in 2004. "Many students joke that we are a drinking school with a football problem," cracks one student, adding quickly that "we still have pride, and those games are still very well attended." Undergrads would also love to see the constant on-campus construction come to an end. Writes one, "A joke around campus is that UCF stands for 'Under Construction Forever,' and it's true. Our school mascot should be the crane because there is so much construction. The campus looks great, though, and we have many nice new facilities."

Student Body

One student describes the UCF student body so neatly we have to include her entire survey response. She writes, "The typical student? You are talking about a campus with 45,000 students; there is no possible way to describe a typical student. There is a vast difference among students not only between the different schools (business, health and public affairs, communication, hospitality, engineering, arts and sciences, etc.), but also within the schools themselves. You have students who have always been at UCF, transfer students, and nontraditional students. We mix so well that one cannot really tell who is who. Of course you can always pick out the athletic students (a huge group) and the Greeks, but mostly, everyone gets along pretty well on campus. And if you don't get along with someone, it is pretty easy to hide among 45,000 other people."

UNIVERSITY OF CENTRAL FLORIDA

FINANCIAL AID: 407-823-2827 • E-MAIL: ADMISSION@MAIL.UCF.EDU • WEBSITE: WWW.UCF.EDU

ADMISSIONS

Very important factors considered include: Secondary school record, standardized test scores. *Important factors considered include:* Essays. *Other factors considered include:* Alumni/ae relation, character/personal qualities, class rank, extracurricular activities, geographical residence, interview, recommendations, state residency, talent/ability, volunteer work, work experience. SAT Reasoning or ACT required; TOEFL required of all international applicants. High school diploma is required and GED is accepted. *Academic units required:* 4 English, 3 math, 3 science, (2 science lab), 2 foreign language, 3 social studies, 4 academic electives.

Inside Word

Over the past decade, UCF has been making a concerted effort to increase its admissions profile, and by and large it has been successful, as the acceptance rate keeps going down while the test scores and average GPAs of newly enrolled students keep ticking up. That means it's virtually nipping at the heels of cross-state rivals Florida State University and University of Florida in terms of selectivity. As is the case at many state schools, it's all a numbers game here; students aren't required to interview or submit essays. It's also worth noting that when calculating your GPA, which is a very important criterion for admission, the admissions committee weights honors, AP, dual enrollment, and International Baccalaureate academic classes more heavily than regular classes.

FINANCIAL AID

Students should submit: FAFSA. Regular filing deadline is June 1. The Princeton Review suggests that all financial aid forms be submitted as soon as possible after January 1. *Need-based scholarships/grants offered:* Pell, SEOG, state scholarships/grants, private scholarships, the school's own gift aid, university scholarships and grants. *Loan aid offered:* FFEL Subsidized Stafford, FFEL Unsubsidized Stafford, FFEL PLUS, Federal Perkins. Applicants will be notified of awards on a rolling basis beginning or about March 15. Federal Work-Study Program available. Institutional employment available. Off-campus job opportunities are excellent.

FROM THE ADMISSIONS OFFICE

"The University of Central Florida offers competitive advantages to its student body. We're committed to teaching, providing advisement, and academic support services for all students. Our undergraduates have access to state-of-the-art wireless buildings, high-tech classrooms, research labs, Web-based classes, and an undergraduate research and mentoring program.

"Our Career Services professionals help students gain practical experiences at NASA, schools, hospitals, high-tech companies, local municipalities, and the entertainment industry. With an international focus to our curricula and research programs, we enroll international students from 122 nations. Our study abroad programs and other study and research opportunities include agreements with 98 institutions and 36 countries.

"UCF's 1,415-acre campus provides a safe and serene setting for learning, with natural lakes and woodlands. The bustle of Orlando lies a short distance away: the pro sport teams, the Kennedy Space Center, film studios, Walt Disney World, Universal Orlando, Sea World, and sandy beaches are all nearby.

"Applicants for summer 2006 and beyond are required to take the new version of the SAT (or the ACT with the writing section), but we will allow students to submit scores from the old SAT or ACT as well, and will use the student's best scores from either test."

SELECTIVITY

Admissions Rating	**89**
# of applicants	22,367
% of applicants accepted	55
% of acceptees attending	48
# accepting a place on wait list	276

FRESHMAN PROFILE

Range SAT Verbal	540-630
Average SAT Verbal	589
Range SAT Math	550-640
Average SAT Math	597
**TPR Projected Range SAT Writing*	*590-650*
Range ACT Composite	24-28
Average ACT Composite	26
Minimum Paper TOEFL	550
Minimum Computer Based TOEFL	213
Average HS GPA	3.8
% graduated top 10% of class	35
% graduated top 25% of class	75
% graduated top 50% of class	91

DEADLINES

Regular application deadline	5/1
Regular notification	rolling
Nonfall registration?	yes

FINANCIAL FACTS

Financial Aid Rating	**77**
Annual in-state tuition	$2,982
Annual out-of-state tuition	$15,488
Room & Board	$7,132
Books and supplies	$828
Required fees	$198
% frosh rec. need-based scholarship or grant aid	19
% UG rec. need-based scholarship or grant aid	19
% frosh rec. need-based self-help aid	16
% UG rec. need-based self-help aid	22
% frosh rec. any financial aid	93
% UG rec. any financial aid	79
Avg. frosh grant	$3,791
Avg. frosh loan	$2,515
Independent 529 member?	No

UNIVERSITY OF CHICAGO

1116 EAST 59TH STREET, CHICAGO, IL 60637 • ADMISSIONS: 773-702-8650 • FAX: 773-702-4199

CAMPUS LIFE

Quality of Life Rating	**83**
Fire Safety Rating	**60**
Type of school	private
Environment	metropolis

STUDENTS

Total undergrad enrollment	4,552
% male/female	50/50
% from out of state	78
% from public high school	60
% live on campus	60
% African American	4
% Asian	15
% Caucasian	56
% Hispanic	8
% international	8
# of countries represented	59

SURVEY SAYS

Small classes
No one cheats
Lab facilities are great
Great computer facilities
Great library
Students love Chicago, IL

ACADEMICS

Academic Rating	**86**
Calendar	quarter
Student/faculty ratio	4:1
Professors interesting rating	82
Professors accessible rating	81
% professors teaching UG courses	90
% classes taught by TAs	0

MOST POPULAR MAJORS

Biology/biological sciences
economics
English language and literature

STUDENTS SPEAK OUT

Academics

"The academic nature of this school is evident everywhere," explains one student, "be it the music performed by the arts groups, the discussions during meals, or even the comments written in the bathroom stalls. It is all highly intellectual." While the workload can be "hard to the point that people cry after chemistry or math finals [and] a returned paper with high praise is about as rare as a total solar eclipse," few students would trade down for a less demanding school. Rather, undergraduates see the university's demands as the best means to gaining "the confidence and intellectual conditioning to not only work through difficult materials, both academic and otherwise, but to thrive in such situations—an invaluable asset put to use for the rest of your life." The school puts students through their paces from day one, challenging them with a broad core curriculum that "is often taught by top professors," including Nobel laureates. One student comments, "The core is a great thing that, despite all the kvetching, gives students a pretty solid foundation in the liberal arts and teaches them how to think about literature, philosophy, and science." As students advance to upper-level courses, they get to choose from a vast selection of professors who are "enthusiastic, exciting, accessible, and incredibly accomplished." They're not spoon feeders, though, they "expect you to know the basic material and will focus much of their time on the more advanced applications of certain theories." One student wraps it up, saying, "If you are seriously academic and don't mind cold winters, Chicago is the best place in the world."

Life

When Chicago students can shake free of the library, they find themselves on a campus abuzz with activity. "The university offers lectures by Nobel laureates and renowned political figures, film screenings, and SCAV HUNT, in which students spend three days without food or sleep trying to do things like build a nuclear reactor or acquire a NASA-certified piece of the Columbia shuttle." Undergraduates also "frequent concerts at Mandel Hall by world-renowned artists. The campus also houses several museums, including the Oriental Institute and the Smart Museum. There is never a lack of fun, as long as one is open to all activities." For one student, the campus itself is "by far one of the most beautiful I have encountered. It's considered a botanical garden." Another student also approves of the dormitories, "the cushiest in the world. I have a kitchen, a walk-in closet, a dining room, and a bathroom that I only have to share with two roommates." Students give Hyde Park mixed reviews. Some say, "The location of the college is also a strength since it is located in a small neighborhood, but still close enough to the city." Still others complain that it offers "a dearth of college hangouts, and the few that we have are sub-par." Fortunately, greater Chicago "has a broad offering of restaurants, theater, opera, dance, art museums, neighborhood festivals, rock concerts, sports games, and so on."

Student Body

Typically "wonkish, nerdy, cloistered, extremely studious, and religiously dedicated to academic performance," Chicago students are "brilliant, on par with those at any other school, but not the kind of people that you want to have a casual conversation with." That is somewhat attributed to "personal hygiene and social skills [that] are sometimes lacking," and partly because "we ask seemingly strange questions. This is only because, after a few years at Chicago, we only see questions in terms of 'useful' or 'useless.' Strange questions are often the most useful, and we eventually forget that normal people avoid asking the strange questions." The school has attempted to recruit beyond its nerdish base, bringing in more students of the frat boy/jock variety. Most agree the efforts are counterproductive. One student writes, "Chicago has a reputation for its antisocial, elitist student body, but when it tries to change this reputation, it just erodes the reason for its greatness."

FINANCIAL AID: 773-702-8666 • WEBSITE: WWW.UCHICAGO.EDU

ADMISSIONS

Very important factors considered include: Character/personal qualities, essays, recommendations, secondary school record, talent/ability. *Important factors considered include:* Class rank, extracurricular activities, volunteer work. *Other factors considered include:* Alumni/ae relation, interview, minority status, standardized test scores, work experience. SAT Reasoning or ACT required. TOEFL required of all international applicants. High school diploma or equivalent is not required. *Academic units recommended:* 4 English, 4 math, 4 science, 3 foreign language, 2 social studies, 2 history.

The Inside Word

While excellent grades in tough courses and high test scores are the norm for applicants to the university, what really counts is what's on your mind. This is a cerebral institution, and thinkers stand out in the admissions process. Think about yourself, think about what you'd like to know more about, think about why you want to attend the university. Once you have some answers, begin writing your essays. And remember that universities that are this selective and recommend interviews should always be taken up on their recommendation.

FINANCIAL AID

Students should submit: FAFSA, institution's own financial aid form, CSS/Financial Aid PROFILE, noncustodial (divorced/separated) parents' statement, business/farm supplement. Regular filing deadline is 2/1. The Princeton Review suggests that all financial aid forms be submitted as soon as possible after 1/1. *Need-based scholarships/grants offered:* Pell, SEOG, state scholarships/grants, private scholarships. *Loan aid offered:* FFEL Subsidized Stafford, FFEL Unsubsidized Stafford, FFEL PLUS, Federal Perkins, private loans. Federal Work-study Program available. Institutional employment available. Off-campus job opportunities are excellent.

FROM THE ADMISSIONS OFFICE

"The University of Chicago is a place where talented young intellectuals, writers, mathematicians, and scientists come to learn in a setting that rewards hard work and prizes initiative and creativity. It's also a place where collegiate life is urban, yet friendly and open, and free of empty traditionalism and snobbishness. Chicago is the right choice for students who know that they would thrive in a intimate classroom setting. Classes at Chicago are small, emphasizing discussion with faculty members whose research is always testing the limits of their chosen fields. Students at U of Chicago take chances—delighting professors when they pursue a topic on their own for the fun of it or display an articulate voice in papers and in discussion. Their good times include the normal collegiate good times—a highly successful Division III sports program, small but active Greek life, 35 student theatrical productions a year, a rich musical life—and the extraordinary opportunities a major city offers our students, who enjoy the politics, music, theater, commerce, architecture, neighborhood life, of Chicago.

"Applicants are asked to submit either the SAT or the ACT. If they are 2006 graduates, we ask that they submit the new version of the SAT Reasoning Test. Chicago does not require SAT Subject Tests. The ACT may be taken without the optional Writing section."

SELECTIVITY

Admissions Rating	**97**
# of applicants	8,751
% of applicants accepted	40
% of acceptees attending	34
# accepting a place on wait list	1,402
% admitted from wait list	16

FRESHMAN PROFILE

Range SAT Verbal	670-770
Range SAT Math	660-760
**TPR Projected Range SAT Writing*	*680-740*
Range ACT Composite	28-33
Minimum Paper TOEFL	600
Minimum Computer Based TOEFL	250
% graduated top 10% of class	82
% graduated top 25% of class	93
% graduated top 50% of class	99

DEADLINES

Regular application deadline	1/1
Regular notification	4/1
Nonfall registration?	no

APPLICANTS ALSO LOOK AT

AND OFTEN PREFER
Columbia College Chicago (IL)
Columbia University—Columbia College
Harvard College
University of Pennsylvania
Yale University

AND SOMETIMES PREFER
Cornell University
Northwestern University
University of California—Berkeley

AND RARELY PREFER
Georgetown University
New York University
University of Michigan—Ann Arbor
Washington University in St. Louis

FINANCIAL FACTS

Financial Aid Rating	**96**
Annual tuition	$31,629
Room & Board	$10,104
Books and supplies	$950
Required fees	$636
% frosh rec. need-based scholarship or grant aid	46
% UG rec. need-based scholarship or grant aid	44
% frosh rec. need-based self-help aid	41
% UG rec. need-based self-help aid	40
% frosh rec. any financial aid	47
% UG rec. any financial aid	58
Avg. frosh grant	$23,405
Avg. frosh loan	$4,474
Independent 529 member?	Yes

UNIVERSITY OF COLORADO—BOULDER

52 UCB, BOULDER, CO 80309-0552 • ADMISSIONS: 303-492-6301 • FAX: 303-492-7115

CAMPUS LIFE

Quality of Life Rating	**88**
Fire Safety Rating	**93**
Type of school	public
Environment	city

STUDENTS

Total undergrad enrollment	25,607
% male/female	53/47
% from out of state	32
% live on campus	22
% in (# of) fraternities	8 (16)
% in (# of) sororities	11 (10)
% African American	2
% Asian	6
% Caucasian	79
% Hispanic	6
% Native American	1
% international	1
# of countries represented	104

SURVEY SAYS

Great computer facilities
Great library
Athletic facilities are great
Students love Boulder, CO
Great off-campus food
Students are happy
Everyone loves the The Golden Buffalos
Lots of beer drinking

ACADEMICS

Academic Rating	**73**
Calendar	semester
Student/faculty ratio	17:1
Professors interesting rating	75
Professors accessible rating	75
% professors teaching UG courses	90
% classes taught by TAs	16
Most common lab size	20-29 students
Most common regular class size	10-19 students

MOST POPULAR MAJORS

English language and literature
journalism
psychology

STUDENTS SPEAK OUT

Academics

Whether you're looking for a backbreaking foray into the world of science, a four-year ski vacation, or something in between, you're likely to find it at the University of Colorado's flagship campus in Boulder. "CU is all about opportunity," explains one undergrad, "from the opportunity to 'Ski and Get D's to Get Degrees' to the opportunity to live your life doing research in a lab." CU boasts strong programs in engineering, the sciences, business, and journalism, all bolstered by "excellent computer resources" and "exceptional laboratory facilities, which can be used by underclassmen (even freshmen)." Like most large state schools, CU is "geared toward research, which results in some teachers who do not have the best teaching skills." Given that, a surprising number of respondents told us that "professors and teaching assistants are usually willing to spend time with you as long as you make the effort to seek them out" and that "teachers are constantly telling us about ways to further our education outside of school, and most make some sort of effort to get to know students personally." Another plus is that "many profs are from industry, so they really know what they are talking about, which makes it easier to pay attention." The Honors Program, students agree, is "exceptional for a large university; the classes are challenging, the discussions are interesting, and the professors are the best on campus." As one undergrad sums it up, "The school gives those students who really want an education a great one, and for those who don't, it's a great place to ski!"

Life

Students come to CU for the peerless quality of life, and by nearly all accounts, that's exactly what they get. The key to it all is "location, location, location." The city of Boulder offers "an endless amount of things to do. From concerts to coffee shops, movies to lecturers, or shopping to parties, as well as just about every sport or outdoor activity, you'll never have an excuse to be bored." And "if that is not enough, Denver is only 30 minutes away." Those willing to travel a little farther harvest what most consider the area's pearl: some of the best skiing and snowboarding to be found anywhere. But students don't have to go anywhere to achieve bliss: "It is hard not to be happy when you live on such a beautiful campus. It's absolutely amazing: open courtyards shaded by beautiful trees, old brick buildings filled with warmth, and the towering Flatirons peering down from the west." The campus is "100 percent pedestrian and bicycle. We have over 15,000 bikes on campus," a testament to the crunchy granola vibe that permeates the university and surrounding town. Add an "awesome rec center," "a multitude of clubs and organizations to belong to," and popular Division I varsity, club, and intramural sports programs, and you begin to understand why so many here agree that "CU is all about having a great time in a beautiful place while learning new and interesting things."

Student Body

The CU student body consists of "a combination of rich kids and hippies, kids who don't care about classwork, and kids who are super-competitive, studying hard during the week and letting loose on the weekends." The typical CU student "is fairly well-off, white, and genuinely nice." The engineering program is more diverse than most here, since "about one-quarter of all the students are foreign." CU has a relatively high out-of-state population; it's "exciting to know so many people from so many different areas." "Many out-of-state students come from California or Texas," and "there is a large visual disparity from the in-state students just lucky to have a chance to get to school here, to your Ms. Beverly Hills decked out in the latest designer wear [and] Tiffany & Co. jewelry and driving her Mercedes that her daddy gave her." Students skew left politically; there are lots of "diversity thugs and enviro-hippies."

UNIVERSITY OF COLORADO—BOULDER

FINANCIAL AID: 303-492-5091 • E-MAIL: APPLY@COLORADO.EDU • WEBSITE: WWW.COLORADO.EDU

ADMISSIONS

Very important factors considered include: Class rank, secondary school record, standardized test scores. *Important factors considered include:* Essays, geographical residence, minority status, recommendations, state residency. *Other factors considered include:* Alumni/ae relation, character/personal qualities, extracurricular activities, talent/ability, volunteer work, work experience. SAT Reasoning or ACT required. TOEFL required of all international applicants. High school diploma is required, and GED is accepted. *Academic units required:* 4 English, 3 math, 3 science (2 science lab), 3 foreign language, 1 social studies, 1 history, 1 geography.

The Inside Word

The University of Colorado—Boulder was in the news quite a bit in the 2003-2004 academic year, first for being named the nation's #1 party school in this publication, then for a series of allegations against the football program concerning sexual misconduct by players during campus visits of recruits, as well as against a former female member of the team. It's too early to tell how the publicity will affect admissions at the school, but it's unlikely that CU will become a less popular destination for students, given the great quality of life and the impressive programs in business and the sciences. Fully one-third of the undergraduate student body is from out-of-state. You can say the same about only a very few other big state schools in this book.

FINANCIAL AID

Students should submit: FAFSA, tax return required. The Princeton Review suggests that all financial aid forms be submitted as soon as possible after 1/1. *Need-based scholarships/grants offered:* Pell, SEOG, state scholarships/grants, private scholarships, the school's own gift aid. *Loan aid offered:* Direct Subsidized Stafford, Direct Unsubsidized Stafford, Direct PLUS, Federal Perkins, college/university loans from institutional funds, private lenders. Applicants will be notified of awards on a rolling basis beginning on or about 2/1. Federal Work-study Program available. Institutional employment available. Off-campus job opportunities are excellent.

FROM THE ADMISSIONS OFFICE

"The University of Colorado at Boulder is a place of beauty and academic prominence at the foot of the Rocky Mountains. A sense of vitality and curiosity fills the campus, and yet it's comfortable and relaxed. It's a place you can be yourself and let your imagination soar.

"We have programs for you if you seek leadership training, research experience, academic honors, international experience (one in four graduates has studied abroad), community involvement, and more. The Undergraduate Academy gives exceptionally talented and intellectually committed students the opportunity to expand their education outside the classroom, build a sense of community, and help prepare for post-graduate opportunities. Residential academic programs (RAPS) in several halls provide undergraduates with shared learning and living experiences.

"Getting involved is easy at CU—Boulder. If you are interested in student government, clubs, athletics, recreation, Greek life, volunteer work, theater, dance, film, exhibits, planetarium shows, or concerts, you will find them here.

"To find out if CU—Boulder is the place for you, we encourage you to visit. Contact the Office of Admissions, or take a virtual tour at www.colorado.edu/prospective.

"The University of Colorado at Boulder requires either SAT or ACT (with or without the Writing component) scores for admission. The university will also accept SAT scores from the old SAT (taken before March 2005), and will use the best scores from either test. SAT Subject Tests are not required."

SELECTIVITY

Admissions Rating	**83**
# of applicants	19,360
% of applicants accepted	85
% of acceptees attending	31
# accepting a place on wait list	179
% admitted from wait list	16

FRESHMAN PROFILE

Range SAT Verbal	530-630
Average SAT Verbal	579
Range SAT Math	550-650
Average SAT Math	596
**TPR Projected Range SAT Writing*	*580-650*
Range ACT Composite	23-28
Average ACT Composite	25
Minimum Paper TOEFL	500
Minimum Computer Based TOEFL	173
Average HS GPA	3.53
% graduated top 10% of class	25
% graduated top 25% of class	58
% graduated top 50% of class	92

DEADLINES

Regular application deadline	1/15
Regular notification	rolling
Nonfall registration?	yes

APPLICANTS ALSO LOOK AT

AND OFTEN PREFER

Stanford University
University of California—Berkeley
University of California—Santa Cruz

AND SOMETIMES PREFER

Arizona State University
Colorado State University
Northwestern University
Oregon State University
University of Arizona

AND RARELY PREFER

University of Oregon
University of Vermont

FINANCIAL FACTS

Financial Aid Rating	**83**
Annual in-state tuition	$3,480
Annual out-of-state tuition	$20,592
Room & Board	$7,564
Books and supplies	$1,187
Required fees	$861
% frosh rec. need-based scholarship or grant aid	22
% UG rec. need-based scholarship or grant aid	20
% frosh rec. need-based self-help aid	35
% UG rec. need-based self-help aid	30
% frosh rec. any financial aid	61
% UG rec. any financial aid	51
Avg. frosh grant	$4,263
Avg. frosh loan	$3,032
Independent 529 member?	No

UNIVERSITY OF CONNECTICUT

2131 HILLSIDE ROAD, UNIT 3088, STORRS, CT 06268-3088 • ADMISSIONS: 860-486-3137 • FAX: 860-486-1476

CAMPUS LIFE

Quality of Life Rating	**65**
Fire Safety Rating	**96**
Type of school	public
Environment	town

STUDENTS

Total undergrad enrollment	15,260
% male/female	48/52
% from out of state	30
% from public high school	85
% live on campus	72
% in (# of) fraternities	10 (14)
% in (# of) sororities	7 (9)
% African American	5
% Asian	7
% Caucasian	75
% Hispanic	4
% international	1
# of countries represented	109

SURVEY SAYS

Great computer facilities
Great library
Athletic facilities are great
Everyone loves the Huskies
Intramural sports are popular
Student publications are popular
Lots of beer drinking
Hard liquor is popular

ACADEMICS

Academic Rating	**76**
Calendar	semester
Student/faculty ratio	17:1
Professors interesting rating	63
Professors accessible rating	69
% professors teaching UG courses	76
% classes taught by TAs	24
Most common lab size	20-29 students
Most common regular class size	10-19 students

MOST POPULAR MAJORS

Nursing/registered nurse training (RN, ASN, BSN, MSN)
political science and government
psychology

STUDENTS SPEAK OUT

Academics

Students at the University of Connecticut's (UConn) flagship campus in Storrs tell us that they chose their school for "the wide variety of opportunities it provides its students to get involved and get ahead." Undergrads here also cite as big pluses "undergraduate research, study abroad, career services/internships, cooperative education programs," "more than 100 majors, including an individualized major which allows students to design their own plan of study, and over 300 clubs and activities. There is literally something for everyone." Business administration, music, theater, education, computer science, and engineering are among the disciplines garnering students' specific praise here. As at many large state schools, many warn that "introductory courses are not that great. It gets better as you progress as a student." Profs are "surprisingly helpful when students go to their office hours and tend to return emails the same day," although "with [UConn] being a research university, you sometimes get stuck with professors that are just too intelligent to be teaching." Of course, for the right student, the presence of so many researchers "provides a great experience. You can find numerous opportunities to get involved in professors' research projects." Many here appreciate the fact that "larger lectures are almost always broken into discussion sections of 20–25 students that meet once a week." Being the flagship university for the state of Connecticut doesn't hurt either. Connecticut profited, not once, but twice from state grants of $1 billion each, first in 1996 and then again in 2002. Students directly benefit from this windfall of dough in that every residence hall, academic building, sports facility, program office, etc. is being completely refurbished, torn down and rebuilt, or simply added anew to campus.

Life

As a large university, UConn has the resources to support a wide variety of campus activities. Big-name acts "come to the university's Jorgensen Auditorium; they're amazing and with student ticket prices are a wonderfully cheap way to see great shows." On a smaller scale, "there are many students who enjoy the concerts of UConn Underground, numerous films, lectures, plays, and other activities going on in the dorms on a nightly basis." Furthermore, "there are so many clubs and organizations to be involved with that if you're bored on campus, it's because of your own laziness." Even so, a surprising number of students here claim that "there is nothing to do here except party." One reason is that many of the nonparty activities end early; explains one student, "UConn has a great campus life, which ends at 10 P.M. every day. Unfortunately because of that, alcohol is a popular late-night substitute. Activities are available . . . if you look hard enough and are open to different cultural and artistic experiences." Don't look in hometown Storrs, though, which "is not a college town. There is nothing to do off campus without driving at least 20 minutes." Do, however, look in the stadiums, arenas, and gymnasiums, as "the University of Connecticut offers strong Division I athletic programs in addition to a vast selection of club and intramural sports." Most here agree that "Spring Weekend is the highlight of the year. Three straight days (starting on a Thursday) of parties with crowds up to and over 10,000 people: just an overall amazing experience."

Student Body

While "the large size of UConn means that there's not one typical student," we're told that most students here "have a good balance of school and social life. They work hard during the week and enjoy the weekend." Many are serious about success but not necessarily about book learning for its own sake; they "know that it's OK to skip at least one or two classes a week and to show up late because no one will say anything." Students are split regarding diversity. While some describe the typical UConn student as "white, middle/upper class, and from Connecticut," others point to "our five cultural centers, [where] it's easy for students to fit in and feel a part of a community."

UNIVERSITY OF CONNECTICUT

FINANCIAL AID: 860-486-2819 • E-MAIL: BEAHUSKY@UCONN.EDU • WEBSITE: WWW.UCONN.EDU

ADMISSIONS

Very important factors considered include: Class rank, secondary school record, standardized test scores, talent/ability. *Important factors considered include:* Character/personal qualities, essays, extracurricular activities, minority status, recommendations, volunteer work. *Other factors considered include:* Alumni/ae relation, geographical residence, state residency, work experience. SAT Reasoning or ACT required. TOEFL required of all international applicants. High school diploma is required, and GED is accepted. *Academic units required:* 4 English, 3 math, 2 science (2 science lab), 2 foreign language, 2 social studies, 3 academic electives. *Academic units recommended:* 3 foreign language.

The Inside Word

While no formulas or cutoffs may be used at UConn in the admissions process, getting in is still simply a matter of decent courses, grades, and tests. The $2.3 billion building program coupled with the recent high national profiles of the UConn men's and women's basketball teams has resulted in an increase in applications and in turn an increase in selectivity. With an incoming freshman class of more than 3,000, UConn is now holding enrollment steady for eager Huskies-to-be.

FINANCIAL AID

Students should submit: FAFSA. The Princeton Review suggests that all financial aid forms be submitted as soon as possible after 1/1. *Need-based scholarships/grants offered:* Pell, SEOG, state scholarships/grants, private scholarships, the school's own gift aid. *Loan aid offered:* FFEL Subsidized Stafford, FFEL Unsubsidized Stafford, FFEL PLUS, Federal Perkins. Applicants will be notified of awards on a rolling basis beginning on or about 3/1.

FROM THE ADMISSIONS OFFICE

"The University of Connecticut provides students with high quality education, personalized attention, and a wide range of social and cultural opportunities. From award-winning actors to the federal reserve board chair, fascinating speakers and world leaders have lectured on campus within the past year, while students have taken in shows by premier dance, jazz, and rock performers. Transportation to campus events is convenient and safe; most students walk to class or ride university shuttlebuses. Through UCONN 2000 and Twenty-first-Century UConn, landmark building programs totaling $2.3 billion, the university is erecting state-of-the-art academic and residential facilities. Among the projects: A new Center for Undergraduate Education, unifying student support services in one central location and providing speedy answers to student concerns. Because of a variety of innovations like this one, UConn is transforming the undergraduate experience and fast becoming a school of choice for a new generation of achievement-oriented students.

"Freshman applicants seeking admittance for fall 2006 are required to submit official score reports from the new SAT or ACT with Writing component."

SELECTIVITY

Admissions Rating	**88**
# of applicants	18,466
% of applicants accepted	50
% of acceptees attending	35
# accepting a place on wait list	2,734
% admitted from wait list	1

FRESHMAN PROFILE

Range SAT Verbal	530-630
Average SAT Verbal	580
Range SAT Math	550-640
Average SAT Math	597
**TPR Projected Range SAT Writing*	*580-650*
Range ACT Composite	22-27
Minimum Paper TOEFL	550
Minimum Computer Based TOEFL	213
% graduated top 10% of class	35
% graduated top 25% of class	79
% graduated top 50% of class	98

DEADLINES

Regular application deadline	2/1
Regular notification	rolling
Nonfall registration?	yes

APPLICANTS ALSO LOOK AT

AND OFTEN PREFER

Boston College, Boston University, Syracuse University, University of Delaware, University of Maryland—College Park

AND SOMETIMES PREFER

Northeastern University, Penn State University Park, Providence College

AND RARELY PREFER

Hofstra University, Marist College, University of Massachusetts—Amherst

FINANCIAL FACTS

Financial Aid Rating	**72**
Annual in-state tuition	$6,096
Annual out-of-state tuition	$18,600
Room & Board	$7,848
Books and supplies	$725
Required fees	$1,816
% frosh rec. need-based scholarship or grant aid	35
% UG rec. need-based scholarship or grant aid	36
% frosh rec. need-based self-help aid	39
% UG rec. need-based self-help aid	40
% frosh rec. any financial aid	48
% UG rec. any financial aid	48
Avg. frosh grant	$6,377
Avg. frosh loan	$2,445
Independent 529 member?	No

UNIVERSITY OF DALLAS

1845 EAST NORTHGATE DRIVE, IRVING, TX 75062 • ADMISSIONS: 972-721-5266 • FAX: 972-721-5017

CAMPUS LIFE

Quality of Life Rating	**79**
Fire Safety Rating	**84**
Type of school	private
Affiliation	Roman Catholic
Environment	metropolis

STUDENTS

Total undergrad enrollment	1,087
% male/female	46/54
% from out of state	44
% from public high school	43
% live on campus	61
% African American	1
% Asian	6
% Caucasian	67
% Hispanic	16
% international	2
# of countries represented	13

SURVEY SAYS

Small classes
Students are friendly
Students are very religious
Students are happy
Frats and sororities are unpopular or nonexistent
(Almost) everyone smokes

ACADEMICS

Academic Rating	**86**
Calendar	semester
Student/faculty ratio	12:1
Professors interesting rating	97
Professors accessible rating	94
% professors teaching UG courses	100
% classes taught by TAs	0
Most common lab size	10-19 students
Most common regular class size	10-19 students

MOST POPULAR MAJORS

Business administration/management
English language and literature

STUDENTS SPEAK OUT

Academics

In their "distinctly Catholic academic and social setting," University of Dallas (UD) students immerse themselves in a core curriculum featuring the poster boys of western thought: "Homer, Virgil, Dante, Milton, Plato, Aristotle, Locke, Aquinas, Shakespeare—you get the idea." The academic experience is intense; "You become the core, and the core becomes you." This course of study "helps me understand my culture, including the political, economic, scientific, and philosophical arenas, by showing me its origins." Even amid these lofty texts, students claim, "the subject matter is never purely theoretical or divorced from morality. I am encouraged to think about how I can use what I've learned to be a better person." Class sizes are kept very small, and the resulting education "surpasses Ivy League schools," according to one fired-up respondent. The "surpassingly excellent" faculty is "the main attraction of the school." These "world-renowned thinkers" reportedly "care deeply about the intellectual growth of their students." An astronomical number of students study abroad, mainly at the university's Rome campus. "The Rome program definitely helps everybody on campus to develop their individuality while creating life-long friends." Students can engage in dialogue with the administrators, who are "very helpful, even [during] the most stressful times of the year." A new president began July 1, 2004.

Life

Though University of Dallas students know how to hit the books, traditional drunken revelry does occur, in the form of parties at upperclassmen apartments or the weekly "Thank God It's Thursday" events. The campus, however, "offers options other than drinking and partying." These include "sword fighting in the courtyard at three in the morning," "reenacting Trojan wars," "crocheting afghans," and "lauding Tolkien." And as we all know, "there is nothing like discussing Dante at two in the morning at the local IHOP with fellow stressed students." Slightly less geeked-out, "the student activities organization always has something planned on campus, be it concerts, comedians, hypnotists, or dances." Students look forward to annual Groundhog Day festivities, which include hayrides and a school-wide party that lasts until the early-morning hours. People with cars can take full advantage of the plentiful Dallas attractions, but those without wheels find themselves mostly campus-bound. As one student sums up the social scene, "UD is about discovering truth through studying the classics and living a complete life, which includes spiritual, emotional, and physical aspects, as well as the intellectual."

Student Body

Most strikingly, UD students are "strongly, almost eccentrically, grounded in orthodox Catholic principles." More than one respondent to our survey offers "sheltered, conservative, middle-class, and white" as appropriate adjectives to describe the undergraduate population. "Unfortunately, there's not much diversity in ethnicity," most here agree. Those who do differ from the norm report some friction: "I'm a pretty liberal Democrat and would support issues like abortion and gay rights, for example, and most people here are appalled by that." Another "minority" student writes, "As one of the few Protestants on campus, I feel like I fit in, and no one forces Catholicism on me." Certain respondents attest that "atypical students are uncommon, but don't have trouble fitting in." Perhaps that owes itself to the fact that "the school tries, with great success, to unify the students in each graduating class." Basically, anyone with "a beer in one hand and the complete works of Plato in the other" can hang. Bottom line, the school stands as a "utopia for the odd," reflected in the rally cry, "We are definitely all geeks here, but we like it that way!"

Financial Aid: 972-721-5266 • E-mail: ugadmis@udallas.edu • Website: www.udallas.edu

ADMISSIONS

Very important factors considered include: Character/personal qualities, essays, recommendations, secondary school record, standardized test scores. *Important factors considered include:* Talent/ability. *Other factors considered include:* Alumni/ae relation, class rank, extracurricular activities, interview, volunteer work, work experience. SAT Reasoning or ACT required. TOEFL required of all international applicants. High school diploma is required, and GED is accepted. *Academic units required:* 4 English, 3 math, 3 science, 2 foreign language, 3 social studies, 3 history, 4 academic electives, 2 art/drama. *Academic units recommended:* 4 English, 4 math, 3 science, 3 foreign language, 4 social studies, 4 history, 4 academic electives, 2 art/drama.

The Inside Word

The university's conservative nature places significant emphasis on "fit" in the admissions process. Having a solid academic background counts, but what kind of match a candidate makes with Dallas can be even more important.

FINANCIAL AID

Students should submit: FAFSA, institution's own financial aid form. Regular filing deadline is 5/30. The Princeton Review suggests that all financial aid forms be submitted as soon as possible after 1/1. *Need-based scholarships/grants offered:* Pell, SEOG, state scholarships/grants, private scholarships, the school's own gift aid. *Loan aid offered:* FFEL Subsidized Stafford, FFEL Unsubsidized Stafford, FFEL PLUS, Federal Perkins, state loans. Applicants will be notified of awards on a rolling basis beginning on or about 3/1.

FROM THE ADMISSIONS OFFICE

"Quite unabashedly, the curriculum at the University of Dallas is based on the supposition that truth and virtue exist and are the proper objects of search in an education. The curriculum further supposes that this search is best pursued through an acquisition of philosophical and theological principles on the part of a student and has for its analogical field a vast body of great literature—perhaps more extensive than is likely to be encountered elsewhere—supplemented by a survey of the sweep of history and an introduction to the political and economic principles of society. An understanding of these subjects, along with an introduction to the quantitative and scientific worldview and a mastery of a language, is expected to form a comprehensive and coherent experience, which, in effect, governs the intellect of a student in a manner that develops independence of thought in its most effective mode.

"Students applying for admission for fall 2006 are required to take the new SAT. Previous SAT scores (prior to March 2005) will also be considered if they are available, but not in place of the new SAT (or the ACT with the Writing section)."

SELECTIVITY

Admissions Rating	**86**
# of applicants	815
% of applicants accepted	87
% of acceptees attending	34
# accepting a place on wait list	15
% admitted from wait list	53

FRESHMAN PROFILE

Range SAT Verbal	560-670
Average SAT Verbal	614
Range SAT Math	540-650
Average SAT Math	590
**TPR Projected Range SAT Writing*	*600-680*
Range ACT Composite	23-28
Average ACT Composite	25
Minimum Paper TOEFL	550
Minimum Computer Based TOEFL	213
Average HS GPA	3.6
% graduated top 10% of class	35
% graduated top 25% of class	67
% graduated top 50% of class	92

DEADLINES

Regular application deadline	8/1
Regular notification	3/1 to 8/1
Nonfall registration?	yes

APPLICANTS ALSO LOOK AT AND OFTEN PREFER

Southern Methodist University
University of Notre Dame

AND SOMETIMES PREFER

Austin College
Texas Christian University
Trinity University

AND RARELY PREFER

Loyola University New Orleans
Saint Louis University
Spring Hill College
Texas A&M University—College Station
The University of Texas—Austin

FINANCIAL FACTS

Financial Aid Rating	**75**
Annual tuition	$19,604
Room & Board	$7,026
Books and supplies	$1,000
Required fees	$807
% frosh rec. need-based scholarship or grant aid	64
% UG rec. need-based scholarship or grant aid	62
% frosh rec. need-based self-help aid	48
% UG rec. need-based self-help aid	52
% frosh rec. any financial aid	96
% UG rec. any financial aid	93
Avg. frosh grant	$11,320
Avg. frosh loan	$5,042
Independent 529 member?	Yes

UNIVERSITY OF DAYTON

300 COLLEGE PARK, DAYTON, OH 45469-1300 • ADMISSIONS: 937-229-4411 • FAX: 937-229-4729

CAMPUS LIFE

Quality of Life Rating	**86**
Fire Safety Rating	**83**
Type of school	private
Affiliation	Roman Catholic
Environment	city

STUDENTS

Total undergrad enrollment	7,008
% male/female	50/50
% from out of state	34
% from public high school	50
% live on campus	79
% in (# of) fraternities	15 (12)
% in (# of) sororities	18 (9)
% African American	4
% Asian	1
% Caucasian	86
% Hispanic	2
% international	1
# of countries represented	25

SURVEY SAYS

Small classes
Great computer facilities
Students are friendly
Students are happy
Lots of beer drinking

ACADEMICS

Academic Rating	**76**
Calendar	semester
Student/faculty ratio	14:1
Professors interesting rating	80
Professors accessible rating	85
% professors teaching UG courses	82
% classes taught by TAs	5
Most common lab size	10-19 students
Most common regular class size	20-29 students

MOST POPULAR MAJORS

Business administration/management
communications studies/speech communication and rhetoric
engineering

STUDENTS SPEAK OUT

Academics

University of Dayton (UD), a midsize university "rooted in the Marianist tradition and Catholic faith," provides its largely career-oriented students with an ethics-based liberal arts education. "My school is all about our 'Learn, Lead, Serve' motto that comes from our Marianist influence," brags one of the many undergraduates who praise a wide array of departments, including engineering, drama, education, and marketing. Students appreciate that their school is large enough to maintain a broad selection of courses, yet small enough to provide mentoring and one-on-one teaching. "Since the undergraduate population is less than 7,000, it is easy to have access to professors," reports one student, "while also having plenty of opportunities, such as those that are found at bigger schools." Better still, "professors are some of the best around. Many work at Wright Patterson Air Force Base, which is nearby." Students give the new administration mixed reviews. Some tell us that administrators "seem to be very upbeat about the future and very interested in the students, what they have to offer seems very promising." Others, however, worry that "the school's administration is out to shed itself of the party school image, and they think that throwing money and technology at the school will solve their problems, instead of getting at the root problems." One of those root problems, writes one undergrad, is that "some teachers and classes are brought down by mediocre students." Even so, most here speak highly of the overall UD experience, satisfied with the sense that "the focus at Dayton is not only grades and learning, but also taking care of us as young adults in need of mentors."

Life

Some kids go to college to escape the ghetto; at UD, the opposite occurs. "The Ghetto, an infamous neighborhood composed of old houses, most of which the University owns, [is] filled with undergrad students, mostly juniors and seniors," explains one undergrad. While "drinking in the Ghetto is the main activity" of many Dayton students, "the experience of the Ghetto is about much more than wild parties . . You learn to live in a community built on respect for one another." Dayton has long had a reputation as a party school, and an especially democratic one at that; "there is no such thing as 'list' parties at Dayton; rather, everyone is accepted everywhere," reports one student. "I know this is hard to believe, but it's the truth, and one of the main reasons I love this place so much." However, "while UD is known as a party school, it really isn't that bad. There are plays, movies, and special activities that Student Government sets up for those who don't want to drink. For fun we go to the movies, out to eat, or to the mall. I think the University of Dayton provides plenty of interesting things to do on the weekend." UD also has "all kinds of intramural sports that students love to play; I think we had hundreds of students play softball last spring."

Student Body

The "J. Crew and Abercrombie" crowd at UD is "dominated by white, Catholic kids from private schools," primarily from Ohio, Illinois, Indiana, and Missouri. Writes one student, "Most students are what my friends and I call the three C's: Caucasian, Catholic (nonpracticing, of course!), and conservative. I am atypical in that I am a liberal Democrat. For students like me, there are student organizations such as Students Allies (gay, lesbian, transgender, etc.), College Democrats, Amnesty International, and Pax Christi (pacifist group)." Many here noted "the university's commitment toward making UD more diverse, reflected in its scholarship and grant-giving this year." Several students told us that "diversity is improving but could still go a long way." Many undergrads are involved in "serving the community of Dayton and reaching out to those less fortunate."

FINANCIAL AID: 937-229-4311 • E-MAIL: ADMISSION@UDAYTON.EDU • WEBSITE: WWW.UDAYTON.EDU

ADMISSIONS

Very important factors considered include: Secondary school record. *Important factors considered include:* Class rank, standardized test scores, talent/ability. *Other factors considered include:* Alumni/ae relation, character/personal qualities, essays, extracurricular activities, interview, minority status, recommendations, volunteer work, work experience. SAT Reasoning or ACT required. TOEFL required of all international applicants. High school diploma is required, and GED is accepted. *Academic units required:* 2 units of foreign language for admission to the College of Arts & Sciences. *Academic units recommended:* 4 English, 3 math, 2 science, 3 social studies, 4 academic electives.

The Inside Word

While Dayton reviews all applicants individually in regard to their potential for success at the university, its high admit rate means that there's little for all but the weakest applicants to worry about concerning admission.

FINANCIAL AID

Students should submit: FAFSA. The Princeton Review suggests that all financial aid forms be submitted as soon as possible after 1/1. *Need-based scholarships/grants offered:* Pell, SEOG, state scholarships/grants, private scholarships. *Loan aid offered:* FFEL Subsidized Stafford, FFEL Unsubsidized Stafford, FFEL PLUS, Federal Perkins, GATE. Applicants will be notified of awards on or about 3/31.

FROM THE ADMISSIONS OFFICE

"The University of Dayton is a Catholic leader in higher education. We offer the resources and diversity of a comprehensive university and the attention and accessibility of a small college.

"More than 70 challenging academic programs are offered in the College of Arts and Sciences and the Schools of Business Administration, Education, and Allied Professions, Engineering, and Law. Classes are small—27 students on average. Our more than 800 full-time and part-time faculty are committed to teaching undergraduate students and involving them in their research projects.

"The University of Dayton Research Institute ranks second in the nation in the amount of materials research performed annually. Technology-enhanced learning and the student computer initiative ensure students gain expertise in the tools that will prepare them for the future. All university-owned housing is fully wired for direct high-speed Internet access, and a wireless network covers several academic buildings, the student union, library, outdoor plazas, and residential buildings.

"Recent campus construction provides a modern home for the University's cutting-edge academic programs. New facilities include ArtStreet, Marianist Hall and the Science Center. Open in January 2006, a new fitness and recreation complex, the RecPlex, provides 130,000 square feet of space for classrooms, courts, a natatorium, offices, and other recreational facilities.

"A strong sense of community is a hallmark feature of the university; a dual emphasis on leadership and service contributes to students' participation in more than 170 clubs and organizations. Division I intercollegiate athletics, and club and intramural sports, are also popular.

"Students applying for admission fall 2006 may provide scores from either version of the SAT, or the ACT. Scores from the new Writing component will be collected but will not be used for admission purposes for 2006. The highest composite scores from either test will be used in admissions decisions."

SELECTIVITY

Admissions Rating	**75**
# of applicants	8,156
% of applicants accepted	80
% of acceptees attending	28
# accepting a place on wait list	213
% admitted from wait list	26

FRESHMAN PROFILE

Range SAT Verbal	510-620
Average SAT Verbal	568
Range SAT Math	520-640
Average SAT Math	583
**TPR Projected Range SAT Writing*	*570-650*
Range ACT Composite	23-27
Average ACT Composite	25
Minimum Paper TOEFL	523
Minimum Computer Based TOEFL	193
% graduated top 10% of class	22
% graduated top 25% of class	46
% graduated top 50% of class	77

DEADLINES

Regular notification	rolling
Nonfall registration?	yes

APPLICANTS ALSO LOOK AT

AND OFTEN PREFER
University of Notre Dame

AND SOMETIMES PREFER
John Carroll University
Marquette University
Miami University
Ohio State University—Columbus
Saint Louis University

AND RARELY PREFER
Ohio University—Athens
Purdue University—West Lafayette
University of Cincinnati
Xavier University (OH)

FINANCIAL FACTS

Financial Aid Rating	**86**
Annual tuition	$21,245
Room & Board	$6,780
Books and supplies	$800
Required fees	$800
% frosh rec. need-based scholarship or grant aid	62
% UG rec. need-based scholarship or grant aid	59
% frosh rec. need-based self-help aid	59
% UG rec. need-based self-help aid	57
% frosh rec. any financial aid	93
% UG rec. any financial aid	90
Avg. frosh grant	$9,505
Avg. frosh loan	$3,683
Independent 529 member?	Yes

UNIVERSITY OF DELAWARE

ADMISSIONS OFFICE, 116 HULLIHEN HALL, NEWARK, DE 19716-6210 • ADMISSIONS: 302-831-8123 • FAX: 302-831-6905

CAMPUS LIFE

Quality of Life Rating	**77**
Fire Safety Rating	**87**
Type of school	public
Environment	town

STUDENTS

Total undergrad enrollment	16,023
% male/female	42/58
% from out of state	58
% from public high school	80
% live on campus	45
% in (# of) fraternities	13 (15)
% in (# of) sororities	13 (15)
% African American	6
% Asian	3
% Caucasian	85
% Hispanic	4
% international	1
# of countries represented	100

SURVEY SAYS

Great computer facilities
Great library
Athletic facilities are great
Students are friendly
Great off-campus food
Students are happy
Everyone loves the Fightin' Blue Hens
Lots of beer drinking
Hard liquor is popular

ACADEMICS

Academic Rating	**79**
Calendar	4-1-4
Student/faculty ratio	13:1
Professors interesting rating	72
Professors accessible rating	74
% professors teaching UG courses	95
% classes taught by TAs	5
Most common lab size	10-19 students
Most common regular class size	20-29 students

MOST POPULAR MAJORS

Biology/biological sciences
elementary education and teaching
psychology

STUDENTS SPEAK OUT

Academics

What students like most about University of Delaware (UD) is that "despite the fact that it's a pretty big school, it doesn't feel that way." One student says, "The school has done a great job making me feel at home and part of an amazing community of people that care about me personally." That sense of engagement permeates the UD academic experience. One undergraduate writes, "Delaware is about opportunities to work hands-on with faculty, either through the honors program, undergraduate research, senior thesis, or simply additional meetings with professors outside of class." Outside the classroom, students, professors, and administrators "keep in close contact via E-mail [and] WebCT," and professors "are extremely accessible." University of Delaware has "a number of excellent faculty members in all of the major fields and an outstanding research program." Undergraduates are especially sanguine about the "strong majors in business and agriculture, [the] great engineering programs, [and] well-developed arts programs, especially in music and theater." The chemistry department is also something to rave about, as it "is a wonderful place for undergraduates." Students also love all the extras, which include a solid study abroad program, an honors program that "gives you a more hands-on approach and allows a much more personal relationship with professors," and a full slate of extracurricular activities. One student sums up, "University of Delaware prides itself on enriching its students while they are here, not only in academics, but also in life experiences, involvement on campus, and preparing for the future."

Life

"There is always something to do on or around campus," UD undergraduates report. "The campus movie theater shows new movies every weekend, and on Main Street there are billiard halls and a bowling alley. There are also a lot of restaurants to go to in the area," and plenty of parties. Students tell us that "Delaware has always had a party-school reputation, which the university is trying to get away from, but the campus is still a great place to go out and party." Where students party depends on their age. "Frat parties are big for the underclassmen. After you're 21, the school turns into a bar school. Everyone is at certain bars on certain nights." Because most students are serious about success, they "know when to stop and get work done, or study for a test. The biggest challenge is to manage the time between partying and studying, but most people handle it pretty well." Not everyone drinks, of course: "For students who don't drink, there are always other options on campus, such as comedy shows, band performances, and a lot of student-run organizations, over 200 of them. The university offers so many activities and organizations to be involved in; someone can always find something that fits them individually." Student groups also organize plenty of bus trips to Philadelphia, Baltimore, Washington, DC, and New York City. With so much to offer, it is no wonder that some students feel that "University of Delaware has achieved the perfect balance between strong and challenging academic work and social events."

Student Body

"There are so many kids at UD that everyone fits in. Whatever you see yourself as: jock, nerd, whatever, there are people like you at UD," students tell us. Most would also agree, however, that you will fit in with the largest part of the population if you "look like you just walked out of an Abercrombie ad. [There are] lots of preppy kids, mostly white and middle to upper class." In general, students tend to self-segregate. As one student puts it, "While we tend to get along, there isn't necessarily interaction between social groups." One clear divide separates Delaware residents and out-of-staters, who actually compose the majority of the student body. "Out-of-state students are, on the whole, very well off, and show it. In-state students, however, are generally viewed as not as well off." Another divide is the "big split between Greek and non-Greek students." Minorities, most agree, are underrepresented at UD.

FINANCIAL AID: 302-831-8761 • E-MAIL: ADMISSIONS@UDEL.EDU • WEBSITE: WWW.UDEL.EDU

ADMISSIONS

Very important factors considered include: Essays, secondary school record, state residency. *Important factors considered include:* Character/personal qualities, class rank, extracurricular activities, geographical residence, recommendations, standardized test scores, talent/ability. *Other factors considered include:* Alumni/ae relation, interview, minority status, volunteer work, work experience. SAT Reasoning or ACT required. TOEFL required of all international applicants. High school diploma is required, and GED is accepted. *Academic units required:* 4 English, 3 math, 3 science (2 science lab), 2 foreign language, 2 social studies, 2 history. *Academic units recommended:* 4 English, 4 math, 4 science (3 science lab), 4 foreign language, 2 social studies, 2 history, 2 academic electives.

Inside Word

Most students applying to Delaware face a moderately selective admissions process focused mainly on grades and tests with some focus on nonacademic characteristics. Those who seek to enter the university's honors program need to be far more thorough in completing their applications and much better prepared academically in order to gain admission. The honors program has high expectations; from what we know, it appears to be well worth it.

FINANCIAL AID

Students should submit: FAFSA. Regular filing deadline is 3/15. The Princeton Review suggests that all financial aid forms be submitted as soon as possible after 1/1. *Need-based scholarships/grants offered:* Pell, SEOG, state scholarships/grants, private scholarships, the school's own gift aid. *Loan aid offered:* Direct Subsidized Stafford, Direct Unsubsidized Stafford, Direct PLUS, Federal Perkins, Federal Nursing. Applicants will be notified of awards on or about 3/15. Federal Work-study Program available. Institutional employment available. Off-campus job opportunities are good.

FROM THE ADMISSIONS OFFICE

"The University of Delaware is a major national research university with a long-standing commitment to teaching and serving undergraduates. It is one of only a few universities in the country designated as a land-grant, sea-grant, urban-grant, and space-grant institution. The academic strength of this university is found in its highly selective Honors Program, nationally recognized Undergraduate Research Program, study abroad opportunities on all seven continents, and its successful alumni, including three Rhodes Scholars since 1998. The University of Delaware offers the wide range of majors and course offerings expected of a university, but in spirit remains a small place where you can interact with your professors and feel at home. The beautiful green campus is ideally located at the very center of the East Coast 'megacity' that stretches from New York City to Washington, DC. All of these elements, combined with an endowment approaching $1 billion and a spirited Division I athletics program, make the University of Delaware a tremendous value.

"Freshman applicants for fall 2006 are required to take the SAT Reasoning Test (or the ACT with the Writing section). If a student takes the new SAT more than once, the best individual scores from each test taken will be combined. Two SAT Subject Tests are recommended for applicants to the University Honors Program."

SELECTIVITY

Admissions Rating	**92**
# of applicants	22,208
% of applicants accepted	45
% of acceptees attending	35
# accepting a place on wait list	3,038
% admitted from wait list	3
# of early decision applicants	615
% accepted early decision	38

FRESHMAN PROFILE

Range SAT Verbal	540-630
Range SAT Math	560-650
**TPR Projected Range SAT Writing*	*590-650*
Range ACT Composite	24-28
Minimum Paper TOEFL	550
Minimum Computer Based TOEFL	213
Average HS GPA	3.5
% graduated top 10% of class	38
% graduated top 25% of class	76
% graduated top 50% of class	97

DEADLINES

Early decision application deadline	11/1
Early decision notification	12/15
Regular application deadline	1/15
Regular notification	3/15
Nonfall registration?	yes

FINANCIAL FACTS

Financial Aid Rating	**78**
Annual in-state tuition	$6,304
Annual out-of-state tuition	$15,990
Room & Board	$6,458
Books and supplies	$800
Required fees	$650
% frosh rec. need-based scholarship or grant aid	36
% UG rec. need-based scholarship or grant aid	30
% frosh rec. need-based self-help aid	31
% UG rec. need-based self-help aid	27
Independent 529 member?	No

UNIVERSITY OF DENVER

UNIVERSITY HALL, ROOM 110, 2197 S. UNIVERSITY BLVD., DENVER, CO 80208 • ADMISSIONS: 303-871-2036 • FAX: 303-871-3301

CAMPUS LIFE

Quality of Life Rating	**76**
Fire Safety Rating	**76**
Type of school	private
Environment	metropolis

STUDENTS

Total undergrad enrollment	4,644
% male/female	45/55
% from out of state	55
% from public high school	81
% live on campus	45
% in (# of) fraternities	20 (8)
% in (# of) sororities	19 (5)
% African American	3
% Asian	5
% Caucasian	80
% Hispanic	7
% Native American	1
% international	4
# of countries represented	87

SURVEY SAYS

Small classes
Lab facilities are great
Great computer facilities
Athletic facilities are great
Students love Denver, CO
Great off-campus food
Campus feels safe
Students are happy

ACADEMICS

Academic Rating	**80**
Calendar	quarter
Student/faculty ratio	10:1
Professors interesting rating	70
Professors accessible rating	81
% professors teaching UG courses	92
% classes taught by TAs	8
Most common lab size	10-19 students
Most common regular class size	10-19 students

MOST POPULAR MAJORS

Business, management, marketing, and related support services
communications studies/speech communication and rhetoric
social sciences

STUDENTS SPEAK OUT

Academics

A little under half of the University of Denver's (UD) undergraduates pursue degrees in business. This pre-MBA focus contributes substantially to the University's overall character. Students are largely diligent workers focused on the prize of a successful career. They are also the type likely to dismiss core classes in the humanities as "ridiculous and having no practical application for reality." The University of Denver appeals to these students by creating "an overall feeling that you are in a business school." That's not to suggest that students pursuing majors other than business receive short shrift at DU. The university also excels in pre-law studies, music, and communications. In fact, students brag that "there is ample funding for all the departments at DU, and therefore undergrads have incredible opportunities to pursue serious academic projects. A dedicated student can get an education equal to that of a student at any top university." They also concede, however, that "Some majors are much, much easier than others." In all departments, "The fact that the school is small benefits everyone. Teachers and students form relationships and work together when in the classroom. Teachers also meet students at The Pub (the on-campus restaurant) for study sessions." The University also "makes it easy and affordable for anyone to study abroad."

Life

The University of Denver offers "tons of different organizations to participate in. DU Programs Board, the Greek system, DU Alpine Club, and Student Government are just a few of the on-campus activities offered." Trouble is, with the exception of the Greek houses (which are quite popular), most of these activities do not inspire the majority of undergraduates. Apparently, there is too much else to distract them: the "shopping and dinner on the 16th Street Mall in downtown Denver, [the] nearby Cherry Creek district for dinner and a movie, [and] the mountains, which are so close by, so we can go skiing every weekend." Many students love to party. One undergraduate jokes, "If there was a degree in business and you could double major in drinking, DU would be it," although there are also plenty of "more mature" students who hang out in the local coffeehouses. Because "the campus is officially dry," a good amount of drinking occurs off campus, either in the "great neighborhood bars located one to three blocks from campus [or] at the two main colleges that are less than an hour away, CU—Boulder and Colorado School of Mines. We often go up to party with those schools." Yet students always return to Denver for sporting events, especially for home games featuring "the great hockey team." Students also love to take advantage of the Ritchie Center, "a great sports facility [for working out] that is gorgeous and free to students." For students, "the campus is beautiful." As one undergraduate puts it, "With a stunning campus and 300 days of sunshine in Denver, you can't go wrong!"

Student Body

The University of Denver is "a perfect size to meet new people all the time, but [also] to run into people you know every time you walk across campus." Its students "are typically relaxed but hardworking people, a large portion of whom (probably about half) are from affluent backgrounds, are trendy, and party a lot." One student notes that not all DU students "are serious about academics, but there are a lot of opportunities for students like this to pursue." The population also includes "a lot of international students and large and active groups of Arab, Jewish, Latino, and other minorities (although there aren't many Blacks)." Students believe the diversity "helps our school face the issues of the day and also helps us have new and different experiences." The university also has a considerable jock population. Students "enjoy being outdoors (anything from a snowball fight to a marathon run to speed skiing) and also like to work out or participate in athletics."

FINANCIAL AID: 303-871-4020 • E-MAIL: ADMISSION@DU.EDU • WEBSITE: WWW.DU.EDU/ADMISSION

ADMISSIONS

Very important factors considered include: Character/personal qualities, interview, secondary school record, standardized test scores. *Important factors considered include:* Essays, recommendations. *Other factors considered include:* Class rank, extracurricular activities, talent/ability, volunteer work, work experience. SAT Reasoning or ACT required. High school diploma is required, and GED is accepted. *Academic units recommended:* 4 English, 4 math, 4 science (2 science lab), 3 foreign language, 2 social studies, 2 history.

The Inside Word

Any good student will find getting admitted to Denver to be a fairly straightforward process.

FINANCIAL AID

Students should submit: FAFSA. Regular filing deadline is 3/1. The Princeton Review suggests that all financial aid forms be submitted as soon as possible after 1/1. *Need-based scholarships/grants offered:* Pell, SEOG, state scholarships/grants, private scholarships, the school's own gift aid. *Loan aid offered:* Direct Subsidized Stafford, Direct Unsubsidized Stafford, Direct PLUS, FFEL Subsidized Stafford, FFEL Unsubsidized Stafford, FFEL PLUS, Federal Perkins, college/university loans from institutional funds. Applicants will be notified of awards on a rolling basis beginning on or about 3/15. Federal Work-study Program available. Off-campus job opportunities are excellent.

FROM THE ADMISSIONS OFFICE

"Founded in 1864, the University of Denver offers an educational experience characterized by adventurous learning and innovative mentoring from a caring faculty. Our undergraduate students come from all across the United States and from more than 90 countries to study in an environment that nurtures potential and passion. The new Hyde Interview requirement provides all applicants the opportunity to give a voice to their application while assisting DU with admission decisions.

"DU is continually developing educational initiatives that help students prepare for an ever-changing world. Among our offerings: residence-based learning communities that provide extracurricular and cocurricular programming in particular areas; a grant program for students that funds everything from research to creative endeavors; and hundreds of internship opportunities that put students in laboratories, corporate offices, government agencies, and cultural settings. In addition, an experimental leadership program emphasizes ethics, community service, and citizenship.

"DU's 25-acre University Park campus, located in a quiet residential neighborhood, is eight miles from downtown Denver and a half-hour's drive from the Rocky Mountain foothills. DU students enjoy an active lifestyle with plenty of opportunities to recreate in the Rockies, cheer on one of the city's many professional sports teams, or enjoy the city's lively arts and entertainment scene.

"Applicants for fall 2006 may submit either version of the ACT or SAT. For this year only, the Writing component of the ACT will not be required. If a student takes the new SAT more than once, the best individual scores from each test taken will be combined."

SELECTIVITY

Admissions Rating	**84**
# of applicants	3,787
% of applicants accepted	87
% of acceptees attending	34
# accepting a place on wait list	41
% admitted from wait list	17

FRESHMAN PROFILE

Range SAT Verbal	510-630
Average SAT Verbal	570
Range SAT Math	520-630
Average SAT Math	576
**TPR Projected Range SAT Writing*	*570-650*
Range ACT Composite	22-27
Average ACT Composite	25
Average HS GPA	3.48
% graduated top 10% of class	33
% graduated top 25% of class	59
% graduated top 50% of class	85

DEADLINES

Regular application deadline	1/15
Regular notification	1/10
Nonfall registration?	yes

APPLICANTS ALSO LOOK AT
AND OFTEN PREFER
Colorado College
Colorado State University
University of Colorado—Boulder
AND SOMETIMES PREFER
Boston University
University of Puget Sound
University of Vermont

FINANCIAL FACTS

Financial Aid Rating	**69**
Annual tuition	$27,756
Room & Board	$8,749
Books and supplies	$1,306
Required fees	$654
% frosh rec. need-based scholarship or grant aid	40
% UG rec. need-based scholarship or grant aid	36
% frosh rec. need-based self-help aid	35
% UG rec. need-based self-help aid	33
% frosh rec. any financial aid	80
% UG rec. any financial aid	78
Avg. frosh grant	$14,582
Avg. frosh loan	$3,581
Independent 529 member?	No

University of Florida

201 Criser Hall, Box 114000, Gainesville, FL 32611-4000 • Admissions: 352-392-1365 • Fax: 904-392-3987

CAMPUS LIFE

Quality of Life Rating	**80**
Fire Safety Rating	**71**
Type of school	public
Environment	city

STUDENTS

Total undergrad enrollment	33,094
% male/female	47/53
% from out of state	4
% live on campus	22
% in (# of) fraternities	15 (29)
% in (# of) sororities	15 (18)
% African American	9
% Asian	7
% Caucasian	72
% Hispanic	12
% Native American	1
% international	1

SURVEY SAYS

Athletic facilities are great
Everyone loves the Gators
Intramural sports are popular
Frats and sororities dominate social scene
Student publications are popular
Lots of beer drinking
Hard liquor is popular

ACADEMICS

Academic Rating	**77**
Calendar	semester
Student/faculty ratio	23:1
Professors interesting rating	68
Professors accessible rating	76
% classes taught by TAs	0
Most common lab size	10-19 students
Most common regular class size	10-19 students

MOST POPULAR MAJORS

Business administration/management
finance
psychology

STUDENTS SPEAK OUT

Academics

Students describe the University of Florida as a school that can be as difficult or easy as they want to make it. Some cruise through by adhering to the principle that "the key to taking classes here is to understand the system and find the scattered easy classes. There are at least two easy teachers in every department. Find them and take every class they offer." Others take a more arduous route; writes one, "UF is very academically challenging, especially when you get into your upper-division courses, and especially in the hard sciences. People who say otherwise are taking doofus electives like 'Insects, Molds, and Mildews' to boost their GPA." Intro level courses are mostly "huge lectures where students sit—silently—and professors lecture indifferently." "The academic experience becomes rewarding," however, "once upper-level classes are reached. Classes are much smaller, and I have been able to know my professors better because I have them for more that one course." Many students love the "TV and WEB classes, which are very convenient. The one good thing about the administration is they put everything online on this thing called ISIS and send a weekly e-mail." Sums up one student, "Because UF is such a large university, it is easy to feel overwhelmed and lost. But if you try to get involved and get to know the facilities you have at hand, UF has soooo many opportunities it's ridiculous."

Life

"What, UF is a school? I thought they were just a football team." So writes one student who pithily sums up many students' reverent attitude toward the Gators' gridiron powerhouse. "Life revolves around Gator football," explains one student, "and on game days the campus is crowded with visitors, alumni, and students, making parking impossible." Students love the men's basketball team, too; in fact, students here just love sports, plain and fancy. "Intramural sports here kick arse," and undergrads participate in "a lot of outdoor activities. The school provides students with a lake of our own where we can use sailboats, canoes, jet skis, etc., all free." When nighttime rolls around, "People go to clubs for fun. There are a lot of raves and keg parties." Also, "the Greek system is extremely popular on campus and they always have stuff going on. It is a good way to meet a ton of people." Much of hometown Gainesville commerce is tailored to serving the large student body, leading students to observe that "Gainesville has pretty much everything, including a ton of bars with something for anyone Greek, non-Greek, gay, Hispanic, Afro-American. If you don't like going out, the Gulf of Mexico is 45 minutes to the west, and the Atlantic is 1.5 hours east. Orlando is 1 hour away. The list goes on. Because of its size, student life at UF is limited only by your imagination, time, and/or course load."

Student Body

At UF "there are so many students that everyone should be able to find a niche." Once students find their niche, most lock in; reports one student, "Different groups don't really mix. Each has its own thing going and doesn't seem to involve others." Among these groups are "large outspoken Christian groups" and a "large Greek population." Notes one student, "The only downfall is that Greek life is pretty dominant, but hey, if you like that kind of thing, you'll be in heaven." Concludes one student, "It's a mixed bag between really amazing people who work hard and have good direction and the spoiled yuppie brats who don't know how lucky they are to be here and what life is all about beyond MTV."

FINANCIAL AID: 352-392-1275 • WEBSITE: WWW.UFL.EDU

ADMISSIONS

SAT Reasoning or ACT required. High school diploma is required, and GED is accepted. *Academic units required:* 4 English, 3 math, 3 science (2 science lab), 2 foreign language, 3 social studies.

The Inside Word

Practically every other high school graduate in the state applies to UF, which gives the admissions staff a huge pool of candidates to choose from. The selection process is driven by numbers, with little personal attention afforded anyone but athletes, legacies, minorities, and National Merit Scholars. Out-of-state students will find that getting into this "party school" isn't at all easy. With budget cuts further restricting enrollment, it won't be long before admission to Florida is as difficult for out-of-staters as it is at such top public universities as North Carolina and Virginia.

FINANCIAL AID

Students should submit: FAFSA. The Princeton Review suggests that all financial aid forms be submitted as soon as possible after 1/1. *Need-based scholarships/grants offered:* Pell, SEOG, state scholarships/grants, private scholarships, the school's own gift aid. *Loan aid offered:* Direct Subsidized Stafford, Direct Unsubsidized Stafford, Direct PLUS, Federal Perkins, college/university loans from institutional funds. Applicants will be notified of awards on a rolling basis beginning on or about 4/1. Federal Work-study Program available. Institutional employment available. Off-campus job opportunities are fair.

FROM THE ADMISSIONS OFFICE

"University of Florida students come from more than 100 countries, all 50 states, and every one of the 67 counties in Florida. Nineteen percent of the student body is comprised of graduate students. Approximately 3,000 African American students, 4,000 Hispanic students, and 2,300 Asian American students attend UF. Ninety percent of the entering freshmen rank above the national mean of scores on standard entrance exams. UF consistently ranks near the top among public universities in the number of new National Merit and Achievement scholars in attendance.

"The new SAT (or ACT with Writing component) is required for all applicants for 2006 and beyond. The old SAT (or ACT tests taken without Writing) will not be accepted. Sub scores (Critical Reading and Math only) on the new SAT will be mixed/matched with other new SAT sub scores to achieve the highest score."

SELECTIVITY	
Admissions Rating	**94**
# of applicants	22,973
% of applicants accepted	52
% of acceptees attending	55
# of early decision applicants	1,778
% accepted early decision	60
FRESHMAN PROFILE	
Range SAT Verbal	560-660
Range SAT Math	580-680
**TPR Projected Range SAT Writing*	*600-670*
Range ACT Composite	24-29
Average HS GPA	3.9
% graduated top 10% of class	79
% graduated top 25% of class	90
% graduated top 50% of class	97
DEADLINES	
Early decision application deadline	10/1
Early decision notification	12/1
Regular application deadline	1/12
Nonfall registration?	yes
FINANCIAL FACTS	
Financial Aid Rating	**81**
Annual in-state tuition	$2,780
Annual out-of-state tuition	$13,808
Room & Board	$5,800
Books and supplies	$790
Required fees	$878
% frosh rec. need-based scholarship or grant aid	18
% UG rec. need-based scholarship or grant aid	21
% frosh rec. need-based self-help aid	14
% UG rec. need-based self-help aid	21
% frosh rec. any financial aid	97
% UG rec. any financial aid	84
Avg. frosh grant	$4,799
Avg. frosh loan	$2,971
Independent 529 member?	No

UNIVERSITY OF GEORGIA

TERRELL HALL, ATHENS, GA 30602 • ADMISSIONS: 706-542-8776 • FAX: 706-542-1466

CAMPUS LIFE

Quality of Life Rating	**86**
Fire Safety Rating	**60**
Type of school	public
Environment	city

STUDENTS

Total undergrad enrollment	24,615
% male/female	43/57
% from out of state	16
% from public high school	76
% live on campus	27
% in (# of) fraternities	19 (32)
% in (# of) sororities	24 (22)
% African American	5
% Asian	5
% Caucasian	89
% Hispanic	2
% international	1
# of countries represented	105

SURVEY SAYS

Great computer facilities
Athletic facilities are great
Students love Athens, GA
Great off-campus food
Everyone loves the Bulldogs
Student publications are popular
Lots of beer drinking
Hard liquor is popular

ACADEMICS

Academic Rating	**74**
Calendar	semester
Student/faculty ratio	18:1
Professors interesting rating	75
Professors accessible rating	68
% classes taught by TAs	0
Most common regular class size	20-29 students

MOST POPULAR MAJORS

Art/art studies
biology/biological sciences
psychology

STUDENTS SPEAK OUT

Academics

The opportunity to "get an unbelievable education at an even more incredible price" figures prominently into students' choices to attend the University of Georgia. The state's HOPE scholarship program (for Georgia residents who attend college in-state) has helped to make the already low tuition and fees even more affordable for most students. Georgia undergraduates praise "the resources provided by the school, such as the new Student Learning Center, which houses innumerable computers." They also enjoy the "wide range of majors offered, with challenging programs of study that can launch a student into a promising future." Classes are taught by "professors who are almost always highly knowledgeable and well-published in their fields." With over 25,000 undergraduates, "UGA is a big state school, and you have to be somewhat aggressive to stand out from the crowd. I believe that UGA is as challenging as you want to make it. You can take honors courses and do research, or you can coast without attending too many classes." Ambitious students should head straight for the honors classes, which "are smaller, taught by more experienced faculty members and more open to class discussion and hands-on learning." One proud and masculine undergraduate sums up, "The University of Georgia is easily the most underrated school in the country. The women are beautiful, the curriculum is challenging, the professors are knowledgeable, our football team is world-class, and any notion that some of your so-called 'party schools' [are] either any more fun, or can out-party us, is not only unfounded, but untrue."

Life

"Going downtown is a must" at UGA, since downtown Athens is, according to students, "hands-down the world's best college town, whether you go to the bars or not. The music scene is awesome, the restaurants are fantastic and unique, and, of course, the bars are the place to be on weekends and Thursday nights." As one student puts it, "There's a saying in Georgia: 'If you lead a good life and say your prayers, when you die you'll go to Athens.' And it is 100 percent true. Athens is heaven on earth; there is something for everyone. There is a huge rock scene, a hippie scene, a jock scene, you name it." Even more popular than hanging in town is UGA football. Students are devoted fans and even more ardent tailgaters. Before games, merry Gaters turns Athens into Mardi Gras." The Greek scene and Dawgs After Dark, the University's late Friday night programming, round out the campus social scene. During the day, students love to "work out (the Ramsey Fitness Center is always a place to go because it has both exercising and racquetball and swimming to choose from), play intramurals, or go camping, kayaking, and hiking." Politics play a large role in many students' lives. Reportedly "the College Republicans is the largest group on campus."

Student Body

The typical UGA student "is from Georgia, is white, has middle- or upper-middle class parents, and loves football and drinking, but still manages to work hard and get the grades he or she wants." A surprising number "look as though they were cut [with] a cookie-cutter mold. They dress the same, have the same hairstyle, and generally drive SUVs." There are also "not a lot of minorities here." With a student body this large, however, there's bound to be some diversity. One student writes, "If you're not a rich kid from metro Atlanta, you'll have a harder time fitting in here. You just have to look a bit harder but you'll find someone with whom you have much in common." Because Athens "is a music town," students observe, "There are a lot of indie-rock types and even a bigger hippie-jam band scene." Students also tell us that "it is hard to be nationally diverse with the HOPE scholarship in effect in Georgia, but we could use more out-of-state students on this campus."

FINANCIAL AID: 706-542-6147 • E-MAIL: UNDERGRAD@ADMISSIONS.UGA.EDU • WEBSITE: WWW.UGA.EDU

ADMISSIONS

Very important factors considered include: Secondary school record, standardized test scores. *Other factors considered include:* Character/personal qualities, class rank, essays, extracurricular activities, recommendations, talent/ability, volunteer work, work experience. SAT Reasoning or ACT required. TOEFL required of all international applicants. High school diploma is required, and GED is accepted. *Academic units required:* 4 English, 4 math, 3 science (2 science lab), 2 foreign language, 1 social studies, 2 history.

The Inside Word

UGA is one of the more popular choices among southern college-bound students. The admissions process is very straightforward, but few large universities have as much success as Georgia in converting admits to enrollees, which makes candidate evaluation fairly selective. So does the fantastically successful Hope Scholarship Program for Georgia residents, now being emulated throughout the United States. Since student satisfaction and interest in the university show no sign of a decline any time soon, look for circumstances to remain the same for the foreseeable future.

FINANCIAL AID

Students should submit: FAFSA, state aid form. Regular filing deadline is 8/1. The Princeton Review suggests that all financial aid forms be submitted as soon as possible after 1/1. *Need-based scholarships/grants offered:* Pell, SEOG, state scholarships/grants, private scholarships, the school's own gift aid. *Loan aid offered:* Direct Subsidized Stafford, Direct Unsubsidized Stafford, Direct PLUS, Federal Perkins, state loans, college/university loans from institutional funds. Applicants will be notified of awards on or about 5/1. Federal Work-study Program available. Institutional employment available. Off-campus job opportunities are good.

FROM THE ADMISSIONS OFFICE

"The University of Georgia's academic reputation continues to rise, largely on the accomplishments of its best undergraduates. In the past three years, students from the University of Georgia have been selected for every major scholarship in national competition: one Rhodes, one Gates Cambridge, two British Marshall, two Mellon, three Truman, five Goldwater, one Udall, and nine Fulbright. UGA offers a large but friendly campus community in a vibrant yet easygoing college town. To experience the excitement of UGA, most prospective students visit Athens, a 90-minute drive northeast of the Atlanta airport. Contact our Visitors Center for tour information and reservations. Visit our website to request information and application materials and view the weekday schedule of admissions information sessions. The first-year application for admission also serves as the initial application for Honors Program membership, most merit scholarships, and Regents Waivers of out-of-state tuition, all highly competitive processes.

"Applicants for first-year admission for summer 2006 or later will be required to submit the Writing component of the new SAT or ACT."

SELECTIVITY

Admissions Rating	**91**
# of applicants	13,267
% of applicants accepted	62
% of acceptees attending	55
# accepting a place on wait list	1,065
% admitted from wait list	50

FRESHMAN PROFILE

Range SAT Verbal	560-660
Average SAT Verbal	616
Range SAT Math	570-660
Average SAT Math	618
**TPR Projected Range SAT Writing*	*600-670*
Range ACT Composite	24-28
Average ACT Composite	27
Minimum Paper TOEFL	550
Minimum Computer Based TOEFL	213
Average HS GPA	3.71
% graduated top 10% of class	50
% graduated top 25% of class	85
% graduated top 50% of class	98

DEADLINES

Regular application deadline	2/1
Regular notification	4/1
Nonfall registration?	yes

APPLICANTS ALSO LOOK AT

AND OFTEN PREFER

Florida State U., Georgia Institute of Technology, U. of North Carolina—Chapel Hill, U. of Virginia, Wake Forest U.

AND SOMETIMES PREFER

College of Charleston, Emory U., Georgia Southern U., Georgia State U., Mercer U.—Atlanta, Vanderbilt U.

AND RARELY PREFER

Auburn U.y, Clemson U., Tulane U., The U. of Alabama—Tuscaloosa, U. of South Carolina—Columbia

FINANCIAL FACTS

Financial Aid Rating	**78**
Annual in-state tuition	$3,368
Annual out-of-state tuition	$14,684
Room & Board	$5,756
Books and supplies	$750
Required fees	$904
% frosh rec. need-based scholarship or grant aid	25
% UG rec. need-based scholarship or grant aid	22
% frosh rec. need-based self-help aid	11
% UG rec. need-based self-help aid	17
% frosh rec. any financial aid	26
% UG rec. any financial aid	26
Avg. frosh grant	$5,768
Avg. frosh loan	$2,505
Independent 529 member?	No

UNIVERSITY OF HAWAII—MANOA

2600 CAMPUS ROAD, QLCSS, ROOM 001, HONOLULU, HI 96822 • ADMISSIONS: 808-956-8975 • FAX: 808-956-4148

CAMPUS LIFE

Quality of Life Rating	**63**
Fire Safety Rating	**60**
Type of school	public
Environment	metropolis

STUDENTS

Total undergrad enrollment	13,070
% male/female	44/56
% from out of state	16
% live on campus	13
% African American	1
% Asian	56
% Caucasian	19
% Hispanic	2
% international	5

SURVEY SAYS

Diverse student types on campus
Great off-campus food
Frats and sororities are unpopular or nonexistent
Student publications are popular
Lots of beer drinking
(Almost) everyone smokes

ACADEMICS

Academic Rating	**70**
Calendar	semester
Student/faculty ratio	12:1
Professors interesting rating	61
Professors accessible rating	61
% classes taught by TAs	0
Most common lab size	10-19 students
Most common regular class size	10-19 students

MOST POPULAR MAJORS

Art history, criticism and conservation
psychology
zoology/animal biology

STUDENTS SPEAK OUT

Academics

The prime location is undoubtedly the chief allure of the University of Hawaii at Manoa. How could it not be? The school, after all, is situated on an island paradise. There's a lot more than fabulous weather and world-class surfing to recommend UHM, though. Students here tout the "excellent technology and the incredible amount of opportunities and programs available," including solid (and site-appropriate) offerings in marine biology, oceanography, geology, and travel industry management. There's also the school's affordability. Tuition rates are low not only for Aloha State natives but also for the majority of out-of-state students who enjoy a reduced tuition rate under the Western Undergraduate Exchange program. Students also love the "fantastic learning assistance centers, great libraries," and the amount of attention lavished on Selected Studies and Honors students. What they dislike are the burdensome curricular requirements: "It's insane. All the unnecessary requirements mean that almost no student can graduate in four years," complains one student, as well as the administration's "laid-back aloha spirit, which is no way to run a premier research institution. It gets them into a lot of messes," as in 2004–2005 when the school came up so short on housing that it had to put students in Waikiki hotels.

Life

"Life here is all about the location," students at UHM agree, adding that "it's great that I can study near the ocean and the city because I can go wherever I want in minutes." A convenient bus system (which, some warn, is "a little expensive") takes those without cars where they need to go, though "hardly anyone is in a hurry around here." In keeping with a laid back, local style that pervades the campus, "dress is casual, usually flip flops and board shorts" and students "typically go to class in the mornings, head to the beach in the afternoon, and drink and socialize in the evenings." One student sums it up by saying, "It is hard work all week and a tropical vacation every weekend. Stress levels drop the moment you land on this island." Parties occur most frequently in off-campus apartments—there are "absolutely no social fraternities or sororities at UH" and on-campus housing is scarce—or, for students over 21, in "a couple of good bars down the street." Undergrads report that "the UH campus is one of the best party spots on the island, or so says a newspaper survey," but add, "there are plenty of activities that do not involve alcohol as well: hiking, going to the beach, paddling, seeing concerts, visiting various museums and historical sites, and going to plays or the opera." Because so many students commute, the campus itself tends to gets neglected ("the facilities are fairly old and they could use updating"), and student life can be a little slow on weekends—except when the football team plays at home. As one student explains, "Football players are gods here. Hawaii does not have professional sports teams, so UH football players take their place. If you're coming to UH to play football, your college social life is set."

Student Body

"White kids are actually the minority for once," at UHM, whose students are "a mixture of students from the mainland U.S. and local white, Asian, and Pacific Islander students." Many point out that "Hawaii has been, for most of its history as a part of the U.S., a liberal state tolerant to all religious, political, sexual, ethnic diversities." Some, however, warn that "whites who aren't from the islands can have a tough time fitting in." There's also a lack of unanimity on the bookworm demographic here. Some tell us that "Hawaii is half and half—half 'study nonstop' and half 'don't know what studying means.'" Others, however, feel that "while there's a handful of students who have ambitious career objectives are focused on studying, the typical student is focused mainly on the beach or going to the clubs. Not that there is anything wrong with having fun, but the typical student is a 24/7 partier."

FINANCIAL AID: 808-956-7251 • E-MAIL: AR-INFO@HAWAII.EDU • WEBSITE: WWW.UHM.HAWAII.EDU

ADMISSIONS

Very important factors considered include: Secondary school record, standardized test scores. *Important factors considered include:* Class rank, state residency. *Other factors considered include:* Character/personal qualities, essays, extracurricular activities, geographical residence, interview, recommendations, talent/ability, volunteer work, work experience. SAT Reasoning or ACT required. TOEFL required of all international applicants. High school diploma is required, and GED is accepted. *Academic units required:* 4 English, 3 math, 3 science, 4 social studies, 4 history, 3 academic electives, 5 Electives. *Academic units recommended:* 2 foreign language.

The Inside Word

A 2.8 high school GPA meets the university's minimum standards for admission. Though preference is given to state residents for admission, in practice there's room for just about any better-than-average student in the freshman class here.

FINANCIAL AID

Students should submit: FAFSA, institution's own financial aid form. The Princeton Review suggests that all financial aid forms be submitted as soon as possible after 1/1. *Need-based scholarships/grants offered:* Pell, SEOG, state scholarships/grants, private scholarships, the school's own gift aid, Federal Nursing scholarships. *Loan aid offered:* FFEL Subsidized Stafford, FFEL Unsubsidized Stafford, FFEL PLUS, Federal Perkins, Federal Nursing, state loans. Applicants will be notified of awards on or about 4/1. Federal Work-study Program available. Institutional employment available. Off-campus job opportunities are fair.

FROM THE ADMISSIONS OFFICE

"Students applying for admission for fall 2006 must submit scores from the new SAT or ACT, including Writing component. Scores from tests without Writing will not be considered. Students who take the new SAT or the ACT more than once will have their best scores considered for admission."

SELECTIVITY	
Admissions Rating	**85**
# of applicants	6,028
% of applicants accepted	59
% of acceptees attending	56
FRESHMAN PROFILE	
Range SAT Verbal	480-580
Average SAT Verbal	537
Range SAT Math	510-620
Average SAT Math	568
**TPR Projected Range SAT Writing*	*540-620*
Range ACT Composite	20-24
Average ACT Composite	23
Minimum Paper TOEFL	500
Minimum Computer Based TOEFL	173
Average HS GPA	3.37
% graduated top 10% of class	26
% graduated top 25% of class	57
% graduated top 50% of class	91
DEADLINES	
Regular application deadline	5/1
Regular notification	rolling
Nonfall registration?	yes
FINANCIAL FACTS	
Financial Aid Rating	**73**
Annual in-state tuition	$3,408
Annual out-of-state tuition	$9,888
Room & Board	$5,675
Books and supplies	$1,017
Required fees	$153
% frosh rec. need-based scholarship or grant aid	24
% UG rec. need-based scholarship or grant aid	26
% frosh rec. need-based self-help aid	19
% UG rec. need-based self-help aid	22
% frosh rec. any financial aid	45
% UG rec. any financial aid	43
Avg. frosh grant	$3,894
Avg. frosh loan	$7,637
Independent 529 member?	No

UNIVERSITY OF IDAHO

UI ADMISSIONS OFFICE, PO BOX 444264, MOSCOW, ID 83844-4264 • ADMISSIONS: 208-885-6326 • FAX: 208-885-9119

CAMPUS LIFE

Quality of Life Rating	**71**
Fire Safety Rating	**83**
Type of school	public
Environment	village

STUDENTS

Total undergrad enrollment	9,047
% male/female	55/45
% from out of state	22
% African American	1
% Asian	2
% Caucasian	85
% Hispanic	4
% Native American	1
% international	2

SURVEY SAYS

Great computer facilities
Great library
Athletic facilities are great
Frats and sororities dominate social scene
Lots of beer drinking
Hard liquor is popular
(Almost) everyone smokes

ACADEMICS

Academic Rating	**72**
Calendar	semester
Student/faculty ratio	20:1
Professors interesting rating	69
Professors accessible rating	63
% professors teaching UG courses	70
% classes taught by TAs	20
Most common lab size	10-19 students
Most common regular class size	fewer than 10 students

STUDENTS SPEAK OUT

Academics

With an academic setting that allows students to "grow in all aspects of life," the University of Idaho (UI) has earned a reputation as a "great school for a great price." Some students point out that fees are on the rise—as it is at most state universities—but they acknowledge that the administration "can't improve anything when they don't have the money." While the budget is being slashed, students feel that the school "runs smoothly" thanks to the "very organized" administration. The "friendly and helpful staff" helps students access the right people, who are "great once you find what building they've moved to." On the academic front, the electrical engineering program garners praise, though students across departments complain about "not being able to understand foreign teachers and TAs." On the whole, students find professors to be "very personable outside of class and very knowledgeable." Instructors "want to be here" and "really do want us to succeed and understand the material." Students also report that they "really get to know their instructors." One undergraduate tells us, "Learning is fun and comes more easily due to the fact that professors don't act superior. They treat you as an equal." The only hitch seems to be problems registering for courses: "I could only get into one class toward my major [during a certain semester]," writes a junior in visual communications.

Life

In the small town of Moscow, Idaho, students report, "there's not much to do but hang out with friends." One undergraduate notes a lusting among his cohorts for a more urban setting: "People are generally happy but want to live in a larger city." Many people seem perfectly content, however, in an "atmosphere that allows the students to be active within the community." Other mellowed-out students concur, with the sentiment "I like to have a laid-back lifestyle, and I am able to do it here." Certain students wish for "more activities to do off campus," but others gladly forgo cheesy techno clubs for the abundant outdoor opportunities: hiking, camping, fishing, and hunting in the area are favorite pastimes. Students use multiple exclamation points when expressing their joy derived from the campus' cushy student recreation center, replete with a new climbing wall. Idaho students can often be found "working out or playing sports for fun," and devoted fans flock to football and basketball games. Students also get out to see "local bands and shows at the Red Hawk," or they "go out to movies or find a party." Fraternities manage to facilitate a steady flow of your standard ragers, and one member diplomatically points out, "Greek life is fun, but I don't know what non-Greeks think about it." Overall, the campus and surrounding environs amount to "a unique college experience" with a "a very homey feel."

Student Body

The most common descriptors of the student population at Idaho would have to be "laid-back" and "easygoing." Among these "down-to-earth" kids, people "don't have to try to fit in." Some students do perceive, however, "a wall between the Greek system and other students," largely based on the sentiment that "some Greeks have a big ego problem on this campus. So do a lot of athletes." This kind of tension makes some students feel that UI is "just like high school all over again." Luckily, undergraduates report more harmony between other groups. "I believe that most students, regardless of race, religion, or year, get along splendidly." Though some students say, "There are students from everywhere, and there is a lot of diversity around our campus," others wish for "more minority and cultural group recognition." Because the university "isn't too big or too small," students report, "everyone gets to know each other pretty well." Overall, undergraduates find their peers "easy to get along with and work with" as well as "very cheerful and friendly."

FINANCIAL AID: 208-885-6312 • E-MAIL: ADMAPPL@UIDAHO.EDU • WEBSITE: WWW.UIDAHO.EDU

ADMISSIONS

Very important factors considered include: Recommendations, secondary school record, standardized test scores, SAT Reasoning or SAT Subject Tests required. TOEFL required of all international applicants. High school diploma is required, and GED is accepted. *Academic units required:* 4 English, 3 math, 3 science (1 science lab), 1 foreign language, 3 social studies, 2 academic electives.

The Inside Word

Idaho's admissions process is typical of large universities and easy to deal with—it doesn't get any more straightforward than this. A small number of college-age students in Idaho means out-of-staters face little in the way of any constraints above and beyond in-state standards.

FINANCIAL AID

Students should submit: FAFSA. The Princeton Review suggests that all financial aid forms be submitted as soon as possible after 1/1. *Need-based scholarships/grants offered:* Pell, SEOG, state scholarships/grants, private scholarships, the school's own gift aid. *Loan aid offered:* Direct Subsidized Stafford, Direct Unsubsidized Stafford, Direct PLUS, Federal Perkins, college/university loans from institutional funds. Applicants will be notified of awards on or about 3/28. Federal Work-study Program available. Institutional employment available. Off-campus job opportunities are good.

FROM THE ADMISSIONS OFFICE

"The University of Idaho combines the best of both worlds. We are the major research university in the state of Idaho, and [we provide] the state's land grant university, and a safe, residential environment. Moscow's small size and the supportive surrounding community provide the ideal atmosphere for a total learning experience.

"Students applying for admission into the fall 2006 entering class are required to take either the SAT or the ACT. Both the new and the old test scores will be accepted. The Writing Test is not required from the ACT. SAT Subject Test scores are not used for admission purposes."

SELECTIVITY

Admissions Rating	**79**
# of applicants	3,973
% of applicants accepted	81
% of acceptees attending	52

FRESHMAN PROFILE

Range SAT Verbal	490-610
Average SAT Verbal	549
Range SAT Math	500-620
Average SAT Math	559
**TPR Projected Range SAT Writing*	*550-640*
Range ACT Composite	20-26
Average ACT Composite	23
Minimum Paper TOEFL	525
Minimum Computer Based TOEFL	193
Average HS GPA	3.4
% graduated top 10% of class	20
% graduated top 25% of class	47
% graduated top 50% of class	78

DEADLINES

Regular notification	rolling
Nonfall registration?	yes

APPLICANTS ALSO LOOK AT AND SOMETIMES PREFER

Boise State University
Washington State University

FINANCIAL FACTS

Financial Aid Rating	**76**
Annual in-state tuition	$3,348
Annual out-of-state tuition	$10,740
Room & Board	$4,868
Books and supplies	$1,248
Required fees	$3,348
% frosh rec. need-based scholarship or grant aid	40
% UG rec. need-based scholarship or grant aid	42
% frosh rec. need-based self-help aid	45
% UG rec. need-based self-help aid	50
Independent 529 member?	No

UNIVERSITY OF ILLINOIS—URBANA-CHAMPAIGN

901 West Illinois Street, Urbana, IL 61801 • Admissions: 217-333-0302 • Fax: 217-333-9758

CAMPUS LIFE

Quality of Life Rating	**79**
Fire Safety Rating	**65**
Type of school	public
Environment	city

STUDENTS

Total undergrad enrollment	28,931
% male/female	53/47
% from out of state	12
% from public high school	75
% live on campus	39
% in (# of) fraternities	20 (58)
% in (# of) sororities	22 (33)
% African American	7
% Asian	13
% Caucasian	68
% Hispanic	6
% international	4
# of countries represented	121

SURVEY SAYS

Great computer facilities
Great library
Everyone loves the Fighting Illini
Frats and sororities dominate social scene
Student publications are popular
Lots of beer drinking
Hard liquor is popular

ACADEMICS

Academic Rating	**76**
Calendar	semester
Student/faculty ratio	14:1
Professors interesting rating	71
Professors accessible rating	71
% professors teaching UG courses	89
% classes taught by TAs	39
Most common lab size	20-29 students
Most common regular class size	20-29 students

MOST POPULAR MAJORS

Biology/biological sciences
finance and financial management services
psychology

STUDENTS SPEAK OUT

Academics

The "big, boisterous, and bureaucratic" University of Illinois at Urbana-Champaign provides a solid range of top-rate programs at a bargain-basement price. Business and engineering are among the best known and most popular programs here; also highly touted are offerings in agriculture, animal sciences, psychology, accounting, and architecture. The liberal arts generally fare less well, although they too are not without their strengths. Students warn that "This school is academically strong across the board. The standards for grades are high, there are very few easy A's, and yes, they will fail you." Intro classes are especially tough and are "good at weeding out the students who do not belong at this university. There is a lot of work, although it's not too overwhelming." Despite the school's considerable size, professors and administrators here earn wide praise. One student writes, "I think everyone is professional and academic. It surprises me that a large school can be run like a small one." Another agrees, "Keeping in mind that there are roughly 29,000 undergraduates, the school's administrators do a decent job of keeping everything together." And the school's size certainly has its benefits; notes one undergrad, "There are so many opportunities to get involved and so many opportunities to build connections and work with professors."

Life

Students at the U of Illinois "like to study, but also have a good time," which is code, it seems, for drinking with friends. One student explains, "Going to school in the middle of cornfields leaves little to do for fun that doesn't involve drinking;" however, the school is looking to improve upon this with the addition of a new Campus Recreation Center and Illinites activities nights." Doing so is no problem, "since you only have to be 19 to enter bars and the same age to bartend. The Greek population is sizable; notes one frat boy, "Illinois is a Greek campus. Most people who are socially adept are associated with a house. Because I'm Greek, I see this as a positive, but I can see how non-Greeks would hate us." Non-Greeks immerse themselves in "the various other subcultures that can be seen throughout campus. You have those people who are interested in politics, others in sports, human rights groups, that sort of thing." Undergrads also enjoy "Frisbee™ or football throwing in the quad" and "watching movies on the Quad at night (Quad Cinema) in the fall, which is definitely a blast. It is kind of like a drive-in, without the cars." And despite the pitiful state of the football team, "Football tailgating is always popular. When you go to a top party school with a bottom 25 football team, what else is there to do on Saturday mornings?"

Student Body

While "Most students seem to be white upper-middle class suburbanites from metropolitan Chicago," "there are many people that contradict that stereotype that diversity isn't really a problem." You'll see more than your fair share of "super-skinny sorority girls and buffed-up frat boys" here—the type who "go to class in pajamas, but out to the bars all decked out"—but you'll also find lots of minorities and "a lot of students from foreign countries, such as China, Taiwan, Korea, Turkey, and the United Arab Emirates." Undergrads report that "Students here at U of I are typical Midwesterners with the joyful addition of international students." If you're looking for the outliers, know that "They can be found in the Living Learning Communities. The LLCs are really nice because they contain both your average white suburbanite and your atypical person and provide a wonderful place for intellectual stimulation and expansion. LLCs rock!"

FINANCIAL AID: 217-333-0100 • E-MAIL: ADMISSIONS@OAR.UIUC.EDU • WEBSITE: WWW.UIUC.EDU

ADMISSIONS

Very important factors considered include: Class rank, essays, secondary school record, standardized test scores. *Important factors considered include:* Character/personal qualities, extracurricular activities, talent/ability, volunteer work, work experience. *Other factors considered include:* Alumni/ae relation, geographical residence, interview, minority status, recommendations, state residency. SAT Reasoning or ACT required. TOEFL required of all international applicants. High school diploma is required, and GED is accepted. *Academic units required:* 4 English, 3 math, 2 science (2 science lab), 2 foreign language, 2 social studies, 2 academic electives.

The Inside Word

Few candidates are deceived by Illinois' relatively high acceptance rate; the university has a well-deserved reputation for expecting applicants to be strong students, and those who aren't usually don't bother to apply. Despite a jumbo applicant pool, the admissions office reports that every candidate is individually reviewed, which deserves mention as rare in universities of this size.

FINANCIAL AID

Students should submit: FAFSA. The Princeton Review suggests that all financial aid forms be submitted as soon as possible after 1/1. *Need-based scholarships/grants offered:* Pell, SEOG, state scholarships/grants, private scholarships, the school's own gift aid, United Negro College Fund. *Loan aid offered:* Direct Subsidized Stafford, Direct Unsubsidized Stafford, Direct PLUS, Federal Perkins, college/university loans from institutional funds, alternative/private loans. Applicants will be notified of awards on or about 3/15. Federal Work-study Program available. Institutional employment available. Off-campus job opportunities are excellent.

FROM THE ADMISSIONS OFFICE

"The campus has been aptly described as a collection of neighborhoods constituting a diverse and vibrant city. The neighborhoods are of many types: students and faculty within a department; people sharing a room or house; the members of a professional organization, a service club, or an intramural team; or simply people who, starting out as strangers sharing a class or a study lounge or a fondness for a weekly film series, have become friends. And the city of this description is the university itself—a rich cosmopolitan environment constructed by students and faculty to meet their educational and personal goals. The quality of intellectual life parallels that of other great universities, and many faculty and students who have their choice of top institutions select Illinois over its peers. While such choices are based often on the quality of individual programs of study, another crucial factor is the 'tone' of the campus life that is linked with the virtues of midwestern culture. There is an informality and a near-absence of pretension which, coupled with a tradition of commitment to excellence, creates an atmosphere that is unique among the finest institutions.

"Applicants for fall 2006 are recommended to take the new SAT or the ACT with the Writing section, but we will allow students to submit scores from the old version (prior to March 2005) of the SAT or ACT. Though strongly recommended, the Writing section of the ACT is not required."

SELECTIVITY

Admissions Rating	**89**
# of applicants	21,914
% of applicants accepted	68
% of acceptees attending	49
# accepting a place on wait list	1,009
% admitted from wait list	16

FRESHMAN PROFILE

Range SAT Verbal	560-670
Average SAT Verbal	614
Range SAT Math	620-730
Average SAT Math	674
**TPR Projected Range SAT Writing*	*600-680*
Range ACT Composite	25-31
Average ACT Composite	28
Minimum Paper TOEFL	550
Minimum Computer Based TOEFL	213
% graduated top 10% of class	50
% graduated top 25% of class	86
% graduated top 50% of class	99

DEADLINES

Regular application deadline	12/15
Regular notification	12/1 to 3/31
Nonfall registration?	yes

APPLICANTS ALSO LOOK AT

AND OFTEN PREFER

Northwestern University
Purdue University—West Lafayette
University of Michigan—Ann Arbor
University of Wisconsin—Madison
Washington University in St. Louis

AND SOMETIMES PREFER

Miami University
Northern Illinois University

AND RARELY PREFER

Illinois State University
Loyola University of Chicago
Southern Illinois University—Edwardsville

FINANCIAL FACTS

Financial Aid Rating	**80**
Annual in-state tuition	$6,460
Annual out-of-state tuition	$19,380
Room & Board	$7,176
Books and supplies	$950
Required fees	$1,582
% frosh rec. need-based scholarship or grant aid	25
% UG rec. need-based scholarship or grant aid	26
% frosh rec. need-based self-help aid	30
% UG rec. need-based self-help aid	33
% frosh rec. any financial aid	41
% UG rec. any financial aid	39
Avg. frosh grant	$8,238
Avg. frosh loan	$3,064
Independent 529 member?	No

UNIVERSITY OF IOWA

107 CALVIN HALL, IOWA CITY, IA 52242 • ADMISSIONS: 319-335-3847 • FAX: 319-333-1535

CAMPUS LIFE

Quality of Life Rating	**84**
Fire Safety Rating	**60**
Type of school	public
Environment	village

STUDENTS

Total undergrad enrollment	19,442
% male/female	46/54
% from out of state	30
% from public high school	91
% live on campus	28
% in (# of) fraternities	8 (21)
% in (# of) sororities	12 (17)
% African American	2
% Asian	4
% Caucasian	87
% Hispanic	2
% international	1
# of countries represented	68

SURVEY SAYS

Great computer facilities
Students love Iowa City, IA
Great off-campus food
Everyone loves the Hawkeyes
Lots of beer drinking
Hard liquor is popular
(Almost) everyone smokes

ACADEMICS

Academic Rating	**74**
Calendar	semester
Student/faculty ratio	14:1
Professors interesting rating	64
Professors accessible rating	67
% professors teaching UG courses	100
% classes taught by TAs	0
Most common lab size	20-29 students
Most common regular class size	10-19 students

MOST POPULAR MAJORS

Communications studies/speech communication and rhetoric
English language and literature
psychology

STUDENTS SPEAK OUT

Academics

Applicants to a big state school like Iowa sometimes fear "drowning in general education classes," but many current Hawkeyes point out, "You can make it personal" with some effort, since "not very many professors have a line of students waiting to hang out at office hours, even though they'd like [them] to." Professors "have a passion for the material," and most complement that with "the passion to teach the material." As at most large state universities, certain undergraduates feel their instructors stay "so buried in their research that they probably wouldn't come to class if a waiting student hadn't called them on their cell." Other students point out that "professors have a presence, but the school does rely on teaching assistants." On the whole, however, "most professors attempt to present lectures in an interesting forum." Respondents single out the writing department as "highly regarded" and tout the honors program as "the ticket to ride for anyone with academic concern." Administrators receive high marks from students, who say they are "readily accessible and extremely supportive—so much so that it borders on mentoring and parental advocacy." Some students, however, see the "very parental" administration as their mortal foe, claiming that they "work with the city council on anti-student policies." Complaints also pop up surrounding the ongoing tuition hikes. In general, however, the campus "seems to run very smoothly," and the people in charge appear "attuned to students' opinions." Overall, the university offers students "a diverse and liberal learning environment" where everyone can "prepare [a] future in an atmosphere of fun and opportunity."

Life

Social life revolves around three things at Iowa: the downtown bars, Hawkeye football, and Christian groups. The "beautiful town" of Iowa City "has a lot to offer," mainly in the form of bars, "packed to capacity every night of the week." The resulting scene is "quite crazy, and most everyone seems to enjoy it." The campus' location right in the thick of things allows the "weekend to start on Tuesday and end on Sunday" even though the on-campus sororities and fraternities are dry. Some people resist the pull and take advantage of the "good restaurants and coffee shops on or near campus." Other alcohol-free options include "improv theater and musical events;" it seems "there's always some sort of live performance going on here." Hawkeye pride abounds—"It's all about sports"—and students congregate for rowdy tailgating sessions on game days during football season. Aside from drinking and cheering, many in the student body keep "involved in campus Christian groups, like, 24/7." Put it all together, and you've got a school that "offers a true big-time college experience in a very unique and exciting town."

Student Body

In the large, somewhat diverse milieu of the University of Iowa, students say, "You can be whoever you want to be and still have a big group of friends." Though many call it "your average white-dominated midwestern university," numerous students claim their school is "surprisingly open-minded, considering the location." One student expands, "The school's reputation of diversity is helped tremendously by the graduate student population." Also, the diversity lies in "social backgrounds rather than racial backgrounds." People may come from the Iowa sticks or the urban spread of Chicago, but the school still "lacks a good social atmosphere for minorities." Several surveys point out the university's intent to attract more students of color. On-campus groups do provide a framework for discussing "various ethnicities, sexual orientations, religious backgrounds, etc." Even if most people are "Christian, middle-class Dave Matthews fans who love the bars," they also share the common traits of "friendliness, enthusiasm, and openness."

FINANCIAL AID: 319-335-1450 • E-MAIL: ADMISSIONS@UIOWA.EDU • WEBSITE: WWW.UIOWA.EDU

ADMISSIONS

Very important factors considered include: Class rank, secondary school record, standardized test scores. *Other factors considered include:* Alumni/ae relation, minority status, state residency, talent/ability. SAT Reasoning or ACT required. TOEFL required of all international applicants. High school diploma is required, and GED is accepted. *Academic units required:* 4 English, 3 math, 3 science, 2 foreign language, 3 social studies. *Academic units recommended:* 4 foreign language.

The Inside Word

On the one hand, Iowa's admissions process is none too personal, but on the other hand, candidates know exactly what is necessary to get admitted. The majority of applicants are fairly good students, most get in, and a lot choose to attend. That helps make Iowa the solid academic community it is.

FINANCIAL AID

Students should submit: FAFSA, institution's own financial aid form. The Princeton Review suggests that all financial aid forms be submitted as soon as possible after 1/1. *Need-based scholarships/grants offered:* Pell, SEOG, state scholarships/grants, private scholarships, the school's own gift aid, Federal Nursing scholarships. *Loan aid offered:* Direct Subsidized Stafford, Direct Unsubsidized Stafford, Direct PLUS, Federal Perkins, Federal Nursing, college/university loans from institutional funds. Applicants will be notified of awards on a rolling basis beginning on or about 3/4. Off-campus job opportunities are excellent.

FROM THE ADMISSIONS OFFICE

"The University of Iowa has outstanding programs in the creative arts, notably the Iowa Writers' Workshop and the world-renowned International Writing Program. It also has strong programs in business, communication studies, journalism, English, engineering, political science, and psychology, and was the birthplace of the discipline of speech pathology and audiology. It offers excellent programs in the basic health sciences and health care programs, led by the top ranked College of Medicine and the closely associated University Hospitals and Clinics.

"The University of Iowa will accept either the new SAT or the old SAT (administered prior to March 2005 and without a Writing component), as well as the ACT with or without the Writing component."

SELECTIVITY

Admissions Rating	**82**
# of applicants	13,874
% of applicants accepted	83
% of acceptees attending	35

FRESHMAN PROFILE

Range SAT Verbal	530-660
Range SAT Math	540-670
**TPR Projected Range SAT Writing*	*580-670*
Range ACT Composite	22-27
Minimum Paper TOEFL	530
Minimum Computer Based TOEFL	197
Average HS GPA	3.55
% graduated top 10% of class	22
% graduated top 25% of class	52
% graduated top 50% of class	91

DEADLINES

Regular application deadline	4/1
Regular notification	rolling
Nonfall registration?	yes

APPLICANTS ALSO LOOK AT

AND OFTEN PREFER

Northwestern University
University of Illinois at Urbana-Champaign

AND SOMETIMES PREFER

Drake University
Grinnell College
Indiana University—Bloomington
Iowa State University
University of Northern Iowa

AND RARELY PREFER

Cornell College
Illinois State University
University of Missouri—Rolla

FINANCIAL FACTS

Financial Aid Rating	**87**
Annual in-state tuition	$4,890
Annual out-of-state tuition	$16,276
Room & Board	$6,560
Books and supplies	$840
Required fees	$722
% frosh rec. need-based scholarship or grant aid	29
% UG rec. need-based scholarship or grant aid	29
% frosh rec. need-based self-help aid	37
% UG rec. need-based self-help aid	39
% frosh rec. any financial aid	81
% UG rec. any financial aid	80
Avg. frosh grant	$4,614
Avg. frosh loan	$4,833
Independent 529 member?	No

UNIVERSITY OF KANSAS

OFFICE OF ADMISSIONS & SCHOLARSHIPS, 1502 IOWA ST., LAWRENCE, KS 66045 • ADMISSIONS: 785-864-3911 • FAX: 785-864-5017

CAMPUS LIFE

Quality of Life Rating	**82**
Fire Safety Rating	**82**
Type of school	public
Environment	city

STUDENTS

Total undergrad enrollment	21,037
% male/female	49/51
% from out of state	24
% live on campus	23
% in (# of) fraternities	14 (24)
% in (# of) sororities	17 (17)
% African American	4
% Asian	4
% Caucasian	84
% Hispanic	3
% Native American	1
% international	3
# of countries represented	113

SURVEY SAYS

Athletic facilities are great
Students love Lawrence, KS
Great off-campus food
Everyone loves the Jayhawks
Student publications are popular
Lots of beer drinking

ACADEMICS

Academic Rating	**73**
Calendar	semester
Student/faculty ratio	19:1
Professors interesting rating	71
Professors accessible rating	69
% professors teaching UG courses	98
% classes taught by TAs	20
Most common lab size	10-19 students
Most common regular class size	20-29 students

MOST POPULAR MAJORS

Biology/biological sciences
engineering science
psychology

STUDENTS SPEAK OUT

Academics

There's a world of options awaiting students at the University of Kansas (KU), "a big school with big opportunities." As one student puts it, "All you have to do is grab them and make the most of your college career by seeking them." The school excels in many diverse areas, from its top business school to its solid programs in education, engineering, nursing, journalism, premedical sciences, communications, music, and the social sciences. As at many large state universities, students can decide for themselves just how challenging a program they want to pursue. One undergraduate writes, "Classes can be either very easy or very hard, depending on your major. A's are hard to come by, but you can slack off and get a B easily." For those who want to push themselves, "the Honors Program is great, and it's not too hard to get into. I like the classes a lot better. They are small and the professors are generally the best teachers who care about their students." Regardless of their program, students appreciate the "strong sense of community among the staff and students, especially in upper-division classes, [the] great study-abroad opportunities, [professors who] are personable and dedicated to education," and GTAs (Graduate Teaching Assistants, who teach or help teach many intro-level courses) who "are usually young enough and into campus groups, [so] you'll run into them at clubs or sporting events and strike up good out-of-the-classroom conversations with them."

Life

The "school spirit is infectious" at KU, especially during basketball season. "Basketball is a way of life from late October to April and the Final Four! Allen Fieldhouse is an awesome experience. I've gotten the chills there countless numbers of times," one student tells us. It is not just the intercollegiate teams that inspire students, though; they love everything about life at KU. Hometown Lawrence "is a godsend to college students, with dozens of bars, great music venues, a rich culture, and literally hundreds of locally owned restaurants." Students appreciate the town's "unique vibe," created by the preponderance of "local businesses that give it an old-fashioned feel," which include the coffeehouses, bookshops, and an old movie theater on Mass Street, the town's main drag. The university "is known as a party school, and it is, [with an] outstanding bar scene," very popular Greek organizations, and "a few dozen house parties to go to every weekend, [but] there are options for everyone," including teetotalers. On campus, the Student Union Association "hosts great speakers from all over the world and tons of activities," while the residential Scholarship Halls "hold social events, such as midnight breakfasts, coffeehouses, speakers, dances, and parties." Add campus ministries, a lively arts community, and "a great new fitness center" to the mix to get some sense of the range of opportunities. No wonder students tell us, "At KU, it's all about enjoying your entire college experience."

Student Body

The 20,000-plus undergraduates at KU "range from Kansas farmers to people from bigger cities (especially Kansas City, and St. Louis) to many international students. [There are] many different groups of students, including Greeks, hippies, and everything in between." While some feel there are divisions among these groups, others tell us "the barriers are more political than [anything else]. Overall, everyone here is very friendly." Although the school is socially and geographically diverse, many students observe that "the minority population is very low. This comes partly from the fact that the minority population in Kansas is low and many minority students who tour campus recognize that it is pretty whitewashed. This problem has been improving recently." The university is "a liberal oasis in the middle of Kansas," but what qualifies as liberal in the Midwest probably does not on either the East or West Coasts. Many students are "very religious and very conservative."

FINANCIAL AID: 785-864-4700 • E-MAIL: ADM@KU.EDU • WEBSITE: WWW.KU.EDU

ADMISSIONS

Very important factors considered include: Class rank, secondary school record, standardized test scores. *Other factors considered include:* Alumni/ae relation, character/personal qualities, essays, extracurricular activities, minority status, recommendations, talent/ability, volunteer work, work experience. SAT Reasoning or ACT required. High school diploma is required, and GED is accepted. *Academic units required:* 4 English, 3 math, 3 science, 3 social studies, 1 computer technology. *Academic units recommended:* 4 English, 4 math, 3 science, 2 foreign language, 3 social studies, 1 computer technology.

The Inside Word

A no-sweat approach to admissions—so who gets denied? Judging from the decreased number of out-of-staters and the increased acceptance rate since the new selective-admissions-for-all standards were introduced in 2001, the weak out-of-staters are the ones who have felt the crunch in recent years.

FINANCIAL AID

Students should submit: FAFSA. Regular filing deadline is 3/1. The Princeton Review suggests that all financial aid forms be submitted as soon as possible after 1/1. *Need-based scholarships/grants offered:* Pell, SEOG, state scholarships/grants, private scholarships, the school's own gift aid. *Loan aid offered:* Direct Subsidized Stafford, Direct Unsubsidized Stafford, Direct PLUS, Federal Perkins, college/university loans from institutional funds. Applicants will be notified of awards on a rolling basis beginning on or about 4/1. Federal Work-study Program available. Institutional employment available. Off-campus job opportunities are excellent.

FROM THE ADMISSIONS OFFICE

"The University of Kansas has a long and distinguished tradition for academic excellence. Outstanding students from Kansas and across the nation are attracted to KU because of its strong academic reputation, beautiful campus, affordable cost of education, and contagious school spirit. KU provides students extraordinary opportunities in honors programs, research, internships, and study abroad. The university is located in Lawrence (40 minutes from Kansas City), a community of 80,000 regarded as one of the nation's best small cities for its arts scene, live music, and historic downtown.

"Students applying for fall 2006 admission may provide scores from either version of the SAT, as well as the ACT. KU will look at the total score of the Math and the Critical Reading (Verbal) section of the exam for admission purposes."

SELECTIVITY

Admissions Rating	**84**
# of applicants	10,442
% of applicants accepted	69
% of acceptees attending	59
# accepting a place on wait list	126
% admitted from wait list	74

FRESHMAN PROFILE

Range ACT Composite	21-27
Average ACT Composite	24
Average HS GPA	3.44
% graduated top 10% of class	28
% graduated top 25% of class	56
% graduated top 50% of class	87

DEADLINES

Regular application deadline	4/1
Regular notification	rolling
Nonfall registration?	yes

FINANCIAL FACTS

Financial Aid Rating	**71**
Annual in-state tuition	$4,163
Annual out-of-state tuition	$12,117
Room & Board	$5,126
Books and supplies	$750
Required fees	$574
% frosh rec. need-based scholarship or grant aid	31
% UG rec. need-based scholarship or grant aid	28
% frosh rec. need-based self-help aid	29
% UG rec. need-based self-help aid	29
% frosh rec. any financial aid	48
% UG rec. any financial aid	47
Avg. frosh grant	$3,385
Avg. frosh loan	$2,544
Independent 529 member?	No

University of Kentucky

100 Funkhouser Building, Lexington, KY 40506 • Admissions: 859-257-2000 • Fax: 859-257-3823

CAMPUS LIFE

Quality of Life Rating	**71**
Fire Safety Rating	**60**
Type of school	public
Environment	city

STUDENTS

Total undergrad enrollment	18,102
% male/female	48/52
% from out of state	17
% live on campus	25
% in (# of) fraternities	15 (19)
% in (# of) sororities	18 (16)
% African American	6
% Asian	2
% Caucasian	89
% Hispanic	1
% international	1
# of countries represented	118

SURVEY SAYS

Great computer facilities
Great library
Athletic facilities are great
Great off-campus food
Everyone loves the Wildcats
Frats and sororities dominate social scene
Student publications are popular
Lots of beer drinking
Hard liquor is popular
(Almost) everyone smokes

ACADEMICS

Academic Rating	**72**
Calendar	semester
Student/faculty ratio	17:1
Professors interesting rating	65
Professors accessible rating	71
% professors teaching UG courses	80
% classes taught by TAs	20
Most common regular class size	20-29 students

STUDENTS SPEAK OUT

Academics

Most students choose University of Kentucky (UK) for its "fun, laid-back lifestyle, blended nicely with an educational experience." For the most part, they get what they came for. Some concede that "the academic experience is very impersonal. You are not given the attention sometimes needed due to class size." "As in every large state university, it is easy to get lost with 30,000 other students in the mix. If you are not a proactive student, the likelihood of you succeeding to get out of here in four years is slim to none." They also report that as in "any big school, you have teachers that care and want to help you learn, and you also have professors that don't give a [expletive] about you, or if you learn, as long as they get paid." And since math and science figure so prominently here, it should come as no surprise that "many of the teachers and the TAs that teach labs and classes are foreign, and that's fine. But when their English is not good enough for a class composed primarily of English-speaking students, this is a serious problem." Despite these drawbacks, students are generally happy here: the academic experience meets their expectations. Plus, many here feel that "the current administration (and especially the current president) have done much to improve the campus for students." Undergraduates are thus hopeful about the university's future.

Life

"Life at UK is very dominated by sports," students agree. Men's varsity football and hockey (a club team) are both well supported, but "basketball reigns supreme. Basketball games in the state of Kentucky are a way of life. If this is news to you, maybe UK isn't the school you want to think about." Undergrads "spend long nights at the ticket lottery just to get tickets to [basketball] games, which are always sold out." On game day, the night's match-ups are just about all anyone on campus discusses. As game time approaches, students gather for pregame parties, then head to Rupp Arena to shout their heads off. While sports are central to UK life, they aren't the alpha and omega. Undergrads tell us that "there is a very popular Greek life;" that "student organizations are popular, with about 300 official clubs;" and that "student government is trying to bring more campus activities than there used to be." "A large number of students also like to do outdoor activities like rock climbing and camping." Hometown Lexington has "lots of excellent restaurants, many theaters, several bowling alleys, a roller-skating rink, ice skating, mini golf—pretty much any activity you can think of, you can probably find it nearby." Students report that drinking is a popular pastime despite the enforced dry-campus policy. This policy, students inform us, encourages them "to party off campus." Few here report any difficulty accessing alcohol, but most agree that the university and town do their best to make drinking a hassle: "Cops around here are not so nice; they bust parties all the time," gripes one student.

Student Body

"Most UK students are friendly natives who share the same southern values and get along very well," undergrads here report. Adds one student, "There are a lot of standard-issue fraternity guys and sorority girls. I can't go ten feet without seeing a girl who completely dresses up for class like it's a fashion show." Still, because of the school's immensity, many feel that "there is no 'typical student' at UK. There are many different types of students here; however, the different types don't usually mix together. Everyone has a niche on campus, and they are all separate." Although there are pockets of hard workers scattered throughout the university, the average student "studies lightly Sunday through Wednesday and parties hard Thursday through Saturday."

FINANCIAL AID: 859-257-3172 • E-MAIL: ADMISSION@UKY.EDU • WEBSITE: WWW.UKY.EDU

ADMISSIONS

Very important factors considered include: Secondary school record, standardized test scores. *Important factors considered include:* Class rank, extracurricular activities, minority status, state residency, talent/ability, volunteer work, work experience. *Other factors considered include:* Character/personal qualities, essays, geographical residence, recommendations. SAT Reasoning and SAT Subject Tests or ACT required. TOEFL required of all international applicants. High school diploma is required, and GED is accepted. *Academic units required:* 4 English, 3 math, 3 science, 2 foreign language, 3 social studies, 5 academic electives. *Academic units recommended:* 4 English, 4 math, 3 science, 2 foreign language, 3 social studies, 4 academic electives.

The Inside Word

The high volume of applications has more to do with Kentucky's selectivity than any other factor. Given the recent successes of the Wildcats in NCAA basketball, more apps are likely to be on the way.

FINANCIAL AID

Students should submit: FAFSA. The Princeton Review suggests that all financial aid forms be submitted as soon as possible after 1/1. *Need-based scholarships/grants offered:* Pell, SEOG, state scholarships/grants, private scholarships, the school's own gift aid. *Loan aid offered:* Direct Subsidized Stafford, Direct Unsubsidized Stafford, Direct PLUS, Federal Perkins, college/university loans from institutional funds. Applicants will be notified of awards on or about 4/1.

FROM THE ADMISSIONS OFFICE

"The University of Kentucky offers you an outstanding learning environment and quality instruction through its excellent faculty. Of the 1,892 full-time faculty, 98 percent hold the doctorate degree or the highest degree in their field of study. Many are nationally and internationally known for their research, distinguished teaching, and scholarly service to Kentucky, the nation, and the world. UK's scholars (students, faculty, and alumni) have been honored by Nobel, Pulitzer, Rhodes, Fulbright, Guggenheim, and Grammy Awards, and most recently the Metropolitan Opera and the Marshall Foundation. Yet, with a student/teacher ratio of only 16:1, UK faculty are accessible and willing to answer your questions and discuss your interests.

"UK will accept either version of the SAT. The new Writing sections of the ACT and SAT will not be used in the admission process. ACT and SAT score requirements will remain the same as the new score will not be figured into the total score used for admission consideration."

SELECTIVITY

Admissions Rating	**82**
# of applicants	10,604
% of applicants accepted	79
% of acceptees attending	47

FRESHMAN PROFILE

Range SAT Verbal	510-620
Average SAT Verbal	564
Range SAT Math	510-640
Average SAT Math	570
**TPR Projected Range SAT Writing*	*570-650*
Range ACT Composite	21-27
Average ACT Composite	24
Minimum Paper TOEFL	527
Minimum Computer Based TOEFL	197
Average HS GPA	3.5
% graduated top 10% of class	26
% graduated top 25% of class	55
% graduated top 50% of class	84

DEADLINES

Regular application deadline	2/15
Regular notification	rolling
Nonfall registration?	yes

APPLICANTS ALSO LOOK AT

AND OFTEN PREFER

Centre College, Indiana University—Bloomington, Miami University, Transylvania University

AND SOMETIMES PREFER

Bellarmine University, Eastern Kentucky University, University of Louisville, University of Tennessee—Knoxville, Western Kentucky University

AND RARELY PREFER

Florida State University, Ohio State University—Columbus, Purdue University—West Lafayette, University of Florida

FINANCIAL FACTS

Financial Aid Rating	**84**
Annual in-state tuition	$4,752
Annual out-of-state tuition	$11,532
Room & Board	$4,735
Books and supplies	$600
Required fees	$563
% frosh rec. need-based scholarship or grant aid	18
% UG rec. need-based scholarship or grant aid	19
% frosh rec. need-based self-help aid	23
% UG rec. need-based self-help aid	27
% frosh rec. any financial aid	40
% UG rec. any financial aid	38
Avg. frosh grant	$5,446
Avg. frosh loan	$2,556
Independent 529 member?	No

UNIVERSITY OF LOUISIANA AT LAFAYETTE

PO DRAWER 41210, LAFAYETTE, LA 70504 • ADMISSIONS: 337-482-6457 • FAX: 337-482-6195

CAMPUS LIFE

Quality of Life Rating	**82**
Fire Safety Rating	**73**
Type of school	public
Environment	city

STUDENTS

Total undergrad enrollment	14,564
% male/female	42/58
% from out of state	4
% from public high school	70
% live on campus	9
% in (# of) fraternities	3 (13)
% in (# of) sororities	4 (8)
% African American	19
% Asian	1
% Caucasian	74
% Hispanic	2
% international	2
# of countries represented	101

SURVEY SAYS

Great library
Diverse student types on campus
Students love Lafayette, LA
Great off-campus food
Lots of beer drinking
(Almost) everyone smokes

ACADEMICS

Academic Rating	**69**
Calendar	semester
Student/faculty ratio	22:1
Professors interesting rating	70
Professors accessible rating	70
% professors teaching UG courses	100
% classes taught by TAs	0
Most common regular class size	20-29 students

MOST POPULAR MAJORS

Business administration/management
general studies
nursing/registered nurse training (RN, ASN, BSN, MSN)

STUDENTS SPEAK OUT

Academics

Students at the University of Louisiana (UL) at Lafayette, the second-largest school in the Pelican State, see a great future for their university, if only they could escape the shadow of LSU. Explains one student, "The university is often overlooked but leads the state academically in the areas of computer science, education, nursing, and often also engineering. The major hindrance is the great, statewide support for the LSU 'flagship' university, and a great deal needs to be done to overcome this." Undergraduates at Lafayette appreciate an "honors program—the largest in the state—that allows even freshmen to have some extremely good teachers, as well as smaller one-on-one class sizes;" a "faculty and staff who love the university, and therefore give it everything they've got;" and "research facilities that are second in the state only to LSU." As at most research-oriented universities, students warn that "many professors are interested in research, not teaching." Most students rely on word-of-mouth to avoid bad profs, whenever possible, noting that "you get your good with your bad here. At UL Lafayette there is more good than bad, but the bad is very powerful."

Life

Students in Lafayette certainly know how to have a good time. Writes a typical undergrad, "Life at my school is crazy! Everyone is always planning a private party or arranging to meet at a different bar a few nights a week. UL Lafayette, I hear, is notorious for its fun-loving students. I'm pretty sure the only time the campus coffee house is full of students actually studying is during finals week." Adds another student, "Nightlife in the community is widespread. There are a high number of bars and dance clubs near campus. Most students frequent 'The Strip,' which is located one block off campus. (There are seven or eight bars on one street). Festivals are frequent here in Lafayette, including a very large International Music Festival as well as a gigantic Mardi Gras celebration." Undergrads love their Ragin' Cajuns, Lafayette's intercollegiate athletic teams, although they love winners more than also-rans. Explains one student, "Due to bad years in football, sports support has been down. However, baseball support is very high. Also, when a major rival is in town for a game—i.e., LSU—there is a great student support. There is also great support for basketball." Students say that UL Lafayette is "quite serious about studies, but also well developed in extracurricular activities," offering "great study groups, awesome clubs, and a variety of other things to keep people busy."

Student Body

According to UL Lafayette undergrads, "the university has a surprising number of minority populations. For instance, there is a very large gay organization that gets great backing by the very conservative local community. In general, the students are extremely friendly and do not discriminate based on artificial stereotypes (how much money you have, what kind of car you drive, are you in a fraternity, is your father a doctor, etc.)." The student body is generally "very diverse, nice, and easy to get along with." An air of southern friendliness permeates the campus: notes one Ragin' Cajun, "Students here are either very serious or very silly. Surprisingly, there is little conflict on the UL Lafayette campus. People are comfortable expressing their views, and after heated classroom discussions, most walk out of class with no hard feelings."

University of Louisiana at Lafayette

FINANCIAL AID: 337-482-6506 • E-MAIL: ADMISSIONS@LOUISIANA.EDU • WEBSITE: WWW.LOUISIANA.EDU

ADMISSIONS

Very important factors considered include: Class rank, secondary school record, standardized test scores. SAT Reasoning or ACT required. TOEFL required of all international applicants. High school diploma is required, and GED is accepted. *Academic units required:* 4 English, 3 math, 3 science, 2 social studies, 1 history, 4 academic electives.

The Inside Word

UL Lafayette is a place where committed students can really put themselves on the map academically. Its students, while not diverse in geographic heritage, are diverse in ethnicity and lifestyle.

FINANCIAL AID

Students should submit: FAFSA, institution's own financial aid form. The Princeton Review suggests that all financial aid forms be submitted as soon as possible after 1/1. *Need-based scholarships/grants offered:* Pell, SEOG, state scholarships/grants, private scholarships, the school's own gift aid, Federal Nursing scholarships. *Loan aid offered:* Direct Subsidized Stafford, FFEL Subsidized Stafford, FFEL Unsubsidized Stafford, FFEL PLUS, Federal Perkins, Federal Nursing. Applicants will be notified of awards on a rolling basis beginning on or about 4/1. Federal Work-study Program available. Institutional employment available. Off-campus job opportunities are good.

FROM THE ADMISSIONS OFFICE

"The University of Louisiana at Lafayette offers students from throughout the United States and more than 90 countries strong academic training and personal enrichment opportunities in a friendly, comfortable, student-centered environment. UL Lafayette students are taught, mentored, and advised by some of the brightest and most accomplished faculty members in the United States. Although UL Lafayette offers more than 100 programs of study and the research opportunities, internship possibilities, and facilities of a major research intensive university, average class size is approximately the same as that at many high schools and smaller higher education institutions.

"UL students receive a good deal of individual attention and support—both personal and academic—from faculty and staff.

"A wide range of cultural, recreational, and social activities are available on and off campus, including more than 150 campus organizations and clubs, NCAA Division I and intramural athletics, a state-of-the-art aquatic center, a thriving arts scene, a wide range of live music venues, shopping, a great variety of excellent restaurants, theaters, the second largest Mardi Gras in the nation, and an international music festival. In fact, *Utne Reader* magazine selected the city of Lafayette as Louisiana's "Most Enlightened Town."

"Our relatively low tuition and generous financial aid and scholarship programs, including an out-of-state tuition waiver for qualified students, make UL Lafayette one of the most affordable universities in the nation.

"Students who have completed the required college preparatory core curriculum in high school may qualify for admission on the basis of a combination of their high school cumulative grade point average and ACT or SAT scores. Writing scores are not required."

SELECTIVITY	
Admissions Rating	**72**
# of applicants	4,903
% of applicants accepted	85
% of acceptees attending	63
FRESHMAN PROFILE	
Range ACT Composite	18-23
Average ACT Composite	21
Minimum Paper TOEFL	450
Minimum Computer Based TOEFL	133
Average HS GPA	3.11
% graduated top 10% of class	16
% graduated top 25% of class	39
% graduated top 50% of class	69
DEADLINES	
Regular notification	rolling
Nonfall registration?	yes
FINANCIAL FACTS	
Financial Aid Rating	**92**
Annual in-state tuition	$3,228
Annual out-of-state tuition	$9,408
Room & Board	$3,386
Books and supplies	$1,000
% frosh rec. need-based scholarship or grant aid	31
% UG rec. need-based scholarship or grant aid	25
% frosh rec. need-based self-help aid	64
% UG rec. need-based self-help aid	31
Independent 529 member?	No

UNIVERSITY OF MAINE

5713 Chadbourne Hall, Orono, ME 04469-5713 • Admissions: 207-581-1561 • Fax: 207-581-1213

CAMPUS LIFE

Quality of Life Rating	**76**
Fire Safety Rating	**60**
Type of school	public
Environment	village

STUDENTS

Total undergrad enrollment	8,397
% male/female	49/51
% from out of state	12
% live on campus	30
% African American	1
% Asian	1
% Caucasian	93
% Hispanic	1
% Native American	2
% international	2
# of countries represented	67

SURVEY SAYS

Great library
Everyone loves the Black Bears
Lots of beer drinking
Hard liquor is popular

ACADEMICS

Academic Rating	**74**
Calendar	semester
Student/faculty ratio	15:1
Professors interesting rating	68
Professors accessible rating	71
% professors teaching UG courses	73
% classes taught by TAs	9
Most common lab size	10-19 students
Most common regular class size	10-19 students

MOST POPULAR MAJORS

Business administration/management
education
engineering

STUDENTS SPEAK OUT

Academics

Combine cheap in-state tuition with top programs, and it's easy to understand why not too many University of Maine students are in any rush to leave the warm embrace (which is at a premium in chilly Maine) of their college after four sweet years. Engineering is tops here, but exciting majors like new media, marine science, and landscape horticulture draw their fair share of undergraduates, too. For those who fear the anonymity of a public school, UM undergrads swear that "It's not overwhelmingly huge." General education classes can be large and impersonal, but a math major writes, "Most of my classes for the past two years have been under 20 people, many under 10. I can actually go to my professors with questions on homework, class, or career." Another undergrad adds, "I have always received attention when I needed it, even in classes of 300-plus." One student who is taking advantage of the tutoring program writes that, thanks to the one-on-one time, "I am now receiving 100's on my tests and quizzes." The administration generally makes a good impression on students from the get-go by "setting up meetings with the first-year students to get to know them and to establish a communication line. If anyone has questions, answers are a phone-call, visit, or e-mail away."

Life

Word on the street is that "people here know how to recreate." Take, for example, flowing pumpkin ale at Oktoberfest, mud volleyball along with campus beautification (in lieu of classes) on Maine Day, and the school-sponsored bonfire celebrating the Red Sox pennant in 2004, which, we are told, "was genius, as it kept the excited student body from doing any damage and gave us all an outlet for our celebratory energy." The Division I athletic teams, hockey in particular, draw a rabid following. "When you say Maine Black Bears, you say all." On the weekends, "You can go dancing at Ushie's or drinking at the Bear Brew, which are almost always packed on Thursdays." Greek life "is slowly getting a better reputation thanks to the fraternities and sororities changing policies and extending out into the community." After the night's revelries are over, kids grab a few hours of sleep before waking in the morning to hike off any hangovers on the extensive network of trails near the campus. There's a lot of alcohol-less cheer to be had at UM too; plenty of people appreciate that "six nights out of the week, somewhere on campus you can find free fun that does not involve alcohol or sports." That means karaoke, comedians, movies in the main lecture hall, board games, and open-mic nights. "There's even a knitting club."

Student Body

The University of Maine's undergraduate population includes a colorful array of more than 8,000 characters: "boozers, stoners, foresters, adventurers, businessmen, and the straight-up Mainers." Just what is a "straight-up Mainer?" The answer depends on whom you ask. Most here agree, though, that he isn't so welcoming to out-of-state folks. That shouldn't upset too many people, though, as only about 15 percent of students hail from beyond the borders of The Pine Tree State. Still, according to students, "every type of person is represented in the student body in some way." A visible Goth contingent mingles with hacky-sacking hippies and anime enthusiasts. Against the backdrop of "white back hill hicks," the "African American athletes from Massachusetts and hockey players from New York or Canada" do stand out. Still, "You can wear what you want, say what you want, think what you want, and it's accepted." Students tend to form cliques "made up of high school friends or people from your area;" in such a small state, people always seem connected by "three or fewer degrees of separation."

FINANCIAL AID: 207-581-1324 • E-MAIL: UM-ADMIT@MAINE.EDU • WEBSITE: WWW.UMAINE.EDU

ADMISSIONS

Very important factors considered include: Secondary school record. *Important factors considered include:* Class rank, standardized test scores. *Other factors considered include:* Alumni/ae relation, character/personal qualities, essays, extracurricular activities, interview, recommendations, talent/ability, volunteer work, work experience. SAT Reasoning or SAT Subject Tests required. TOEFL required of all international applicants. High school diploma is required, and GED is accepted. *Academic units required:* 4 English, 3 math, 2 science (2 science lab), 2 foreign language, 2 social studies, 3 academic electives, 1 physical education. *Academic units recommended:* 4 English, 4 math, 3 science (3 science lab), 2 foreign language, 3 social studies, 1 history, 3 academic electives, 1 physical education.

The Inside Word

The University of Maine is much smaller than most public flagship universities, and its admissions process reflects this; it is a much more personal approach than most others use. Candidates are reviewed carefully for fit with their choice of college and major, and the committee will contact students regarding a second choice if the first doesn't seem to be a good match. Prepare your application as if you are applying to a private university.

FINANCIAL AID

Students should submit: FAFSA. The Princeton Review suggests that all financial aid forms be submitted as soon as possible after 1/1. *Need-based scholarships/grants offered:* Pell, SEOG, state scholarships/grants, private scholarships, the school's own gift aid. *Loan aid offered:* FFEL Subsidized Stafford, FFEL Unsubsidized Stafford, FFEL PLUS, Federal Perkins, state loans. Applicants will be notified of awards on a rolling basis beginning on or about 3/15. Federal Work-study Program available. Institutional employment available. Off-campus job opportunities are good.

FROM THE ADMISSIONS OFFICE

"The University of Maine offers students a wide array of academic and social programs, including clubs, organizations, professional societies, and religious groups. We strive to help students feel welcome and to provide opportunities for them to become an integral part of the campus community. Visit our beautiful campus and become better acquainted with this community. Take a guided campus tour and learn about campus facilities, services and technologies, and living and dining. Our student tour guides give a firsthand view of the Black Bear experience. During your visit, meet with faculty and admission staff to learn more about your program of interest and our academic climate. The University of Maine's commitment to educational excellence and community building will be reinforced when you visit our campus!

"Students applying for admission into the fall 2006 class are required to submit official scores from either the SAT or ACT. Students are not required to submit the Writing component from either test. In making admission decisions, UMaine will use the student's best scores from either test."

SELECTIVITY

Admissions Rating	**78**
# of applicants	5,622
% of applicants accepted	79
% of acceptees attending	38

FRESHMAN PROFILE

Range SAT Verbal	480-590
Average SAT Verbal	539
Range SAT Math	480-600
Average SAT Math	543
**TPR Projected Range SAT Writing*	*540-620*
Range ACT Composite	20-26
Average ACT Composite	24
Minimum Paper TOEFL	530
Minimum Computer Based TOEFL	197
Average HS GPA	3.21
% graduated top 10% of class	21
% graduated top 25% of class	51
% graduated top 50% of class	88

DEADLINES

Regular notification	rolling
Nonfall registration?	yes

APPLICANTS ALSO LOOK AT AND OFTEN PREFER

University of New Hampshire
University of Southern Maine
University of Vermont

AND SOMETIMES PREFER

University of Connecticut
University of Maine at Farmington
University of Massachusetts—Amherst
University of Rhode Island

FINANCIAL FACTS

Financial Aid Rating	**75**
Annual in-state tuition	$5,520
Annual out-of-state tuition	$15,660
Room & Board	$6,732
Books and supplies	$700
Required fees	$1,390
% frosh rec. need-based scholarship or grant aid	57
% UG rec. need-based scholarship or grant aid	45
% frosh rec. need-based self-help aid	59
% UG rec. need-based self-help aid	53
% frosh rec. any financial aid	83
% UG rec. any financial aid	81
Avg. frosh grant	$5,760
Avg. frosh loan	$4,172
Independent 529 member?	No

UNIVERSITY OF MARY WASHINGTON

1301 College Avenue, Fredericksburg, VA 22401 • Admissions: 540-654-2000 • Fax: 540-654-1857

CAMPUS LIFE

Quality of Life Rating	**64**
Fire Safety Rating	**60**
Type of school	public
Environment	city

STUDENTS

Total undergrad enrollment	4,130
% male/female	34/66
% from out of state	35
% from public high school	76
% live on campus	70
% African American	5
% Asian	5
% Caucasian	100
% Hispanic	4
% international	1
# of countries represented	11

SURVEY SAYS

Small classes
No one cheats
Great computer facilities
Diversity lacking on campus
Frats and sororities are unpopular or nonexistent

ACADEMICS

Academic Rating	**78**
Calendar	semester
Student/faculty ratio	17:1
Professors interesting rating	80
Professors accessible rating	77
% professors teaching UG courses	100
% classes taught by TAs	0
Most common lab size	20-29 students
Most common regular class size	20-29 students

MOST POPULAR MAJORS

Business administration/management
English language and literature
psychology

STUDENTS SPEAK OUT

Academics

With the rapid growth of its graduate programs, Mary Washington College has been poised for an upgrade to university status for several years. The school finally pulled the big move in the summer of 2004, changing its name to University of Mary Washington. Despite the new moniker, little will change for traditional undergraduates, who will continue to receive a demanding, personalized education on UMW's Fredericksburg campus. They tell us that Mary Washington will remain "a school with excellent academic programs." Students sometimes balk at "so many core requirements!" but appreciate the university's strong offerings in history, education, psychology, English, and the life sciences. Just as important, the school's honor code will continue to "permeate the campus and underlie everything; you trust everyone, so you are nicer to people. People leave their purses, backpacks, and cell phones unattended for hours and nothing is stolen. Most people leave their doors unlocked. It goes way beyond not cheating in the classroom. There is a constant foundation of trust." Undergrads here will rarely see the graduate students and the nontraditional undergraduates seeking professional training, who now attend the school's second campus (the College of Graduate and Professional Studies, formerly the James Monroe Center for Graduate and Professional Studies) in Stafford County.

Life

The pace of life at UMW is "pretty relaxed, [with] a lot of small activities that go on [but] no Greek life" to create a happening party scene. It's the kind of place where "after a while students find their niche," whether it be with a clique of friends or an extracurricular organization, "and, if not, they transfer." How easily students find their comfort zone depends largely on how they perceive hometown Fredericksburg. Some praise its "great downtown shopping area completely devoid of chain shops; instead you get a mom-and-pop feel and really cute stores [and] great restaurants." Others feel the city is "pretty dead," telling us that "downtown Fredericksburg is historic and quaint, but not exactly the stuff of which college entertainment dreams are made." Without a Greek scene, parties tend to be pretty small, because larger ones get "broken up by the cops almost immediately." Some students cope by heading elsewhere whenever possible; Washington DC, Richmond, Virginia Beach, and Charlottesville are all potential weekend destinations. Then there are the outdoorsy types, grateful that "a two-hour drive to Shenandoah provides days of hiking, biking, climbing, and camping, and even skiing in the winter."

Students

With a two-to-one female-to-male ratio, UMW continues to have an estrogen-laced campus, its switch to coeducation over 30 years ago notwithstanding. Your standard-issue UMW woman is "majoring in a liberal art, education, or historic preservation, or even possibly a mixture...lives on campus, but goes home a lot, and balances her out-of-class time by either studying, hanging out with friends, or playing a sport." She's also likely to be a conservative Republican from Virginia or Maryland—although "we have a lot of students from New England and New York"—blond-haired and blue-eyed, and the type of preppy who "loves her polo shirts and khakis and pearls and ribbons in her hair." The guys are "split between the studious and athletic," and are less likely to be as serious about their schoolwork, "due to the fact that it's easier to get in if you're male." UMW is home to "very few minorities (especially African Americans and Hispanics), but they generally fit in." The school "has a very large Christian population...but non-Christians don't feel pressured because there are plenty of non-Christians as well."

University of Mary Washington

Financial Aid: 800-468-5614 • E-mail: admit@mwc.edu • Website: www.mwc.edu

ADMISSIONS

Very important factors considered include: Secondary school record. *Important factors considered include:* Class rank, essays, standardized test scores. *Other factors considered include:* Alumni/ae relation, character/personal qualities, extracurricular activities, geographical residence, minority status, recommendations, state residency, talent/ability, volunteer work, work experience. SAT Reasoning or ACT required. TOEFL required of all international applicants. High school diploma is required, and GED is accepted. *Academic units required:* 4 English, 3 math, 3 science (3 science lab), 2 foreign language, 2 social studies, 1 history. *Academic units recommended:* 4 English, 4 math, 4 science (4 science lab), 4 foreign language, 2 social studies, 2 history.

The Inside Word

It's hard to beat small, selective public colleges like Mary Washington for quality and cost, and more and more students are discovering this. The admissions process is very selective and, with the exception of preferential treatment for Virginia residents, functions in virtually the same manner as small private college admissions committees do. Students who are interested need to focus on putting their best into all aspects of the application.

FINANCIAL AID

Students should submit: FAFSA. The Princeton Review suggests that all financial aid forms be submitted as soon as possible after 1/1. *Need-based scholarships/grants offered:* Pell, SEOG, state scholarships/grants, private scholarships, the school's own gift aid. *Loan aid offered:* FFEL Subsidized Stafford, FFEL Unsubsidized Stafford, FFEL PLUS, Federal Perkins. Applicants will be notified of awards on or about 4/15. Institutional employment available. Off-campus job opportunities are good.

FROM THE ADMISSIONS OFFICE

"Among institutions of higher learning in Virginia, the University of Mary Washington stands alone. We have distinctive academic programs, a breathtakingly beautiful campus, a sharp and diverse student body, and a unique sense of friendship and camaraderie that make the university very special. In fact, we have one of the best combinations of strong academics, personal attention, low cost, and impressive graduate school and job placement of any school in the country. Our students come from all over the country and the world, and are instructed by a faculty that considers teaching its primary objective—research and publishing come second. Committed to providing a well-rounded liberal arts and sciences education, the university offers its students the opportunity to pursue individual or collaborative research projects. Supportive faculty and more than $186,000 in student research funds annually make ours one of the most ambitious undergraduate research programs in the country. There are 17 residence halls on the Mary Washington campus with a university-owned apartment complex located adjacent to the main campus. The "Apartments at UMW" provide the opportunity for 350 junior and senior students to experience apartment-style living while enjoying the amenities of on-campus living. Recently, the Jepson Executive Alumni Center, a new fitness center, and an indoor tennis facility were added to the university landscape.

"Applicants are required to submit official results of either the old or new SAT, or the ACT. The highest composite score will be used in admissions decisions. In addition, we strongly recommend that applicants submit results of two or more SAT Subject Tests of each applicant's choosing."

SELECTIVITY

Admissions Rating	**91**
# of applicants	4,462
% of applicants accepted	64
% of acceptees attending	31
# accepting a place on wait list	300
% admitted from wait list	42

FRESHMAN PROFILE

Range SAT Verbal	580-670
Average SAT Verbal	628
Range SAT Math	560-640
Average SAT Math	602
**TPR Projected Range SAT Writing*	*620-680*
Range ACT Composite	25-29
Average ACT Composite	27
Minimum Paper TOEFL	550
Minimum Computer Based TOEFL	230
Average HS GPA	3.64
% graduated top 10% of class	43
% graduated top 25% of class	87
% graduated top 50% of class	99

DEADLINES

Regular application deadline	2/1
Regular notification	4/1
Nonfall registration?	yes

APPLICANTS ALSO LOOK AT

AND OFTEN PREFER
College of William and Mary
University of Virginia

AND SOMETIMES PREFER
James Madison University
University of Richmond

AND RARELY PREFER
George Mason University
Longwood University

FINANCIAL FACTS

Financial Aid Rating	**61**
Annual in-state tuition	$5,128
Annual out-of-state tuition	$13,534
Room & Board	$5,744
Books and supplies	$800
% frosh rec. need-based scholarship or grant aid	40
% UG rec. need-based scholarship or grant aid	45
% frosh rec. need-based self-help aid	37
% UG rec. need-based self-help aid	37
% frosh rec. any financial aid	57
% UG rec. any financial aid	59
Avg. frosh grant	$4,450
Avg. frosh loan	$2,700
Independent 529 member?	No

UNIV. OF MARYLAND—BALTIMORE COUNTY

1000 HILLTOP CIRCLE, BALTIMORE, MD 21250 • ADMISSIONS: 410-455-2291 • FAX: 410-455-1094

CAMPUS LIFE

Quality of Life Rating	**70**
Fire Safety Rating	**88**
Type of school	public
Environment	metropolis

STUDENTS

Total undergrad enrollment	9,668
% male/female	53/47
% from out of state	9
% from public high school	87
% live on campus	33
% in (# of) fraternities	4 (12)
% in (# of) sororities	4 (9)
% African American	14
% Asian	19
% Caucasian	55
% Hispanic	3
% international	4
# of countries represented	106

SURVEY SAYS

Great computer facilities
Great library
Diverse student types on campus
Campus feels safe

ACADEMICS

Academic Rating	**76**
Calendar	4-1-4
Student/faculty ratio	19:1
Professors interesting rating	70
Professors accessible rating	65
% professors teaching UG courses	100
% classes taught by TAs	2
Most common lab size	10-19 students
Most common regular class size	10-19 students

MOST POPULAR MAJORS

Information technology
psychology
visual and performing arts

STUDENTS SPEAK OUT

Academics

The University of Maryland—Baltimore County is primarily known as a great "science and engineering school" with superb "research opportunities"—but this justly earned reputation tells only part of the story. Many here report that "the humanities are wonderful," even though some concede that they "are not very well funded or respected." Offerings here are enhanced by the "focus on research. There are so many opportunities for students to learn the latest tidbits of up-to-date research done on campus and to work with professors for credit." "The professors seem to be a mixed bag," getting reviews that range from "very inspiring" and "excellent" to "crappy" and "awful," with some falling "in the middle." Students here enjoy "really great opportunities for internships. The proximity to Washington, DC, and Baltimore provides easy access to jobs other people around the country would love to have." UMBC's career services office also facilitates "great placement opportunities. The methods of getting your resume around in your field of interest are easy and very effective." In all areas, UMBC adheres to an "honors college philosophy of smaller classes and more professor interaction."

Life

Campus life at UMBC has many hurdles to clear. One of the biggest is the campus itself, which students complain "has no atmosphere," griping that "it's just a bunch of buildings" that are "disconnected from the surrounding community." Explains one undergrad, "The campus is not very inviting...There's almost nowhere to relax or study outdoors between classes. The dorms are on the outskirts of campus, [so] the part where classrooms are located is pretty desolate. It's rare to see people socializing, sunbathing, playing Frisbee™, etc. on campus between classes." Compounding these problems is the fact that it has "the reputation of being a commuter campus." A growing number of underclassmen—over 70 percent of last year's freshman class—also live on campus, which has bolstered a sense of community at UMBC. There is fun to be had, though. Several students write that "fun at UMBC usually consists of hanging out at the Commons and eating food, playing in the game room, or just relaxing in a friend's dorm room." Some note optimistically that "campus life is improving, especially with the addition of our on-campus bar," and others point out that the Student Events Board (which "tries to give us something cool to do as much as possible") has booked "many great events, such as Dave Chappelle, Good Charlotte, Kanye West, Third Eye Blind, Tracey Morgan, and most recently, Yellowcard." While "there are many students that go out to drink," this is not true of "everyone by any means." And while "most weekends are still pretty much dead here," students can take comfort in the fact that "Baltimore's Inner Harbor is only five minutes away."

Student Body

With minorities making up about one-third of the student body, UMBC is a "truly diverse" place. "The diversity is wonderful," writes one junior. "It gives everyone a chance to learn about different cultures, religions, etc." A few students also note that while "the ethnic, religious and ideological diversity on the campus means that most people can find some small set of friends or acquaintances with whom they can comfortably spend what free time they have," it also "contributes to a certain cliquishness...which is easily seen by the lack of great interaction between students of different nationalities and races." More than half the students are commuters "like to go to school and go home." While commuters are "typically poorly integrated into the social fabric of the campus," they aren't totally isolated: they have a "commuter lounge where breakfast is offered for free for commuters on Tuesdays and Thursdays." UMBC's students "try to eke out a social existence however they can. Even those who live on-campus, however, are typically mostly dedicated to completing their work, rapidly earning their degrees, and quickly leaving the school."

FINANCIAL AID: 410-455-2387 • E-MAIL: ADMISSIONS@UMBC.EDU • WEBSITE: WWW.UMBC.EDU

ADMISSIONS

Very important factors considered include: Secondary school record, standardized test scores. *Important factors considered include:* Class rank, essays, recommendations. *Other factors considered include:* Character/personal qualities, extracurricular activities, interview, talent/ability, volunteer work, work experience. SAT Reasoning or ACT required. TOEFL required of all international applicants. High school diploma is required, and GED is accepted. *Academic units required:* 4 English, 3 math, 3 science (2 science lab), 2 foreign language, 2 social studies, 2 history, 4 academic electives. *Academic units recommended:* 4 English, 4 math, 3 science (2 science lab), 2 foreign language, 2 social studies, 2 history, 4 academic electives.

The Inside Word

The State of Maryland seems blessed with several strong, small, public universities in addition to its flagship campus at College Park. UMBC is one of those to watch; its national visibility and admissions standards are on the rise. Strong students are attracted by UMBC's emphasis on academic achievement. As a result, the admissions committee has grown to expect evidence of challenging academic course work throughout high school from its candidates, preferably at the honors or AP level. This competitive path will give you the best shot for admission if you're an eager learner looking for a campus where the academic experience is engaging.

FINANCIAL AID

Students should submit: FAFSA. The Princeton Review suggests that all financial aid forms be submitted as soon as possible after 1/1. *Need-based scholarships/grants offered:* Pell, SEOG, state scholarships/grants, private scholarships. *Loan aid offered:* FFEL Subsidized Stafford, FFEL Unsubsidized Stafford, FFEL PLUS, Federal Perkins. Applicants will be notified of awards on a rolling basis beginning on or about 3/15. Off-campus job opportunities are excellent.

FROM THE ADMISSIONS OFFICE

"When it comes to universities, a midsized school can be just right. Some students want the resources of a large community. Others are looking for the attention found at a smaller one. With an undergraduate population of 8,000, UMBC can offer the best of both. There are always new people to meet and things to do—from Division 1 sports to more than 170 student clubs. As a research university, we offer an abundance of programs, technology, and opportunities for hands-on experiences. Yet we are small enough that students don't get lost in the shuffle. More than 80 percent of our classes have fewer than 40 students. Among public research universities, UMBC is recognized for its success in placing students in the most competitive graduate programs and careers. Of course, much of the success of UMBC has to do with the students themselves—highly motivated students who get involved in their education.

"Freshman applicants for falls 2006 are strongly encouraged to take the new SAT or ACT (with Writing component); however, the admissions committee will consider scores from the old SAT or ACT if no new scores are available."

SELECTIVITY

Admissions Rating	**86**
# of applicants	5,446
% of applicants accepted	70
% of acceptees attending	37
# accepting a place on wait list	90
% admitted from wait list	6

FRESHMAN PROFILE

Range SAT Verbal	540-640
Average SAT Verbal	597
Range SAT Math	580-670
Average SAT Math	624
**TPR Projected Range SAT Writing*	*590-660*
Range ACT Composite	22-28
Average ACT Composite	25
Minimum Paper TOEFL	550
Minimum Computer Based TOEFL	220
Average HS GPA	3.5
% graduated top 10% of class	30
% graduated top 25% of class	58
% graduated top 50% of class	86

DEADLINES

Regular application deadline	2/1
Regular notification	rolling
Nonfall registration?	yes

APPLICANTS ALSO LOOK AT

AND OFTEN PREFER
Johns Hopkins University
Virginia Tech

AND SOMETIMES PREFER
Penn State University Park
University of Delaware
University of Maryland—College Park
University of Virginia

AND RARELY PREFER
St. Mary's College of Maryland
Towson University

FINANCIAL FACTS

Financial Aid Rating	**71**
Annual in-state tuition	$8,020
Annual out-of-state tuition	$15,620
Room & Board	$7,845
Books and supplies	$1,000
% frosh rec. need-based scholarship or grant aid	27
% UG rec. need-based scholarship or grant aid	27
% frosh rec. need-based self-help aid	45
% UG rec. need-based self-help aid	44
% frosh rec. any financial aid	53
% UG rec. any financial aid	53
Avg. frosh grant	$6,000
Avg. frosh loan	$2,500
Independent 529 member?	No

University of Maryland—College Park

Mitchell Building, College Park, MD 20742-5235 • Admissions: 301-314-8385 • Fax: 301-314-9693

CAMPUS LIFE

Quality of Life Rating	**69**
Fire Safety Rating	**68**
Type of school	public
Environment	metropolis

STUDENTS

Total undergrad enrollment	24,590
% male/female	51/49
% from out of state	24
% live on campus	33
% in (# of) fraternities	11 (30)
% in (# of) sororities	11 (26)
% African American	12
% Asian	14
% Caucasian	58
% Hispanic	6
% international	2
# of countries represented	169

SURVEY SAYS

Great library
Athletic facilities are great
Diverse student types on campus
Everyone loves the Terrapins
Student publications are popular
Lots of beer drinking
Hard liquor is popular

ACADEMICS

Academic Rating	**76**
Calendar	semester
Student/faculty ratio	18:1
Professors interesting rating	69
Professors accessible rating	66
% classes taught by TAs	0
Most common lab size	20-29 students
Most common regular class size	20-29 students

MOST POPULAR MAJORS

Computer and information sciences
criminology
political science and government

STUDENTS SPEAK OUT

Academics

The University of Maryland—College Park (UMCP) contains boosters that proudly proclaim, "[it] has it all: a beautiful campus, a diverse student body (but always plenty of people like yourself), awesome athletics, an incredible array of great classes, and a million and one ways to get involved and pursue what you love." The school is a winner in students' eyes, even when they focus solely on academics. "Maryland has the kind of academic reputation that you'd like to see on a resume," reports one undergraduate. "We have awesome resources available to students, and there are even opportunities to work one-on-one with professors on research projects." Engineering and business offerings earn high marks. The school's proximity to Washington, DC makes it a solid choice for those interested in government and political science as well. Like the federal government (for which many grads will ultimately work), UMCP is "so large that a student is nothing more than a number." (Honors Programs remedy this problem for those ambitious enough to take on some extra work.) To help students deal with their often-impersonal educations, "all courses have an online component, with syllabi, announcements, message boards to contact teachers and other students, and often quizzes and class discussions, which is very helpful." Large classes offer "labs and discussions, usually run by TAs, but they [the TAs] are very knowledgeable and personable. They're also easy to contact and easy to relate to on an academic and personal level." Students conclude that "courses at UMCP are challenging, and many times incredibly difficult, but with great teachers, thousands of campus resources, and some good hard work, it is a great place to be."

Life

"Having a huge campus gives Maryland one advantage over the rest," students tell us. They also point out, "There's everything in the world to do here. From a number one nationally ranked Mock Trial Team to chorus groups and the highly visible Pride Alliance, there's something for everyone, if you can find it." Not to mention the school's many nationally ranked athletic teams. Undergraduates report that "basketball season is particularly fun, as the men's basketball games will make a sports fan out of anyone!" The university's location gets mixed reviews. Students dislike hometown College Park ("ugly and a little dangerous" and say "residents do not like students"), but love the campus (they think it is "beautiful," and there is "easy access to a variety of food") and its proximity to both Baltimore and Washington, DC. One student writes, "If you can't find something to do locally, there are tons of places to go in DC and Baltimore for students of all ages and interests. The metro trains and buses offer ways for students to get around without needing a car. The cities offer so many cultural things to do!"

Student Body

"You definitely see all kinds of people when you are walking across campus" at the University of Maryland. As one student puts it, "Nothing shocks me anymore. Each person seems to find her place, whether it's with the Satanic Mechanics (i.e., *Rocky Horror Picture Show* people), the Greeks, or the Solar House team." But while "Maryland has a very diverse student population, students tend to gravitate toward students more like them, mostly because the school is so large. It can become somewhat cliquish." Once you learn the lay of the land, "you can really tell where people fit in. All the sorority girls look the same (think headbands, Saucony sneakers, and Juicy Couture sweats). There is definitely a preppy-suburban look to most of the student body. Then there's still a bunch of people who have their own thing. So basically anyone can fit in."

ADMISSIONS

Very important factors considered include: Secondary school record, standardized test scores. *Important factors considered include:* Class rank, essays, recommendations, state residency, talent/ability. *Other factors considered include:* Alumni/ae relation, character/personal qualities, extracurricular activities, geographical residence, minority status, volunteer work, work experience. SAT Reasoning or SAT Subject Tests required. TOEFL required of all international applicants. High school diploma is required, and GED is accepted. *Academic units required:* 4 English, 3 math, 3 science (2 science lab), 2 foreign language, 3 social studies. *Academic units recommended:* 4 math.

The Inside Word

Maryland's initial candidate review process emphasizes academic credentials and preparedness. Through this first review, roughly 20 percent of the applicant pool is either admitted or denied. The remaining 80 percent are then evaluated in depth by admissions officers and reviewed by an admissions committee of seven, who collectively decide upon each candidate. Don't take essays and the compilation of other personal material that is required of applicants lightly. It's uncommon for a large university to devote this kind of attention to candidate selection. Perhaps this explains why so many of the students here made Maryland their first choice.

FINANCIAL AID

Students should submit: FAFSA. The Princeton Review suggests that all financial aid forms be submitted as soon as possible after 1/1. *Need-based scholarships/grants offered:* Pell, SEOG, state scholarships/grants, private scholarships, the school's own gift aid. *Loan aid offered:* FFEL Subsidized Stafford, FFEL Unsubsidized Stafford, FFEL PLUS, Federal Perkins. Applicants will be notified of awards on a rolling basis beginning on or about 4/1.

FROM THE ADMISSIONS OFFICE

"Commitment to excellence, to diversity, to learning—these are the hallmarks of a Maryland education. As the state's flagship campus and one of the nation's leading public universities, Maryland offers students and faculty the opportunity to come together to explore and create knowledge, to debate and discover our similarities and our differences, and to serve as a model of intellectual and cultural excellence for the state and the nation's capital. With leading programs in engineering, business, journalism, architecture, and the sciences, the university offers an outstanding educational value.

"University of Maryland—College Park will require the new SAT Reasoning Test. For students submitting an ACT score, the ACT with the Writing component is required."

SELECTIVITY

Admissions Rating	**93**
# of applicants	22,292
% of applicants accepted	52
% of acceptees attending	37
# accepting a place on wait list	2,530
% admitted from wait list	7

FRESHMAN PROFILE

Range SAT Verbal	560-670
Range SAT Math	590-700
**TPR Projected Range SAT Writing*	*600-680*
Minimum Paper TOEFL	575
Minimum Computer Based TOEFL	233
Average HS GPA	3.85
% graduated top 10% of class	53
% graduated top 25% of class	87
% graduated top 50% of class	99

DEADLINES

Regular application deadline	1/20
Regular notification	4/1
Nonfall registration?	yes

APPLICANTS ALSO LOOK AT

AND OFTEN PREFER
Cornell University

AND SOMETIMES PREFER
New York University

AND RARELY PREFER
University of Maryland—Baltimore County

FINANCIAL FACTS

Financial Aid Rating	**65**
Annual in-state tuition	$6,200
Annual out-of-state tuition	$17,500
Room & Board	$7,791
Books and supplies	$909
Required fees	$1,210
% frosh rec. need-based scholarship or grant aid	26
% UG rec. need-based scholarship or grant aid	27
% frosh rec. need-based self-help aid	24
% UG rec. need-based self-help aid	28
% frosh rec. any financial aid	70
% UG rec. any financial aid	60
Avg. frosh grant	$5,826
Avg. frosh loan	$4,691
Independent 529 member?	No

University of Massachusetts—Amherst

University Admissions Center, Amherst, MA 01003-9291 • Admissions: 413-545-0222 • Fax: 413-545-4312

CAMPUS LIFE

Quality of Life Rating	**68**
Fire Safety Rating	**72**
Type of school	public
Environment	village

STUDENTS

Total undergrad enrollment	18,378
% male/female	50/50
% from out of state	15
% from public high school	90
% live on campus	61
% in (# of) fraternities	3 (17)
% in (# of) sororities	7 (15)
% African American	4
% Asian	7
% Caucasian	75
% Hispanic	3
% international	1
# of countries represented	98

SURVEY SAYS

Great library
Students love Amherst, MA
Great off-campus food
Student publications are popular
Lots of beer drinking
Hard liquor is popular

ACADEMICS

Academic Rating	**69**
Calendar	semester
Student/faculty ratio	17:1
Professors interesting rating	64
Professors accessible rating	66
% professors teaching UG courses	87
% classes taught by TAs	13
Most common lab size	20-29 students
Most common regular class size	20-29 students

MOST POPULAR MAJORS

Communications studies/speech communication and rhetoric
psychology

STUDENTS SPEAK OUT

Academics

It is no secret to Massachusetts residents that their entire state university system, including its flagship campus at Amherst, has struggled with deep budget cuts in recent years. The school is doing its best under such less-than-ideal fiscal circumstances. As one student reports, "While struggling against major budget deficits in the state, UMass has done an excellent job keeping a strong faculty. And while classes are often too large, many professors compensate for this with abundant office hours and interesting teaching styles." The biggest problem caused by the cuts is "getting into classes that you want can be nearly impossible." One undergraduate explains further, "Students are now informed that they most likely will be here for more then four years because it is so hard to get into courses you want." For those willing to endure these inconveniences, the university has plenty to offer: still-reasonable tuition and fees, a universe of excellent departments, a faculty that includes "many leading thinkers," and access to the Five College Consortium, which broadens available offerings even further. Some appreciate another choice provided by the school: "The ability to choose to party every night or advance one's intellect with the incredible minds that are around (both students and professors alike)." Class sizes vary by major, but "all intro-level classes are large." The University takes a variety of steps to make the experience a little easier. Some professors, for example, "are great when it comes to e-mail response and personal help, if students needed it, [and] most of the text offerings are available on the Internet, which is a big help."

Life

"I have to give credit for the location of UMass," writes one student of the school's western Massachusetts Pioneer Valley setting. "It's in the middle of nowhere, but there are so many other colleges around it that you can always find people. It's also close to New York City, Boston, Hartford, and skiing up in Vermont." Students have no trouble finding entertainment in Amherst and its environs. The school's hometown offers "Uptown, which is what we call the downtown area, and it is always busy," while nearby Northampton offers a music scene and quaint shops. A little farther down the road sits Springfield, home to numerous dance clubs and the Basketball Hall of Fame. Not that anyone needs to travel that far to find entertainment. The University is home to so many parties that some students refer to the school as "ZooMass." One student explains, "Off-campus keg parties are huge at our school. Smoking marijuana is also very popular." There are also plenty of "intramurals, organizations, political protests," and all the other standard trappings of a large college campus. The Pioneer Valley, many students note, is ideal for "biking and hiking; the area also has awesome places to eat, shop, and just hang out."

Student Body

As at most large universities, there is a little of everything at the University of Massachusetts. Different groups are easily identified by their residences, undergraduates tell us. One student writes, "Those who enjoy normal mainstream culture live in the high-rises of Southwest. (It is also where the booze usually is.) Students who are more socially conscious and are open to diversity live in Central. (It is also where most of the drugs are.) Orchard Hill is usually more quiet and is filled with people who have a hard time in social situations, or those that would rather study than party. Northeast is filled with mainly computer science majors and Asian students. (The Asian-cuisine-influenced dining hall is also there.)" Despite such segregation by domicile, "everyone is forced to mix during the day on campus, and everyone seems to get along well," observes one student. "It is a good social environment, as you can meet any imaginable type of person, from anarchist to über-conservative, and can encounter everything from blank, unintelligent conversation to ones of brilliance that are difficult to wrap one's mind around."

University of Massachusetts—Amherst

Financial Aid: 413-545-0801 • E-mail: mail@admissions.umass.edu • Website: www.umass.edu

ADMISSIONS

Very important factors considered include: Secondary school record. *Important factors considered include:* Standardized test scores. *Other factors considered include:* Alumni/ae relation, character/personal qualities, class rank, essays, extracurricular activities, geographical residence, minority status, recommendations, talent/ability, volunteer work, work experience. SAT Reasoning or ACT required. TOEFL required of all international applicants. High school diploma is required, and GED is accepted. *Academic units required:* 4 English, 3 math, 3 science (2 science lab), 2 foreign language, 2 social studies, 2 academic electives.

The Inside Word

Gaining admission to UMass is generally not particularly difficult, but an increase in applications last year resulted in the university increasing its selectivity. Still, most applicants with solid grades in high school should be successful. UMass is a great choice for students who might have a tougher time getting in at the other Five College Consortium members.

FINANCIAL AID

Students should submit: FAFSA. The Princeton Review suggests that all financial aid forms be submitted as soon as possible after 1/1. *Need-based scholarships/grants offered:* Pell, SEOG, state scholarships/grants, private scholarships, the school's own gift aid. *Loan aid offered:* Direct Subsidized Stafford, Direct Unsubsidized Stafford, Direct PLUS, Federal Perkins, state loans. Applicants will be notified of awards on a rolling basis beginning on or about 4/1. Federal Work-study Program available. Institutional employment available. Off-campus job opportunities are good.

FROM THE ADMISSIONS OFFICE

"The University of Massachusetts—Amherst is the largest public university in New England, offering its students an almost limitless variety of academic programs and activities. Nearly 100 majors are offered, including a unique program called Bachelor's Degree with Individual Concentration (BDIC) in which students create their own program of study. The outstanding faculty of 1,100 includes novelist John Wideman, Pulitzer Prize winners Madeleine Blais and James Tate, National Medal of Science winner Lynn Margulis, and five members of the prestigious National Academy of Sciences. Students can take courses through the honors program and sample classes at nearby Amherst, Hampshire, Mount Holyoke, and Smith Colleges at no extra charge. Students can take classes in the residence halls with other dorm residents through Residential Academic Programs (RAP), and first-year students may be asked to participate in the Talent Advancement Programs (TAP) in which students with the same majors live and take classes together. And the university's extensive library system is the largest at any public institution in the Northeast. Extracurricular activities include more than 200 clubs and organizations, fraternities and sororities, multicultural and religious centers, and NCAA Division I sports for men and women. Award-winning student-operated businesses, the largest college daily newspaper in the region, and an active student government provide hands-on experiences. About 5,000 students a year participate in the intramural sports program. The picturesque New England town of Amherst offers shopping and dining, and the ski slopes of western Massachusetts and southern Vermont are close by.

"SAT or ACT scores are required for admission to the university. The school takes a holistic view of the student's application package, and considers these scores as only part of the evaluation criteria. Additionally, any Advanced Placement, Honors, and SAT Subject Test scores are considered when reviewing each applicant."

SELECTIVITY

Admissions Rating	**78**
# of applicants	17,930
% of applicants accepted	81
% of acceptees attending	29
# accepting a place on wait list	200
% admitted from wait list	50

FRESHMAN PROFILE

Range SAT Verbal	510-610
Average SAT Verbal	561
Range SAT Math	520-630
Average SAT Math	576
**TPR Projected Range SAT Writing*	*570-640*
Minimum Paper TOEFL	550
Minimum Computer Based TOEFL	213
Average HS GPA	3.29
% graduated top 10% of class	15
% graduated top 25% of class	45
% graduated top 50% of class	84

DEADLINES

Regular application deadline	1/15
Regular notification	rolling
Nonfall registration?	yes

APPLICANTS ALSO LOOK AT

AND OFTEN PREFER
Boston College
Boston University
Tufts University

AND SOMETIMES PREFER
Northeastern University
Syracuse University
University of Connecticut

AND RARELY PREFER
Quinnipiac University
University of Hartford
University of Rhode Island

FINANCIAL FACTS

Financial Aid Rating	**71**
Annual in-state tuition	$1,714
Annual out-of-state tuition	$9,937
Room & Board	$6,189
Books and supplies	$1,000
Required fees	$7,294
% frosh rec. need-based scholarship or grant aid	36
% UG rec. need-based scholarship or grant aid	47
% frosh rec. need-based self-help aid	34
% UG rec. need-based self-help aid	46
% frosh rec. any financial aid	61
% UG rec. any financial aid	76
Avg. frosh grant	$5,931
Avg. frosh loan	$7,052
Independent 529 member?	No

UNIVERSITY OF MIAMI

OFFICE OF ADMISSION, PO BOX 248025, CORAL GABLES, FL 33124-4616 • ADMISSIONS: 305-284-4323 • FAX: 305-284-2507

CAMPUS LIFE

Quality of Life Rating	**81**
Fire Safety Rating	**60**
Type of school	private
Environment	town

STUDENTS

Total undergrad enrollment	9,741
% male/female	41/59
% from out of state	45
% live on campus	42
% in (# of) fraternities	13 (14)
% in (# of) sororities	13 (10)
% African American	9
% Asian	6
% Caucasian	52
% Hispanic	24
% international	6

SURVEY SAYS

Great computer facilities
Great library
Athletic facilities are great
Diverse student types on campus
Students love Coral Gables, FL
Great off-campus food
Everyone loves the Hurricanes
Lots of beer drinking

ACADEMICS

Academic Rating	**83**
Calendar	semester
Student/faculty ratio	13:1
Professors interesting rating	76
Professors accessible rating	75
% classes taught by TAs	0
Most common lab size	10-19 students
Most common regular class size	10-19 students

STUDENTS SPEAK OUT

Academics

Fine academics, coupled with an unbeatable quality of life, are what draw students to the University of Miami (UM). "Studying doesn't seem like such a chore when you're studying in the sun, under palm trees, with an ocean breeze blowing," explains one student. Agrees another, "Attending University of Miami is like being on vacation all year long while at the same time having to put in a fair amount of work time." Pre-medical studies are a key drawing card here, as are the "good music and film programs." Students tell us that "for a large research university, UM is run efficiently," although they warn that "in the larger departments, where professors have more classes to teach, some simply have no time to meet students outside the classroom." Professors are generally good; "sure, you get a dud somewhere in between the outstanding ones, but overall the faculty is very impressive," writes one undergrad. Students also appreciate how "classes are taught in an interesting fashion with extra learning methods, such as trips to courts, films, the school's museum visits, etc., to keep it fun."

Life

University of Miami, students tell us, "is like a resort. You walk to class, and you pass the lake and all the palm trees, and it's just gorgeous." In fact, the idyllic tropical setting is the primary reason many choose UM. Students love the "amazing weather, as long as you don't mind buttloads of rain every once in a while;" the easy access to the beach; the "state-of-the-art fitness center that offers free exercise classes, an indoor pool, and a Jacuzzi;" and the hopping club scene in South Beach. "On Friday and Saturday nights, there's a shuttle to both South Beach and Coconut Grove, so a lot of people will go hang out there," students tell us; even so, most agree that a car is pretty close to a necessity here. "If you don't have a car to get out of Coral Gables, you have to lock yourself in your room and do some mind-altering substance," warns one student. Alcohol and drugs, students tell us, are easy to come by. Even so, many insist that "while there are lots of fun parties, this is not as big a party school as the rest of the world thinks." It is, however, a huge football school. Writes one student, "Football is life at UM. We have the best football team in the country. Every Saturday, the entire student body converges at the Orange Bowl to watch our Hurricanes romp their opponents."

Student Body

At "Club UM," the typical student "wears designer clothes to class and heels (if female), drives a BMW, has a cell phone attached to her ear (probably speaking another language, such as Spanish or Portuguese), works out every day of the week, parties at least three times a week, and (if female) has her books tucked away in her Coach backpack." This student "tends to be more concerned with their appearance than average and tends to be self-absorbed." Many "come from New York or New Jersey. There is a strong Hispanic population and a strong Jewish population." However, "there are a good number of atypical students as well, and they fit in simply by wearing normal clothes to class, less makeup, and not conforming to the superficial tendencies of the rest of the students." Many agree that the student body's most compelling asset is its sizable international population. "You learn a lot from classes, but you end up learning more from the people that you associate yourself with, so in the case of UM with its huge international population and range of students, you end up with a first-class education about the world," writes one student.

FINANCIAL AID: 305-284-5212 • WEBSITE: WWW.MIAMI.EDU/ADMISSIONS

ADMISSIONS

Very important factors considered include: Character/personal qualities, class rank, essays, extracurricular activities, recommendations, secondary school record, standardized test scores, talent/ability. *Important factors considered include:* Alumni/ae relation, volunteer work. *Other factors considered include:* Geographical residence, minority status, work experience. SAT Reasoning or ACT required. TOEFL required of all international applicants. High school diploma is required, and GED is accepted. *Academic units recommended:* 4 English, 4 math, 3 science (2 science lab), 2 foreign language, 3 social studies, 2 history.

The Inside Word

Over the years Miami has gotten far more national attention for the escapades of the 'Canes on and off the football field than it has for academic excellence. But anyone who takes a closer look will find national-caliber programs in several areas. Candidates who apply for the schools of music and marine sciences will face lots of competition and rigorous screening from the admissions committee.

FINANCIAL AID

Students should submit: FAFSA. The Princeton Review suggests that all financial aid forms be submitted as soon as possible after 1/1. *Need-based scholarships/grants offered:* Pell, SEOG, state scholarships/grants, private scholarships, the school's own gift aid, Federal Nursing scholarships. *Loan aid offered:* FFEL Subsidized Stafford, FFEL Unsubsidized Stafford, FFEL PLUS, Federal Perkins, Federal Nursing, Signature Loan. Applicants will be notified of awards on a rolling basis beginning on or about 3/15. Federal Work-study Program available. Institutional employment available. Off-campus job opportunities are excellent.

FROM THE ADMISSIONS OFFICE

"The University of Miami in Coral Gables, Florida, is an innovative private research university in a location unlike any other in the country. Located 10 miles from the vibrant international city of Miami, UM's 9,000 undergraduates come from every state and 114 nations, allowing people of many cultures to challenge and champion each other. Faculty work closely with students, and internships and research experiences are integral to academic life. Students work hard as community volunteers and exert leadership in a range of lively clubs and organizations, including the student-managed TV station, radio station, and newspaper.

"The University of Miami will accept either the new SAT or the old SAT (administered prior to March 2005 and without a Writing component), as well as the ACT with or without the Writing component."

SELECTIVITY

Admissions Rating	**95**
# of applicants	18,507
% of applicants accepted	42
% of acceptees attending	26
# of early decision applicants	380
% accepted early decision	47

FRESHMAN PROFILE

Range SAT Verbal	570-670
Range SAT Math	590-680
**TPR Projected Range SAT Writing*	*610-680*
Range ACT Composite	25-30
Minimum Paper TOEFL	550
Minimum Computer Based TOEFL	213
Average HS GPA	4.0
% graduated top 10% of class	62
% graduated top 25% of class	88
% graduated top 50% of class	98

DEADLINES

Early decision application deadline	11/1
Early decision notification	12/20
Regular application deadline	2/1
Regular notification	4/15
Nonfall registration?	yes

APPLICANTS ALSO LOOK AT

AND OFTEN PREFER
Duke University

AND SOMETIMES PREFER
Boston University
New York University
University of Southern California
Vanderbilt University

AND RARELY PREFER
Florida State University

FINANCIAL FACTS

Financial Aid Rating	**76**
Annual tuition	$14,510
Room & Board	$8,906
Books and supplies	$830
Required fees	$483
% frosh rec. need-based scholarship or grant aid	55
% UG rec. need-based scholarship or grant aid	52
% frosh rec. need-based self-help aid	41
% UG rec. need-based self-help aid	43
Independent 529 member?	Yes

UNIVERSITY OF MICHIGAN—ANN ARBOR

1220 STUDENT ACTIVITIES BUILDING, ANN ARBOR, MI 48109-1316 • ADMISSIONS: 734-764-7433 • FAX: 734-936-0740

CAMPUS LIFE

Quality of Life Rating	**83**
Fire Safety Rating	**60**
Type of school	public
Environment	city

STUDENTS

Total undergrad enrollment	24,677
% male/female	49/51
% from out of state	31
% from public high school	80
% live on campus	37
% in (# of) fraternities	16 (37)
% in (# of) sororities	15 (23)
% African American	8
% Asian	12
% Caucasian	64
% Hispanic	5
% Native American	1
% international	5
# of countries represented	117

SURVEY SAYS

Great computer facilities
Great library
Great off-campus food
Everyone loves the Wolverines
Student publications are popular
Lots of beer drinking

ACADEMICS

Academic Rating	**83**
Calendar	trimester
Student/faculty ratio	15:1
Professors interesting rating	71
Professors accessible rating	72
% professors teaching UG courses	72
% classes taught by TAs	0
Most common lab size	20-29 students
Most common regular class size	10-19 students

MOST POPULAR MAJORS

Economics
English language and literature
mechanical engineering

STUDENTS SPEAK OUT

Academics

"Steeped in academics, brimming with extracurriculars, full of opportunity for internships, happily obsessed with partying and football, and set in a fantastically beautiful city." That's the University of Michigan (U-M) at Ann Arbor in a nutshell, its students tell us. Academically, the university's "strong suits are its research and its diverse offerings. You can find any club, any class, any research job you'd like. If you can't? Start it. There's funding available for student organizations, and many departments also help others." As at most large universities, "it's hard to imagine a school that provides more academically, politically, and socially than Michigan. At the same time, there isn't anyone who will hunt you down to make sure you're taking advantage of what's around you. To succeed here, you need a certain degree of self-motivation to capitalize on all the opportunities." The reward for your work comes from "excellent academics, with nearly all the academic majors rated nationally near the top." Students warn to expect a "challenge from the rigor of the academics." They say, "Most students come here expecting to be blown away by their classes—and they are." Students who brave the challenge and see their way through to graduation experience another windfall of the Michigan experience, a "strong network of proud alumni. Graduates of the University of Michigan are proud to admit their alma mater and do everything they can to help out students and graduates."

Life

"There is definitely something for everyone" at the massive University of Michigan flagship campus, including "a vast abundance of organizations and athletics that give students opportunities to get involved. Also, the party scene is pretty big, especially in the warmer months." Athletics have a firm grip on the campus; students describe the intercollegiate teams as "amazing! What other school in the country has very good basketball, football, and hockey teams?" Intramurals are "also huge. Most students are very physically active; the gym's always packed." Campus entertainment offers a lot more than ballgames, though. One undergraduate reports, "This year there was the Royal Shakespeare Company's residency on campus and the opportunity to see the Bolshoi Ballet perform for a student discount rate of less than ten dollars." Hometown Ann Arbor earns students' applause. They tell us it is "a great city, lots of fun, [and] an ideal college town. Lots of little quaint shops, a good shopping mall, hundreds of amazing restaurants, and two movie theaters are in town. Plus, Ann Arbor is a very socially active town. If there's a cause, there's someone at U-M fighting for it." Students will put down the protest signs, however, to pick up a beer. "On the weekends," students tell us, "all people think about is partying! During the week, people are trying to get work done, so they can relax on the weekends, go to the football games, and go partying. Most people are pretty good at leaving the partying to the weekend."

Student Body

"It's amazing how diverse U-M is," students tell us, pointing out that "there are tons of East Coast/New York/Long Island kids," along with the "rich kids from the Detroit suburbs, people from all over the world, [and] everything from the trendy, work-hard play/hard Greek to the strictly nerdy study type to the earthy, hippie type." However, they also tell us, "Michigan seems to be more of a salad bowl than a melting pot. There is a variety of diverse students, but they oftentimes gravitate toward those of similar interest." While not all students are affluent, the well heeled are among the student body's most conspicuous individuals. One undergraduate writes, "Many students flaunt their wealth, from the frat boy or rich kid that dresses like a *Queer Eye for the Straight Guy* makeover to the rich girl who walks with a trendy cup of coffee in her right hand and a cell phone in her left."

FINANCIAL AID: 734-763-6600 • WEBSITE: WWW.ADMISSIONS.UMICH.EDU, WWW.FINAID.UMICH.EDU

ADMISSIONS

Very important factors considered include: Secondary school record. *Important factors considered include:* Character/personal qualities, essays, minority status, recommendations, standardized test scores, state residency, talent/ability. *Other factors considered include:* Alumni/ae relation, class rank, extracurricular activities, geographical residence, volunteer work, work experience. SAT Reasoning or ACT required. TOEFL required of all international applicants. High school diploma is required, and GED is accepted. *Academic units required:* 4 English, 3 math, 2 science, 2 foreign language, 3 social studies. *Academic units recommended:* 4 English, 4 math, 3 science (1 science lab), 4 foreign language, 3 social studies, 2 history, 2 academic electives.

The Inside Word

Making the cut at Michigan is tough—and is getting even tougher for out-of-state applicants, though the university definitely wants them in large numbers. There are simply loads of applicants from outside the state. If being a Wolverine is high on your list of choices, make sure you're well prepared, and since Michigan admits on a rolling basis—apply early! Michigan establishes an enormous waitlist each year. Controversies surrounding Michigan's approach to affirmative action have resulted in significant changes in the manner in which candidates are evaluated, with greater emphasis now given to aspects of candidates' backgrounds that are not quantified by grades and scores.

FINANCIAL AID

Students should submit: FAFSA, parent and student 1040 forms. Regular filing deadline is 4/30. The Princeton Review suggests that all financial aid forms be submitted as soon as possible after 1/1. *Need-based scholarships/grants offered:* Pell, SEOG, state scholarships/grants, private scholarships, the school's own gift aid. *Loan aid offered:* Direct Subsidized Stafford, Direct Unsubsidized Stafford, Direct PLUS, Federal Perkins, Federal Nursing, state loans, college/university loans from institutional funds, Michigan Loan Program, Health Professional student loans. Applicants will be notified of awards on a rolling basis beginning on or about 3/15. Federal Work-study Program available. Institutional employment available. Off-campus job opportunities are excellent.

FROM THE ADMISSIONS OFFICE

"Michigan is a place of incredible possibility. Students shape that possibility according to their diverse interests, goals, energy, and initiative. Undergraduate education is in the academic spotlight at Michigan, offering more than 226 fields of study in 11 schools and colleges; more than 150 first-year seminars with 20 or fewer students taught by senior faculty; composition classes of 20 or fewer students; more than 1,200 first- and second-year students in undergraduate research partnerships with faculty; and numerous service learning programs linking academics with volunteerism. Some introductory courses have large lectures, but these are combined with labs or small group discussions where students get plenty of individualized attention. A Michigan degree is one of distinction and promise; graduates are successful in medical, law, and graduate schools all over the nation and world. A year after graduation, more than 95 percent of U-M alumni report that they are in the "next step" of their career—whether that is graduate or professional school, working, or volunteering.

"Students applying as freshmen for summer 2006 or later will be required to submit the results from the new SAT or ACT (with Writing component). At this time, it has not been determined by the university how the Writing sub score will be integrated into the school's review process."

SELECTIVITY

Admissions Rating	**95**
# of applicants	21,293
% of applicants accepted	62
% of acceptees attending	46
# accepting a place on wait list	4,836

FRESHMAN PROFILE

Range SAT Verbal	580-680
Range SAT Math	630-720
**TPR Projected Range SAT Writing*	*620-680*
Range ACT Composite	26-30
Minimum Paper TOEFL	570
Minimum Computer Based TOEFL	230
Average HS GPA	3.72
% graduated top 10% of class	90
% graduated top 25% of class	99
% graduated top 50% of class	100

DEADLINES

Regular application deadline	2/1
Regular notification	rolling
Nonfall registration?	yes

APPLICANTS ALSO LOOK AT AND OFTEN PREFER

Brown University
Duke University
Harvard College
Princeton University
Stanford University
University of Pennsylvania

AND SOMETIMES PREFER

Cornell University
New York University
Northwestern University
University of Notre Dame
Washington University in St. Louis

AND RARELY PREFER

Boston University
Penn State University Park

FINANCIAL FACTS

Financial Aid Rating	**91**
Annual in-state tuition	$8,535
Annual out-of-state tuition	$26,754
Room & Board	$7,030
Books and supplies	$956
Required fees	$187
% frosh rec. need-based scholarship or grant aid	24
% UG rec. need-based scholarship or grant aid	24
% frosh rec. need-based self-help aid	50
% UG rec. need-based self-help aid	44
% frosh rec. any financial aid	50
% UG rec. any financial aid	44
Avg. frosh grant	$8,479
Avg. frosh loan	$4,311
Independent 529 member?	No

UNIVERSITY OF MINNESOTA—TWIN CITIES

240 WILLIAMSON HALL, 231 PILLSBURY DRIVE. SE, MINNEAPOLIS, MN 55455-0213 • ADMISSIONS: 612-625-2008 • FAX: 612-626-1693

CAMPUS LIFE

Quality of Life Rating	**79**
Fire Safety Rating	**60**
Type of school	public
Environment	metropolis

STUDENTS

Total undergrad enrollment	28,103
% male/female	48/52
% from out of state	18
% live on campus	22
% African American	4
% Asian	8
% Caucasian	80
% Hispanic	2
% Native American	1
% international	2

SURVEY SAYS

Great library
Athletic facilities are great
Students love Minneapolis, MN
Great off-campus food
Student publications are popular
Lots of beer drinking

ACADEMICS

Academic Rating	**74**
Calendar	semester
Student/faculty ratio	15:1
Professors interesting rating	65
Professors accessible rating	68
% classes taught by TAs	0
Most common lab size	10-19 students
Most common regular class size	10-19 students

STUDENTS SPEAK OUT

Academics

At the University of Minnesota—Twin Cities, students love "the opportunities and resources available by being a Big Ten school. We have amazing research, highly awarded faculty, lots of school spirit, internship opportunities, and a high public visibility." It's "up to you to carve your own path" here—no one is going to hold your hand, although at least "the advising facilities are excellent and the people who work there really do want to help"—but in return for their independent efforts, students enjoy "sooo many options and opportunities." A "strong medical program," a "great veterinary program," and an "excellent business school" are just some of the many top choices here; explains one student, "There really seems to be something for everyone. For students, that means you can come here not knowing what you want to do with your life, try out a bunch of stuff, and figure it out." The U's location yields some plum benefits, including "access to lots of local businesses, which translates into lots of opportunities after graduation." Students report that "the U does a great job trying to help students obtain enough experience and opportunities to make their post-college life better" through research opportunities and internships. Undergrads also love the "great study abroad and exchange programs."

Life

"The greatest thing about the U is always having something different to do," students tell us. They enumerate their many options: "In Minneapolis–St. Paul, the choices are endless: we've got Twins, Vikings, Timberwolves, and Wild games; Gopher athletics (hockey is huge here); concerts; movie theaters; special events like the St. Paul Winter Carnival; and tons of lakes and parks to visit during the summer. We also have our own separate campus community, where you just have regular old college students, hanging out at their house or the bar with friends." The school also has "student groups for every imaginable interest, and if you don't find one you like, you can start your own with three people and $15." Some here feel that "the social life is a little hurting" due to the large, diffuse nature of the student body, and they are glad that the University increased support for the Greek community, "because it helps in centralizing the social scene." Others are good with things as they stand. Just about everyone appreciates the "great infrastructure of tunnels and skyways to get between buildings" and "the wonderful campus bus system, without which it would be impossible to get around this big, spread-out campus." These assets are especially important during the long, cold winters, which definitely put a damper on certain extracurricular activities. "Party-hopping is difficult during the winter because it is so cold outside," one undergrad explains.

Student Body

"There are like 43,000 students here counting undergrad and grad students," writes one U undergrad. "The campus is a city to itself. There is every type of person here." Observes another, "One good thing about a school this size is that there is a little something for everyone. You can show up to class in sweats or in a suit, with blonde hair or green, and no one will look at you funny. Everyone can find a place here where they will fit in. The only problem you will encounter is that if you meet someone cool, you'll probably never see them again. You really have to make an effort if you want to make new friends." Because of its location, "nearly everyone is from either Minnesota or Wisconsin" and "there are many Somalis and Hmong among the minority population." The standard outfit here? "Backpack, coat, mittens, and a funny hat."

UNIVERSITY OF MINNESOTA—TWIN CITIES

FINANCIAL AID: 612-624-1665 • E-MAIL: ADMISSIONS@TC.UMN.EDU • WEBSITE: ADMISSIONS.TC.UMN.EDU

ADMISSIONS

Very important factors considered include: Class rank, secondary school record, standardized test scores. *Other factors considered include:* Character/personal qualities, essays, extracurricular activities, geographical residence, interview, minority status, state residency, talent/ability, volunteer work, work experience. SAT Reasoning or ACT required. TOEFL required of all international applicants. High school diploma is required, and GED is accepted. *Academic units required:* 4 English, 3 math, 3 science, 2 foreign language, 3 social studies, 1 history.

The Inside Word

Despite what looks to be a fairly choosy admissions rate, it's the sheer volume of applicants that creates a selective situation at Minnesota. Only those with weak course selections and inconsistent academic records need to work up a sweat over getting admitted.

FINANCIAL AID

Students should submit: FAFSA. The Princeton Review suggests that all financial aid forms be submitted as soon as possible after 1/1. *Need-based scholarships/grants offered:* Pell, SEOG, state scholarships/grants, private scholarships, the school's own gift aid, NSS, ROTC scholarships, academic merit scholarships, athletic scholarships, and aid for undergraduate international students. *Loan aid offered:* Direct Subsidized Stafford, Direct Unsubsidized Stafford, Direct PLUS, Federal Perkins, Federal Nursing, state loans, college/university loans from institutional funds, NSL, private loans. Federal Work-study Program available. Institutional employment available. Off-campus job opportunities are excellent.

FROM THE ADMISSIONS OFFICE

"Great academics: The University of Minnesota is one of the nation's top research universities. That means your college experience will be enhanced by world-renowned faculty, state-of-the-art learning facilities, and an unprecedented variety of options (150 majors and thousands of challenging courses).

"Great opportunities: Hands-on courses, mentor programs, volunteer opportunities, career counseling, internships, and research opportunities are part of the U of M experience. Plus, our Learning Abroad Center offers one of the nation's largest study abroad programs, with more than 250 opportunities in 60 countries: you can study art in Florence, agriculture in Morocco, or development in Kenya.

"Great location: Right on campus, you will find rolling green space, historic architecture, and breathtaking views of the skyline and river. And with a wealth of cultural, career, social, and recreational opportunities in the Twin Cities, there's no better place to earn your college degree! The Twin Cities metro is home to 18 Fortune 500 companies, and a recent survey ranked our area in the nation's top 10 in the "Bohemian Index" for the concentration of creative people.

"Great value: The University of Minnesota is a world-class, Big Ten, research university. We offer a fantastic education and prestigious degree at a competitive price. Residents of Minnesota benefit from in-state tuition. Residents of Kansas, Michigan, Missouri, Nebraska, North Dakota, South Dakota, Wisconsin, or Manitoba pay tuition rates significantly below nonresident tuition. Last year, we also awarded over $9 million in four-year scholarship packages.

"Freshman applicants for fall 2006 must take the new SAT (or the ACT with the Writing component). In addition, students may submit scores from the old SAT (before March 2005or ACT), and the best scores from either test will be used."

SELECTIVITY

Admissions Rating	**81**
# of applicants	14,724
% of applicants accepted	74
% of acceptees attending	47

FRESHMAN PROFILE

Range SAT Verbal	540-660
Average SAT Verbal	593
Range SAT Math	550-670
Average SAT Math	612
**TPR Projected Range SAT Writing*	*590-670*
Range ACT Composite	22-28
Average ACT Composite	25
Minimum Paper TOEFL	550
% graduated top 10% of class	30
% graduated top 25% of class	65
% graduated top 50% of class	92

DEADLINES

Regular notification	rolling
Nonfall registration?	yes

APPLICANTS ALSO LOOK AT AND OFTEN PREFER

Northwestern University
University of Michigan—Ann Arbor

AND SOMETIMES PREFER

Iowa State University
University of Wisconsin—Madison

FINANCIAL FACTS

Financial Aid Rating	**76**
Annual in-state tuition	$5,420
Annual out-of-state tuition	$15,994
Room & Board	$5,696
Books and supplies	$730
Required fees	$860
% frosh rec. need-based scholarship or grant aid	37
% UG rec. need-based scholarship or grant aid	34
% frosh rec. need-based self-help aid	40
% UG rec. need-based self-help aid	40
Avg. frosh grant	$6,346
Avg. frosh loan	$3,874
Independent 529 member?	No

UNIVERSITY OF MISSISSIPPI

145 MARTINDALE, UNIVERSITY, MS 38677 • ADMISSIONS: 662-915-7226 • FAX: 662-915-5869

CAMPUS LIFE

Quality of Life Rating	**84**
Fire Safety Rating	**60**
Type of school	public
Environment	village

STUDENTS

Total undergrad enrollment	11,765
% male/female	47/53
% from out of state	34
% from public high school	70
% live on campus	28
% African American	13
% Asian	1
% Caucasian	83
% Hispanic	1
% international	1
# of countries represented	68

SURVEY SAYS

Great off-campus food
Everyone loves the Ole Miss Rebels
Frats and sororities dominate social scene
Student publications are popular
Lots of beer drinking
Hard liquor is popular
(Almost) everyone smokes

ACADEMICS

Academic Rating	**70**
Calendar	semester
Student/faculty ratio	21:1
Professors interesting rating	66
Professors accessible rating	68
% classes taught by TAs	0
Most common lab size	20-29 students
Most common regular class size	10-19 students

MOST POPULAR MAJORS

Business administration/management
elementary education and teaching
marketing/marketing management

STUDENTS SPEAK OUT

Academics

For many, University of Mississippi—"Ole Miss" to friends—is as much a lifestyle choice as an academic one. "The best aspect of Ole Miss is the southern pride and the beauty that you experience," explains one undergrad. Students here single out the business school and programs in pharmacology and accounting for special praise; education is also a popular major. Professors, many agree, "are highly accessible and are willing to work with you and meet with you whenever you need to speak with them. They are also extraordinarily friendly, making an effort to talk to you if there seems to be something wrong." Administrators also receive remarkably high grades for a large state school: "The administration is incredibly supportive as well. I am so comfortable with the administration that I can walk up to the chancellor and start a conversation without a second thought," writes a typical undergrad. Students also love the strong alumni network and the McDonnell-Barksdale Honors College ("small, discussion-oriented classes"). Although the subject of some debate, the school's efforts to update its image wins many students' support; writes one, "The school is getting rid of the old symbols like the Confederate battle flag and things like that. They really are trying to make things better for all people," notes one student approvingly.

Life

You should know that "people either really like Ole Miss or really hate Ole Miss," and that the heavily Greek-oriented student population is "either studying or partying." One student says, "I've witnessed abstain from either or both." Football is the alpha and omega of fall semester; on game day "the Grove, a 15-acre park in the center of campus, is packed with tents. Under each tent, friends and family gather to eat and drink. Some people bring candelabras, white linen, and fine china. This is without doubt the greatest tradition in college football; it's Mississippi Mardi Gras." The Greeks, who claim one-third of the student body, are integral to the action. "On game nights fraternities have big parties at their houses with kegs and hooch." Students tell us that Ole Miss is "a huge party school." Students also note the "unbelievably beautiful campus. The trees [and] green grass in the Grove, the old historic buildings on the circle . . . there is nothing else quite like the atmosphere here at Ole Miss."

Student Body

"Ole Miss is the central meeting place of well-to-do southerners," a place where "everybody's father is somebody and every girl is beautiful and expects to get her way." "There are a lot of rich kids here," explains one student. "It seems like every other car in the parking lot is an Infiniti or a Jaguar or a Range Rover." Students extend the courtesies of southern hospitality, however, as "everyone is always greeting one another with a common 'Hello' or 'Hey, how are you doing?'" Under this veneer of cordiality, however, the student body is divided by "a very strong Greek system." Writes one independent, "You are an oddball if you are not in a sorority or a fraternity. We call them 'packs,' the groups of Greek guys and girls that roam around the town square and campus." While a demanding education can certainly be had at Ole Miss, it's also possible to glide through. "A lot of students don't come here to get an education. That's a major problem, but probably not the university's fault," writes one undergrad.

FINANCIAL AID: 662-915-7175 • E-MAIL: ADMISSIONS@OLEMISS.EDU • WEBSITE: WWW.OLEMISS.EDU

ADMISSIONS

Very important factors considered include: Secondary school record. *Important factors considered include:* Class rank, standardized test scores. *Other factors considered include:* Alumni/ae relation, state residency, talent/ability. TOEFL required of all international applicants. High school diploma is required, and GED is accepted. *Academic units required:* 4 English, 3 math, 3 science (3 science lab), 1 foreign language, 1 social studies, 2 history, 1 academic elective. *Academic units recommended:* 4 math, 4 science, 2 foreign language, 2 social studies.

The Inside Word

The admissions process at Ole Miss is relatively stress-free. Solid high school achievement in college-prep courses will open the doors for most applicants.

FINANCIAL AID

Students should submit: FAFSA. The Princeton Review suggests that all financial aid forms be submitted as soon as possible after 1/1. *Need-based scholarships/grants offered:* Pell, SEOG, state scholarships/grants, private scholarships, the school's own gift aid. *Loan aid offered:* FFEL Subsidized Stafford, FFEL Unsubsidized Stafford, FFEL PLUS, Federal Perkins, college/university loans from institutional funds. Applicants will be notified of awards on a rolling basis beginning on or about 4/1.

FROM THE ADMISSIONS OFFICE

"The flagship university of the state, The University of Mississippi, widely known as Ole Miss, offers extraordinary opportunities through more than 100 areas of study, including programs such as the Sally McDonnell Barksdale Honors College and the Croft Institute for International Studies. UM students are the only public university students in the state who have the opportunity to be tapped by the nation's oldest and most prestigious honor society, Phi Beta Kappa. Strong academic programs and a rich and varied campus life have helped Ole Miss graduate 24 Rhodes Scholars.

"The campus is diverse; 34 percent come from other states and countries and 13 percent are African American. Recent significant campus improvements include the $25 million Gertrude Ford Performing Arts Center and the privately funded Paris-Yates Chapel and Peddle Bell Tower. UM ranks 32nd in the nation among public universities for endowment per student. Ole Miss is home to 20 research centers, including the National Center for Justice and the Rule of Law, which provides training on investigating and prosecuting cybercrime; the William Winter Institute for Racial Reconciliation; and the National Center for Natural Products Research.

"The university is located in Oxford, consistently recognized as a great college town and as a center for writers and other artists. Like Ole Miss, Oxford is modest in size and large in the opportunities it provides residents, offering many of the advantages of a larger place in a friendly and open environment.

"Students applying for fall 2006 will be allowed to take either version of the SAT and are not required to take the ACT Writing section. The university will not consider the writing section of either exam when evaluated students for admission, but certain specialty programs may request these scores."

SELECTIVITY

Admissions Rating	**80**
# of applicants	6,999
% of applicants accepted	80
% of acceptees attending	42

FRESHMAN PROFILE

Range ACT Composite	20-26
Average ACT Composite	23
Minimum Paper TOEFL	550
Minimum Computer Based TOEFL	213
Average HS GPA	3.37
% graduated top 10% of class	35
% graduated top 25% of class	50
% graduated top 50% of class	77

DEADLINES

Regular application deadline	7/20
Regular notification	rolling
Nonfall registration?	yes

FINANCIAL FACTS

Financial Aid Rating	**70**
Annual in-state tuition	$4,110
Annual out-of-state tuition	$9,264
Room & Board	$5,610
Books and supplies	$900
% frosh rec. need-based scholarship or grant aid	21
% UG rec. need-based scholarship or grant aid	24
% frosh rec. need-based self-help aid	23
% UG rec. need-based self-help aid	30
% frosh rec. any financial aid	66
% UG rec. any financial aid	75
Avg. frosh grant	$4,243
Avg. frosh loan	$2,757
Independent 529 member?	No

UNIVERSITY OF MISSOURI—ROLLA

106 PARKER HALL, ROLLA, MO 65409 • ADMISSIONS: 573-341-4165 • FAX: 573-341-4082

CAMPUS LIFE

Quality of Life Rating	**63**
Fire Safety Rating	**78**
Type of school	public
Environment	town

STUDENTS

Total undergrad enrollment	4,023
% male/female	78/22
% from out of state	23
% from public high school	85
% live on campus	58
% in (# of) fraternities	27 (20)
% in (# of) sororities	24 (5)
% African American	4
% Asian	3
% Caucasian	83
% Hispanic	2
% international	2
# of countries represented	54

SURVEY SAYS

Class discussions are rare
Small classes
Registration is a breeze
Great computer facilities
Great library
Campus feels safe
Lots of beer drinking
Very little drug use

ACADEMICS

Academic Rating	**75**
Calendar	semester
Student/faculty ratio	14:1
Professors interesting rating	65
Professors accessible rating	68
% professors teaching UG courses	88
% classes taught by TAs	12
Most common lab size	10-19 students
Most common regular class size	20-29 students

MOST POPULAR MAJORS

Computer and information sciences and support services
electrical, electronics, and communications engineering
mechanical engineering

STUDENTS SPEAK OUT

Academics

Students looking for "serious, engineering studies" flock to Rolla, where "research programs and post-graduation job placement" are often listed among the school's strengths. The course work is "not designed for the lazy," and a senior tells us, "Most people here are highly dedicated, [which is] reflected by our average graduating GPA." Students relish this academic community, relieved "finally to be among my [intellectual] peers." Most students find their professors "very knowledgeable and easy to talk to" as well as "interesting and experienced." Certain respondents see the faculty as "research oriented," but others say they are "very involved with undergraduates." Instructors are known to "act tough," but a junior writes that those who are "aloof in class" can be "laid-back and human in the office." Students find themselves slaving for those top grades: "Nobody cares if you spend 30 hours a week in a two-credit-hour lab." Some students wish for more discussion in classes, complain about understaffing, and lament certain outdated facilities. But the "programs offered that assist students with their academic program and overall well-being" more than compensate for any shortcomings. However, they succeed in creating an atmosphere that "teaches great leadership qualities" and produces "graduates who know what they're doing," according to a junior in the computer engineering department.

Life

Life at University of Missouri—Rolla (UMR) revolves around academics, which is reflected in the buildings themselves, "built for utility, not art." One student writes, "The reason people come to school here is not to have fun," but many people appreciate that "the environment provides very few distractions from the education that I am paying for." Those looking for a respite from the "strictly business" vibe are "forced to be creative." That translates to "climbing the abandoned nine-story building or building flame throwers" with surprising frequency. Magic tournaments, computer games, and engineering design teams such as the "SAE formula car group" also occupy students' time when they aren't studying, and one respondent reports, "Role playing happens around the clock." (Meaning avatars, not French maids, we assume.) Rolla "ain't no place to party," and "people who like to drink a lot are unsatisfied because there aren't many bars," aside from the campus pub, The Grotto. The Student Union Board attempts to lure people away from the monitor's glow, but "a lot of people don't support campus activities;" however students seem to be gung ho about the school's annual St. Pat's celebration. Though the surrounding city offers "no malls or clubs," the Ozarks provide an outdoor playground, with plenty of places for caving, fishing, hunting, and hiking. In a typically practical Rolla statement, one student concludes, "We came for the engineering degree, not the city."

Student Body

At a school full of engineers and computer scientists, it's not surprising to find high representation of "somewhat introverted white males who rarely tear themselves away from the computer." Although they may "not get out much," certain students assure us that they can be "very nice and social when necessary." "Frat boys" add some diversity of personality to the student body, but some respondents feel that, at 30 percent, "too much of the campus population is Greek." Many of Rolla's young men complain about the paucity of women, but one Don Juan quips, "If you eliminate all the guys who are attached or just plain pathetic, the odds are pretty even." The ladies themselves mostly enjoy the advantageous ratio, but a female student writes, "Sometimes a female will run into a person who doesn't believe that girls can be engineers." Students perceive "factions of each minority," noting that "foreign students flock together and rarely interact with the rest of us." Overall, Rolla enjoys the harmony that comes from common purpose: "Despite the diverse campus, everybody seems to get along."

UNIVERSITY OF MISSOURI—ROLLA

FINANCIAL AID: 800-522-0938 • E-MAIL: ADMISSIONS@UMR.EDU • WEBSITE: WWW.UMR.EDU

ADMISSIONS

Very important factors considered include: Class rank, secondary school record, standardized test scores. *Important factors considered include:* Essays, recommendations. *Other factors considered include:* Character/personal qualities, extracurricular activities, interview, talent/ability, volunteer work, work experience. SAT Reasoning or ACT required. TOEFL required of all international applicants. High school diploma is required, and GED is accepted. *Academic units required:* 4 English, 4 math, 3 science (1 science lab), 2 foreign language, 3 social studies, 1 fine arts.

The Inside Word

This public university admissions committee functions pretty much the same as most others; admission is based on numbers and course distribution requirements. The applicant pool is small, well-qualified, and self-selected; despite the extremely high admit rate, only strong students are likely to be successful.

FINANCIAL AID

Students should submit: FAFSA. The Princeton Review suggests that all financial aid forms be submitted as soon as possible after 1/1. *Need-based scholarships/grants offered:* Pell, SEOG, state scholarships/grants, private scholarships, the school's own gift aid, United Negro College Fund. *Loan aid offered:* Direct Subsidized Stafford, Direct Unsubsidized Stafford, FFEL PLUS, Federal Perkins, state loans, college/university loans from institutional funds. Applicants will be notified of awards on a rolling basis beginning on or about 4/1.

FROM THE ADMISSIONS OFFICE

"Widely recognized as one of our nation's best universities for engineering, sciences, computer science, and technology, the University of Missouri—Rolla also offers programs in information science, business, and liberal arts. Personal attention, access to leadership opportunities, research projects, and co-ops and internships mean students are well prepared for the future. A 96 percent career placement rate across all majors and a 90-plus percent placement rate to medical, law, and other professional schools tell the tale; UMR offers a terrific undergraduate experience and value for your money.

"As of this book's publication, the University of Missouri, Rolla did not have information available about their policy regarding the new SAT."

SELECTIVITY

Admissions Rating	**88**
# of applicants	1,887
% of applicants accepted	79
% of acceptees attending	57

FRESHMAN PROFILE

Range ACT Composite	25-30
Average ACT Composite	27
Minimum Paper TOEFL	550
Minimum Computer Based TOEFL	213
Average HS GPA	3.5
% graduated top 10% of class	41
% graduated top 25% of class	71
% graduated top 50% of class	93

DEADLINES

Regular application deadline	7/1
Regular notification	rolling
Nonfall registration?	yes

APPLICANTS ALSO LOOK AT AND OFTEN PREFER

Massachusetts Institute of Technology
Truman State University
University of Illinois at Urbana-Champaign
University of Missouri—Columbia
University of Wisconsin—Madison
Washington University in St. Louis

AND SOMETIMES PREFER

Georgia Institute of Technology
Iowa State University
Purdue University—West Lafayette
Saint Louis University

FINANCIAL FACTS

Financial Aid Rating	**75**
Annual in-state tuition	$6,276
Annual out-of-state tuition	$15,723
Room & Board	$5,646
Books and supplies	$875
Required fees	$1,023
% frosh rec. need-based scholarship or grant aid	53
% UG rec. need-based scholarship or grant aid	50
% frosh rec. need-based self-help aid	39
% UG rec. need-based self-help aid	45
Avg. frosh grant	$5,900
Avg. frosh loan	$3,400
Independent 529 member?	No

UNIVERSITY OF MONTANA—MISSOULA

103 Lodge Building, Missoula, MT 59812 • Admissions: 406-243-6266 • Fax: 406-243-5711

CAMPUS LIFE

Quality of Life Rating	**92**
Fire Safety Rating	**99**
Type of school	public
Environment	city

STUDENTS

Total undergrad enrollment	11,302
% male/female	47/53
% from out of state	23
% from public high school	44
% live on campus	24
% in (# of) fraternities	6 (6)
% in (# of) sororities	6 (4)
% African American	1
% Asian	1
% Caucasian	83
% Hispanic	1
% Native American	4
% international	1
# of countries represented	60

SURVEY SAYS

Athletic facilities are great
Students are friendly
Students love Missoula, MT
Great off-campus food
Students are happy
Everyone loves the Grizzlies

ACADEMICS

Academic Rating	**73**
Calendar	semester
Student/faculty ratio	20:1
Professors interesting rating	71
Professors accessible rating	66
% professors teaching UG courses	99
% classes taught by TAs	9
Most common lab size	20-29 students
Most common regular class size	10-19 students

MOST POPULAR MAJORS

Business administration and management
education
psychology

STUDENTS SPEAK OUT

Academics

Students at University of Montana—Missoula (UM) love the gestalt of their school, telling us that "Missoula is one of the best places to be: friendly people, supportive faculty, a great sense of community, fantastic educational opportunities, and beautiful, beautiful scenery!" Montana receives praise for its offerings in a broad range of subjects—English literature, wildlife biology, business, and communications are just a few our respondents named—although students worry that recent state financial problems will cause some departments to shrink or even disappear. In the wake of budget cuts, many here resent the school's focus on intercollegiate athletics; "the contrast of the buildings on campus is ridiculous," complained a typical undergrad. "We have [a] fancy stadium and sport center, but we have [a] crappy and dilapidated math building, for example." Others gripe that UM sets the academic bar too low; "if you want to learn a lot, you must pay attention and study a lot out of desire. The course load is not very demanding," writes one student. For students seeking a greater challenge, "The honors college is a lifesaver. Honors classes are small and taught by many of the university's best professors. All the resources for an unmatched education are here, as long as you are willing to take responsibility for finding them." UM professors "are easy to relate to because they are in Montana for the same reason we are. Outdoor recreation!" They are also "very accessible and grade reasonably."

Life

"Missoula is definitely a granola town," students at UM agree. "Everyone is very earthy, into the environment and the outdoors." Campus life mirrors the life of the town; UM students tend to be hippie-ish, outdoorsy types who, atypically, love football. When not immersed in their studies, undergrads "are usually enjoying the amazing outdoor possibilities. Missoula is known for its beautiful mountains and streams, which lend themselves to almost any outdoor activity." Despite "three ski mountains within an hour," during the cold winters "activities are harder to come by." The social scene kicks up after the "Montana winter retreats in time for the summer-fire season." Students of drinking age enjoy a lively bar scene; "the nightlife for those over 21 is great. There are bars and places for you to hang out no matter what kind of person you are," explains one student. Life is less active for the under-21 set; as one student told us, "UM needs to improve on entertainment for students on and off campus who are under 21. There is nowhere to really go to dance if you are not of age. Besides going to the movies, bowling, and maybe ice skating, you are limited." Underclassmen can't simply fall back on the frat-party scene since "Greek life is not a huge thing here." In the fall, it's all about football; "Griz football is huge here. People live and die for their football around here."

Student Body

Students at UM are "very open and friendly. It is easy to meet people in any class or just out in the open oval." The student body includes "lots of people from the East Coast. Kids come out here, get into the laid-back vibe, turn into hippies (trustafarians, they're called), and 30 years down the road, they still live in Missoula. No one ever wants to leave!" Like hometown Missoula (but unlike the rest of Montana), "there is a very liberal sense of politics at UM. The town reinforces that, making it easy for a person to hold and stick to their personal values." Fortunately, "while people out here tend to be pretty opinionated, everyone still gets along royally. Students are very respectful of others." Most here agree that "the school community could use a little more diversity."

UNIVERSITY OF MONTANA—MISSOULA

FINANCIAL AID: 406-243-5373 • E-MAIL: ADMISS@SELWAY.UMT.EDU • WEBSITE: WWW.UMT.EDU

ADMISSIONS

Very important factors considered include: Class rank, secondary school record, standardized test scores. *Important factors considered include:* Extracurricular activities, talent/ability. *Other factors considered include:* Essays, recommendations. SAT Reasoning or ACT required. TOEFL required of all international applicants. High school diploma is required, and GED is accepted. *Academic units required:* 4 English, 3 math, 2 science (2 science lab), 3 social studies, 2 history, 2 academic electives. *Academic units recommended:* 2 foreign language.

The Inside Word

Montana's rolling admissions process places few demands on its applicants. Most students with a college-prep curriculum in high school and average grades should encounter no trouble gaining admission.

FINANCIAL AID

Students should submit: FAFSA, UM supplemental information sheet. The Princeton Review suggests that all financial aid forms be submitted as soon as possible after 1/1. *Need-based scholarships/grants offered:* Pell, SEOG, state scholarships/grants, private scholarships, the school's own gift aid. *Loan aid offered:* FFEL Subsidized Stafford, FFEL Unsubsidized Stafford, FFEL PLUS, Federal Perkins. Applicants will be notified of awards on a rolling basis beginning on or about 4/1.

FROM THE ADMISSIONS OFFICE

"There's something special about this place. It's something different for each person. For some, it's the blend of academic quality and outdoor recreation. The University of Montana ranks fifth in the nation among public institutions for producing Rhodes scholars and *Outside Magazine* lists Missoula in its top ten amazing places for outdoor recreation. For others, it's size—not too big, not too small. University of Montana is a midsized university in the heart of the Rocky Mountains—accessible in both admission and tuition bills—that produces graduates considered among the best and brightest in the world. It is located in a community that could pass for a cozy college town or a bustling big city, depending on your point of view. There's a lot happening, but you won't get lost. People are friendly and diverse. They come from all over the world to study and learn and to live a good life. They come to a place to be inspired, a place where they feel comfortable yet challenged. Some never leave. Most never want to.

"As of this book's publication, the University of Montana, Missoula did not have information available about their policy regarding the new SAT."

SELECTIVITY	
Admissions Rating	**74**
# of applicants	4,452
% of applicants accepted	93
% of acceptees attending	52

FRESHMAN PROFILE	
Range SAT Verbal	515-562
Average SAT Verbal	547
Range SAT Math	491-552
Average SAT Math	540
**TPR Projected Range SAT Writing*	*570-600*
Range ACT Composite	20-25
Average ACT Composite	23
Minimum Paper TOEFL	500
Minimum Computer Based TOEFL	173
Average HS GPA	3.29
% graduated top 10% of class	17
% graduated top 25% of class	41
% graduated top 50% of class	73

DEADLINES	
Regular notification	rolling
Nonfall registration?	yes

FINANCIAL FACTS	
Financial Aid Rating	**79**
Annual in-state tuition	$3,653
Annual out-of-state tuition	$12,642
Room & Board	$5,646
Books and supplies	$800
Required fees	$1,229
% frosh rec. need-based scholarship or grant aid	40
% UG rec. need-based scholarship or grant aid	42
% frosh rec. need-based self-help aid	47
% UG rec. need-based self-help aid	48
% frosh rec. any financial aid	81
% UG rec. any financial aid	85
Avg. frosh grant	$3,744
Avg. frosh loan	$2,807
Independent 529 member?	No

UNIVERSITY OF NEBRASKA—LINCOLN

313 N. 13TH STREET, VAN BRUNT VISITORS' CENTER, LINCOLN, NE 68588-0256 • ADMISSIONS: 402-472-2023 • FAX: 402-472-0670

CAMPUS LIFE

Quality of Life Rating	**84**
Fire Safety Rating	**74**
Type of school	public
Environment	city

STUDENTS

Total undergrad enrollment	17,137
% male/female	53/47
% from out of state	20
% live on campus	24
% in (# of) fraternities	13 (21)
% in (# of) sororities	18 (14)
% African American	2
% Asian	2
% Caucasian	86
% Hispanic	2
% Native American	1
% international	3
# of countries represented	115

SURVEY SAYS

Great library
Athletic facilities are great
Great off-campus food
Students are happy
Everyone loves the Cornhuskers
Intramural sports are popular

ACADEMICS

Academic Rating	**71**
Calendar	semester
Student/faculty ratio	19:1
Professors interesting rating	66
Professors accessible rating	70
% classes taught by TAs	14
Most common lab size	10-19 students
Most common regular class size	20-29 students

MOST POPULAR MAJORS

Business administration/management
psychology
teacher education, multiple levels

STUDENTS SPEAK OUT

Academics

Students at University of Nebraska—Lincoln (UNL) tell us that their school offers "the opportunities of a large school, but with a small school feel." Nebraska achieves its "small school feel" by dividing its 18,000 undergraduates into its undergraduate colleges: Agricultural Sciences and Natural Resources; Architecture, Arts & Sciences; Business Administration; Engineering and Technology; College of Education & Human Sciences; Fine & Performing Arts; Human Resources and Family Sciences, Journalism and Mass Communication, and Teachers. Further personal touches are supplied by "a very strong and prominent Greek system as well as one of the best residence hall systems in the area." Students brag that UNL offers "great access to research opportunities combined with good access to professors and community" and that "the full professors are quite good, although the TAs and graduate assistants often leave something to be desired." Even with all the intimate touches, UNL's scope can be a little intimidating; the resultant fears, however, are relatively easy to overcome. As one student put it, "My freshman year, I was scared to death of the large lecture halls. I took my parents' advice, though, and got to know my professors. I have discovered that they are there to help you if you just make a little effort to show that you need or want it." Surprisingly (considering this is a state school), undergrads report "very little red tape to deal with. Bills are easy to pay in person or online, class registration is a breeze, and any concerns I have had have been answered promptly by administration."

Life

Lincoln's nation of 18,000 Cornhuskers agrees that "athletics, both intramural and intercollegiate, are a big part of the culture at Nebraska. It has a unifying effect among students and impacts the social life of most. The best part of the school year is definitely the football season." There's more to life in Lincoln than game day, however. Students here enjoy an active social life that centers on the Greek houses (especially for those under 21) and O Street and its "30+ bars that are packed with college kids on weekends." Our respondents report that alcohol is popular "even though UNL is a dry campus. The rule is strictly enforced." Student opinions vary on hometown Lincoln. Some brag that "Lincoln is definitely a 'college town'" because "less than two blocks away [from campus] are the historic HayMarket, movie theaters, the Lied Center for Performing Arts, and the bar and club district." Others, noting that much of the entertainment near campus is limited to the 21-and-over crowd, complain that "there's not a lot to do in this town, so it helps to have good friends to spend time with." Summing up campus life, one student writes the following: "Sports and beer—that's Nebraska nightlife. People try to change and do different things, but it always comes back to sports and beer." Adds another, "Either you drink or you go to Bible study. That's it. And some people do both!"

Student Body

While most students at UNL "are from Nebraska or surrounding areas," "there are students from every state and many, many countries" at the university. "There are more minority and international students now than when I first started college in 1999," notes one senior, although most here agree that "there is not a lot of diversity on campus." A sizable number of students are "very religious," and "many of them try and force this on others, who do not wish it." On the upside, "most students are involved with at least one organization on campus," and "because football is so big and many of our other athletic teams are excellent (volleyball, wrestling, gymnastics, and bowling), there's a real emphasis among the student body on exercise and athletics."

FINANCIAL AID: 402-472-2030 • E-MAIL: NUHUSKER@UNL.EDU • WEBSITE: WWW.UNL.EDU

ADMISSIONS

Very important factors considered include: Class rank, secondary school record, standardized test scores. *Important factors considered include:* Talent/ability. *Other factors considered include:* Alumni/ae relation, geographical residence, minority status, recommendations. TOEFL required of all international applicants. High school diploma is required, and GED is accepted. *Academic units required:* 4 English, 4 math, 3 science (1 science lab), 2 foreign language, 3 social studies. *Academic units recommended:* 1 history.

The Inside Word

Like most large-scale universities, Nebraska—Lincoln admits a huge freshman class each year. The need for numbers is reflected in an admissions process that concentrates on them—your course selection, GPA, and test scores will be all they need to see. Unless you've had troubles academically, they're likely to welcome you aboard, though some programs have higher expectations than others.

FINANCIAL AID

Students should submit: FAFSA. The Princeton Review suggests that all financial aid forms be submitted as soon as possible after 1/1. *Need-based scholarships/grants offered:* Pell, SEOG, state scholarships/grants, private scholarships, the school's own gift aid. *Loan aid offered:* Direct Subsidized Stafford, Direct Unsubsidized Stafford, Direct PLUS, Federal Perkins, college/university loans from institutional funds. Applicants will be notified of awards on a rolling basis beginning on or about 4/15. Federal Work-study Program available. Institutional employment available. Off-campus job opportunities are excellent.

FROM THE ADMISSIONS OFFICE

"The University of Nebraska—Lincoln offers one of today's most dynamic college experiences.

"The university has developed a national reputation for its substantial out-of-state scholarship program. As a result, more students nationwide are finding that the university, with its strength in undergraduate education, its tradition of student engagement, its lively campus atmosphere and its connection to downtown Lincoln, is uniquely suited to provide an enriching student experience. The university delivers on the all-too-often empty promise of the friendliness of a private college with major university resources. It is no wonder alumni stay connected years after graduating and thousands of miles from campus.

"Established in 1869, the University of Nebraska—Lincoln has a rich tradition of excellence. Students join more than 200,000 alumni who have made their mark as industry leaders in business, engineering, the arts, journalism, education and the sciences. A degree from Nebraska opens doors. UN—Lincoln graduates recently interviewed on campus with major national companies like Abercrombie and Fitch, the Central Intelligence Agency (CIA), IBM, Microsoft, Sprint, Target, and The Washington Post. Attending UN—Lincoln also means you will have built-in connections with 116 graduate degree programs, including those in University of Nebraska Law, Dental, and Medical Centers located either on campus or 50 miles east in Omaha.

"Freshmen students seeking admission should either be ranked in the upper one-half of their high school class, or have received an ACT composite score of 20 or higher or an SAT total score of 950 or higher (Critical Reading and Math only, Writing portion not considered)."

SELECTIVITY

Admissions Rating	**78**
# of applicants	6,871
% of applicants accepted	74
% of acceptees attending	64

FRESHMAN PROFILE

Range SAT Verbal	510-640
Average SAT Verbal	576
Range SAT Math	530-660
Average SAT Math	596
**TPR Projected Range SAT Writing*	*570-660*
Range ACT Composite	22-28
Average ACT Composite	25
Minimum Paper TOEFL	525
Minimum Computer Based TOEFL	193
% graduated top 10% of class	28
% graduated top 25% of class	54
% graduated top 50% of class	85

DEADLINES

Regular application deadline	5/1
Regular notification	rolling
Nonfall registration?	yes

FINANCIAL FACTS

Financial Aid Rating	**79**
Annual in-state tuition	$5,268
Annual out-of-state tuition	$13,759
Room & Board	$6,008
Books and supplies	$850
Required fees	$675
% frosh rec. need-based scholarship or grant aid	43
% UG rec. need-based scholarship or grant aid	34
% frosh rec. need-based self-help aid	38
% UG rec. need-based self-help aid	39
% frosh rec. any financial aid	51
% UG rec. any financial aid	45
Avg. frosh grant	$4,995
Avg. frosh loan	$2,891
Independent 529 member?	No

UNIVERSITY OF NEW HAMPSHIRE

4 GARRISON AVENUE, DURHAM, NH 03824 • ADMISSIONS: 603-862-1360 • FAX: 603-862-0077

CAMPUS LIFE

Quality of Life Rating	**69**
Fire Safety Rating	**78**
Type of school	public
Environment	village

STUDENTS

Total undergrad enrollment	10,942
% male/female	43/57
% from out of state	41
% from public high school	78
% live on campus	56
% in (# of) fraternities	4 (9)
% in (# of) sororities	5 (5)
% African American	1
% Asian	2
% Caucasian	87
% Hispanic	1
% international	1
# of countries represented	28

SURVEY SAYS

Great library
Athletic facilities are great
Frats and sororities dominate social scene
Lots of beer drinking
Hard liquor is popular

ACADEMICS

Academic Rating	**73**
Calendar	semester
Student/faculty ratio	14:1
Professors interesting rating	63
Professors accessible rating	65
% professors teaching UG courses	90
% classes taught by TAs	1
Most common lab size	20-29 students
Most common regular class size	10-19 students

MOST POPULAR MAJORS

Business administration/management
English language and literature
psychology

STUDENTS SPEAK OUT

Academics

"University of New Hampshire captures the social appeal every student wants and provides every academic opportunity he or she needs," students at this midsize state university agree. With "so many students and majors it is impossible not to find some activity or major to interest you." UNH allows students to pursue their ambitions as aggressively as they like. Some choose to take advantage of the "excellent nursing and nutrition programs," "the awesome business school," "a great education program," "strong departments in music and computer science," an "incredible aggie school," and "one of the best programs for marine biology on the East Coast." These students tout the "excellent internships and study abroad programs" available here, as well as the "great research opportunities. The business kids are always working on outside projects, and every class I have had has ended with some type of individual research project. There are tons of opportunities for research grants from your sophomore year on. . . . The list is endless." Others pursue an "all play, no work" option, cruising through with a carefully chosen curriculum of easy courses. The presence of this latter group partly accounts for the perception that "UNH is really underrated academically." Undergrads warn that the school "lacks a personal touch at times, but in general, it works well for a university of its size."

Life

"The social scene is great" at UNH, where "the Greek system is strong and very involved in the campus community," and "there are also numerous sports clubs, intramurals, and other groups to get involved in." Undergrads generally "like to party, and the opportunities are plentiful. Along with UMass we're probably the place to go and party if you're going to school in the New England region." Observes one student, "Life is all about going to class in sweats and getting dressed up to drink. Classes later in the day are preferred and drinking isn't reserved just for the weekends; it's a week-long ordeal." While some here pride themselves on their partying prowess, others are not impressed; writes one, "I'm from the South, so I've seen what partying is really like at state schools like Georgia and Tennessee. UNH kind of pales in comparison." No one disputes UNH's primacy in college hockey, though; the men's team "is practically an annual participant in the Frozen Four. It's hard not to get caught up in the excitement of the UNH hockey season." The campus also plays host to "constant theatrical productions, comedians, fairs, and sports. Every weekend movies are playing for 3 bucks in the MUB (Memorial Union Building); they range from *Star Wars* to sneak previews of movies that aren't in theatres yet." Outdoor enthusiasts enjoy "at least one student-led hiking/ biking/ kayaking/rock climbing/ canoeing/ sky-diving trip per week, organized by the Outing Club." The nearby White Mountains ensure "great skiing," while the charming oceanfront town of Portsmouth and the Kittery Outlets in Maine mean great dining and shopping is just down the road.

Student Body

"Since we are a state university in New England, sort of in the center of the region, our demographics generally reflect that of New England itself," explains one UNH undergrad. Undergrads "are pretty run-of-the-mill, with a lot of them being local suburban kids from Concord and Manchester. There are some extremes—the hippies, the preps, the hicks, the nerds, the wannabe gangstas—but overall, there is not too much diversity at UNH. Just a lot of average-Joes." The student body includes "a lot of jock types. Athletics in all forms (varsity, club, and intramurals) is huge."

UNIVERSITY OF NEW HAMPSHIRE

FINANCIAL AID: 603-862-3600 • E-MAIL: ADMISSIONS@UNH.EDU • WEBSITE: WWW.UNH.EDU

ADMISSIONS

Very important factors considered include: Secondary school record. *Important factors considered include:* Class rank, essays, recommendations, standardized test scores, state residency. *Other factors considered include:* Alumni/ae relation, character/personal qualities, extracurricular activities, geographical residence, minority status, talent/ability, volunteer work, work experience. SAT Reasoning or ACT required. TOEFL required of all international applicants. High school diploma is required, and GED is accepted. *Academic units recommended:* 4 English, 4 math, 4 science (4 science lab), 3 foreign language, 3 social studies.

The Inside Word

New Hampshire's emphasis on academic accomplishment in the admissions process makes it clear that the admissions committee is looking for students who have taken high school seriously. Standardized tests take as much of a backseat here as is possible at a large public university.

FINANCIAL AID

Students should submit: FAFSA. The Princeton Review suggests that all financial aid forms be submitted as soon as possible after 1/1. *Need-based scholarships/grants offered:* Pell, SEOG, state scholarships/grants, private scholarships, the school's own gift aid. *Loan aid offered:* FFEL Subsidized Stafford, FFEL Unsubsidized Stafford, FFEL PLUS, Federal Perkins, state loans, college/university loans from institutional funds. Applicants will be notified of awards on a rolling basis beginning on or about 3/1. Federal Work-study Program available. Institutional employment available. Off-campus job opportunities are excellent.

FROM THE ADMISSIONS OFFICE

"The University of New Hampshire is a public university founded in 1866 with an undergraduate population of 11,000 students. UNH offers an excellent education at a reasonable cost to students with a broad range of interests. Over 100 majors, 2,000 courses, and 130 student clubs and organizations are offered. Programs that provide valuable experience include the honors program, undergraduate research, internships, study abroad, and national exchange. UNH's location also caters to a wide range of interests. The campus itself is in a small town setting, surrounded by woods and farms; within 20 minutes is the Atlantic coastline, and just over an hour away are the White Mountains, Boston, and Portland.

"University of New Hampshire will require all 2006 high school graduates to submit results from the new SAT or the ACT (with the Writing component). The first administration of the new SAT will be in March 2005 and the ACT in February 2005. The Writing portions will not be used for admissions decisions during the first 2–3 admissions cycles."

SELECTIVITY

Admissions Rating	**80**
# of applicants	11,587
% of applicants accepted	68
% of acceptees attending	31
# accepting a place on wait list	347
% admitted from wait list	9

FRESHMAN PROFILE

Range SAT Verbal	500-610
Average SAT Verbal	550
Range SAT Math	510-620
Average SAT Math	561
**TPR Projected Range SAT Writing*	*560-640*
Minimum Paper TOEFL	550
Minimum Computer Based TOEFL	213
% graduated top 10% of class	22
% graduated top 25% of class	63
% graduated top 50% of class	97

DEADLINES

Regular application deadline	2/1
Regular notification	4/15
Nonfall registration?	yes

APPLICANTS ALSO LOOK AT

AND OFTEN PREFER

University of Connecticut
University of Massachusetts—Amherst
University of Vermont

AND SOMETIMES PREFER

Boston University
Northeastern University
Providence College
University of Rhode Island

AND RARELY PREFER

Boston College
Syracuse University
University of Maine

FINANCIAL FACTS

Financial Aid Rating	**71**
Annual in-state tuition	$7,210
Annual out-of-state tuition	$18,240
Room & Board	$6,612
Books and supplies	$1,400
Required fees	$2,016
% frosh rec. need-based scholarship or grant aid	42
% UG rec. need-based scholarship or grant aid	36
% frosh rec. need-based self-help aid	56
% UG rec. need-based self-help aid	55
% frosh rec. any financial aid	83
% UG rec. any financial aid	78
Avg. frosh grant	$6,966
Avg. frosh loan	$6,203
Independent 529 member?	No

UNIVERSITY OF NEW MEXICO

OFFICE OF ADMISSIONS, PO BOX 4895, ALBUQUERQUE, NM 87196-4895 • ADMISSIONS: 505-277-2446 • FAX: 505-277-6686

CAMPUS LIFE

Quality of Life Rating	**73**
Fire Safety Rating	**61**
Type of school	public
Environment	metropolis

STUDENTS

Total undergrad enrollment	17,442
% male/female	43/57
% live on campus	11
% African American	3
% Asian	3
% Caucasian	49
% Hispanic	34
% Native American	7
% international	1
# of countries represented	56

SURVEY SAYS

Great computer facilities
Great library
Diverse student types on campus
Great off-campus food
Student publications are popular
Lots of beer drinking
(Almost) everyone smokes

ACADEMICS

Academic Rating	**72**
Calendar	semester
Student/faculty ratio	19:1
Professors interesting rating	63
Professors accessible rating	62
% classes taught by TAs	0
Most common lab size	10-19 students
Most common regular class size	20-29 students

MOST POPULAR MAJORS

Business administration/management
elementary education and teaching

STUDENTS SPEAK OUT

Academics

The University of New Mexico "offers a strong academic community with all of its many research opportunities [for] a bargain price," students at this large state university tell us. Excellent graduate programs in law, business, and medicine exert a trickle-down effect on the undergraduate divisions. Explains one undergrad, "We have one of the top 10 law schools and medical schools in the nation right now, and the undergraduate programs that lead into those schools want to make sure that at least some of their students get accepted and decide to attend one of these graduate programs." Students also praise UNM's offerings in pharmacy, psychology, architecture, anthropology, engineering, and sociology. With this many options, "even if you don't know what you want, you are bound to find something that you love." Students may find that something through UNM's interesting freshman-year options, which include courses designed to get students up to speed in writing, math, and research skills; freshman learning communities, a pair of team-taught interdisciplinary classes; and freshman interest groups, theme-based seminars that allow students to delve a little deeper into one of their core curriculum requirements. For top-ranked students, UNM's University Honors Program places students in small, seminar-style classes with an intensive focus on writing and reading.

Life

"Campus life can be as full of activities as one wants it to be" at UNM. A large student population means there are always plenty of extracurricular options. Sizeable commuter and nontraditional populations, on the other hand, ensure that many students aren't interested in them, as they visit campus only to attend classes. Commuters do appreciate the university's addition of a new student union building, "with three floors that include a movie theater, pool tables, computer labs, art studios, tons of food options, and many ballrooms and conference rooms. Lots of students hang out in the SUB in between classes." For residents and those who live close by, "there is always something going on, whether it's a dance show, a movie on the field, a cultural event, a sporting event, or any other casual activity. There are also a lot of opportunities for community service projects and political activism." Everyone gets behind UNM's "amazing athletics," embraced as enthusiastically by the city of Albuquerque as by UNM students. Basketball has a huge fan base here, while football draws tailgaters regardless of the quality of the team. Because UNM's campus is officially dry, "many students choose to go to local bars and downtown Albuquerque where there are many bars in one area" to socialize. Most students agree that there's much fun to be had in Albuquerque, "a fairly large city with frequent cultural activities (Zozobra, Balloon Fiesta, State Fair) that are really fun and interesting, especially if you are from out of state and haven't experienced them before."

Student Body

"UNM has students from all walks of life," which isn't so surprising given its undergraduate population of nearly 20,000. Many are nontraditional, are "roughly 25 years old, approach studies from a very practical perspective, and work a full-time job or close to it to pay for school." Observes one undergrad, "Because of its many nontraditional students, the school can sometimes feel too old or too young. UNM needs to work on integrating all students and finding activities that allow all age groups to interact." (Though any such efforts may be hampered by the fact that "most students are commuters, who are solely focused on earning their degree.") With "many Hispanic, Native American, Anglo, and other students," UNM is "extremely diverse." Notes one student, "There are so many different ethnicities here that racial discrimination really isn't an issue."

UNIVERSITY OF NEW MEXICO

FINANCIAL AID: 505-277-2041 • E-MAIL: APPLY@UNM.EDU • WEBSITE: WWW.UNM.EDU

ADMISSIONS

Very important factors considered include: Secondary school record. *Important factors considered include:* Class rank. *Other factors considered include:* Standardized test scores. SAT Reasoning or ACT required. TOEFL required of all international applicants. High school diploma is required, and GED is accepted. *Academic units required:* 4 English, 3 math, 2 science (1 science lab), 2 foreign language, 1 social studies, 1 history.

The Inside Word

UNM's rolling admissions process is quite typical of large public universities. Consideration is based nearly entirely on courses, grades, and test scores, though recommendations can sometimes help a candidate. Solid average students should encounter no difficulty in gaining an offer of admission.

FINANCIAL AID

Students should submit: FAFSA. The Princeton Review suggests that all financial aid forms be submitted as soon as possible after 1/1. *Need-based scholarships/grants offered:* Pell, SEOG, state scholarships/grants, private scholarships, the school's own gift aid, United Negro College Fund, Federal Nursing scholarships. *Loan aid offered:* Direct Subsidized Stafford, Direct Unsubsidized Stafford, Direct PLUS, Federal Perkins, Federal Nursing, state loans, college/university loans from institutional funds. Applicants will be notified of awards on a rolling basis beginning on or about 4/15. Federal Work-study Program available. Institutional employment available. Off-campus job opportunities are excellent.

FROM THE ADMISSIONS OFFICE

"The University of New Mexico is a major research institution nestled in the heart of multi-cultural Albuquerque on one of the nation's most beautiful and unique campuses. Students learn in an environment graced by distinctive southwestern architecture, beautiful plazas and fountains, spectacular art and a national arboretum . . . all within view of the 10,000-foot Sandia Mountains. At UNM, diversity is a way of learning with education enriched by a lively mix of students being taught by a world-class research faculty that includes a Nobel laureate, a MacArthur Fellow, and members of several national academies. UNM offers more than 225 degree programs and majors and has earned national recognition in dozens of disciplines, ranging from primary care medicine and clinical law to engineering, photography, Latin American history, and intercultural communications. Research and the quest for new knowledge fuels the university's commitment to an undergraduate education where students work side by side with many of the finest scholars in their fields.

"The university will continue to accept SAT or ACT scores, but does not require the Writing component at this time. The SAT Critical Reading portion will be used with the SAT Math to be considered in any admission decision based on formula. The use of ACT composite remains unchanged. These requirements are subject to change."

SELECTIVITY

Admissions Rating	**84**
# of applicants	9,752
% of applicants accepted	52
% of acceptees attending	59

FRESHMAN PROFILE

Range SAT Verbal	480-600
Average SAT Verbal	536
Range SAT Math	460-590
Average SAT Math	529
**TPR Projected Range SAT Writing*	*540-630*
Range ACT Composite	19-24
Average ACT Composite	22
Minimum Paper TOEFL	520
Minimum Computer Based TOEFL	190
Average HS GPA	3.31
% graduated top 10% of class	17
% graduated top 25% of class	44
% graduated top 50% of class	79

DEADLINES

Regular application deadline	6/15
Regular notification	rolling
Nonfall registration?	yes

FINANCIAL FACTS

Financial Aid Rating	**60**
Annual in-state tuition	$2,740
Annual out-of-state tuition	$11,381
Room & Board	$5,450
Books and supplies	$768
Required fees	$573
Independent 529 member?	No

UNIVERSITY OF NEW ORLEANS

AD 103, LAKEFRONT, NEW ORLEANS, LA 70148 • ADMISSIONS: 504-280-6595 • FAX: 504-280-5522

CAMPUS LIFE

Quality of Life Rating	**68**
Fire Safety Rating	**60**
Type of school	public
Environment	metropolis

STUDENTS

Total undergrad enrollment	13,225
% male/female	44/56
% from out of state	4
% from public high school	62
% live on campus	9
% in (# of) fraternities	2 (8)
% in (# of) sororities	2 (6)
% African American	25
% Asian	6
% Caucasian	55
% Hispanic	7
% international	2
# of countries represented	92

SURVEY SAYS

Small classes
Athletic facilities are great
Diverse student types on campus
Students love New Orleans, LA
Great off-campus food
(Almost) everyone smokes

ACADEMICS

Academic Rating	**69**
Calendar	semester
Student/faculty ratio	21:1
Professors interesting rating	66
Professors accessible rating	66
% professors teaching UG courses	80
% classes taught by TAs	3
Most common regular class size	20-29 students

MOST POPULAR MAJORS

Business administration/management
communications studies/speech communication and rhetoric
general studies

STUDENTS SPEAK OUT

Academics

"In the past, University of New Orleans wasn't always seen as a great public school," students at this mid-size state school note, "but in the last couple of decades, its reputation has improved greatly owing to the incorporation of cohesive courses of study, accumulation of progressive and insightful instructors, and low-cost tuition." Today UNO excels in a number of areas, including business (alumni "go on to do wonderful things in the business world," and students boast about the "high average of students passing the CPA exam"), English (the department is deemed "rigorous" by students, some of whom cite the demanding freshman writing program as a case in point), music (called "stellar"), engineering (UNO earns kudos as being "great for engineering"), and psychology (whose programs students rate "excellent"). Smaller but equally impressive offerings in naval architecture and marine engineering as well as film production demonstrate just how aggressively UNO "strives to provide educational opportunities to enhance the college experience" in a broad range of disciplines. "Like any school, there are great professors and terrible ones," points out a junior. That said, a number of profs here "go above and beyond to help students to succeed, including allowing the students to contact them outside of school if they need to, and including setting office hours around the times a student may need." The administration gets mixed reviews; many students grumble that it "is not as great as it could be" and that "paperwork is slow." A senior mitigates that with the affirmation that "the professors completely make it up to you by acting as dedicated mentors and advocates." Don't expect to slide by here, though; one freshman warns: "It's easy to get into, but hard to get out," undergrads warn. But for those who can make the grade, "UNO provides an equal opportunity for all people to get a superior education at an affordable price."

Life

"Student life at UNO is best enjoyed off campus," nearly everyone at this school agrees. Because most of the student population lives in New Orleans and commute to classes, the on-campus activities are limited"; "there is really no organized student life like you find on other campuses." Further, students gripe that dorms are "not in very good shape at all." Most here think that the addition of new student residences will "create more enthusiasm about campus life" but note that while new dorms are being planned, "they are years in the future." Another deterrent to campus life is the campus itself, which has "a lot of cement." Given the campus's lakefront location, some are disappointed that the university doesn't "capitalize on" its "many aesthetic assets." On a positive note, "the environment on campus gives no indication that Bourbon Street is minutes away…It's easier to separate school and play." When playtime rolls around, the great city of New Orleans beckons, tempting undergrads with "some of the best restaurants in the nation," not to mention "Bourbon Street, Harrah's Casino, the French Market, Riverwalk, and Jackson's Square. You can take a tour of Anne Rice's house, visit haunted plantations, hear great music at House of Blues, eats some crayfish, (pronounced 'crawfish'), and experience Mardi Gras for the best two weeks of your life."

Student Body

The "racial, and therefore cultural, diversity" of University of New Orleans is "the school's greatest strength," some here feel. UNO has a large nontraditional population—including graduate students, half the student body is older than 25—and "most students work either full- or part-time, except for the international students." A fair number of students "are already married and have children." Writes one junior, "The incredible diversity makes it possible for people of such wide ages and backgrounds to become friends and work together." Most students are New Orleans locals who are "pretty friendly," but because "this is basically a commuter school," students tend to come to campus "only to attend classes." That being said, "Everyone can find their niche here."

University of New Orleans

Financial Aid: 504-280-6603 • E-mail: admissions@uno.edu • Website: www.uno.edu

ADMISSIONS

Very important factors considered include: Class rank, secondary school record, standardized test scores. *Other factors considered include:* Alumni/ae relation, character/personal qualities, essays, extracurricular activities, interview, recommendations, state residency, talent/ability, volunteer work, work experience. SAT Reasoning or ACT required. TOEFL required of all international applicants. High school diploma is required, and GED is accepted. *Academic units required:* 4 English, 3 math, 3 science, 2 foreign language, 3 history, 1 academic elective.

The Inside Word

It doesn't really get any more direct than the admissions process at UNO. The primary emphasis in candidate evaluation at this public university on the shores of Lake Ponchartrain is on test scores. If you've got a 950 combined SAT or a 20 composite on the ACT, you'll get in with minimal hassle. Course selection and GPA get the rest of the admissions committee's attention.

FINANCIAL AID

Students should submit: FAFSA, institution's own financial aid form. The Princeton Review suggests that all financial aid forms be submitted as soon as possible after 1/1. *Need-based scholarships/grants offered:* Pell, SEOG, state scholarships/grants, private scholarships, the school's own gift aid. *Loan aid offered:* FFEL Subsidized Stafford, FFEL Unsubsidized Stafford, FFEL PLUS, Federal Perkins, college/university loans from institutional funds. Applicants will be notified of awards on a rolling basis beginning on or about 4/20. Federal Work-study Program available. Institutional employment available. Off-campus job opportunities are good.

FROM THE ADMISSIONS OFFICE

"Knowledge is perishable and careers inconstant. Corporate and government leaders are looking to higher education for solutions to their immediate needs. The University of New Orleans provides these leaders with graduates who can contribute to the economic, social, and academic growth of their industries now and into the future. UNO embraces its mission by providing the best educational opportunities for undergraduate and graduate students, conducting world-class research, and serving a diverse community in critical areas. The university's general level of excellence is reflected in its students and faculty. Its Centers of Excellence, which address important community needs, are recognized as among the best in the world. UNO's most outstanding offerings include a doctoral program in conservation biology providing training in the most advanced molecular biological techniques; the largest U.S. undergraduate program in naval architecture and marine engineering; one of the top 25 film programs in the country; and the only graduate arts administration program in the Gulf South.

"UNO will use the total score from the Critical Reading/Verbal and Math sub sections of both the old and new SAT or the composite score for the ACT. The Writing components of the ACT and SAT will be used for placement purposes, but not for admission purposes, at the current time."

SELECTIVITY

Admissions Rating	**75**
# of applicants	6,197
% of applicants accepted	63
% of acceptees attending	52

FRESHMAN PROFILE

Range SAT Verbal	450-590
Average SAT Verbal	524
Range SAT Math	450-580
Average SAT Math	517
**TPR Projected Range SAT Writing*	*520-620*
Range ACT Composite	18-23
Average ACT Composite	21
Minimum Paper TOEFL	550
Minimum Computer Based TOEFL	213
Average HS GPA	2.94
% graduated top 10% of class	11
% graduated top 25% of class	32
% graduated top 50% of class	60

DEADLINES

Regular application deadline	8/30
Regular notification	rolling
Nonfall registration?	yes

APPLICANTS ALSO LOOK AT AND OFTEN PREFER

Louisiana State University

FINANCIAL FACTS

Financial Aid Rating	**63**
Annual in-state tuition	$3,184
Annual out-of-state tuition	$10,228
Room & Board	$4,590
Books and supplies	$1,000
Required fees	$518
% frosh rec. need-based scholarship or grant aid	43
% UG rec. need-based scholarship or grant aid	38
% frosh rec. need-based self-help aid	36
% UG rec. need-based self-help aid	39
% frosh rec. any financial aid	85
% UG rec. any financial aid	70
Avg. frosh grant	$3,845
Avg. frosh loan	$3,427
Independent 529 member?	No

UNIV. OF NORTH CAROLINA—ASHEVILLE

CPO #2210, 117 LIPINSKY HALL, ASHEVILLE, NC 28804-8510 • ADMISSIONS: 828-251-6481 • FAX: 828-251-6482

CAMPUS LIFE

Quality of Life Rating	**89**
Fire Safety Rating	**97**
Type of school	public
Environment	town

STUDENTS

Total undergrad enrollment	3,232
% male/female	42/58
% from out of state	14
% from public high school	87
% live on campus	39
% in (# of) fraternities	3 (4)
% in (# of) sororities	3 (2)
% African American	3
% Asian	1
% Caucasian	90
% Hispanic	2
% international	1
# of countries represented	28

SURVEY SAYS

Small classes
Great library
Students are friendly
Students love Asheville, NC
Great off-campus food
Campus feels safe
Students are happy

ACADEMICS

Academic Rating	**84**
Calendar	semester
Student/faculty ratio	14:1
Professors interesting rating	94
Professors accessible rating	86
% professors teaching UG courses	100
% classes taught by TAs	0
Most common lab size	10-19 students
Most common regular class size	20-29 students

MOST POPULAR MAJORS

Business administration/management
environmental studies
psychology

STUDENTS SPEAK OUT

Academics

At the University of North Carolina (UNC)—Asheville, the emphasis lies on the "freedom of the individual mind." The "challenging liberal arts curriculum," with a "major emphasis on the humanities and social sciences," provides an environment that "encourages you to think." The professors "know who you are and care about how you do," displaying not only impressive academic credentials but "a desire to actually teach and help their students in and out of class." Many faculty members "keep in active contact with their students through e-mail" and take time to address personal concerns as well as classroom issues. When the material gets overwhelming, "help is always available, and professors do not mind putting in overtime to help you understand a concept." One student reports easy interpersonal relations, assuring readers, "I could ask a prof to have coffee and this would not be weird." The administration functions transparently according to students: "They're there, but you would hardly know it unless you need to find them." The chancellor garners popularity by showing up "not only at events, but sometimes just in the dining hall. He is very warm and keeps a good relationship with the student body." Generally, the higher-ups "do not interfere in the lives of students," and the only complaint we hear is that "the state school penny-pinching is extremely evident." Finances aside, the staff, administration, and faculty combine to facilitate a "liberating education based on what life really means."

Life

Students flock to this UNC campus "for the liberal atmosphere that Asheville provides." Known as a progressive and "completely college-friendly" town, Asheville "caters to the granola heads" and ensures that "there is a new cause on campus every week, from Amnesty International to trout ponds. Capitalism is a dirty word, and the views are socialistic." The picturesque mountain setting only adds to this bohemian lifestyle. Some students gripe, "The weekends are generally kind of dead around here" because people go home or hang out off campus. Other respondents qualify that judgment: "Those who complain of having nothing to do are only looking on campus, so if that is what a potential student is looking for, they may get bored here." On the fiesta front, "getting drunk is, like, a pastime, and frat parties are widely known," but many students agree that "drinking and partying are not really a priority because of all the other things offered either on campus or in town." Options include "plenty of pizza places and movie theatres," "lots of art galleries," "hanging out and watching TV," and "studying the *Bible*." Student organizations occupy free time, and many undergraduates join them "not only to become involved, but [also] to rise to leadership positions."

Student Body

Students at UNC—Asheville manage to strike the typically elusive balance of being "very mellow and down to earth, but surprisingly driven." These "children of Deadheads" and "mountain people" tend to be "environmentally friendly types," but "plenty of nonhippies, some rednecks, and a small but growing population of ethnic minorities" round out the student body. To put it bluntly, "this school is extremely white and unaware of the lack of race relations," according to one student, and many people would encourage the school to "make itself available to more students of varying ethnic backgrounds." Others contend, "We don't have many minorities, but we have a broad diversity in the types of people we do have." Reportedly, atypical students "are accepted here without question," but though they "fit in fine," they "tend not to mingle." Thanks to an open-minded atmosphere and common interests among the population, "most of the time one sees smiles on the faces of the students here."

UNIVERSITY OF NORTH CAROLINA—ASHEVILLE

FINANCIAL AID: 828-251-6535 • E-MAIL: ADMISSIONS@UNCA.EDU • WEBSITE: WWW.UNCA.EDU

ADMISSIONS

Very important factors considered include: Class rank, secondary school record. *Important factors considered include:* Standardized test scores. *Other factors considered include:* Alumni/ae relation, character/personal qualities, essays, extracurricular activities, geographical residence, interview, minority status, recommendations, state residency, talent/ability, volunteer work, work experience. SAT Reasoning or ACT required. TOEFL required of all international applicants. High school diploma is required, and GED is not accepted. *Academic units required:* 4 English, 3 math, 3 science (2 science lab), 2 foreign language, 1 social studies, 1 history. *Academic units recommended:* 4 English, 4 math, 4 science (3 science lab), 3 foreign language, 1 social studies, 1 history, 4 academic electives.

The Inside Word

UNC—Asheville is one of those relatively unknown gems in higher education. Recent publicity has fueled increases in applications and in turn boosted selectivity. The university is dynamic and eager to take advantage of this newfound recognition. No doubt admissions will become more and more competitive as the cycle repeats itself. For students who seek a public education in a smaller campus environment than places like Chapel Hill, this is a great choice.

FINANCIAL AID

Students should submit: FAFSA. The Princeton Review suggests that all financial aid forms be submitted as soon as possible after 1/1. *Need-based scholarships/grants offered:* Pell, SEOG, state scholarships/grants, private scholarships, the school's own gift aid. *Loan aid offered:* Direct Subsidized Stafford, Direct Unsubsidized Stafford, Direct PLUS, Federal Perkins, state loans, college/university loans from institutional funds. Applicants will be notified of awards on a rolling basis beginning on or about 3/15. Federal Work-study Program available. Off-campus job opportunities are good.

FROM THE ADMISSIONS OFFICE

"If you want to learn how to think, how to analyze and solve problems on your own, and how to become your own best teacher, a broad-based liberal arts education is the key. UNC—Asheville focuses on undergraduates, with a core curriculum covering humanities, language and culture, arts and ideas, and health and fitness. Students thrive in small classes, with a faculty dedicated first of all to teaching. The liberal arts emphasis develops discriminating thinkers, expert and creative communicators with a passion for learning. These are qualities you need for today's challenges and the changes of tomorrow.

"The University of North Carolina—Asheville will require the new SAT Reasoning Test. For students submitting an ACT score, the ACT with the Writing component is required."

SELECTIVITY

Admissions Rating	**84**
# of applicants	2,571
% of applicants accepted	73
% of acceptees attending	38

FRESHMAN PROFILE

Range SAT Verbal	540-650
Average SAT Verbal	593
Range SAT Math	520-620
Average SAT Math	576
**TPR Projected Range SAT Writing*	*590-670*
Range ACT Composite	22-27
Average ACT Composite	24
Minimum Paper TOEFL	550
Minimum Computer Based TOEFL	213
Average HS GPA	3.7
% graduated top 10% of class	21
% graduated top 25% of class	58
% graduated top 50% of class	94

DEADLINES

Regular application deadline	3/1
Regular notification	4/1
Nonfall registration?	yes

FINANCIAL FACTS

Financial Aid Rating	**79**
Annual in-state tuition	$1,897
Annual out-of-state tuition	$11,097
Room & Board	$5,212
Books and supplies	$850
Required fees	$1,495
% frosh rec. need-based scholarship or grant aid	36
% UG rec. need-based scholarship or grant aid	36
% frosh rec. need-based self-help aid	30
% UG rec. need-based self-help aid	33
% frosh rec. any financial aid	61
% UG rec. any financial aid	59
Avg. frosh grant	$3,780
Avg. frosh loan	$4,928
Independent 529 member?	No

UNIV. OF NORTH CAROLINA—CHAPEL HILL

JACKSON HALL 153A, CAMPUS BOX #2200, CHAPEL HILL, NC 27599 • ADMISSIONS: 919-966-3621 • FAX: 919-962-3045

CAMPUS LIFE

Quality of Life Rating	**94**
Fire Safety Rating	**87**
Type of school	public
Environment	town

STUDENTS

Total undergrad enrollment	16,065
% male/female	42/58
% from out of state	18
% from public high school	85
% live on campus	43
% African American	11
% Asian	6
% Caucasian	74
% Hispanic	3
% Native American	1
% international	1
# of countries represented	102

SURVEY SAYS

Great library
Students love Chapel Hill, NC
Students are happy
Everyone loves the Tar Heels
Student publications are popular

ACADEMICS

Academic Rating	**80**
Calendar	semester
Student/faculty ratio	14:1
Professors interesting rating	79
Professors accessible rating	72
% classes taught by TAs	0
Most common lab size	10-19 students
Most common regular class size	10-19 students

MOST POPULAR MAJORS

Biology/biological sciences
mass communications/media studies
psychology

STUDENTS SPEAK OUT

Academics

The University of North Carolina—Chapel Hill "is so well rounded," according to students who make their case by pointing to the "very highly recognized academics, sports, and quality students who are here to get a great education and have fun doing it." With a typically Southern approach, UNC "creates a very balanced atmosphere to live in. The workload isn't so overwhelming that you can't go out and do anything.... It makes for a good place to live because people aren't always stressed out." Undergrads report that "You won't find a better combination of quality, cost, and environment for any student specifically interested in undergraduate programs in business, journalism, or education," and that "the humanities and social sciences have a huge presence here" as well. The sciences aren't too shabby either; in fact, pretty much across the board "the academic life is very rigorous" and professors "are not only educated in their fields but have life experiences that add to the flavor of their courses." Many students warn that academic advising is a weak point; reports one student, "We have complicated requirements for majors and...sometimes students end up taking classes that don't count toward their major. Or, they end up not realizing they had to take a particular class until senior year." The Constitution of the state of North Carolina keeps UNC's in-state tuition rates very low; some out-of-state students complain that the cost of this guarantee falls disproportionately to them.

Life

"UNC has a great nightlife" with plenty of options. Franklin Street, the main drag of Chapel Hill, runs along one side of the campus and "has tons of restaurants," "packed bars," and college-oriented shopping. "Students from Duke and NC State will often come party on Franklin Street" because it's the most student-friendly stretch in the Triangle. The campus offers "tons of clubs and organizations—almost 600—so there is plenty of stuff to do." The dorms "are wonderful, and there is always something going on," although "dorm parties are hard to pull off on South Campus, where most of the freshmen live. Just about anything goes on North Campus, though." The active Greek scene also provides plenty of party options; GDIs note that "it's really easy to have a social life and be an independent." But what truly binds the campus are the Tar Heel athletic teams, with the men's basketball team paramount among them. Reports one student, "People look forward to basketball season more than anything. The rivalries are intense" and the quality of play is excellent: the Atlantic Coast Conference is arguably the NCAA's strongest in basketball. Students also enjoy a "beautiful campus" and great weather; observes one student, "One of the most relaxing things to do is to sit outside on the grass in the quad studying in the 70 degree weather and sun in November."

Student Body

By state law, native Tar Heels must make up 82 percent of each incoming undergraduate class at UNC, so "the typical student is a North Carolina resident." Out-of-state students "blend seamlessly into this mix, and are often the ones to take the helm of leadership opportunities." Undergraduates here "are very involved, whether it's in the Greek scene, the religious scene, playing intramural sports, or starting their own club. Philanthropic involvement is also high." Students typically "are academically oriented but aren't dominated by it. You can't 'feel' midterms in the air, as you can at other schools." You'll "find every stereotype represented here: the J. Crew snob, the polo shirt & sunglass-wearing frat boy, the emo/punk rocker, the Southern belle, etc." The most apparent stereotypes, though, are "the ones who look like they stepped out of the Carolina catalogue, sporting Carolina-blue laptop bags, polo shirts, and sneakers." UNC is liberal by Southern standards, although no one would ever confuse a UNC undergrad for a Reed College or Wesleyan University student.

FINANCIAL AID: 919-962-8396 • E-MAIL: UADM@EMAIL.UNC.EDU • WEBSITE: WWW.UNC.EDU

ADMISSIONS

Very important factors considered include: Character/personal qualities, class rank, essays, extracurricular activities, recommendations, secondary school record, standardized test scores, state residency, talent/ability. *Important factors considered include:* Alumni/ae relation, minority status, volunteer work, work experience. SAT Reasoning or ACT required. TOEFL required of all international applicants. High school diploma is required, and GED is not accepted. *Academic units required:* 4 English, 3 math, 3 science (1 science lab), 2 foreign language, 2 social studies, 2 academic electives. *Academic units recommended:* 4 English, 4 math, 4 science (1 science lab), 4 foreign language, 3 social studies.

The Inside Word

UNC's admissions process is highly selective. North Carolina students compete against other students from across the state for 82 percent of all spaces available in the freshman class; out-of-state students compete for the remaining 18 percent of the spaces. State residents will find the admissions standards high, and out-of-state applicants will find that it's one of the hardest offers of admission to come by in the country.

FINANCIAL AID

Students should submit: FAFSA, CSS/Financial Aid PROFILE. The Princeton Review suggests that all financial aid forms be submitted as soon as possible after 1/1. *Need-based scholarships/grants offered:* Pell, SEOG, state scholarships/grants, private scholarships, the school's own gift aid, State grants. *Loan aid offered:* FFEL Subsidized Stafford, FFEL Unsubsidized Stafford, FFEL PLUS, Federal Perkins, state loans, college/university loans from institutional funds, alternative loans. Applicants will be notified of awards on a rolling basis beginning on or about 3/15. Federal Work-study Program available. Institutional employment available. Off-campus job opportunities are good.

FROM THE ADMISSIONS OFFICE

"One of the leading research and teaching institutions in the world, UNC—Chapel Hill offers first-rate faculty, innovative academic programs, and students who are smart, friendly, and committed to public service. Students take full advantage of extensive undergraduate research opportunities, a study abroad program with programs on every continent except Antarctica, and 500 plus clubs and organizations. We offer all this in Chapel Hill, one of the greatest and most welcoming college towns anywhere.

"Carolina's commitment to excellence, access, and affordability is reflected in premier scholarships, such as the prestigious Morehead and Robertson Scholarships, as well the Carolina Covenant, a landmark program that enables students from low-income families to graduate from Carolina debt-free. We invite you to visit—talk with our professors, attend a class, spend time with some students, and walk across the campus on which public education was born.

"All freshman applicants are required to submit an SAT or an ACT Writing component score. If students took the SAT or ACT before the Writing section was offered, the SAT or ACT Writing score is still required. Our holistic application review process considers more than standardized test scores."

SELECTIVITY

Admissions Rating	**96**
# of applicants	18,850
% of applicants accepted	36
% of acceptees attending	53
# accepting a place on wait list	1,125
% admitted from wait list	22

FRESHMAN PROFILE

Range SAT Verbal	590-690
Average SAT Verbal	638
Range SAT Math	600-700
Average SAT Math	649
**TPR Projected Range SAT Writing*	*620-690*
Range ACT Composite	25-30
Average ACT Composite	27
Minimum Paper TOEFL	600
Minimum Computer Based TOEFL	250
Average HS GPA	4.19
% graduated top 10% of class	74
% graduated top 25% of class	95
% graduated top 50% of class	99

DEADLINES

Regular application deadline	1/15
Regular notification	1/31, 3/31
Nonfall registration?	no

FINANCIAL FACTS

Financial Aid Rating	**91**
Annual in-state tuition	$3,205
Annual out-of-state tuition	$16,303
Room & Board	$6,245
Books and supplies	$900
Required fees	$1,246
% frosh rec. need-based scholarship or grant aid	32
% UG rec. need-based scholarship or grant aid	32
% frosh rec. need-based self-help aid	15
% UG rec. need-based self-help aid	19
% frosh rec. any financial aid	53
% UG rec. any financial aid	51
Avg. frosh grant	$6,208
Avg. frosh loan	$3,281
Independent 529 member?	No

THE UNIVERSITY OF NORTH CAROLINA—GREENSBORO

1400 Spring Garden Street, Greensboro, NC 27402-6170 • Admissions: 336-334-5243 • Fax: 336-334-4180

CAMPUS LIFE

Quality of Life Rating	**81**
Fire Safety Rating	**60**
Type of school	public

STUDENTS

Total undergrad enrollment	11,241
% male/female	32/68
% from out of state	8
% from public high school	95
% live on campus	32
% African American	19
% Asian	3
% Caucasian	69
% Hispanic	2
% international	1

SURVEY SAYS

Great computer facilities
Great library
Athletic facilities are great
Diverse student types on campus
Great off-campus food
(Almost) everyone smokes

ACADEMICS

Academic Rating	**75**
Calendar	semester
Student/faculty ratio	16:1
Professors interesting rating	76
Professors accessible rating	74
% professors teaching UG courses	100
% classes taught by TAs	0
Most common lab size	20-29 students
Most common regular class size	20-29 students

MOST POPULAR MAJORS

Business administration/management
elementary education and teaching
nursing/registered nurse training (RN, ASN, BSN, MSN)

STUDENTS SPEAK OUT

Academics

Students describe The University of North Carolina—Greensboro as "about a half-and-half commuter school with great specialized programs and schools such as nursing, education, dance, and music." Undergrads here praise the "high quality of education at a significantly reduced rate, while having the smaller classes allowing closer bonds between faculty and students" than one could reasonably expect for the tuition charged. The key here is the faculty; "UNCG places a big emphasis on having great teachers. There are some duds, but overall, more of them are fantastic than anything else." The school excels in some off-the-beaten-path areas; programs in exercise and sports science, deaf education, and human development and family studies all receive enthusiastic praise from current students. Undergrads also love the "opportunities that are given to network with businesses and people outside of campus" and the "great internships" the school helps them find. Nontraditional students appreciate the "great support system for adult students." As the school's reputation continues to improve, some here worry that this "historically moderate-sized university where student well-being was the first priority...will change into a large research university where the focus is raising more and more money instead of concentrating on what is really best for students." One undeniable upside of the school's increased stature is that "You feel like you are respected in the community when you tell someone that you are a student at UNCG."

Life

UNCG is conveniently located "a mile from downtown and close to surrounding schools: Guilford College, NC A&T, Greensboro College, Elon, UNC, NC State." Observes one student, "With six colleges around UNCG, a metropolis of 250,000+ (1.1 million in the metro area), and access within a three-hour drive to both beaches and mountains, there is always something to do." On campus, "UNCG makes it easy for anyone and everyone to fit in and feel included. Through clubs, students have the ability to offer ideas and have them implemented. There's also intramural sports and free events." The high-profile arts programs on campus yield some wonderful cultural opportunities. "The Weatherspoon Museum of Art is amazing at showcasing the most modern American art and keeps this provincial little town on its toes," writes one artist. A performing arts student adds, "There are wonderful concerts and plays and lectures here. It's a great cultural center and you can always have something to do as long as you look for it." Intercollegiate athletics, students tell us, "are not as popular as they could be, even though they are often ranked nationally, or at least ranked in the conference." Many here feel the addition of a football team (the school has none) would change that; "It would really bring the school spirit up," opines one undergrad. The school's many commuters warn that "parking is horrendous. Prepare to get here an hour before class if you want to find a space on time."

Student Body

UNCG is a big school with "many people from all walks of life, social/cultural backgrounds, etc. The university promotes cultural diversity and acceptance and tolerance of people of different backgrounds." One student reports, "One minute you see a bunch of music majors talking about how much Bach has affected their life and the next minute, you see a bunch of sorority girls discussing the Gap. Mainly, I have observed that sorority girls stick together, jocks stick together, etc." Two in three students are female, and there is a widespread perception that "many of the males are either married or gay. The straight young chill male is a minority here." As at many state schools, "about half of the students at UNCG came here to party. The other half consists of hard working students who are generally frustrated with the slacker mentality in a lot of our classes. This is less of a problem once you get past the intro-level lectures."

UNIVERSITY OF NORTH CAROLINA—GREENSBORO

FINANCIAL AID: 336-334-5702 • E-MAIL: UNDERGRAD_ADMISSIONS@UNCG.EDU • WEBSITE: WWW.UNCG.EDU

ADMISSIONS

Important factors considered include: Secondary school record, standardized test scores. *Other factors considered include:* Class rank. SAT Reasoning or SAT Subject Tests required. TOEFL required of all international applicants. High school diploma is required, and GED is accepted. *Academic units required:* 4 English, 3 math, 3 science (1 science lab), 2 foreign language, 1 social studies, 1 history, 1 academic elective.

The Inside Word

UNCG has yet to gain much attention outside of regional circles so, at least for the moment, gaining admission is not particularly difficult. The usual public university considerations apply; expect the admissions office to focus on grades and test scores, and not much else. Out-of-staters will find a much smoother path to admission here than at Chapel Hill and will still be within reasonable reach of internship and career possibilities in the Research Triangle.

FINANCIAL AID

Students should submit: FAFSA. The Princeton Review suggests that all financial aid forms be submitted as soon as possible after 1/1. *Need-based scholarships/grants offered:* Pell, SEOG, state scholarships/grants, private scholarships, the school's own gift aid. *Loan aid offered:* FFEL Subsidized Stafford, FFEL Unsubsidized Stafford, FFEL PLUS, Federal Perkins, state loans. Applicants will be notified of awards on or about 4/1. Federal Work-study Program available. Institutional employment available. Off-campus job opportunities are good.

FROM THE ADMISSIONS OFFICE

"UNCG is committed to helping students discover how they can make their mark in the world. Exceptional teaching and first-rate academic programs provide a solid learning foundation. Hands-on experiences in internships, leadership opportunities, and service-learning programs prepare students to take on the challenges of the twenty-first century. Students can broaden their experience by taking advantage of one of the most extensive and affordable study abroad programs in the country. Beginning in 2006, the International Honors College will offer a genuinely unique opportunity for talented students. UNCG's ideal size and supportive campus environment enable students to excel as individuals while discovering how they can have an impact on the larger community. Students get connected through more than 170 student organizations, intramural, club and intercollegiate sports, Greeks, outdoor adventures, residential colleges, and a friendly southern city that quickly starts to feel like home.

"Students applying for admission into the fall 2006 entering class are required to take the new SAT (or the ACT with the Writing section), but students may submit scores from the old version of the SAT (prior to March 2005) or ACT as well, and the student's best scores from either test will be used."

SELECTIVITY

Admissions Rating	**76**
# of applicants	7,532
% of applicants accepted	78
% of acceptees attending	37

FRESHMAN PROFILE

Range SAT Verbal	470-570
Average SAT Verbal	522
Range SAT Math	470-570
Average SAT Math	523
**TPR Projected Range SAT Writing*	*530-610*
Minimum Paper TOEFL	550
Average HS GPA	3.44
% graduated top 10% of class	13
% graduated top 25% of class	44
% graduated top 50% of class	85

DEADLINES

Regular application deadline	8/1
Nonfall registration?	yes

FINANCIAL FACTS

Financial Aid Rating	**71**
Annual in-state tuition	$4,056
Annual out-of-state tuition	$25,992
Room & Board	$5,000
Books and supplies	$1,314
Required fees	$2,838
% frosh rec. need-based scholarship or grant aid	46
% UG rec. need-based scholarship or grant aid	50
% frosh rec. need-based self-help aid	37
% UG rec. need-based self-help aid	42
Independent 529 member?	No

UNIVERSITY OF NORTH DAKOTA

PO BOX 8135, GRAND FORKS, ND 58202 • ADMISSIONS: 800-225-5863 • FAX: 701-777-4857

CAMPUS LIFE

Quality of Life Rating	**78**
Fire Safety Rating	**82**
Type of school	public
Environment	town

STUDENTS

Total undergrad enrollment	10,710
% male/female	53/47
% from out of state	46
% from public high school	92
% live on campus	31
% in (# of) fraternities	10 (13)
% in (# of) sororities	8 (7)
% African American	1
% Asian	1
% Caucasian	92
% Hispanic	1
% Native American	3
% international	2
# of countries represented	61

SURVEY SAYS

Athletic facilities are great
Students are friendly
Students are happy
Everyone loves the Fighting Sioux
Lots of beer drinking
Hard liquor is popular

ACADEMICS

Academic Rating	**70**
Calendar	semester
Student/faculty ratio	18:1
Professors interesting rating	68
Professors accessible rating	61
% professors teaching UG courses	90
% classes taught by TAs	0
Most common lab size	20-29 students
Most common regular class size	20-29 students

MOST POPULAR MAJORS

Aeronautics/aviation/aerospace science and technology
elementary education and teaching
nursing/registered nurse training (RN, ASN, BSN, MSN)

STUDENTS SPEAK OUT

Academics

"A history of producing hardworking professionals and a strong alumni association" are just two of the many reasons students choose to come to the University of North Dakota (UND). Affordability and the chance to "receive a great education while still having tons of fun" are two more. Students here brag about a variety of programs, the nationally renowned aviation program ("one of the best anywhere"), the "super business and engineering schools, and a great social work program" among them. Like most large state universities, UND offers a wide range of options, making it "great for students who definitely know what their career path is, and great for those students who are still searching for their direction." Atypically for a big school, "classes are small, which makes learning easier," and "there are a large number of professors and other faculty members dedicated to making sure every student receives the best possible education. If there is a problem or a student needs assistance, people are willing to listen and help out." To many, though, UND's large and active alumni network is the school's chief asset. Explains one student, "Alumni are amazing. They really look out for one another. It establishes an immediate connection. You say to someone in Florida, 'I graduated from UND,' and they will give you a job or find you one."

Life

North Dakota, its students brag, is home to "the best hockey team on earth," and most here would agree that intercollegiate sports—not just hockey, but also football, women's basketball, and swimming—are central to campus life. Some think sports are a little too central; complains one, "Don't get me wrong; I love hockey and football as much as the next guy. But when some faculty on campus literally have their offices in closets, and UND is buying the hockey players engraved suitcases and matching jackets, it's a little pathetic." When there's no game to attend, students enjoy a lively party scene. "Life at UND is study during the week and party on the weekend," explains one student. "Frats have many parties, and the college has events going most weekends." Undergrads also report that "the university programming is usually really good. In the dorms, there is Residence Life Cinema, which has great movies. They have concerts at the new arena." Hometown Grand Forks "isn't a huge city, so there's not a whole lot of places for students under 21 to go to." However, "once a student turns 21, there are a lot of bars, and most of them are pretty fun." Students appreciate how "the campus and the town are pretty safe," but wish the school would build some underground walkways: "It's subzero most of the year and we must often walk 10 to 15 minutes around campus!" writes one student. Road trips to Canada are popular among students with access to vehicles.

Student Body

According to some students here, geography is destiny; as one put it, "In North Dakota, the land is flat and unchanging. At UND, most of the students are the same way: everyone looks and basically acts the same. This is good and bad, and stems from the fact that most of the students here are from the tri-state region. Not many kids from other parts of the country want to go to school so far north." The exceptions to the rule "are athletes and aviation students, who add diversity. Everyone else is a Caucasian with blonde hair. We live in a Scandinavian area. It's bound to happen!" Students also note that many of their classmates "are from farms or the city of Grand Forks." Most agree that a friendly, midwestern vibe pervades the campus. Writes one undergrad, "Students here are extremely nice and never put anyone down."

FINANCIAL AID: 701-777-3121 • E-MAIL: ENROLSER@SAGE.UND.NODAK.EDU • WEBSITE: WWW.UND.EDU

ADMISSIONS

Very important factors considered include: Secondary school record, standardized test scores. *Other factors considered include:* Class rank, essays, recommendations. SAT Reasoning or ACT required. TOEFL required of all international applicants. High school diploma is required, and GED is accepted. *Academic units required:* 4 English, 3 math, 3 science (3 science lab), 3 social studies. *Academic units recommended:* 1 foreign language.

The Inside Word

North Dakota shapes up as a low-stress choice with little pressure on applicants. Its sound reputation serves as a reminder that a highly selective admissions profile isn't an indicator of the quality of a university. Who graduates is much more important than who gets admitted or denied.

FINANCIAL AID

Students should submit: FAFSA. The Princeton Review suggests that all financial aid forms be submitted as soon as possible after 1/1. *Need-based scholarships/grants offered:* Pell, SEOG, state scholarships/grants, private scholarships, the school's own gift aid, Federal Nursing scholarships. *Loan aid offered:* FFEL Subsidized Stafford, FFEL Unsubsidized Stafford, FFEL PLUS, Federal Perkins, Federal Nursing, alternative commercial loans. Applicants will be notified of awards on or about 5/15. Federal Work-study Program available. Institutional employment available. Off-campus job opportunities are good.

FROM THE ADMISSIONS OFFICE

"More than 13,000 students come to the University of North Dakota each year, from every state in the nation and more than 60 countries. They're impressed by our academic excellence, about 180 major fields of study, our dedication to the liberal arts mission, and alumni success record. Nearly all of the university's new students rank in the top half of their high school classes, with about half in the top quarter. As the oldest and most diversified institution of higher education in the Dakotas, Montana, Wyoming, and western Minnesota, UND is a comprehensive teaching and research university. Yet the university provides individual attention that may be missing at very large universities. UND graduates are highly regarded among prospective employers. Representatives from more than 200 regional and national companies recruit UND students every year. Our campus is approximately 98 percent accessible.

"Students applying for admission to UND are required to take either the ACT or SAT unless they are older than 25. The ACT Writing component is not a requirement for admission, and SAT results considered include only the Math and Verbal sections."

SELECTIVITY

Admissions Rating	**78**
# of applicants	4,255
% of applicants accepted	69
% of acceptees attending	75

FRESHMAN PROFILE

Range ACT Composite	20-25
Average ACT Composite	23
Minimum Paper TOEFL	525
Minimum Computer Based TOEFL	195
Average HS GPA	3.36
% graduated top 10% of class	16
% graduated top 25% of class	38
% graduated top 50% of class	72

DEADLINES

Regular application deadline	7/1
Regular notification	rolling
Nonfall registration?	yes

APPLICANTS ALSO LOOK AT

AND OFTEN PREFER

Minnesota State University Moorhead
Saint Cloud State University
University of Minnesota Duluth
University of Minnesota—Twin Cities
University of Wisconsin—Madison

AND SOMETIMES PREFER

Concordia College (Moorhead, MN)
Minot State University
University of Minnesota—Crookston

FINANCIAL FACTS

Financial Aid Rating	**78**
Annual in-state tuition	$4,009
Annual out-of-state tuition	$10,703
Room & Board	$4,454
Books and supplies	$700
Required fees	$819
% frosh rec. need-based scholarship or grant aid	20
% UG rec. need-based scholarship or grant aid	24
% frosh rec. need-based self-help aid	47
% UG rec. need-based self-help aid	49
% frosh rec. any financial aid	78
% UG rec. any financial aid	76
Avg. frosh grant	$2,830
Avg. frosh loan	$5,418
Independent 529 member?	No

UNIVERSITY OF NOTRE DAME

220 MAIN BUILDING, NOTRE DAME, IN 46556 • ADMISSIONS: 574-631-7505 • FAX: 574-631-8865

CAMPUS LIFE

Quality of Life Rating	**87**
Fire Safety Rating	**90**
Type of school	private
Affiliation	Roman Catholic
Environment	city

STUDENTS

Total undergrad enrollment	8,322
% male/female	53/47
% from out of state	87
% from public high school	50
% live on campus	76
% African American	4
% Asian	5
% Caucasian	78
% Hispanic	8
% Native American	1
% international	4
# of countries represented	100

SURVEY SAYS

Athletic facilities are great
Campus feels safe
Everyone loves the Fighting Irish
Intramural sports are popular
Frats and sororities are unpopular or nonexistent
Lots of beer drinking
Very little drug use

ACADEMICS

Academic Rating	**93**
Calendar	semester
Student/faculty ratio	13:1
Professors interesting rating	86
Professors accessible rating	85
% professors teaching UG courses	94
% classes taught by TAs	7
Most common lab size	10-19 students
Most common regular class size	10-19 students

MOST POPULAR MAJORS

Business administration/management
engineering
premedicine/premedical studies

STUDENTS SPEAK OUT

Academics

"Tradition is the greatest strength" of University of Notre Dame (ND). It is a place where "you become part of something that cannot be rivaled. The history and image of the school are untouched and unique. People leave proud of where they are from." One undergraduate says, "At Notre Dame, the term 'family' is used a lot. You really do feel like part of a big family when you come here." The workload can be "intense, but not overwhelmingly so [at this] academically challenging school with a conservative, hardworking, overachieving student body whose lives are structured around studying and sports." Because of the family atmosphere, "students here are really willing to help each other out. It's definitely not cutthroat." Professors, too, "are very accessible and very helpful. Every professor is paid to help us outside of class. I can even go to my economics teacher, not a TA, if I find it necessary, and I'm in a class of about two hundred students!" Not only are professors there to help, "they actually get excited if you visit them during office hours, encourage discussion and questions, and often use humor to remind students that a test, in the overall scheme of things, is just a test." Students are a bit more reserved in their praise of the administration, which is "good, but rather strict. Example: the administration successfully banned the new [and short-lived] NBC show *Coupling* from airing in the South Bend region. They apparently feel they have the right to restrict our viewing privileges and pretend to be our parents."

Life

Life at Notre Dame revolves around the residence halls. One student explains, "Notre Dame is a very residential campus. Most students live on campus and stay in the same single-sex dorms throughout their years at the university. Your dorm is a major part of your experience at Notre Dame, and most of your good friends come from the dorm." Another undergraduate puts it this way: "No frats or sororities means that your residence hall will be like your frat or sorority. Each hall has its own mascot, colors, rivalries, signature events, [and] sports teams." The system apparently works well, nurturing a campus that remains lively 24/7. "There is always something to do here," writes one student. "We've had some amazing concerts in the last couple years: U2, Guster, Matchbox 20, George Clinton, Nine Days, SR71, Black Eyed Peas. There's always inter-hall sporting events, dances, and volunteer activities." And then, of course, there's also football. "Football season is the most fun time of the year," undergrads agree. "Thousands of people come on football game weekends, and it is mass chaos, but very enjoyable." It's a good thing the campus is so vibrant because "South Bend sucks, offering chain restaurants, bowling, movies, and that's it." While "Notre Dame students do like to party," they are sometimes thwarted by an administration that "holds true to Catholic values."

Student Body

Don't expect to sit on the sidelines if you attend Notre Dame. "The typical ND student loves life and getting involved, even if that means sacrificing sleep. The classrooms are full, the library is packed, the entire student body is standing on the benches at the football games, theater performances and concerts are sold out, everyone reads the daily student-run newspaper *The Observer*, the athletic fields and gyms are bustling with activity, about 85 percent of students are involved in some form of service, and masses in the Basilica on Sunday are often standing room only." Religion plays a large role in many people's lives. One student writes, "Notre Dame is very big on the spiritual aspect of a student's life, and so there is a big emphasis on religion and spirituality in general," explains one undergrad. Another adds, "There are mostly two kinds of people at Notre Dame. There is the jock type and the religious type." The vast majority are "white, Catholic, and conservative and come from upper-middle-class families."

FINANCIAL AID: 574-631-6436 • E-MAIL: ADMISSIO.1@ND.EDU • WEBSITE: WWW.ND.EDU

ADMISSIONS

Very important factors considered include: Character/personal qualities, class rank, essays, extracurricular activities, recommendations, secondary school record, standardized test scores, talent/ability. *Other factors considered include:* Alumni/ae relation, minority status, religious affiliation/commitment, volunteer work, work experience. SAT Reasoning or ACT required. TOEFL required of all international applicants. High school diploma is required, and GED is not accepted. *Academic units required:* 4 English, 3 math, 2 science (1 science lab), 2 foreign language, 2 history, 3 academic electives. *Academic units recommended:* 4 English, 4 math, 4 science, 4 foreign language, 4 history.

The Inside Word

For most candidates, getting admitted to Notre Dame is pretty tough. Legacies, however, face some of the most favorable admissions conditions to be found at any highly selective university. Unofficially, athletic talents seem to have some influence on the committee as well: An enormous percentage of the total student body holds at least one varsity letter from high school, and many were team captains. Perhaps it's merely coincidence, but even so, candidates who tap well into the Notre Dame persona are most likely to succeed.

FINANCIAL AID

Students should submit: FAFSA, CSS/Financial Aid PROFILE, noncustodial (divorced/separated) parents' statement, business/farm supplement, federal income tax return and W-2 forms, student federal income tax return. The Princeton Review suggests that all financial aid forms be submitted as soon as possible after 1/1. *Need-based scholarships/grants offered:* Pell, SEOG, state scholarships/grants, private scholarships, the school's own gift aid, alumni club scholarships. *Loan aid offered:* FFEL Subsidized Stafford, FFEL Unsubsidized Stafford, FFEL PLUS, Federal Perkins, privately funded student loan. Applicants will be notified of awards on a rolling basis beginning on or about 3/15.

FROM THE ADMISSIONS OFFICE

"Notre Dame is a Catholic university, which means it offers unique opportunities for academic, ethical, spiritual, and social service development. The First Year of Studies program provides special assistance to our students as they make the adjustment from high school to college. The first-year curriculum includes many core requirements, while allowing students to explore several areas of possible future study. Each residence hall is home to students from all classes; most will live in the same hall for all their years on campus. An average of 93 percent of entering students will graduate within five years.

"Scores from either the old or new SAT are accepted. The highest Verbal score and the highest Math score from either test will be accepted; the Writing component score is not required. The ACT is also accepted (with or without Writing component) in lieu of the SAT."

SELECTIVITY

Admissions Rating	**98**
# of applicants	11,490
% of applicants accepted	30
% of acceptees attending	57
# accepting a place on wait list	840
% admitted from wait list	15

FRESHMAN PROFILE

Range SAT Verbal	630-730
Average SAT Verbal	676
Range SAT Math	650-740
Average SAT Math	693
**TPR Projected Range SAT Writing*	*650-720*
Range ACT Composite	30-33
Average ACT Composite	31
Minimum Paper TOEFL	600
Minimum Computer Based TOEFL	250
% graduated top 10% of class	85
% graduated top 25% of class	95
% graduated top 50% of class	100

DEADLINES

Regular application deadline	12/31
Regular notification	4/1
Nonfall registration?	no

APPLICANTS ALSO LOOK AT

AND OFTEN PREFER
Princeton University
Stanford University

AND SOMETIMES PREFER
Cornell University
Duke University
Georgetown University
Northwestern University

AND RARELY PREFER
Boston College
University of Illinois at Urbana-Champaign
University of Michigan—Ann Arbor

FINANCIAL FACTS

Financial Aid Rating	**96**
Annual tuition	$31,100
Room & Board	$8,010
Books and supplies	$850
Required fees	$442
% frosh rec. need-based scholarship or grant aid	51
% UG rec. need-based scholarship or grant aid	46
% frosh rec. need-based self-help aid	41
% UG rec. need-based self-help aid	41
Independent 529 member?	Yes

UNIVERSITY OF OKLAHOMA

1000 ASP AVENUE, NORMAN, OK 73019-4076 • ADMISSIONS: 405-325-2252 • FAX: 405-325-7124

CAMPUS LIFE

Quality of Life Rating	**84**
Fire Safety Rating	**86**
Type of school	public
Environment	city

STUDENTS

Total undergrad enrollment	20,843
% male/female	50/50
% from out of state	22
% live on campus	20
% in (# of) fraternities	16 (24)
% in (# of) sororities	25 (17)
% African American	5
% Asian	5
% Caucasian	76
% Hispanic	4
% Native American	8
% international	2
# of countries represented	97

SURVEY SAYS

Great library
Athletic facilities are great
Everyone loves the Sooners
Frats and sororities dominate social scene
Lots of beer drinking

ACADEMICS

Academic Rating	**74**
Calendar	semester
Student/faculty ratio	21:1
Professors interesting rating	72
Professors accessible rating	74
% classes taught by TAs	20
Most common lab size	20-29 students
Most common regular class size	20-29 students

MOST POPULAR MAJORS

Psychology
sociology
zoology/animal biology

STUDENTS SPEAK OUT

Academics

The University of Oklahoma "prides itself on the leadership and ingenuity of its students," a number of whom credit the school's president, David Boren, with transforming OU "from well-known in the state of Oklahoma to well-known across the nation" in the past decade. Students call their academic experiences at OU "exceptional"—both in and out of the classroom. "We are encouraged to get not only a great academic base but also life experiences, through lab research, internships, and campus leadership positions." Not to be eclipsed by the famous meteorology department, the business and drama programs are starting to get attention, as well. When it comes to teaching, some students see "a clear distinction between two types of professors: those who have been here forever and have tenure (they're boring and don't really 'teach'), and new professors, who have real-life experience and give students a feel for what the real world is like." More often than not, we read that the professors are "very helpful and knowledgeable." An economics student boasts that after e-mailing homework assignments to a calculus professor, she "received the answers back promptly." Undergrads wish the school would address the "definite need for more professors and more classes for the ever-growing number of students here at OU." A handful also gripes about having to jump through bureaucratic hoops; writes an all-too experienced senior: "There's a lot of standing in lines for everything." That said, many students find the administration members "available and helpful." Those in the honors program experience "a wonderful dynamic. It's nice to be at a big university but still get to take small, discussion-centered classes." One content sophomore writes, "I believe I am getting not only a great education, but also meeting people who make huge impressions in my life."

Life

To some, OU has a party school reputation, perhaps made possible by its "huge Greek population" (in total, OU offers 42 fraternities and sororities). A senior notes that "there are plenty of things to do on OU's campus besides partying," and students repeatedly point out that Greeks "work hard to co-program with various events and encourage members to attend activities out of their regular spectrum." For example, "In my sorority," writes one senior, "we have different groups come over for dinner and exchanges." This "ongoing process" of increasing interaction among all factions is starting to pay off in some campus-wide participation. A senior recounts how OU started "a one-day community service project called the Big Event that now, in its sixth year, attracts nearly one in every four students." The student union sponsors free new-release movies "just about every Friday night," and the Campus Activities Council organizes "free events like Homecoming, Howdy Week, pep rallies, and concert series (including the Dixie Chicks)." People call the town of Norman, 15 miles from Oklahoma City, "pretty bland to say the least," though it does have a museum, dollar theater, and popular 1950s-style diner. Of course, students and Norman locals come together in their undying love of Sooner football, packing the stadium to see the team and the talented marching band all through the fall.

Student Body

Most students hail from Oklahoma or Texas, and several comment that "you definitely feel the Bible Belt" at OU. Students describe typical classmates as "conservative"; however, in the words of a sophomore, "most people here are not judgmental, at least openly, and tend to either ignore or respect foreign views and beliefs." In this welcoming group, "if you were to go to a football game by yourself and sit in the middle of the student section, everyone would give you a high five and yell along with you while you were there." One student observes a shift in his classmates: "People are still always talking about what they are doing that night; but surprisingly, students are starting to get more serious about school, which I think is really good."

UNIVERSITY OF OKLAHOMA

FINANCIAL AID: 405-325-4521 • E-MAIL: ADMREC@OU.EDU • WEBSITE: WWW.OU.EDU

ADMISSIONS

Very important factors considered include: Class rank, secondary school record, standardized test scores. *Other factors considered include:* Essays, recommendations, state residency. SAT Reasoning or ACT required. TOEFL required of all international applicants. High school diploma is required, and GED is accepted. *Academic units required:* 4 English, 3 math, 2 science (2 science lab), 2 social studies, 1 history, 3 academic electives. *Academic units recommended:* 3 foreign language, 1 computer science.

The Inside Word

It's plain from the approach of Oklahoma's evaluation process that candidates needn't put much energy into preparing supporting materials for their applications. This is one place that is going to get you a decision pronto—your numbers will call the shots.

FINANCIAL AID

Students should submit: FAFSA. The Princeton Review suggests that all financial aid forms be submitted as soon as possible after 1/1. *Need-based scholarships/grants offered:* Pell, SEOG, state scholarships/grants, private scholarships, the school's own gift aid, United Negro College Fund. *Loan aid offered:* FFEL Subsidized Stafford, FFEL Unsubsidized Stafford, FFEL PLUS, Federal Perkins, college/university loans from institutional funds. Applicants will be notified of awards on a rolling basis beginning on or about 3/15. Off-campus job opportunities are excellent.

FROM THE ADMISSIONS OFFICE

"Ask yourself some significant questions. What are your ambitions, goals, and dreams? Do you desire opportunity, and are you ready to accept challenge? What do you hope to gain from your educational experience? Are you looking for a university that will provide you with the tools, resources, and motivation to convert ambitions, opportunities, and challenges into meaningful achievement? To effectively answer these questions you must carefully seek out your options, look for direction, and make the right choice. The University of Oklahoma combines a unique mixture of academic excellence, varied social cultures, and a variety of campus activities to make your educational experience complete. At OU, comprehensive learning is our goal for your life. Not only do you receive a valuable classroom learning experience, but OU is also one of the finest research institutions in the United States. This allows OU students the opportunity to be a part of technology in progress. It's not just learning, it's discovery, invention, and dynamic creativity, a hands-on experience that allows you to be on the cutting edge of knowledge. Make the right choice and consider the University of Oklahoma!

"Both versions of the SAT (or ACT) will be used when considering freshman applicants for admission. The new Writing component of either test is not required of students and is not used in determining admission to the university. The student's best composite score from any one test will be used."

SELECTIVITY

Admissions Rating	**86**
# of applicants	8,165
% of applicants accepted	82
% of acceptees attending	54
# accepting a place on wait list	836
% admitted from wait list	33

FRESHMAN PROFILE

Average SAT Verbal	589
Average SAT Math	597
Range ACT Composite	23-28
Average ACT Composite	26
Minimum Paper TOEFL	550
Minimum Computer Based TOEFL	213
Average HS GPA	3.59
% graduated top 10% of class	36
% graduated top 25% of class	71
% graduated top 50% of class	92

DEADLINES

Regular application deadline	4/1
Nonfall registration?	yes

APPLICANTS ALSO LOOK AT AND OFTEN PREFER

Rice University
Washington University in St. Louis

AND SOMETIMES PREFER

Baylor University
University of Kansas
The University of Texas—Austin

FINANCIAL FACTS

Financial Aid Rating	**80**
Annual in-state tuition	$2,778
Annual out-of-state tuition	$10,296
Room & Board	$5,814
Books and supplies	$953
Required fees	$1,362
% frosh rec. need-based scholarship or grant aid	9
% UG rec. need-based scholarship or grant aid	16
% frosh rec. need-based self-help aid	27
% UG rec. need-based self-help aid	33
% frosh rec. any financial aid	77
% UG rec. any financial aid	74
Avg. frosh grant	$4,150
Avg. frosh loan	$5,930
Independent 529 member?	No

UNIVERSITY OF OREGON

1217 UNIVERSITY OF OREGON, EUGENE, OR 97403-1217 • ADMISSIONS: 541-346-3201 • FAX: 541-346-5815

CAMPUS LIFE

Quality of Life Rating	**80**
Fire Safety Rating	**73**
Type of school	public
Environment	city

STUDENTS

Total undergrad enrollment	16,024
% male/female	47/53
% from out of state	22
% from public high school	90
% live on campus	21
% in (# of) fraternities	8 (13)
% in (# of) sororities	10 (8)
% African American	2
% Asian	6
% Caucasian	76
% Hispanic	3
% Native American	1
% international	4
# of countries represented	86

SURVEY SAYS

Great library
Athletic facilities are great
Everyone loves the Ducks
Political activism is popular

ACADEMICS

Academic Rating	**75**
Calendar	quarter
Student/faculty ratio	19:1
Professors interesting rating	72
Professors accessible rating	75
% professors teaching UG courses	100
% classes taught by TAs	22
Most common lab size	20-29 students
Most common regular class size	20-29 students

MOST POPULAR MAJORS

Business administration/management
journalism
psychology

STUDENTS SPEAK OUT

Academics

For applicants looking for "a good balance of fun and studies," the University of Oregon offers top programs in journalism, sports marketing, business, architecture, and education in a laid-back academic atmosphere. Within these popular disciplines, "demand is so high for classes that even as an upper-level student with significant credits and coursework, I have had trouble getting into classes," says a journalism student. Those looking to cruise through college "can skim by with B's and C's in the social sciences," but departments like biochemistry "weed out the drifters and demand a lot of work." Across disciplines, professors exude "a jovial attitude" from the lectern, and students will occasionally "go to an independent film in a small group with a professor or talk politics with them over dinner." One junior recalls, "I did not think that I would get the love and caring behavior that I have received from teachers by going to a big university." Participants in the Clark Honors College feel like they're "attending a small liberal arts school within a larger university" and tout the opportunities for "small classes with heated discussions" and interaction with top faculty. On the downside, "especially for science majors, the rigid Honors College requirements cut into time that could be well spent elsewhere." While some see U of O as simply a "decent education at a decent price," most feel challenged "to become well-rounded thinkers and educated, active participants in the world."

Life

Throw together "hippies, conservatives, sick parties, and rain like no other," and you've got a decent picture of Oregon life. The large Greek system paired with the "typical student who goes to most of their classes and does most of their work but likes partying a lot" accounts for a well-lubricated social scene. However, some students maintain that it's "not nearly the party school that a lot of the California beach and Arizona schools are." Whether students want to have a pint at the local brewpub, talk politics at "a small, international party with yummy food," or rage on at "huge dance parties with hundreds of people," a destination awaits them. On this "very athletic campus," students like to hit the "amazing workout facilities and intramural fields" during the week and spend the weekends camping, hiking, surfing, skiing, and rock climbing. Many also turn out to cheer on the Ducks in Pac-10 action. The "sweet little hippie town" of Eugene, home to many a WTO protester, offers an "extremely fun downtown area that's a different experience from what most college kids are used to." According to a junior, "It is easy to become an active citizen and enjoy the great cultural benefits of the area if one is willing to put in the effort to explore."

Student Body

Most students feel challenged to summarize their 20,000 classmates, since "a very eclectic vibe" pervades the campus. Overall, "U of O is a very liberal school within a very liberal community. As a whole, the area is very accepting of people from different backgrounds." Various subgroups thrive within the university "with their own student organizations and cultures," but the hippies make the reputation. Some believe "the problem is that the hippies get the press and are so outlandish that the majority of students are overlooked." But freshmen marvel that the majority of roommate postings "openly ask for people who are 'herb friendly.'" Another student clarifies, "The hippie population is present—and there are probably more here than at other schools—but there are also plenty of people who are not," and are able to "break away from that mold." U of O students, mostly from in-state or somewhere on the West coast, maintain their idealism and an "interest in learning how and where they can make an impact in the world." They ponder questions like "Why are we here? What is our purpose?" which too often lead to, "Why should we bother studying for our history final when we'll all eventually die anyway?"

UNIVERSITY OF OREGON

FINANCIAL AID: 541-346-3211 • E-MAIL: UOADMIT@OREGON.UOREGON.EDU • WEBSITE: WWW.UOREGON.EDU

ADMISSIONS

Very important factors considered include: Secondary school record. *Other factors considered include:* Class rank, essays, geographical residence, minority status, recommendations, standardized test scores, state residency, talent/ability, volunteer work, work experience. SAT Reasoning or ACT required. TOEFL required of all international applicants. High school diploma is required, and GED is accepted. *Academic units required:* 4 English, 3 math, 2 science, 2 foreign language, 3 social studies. *Academic units recommended:* (1 science lab), 2 college preparatory recommended.

The Inside Word

Oregon's admissions process is essentially a formula; it's not likely that anything beyond your grades, rank, and tests will play much of a part in getting you admitted.

FINANCIAL AID

Students should submit: FAFSA. The Princeton Review suggests that all financial aid forms be submitted as soon as possible after 1/1. *Need-based scholarships/grants offered:* Pell, SEOG, state scholarships/grants, private scholarships, the school's own gift aid. *Loan aid offered:* Direct Subsidized Stafford, Direct Unsubsidized Stafford, Direct PLUS, Federal Perkins, college/university loans from institutional funds. Applicants will be notified of awards on or about 4/1. Federal Work-study Program available. Institutional employment available. Off-campus job opportunities are good.

FROM THE ADMISSIONS OFFICE

"Many of the UO's over 125 academic programs are internationally recognized for academic excellence. The College of Education and individual departments in architecture, chemistry, economics, English, psychology, molecular biology, biochemistry, physics, and neuroscience all rank among the top ten in the United States. The UO's School of Journalism and Communication and the College of Business rank in the top twenty in the United States. Three separate ranking organizations recognize the UO as one of the nation's best buys in higher education. Eugene is the classic U.S. college town, small enough to bike across, but large enough to offer cafés, clubs, and culture. The UO is located in a vast outdoor recreation area, with hundreds of miles of bike paths and hiking trails inside the city limits. With the Pacific Ocean an hour to the west and the Cascade Mountains an hour to the east, you'll have surfing, skiing, snowboarding, river rafting, and rock-climbing areas close to home. The UO has been recognized by the American Council on Education as one of the country's leaders in internationalization. Over 14 percent of UO students study abroad in more than 70 countries around the world. You'll attend classes alongside students from all fifty states and eighty-two countries. At the University of Oregon, you'll live the university motto, Minds Move Mountains. Whether you want to change a community, a law, or one person's mind, the UO will provide you with all the inspiration and resources you'll need to succeed.

"Applicants for fall 2006 are required to take the new version of the SAT, or the ACT with the Writing section. Students may submit additional test scores from the old version of the SAT (prior to March 2005) or ACT in addition to the new SAT scores, and the student's best test scores will be used."

SELECTIVITY

Admissions Rating	**78**
# of applicants	9,623
% of applicants accepted	91
% of acceptees attending	36

FRESHMAN PROFILE

Range SAT Verbal	496-613
Average SAT Verbal	555
Range SAT Math	503-615
Average SAT Math	559
**TPR Projected Range SAT Writing*	*560-640*
Minimum Paper TOEFL	500
Minimum Computer Based TOEFL	173
Average HS GPA	3.49
% graduated top 10% of class	21
% graduated top 25% of class	52
% graduated top 50% of class	87

DEADLINES

Regular application deadline	1/15
Regular notification	rolling
Nonfall registration?	yes

APPLICANTS ALSO LOOK AT AND OFTEN PREFER

University of California—Berkeley
University of California—Davis

AND SOMETIMES PREFER

University of Arizona
University of California—Santa Cruz
University of Colorado—Boulder
University of Portland
University of Washington

AND RARELY PREFER

Willamette University

FINANCIAL FACTS

Financial Aid Rating	**67**
Annual in-state tuition	$4,077
Annual out-of-state tuition	$15,501
Room & Board	$6,570
Books and supplies	$900
Required fees	$1,413
% frosh rec. need-based scholarship or grant aid	19
% UG rec. need-based scholarship or grant aid	25
% frosh rec. need-based self-help aid	34
% UG rec. need-based self-help aid	39
% frosh rec. any financial aid	62
% UG rec. any financial aid	63
Avg. frosh grant	$3,588
Avg. frosh loan	$3,467
Independent 529 member?	No

UNIVERSITY OF THE PACIFIC

3601 PACIFIC AVENUE, STOCKTON, CA 95211 • ADMISSIONS: 209-946-2211 • FAX: 209-946-2413

CAMPUS LIFE

Quality of Life Rating	**66**
Fire Safety Rating	**89**
Type of school	private
Environment	city

STUDENTS

Total undergrad enrollment	3,446
% male/female	43/57
% from out of state	13
% from public high school	82
% live on campus	58
% in (# of) fraternities	20 (8)
% in (# of) sororities	21 (6)
% African American	3
% Asian	29
% Caucasian	46
% Hispanic	10
% Native American	1
% international	2
# of countries represented	46

SURVEY SAYS

Small classes
Great library
Students are friendly
Frats and sororities dominate social scene
Lots of beer drinking

ACADEMICS

Academic Rating	**71**
Calendar	semester
Student/faculty ratio	14:1
Professors interesting rating	79
Professors accessible rating	83
% professors teaching UG courses	91
% classes taught by TAs	0
Most common lab size	10-19 students
Most common regular class size	fewer than 10 students

MOST POPULAR MAJORS

Biology/biological sciences
Business administration/ management
engineering

STUDENTS SPEAK OUT

Academics

For those teenagers who already know what they want to be when they grow up, the University of the Pacific offers accelerated "Advantage" programs that cram those pesky undergrad and graduate degrees into less time. Options in pharmacy, dentistry, business, and engineering all "attract competitive students that promote academic achievement and motivate others to study hard as well." With all these high-powered types, tourists are quickly culled. A future pharmacist writes, "The toughness of the science classes made it necessary for me to seek a tutor, which was readily available." The entire biological sciences faculty works hard to herd everyone through their health-profession requirements; occasional complaints pop up regarding the teaching in chemistry classes. Before reducing Pacific to a dentist factory, consider the international relations, speech pathology, special education, and music programs. Students in the School for International Studies embrace the compulsory stint abroad, and they call their popular dean "an incredible humanitarian." A junior says, "I basically want to be her." Students commonly find department chairs teaching introductory classes, and most majors "encourage undergrad research," according to an engineering major. Pacific guarantees that students will graduate in four years if they follow the plan laid out for each course of study. Beyond the degree, professors "support their students to become good citizens and role models." The school publicizes their belief that the 2005 matriculates represent "the most talented and academically prepared class ever." That kind of momentum may propel this "small Pacific coast private college with a lot of big thinking going on" to great things in its second century.

Life

Students are now entering Stockton, California, hometown of indie rock legends Pavement and official armpit of the Golden State. This is where produce comes from, and you can smell the pesticides on the wind. Pacific is like a gated community in Tijuana. Everyone calls the surrounding area "a little sketchy." Put bluntly, "The neighborhood feels very unsafe and the crime rates seem to be high." Unfortunately, the campus anti-alcohol policies "force people to go off campus to find entertainment, which means more risk." Pacific addresses the issue with programs like "a day when freshman go out during orientation and volunteer in the community." As frequently as class allows, students flee their "drug-infested, gang-ridden, loathsome little town" for the glorious surrounding areas: San Francisco, Lake Tahoe, Yosemite, and the rest of northern California. On campus, students go to Big West basketball and volleyball games or just hang out at the Summit student lounge. Though "Greeks can barely do anything" under the rules, they still manage to "control the weekends" for everyone who sticks around.

Student Body

The Pacific student body prides itself on a measure of worldliness not always found at pricey, private schools. They may be mainstream and preppy, but "there is a lot of awareness about people who are not necessarily 'average Americans.'" Revealing demographic statistics include the girl-heavy gender imbalance and the Christian-heavy religious imbalance. A sophomore thinks, "Other religions seem to be represented as well, which is really cool, because there's always some sort of holiday for someone going on." Students note the existence of some loose cliques based on race, major, Greek affiliation, religion, and athletics, but are quick to add that "there is movement between groups. It is easy to be part of different groups and everyone gets along." Pacific's small population also ensures that plenty of people make connections across these lines. "You end up recognizing everyone, and there are even people that have gotten kind of famous. 'There goes that running boy,' or 'He's the prince of Thailand.'" Though the high tuition forces a polarized mix of rich and poor students, "pajamas, flip flops, and a skateboard," serve as common denominators.

FINANCIAL AID: 209-946-2421 • E-MAIL: ADMISSIONS@PACIFIC.EDU • WEBSITE: WWW.PACIFIC.EDU

ADMISSIONS

Very important factors considered include: Secondary school record. *Important factors considered include:* Essays, extracurricular activities, recommendations, standardized test scores. *Other factors considered include:* Alumni/ae relation, character/personal qualities, class rank, geographical residence, minority status, talent/ability, volunteer work, work experience. SAT Reasoning or ACT required. TOEFL required of all international applicants. High school diploma is required, and GED is accepted. *Academic units recommended:* 4 English, 3 math, 2 science (2 science lab), 2 foreign language, 1 history, 3 academic electives, 1 fine arts/performing arts.

The Inside Word

Pacific's small applicant pool and average yield of admits who enroll results in an admissions profile that is less competitive than the academic quality of the freshmen might predict. Test scores count less than a consistently solid academic performance in high school toward getting admitted. The out-of-state population is small; candidates from far afield can expect this to benefit them to a minor degree.

FINANCIAL AID

Students should submit: FAFSA. The Princeton Review suggests that all financial aid forms be submitted as soon as possible after 1/1. *Need-based scholarships/grants offered:* Pell, SEOG, state scholarships/grants, private scholarships, the school's own gift aid. *Loan aid offered:* Direct Subsidized Stafford, Direct Unsubsidized Stafford, Direct PLUS, FFEL Subsidized Stafford, FFEL Unsubsidized Stafford, FFEL PLUS, Federal Perkins, state loans. Applicants will be notified of awards on a rolling basis beginning on or about 3/15. Federal Work-study Program available. Institutional employment available. Off-campus job opportunities are good.

FROM THE ADMISSIONS OFFICE

"One of the most concise ways of describing the University of the Pacific is that it is 'a major university in a small college package.' Our 3,400 undergraduates get the personal attention that you would expect at a small, residential college. But they also have the kinds of opportunities offered at much larger institutions, including more than 90 majors and programs; hundreds of student organizations; drama, dance, and musical productions; 16 NCAA Division I athletic teams; and two dozen club and intramural sports. We offer undergraduate major programs in the arts, sciences and humanities, business, education, engineering, international studies, music, pharmacy, and health sciences. Some of the more unique aspects of our academic programs include the following: we have the only independent, coed, nonsectarian liberal arts and sciences college located between Los Angeles and central Oregon; we have the only undergraduate professional school of international studies in California—and it's the only one in the nation that actually requires you to study abroad; we have the only engineering program in the West that requires students to complete a year's worth of paid work experience as part of their degree; our Conservatory of Music focuses on performance but also offers majors in music management, music therapy, and music education; and we offer several accelerated programs in business, dentistry, dental hygiene, education, law, engineering, and pharmacy. Our beautiful New England–style main campus is located in Stockton (population 250,000) and is within two hours or less of San Francisco, Santa Cruz, Yosemite National Park, and Lake Tahoe.

"Applicants must submit Writing scores from either the SAT or ACT. Students may also submit scores from tests taken before spring 2005; the best scores submitted will be used for admission decisions. SAT Subject Tests recommended: Mathematics, Chemistry, (natural science majors only)."

SELECTIVITY

Admissions Rating	**88**
# of applicants	5,255
% of applicants accepted	64
% of acceptees attending	26

FRESHMAN PROFILE

Range SAT Verbal	520-620
Average SAT Verbal	574
Range SAT Math	540-660
Average SAT Math	600
**TPR Projected Range SAT Writing*	*570-650*
Range ACT Composite	22-27
Average ACT Composite	25
Minimum Paper TOEFL	475
Minimum Computer Based TOEFL	150
Average HS GPA	3.47
% graduated top 10% of class	37
% graduated top 25% of class	72
% graduated top 50% of class	92

DEADLINES

Regular notification	3/15
Nonfall registration?	yes

AND SOMETIMES PREFER

California Polytechnic State University—San Luis Obispo
University of California—Berkeley
University of California—Davis
University of California—Los Angeles
University of Southern California

FINANCIAL FACTS

Financial Aid Rating	**72**
Annual tuition	$24,320
Room & Board	$7,858
Books and supplies	$1,260
Required fees	$430
% frosh rec. need-based scholarship or grant aid	67
% UG rec. need-based scholarship or grant aid	63
% frosh rec. need-based self-help aid	61
% UG rec. need-based self-help aid	61
% frosh rec. any financial aid	68
% UG rec. any financial aid	67
Avg. frosh grant	$16,710
Avg. frosh loan	$3,331
Independent 529 member?	Yes

University of Pennsylvania

1 College Hall, Philadelphia, PA 19104 • Admissions: 215-898-7507 • Fax: 215-898-9670

CAMPUS LIFE

Quality of Life Rating	**75**
Fire Safety Rating	**60**
Type of school	private
Environment	metropolis

STUDENTS

Total undergrad enrollment	9,719
% male/female	50/50
% from out of state	81
% from public high school	53
% live on campus	64
% in (# of) fraternities	24 (33)
% in (# of) sororities	18 (12)
% African American	6
% Asian	18
% Caucasian	49
% Hispanic	6
% international	9
# of countries represented	113

SURVEY SAYS

Registration is a breeze
Great computer facilities
Great library
Athletic facilities are great
Great off-campus food
Student publications are popular
Lots of beer drinking
Hard liquor is popular

ACADEMICS

Academic Rating	**92**
Calendar	semester
Student/faculty ratio	6:1
Professors interesting rating	73
Professors accessible rating	75
% professors teaching UG courses	100
% classes taught by TAs	6
Most common regular class size	fewer than 10 students

MOST POPULAR MAJORS

Business administration/management
economics
finance

STUDENTS SPEAK OUT

Academics

The University of Pennsylvania is perhaps best known for its Wharton School of Business ("the number one undergraduate business program in the country," students claim), but this Ivy League institution "is strong in all divisions, a fact that one can take advantage of very easily through dual degree programs across schools." Wharton, the engineering school and science programs "require students to study a lot, as the courses move fast and cover a lot of material," while "students in the College studying liberal arts don't have it as bad." With a world-class faculty in nearly all disciplines, "Penn offers access to the best and brightest minds in the world, people who are always willing and available to discuss any topic, whether or not you are enrolled in one of their classes." Students tell us that "among the Ivies, Penn seems to be the most career-oriented, as fewer students here are on the academia track than at other schools. Many students take jobs right out after graduation rather than go to graduate school, and Penn does an excellent job of placing these students." Indeed, "a very large number of students grab the country's most prestigious jobs for undergrads: investment banking, consulting, and private equity." As at many large schools, "the administration tends to feel a bit remote to most students" and "the school can be a little bureaucratic, with little communication among administrative departments."

Life

There's a common arc to most students' extracurricular lives during their four years at Penn. When they first arrive they stick close to campus; "The social scene for most freshmen consists of frat parties, period," explains one student. As they get older, "they leave the bubble of campus and explore more of Philadelphia. There are a lot of awesome places in the city in terms of the nightlife, but you can't really get in unless you're of age." Options abound both on and off campus; notes one student, "Having Center City (and many bars/clubs/activities) just 20 blocks away is a plus, though there is also tons to do on campus as well." Campus options include "parties, theater, a cappella shows, sporting events, guest lectures, sketch comedy, movie showings, etc." Students point out that "Penn's campus is located in West Philly, which doesn't have the best reputation, but the campus itself is a vast improvement from the local area and security is a moderate concern." They also note that "for being a city school, Penn's campus is so nice, it looks more like a plush suburban park... Walking down Locust Walk (the main artery of campus) one can always see people stopping to say hello to their fellow students, student groups handing out fliers promoting an event or trying to draw attention to an issue, students enjoying an outdoor lunch while sitting at one of the many benches or tables set up outside, or standing in line at one of the lunch trucks (a staple of any Penn student's diet)."

Student Body

"There are distinct stereotypes for each of the four undergraduate schools" at Penn—brainy engineer, ambitious Wharton student, artsy college kid, hardworking nurse—although "generally students from all four schools interact quite smoothly." The student body includes "a surprising number of very religious people, including some staunch Christians and many Jews. There are far fewer agnostics and atheists than you would expect." Penn is known among the Ivies as the school where students unwind most enthusiastically; "Everyone at Penn is very stressed out, all the time, which is why most people have to let loose on the weekend," explains one student. Adds another, "The average Penn student is a thinker and a drinker. Everybody studies really hard all week long and lets loose on the weekends at wild parties. But the students are also insanely smart. On our first day, the dean asked everyone to stand up in the auditorium who had been valedictorian. The number of people who stood up almost scared me to death."

UNIVERSITY OF PENNSYLVANIA

FINANCIAL AID: 215-898-1988 • E-MAIL: INFO@ADMISSIONS.UGAO.UPENN.EDU • WEBSITE: WWW.UPENN.EDU

ADMISSIONS

Very important factors considered include: Character/personal qualities, essays, recommendations, secondary school record. *Important factors considered include:* Extracurricular activities, standardized test scores. *Other factors considered include:* Alumni/ae relation, class rank, geographical residence, interview, minority status, talent/ability, volunteer work, work experience. SAT Reasoning and SAT Subject Tests or ACT required. TOEFL required of all international applicants. High school diploma is required, and GED is accepted. *Academic units recommended:* 4 English, 4 math, 4 science, 4 foreign language, 1 social studies, 3 history.

The Inside Word

After a small decline three cycles ago, applications are once again climbing at Penn—the fourth increase in five years. The competition in the applicant pool is formidable. Applicants can safely assume that they need to be one of the strongest students in their graduating class in order to be successful.

FINANCIAL AID

Students should submit: FAFSA, institution's own financial aid form, CSS/Financial Aid PROFILE, state aid form, noncustodial (divorced/separated) parents' statement, business/farm supplement, parent and student federal income tax returns (for verification). The Princeton Review suggests that all financial aid forms be submitted as soon as possible after 1/1. *Need-based scholarships/grants offered:* Pell, SEOG, state scholarships/grants, private scholarships, the school's own gift aid. *Loan aid offered:* FFEL Subsidized Stafford, FFEL Unsubsidized Stafford, FFEL PLUS, Federal Perkins, Federal Nursing, college/university loans from institutional funds, Penn Guaranteed loan. Applicants will be notified of awards on or about 4/1. Federal Work-study Program available. Institutional employment available. Off-campus job opportunities are excellent.

FROM THE ADMISSIONS OFFICE

"The nation's first university, the University of Pennsylvania had its beginnings in 1740, some 36 years before Thomas Jefferson, Benjamin Franklin (Penn's founder), and their fellow revolutionaries went public in Philadelphia with incendiary notions about life, liberty and the pursuit of happiness. Today, Penn continues in the spirit of the Founding Fathers, developing the intellectual, discussion-oriented seminars that comprise the majority of our course offerings, shaping innovative new courses of study, and allowing a remarkable degree of academic flexibility to its undergraduate students.

"Penn is situated on a green, tree-lined, 260-acre, urban campus, four blocks west of the Schuylkill River in Philadelphia. The broad lawns that connect Penn's stately halls embody a philosophy of academic freedom within our undergraduate schools. Newly developed interdisciplinary programs fusing classical disciplines with practical, professional options enable Penn to define cutting-edge academia in and out of the classroom. Students are encouraged to partake in study and research that may extend into many of the graduate and professional schools. As part of our College House system, Penn's Faculty Masters engage students in academic and civic experience while leading residential programs that promote an environment where living and learning intersect around the clock.

"Penn students are part of a dynamic community that includes a traditional campus, a lively neighborhood, and a city rich in culture and diversity. Whether your interests include artistic performance, community involvement, student government, athletics, fraternities and sororities, or cultural and religious organizations, you'll find many different options. Most importantly, students at Penn find that their lives in and out of the classroom compliment each other and are full, interesting and busy. We invite you to visit Penn in Philadelphia. You'll enjoy the revolutionary spirit of the campus and city.

"Penn requires either the new SAT plus two SAT Subject Tests (in different fields) or the ACT. Scores from older versions of the SAT (pre-March 2005 version) and the ACT are acceptable. For the old SAT, scores must be submitted with the results of three SAT Subject Tests, one of which must be the writing test."

SELECTIVITY

Admissions Rating	**99**
# of applicants	18,282
% of applicants accepted	21
% of acceptees attending	63
# accepting a place on wait list	1,149
% admitted from wait list	7
# of early decision applicants	1,120
% accepted early decision	34

FRESHMAN PROFILE

Range SAT Verbal	650-740
Average SAT Verbal	694
Range SAT Math	680-760
Average SAT Math	718
**TPR Projected Range SAT Writing*	*670-720*
Range ACT Composite	28-33
Average ACT Composite	30
Minimum Paper TOEFL	550
Minimum Computer Based TOEFL	220
Average HS GPA	3.84
% graduated top 10% of class	94
% graduated top 25% of class	99
% graduated top 50% of class	100

DEADLINES

Early decision application deadline	11/1
Early decision notification	12/15
Regular application deadline	1/1
Regular notification	4/1
Nonfall registration?	no

APPLICANTS ALSO LOOK AT

AND OFTEN PREFER
Harvard College, Princeton U., Stanford U., Yale U.

AND SOMETIMES PREFER
Brown U., Columbia U.—Columbia College, Duke U.

AND RARELY PREFER
Cornell U., Georgetown U., Northwestern U.

FINANCIAL FACTS

Financial Aid Rating	**94**
Annual tuition	$27,544
Room & Board	$8,918
Books and supplies	$830
Required fees	$3,172
% frosh rec. need-based scholarship or grant aid	42
% UG rec. need-based scholarship or grant aid	40
% frosh rec. need-based self-help aid	45
% UG rec. need-based self-help aid	44
% frosh rec. any financial aid	62
% UG rec. any financial aid	58
Avg. frosh grant	$26,256
Avg. frosh loan	$3,001
Independent 529 member?	No

UNIVERSITY OF PITTSBURGH—PITTSBURGH

4227 FIFTH AVENUE, FIRST FLOOR, ALUMNI HALL, PITTSBURGH, PA 15260 • ADMISSIONS: 412-624-7488 • FAX: 412-648-8815

CAMPUS LIFE

Quality of Life Rating	**80**
Fire Safety Rating	**60**
Type of school	public

STUDENTS

Total undergrad enrollment	16,677
% male/female	48/52
% from out of state	6
% live on campus	36
% in (# of) fraternities	8 (15)
% in (# of) sororities	7 (11)
% African American	9
% Asian	4
% Caucasian	82
% Hispanic	1
% international	1
# of countries represented	48

SURVEY SAYS

Great computer facilities
Great library
Athletic facilities are great
Students love Pittsburgh, PA
Great off-campus food
Everyone loves the Panthers
Student publications are popular
Lots of beer drinking

ACADEMICS

Academic Rating	**81**
Calendar	semester
Student/faculty ratio	16:1
Professors interesting rating	72
Professors accessible rating	80
% classes taught by TAs	0
Most common lab size	20-29 students
Most common regular class size	10-19 students

MOST POPULAR MAJORS

Finance
marketing/marketing management
speech and rhetorical studies

STUDENTS SPEAK OUT

Academics

Many University of Pittsburgh students feel "happy that we discovered this amazing yet quite underrated school." They cite the English and science programs as two of the strongest, and one student tells us, "The nursing program is excellent and prepares you for the real world." The university offers "tons of diverse courses in any one semester," and students are encouraged to take a term abroad, "which is the best thing you can do." Some people see Pitt as "primarily a research school," but "it's stated university policy that professors are easy to see." The faculty "urges us to question things and provides an environment where we feel comfortable doing that." These "instructors and mentors" are known for being "passionate about what they teach" and "helpful both during lecture and during their office hours." Students appreciate that they "draw from real world experience as a complement to their academic knowledge." Advisors provide additional academic support: "We meet one-on-one with our advisors at least twice a semester, and mine has always gotten me the classes I needed at the times I needed with the professors I want." The administration receives high marks "for advancing the university, raising money, recruiting strong applicants, and managing public affairs." Though they may "look out for our best interests," administrators are seen as "a bit detached," "extremely inaccessible," and "nearly impossible to reach." Recent tuition hikes only exacerbate this unfavorable assessment. Nonetheless, Pitt provides a scholastic climate where undergraduates "learn so much and grow as people." A senior writes, "It has been quite challenging, but I am thankful for my time here. It just goes to prove that I have a strong degree behind me."

Life

The Pitt existence can be "extremely busy with academics, extracurricular activities, internships, part-time jobs, work-study positions, and social life." With more than 300 student organizations, there's room for everyone to "do their own thing." Students love their location in the Oakland section of Pittsburgh, "home to many restaurants and bars, making for a very social atmosphere." Students looking to enrich themselves take advantage of the "Carnegie Museums across the street" and the popular PITT ARTS program, which "provides discounted or free tickets to various cultural events around Pittsburgh." Couple that with free public transit for students, and one student writes, "What can beat free transportation, dinner, a symphony ticket, and dessert afterward?" The only better plan could be cheering on the top-notch football and basketball squads—season tickets set students back only 40 bucks. On campus, "the weekends are full of fun with activities planned through different student organizations and great parties." Though some students claim "the majority of students drink on the weekends," many people think the "novelty of fraternity parties tends to wear off pretty fast."

Student Body

The 17,000 undergarduate students attending Pitt form "a diverse group of students that, from what I have seen, interact easily and on a regular basis." One student observes, "We are amazingly diverse, and everyone is not only respectful, but also curious and excited to learn about and meet new people." Other respondents report that "people of the same ethnic group or background usually hang together." Even with approximately 14 percent of the student body members of minorities, one student points out, "Unfortunately, that is low for a city school." The minority populations organize effectively, in groups including the Black Action Society, Rainbow Alliance, and Asian Students Alliance. Amid this "wide spectrum of students" with a "broad range of interests," most are "friendly, outgoing, involved, motivated, and responsible." Most people seem to find their niche among "academically focused and open-minded" peers.

FINANCIAL AID: 412-624-7488 • E-MAIL: OAFA@PITT.EDU • WEBSITE: WWW.PITT.EDU

ADMISSIONS

Very important factors considered include: Class rank, secondary school record, standardized test scores. *Important factors considered include:* Essays, recommendations. *Other factors considered include:* Character/personal qualities, extracurricular activities, geographical residence, interview, minority status, state residency, talent/ability, volunteer work, work experience. SAT Reasoning, SAT Subject Tests, or ACT required. TOEFL required of all international applicants. High school diploma is required, and GED is not accepted. *Academic units required:* 4 English, 3 math, 3 science (3 science lab), 1 social studies, 4 academic electives. *Academic units recommended:* 3 foreign language, 3 social studies.

The Inside Word

Applicants to Pitt, as at most large public universities, are admitted primarily on the strength of basic qualifiers like grades and test scores. If you are serious about Pitt, rolling admissions allows you to get a decision earlier than most colleges notify their applicants.

FINANCIAL AID

Students should submit: FAFSA, institution's own financial aid form. Regular filing deadline is 6/1. The Princeton Review suggests that all financial aid forms be submitted as soon as possible after 1/1. *Need-based scholarships/grants offered:* Pell, SEOG, state scholarships/grants, private scholarships, the school's own gift aid. *Loan aid offered:* FFEL Subsidized Stafford, FFEL Unsubsidized Stafford, FFEL PLUS, Federal Perkins, Federal Nursing, college/university loans from institutional funds. Applicants will be notified of awards on a rolling basis beginning on or about 3/1. Federal Work-study Program available. Off-campus job opportunities are excellent.

FROM THE ADMISSIONS OFFICE

"The University of Pittsburgh is one of 62 members of the Association of American Universities, a prestigious group whose members include the major research universities of North America. There are nearly 400 degree programs available at the 16 Pittsburgh campus schools (two offering only undergraduate degree programs, four offering graduate degree programs, and ten offering both) and four regional campuses, allowing students a wide latitude of choices, both academically and in setting and style, size and pace of campus. Programs ranked nationally include philosophy, history and philosophy of science, chemistry, economics, English, history, physics, political science, and psychology. The University Center for International Studies is ranked one of the exemplary international programs in the country by the Council on Learning; and the Semester at Sea Program takes students to different ports of call around the world on an ocean liner.

"Freshman applicants for fall 2006 are required to take the new SAT, or the ACT with the Writing section, but we students may also submit scores from the old SAT (prior to March 2005) or ACT as well, and the best scores (Verbal/Critical Reading and Math) from either test will be used. "

SELECTIVITY

Admissions Rating	**89**
# of applicants	18,973
% of applicants accepted	49
% of acceptees attending	32

FRESHMAN PROFILE

Range SAT Verbal	560-660
Average SAT Verbal	610
Range SAT Math	580-670
Average SAT Math	621
**TPR Projected Range SAT Writing*	*600-670*
Range ACT Composite	24-28
Average ACT Composite	26
Minimum Paper TOEFL	550
Minimum Computer Based TOEFL	213
% graduated top 10% of class	46
% graduated top 25% of class	83
% graduated top 50% of class	98

DEADLINES

Regular notification	rolling
Nonfall registration?	yes

APPLICANTS ALSO LOOK AT

AND OFTEN PREFER
Boston University
Carnegie Mellon University
New York University
University of Pennsylvania
Virginia Tech

AND SOMETIMES PREFER
Penn State University Park
University of Delaware
University of Maryland—College Park

AND RARELY PREFER
Duquesne University
Indiana University of Pennsylvania
Slippery Rock University of Pennsylvania
Temple University

FINANCIAL FACTS

Financial Aid Rating	**78**
Annual in-state tuition	$8,218
Annual out-of-state tuition	$17,098
Room & Board	$7,090
Books and supplies	$700
Required fees	$700
% frosh rec. need-based scholarship or grant aid	41
% UG rec. need-based scholarship or grant aid	36
% frosh rec. need-based self-help aid	54
% UG rec. need-based self-help aid	41
Independent 529 member?	No

UNIVERSITY OF PUGET SOUND

1500 NORTH WARNER STREET, TACOMA, WA 98416-1062 • ADMISSIONS: 253-879-3211 • FAX: 253-879-3993

CAMPUS LIFE

Quality of Life Rating	**89**
Fire Safety Rating	**65**
Type of school	private
Environment	city

STUDENTS

Total undergrad enrollment	2,595
% male/female	42/58
% from out of state	70
% from public high school	78
% live on campus	59
% in (# of) fraternities	22 (4)
% in (# of) sororities	23 (4)
% African American	2
% Asian	8
% Caucasian	77
% Hispanic	3
% Native American	1

SURVEY SAYS

Small classes
Great library

ACADEMICS

Academic Rating	**91**
Calendar	semester
Student/faculty ratio	12:1
Professors interesting rating	95
Professors accessible rating	96
% professors teaching UG courses	96
% classes taught by TAs	0
Most common lab size	10-19 students
Most common regular class size	10-19 students

MOST POPULAR MAJORS

Business administration/management
English language and literature
psychology

STUDENTS SPEAK OUT

Academics

Set "in the shadows of the Cascades" and just down the road from Washington State's Commencement Bay, the University of Puget Sound "offers a strong (and getting stronger) liberal arts education." A junior explains, "We are a very student-centered school," which means that teaching is top priority for this highly qualified faculty. Not only are professors "intelligent, well-versed, [and] articulate," they're also concerned about the well-being of their students. "Many professors want to have conversations about what is going on in your life," writes a senior. "They make this school." So does the strong allotment of academic offerings. Students point to the Asian studies, biology, international political economy, and music offerings as the crème de la crème. You won't find the standard "huge lecture classes" at UPS; "even intro-level lectures have maybe 30 people in them." Despite the friendly atmosphere in class, professors tend to set high expectations for their students. "Coasting by on natural ability doesn't work anymore," warns a senior. Opinions of the administration vary, but most find it to be "caring and supportive of the students. If you have an idea, they say go for it." Students are hoping that the new president of the university will help put the place on the map. As a psychology major puts it, "The university is academically strong, but needs to be recognized for that across the country, not just in the Pacific Northwest."

Life

Whether you're a city slicker or a rugged outdoorsman, UPS's location ensures you'll find something to satisfy your interests. Seattle is a short drive away and has everything from pro sports teams to world-class art exhibits. With beaches, the Sound, the Cascades, and the Olympic Rain Forest all nearby, outdoor enthusiasts are never at a loss for adventure. "Outdoor interests are really popular, [including] ultimate Frisbee™, soccer, biking, and hiking." "Athletics are huge," too, and with 21 varsity teams, 14 intramural sports, and three club sports, athletes have plenty of opportunities to flex their muscles. Sports aside, "there are tons of activities (presentations, volunteer opportunities, meetings, movies, talks, concerts, and clubs) every night of the week." In total, UPS offers about 75 student clubs, and "most people are involved in a ton of groups." When they're not involved in parties, that is. And "there are always plenty going on, either at Greek houses or in other nearby campus houses." But beware, warns an undergrad: "The administration can have a Gestapo-esque feel when it comes to parties and drinking on campus." Nonetheless, some students line up at the keg, while others fill the seats for the popular "one-dollar movies" on campus. Regardless of what you're doing, "if you're not doing anything in the evening, you're either lazy or antisocial…or dead."

Student Body

"There are three groups of students" at UPS, according to a senior: "(1) the preppies, (2) the hippies, (3) the Hawaiians." Among groups (1) and (2), you're likely to find "a lot of 'trustafarians' and rich kids." There's no doubt that liberalism rules the roost here, which causes one junior to note that "the least accepted student organization is, ironically, the Republican Majority." But political differences—or any differences, for that matter—don't cause irreparable rifts in this student body. According to a sophomore, "Everyone gets along extremely well, no matter what gender, religion, race, ethnicity, [or] social class. UPS has a great atmosphere that I sincerely appreciate." Another classmate adds, "Overall, students are accepting and curious about other beliefs. And students here are open-minded." They're open-hearted, as well. Many students reported participating in community service.

FINANCIAL AID: 800-396-7192 • E-MAIL: ADMISSION@UPS.EDU • WEBSITE: WWW.UPS.EDU

ADMISSIONS

Very important factors considered include: Secondary school record, standardized test scores. *Important factors considered include:* Alumni/ae relation, character/personal qualities, essays, extracurricular activities, minority status, recommendations, talent/ability. *Other factors considered include:* Class rank, interview, volunteer work, work experience. SAT Reasoning or ACT required. TOEFL required of all international applicants. High school diploma is required, and GED is accepted. *Academic units recommended:* 4 English, 4 math, 4 science (4 science lab), 3 foreign language, 3 social studies, 3 history, 1 fine/visual and performing arts

The Inside Word

The University of Puget Sound is on the right track with its willingness to supply students with detailed information about how the selection process works. If universities in general were more forthcoming about candidate evaluation, college admission wouldn't be the angst-ridden exercise that it is for so many students. All students are aware that their academic background is the primary consideration of every admissions committee. How they are considered as individuals remains mysterious. At Puget Sound, it is clear that people mean more to the university than its freshman profile and that candidates can count on a considerate and caring attitude before, during, and after the review process.

FINANCIAL AID

Students should submit: FAFSA. The Princeton Review suggests that all financial aid forms be submitted as soon as possible after 1/1. *Need-based scholarships/grants offered:* Pell, SEOG, state scholarships/grants, private scholarships, the school's own gift aid. *Loan aid offered:* FFEL Subsidized Stafford, FFEL Unsubsidized Stafford, FFEL PLUS, Federal Perkins, state loans. Applicants will be notified of awards on a rolling basis beginning on or about 3/15. Federal Work-study Program available. Institutional employment available. Off-campus job opportunities are excellent.

FROM THE ADMISSIONS OFFICE

"For over 100 years, students from many locations and backgrounds have chosen to join our community. It is a community committed to excellence—excellence in the classroom and excellence in student organizations and activities. Puget students are serious about rowing and writing, management and music, skiing and sciences, leadership and languages. At Puget Sound you'll be challenged—and helped—to perform at the peak of your ability.

"Applicants are required to submit the SAT or the ACT. For the foreseeable future, Puget Sound will record the SAT or ACT Writing component score, but will not require it as a part of a completed freshman admission application."

SELECTIVITY

Admissions Rating	**90**
# of applicants	4,554
% of applicants accepted	70
% of acceptees attending	21
# accepting a place on wait list	308
% admitted from wait list	4
# of early decision applicants	148
% accepted early decision	92

FRESHMAN PROFILE

Range SAT Verbal	580-685
Average SAT Verbal	631
Range SAT Math	575-670
Average SAT Math	621
**TPR Projected Range SAT Writing*	*620-690*
Range ACT Composite	25-29
Average ACT Composite	27
Minimum Paper TOEFL	550
Minimum Computer Based TOEFL	213
Average HS GPA	3.57
% graduated top 10% of class	38
% graduated top 25% of class	74
% graduated top 50% of class	95

DEADLINES

Early decision application deadline	11/15
Early decision notification	12/15
Regular application deadline	5/1
Regular notification	4/1
Nonfall registration?	yes

APPLICANTS ALSO LOOK AT

AND OFTEN PREFER

Pomona College, Stanford U., Washington U. in St. Louis

AND SOMETIMES PREFER

Colorado College, Lewis & Clark College, U. of Washington, Whitman College, Willamette U.

AND RARELY PREFER

Albertson College of Idaho, Gonzaga U., Linfield College

FINANCIAL FACTS

Financial Aid Rating	**77**
Annual tuition	$28,270
Room & Board	$7,140
Required fees	$190
% frosh rec. need-based scholarship or grant aid	60
% UG rec. need-based scholarship or grant aid	59
% frosh rec. need-based self-help aid	47
% UG rec. need-based self-help aid	50
% frosh rec. any financial aid	88
% UG rec. any financial aid	89
Avg. frosh grant	$12,094
Avg. frosh loan	$5,344
Independent 529 member?	No

UNIVERSITY OF REDLANDS

1200 E. Colton Avenue, Redlands, CA 92373 • Admissions: 909-335-4074 • Fax: 909-335-4089

CAMPUS LIFE

Quality of Life Rating	**83**
Fire Safety Rating	**83**
Type of school	private
Environment	city

STUDENTS

Total undergrad enrollment	2,345
% male/female	41/59
% from out of state	28
% live on campus	73
% in (# of) fraternities	5 (5)
% in (# of) sororities	8 (5)
% African American	2
% Asian	6
% Caucasian	61
% Hispanic	12
% Native American	1
% international	1
# of countries represented	16

SURVEY SAYS

Small classes
Lab facilities are great
Great computer facilities
Athletic facilities are great
Students are friendly
Lots of beer drinking

ACADEMICS

Academic Rating	**84**
Calendar	4-4-1
Student/faculty ratio	11:1
Professors interesting rating	86
Professors accessible rating	83
% professors teaching UG courses	100
% classes taught by TAs	0
Most common regular class size	10-19 students

MOST POPULAR MAJORS

Business administration/management
psychology

STUDENTS SPEAK OUT

Academics

The University of Redlands is essentially two undergraduate programs in one. Through the College of Arts and Sciences (CAS), the majority of students follow a relatively conventional undergraduate curriculum, declaring majors and meeting the related requirements in order to graduate. About 200 students take a more independent approach through the Johnston Center for Integrative Studies, "where students who are accepted can create their own major with the help of their professors." These Johnston students write contracts for their courses and receive narrative evaluations of their work (rather than letter grades). This structure "allows students to learn in a way that is the most efficient for each individual." Because Johnston is a residential community, "everyone works together to strengthen their education," much to the delight of participants. But regardless of the track they choose, Redlands undergrads enjoy a "personable, student-oriented" school that's "just small enough to have incredible personal attention, yet large enough to still see different people almost every day." Students also appreciate a study abroad program that "is strongly emphasized and encouraged. If there's anywhere in the world that you've had an interest in going—for a month or semester to a year—the University of Redlands is the perfect place to do it. Many students go to Austria because it's a wonderful program and all your credits transfer when you come back." Redlands excels in a number of areas, including business, music, creative writing, and biology, but they don't do it without a bit of sweat. Undergrads warn, "The academics are Redlands are demanding; I find myself reading, writing, and studying with extremely high degrees of intensity."

Life

Redlands is close to a lot of great places, but the town of Redlands itself "isn't much," students say. A number of them use the nickname "Dead Lands" to sum up their attitude, and a freshman gripes that "we can't just go into town to read at a coffee shop because there is no town!" So while "there's not much to do if you don't have a car," for the automobile-enabled, "everything is within an hour: the beach, LA, Palm Springs, and the mountains. Trips to the desert in Joshua Tree National Park are also common. Many people like to snowboard or ski in Big Bear in the winter." This nature-rich setting attracts outdoorsy types, and unsurprisingly Redlands "has a very involved outdoor activities group on campus that takes students kayaking, rock climbing and backpacking to destinations throughout the country." The Redlands campus "is beautiful for its Roman-style buildings and pillars, especially in the winter with the snow-capped mountains in the background," and it stays reasonably busy for a school of Redland's size. "Usually, there's something happening on campus, whether it's a philosophical discussion, a screening of a movie, karaoke night, or a basketball game." Still, "on weekends, most people end up drinking and going to parties," which the school frowns upon. Students wish the administration would be "a little more relaxed when it comes to party scenes. It seems like everyone is always getting in trouble. And even the frats have to be really careful and always have huge fines."

Student Body

Because of the CAS/Johnston academic fault line at Redlands, "The school is somewhat divided," with "ultra-liberal Johnston students who meander about the campus on long boards, leaving behind a perpetual smell of hemp and patchouli" on one side, and "more conservative Abercrombie-wearing NCAA athletes, Greeks, and California-skater types" on the other. The CAS student body also includes "math/science geeks, the philosophy brains, the artists and musicians, the business people and the whimsical lit majors," about half of whom "regard the Johnston kids with complete suspicion and mistrust," in part because some of the Johnston kids seem to look down on the CAS majority. Johnston undergrads are known for being drawn to "a high-energy community of creativity, inhibition, and at times, spurts of college randomness. They are notorious for doing strange things!"

University of Redlands

Financial Aid: 909-335-4047 • E-mail: admissions@redlands.edu • Website: www.redlands.edu

ADMISSIONS

Very important factors considered include: Character/personal qualities, recommendations, secondary school record, talent/ability. *Important factors considered include:* Essays, standardized test scores. *Other factors considered include:* Alumni/ae relation, extracurricular activities, geographical residence, interview, minority status, volunteer work, work experience. SAT Reasoning or ACT required. TOEFL required of all international applicants. High school diploma is required, and GED is accepted. *Academic units required:* 4 English, 3 math, 2 science (1 science lab), 2 foreign language, 2 social studies. *Academic units recommended:* 4 English, 4 math, 3 science (1 science lab), 3 foreign language, 2 social studies, 1 history.

The Inside Word

The University of Redlands is a solid admit for any student with an above average high school record. Candidates who are interested in pursuing self-designed programs through the University's Johnston Center will find the admissions process to be distinctly more personal than it generally is; the center is interested in intellectually curious, self-motivated students and puts a lot of energy into identifying and recruiting them.

FINANCIAL AID

Students should submit: FAFSA, GPA verification form for California residents. The Princeton Review suggests that all financial aid forms be submitted as soon as possible after 1/1. *Need-based scholarships/grants offered:* Pell, SEOG, state scholarships/grants, private scholarships, the school's own gift aid. *Loan aid offered:* FFEL Subsidized Stafford, FFEL Unsubsidized Stafford, FFEL PLUS, Federal Perkins, college/university loans from institutional funds. Applicants will be notified of awards on or about 2/28. Federal Work-study Program available.

FROM THE ADMISSIONS OFFICE

"We've created an unusually blended curriculum of the liberal arts and preprofessional study because we think education is about learning how to think and learning how to do. For example, our environmental studies students have synthesized their study of computer science, sociology, biology, and economics to develop an actual resource management plan for the local mountain communities. Our creative writing program encourages internships with publishing or television production companies so that when our graduates send off their first novel, they can pay the rent as magazine writers. We educate managers, poets, environmental scientists, teachers, musicians, and speech therapists to be reflective about culture and society so that they can better understand and improve the world they'll enter upon graduation.

"First-year students applying for admission for fall 2006 are required to submit the results of either the SAT or the ACT. We do not require the Writing section of either test. Students may also submit scores from the old SAT (prior to March 2005) or ACT and the student's best scores from either test will be used."

SELECTIVITY

Admissions Rating	**86**
# of applicants	2,934
% of applicants accepted	75
% of acceptees attending	27

FRESHMAN PROFILE

Range SAT Verbal	540-640
Average SAT Verbal	584
Range SAT Math	530-630
Average SAT Math	580
**TPR Projected Range SAT Writing*	*590-660*
Range ACT Composite	22-27
Average ACT Composite	24
Minimum Paper TOEFL	550
Minimum Computer Based TOEFL	213
Average HS GPA	3.54
% graduated top 10% of class	32
% graduated top 25% of class	66
% graduated top 50% of class	93

DEADLINES

Regular application deadline	5/1
Regular notification	rolling
Nonfall registration?	yes

APPLICANTS ALSO LOOK AT

AND OFTEN PREFER

University of California—San Diego
University of California—Santa Barbara
University of Southern California

AND SOMETIMES PREFER

Chapman University
Loyola Marymount University
Pitzer College
University of San Diego

AND RARELY PREFER

Boston University
Colorado State University
University of Hawaii at Hilo

FINANCIAL FACTS

Financial Aid Rating	**85**
Annual tuition	$25,224
Room & Board	$8,696
Books and supplies	$1,000
Required fees	$300
% frosh rec. need-based scholarship or grant aid	68
% UG rec. need-based scholarship or grant aid	69
% frosh rec. need-based self-help aid	63
% UG rec. need-based self-help aid	66
% frosh rec. any financial aid	91
% UG rec. any financial aid	90
Avg. frosh grant	$13,381
Avg. frosh loan	$4,275
Independent 529 member?	Yes

UNIVERSITY OF RHODE ISLAND

14 UPPER COLLEGE ROAD, KINGSTON, RI 02881-1391 • ADMISSIONS: 401-874-7100 • FAX: 401-874-5523

CAMPUS LIFE

Quality of Life Rating	**64**
Fire Safety Rating	**84**
Type of school	public
Environment	rural

STUDENTS

Total undergrad enrollment	10,957
% male/female	44/56
% from out of state	39
% from public high school	90
% live on campus	39
% in (# of) fraternities	9 (9)
% in (# of) sororities	10 (8)
% African American	4
% Asian	3
% Caucasian	76
% Hispanic	4

SURVEY SAYS

Great library
Great off-campus food
Students are happy
Student publications are popular
Lots of beer drinking
Hard liquor is popular
(Almost) everyone smokes

ACADEMICS

Academic Rating	**61**
Calendar	semester
Student/faculty ratio	19:1
Professors interesting rating	62
Professors accessible rating	61
% professors teaching UG courses	83
% classes taught by TAs	8
Most common lab size	10-19 students
Most common regular class size	20-29 students

MOST POPULAR MAJORS

Communications studies/speech communication and rhetoric
nursing/registered nurse training (RN, ASN, BSN, MSN)
psychology

STUDENTS SPEAK OUT

Academics

In square miles, Rhode Island is the smallest of the 50 states, but at the University of Rhode Island, a large-scale academic experience is offered to the school's 10,000-plus undergrads. Popular majors include psychology, communication studies, pharmacy, and human development and family studies and "most professors go out of their way to help their students." A junior in the communications studies programs appreciates that, "Professors actually know what they're talking about. They've had out of the classroom experience and have held jobs in the fields they're teaching. It's reassuring to know that what I'm learning will still be applicable once I leave my classroom." A student in the political science department confirms, "There are some amazing professors that really get you thinking, but others are not so passionate." We've also heard several rumblings from students who've struggled "to understand the professor due to a lack of the English language." Among this community of pre-professional students, though, most feel that they're receiving a strong, vocation-minded education at "a good price." As one student says, URI is all about "preparing students for the real world." In the meantime, students wrangle with an administration that "puts meaning to the quote, 'In the land of the blind, the man with one eye leads.'" "Registering for classes can be a huge pain, [and] "the Internet system is terrible."

Life

The Oliver Watson House—the oldest building at URI—was built around 1796, and when students reflect on the relatively dry campus here (students 21+ can drink in their room), they feel as if they're living back in the era of Oliver Watson himself. "Campus liquor rules are very strict," sighs one student. "Everyone goes home on the weekends [because] there isn't much going on." Those who stick around "are here to party," and head to off-campus ragers or cruise into nearby Providence or Newport. If you find the parties, says a sophomore, the "social life at URI can be a lot of sloppy fun." Even if that's not your scene, students assure us there's "a peaceful, friendly environment [on a] beautiful campus" with opportunities to satisfy a range of tastes. Make an effort to "get involved and it's a great place to be." Upwards of 80 campus organizations are offered, and the new, state-of-the-art Ryan Center hosts entertainment and athletic events. The school "definitely takes care of their athletes," and athletics are serious business around here. The Rhode Island Rams' men's basketball team makes a fair share of headlines, and a sophomore asserts, "The ice hockey club team is the best in the nation!" Aside from the "horrific" parking situation—the many students who commute have been known "to skip class because there are literally no spots to park"—students find that life at URI is pretty good; many of them say they chose the school for its beach locale. As one Rhode Island native yelps, "RI born! RI die!"

Student Body

The majority of URI's student body comes from Rhode Island—attracted by the close proximity to home and the nice in-state price—though Massachusetts, New Jersey, Connecticut, and New York contribute noteworthy numbers to the population, too. One student gripes that "local RI students come with their friends from high school and they aren't really interested in making new friends," but at least there's "a mixture of students socioeconomically." Among this mix, "many students are extremely involved in campus life, but there are still those who are apathetic and refuse to do anything outside of themselves." The majority of URI students are "white and middle class," and one senior warns that "ethnic groups do not mix. People here tend to hang out with people who look and act like they do." But this tendency, of course, is not law. A business administration major sums up his experience by saying, "At URI you can enjoy the best of what college life has to offer."

University of Rhode Island

Financial Aid: 401-874-9500 • E-mail: uriadmit@etal.uri.edu • Website: www.uri.edu/admissions

ADMISSIONS

Very important factors considered include: Class rank, secondary school record. *Important factors considered include:* Standardized test scores. *Other factors considered include:* Alumni/ae relation, character/personal qualities, essays, extracurricular activities, geographical residence, interview, minority status, recommendations, state residency, talent/ability, volunteer work, work experience. SAT Reasoning or ACT required. TOEFL required of all international applicants. High school diploma is required, and GED is accepted. *Academic units required:* 4 English, 3 math, 2 science (2 science lab), 2 foreign language, 2 social studies, 5 academic electives. *Academic units recommended:* 4 English, 4 math, 4 science, 4 foreign language, 4 social studies.

The Inside Word

Any candidate with solid grades is likely to find the university's admissions committee to be welcoming. The yield of admits who enroll is low and the state's population small. Out-of-state students are attractive to URI because they are sorely needed to fill out the student body. Students who graduate in the top 10 percent of their class are good scholarship bets.

FINANCIAL AID

Students should submit: FAFSA. The Princeton Review suggests that all financial aid forms be submitted as soon as possible after 1/1. *Need-based scholarships/grants offered:* Pell, SEOG, state scholarships/grants, private scholarships, the school's own gift aid. *Loan aid offered:* Direct Subsidized Stafford, Direct Unsubsidized Stafford, Direct PLUS, Federal Perkins, Federal Nursing, state loans, college/university loans from institutional funds. Applicants will be notified of awards on a rolling basis beginning on or about 3/31. Federal Work-study Program available.

FROM THE ADMISSIONS OFFICE

"Outstanding freshmen candidates with minimum SAT scores of 1150 or ACT composite of 25 who rank in the top third of their high school class are eligible to be considered for a Centennial Scholarship. These merit based scholarships range up to full tuition and are renewable each semester if the student maintains full-time continuous enrollment and a 3.00 average or better. Eligibility requires that a completed admissions application be RECEIVED by our December 15, 2005 Early Action deadline. Applications filed electronically are NOT considered complete until the application fee, official secondary school transcript(s), and SAT or ACT scores are received. To qualify for consideration for the Centennial Scholarship, everything must arrive in the Undergraduate Admissions Office by December 15, 2005. No extra form is required. If a student's residency status changes from out-of-state to regional or in-state, the Centennial award will be reduced because tuition varies on the basis of residency classification. Secondary school students with more than 23 college credits (excluding AP credits) and secondary school graduates who have matriculated at other postsecondary institutions are not eligible for Centennial Scholarships.

"Both the old and new version of the SAT is accepted. While the Verbal and Math scores will continue to be used for admission evaluation and Centennial scholarship consideration, the new Writing score will not be used for admission purposes."

SELECTIVITY	
Admissions Rating	**60**
# of applicants	13,110
% of applicants accepted	70
% of acceptees attending	29
FRESHMAN PROFILE	
Range SAT Verbal	510-600
Average SAT Verbal	556
Range SAT Math	520-610
Average SAT Math	568
**TPR Projected Range SAT Writing*	*570-630*
Average ACT Composite	24
Minimum Paper TOEFL	550
Minimum Computer Based TOEFL	213
% graduated top 10% of class	18
% graduated top 50% of class	89
DEADLINES	
Regular application deadline	2/1
Regular notification	rolling
Nonfall registration?	yes
FINANCIAL FACTS	
Financial Aid Rating	**65**
Annual in-state tuition	$4,680
Annual out-of-state tuition	$16,266
Room & Board	$7,810
Books and supplies	$800
Required fees	$2,072
% frosh rec. need-based scholarship or grant aid	51
% UG rec. need-based scholarship or grant aid	51
% frosh rec. need-based self-help aid	47
% UG rec. need-based self-help aid	48
% frosh rec. any financial aid	51
% UG rec. any financial aid	52
Avg. frosh grant	$5,481
Avg. frosh loan	$5,178
Independent 529 member?	No

UNIVERSITY OF RICHMOND

28 WESTHAMPTON WAY, RICHMOND, VA 23173 • ADMISSIONS: 804-289-8640 • FAX: 804-287-6003

CAMPUS LIFE

Quality of Life Rating	**85**
Fire Safety Rating	**75**
Type of school	private
Environment	city

STUDENTS

Total undergrad enrollment	2,909
% male/female	49/51
% from out of state	84
% from public high school	63
% live on campus	92
% in (# of) fraternities	45 (7)
% in (# of) sororities	45 (8)
% African American	5
% Asian	4
% Caucasian	86
% Hispanic	2
% international	1
# of countries represented	75

SURVEY SAYS

Small classes
No one cheats
Great off-campus food
Campus feels safe
Frats and sororities dominate social scene
Lots of beer drinking

ACADEMICS

Academic Rating	**94**
Calendar	semester
Student/faculty ratio	10:1
Professors interesting rating	89
Professors accessible rating	89
% professors teaching UG courses	100
% classes taught by TAs	0
Most common lab size	10-19 students
Most common regular class size	10-19 students

MOST POPULAR MAJORS

Business administration/management
political science and government

STUDENTS SPEAK OUT

Academics

With a strong liberal arts core that integrates a "great business school and equally strong leadership school" and "amazing and challenging premed programs," the University of Richmond serves well a student population that "knows that after college they will go to med, law, or grad school and end up with a high-paying job." Undergrads tell us that UR "is the perfect size. It's small enough where it's easy to get involved in lots of different things and to play a leadership role in that group. However, you always have plenty of options and are constantly meeting new people." The school "encourages undergraduate research, both in the sciences and in other fields, and most appealing is that students are often paid for their research," although the benefits to students' resumes aren't half bad either. Classes are "challenging and the workload can be difficult," but "professors tend to be understanding" and "really do care about their students." Undergrads love the academics, although many complain that the required writing-intensive, first-year course "is a pain that many students find annoying and pointless." Some here warn that due to the size of the school, "there are a limited number of classes offered. Especially in the less-popular departments, interesting classes that were in the catalogue were hardly offered, and were almost impossible to get into for underclassmen." Support systems are strong; they include "academic advisors to ensure that the student is getting a quality education with opportunities to do internships and study abroad," "an effective career development center," "speech, writing and academic skills centers (all excellent)," "free tutoring," and "a great alumni network."

Life

UR's coordinate system divides men and women into coordinate colleges: Richmond for men, Westhampton for women. Students dine and attend classes together and share some student organizations, but they function under separate governance systems. The benefits of this system include "great leadership opportunities for tons of men and women." Many here complain, though, that the system "makes dating on campus difficult. It makes relationships between men and women (whether intimate or just friends) awkward and unlike real life." The problem is exacerbated by the fact that "there aren't enough common get-together spaces for men and women. We need a space to hang out that is not just a mediocre dorm lounge." The Greek houses help; students report that "the fraternity scene is central to the culture of the school, almost at the exclusion of every other weekend activity." Students might take greater advantage of their proximity to a big city except that "it is very difficult to go anywhere without a car because the university as well as the city has limited public transportation." One student explains, "This campus is located near a great city that many students never explore, outside of bars." Perhaps students stick so close to school because it's just so beautiful; everyone here agrees that "our campus is quite obviously one of the most gorgeous in the world. Everything from the lake and gazebo to the architecture of the buildings are breathtaking."

Student Body

UR, most students agree, "is extremely preppy, with a lot of very wealthy students. It is also very fraternity/sorority-oriented. If you aren't in one of those groups, it is definitely harder to find close friends because the school is so small." Harder, but not impossible; notes one outsider, "There is a decided proportion of students who don't fit this mold, who are easy to find and certainly fit in, but if you are one of this latter group, it may seem on occasion as though you are starring in 'Operation J. Crew Invasion.'" Most students "live, eat, study, and party on campus; they enjoy a sense of belonging here. Everyone you pass waves, nods, smiles or says 'hello,' even if you've never met them before. Walking to class can really put you in a good mood, no matter how late you were up cramming for a test."

UNIVERSITY OF RICHMOND

FINANCIAL AID: 804-289-8438 • E-MAIL: ADMISSIONS@RICHMOND.EDU • WEBSITE: WWW.RICHMOND.EDU

ADMISSIONS

Very important factors considered include: Secondary school record. *Important factors considered include:* Character/personal qualities, class rank, essays, standardized test scores, talent/ability. *Other factors considered include:* Alumni/ae relation, extracurricular activities, geographical residence, minority status, recommendations, state residency, volunteer work, work experience. SAT Reasoning or ACT required. TOEFL required of all international applicants. High school diploma is required, and GED is accepted. *Academic units required:* 4 English, 3 math, 2 science (2 science lab), 2 foreign language, 2 history. *Academic units recommended:* 4 English, 4 math, 4 science (4 science lab), 4 foreign language, 4 history.

The Inside Word

There may not be an admissions formula, but two SAT Subject Tests are an important application requirement; we'd advise candidates to prepare for them thoroughly, since they outweigh the SAT I. When used with a measure of flexibility and a willingness to consider other factors, as Richmond does, there is nothing inherently wrong with such an approach. There does appear to be an effort to look at the candidate's record carefully and thoroughly. Make no mistake: Course of study, high school performance, and test scores are the most important parts of your application, but Richmond also makes sure that all files are read at least three times before a final decision has been rendered.

FINANCIAL AID

Students should submit: FAFSA, institution's own financial aid form. Regular filing deadline is 2/25. The Princeton Review suggests that all financial aid forms be submitted as soon as possible after 1/1. *Need-based scholarships/grants offered:* Pell, SEOG, state scholarships/grants, private scholarships. *Loan aid offered:* Direct Subsidized Stafford, Direct Unsubsidized Stafford, Direct PLUS, Federal Perkins, Charles B. Keesee Educational Loans (VA & NC residents). Applicants will be notified of awards on or about 4/1. Off-campus job opportunities are good.

FROM THE ADMISSIONS OFFICE

"The University of Richmond combines the characteristics of a small college with the dynamics of a large university. The unique size, beautiful suburban campus, and world-class facilities offer students an extraordinary mix of opportunities for personal growth and intellectual achievement. At Richmond, students are encouraged to engage themselves in their environment. Discussion and dialogue are the forefront of the academic experience, while research, internships, and international experiences are important components of students' cocurricular lives. The university is committed to providing undergraduate students with a rigorous academic experience, while integrating these studies with opportunities for experiential learning and promoting total individual development. The university also places a high value on diversity and believes in taking full advantage if the rich benefits of learning in a community of individuals from varied backgrounds.

"For fall 2006, students will meet admission requirements one of three ways: by taking the new SAT, the old SAT (plus the SAT Subject Test in Writing), or the ACT (the Writing component is optional). If multiple tests are submitted, the evaluation considers those results which are most favorable to the applicant."

SELECTIVITY

Admissions Rating	**95**
# of applicants	6,236
% of applicants accepted	40
% of acceptees attending	32
# accepting a place on wait list	1,603
% admitted from wait list	6
# of early decision applicants	182
% accepted early decision	47

FRESHMAN PROFILE

Range SAT Verbal	620-690
Range SAT Math	630-700
**TPR Projected Range SAT Writing*	*650-690*
Range ACT Composite	27-30
Minimum Paper TOEFL	550
Minimum Computer Based TOEFL	213
Average HS GPA	3.52
% graduated top 10% of class	60
% graduated top 25% of class	92
% graduated top 50% of class	99

DEADLINES

Early decision application deadline	11/15
Early decision notification	12/15
Regular application deadline	1/15
Regular notification	4/1
Nonfall registration?	no

APPLICANTS ALSO LOOK AT AND OFTEN PREFER

College of William and Mary
U. of North Carolina—Chapel Hill
University of Virginia

AND SOMETIMES PREFER

Boston College
Duke University
Georgetown University
Vanderbilt University
Wake Forest University

AND RARELY PREFER

Bucknell University
Lafayette College

FINANCIAL FACTS

Financial Aid Rating	**92**
Annual tuition	$34,850
Room & Board	$5,660
Books and supplies	$1,050
% frosh rec. need-based scholarship or grant aid	37
% UG rec. need-based scholarship or grant aid	33
% frosh rec. need-based self-help aid	29
% UG rec. need-based self-help aid	26
% frosh rec. any financial aid	67
% UG rec. any financial aid	68
Avg. frosh grant	$16,725
Avg. frosh loan	$2,820
Independent 529 member?	Yes

University of Rochester

300 Wilson Boulevard, PO Box 270251, Rochester, NY 14627-0251 • Admissions: 585-275-3221 • Fax: 585-461-4595

CAMPUS LIFE

Quality of Life Rating	**78**
Fire Safety Rating	**60**
Type of school	private
Environment	village

STUDENTS

Total undergrad enrollment	4,449
% male/female	53/47
% live on campus	87
% African American	4
% Asian	11
% Caucasian	64
% Hispanic	4
% international	4

SURVEY SAYS

Lab facilities are great
Great computer facilities
Great library
Athletic facilities are great
Student publications are popular

ACADEMICS

Academic Rating	**88**
Calendar	semester
Student/faculty ratio	9:1
Professors interesting rating	78
Professors accessible rating	77
% classes taught by TAs	0
Most common regular class size	10-19 students

STUDENTS SPEAK OUT

Academics

Those seeking "a small, quantitative, team-oriented environment with a lot of diversity, challenges, and customization" might want to consider the University of Rochester (U of R), a math and science heavy hitter that also "has well-recognized economics and political science programs [and] a top-notch optics program." Many students insist that "U of R has strengths in all aspects of the school," reporting that "there is so much diversity within the academic departments. It's wonderful to have friends in the humanities and also in engineering." Despite its breadth of offerings, U of R maintains a small-school feel. Students think, "It's the perfect size, so that you can see familiar faces." They say professors "are extremely approachable for both academic and nonacademic matters, are very flexible in setting up a meeting, [and] are not only amazing thinkers, but [also] they also genuinely care that you leave the institution with a firm grasp of concepts." Administrators also earn raves because they "seem to genuinely care about the student body. The deans and faculty make sure that they roam the campus and dining halls, and typically invite students to eat with them."

Life

"There are all different types of people who are into all different types of things" at the University of Rochester. In terms of student involvement, "there is definitely a large population of students at Rochester who are not involved with many campus, community, or social activities." However, "there are also a lot of other students who do like to be active and have fun, so you need to get out and do things to meet these people." Many students "work hard during the week, and on the weekends they relax on the fraternity quad, regardless of affiliation." While students observe, "Fraternities and sororities have a large presence on campus," they follow up by saying, "[they] are certainly not the only social outlets." There are also sports—Rochester's Division III standing allows serious scholars to compete at the intercollegiate level and still have time for the copious amount of schoolwork—as well as "dances, balls, movies, and guest speakers." Weather plays a role in determining how active the campus is. Because winters at U of R are very long and very cold, "people tend to stay inside more, and there are more dorm-related activities held." Although the city of Rochester "can be a lot of fun," the school "is not located well in the city. There's a huge cemetery on one side, a large medical center on another, and a river along the other two sides." Unfortunately, some students see the location as a disincentive to leaving campus.

Student Body

University of Rochester is "small enough to find your niche, but large enough to have enough people [so that] you are bound to find a group you like," students tell us. The "smart, intellectual, nicely-dressed" U of R undergraduates "take academics very seriously." They must to survive the challenges of the curriculum. Although the school has taken some knocks for its failure to recruit minorities more successfully, students tell us that "there are plenty of blacks, Hispanics, and Asians on campus" and that "University of Rochester is much more diverse than I would have ever expected. The people one meets around campus are as varied as a large box of Crayolas," in part because they bring "different views and upbringings" to the table. Despite their differences, "all have a common willingness to meet new people and learn to live with those that are different."

FINANCIAL AID: 716-275-3226 • E-MAIL: ADMIT@ADMISSIONS.ROCHESTER.EDU • WEBSITE: WWW.ROCHESTER.EDU

ADMISSIONS

Very important factors considered include: Character/personal qualities, interview, secondary school record. *Important factors considered include:* Class rank, essays, minority status, recommendations, talent/ability. *Other factors considered include:* Alumni/ae relation, extracurricular activities, standardized test scores, volunteer work, work experience. SAT Reasoning or ACT required. SAT Subject Tests recommended. TOEFL required of all international applicants. High school diploma is required, and GED is accepted.

The Inside Word

The University of Rochester is definitely a good school, but the competition takes away three-fourths of the university's admits. Many students use Rochester as a safety; this hinders the university's ability to move up among top national institutions in selectivity. It also makes U of R a very solid choice for above-average students who aren't Ivy material.

FINANCIAL AID

Students should submit: FAFSA, CSS/Financial Aid PROFILE, state aid form, noncustodial (divorced/separated) parents' statement, business/farm supplement. Regular filing deadline is 2/1. The Princeton Review suggests that all financial aid forms be submitted as soon as possible after 1/1. *Need-based scholarships/grants offered:* Pell, SEOG, state scholarships/grants, the school's own gift aid. *Loan aid offered:* Direct Subsidized Stafford, Direct Unsubsidized Stafford, Direct PLUS, Federal Perkins, Federal Nursing, college/university loans from institutional funds. Applicants will be notified of awards on or about 4/1. Federal Work-study Program available. Institutional employment available. Off-campus job opportunities are excellent.

FROM THE ADMISSIONS OFFICE

"A campus visit can be one of the most important (and most enjoyable) components of a college search. Visiting Rochester can provide you with the opportunity to experience for yourself the traditions and innovations of our university. Whether you visit a class, tour the campus, or meet with a professor or coach, you'll learn a great deal about the power of a Rochester education—with advantages that begin during your undergraduate years and continue after graduation. No other school combines the wealth of academic programs on the personal scale that the University of Rochester offers. Our students achieve academic excellence in a university setting that encourages frequent, informal contact with distinguished faculty. Our faculty-designed 'Rochester Renaissance Curriculum' allows students to spend as much of their time as possible studying subjects they enjoy so much that they stop watching the clock,' says William Scott Green, dean of the undergraduate college. At the heart of the Renaissance Curriculum is the Quest Program. Quest courses are seminar-sized offerings that encourage you to solve problems through investigations and exploration . . . much the same way our faculty do. Working alongside your professor, you will test theories and explore education frontiers on a campus with some of the best resources in the world, driven by a curriculum that is truly unprecedented.

"Students applying to Rochester for 2006, 2007, and 2008 admission may submit the results from the old SAT or the ACT (with or without Writing component). In addition to one of these tests, optional submissions such as SAT Subject Tests, AP or IB exam results, and additional high school writing samples are wecomed and will be reviewed."

SELECTIVITY

Admissions Rating	**96**
# of applicants	11,052
% of applicants accepted	48
% of acceptees attending	18
# accepting a place on wait list	1,123
% admitted from wait list	14
# of early decision applicants	231
% accepted early decision	44

FRESHMAN PROFILE

Range SAT Verbal	600-700
Average SAT Verbal	665
Range SAT Math	630-710
Average SAT Math	687
**TPR Projected Range SAT Writing*	*630-700*
Range ACT Composite	27-32
Average ACT Composite	30
Minimum Paper TOEFL	550
Average HS GPA	3.75
% graduated top 10% of class	76
% graduated top 25% of class	95

DEADLINES

Early decision application deadline	11/1
Early decision notification	12/15
Regular application deadline	1/20
Regular notification	rolling
Nonfall registration?	yes

APPLICANTS ALSO LOOK AT

AND OFTEN PREFER
Cornell University
SUNY at Binghamton
SUNY at Buffalo
Washington University in St. Louis

AND SOMETIMES PREFER
Boston University
New York University
SUNY at Albany
Syracuse University
University of Vermont

AND RARELY PREFER
Franklin & Marshall College

FINANCIAL FACTS

Financial Aid Rating	**85**
Annual tuition	$28,250
Room & Board	$9,845
Books and supplies	$550
Required fees	$732
% frosh rec. need-based scholarship or grant aid	56
% UG rec. need-based scholarship or grant aid	55
% frosh rec. need-based self-help aid	41
% UG rec. need-based self-help aid	43
Independent 529 member?	Yes

UNIVERSITY OF SAN DIEGO

5998 ALCALA PARK, SAN DIEGO, CA 92110-2492 • ADMISSIONS: 619-260-4506 • FAX: 619-260-6836

CAMPUS LIFE

Quality of Life Rating	**89**
Fire Safety Rating	**60**
Type of school	private
Affiliation	Roman Catholic
Environment	metropolis

STUDENTS

Total undergrad enrollment	4,904
% male/female	39/61
% from out of state	38
% from public high school	65
% live on campus	49
% in (# of) fraternities	10 (4)
% in (# of) sororities	19 (5)
% African American	2
% Asian	7
% Caucasian	68
% Hispanic	15
% Native American	1
% international	2
# of countries represented	63

SURVEY SAYS

Small classes
Lab facilities are great
Students love San Diego, CA
Great off-campus food
Campus feels safe

ACADEMICS

Academic Rating	**82**
Calendar	4-1-4
Student/faculty ratio	16:1
Professors interesting rating	85
Professors accessible rating	85
% professors teaching UG courses	100
% classes taught by TAs	0
Most common lab size	10-19 students
Most common regular class size	30-39 students

MOST POPULAR MAJORS

Business administration/management
communications studies/speech communication and rhetoric
psychology

STUDENTS SPEAK OUT

Academics

Approximately one in three undergraduates major in business, management, or marketing at the University of San Diego, a small, prestigious, Catholic school perched on the Pacific Ocean's edge. But there's a whole lot more to a USD education than prepping for a successful corporate career. All undergraduates here must complete the demanding general education requirements that ensure a "values-based education for everyone. You not only learn about Plato's Republic, but also how its themes are relevant to our socio-political situation today in this country and around the world. There is exploration beyond the here and now and spiritual adventure here." Adding to that sort of experience is USD's community service-learning, which "provides opportunities for community relations and student 'hands on experience' in different fields (sociology, psychology, political science)." USD also offers solid, popular programs in communications, psychology, nursing, and education. Smaller departments like engineering and the sciences earn praise, too, the latter which benefits from "a great facility with brand-new labs." Undergrads in all departments embrace the small school environment in which "professors know you by name and expect you to be in class and doing your work." USD professors "are enthusiastic and you can tell they love teaching at a small school rather than a huge state university." And just so you know, they expect a lot from their students. Cautions one student: "This school is very academically challenging and you have to work hard for your grades. The results, though, are more satisfying because you actually did work hard and put in the effort and you learned something."

Life

"USD is a place where you can be in an engaging and stimulating class one minute, and five minutes later you're sitting on the beach with your friends," writes one student, summing up the near-idyllic situation here. "To be able to study and surf at the same time: that's what college is about!" USD students love their campus, which is "beautiful and immaculate. The grounds are perfectly kept at all times, and the architecture is gorgeous. Just being here will make you happy and wanting to learn." They're also crazy for the "awesome weather," the "great opportunities to get involved, and the tremendous resources to become a leader on campus, if you have the personal drive to take on the challenge." Most of all, they love San Diego, "one of the coolest, most interactive cities in the world. Along with its beaches, babes, nightlife, and abundant outdoor activities, San Diego is a multi-cultural epicenter, attracting all kinds of different people." Undergrads recommend the Gaslamp District for fun and food, Mission Beach for the ocean, La Jolla and Fashion Valley for shopping, and Tijuana for wild weekends. About the only thing USD undergrads don't love is the school's public safety policy, which is "very strict. Every week numerous people are written up for not only drinking but even for being in the presence of alcohol. It is as if they have to fill a quota of how many people they write up each weekend." As a result, "there are not many things to do on campus on the weekend. It can get pretty boring if you're stuck there."

Student Body

USD's student body "has the general southern California 'feeling,' meaning that pretty much everyone is laid back and easygoing." Many here "come from very affluent families. They drive the best, wear the best, and just have the best of everything. All the girls dress the same," decking themselves out in a tank top, a miniskirt, Ugg boots, and a Louis Vuitton bag. Some observers add that "there are a good number of atypical students at USD, very down-to-earth students with caring and fun personalities. Virtually anyone can find a comfortable group of friends to surround them." Students point out that "even though the campus is pretty religious, almost everyone is accepting of the PRIDE organization. Also, the organizations for minority groups are extremely active on campus (even though the school is not very diverse)."

UNIVERSITY OF SAN DIEGO

FINANCIAL AID: 619-260-4514 • E-MAIL: ADMISSIONS@SANDIEGO.EDU • WEBSITE: WWW.SANDIEGO.EDU/UGADMISS

ADMISSIONS

Very important factors considered include: Secondary school record, standardized test scores. *Important factors considered include:* Character/personal qualities, essays, extracurricular activities, talent/ability. *Other factors considered include:* Alumni/ae relation, class rank, minority status, recommendations, religious affiliation/commitment, volunteer work, work experience. SAT Reasoning or ACT required. SAT Subject Tests recommended. TOEFL required of all international applicants. High school diploma is required, and GED is accepted. *Academic units recommended:* 4 English, 4 math, 4 science (4 science lab), 4 foreign language, 4 social studies.

The Inside Word

Applicants to the University of San Diego will find a unique place with a remarkable amount of diversity in its 4,000-student population. Academically, the school offers a solid liberal arts core with close interaction between professors—all in one of the most livable cities anywhere. Solid test scores and high schools grades should be a given for applicants.

FINANCIAL AID

Students should submit: FAFSA. Regular filing deadline is 2/20. The Princeton Review suggests that all financial aid forms be submitted as soon as possible after 1/1. *Need-based scholarships/grants offered:* Pell, SEOG, state scholarships/grants, private scholarships, the school's own gift aid. *Loan aid offered:* FFEL Subsidized Stafford, FFEL Unsubsidized Stafford, FFEL PLUS, Federal Perkins, state loans, college/university loans from institutional funds, nonfederal loan programs. Applicants will be notified of awards on a rolling basis beginning on or about 3/1. Federal Work-study Program available. Institutional employment available. Off-campus job opportunities are excellent.

FROM THE ADMISSIONS OFFICE

"Looking at the University of San Diego is easy on the eyes. But really seeing our true character demands a little work.

"It is easy to focus on the obvious: the incredible beauty of the campus, the region's unparalleled climate and livability, long lists of recreational and cocurricular opportunities, the vitality of students walking through the central plaza, or even the obvious expressions of USD's Catholic character. But to focus on the superficial would be misleading.

"While the beach is nearby, USD is a serious academic institution. And while the campus is stunning, the people make the difference. More than 7,000 candidates vie for 1,000 freshman openings. But to see the 'average' freshman as a 3.8 GPA or a 1210 SAT score would miss the person. Each is unique—selected on expressions of diversity, leadership, service, talent, and essential human character. Faculty, too, are rigorously screened. USD draws over 100 candidates for every faculty opening, and this screening goes well beyond their lists of publications or the names on their diplomas. To challenge and inspire, they bring innovative approaches to undergraduate research, experiential learning, and faculty mentoring.

"While often compared to much larger institutions, USD seeks to be recognized for undergraduate teaching and residential learning. In comparison to schools of similar character, USD's academic offerings are truly impressive; a small sample includes marine biology, environmental studies, Latino studies, communication studies, e-commerce, and professional programs in engineering, business, nursing, and education, each of which complements a rigorous liberal arts base. New facilities demonstrate this diversity, including a state-of-the-art science center, the Kroc Institute for Peace and Justice, and the Jenny Craig Sports Pavilion.

"Freshman applicants must submit scores from the new SAT or the ACT exam with Writing. Scores on the previous exams will not be considered. As always, these scores will be used in conjunction with many other factors; in particular, the student's grade point average, curriculum, extra curricular activities, and letters of recommendation."

SELECTIVITY

Admissions Rating	**88**
# of applicants	7,623
% of applicants accepted	66
% of acceptees attending	23
# accepting a place on wait list	458
% admitted from wait list	1

FRESHMAN PROFILE

Range SAT Verbal	530-620
Average SAT Verbal	570
Range SAT Math	550-640
Average SAT Math	595
**TPR Projected Range SAT Writing*	*580-650*
Range ACT Composite	23-28
Average ACT Composite	26
Minimum Paper TOEFL	550
Minimum Computer Based TOEFL	213
Average HS GPA	3.66
% graduated top 10% of class	34
% graduated top 25% of class	70
% graduated top 50% of class	95

DEADLINES

Regular application deadline	1/5
Regular notification	4/15
Nonfall registration?	yes

APPLICANTS ALSO LOOK AT

AND OFTEN PREFER

University of California—Los Angeles

AND SOMETIMES PREFER

University of California—San Diego

AND RARELY PREFER

San Diego State University

FINANCIAL FACTS

Financial Aid Rating	**81**
Annual tuition	$14, 380
Room & Board	$7,640
% frosh rec. need-based scholarship or grant aid	52
% UG rec. need-based scholarship or grant aid	49
% frosh rec. need-based self-help aid	41
% UG rec. need-based self-help aid	43
% UG rec. any financial aid	69
Avg. frosh grant	$15,896
Avg. frosh loan	$4,661
Independent 529 member?	Yes

UNIVERSITY OF SAN FRANCISCO

2130 FULTON STREET, SAN FRANCISCO, CA 94117 • ADMISSIONS: 415-422-6563 • FAX: 415-422-2217

CAMPUS LIFE

Quality of Life Rating	**90**
Fire Safety Rating	**60**
Type of school	private
Affiliation	Roman Catholic

STUDENTS

Total undergrad enrollment	4,274
% male/female	35/65
% from out of state	38
% from public high school	51
% live on campus	54
% in (# of) fraternities	2 (4)
% in (# of) sororities	2 (4)
% African American	5
% Asian	26
% Caucasian	37
% Hispanic	13
% international	7
# of countries represented	78

SURVEY SAYS

Small classes
Great library
Athletic facilities are great
Diverse student types on campus
Students love San Francisco, CA
Great off-campus food

ACADEMICS

Academic Rating	**83**
Calendar	4-1-4
Student/faculty ratio	14:1
Professors interesting rating	85
Professors accessible rating	83
% professors teaching UG courses	75
% classes taught by TAs	0
Most common lab size	10-19 students
Most common regular class size	10-19 students

MOST POPULAR MAJORS

Business administration/management
nursing/registered nurse training (RN, ASN, BSN, MSN)
psychology

STUDENTS SPEAK OUT

Academics

"Educating minds and hearts to change the world," the Jesuit-led University of San Francisco "prides itself in its dedication to social justice." As one student puts it, "The underlying spiritual mission of the school is really positive, and it integrates itself into our coursework in the form of a strong community-service ethic." Although small, USF offers a breadth of options typical of a larger university, including a business school that "provides a great education for those who want to work in San Francisco and the Bay area" and that arms "students with an ethical approach to business;" a nursing program with excellent clinicals that "allow you to schmooze all the right people even before you graduate;" and "a plethora of global awareness programs and seminars." Given the university's location, "There are so many opportunities to take advantage of: internships, research experience, and so forth that might not be readily available" in a smaller city. Classes at USF are often "75 percent lecture, with the last 25 percent of the class reserved for discussion," which students use with enthusiasm. Core requirements include "one class in each of a variety of subject areas (science, math, history, literature, philosophy, and theology) in order to give students a solid liberal arts background." Students may circumvent these requirements by entering the Saint Ignatius Institute, a "great books program" that is also "a great community." Another plus: "A high percentage of our student body studies abroad at some point, usually in their junior year. There are so many options for studying abroad!"

Life

"Nestled in a quiet spot of a bustling city," the USF campus is "amazing. You could stay around here your entire college career and never know there was a big city around you. Yet it's close to shops, restaurants, and all the other advantages of urban living, just a few blocks off Golden Gate Park." The campus itself is "small but gorgeous. Every morning as you walk to class, there is the beautiful St. Ignatius Church, big redwood trees, a sprawling grass lawn, gorgeous landscaping, and, often, the fog rolling out in the distance." Just beyond the campus gates, of course, is one of America's great cities. As one student notes, "The best thing about USF is that it's in the middle of San Francisco! And the school definitely takes advantage of that." For recreation, undergrads "can just take the bus and in five minutes, we're walking along popular Haight Street. Everything is accessible." The only downside: "The Bay area is incredibly expensive, and the cost can hamper the ability to have fun as a student." Oddly enough, the allure of the big city dampens campus life. "There's not much school spirit here," undergrads tell us, manifesting in "the lack of a collective backing of sports on campus."

Student Body

"The student body at USF is like a scaled-down version of the people you will meet in San Francisco, [with] plenty of stylish students, the type who wears heels, miniskirts, and tube tops to an 8:00 A.M. class. One only needs to perch on a bench outside the cafeteria to see all the goths, punks, divas, slackers, jocks, prepsters, and wanna-be-prepsters." Most here "have a passionate interest in something. Almost no one is apathetic. Many people have music as their passion, while others have acting, community service, dancing, writing, and athletics." A large number "are concerned with the political and social affairs on all levels: local, national, and international, [and] although USF may be a conservative Jesuit school at the core, the generally liberal attitude of San Francisco is heavily reflected in the student body." With "a wide variety of feeder schools, including internationally," USF is "incredibly diverse." It suffers, however, from a dearth of straight men. Explains one woman, "There's a high female to male ratio in the freshmen class, and we've figured it's much, much higher when you factor out the guys in relationships and gay guys."

UNIVERSITY OF SAN FRANCISCO

FINANCIAL AID: 415-422-6303 • E-MAIL: ADMISSION@USFCA.EDU • WEBSITE: WWW.USFCA.EDU

ADMISSIONS

Very important factors considered include: Recommendations, secondary school record, standardized test scores. *Important factors considered include:* Class rank, essays. *Other factors considered include:* Alumni/ae relation, character/personal qualities, extracurricular activities, interview, minority status, talent/ability, volunteer work. SAT Reasoning or ACT required. TOEFL required of all international applicants. High school diploma is required, and GED is accepted. *Academic units required:* 1 chemistry, 1 biology or physics of nursing and science applicants. *Academic units recommended:* 4 English, 3 math, 2 science (2 science lab), 2 foreign language, 3 social studies, 6 academic electives.

The Inside Word

The admissions committee at USF is not purely numbers-focused. They'll evaluate your full picture here, using your academic strengths and weaknesses along with your personal character strengths, essays, and recommendations to assess your suitability for admission. It's matchmaking. If you fit well in the USF community, you'll be welcome

FINANCIAL AID

Students should submit: FAFSA. The Princeton Review suggests that all financial aid forms be submitted as soon as possible after 1/1. *Need-based scholarships/grants offered:* Pell, SEOG, state scholarships/grants, private scholarships, the school's own gift aid, Federal Nursing scholarships. *Loan aid offered:* Direct Subsidized Stafford, Direct Unsubsidized Stafford, Direct PLUS, FFEL PLUS, Federal Perkins, Federal Nursing, college/university loans from institutional funds. Applicants will be notified of awards on a rolling basis beginning on or about 3/24. Federal Work-study Program available. Institutional employment available. Off-campus job opportunities are excellent.

FROM THE ADMISSIONS OFFICE

"The University of San Francisco has experienced a significant increase in applications for admission over the past two years. This has made the application evaluation process more challenging and exciting. Ultimately, it gives those who read the applications the opportunity to find applicants who can make the most of the university's location in San Francisco and its mission to educate minds and hearts to change the world. Community outreach and service to others, along with academic excellence are characteristics that help distinguish those offered admission.

"Applicants for fall 2006 are required to take the new SAT Reasoning test (or the ACT with the Writing section). The Writing sections will be used for advising and placement purposes. SAT Subject Test scores will also be accepted. If scores from both the old and new SAT are submitted, the higher of the scores will be used."

SELECTIVITY

Admissions Rating	**84**
# of applicants	5,338
% of applicants accepted	74
% of acceptees attending	24

FRESHMAN PROFILE

Range SAT Verbal	510-620
Range SAT Math	500-620
**TPR Projected Range SAT Writing*	*570-650*
Range ACT Composite	21-26
Minimum Paper TOEFL	550
Minimum Computer Based TOEFL	213
Average HS GPA	3.45
% graduated top 10% of class	25
% graduated top 25% of class	57
% graduated top 50% of class	90

DEADLINES

Regular notification	within 4 weeks of completed application
Nonfall registration?	yes

APPLICANTS ALSO LOOK AT

AND OFTEN PREFER

Santa Clara University
University of California—Berkeley
University of California—Davis
University of Southern California

AND SOMETIMES PREFER

Loyola Marymount University
Saint Mary's College of California
University of California—Santa Cruz

AND RARELY PREFER

Boston College
Fordham University

FINANCIAL FACTS

Financial Aid Rating	**70**
Annual tuition	$26,680
Room & Board	$10,240
Books and supplies	$900
Required fees	$160
% frosh rec. need-based scholarship or grant aid	48
% UG rec. need-based scholarship or grant aid	50
% frosh rec. need-based self-help aid	52
% UG rec. need-based self-help aid	53
Avg. frosh grant	$14,867
Avg. frosh loan	$4,094
Independent 529 member?	No

UNIVERSITY OF SCRANTON

800 LINDEN STREET, SCRANTON, PA 18510-4699 • ADMISSIONS: 570-941-7540 FAX: 570-941-5928

CAMPUS LIFE

Quality of Life Rating	**83**
Fire Safety Rating	**77**
Type of school	private
Affiliation	Roman Catholic
Environment	city

STUDENTS

Total undergrad enrollment	3,982
% male/female	43/57
% from out of state	49
% from public high school	55
% live on campus	52
% African American	1
% Asian	2
% Caucasian	83
% Hispanic	4
% international	1

SURVEY SAYS

Small classes
Great computer facilities
Great library
Frats and sororities are unpopular or nonexistent
Lots of beer drinking

ACADEMICS

Academic Rating	**82**
Calendar	semester
Student/faculty ratio	13:1
Professors interesting rating	81
Professors accessible rating	83
% professors teaching UG courses	98
% classes taught by TAs	0
Most common lab size	10-19 students
Most common regular class size	10-19 students

MOST POPULAR MAJORS

Communications studies/speech communication and rhetoric
elementary education and teaching
marketing/marketing management

STUDENTS SPEAK OUT

Academics

With "an outstanding record for admission to graduate programs, not only in law and medicine but also in several other fields," the University of Scranton is a good fit for ambitious students seeking "a Jesuit school in every sense of the word. If you come here, expect to be challenged to become a better person, to develop a strong concern for the poor and marginalized, and to grow spiritually and intellectually." The school manages to accomplish this without "forcing religion upon you, which is nice." Undergraduates also approve of the mandatory liberal-arts-based curriculum that "forces you to learn about broader things than your own major." Strong majors here include "an amazing occupational therapy program, [an] excellent special education program," business, and biology. "This is a great place for premeds and other sciences," students agree. While the workload can be difficult, "a tutoring center provides free tutoring for any students who may need it, and also provides work-study positions for students who qualify to tutor." Need more help? Professors "are extremely accessible. They will go to any lengths to help you understand material and do well," while administrators "are here for the students, and show that every day inside and outside of the classroom." Community ties here are strong; as one student points out, "The Jesuits live in our dorms, creating an even greater sense of community, because we don't view them as just priests, we view them as real people who can relate on our level."

Life

"There is a whole range of activities to do on the weekends" at University of Scranton, including "frequent trips, dances, and movies that are screened for free." Students tell us that "the school and student organizations provide plenty of options, such as retreats, talent shows, and other various activities." There are also "many intramurals to become involved in, and the varsity sports (specifically the women's) are very successful." Furthermore, "Being a Jesuit school, social justice issues are huge. They are taught in the classroom, and students spend a lot of time volunteering." Hometown Scranton is big enough to provide "movie theaters, two malls, parks, a zoo, a bowling alley, and a skiing/snowboarding mountain." In short, there are plenty of choices for the non-partier at Scranton; the many we heard from in our survey reported busy extracurricular schedules. But those seeking a party won't be disappointed here, either. Scranton undergrads "party a lot, but they balance it with studying. Parties are chances to go out, see people, dance, and drink if you want." You "can find a party any time of day, seven days a week" here, usually with a keg tapped and pouring. Few here feel the party scene is out of hand, however; a typical student writes, "It's very different than at schools with Greek systems. It is a lot more laid back, and all about everyone having a good time."

Students

While "the typical Scranton student is white, Catholic, and from the suburbs," students hasten to point out that "Within this sameness, there is much diversity. There are people who couldn't care at all about religion, and there are people who are deeply religious. Even in the Catholic atmosphere of the school, the school only requires that you learn about Catholicism as it stands. Theology classes…are prefaced with the idea that 'You do not have to believe this!'" Undergrads here are generally "friendly and welcoming. Cliques are pretty much nonexistent, and anyone who would be classified as 'popular' is only considered so because they are extremely friendly, outgoing, and seek out friendships with as many people as possible." Students tend to be on the Abercrombie-preppy side, with lots of undergrads of Italian, Irish, and Polish descent.

ADMISSIONS

Very important factors considered include: Secondary school record. *Important factors considered include:* Class rank, standardized test scores. *Other factors considered include:* Alumni/ae relation, character/personal qualities, essays, extracurricular activities, interview, minority status, recommendations, talent/ability, volunteer work, work experience. SAT Reasoning or ACT required. TOEFL required of all international applicants. High school diploma is required, and GED is accepted. *Academic units required:* 4 English, 3 math, 1 science, 2 foreign language, 2 social studies, 4. *Academic units recommended:* 4 English, 4 math, 2 science, 2 foreign language, 3 social studies.

The Inside Word

Admission to Scranton gets harder each year. A steady stream of smart kids from the tri-state area keeps classes full and the admit rate low. Successful applicants will need solid grades and test scores. As with many religiously affiliated schools, students should be a good match philosophically as well.

FINANCIAL AID

Students should submit: FAFSA. The Princeton Review suggests that all financial aid forms be submitted as soon as possible after 1/1. *Need-based scholarships/grants offered:* Pell, SEOG, state scholarships/grants, private scholarships, the school's own gift aid. *Loan aid offered:* FFEL Subsidized Stafford, FFEL Unsubsidized Stafford, FFEL PLUS, Federal Perkins, Federal Nursing. Applicants will be notified of awards on a rolling basis beginning on or about 3/1.

FROM THE ADMISSIONS OFFICE

"A Jesuit institution in Pennsylvania's Pocono northeast, The University of Scranton is known for its outstanding academics, state-of-the art campus and technology, and exceptional sense of community. Founded in 1888, the university offers more than 80 undergraduate and graduate academic programs of study through five colleges and schools.

"For the tenth consecutive year, *U.S. News & World Report* named Scranton among the top 10 comprehensive universities in the North. In the 2004 edition, Scranton ranked sixth and was spotlighted among schools in the north with the "Highest Graduate Rate."

"The Princeton Review included Scranton among *The Best 351 Colleges* in the nation in its 2004 edition. Princeton Review also ranked Scranton thirtieth among the nation's most connected campuses in a listing published in *Forbes* magazine. Intel Corporation focused attention on Scranton's increasing commitment to wireless technology, ranking the university eighty-seventh on its list of the nation's most "Most Unwired Campus Colleges."

"For two consecutive years, *USA Today* included Scranton students on its All-USA College Academic Team. In 2004, Scranton was the only college in Pennsylvania and the only Jesuit university to have two students listed and to have a student placed on the first academic team.

"In other national recognition, Kaplan Publishing counted Scranton among the nation's 328 Most Interesting Colleges and *The Washington Post Magazine* included the university in a national list of just "100 Colleges Worth Considering."

"Students are encouraged to apply early for admission and can do so online with no application fee at www.scranton.edu/apply.

"Freshman applicants for fall 2006 must take the new SAT (or the ACT with Writing), but the Writing scores will not be considered in the admissions decision process. Students may submit scores from the old SAT (before March 2005) or ACT, and the best scores from either test will be used."

SELECTIVITY

Admissions Rating	**84**
# of applicants	6,133
% of applicants accepted	75
% of acceptees attending	21
# accepting a place on wait list	798
% admitted from wait list	5

FRESHMAN PROFILE

Range SAT Verbal	510-600
Average SAT Verbal	559
Range SAT Math	510-610
Average SAT Math	562
**TPR Projected Range SAT Writing*	*570-630*
Minimum Paper TOEFL	500
Minimum Computer Based TOEFL	173
Average HS GPA	3.33
% graduated top 10% of class	22
% graduated top 25% of class	61
% graduated top 50% of class	93

DEADLINES

Regular application deadline	3/1
Regular notification	rolling
Nonfall registration?	yes

APPLICANTS ALSO LOOK AT AND OFTEN PREFER

Fairfield University
Saint Joseph's University (PA)
University of Delaware
Villanova University

AND SOMETIMES PREFER

Fordham University
Loyola College in Maryland
Penn State University Park

FINANCIAL FACTS

Financial Aid Rating	**70**
Annual tuition	$22,214
Room & Board	$9,524
Books and supplies	$900
Required fees	$260
% frosh rec. need-based scholarship or grant aid	68
% UG rec. need-based scholarship or grant aid	64
% frosh rec. need-based self-help aid	63
% UG rec. need-based self-help aid	57
% frosh rec. any financial aid	90
% UG rec. any financial aid	83
Avg. frosh grant	$12,130
Avg. frosh loan	$3,688
Independent 529 member?	No

UNIVERSITY OF SOUTH CAROLINA—COLUMBIA

UNIVERSITY OF SOUTH CAROLINA, COLUMBIA, SC 29208 • ADMISSIONS: 803-777-7700 • FAX: 803-777-0101

CAMPUS LIFE

Quality of Life Rating	**81**
Fire Safety Rating	**87**
Type of school	public
Environment	city

STUDENTS

Total undergrad enrollment	17,016
% male/female	46/54
% from out of state	12
% live on campus	40
% in (# of) fraternities	17 (17)
% in (# of) sororities	17 (12)
% African American	15
% Asian	3
% Caucasian	71
% Hispanic	2
% international	1

SURVEY SAYS

Great library
Athletic facilities are great
Great off-campus food
Everyone loves the Fighting Gamecocks
Lots of beer drinking
(Almost) everyone smokes

ACADEMICS

Academic Rating	**70**
Calendar	semester
Student/faculty ratio	17:1
Professors interesting rating	70
Professors accessible rating	69
% professors teaching UG courses	63
% classes taught by TAs	12
Most common lab size	20-29 students
Most common regular class size	10-19 students

MOST POPULAR MAJORS

Biology/biological sciences
experimental psychology
nursing/registered nurse training (RN, ASN, BSN, MSN)

STUDENTS SPEAK OUT

Academics

Affordable tuition and a wide range of programs make the University of South Carolina—Columbia (USC) an attractive value proposition for the educational bargain hunter. Academic opportunities are diverse, although somewhat impersonal. The undergraduate business, nursing, and hospitality programs are especially popular. The school's general education requirements include courses in liberal arts, plus demonstrated proficiency in a foreign language. Snagging a seat in these courses may be difficult. One student agrees, "The classes are great. If you can get into them!" Although congested classrooms are one downside of a big time state school, students say professors "really care about your learning. They are available outside of class by request and respond by E-mail frequently." Adds one freshman, "Most [professors] even give out their home phone numbers." Some undergraduates, however, complain that professors place too much emphasis on research and publishing and not enough emphasis on good teaching. One senior reports, "Academics are second to research and football." For the exceptionally motivated undergraduate, the university's Honors College is just the ticket: smaller, more intimate, and highly competitive. Writes one participant, "As we say in the Honors College, our students are barracudas, not sponges." Students would like to see an improved freshman advising system—one that better guides students through the sometimes overwhelming process of choosing classes.

Life

Work hard enough, and play a little harder seems to be the motto in Columbia. One student describes USC as "school, but with a twist of summer camp." Students take their fun and their drinking seriously. "Class, party, eat, sleep—in that order," writes a freshman. The "hugely popular" Greek system rules this social scene. But if you don't want to follow the Greek life, it doesn't mean you won't find your niche. "A lot of people just go out and get drunk," writes one freshman, "but there are a lot of other things to do—cultural events such as theater, concerts, ballet, [and guest] speakers." Student organizations and an on-campus cinema add to the list of available activities. Columbia allows students to enjoy dynamic city life—and all its possibilities—and it's only steps away from campus. The university describes its setting as an urban countryside. Students agree, bragging that one can experience the "beach, mountains, area nightlife, outdoor sports, [and] restaurants," all in one weekend. The sprawling Five Points Mall is a popular off-campus destination and has a wealth of restaurants, shops, bars, and nightclubs. And let's not forget football. "Life at USC centers around Saturday, when the locally worshipped Gamecocks take the field," writes one student. The campus shuts down on game days, and "tailgating is huge here!" Students say their "crazy" school spirit is one of things that make this campus special. Freshman dorms, however, leave something to be desired. Although the university did recently complete a brand-new fitness and recreation center, many other campus facilities could use some refurbishing. Parking is also an issue, as is campus security.

Student Body

The typical student is "polite, courteous, holds doors, [and] smiles when a stranger walks by." Yes, chivalry is alive and well at USC, where "southern hospitality prevails." For many of the students, school is "close to home"—and its regional character largely defines the student body. The vast majority of students are South Carolinians, and most of them are white, conservative, and Christian. Many students also pledge fraternities and sororities. One freshman says, "There are frat boys and sorority girls everywhere and little interracial interaction." Another student adds, "Greeks and non-Greeks do not get along at all." But this freshman says students are more laid-back about their differences: "Yeah, there are some weird and pierced people here, and then there are athletes and Greek kids, but everyone gets along well enough."

UNIVERSITY OF SOUTH CAROLINA—COLUMBIA

FINANCIAL AID: 803-777-8134 • E-MAIL: ADMISSIONS-UGRAD@SC.EDU • WEBSITE: WWW.SC.EDU

ADMISSIONS

Very important factors considered include: Secondary school record, standardized test scores. *Other factors considered include:* Recommendations, talent/ability. SAT Reasoning or ACT required. TOEFL required of all international applicants. High school diploma is required, and GED is accepted. *Academic units required:* 4 English, 3 math, 3 science (3 science lab), 2 foreign language, 2 social studies, 1 history, 4 academic electives, 1 physical education or ROTC.

The Inside Word

The admissions process at South Carolina is formula-driven and not particularly demanding. A solid academic performance in high school should do the trick. For the past three years, USC has had to close its admissions to the freshman class early, as the number of applicants has risen. So it is important to meet the application deadline.

FINANCIAL AID

Students should submit: FAFSA. The Princeton Review suggests that all financial aid forms be submitted as soon as possible after 1/1. *Need-based scholarships/grants offered:* Pell, SEOG, state scholarships/grants, private scholarships, the school's own gift aid, United Negro College Fund, Federal Nursing scholarships. *Loan aid offered:* FFEL Subsidized Stafford, FFEL Unsubsidized Stafford, FFEL PLUS, Federal Perkins, Federal Nursing. Applicants will be notified of awards on or about 4/1.

FROM THE ADMISSIONS OFFICE

"Nestled among ancient oaks and beautiful green spaces, University of South Carolina sits in the center of Columbia, South Carolina, the state's capital city. A major research university, USC awards baccalaureate, master's, and doctoral degrees, and is known for its top-ranked academic programs. For example, USC is currently ranked number one in the nation for undergraduate international business by *U.S. News & World Report*. Other programs are regularly listed in the top 25, including advertising, public relations, and marine science. Additionally, the magazine recognizes USC's pioneering efforts in freshman outreach as number one for 'Programs That Really Work.' USC's Honors College is one of the nation's best, offering Ivy League quality at state college costs. Academic major choices are plentiful, with more than 70 options available. USC also has a graduate school, school of law, school of medicine, and professional degree programs. The university offers quality student support in such areas as career development, disability services, and computer lab access. The campus and surrounding community also have great entertainment, cultural, and recreational outlets. A new 18,000-seat arena brings national concerts to town and serves as home to USC basketball. And students enjoy USC's newly opened, $40 million fitness center featuring state-of-the-art equipment and amenities. Beyond city borders, South Carolina's world-famous beaches and the Blue Ridge Mountains are each less than a three-hour drive away. Growing numbers of students are discovering that the University of South Carolina is the right choice for them.

"Applicants are required to take the Writing section of the SAT (or ACT) for any tests taken after March 2000, We will use the highest scores from either test for evaluation purposes."

SELECTIVITY

Admissions Rating	**86**
# of applicants	12,379
% of applicants accepted	67
% of acceptees attending	41

FRESHMAN PROFILE

Range SAT Verbal	520-620
Average SAT Verbal	569
Range SAT Math	520-630
Average SAT Math	582
**TPR Projected Range SAT Writing*	*570-650*
Range ACT Composite	22-27
Average ACT Composite	24
Minimum Paper TOEFL	550
Minimum Computer Based TOEFL	210
Average HS GPA	3.8
% graduated top 10% of class	26
% graduated top 25% of class	58
% graduated top 50% of class	90

DEADLINES

Regular application deadline	2/15
Regular notification	rolling
Nonfall registration?	yes

APPLICANTS ALSO LOOK AT AND OFTEN PREFER
University of North Carolina—Chapel Hill
AND SOMETIMES PREFER
Clemson University
AND RARELY PREFER
Wake Forest University

FINANCIAL FACTS

Financial Aid Rating	**78**
Annual in-state tuition	$5,548
Annual out-of-state tuition	$14,886
Room & Board	$5,590
Books and supplies	$720
Required fees	$200
% frosh rec. need-based scholarship or grant aid	22
% UG rec. need-based scholarship or grant aid	26
% frosh rec. need-based self-help aid	35
% UG rec. need-based self-help aid	39
% frosh rec. any financial aid	94
% UG rec. any financial aid	81
Avg. frosh grant	$6,660
Avg. frosh loan	$2,535
Independent 529 member?	No

THE UNIVERSITY OF SOUTH DAKOTA

414 EAST CLARK, VERMILLION, SD 57069 • ADMISSIONS: 605-677-5434 • FAX: 605-677-6323

CAMPUS LIFE

Quality of Life Rating	**70**
Fire Safety Rating	**72**
Type of school	public
Environment	village

STUDENTS

Total undergrad enrollment	5,315
% male/female	38/62
% from out of state	27
% from public high school	90
% live on campus	31
% in (# of) fraternities	22 (8)
% in (# of) sororities	14 (4)
% African American	1
% Asian	1
% Caucasian	90
% Hispanic	1
% Native American	2
% international	1
# of countries represented	23

SURVEY SAYS

Small classes
Great computer facilities
Great library
Frats and sororities dominate social scene
Lots of beer drinking
Hard liquor is popular
(Almost) everyone smokes

ACADEMICS

Academic Rating	**74**
Calendar	semester
Student/faculty ratio	16:1
Professors interesting rating	74
Professors accessible rating	70
% professors teaching UG courses	95
% classes taught by TAs	5
Most common regular class size	10-19 students

MOST POPULAR MAJORS

Business administration/management
psychology

STUDENTS SPEAK OUT

Academics

Tucked into the southeast corner of its home state, The University of South Dakota provides both in- and out-of-state students with "a quality education at an exceptionally affordable price." With highly touted offerings in media, law, political science, business, and pre-health majors, The U "is all about preparing students for their future careers. The school puts a heavy emphasis not only on the material, but also on how it applies to real-life situations, as opposed to a merely academic abstraction." Students apply their learning across subjects through the school's IdEA (Interdisciplinary Education and Action) program. Required of all undergraduates, IdEA consists of nine course credits in thematically linked subject areas (e.g., Global Health, Wealth & Justice in America, and Living a Life of Leadership are three of the nine areas), participation in co-curricular events and activities (like giving presentations or attending exhibitions), and an Action project (such as service-learning, research, or creative activity). With fewer than 6,000 undergraduates, The U can offer an unusual amount of student-teacher interaction for a state university; one undergrad writes, "All of my professors have an open-door policy and are usually very willing to work with students outside of the classroom."

Life

The Vermillion campus of The U is "typical" of a smaller state university, with "parties, coffee shops, bar hopping, frats, and sororities" as well as "organizations for virtually anything you can think of, from sports to self-defense, to art to GLBA." During the week, the campus buzzes with activity. One student reports, "The fine arts college regularly has art shows and theatrical performances. The Dakota Dome is host to any number of sporting events [and has] a full gym, pool, tennis, and racquetball courts available to students." Weekends are another matter, however (except when the Division II Coyotes football squad is playing at home). Many here report that USD is "a backpack school [since] there's nothing to keep us here on the weekends." The countryside surrounding Vermillion is a paradise for hunters, fishers, and campers, but others find the town "incredibly boring. It has a Hy-Vee and a Pamida. That's basically it, except for the small shops downtown. There's a bowling alley and several bars. Not much to do for underage students." To the town's credit, it is "supportive and proud of the university. There are few businesses that don't offer discounts for students and hang banners for the sports activities." Problem is, it just isn't very much fun, so students road trip to Sioux Falls or Sioux City when they can, or they simply head home once classes are done.

Student Body

Many U students "are from small communities from the Midwest (mainly South Dakota and surrounding states), [and are] blonde or brunette, Caucasian, blue- or brown-eyed, have Germanic or Norwegian names." Students are "good to one another and friendly for the most part. We are pretty interested in our university, and even more so in our friends." The school has a growing population of nontraditional students, as well as a "small percentage of students from Africa, Europe, and other continents, countries, and states on exchange programs." One undergrad writes, "Virtually every Midwesterner has a grandparent or great aunt who still doesn't speak English fluently since they immigrated to the U.S., so attitudes against immigrants are hard to find. Perhaps the only thing we wonder is why anyone would be willing to come here and deal with our harsh winters!" The university is "one of the most liberal places in South Dakota," so "most atypical students fit right in. Alternate sexual orientation is becoming increasingly accepted, for example."

FINANCIAL AID: 605-677-5446 • E-MAIL: ADMISS@USD.EDU • WEBSITE: WWW.USD.EDU

ADMISSIONS

Very important factors considered include: Class rank, secondary school record, standardized test scores. *Other factors considered include:* Essays, extracurricular activities, minority status, recommendations, talent/ability. SAT Reasoning and SAT Subject Tests or ACT required. TOEFL required of all international applicants. High school diploma is required, and GED is accepted. *Academic units required:* 4 English, 3 math, 3 science (3 science lab), 3 social studies, 1 fine arts. *Academic units recommended:* 4 English, 4 math, 4 science (3 science lab), 2 foreign language, 3 social studies, 1 fine arts.

The Inside Word

Given the relatively small numbers of high school graduates coming from South Dakota's high schools each year, the university's rolling admission policy is nearly open admission, though admissions standards are expected to increase starting in 2007. Solid college-prep students should encounter no trouble in gaining admission.

FINANCIAL AID

Students should submit: FAFSA. The Princeton Review suggests that all financial aid forms be submitted as soon as possible after 1/1. *Need-based scholarships/grants offered:* Pell, SEOG, private scholarships, the school's own gift aid, Federal Nursing scholarships. *Loan aid offered:* FFEL Subsidized Stafford, FFEL Unsubsidized Stafford, FFEL PLUS, Federal Perkins, Federal Nursing, college/university loans from institutional funds. Applicants will be notified of awards on or about 4/5.

FROM THE ADMISSIONS OFFICE

"The University of South Dakota is the perfect fit for students looking for a smart educational investment. USD is nationally ranked in academics and research, and seventh in the nation for value among public colleges and universities. USD annually awards scholarships to more than 800 first-year students, and over 80 percent of all students receive some form of financial aid through grants, loans, and work-study jobs.

"When it comes to producing top scholars, USD's quality of teaching and research prepares students for continuing education. U graduates have gone on to institutions such as Harvard, Johns Hopkins, Northwestern, and beyond. Thirty-five USD students have been awarded prestigious Fulbright, Rhodes, Truman, Udall, Jack Kent Cooke, and Goldwater scholarships and grants for graduate study. USD offers personal attention and a welcoming atmosphere that makes students feel right at home.

"As the flagship liberal arts institution in South Dakota, The University of South Dakota, founded in 1862 has long been regarded as a leader in the state and the region. Notable undergraduate and postgraduate alumni include journalist Ken Bode, former NBC news anchor Tom Brokaw, writer and Emmy Award winner Dorothy Cooper Foote, U.S. Senator Tim Johnson, USA TODAY Founder Al Neuharth, and U.S. Senator John Thune.

"Applicants for fall 2006 are not required to take the new writing test for either SAT or ACT. USD recommends taking the ACT over the SAT. Students who wish to send their SAT scores will have their scores converted to ACT scores for placement and scholarship consideration."

SELECTIVITY

Admissions Rating	**75**
# of applicants	2,632
% of applicants accepted	83
% of acceptees attending	49

FRESHMAN PROFILE

Range SAT Verbal	460-610
Range SAT Math	470-620
**TPR Projected Range SAT Writing*	*530-640*
Range ACT Composite	20-25
Average ACT Composite	23
Minimum Paper TOEFL	550
Minimum Computer Based TOEFL	213
Average HS GPA	3.27
% graduated top 10% of class	12
% graduated top 25% of class	34
% graduated top 50% of class	67

DEADLINES

Regular notification	rolling
Nonfall registration?	yes

APPLICANTS ALSO LOOK AT

AND OFTEN PREFER

Minnesota State University—Mankato
University of Nebraska—Lincoln

AND SOMETIMES PREFER

Augustana College (SD)
South Dakota State University

AND RARELY PREFER

Dakota State University
Mount Marty College
Northern State University

FINANCIAL FACTS

Financial Aid Rating	**76**
Annual in-state tuition	$2,291
Annual out-of-state tuition	$7,278
Room & Board	$4,239
Books and supplies	$750
Required fees	$2,538
% frosh rec. need-based scholarship or grant aid	30
% UG rec. need-based scholarship or grant aid	34
% frosh rec. need-based self-help aid	50
% UG rec. need-based self-help aid	6
% frosh rec. any financial aid	93
% UG rec. any financial aid	88
Avg. frosh grant	$3,138
Avg. frosh loan	$3,076
Independent 529 member?	No

UNIVERSITY OF SOUTH FLORIDA

4202 EAST FOWLER AVENUE, SVC-1036, TAMPA, FL 33620-9951 • ADMISSIONS: 813-974-3350 • FAX: 813-974-9689

CAMPUS LIFE

Quality of Life Rating	**80**
Fire Safety Rating	**85**
Type of school	public
Environment	metropolis

STUDENTS

Total undergrad enrollment	32,458
% male/female	41/59
% from out of state	4
% from public high school	91
% live on campus	13
% in (# of) fraternities	6 (13)
% in (# of) sororities	4 (11)
% African American	13
% Asian	6
% Caucasian	66
% Hispanic	11
% international	3
# of countries represented	133

SURVEY SAYS . . .

Great library
Athletic facilities are great
Diverse student types on campus
Great off-campus food
Student publications are popular

ACADEMICS

Academic Rating	**74**
Calendar	semester
Student/faculty ratio	18:1
Profs interesting rating	73
Profs accessible rating	73
% profs teaching UG courses	85
% classes taught by TAs	15
Most common lab size	20-29 students
Most common reg class size	20-29 students

MOST POPULAR MAJORS

curriculum and instruction
marketing/marketing management
social sciences

Academics

It is an exciting time to be a part of the community of the University of South Florida, "an up-and-coming public university that is just about to make [its] mark." Founded in 1956, a sense of freshness and opportunity still permeates the college. "As a relatively young school, we are still growing and forming our own personality," writes a senior. "New traditions are continually being created and school spirit is growing." Academically, students praise the premed program as well as psychology, engineering, communication, and environmental science. If you can get into it, undergrads recommend the Honors College, which "is run very smoothly, with great teachers who are easily accessible and helpful, classes that are small and interesting, and privileges that other students don't get (like early registration for classes)." Even in large lecture courses, professors are reputed to be intelligent, friendly, and available outside the classroom. As USF is a respected educational pillar of the Tampa Bay community, students can easily translate academics into career and internship opportunities in the city; "I had the opportunity to work with companies in the area on projects such as alternative buses, methane microturbine generators and solar cells," writes one senior. While some complain that "the administration is shaky," well-leveraged technology, like the university's website, which "is a thing of beauty and makes almost all personal contact unnecessary," helps USF keep up with the needs of its 30,000 undergraduates.

Life

On the huge and social campus of USF, there is truly something for everyone. For example, "if it's comic books that tickle your fancy, we have a club for that; if it's surfing, we have a club for that, too." While the vast majority of undergraduates commute to USF, there is a surprisingly strong sense of campus community, and many students participate in clubs, sports and social groups. In addition "there are music concerts almost every weekend on and off campus, and new movies on Wednesdays on the lawn on campus." In particular, many undergrads believe that "The Marshall Center is a great place for students, especially those under 21, to hang out; there is always something going on in there, like bands, tournaments, and get-togethers." As "the weather is great…outdoor activities are very popular," making it easy to "play beach volleyball right outside my dorm room." Also, "Since Tampa is a large community, many students find lots to do off campus," such as attending sporting events, or going to shows at Busch Gardens. And be aware that "Ybor City, a historic-district-turned-night-clubbing-district, is a very popular night spot for college students." USF is "definitely a major party school," and "Greek life is very prominent." A sophomore avers, "The weekends consist mainly of parties…. Weekdays consist of much of the same…plus some classes."

Student Body

The University of South Florida draws students who are "young, older, middle-aged, skinny, average, overweight, bald, hairy, black, white, or tan." We assume this means the place is diverse. A not-so-literal senior clarifies: "Everyone here is from different walks of life and everyone here is open to it, accepts it, and loves it." Undergrads generally describe their classmates as friendly and studious, and they tell us that at a school of more than 32,000, "you can always find somewhere to fit in." Some would like to see more interaction between ethnic groups outside of class, but in class, "most of the students are highly intelligent and contribute to class discussions, putting [forth] a different perspective on issues." Even nontraditional students feel comfortable within the undergraduate community; "I find it amazing that as an older student, I don't feel cut off from the events on campus," writes one senior.

ADMISSIONS

Very important factors considered include: Secondary school record. *Important factors considered include:* Standardized test scores. *Other factors considered include:* Character/personal qualities, essays, extracurricular activities, minority status, recommendations, talent/ability. SAT Reasoning and SAT Subject Tests or ACT required; TOEFL required of all international applicants. High school diploma is required and GED is accepted. *Academic units required:* 4 English, 3 math, 3 science, (2 science lab), 2 foreign language, 3 social studies, 3 academic electives.

Inside Word

A traditional college-prep high school course load is required for admission to USF. Beyond making sure that you complete all prerequisite classes, however, keep two other things in mind when applying to USF. First, admissions decisions are made on a rolling basis, so the earlier one applies, the better his chances of acceptance since there are more unfilled seats early in the admissions cycle. Second, Advanced Placement (AP) and International Baccalaureate (IB) classes are looked upon favorably in the admissions office here, so if your school offers them, load up on them and do well.

FINANCIAL AID

Students should submit: FAFSA. The Princeton Review suggests that all financial aid forms be submitted as soon as possible after January 1. *Need-based scholarships/grants offered:* Pell, SEOG, state scholarships/grants, private scholarships, the school's own gift aid, United Negro College Fund, Federal Nursing Scholarships. *Loan aid offered:* FFEL Subsidized Stafford, FFEL Unsubsidized Stafford, FFEL PLUS, Federal Perkins, Federal Nursing Loans, college/university loans from institutional funds. Applicants will be notified of awards on a rolling basis beginning or about March 1.

FROM THE ADMISSIONS OFFICE

"Two of the most distinguishing features of USF are the Honors College and the undergraduate research experience. The Honors College has a specially designed Honors major. The program is offered to students who have demonstrated excellent scholarship potential. The undergraduate research experience is designed for all students who are interested in an intensive research experience.

"Admission to the university is based on the strength of an applicant's high school background, including the degree of difficulty of courses selected, record of academic achievement and SAT or ACT scores. USF also takes into account the student's profile and special talents in and outside of the classroom.

"Students are encouraged to use academic electives to better enhance their preparation for entrance into a selected major. USF also encourages students with talent in music, art, dance, and theater to balance their high school experience with advanced courses in the visual and performing arts.

"USF encourages high school students to apply early in their senior year. USF makes admissions decisions on a rolling basis. No essay is required, however first time in college students entering in 2006 will be required to submit the new SAT and/or ACT with writing sample.

"It's always a great time to visit USF. Campus tours, information sessions and tours of the residence halls are offered daily and the first Saturday of each month. Reservations are strongly encouraged.

"Applicants into the entering class for summer 2006 class are required to take the new version of the SAT (or the ACT with the writing section). USF will mix sub section scores from the SAT prior to March 2005 (ACT prior to February 2005) but will not use the composite score from the old version to make the admissions decision."

SELECTIVITY

Admissions Rating	**87**
# of applicants	16,985
% of applicants accepted	51
% of acceptees attending	55

FRESHMAN PROFILE

Range SAT Verbal	490-590
Average SAT Verbal	540
Range SAT Math	490-600
Average SAT Math	545
**TPR Projected Range SAT Writing*	*550-620*
Range ACT Composite	20-25
Average ACT Composite	23
Minimum Paper TOEFL	550
Minimum Computer Based TOEFL	213
Average HS GPA	3.74
% graduated top 10% of class	24
% graduated top 25% of class	58
% graduated top 50% of class	89

DEADLINES

Regular application deadline	4/15
Regular notification	continuous
Nonfall registration?	yes

FINANCIAL FACTS

Financial Aid Rating	**62**
Annual in-state tuition	$3,090
Annual out-of-state tuition	$15,960
Room & Board	$6,730
Books and supplies	$800
Required fees	$74
% frosh rec. need-based scholarship or grant aid	28
% UG rec. need-based scholarship or grant aid	31
% frosh rec. need-based self-help aid	15
% UG rec. need-based self-help aid	23
Independent 529 member?	No

UNIVERSITY OF SOUTHERN CALIFORNIA

700 CHILDS WAY, LOS ANGELES, CA 90089-0911 • ADMISSIONS: 213-740-1111 • FAX: 213-740-6364

CAMPUS LIFE

Quality of Life Rating	**85**
Fire Safety Rating	**96**
Type of school	private
Environment	metropolis

STUDENTS

Total undergrad enrollment	16,271
% male/female	49/51
% from out of state	32
% from public high school	59
% live on campus	36
% in (# of) fraternities	18 (25)
% in (# of) sororities	21 (18)
% African American	7
% Asian	21
% Caucasian	48
% Hispanic	13
% Native American	1
% international	9
# of countries represented	148

SURVEY SAYS

Great computer facilities
Great library
Diverse student types on campus
Everyone loves the Trojans
Frats and sororities dominate social scene

ACADEMICS

Academic Rating	**88**
Calendar	semester
Student/faculty ratio	10:1
Professors interesting rating	85
Professors accessible rating	80
% professors teaching UG courses	75
% classes taught by TAs	0
Most common lab size	20-29 students
Most common regular class size	10-19 students

MOST POPULAR MAJORS

Business administration/management
communications studies/speech communication and rhetoric
psychology

STUDENTS SPEAK OUT

Academics

"In a city that 'pays a thousand dollars for a kiss and fifty cents for your soul,' [University of Southern California)] is a hip, urban oasis where the creative theater/film/artsy types easily befriend business/accounting/premed types in the name of the Trojan family," writes one student. We couldn't have said it better ourselves. A hip environment, a broad range of academic offerings (including one of the nation's preeminent film schools), and a sense of school pride fermented by success on the football field and reaching perfect vintage in the alumni network are the central ingredients of the USC formula. It is one that engenders a ton of school spirit. "Once a Trojan, always a Trojan. School spirit is by far this school's greatest strength," asserts one of the university's many boosters. Those who disagree wouldn't downplay Trojan fervor. Rather, they'd simply prefer to single out "the fact that USC is academically strong in so many diverse fields." The school's "interdisciplinary approach to academics;" or the "hands-on learning experience, which brings professors and administrators (most of whom are required to teach an undergraduate course, including our president) together with students on a regular basis," are all popular among the student body. Best of all—as far as the many career-minded undergraduates are concerned—USC is the school that keeps on giving long after graduation because "USC is all about the connections. Our alumni network is amazing, and the alumni are so successful."

Life

"We're in a large city, so much of the 'student life' is off campus," USC undergraduates tell us, adding, "You get bored quickly if you don't have a car or access to friends who have cars." As one student puts it, "LA is a Trojan's playground, if you don't mind driving to get there. There's very little to do in USC's part of Los Angeles, so Trojans usually drive to Beverly Hills, Hollywood, and Santa Monica." Westwood, "UCLA's backyard, is another popular site for Trojans. It's hard to tell the Bruins apart from the Trojans, besides that Trojans are wearing cardinal and gold, and we just tend to look better." The neighborhood surrounding USC is not a favored destination. Students comment that the "seedy downtown LA [locale] is not that bad, and as long as you stay within a five-block radius and stay smart, you'll be okay." Unfortunately, the surrounding area offers little in the way of student-friendly diversion, except for "The Row, [or] to LA kids, 28th Street. Almost all Greek houses are located on one street, with nothing else. It is famous for its parties on Thursday nights because campus dies down on Friday." Students are also "very involved in collegiate sports (especially football)" and on-campus lectures and movie showings. One undergraduate writes, "There's always an advance screening somewhere that you get handed tickets to on the way to class."

Student Body

"There is a huge mix of students at USC," undergraduates tell us. "You have everything from rich daddy's girls to minority students from the poorest LA neighborhoods on scholarships." The most conspicuous campus contingent is "the beautiful people," the wealthy kids referenced by those who dub USC "the University of Spoiled Children." While it is difficult to walk across campus without spotting "the blond-haired, blue-eyed surfer types who are either ridiculously skinny and tan or finely built and tan, who ride skateboards, go to frat parties, talk on cell phones, and wear Abercrombie and Fitch," they only represent part of the story. According to the *Irvine Quarterly*, USC culls more than one-quarter of its enrollment from families in the bottom third of annual income. Also mixed in among California's future business elite are "thousands of cinema students, atypical students who happen to be a large percentage of the population, so there's a great mixing of the whole spectrum of people."

FINANCIAL AID: 213-740-1111 • E-MAIL: ADMITUSC@USC.EDU • WEBSITE: WWW.USC.EDU

ADMISSIONS

Very important factors considered include: Essays, recommendations, secondary school record, standardized test scores. *Important factors considered include:* Extracurricular activities, talent/ability. *Other factors considered include:* Alumni/ae relation, character/personal qualities, class rank, interview, minority status, volunteer work, work experience. SAT Reasoning or ACT required. SAT Subject Tests recommended. High school diploma is required, and GED is not accepted. *Academic units required:* 4 English, 3 math, 3 science (2 science lab), 2 foreign language, 2 social studies. *Academic units recommended:* 4 math, 4 science (3 science lab), 3 foreign language, 3 social studies.

The Inside Word

The high national visibility of its athletic teams and glamorous images has long enabled USC to maintain a large applicant pool. Recently, though, this athletic powerhouse has become an academic powerhouse. Admission is solidly competitive. USC is looking for top students who are motivated and ready to take advantage of all the resources of a large, urban research university.

FINANCIAL AID

Students should submit: FAFSA, CSS/Financial Aid PROFILE, parent and student federal income tax form with all schedules and W-2 forms. Income documentation for nonfilers. The Princeton Review suggests that all financial aid forms be submitted as soon as possible after 1/1. *Need-based scholarships/grants offered:* Pell, SEOG, state scholarships/grants, private scholarships, the school's own gift aid. *Loan aid offered:* FFEL Subsidized Stafford, FFEL Unsubsidized Stafford, FFEL PLUS, Federal Perkins, credit-ready and credit-based loans. Applicants will be notified of awards on a rolling basis beginning on or about 3/15. Federal Work-study Program available. Institutional employment available. Off-campus job opportunities are excellent.

FROM THE ADMISSIONS OFFICE

"One of the best ways to discover if USC is right for you is to walk around campus, talk to students, and get a feel for the area both as a place to study and a place to live. If you can't visit, we hold admission information programs around the country. Watch your mailbox for an invitation, or send us an e-mail if you're interested.

"Freshman applicants are required to submit a standardized Writing exam. We will accept either the new SAT or the ACT with its optional Writing section. In rare cases we will accept the old SAT if accompanied by a score from the SAT Subject Test in Writing."

SELECTIVITY

Admissions Rating	**97**
# of applicants	29,792
% of applicants accepted	27
% of acceptees attending	34

FRESHMAN PROFILE

Range SAT Verbal	620-710
Average SAT Verbal	665
Range SAT Math	640-730
Average SAT Math	685
**TPR Projected Range SAT Writing*	*650-700*
Range ACT Composite	27-31
Average ACT Composite	29
Average HS GPA	4
% graduated top 10% of class	84
% graduated top 25% of class	94
% graduated top 50% of class	100

DEADLINES

Regular application deadline	1/10
Regular notification	4/1
Nonfall registration?	yes

APPLICANTS ALSO LOOK AT

AND OFTEN PREFER
Stanford University
University of California—Berkeley

AND SOMETIMES PREFER
New York University
Northwestern University
University of California—Los Angeles

AND RARELY PREFER
University of California—Irvine
University of California—Santa Barbara

FINANCIAL FACTS

Financial Aid Rating	**96**
Annual tuition	$29,988
Room & Board	$8,998
Books and supplies	$650
Required fees	$524
% frosh rec. need-based scholarship or grant aid	45
% UG rec. need-based scholarship or grant aid	42
% frosh rec. need-based self-help aid	50
% UG rec. need-based self-help aid	47
% frosh rec. any financial aid	72
% UG rec. any financial aid	66
Avg. frosh grant	$18,073
Avg. frosh loan	$3,756
Independent 529 member?	No

UNIVERSITY OF TENNESSEE—KNOXVILLE

320 STUDENT SERVICE BLDG., CIRCLE PARK DRIVE, KNOXVILLE, TN 37996-0230 • ADMISSIONS: 865-974-2184 • FAX: 865-974-6341

CAMPUS LIFE

Quality of Life Rating	**72**
Fire Safety Rating	**60**
Type of school	public
Environment	city

STUDENTS

Total undergrad enrollment	19,308
% male/female	49/51
% from out of state	13
% live on campus	33
% in (# of) fraternities	15 (26)
% in (# of) sororities	20 (17)
% African American	8
% Asian	3
% Caucasian	86
% Hispanic	1
% international	1
# of countries represented	90

SURVEY SAYS

Great library
Athletic facilities are great
Great off-campus food
Everyone loves the Volunteers
Intramural sports are popular
Frats and sororities dominate social scene
Student publications are popular
Lots of beer drinking
Hard liquor is popular
(Almost) everyone smokes

ACADEMICS

Academic Rating	**71**
Calendar	semester
Student/faculty ratio	15:1
Professors interesting rating	63
Professors accessible rating	63
% professors teaching UG courses	88
% classes taught by TAs	18
Most common lab size	10-19 students
Most common regular class size	20-29 students

MOST POPULAR MAJORS

Accounting
English language and literature
psychology

STUDENTS SPEAK OUT

Academics

Academics at the University of Tennessee Knoxville can be as challenging as you want to make them, students here tell us. This "great institution [offers] ample opportunity for leadership development, involvement, and travel to conferences." The school "has the money to provide top facilities, and they have done so and continue to upgrade facilities." The school also offers "all kinds of majors," including "the best undergraduate Engineering program in the state, [a] good journalism program, [and] exceptional business and communications departments." Professors are accomplished and "tend to be really supportive if you are willing to try." Students also report that "there is consistent support for improvement in academic performance through various tutorial programs and extra study sessions that are often available from professors and teaching assistants." The only caveat is that some students here care a lot more about football and parties than academics. "These undergraduates seek mediocre grades and an average experience, and the school lays out a path for them with little, if any, obstacle." At the other end of the spectrum, a few students wish that more were demanded of them academically, claiming, "You'd have to try to flunk out of UT." Those seeking the most rigorous program available should apply to the Honors Program, which provides "excellent assistance in all academic endeavors." Students warn that UT is administratively challenged and does little to assist students.

Life

"Weekends are when the biggest events occur" at UT, and "weekends start on Wednesday here, and end on Monday," which means lots of big events, both on and off campus. The biggest of all, without question, is Volunteer football: "Everyone comes together on Saturdays, as the student body, faculty, staff, alumni, and fans all unite in high spirits and pride," students tell us. While football is king, "The whole athletic program at UT is second-to-none. Not only is the football team consistently ranked in the Top 25 each season, but the women's basketball team has consistently made it to the Final Four in recent years." Intramurals are almost as big and almost as fiercely fought as the intercollegiate games; "Everything is a big deal, there is no casual game," writes one undergrad. Athletics may be first at UT, but for many undergrads partying runs a close second. "The drinking starts at dusk and doesn't end 'til dawn" at the school's many house parties and Greek parties. Students over 21 hit 'the Strip,' where there are "lots of bars." Younger students can't join them, however, because "the police have gotten really hard on fake IDs." The twin allures of athletics and partying leads students to opine that "Knoxville is a drinking town with a serious football problem." Life isn't just booze and ballgames, though; "We are in the Bible Belt, so religious activities like Campus Crusade are highly attended and interesting," students tell us. The university is also home to a wide range of student clubs and organizations.

Student Body

UT's student body "avidly practices Southern politeness and Republican-ism, since most of us were raised in the South…There is no such thing as a serious atmosphere, and usually the most threatening arguments involve people in a drunken discussion of football." Students are "extremely friendly," to the point that "if you're walking down the road at night, people will say, 'Are you looking for a party? Come to ours.'" There's a sense among some that UT has a "homogenous population of white, southern, middle- to upper-class, BMW-driving, Abercrombie and Fitch-wearing conservatives," with a few "nerds, video gamers, and just plain weird dudes" thrown in for good measure. But "in a public school of 20,000 people, there is no such thing as a typical student. There are all types here and everyone finds a group of people they connect with," even "Yankees who are teased for their accent." Many here agree, "We could definitely use improvement in the area of diversity, not only ethnically, but also socially and ideologically."

FINANCIAL AID: 865-974-3131 • E-MAIL: ADMISSIONS@TENNESSEE.EDU • WEBSITE: WWW.UTK.EDU

ADMISSIONS

Very important factors considered include: Secondary school record, standardized test scores. *Important factors considered include:* Essays, state residency, talent/ability. *Other factors considered include:* Alumni/ae relation, character/personal qualities, class rank, extracurricular activities, interview, minority status, recommendations, volunteer work, work experience. SAT Reasoning and SAT Subject Tests or ACT required. TOEFL required of all international applicants. High school diploma is required, and GED is accepted. *Academic units required:* 4 English, 3 math, 2 science (1 science lab), 2 foreign language, 1 social studies, 1 history, 1 visual and performing arts.

The Inside Word

Don't expect any attention to be given to your essays or extracurriculars at Tennessee unless you are not "automatically admissible." The university takes in a jumbo freshman class and has to use a fairly straightforward approach to getting these kids admitted. Standards are the same for out-of-state applicants as for in-state, but the school's mix of in-state/out-of-state students is firm, since it is set by policy of the Board of Trustees.

FINANCIAL AID

Students should submit: FAFSA, institution's own financial aid form, academic college scholarship application. The Princeton Review suggests that all financial aid forms be submitted as soon as possible after 1/1. *Need-based scholarships/grants offered:* Pell, SEOG, state scholarships/grants, private scholarships, the school's own gift aid. *Loan aid offered:* FFEL Subsidized Stafford, FFEL Unsubsidized Stafford, FFEL PLUS, Federal Perkins, college/university loans from institutional funds. Applicants will be notified of awards on a rolling basis beginning on or about 4/1. Institutional employment available. Off-campus job opportunities are good.

FROM THE ADMISSIONS OFFICE

"The University of Tennessee—Knoxville is the place where you belong if you're interested in outstanding resources and unlimited opportunities to foster your personal and academic growth. Nine colleges offer more than 120 majors to students from all 50 states and 95 foreign countries. More than 300 clubs and organizations on campus offer opportunities for fun, challenge, and service. UTK is a place where students take pride in belonging to a 200-year-old tradition and celebrate the excitement of 'the Volunteer spirit.' We invite you to explore the many advantages UTK has to offer.

"Freshman applicants to the University of Tennessee are required to submit scores from either the old or new SAT (or ACT). Students submitting SAT scores are also required to submit results from SAT Subject Tests."

SELECTIVITY

Admissions Rating	**88**
# of applicants	10,832
% of applicants accepted	44
% of acceptees attending	92

FRESHMAN PROFILE

Range SAT Verbal	500-610
Average SAT Verbal	551
Range SAT Math	500-610
Average SAT Math	549
**TPR Projected Range SAT Writing*	*560-640*
Range ACT Composite	22-27
Average ACT Composite	25
Minimum Paper TOEFL	523
Minimum Computer Based TOEFL	193
Average HS GPA	3.45
% graduated top 10% of class	29
% graduated top 25% of class	56
% graduated top 50% of class	86

DEADLINES

Regular application deadline	2/1
Regular notification	rolling
Nonfall registration?	yes

APPLICANTS ALSO LOOK AT

AND OFTEN PREFER
Auburn University
Emory University
Middle Tennessee State University

AND SOMETIMES PREFER
University of Florida
University of Georgia
Vanderbilt University

AND RARELY PREFER
Clemson University
East Tennessee State University
Sewanee—The University of the South
University of Kentucky

FINANCIAL FACTS

Financial Aid Rating	**63**
Annual in-state tuition	$4,714
Annual out-of-state tuition	$9,780
Room & Board	$5,398
Books and supplies	$1,156
Required fees	$662
% frosh rec. need-based scholarship or grant aid	3
% UG rec. need-based scholarship or grant aid	25
% frosh rec. need-based self-help aid	29
% UG rec. need-based self-help aid	30
Independent 529 member?	No

UNIVERSITY OF TEXAS—AUSTIN

PO BOX 8058, AUSTIN, TX 78713-8058 • ADMISSIONS: 512-475-7440 • FAX: 512-475-7475

CAMPUS LIFE

Quality of Life Rating	**85**
Fire Safety Rating	**86**
Type of school	public
Environment	metropolis

STUDENTS

Total undergrad enrollment	36,473
% male/female	48/52
% from out of state	5
% live on campus	18
% in (# of) fraternities	9 (26)
% in (# of) sororities	12 (22)
% African American	4
% Asian	17
% Caucasian	60
% Hispanic	15
% international	3
# of countries represented	121

SURVEY SAYS

Great library
Athletic facilities are great
Students love Austin, TX
Everyone loves the Longhorns
Student publications are popular
Lots of beer drinking

ACADEMICS

Academic Rating	**76**
Calendar	semester
Student/faculty ratio	19:1
Professors interesting rating	68
Professors accessible rating	63
% professors teaching UG courses	100
% classes taught by TAs	0
Most common lab size	10-19 students
Most common regular class size	10-19 students

MOST POPULAR MAJORS

Economics
political science and government

STUDENTS SPEAK OUT

Academics

The University of Texas at Austin is one of the largest universities in the nation, with more than 50,000 students (undergraduate plus grad), and the school "really capitalizes on its size and funds" with "so many libraries, its state-of-the-art technology, and student programs galore," as well as "tons of opportunities to get involved in research." The school poses near-limitless options for undergrads willing to seek them out; writes one, "You can plan your college experience exactly as you want it. Basically the attitude is: If you can fit it in in four years and you meet the prerequisites, go for it. And if they don't offer what you want, figure out how to take it and it's yours." As one student puts it, "Academically, UT is what you make of it. If you want to register for courses that are challenging (but worth it) you can. If you want to register for easy A courses, you can do that too." Of course, "it is easy to get lost in the shuffle" at a school this big, and "when you run into a problem, dealing with the bureaucracy can be difficult and frustrating." Fortunately, "for a school of this size, UT runs pretty well." Professors here are often surprisingly good and engaged, although "students often have to take the initiative because the professors don't have the time to seek out every student individually." A course instructor survey system allows students to check other students' ratings of professors online; there are also "tons of teaching awards at UT as incentives to focus on that aspect," and they seem to be doing the job.

Life

Lots of self-respecting cities have smaller populations than UT, but they're not surrounded by "the coolest college town that ever existed," so as you might imagine "there is so much available to do here that fits the bill for just about anyone." The campus hosts "a huge college scene that translates into lots of parties (and drinking) every weekend, from the Greek houses to off-campus houses, apartments, co-ops, etc." "Football games and other sporting events are also a lot of fun," and the "900+ registered student organizations" allow undergrads to explore any and all extracurricular interests. Beyond campus is the capital of Texas, a city that "never sleeps. If you can't find anything to do in Austin, you're crazy." Students report that "Restaurants are very popular—you can get the best Tex-Mex in the world here," and "Sixth Street is very big with the older students, as it hosts bar after bar and an interesting scene. It's like Austin's version of Bourbon Street," right down to the "tons of concerts; this city is the live music capital of the world." Outdoor enthusiasts also "have lots to do, with the many hike and bike trails in and around Austin. Barton Springs and Zilker Park are favorites for natural recreation. Most UT students love to be outside enjoying the sunshine, be it playing sports, exercising, horseback riding, studying, reading, tanning or just lounging." Don't have a car? Don't worry; "the public transportation is readily available."

Student Body

"There's really no typical student at UT" due to the school's enormous size and the diversity of its home state. One student writes, "It would be really hard to not fit in. In fact, even if you're a left-handed vegetarian lesbian who wants to be an astronaut, there are probably enough people like you to start the 3,000th club on campus. I guess out of over 50,000 students, your odds are pretty good" of finding multiple kindred spirits. UT "is known as the 'liberal' school in Texas, and we do have a large GLBT population, as well as the 'Austin-type' bohemian culture. Of course we have our fair share of cute Texas blondes and frat boys, so a typical student could be any or all of the above."

FINANCIAL AID: 512-475-6282 • WEBSITE: WWW.UTEXAS.EDU

ADMISSIONS

Very important factors considered include: Class rank, secondary school record. *Important factors considered include:* Essays, extracurricular activities, standardized test scores, talent/ability, volunteer work, work experience. *Other factors considered include:* Character/personal qualities, geographical residence, minority status, recommendations, state residency. SAT Reasoning or ACT required. TOEFL required of all international applicants. High school diploma is required, and GED is accepted. *Academic units required:* 4 English, 3 math, 2 science, 2 foreign language, 3 social studies, 2 academic electives. *Academic units recommended:* 4 math, 3 science, 3 foreign language, 1 fine arts.

The Inside Word

Top faculty and super facilities draw a mega-sized applicant pool to UT, as does Longhorn football. Texas wants top athletes in each entering class, to be sure. But it also seeks students who are well qualified academically, and it gets loads of them. Both the university and Austin are thriving intellectual communities; Austin has the highest per capita book sales of any city in the United States. Many students continue on to grad school without ever leaving, which is understandable—it's hard to spend any time without developing an affinity for the school and the city.

FINANCIAL AID

Students should submit: FAFSA. The Princeton Review suggests that all financial aid forms be submitted as soon as possible after 1/1. *Need-based scholarships/grants offered:* Pell, SEOG, state scholarships/grants, private scholarships, the school's own gift aid, Federal Nursing scholarships. *Loan aid offered:* FFEL Subsidized Stafford, FFEL Unsubsidized Stafford, FFEL PLUS, Federal Perkins, state loans. Applicants will be notified of awards on a rolling basis beginning on or about 4/1. Federal Work-study Program available. Institutional employment available. Off-campus job opportunities are fair.

FROM THE ADMISSIONS OFFICE

"UT Austin is a large, research-oriented university located in the capital of Texas, at the edge of the beautiful hill country of Texas. More than 50,000 students representing 50 states and 126 foreign countries live and learn in a competitive academic environment. A strong intercollegiate athletic program for both men and women is supplemented by an intramural athletic program that is available to all students as well as faculty and staff. An undergraduate advising center for undeclared majors, a career choice information center, and college placement centers provide advising, career counseling, and placement. Other student services include an honors center, counseling and student health centers, and a study abroad office. The university serves as a cultural center to the community at large as well as to students, faculty, and staff. A performing arts center is host to Broadway plays, the Austin Civic Opera, the Austin Symphony, and visiting musical and dance groups throughout the year. A strong faculty, fine facilities and student services, and a commitment to undergraduate education make UT Austin one of the truly great universities in America and in the world.

"Freshman applicants must submit official scores from the new version of the SAT or the ACT with the optional Writing exam. SAT Subject Test scores are required only for applicants to the College of Engineering who need to submit scores to meet the Math Readiness Requirement."

SELECTIVITY

Admissions Rating	**92**
# of applicants	23,008
% of applicants accepted	51
% of acceptees attending	58

FRESHMAN PROFILE

Range SAT Verbal	540-660
Average SAT Verbal	603
Range SAT Math	570-680
Average SAT Math	627
**TPR Projected Range SAT Writing*	*590-670*
Range ACT Composite	23-28
Average ACT Composite	26
Minimum Paper TOEFL	550
Minimum Computer Based TOEFL	213
% graduated top 10% of class	66
% graduated top 25% of class	93
% graduated top 50% of class	99

DEADLINES

Regular application deadline	2/1
Regular notification	rolling
Nonfall registration?	yes

FINANCIAL FACTS

Financial Aid Rating	**92**
Annual in-state tuition	$7,438
Annual out-of-state tuition	$17,474
Room & Board	$7,638
Books and supplies	$800
% frosh rec. need-based scholarship or grant aid	49
% UG rec. need-based scholarship or grant aid	36
% frosh rec. need-based self-help aid	46
% UG rec. need-based self-help aid	44
% frosh rec. any financial aid	77
% UG rec. any financial aid	74
Avg. frosh grant	$6,650
Avg. frosh loan	$3,650
Independent 529 member?	No

UNIVERSITY OF TORONTO

315 Bloor Street West, Toronto, ON M5S1A3 • Admissions: 416-978-2190 • Fax: 416-978-7022

CAMPUS LIFE

Quality of Life Rating	**66**
Fire Safety Rating	**60**
Type of school	public
Environment	metropolis

STUDENTS

Total undergrad enrollment	40,341
% male/female	44/56
% from out of state	4
% live on campus	23
% international	4

SURVEY SAYS

Class discussions are rare
Great computer facilities
Great library
Athletic facilities are great
Diverse student types on campus
Students love Toronto, ON
Great off-campus food
Campus feels safe

ACADEMICS

Academic Rating	**61**
Calendar	semesters
Student/faculty ratio	26:1
Professors interesting rating	62
Professors accessible rating	61
% classes taught by TAs	0
Most common regular class size	10-19 students

MOST POPULAR MAJORS

Computer science
English language and literature
environmental studies

STUDENTS SPEAK OUT

Academics

University of Toronto (U of T) is the quintessential large public university, offering its students "excellent research opportunities," "a wide variety of co-op programs," "multiculturalism and a huge selection of courses," and, unfortunately, "a huge student body that makes one feel like just one more in a crowd." Students warn that there's "not much outreach to us students" and "not enough staff to run the school smoothly." In other words, self-sufficiency is a requirement to succeed here. Making the U of T experience even more stressful is its notoriously demanding academics. Students warn that "professors are extremely difficult graders. They require immense commitment to studying. You can't ever slack off or fall behind." As a result, "students are extremely competitive. Grades are all-important to many." Upping the ante is the fact that "everyone wants to get a good GPA to get into the 'specialist' programs, which I think should be open to everyone who is interested, not only to those who have a specific GPA." Toronto profs are a mixed bag; writes one student, "Professors are either extremely helpful, or they don't give a hoot about you." Many note that "professors seem more personable and approachable in higher-level courses." Summing up the U of T experience, one student writes, "The strength of this school is also its biggest weakness: it is really, really big. That means we get the best academics, researchers, city, etc. However, if you like the small-town experience, don't come here."

Life

Toronto students generally agree that their school is not conducive to an active social scene. Many factors, they report, contribute to the dearth of extracurricular life here. As one student puts it, "Since U of T is extremely large, it has a huge student population, and it is hard to feel like you actually belong and are wanted here." The large commuter population means that "many here are already in their own cliques formed previously, and it is very hard to find a good group of people to spend time with on campus." Finally, there's the intensity of the academic pressure and the competitiveness among students, which means that a student's schedule typically consists of nothing more than "going to class, studying, procrastinating, cramming before a test, drinking to celebrate afterward, and sleeping a lot." On a positive note, some tell us that "if you make an effort to participate, you'll probably find an organization that is suitable for you because the school is so large. There are revolver clubs and Kendo clubs, for example, to name just two." Fortunately, hometown Toronto is a major metropolis offering a near-endless stream of options. As one student put it, "The best thing about U of T is that it is right in the middle of Toronto." Students here also like the fact that "all the buildings are connected. Therefore there is no need to go outside in the roaring winds to run from class to class."

Student Body

"There is no typical student" at U of T because "Toronto is a multicultural city, and the university is in the middle of that." The school is home to "a high concentration of Indian and East Asian students. Most stay within their own ethnic groups." Because the majority of students live off campus, "the typical student is a commuter who spends most of her time on the bus or subway going from the university to where [she lives]. I think students feel very isolated, and it is hard for them to get involved with school activities." That sense of isolation is further intensified by the sense that "many of the students are very competitive and do not help each other out." Competition is most pronounced, students agree, in the sciences and engineering; humanities students, conversely, report a more friendly, cooperative atmosphere. Because of the relatively small population of campus residents, "there is a lack of participation in anything nonacademic, and there is very little (if any) school spirit."

FINANCIAL AID: 416-978-2190 • E-MAIL: ASK@ADM.UTORONTO.CA • WEBSITE: WWW.UTORONTO.CA

ADMISSIONS

Very important factors considered include: Class rank, secondary school record, standardized test scores, SAT Subject Tests required. TOEFL required of all international applicants. High school diploma is required, and GED is accepted.

The Inside Word

The University of Toronto is one of Canada's best, and its admissions process is appropriately selective. U.S. candidates: Give yourself extra time to research and prepare for filing an application. You're an international student here, and some additional paperwork is required to attend—although the hassles are ultimately minimal, and the financial bargain substantial.

FINANCIAL AID

The Princeton Review suggests that all financial aid forms be submitted as soon as possible after 1/1.

FROM THE ADMISSIONS OFFICE

"The University of Toronto is committed to being an internationally significant research university with undergraduate, graduate, and professional programs of study.

"Students educated at U.S. schools should present the new SAT or the ACT with the Writing section. Scores from the old SAT or ACT will be accepted. Students must also present at least three SAT Subject Tests or Advanced Placement Examinations appropriate to the student's intended area of study at university."

SELECTIVITY

Admissions Rating	**60**
# of applicants	59,161
% of applicants accepted	66

FRESHMAN PROFILE

Minimum Paper TOEFL	600
Minimum Computer Based TOEFL	250
Average HS GPA	3.0

DEADLINES

Regular application deadline	3/1
Regular notification	rolling
Nonfall registration?	no

FINANCIAL FACTS

Financial Aid Rating	**60**
In-province tuition	$3,991-$6,417
Out-of-province tuition	$3,991-$6,417
International tuition	$10,195-$13,659
Room & Board	$5,000
Books and supplies	$1,050
Required fees	$650
Independent 529 member?	No

UNIVERSITY OF TULSA

600 SOUTH COLLEGE AVENUE, TULSA, OK 74104 • ADMISSIONS: 918-631-2307 • FAX: 918-631-5003

CAMPUS LIFE

Quality of Life Rating	**98**
Fire Safety Rating	**88**
Type of school	private
Affiliation	Presbyterian
Environment	metropolis

STUDENTS

Total undergrad enrollment	2,699
% male/female	50/50
% from out of state	28
% from public high school	78
% live on campus	64
% in (# of) fraternities	21 (6)
% in (# of) sororities	23 (9)
% African American	7
% Asian	2
% Caucasian	66
% Hispanic	3
% Native American	5
% international	9
# of countries represented	41

SURVEY SAYS

Small classes
Great computer facilities
Athletic facilities are great
Students are happy

ACADEMICS

Academic Rating	**87**
Calendar	semester
Student/faculty ratio	11:1
Professors interesting rating	95
Professors accessible rating	95
% professors teaching UG courses	100
% classes taught by TAs	4
Most common lab size	10-19 students
Most common regular class size	10-19 students

MOST POPULAR MAJORS

Business administration/management
computer and information sciences
fine/studio arts

STUDENTS SPEAK OUT

Academics

The University of Tulsa is one of the sleeper gems of the Great Plains, a private school large enough to house numerous top-flight programs but small enough to facilitate one-on-one instruction provided in a homey atmosphere. TU is justly recognized for its excellent offerings in computer science, athletic training, and for its "incredible engineering program with a focus on undergraduate research." Students tell us the school is uniformly solid across all popular departments, and that "because of the smaller graduate programs, undergrads get the experiences that only grad students get at larger state schools or seriously research-driven universities." All students here complete the cross-discipline Tulsa curriculum that one student says "has been incredible in helping me learn to think in a variety of ways, and connect thoughts across curricula. In every one of my classes, I think back to what I've been learning in another class and that adds to my understanding of my overall education." While "classes are quite strenuous, [a] friendly and helpful atmosphere—with tutoring for all students who need help—and lots of study groups" help students to survive the demanding workload. As for the teachers, "TU professors can be top-notch or so-so. Some of them need to work on their teaching skills. Despite that, every teacher seems to genuinely care about his students, is readily accessible, encourages his students to get involved, and demands quality. If you get out of a class with an A here, you will know the material."

Life

"In general, academics come first for most students" at TU, "but many students enjoying unwinding on the weekends by going out to local bars (to hear several popular local bands), or heading to nearby party." The Greek houses are popular party destinations, but so, too, are dorm rooms, off-campus apartments, and greater Tulsa, where "there is a burgeoning bar and nightclub scene downtown." The party scene is happening without getting out of hand, students tell us. Explains one undergrad, "TU is pretty laid back in my opinion because they trust us to be adults, and we haven't abused their confidence so far." Athletic events—and the "amazing" facilities that host them—draw big crowds, too. "The football team improved greatly last year and our basketball team has high hopes this year. Most of our other sports have always done well and have great attendance, such as soccer." Intramurals and recreational sports are "very big; on any given afternoon there are multiple pick-up games of soccer, football, basketball going on around campus." Campus clubs and organizations are also active, with strong enrollment in religious and service organizations. As a bonus, "the new administration of the student government decided they wanted to really create things to do around campus, so now there are events on campus almost every night." So, what's the down side? "It is so small we call it Tulsa High School. Everyone knows everyone's business."

Student Body

There are "kids from all over the world" at TU, making it "really neat to walk down the sidewalk because you see so many different kids, each with their own beliefs and morals. We all come from different backgrounds, from Christian to Jewish, to Muslim to atheist and everything in between." International students provide most of the diversity, as the majority of Americans are "white Christians from Oklahoma, Texas, Missouri, and Arkansas [who are] usually reasonably well off." A freshman from California says she had a bit of "culture shock. The fried food and the popularity of football freaked me out at first. But the Oakies take you in." Nearly everyone is "very serious and passionate about what we are studying. Most of us were in the top 20 percent of our high school class and work very hard in school."

Financial Aid: 918-631-2526 • E-mail: admission@utulsa.edu • Website: www.utulsa.edu

ADMISSIONS

Very important factors considered include: Class rank, interview, secondary school record. *Important factors considered include:* Extracurricular activities, recommendations, standardized test scores, talent/ability. *Other factors considered include:* Alumni/ae relation, character/personal qualities, essays, minority status, volunteer work, work experience. SAT Reasoning or ACT required. TOEFL required of all international applicants. High school diploma is required, and GED is accepted. *Academic units recommended:* 4 English, 3 math, 3 science (2 science lab), 2 foreign language, 1 social studies, 2 history, 1 academic elective.

The Inside Word

TU is a university with solid academic offerings, a strong sense of community, lots of student-faculty interaction, and attainable admission standards. The school's commitment to undergrads is clear. One of TU's most impressive programs, The Tulsa Undergraduate Research Challenge (TURC), allows undergrads to complete research along with faculty.

FINANCIAL AID

Students should submit: FAFSA, institution's own financial aid form. The Princeton Review suggests that all financial aid forms be submitted as soon as possible after 1/1. *Need-based scholarships/grants offered:* Pell, SEOG, state scholarships/grants, private scholarships, the school's own gift aid. *Loan aid offered:* FFEL Subsidized Stafford, FFEL Unsubsidized Stafford, FFEL PLUS, Federal Perkins. Applicants will be notified of awards on a rolling basis beginning on or about 3/1. Federal Work-study Program available. Institutional employment available. Off-campus job opportunities are good.

FROM THE ADMISSIONS OFFICE

"The University of Tulsa is a private university with a comprehensive scope. Students choose from more than 80 majors offered through three undergraduate colleges—Arts and Sciences, Business Administration, and Engineering, and Natural Sciences. Their curriculum can be customized with collaborative research, joint BA/MBA and BA/law degree programs, and an honors program, among other options. Professors are equally committed to teaching undergraduates and to scholarly research. This results in extraordinary individual achievement, as demonstrated by the nationally competitive scholarships TU students have won since 1995: 36 Goldwater scholars, 8 Truman scholars, 3 Udall scholars, and 4 Marshall scholars. Since 1994 campus life has benefited from more than $35 million in new student apartments and residence hall renovations. Over 160 registered clubs, organizations, special interest groups, and intramural and recreational sports exist on campus as well as 6 fraternities and 9 sororities. The 8,300-seat Reynolds Arena is home to the standout Golden Hurricane NCAA Division I men's basketball team, campus events, and concerts. A 40-acre sports complex includes a student fitness center and indoor tennis center that will host the 2008 NCAA Division I Men's and Women's tennis finals. An outdoor adventure freshman orientation program launches an entire first-year experience dedicated to developing students' full potential. Ninety-four percent of undergraduates receive financial aid: need-based, merit, or both.

"Applicants for fall 2006 term are required to submit the SAT or ACT. The Writing component is not required. For admission and scholarship consideration, the best composite score of submitted tests will be used."

SELECTIVITY

Admissions Rating	**90**
# of applicants	2,621
% of applicants accepted	74
% of acceptees attending	35
# accepting a place on wait list	147
% admitted from wait list	48

FRESHMAN PROFILE

Range SAT Verbal	540-690
Average SAT Verbal	610
Range SAT Math	540-690
Average SAT Math	610
**TPR Projected Range SAT Writing*	*590-690*
Range ACT Composite	23-30
Average ACT Composite	26
Minimum Paper TOEFL	500
Minimum Computer Based TOEFL	173
Average HS GPA	3.7
% graduated top 10% of class	56
% graduated top 25% of class	76
% graduated top 50% of class	94

DEADLINES

Regular notification	rolling
Nonfall registration?	yes

APPLICANTS ALSO LOOK AT

AND OFTEN PREFER
Oklahoma State University
Southern Methodist University
Texas Christian University
University of Oklahoma

AND SOMETIMES PREFER
Baylor University
Trinity University
Tulane University
Washington University in St. Louis

AND RARELY PREFER
Texas A&M University—College Station
University of Kansas
University of Missouri—Columbia

FINANCIAL FACTS

Financial Aid Rating	**93**
Annual tuition	$18,780
Room & Board	$6,488
Books and supplies	$1,200
Required fees	$80
% frosh rec. need-based scholarship or grant aid	28
% UG rec. need-based scholarship or grant aid	30
% frosh rec. need-based self-help aid	42
% UG rec. need-based self-help aid	39
% frosh rec. any financial aid	92
% UG rec. any financial aid	86
Avg. frosh grant	$11,184
Avg. frosh loan	$4,735
Independent 529 member?	Yes

UNIVERSITY OF UTAH

201 South 1460 East, Room 250 S, Salt Lake City, UT 84112 • Admissions: 801-581-7281 • Fax: 801-585-7864

CAMPUS LIFE

Quality of Life Rating	**80**
Fire Safety Rating	**74**
Type of school	public
Environment	metropolis

STUDENTS

Total undergrad enrollment	21,626
% male/female	56/44
% from out of state	8
% from public high school	95
% live on campus	7
% in (# of) fraternities	1 (7)
% in (# of) sororities	2 (7)
% African American	1
% Asian	5
% Caucasian	81
% Hispanic	4
% Native American	1
% international	2

SURVEY SAYS

Great computer facilities
Great library
Students are very religious
Students love Salt Lake City, UT
Great off-campus food
Campus feels safe
Students are happy
Everyone loves the Utes

ACADEMICS

Academic Rating	**73**
Calendar	semester
Student/faculty ratio	15:1
Professors interesting rating	68
Professors accessible rating	61
% professors teaching UG courses	64
% classes taught by TAs	10
Most common lab size	20-29 students
Most common regular class size	fewer than 10 students

MOST POPULAR MAJORS

Business administration/management
elementary education and teaching
psychology

STUDENTS SPEAK OUT

Academics

The U, as people here like to call it, "provides the highest quality education at the lowest possible price in the state of Utah." So if you want to be in Utah and affordability is high on your checklist, this university has a good deal to offer. It helps, though, if you are enterprising. "You really have to take care of yourself," one student writes, "and YOU have to approach the instructors." If you can actually get into class with a professor, that is. "In my four years at the University of Utah, I have only had four REAL professors," one student writes. "The rest of my teachers have been graduate students." Because this is primarily a research institution, sometimes "professors lack teaching ability and make up for it in their research, which isn't always the greatest for us students." Others tell of more personalized classroom experiences and say professors "strive to help us understand the material, rather than move on with the syllabus." One student notes, "Some classes are very, very good, especially upper-division and honors classes." Another student continues that sentiment by saying, "The education here really is top-notch, tons of opportunities for undergraduate research." Students also say the administration generally knows what it is doing. Administrators "are always looking out for the good of the students [and are] very dedicated to education, leadership, and diversity."

Life

Cradled by the majestic Wasatch Mountains, the campus provides easy access to a range of outdoor sports. "The mountains right by the school are awesome for biking, hiking, or skiing," writes one student. However, life on the campus itself is decidedly less awesome. Though more than 22,000 students are enrolled, only a small percentage actually live on campus. (According to the University, about 3,500 students live in the dorms and campus apartments.) Since the vast majority of enrolled students are commuters, "there is not a lot of excitement on campus," reports one student. Most of these commuters "don't have time or resources to return to campus several times a week for meetings or other activities." The result? Very little school spirit or social life, though a "relatively small but notable frat scene" does keep students entertained on campus. Still, most turn elsewhere, that elsewhere being Salt Lake City. Those who do won't be disappointed, though they probably won't be thrilled, either. One student writes, "Salt Lake isn't the greatest college town, but [the University] is located near malls, restaurants, movie theaters, and bars." By most accounts, the social pulse at the U and in town is pretty chaste, a reflection, students say, of the state's Mormon values.

Student Body

"If you're not Mormon, all you ever think about is how many Mormons there are," one student writes. Indeed, like the state that houses it, a great many of the students at this university are Mormons—and most are also from Utah. "It's true that the majority of students come from a middle-class, Mormon, white-bread home, but people are very friendly and minority groups fit in easily," writes a student. Another student agrees, "Students are generally accepting of anyone, regardless of race or religion." Take, for example, this student's experience: "I am not a Mormon, and I have no problem fitting in. Walking across campus, you will hear four or five different languages." Another student says, "I don't catch the religious vibe very much anymore." The reality may just be that the "University of Utah is the closest thing to diversity in a [Latter-day Saints]-dominated state." One student writes, "With 23,000 of us, we get people from all walks of life." And the cliché is truer at this college than at others, since so many of the students are nontraditional—meaning they are married, part-time attendees, or commuters.

FINANCIAL AID: 801-581-6211 • E-MAIL: FAWIN1@SA.UTAH.EDU • WEBSITE: WWW.UTAH.EDU

ADMISSIONS

Very important factors considered include: Secondary school record, standardized test scores. *Important factors considered include:* Talent/ability. *Other factors considered include:* Class rank, extracurricular activities, interview, minority status, recommendations. SAT Reasoning and SAT Subject Tests or ACT required. TOEFL required of all international applicants. High school diploma is required, and GED is accepted. *Academic units required:* 4 English, 2 math, 2 science (1 science lab), 2 foreign language, 1 history, 4 academic electives.

The Inside Word

Utah is another state in which low numbers of high school grads keep selectivity down at its public flagship university. Admission is based primarily on the big three: course selection, grades, and test scores; if you've got a 3.0 GPA or better and average test scores, you're close to a sure bet for admission.

FINANCIAL AID

Students should submit: FAFSA, institution's own financial aid form. The Princeton Review suggests that all financial aid forms be submitted as soon as possible after 1/1. *Need-based scholarships/grants offered:* Pell, SEOG, state scholarships/grants, private scholarships, the school's own gift aid. *Loan aid offered:* FFEL Subsidized Stafford, FFEL Unsubsidized Stafford, FFEL PLUS, Federal Perkins, Federal Nursing, college/university loans from institutional funds, private alternative loans. Applicants will be notified of awards on a rolling basis beginning on or about 4/15. Federal Work-study Program available. Institutional employment available. Off-campus job opportunities are fair.

FROM THE ADMISSIONS OFFICE

"The University of Utah is a distinctive community of learning in the American West. Today's 28,000 students are from every state and 109 foreign countries. The U has research ties worldwide, with national standing among the top comprehensive research institutions. The U offers majors in 73 undergraduate and 94 graduate subjects. Nationally recognized honors and undergraduate research programs stimulate intellectual inquiry. Undergraduates collaborate with faculty on important investigations. The U's intercollegiate athletes compete in the NCAA Division I Mountain West Conference. The men's basketball team has been nationally ranked for several years, as have our women's gymnastics and skiing teams. The U's location in Salt Lake City provides easy access to the arts, theater, Utah Jazz basketball, and hockey. Utah's Great Outdoors—skiing, hiking, and five national parks—are nearby. The university was the site for the opening and closing ceremonies and the Athletes Village for the 2002 Winter Olympic Games.

"Residential Living has greatly expanded the opportunity for students to live on campus with a new and wide variety of housing. Heritage Commons, located in historic Fort Douglas on campus, consists of 21 newly constructed buildings, including three residence hall–style facilities, which accommodate more than 2,500 students.

"Applicants are required to submit ACT scores. SAT scores are also accepted, although ACT scores are preferred. Students are urged to take the ACT near the end of their junior year or early in the senior year of high school."

SELECTIVITY

Admissions Rating	**78**
# of applicants	6,251
% of applicants accepted	86
% of acceptees attending	49

FRESHMAN PROFILE

Range ACT Composite	21-26
Average ACT Composite	24
Minimum Paper TOEFL	500
Minimum Computer Based TOEFL	173
Average HS GPA	3.51
% graduated top 10% of class	27
% graduated top 25% of class	51
% graduated top 50% of class	84

DEADLINES

Regular application deadline	4/1
Regular notification	rolling basis, within 2 weeks of file completion
Nonfall registration?	yes

FINANCIAL FACTS

Financial Aid Rating	**66**
Annual in-state tuition	$2,986
Annual out-of-state tuition	$9,495
Room & Board	$5,636
Books and supplies	$1,086
Required fees	$359
% frosh rec. need-based scholarship or grant aid	26
% UG rec. need-based scholarship or grant aid	33
% frosh rec. need-based self-help aid	22
% UG rec. need-based self-help aid	31
% frosh rec. any financial aid	53
% UG rec. any financial aid	38
Avg. frosh grant	$3,963
Avg. frosh loan	$4,794
Independent 529 member?	No

UNIVERSITY OF VERMONT

194 SOUTH PROSPECT STREET., BURLINGTON, VT 05401-3596 • ADMISSIONS: 802-656-3370 • FAX: 802-656-8611

CAMPUS LIFE

Quality of Life Rating	**82**
Fire Safety Rating	**80**
Type of school	public
Environment	town

STUDENTS

Total undergrad enrollment	8,143
% male/female	45/55
% from out of state	63
% from public high school	70
% live on campus	52
% in (# of) fraternities	7 (8)
% in (# of) sororities	6 (5)
% African American	1
% Asian	2
% Caucasian	93
% Hispanic	2
% international	1
# of countries represented	40

SURVEY SAYS

Students are friendly
Students love Burlington, VT
Great off-campus food
Lots of beer drinking
Hard liquor is popular

ACADEMICS

Academic Rating	**77**
Calendar	semester
Student/faculty ratio	15:1
Professors interesting rating	76
Professors accessible rating	76
% professors teaching UG courses	85
% classes taught by TAs	2
Most common lab size	10-19 students
Most common regular class size	10-19 students

MOST POPULAR MAJORS

Business administration/management
psychology

STUDENTS SPEAK OUT

Academics

The University of Vermont, students tell us, is the perfect size: "Small enough to allow for close relationships between friends and faculty, yet large enough for a diverse academic experience, all while being set in one of the most beautiful locations in the Northeast." Unlike most state universities, the trend at UVM is toward smaller classes, not larger. One student writes, "The class sizes have gotten much smaller over the past few years, and I feel that is very impressive. Sure, we have a few large classes, but the majority of mine have less than 50 students in them." The university excels in areas both mainstream—education, political science, English, nursing, business administration, and sociology—and extraordinary. The university's Rubenstein School for the Environment and Natural Resources, for example, "is wonderful. The school has an amazing diversity of course offerings for the size (100 per class)." The department of animal science, which offers degrees in dairy production, equine sciences, and pre-veterinary medicine, is another standout. If there is any knock on UVM, it's the quality of some of its students; many are drawn to UVM more by the school's surroundings than by a genuine desire for a first-rate education. As one undergraduate puts it, "Overall, the school is hamstrung by its deserved reputation as a party school."

Life

The University of Vermont "is in one of the best college towns in the U.S.," according to students, who love that the university is "a strong academic school but still has a raging social scene." Undergraduates feel they "are typically very focused during the first three days of the week and Sunday. This is the time when people finish up any papers, big projects, and homework. When Thursday arrives, though, it's time to have fun." The town of Burlington "has something for everyone to do: movies, dining, the waterfront, the gym, shopping, and coffee shops." It's especially good "if you like music. All sorts of bands come here; Phish-y stuff to hard-core hip-hop and everything between." Just beyond the town are the mountains, providing all manner of outdoor activity. "A majority of students ski or snowboard often [since] the best skiing and snowboarding on the East Coast is just minutes away." Other students "climb in the Green, White, or Adirondack Mountains, fish nearby trout streams, or simply relax down by the waterfront of Lake Champlain." On campus, "frat parties are popular, but they're very selective as to who they allow in" and often lose their appeal as students get older. Upperclassmen tend to move off campus and "host smaller, more intimate parties with 10 to 25 people [or] hit the bars downtown." The university offers "many intramural, club and varsity athletics, as well as a variety of student organizations." The Canadian city of Montreal "is not too far away for those who need a dose of city life on occasion."

Student Body

The student body at University of Vermont consists of "two main types: preppies and hippies." Skiing and the beautiful location seem to be the chief attractions for preppy undergraduates, who "sport polo shirts (collars up), Patagonia/North Face new seasonal outerwear, designer jeans, shoes, jewelry, and accessories (down to the Louis Vuitton bags). The girls tend to sport pearls and hair ribbons." The hippies, in contrast, favor "Birkenstocks, dreadlocks, hemp necklaces, and glass beads; they speak freely about left-wing politics and marijuana, wear natural scents, and eat vegetarian foods that are organically grown." Many students come from well-off families, leading some to comment caustically that "lots of people preach a simplistic way of life and pretend they are hippies, yet drive SUVs and have a trust fund set up by their parents." A third, more conservative group, consisting largely of native Vermonters, can be found "in the college of business and the department of animal science. Mostly, these students tolerate or ignore the liberals who primarily do the same, although there are some who propagandize in front of the library."

FINANCIAL AID: 802-656-3156 • E-MAIL: ADMISSIONS@UVM.EDU • WEBSITE: WWW.UVM.EDU

ADMISSIONS

Very important factors considered include: Secondary school record. *Important factors considered include:* Character/personal qualities, class rank, essays, standardized test scores, state residency. *Other factors considered include:* Alumni/ae relation, extracurricular activities, geographical residence, interview, minority status, recommendations, talent/ability, volunteer work, work experience. SAT Reasoning or ACT required. TOEFL required of all international applicants. High school diploma is required, and GED is accepted. *Academic units required:* 4 English, 3 math, 2 science (1 science lab), 2 foreign language, 3 social studies.

The Inside Word

UVM is one of the most popular public universities in the country, and its admissions standards are significantly more competitive for out-of-state students. Nonresidents shouldn't get too anxiety-ridden about getting in; more than half of the student body comes from elsewhere. Candidates with above-average academic profiles should be in good shape.

FINANCIAL AID

Students should submit: FAFSA. The Princeton Review suggests that all financial aid forms be submitted as soon as possible after 1/1. *Need-based scholarships/grants offered:* Pell, SEOG, state scholarships/grants, private scholarships, the school's own gift aid, Federal Nursing scholarships. *Loan aid offered:* FFEL Subsidized Stafford, FFEL Unsubsidized Stafford, FFEL PLUS, Federal Perkins, Federal Nursing, college/university loans from institutional funds. Applicants will be notified of awards on a rolling basis beginning on or about 3/15. Federal Work-study Program available. Institutional employment available. Off-campus job opportunities are good.

FROM THE ADMISSIONS OFFICE

"The University of Vermont blends the close faculty-student relationships most commonly found in a small liberal arts college with the dynamic exchange of knowledge associated with a research university. This is not surprising because UVM is both. A comprehensive research university offering nearly 100 undergraduate majors and extensive offerings through its Graduate College and College of Medicine, UVM is one of the nation's premier public research universities. UVM prides itself on the richness of its undergraduate experience. Distinguished senior faculty teach introductory courses in their fields. They also advise not only juniors and seniors, but also first- and second-year students, and work collaboratively with undergraduates on research initiatives. Students find extensive opportunities to test classroom knowledge in field through practicums, academic internships, and community service. More than 100 student organizations (involving 80 percent of the student body), 20 Division I varsity teams, 15 intercollegiate club and 14 intramural sports programs, and a packed schedule of cultural events fill in where the classroom leaves off.

"Applicants for the entering class of fall 2006 class and beyond are required to take the new version of the SAT, or the ACT with the writing section, and must submit official test scores. SAT Subject Tests are neither required nor recommended for the admission application."

SELECTIVITY

Admissions Rating	**79**
# of applicants	11,384
% of applicants accepted	76
% of acceptees attending	23
# accepting a place on wait list	977
% admitted from wait list	9

FRESHMAN PROFILE

Range SAT Verbal	530-620
Average SAT Verbal	577
Range SAT Math	530-630
Average SAT Math	578
**TPR Projected Range SAT Writing*	*580-650*
Range ACT Composite	22-27
Average ACT Composite	24
Minimum Paper TOEFL	550
Minimum Computer Based TOEFL	213
% graduated top 10% of class	23
% graduated top 25% of class	57
% graduated top 50% of class	93

DEADLINES

Regular application deadline	1/15
Regular notification	3/31
Nonfall registration?	yes

FINANCIAL FACTS

Financial Aid Rating	**79**
Annual in-state tuition	$9,088
Annual out-of-state tuition	$22,728
Room & Board	$7,016
Books and supplies	$832
Required fees	$1,138
% frosh rec. need-based scholarship or grant aid	52
% UG rec. need-based scholarship or grant aid	50
% frosh rec. need-based self-help aid	48
% UG rec. need-based self-help aid	47
% frosh rec. any financial aid	81
% UG rec. any financial aid	77
Avg. frosh grant	$10,721
Avg. frosh loan	$6,059
Independent 529 member?	No

University of Virginia

Office of Admission, PO Box 400160, Charlottesville, VA 22906 • Admissions: 434-982-3200 • Fax: 434-924-3587

CAMPUS LIFE

Quality of Life Rating	**83**
Fire Safety Rating	**80**
Type of school	public
Environment	city

STUDENTS

Total undergrad enrollment	13,231
% male/female	46/54
% from out of state	28
% from public high school	74
% live on campus	46
% in (# of) fraternities	30 (31)
% in (# of) sororities	30 (16)
% African American	9
% Asian	11
% Caucasian	67
% Hispanic	3
% international	5
# of countries represented	119

SURVEY SAYS

Great computer facilities
Great library
Athletic facilities are great
Everyone loves the Cavaliers, Wahoos, Hoos
Frats and sororities dominate social scene
Student publications are popular
Lots of beer drinking

ACADEMICS

Academic Rating	**87**
Calendar	semester
Student/faculty ratio	15:1
Professors interesting rating	82
Professors accessible rating	77
% classes taught by TAs	15
Most common lab size	10-19 students
Most common regular class size	10-19 students

MOST POPULAR MAJORS

Business administration/management
economics
psychology

STUDENTS SPEAK OUT

Academics

Regarded as one of the country's premier state universities, University of Virginia (UVA) offers an "excellent all-around college experience: great, intelligent students; wonderful intercollegiate sports; phenomenal faculty; and, of course, excellent academics." Students appreciate that "unlike other publics, there is not a tendency for students at UVA to be lost in paperwork and bureaucracy. The people who work in the administrative offices are very nice and understanding; perhaps this is a product of 'southern hospitality.' Also, professors at UVA are not only accessible but hospitable." Indeed, "most professors at UVA are eager to get to know the students. Many bend over backward to help students and understand what is important to the students." Additionally, "UVA has an extraordinary number of professors who are both dedicated teachers and [at the] top of their fields." Students also tell us that "your education does not end at the classroom. There are numerous opportunities related to service in which you can learn to become part of your community and give back to people who need help. In addition, there are numerous cultural, social, and athletic organizations, all of which allow you to pursue a well-rounded education."

Life

"For all the hard-core nature of academics at UVA, it is still a really fun place to be," students here agree, especially if you love frat parties ("Greek life is very prominent at the university"). For students who "do not enjoy alcohol . . . There are many other things to do. The University of Virginia is located about 20 miles from the Blue Ridge Mountains, where you can go for a nice hike. Winter Green is about an hour away from Charlottesville (for those who enjoy skiing or playing golf). The James River is about 40 minutes away for those who enjoy tubing or rafting." Nor is travel off campus necessary, as the school itself offers a "diversity of activities! If you play sports, dance, act, like intellectual activities, [or] participate in the strong student self-governance, you can do it at UVA." The school also attracts "awesome speakers, including Isabel Allende, Ralph Nader, the Dalai Lama, and Archbishop Desmond Tutu, to name a few that have come while I've been here." Students may just choose to sit back and enjoy the beautiful campus itself; writes one student, "When I finished my last final first year, I walked out of my classroom elated. But as I passed the historical Lawn and the beautiful amphitheater, my heart dropped at the thought of having to leave such gorgeous surroundings." Virginia is a school rich in tradition, a fact appreciated by most students. Traditions include streaking across the Lawn ("The tradition is to start from the Rotunda, sprint down to Homer—located in front of Old Cabell hall—and kiss his butt, and sprint back. Then you look through the keyhole at the top of the steps of the rotunda to see if you can see Thomas Jefferson"), "dressing up to go to athletic events," and the Honor Code.

Student Body

Virginia has long had a reputation as a preppy haven, a reputation students tell us is well deserved. "UVA is quite a preppy, well-to-do school," writes one undergrad. "It's the perfect school for frat boys who like to wear Gucci shoes and sorority girls who dig Versace." Not everyone fits the mold; explains one student, "Upon closer inspection, you'll realize that the student population includes people of all walks of life." The student body has its share of "gun-toting, abortion-hating, Confederacy-loving students; insane-worker, dedicated-to-a-fault, anal-about-cleanliness students; and 'eccentric to a point that begs the question not of whether, but of when they'll be committed' students." Although fairly diverse, "UVA is very segregated. Different ethnic groups do not mix very much, and the Greek population is an entity unto [itself]." Political activism "is not big at the university at all. The student body is largely more conservative-leaning, and the flaming liberals don't have too much of an impact of student life."

FINANCIAL AID: 434-982-6000 • E-MAIL: UNDERGRADADMISSION@VIRGINIA.EDU • WEBSITE: WWW.VIRGINIA.EDU

ADMISSIONS

Very important factors considered include: Alumni/ae relation, class rank, recommendations, secondary school record, state residency. *Important factors considered include:* Character/personal qualities, essays, extracurricular activities, standardized test scores, talent/ability. *Other factors considered include:* Geographical residence, minority status, volunteer work, work experience. SAT Reasoning and SAT Subject Tests or ACT required. TOEFL required of all international applicants. High school diploma is required, and GED is accepted. *Academic units required:* 4 English, 4 math, 2 science (2 science lab), 2 foreign language, 1 social studies, 5 college preparatory courses. *Academic units recommended:* 5 math, 4 science, 5 foreign language, 4 social studies.

The Inside Word

Even many Virginia residents regard trying to get into UVA as a feeble attempt. The competition doesn't get much more severe, and only the most capable and impressive candidates stand to be offered admission. The volume of out-of-state applications borders on enormous when considered in conjunction with available spots in the entering class.

FINANCIAL AID

Students should submit: FAFSA, institution's own financial aid form. The Princeton Review suggests that all financial aid forms be submitted as soon as possible after 1/1. *Need-based scholarships/grants offered:* Pell, SEOG, state scholarships/grants, private scholarships, the school's own gift aid. *Loan aid offered:* Direct Subsidized Stafford, Direct Unsubsidized Stafford, Direct PLUS, Federal Perkins, Federal Nursing, college/university loans from institutional funds. Applicants will be notified of awards on or about 4/5.

FROM THE ADMISSIONS OFFICE

"Admission to competitive schools requires strong academic credentials. Students who stretch themselves and take rigorous courses (honors-level and Advanced Placement courses, when offered) are significantly more competitive than those who do not. Experienced admission officers know that most students are capable of presenting superb academic credentials, and the reality is that a very high percentage of those applying do so. Other considerations, then, come into play in important ways for academically strong candidates, as they must be seen as 'selective' well as academically competitive.

"Students applying for first-year admission for fall 2006 are required to take the new SAT or the ACT with the Writing section, but students may submit scores from the old version of the SAT (prior to March 2005) or ACT as well. It is recommended that applicants take two SAT Subject Tests, one in Math for math and science students."

SELECTIVITY

Admissions Rating	**97**
# of applicants	14,822
% of applicants accepted	39
% of acceptees attending	54
# accepting a place on wait list	3,017
% admitted from wait list	1
# of early decision applicants	924
% accepted early decision	39

FRESHMAN PROFILE

Range SAT Verbal	610-710
Average SAT Verbal	659
Range SAT Math	620-720
Average SAT Math	671
**TPR Projected Range SAT Writing*	*640-700*
Range ACT Composite	25-31
Average ACT Composite	28
Minimum Paper TOEFL	600
Minimum Computer Based TOEFL	250
Average HS GPA	4.0
% graduated top 10% of class	84
% graduated top 25% of class	96
% graduated top 50% of class	100

DEADLINES

Early decision application deadline	11/1
Early decision notification	12/1
Regular application deadline	1/2
Regular notification	4/1
Nonfall registration?	no

APPLICANTS ALSO LOOK AT AND OFTEN PREFER

College of William and Mary, Duke University

AND SOMETIMES PREFER

Cornell University, Georgetown College, Harvard College, Notre Dame College (OH), Penn State Lehigh Valley, Princeton University, University of North Carolina—Chapel Hill, Virginia Tech, Yale University

FINANCIAL FACTS

Financial Aid Rating	**85**
Annual in-state tuition	$3,492
Annual out-of-state tuition	$11,352
% frosh rec. need-based scholarship or grant aid	20
% UG rec. need-based scholarship or grant aid	19
% frosh rec. need-based self-help aid	15
% UG rec. need-based self-help aid	17
% frosh rec. any financial aid	50
% UG rec. any financial aid	44
Avg. frosh grant	$7,430
Avg. frosh loan	$3,592
Independent 529 member?	No

UNIVERSITY OF WASHINGTON

1410 NE Campus Parkway, 320 Schmitz Box 355840, Seattle, WA 98195-5840 • Admissions: 206-543-9686 • Fax: 206-685-3655

CAMPUS LIFE

Quality of Life Rating	**85**
Fire Safety Rating	**97**
Type of school	public
Environment	city

STUDENTS

Total undergrad enrollment	26,042
% male/female	49/51
% from out of state	13
% live on campus	17
% in (# of) fraternities	12 (30)
% in (# of) sororities	11 (18)
% African American	3
% Asian	24
% Caucasian	48
% Hispanic	3
% Native American	1
% international	3

SURVEY SAYS

Great computer facilities
Great library
Athletic facilities are great
Students love Seattle, WA
Great off-campus food
Student publications are popular

ACADEMICS

Academic Rating	**79**
Calendar	quarter
Student/faculty ratio	11:1
Professors interesting rating	74
Professors accessible rating	71
% classes taught by TAs	0
Most common lab size	20-29 students
Most common regular class size	20-29 students

MOST POPULAR MAJORS

Economics
political science and government
psychology

STUDENTS SPEAK OUT

Academics

University of Washington enthusiasts, of whom there are many, believe "it's impossible to spend a day on campus and not fall in love with this school. It offers everything to everyone: diverse and respected programs, good climate, good location, and a student population that is informed enough to give a damn about the world around them." "Independent research and intellectual initiative are encouraged" at UW, where "professors are surprisingly accessible," especially to those who "show the interest to approach them." Reports one student, "Most of the professors are excellent teachers who want to make sure you are learning and understanding the material. Most are also very passionate about the subject they teach and make it a great learning experience." UW's strengths include "some of the top graduate programs in the nation," an "amazing pre-med program associated with one of the top hospitals in the country," a "cheap, big, good engineering program," and computer-related offerings strengthened by "a lot of financial benefits from our relationship with Microsoft." UW students also profit from "an amazing library program. Not only is it huge, but the main library, Suzallo, is beautiful. It looks like something straight out of a Harry Potter movie—it's gorgeous." Administration is typically labyrinthine, but students see the glass as half full. Writes one, "Considering the budget crisis in this country, they are doing a phenomenal job with the balancing act."

Life

Students can find "pretty much everything and anything at the UW," and though "nothing is widely advertised or known about, if you do some looking you'll find Ultimate Frisbee™ groups, 'boffers' staging medieval warfare at the campus center using Nerf bats, intramural sports played at three levels (beginner, intermediate, and advanced), clubs for every interest and hobby, honor societies, and activist groups all over the political spectrum. There are even two unofficial campus newspapers in addition to the UW-sponsored paper." Greek life with its "nonstop parties," "is huge" on campus, and "students regularly attend the gym, especially since there are a number of things to do there aside from your basic cardio and lifting." Aesthetically, "the campus is beautiful: clean and green with lots of grassy spaces to hang out, study, or just enjoy the odd sunny day." While life on campus is extremely active, the surrounding city of Seattle is even more so. Near campus, "people go to the Avenue, the road next to campus with funky stores and good restaurants, or U Village, the shopping center with more mainstream/nice stores." Beyond these destinations, "there is plenty to do around town, and with the great bus system, there is absolutely no need for a vehicle. Within the city, there are amazing restaurants, concerts, movie previews, Broadway plays, etc." The city also provides access to excellent outdoor options. "We are close to the mountains, so people who love to ski or board in the winter and hike during summer are really close. We basically live on two lakes, so lake activities like boating are really accessible," explains one undergrad.

Student Body

"Being such a huge school, there are people of every single type at UW," but "most fall into either the coffee-drinking, indie rock group or the engineering or medical majors who spend eight years or more in college." Whether you're one, both, or neither, "because of the sheer size of the campus, there is a niche for everybody, and there is bound to be somebody just like you—be that nerd, jock, foreign, or hippie." That might be why "even though the school is socially and ethnically diverse, groups tend to stick together in cliques." Undergrads tend to be left-coast friendly and "laid back," "sport a larger than average number of piercings" and are, "for the most part, liberals and Democrats--but there are still UWCR (UW College Republicans) and the LaRouche campaigners." The student body has a definite look of "Northwest fashion" to them. Notes one student, "Some friends of mine joke that the UW 'starter pack' includes a North Face jacket, a Nalgene water bottle, and an iPod."

ADMISSIONS

Very important factors considered include: Secondary school record. *Important factors considered include:* Essays, standardized test scores. *Other factors considered include:* Alumni/ae relation, character/personal qualities, extracurricular activities, state residency, talent/ability, volunteer work, work experience. SAT Reasoning or ACT required. High school diploma or equivalent is not required. *Academic units required:* 4 English, 3 math, 2 science (1 science lab), 2 foreign language, 3 social studies. *Academic units recommended:* 4 English, 4 math, 3 science (3 science lab), 3 foreign language, 4 social studies, 1 fine arts.

The Inside Word

Like the other five public colleges in Washington, UW uses an admissions index (AI) as part of its initial review of applications, taking into account the student's GPA, as well as combined SAT I or composite ACT scores, course selection, personal statements, and essays. A student whose qualifications exceed expectations in all of these areas may be a "turbo admit"; all other applications receive an intensive review, which evaluates evidence of academic rigor in the student's curriculum, a challenging senior year, academic awards, personal statement, school and community activities, educational and economic disadvantage, personal adversity, grade trends, special talents in the arts, and cultural awareness. UW notes the importance of these qualitative factors as it moves away from AI-driven decisions.

FINANCIAL AID

Students should submit: FAFSA. The Princeton Review suggests that all financial aid forms be submitted as soon as possible after 1/1. *Need-based scholarships/grants offered:* Pell, SEOG, state scholarships/grants, private scholarships, the school's own gift aid. *Loan aid offered:* Direct Subsidized Stafford, Direct Unsubsidized Stafford, Direct PLUS, Federal Perkins, Federal Nursing, college/university loans from institutional funds. Applicants will be notified of awards on or about 4/1.

FROM THE ADMISSIONS OFFICE

"Are you curious about everything, from comet dust to computer game design, salmon to Salman Rushdie, ancient Rome to the atmospherics of Mars? Do you seek the freedom to chart your own course—and work on breakthrough research? Are you ready to cheer on the Division I Huskies and spend your weekends sea kayaking? Would you like to walk to class on a 700-acre stunning, ivy-covered campus, yet be only 15 minutes from downtown Seattle? If the answers are yes, then the University of Washington may be the place for you. Offering more than 140 majors and 450 student organizations, the UW is looking for students who are both excited about the vast academic and social possibilities available to them and eager to contribute to the campus' cultural and intellectual life.

"We encourage you to take advantage of every opportunity in the application, especially the personal statement and activities summary, to tell us why Washington would be good fit for you and how you will contribute to the freshman class.

"Good luck in your senior year and with your college search!

"Freshman applicants to the University of Washington are required to submit scores from either the new SAT or ACT (with the Writing component)."

SELECTIVITY

Admissions Rating	**91**
# of applicants	15,402
% of applicants accepted	69
% of acceptees attending	45
# accepting a place on wait list	1,205
% admitted from wait list	2

FRESHMAN PROFILE

Range SAT Verbal	520-640
Range SAT Math	550-670
**TPR Projected Range SAT Writing*	*570-660*
Range ACT Composite	23-28
Average HS GPA	3.69
% graduated top 10% of class	66
% graduated top 25% of class	86
% graduated top 50% of class	99

DEADLINES

Regular application deadline	1/15
Regular notification	rolling
Nonfall registration?	yes

APPLICANTS ALSO LOOK AT

AND OFTEN PREFER

University of Southern California

AND SOMETIMES PREFER

Seattle University
University of Oregon
Western Washington University

AND RARELY PREFER

University of Colorado—Boulder
University of Puget Sound
Washington State University

FINANCIAL FACTS

Financial Aid Rating	**73**
Annual in-state tuition	$4,770
Annual out-of-state tuition	$17,400
Room & Board	$6,663
Books and supplies	$900
Required fees	$516
% frosh rec. need-based scholarship or grant aid	6
% UG rec. need-based scholarship or grant aid	34
% frosh rec. need-based self-help aid	5
% UG rec. need-based self-help aid	38
Avg. frosh grant	$9,000
Avg. frosh loan	$3,200
Independent 529 member?	No

UNIVERSITY OF WISCONSIN—MADISON

716 LANGDON STREET, MADISON, WI 53706-1481 • ADMISSIONS: 608-262-3961 • FAX: 608-262-7706

CAMPUS LIFE

Quality of Life Rating	**89**
Fire Safety Rating	**76**
Type of school	public
Environment	city

STUDENTS

Total undergrad enrollment	28,217
% male/female	47/53
% from out of state	29
% live on campus	24
% in (# of) fraternities	9 (26)
% in (# of) sororities	8 (11)
% African American	2
% Asian	5
% Caucasian	84
% Hispanic	3
% Native American	1
% international	3
# of countries represented	110

SURVEY SAYS

Great library
Athletic facilities are great
Students love Madison, WI
Great off-campus food
Everyone loves the Badgers
Student publications are popular
Lots of beer drinking
Hard liquor is popular

ACADEMICS

Academic Rating	**81**
Calendar	semester
Student/faculty ratio	13:1
Professors interesting rating	71
Professors accessible rating	72
% professors teaching UG courses	90
% classes taught by TAs	25
Most common lab size	20-29 students
Most common regular class size	10-19 students

MOST POPULAR MAJORS

History
political science and government
psychology

STUDENTS SPEAK OUT

Academics

"Choices are the biggest asset at the University of Wisconsin—Madison," where "we have every major under the sun, every kind of club, every kind of person, every kind of activity you can imagine. All you have to do is get out there and find what's right for you." The university is especially strong in "research, research, and research, along with any undergrad programs that lead into some type of research," such as engineering and the sciences. The business program is also "among the best in the country" with "state-of-the-art facilities and equipment." Caution some students outside these disciplines, "UW could improve by putting more emphasis on the arts and humanities rather than always relying on UW as a 'research' school. Facilities for the humanities and social sciences need improvement." Undergrads also tell us that "at times, due to the sheer size, the university can feel a little impersonal. You have to grab the bull by the horns and get yourself involved because nobody is going to do it for you." Those in large lecture classes "spend more time with their TAs than the actual professors teaching the courses," which isn't necessarily a bad thing. "Professors' lectures can be hard to follow," writes a biology major, "but discussion sections led by TAs help to clarify information from the lecture and allow more one-on-one attention." Advises one student, "Overall the school runs surprisingly smoothly, but the way in which things are organized makes it essential that you have a good relationship with your advisor, so you know what the heck to do as far as taking the right classes to earn a degree. It can be confusing."

Life

UW's hometown of Madison, most agree, "is the perfect spot for anyone hoping for a small-town atmosphere while being a part of a large-campus lifestyle." One undergrad writes, "If you take the time to look into some of the options, you'll never get bored. But if you're looking for a relaxing day, Madison is great for that, too. Just take a walk through its beautiful setting." The city is "especially great in the warm months. At any given time, walk down State Street and you will pass an inordinate number of diners and unique stores, a good number of homeless people—many of whom the students have nicknames for—musicians showing off their talents, a bunch of food vendors, some Christian dude preaching and reading parts of the Bible to everyone who walks by, a group of atheists yelling at him, and a bunch of other people advertising protests and student organizations." All year round "the access to government, politics, and history is perfect for any liberal arts major." On campus, UW "has a group to represent every segment of the population. There are groups here for every race, religion, gender, sexual orientation, political affiliation, and anything else you could think of. A campus center helps people to find volunteer opportunities." Intercollegiate athletics are huge. Reports one student, "Our level of enthusiasm for multiple sports cannot be beat. We don't suck up to just one sport because we don't have to." Another student agrees, "One of the most fun things at our school is our Badger game days. There's nothing like getting up at 9 A.M. to drink before an 11:00 A.M. football game. The streets are lined with parties and blasting music by early morning."

Student Body

According to the undergrads we contacted, "One of the greatest strengths of Madison is the people themselves. Madison draws a wide array of people with one thing in common, and that is their talent. Not just academic talent—although that is prevalent—but talents that extend in all directions and make meeting people every day an exciting thing to do." It is "easy to find people you are compatible with here, both because of the size of the student population and the many interest groups you can join." With over 40,000 students, UW "has people of every ethnic, social, economic, and religious background. You can always find someone to relate to."

FINANCIAL AID: 608-262-3060 • E-MAIL: ONWISCONSIN@ADMISSIONS.WISC.EDU • WEBSITE: WWW.WISC.EDU

ADMISSIONS

Very important factors considered include: Class rank, secondary school record. *Important factors considered include:* Recommendations, standardized test scores, state residency, talent/ability. *Other factors considered include:* Alumni/ae relation, character/personal qualities, essays, extracurricular activities, interview, minority status, volunteer work, work experience. SAT Reasoning or ACT required. TOEFL required of all international applicants. High school diploma is required, and GED is accepted. *Academic units required:* 4 English, 3 math, 3 science, 2 foreign language, 3 social studies, 2 academic electives. *Academic units recommended:* 4 English, 4 math, 4 science, 2 foreign language, 4 social studies.

The Inside Word

Wisconsin has high expectations of its candidates and virtually all of them relate to numbers. Though not at the top tier of selectivity and not quite entirely admissions-by-formula, UW does look at each application individually.

FINANCIAL AID

Students should submit: FAFSA, institution's own financial aid form. The Princeton Review suggests that all financial aid forms be submitted as soon as possible after 1/1. *Need-based scholarships/grants offered:* Pell, SEOG, state scholarships/grants, private scholarships, the school's own gift aid. *Loan aid offered:* FFEL Subsidized Stafford, FFEL Unsubsidized Stafford, FFEL PLUS, Federal Perkins, Federal Nursing, state loans, college/university loans from institutional funds. Applicants will be notified of awards on a rolling basis beginning on or about 4/1. Federal Work-study Program available. Institutional employment available. Off-campus job opportunities are excellent.

FROM THE ADMISSIONS OFFICE

"UW-Madison is the university of choice for some of this country's (and the world's) best and brightest. Our freshman class has an average ACT score of 27.5 and an average SAT of 1260. Over half come from the top 10 percent of their high school class, and nearly 95 percent come from the top quarter.

"These factors combine to make admission to UW—Madison both competitive and selective. We consider academic record, course selection, strength of curriculum (honors, AP, IB, etc.), grade trend, class rank, results of the ACT and/or SAT, and nonacademic factors. We do not have a prescribed minimum test score, GPA, or class rank criteria. Rather we admit the best and most well-prepared students-students who have challenged themselves and who will contribute to Wisconsin's strength and diversity-for the limited space available.

"Each application is personally reviewed by our admission counselors. Admission decisions are made within six weeks of the time when an applicant's admission file is complete. A complete file includes the application for admission, application fee, official high school transcript, and official test score report(s). Supplemental application materials may include a personal statement and letters of recommendation.

"We practice rolling admissions and applications are accepted beginning September 15. For full consideration for fall and summer terms, complete applications must be received by February 1. The deadline for the spring term is October 1. Applications received after these deadlines will be considered on a space-available basis.

"Starting in fall 2006, all freshman applicants must submit results from either the new SAT or the ACT with the Writing component. Students who took either test before February 2005 must take at least one of the exams again in order to provide a Writing score and be eligible for admission."

SELECTIVITY

Admissions Rating	**93**
# of applicants	20,495
% of applicants accepted	66
% of acceptees attending	42

FRESHMAN PROFILE

Range SAT Verbal	560-670
Average SAT Verbal	611
Range SAT Math	600-700
Average SAT Math	649
**TPR Projected Range SAT Writing*	*600-680*
Range ACT Composite	26-30
Average ACT Composite	28
Minimum Paper TOEFL	550
Minimum Computer Based TOEFL	213
Average HS GPA	3.68
% graduated top 10% of class	58
% graduated top 25% of class	93
% graduated top 50% of class	99

DEADLINES

Regular application deadline	2/1
Regular notification	rolling
Nonfall registration?	yes

APPLICANTS ALSO LOOK AT AND OFTEN PREFER

Marquette University
University of Illinois at Urbana-Champaign
University of Michigan—Ann Arbor
University of Minnesota—Twin Cities

AND SOMETIMES PREFER

Northwestern University
University of Colorado—Boulder
University of Iowa
University of Wisconsin — La Crosse, University of Wisconsin—Milwaukee

FINANCIAL FACTS

Financial Aid Rating	**66**
Annual in-state tuition	$6,220
Annual out-of-state tuition	$21,060
Room & Board	$6,500
Books and supplies	$860
% frosh rec. need-based scholarship or grant aid	12
% UG rec. need-based scholarship or grant aid	14
% frosh rec. need-based self-help aid	24
% UG rec. need-based self-help aid	27
Independent 529 member?	No

UNIVERSITY OF WYOMING

DEPT 3435, 1000 E. UNIVERSITY AVENUE, LARAMIE, WY 82071 • ADMISSIONS: 307-766-5160 • FAX: 307-766-4042

CAMPUS LIFE

Quality of Life Rating	**79**
Fire Safety Rating	**60**
Type of school	public
Environment	town

STUDENTS

Total undergrad enrollment	9,102
% male/female	48/52
% from out of state	27
% from public high school	91
% live on campus	20
% in (# of) fraternities	7 (9)
% in (# of) sororities	4 (4)
% African American	1
% Asian	1
% Caucasian	87
% Hispanic	4
% Native American	1
% international	1
# of countries represented	67

SURVEY SAYS

Great computer facilities
Students are friendly
Students are happy
Everyone loves the Cowboys
Student publications are popular
Lots of beer drinking
Hard liquor is popular

ACADEMICS

Academic Rating	**73**
Calendar	semester
Student/faculty ratio	16:1
Professors interesting rating	74
Professors accessible rating	77
% professors teaching UG courses	97
% classes taught by TAs	9
Most common lab size	10-19 students
Most common regular class size	20-29 students

MOST POPULAR MAJORS

Business administration and management
elementary education and teaching
nursing/registered nurse training (RN, ASN, BSN, MSN)

STUDENTS SPEAK OUT

Academics

"Large enough to offer big-school opportunities to all students but small enough that those opportunities are not competitive," the University of Wyoming optimizes the advantages of its midsize status. The university attracts enough students to host a wide range of strong majors, including those with wide appeal (biology, education, pharmacy, nursing, criminal justice), as well as those aimed at more idiosyncratic populations (rangeland ecology and waste-land management; textiles and merchandising; and, "one of the very few agricultural economics programs in the nation"). At the same time, the school has been able to keep class sizes manageable and student-teacher interaction frequent. Unfortunately, some students feel that although UW has mandatory advising, some students feel that "it sucks. It seems like any person can sign up for any class." On the whole, the secret to the university's success, we're told, is that "UW is well-funded. This means there are a lot of extracurricular opportunities available to everyone. Every day I hear about some amazing program that is looking for applicants...summer drawing classes in India, research opportunities on a glacier in Alaska, language study in Peru, field trips to natural gas fields and conservation ranches, and the list goes on. It also means that tuition isn't too high—another plus." Add to the mix "phenomenal research opportunities [and] classrooms constantly under a state of upgrade to integrate the latest technologies and teaching aids" and you'll understand why so many here give UW an unqualified thumbs up.

Life

Numerous "outdoor events lie at the students' fingertips" at UW where, thanks to the proximity of the "beautiful Snowy Mountains," undergrads regularly enjoy high-quality "skiing, snowboarding, camping, hiking, canoeing, rock climbing, hunting, and fishing." In fact, many choose the school primarily for its myriad outdoor opportunities; those who do either have a high tolerance for cold weather or grow greatly disappointed in their choice. For those who prefer to keep warm indoors, UW has "a lot of activities affiliated with the school and off campus. There are over 100 different student life organizations, so if you are looking to get involved you most certainly can." Wyoming often hosts "free activities, like comedy nights, concerts, and film festivals," too. Best of all, "students get in free to all sporting events, and Wyoming fans are crazy. We almost always storm the field when we win a football game." Basketball, volleyball, and soccer are also "really popular during their respective seasons." Hometown Laramie "is a small town, so people tend to think the only thing you can do here is drink. However, there are many volunteer services and research opportunities here that other schools don't have." There are also plenty of opportunities to tie one on, with "lots of house parties" and "Fort Collins (home to Colorado State University) and its hopping club scene only 45 minutes away." For students who crave big-city life, "Denver is only a couple hours [away]."

Student Body

Sometimes the clichés are true: there is indeed a "large population of truck-driving, rifle shooting, rodeoing, snoose-spitting, belt buckle-wearing ranch kids" at UW. There are, however, also a lot of students who don't fit that mold. Undergrads point out that Laramie's size means you can "easily get to know every corner of the town and campus." It is also "by far the most liberal city in the state, by virtue of the university," and that "there were as many Kerry bumper stickers as Bush stickers here in 2004." Students also point out that all factions here share a common trait: "Basically, Wyomingites don't want to be told what to do. If either Republicans or Democrats tell them what to do, they will be pissed." Accordingly, most here "adopt a live-and-let-live attitude, respect each others' views, and mind their own business, creating a remarkably tolerant atmosphere." A large nontraditional population—from older students to those with families—"fits in fairly well." In fact, "everyone fits in here, as long as they don't care that there isn't a mall in town!"

FINANCIAL AID: 307-766-2116 • E-MAIL: WHY-WYO@UWYO.EDU • WEBSITE: WWW.UWYO.EDU

ADMISSIONS

Very important factors considered include: Secondary school record, standardized test scores. *Important factors considered include:* Essays, extracurricular activities, geographical residence, recommendations, state residency. *Other factors considered include:* Character/personal qualities, interview, talent/ability. TOEFL required of all international applicants. High school diploma is required, and GED is accepted. *Academic units required:* 4 English, 3 math, 3 science (3 science lab), 3 cultural context electives. *Academic units recommended:* 4 English, 3 math, 3 science, 9 cultural context electives.

The Inside Word

The admissions process at Wyoming is fairly formula-driven. State residents need a minimum 2.75 high school GPA to gain admission. Nonresidents have to have a 3.0 GPA. That and some solid test scores will open the door to Laramie.

FINANCIAL AID

Students should submit: FAFSA. The Princeton Review suggests that all financial aid forms be submitted as soon as possible after 1/1. *Need-based scholarships/grants offered:* Pell, SEOG, state scholarships/grants, private scholarships, the school's own gift aid. *Loan aid offered:* FFEL Subsidized Stafford, FFEL Unsubsidized Stafford, FFEL PLUS, Federal Perkins. Applicants will be notified of awards on or about 3/15. Off-campus job opportunities are good.

FROM THE ADMISSIONS OFFICE

"The entire admission staff have analyzed why we love UW and Laramie. We think it primarily boils down to size and location. The University of Wyoming and Laramie are relatively small, affording students the opportunity to get personal attention and develop a close rapport with their professors. They can easily make friends and find peers with similar interests and values. Over 200 student organizations offer students a great way to get involved and encourage growth and learning. Couple the small size with a great location and you have a winning combination. Laramie sits between the Laramie and the Snowy Range Mountains. There are numerous outdoor activities in which one can participate. Furthermore, the university works hard to attract other great cultural events. Major label recording artists come to UW as well as some of today's great minds. In all, the University of Wyoming is a great place to be because of its wonderful blend of a small town atmosphere with 'big city' activities.

"University of Wyoming requires freshman applicants may submit scores from the old or new SAT. Students may also choose to submit scores from the ACT (with or without the Writing component) in lieu of the SAT."

SELECTIVITY	
Admissions Rating	**76**
# of applicants	3,211
% of applicants accepted	95
% of acceptees attending	50

FRESHMAN PROFILE	
Range SAT Verbal	480-600
Average SAT Verbal	535
Range SAT Math	480-610
Average SAT Math	544
**TPR Projected Range SAT Writing*	*540-630*
Range ACT Composite	20-26
Average ACT Composite	23
Minimum Paper TOEFL	525
Minimum Computer Based TOEFL	197
Average HS GPA	3.4
% graduated top 10% of class	21
% graduated top 25% of class	48
% graduated top 50% of class	77

DEADLINES	
Regular application deadline	8/10
Regular notification	rolling
Nonfall registration?	yes

FINANCIAL FACTS	
Financial Aid Rating	**86**
Annual in-state tuition	$2,610
Annual out-of-state tuition	$8,640
Room & Board	$5,953
Books and supplies	$1,000
Required fees	$633
% frosh rec. need-based scholarship or grant aid	19
% UG rec. need-based scholarship or grant aid	19
% frosh rec. need-based self-help aid	30
% UG rec. need-based self-help aid	42
Avg. frosh grant	$3,321
Avg. frosh loan	$1,188
Independent 529 member?	No

URSINUS COLLEGE

URSINUS COLLEGE, ADMISSIONS OFFICE, COLLEGEVILLE, PA 19426 • ADMISSIONS: 610-409-3200 • FAX: 610-409-3662

CAMPUS LIFE

Quality of Life Rating	**88**
Fire Safety Rating	**93**
Type of school	private
Environment	metropolis

STUDENTS

Total undergrad enrollment	1,481
% male/female	47/53
% from out of state	36
% from public high school	61
% live on campus	93
% in (# of) fraternities	17 (7)
% in (# of) sororities	28 (7)
% African American	7
% Asian	4
% Caucasian	79
% Hispanic	3
% international	2

SURVEY SAYS

Small classes
Lab facilities are great
Athletic facilities are great
Lots of beer drinking

ACADEMICS

Academic Rating	**92**
Calendar	semester
Student/faculty ratio	11:1
Professors interesting rating	88
Professors accessible rating	86
% professors teaching UG courses	100
% classes taught by TAs	0
Most common lab size	10-19 students
Most common regular class size	fewer than 10 students

MOST POPULAR MAJORS

Economics
English language and literature

STUDENTS SPEAK OUT

Academics

Ursinus College is justly renowned for its biology and chemistry departments. The school's graduates—about one in eight proceed to medical school—boast an impressive 90-plus percent acceptance rate with medical programs. A program this successful, of course, does a good job of winnowing out any slackers, which explains why "Ursinus has many 'ex-biology' students as well as biology students." Those who survive the ordeal benefit from "some of the best chemistry and biology labs around, where really interesting research is being done by undergraduate students and professors. It's nice to have that opportunity, rather than giving up all the research opportunities to graduate students." "Passionate" professors who "care about you and your education" are very accessible to students," as well as an "administration that runs smoothly." A laptop for every student is also part of the deal. Ursinus isn't exclusively about premeds, either. In fact, just as many graduates go on to law school, thanks to "strong humanities programs, especially in history, politics, philosophy, and religion." A brand-new performing arts center that will open in April 2005, promising a flowering of music, dance, and theater on campus. In all areas, "Ursinus College does a great job at preparing its students for future education or jobs by focusing on independent learning, discussions, and providing a ton of learning resources."

Life

"Ursinus is all about having a great learning atmosphere while at the same time providing a place for sports and many other kinds of social events where one can get a true and complete liberal arts education," undergraduates here agree. Even the overworked premeds occasionally find time to work out, play on a team, participate in a student organization, and attend the occasional frat party, we're told. "Greek organizations run the social life and all the big parties" at Ursinus, with about one-third of all students pledging. At the same time, there are "both registered and unregistered parties every weekend," so there's always a party for unaffiliated students to attend. Students like to drink—beer pong is a popular pastime—and smoke herb, but will point out that "while Ursinus College students do party very hard, they are reasonably responsible about it. The college has very loose rules which allow students to make up for the difficult academics with an active social life, while still being held responsible for their actions." For those who abjure intoxication, "there are usually plenty of non-alcoholic activities on campus to attend like movies, concerts, etc." Just don't expect much from Collegeville (yes, the town's real name) other than a Dunkin' Donuts. That's why when students leave campus, they usually head to Philly about half an hour away. A bus or train can "get you to the hot spots of the city," although automobile is the preferred mode of transportation.

Students

The "motivated and ambitious" undergraduates of Ursinus "have a desire to succeed, but also want to have a good time while in college." Many "are white and from the middle to upper classes of society," but students claim that Ursinus "has a larger minority component than most liberal arts colleges in the this area." We're a good-looking school." Students note however, that "the typical student at Ursinus is generally very well-rounded. There are no typical 'jocks' because so many people play sports, and there are no typical 'nerds' because a lot of the same kids excelling in the playing fields are excelling in the classroom as well." In the past, Ursinus has had a large preppy population ("Most of the kids want to be Abercrombie models"), but these days it's starting to attract "a lot of students who have different tastes." "We're a good looking school," says one. A senior describes her school as "one huge clique. Students here may not be diverse in ethnicity, but they are at least diverse in their interests." Undergrads report approvingly that "the tolerant atmosphere on campus is rather amazing. The Gay-Straight Alliance, for example, is a vivacious group coming up with a lot of activities that involve the whole campus."

ADMISSIONS

Very important factors considered include: Class rank, extracurricular activities, secondary school record. *Important factors considered include:* Alumni/ae relation, essays, minority status, recommendations, standardized test scores, talent/ability, volunteer work, work experience. *Other factors considered include:* Character/personal qualities, geographical residence, interview. TOEFL required of all international applicants. High school diploma is required, and GED is accepted. *Academic units required:* 4 English, 3 math, 1 science (1 science lab), 2 foreign language, 1 social studies, 5 academic electives. *Academic units recommended:* 4 math, 3 science, 4 foreign language, 3 social studies.

The Inside Word

The admission process at Ursinus is very straightforward; about 70 percent of those who apply get in. Grades, test scores, and class rank count for more than anything else, and unless you are academically inconsistent, you'll likely get good news.

FINANCIAL AID

Students should submit: FAFSA, institution's own financial aid form, CSS/Financial Aid PROFILE. Regular filing deadline is 2/15. The Princeton Review suggests that all financial aid forms be submitted as soon as possible after 1/1. *Need-based scholarships/grants offered:* Pell, SEOG, state scholarships/grants, private scholarships, the school's own gift aid. *Loan aid offered:* FFEL Subsidized Stafford, FFEL Unsubsidized Stafford, FFEL PLUS, Federal Perkins, college/university loans from institutional funds. Applicants will be notified of awards on or about 4/1. Federal Work-study Program available. Off-campus job opportunities are excellent.

FROM THE ADMISSIONS OFFICE

"Located one-half hour from center-city Philadelphia, the college boasts a beautiful 168-acre campus that includes the Residential Village (renovated Victorian-style homes that decorate the Main Street and house our students) and the nationally recognized Berman Museum of Art. Ursinus is a member of the Centennial Conference, competing both in academics and in intercollegiate athletics with institutions such as Dickinson, Franklin and Marshall, Gettysburg, and Muhlenberg. The academic environment is enhanced with such fine programs as a chapter of Phi Beta Kappa, an Early Assurance Program to medical school with the Medical College of Pennsylvania, and myriad student exchanges both at home and abroad. A heavy emphasis is placed on student research—an emphasis that can only be carried out with the one-on-one attention Ursinus students receive from their professors.

"Ursinus will continue to ask applicants for writing samples—both a series of application essays and a graded high school paper. Pending further examination, the Writing portion of the new SAT will not initially affect admissions decisions."

SELECTIVITY

Admissions Rating	**89**
# of applicants	1,801
% of applicants accepted	73
% of acceptees attending	30
# accepting a place on wait list	67
% admitted from wait list	27
# of early decision applicants	131
% accepted early decision	80

FRESHMAN PROFILE

Range SAT Verbal	550-660
Average SAT Verbal	605
Range SAT Math	560-660
Average SAT Math	609
**TPR Projected Range SAT Writing*	*600-670*
Range ACT Composite	22-28
Average ACT Composite	26
Minimum Paper TOEFL	500
Minimum Computer Based TOEFL	173
Average HS GPA	3.5
% graduated top 10% of class	48
% graduated top 25% of class	75
% graduated top 50% of class	94

DEADLINES

Early decision application deadline	1/15
Early decision notification	1/31
Regular application deadline	2/15
Regular notification	4/1
Nonfall registration?	yes

APPLICANTS ALSO LOOK AT AND OFTEN PREFER

Brown University
Haverford College
Johns Hopkins University
Princeton University
Swarthmore College

AND SOMETIMES PREFER

Dickinson College
Franklin & Marshall College
Gettysburg College

FINANCIAL FACTS

Financial Aid Rating	**89**
Annual tuition	$31,450
Room & Board	$7,350
Books and supplies	$600
% frosh rec. need-based scholarship or grant aid	82
% UG rec. need-based scholarship or grant aid	83
% frosh rec. need-based self-help aid	82
% UG rec. need-based self-help aid	83
% frosh rec. any financial aid	82
% UG rec. any financial aid	83
Avg. frosh grant	$18,117
Avg. frosh loan	$4,018
Independent 529 member?	Yes

Valparaiso University

Kretzmann Hall, 1700 Chapel Drive, Valparaiso, IN 46383 • Admissions: 219-464-5011 • Fax: 219-464-6898

CAMPUS LIFE

Quality of Life Rating	**74**
Fire Safety Rating	**67**
Type of school	private
Affiliation	Lutheran
Environment	town

STUDENTS

Total undergrad enrollment	3,041
% male/female	47/53
% from out of state	65
% from public high school	80
% live on campus	65
% in (# of) fraternities	25 (10)
% in (# of) sororities	18 (6)
% African American	4
% Asian	2
% Caucasian	86
% Hispanic	3
% international	1
# of countries represented	38

SURVEY SAYS

Small classes
No one cheats
Great library
Students are friendly

ACADEMICS

Academic Rating	**85**
Calendar	semester
Student/faculty ratio	13:1
Professors interesting rating	78
Professors accessible rating	82
% professors teaching UG courses	100
% classes taught by TAs	0
Most common lab size	10-19 students
Most common regular class size	10-19 students

MOST POPULAR MAJORS

Biology/biological sciences
elementary education and teaching
nursing/registered nurse training (RN, ASN, BSN, MSN)

STUDENTS SPEAK OUT

Academics

Valparaiso's brand-new Christopher Center library complex stands as a shiny monument to the university's dedication to academics. Once freshmen get through the Valpo core curriculum, they choose from a host of strong major programs, with nursing, and biology specifically called out quite often. Nearly all students agree that professors "put the human, caring relationship first, rather than the teacher-pupil, formal relationship." In addition to conducting tutoring sessions and study groups, professors extend holiday invitations, make appearances at non-academic events, and call students to check on them when they're sick. The administration also demonstrates dedication to enriching the undergraduate experience. Check this out: "During my year abroad, I received a scholarship for which I didn't even apply. I had complained to the International Studies Director about money, and he went to bat for me. The next month, without my knowing it, I began to receive a monthly scholarship from a foreign government! That shows the kind of support I've gotten." The less optimistic see the administration as "hopelessly anachronistic [or] stuffy and conservative." Ultimately, however, students support the school's "high morals and standards." Governed by an honor code, cheating has all but disappeared on this campus of 3,000 undergraduates. With the combination of mental and spiritual enrichment as the goals of a Valpo education, it's hardly surprising that "The main focus is academics."

Life

It's pretty easy to guess which things are encouraged and discouraged at Valpo. For example: chapel good, kegs bad. Dorm visitation privileges between men and women are restricted, and the campus is officially dry. Also, this school is not kidding around when it comes to enforcement. "The police are really strict. They should focus more on keeping students safe, [rather] than busting everyone for alcohol." Despite these deterrents, many students drink, enough so that "we think of ourselves as 'The Lutheran Party School.'" Many students mention the activities common to other sober campuses: scavenger hunts, comedians, late-night bingo, sledding on lunch trays, and Mario Kart 64 tournaments. Caffeine addicts with a conscience gather over Fair Trade coffee at the popular coffee shop in the library. Everyone turns out for the Union Board's annual major concert and "to watch Homer Drew coach the Crusader basketball team" to sweet victory. When the campus and small-town life start to feel like they're closing in, students head to Chicago or the beaches at Indiana Dunes.

Student Body

The Valpo population largely comprises white, studious, middle-class students forever flashing that famously genuine Valpo smile. Some students say that "Most of the people here believe in the Bible and follow the guidelines set forth in [it]," but others claim that "Less than half of the students could be described as 'religious' by any stretch of the imagination." Amid this mix of Lutherans and Catholics, lapsed or practicing, students generally agree that they have not "personally experienced any problems due to religious differences." A senior tells us, "You do not have to be a Lutheran or believe in God to enjoy Valpo." Overall, the campus leans conservative, but "there is a very visible population of student Democrats and politically aware activists." The Office of Multicultural Programs "is doing a lot to bring more culture to campus, and minority organizations have decent clout on campus." A business student says, "Minorities here are in fact scarce, so we find ourselves fighting ignorance, and it just gives us a reason for being here." Sexual orientation, described as "a sore point," seems to be the last frontier of tolerance. "I was really disappointed to find out that all of the notices about national coming out week were vandalized," writes a freshman. Another student cites the ongoing dialogue as a positive aspect of campus life, pointing out that "it is rare, in a university setting, that those who disagree morally with homosexuality would actually be allowed to speak."

FINANCIAL AID: 219-464-5015 • E-MAIL: UNDERGRAD.ADMISSIONS@VALPO.EDU • WEBSITE: WWW.VALPO.EDU

ADMISSIONS

Very important factors considered include: Secondary school record. *Important factors considered include:* Class rank, extracurricular activities, standardized test scores, talent/ability. *Other factors considered include:* Alumni/ae relation, character/personal qualities, essays, interview, minority status, recommendations, religious affiliation/commitment, volunteer work. SAT Reasoning or ACT required. TOEFL required of all international applicants. High school diploma is required, and GED is accepted. *Academic units required:* 4 English, 3 math, 2 science (2 science lab), 3 social studies, 3 academic electives. *Academic units recommended:* 4 math, 3 science (3 science lab), 2 foreign language, 3 social studies, 3 academic electives.

The Inside Word

Valparaiso admits the vast majority of those who apply, but candidates should not be overconfident. Places like this fill a special niche in higher education and spend a good deal of time assessing the match a candidate makes with the university, even if the expected better-than-average high school record is present. Essays and extracurriculars can help you get admitted if your transcript is weak.

FINANCIAL AID

Students should submit: FAFSA. The Princeton Review suggests that all financial aid forms be submitted as soon as possible after 1/1. *Need-based scholarships/grants offered:* Pell, SEOG, state scholarships/grants, private scholarships, the school's own gift aid. *Loan aid offered:* Direct Subsidized Stafford, Direct Unsubsidized Stafford, Direct PLUS, Federal Perkins, college/university loans from institutional funds. Applicants will be notified of awards on a rolling basis beginning on or about 3/1. Federal Work-study Program available. Institutional employment available. Off-campus job opportunities are good.

FROM THE ADMISSIONS OFFICE

"Valpo provides students a blend of academic excellence, social experience, and spiritual exploration. The concern demonstrated by faculty and administration for the total well-being of students reflects a long history as a Lutheran-affiliated university.

"All first-time students from the high school graduating class of 2006 must submit an SAT or ACT score with the new Writing component with their application. If they previously took the SAT or ACT without the Writing portion, they must take the test again."

SELECTIVITY

Admissions Rating	**87**
# of applicants	3,567
% of applicants accepted	81
% of acceptees attending	26

FRESHMAN PROFILE

Range SAT Verbal	530-630
Average SAT Verbal	578
Range SAT Math	530-640
Average SAT Math	587
**TPR Projected Range SAT Writing*	*580-650*
Range ACT Composite	23-29
Average ACT Composite	26
Minimum Paper TOEFL	550
Minimum Computer Based TOEFL	213
Average HS GPA	3.38
% graduated top 10% of class	35
% graduated top 25% of class	65
% graduated top 50% of class	91

DEADLINES

Regular application deadline	8/15
Regular notification	rolling
Nonfall registration?	yes

APPLICANTS ALSO LOOK AT

AND OFTEN PREFER

Ball State University, Bradley University, Butler University, Indiana University—Bloomington, Purdue University—West Lafayette, University of Illinois at Urbana-Champaign, University of Wisconsin—Madison

AND SOMETIMES PREFER

Augustana College (IL), Illinois Wesleyan University, Marquette University, Miami University, Michigan State University, University of Notre Dame

AND RARELY PREFER

Loyola University of Chicago

FINANCIAL FACTS

Financial Aid Rating	**88**
Annual tuition	$22,000
Room & Board	$6,220
Books and supplies	$1,000
Required fees	$750
% frosh rec. need-based scholarship or grant aid	73
% UG rec. need-based scholarship or grant aid	67
% frosh rec. need-based self-help aid	60
% UG rec. need-based self-help aid	57
% frosh rec. any financial aid	97
% UG rec. any financial aid	95
Avg. frosh grant	$13,423
Avg. frosh loan	$4,903
Independent 529 member?	Yes

VANDERBILT UNIVERSITY

2305 WEST END AVENUE, NASHVILLE, TN 37203 • ADMISSIONS: 615-322-2561 • FAX: 615-343-7765

CAMPUS LIFE

Quality of Life Rating	**85**
Fire Safety Rating	**60**
Type of school	private
Environment	metropolis

STUDENTS

Total undergrad enrollment	6,231
% male/female	49/51
% from out of state	76
% from public high school	60
% live on campus	83
% in (# of) fraternities	34 (19)
% in (# of) sororities	50 (12)
% African American	7
% Asian	6
% Caucasian	73
% Hispanic	4
% international	2
# of countries represented	52

SURVEY SAYS

Registration is a breeze
Athletic facilities are great
Students love Nashville, TN
Great off-campus food
Frats and sororities dominate social scene
Lots of beer drinking
Hard liquor is popular

ACADEMICS

Academic Rating	**72**
Calendar	semester
Professors interesting rating	83
Professors accessible rating	82
% classes taught by TAs	0
Most common lab size	10-19 students
Most common regular class size	10-19 students

MOST POPULAR MAJORS

Engineering science
psychology
sociology

STUDENTS SPEAK OUT

Academics

Based on students' comments, Vanderbilt University might want to consider changing its name to Feng Shui University. After all, keeping all the elements of a great education in proper balance, undergraduates agree, is what makes the school great. "It's a balance between small college and large university. It's the perfect size," writes one student. Another student adds, "I also feel like the size provides me with opportunities that I would never have elsewhere (e.g., research position in a lab, leadership in different organizations that have great influence on campus, etc.)." Vanderbilt is small enough that "the administration is extremely involved in all aspects of student life," yet large enough to "offer a wide range of subjects that may not be offered elsewhere." Students also appreciate how Vanderbilt provides "a great academic environment with a good balance of social activities." As one student puts it, "Vanderbilt presents a balance of academics and extracurricular activities in a thriving urban environment." Professors at Vanderbilt "can be tough sometimes, but on the whole, they are interesting and fair, [and they] are extremely accessible, holding weekly office hours. They provide home numbers, often cell phone numbers, and it is not unusual to go out as a class to dinner or to [a professor's] house for a homemade meal." One undergraduate sums up, "I can't imagine a place with a better academic experience, especially for someone in the sciences."

Life

"People are very concerned about their academics" at Vanderbilt, "but everyone is also very concerned with his social life or activities outside of the classroom, whether it involves working or leisure." For many, "frats are the weekend social entertainment." Students point out that "Greek life is not as exclusive as people make it out to be. The frats/sororities are non-residential, and all on-campus parties are open to any student." Plus, "there are many other opportunities on campus for social activities. There are hundreds of organizations on campus for students to participate in." Among the most popular are service groups and religious organizations ("A good portion of the population is involved in religious groups, Bible studies, Young Life (as leaders), or churches/synagogues," explains one student). The campus offers plenty of "movies to see, concerts to go to, plays to attend (all on campus), sporting events, and a great rec. center." Hometown Nashville offers more of the same, plus, of course, a huge music scene. One music enthusiast advises, "12th and Porter and the Bluebird Cafe are two popular music spots on the weekend, and big names, such as Pete Yorn and Guster, are downtown at the Ryman or Gaylord Entertainment Center often. I enjoy the local talent as well." Those who just want to stay home will be happy to hear that "Vanderbilt does know how to pamper. Our dorms are unbeatable; single dorm rooms are available for first-year students, beer is available on campus, and the Baseball Glove Lounge is equipped with numerous comfy leather chairs and sofas."

Student Body

Vanderbilt students are renowned for "the Vandy 'look': Louis V purse, pearls, and flipped collar." Students concede that the typical Vandy student has a "preppy, country-club style [and] is well put together and always looks polished and professional." They add, however, "A lot of people here look similar on the outside—they have money, they are pretty, they seem smart—but really, everyone is still learning about life. Too many people are scared to break the bubble of the traditional student until they are a junior or senior." Most students are "religious, conservative, Republican," and active, both on campus and in the community. In their approach to schoolwork, "students apply the law of diminishing returns to all aspects of their lives. They carefully weigh their goals and how much effort they want to put forth and will cease to pursue anything the minute they feel they're gaining less than they're putting in."

FINANCIAL AID: 615-322-3591 • E-MAIL: ADMISSIONS@VANDERBILT.EDU • WEBSITE: WWW.VANDERBILT.EDU

ADMISSIONS

Very important factors considered include: Character/personal qualities, class rank, essays, extracurricular activities, recommendations, secondary school record, standardized test scores, talent/ability. *Other factors considered include:* Alumni/ae relation, minority status. SAT Reasoning or ACT required. SAT Subject Tests recommended. TOEFL required of all international applicants. High school diploma or equivalent is not required. *Academic units required:* 4 English, 3 math, 2 science (2 science lab), 2 foreign language, 2 social studies, 2 history. *Academic units recommended:* 4 English, 4 math, 3 science (3 science lab), 3 foreign language, 3 social studies, 2 history, 2 academic electives.

The Inside Word

Vanderbilt's strong academic reputation has positioned the university among the most selective in the South. Make no mistake, the applicant pool is competitive, and all apps are read by at least three admissions counselors; students should not downplay the importance of submitting strong essays and recommendations—they make the difference for some candidates.

FINANCIAL AID

Students should submit: FAFSA, CSS/Financial Aid PROFILE, noncustodial (divorced/separated) parents' statement. The Princeton Review suggests that all financial aid forms be submitted as soon as possible after 1/1. *Need-based scholarships/grants offered:* Pell, SEOG, state scholarships/grants, private scholarships, the school's own gift aid. *Loan aid offered:* FFEL Subsidized Stafford, FFEL Unsubsidized Stafford, FFEL PLUS, Federal Perkins, Federal Nursing, college/university loans from institutional funds, Undergrad Educaton Laon. Applicants will be notified of awards on or about 4/1. Federal Work-study Program available. Institutional employment available. Off-campus job opportunities are excellent.

FROM THE ADMISSIONS OFFICE

"Exceptional accomplishment and high promise in some field of intellectual endeavor are essential. The student's total academic and nonacademic record is reviewed in conjunction with recommendations and personal essays. For students at Blair School of Music, the audition is a prime consideration.

"Freshman applicants for fall 2006 are required to submit Writing scores from the new SAT or ACT as part of their application. If a 2006 graduate has taken the old version of the SAT, they may submit Verbal and Math scores and the best scores will be combined regardless of test date."

SELECTIVITY

Admissions Rating	**60**
# of applicants	11,170
% of applicants accepted	38
% of acceptees attending	37

FRESHMAN PROFILE

Range SAT Verbal	620-710
Range SAT Math	650-730
**TPR Projected Range SAT Writing*	*650-700*
Range ACT Composite	28-32
Minimum Paper TOEFL	570

DEADLINES

Early decision application deadline	11/1
Early decision notification	12/15
Nonfall registration?	yes

APPLICANTS ALSO LOOK AT

AND OFTEN PREFER

Cornell University
Georgetown University
Princeton University
University of Notre Dame
University of Virginia

AND SOMETIMES PREFER

Dartmouth College
Duke University
Emory University
Northwestern University
Wake Forest University

AND RARELY PREFER

Boston College
Rhodes College
Southern Methodist University
Tulane University
Washington University in St. Louis

FINANCIAL FACTS

Financial Aid Rating	**98**
Annual tuition	$29,240
Room & Board	$9,736
Books and supplies	$1,030
Required fees	$750
% frosh rec. need-based scholarship or grant aid	40
% UG rec. need-based scholarship or grant aid	37
% frosh rec. need-based self-help aid	27
% UG rec. need-based self-help aid	27
Independent 529 member?	Yes

VASSAR COLLEGE

124 RAYMOND AVENUE, POUGHKEEPSIE, NY 12604 • ADMISSIONS: 845-437-7300 • FAX: 845-437-7063

CAMPUS LIFE

Quality of Life Rating	**79**
Fire Safety Rating	**89**
Type of school	private
Environment	town

STUDENTS

Total undergrad enrollment	2,428
% male/female	40/60
% from out of state	73
% from public high school	65
% live on campus	95
% African American	5
% Asian	9
% Caucasian	75
% Hispanic	5
% international	5
# of countries represented	49

SURVEY SAYS

Small classes
Great library
Frats and sororities are unpopular or nonexistent
Theater is popular

ACADEMICS

Academic Rating	**95**
Calendar	semester
Student/faculty ratio	8:1
Professors interesting rating	90
Professors accessible rating	89
% professors teaching UG courses	100
% classes taught by TAs	0
Most common lab size	10-19 students
Most common regular class size	10-19 students

MOST POPULAR MAJORS

English language and literature
political science and government
psychology

STUDENTS SPEAK OUT

Academics

Students say that Vassar's goal is "teaching students to think" and that the college achieves this end by affording undergraduates a high degree of academic freedom. "Vassar trusts that I can achieve my academic goals without strict guidance" is one common sentiment among students. Most students "love that we have no core curriculum," leaving them time to pursue their "genuine interests." Though the "workload is very challenging," students feel supported by their "impressive, friendly, empathetic," and "very encouraging" professors. "If you had a question for one of my professors after class, she would talk to you for half an hour and not realize how much time had gone by," writes a sophomore. Instructors "love what they do and want you to do well," and the small class sizes "force us to contribute to discussions." Students perceive "significant academic competitiveness" among undergraduates; writes one, "Sometimes Vassar students are a bit too intense about academics." A few complaints arise regarding the "limited number of classes and sections." Certain students groan that the administration "likes to maintain absurd amounts of authority." Still others call for "increased communication between administration and students." But a sophomore offers the following challenge: "Tell me any other college where the president would take the time to e-mail me personally to tell me that she's a fan of my newspaper column." In the end, a student in the American culture department avers that a Vassar education is "about self-development and intellectual glory."

Life

In their fairly isolated location in the Hudson Valley, most students feel "restricted to on-campus activities." Luckily, "on any given Friday, there's usually a concert, lecture, play, and comedy performance." Other students frequent The Mug, the college's dance club and bar, or hit the live music performances at the campus café every Thursday. One student writes, "For fun, most people are drinking," and another adds that students have "no social life if you don't drink or take drugs recreationally." The administration, however, has been "cracking down lately with new party rules," putting a damper on the scene. As an alternative, students happily resort to sledding on cafeteria trays, also known as "tray-ing." When this grows tiresome—or when the snow melts—students take advantage of their "great location close to New York City." Several respondents note the abundant "opportunities for leadership positions and internships" at Vassar, emphasizing that "the activist groups here are great." Surveys repeatedly praise the beautiful campus, the perfect surroundings in which to pursue Vassar students' favorite pastime of all: "finding yourself."

Student Body

The most common opinion regarding the undergraduate population of Vassar goes something like, "An atypical student here is the sort who would be a typical student elsewhere." In a place where students "conform by not conforming," the climate remains "very accepting of individuality," prompting one student to describe her peers as "tolerant, almost to the point of apathy." If forced to pin down a stereotype, one might try one or all of: "hippie, style conscious, smart, left wing, idealist, East-Village-y." Less generous characterizations call students "white, rich kids with holes in their clothes" or "liberal people feeling good about it." Though some people see "no ideological diversity," others are quick to point out that the campus is "getting more conservative" and that "there are spiritual and religious people here." The student body is "very accepting in terms of sexuality," which can be a boon, considering that 60 percent of the population is female. Basically, these "pretty people with lots of talent" will continue to "pride themselves on being unique and involved" and "overthinking virtually everything."

FINANCIAL AID: 845-437-5230 • E-MAIL: ADMISSIONS@VASSAR.EDU • WEBSITE: WWW.VASSAR.EDU

ADMISSIONS

Very important factors considered include: Secondary school record. *Important factors considered include:* Class rank, essays, recommendations, standardized test scores. *Other factors considered include:* Alumni/ae relation, character/personal qualities, extracurricular activities, geographical residence, minority status, talent/ability, volunteer work, work experience. SAT Reasoning and SAT Subject Tests or ACT required. TOEFL required of all international applicants. High school diploma is required, and GED is accepted. *Academic units required:* 4 English, 4 math, 3 science (3 science lab), 3 foreign language, 2 social studies, 2 history, 4 academic electives. *Academic units recommended:* 4 English, 4 math, 3 science (4 science lab), 4 foreign language, 3 social studies, 2 history.

The Inside Word

Vassar is relatively frank about its standards; you won't get much more direct advice from colleges about how to get admitted. The admissions process here follows very closely the practices of most prestigious northeastern schools. Your personal side—essays, extracurriculars, interview, etc.—is not going to do a lot for you if you don't demonstrate significant academic accomplishments. Multiple applicants from the same high school will be compared against each other as well as the entire applicant pool. Males and minorities are actively courted by the admissions staff, and the college is sincere in its commitment.

FINANCIAL AID

Students should submit: FAFSA, institution's own financial aid form, CSS/Financial Aid PROFILE, state aid form, noncustodial (divorced/separated) parents' statement, business/farm supplement. Regular filing deadline is 2/1. The Princeton Review suggests that all financial aid forms be submitted as soon as possible after 1/1. *Need-based scholarships/grants offered:* Pell, SEOG, state scholarships/grants, private scholarships, the school's own gift aid. *Loan aid offered:* FFEL Subsidized Stafford, FFEL Unsubsidized Stafford, FFEL PLUS, Federal Perkins, loans for noncitizens with need. Applicants will be notified of awards on or about 3/30. Federal Work-study Program available. Off-campus job opportunities are good.

FROM THE ADMISSIONS OFFICE

"Vassar presents a rich variety of social and cultural activities, clubs, sports, living arrangements, and regional attractions. Vassar is a vital, residential college community recognized for its respect for the rights and individuality of others.

"Candidates for admission to the Class of 2010 (high school graduates in 2006) may submit either the old SAT along with three SAT Subject Tests or the new SAT Reasoning Test and two SAT Subject Tests. Alternatively, students may submit the ACT (the Writing component is recommended)."

SELECTIVITY

Admissions Rating	**97**
# of applicants	6,193
% of applicants accepted	29
% of acceptees attending	37
# accepting a place on wait list	1,014
# of early decision applicants	247
% accepted early decision	44

FRESHMAN PROFILE

Range SAT Verbal	660-740
Average SAT Verbal	698
Range SAT Math	660-720
Average SAT Math	679
**TPR Projected Range SAT Writing*	*670-720*
Range ACT Composite	28-32
Average ACT Composite	30
Minimum Paper TOEFL	600
Minimum Computer Based TOEFL	250
Average HS GPA	3.8
% graduated top 10% of class	68
% graduated top 25% of class	95
% graduated top 50% of class	100

DEADLINES

Early decision application deadline	11/15
Early decision notification	12/15
Regular application deadline	1/1
Regular notification	4/1
Nonfall registration?	no

APPLICANTS ALSO LOOK AT

AND OFTEN PREFER
Brown University
Yale University

AND SOMETIMES PREFER
Columbia University—Columbia College
New York University
Wesleyan University

AND RARELY PREFER
Skidmore College

FINANCIAL FACTS

Financial Aid Rating	**98**
Annual tuition	$30,895
Room & Board	$7,680
Books and supplies	$820
Required fees	$455
% frosh rec. need-based scholarship or grant aid	50
% UG rec. need-based scholarship or grant aid	52
% frosh rec. need-based self-help aid	50
% UG rec. need-based self-help aid	53
% frosh rec. any financial aid	50
% UG rec. any financial aid	52
Avg. frosh grant	$22,009
Avg. frosh loan	$1,890
Independent 529 member?	Yes

VILLANOVA UNIVERSITY

800 LANCASTER AVENUE, VILLANOVA, PA 19085-1672 • ADMISSIONS: 610-519-4000 • FAX: 610-519-6450

CAMPUS LIFE

Quality of Life Rating	**82**
Fire Safety Rating	**87**
Type of school	private
Affiliation	Roman Catholic
Environment	village

STUDENTS

Total undergrad enrollment	6,892
% male/female	49/51
% from out of state	71
% from public high school	55
% live on campus	75
% in (# of) fraternities	18 (9)
% in (# of) sororities	28 (9)
% African American	3
% Asian	6
% Caucasian	82
% Hispanic	5
% international	2
# of countries represented	30

SURVEY SAYS

Small classes
Great off-campus food
Campus feels safe
Everyone loves the Wildcats
Lots of beer drinking

ACADEMICS

Academic Rating	**82**
Calendar	semester
Student/faculty ratio	12:1
Professors interesting rating	78
Professors accessible rating	80
% professors teaching UG courses	100
% classes taught by TAs	0
Most common lab size	10-19 students
Most common regular class size	10-19 students

MOST POPULAR MAJORS

Finance
nursing/registered nurse training (RN, ASN, BSN, MSN)

STUDENTS SPEAK OUT

Academics

Students at Villanova feel that their university "helps everyone to be their best on a personal and academic level." The challenging course work and Catholic environment draw young scholars eager to jump in on "great class discussions" and work with professors who are "easy to approach." Instructors are known to "go out of their way to accommodate students," whether that means "inviting everyone who was going to be on campus over for Thanksgiving" or "giving out their cell phone numbers in case we are screwed on an assignment." This "great rapport" allows professors to "help you learn about the material and about yourself." Undergraduates see that the faculty "reaches out and wants to meet their students," which is part of what helps them all to be "good at their job and enjoy what they're doing." We get mixed reviews regarding the administration, with some students calling them "extremely helpful" and others "a big hassle." Overall, however, the campus seems to "run pretty smoothly," and students feel they are "a face with a name, not a number."

Life

The Villanova lifestyle combines academics with top-notch athletics and plenty of opportunities for fun. The typical schedule runs "learn four days a week, get hammered two days a week, and save the world on the other day." The get-hammered portion is brought to you by your friendly neighborhood frat house. "Greeks provide a great social life, but you don't have to be a brother or a sister to have a good time." Students say, "I always manage to drink in some dorm room," but it can be "hard to have a lot of fun because of strict [alcohol] policies." Some think that "the rules are too strict," but they can still head to "the Brick Bar, which is pretty popular when the beer is cheap." For those not interested in bending the hooch regulations, "there are a lot of nonalcohol activities, too," including "late-night movies," theater performances, supporting the perennially successful basketball team, and listening to the ever-popular radio station. Some undergrads complain that "the campus is secluded," meaning they "must go to Philly for fun," but creative fun seekers claim "the town around campus has some good surprises." Student life is rounded out by "so many volunteer opportunities [that] it's overwhelming." Many people participate in the campus ministry, and many agree that "the religious presence here is completely optional but really adds to the sense of community and charity."

Student Body

A field guide to Villanova students might describe them as "white kids from different suburbs across the country," the progeny of "upper-middle-class, Catholic" families. Sometimes known as "Vanilla-nova," the university is "hurting for diversity," but also seems to be "making good progress to diversify the school." For now, the majority of students either are "pretty preppy, or they're guidos." Certain plebeians call their peers "snobbish" and snipe that "being academic comes second to looking good." The "motivated, bright, and outgoing" population includes "very few atypical students." Those who deviate from the "fun-loving, studious, career-oriented" norm may be few in number, but they "find their own niche." Others argue that within this "family environment" of "involved, intelligent, and witty" students, they do count a "decent number of interesting/quirky people."

VILLANOVA UNIVERSITY

FINANCIAL AID: 610-519-4010 • E-MAIL: GOTOVU@VILLANOVA.EDU • WEBSITE: WWW.VILLANOVA.EDU

ADMISSIONS

Factors considered include: Alumni/ae relation, character/personal qualities, class rank, essays, extracurricular activities, geographical residence, minority status, recommendations, secondary school record, standardized test scores, volunteer work, work experience. SAT Reasoning or ACT required. TOEFL required of all international applicants. High school diploma is required, and GED is accepted. *Academic units required:* 4 English, 4 math, 4 science (2 science lab), 2 foreign language. *Academic units recommended:* 4 English, 4 math, 4 science (3 science lab), 4 foreign language.

The Inside Word

Villanova has a very solid and growing reputation among Catholic universities nationally, yet is less competitive for admissions than the top tier of schools like Georgetown and Notre Dame. If Villanova is your first choice, be careful. As is the case at many universities, Early Action applicants face higher academic standards than those for the regular pool. This university is a very sound option, whether high on your list of choices or as a safety school.

FINANCIAL AID

Students should submit: FAFSA, institution's own financial aid form. Regular filing deadline is 2/7. The Princeton Review suggests that all financial aid forms be submitted as soon as possible after 1/1. *Need-based scholarships/grants offered:* Pell, SEOG, state scholarships/grants, private scholarships, the school's own gift aid. *Loan aid offered:* FFEL Subsidized Stafford, FFEL Unsubsidized Stafford, FFEL PLUS, Federal Perkins, Federal Nursing. Applicants will be notified of awards on or about 4/1. Federal Work-study Program available. Off-campus job opportunities are excellent.

FROM THE ADMISSIONS OFFICE

"The university is a community of persons of diverse professional, academic, and personal interests who in a spirit of collegiality cooperate to achieve their common goals and objectives in the transmission, the pursuit, and the discovery of knowledge. Villanova attempts to enroll students with diverse social, geographic, economic, and educational backgrounds. Villanova welcomes students who consider it desirable to study within the philosophical framework of Christian Humanism. Finally, this community seeks to reflect the spirit of St. Augustine by the cultivation of knowledge, by respect for individual differences, and by adherence to the principle that mutual love and respect should animate every aspect of university life."

—*Villanova University Mission Statement*

"Freshman applicants to the Villanova University are required to submit scores from either the new SAT or ACT with Writing component. "

SELECTIVITY

Admissions Rating	**92**
# of applicants	9,175
% of applicants accepted	58
% of acceptees attending	31
# accepting a place on wait list	2,084

FRESHMAN PROFILE

Range SAT Verbal	580-660
Average SAT Verbal	605
Range SAT Math	600-680
Average SAT Math	633
**TPR Projected Range SAT Writing*	*620-670*
Range ACT Composite	27-30
Average ACT Composite	27
Minimum Paper TOEFL	550
Minimum Computer Based TOEFL	213
Average HS GPA	3.67
% graduated top 10% of class	48
% graduated top 25% of class	72
% graduated top 50% of class	98

DEADLINES

Regular application deadline	1/7
Regular notification	4/1
Nonfall registration?	no

APPLICANTS ALSO LOOK AT

AND OFTEN PREFER
Georgetown University
University of Notre Dame

AND SOMETIMES PREFER
Boston College
College of the Holy Cross

AND RARELY PREFER
Fairfield University
Loyola College in Maryland
Providence College

FINANCIAL FACTS

Financial Aid Rating	**71**
Annual tuition	$27,175
Room & Board	$9,067
Books and supplies	$950
Required fees	$550
% frosh rec. need-based scholarship or grant aid	43
% UG rec. need-based scholarship or grant aid	41
% frosh rec. need-based self-help aid	46
% UG rec. need-based self-help aid	41
% frosh rec. any financial aid	66
% UG rec. any financial aid	63
Avg. frosh grant	$18,298
Avg. frosh loan	$3,089
Independent 529 member?	No

VIRGINIA TECH

UNDERGRADUATE ADMISSIONS, 201 BURRUSS HALL, BLACKSBURG, VA 24061 • ADMISSIONS: 540-231-6267 • FAX: 540-231-3242

CAMPUS LIFE

Quality of Life Rating	**89**
Fire Safety Rating	**83**
Type of school	public
Environment	village

STUDENTS

Total undergrad enrollment	21,272
% male/female	59/41
% from out of state	29
% from public high school	95
% live on campus	41
% African American	6
% Asian	7
% Caucasian	75
% Hispanic	2
% international	3
# of countries represented	92

SURVEY SAYS

Great computer facilities
Great library
Athletic facilities are great
Great food on campus
Campus feels safe
Everyone loves the Hokies
Student publications are popular
Lots of beer drinking

ACADEMICS

Academic Rating	**75**
Calendar	semester
Student/faculty ratio	16:1
Professors interesting rating	72
Professors accessible rating	74
% professors teaching UG courses	75
% classes taught by TAs	0
Most common lab size	20-29 students
Most common regular class size	20-29 students

MOST POPULAR MAJORS

Communications studies/speech communication and rhetoric
engineering

STUDENTS SPEAK OUT

Academics

For 20,000-plus bright, goal-oriented Virginia undergraduates, Virginia Polytechnic and State University (VT) offers the perfect mixture of academic theory and practical application (and, of course, football). As one student explains, "I feel that many schools, like University of Virginia, have excellent academics, but do not offer a real-world mentality attached to that education. Virginia Tech has the best of both worlds. I feel that upon graduation I will have a successful professional life that will be easily transitioned into." Tech students also appreciate how their school "is a place where people really care about learning and are proud of their studies, but they also know how to enjoy life and not just spend all their time in the books." Undergrads here speak highly of the "excellent engineering department," "the state's only veterinary school," and "solid business and computer science departments." Profs here, as at most tech schools, are a mixed bag; "some professors are great, while others are dreadful," reports one engineer. "Fortunately, there's this really useful website where you can evaluate teachers that you have had, and check up on what teachers that you may have are like." Most here agree that the quality of instruction—as well as the interest level of the material—improves as they progress through school. "All professors are helpful, but the more high-level classes you take, the even-more-helpful the professors are. I have had a very good academic experience here." Students note that VT has not been immune to the nationwide epidemic of state budget-cutting; reports one undergrad, "With the recent huge budget cuts in Virginia, students will be paying more and getting less."

Life

Students tell us that "life at VT is pretty laid-back, for the most part. Students are expected to work hard for good grades, and they generally do. Monday through Thursday is pretty academically geared. But come Thursday night, it's all about the party." Notes one student, "Most people start partying on Thursday night. They go downtown to one of the many local bars, go to a frat party, or go to an apartment party. There are so many apartments off campus that there are at least ten parties at anyone's fingertips at one time. We party hard, and we love our sports." Hokie football reigns supreme on the Blacksburg campus; volleyball and women's basketball both have also fielded competitive squads in recent seasons. If you're not into partying or sports, students warn, "There's not much more available aside from the restaurants and local theater. Since most of the things to do, like bowling or the big movie theater, are located in the next town (about 15 minutes by car), they are somewhat uncompelling." Agrees one student, "Wal-Mart is about as much fun as it gets for the nonpartiers, as there are pretty slim pickings if you don't party." Hometown Blacksburg, most admit, "doesn't offer much." The closest city, Roanoke, is about an hour's drive from campus.

Student Body

Students at VT are bright but not necessarily intellectually curious: "We're very concerned about doing well, though not necessarily learning" is how one student puts it. While "the typical student is white, dresses in clothes from Abercrombie, Structure, Gap, American Eagle, etc. and obviously comes from a white-collar family," there are "many atypical students, probably just under 50 percent of the student body. The school is big enough so that cliques are impossible." As one student put it, "The campus is really diverse, and everyone can find a place not just with people like them, but with almost anyone." As a rule, "people here are generally pretty laid-back and friendly," eschewing the cutthroat competitiveness that characterizes many engineering and tech schools.

FINANCIAL AID: 540-231-5179 • E-MAIL: VTADMISS@VT.EDU • WEBSITE: WWW.VT.EDU

ADMISSIONS

Very important factors considered include: Secondary school record, standardized test scores. *Important factors considered include:* Class rank. *Other factors considered include:* Alumni/ae relation, essays, extracurricular activities, geographical residence, minority status, recommendations, state residency, talent/ability, volunteer work, work experience. SAT Reasoning or ACT required. TOEFL required of all international applicants. High school diploma is required, and GED is accepted. *Academic units required:* 4 English, 3 math, 2 science (2 science lab), 1 social studies, 1 history, 3 academic electives, 4. *Academic units recommended:* 3 science, 3 foreign language.

The Inside Word

When compared to applying to UVA or William and Mary, getting into Virginia Tech is a cakewalk. Tech has a great reputation, which from a careerist point of view makes it well worth considering.

FINANCIAL AID

Students should submit: FAFSA Scholarship. Regular filing deadline is 3/11. The Princeton Review suggests that all financial aid forms be submitted as soon as possible after 1/1. *Need-based scholarships/grants offered:* Pell, SEOG, state scholarships/grants, private scholarships, the school's own gift aid, cadet scholarships/grants. *Loan aid offered:* Direct Subsidized Stafford, Direct Unsubsidized Stafford, Direct PLUS, FFEL PLUS, Federal Perkins, college/university loans from institutional funds. Applicants will be notified of awards on or about 3/30. Off-campus job opportunities are excellent.

FROM THE ADMISSIONS OFFICE

"Virginia Tech offers the opportunities of a large research university in a small-town setting. Undergraduates choose from more than 70 majors in 7 colleges, including nationally ranked business, forestry, and engineering schools, as well as excellent computer science, biology, communication studies, and architecture programs. Technology is a key focus, both in classes and in general. All first-year students are required to own a personal computer, each residence hall room has Ethernet connections, and every student is provided e-mail and Internet access. Faculty incorporate a wide variety of technology into class, utilizing chat rooms, online lecture notes, and multimedia presentations. The university offers cutting-edge facilities for classes and research, abundant opportunities for advanced study in the Honors Program, undergraduate research opportunities, study abroad, internships, and cooperative education. Students enjoy more than 500 organizations, which offer something for everyone. Tech offers the best of both worlds—everything a large university can provide and a small-town atmosphere.

"Fall 2006 freshman applicants must take the new SAT or ACT with Writing section unless they are satisfied with SAT or ACT scores received prior to March 2005. We will use the highest scores from any SAT or ACT test scores submitted."

SELECTIVITY

Admissions Rating	**88**
# of applicants	17,796
% of applicants accepted	71
% of acceptees attending	47
# accepting a place on wait list	600
% admitted from wait list	17
# of early decision applicants	1,175
% accepted early decision	55

FRESHMAN PROFILE

Range SAT Verbal	540-630
Average SAT Verbal	587
Range SAT Math	560-660
Average SAT Math	611
**TPR Projected Range SAT Writing*	*590-650*
Average ACT Composite	25
Minimum Paper TOEFL	550
Minimum Computer Based TOEFL	207
Average HS GPA	3.67
% graduated top 10% of class	31
% graduated top 25% of class	67
% graduated top 50% of class	93

DEADLINES

Early decision application deadline	11/1
Early decision notification	12/15
Regular application deadline	1/15
Regular notification	4/1
Nonfall registration?	yes

APPLICANTS ALSO LOOK AT

AND OFTEN PREFER

James Madison University
University of Virginia

AND SOMETIMES PREFER

Virginia Commonwealth University

AND RARELY PREFER

College of William and Mary
University of North Carolina—Chapel Hill

FINANCIAL FACTS

Financial Aid Rating	**68**
Annual in-state tuition	$4,512
Annual out-of-state tuition	$15,206
Room & Board	$4,288
Books and supplies	$900
Required fees	$1,324
% frosh rec. need-based scholarship or grant aid	30
% UG rec. need-based scholarship or grant aid	28
% frosh rec. need-based self-help aid	32
% UG rec. need-based self-help aid	33
% frosh rec. any financial aid	30
% UG rec. any financial aid	28
Avg. frosh grant	$8,143
Avg. frosh loan	$10,596
Independent 529 member?	No

Wabash College

PO Box 352, 301 W. Wabash Avenue, Crawfordsville, IN 47933 • Admissions: 765-361-6225 • Fax: 765-361-6437

CAMPUS LIFE

Quality of Life Rating	**93**
Fire Safety Rating	**75**
Type of school	private
Environment	village

STUDENTS

Total undergrad enrollment	845
% male/female	100/0
% from out of state	25
% from public high school	91
% live on campus	87
% in (# of) fraternities	60 (10)
% African American	7
% Asian	3
% Caucasian	80
% Hispanic	4
% international	4
# of countries represented	24

SURVEY SAYS

Small classes
Lab facilities are great
Athletic facilities are great
Frats and sororities dominate social scene

ACADEMICS

Academic Rating	**97**
Calendar	semester
Student/faculty ratio	10:1
Professors interesting rating	99
Professors accessible rating	99
% professors teaching UG courses	100
% classes taught by TAs	0
Most common lab size	10-19 students
Most common regular class size	10-19 students

MOST POPULAR MAJORS

English language and literature
history
political science and government

STUDENTS SPEAK OUT

Academics

Undertaking higher education at Wabash College entails a lot of "thinking about what it means to be a man, challenging current definitions, and graduating as a gentleman." Students feel comfortable in the traditional academic framework that encourages responsible action and critical thinking. A junior history major believes, "The all-male environment makes us more open to frank discussion of issues that would not be raised at a large coed school." The science, language, math, and economics departments rank highly, while courses in the speech, psychology, and history programs are considered lightweight. Rather than "spoon-feed" their students, professors employ "the Socratic Method, meaning that they drill you on what you read the night before to make sure you are prepared for class." Faculty members retain their authority while routinely participating in campus clubs and sporting events alongside their students. A chemistry major says, "I have been to the home of every professor in my department," and all freshmen are invited to the president's house soon after their arrival. These rapport-building interactions create an environment where "crime, insubordination, and plagiarism are almost non-existent." Graduates are released into the real world cushioned with alumni contacts and career placement support. "I knew there was not another school in the Midwest that would take care of me the way Wabash College does."

Life

Life at Wabash is governed by the Gentleman's Rule, which basically says, "Don't be an idiot," trusting students to define "idiot" for themselves. "Everyone enjoys freedom to an amazing extent but also knows where the limits are." New rules are starting to appear, however, rankling students who think "it's only going to create more rebellion." Wabash loves a good tradition, particularly of the gladiatorial variety. The Monon Bell Game against DePauw is officially the "oldest football rivalry west of the Alleghenies." Fraternities also perpetuate long-standing, testosterone-fueled intramural competition. "We are constantly pitted against each other for some type of honor that has been around since forever. Your fraternity's honor is on the line." Though Greek bonds run deep at Wabash, "independent men" insist they lead a viable social life, too. The weekly books/booze cycle dictates "from Sunday to Thursday, we study like monastic initiates. On the weekends, we're as libertine as any Bohemian." At times, the line blurs: "It is the weirdest thing. A bunch of guys will be drinking and all of a sudden a political or religious debate breaks out." Students also spend time "writing for the newspaper, editing a student journal, playing collegiate sports, learning a musical instrument, writing and reciting poetry, or acting in a theater production." And why shouldn't they? "Wabash has a lot of money" to fund any student's interest or whim.

Student Body

Despite ongoing efforts to diversify the student body, Wabash remains "a monochromatic sea of Indiana WASPs." That said, tolerance and open-mindedness are considered part of being a gentlemanly Indiana WASP. "I'm a practicing Buddhist myself, and even though there are many students who feel very strongly about their own faith, never once have I felt that a student or professor was judging me because my faith was different then theirs." Universal school identification trumps even the most contentious dividing line of all: "While the cracks at his masculinity from those who know nothing of Wabash may have chafed him, a Wabash man accepts homosexuals as members of the same grand school." Several students comment that African American students "create their own close-knit community." All Wabash men relate to each other based on shared interests in studies and career, politics, social events, and community service, as well as "a common feeling of invincibility among us."

FINANCIAL AID: 765-361-6370 • E-MAIL: ADMISSIONS@WABASH.EDU • WEBSITE: WWW.WABASH.EDU

ADMISSIONS

Very important factors considered include: Class rank, secondary school record. *Important factors considered include:* Character/personal qualities, extracurricular activities, recommendations, standardized test scores, talent/ability. *Other factors considered include:* Alumni/ae relation, essays, geographical residence, interview, minority status, volunteer work, work experience. SAT Reasoning or ACT required. TOEFL required of all international applicants. High school diploma is required, and GED is accepted. *Academic units recommended:* 4 English, 4 math, 3 science (2 science lab), 2 foreign language, 2 social studies, 2 history.

The Inside Word

Wabash is one of the few remaining all-male colleges in the country, and like the rest it has a small applicant pool. The pool is highly self-selected, and the academic standards for admission, while selective, are not particularly demanding. However, Wabash is tough to graduate from—don't consider it if you aren't prepared to work.

FINANCIAL AID

Students should submit: FAFSA, CSS/Financial Aid PROFILE, federal tax returns and W-2 forms. Regular filing deadline is 3/1. The Princeton Review suggests that all financial aid forms be submitted as soon as possible after 1/1. *Need-based scholarships/grants offered:* Pell, state scholarships/grants, private scholarships, the school's own gift aid. *Loan aid offered:* FFEL Subsidized Stafford, FFEL Unsubsidized Stafford, FFEL PLUS, college/university loans from institutional funds. Applicants will be notified of awards on or about 4/1. Institutional employment available. Off-campus job opportunities are good.

FROM THE ADMISSIONS OFFICE

"Wabash College is different—and distinctive—from other liberal arts colleges. Different in that Wabash is an outstanding college for men only. Distinctive in the quality and character of the faculty, in the demanding nature of the academic program, in the farsightedness and maturity of the men who enroll, and in the richness of the traditions that have evolved throughout its 173-year history. Wabash is preeminently a teaching institution, and fundamental to the learning experience is the way faculty and students talk to each other: with mutual respect for the expression of informed opinion. For example, students who collaborate with faculty on research projects are considered their peers in the research—an esteem not usually extended to undergraduates. The college takes pride in the sense of community that such a learning environment fosters. But perhaps the single most striking aspect of student life at Wabash is personal freedom. The college has only one rule: 'The student is expected to conduct himself at all times, both on and off the campus, as a gentleman and a responsible citizen.' Wabash College treats students as adults, and such treatment attracts responsible freshmen and fosters their independence and maturity.

"For students applying for admission into the fall 2006 entering class, Wabash will accept either the new version of the SAT or the old version; the same policy applies for the ACT. Wabash will use the student's best scores from either examination. Wabash does not accept SAT Subject Tests."

SELECTIVITY

Admissions Rating	**90**
# of applicants	1,376
% of applicants accepted	49
% of acceptees attending	37
# accepting a place on wait list	82
% admitted from wait list	10
# of early decision applicants	47
% accepted early decision	75

FRESHMAN PROFILE

Range SAT Verbal	530-650
Average SAT Verbal	592
Range SAT Math	550-660
Average SAT Math	604
**TPR Projected Range SAT Writing*	*580-670*
Range ACT Composite	23-28
Average ACT Composite	26
Minimum Paper TOEFL	550
Minimum Computer Based TOEFL	213
Average HS GPA	3.6
% graduated top 10% of class	37
% graduated top 25% of class	68
% graduated top 50% of class	94

DEADLINES

Early decision application deadline	11/15
Early decision notification	12/15
Regular notification	rolling
Nonfall registration?	no

APPLICANTS ALSO LOOK AT

AND OFTEN PREFER
Indiana University—Bloomington
Purdue University—West Lafayette

AND SOMETIMES PREFER
Butler University
DePauw University
Hanover College

AND RARELY PREFER
Franklin College
Miami University

FINANCIAL FACTS

Financial Aid Rating	**83**
Annual tuition	$21,870
Room & Board	$7,050
Books and supplies	$700
Required fees	$404
% frosh rec. need-based scholarship or grant aid	70
% UG rec. need-based scholarship or grant aid	67
% frosh rec. need-based self-help aid	69
% UG rec. need-based self-help aid	63
% frosh rec. any financial aid	98
% UG rec. any financial aid	97
Avg. frosh grant	$11,908
Avg. frosh loan	$3,812
Independent 529 member?	Yes

WAGNER COLLEGE

1 CAMPUS ROAD, STATEN ISLAND, NY 10301-4495 • ADMISSIONS: 718-390-3411 • FAX: 718-390-3105

CAMPUS LIFE

Quality of Life Rating	**70**
Fire Safety Rating	**60**
Type of school	private
Affiliation	Lutheran
Environment	metropolis

STUDENTS

Total undergrad enrollment	1,929
% male/female	39/61
% from out of state	51
% live on campus	76
% in (# of) fraternities	10 (7)
% in (# of) sororities	11 (7)
% African American	5
% Asian	3
% Caucasian	79
% Hispanic	5

SURVEY SAYS

Small classes
Athletic facilities are great
Theater is popular
Lots of beer drinking
Hard liquor is popular
(Almost) everyone smokes

ACADEMICS

Academic Rating	**77**
Calendar	semester
Student/faculty ratio	16:1
Professors interesting rating	73
Professors accessible rating	76
% professors teaching UG courses	100
% classes taught by TAs	0
Most common lab size	10-19 students
Most common regular class size	10-19 students

MOST POPULAR MAJORS

Business administration/management
drama and dramatics/theater arts
psychology

STUDENTS SPEAK OUT

Academics

In theory, the Wagner Plan for the Practical Liberal Arts educates free thinkers who can also pay the rent. Required senior-year internships and active volunteering programs mean "a head start on post-graduation plans." First-year learning communities incorporate experiential learning, creative expression, interdisciplinary connections, and frequent trips to the "classroom of New York City." A freshman writes, "They force you to look at the way two subjects relate to each other in a new way." Some people think the four-year-old program still needs to work out a few kinks. "It is difficult for students to have confidence in what they are doing if there is no one to encourage them," an English major writes, referring to the self-guided assignments. Theater is a big thing here, too, but even with its liberal and fine arts focus, Wagner manages to also attract students interested in health professions with top nursing and physician's assistant programs. Regardless of major, writing skills are emphasized. "If you don't like doing papers, this is not the place for you. Even the dance classes have tons of them assigned," students warn. Professors are said to be available for academic advice, problem solving, or casual conversation. Reviews of the efficacy of the administration are mixed, but one sage senior adds some helpful context, noting that "since coming to Wagner the administration has gotten better (more involved) and the professors are still about the same (sometimes you get old, boring ones; other times you get good, interesting ones). The more I've gotten involved on campus, the better my experience has been as a whole,"—advice that a student at any college could employ to good effect.

Life

Visually, imagine "a classic TV high school"—a large, well-endowed, private high school—and you've got Wagner College. Students relish their dorm-room views of the skyline of Lower Manhattan and make frequent trips to "the greatest metropolis on Earth." One grumpy junior points out that Wagner is "supposedly close to NYC," but cites the time it takes to get to the Staten Island ferry, ride it, and hop the subway to midtown to back up his case. Commuters mingle with residents, though on-campus students maintain that they "have more fun living the ultimate college life." Nighttime hours are typically reserved for social activities, sometimes involving alcohol, rather than sleeping, resulting in a culture prone to cat-napping. Other popular activities include movie nights, hanging out at the coffee house, and using open studio space for ceramics and sculpture. The annual Wagnerstock festivities bring barbecues, bands, and booths. With only 20 percent Greek participation, it's up to the "theater people" to throw the risqué theme parties, like "Schoolgirls and Professors." Tension does arise between the school's main interests, sports and theater—"two things that don't go together at all." Students at Wagner are the first to admit they love to gripe when opportunity presents itself, but underneath the East Coast attitude, they admit, "We're spoiled here."

Student Body

Pull a Wagner student from the crowd and you'll typically find wrinkled clothes, flip flops, and dark circles under the eyes. A senior psychology major sees everyone as "white, young, and skinny." "A different Coach purse every day seems to be the norm, and when you don't come from that, or have the resources for it, fitting in is a little difficult," reports one woman. A large percentage of Wagner kids "dream of making it on Broadway," and this show-tune-humming theater contingent does feel some animosity from the jocks. "Ultimately, they all get along pretty well. Just don't ask different categories to sit together in the dining hall." Single straight women complain about "a really low ratio of guys to girls" and the fact that "a lot of the guys here are gay." A small-town transplant writes, "Wagner has really opened my eyes to the issues facing the homosexual community." The college's "commitment to teaching us to accept diversity" seems to be working.

FINANCIAL AID: 718-390-3183 • E-MAIL: ADMISSIONS@WAGNER.EDU • WEBSITE: WWW.WAGNER.EDU

ADMISSIONS

Very important factors considered include: Class rank, secondary school record, standardized test scores. *Important factors considered include:* Essays, extracurricular activities, interview, recommendations. *Other factors considered include:* Character/personal qualities, talent/ability, volunteer work, work experience. TOEFL required of all international applicants. High school diploma is required, and GED is accepted. *Academic units required:* 4 English, 3 math, 2 science (1 science lab), 2 foreign language, 1 social studies, 3 history, 6 academic electives.

The Inside Word

Wagner has profited in recent years from a renewed interest in urban colleges. In other words, don't take the application process too lightly. Applicants are met with a college admissions staff dedicated to finding the right students for their school. Wagner's pioneering efforts in experiential learning for all students make its recent resurgence well earned.

FINANCIAL AID

Students should submit: FAFSA, institution's own financial aid form, state aid form. The Princeton Review suggests that all financial aid forms be submitted as soon as possible after 1/1. *Need-based scholarships/grants offered:* Pell, SEOG, state scholarships/grants, private scholarships, the school's own gift aid. *Loan aid offered:* FFEL Subsidized Stafford, FFEL Unsubsidized Stafford, FFEL PLUS, Federal Perkins, Federal Nursing. Applicants will be notified of awards on or about 3/1. Federal Work-study Program available. Institutional employment available. Off-campus job opportunities are good.

FROM THE ADMISSIONS OFFICE

"At Wagner College, we attract and develop active learners and future leaders. Wagner College has received national acclaim (*Time* magazine, American Association of Colleges and Universities) for its innovative curriculum, 'The Wagner Plan for the Practical Liberal Arts.' At Wagner, we capitalize on our unique geography; we are a traditional, scenic, residential campus, which happens to sit atop a hill on an island overlooking lower Manhattan. Our location allows us to offer a program that couples required off-campus experiences (experiential learning), with 'learning community' clusters of courses. This program begins in the first semester and continues through the senior capstone experience in the major. Fieldwork and internships, writing-intensive reflective tutorials, connected learning, 'reading, writing, and doing' . . . at Wagner College our students truly discover 'the practical liberal arts in New York City.'

"Applicants for fall 2006 are required to take the new version of the SAT, or the ACT with the Writing section. Students may submit scores from the old version of the SAT (prior to March 2005) or ACT as well, and the best scores from either test will be used."

SELECTIVITY

Admissions Rating	**79**
# of applicants	2,516
% of applicants accepted	67
% of acceptees attending	29
# accepting a place on wait list	93
% admitted from wait list	13
# of early decision applicants	30
% accepted early decision	37

FRESHMAN PROFILE

Range SAT Verbal	530-620
Average SAT Verbal	560
Range SAT Math	530-630
Average SAT Math	560
**TPR Projected Range SAT Writing*	*580-650*
Range ACT Composite	23-28
Average ACT Composite	26
Minimum Paper TOEFL	550
Minimum Computer Based TOEFL	217
% graduated top 10% of class	12
% graduated top 25% of class	61
% graduated top 50% of class	91

DEADLINES

Early decision application deadline	1/1
Early decision notification	1/10
Regular application deadline	3/15
Regular notification	rolling
Nonfall registration?	yes

APPLICANTS ALSO LOOK AT

AND OFTEN PREFER

Fairfield University
Muhlenberg College
New York University

AND SOMETIMES PREFER

Drew University
Fordham University
Hobart and William Smith Colleges

AND RARELY PREFER

Manhattan College
Marist College

FINANCIAL FACTS

Financial Aid Rating	**70**
Annual tuition	$23,900
Room & Board	$7,500
Books and supplies	$701
% frosh rec. need-based scholarship or grant aid	63
% UG rec. need-based scholarship or grant aid	57
% frosh rec. need-based self-help aid	48
% UG rec. need-based self-help aid	44
% frosh rec. any financial aid	89
% UG rec. any financial aid	80
Avg. frosh grant	$11,941
Avg. frosh loan	$3,508
Independent 529 member?	No

WAKE FOREST UNIVERSITY

BOX 7305, REYNOLDA STATION, WINSTON-SALEM, NC 27109 • ADMISSIONS: 336-758-5201 • FAX: 336-758-4324

CAMPUS LIFE

Quality of Life Rating	**77**
Fire Safety Rating	**91**
Type of school	private
Environment	city

STUDENTS

Total undergrad enrollment	4,104
% male/female	49/51
% from out of state	71
% from public high school	65
% live on campus	78
% in (# of) fraternities	33 (14)
% in (# of) sororities	53 (9)
% African American	6
% Asian	4
% Caucasian	87
% Hispanic	2
% international	1

SURVEY SAYS

Small classes
Great computer facilities
Great library
Everyone loves the Demon Deacons
Frats and sororities dominate social scene
Lots of beer drinking

ACADEMICS

Academic Rating	**89**
Calendar	semester
Student/faculty ratio	10:1
Professors interesting rating	80
Professors accessible rating	86
% professors teaching UG courses	100
% classes taught by TAs	0
Most common lab size	10-19 students
Most common regular class size	10-19 students

MOST POPULAR MAJORS

Business administration/management
communications studies/speech communication and rhetoric
political science and government

STUDENTS SPEAK OUT

Academics

Students at Wake Forest agree that "lots of opportunities and resources that are typically available only at larger schools," "great technology (everyone gets a laptop upon entering)," a "small student population, and small classes" are what distinguish their school from the pack—that, and a wicked-hard grading system; many here warn that "grading is extremely rigid, with no curves, extra credit, or other benefits to the students. Overall, I have found that a C can be achieved with little to no effort, B's are possible with a significant amount of work, and A's are virtually impossible." They love their professors, whom they describe as "down to earth and easy to talk to," "at the top of their fields, and very knowledgeable in their respective areas of expertise." The administration earns similar plaudits ("Friendly through-and-through. Must be that southern hospitality" is how one student puts it). Many here wish the school would reduce the number of core requirements, telling us that "the amount of core courses leaves little room to explore interests outside a major/minor. Forget about electives if you're double majoring or have a minor."

Life

As one student puts it, "I can sum up fun at Wake pretty easily: Monday through Wednesday everyone works, Wednesday night everyone drinks, Thursday people study for Friday tests, Friday through Sunday everyone drinks like rock stars, and Sunday everyone goes to the library." The lively party scene here revolves around the Greeks and area bars and clubs. Frat parties "are completely open and welcoming to all students and provide dancing and free beer," but upperclassmen eventually "tire of the frat scene. Even so, we are comfortable with the social options at Wake." Many complain about the university's restrictive regulations, especially those concerning alcohol. Beyond the party scene, "opportunities to get involved on campus abound: there are a ton of clubs, teams, and organizations to join." Students brag that "we're in the ACC, so we have some of the best athletics in the nation" and also note that "there is always so much going on on campus, whether that is a local/school band in the coffeehouse, a play in the theater, or just a movie playing in your suite." Most here agree that "student life is very campus-centered . . . in spite of the fact that there are good things to do in the surrounding area. For example, the NC School of the Arts is in town and puts on fantastic works, but most students are unaware of it." They also agree that the campus is "gorgeous." Opinion is split on hometown Winston-Salem; the town has its boosters, but most here feel that it "isn't exactly a college town."

Student Body

"Most students are conservative, clean-cut, studious, easygoing, and involved in many activities on campus and in the community." The majority are also "white, upper-middle-class, very Christian, Republican, and Greek." Adds one student, "'Diversified' is the last word that could ever be used to describe Wake, but honestly, most like it that way. The few that do stand out are pointed out and would hardly be said to fit in." Some disagree, telling us that "more and more students here are choosing to pull away from the stereotype, and so atypical students fit in fairly well." Nearly all concede, however, that "The school is hugely lacking in a minority presence. What minorities there are tend to self-segregate, and the social separation perpetuates itself." Athletics form a common bond for most here; "anyone overweight really stands out as an oddity," writes one undergrad.

WAKE FOREST UNIVERSITY

FINANCIAL AID: 336-758-5154 • E-MAIL: ADMISSIONS@WFU.EDU • WEBSITE: WWW.WFU.EDU

ADMISSIONS

Very important factors considered include: Character/personal qualities, class rank, secondary school record, standardized test scores. *Important factors considered include:* Alumni/ae relation, essays, extracurricular activities, minority status, recommendations, religious affiliation/commitment, talent/ability, volunteer work. *Other factors considered include:* Geographical residence, state residency. SAT Reasoning Test required. SAT Subject Tests recommended. TOEFL required of all international applicants. High school diploma is required, and GED is accepted. *Academic units required:* 4 English, 3 math, 1 science, 2 foreign language, 2 social studies. *Academic units recommended:* 4 English, 4 math, 4 science, 4 foreign language, 4 social studies.

The Inside Word

An applicant to Wake Forest undergoes very close scrutiny from the admissions committee; many very solid candidates wind up on the wait list. Fortunately, the admissions staff is as friendly and accessible as the university's students rate the whole place. Successful candidates typically show impressive extracurricular accomplishments as well as academic excellence and are good matches with the university's personality.

FINANCIAL AID

Students should submit: FAFSA, CSS/Financial Aid PROFILE, state aid form, noncustodial (divorced/separated) parents' statement. The Princeton Review suggests that all financial aid forms be submitted as soon as possible after 1/1. *Need-based scholarships/grants offered:* Pell, SEOG, state scholarships/grants, private scholarships, the school's own gift aid. *Loan aid offered:* FFEL Subsidized Stafford, FFEL Unsubsidized Stafford, FFEL PLUS, Federal Perkins, state loans, college/university loans from institutional funds, private alternative loans. Applicants will be notified of awards on or about 4/1. Federal Work-study Program available. Institutional employment available. Off-campus job opportunities are excellent.

FROM THE ADMISSIONS OFFICE

"Wake Forest University has been dedicated to the liberal arts for over a century and a half; this means education in the fundamental fields of human knowledge and achievement. It seeks to encourage habits of mind that ask why, that evaluate evidence, that are open to new ideas, that attempt to understand and appreciate the perspective of others, that accept complexity and grapple with it, that admit error, and that pursue truth. Wake Forest is among a small, elite group of American colleges and universities recognized for their outstanding academic quality. It offers small classes taught by full-time faculty—not graduate assistants—and a commitment to student interaction with those professors. Students are all provided IBM ThinkPads and color printers. Classrooms and residence halls are fully networked. Wake Forest maintains a need-blind admissions policy by which qualified students are admitted regardless of their financial circumstances.

"Applicants for fall 2006 are required to submit scores from the new version of the SAT. Students may also submit scores taken prior to March 2005 from the older version of the test. SAT Subject Tests are strongly recommended for students planning to apply for merit-based scholarships."

SELECTIVITY

Admissions Rating	**95**
# of applicants	6,289
% of applicants accepted	47
% of acceptees attending	38
# of early decision applicants	309
% accepted early decision	53

FRESHMAN PROFILE

Range SAT Verbal	610-700
Range SAT Math	630-710
**TPR Projected Range SAT Writing*	*640-700*
Minimum Paper TOEFL	600
Minimum Computer Based TOEFL	250
% graduated top 10% of class	65
% graduated top 25% of class	94
% graduated top 50% of class	99

DEADLINES

Early decision application deadline	11/15
Early decision notification	12/15
Regular application deadline	1/15
Regular notification	4/1
Nonfall registration?	yes

APPLICANTS ALSO LOOK AT AND SOMETIMES PREFER

Duke University
University of North Carolina—Chapel Hill
University of Virginia
Vanderbilt University

FINANCIAL FACTS

Financial Aid Rating	**81**
Annual tuition	$30,110
Room & Board	$8,500
Books and supplies	$800
Required fees	$100
% frosh rec. need-based scholarship or grant aid	37
% UG rec. need-based scholarship or grant aid	33
% frosh rec. need-based self-help aid	32
% UG rec. need-based self-help aid	30
% frosh rec. any financial aid	68
% UG rec. any financial aid	69
Avg. frosh grant	$14,757
Avg. frosh loan	$5,511
Independent 529 member?	Yes

WARREN WILSON COLLEGE

PO BOX 9000, ASHEVILLE, NC 28815-9000 • ADMISSIONS: 828-771-2073 • FAX: 828-298-1440

CAMPUS LIFE

Quality of Life Rating	**88**
Fire Safety Rating	**60**
Type of school	private
Affiliation	Presbyterian
Environment	village

STUDENTS

Total undergrad enrollment	781
% from out of state	80
% from public high school	65
% live on campus	90
% African American	2
% Asian	1
% Caucasian	91
% Hispanic	1
% Native American	1
% international	5

SURVEY SAYS

Small classes
Students are friendly
Frats and sororities are unpopular or nonexistent
Political activism is popular

ACADEMICS

Academic Rating	**80**
Calendar quarter/semester system of 2 quarters per semester	
Student/faculty ratio	12:1
Professors interesting rating	81
Professors accessible rating	85
% professors teaching UG courses	100
% classes taught by TAs	0
Most common lab size	10-19 students
Most common regular class size	10-19 students

MOST POPULAR MAJORS

Environmental science
fine/studio arts
parks, recreation, leisure, and fitness studies

STUDENTS SPEAK OUT

Academics

"It's all about the Triad" at Warren Wilson College. No, our respondents aren't talking about the Greensboro/High Point/Winston-Salem metropolitan area, but rather Wilson's "unique requirements to work 15 hours a week and perform community service" as integral parts of the curriculum. The goal of the Triad, according to the school, is to foster "community, creativity, learning, and a sense of harmony with the environment." Most here feel it achieves that goal handily. "Work and service are very important," explains one undergrad. "People here are realistic, yet willing to work hard toward making positive change in the world." Students also appreciate the strong community ties that the Wilson program creates: "Our professors are our peers. We teach and learn together" is how one student puts it. Writes another, "Professors are understanding and treat you like an actual person; they notice your bad days, are genuinely concerned if you are not working up to your potential, and are always available for help outside of class." Similarly, "the administration is exceptionally interested in the students and student wellness." Some here feel, however, that "the focus on academics could be stronger." Warns one student, "Some profs can make you laugh for hours and never actually teach you anything." Adds another, "The real excitement is in seminar/discussion classes, where you actually get to interact with the people around you. If it weren't for the average academics at this school, it'd be Valhalla." Even so, most feel that Wilson offers an enriching, empowering academic experience. As one student puts it, "It's all about the kids. We are this place; we own it."

Life

Life under the Triad program takes some getting used to. Explains one freshman, "When I first got here, it felt like summer camp, too much fun. Now I've settled into academics, and it's excellent. Life of the Mind and Life of the Bawdy Politic blended into a great experience." Fun, maybe, but definitely time- and labor-intensive. As one student tells us, "Since we're a work school, there isn't a lot of time to hang out. We kind of hang out and walk around campus." Students also "watch movies, drink, go to town, cook, etc. for fun. Life's pretty fun and laid-back here." Others enjoy "school-sponsored and community-sponsored activities. They're very popular." Some even "go for hikes in the woods, swim in the pond, and be children of Mother Earth." Mother Earth, hmm? No wonder "some call it a 'hippie' school. But that doesn't mean it's a bunch of kids getting stoned all the time. It's very progressive. People here are very conscious about current issues, locally and worldwide. Many students here are activist types." Wilson's hometown, Asheville, is a quaint mountain city long regarded as a North Carolina liberal haven.

Student Body

"Wilson is known as a hippie college," students tell us, "but there is a startling diversity of other kinds of alterna-creatures here. We have our punk rockers; we have our socialists; we have girls who shave. Everybody here smiles and says 'hello.'" Politically, the school is not quite so diverse: "This college consists of various facets of the left wing: the Democrats, the Greens, and the anarchists. No Republican has ever set foot on this campus—ever. If they did, they'd probably be pelted to death with hand-rolled cigarette butts," writes one undergrad. Students share another common characteristic: "We all come to class all covered in dirt from being working young lads and lasses. We don't usually brush our hair." Notes another student, "We're a stinky bunch of kids, that's for damned sure, but we're all united by this idealism that would get us accosted at any other school. Just the fact that the person goes to Wilson, a school with such a unique vision of education, is enough to automatically classify them as cool."

Warren Wilson College

Financial Aid: 828-298-3325 • E-mail: admit@warren-wilson.edu • Website: www.warren-wilson.edu

ADMISSIONS

Very important factors considered include: Character/personal qualities, essays, interview, secondary school record, standardized test scores, volunteer work, work experience. *Important factors considered include:* Class rank, recommendations. *Other factors considered include:* Alumni/ae relation, extracurricular activities, state residency, talent/ability. SAT Reasoning or ACT required. TOEFL required of all international applicants. High school diploma is required, and GED is accepted. *Academic units required:* 4 English, 3 math, 2 science (2 science lab), 1 history. *Academic units recommended:* 2 foreign language.

The Inside Word

Warren Wilson is a college for thinkers with a deep sense of social commitment. The admissions process clearly reflects the committee's desire for solid academic achievement in successful candidates, but they also take a close and careful look at the person being considered. It isn't supercompetitive to get in here, but only candidates who make good matches with the college are offered admission.

FINANCIAL AID

Students should submit: FAFSA, institution's own financial aid form. The Princeton Review suggests that all financial aid forms be submitted as soon as possible after 1/1. *Need-based scholarships/grants offered:* Pell, SEOG, state scholarships/grants, private scholarships, the school's own gift aid. *Loan aid offered:* FFEL Subsidized Stafford, FFEL Unsubsidized Stafford, FFEL PLUS, Federal Perkins, college/university loans from institutional funds. Applicants will be notified of awards on a rolling basis beginning on or about 3/2. Federal Work-study Program available. Institutional employment available. Off-campus job opportunities are good.

FROM THE ADMISSIONS OFFICE

"This book is *The Best 361 Colleges*, but Warren Wilson College may not be the best college for many students. There are 3,500 colleges in the U.S., and there is a best place for everyone. The 'best college' is one that has the right size, location, programs, and above all, the right feel for you, even if it is not listed here. Warren Wilson College may be the best choice if you think and act independently, actively participate in your education, and want a college that provides a sense of community. Your hands will get dirty here, your mind will be stretched, and you'll not be anonymous. If you are looking for the traditional college experience with football and frats and a campus-on-a-quad, this probably is not the right place. However, if you want to be a part of an academic community that works and serves together, this might be exactly what you are looking for.

"Students applying for admission for fall 2006 are strongly advised to take the new version of the SAT (or the ACT with the Writing section), but students may submit scores from the old version of either test, and we will use the student's best scores from either test."

SELECTIVITY

Admissions Rating	**83**
# of applicants	753
% of applicants accepted	81
% of acceptees attending	35
# accepting a place on wait list	6
% admitted from wait list	33
# of early decision applicants	48
% accepted early decision	83

FRESHMAN PROFILE

Range SAT Verbal	560-670
Average SAT Verbal	605
Range SAT Math	500-620
Average SAT Math	563
**TPR Projected Range SAT Writing*	*600-680*
Range ACT Composite	22-28
Average ACT Composite	24
Minimum Paper TOEFL	550
Average HS GPA	3.32
% graduated top 10% of class	20
% graduated top 25% of class	48
% graduated top 50% of class	76

DEADLINES

Early decision application deadline	11/15
Regular application deadline	3/15
Regular notification	Notification begins 2/01
Nonfall registration?	yes

APPLICANTS ALSO LOOK AT

AND OFTEN PREFER
Earlham College

AND SOMETIMES PREFER
The Evergreen State College
Northland College

AND RARELY PREFER
Antioch College
Arizona State University
Guilford College

FINANCIAL FACTS

Financial Aid Rating	**71**
Annual tuition	$18,916
Room & Board	$5,466
Books and supplies	$724
Required fees	$200
% frosh rec. need-based scholarship or grant aid	45
% UG rec. need-based scholarship or grant aid	43
% frosh rec. need-based self-help aid	49
% UG rec. need-based self-help aid	50
Avg. frosh loan	$2,325
Independent 529 member?	No

WASHINGTON AND LEE UNIVERSITY

LETCHER AVENUE, LEXINGTON, VA 24450-0303 • ADMISSIONS: 540-458-8710 • FAX: 540-458-8062

CAMPUS LIFE

Quality of Life Rating	**88**
Fire Safety Rating	**60**
Type of school	private
Environment	village

STUDENTS

Total undergrad enrollment	1,754
% male/female	51/49
% from out of state	85
% live on campus	61
% in (# of) fraternities	79 (14)
% in (# of) sororities	74 (5)
% African American	4
% Asian	3
% Caucasian	87
% Hispanic	1
% international	4
# of countries represented	47

SURVEY SAYS

Small classes
No one cheats
Campus feels safe
Frats and sororities dominate social scene
Lots of beer drinking
Hard liquor is popular

ACADEMICS

Academic Rating	**98**
Calendar	4-4-2
Professors interesting rating	99
Professors accessible rating	99
% professors teaching UG courses	100
% classes taught by TAs	0
Most common lab size	fewer than 10 students
Most common regular class size	10-19 students

MOST POPULAR MAJORS

Business administration/management
economics
history

STUDENTS SPEAK OUT

Academics

Washington and Lee, according to one student with a knack for turning phrases, is "the best conservative, Republican liberal arts education available, in the smallest town possible." Although open to all comers (thanks to a generous financial aid office), W & L typifies the genteel South, exemplified perfectly by the school's honor code, which one student describes this way: "W & L only has one rule, established by Robert E. Lee himself: that every student should be a gentleman (or lady). Don't lie, cheat, or steal. And the amazing thing is, it works! We leave our dorm rooms unlocked, our laptops in our study carrels at the library, our jackets on hooks in classrooms, etc. We take unproctored exams on our own schedule. It's great." Academically, the University offers a surprisingly broad range of courses for a school of its size. One undergraduate writes, "I'm a double major because there are so many major options, strong departments, and passionate professors." The university works students hard. Everyone is adamant that "we have no grade inflation, and our classes are actually difficult. That makes it a different experience than at other schools." With the difficult work comes the respect of the university's highly praised faculty, which students cherish. One student believes "W & L students have such a unique opportunity to be peers—not underlings—of their professors. Close contact, assistance in research, and open discussion really creates an environment much like that of many graduate schools."

Life

"Picture this: You are standing in a sweaty frat basement sipping grain that originated from a large trash can receptacle and listening to a jam band out of Alabama that you've never heard of in your life, while mingling with soon-to-be investment bankers wearing bright pink polo shirts with pastel madras shorts and Wallabies—and you're loving every minute of it." Sound good? That's not everyone's experience, but it can be for anyone who wants it, students assure us. "The Greek system is the defining characteristic of life at this school," according to students. This assertion is borne out by the high percentage of students who join frats and sororities. "One's social life is very limited if not involved with the Greek system," most students agree, pointing out that hometown Lexington "is not exactly a Mecca of 18- to 22-year-old activity. We have one bar, one movie theater, one bowling alley, and a few decent restaurants." For those few who shun the Greek scene, "there are school- or student-organization-sponsored activities every single day: movies, guest speakers, poetry readings, concerts, [and] national performances." Another student continues the praise by saying there is "so much outdoor stuff to do, and the area is so beautiful. There are many rivers for canoeing, kayaking, fishing, and tubing. There are great running trails, and also amazing rock climbing." Students also road trip to Charlottesville, Roanoke, and occasionally Washington, DC.

Student Body

Washington and Lee has long held a reputation as the school for kids who are "rich, white, and Southern," and according to the current crop of undergraduates, the stereotype remains largely true. One student writes, "Walk into the nicest country club in a suburb near you and you will probably discover a population similar to that of the students at Washington and Lee." Another student notes, "This may be the only place where I think pearls are actually popular among girls ages 18 to 22." Undergraduates "study hard during the week but go out on the weekend. Every student understands the balance between work and play—both of which we do plenty." Typical students are "very intelligent, although not very intellectual, and very ambitious and sincere in their endeavors." Students are also very Republican. One student writes, "Being a Democrat at W & L is like being a part of a secret underground society."

FINANCIAL AID: 540-463-8715 • E-MAIL: ADMISSIONS@WLU.EDU • WEBSITE: WWW.WLU.EDU

ADMISSIONS

Very important factors considered include: Character/personal qualities, extracurricular activities, secondary school record, standardized test scores. *Important factors considered include:* Class rank, recommendations. *Other factors considered include:* Alumni/ae relation, essays, geographical residence, minority status, state residency, talent/ability, volunteer work, work experience. SAT Reasoning or ACT required. TOEFL required of all international applicants. High school diploma or equivalent is not required. *Academic units required:* 4 English, 3 math, 1 science (1 science lab), 2 foreign language, 1 social studies, 1 history, 4 academic electives. *Academic units recommended:* 4 math, 3 science, 3 foreign language, 2 history.

The Inside Word

If you're looking for a bastion of southern tradition, Washington and Lee is one of the foremost. Its admissions process is appropriately traditional and highly selective. Under these circumstances, it is always best to take a cautious and conservative approach to preparing your candidacy. Smart applicants have taken the toughest courses available to them in high school—the minimum requirements aren't likely to help you gain admission. Neither will a glib approach to the personal side of the application; a well-written essay is what they're after.

FINANCIAL AID

Students should submit: FAFSA, CSS/Financial Aid PROFILE, noncustodial (divorced/separated) parents' statement, business/farm supplement. The Princeton Review suggests that all financial aid forms be submitted as soon as possible after 1/1. *Need-based scholarships/grants offered:* Pell, SEOG, state scholarships/grants, private scholarships, the school's own gift aid. *Loan aid offered:* FFEL Subsidized Stafford, FFEL Unsubsidized Stafford, FFEL PLUS, Federal Perkins, college/university loans from institutional funds. Applicants will be notified of awards on or about 4/3. Federal Work-study Program available. Institutional employment available. Off-campus job opportunities are fair.

FROM THE ADMISSIONS OFFICE

"Washington and Lee University is a small, private, liberal arts institution located in the beautiful Shenandoah Valley, in Lexington, Virginia. The nation's ninth oldest university, W & L has been touched and shaped by major men, women, and moments in U.S. history. Today, W & L enjoys national appeal, with undergraduates representing 46 states and 38 countries. Small classes, state-of-the-art facilities, and outstanding teachers combine to prepare W & L students for success in both graduate school and the workplace. Professors are committed to mentoring their students in and out of the classroom, often forming lifelong relationships in the process. Over 90 percent of faculty hold earned doctoral or terminal degrees and remain active researchers in their chosen fields. W & L's curriculum offers unique breadth among the nation's leading undergraduate colleges, boasting such majors as accounting, business, engineering, journalism, and public policy, in addition to the traditional arts and sciences. Interdisciplinary courses are common at W & L and employ the latest technology and research techniques. The fully accredited Williams School of Commerce, Economics, and Politics and the nationally ranked School of Law afford undergraduates with remarkable opportunities more typically found in comprehensive research universities. Student autonomy is a hallmark of a W & L education and the student-run honor system yields high expectations that students internalize and live out in a community of trust. With exams not proctored and facilities open 24/7, this pervasive trust engenders a commitment to honor and civility that continues to inform students' decisions well beyond graduation.

"High school graduates of 2006 will have four options for fulfilling testing requirements: new SAT plus two SAT Subject exams in unrelated areas; old SAT plus three SAT Subject Tests, one of which must be in Writing; new ACT with essay plus two SAT Subject exams in unrelated areas; old ACT plus three SAT Subject exams, one of which must be in Writing."

SELECTIVITY

Admissions Rating	**98**
# of applicants	3,649
% of applicants accepted	30
% of acceptees attending	43
# accepting a place on wait list	709
% admitted from wait list	4
# of early decision applicants	194
% accepted early decision	48

FRESHMAN PROFILE

Range SAT Verbal	660-730
Range SAT Math	660-720
**TPR Projected Range SAT Writing*	*670-720*
Range ACT Composite	28-31
% graduated top 10% of class	86
% graduated top 25% of class	99
% graduated top 50% of class	100

DEADLINES

Early decision application deadline	11/15
Early decision notification	12/22
Regular application deadline	1/15
Regular notification	4/1
Nonfall registration?	no

APPLICANTS ALSO LOOK AT

AND OFTEN PREFER

Duke University
University of Virginia

AND SOMETIMES PREFER

College of William and Mary
Davidson College
Georgetown University
University of North Carolina—Chapel Hill

AND RARELY PREFER

Rhodes College
University of Georgia
University of Richmond
Vanderbilt University
Wake Forest University

FINANCIAL FACTS

Financial Aid Rating	**96**
Annual tuition	$27,960
Room & Board	$8065
Required fees	$860
% frosh rec. need-based scholarship or grant aid	24
% UG rec. need-based scholarship or grant aid	22
% frosh rec. need-based self-help aid	12
% UG rec. need-based self-help aid	13
Independent 529 member?	No

WASHINGTON STATE UNIVERSITY

370 LIGHTY STUDENT SERVICES, PULLMAN, WA 99164-1067 • ADMISSIONS: 509-335-5586 • FAX: 509-335-4902

CAMPUS LIFE

Quality of Life Rating	**74**
Fire Safety Rating	**78**
Type of school	public
Environment	village

STUDENTS

Total undergrad enrollment	18,825
% male/female	47/53
% from out of state	8
% from public high school	99
% live on campus	37
% in (# of) fraternities	13 (23)
% in (# of) sororities	16 (16)
% African American	3
% Asian	6
% Caucasian	76
% Hispanic	4
% Native American	1
% international	3
# of countries represented	94

SURVEY SAYS

Great computer facilities
Great library
Athletic facilities are great
Everyone loves the Cougars
Student publications are popular
Lots of beer drinking
Hard liquor is popular

ACADEMICS

Academic Rating	**74**
Calendar	semester
Student/faculty ratio	18:1
Professors interesting rating	68
Professors accessible rating	64
% professors teaching UG courses	100
% classes taught by TAs	0
Most common regular class size	10-19 students

MOST POPULAR MAJORS

Business administration/management
communications studies/speech communication and rhetoric
social sciences

STUDENTS SPEAK OUT

Academics

Washington State University (WSU), a large public school near the Idaho border, offers a lot "for its price and cost of living." The university endeavors to foster more personalized learning by dividing its academic programs into ten separate colleges, within which students may pursue their chosen majors. Each college also controls its own scholarship resources. The result is "fairly small classes" for a state school of a fairly large size. "Most of my classes are small and professors are accessible," writes a freshman. Whether you want to contact them outside of class, though, depends on which professors you get. "Professors are either hit or miss," writes a sophomore. "I've had fabulous ones and a few terrible ones." Some of the better ones "really encourage critical thinking in their classes." The university's standout departments include its Edward R. Murrow School of Communication (within the College of Liberal Arts) and its pre-professional programs. For those nationally recognized students who make good grades and want to give themselves even more of a challenge academically, there is the oft-touted Honors College. "If it wasn't for the excellent Honors College, I wouldn't have applied here," writes one academically ambitious sophomore. Though most students express satisfaction with WSU's advising system, the administration has dedicated new resources to enhancing it. Students also want to see more funding for programs in the arts. Finally, some students resent the preferential treatment of athletes at this Pac-10 school.

Life

The campus of WSU is in the middle of what students describe as "wheat fields," and the ubiquitous golden grain makes it a beautiful place to go to school. Student opinion seems evenly split on what kind of social scene this Pullman campus really has. One student writes, "Everyone thinks WSU is a party school. That is a myth!" Another undergraduate offers a list of the various pastimes that keep many busy: "In the summer there's always ultimate Frisbee™ and football games. In the winter everyone crowds around inside with coffee and cocoa to hang out and talk. [The community] has an eight-plex theater, which is a popular place to go on dates." One junior adds, "Intramural sports are a good way to fight the boredom." But a sophomore counters, "I always thought the 'party school' reputation was overhyped, but once I got here I found out it's all true." One junior adds, "We sneak in some solid studying in between parties." Whatever the case may be, the Greeks have a large hand in the campus social scene, and it "basically breaks down to Greeks vs. non-Greeks." Though Greeks have a "bad rep" as lawless partiers, "the minority of Greeks provide this reputation," reassures one sophomore. There's no boredom during football season, however. "Football season is the best part of the year," writes a senior. Another student continues, "We are all Cougs. It's good to be one!" Students also exercise at the giant, state-of-the-art recreation center in their free time. Moscow, Idaho, home of the University of Idaho—and, by extension, a whole other undergraduate student population—is a fifteen-minute car drive away.

Student Body

An "abundance of middle-class white kids" from the area is how students tend to describe their peers at Washington State most of whom are Washingtonians. "Students of color are underrepresented," writes a junior, but the university is trying to change that situation, and "everyone gets along pretty easily: students of all backgrounds turn out for cultural events like pow wows and step shows." There are also a lot of preppy students. One junior wishes there were "more political awareness and activism" on campus. For now, though, she will have to settle for school spirit, which in large part is associated with the football program [see "Life," above].

FINANCIAL AID: 509-335-9711 • E-MAIL: ADMISS2@WSU.EDU • WEBSITE: WWW.WSU.EDU

ADMISSIONS

Very important factors considered include: Secondary school record, standardized test scores. *Important factors considered include:* Essays. *Other factors considered include:* Extracurricular activities, recommendations, talent/ability, volunteer work, work experience. SAT Reasoning or ACT required. TOEFL required of all international applicants. High school diploma is required, and GED is accepted. *Academic units required:* 4 English, 3 math, 2 science (1 science lab), 2 foreign language, 2 social studies, 1 history, 1 academic elective. *Academic units recommended:* 4 English, 4 math, 2 science (1 science lab), 2 foreign language, 2 social studies, 1 history, 1 academic elective.

The Inside Word

Admission is based on a combination of high school GPA, standardized test scores, completion of appropriate college prep courses in high school ("core requirements" for students in the state of Washington), and an application essay, which receives particular scrutiny. The successful high school candidate will have at least a 3.4 GPA and 1150 SAT score. High-ability early applicants (those who apply in early fall) may be eligible for admission awards worth thousands of dollars.

FINANCIAL AID

Students should submit: FAFSA. The Princeton Review suggests that all financial aid forms be submitted as soon as possible after 1/1. *Need-based scholarships/grants offered:* Pell, SEOG, state scholarships/grants, private scholarships, the school's own gift aid, Federal Nursing scholarships. *Loan aid offered:* FFEL Subsidized Stafford, FFEL Unsubsidized Stafford, FFEL PLUS, Federal Perkins, Federal Nursing, college/university loans from institutional funds, alternative loans. Applicants will be notified of awards on a rolling basis beginning on or about 4/15. Federal Work-study Program available. Off-campus job opportunities are good.

FROM THE ADMISSIONS OFFICE

"At Washington State University, you can work side by side with nationally renowned faculty who will help you succeed. Many of the university's academic programs are ranked among the best in the nation. Programs are designed to give you real-world experience through internships, fieldwork, community service, and in-depth labs. You can take part in faculty research, or even conduct your own. Washington State University graduates are considered the best prepared in the state in many fields and are actively recruited by Fortune 500 employers.

"The campus forms the heart of a warm, supportive college town—a community of faculty and friends who can help you achieve your greatest potential. You'll have opportunities to build your leadership skills by getting involved in any of a wide selection of campus organizations. If you have top grades and a passion for learning, apply to the highly acclaimed Honors College. It will challenge you with interdisciplinary studies, rich discussions, and opportunities to study abroad. The priority deadline to apply for admission to Washington State University and the deadline to apply for scholarships is January 31.

"In addition to the Pullman campus, WSU has three nonresidential urban campuses in Spokane, the TriCities (Richland), and Vancouver.

"High school graduates from 2006 or later must provide official scores from the new SAT or the ACT with the Writing Test. For both exams, the assessment and the Writing Test must be completed during the same sitting. Students graduating high school before 2006 may provide scores from either the old or new SAT or ACT examinations."

SELECTIVITY	
Admissions Rating	**83**
# of applicants	9,508
% of applicants accepted	75
% of acceptees attending	43
FRESHMAN PROFILE	
Range SAT Verbal	470-580
Average SAT Verbal	527
Range SAT Math	490-600
Average SAT Math	545
**TPR Projected Range SAT Writing*	*530-620*
Range ACT Composite	19-25
Average ACT Composite	23
Minimum Paper TOEFL	520
Minimum Computer Based TOEFL	190
Average HS GPA	3.46
% graduated top 10% of class	34
% graduated top 25% of class	59
% graduated top 50% of class	90
DEADLINES	
Regular notification	12/1
Nonfall registration?	yes
FINANCIAL FACTS	
Financial Aid Rating	**79**
Annual in-state tuition	$4,836
Annual out-of-state tuition	$12,938
Room & Board	$6,196
Books and supplies	$912
Required fees	$444
% frosh rec. need-based scholarship or grant aid	26
% UG rec. need-based scholarship or grant aid	37
% frosh rec. need-based self-help aid	32
% UG rec. need-based self-help aid	46
% frosh rec. any financial aid	80
% UG rec. any financial aid	82
Avg. frosh grant	$5,860
Avg. frosh loan	$9,895
Independent 529 member?	No

WASHINGTON UNIVERSITY IN ST. LOUIS

CAMPUS BOX 1089, ONE BROOKINGS DRIVE, ST. LOUIS, MO 63130-4899 • ADMISSIONS: 314-935-6000 • FAX: 314-935-4290

CAMPUS LIFE

Quality of Life Rating	**99**
Fire Safety Rating	**87**
Type of school	private
Environment	city

STUDENTS

Total undergrad enrollment	6,355
% male/female	49/51
% from out of state	88
% from public high school	61
% live on campus	75
% in (# of) fraternities	25 (12)
% in (# of) sororities	25 (6)
% African American	9
% Asian	9
% Caucasian	64
% Hispanic	3
% international	5
# of countries represented	106

SURVEY SAYS

Lab facilities are great
Great library
Students are friendly
Great food on campus
Great off-campus food
Dorms are like palaces

ACADEMICS

Academic Rating	**95**
Calendar	semester
Student/faculty ratio	7:1
Professors interesting rating	81
Professors accessible rating	88
% professors teaching UG courses	92
% classes taught by TAs	0
Most common lab size	10-19 students
Most common regular class size	10-19 students

MOST POPULAR MAJORS

Biology/biological sciences
finance
psychology

STUDENTS SPEAK OUT

Academics

Students at Washington University find Ivy-caliber academics free of psychotic premeds or other bothersome nerds. A sophomore in the humanities says, "A lot of great students decide to come here because you can be serious about academics yet laid-back." The strong science departments support their students in terms of research opportunities and pre-professional advising but bury them with the workload. In other words, "you'll definitely learn chemistry, but your grade might reflect the opposite." Advisors in every department come well-armed with information. A sophomore writes, "For every class I've ever asked about, my advisor has had a story or a piece of advice." Incoming students balk at the arts and sciences "cluster" system, but an upperclassman assures that "once you get a sense of what they want, it's not too tough to get your distribution requirements done." Faculty members and students genuinely enjoy their time together and choose to extend their classroom relationship. "I just finished a five-hour class dinner at my professor's house—we didn't want to leave!" writes one student. "She always has her class over at the end of the semester to eat, have fun, and discuss our final papers. What more could you want?" Alas, not everyone sings similar praise. One in six students attends the engineering school, where you're wise to "research your professors, as some only care about their research." These gripes find audience during the free-lunch Dean's Forums, though taking action is another issue. The school's leadership, "dignified, but willing to smile," is getting serious about Washington's reputation and ranking, and "this has lead to a concerted effort to eliminate the more relaxed atmosphere of the school." For now, the low-stress attitude remains. "People here are smart, there's no doubt, but there's also a common goal to make it fun and a willingness to take breaks...often."

Life

Washington life strikes a balance of "great academics, good sports, a medium size, yummy food, a breathtaking campus, nice dorms, friendly people, and financial assistance." Students here are "extremely bright" and believe they have brains to spare if they decide to drink their weekends away. Though management has started down "a path to make the campus dry," undergrads are currently able to "break into a philosophical or political debate in the middle of a game of beer pong." Casual hanging out or dining with friends break up the party scene. "Often I'll come back to my dorm and find half of my floor doing something together, whether it's playing a game or helping each other study for exams." The campus abuts two idyllic student-friendly areas: the Loop, for cute shops, ethnic restaurants, and independent movies, and Forest Park, with its free museums, zoo, and science center. Students consider the park, which is 500 acres larger than Manhattan's Central Park, their "front yard" and make frequent use of the skating rink, paddleboats, and shade trees. More than 200 student organizations, ranging from club sports to community service groups, benefit from a whopping shared budget of more than $2 million each year.

Student Body

Washington hosts a student population roughly "one-third Jewish, one-third Catholic, and the rest are Protestant, Buddhist, Muslim, or don't care." Most people come from New Jersey or New York, but shed their East Coast intensity upon arrival in the Midwest. The majority espouses strong leftist views and backs them up with political involvement. "Everyone is pretty passionate about something, and that's inspiring," says a first-year. Different groups interact easily, as students attest: "My boyfriend is black, my best friends are Korean and half Indian, and I am a white woman." Though many Washington students come from boatloads of money, people observe "no segregation between the haves and the have-nots." A junior emphasizes, "This is a very rich school, but most people aren't in your face about their wealth." The average Washington student isn't used to being average, but these "over-committed, fun-loving, high-school all-stars" still coexist with "very little animosity or competitiveness."

FINANCIAL AID: 888-547-6670 • E-MAIL: ADMISSIONS@WUSTL.EDU • WEBSITE: WUSTL.EDU

ADMISSIONS

Very important factors considered include: Character/personal qualities, class rank, essays, extracurricular activities, recommendations, secondary school record, standardized test scores, talent/ability, volunteer work, work experience. *Other factors considered include:* Alumni/ae relation, interview, minority status. SAT Reasoning or ACT required. TOEFL required of all international applicants. High school diploma or equivalent is not required. *Academic units recommended:* 4 English, 4 math, 4 science (4 science lab), 2 foreign language, 4 social studies, 4 history.

The Inside Word

The fact that Washington U. doesn't have much play as a nationally respected car-window decal is about all that prevents it from being among the most selective universities. In every other respect—that is, in any way which really matters—this place is hard to beat and easily ranks as one of the best. No other university with as impressive a record of excellence across the board has a more accommodating admissions process. Not that it's easy to get in here, but lack of instant name recognition does affect Washington's admission rate. Students with above-average academic records who are not quite Ivy material are the big winners. Marginal candidates with high financial need may find difficulty; the admissions process at Washington U. is not need-blind and may take into account candidates' ability to pay if they are not strong applicants.

FINANCIAL AID

Students should submit: FAFSA, CSS/Financial Aid PROFILE, noncustodial (divorced/separated) parents' statement, student and parent 1040 tax return or signed waiver if there is no tax return. Regular filing deadline is 2/15. The Princeton Review suggests that all financial aid forms be submitted as soon as possible after 1/1. *Need-based scholarships/grants offered:* Pell, SEOG, state scholarships/grants, private scholarships, the school's own gift aid, United Negro College Fund. *Loan aid offered:* FFEL Subsidized Stafford, FFEL Unsubsidized Stafford, FFEL PLUS, Federal Perkins, state loans, college/university loans from institutional funds. Applicants will be notified of awards on or about 4/1. Federal Work-study Program available. Institutional employment available. Off-campus job opportunities are excellent.

FROM THE ADMISSIONS OFFICE

"Washington University students learn in a flexible academic atmosphere that encourages them to cross disciplines, taking courses in any of our five undergraduate divisions: arts & sciences, architecture, art, business, and engineering. We also offer graduate programs in these divisions as well as law; medicine, including occupational therapy and physical therapy; and social work. This interdisciplinary environment allows students to study alongside other academically talented students from across the country and around the world in any subject that interests them. Through research projects that start as early as the freshman year, students can participate with our world-class faculty in the creation of knowledge. This academic exploration takes place in a supportive, friendly community that provides the resources to ensure success. Outside the classroom, students participate in nearly 200 activities, including community service and multicultural groups; musical, dance, and theater groups; fraternities and sororities; intramural sports; student government; and literary groups. We invite you to visit Washington University any time to experience these outstanding opportunities firsthand.

"Applicants for fall 2006 are required to submit scores from either the SAT or ACT test. Both old and new versions are accepted. If a student submits both the old and new SAT exams, their best scores from either test will be used."

SELECTIVITY

Admissions Rating	**99**
# of applicants	19,822
% of applicants accepted	22
% of acceptees attending	33

FRESHMAN PROFILE

Range SAT Verbal	660-740
Range SAT Math	690-780
**TPR Projected Range SAT Writing*	*670-720*
Range ACT Composite	30-33
Minimum Paper TOEFL	550
Minimum Computer Based TOEFL	213
% graduated top 10% of class	93
% graduated top 25% of class	99
% graduated top 50% of class	100

DEADLINES

Early decision application deadline	11/15
Early decision notification	12/15
Regular application deadline	1/15
Regular notification	4/1
Nonfall registration?	no

APPLICANTS ALSO LOOK AT

AND OFTEN PREFER
Harvard College
Princeton University
Stanford University
University of Pennsylvania
Yale University

AND SOMETIMES PREFER
Cornell University
Duke University
Northwestern University
University of Chicago

AND RARELY PREFER
Emory University
Tulane University
University of Michigan—Ann Arbor
University of Rochester

FINANCIAL FACTS

Financial Aid Rating	**98**
Annual tuition	$31,100
Room & Board	$10,064
Books and supplies	$1,050
Required fees	$942
% frosh rec. need-based scholarship or grant aid	36
% UG rec. need-based scholarship or grant aid	43
% frosh rec. need-based self-help aid	30
% UG rec. need-based self-help aid	34
% frosh rec. any financial aid	38
% UG rec. any financial aid	43
Avg. frosh grant	$25,095
Avg. frosh loan	$4,239
Independent 529 member?	Yes

WEBB INSTITUTE

298 CRESCENT BEACH ROAD, GLEN COVE, NY 11542 • ADMISSIONS: 516-671-2213 • FAX: 516-674-9838

CAMPUS LIFE

Quality of Life Rating	**97**
Fire Safety Rating	**60**
Type of school	private
Environment	village

STUDENTS

Total undergrad enrollment	72
% male/female	79/21
% from out of state	68
% from public high school	88
% live on campus	100
% African American	1
% Asian	3
% Caucasian	96

SURVEY SAYS

Small classes
No one cheats
Registration is a breeze
Dorms are like palaces
Campus feels safe
Frats and sororities are unpopular or nonexistent
Very little drug use

ACADEMICS

Academic Rating	**96**
Calendar	semester
Student/faculty ratio	7:1
Professors interesting rating	72
Professors accessible rating	98
% professors teaching UG courses	100
% classes taught by TAs	0
Most common regular class size	10-19 students

STUDENTS SPEAK OUT

Academics

Offering a full-tuition scholarship to every student and boasting a "100 percent placement rate in grad schools and careers," Long Island's Webb Institute would be the ideal school for everyone, but for one catch: only one major, Naval Architecture and Marine Engineering, is available here. For the "shipbuilders of tomorrow," though, Webb is a dream come true—a "rigorously academic experience tempered by a spirit of cooperation amongst the students and professors who are always willing to help out." Like most engineering schools, Webb demands a lot from its students; writes one, "This school is about keeping a positive attitude in the face of long days and nights of plentiful and difficult work." That task is made easier by the fact that students and faculty form "a tight knit community with strong social bonds. It is not competitive amongst the students, which makes the overall academic experience good." Webb professors "are readily available and often hold review sessions outside of class hours," and while "some introductory professors just don't know how to teach, all courses important to the major are taught by knowledgeable and good professors." Administrators are "readily available and responsive to suggestions, [and] because our school is run on an honor code, the administration has little to do with the overall social lives of the students. So in essence the students run the school." Concludes one engineer, "For the major they offer, it's the best school in the world. The professors are great, the other students are great, and overall the school is great."

Life

"The class load is brutal" at Webb Institute, and "schoolwork has a tendency to take over everything," including leisure time. "We get hours of homework each night," students explain, "so we have to work together and make homework fun in order to survive." All students live together, too, in a remodeled mansion on a 26-acre beachfront estate. As a result, "you get to know your classmates very well because you spend all day with them. All of the classes intermingle a lot too." Webb engineers "joke that we function on our own time zone here. We stay up until 2:00 or 3:00 A.M. regularly, but classes don't start until 9:00 A.M., so we sleep later than the rest of the Eastern Seaboard too." When students can muster some spare time, they enjoy typical college fun. One student reports, "There are many school-sponsored parties every semester, as well as a pub, a TV room, and game room in the main building. Watching movies is pretty popular, as well as video games. Also, there are annual white water rafting and ski trips. Basketball and other sports are played pretty often, just for fun." Because the administration "is very strict about drinking on campus," students head to the local pub or travel into New York City when they feel the need to tie one on. "One must make every effort possible to go to New York City, an easy one-hour train ride away," students insist.

Student Body

"All of the students are very hard working" at Webb, because "if you're not then you won't stay for very long." There are "two types of students at Webb: those who are bookworms and study all the time and are always working, and those who do the work when needed but also enjoy themselves on campus by playing sports or going out and having a good time." As at most engineering schools, most students are male; atypical of engineering schools, nearly all students are white. "We're all nerdy white boys, except for the few nerdy white girls," sums up one student, adding that "minority students aren't social outcasts or anything like that. We don't care what you look like; we care what's going on inside and upstairs. We treat each other with mutual respect."

FINANCIAL AID: 516-671-2213 • E-MAIL: ADMISSIONS@WEBB-INSTITUTE.EDU • WEBSITE: WWW.WEBB-INSTITUTE.EDU

ADMISSIONS

Very important factors considered include: Class rank, interview, secondary school record, standardized test scores. *Important factors considered include:* Character/personal qualities, recommendations, talent/ability. *Other factors considered include:* Extracurricular activities, volunteer work, work experience. SAT Reasoning Test and SAT Subject Tests required. High school diploma is required, and GED is not accepted. *Academic units required:* 4 English, 4 math, 2 science (2 science lab), 2 social studies, 4 academic electives.

The Inside Word

Let's not mince words; admission to Webb is mega-tough. Webb's admissions counselors are out to find the right kid for their curriculum—one that can survive the school's rigorous academics. The applicant pool is highly self-selected because of the focused program of study: naval architecture and marine engineering.

FINANCIAL AID

Students should submit: FAFSA. Regular filing deadline is 7/1. The Princeton Review suggests that all financial aid forms be submitted as soon as possible after 1/1. *Need-based scholarships/grants offered:* Pell, state scholarships/grants, private scholarships, the school's own gift aid. *Loan aid offered:* FFEL Subsidized Stafford, FFEL Unsubsidized Stafford, FFEL PLUS. Applicants will be notified of awards on or about 8/1. Off-campus job opportunities are good.

FROM THE ADMISSIONS OFFICE

"Webb, the only college in the country that specializes in the engineering field of Naval Architecture and Marine Engineering, seeks young men and women of all races from all over the country who are interested in receiving an excellent engineering education with a full-tuition scholarship. Students don't have to know anything about ships, they just have to be motivated to study how mechanical, civil, structural, and electrical engineering come together with the design elements that make up a ship and all its systems. Being small and private has its major advantages. Every applicant is special and the President will interview all entering students personally. The student/faculty ratio is 6:1, and since there are no teaching assistants, interaction with the faculty occurs daily in class and labs at a level not found at most other colleges. The college provides each student with a high-end laptop computer. The entire campus operates under the Student Organization's Honor System that allows unsupervised exams and 24-hour access to the library, every classroom and laboratory, and the shop and gymnasium. Despite a total enrollment of between 70 and 80 students and a demanding workload, Webb manages to field six intercollegiate teams. Currently more than 60 percent of the members of the student body play on one or more intercollegiate teams. Work hard, play hard and the payoff is a job for every student upon graduation. The placement record of the college is 100 percent every year.

"Freshman applicants must take the new SAT. In addition, students may submit scores from the old SAT (before March 2005), and the best scores from either test will be used. We also require scores from two SAT Subject Tests: Math Level 1 or 2 and either Physics or Chemistry."

SELECTIVITY

Admissions Rating	**98**
# of applicants	103
% of applicants accepted	32
% of acceptees attending	79
# of early decision applicants	8
% accepted early decision	33

FRESHMAN PROFILE

Range SAT Verbal	640-710
Average SAT Verbal	670
Range SAT Math	700-760
Average SAT Math	720
**TPR Projected Range SAT Writing*	*660-700*
Average HS GPA	3.9
% graduated top 10% of class	83
% graduated top 25% of class	100
% graduated top 50% of class	100

DEADLINES

Early decision application deadline	10/15
Early decision notification	12/15
Regular application deadline	2/15
Regular notification	3/15-4/30
Nonfall registration?	no

APPLICANTS ALSO LOOK AT

AND OFTEN PREFER
United States Coast Guard Academy
United States Naval Academy

AND SOMETIMES PREFER
Cooper Union
Virginia Tech

AND RARELY PREFER
SUNY Maritime College
University of Michigan—Ann Arbor

FINANCIAL FACTS

Financial Aid Rating	**83**
Annual tuition	$0
Room & Board	$7,550
Books and supplies	$600
% frosh rec. need-based scholarship or grant aid	4
% UG rec. need-based scholarship or grant aid	3
Avg. frosh grant	$2,750
Avg. frosh loan	$2,625
Independent 529 member?	No

WELLESLEY COLLEGE

BOARD OF ADMISSION, 106 CENTRAL STREET, WELLESLEY, MA 02481-8203 • ADMISSIONS: 781-283-2270 • FAX: 781-283-3678

CAMPUS LIFE

Quality of Life Rating	**96**
Fire Safety Rating	**60**
Type of school	private
Environment	town

STUDENTS

Total undergrad enrollment	2,229
% male/female	0/100
% from out of state	84
% from public high school	63
% live on campus	97
% African American	6
% Asian	28
% Caucasian	43
% Hispanic	6
% international	8
# of countries represented	66

SURVEY SAYS

Small classes
No one cheats
Lab facilities are great
Great computer facilities
Great library
Diverse student types on campus
Campus feels safe
Frats and sororities are unpopular or nonexistent

ACADEMICS

Academic Rating	**98**
Calendar	semester
Student/faculty ratio	9:1
Professors interesting rating	99
Professors accessible rating	98
% professors teaching UG courses	100
% classes taught by TAs	0
Most common lab size	10-19 students
Most common regular class size	10-19 students

MOST POPULAR MAJORS

Economics
English language and literature
psychology

STUDENTS SPEAK OUT

Academics

"It's plastered all over campus, but that doesn't make it any less true: 'Wellesley—women who will make a difference in the world.'" Not that Wellesley students need to see their school's unofficial motto (its official motto is *Non ministrari sed ministrare*; "Not to be served, but to serve") to remember their school's mission. It is evidenced in the intensity and scope of the curriculum, the "amazing, inspiring faculty," and the school's success in sending students on to graduate school and careers in a wide variety of areas. Wellesley classes often "resemble high-school classes or seminars, in that the numbers are usually pretty low, and there is more discussion than you would expect in a college class." Frequent discussion keeps students honest, ensuring that they keep up with the syllabus. One student adds, "Academics are hard and time-consuming, but so rewarding." Those who put in the hours reap the rewards. Students tell us, "The faculty will do everything to assure you get into grad school and help you prepare for your future, [while] the Alumnae Association is also full of amazing people who are constantly giving us advice and help with internships, jobs, and just Wellesley in general." Students are satisfied with the Wellesley experience, telling us that it is "all about finding out who you are, even when the world tells you something otherwise."

Life

"There is something for everyone at Wellesley College," women at Wellesley report, adding, "Your social life is really what you make of it." While some will "go out on weekends and go to frat parties," others say they "will go into Boston or Cambridge and go out for dinner, or see a concert, or just go shopping." Another majority of students "will stay on campus and watch movies, surf the Internet, order takeout, do homework or laundry, or just stay in and study." Despite students' tendency to "do their own thing," the campus unites for "Wellesley's special traditions, such as Stepsinging (classes compete to have the loudest cheers), Spring Weekend (concerts, cookouts, and other fun activities), Tower Court (our biggest party of the year, guys come from other schools in U-Hauls), and Lake Day (students skip classes and hang out by Lake Waban)." Though Boston and all that it offers are a mere ten miles away, the school "makes a solid effort to entertain students who remain on campus. There are many lecturers throughout the year, and last year [there were] such visitors as Amiri Baraka, Seamus Heaney, and Phyllis Schlafly. There have also been movie screenings outdoors on Severance Green, and other college-sponsored events meant to entertain (or enlighten) the students at Wellesley College." When these hardworking students can cobble together more than a few hours for fun, they often "walk into the town (the 'Ville') or take buses to Cambridge or the T [Boston's subway]."

Student Body

"The typical student in Wellesley is studious, laborious, and loquacious," undergraduates tell us. "One of the things I love about Wellesley," explains one undergraduate, "is that when you arrive for orientation, you see that the women in the seats around you are just the type of people you liked in high school, and that you won't have to deal with the ditzy popular girls or the macho dumb boys here. We have the cream of the crop, the women who take their education seriously and enjoy every minute of it." Wellesley women love "the incredible diversity of the school, including (but not limited to) ethnicity, socioeconomic class, sexual orientation, and race." One student notes, "Women come from all over the world and the country. My roommate is from Florida, my best friend is from Chicago, a girl down the hall is from Thailand, another from South Africa." Most Wellesley women, we're told, are "rather strong-willed and independent," politically to the left, and vocal about their beliefs. "The college can overload on political correctness. Sometimes students at Wellesley are too easily offended and too uptight," warn some.

Wellesley College

FINANCIAL AID: 781-283-2360 • E-MAIL: ADMISSION@WELLESLEY.EDU • WEBSITE: WWW.WELLESLEY.EDU

ADMISSIONS

Very important factors considered include: Essays, recommendations, secondary school record, standardized test scores. *Important factors considered include:* Character/personal qualities, class rank, extracurricular activities. *Other factors considered include:* Alumni/ae relation, geographical residence, interview, minority status, state residency, talent/ability, volunteer work, work experience. SAT Reasoning and SAT Subject Tests or ACT required. TOEFL required of all international applicants. High school diploma or equivalent is not required. *Academic units recommended:* 4 English, 4 math, 3 science (2 science lab), 4 foreign language, 4 social studies, 4 history.

The Inside Word

While the majority of women's colleges have gone coed or even closed over the past two decades, Wellesley has continued with vigor. As a surviving member of the Seven Sisters, the nation's most prestigious women's colleges, Wellesley enjoys even more popularity with students who choose the single-sex option. Admissions standards are rigorous, but among institutions of such high reputation, Wellesley's admissions staff is friendlier and more open than the majority. Their willingness to conduct preliminary evaluations for candidates is especially commendable and in some form or another should be the rule rather than an exception at highly selective colleges.

FINANCIAL AID

Students should submit: FAFSA, institution's own financial aid form, CSS/Financial Aid PROFILE, noncustodial (divorced/separated) parents' statement, business/farm supplement, parents' and student' tax returns and W-2 forms. The Princeton Review suggests that all financial aid forms be submitted as soon as possible after 1/1. *Need-based scholarships/grants offered:* Pell, SEOG, state scholarships/grants, private scholarships, the school's own gift aid. *Loan aid offered:* FFEL Subsidized Stafford, FFEL Unsubsidized Stafford, FFEL PLUS, Federal Perkins, state loans, college/university loans from institutional funds. Applicants will be notified of awards on or about 4/1. Federal Work-study Program available. Institutional employment available. Off-campus job opportunities are good.

FROM THE ADMISSIONS OFFICE

"A student's years at Wellesley are the beginning—not the end—of an education. A Wellesley College degree signifies not that the graduate has memorized certain blocks of material, but that she has acquired the curiosity, the desire, and the ability to seek and assimilate new information. Four years at Wellesley can provide the foundation for the widest possible range of ambitions and the necessary self-confidence to fulfill them. At Wellesley, a student has every educational opportunity. Above all, it is Wellesley's purpose to teach students to apply knowledge wisely and to use the advantages of talent and education to seek new ways to serve the wider community.

"First-year applicants for fall 2006 must take the SAT and two SAT Subject Tests; Wellesley prefers one Subject Test in Math or Science. The ACT with Writing component is also accepted."

SELECTIVITY

Admissions Rating	**97**
# of applicants	3,944
% of applicants accepted	37
% of acceptees attending	42
# accepting a place on wait list	920
# of early decision applicants	133
% accepted early decision	61

FRESHMAN PROFILE

Range SAT Verbal	640-740
Average SAT Verbal	689
Range SAT Math	640-720
Average SAT Math	678
**TPR Projected Range SAT Writing*	*660-720*
Range ACT Composite	27-31
Average ACT Composite	29
Minimum Paper TOEFL	600
Minimum Computer Based TOEFL	270
% graduated top 10% of class	75
% graduated top 25% of class	95
% graduated top 50% of class	100

DEADLINES

Early decision application deadline	11/1
Early decision notification	12/15
Regular application deadline	1/15
Regular notification	4/1
Nonfall registration?	no

FINANCIAL FACTS

Financial Aid Rating	**80**
Room & Board	$9,202
Books and supplies	$800
Required fees	$620
% frosh rec. need-based scholarship or grant aid	55
% UG rec. need-based scholarship or grant aid	57
% frosh rec. need-based self-help aid	51
% UG rec. need-based self-help aid	54
% frosh rec. any financial aid	57
% UG rec. any financial aid	59
Avg. frosh grant	$24,015
Avg. frosh loan	$2,488
Independent 529 member?	Yes

Wells College

Route 90, Aurora, NY 13026 • Admissions: 315-364-3264 • Fax: 315-364-3227

CAMPUS LIFE

Quality of Life Rating	**73**
Fire Safety Rating	**85**
Type of school	private
Environment	rural

STUDENTS

Total undergrad enrollment	384
% male/female	0/100
% from out of state	31
% from public high school	88
% live on campus	87
% African American	5
% Asian	3
% Caucasian	67
% Hispanic	4
% Native American	1
% international	2
# of countries represented	5

SURVEY SAYS

Small classes
No one cheats
Students are friendly
Campus feels safe
Frats and sororities are unpopular or nonexistent

ACADEMICS

Academic Rating	**88**
Calendar	semester
Student/faculty ratio	8:1
Professors interesting rating	93
Professors accessible rating	81
% professors teaching UG courses	100
% classes taught by TAs	0
Most common regular class size	10-19 students

MOST POPULAR MAJORS

Psychology
visual and performing arts

STUDENTS SPEAK OUT

Academics

The women of Wells College enrolled expecting "a single-sex education" designed to "form a strong community and strong female leaders." Recently, however, they were rocked by the administration's decision to go coed. Most students adamantly believe "the decision will seriously impair the school's ability to achieve its most important goal: teaching women to be independent, free-thinking individuals." Trust between students and administrators has been damaged, "creating an unhealthy divide." The good news is that professors still enjoy a close relationship with students and employ an honor code that rewards responsibility with freedom. "Students are allowed to take exams out of the classroom and leave it in the professor's office when they're done." Due to small classes, teachers notice class participation and "will approach you afterwards if they think you did well or saw that you were unprepared. Three-hour seminars pause for a mid-session tea break "when the dining hall brings cookies and coffee." Students call for improvements in "our science, art, and music programs, athletic facilities, library sources, and website," but they praise the sociology and language departments. Throw in extensive study abroad opportunities and the "very interesting and very rare" book arts center, and we predict Wells will continue to attract students into their coed halls.

Life

The Wells existence "can be summarized in one word: isolation." Hometown Aurora, shuts down by 8:00 P.M. One student warns: "If you are from NYC, you may be culture shocked" when you find yourself spending "Friday and Saturday nights doing homework." Besides the farms and barns, "there's a bar where the entire senior class congregates on Fridays, a wickedly expensive inn, and a pizza place." At least "the Office of Campus Events is really good about giving us stuff to do. But the most fun comes from the traditions: The Even/Odd rivalry, Junior Blast, Freshman Elves, . . . These are really what give Wells its fabulous life." Civilization, meaning malls and Cornell boys, lies 45 minutes away in Ithaca, but some people prefer to stay put, swimming in Cayuga Lake, sledding down Student Union hill, exploring the local cemetery, and involving themselves with campus organizations. "Being creative and willing to try new things makes for interesting weekends," as long as you can "make your own fun." For the Wells crowd, that can range from "hallway soccer" to a good "wine and Cheez-Its party." Off campus, "there's a 24 hour Wal-Mart that always produces some good stories." Other students emphasize the luxury of "the safe space we have here. You can walk back to your dorm across campus at 3:00 A.M. alone, and your biggest worry is bumping into the campus skunk."

Student Body

"Whether a radical feminist or a quiet feminist, this school is full of feminists," asserts a senior. And plenty of them are happy to show up at their morning classes "in their PJ bottoms, flip-flops, a hoodie, and no make-up." These 400 women are typically "liberal, confident, outgoing, and willing to share [their] thoughts," which might just center on "queer and gender theory." Lesbians represent at Wells, and most students agree that everyone gets along well, regardless of sexual preferences.students come from "working-class, white, New York state families," but wherever they are from, "you will rarely find someone who belonged to the popular crowd in high school." The coed crisis has brought out differences of opinion. "Our amazing sisterhood has fractured, and the community has become more like a brood of disgruntled women," writes one student. Others are optimistic that the student body can "keep the same feeling of community even though it is no longer a women's college."

FINANCIAL AID: 315-364-3289 • E-MAIL: ADMISSIONS@WELLS.EDU • WEBSITE: WWW.WELLS.EDU

ADMISSIONS

Very important factors considered include: Extracurricular activities, recommendations, secondary school record, standardized test scores. *Important factors considered include:* Essays, interview. *Other factors considered include:* Alumni/ae relation, character/personal qualities, class rank, talent/ability, volunteer work, work experience. SAT Reasoning or ACT required. TOEFL required of all international applicants. High school diploma is required, and GED is accepted. *Academic units required:* 4 English, 3 math, 2 science (2 science lab), 2 social studies, 2 academic electives. *Academic units recommended:* 4 English, 4 math, 3 science (3 science lab), 2 foreign language, 3 social studies, 3 academic electives.

The Inside Word

Wells is engaged in that age-old admissions game called matchmaking. There are no minimums or cutoffs in the admissions process here. But don't be fooled by the high admit rate. The admissions committee will look closely at your academic accomplishments, but also gives attention to your essay, recommendations, and extracurricular pursuits. The committee also recommends an interview; we suggest taking them up on it.

FINANCIAL AID

Students should submit: FAFSA, CSS/Financial Aid Profile for Early Decision Applicants only. The Princeton Review suggests that all financial aid forms be submitted as soon as possible after 1/1. *Need-based scholarships/grants offered:* Pell, SEOG, state scholarships/grants, private scholarships, the school's own gift aid. *Loan aid offered:* FFEL Subsidized Stafford, FFEL Unsubsidized Stafford, FFEL PLUS, Federal Perkins. Applicants will be notified of awards on a rolling basis beginning on or about 3/1.

FROM THE ADMISSIONS OFFICE

"Wells College believes the twenty-first century needs well-educated individuals with the ability, self-confidence, and vision to contribute to an ever-changing world. Wells offers an outstanding classroom experience and innovative liberal arts curriculum that prepares students for leadership in a variety of fields, including business, government, the arts, sciences, medicine, and education. By directly connecting the liberal arts curriculum to experience and career development through internships, off-campus study, study abroad, research with professors, and community service, each student has an ideal preparation for graduate and professional school as well as for the twenty-first century.

"Wells College requires freshman applicants to submit scores from the old or new SAT. Students may also choose to submit scores from the ACT (with or without the Writing component) in lieu of the SAT."

SELECTIVITY

Admissions Rating	**88**
# of applicants	381
% of applicants accepted	77
% of acceptees attending	30
# of early decision applicants	11
% accepted early decision	100

FRESHMAN PROFILE

Range SAT Verbal	520-640
Average SAT Verbal	580
Range SAT Math	470-590
Average SAT Math	530
**TPR Projected Range SAT Writing*	*570-660*
Range ACT Composite	20-28
Average ACT Composite	24
Minimum Paper TOEFL	550
Minimum Computer Based TOEFL	213
Average HS GPA	3.5
% graduated top 10% of class	45
% graduated top 25% of class	76
% graduated top 50% of class	91

DEADLINES

Early decision application deadline	12/15
Early decision notification	1/15
Regular application deadline	3/1
Regular notification	4/1
Nonfall registration?	no

APPLICANTS ALSO LOOK AT

AND OFTEN PREFER
Hobart and William Smith Colleges
Mount Holyoke College
Smith College

AND SOMETIMES PREFER
SUNY at Binghamton
SUNY College at Geneseo
Syracuse University

AND RARELY PREFER
Elmira College
Le Moyne College

FINANCIAL FACTS

Financial Aid Rating	**84**
Annual tuition	$14,000
Room & Board	$7,000
Books and supplies	$700
Required fees	$900
% frosh rec. need-based scholarship or grant aid	73
% UG rec. need-based scholarship or grant aid	72
% frosh rec. need-based self-help aid	73
% UG rec. need-based self-help aid	72
% frosh rec. any financial aid	66
% UG rec. any financial aid	274
Avg. frosh grant	$12,595
Avg. frosh loan	$2,626
Independent 529 member?	Yes

WESLEYAN COLLEGE

4760 FORSYTH ROAD, MACON, GA 31210-4462 • ADMISSIONS: 912-757-5206 • FAX: 912-757-4030

CAMPUS LIFE

Quality of Life Rating	**89**
Fire Safety Rating	**60**
Type of school	private
Affiliation	Methodist
Environment	city

STUDENTS

Total undergrad enrollment	567
% male/female	0/100
% from out of state	8
% from public high school	81
% live on campus	61
% African American	31
% Asian	2
% Caucasian	44
% Hispanic	2
% international	18
# of countries represented	28

SURVEY SAYS

Small classes
Students are friendly
Diverse student types on campus
Dorms are like palaces
Campus feels safe
Frats and sororities are unpopular or nonexistent
Student government is popular
Very little drug use

ACADEMICS

Academic Rating	**90**
Calendar	semester
Student/faculty ratio	8:1
Professors interesting rating	91
Professors accessible rating	80
% professors teaching UG courses	100
% classes taught by TAs	0
Most common lab size	10-19 students
Most common regular class size	10-19 students

MOST POPULAR MAJORS

Business/managerial operations
communications, journalism, and related fields
psychology

STUDENTS SPEAK OUT

Academics

"Tradition, community, sisterhood, and southern charm are the heart of Wesleyan College," a small, all-women's liberal arts school in the heart of the Cotton Belt. Students are attracted to Wesleyan by its mission to "teach women of all ages, races, creeds, and colors to think analytically, be independent, and go out into the workplace prepared and with a lot of self-esteem." Once they arrive, however, it is "the experience in the class—the discussions and passion of each of the professors—that has kept me enthralled with the Wesleyan experience." Students agree that profs here "are all extremely well educated, very interested in passing on knowledge to current students, and very available for meetings, study sessions, etc." and that "the curriculum is challenging but satisfying: You sure get your money's worth." Undergrads also love the new president, Ruth Knox, describing her as "an absolute gem to the school" who is "quite easy to carry on a conversation with. You always see her about the school taking care of everyday matters." Student complaints center on budget concerns ("The school could stand to have more money to spend on technology and renovations around campus. I think a lack of available funds is our weakest area," writes a typical undergrad) and the constraints of life in Macon.

Life

Wesleyan operates on a unique class system in which "each entering class is assigned a color and a mascot." Students love it, telling us it "helps to encourage sisterhood. Without the typical sororities, this provides a way for students to bond with each other." Sisterhood—the spirit that bonds classes as well as the entire student body here—is reinforced by "tons of traditions," including STUNT ("a musical that five members from each class write and direct"); Bandfest ("where local bands come onto campus for an entire day of fun"); Funday ("We basically bring a mini-carnival of blow-up rides and stuff onto campus"); and Sister Sports ("The most popular is class soccer"). A large minority of this tiny student body is "actively involved in student government," under whose auspices the "Student Recreation Council and Campus Activities Board bring new things to campus, and they do an awesome job." All this helps make up for the fact that "there isn't much to do in the town of Macon." Male visitors are kept at bay by "very strict rules," which is why "the majority of social interactions take place off campus." Sometimes way off campus: students tell us that road trips to Atlanta (about 90 minutes away by car) are fairly common. "We often go there and shop, go to the clubs [and] restaurants, or just hang out," explains one student.

Student Body

Students at Wesleyan College strongly believe that "there is no 'typical' Wesleyan student. There are feminists and those who aren't, there are lesbians and those who aren't, there are churchgoers and those who aren't." Students do tend to share a few common traits, however; they are all "incredibly involved, love to have a good time, and we all know how to get serious when it is time to get serious. Everybody here has her own niche, and we all fit very well together." They also share a sense of "sisterhood" that they describe as "unbelievable—it is something that, until you experience it for yourself, you can never know exactly what it is." The "large international community" and "great ethnic diversity" leave students wondering "if there is any other place in the world where so many different women can come to one place and fit so well together." Although Wesleyan is a Methodist school, the student body includes "numerous Catholics, Baptists, Muslims, and probably any other religion you could possibly think of. People of [different] races or religions or people of different sexual orientations are accepted with open arms."

FINANCIAL AID: 800-447-6610 • E-MAIL: ADMISSIONS@WESLEYANCOLLEGE.EDU • WEBSITE: WWW.WESLEYANCOLLEGE.EDU

ADMISSIONS

Very important factors considered include: Secondary school record. *Important factors considered include:* Character/personal qualities, class rank, extracurricular activities, recommendations, standardized test scores, talent/ability, volunteer work. *Other factors considered include:* Alumni/ae relation, essays, interview, work experience. SAT Reasoning or ACT required. TOEFL required of all international applicants. High school diploma is required, and GED is accepted. *Academic units required:* 4 English, 3 math, 3 science (2 science lab), 2 foreign language, 3 social studies. *Academic units recommended:* 4 English, 4 math, 4 science (3 science lab), 4 foreign language, 4 social studies, 2 academic electives.

The Inside Word

The college has gotten lots of national publicity of late, but its applicant pool is still primarily southeastern in origin. Candidates from outside the usual sphere of influence of any college draw the attention of admissions officers, and it's no exception here. Recommendations are important at Wesleyan; we'd advise that such letters make at least some reference to your interest in and suitability for a women's college; your own essay won't carry nearly as much weight.

FINANCIAL AID

Students should submit: FAFSA, institution's own financial aid form, state aid form. Regular filing deadline is 6/30. The Princeton Review suggests that all financial aid forms be submitted as soon as possible after 1/1. *Need-based scholarships/grants offered:* Pell, SEOG, state scholarships/grants, private scholarships, the school's own gift aid. *Loan aid offered:* FFEL Subsidized Stafford, FFEL Unsubsidized Stafford, FFEL PLUS, Federal Perkins, college/university loans from institutional funds, CitiAssist, Wells FARGO, Collegiate Loans, Key Alternative Loans. Applicants will be notified of awards on a rolling basis beginning on or about 3/1.

FROM THE ADMISSIONS OFFICE

"Mention the term 'women's college,' and most people envision ivy-covered towers in the U.S. northeast. However, Wesleyan College in Macon, Georgia, a four-year liberal arts college founded in 1836, has the distinction of having been the world's first degree-granting college for women. Today it is recognized as one of the nation's most diverse and affordable selective colleges. Students value the college's tradition of service, small classes, beautiful residence halls, and a picturesque campus. Wesleyan is committed to the goals of training women to understand and appreciate the liberal and fine arts and preparing them for careers through high-quality professional programs.

"First-year applicants for fall 2006 must take the SAT and two SAT Subject Tests; Wellesley prefers one Subject Test in Math or Science. The ACT with Writing component is also accepted."

SELECTIVITY

Admissions Rating	**88**
# of applicants	516
% of applicants accepted	55
% of acceptees attending	26
# of early decision applicants	30
% accepted early decision	47

FRESHMAN PROFILE

Range SAT Verbal	500-630
Average SAT Verbal	574
Range SAT Math	490-600
Average SAT Math	562
**TPR Projected Range SAT Writing*	*560-650*
Range ACT Composite	21-27
Average ACT Composite	24
Minimum Paper TOEFL	550
Minimum Computer Based TOEFL	213
Average HS GPA	3.5
% graduated top 10% of class	34
% graduated top 25% of class	66
% graduated top 50% of class	83

DEADLINES

Early decision application deadline	11/15
Early decision notification	12/15
Regular application deadline	8/1
Regular notification	rolling
Nonfall registration?	no

APPLICANTS ALSO LOOK AT AND SOMETIMES PREFER

Agnes Scott College
Emory University
Mercer University—Macon
University of Georgia

AND RARELY PREFER

Berry College
Florida State University
Rhodes College
University of Florida

FINANCIAL FACTS

Financial Aid Rating	**77**
Annual tuition	$11,260
Room & Board	$7,450
Books and supplies	$800
Required fees	$850
% frosh rec. need-based scholarship or grant aid	65
% UG rec. need-based scholarship or grant aid	43
% frosh rec. need-based self-help aid	45
% UG rec. need-based self-help aid	34
% frosh rec. any financial aid	96
% UG rec. any financial aid	91
Avg. frosh grant	$9,852
Avg. frosh loan	$4,644
Independent 529 member?	Yes

WESLEYAN UNIVERSITY

STEWART M. REID HOUSE, 70 WYLLYS AVENUE, MIDDLETOWN, CT 06459-0265 • ADMISSIONS: 860-685-3000 • FAX: 860-685-3001

CAMPUS LIFE

Quality of Life Rating	**82**
Fire Safety Rating	**60**
Type of school	private
Environment	town

STUDENTS

Total undergrad enrollment	2,755
% male/female	48/52
% from out of state	92
% from public high school	56
% live on campus	92
% in (# of) fraternities	3 (9)
% in (# of) sororities	1 (4)
% African American	7
% Asian	9
% Caucasian	62
% Hispanic	7
% international	6
# of countries represented	48

SURVEY SAYS

Great library
Students are friendly
Theater is popular
Political activism is popular

ACADEMICS

Academic Rating	**93**
Calendar	semester
Student/faculty ratio	9:1
Professors interesting rating	84
Professors accessible rating	81
% professors teaching UG courses	100
% classes taught by TAs	1
Most common lab size	10-19 students
Most common regular class size	10-19 students

STUDENTS SPEAK OUT

Academics

Prestigious Wesleyan University serves a unique demographic. Students tell us it is "a place for those wacky hippie types who would be interested in participating in a Jewish a cappella group, coteaching at a high school, working towards a 'third path' to break outside of the current binary Israel/Palestine debate, singing in the campus gospel choir, and starring in a rock opera in which he/she/ze runs across the stage screaming his/her/hir lines wearing nothing but yellow suspenders and a rainbow-colored belt; or, for those who like a good film department." Actually, others find a comfortable niche at Wesleyan as well, but those who love it mostly fall into the general category implied above: creative, active, extremely bright, and more than a little liberal. Undergraduates are a demanding lot. Fortunately, their school delivers, offering solid academics, attentive professors, and a caring (if not always accommodating) administration. Professors "tend to be brilliant. For example, my chemistry teacher can talk intelligently about chemistry, as well as advanced physics, mathematics, and literature. There is an amazing level of experience there. My academic experience has so far been wonderful," explains an undergrad. Coursework is tough. As one student puts it, "The only complaint I have about academics at Wesleyan is that my classes constantly interfere with my extracurricular activities, which is to say classes are hard!" Fortunately, "professors are very encouraging and they want to see their students succeed. They are almost always available if you need to talk to them about homework, a test, or just need help."

Life

Students at Wesleyan "work very hard, but they also know when to have fun. There are parties, concerts, plays, movies, dances, games, protests, and anything else you can think of nearly every time you turn around." There are also "so many different student groups on campus that a lot of people are involved in. These include every activist group you could imagine, many student-run dance groups, a storytelling club, a cappella groups galore, improvisational comedy, etc. There are lots of performances to go to on weekends." And, of course, there are parties, some "big frat parties" and lots of "small parties at students' houses. The wood frame houses that are given to upperclassmen make for a great house party scene." This scene, while active, is not out of hand. "There are definitely a lot of people here who drink, smoke pot, and trip, but no one will ever look down on you if you don't do any of these things," one student tells us. Overall, the "good amount of stuff going on on campus [helps] make up for the relative lack of activity in Middletown," which students say is "not a ghost town, but not a big city, either. It doesn't offer much in the way of entertainment."

Student Body

Thanks to the efforts of its fine admissions department, Wesleyan's student population is one of the most diverse in the nation among highly selective universities. Students recognize the benefits of such a population, telling us, "Wesleyan's greatest strength is its diverse student body. The huge range of perspectives and the intellectual hunger make Wes the vibrant and amazing community that it is." The high degree of selectivity means "Wesleyan students have got their [you-know-what] together like no one you ever meet. They're those ideal college kids who are every bit as intellectual and driven as any Ivy Leaguer, every bit as snobby about it as a Reed student, every bit as hip as a RISD student, and yet as crunchy and earthy as a UC—Berkeley student. It's a campus of total badass intellectuals." Politically, students say, "The atmosphere is open to many views, as long as they're radical."

FINANCIAL AID: 860-685-2800 • E-MAIL: ADMISS@WESLEYAN.EDU • WEBSITE: WWW.WESLEYAN.EDU/

ADMISSIONS

Very important factors considered include: Class rank, secondary school record. *Important factors considered include:* Alumni/ae relation, character/personal qualities, essays, extracurricular activities, minority status, recommendations, standardized test scores, talent/ability, volunteer work. *Other factors considered include:* Geographical residence, interview, work experience. SAT Reasoning and SAT Subject Tests or ACT required. TOEFL required of all international applicants. High school diploma is required, and GED is not accepted. *Academic units required:* 4 English, 3 math, 3 science, 3 foreign language, 3 social studies. *Academic units recommended:* 4 math, 4 science (3 science lab), 4 foreign language, 4 social studies.

The Inside Word

Wesleyan stacks up well against its very formidable competitors academically, yet due to these same competitors the university admits at a fairly high rate for an institution of its high caliber. Candidate evaluation is nonetheless rigorous. If you aren't one of the best students in your graduating class, it isn't likely that you will be very competitive in Wesleyan's applicant pool. Strong communicators can help open the doors by submitting persuasive essays and interviews that clearly demonstrate an effective match with the university.

FINANCIAL AID

Students should submit: FAFSA, CSS/Financial Aid PROFILE, noncustodial (divorced/separated) parents' statement, business/farm supplement. Regular filing deadline is 2/1. The Princeton Review suggests that all financial aid forms be submitted as soon as possible after 1/1. *Need-based scholarships/grants offered:* Pell, SEOG, state scholarships/grants, private scholarships, the school's own gift aid. *Loan aid offered:* FFEL Subsidized Stafford, FFEL Unsubsidized Stafford, FFEL PLUS, Federal Perkins, college/university loans from institutional funds. Applicants will be notified of awards on or about 4/1. Federal Work-study Program available. Off-campus job opportunities are good.

FROM THE ADMISSIONS OFFICE

"Wesleyan faculty believe in an education that is flexible and affords individual freedom and that a strong liberal arts education is the best foundation for success in any endeavor. The broad curriculum focuses on essential communication skills and analytical abilities through course content and teaching methodology, allowing students to pursue their intellectual interests with passion while honing those capabilities. As a result, Wesleyan students achieve a very personalized but broad education. Wesleyan's dean of admission and financial aid, Nancy Hargrave Meislahn, describes the qualities Wesleyan seeks in its students: 'Our very holistic process seeks to identify academically accomplished and intellectually curious students who can thrive in Wesleyan's rigorous and vibrant academic environment; we look for personal strengths, accomplishments, and potential for real contribution to our diverse community.'

"Applicants will meet standardized testing requirements one of two ways: by taking the new SAT plus two SAT Subject Tests of the student's choice, or by taking the old SAT plus three SAT Subject Tests (one of which must be Writing)."

SELECTIVITY

Admissions Rating	**97**
# of applicants	6,538
% of applicants accepted	28
% of acceptees attending	40
# accepting a place on wait list	1,000
% admitted from wait list	4
# of early decision applicants	283
% accepted early decision	48

FRESHMAN PROFILE

Range SAT Verbal	660-750
Average SAT Verbal	700
Range SAT Math	650-740
Average SAT Math	700
**TPR Projected Range SAT Writing*	*670-730*
Range ACT Composite	28-32
Average ACT Composite	32
Minimum Paper TOEFL	600
Minimum Computer Based TOEFL	250
% graduated top 10% of class	66
% graduated top 25% of class	95
% graduated top 50% of class	99

DEADLINES

Early decision application deadline	11/15
Early decision notification	12/15
Regular application deadline	1/1
Regular notification	4/1
Nonfall registration?	no

APPLICANTS ALSO LOOK AT

AND OFTEN PREFER

Brown U., Columbia U.—Columbia College, Harvard College, Stanford U., Yale U.

AND SOMETIMES PREFER

Amherst College, Bowdoin College, Princeton U., Swarthmore College, Williams College

AND RARELY PREFER

Brandeis U., Middlebury College, Oberlin College, Tufts U.

FINANCIAL FACTS

Financial Aid Rating	**96**
Annual tuition	$32,976
Room & Board	$8,932
Books and supplies	$2,310
Required fees	$214
% frosh rec. need-based scholarship or grant aid	45
% UG rec. need-based scholarship or grant aid	45
% frosh rec. need-based self-help aid	47
% UG rec. need-based self-help aid	48
% UG rec. any financial aid	43
Avg. frosh grant	$23,645
Avg. frosh loan	$2,466
Independent 529 member?	Yes

WEST VIRGINIA UNIVERSITY

ADMISSIONS OFFICE, PO BOX 6009, MORGANTOWN, WV 26506-6009 • ADMISSIONS: 304-293-2121 • FAX: 304-293-3080

CAMPUS LIFE

Quality of Life Rating	**87**
Fire Safety Rating	**91**
Type of school	public
Environment	town

STUDENTS

Total undergrad enrollment	18,653
% male/female	53/47
% from out of state	41
% live on campus	27
% in (# of) fraternities	5 (15)
% in (# of) sororities	5 (13)
% African American	4
% Asian	2
% Caucasian	90
% Hispanic	1
% international	2
# of countries represented	85

SURVEY SAYS

Great computer facilities
Great library
Athletic facilities are great
Students are friendly
Everyone loves the WV Mountaineers
Student publications are popular
Lots of beer drinking
Hard liquor is popular

ACADEMICS

Academic Rating	**71**
Calendar	semester
Student/faculty ratio	22:1
Professors interesting rating	70
Professors accessible rating	73
% classes taught by TAs	0
Most common lab size	20-29 students
Most common regular class size	20-29 students

MOST POPULAR MAJORS

Business administration/management
engineering
psychology

STUDENTS SPEAK OUT

Academics

There are two West Virginia Universities, students tell us. There is the legendary party school enjoyed by those who somehow manage to stagger bleary-eyed through the five or more years it takes them to complete degrees, and there is the serious academic school, which boasts a "wide array of majors," many of them extremely good. An undergraduate attending the latter institution writes, "After getting used to students who don't take their educations very seriously, I began to enjoy my life here." Among the school's many strengths are offerings in journalism, engineering, biochemistry, physical therapy, nursing, business, and communications/broadcasting. Students note, "There is a major difference in the way a professor will deal with a good student as opposed to a bad one. Good students can get away with a lot if the privilege is not abused (and if you are a good student it won't be)." Although WVU's large intro classes are enormous, class sizes reduce dramatically "once you get into the higher-level classes." That's when undergraduates start to realize that "WVU has all of the perks of a large university—a diverse student body, a vast array of extracurricular activities, superior instructors—but has the same 'caring' atmosphere as a small school." Recent upgrades include a new library ("with state-of-the-art digital facilities"), a new life sciences building, and new computer labs.

Life

If you are looking for a party, you needn't look too far at WVU, since, as one student tells us, "There is a party every night at this school. It would be hard to get bored here unless you locked yourself in a room like a hermit." In an effort to offer an alternative to the never-ending party scene, the University instituted WVUp All Night, an alcohol-free event offered every Thursday through Saturday night. Some students see the program as an unqualified success. One such student writes, "I think Up All Night is one of the best things that WVU ever did! It gives a fun alternative to the bars." Others point out that "WV Up All Night, which was started to curb the drinking, has actually turned into a place for drunk kids to get free food and sober up when they're done partying." However, everyone agrees, "You don't have to do anything that you don't want to do here; there are many other things to do besides drink, like the mall, movies, sports, clubs, and hanging out with friends, to name a few." Students love hometown football and basketball games—the games are great and provide an excuse to tailgate—as well as "outdoor recreation (skiing, whitewater rafting) and trips to large cities (Washington, DC, Pittsburgh, New York City, Cleveland)." While many students feel that "the greatest strength of our school is its homey environment, with its relaxed, small-town atmosphere," most also concede that "the townspeople don't really like the students. No one is outright mean, and they certainly need the money students provide."

Student Body

The student body of WVU consists of "city people trying to mesh with country people. At times, it is rough." As one New Yorker put it, "It was interesting at first. There's a lot of difference in attitude. But I get along with my fellow students, [in part because] this school has the friendliest population in the country, so long as you're another Mountaineer or you like West Virginia." While the typical Mountaineer is your "normal frat boy or sorority girl," there are "lots of hippies, too." Another student observes "a large international population," as well. By and large, "people here really aren't very intellectual, nor politically active. Many seem like they are here to get their degree and have a good time before doing so."

FINANCIAL AID: 304-293-5242 • E-MAIL: WVUADMISSIONS@ARC.WVU.EDU • WEBSITE: WWW.WVU.EDU

ADMISSIONS

Very important factors considered include: Secondary school record, standardized test scores. SAT Reasoning or ACT required. TOEFL required of all international applicants. High school diploma is required, and GED is accepted. *Academic units required:* 4 English, 3 math, 3 science (2 science lab), 3 social studies. *Academic units recommended:* 2 foreign language.

The Inside Word

West Virginia's admissions office made an excellent point about rolling admission in their response to us, which applies to candidates for admission at any university that uses such an approach. As the admissions committee gets closer to its enrollment targets, the admissions process becomes progressively more selective. At West Virginia the early bird usually gets a worm, and there is often another one for a late bird. Still, don't hold off on rolling admission applications just because others have more pressing deadlines. Forget that there's a rolling plan, and complete your application as if it has to be in at the same time as all the rest.

FINANCIAL AID

Students should submit: FAFSA. Regular filing deadline is 3/1. The Princeton Review suggests that all financial aid forms be submitted as soon as possible after 1/1. *Need-based scholarships/grants offered:* Pell, SEOG, state scholarships/grants, private scholarships, the school's own gift aid. *Loan aid offered:* Direct Subsidized Stafford, Direct Unsubsidized Stafford, Direct PLUS, Federal Perkins, college/university loans from institutional funds. Applicants will be notified of awards on a rolling basis beginning on or about 3/15. Federal Work-study Program available. Institutional employment available. Off-campus job opportunities are good.

FROM THE ADMISSIONS OFFICE

"From quality academic programs and outstanding, caring faculty to incredible new facilities and a campus environment that focuses on students' needs, WVU is a place where dreams can come true. The university's tradition of academic excellence attracts some of the region's best high school seniors. WVU has produced 25 Rhodes Scholars, 25 Goldwater Scholars, 14 Truman Scholars, 5 members of *USA Today*'s All-USA College Academic First Team, and 2 Udall Scholarship winners. Whether your goal is to be an aerospace engineer, reporter, physicist, athletic trainer, opera singer, forensic investigator, pharmacist, or CEO, WVU's 174 degree choices can make it happen. Unique student-centered initiatives include Operation Jump Start, which helps students experience true education extending beyond the classroom. Resident Faculty Leaders live next to the residence halls to mentor students, and WVU Up All Night provides a way to relax and have fun with free food and activities nearly every weekend. The Mountaineer Parents' Club connects more than 11,000 WVU families, and a parents' helpline (800-WVU-0096) leads to a full-time parent advocate. A new Student Recreation Center includes athletic courts, pools, weight/fitness equipment, and a 50-foot indoor climbing wall. Also, a brand-new life sciences building and completely renovated library complex just opened. With programs for studying abroad, a Center for Black Culture and Research, an Office of Disability Services, and a student body that comes from every WV county, 49 states, and 85 different countries, WVU encourages and nurtures diversity. More than $140 million in annual grant funding makes WVU a major research institution where undergraduates can participate. The main campus is one of the safest in the nation, and the area's natural beauty provides chances to ski, bike, hike, and go whitewater rafting.

"Applicants for fall 2006 are required to take the Writing section of the ACT or the new version of the SAT. However, if a student has taken either the ACT or the SAT prior to March 2005, we will accept the older version and use the student's best composite score from either test."

SELECTIVITY

Admissions Rating	**76**
# of applicants	10,523
% of applicants accepted	89
% of acceptees attending	46

FRESHMAN PROFILE

Range SAT Verbal	480-570
Average SAT Verbal	529
Range SAT Math	500-590
Average SAT Math	543
**TPR Projected Range SAT Writing*	*540-610*
Range ACT Composite	20-25
Average ACT Composite	23
Minimum Paper TOEFL	550
Minimum Computer Based TOEFL	173
Average HS GPA	3.3
% graduated top 10% of class	17
% graduated top 25% of class	45
% graduated top 50% of class	78

DEADLINES

Regular application deadline	8/1
Regular notification	rolling
Nonfall registration?	yes

APPLICANTS ALSO LOOK AT

AND OFTEN PREFER

Penn State University Park
University of Pittsburgh—Pittsburgh Campus
Virginia Tech

AND SOMETIMES PREFER

James Madison University
Ohio State University—Columbus
Towson University
University of Maryland—College Park

AND RARELY PREFER

Duquesne University
Kent State University—Kent Campus
University of Kentucky

FINANCIAL FACTS

Financial Aid Rating	**77**
Annual in-state tuition	$3,938
Annual out-of-state tuition	$12,060
Room & Board	$5,894
Books and supplies	$800
% frosh rec. need-based scholarship or grant aid	21
% UG rec. need-based scholarship or grant aid	33
% frosh rec. need-based self-help aid	24
% UG rec. need-based self-help aid	39
% frosh rec. any financial aid	71
% UG rec. any financial aid	86
Avg. frosh grant	$4,240
Avg. frosh loan	$3,518
Independent 529 member?	No

WESTMINSTER COLLEGE (PA)

319 SOUTH MARKET STREET, NEW WILMINGTON, PA 16172 • ADMISSIONS: 800-942-8033 • FAX: 724-946-7171

CAMPUS LIFE

Quality of Life Rating	**78**
Fire Safety Rating	**60**
Type of school	private
Affiliation	Presbyterian
Environment	village

STUDENTS

Total undergrad enrollment	1,261
% male/female	34/66
% from out of state	21
% from public high school	90
% live on campus	78
% in (# of) fraternities	50 (5)
% in (# of) sororities	50 (5)
% African American	3
% Caucasian	81

SURVEY SAYS

Small classes
Students are friendly
Frats and sororities dominate social scene
Lots of beer drinking

ACADEMICS

Academic Rating	**82**
Calendar	semester
Student/faculty ratio	12:1
Professors interesting rating	80
Professors accessible rating	85
% professors teaching UG courses	100
% classes taught by TAs	0
Most common lab size	10-19 students
Most common regular class size	10-19 students

MOST POPULAR MAJORS

Biology/biological sciences
Business administration/management
education

STUDENTS SPEAK OUT

Academics

At most schools, if your alarm clock doesn't go off the morning of your final exam, you miss the test, fail the class, and enter therapy. Not so for a freshman at Westminster: "I received a phone call from my professor at quarter after nine saying, 'The exam has started! Where are you? Get down here!'" This type of personal attention is the norm at Westminster, where students site the faculty and administrators as one of the school's greatest assets. "My sister who had just graduated introduced me to the professors in her education major. They hugged me, shook my hand, and treated me like family." Clearly, many of the teachers here "relate well to the students and their needs," cultivating a "personal and comfortable atmosphere in the classroom," which extends outside of class as well. It's not unusual to be invited to a professor's house for a meal; even the president hosts picnics and dinners to get to know the students. A sophomore now majoring in communications was appreciative when "the Dean of Academic Affairs took me under his wing last year because I was undecided." Undergrads aspiring to be doctors one day hope to cash in on the school's exceptional medical school acceptance rates. But they don't complete the premed program easily; these students will tell you that "slacking is not an option." Other top programs include English, business, elementary education, and music. In addition, "the education experience in physics here competes with some of the biggest name schools, even though we lack equipment and opportunity." Overall, the Westminster academic experience aims to "expand your views on the world" and make students "think more clearly and analytically." The Career Center "offers amazing career placements, and they are always willing to help students improve resumes and job skills." A graduating senior sums it up well, saying her school is "loaded with people looking to make each student's life a little easier."

Life

"People think we don't do anything here because our college is located in a small, dry town." Rural New Wilmington shuts down at 7:00 P.M., precluding much excitement "unless an Amish revolt should break out." Most people head to nearby megalopolises Grove City and New Castle "because this town is stuck in 1950." On-campus activities occasionally suffer from low attendance, but movies and sports draw a crowd. Religious students take part in "varied opportunities for Christian fellowship and worship. There are organizations for athletes; Gospel Choir and Praise Band for singers and musicians; and Bible study groups, chapel services, a weekly informal, student-led worship, and weekly Vespers for everyone else." Though the campus is "supposedly dry," students still find a way to drink. "I feel that by following the rules and applying myself to my studies I am in the minority of kids who take college seriously," reports a resident assistant. Several students comment that rivalries between fraternities and tensions between Greeks and independent students have been overemphasized in the past. They claim all groups come together "for fun and philanthropy." A chorus of voices also agree that both the food and the parking situations could use some improvement.

Student Body

Westminster students jump to point out that "things have really improved here in terms of diversity, especially in the past two years." For example, "there has been a dramatic spike in the number of open homosexuals and people who support that community. A gay student was even elected as homecoming king." On the other hand, many still complain that the small percentage of minorities is disheartening. Undergraduates separate into straight-laced religious types, rowdy bacchanalian slackers, and a few black-clad "protestors of modern society." Most are Caucasian and come from rural towns in western Ohio or eastern Pennsylvania—with a few Pittsburgh suburbanites mixed in—and families with money and college degrees. Many respondents emphasize "the interpersonal aspect" of the community—the say-hi-to-everyone culture, rooted in Christian conservative values without being all the way religious right.

Financial Aid: 724-946-7102 • E-mail: admis@westminster.edu • Website: www.westminster.edu

ADMISSIONS

Very important factors considered include: Interview, secondary school record, standardized test scores. *Important factors considered include:* Character/personal qualities, class rank, essays, recommendations. *Other factors considered include:* Alumni/ae relation, extracurricular activities, minority status, talent/ability, volunteer work, work experience. SAT Reasoning or ACT required. TOEFL required of all international applicants. High school diploma is required, and GED is accepted. *Academic units required:* 4 English, 3 math, 2 science (2 science lab), 2 foreign language, 2 social studies, 1 history, 3 academic electives.

The Inside Word

The vast majority of those who apply to Westminster gain admission, but the applicant pool is strong enough to enable the college to weed out those who don't measure up to the solid entering class academic profile. Candidates who are shooting for academic scholarships should play the admissions game all the way and put a solid effort into the completion of their applications.

FINANCIAL AID

Students should submit: FAFSA, institution's own financial aid form. The Princeton Review suggests that all financial aid forms be submitted as soon as possible after 1/1. *Need-based scholarships/grants offered:* Pell, SEOG, state scholarships/grants, private scholarships, the school's own gift aid. *Loan aid offered:* FFEL Subsidized Stafford, FFEL Unsubsidized Stafford, FFEL PLUS, Federal Perkins. Federal Work-study Program available. Off-campus job opportunities are good.

FROM THE ADMISSIONS OFFICE

"Since its founding, Westminster has been dedicated to a solid foundation in today's most crucial social, cultural, and ethical issues. Related to the Presbyterian Church (U.S.A.), Westminster is home to people of many faiths. Our students and faculty, tradition of campus, and small-town setting all contribute to an enlightening educational experience.

"For purposes of admission and merit scholarships Westminster College will evaluate applicants for fall 2006 using the composite score of the Math and Critical Reading sections of the new SAT. Westminster will collect new Writing section scores and compare with national percentiles for possible inclusion in admission and scholarship criteria for the Fall of 2007."

SELECTIVITY

Admissions Rating	**80**
# of applicants	1,444
% of applicants accepted	75
% of acceptees attending	32

FRESHMAN PROFILE

Range SAT Verbal	490-590
Average SAT Verbal	544
Range SAT Math	480-600
Average SAT Math	543
**TPR Projected Range SAT Writing*	*550-620*
Range ACT Composite	20-26
Average ACT Composite	24
Minimum Paper TOEFL	500
Average HS GPA	3.3
% graduated top 10% of class	20
% graduated top 25% of class	55
% graduated top 50% of class	87

DEADLINES

Early decision application deadline	11/15
Early decision notification	11/15
Regular application deadline	4/15
Regular notification	rolling
Nonfall registration?	no

APPLICANTS ALSO LOOK AT

AND OFTEN PREFER

Baldwin—Wallace College
The College of Wooster

AND SOMETIMES PREFER

Duquesne University
Grove City College
University of Pittsburgh—Pittsburgh Campus

AND RARELY PREFER

Allegheny College
Slippery Rock University of Pennsylvania
Thiel College
Washington & Jefferson College

FINANCIAL FACTS

Financial Aid Rating	**84**
Annual tuition	$21,700
Room & Board	$6,600
Required fees	$980
% frosh rec. need-based scholarship or grant aid	66
% UG rec. need-based scholarship or grant aid	68
% frosh rec. need-based self-help aid	57
% UG rec. need-based self-help aid	61
Avg. frosh grant	$7,500
Avg. frosh loan	$3,100
Independent 529 member?	Yes

Wheaton College (IL)

501 College Avenue, Wheaton, IL 60187 • Admissions: 630-752-5005 • Fax: 630-752-5285

CAMPUS LIFE

Quality of Life Rating	**96**
Fire Safety Rating	**89**
Type of school	private
Affiliation	Christian nondenominational
Environment	town

STUDENTS

Total undergrad enrollment	2,408
% male/female	48/52
% from out of state	67
% from public high school	63
% live on campus	87
% African American	2
% Asian	7
% Caucasian	85
% Hispanic	3
% international	1
# of countries represented	15

SURVEY SAYS

Small classes
Athletic facilities are great
Students are very religious
Great food on campus
Frats and sororities are unpopular or nonexistent

ACADEMICS

Academic Rating	**87**
Calendar	semester
Student/faculty ratio	13:1
Professors interesting rating	89
Professors accessible rating	89
% professors teaching UG courses	90
% classes taught by TAs	0
Most common lab size	10-19 students
Most common regular class size	10-19 students

MOST POPULAR MAJORS

Business/managerial economics
communications studies/speech communication and rhetoric
English language and literature

STUDENTS SPEAK OUT

Academics

At Wheaton, ask a faculty member to lunch and the student government will pick up the tab. "Most professors are more than happy to go with you!" The emphasis on teacher-student interaction starts early, since the school likes to see professors put "a lot of effort into the introductory classes. They believe it is their duty to present students with the most engaging education possible." Even established slackers admit that "classes and texts are so stimulating that sometimes I actually want to study." Many students emphasize the workload is heavy with rich content rather than busywork. Courses are "usually well-organized and well-taught," making it nearly impossible for students to "name an absolute favorite because there are too many." The conservatory of music is especially well known for academic quality. Instructors all around "strive to present information honestly, with the least possible degree of bias, in order to equip students to discover the truth for themselves." Students call the administration "generally knowledgeable and effective, but also overbearing and sometimes paranoid." A senior reports, "They work hard to maintain this holy, Christian atmosphere while often overlooking or neglecting the problems of the school and student body." Still, Wheaton succeeds at its goal of "integrating the Christian faith into all areas of academia with the purpose of making Christian workers who will infiltrate every part of the world and affect it for Christ and his kingdom."

Life

Wheaton life is governed by a community covenant, signed by all, aiming to "control everyone's life so they stay Christian," according to some undergraduate agitators. "While there is some underground smoking and drinking, I would say that it is less than two percent of the students who would partake over their four years," estimates one student. Entertainment centers more on the wholesome, dorm-based life: raids on brother/sister floors, miniature golf courses set up in the halls, or an innocent game of sardines. The recent legalization of dancing, as long as it's not "immodest, sinfully erotic, or harmfully violent," has spawned a frenzy of square dancing and swing dancing events. As far as the "somewhat strange dating scene," most coed events organized by the school are called "a joke." Other students think, "It actually reminds me of a more normalized form of high school dating, one with far less rumor-mongering, fighting, and drama." Many kids avoid the dating scene altogether, spending time at Bible study, staying up late watching movies, talking theology, or immersing themselves in the chaste haven of a philosophy paper on a Friday night. For variety, students can escape to the North Woods campus, explore Chicago, or participate in urban social justice ministries.

Student Body

Wheaton students form "strong social support networks" based mainly on sports teams, dormitory floors, major, or artistic involvement. A senior who had a single room in one of the dorms said of the building, "We treated our small population of 50 guys like a sort of alternative community—not quite monastic though." Christianity operates as the default denominator, to the extent that some students feel "you have to be a Christian here or you won't fit in." At the forefront of the "strictly mono-cultural" population, we find preppy, type-A, conservative WASPs, who are "obsessed with their GPA and being the perfect Christian." The commonly held concern with social issues has triggered "a recent emphasis on diversity issues and racial relations." A junior says of his peers, "While they are mostly good people, their cultural exposure is close to nil. They tend to believe that all Asians know martial arts, all African Americans can rap well, and that anyone not from the conservative part of the U.S. is weird." A degree of diversity and worldliness comes from students who grew up overseas "either as missionary kids or military brats."

WHEATON COLLEGE (IL)

FINANCIAL AID: 630-752-5021 • E-MAIL: ADMISSIONS@WHEATON.EDU • WEBSITE: WWW.WHEATON.EDU

ADMISSIONS

Very important factors considered include: Essays, recommendations, religious affiliation/commitment, secondary school record, standardized test scores. *Important factors considered include:* Alumni/ae relation, character/personal qualities, minority status, talent/ability. *Other factors considered include:* Class rank, extracurricular activities, geographical residence, interview, volunteer work, work experience. SAT Reasoning or ACT required. TOEFL required of all international applicants. High school diploma is required, and GED is accepted. *Academic units recommended:* 4 English, 3 math, 3 science, 2 foreign language, 3 social studies.

The Inside Word

The admissions process at Wheaton is quite rigorous. As at most small colleges, the review of candidates focuses on far more than courses, grades, and test scores. The admissions committee will also carefully consider your essays, recommendations, and other indicators of your character as they assess how well suited you are to the campus community. Wheaton limits acceptance to students who profess Christian faith.

FINANCIAL AID

Students should submit: FAFSA, institution's own financial aid form. The Princeton Review suggests that all financial aid forms be submitted as soon as possible after 1/1. *Need-based scholarships/grants offered:* Pell, SEOG, state scholarships/grants, the school's own gift aid. *Loan aid offered:* FFEL Subsidized Stafford, FFEL Unsubsidized Stafford, FFEL PLUS, Federal Perkins, college/university loans from institutional funds. Applicants will be notified of awards on a rolling basis beginning on or about 3/1. Federal Work-study Program available. Institutional employment available. Off-campus job opportunities are excellent.

FROM THE ADMISSIONS OFFICE

"At Wheaton, we're commited to being a community that fearlessly pursues truth, upholds an academically rigorous curriculum, and promotes virtue. The college takes seriously its impact on society. The influence of Wheaton is seen in fields ranging from government (the speaker of the house) to sports (two NBA coaches) to business (the CEO of John Deere) to music (Metropolitan Opera National Competition winners) to education (over 40 college presidents) to global ministry (Billy Graham). Wheaton seeks students who want to make a difference and are passionate about their Christian faith and rigorous academic pursuit.

"Fall 2006 applicants are required to submit results from the New SAT, or ACT with Writing section. Wheaton will use the highest of these scores from either test in evaluating a student's application. Additionally, since the multiple choice sections of the ACT have not been changed, Wheaton College will accept the composite score from the old ACT."

SELECTIVITY

Admissions Rating	**94**
# of applicants	2,133
% of applicants accepted	50
% of acceptees attending	56
# accepting a place on wait list	414
% admitted from wait list	1

FRESHMAN PROFILE

Range SAT Verbal	620-720
Average SAT Verbal	664
Range SAT Math	610-700
Average SAT Math	655
**TPR Projected Range SAT Writing*	*650-710*
Range ACT Composite	26-31
Average ACT Composite	29
Minimum Paper TOEFL	550
Minimum Computer Based TOEFL	215
Average HS GPA	3.7
% graduated top 10% of class	54
% graduated top 25% of class	82
% graduated top 50% of class	96

DEADLINES

Regular application deadline	1/15
Regular notification	4/10
Nonfall registration?	yes

APPLICANTS ALSO LOOK AT AND SOMETIMES PREFER

Calvin College
Grove City College
Northwestern University
University of Illinois at Urbana-Champaign

AND RARELY PREFER

Baylor University
Taylor University

FINANCIAL FACTS

Financial Aid Rating	**73**
Annual tuition	$21,100
Room & Board	$6,660
Books and supplies	$714
% frosh rec. need-based scholarship or grant aid	39
% UG rec. need-based scholarship or grant aid	41
% frosh rec. need-based self-help aid	48
% UG rec. need-based self-help aid	49
% frosh rec. any financial aid	75
% UG rec. any financial aid	68
Avg. frosh grant	$9,278
Avg. frosh loan	$4,519
Independent 529 member?	No

WHEATON COLLEGE (MA)

OFFICE OF ADMISSION, NORTON, MA 02766 • ADMISSIONS: 508-286-8251 • FAX: 508-286-8271

CAMPUS LIFE

Quality of Life Rating	**69**
Fire Safety Rating	**60**
Type of school	private
Environment	village

STUDENTS

Total undergrad enrollment	1,524
% male/female	37/63
% from out of state	65
% from public high school	61
% live on campus	97
% African American	3
% Asian	3
% Caucasian	78
% Hispanic	4
% international	3
# of countries represented	31

SURVEY SAYS

Small classes
Frats and sororities are unpopular or nonexistent
Lots of beer drinking

ACADEMICS

Academic Rating	**91**
Calendar	semester
Student/faculty ratio	11:1
Professors interesting rating	87
Professors accessible rating	84
% professors teaching UG courses	100
% classes taught by TAs	0
Most common lab size	10-19 students
Most common regular class size	10-19 students

MOST POPULAR MAJORS

Economics
English language and literature
psychology

STUDENTS SPEAK OUT

Academics

"The greatest strengths of Wheaton are the opportunities that come as a result of being such a small school," students at this New England liberal arts stronghold agree. Those opportunities include "close relationships with faculty, chances to study something independently if the subject is not specifically offered," and the encouragement students receive, "for studying abroad and getting internships, which is really awesome at the undergraduate level." Students get personal-touch treatment from the moment they arrive. Their first academic experience is the First Year Seminar, "in which students learn to read, write, and study at a college level. It serves as an introductory course for the way most classes will run. The professor of this course will be the student's advisor until that student declares his/her major...Each first-year student is also assigned two upper-class students who serve as mentors to the freshmen, guiding them through their adjustments to college life and answering any questions that need answering. The transition into college life couldn't have been easier because of this program." The personal attention continues right through to graduation and beyond, with help from the exceptional Filene Center, "a career and job placement services office that is the best institution available to students and graduates of Wheaton. It opens many doors for students to obtain internships as well as jobs after college, and from freshman year on they help you build your resume and interests." The school's size also has its drawbacks; "It is very difficult to get into the classes of your choice here, especially if you are a psychology major," warns a student in one of the school's more popular majors.

Life

"Wheaton is cursed by geography," students agree, complaining that hometown Norton "has nothing to offer college students." Couple this with the school's aggressively enforced dry-campus policy and you can see why "Wheaton is a suitcase school. Too many people go home on the weekends, and college shouldn't be like that." Students wish it were otherwise. "You don't get the full experience by going home every weekend," grouses one. On the up side, the school is making efforts to address the situation. One undergrad explains, "The school has tried having dances and more on-campus events, but the reality of it is that campus life over the weekend here will never be fabulous." As a result, students bug out on Fridays, "going into Boston and Providence for dinner or just to hang out." Things are pretty busy during the week, as "there are over 50 student run organizations on campus. Literally, there is something for everybody, and if you don't find a club for you, start one! The process is very easy!" Weekends, however, are a different story. Also, "athletics are a big part of life here, since such a big proportion of students are athletes." A few students note the benefits of living in quiet seclusion: "Our small, suburban town means that students concentrate on their studies, sans distractions, on a beautiful campus," explains one undergrad.

Student Body

"There are no 'typical' students on campus, unless you count white, upper-middle class, sweater-and-jeans wearing, white-teeth blazing, upstanding men and women," jokes a typical Wheatie. This same student adds that "realistically, we are a predominately wealthy, educated student body whose parents are usually educated as well. We have a pitifully small racial and ethnic population, and those who are diverse tend to group together." A former women's school, Wheaton is still predominantly female. Observes one male, "I can't complain about the male to female ratio—67 percent female is 67 percent female no matter how you look at it. The benefits…just think about the benefits." Most undergraduates "fall into the category of liberal when it comes to many issues [and] are very intellectually and artistically active. Students are really encouraged to explore their interests and passions here," regardless of the health impact. "Almost 100 percent of the campus exercises regularly, [yet] many students smoke like chimneys."

FINANCIAL AID: 508-286-8232 • E-MAIL: ADMISSION@WHEATONCOLLEGE.EDU • WEBSITE: WWW.WHEATONCOLLEGE.EDU

ADMISSIONS

Very important factors considered include: Character/personal qualities, essays, extracurricular activities, secondary school record, talent/ability. *Important factors considered include:* Alumni/ae relation, class rank, interview, recommendations, volunteer work, work experience. *Other factors considered include:* Geographical residence, minority status, state residency. TOEFL required of all international applicants. High school diploma is required, and GED is accepted. *Academic units recommended:* 4 English, 4 math, 3 science (2 science lab), 4 foreign language, 2 social studies.

The Inside Word

Wheaton is to be applauded for periodically re-examining its admissions process; some colleges use virtually the same application process eternally, never acknowledging the fluid nature of societal attitudes and institutional circumstances. Approaches that emphasize individuals, or even their accomplishments, over their numbers are unfortunately rare in the world of college admission, where GPA and SAT I reign supreme. Wheaton has an easier time than some colleges in taking this step because it isn't prohibitively selective.

FINANCIAL AID

Students should submit: FAFSA, CSS/Financial Aid PROFILE, noncustodial (divorced/separated) parents' statement, business/farm supplement, parent and student federal tax returns and W-2 forms. Regular filing deadline is 2/1. The Princeton Review suggests that all financial aid forms be submitted as soon as possible after 1/1. *Need-based scholarships/grants offered:* Pell, SEOG, state scholarships/grants, private scholarships, the school's own gift aid. *Loan aid offered:* FFEL Subsidized Stafford, FFEL Unsubsidized Stafford, FFEL PLUS, Federal Perkins, state loans, MEFA, TERI, CitiAssist, Signature, and other private loans. Applicants will be notified of awards on or about 4/1. Federal Work-study Program available. Institutional employment available. Off-campus job opportunities are good.

FROM THE ADMISSIONS OFFICE

"What makes for a 'best college'? Is it merely the hard-to-define notions of prestige or image? We don't think so. We think what makes college 'best' and best for you is a school that will make you a first-rate thinker and writer, a pragmatic professional in your work, and an ethical practitioner in your life. To get you to all these places, Wheaton takes advantage of its great combinations: a beautiful, secluded New England campus combined with access to Boston and Providence; a high quality, classic liberal arts and sciences curriculum combined with award-winning internship, job, and community service programs; and a campus that respects your individuality in the context of the larger community. What's the 'best' outcome of a Wheaton education? A start on life that combines meaningful work, significant relationships, and a commitment to your local and global community. Far more than for what they've studied or for what they've gone on to do for a living, we're most proud of Wheaton graduates for who they become.

"Wheaton does not require students to submit the results of any standardized testing. The only exception is the TOEFL for students for whom English is a second language. Students who choose to submit standardized testing may use results from the historic SAT, its revised version, or from the ACT."

SELECTIVITY

Admissions Rating	**92**
# of applicants	3,460
% of applicants accepted	45
% of acceptees attending	28
# accepting a place on wait list	763
% admitted from wait list	3
# of early decision applicants	202
% accepted early decision	86

FRESHMAN PROFILE

Range SAT Verbal	560-650
Average SAT Verbal	620
Range SAT Math	580-650
Average SAT Math	610
**TPR Projected Range SAT Writing*	*600-670*
Range ACT Composite	24-30
Average ACT Composite	27
Minimum Paper TOEFL	550
Minimum Computer Based TOEFL	213
Average HS GPA	3.45
% graduated top 10% of class	42
% graduated top 25% of class	76
% graduated top 50% of class	93

DEADLINES

Early decision application deadline	11/15
Early decision notification	12/15
Regular application deadline	1/15
Regular notification	4/1
Nonfall registration?	yes

APPLICANTS ALSO LOOK AT AND OFTEN PREFER

Bates College, Connecticut College

AND SOMETIMES PREFER

Hamilton College, Skidmore College, University of Vermont

AND RARELY PREFER

Boston University, Brandeis University, Clark University

FINANCIAL FACTS

Financial Aid Rating	**83**
Annual tuition	$30,355
Room & Board	$7,580
Books and supplies	$940
Required fees	$225
% frosh rec. need-based scholarship or grant aid	47
% UG rec. need-based scholarship or grant aid	49
% frosh rec. need-based self-help aid	47
% UG rec. need-based self-help aid	49
% frosh rec. any financial aid	62
% UG rec. any financial aid	63
Avg. frosh grant	$16,678
Avg. frosh loan	$3,568
Independent 529 member?	Yes

WHITMAN COLLEGE

345 BOYER AVENUE, WALLA WALLA, WA 99362-2083 • ADMISSIONS: 509-527-5176 • FAX: 509-527-4967

CAMPUS LIFE

Quality of Life Rating	**99**
Fire Safety Rating	**84**
Type of school	private
Environment	town

STUDENTS

Total undergrad enrollment	1,452
% male/female	45/55
% from out of state	58
% from public high school	25
% live on campus	56
% in (# of) fraternities	34 (4)
% in (# of) sororities	32 (4)
% African American	2
% Asian	9
% Caucasian	69
% Hispanic	3
% Native American	1
% international	3
# of countries represented	26

SURVEY SAYS

Small classes
Great library
Students are friendly
Intramural sports are popular

ACADEMICS

Academic Rating	**98**
Calendar	semester
Student/faculty ratio	10:1
Professors interesting rating	97
Professors accessible rating	97
% professors teaching UG courses	100
% classes taught by TAs	0
Most common lab size	10-19 students
Most common regular class size	10-19 students

MOST POPULAR MAJORS

English language and literature
psychology
sociology

STUDENTS SPEAK OUT

Academics

With "a tight community that has approachable professors, small class sizes, and a rigorous academic course to prepare well-rounded, well-educated students," Whitman College is a comfortable fit for its "intelligent and passionate" student body. Undergrads here especially appreciate "the great length to which the staff, faculty, and administration go to make sure that we are happy, healthy, and doing well in school. It's a very homey place." The school offers "tons of great study areas and learning facilities to take advantage of, like computer labs in every building and a 24-hour library." Students are particularly impressed with the "strong biology department, which offers a great BBMB program (biophysics, biochemistry, molecular biology)." The workload is heavy, and "some Whitman kids wear themselves thin doing too much. There's almost the social expectation that you will participate in a million activities, have a job, volunteer, have tons of friends, party hard, and—of course—excel academically, which can be really stressful." Most here don't mind, however. In fact, they relish the challenge, which is why they chose Whitman in the first place. "This school demands an intense amount of effort, time, and commitment," writes one senior. "But it pays off socially and academically if you have the motivation." Students also love that they "have a big say in what is going on. We get a voice in choosing the new college president, in reviewing teachers, and even in the admissions process (if an overnight host had a negative experience with a visiting prospective student, the host can report it to the admissions office and the comments go on the student's record during the admissions proceedings)."

Life

Hometown Walla Walla "is cute and quaint, but as far as activities that college students want to do, fairly limited. There's bowling, wheat fields, a movie theatre, some good restaurants, and not much more." Some here feel the town is "Whitman's biggest drawback" and observe that "being in such a small town forces the campus life to be amazing." And, by most accounts, campus life is just that. One student reports, "There are always a ridiculous amount of things going on on campus. Sometimes the trouble is choosing what you are going to do or having time to do all of the things you are interested in. There are tons of clubs (and some really odd ones, like the Ender's Game Alliance and the Flight Club) to get involved in and lots of musical performances, plays, parties, speakers, etc." As a result, students stick close to home, which is why "the campus here is often referred to as 'The Whitman Bubble.' Often you forget there is a world outside of Whitman just because you are so overwhelmed with all that is here." To break up long nights spent on homework, "every dorm has a planned "study break once a week, in which we do things like finger-paint, have pillow fights, or invite one of the insanely popular a cappella groups to sing to us." Undergrads appreciate that "Whitman is a very green campus, and aware of the environment. There are always numerous vegetarian and vegan options in the dining halls."

Student Body

"Everyone is passionate and active about both academics and extracurricular activities," at Whitman, "whether it's music, volunteering, intramural sports, a political group, or something else. People aren't content with just sitting around doing nothing." Undergrads here identify the typical student as "a high middle- to upper-class white kid who attended private school and grew up near Seattle or Portland," but they also detect "a surprising number of students from lower-income families." There are lots of "granola hippies" here who are "hard workers, environmentally and politically-conscious, vegetarian, Birkenstock-wearing, bicycling, happy people." Most here agree that "Whitman needs to work on diversity. There is not enough racial diversity on campus, although the school is working hard to encourage diversity. There are diversity clubs on campus that help minority students and increase awareness about diversity on and off campus." The student body is "heavy on Democrats."

WHITMAN COLLEGE

FINANCIAL AID: 509-527-5178 • E-MAIL: ADMISSION@WHITMAN.EDU • WEBSITE: WWW.WHITMAN.EDU

ADMISSIONS

Very important factors considered include: Character/personal qualities, essays, secondary school record. *Important factors considered include:* Extracurricular activities, minority status, recommendations, standardized test scores, talent/ability. *Other factors considered include:* Alumni/ae relation, class rank, geographical residence, interview, state residency, volunteer work, work experience. SAT Reasoning or ACT required. TOEFL required of all international applicants. High school diploma is required, and GED is accepted. *Academic units recommended:* 4 English, 4 math, 3 science (3 science lab), 2 foreign language, 2 social studies, 2 history, 1 arts.

The Inside Word

Whitman's admissions committee is to be applauded; any admissions process that emphasizes essays and extracurriculars over the SAT has truly gotten it right. The college cares much more about who you are and what you have to offer if you enroll than it does about what your numbers will do for the freshman academic profile. Whitman is a mega-sleeper. Educators all over the country know it as an excellent institution, and the college's alums support it at one of the highest rates of giving at any college in the nation. Student seeking a top-quality liberal arts college owe it to themselves to take a look.

FINANCIAL AID

Students should submit: FAFSA, institution's own financial aid form, CSS/Financial Aid PROFILE, parent tax return. Regular filing deadline is 2/1. The Princeton Review suggests that all financial aid forms be submitted as soon as possible after 1/1. *Need-based scholarships/grants offered:* Pell, SEOG, state scholarships/grants, private scholarships, the school's own gift aid. *Loan aid offered:* Direct Subsidized Stafford, Direct Unsubsidized Stafford, Direct PLUS, FFEL Subsidized Stafford, private alternative loans. Applicants will be notified of awards on or about 2/1. Off-campus job opportunities are good.

FROM THE ADMISSIONS OFFICE

"Whitman is a place that encourages you to explore past the boundaries of disciplines because learning and living don't always fall neatly into tidy little compartments. Many students choose Whitman specifically because they're interested in a particular career such as business or engineering but want the well-rounded preparation that only a liberal arts education provides.

"Applicants for fall 2006 are required to take the new version of the SAT or the ACT with the Writing section, but students may submit scores from the old version of the SAT (prior to March 2005) or ACT as well, and the best scores from either test will be used."

SELECTIVITY

Admissions Rating	**95**
# of applicants	2,497
% of applicants accepted	50
% of acceptees attending	31
# accepting a place on wait list	398
% admitted from wait list	1
# of early decision applicants	110
% accepted early decision	76

FRESHMAN PROFILE

Range SAT Verbal	610-710
Average SAT Verbal	612
Range SAT Math	600-700
Average SAT Math	619
**TPR Projected Range SAT Writing*	*640-700*
Range ACT Composite	27-31
Average ACT Composite	26
Minimum Paper TOEFL	560
Minimum Computer Based TOEFL	220
Average HS GPA	3.77
% graduated top 10% of class	59
% graduated top 25% of class	92
% graduated top 50% of class	98

DEADLINES

Early decision application deadline	11/15
Early decision notification	12/15
Regular application deadline	1/15
Regular notification	4/1
Nonfall registration?	yes

APPLICANTS ALSO LOOK AT

AND OFTEN PREFER

Carleton College, Middlebury College, Pomona College, U. of California—Berkeley

AND SOMETIMES PREFER

Colorado College, Lewis—Clark State College, Occidental College

AND RARELY PREFER

Reed College, Scripps College, U. of Oregon, U. of San Diego

FINANCIAL FACTS

Financial Aid Rating	**91**
Annual tuition	$28,400
Room & Board	$7,470
Books and supplies	$1,250
Required fees	$240
% frosh rec. need-based scholarship or grant aid	48
% UG rec. need-based scholarship or grant aid	45
% frosh rec. need-based self-help aid	35
% UG rec. need-based self-help aid	41
% frosh rec. any financial aid	48
% UG rec. any financial aid	45
Avg. frosh grant	$15,080
Avg. frosh loan	$2,606
Independent 529 member?	No

WHITTIER COLLEGE

13406 PHILADELPHIA STREET, PO BOX 634, WHITTIER, CA 90608 • ADMISSIONS: 562-907-4238 • FAX: 562-907-4870

CAMPUS LIFE

Quality of Life Rating	**75**
Fire Safety Rating	**87**
Type of school	private
Environment	city

STUDENTS

Total undergrad enrollment	1,304
% male/female	43/57
% from out of state	33
% live on campus	68
% in (# of) fraternities	5 (4)
% in (# of) sororities	11 (5)
% African American	4
% Asian	10
% Caucasian	45
% Hispanic	25
% Native American	1
% international	6
# of countries represented	21

SURVEY SAYS

Small classes
Great computer facilities
Great library
Lots of beer drinking
Hard liquor is popular

ACADEMICS

Academic Rating	**86**
Calendar	4-1-4
Student/faculty ratio	13:1
Professors interesting rating	86
Professors accessible rating	87
% professors teaching UG courses	100
% classes taught by TAs	0
Most common lab size	10-19 students
Most common regular class size	10-19 students

MOST POPULAR MAJORS

Business administration/management
child development

STUDENTS SPEAK OUT

Academics

A Whittier College education is a paradigmatic small-school experience, with all its many benefits and occasional drawbacks. Students enthusiastically tell us that "the greatest strength of the school is its small size," which allows for "discussion-based classes that are always taught by a full professor, the freedom to move around on your own and challenge yourself as much as you want, [and] countless opportunities to get involved and explore your interests and talents." It also means professors have time to "genuinely care about their students and their student's success. They wonder why you are not in class and are always open for a knock at their office door and hour-long discussions." Notes one undergrad, "We get strong support from the faculty and upperclassman, who help the students with everything from writing papers to organizing schedules to adjusting to life on your own." On the downside, "There's no mega-stadium or brand new lab equipment. The school was built in the early 1900s so some of the buildings are old. But you'd be amazed how the teachers make use of everything they have." The school is upgrading facilities whenever it can; one student reports, "We have this brand-spanking new library facility that is pretty sweet, and an all-new computer lab. Not to mention the Center for Academic Success, which provides free tutoring (very helpful) and has really comfortable beanbags to chill out in." Many here warn that, "The administration side of the school is a mess! It takes students months to receive financial aid, offices do not interact to help make the process better for students, and administrators seem bothered with student requests."

Life

Whittier's size has as powerful an impact on its social life as on its academics. As one student puts it, "The joke on campus is that the school's so small that everyone knows what you did before you even do it." Undergrads report that, "Campus life seems very calm because it is such a small school and there aren't that many students. However, that does not mean it's not fun. There are campus events constantly and students participate religiously." There are also "parties just about every night" and lots of "ultra-competitive beer pong" for those so inclined. Nondrinkers in our survey say that, "As easy as it is to find them, it is also just as easy to avoid them." Like Randy Newman, students love LA, "a great place to go to college. Whittier allows you to mix suburban and urban life. You can either stay in Whittier for a movie and dinner, or go to LA for a great concert or a night at the clubs." There's also "Disneyland, Huntington Beach, and Knott's Berry Farm, all just a close drive from school." Best of all, according to many here, "The beaches are only 20 minutes away. Lots of people surf." Nearly all these activities require a car, or a friend with a car; warns one undergrad, "If you don't have a car, prepared to be completely bored on weekends and at a real disadvantage when you need to run errands such as buying food." You won't be completely stranded, though, since "Uptown Whittier is just down the street from school and has a number of shops and restaurants: several great Asian restaurants, Mexican restaurants, BBQ, pizza, burgers, gelato, a Starbucks, and a movie theater along with miscellaneous other shops."

Student Body

A lot of schools brag about the diversity of their student body, but few can match Whittier, where "we have blacks, whites, Hispanics, Asians, gays, straights, Christians, Muslims, the poor, and the very rich. The greatest thing is that even with such diversity among such a small school, everyone is extremely friendly, open to new ideas, and accepts people for who they are." Students also vary widely in the degrees of their ambition and curiosity; notes one undergrad, "There are some students that do not take advantage of the opportunities here and make you wonder how they even passed high school. But then we have Marshall and Rhodes Scholar nominees, and a majority of students who have plans for graduate school."

WHITTIER COLLEGE

FINANCIAL AID: 562-907-4285 • E-MAIL: ADMISSION@WHITTIER.EDU • WEBSITE: WWW.WHITTIER.EDU

ADMISSIONS

Very important factors considered include: Essays, secondary school record. *Important factors considered include:* Character/personal qualities, extracurricular activities, interview, recommendations, standardized test scores, talent/ability, volunteer work. *Other factors considered include:* Alumni/ae relation, class rank, geographical residence, minority status, state residency, work experience. SAT Reasoning or SAT Subject Tests required. TOEFL required of all international applicants. High school diploma is required, and GED is accepted. *Academic units required:* 4 English, 3 math, 1 science, 2 foreign language, 1 social studies. *Academic units recommended:* 3 science (2 science lab), 3 foreign language, 2 social studies, 3 history.

The Inside Word

The admissions committee at Whittier subjects each candidate to very close scrutiny. Their academic expectations aren't too high, but their interest in making good solid matches between candidates and the college is paramount. If Whittier is high on your list, make sure you put forth a serious effort to demonstrate what you want out of the college and what you'll bring to the table in return.

FINANCIAL AID

Students should submit: FAFSA, CSS/Financial Aid PROFILE. Regular filing deadline is 6/30. The Princeton Review suggests that all financial aid forms be submitted as soon as possible after 1/1. *Need-based scholarships/grants offered:* Pell, SEOG, state scholarships/grants, private scholarships, the school's own gift aid. *Loan aid offered:* Direct PLUS, FFEL Subsidized Stafford, FFEL Unsubsidized Stafford, FFEL PLUS, Federal Perkins, alternative financing loans. Applicants will be notified of awards on a rolling basis beginning on or about 2/15. Federal Work-study Program available. Institutional employment available. Off-campus job opportunities are good.

FROM THE ADMISSIONS OFFICE

"Faculty and students at Whittier share a love of learning and delight in the life of the mind. They join in understanding the value of the intellectual quest, the use of reason, and a respect for values. They seek knowledge of their own culture and the informed appreciation of other traditions, and they explore the interrelatedness of knowledge and the connections among disciplines. An extraordinary community emerges from teachers and students representing a variety of academic pursuits, individuals who have come together at Whittier in the belief that study within the liberal arts forms the best foundation for rewarding endeavor throughout a lifetime.

"Freshman applicants for fall 2006 must take the new SAT (or the ACT with the Writing component). In addition, students may submit scores from the old SAT (before March 2005) or ACT, and we will use their best scores from either test."

SELECTIVITY

Admissions Rating	**78**
# of applicants	1,987
% of applicants accepted	78
% of acceptees attending	25

FRESHMAN PROFILE

Range SAT Verbal	480-590
Average SAT Verbal	547
Range SAT Math	470-590
Average SAT Math	553
**TPR Projected Range SAT Writing*	*540-620*
Range ACT Composite	20-26
Average ACT Composite	23
Minimum Paper TOEFL	550
Minimum Computer Based TOEFL	230
Average HS GPA	3.4
% graduated top 10% of class	20
% graduated top 25% of class	39
% graduated top 50% of class	78

DEADLINES

Regular notification	rolling
Nonfall registration?	no

APPLICANTS ALSO LOOK AT

AND OFTEN PREFER
Occidental College
University of Redlands

AND SOMETIMES PREFER
Loyola Marymount University
Pitzer College

AND RARELY PREFER
Chapman University
Claremont McKenna College

FINANCIAL FACTS

Financial Aid Rating	**78**
Annual tuition	$25,838
Room & Board	$7,928
Books and supplies	$720
Required fees	$300
% frosh rec. need-based scholarship or grant aid	50
% UG rec. need-based scholarship or grant aid	56
% frosh rec. need-based self-help aid	59
% UG rec. need-based self-help aid	64
% frosh rec. any financial aid	66
% UG rec. any financial aid	69
Avg. frosh grant	$16,531
Avg. frosh loan	$7,497
Independent 529 member?	Yes

WILLAMETTE UNIVERSITY

900 STATE STREET, SALEM, OR 97301 • ADMISSIONS: 503-370-6303 • FAX: 503-375-5363

CAMPUS LIFE

Quality of Life Rating	**80**
Fire Safety Rating	**77**
Type of school	private
Affiliation	Methodist
Environment	city

STUDENTS

Total undergrad enrollment	1,876
% male/female	45/55
% from out of state	58
% from public high school	69
% live on campus	69
% in (# of) fraternities	30 (5)
% in (# of) sororities	29 (3)
% African American	2
% Asian	6
% Caucasian	62
% Hispanic	5
% Native American	1

SURVEY SAYS

Small classes
Lab facilities are great
Great computer facilities
Great library
Students are friendly

ACADEMICS

Academic Rating	**84**
Calendar	semester
Student/faculty ratio	11:1
Professors interesting rating	89
Professors accessible rating	87
% professors teaching UG courses	100
% classes taught by TAs	0
Most common lab size	fewer than 10 students
Most common regular class size	10-19 students

MOST POPULAR MAJORS

Political science and government
psychology

STUDENTS SPEAK OUT

Academics

"Willamette is about balance," writes one of the many satisfied undergraduates we surveyed at this small liberal arts school in Oregon. "The academics are outstanding, music is huge, sports are great, and fun is abounding." Completing the picture is a healthy complement of "community service and political awareness." Students at Willamette (WU) have many opportunities to share their experiences and opinions, since "the classes are mostly discussion-based and the professors are really open. There is not a professor in my major that I don't know by first name or by nickname even," notes one satisfied student. The professors, "brilliant individuals who are at the same time laid-back and humorous," administer an academic regimen that "can be very rigorous, depending on your course load for the semester." Those who fall behind find that "there is a lot of one-on-one advising that clears up any confusion that a student might be experiencing in a class." Noted one undergrad, "I never thought it would actually be easier to meet professors for coffee and chat about assignments or current events than it was at my high school of 120 students—but it is!" Students also praise the "great study abroad experiences" and internship opportunities, especially in government. "Many of us intern at the State Capitol right across the street. It's a good source of internships and development," reports one student.

Life

About one-third of the Willamette student body belongs to a fraternity or sorority. It is no wonder, then, that "the Greek system seems to be the nucleus of the social life, at WU. Still, there's a lot of other ways to get involved socially, for example, through student government and intramural sports." Another undergraduate agrees, "We have lots of entertainment for such a small school." Those events are remarkably varied. Students report, "There are music-department events typically twice a month and two plays a semester on campus, as well as an amateur open-mic night at the student-run coffee shop every month. You can watch an outdoor movie, go to a Slip 'N Slide in the quad, or play a pickup game of ultimate Frisbee or soccer. In the spring, we like to wade in the Mill Stream that flows through campus." Most students have no trouble finding ways to fill their time; as one student tells us, "It seems like everyone at Willamette has at least one or two causes that sort of become their lives, whether it's political/social, or something more general, like a major, and that's kind of how people are known. 'Oh, that's so-and-so. She's a sociology major, and she's really involved in the College Democrats.'" The city of Portland is only half an hour away, and many students head there on weekends. Others take advantage of the many opportunities for outdoor activities in the surrounding area.

Student Body

The Willamette student body includes "lots of hippies, lots of preps, lots of nerds, and meatheads, like any other school. But I'd say that most of the students here want to learn, want to grow, want to challenge themselves." This does not apply just in the classrooms. "Most students are very busy and involved in a variety of activities: academic, religious, social, athletic, internships, jobs, clubs, etc." The hefty price tag attached to a Willamette education means that "the typical student has lots of money and worries about whether or not they have the latest clothing or enough extracurriculars to make an impression. Atypical students are plentiful, and they tend to all socialize amongst each other." Similarly, another student adds that many students at "Willamette are strongly conservative, but there is a rampant liberal underground." Asian students make up the largest minority in the student body; "there are many Japanese students because Willamette is associated with the Tokyo International University Academy (TIUA)," explains one undergrad.

FINANCIAL AID: 503-370-6273 • E-MAIL: LIBARTS@WILLAMETTE.EDU • WEBSITE: WWW.WILLAMETTE.EDU

ADMISSIONS

Very important factors considered include: Class rank, recommendations, secondary school record, standardized test scores. *Important factors considered include:* Character/personal qualities, essays, extracurricular activities, interview, talent/ability. *Other factors considered include:* Alumni/ae relation, geographical residence, minority status, volunteer work, work experience. SAT Reasoning or ACT required. TOEFL required of all international applicants. High school diploma is required, and GED is accepted. *Academic units recommended:* 4 English, 4 math, 3 science, 3 foreign language, 3 social studies.

The Inside Word

Willamette's admissions process is relatively standard for small liberal arts colleges. Extracurriculars, recommendations, and essays help the admissions committee do some matchmaking, but ultimately it's a candidate's grades that determine admissibility.

FINANCIAL AID

Students should submit: FAFSA, CSS/Financial Aid PROFILE. The Princeton Review suggests that all financial aid forms be submitted as soon as possible after 1/1. *Need-based scholarships/grants offered:* Pell, SEOG, state scholarships/grants, private scholarships, the school's own gift aid, United Negro College Fund. *Loan aid offered:* FFEL Subsidized Stafford, FFEL Unsubsidized Stafford, FFEL PLUS, Federal Perkins, state loans, private loans. Applicants will be notified of awards on or about 4/1. Federal Work-study Program available. Institutional employment available. Off-campus job opportunities are good.

FROM THE ADMISSIONS OFFICE

"And here are what other students have to say about the Willamette experience: 'What I like most about Willamette is the feeling of openness. The professors are open to new ideas and students challenging them,' says Fulbright Scholar Alex Dukalskis 2004, 'and the students are generally curious and interested in learning.' Freshman Jessa Fox concurs: 'I think the people here are very passionate—they all have something they really care about.' Reflecting on the university's motto, sociology major Amber Simonton agrees: 'I think the idea behind the school—existing in order to serve others and to impact the greater world and society around you—is a wonderful basis for an education.' Graduating senior Justin Brown reflected on the value of his Willamette experience and concluded, 'I've totally changed since I came here. I'm a lot more independent-minded and I feel like my perspective has widened. I've learned to look at the world and see what needs to be changed.'

"All freshman applicants for fall 2006 must submit either the new SAT or the ACT with Writing section."

SELECTIVITY

Admissions Rating	**90**
# of applicants	2,489
% of applicants accepted	76
% of acceptees attending	27
# accepting a place on wait list	161
% admitted from wait list	16

FRESHMAN PROFILE

Range SAT Verbal	580-680
Average SAT Verbal	619
Range SAT Math	580-660
Average SAT Math	628
**TPR Projected Range SAT Writing*	*620-680*
Range ACT Composite	25-30
Average ACT Composite	27
Minimum Paper TOEFL	550
Minimum Computer Based TOEFL	213
Average HS GPA	3.75
% graduated top 10% of class	47
% graduated top 25% of class	79
% graduated top 50% of class	96

DEADLINES

Regular application deadline	2/1
Regular notification	4/1
Nonfall registration?	yes

APPLICANTS ALSO LOOK AT

AND OFTEN PREFER
Whitman College

AND SOMETIMES PREFER
Lewis & Clark College
University of Oregon
University of Puget Sound

AND RARELY PREFER
Pacific University
Portland State University
Seattle University
Southern Oregon University

FINANCIAL FACTS

Financial Aid Rating	**78**
Annual tuition	$28,416
Room & Board	$7,000
Books and supplies	$800
% frosh rec. need-based scholarship or grant aid	65
% UG rec. need-based scholarship or grant aid	64
% frosh rec. need-based self-help aid	54
% UG rec. need-based self-help aid	56
Independent 529 member?	Yes

WILLIAM JEWELL COLLEGE

500 COLLEGE HILL, LIBERTY, MO 64068 • ADMISSIONS: 816-415-7511 • FAX: 816-415-5040 • 888-2-JEWELL

CAMPUS LIFE

Quality of Life Rating	**96**
Fire Safety Rating	**60**
Type of school	private
Affiliation	Baptist
Environment	town

STUDENTS

Total undergrad enrollment	1,310
% male/female	41/59
% from out of state	16
% from public high school	90
% live on campus	62
% in (# of) fraternities	33 (3)
% in (# of) sororities	35 (4)
% African American	4
% Asian	1
% Caucasian	90
% Hispanic	2
% Native American	1
% international	1
# of countries represented	12

SURVEY SAYS

Small classes
Students are friendly
Students get along with local community
Students are happy
Frats and sororities dominate social scene
Very little drug use

ACADEMICS

Academic Rating	**89**
Calendar	semester
Student/faculty ratio	11:1
Professors interesting rating	95
Professors accessible rating	92
% professors teaching UG courses	100
% classes taught by TAs	0
Most common lab size	10-19 students
Most common regular class size	fewer than 10 students

MOST POPULAR MAJORS

Business administration/management
communications studies/speech communication and rhetoric
psychology

STUDENTS SPEAK OUT

Academics

A freshman majoring in political science reports, "Students at William Jewell College often believe that they are attending one of the top colleges in the Midwest, if not the United States, and receiving an Ivy League-quality education. That may be stretching it a bit, but I don't think that it's too far from the truth." This historically Baptist college offers a "highly selective and extremely intense" Oxbridge Honors Program, which subjects students to instruction English tutorial style. The nursing, music, education, and political science departments draw the most students, though class sizes across disciplines are often kept under 20. Nearly everyone emphasizes how actively welcomed they are made to feel by Jewell administrators. A freshman remembers, "They were so concerned with whether or not I was going to be happy." The President and his wife host a Christmas party complete with snickerdoodles, and professors are known for their "understanding of personal issues." One sophomore writes, "If you have something come up in your life or need a little break for some reason, professors will work with you to help you through." Some students accuse professors of "pushing their beliefs on everyone [or] trying to convert people" religiously and politically. Other undergraduates see just the opposite taking place: "My professors like to spark a conversation then get out of it and let the students hash it out," recounts a chemistry major. Either way, by getting through WJC, "You can't help but be a more informed and complete contributor to the world around you."

Life

Students who arrive expecting an oasis of godly behavior in a heathen world may be disappointed. "I thought it was a Christian School—as it turns out I was wrong." In this semi-religious environment, rules may govern visitation, but you can get a beer if you want one. Members of fraternities claim, "It is not your typical party-hard/bad grades Greek life." Watch for the new Greek Strategic Plan to "help all of us become undivided" and present a milder Greek image. A senior reminds readers, "Just because I am a Christian doesn't mean I don't get out and have good, clean fun." Students frequent something called "Worship Jams," as well as on-campus concerts booked by College Union Activities. A freshman's typical evening entails "hanging out in the dorm because we are all broke. We also play a lot of pranks." Off-campus destinations in Liberty include the Corner Bar for drinks or Steak and Shake for late-night eats. For the culturally inclined, the Harriman Arts Program arranges student tickets for ballet and orchestra performances 20 minutes away in Kansas City.

Student Body

The distinctive quality of the Jewell student body is a repeated emphasis on thoughtfulness and self-reflection. "Overall, I live with students who want to use their passions in life to positively change society." Another student adds, "It doesn't matter what it is that you believe, as long as you have looked down every road and sought out every option before reaching a complete and final decision." It seems that Jewell conservatives think the school is too liberal, and vice versa. "We all have some sort of political views and talk about the world and the state of the country." Discussions get interesting because the split is about 50/50 between actively practicing Christians and the Baptists by birth only. The Republican/Democrat line doesn't coincide exactly, but close. An African American student finds it "exhausting being black here," and many people recognize a need for improved representation "of our pluralistic society." Finally, with a slightly lopsided gender ratio, it sometimes feels more like an all-girls' school than a coed one.

FINANCIAL AID: 888-2-JEWELL • E-MAIL: ADMISSION@WILLIAM.JEWELL.EDU • WEBSITE: WWW.JEWELL.EDU

ADMISSIONS

Very important factors considered include: Class rank, secondary school record, standardized test scores. *Important factors considered include:* Character/personal qualities, essays, extracurricular activities, interview, recommendations, talent/ability. *Other factors considered include:* Alumni/ae relation, minority status, volunteer work, work experience. SAT Reasoning or ACT required. TOEFL required of all international applicants. High school diploma is required, and GED is accepted. *Academic units recommended:* 4 English, 3 math, 3 science (1 science lab), 2 foreign language, 4 social studies.

The Inside Word

Admission to William Jewell requires the usual suspects: solid grades and test scores. The college is competitive, but admission is not out of reach for the average student. Once admitted, undergrads benefit from William Jewell's leading efforts in experiential learning.

FINANCIAL AID

Students should submit: FAFSA, institution's own financial aid form. The Princeton Review suggests that all financial aid forms be submitted as soon as possible after 1/1. *Need-based scholarships/grants offered:* Pell, SEOG, state scholarships/grants, the school's own gift aid. *Loan aid offered:* FFEL Subsidized Stafford, FFEL Unsubsidized Stafford, FFEL PLUS, Federal Perkins, Federal Nursing, nonfederal alternative loans. Applicants will be notified of awards on a rolling basis beginning on or about 1/31. Federal Work-study Program available. Off-campus job opportunities are good.

FROM THE ADMISSIONS OFFICE

"'Founded in 1849, William Jewell College offers students an outstanding liberal arts education and a unique focus on cultivating leadership within an environment that values Christian ideals and spiritual growth. Its' beautiful campus is perched above the town of Liberty, Missouri, and offers students all the amenities of a beautiful residential campus with exceptional recreational and athletic facilities. The college is just 20 minutes from downtown Kansas City.

"Enrollment stands at approximately 1,300 full-time students. The student body has representation from approximately 36 states and 12 foreign countries. International programs in Europe, Australia, Central and South America, and Asia, allow Jewell students to study at some of the world's great universities. The Oxbridge Honors Program, recognized as one of the best study abroad opportunities in the nation, combines British tutorial methods of instruction with opportunities for a year of study in Oxford or Cambridge.

"Jewell continues to earn it reputation as a campus of achievement. Since being named Time Magazine's "Liberal Arts College of the Year" in 2001–2002, the school has seen its students earn one Marshall Scholarship, two Truman Scholarships, two Goldwater Scholarships and two spots on USA Today's All USA College Academic Team. The college's Harriman Arts Program is considered the Midwest's premiere program in the performing arts. The renowned Pryor Leadership Studies Program allows students to enhance their leadership skills across the curriculum.

"William Jewell College will not require the new Writing section of the ACT or SAT. As a part of the application process students will be required to submit a separate essay. William Jewell does not use SAT Subject Tests."

SELECTIVITY

Admissions Rating	**87**
# of applicants	1,127
% of applicants accepted	73
% of acceptees attending	40

FRESHMAN PROFILE

Range SAT Verbal	550-700
Range SAT Math	540-670
**TPR Projected Range SAT Writing*	*600-700*
Range ACT Composite	22-27
Average ACT Composite	25
Minimum Paper TOEFL	550
Minimum Computer Based TOEFL	213
Average HS GPA	3.7
% graduated top 10% of class	32
% graduated top 25% of class	60
% graduated top 50% of class	91

DEADLINES

Regular application deadline	8/15
Regular notification	rolling
Nonfall registration?	yes

FINANCIAL FACTS

Financial Aid Rating	**60**
Annual tuition	$18,500
Room & Board	$5,350
Books and supplies	$750
Required fees	$300
% frosh rec. need-based scholarship or grant aid	66
% UG rec. need-based scholarship or grant aid	66
% frosh rec. need-based self-help aid	51
% UG rec. need-based self-help aid	51
% frosh rec. any financial aid	98
% UG rec. any financial aid	98
Avg. frosh grant	$9,834
Avg. frosh loan	$3,633
Independent 529 member?	No

WILLIAMS COLLEGE

33 STETSON COURT, WILLIAMSTOWN, MA 01267 • ADMISSIONS: 413-597-2211 • FAX: 413-597-4052

CAMPUS LIFE

Quality of Life Rating	**96**
Fire Safety Rating	**94**
Type of school	private
Environment	village

STUDENTS

Total undergrad enrollment	1,931
% male/female	50/50
% from out of state	84
% from public high school	54
% live on campus	93
% African American	10
% Asian	9
% Caucasian	67
% Hispanic	8
% international	6
# of countries represented	63

SURVEY SAYS

Small classes
Campus feels safe
Everyone loves the Ephs
Frats and sororities are unpopular or nonexistent

ACADEMICS

Academic Rating	**99**
Calendar	4-1-4
Student/faculty ratio	7:1
Professors interesting rating	96
Professors accessible rating	91
% professors teaching UG courses	100
% classes taught by TAs	0
Most common lab size	10-19 students
Most common regular class size	fewer than 10 students

MOST POPULAR MAJORS

Art/art studies
economics
political science and government

STUDENTS SPEAK OUT

Academics

"The academics are quite rigorous—expect to spend six hours a day studying—and the professors definitely challenge you" at Williams College, a small liberal arts school in the northwestern corner of Massachusetts. Undergrads insist, however, that "that's what you come here for." A strong campus community makes Williams "a perfect stepping stone from high school to the real world. If you feel you can become obscenely excited at the sight of a purple cow (our mascot); love to get to know professors, classmates and staff on a personal level; and enjoy sports at all, be it as a spectator, athlete, or would-be athlete, Williams is your nirvana." Undergrads assure us that "there's absolutely no place better for an undergraduate to study any of the hard sciences or art history" and that "math, English, economics, and the visual and performing arts are also very strong." Coursework "really pushes you to delve deep into the material and encourages original thinking," allowing students "to learn a lot, more maybe than you even think possible." Undergrads are especially enthusiastic about Williams' winter study program, "a month where you take one relatively low-stress class and get to go snowboarding and hang out a lot. My friends and I like to think of it as our reward for having lived through finals." One student says, "Williams combines stellar academics with a beautiful campus, friendly atmosphere, and caring administration that jump to make students as happy as possible. I've never seen a happier group of people in my life."

Life

"Williams is in the middle of some very beautiful, although very isolated, countryside" in Williamstown, which "is not exactly a metropolis." Reports one student, "Because Williamstown pretty much closes at 5:00 P.M., the college knows it has to provide all of our entertainment, and it does a pretty great job of it. Movies, plays, concerts, and lectures can be found on campus almost every night of the week, and each weekend a few student organizations get $500 to throw all-campus parties." Athletics occupy the minds of many undergrads; the intercollegiate teams "are particularly strong," "intramural sports are big, as is just playing for fun," and the surrounding area is especially amenable to outdoor fun. One student notes, "We enjoy the outdoors year round. On a random Friday in October, the President continues a two-hundred-year tradition by declaring it 'Mountain Day'; classes are cancelled and the majority of the student body heads to the top of our mountain to enjoy the fall colors, the outdoors, and each other! In Winter, most everyone skis or snowboards at a local ski mountain, 15 minutes away from campus." As one student puts it, "I've never seen so many physically active people in my life. It's actually inspired me to start going to the gym." Williams' strong sense of community receives a boost from the "JA entry system, under which 15 to 25 freshmen live in 'entries' with two 'JAs.' The JAs are basically upperclassmen who volunteer to be cool junior friends to all of the frosh on campus. The entry system eases the transition from high school to college, as you have a core group of friends from the first day of school on." The dorms, we're told, "are awesome, with nice touches that make dorm life very comfortable and non-institutional."

Student Body

Williams undergrads describe themselves as "exceptionally driven and intelligent, yet not dorky or unsociable." Ephs (pronounced "Eefs," short for the school's founder, Ephraim Williams) "love politics, scientific research, reading," and for some, "getting plastered after a rough week." Because of the school's secluded mountain location, "students tend to be outdoors-types, and sports are big, although we don't have typical college 'jocks.' Everyone participates at their level. The presence of sports on campus means that most students are tremendously motivated, disciplined, and hard-working, not to mention fit." While "there is a bit of segregation between the jocks and the artsy students, there isn't ever any tension" between the two groups.

Williams College

Financial Aid: 413-597-4181 • E-mail: admission@williams.edu • Website: www.williams.edu

ADMISSIONS

Very important factors considered include: Essays, recommendations, secondary school record, standardized test scores. *Important factors considered include:* Class rank, extracurricular activities, talent/ability. *Other factors considered include:* Alumni/ae relation, character/personal qualities, geographical residence, minority status, volunteer work, work experience. SAT Reasoning and SAT Subject Tests or ACT required. High school diploma or equivalent is not required. *Academic units recommended:* 4 English, 4 math, 3 science (3 science lab), 4 foreign language, 3 social studies.

The Inside Word

As is typical of highly selective colleges, at Williams high grades and test scores work more as qualifiers than to determine admissibility. Beyond a strong record of achievement, evidence of intellectual curiosity, noteworthy nonacademic talents, and a noncollege family background are some aspects of a candidate's application that might make for an offer of admission. But there are no guarantees—the evaluation process here is rigorous. The admissions committee (the entire admissions staff) discusses each candidate in comparison to the entire applicant pool. The pool is divided alphabetically for individual reading; after weak candidates are eliminated, those who remain undergo additional evaluations by different members of the staff. Admission decisions must be confirmed by the agreement of a plurality of the committee. Such close scrutiny demands a well-prepared candidate and application.

FINANCIAL AID

Students should submit: FAFSA, CSS/Financial Aid PROFILE. The Princeton Review suggests that all financial aid forms be submitted as soon as possible after 1/1. *Need-based scholarships/grants offered:* Pell, SEOG, state scholarships/grants, private scholarships, the school's own gift aid. *Loan aid offered:* Direct Subsidized Stafford, Direct Unsubsidized Stafford, Direct PLUS, Federal Perkins, college/university loans from institutional funds. Applicants will be notified of awards on or about 4/1. Federal Work-study Program available. Institutional employment available. Off-campus job opportunities are fair.

FROM THE ADMISSIONS OFFICE

"Special course offerings at Williams include Oxford-style tutorials, where students (in teams of two) research and defend ideas, engaging in weekly debate with a faculty tutor.Annually 30 Williams students devote a full year to the tutorial method of study at Oxford; half of Williams students pursue overseas education. Four weeks of Winter Study each January provide time for individualized projects, research, and novel fields of study. Students compete in 32 Division III athletic teams, perform in 25 musical groups, stage 10 theatrical productions, and volunteer in 30 service organizations. The college receives several million dollars annually for undergraduate science research and equipment. The town offers two distinguished art museums, and 2,200 forest acres—complete with a treetop canopy walkway—for environmental research and recreation.

"For fall 2006, students are required to submit either the new SAT or the ACT including the optional Writing section. Students may also submit scores from the old SAT and ACT. Applicants should also submit scores from any two SAT Subject Tests."

SELECTIVITY

Admissions Rating	**98**
# of applicants	5,705
% of applicants accepted	19
% of acceptees attending	49
# of early decision applicants	214
% accepted early decision	38

FRESHMAN PROFILE

Range SAT Verbal	660-760
Average SAT Verbal	705
Range SAT Math	670-760
Average SAT Math	708
**TPR Projected Range SAT Writing*	*670-740*
Average ACT Composite	32
% graduated top 10% of class	85
% graduated top 25% of class	97
% graduated top 50% of class	100

DEADLINES

Early decision application deadline	11/10
Early decision notification	12/15
Regular application deadline	1/1
Regular notification	4/9
Nonfall registration?	no

APPLICANTS ALSO LOOK AT

AND OFTEN PREFER

Harvard College
Massachusetts Institute of Technology
Princeton University
Stanford University
Yale University

AND SOMETIMES PREFER

Amherst College
Brown University
Dartmouth College

AND RARELY PREFER

Colgate University
Hamilton College
Haverford College
Middlebury College

FINANCIAL FACTS

Financial Aid Rating	**99**
Annual tuition	$29,786
Room & Board	$8,110
Books and supplies	$800
Required fees	$204
% frosh rec. need-based scholarship or grant aid	41
% UG rec. need-based scholarship or grant aid	40
% frosh rec. need-based self-help aid	41
% UG rec. need-based self-help aid	42
% frosh rec. any financial aid	64
% UG rec. any financial aid	70
Avg. frosh grant	$26,700
Avg. frosh loan	$2,468
Independent 529 member?	No

WITTENBERG UNIVERSITY

PO Box 720, Springfield, OH 45501 • Admissions: 800-677-7558 • Fax: 937-327-6379

CAMPUS LIFE

Quality of Life Rating	**85**
Fire Safety Rating	**75**
Type of school	private
Affiliation	Lutheran
Environment	town

STUDENTS

Total undergrad enrollment	2,051
% male/female	44/56
% from out of state	25
% from public high school	78
% live on campus	86
% in (# of) fraternities	16 (6)
% in (# of) sororities	29 (6)
% African American	6
% Asian	2
% Caucasian	81
% Hispanic	1

SURVEY SAYS

Small classes
Lab facilities are great
Students are friendly
Students are happy
Lots of beer drinking

ACADEMICS

Academic Rating	**84**
Calendar	semester
Student/faculty ratio	12:1
Professors interesting rating	93
Professors accessible rating	96
% professors teaching UG courses	100
% classes taught by TAs	0
Most common lab size	10-19 students
Most common regular class size	10-19 students

MOST POPULAR MAJORS

Biological and physical sciences
business/commerce
teacher education, multiple levels

STUDENTS SPEAK OUT

Academics

Often described as "a small university with a family feel," Wittenberg offers the "opportunities and challenges of a large school on a small, close-knit campus," students here report. Explains one satisfied undergrad, "Academically, Witt gives me what I wanted in high school but never received: highly focused and intense courses that challenge me but don't destroy the confidence in how I'm handling the class." Witt achieves this happy balance by providing "small classes, accessible faculty, a friendly staff, the personal attention needed to grow as a person and an academic, and a great social scene." Popular programs in biology, political science, and education all rank high here; students also praise the less-popular but equally strong marine and aquatic biology program. Undergrads point out that "since this is a liberal arts school, we are required to take general education courses. Professors are extremely helpful in getting all of your requirements filled, not only for generals but for the intended major." Profs also "all absolutely love to teach, are intrigued by class discussions, and are willing to work with you as an individual student." As a result, "this is definitely not a school where you are only known by your student ID number." The administration is "always open to students' input and ideas" and Witt's learning environment "is one that fosters motivated and high-achieving students."

Life

At Wittenberg, you'll find "the perfect balance of academics and extracurriculars," students agree, reporting that Witt is "a very social campus that is all about hanging out and having a good time." Undergrads "study pretty hard during the week," then "Saturday nights are the party nights because all the athletic teams have parties after their games." That's when "everyone parties pretty hard, but only if they want to." We're told that most RAs here are willing to let their residents enjoy a party or two," which makes good times easy to come by. Campus life offers "clubs and groups for whatever you are interested in and more," as well as "an awesome Frisbee™ golf course" and "sororities and frats that are pretty popular." In addition, the school boasts "really strong sports for a Division III school and we take our athletics pretty seriously." As proof, "we have a lot of students who could play at Division I schools who choose to come here." In 2002–2003, women's teams won championships in field hockey, volleyball, and basketball. Undergrads brag that Witt's campus is "gorgeous all year round; in the spring there are flowers everywhere, and in the fall the trees turn amazing colors." Even so, most agree that it's "nice to get off campus occasionally. The Kuss Performing Arts Center in Springfield brings in great entertainment. There's also putt-putt, movies, restaurants, shopping, and a great bike trail in town. Yellow Springs, a small town only about 20 minutes away, has a great arts theater and quaint shops." Dayton and Columbus "are just down the road for bigger-city entertainment."

Student Body

Witt undergrads "are generally well-rounded and have strengths and interests in many areas; arts, politics, athletics, etc. It's not uncommon to find a jock that plays the trumpet and is involved in social awareness organizations." Witt fields 23 intercollegiate teams, which means lots of athletic-types mixed among the small student population. "Friendly and outgoing" describe most Witt students, regardless of their interests: "You can't walk to class without seeing 10 people you know and saying hi to about 20 more." "Preppy but not over-the-top preppy" is the overwhelming style and "many students at Witt are wealthy and (some are) legacies." Overall, "people are free-spirited and laid back." They "work hard for their classes but also like to have a good time." There is a sizeable group of very religious students who shun the party scene but enjoy extracurricular life all the same. Students say it is refreshing that at Witt, just about everyone "is proud of the school. When you walk into your class, over three-fourths the students will have on some school apparel."

FINANCIAL AID: 800-677-7558 • E-MAIL: ADMISSION@WITTENBERG.EDU • WEBSITE: WWW.WITTENBERG.EDU

ADMISSIONS

Very important factors considered include: Class rank, essays, interview, recommendations, secondary school record. *Important factors considered include:* Character/personal qualities, extracurricular activities, talent/ability, volunteer work. *Other factors considered include:* Alumni/ae relation, work experience. SAT Reasoning or ACT required. TOEFL required of all international applicants. High school diploma is required, and GED is accepted. *Academic units required:* 4 English, 3 math, 3 science (2 science lab), 2 foreign language, 2 history. *Academic units recommended:* 4 English, 4 math, 4 science (2 science lab), 3 foreign language, 3 history.

The Inside Word

Wittenberg's applicant pool is small but quite solid coming off of a couple of strong years. Students who haven't successfully reached an above-average academic level in high school will meet with little success in the admissions process. Candidate evaluation is thorough and personal; applicants should devote serious attention to all aspects of their candidacy.

FINANCIAL AID

Students should submit: FAFSA. The Princeton Review suggests that all financial aid forms be submitted as soon as possible after 1/1. *Need-based scholarships/grants offered:* Pell, SEOG, state scholarships/grants, private scholarships, the school's own gift aid. *Loan aid offered:* FFEL Subsidized Stafford, FFEL Unsubsidized Stafford, FFEL PLUS, Federal Perkins, college/university loans from institutional funds. Applicants will be notified of awards on or about 3/1. Off-campus job opportunities are excellent.

FROM THE ADMISSIONS OFFICE

"At Wittenberg, we believe that helping you to achieve symmetry demands a special environment, a setting where you can refine your definition of self yet gain exposure to the varied kinds of knowledge, people, views, activities, options, and ideas that add richness to our lives. Wittenberg is a university where students are able to thrive in a small campus environment with many opportunities for intellectual and personal growth in and out of the classroom. Campus life is as diverse as the interests of our students. Wittenberg attracts students from all over the United States and from many other countries. Historically, the university has been committed to geographical, educational, cultural, and religious diversity. With their varied backgrounds and interests, Wittenberg students have helped initiate many of the more than 125 student organizations that are active on campus. The students will be the first to tell you there's never a lack of things to do on or near the campus any day of the week, if you're willing to get involved.

"Wittenberg University requires freshman applicants to submit scores from the old or new SAT. Students may also choose to submit scores from the ACT (with or without the Writing component) in lieu of the SAT."

SELECTIVITY

Admissions Rating	**82**
# of applicants	2,903
% of applicants accepted	81
% of acceptees attending	25
# of early decision applicants	31
% accepted early decision	69

FRESHMAN PROFILE

Range SAT Verbal	510-630
Average SAT Verbal	566
Range SAT Math	510-620
Average SAT Math	568
**TPR Projected Range SAT Writing*	*570-650*
Range ACT Composite	21-27
Average ACT Composite	24
Minimum Paper TOEFL	550
Minimum Computer Based TOEFL	213
Average HS GPA	3.42
% graduated top 10% of class	28
% graduated top 25% of class	56
% graduated top 50% of class	85

DEADLINES

Early decision application deadline	11/15
Early decision notification	11/15
Regular application deadline	3/15
Regular notification	rolling
Nonfall registration?	yes

APPLICANTS ALSO LOOK AT

AND OFTEN PREFER
Miami University

AND SOMETIMES PREFER
Allegheny College, The College of Wooster, Denison University, DePauw University, Ohio State University—Columbus, Ohio Wesleyan University

AND RARELY PREFER
Capital University, Gettysburg College, Ohio Northern University

FINANCIAL FACTS

Financial Aid Rating	**69**
Annual tuition	$27,342
Room & Board	$7,054
Books and supplies	$800
Required fees	$200
% frosh rec. need-based scholarship or grant aid	75
% UG rec. need-based scholarship or grant aid	72
% frosh rec. need-based self-help aid	56
% UG rec. need-based self-help aid	55
% frosh rec. any financial aid	98
% UG rec. any financial aid	99
Avg. frosh grant	$16,150
Avg. frosh loan	$3,226
Independent 529 member?	Yes

WOFFORD COLLEGE

429 North Church Street, Spartanburg, SC 29303-3663 • Admissions: 864-597-4130 • Fax: 864-597-4147

CAMPUS LIFE

Quality of Life Rating	**83**
Fire Safety Rating	**60**
Type of school	private
Affiliation	Methodist
Environment	city

STUDENTS

Total undergrad enrollment	1,158
% male/female	51/49
% from out of state	35
% from public high school	72
% live on campus	88
% in (# of) fraternities	50 (8)
% in (# of) sororities	60 (4)
% African American	7
% Asian	2
% Caucasian	89
% Hispanic	1

SURVEY SAYS

Small classes
Lab facilities are great
Great computer facilities
Athletic facilities are great
Frats and sororities dominate social scene
Lots of beer drinking
Hard liquor is popular

ACADEMICS

Academic Rating	**89**
Calendar	4-1-4
Student/faculty ratio	12:1
Professors interesting rating	95
Professors accessible rating	94
% professors teaching UG courses	94
% classes taught by TAs	0
Most common regular class size	10-19 students

MOST POPULAR MAJORS

Biology/biological sciences
business/managerial economics
political science and government

STUDENTS SPEAK OUT

Academics

Wofford College, which has a strong history of preparing students for careers in law, the ministry, medicine, and other health sciences, continues to enjoy "a very good regional reputation," well after it passed its 150th anniversary. While this Old South school is also well known for its aristocratic student body, Wofford is by no means a country club. On the contrary, "The school is known as rigorous, and it lives up to its reputation. There's one thing for sure: When you finish a class after a final, you never think to yourself, 'Hey, that wasn't that bad.'" Students warn that "the workload is huge, and most classes involve a lot of time outside class" and that "the conflicts with tests and papers are sometimes bad when they all come due at once." Most, however, approve of the "Wofford way," explaining that "tough studies and hard teachers make the student better prepared for life." Students here know that whatever support they need to make it through will be provided them. "Wofford is a place where you are encouraged to do your best because you know that the administration and faculty care about you and expect your best," explains one student. "I'm challenged here every day, but I know that if I ever have trouble I can call my professor or go by his/her office, and they're more than willing to help." Also, "tutors are easily accessible." "Great opportunity to travel abroad" further helps to take the sting off the demands of Wofford academics. Sums up one undergrad, "Wofford has been the most difficult challenge that I have faced in my life. I have had to fight for every grade that I've gotten, but it's taught me a lot about myself and life."

Life

"Not many people go out during the week because there is so much studying that has to be done," students at Wofford agree. Weekends, however, are a different story. "From Thursday night to Saturday night everyone drinks well into the night and sleeps during the day to go back out and drink that night." And where does all this partying occur? At the Greek houses, mostly; students tell us that "social life revolves around the fraternity row on the weekends." Those with less bibulous inclinations appreciate the fact that "it's not like you are totally out of it here if you don't drink. There are plenty of students who don't drink and still have a good time." Some here skip the Greek houses entirely and "simply unwind at the end of the week by going to a movie or to the mall or just out to eat with friends." Others "are very active in the community-service projects, Habitat for Humanity, lots of stuff." Still others "may go mountain climbing or kayaking for the day on the weekend. On weekdays, we'll head to the movies, out to eat, possibly a pickup game of soccer, or even just grab some friends and head to the gym to socialize while pretending to work out." Students tout the "top-notch athletic facilities" and list the "athletic programs and reputations," especially varsity football and basketball, among the school's strengths. Hometown Spartanburg, unfortunately, doesn't offer much in the way of diversion. "People also sometimes go to Greenville for a little bigger city. Sometimes they go to Asheville or Charlotte." And sometimes those places come to them: "Students from surrounding larger universities come to Wofford a lot for various parties/special weekends," reports one student.

Student Body

"Most of the students here are alike," Wofford undergrads readily concede. "The atypical student really stands out." Nearly all the "well-dressed and well-put-together," "preppy" students here are "rich, Republican, and very southern. They generally come from good, well-established families." The men are "shaggy-haired, preppy-as-it-gets, frat-tastic guys: pink golf shirts, oxford shirts with their initials on the pocket, and boat shoes required! They study hard, but live to drink and party." The women are "Baptist; blond-haired; 'Father, I love you, I need more money;' dot-the-i's-with-hearts girls." Wofford is home to lots of "second- or third-generation Wofford students."

WOFFORD COLLEGE

FINANCIAL AID: 864-597-4160 • E-MAIL: ADMISSIONS@WOFFORD.EDU • WEBSITE: WWW.WOFFORD.EDU

ADMISSIONS

Very important factors considered include: Secondary school record. *Important factors considered include:* Alumni/ae relation, character/personal qualities, class rank, essays, extracurricular activities, minority status, standardized test scores, talent/ability, volunteer work. *Other factors considered include:* Geographical residence, interview, recommendations, work experience. SAT Reasoning or ACT required. TOEFL required of all international applicants. High school diploma is required, and GED is accepted. *Academic units recommended:* 4 English, 4 math, 3 science lab, 3 foreign language, 3 social studies, 3 academic electives.

The Inside Word

Wofford is under-recognized among excellent college options in the South. Matchmaking plays a large part in the decisions of the admissions committee, which means that it takes much more than just above-average grades and solid test scores to get admitted. The admissions staff is friendly and eager to help students put their best foot forward in the process. Wofford is a particularly good choice for those who, while strong academically, are not likely candidates for admission to Duke and other top southern schools.

FINANCIAL AID

Students should submit: FAFSA. The Princeton Review suggests that all financial aid forms be submitted as soon as possible after 1/1. *Need-based scholarships/grants offered:* Pell, SEOG, state scholarships/grants, private scholarships, the school's own gift aid. *Loan aid offered:* FFEL Subsidized Stafford, FFEL Unsubsidized Stafford, FFEL PLUS, Federal Perkins, state loans. Applicants will be notified of awards on or about 3/31.

FROM THE ADMISSIONS OFFICE

"Approaching the end of his first year in office in the spring of 2001, Wofford President Benjamin Dunlap (a Rhodes scholar and Harvard PhD) asked the faculty, 'If you had the assurance of sufficient time and institutional support to teach the sort of course you've always dreamed of, what would you do?' In response, using grants from the Andrew Mellon and National Science Foundations, Wofford faculty created approximately 50 new courses and almost a dozen new interdisciplinary course sequences. Some of the new courses are 'learning communities,' the prototype for which was fashioned by a biologist and an English professor on 'the nature and culture of water.' A Spanish language course is taught in conjunction with a Latin American and Caribbean history course and a sociology course featuring fieldwork in the local Hispanic community. Handsomely appointed rooms suitable for meetings, meals, and seminars have been included in an ongoing series of major building projects and renovations to forge even closer relationships between faculty and students. Blessed with a Phi Beta Kappa academic tradition, a nationally ranked program of studies abroad, and an economy of scale that encourages innovation and collaboration among faculty and students, Wofford is positioning itself among the national leaders in redefining the liberal arts. More importantly, however, the college community is vigorously pursuing a goal of educating young leaders who can make connections, cross boundaries, and negotiate a world no longer neatly divided into categories of endeavor.

"Wofford College requires freshman applicants to submit scores from either the old or new SAT. Students may also choose to submit scores from the ACT in lieu of the SAT."

SELECTIVITY

Admissions Rating	**93**
# of applicants	1,632
% of applicants accepted	66
% of acceptees attending	30
# accepting a place on wait list	100
% admitted from wait list	1
# of early decision applicants	276
% accepted early decision	69

FRESHMAN PROFILE

Range SAT Verbal	570-670
Average SAT Verbal	616
Range SAT Math	590-680
Average SAT Math	631
**TPR Projected Range SAT Writing*	*610-680*
Range ACT Composite	22-27
Average ACT Composite	25
Minimum Paper TOEFL	550
Minimum Computer Based TOEFL	213
Average HS GPA	4.05
% graduated top 10% of class	57
% graduated top 25% of class	82
% graduated top 50% of class	98

DEADLINES

Early decision application deadline	11/15
Early decision notification	12/1
Regular application deadline	2/1
Regular notification	3/15
Nonfall registration?	yes

APPLICANTS ALSO LOOK AT

AND OFTEN PREFER
Wake Forest University

AND SOMETIMES PREFER
Furman University

AND RARELY PREFER
Clemson University
University of South Carolina—Columbia

FINANCIAL FACTS

Financial Aid Rating	**87**
Annual tuition	$24,130
Room & Board	$6,805
Books and supplies	$851
% frosh rec. need-based scholarship or grant aid	52
% UG rec. need-based scholarship or grant aid	54
% frosh rec. need-based self-help aid	26
% UG rec. need-based self-help aid	29
% frosh rec. any financial aid	92
% UG rec. any financial aid	89
Avg. frosh grant	$10,122
Avg. frosh loan	$2,984
Independent 529 member?	Yes

Worcester Polytechnic Institute

100 Institute Road, Worcester, MA 01609 • Admissions: 508-831-5286 • Fax: 508-831-5875

CAMPUS LIFE

Quality of Life Rating	**77**
Fire Safety Rating	**79**
Type of school	private
Environment	city

STUDENTS

Total undergrad enrollment	2,805
% male/female	76/24
% from out of state	38
% live on campus	60
% in (# of) fraternities	38 (12)
% in (# of) sororities	28 (2)
% African American	2
% Asian	6
% Caucasian	8
% Hispanic	3
% Native American	1
% international	4
# of countries represented	70

SURVEY SAYS

Small classes
Registration is a breeze
Great computer facilities
Campus feels safe
Frats and sororities dominate social scene
Lots of beer drinking
Hard liquor is popular

ACADEMICS

Academic Rating	**85**
Calendar	quarter
Student/faculty ratio	13:1
Professors interesting rating	74
Professors accessible rating	81
% professors teaching UG courses	100
% classes taught by TAs	0
Most common lab size	10-19 students
Most common regular class size	fewer than 10 students

MOST POPULAR MAJORS

Computer and information sciences
electrical, electronics, and communications engineering
mechanical engineering

STUDENTS SPEAK OUT

Academics

For "engineering taught in terms of both theory and practice, with unique opportunities and special attention paid to undergraduate students," consider Worcester Polytechnic Institute (WPI). Instruction at this student-friendly university centers on the three-project system, "which requires that each student completes three projects in order to graduate. The first is done in the humanities, the second relates science and technology with society and real-world problems, and the third is within your major." The second project, called the Interactive Project, sends about half the student body abroad "to analyze and solve real-life problems unrelated to their major." One engineer notes, "The global projects have allowed me to gain a more realistic view of the world outside of the United States The project system also promotes gaining practical knowledge in engineering, along with group dynamics and technological problem solving and management. And you can actually help society." As at most tech schools, the workload at WPI is difficult, the challenges are amplified by a quarterly schedule "where we have new classes every seven weeks, [which] makes it impossible to procrastinate." Yet such a schedule offers several noteworthy benefits, like forcing "students to adapt to a daily schedule that more closely resembles the real world." Professors are a mixed bag. "Some are excellent, some are more concerned with research, and some have a language barrier." All, however, "encourage students to utilize office hours for personal and academic concerns."

Life

"There is a big diversity of what people do for fun" at WPI; what they choose to do seems to depend on how anxious they are to abandon their computers. One student writes, "Some people never leave their rooms and play video games all day, while others party every night. It all depends on what you are into." Some are into tinkering. One such student writes, "For fun, we FIX things. We hook up homemade stereo systems to our televisions, we rig washing machines, we program computers, we play Risk, Warcraft, and any other strategy game on the market." Worcester is not a pure Nerdvana, though; there is also "Greek life, which is really big for about a third of campus. Frat parties are a big part of the social scene, but the other half of campus probably wouldn't know what to do with a beer if they saw one." There are also "literally hundreds of organizations with all kinds of people in them. Any interest you have will be represented by a group, some large, some small, but there are always a few people around who are more than willing to share experiences." Students rarely leave campus except to travel to other area schools, since Worcester "doesn't have much to do in terms of nightlife. The clubs and aren't safe, and there aren't any late night diners within walking distance." The campus confines, fortunately, are comfy, since the "dorms are amazing, [and] the food is excellent."

Student Body

"There are two types of typical students at WPI," undergraduates tell us. "The first type is a very outgoing person who has joined at least two or three different clubs and organizations and/or is in a fraternity or sorority. The second type of person is very introverted and doesn't leave his room very often to socialize." Some students are, by their own admission, awfully nerdy. One undergraduate writes, "Looking out the window right now, I see a kid with welder goggles and a foam sword. He is a 'wedge rat.' Perhaps he is socially inept. Fortunately there are many people here just like him." The ratio of males to females is a bit lopsided; "the 25 percent female population consists of mostly engineering majors, so the selection is rather poor. However, with WPI having the only Greek scene in the Worcester area, finding a girl is hardly an issue at large fraternity parties."

WORCESTER POLYTECHNIC INSTITUTE

FINANCIAL AID: 508-831-5469 • E-MAIL: ADMISSIONS@WPI.EDU • WEBSITE: WWW.WPI.EDU

ADMISSIONS

Very important factors considered include: Class rank, secondary school record, standardized test scores. *Important factors considered include:* Essays, extracurricular activities, recommendations. *Other factors considered include:* Alumni/ae relation, character/personal qualities, geographical residence, interview, minority status, state residency, talent/ability, volunteer work, work experience. SAT Reasoning or ACT required. SAT Subject Tests recommended. TOEFL required of all international applicants. High school diploma is required, and GED is not accepted. *Academic units required:* 4 math, 2 science (2 science lab). *Academic units recommended:* 4 English.

The Inside Word

Worcester's applicant pool is small but very well qualified. Its high acceptance rate makes it a good safety choice for those aiming at more difficult tech schools and for those who are solid but aren't MIT material. As is the case at most technical institutes, women will meet with a very receptive admissions committee.

FINANCIAL AID

Students should submit: FAFSA, CSS/Financial Aid PROFILE, noncustodial (divorced/separated) parents' statement, parents' and student's prior year federal tax return and W-2 forms. Regular filing deadline is 3/1. The Princeton Review suggests that all financial aid forms be submitted as soon as possible after 1/1. *Need-based scholarships/grants offered:* Pell, SEOG, state scholarships/grants, the school's own gift aid. *Loan aid offered:* FFEL Subsidized Stafford, FFEL Unsubsidized Stafford, FFEL PLUS, Federal Perkins, state loans, college/university loans from institutional funds. Applicants will be notified of awards on or about 4/1. Federal Work-study Program available. Institutional employment available. Off-campus job opportunities are good.

FROM THE ADMISSIONS OFFICE

"Projects and research enrich WPI's academic program. WPI believes that in these times simply passing courses and accumulating theoretical knowledge is not enough to truly educate tomorrow's leaders. Tomorrow's professionals ought to be involved in project work that prepares them today for future challenges. Projects at WPI come as close to professional experience as a college program can possibly achieve. In fact, WPI works with more than 200 companies, government agencies, and private organizations each year. These groups provide opportunities where students get a chance to work in real, professional settings. Students gain invaluable experience in planning, coordinating team efforts, meeting deadlines, writing proposals and reports, making oral presentations, doing cost analyses, and making decisions.

"Applicants for fall 2006 are required to take either the new SAT or the ACT (the Writing section is optional). We will allow students to submit scores from the old SAT (prior to March 2005) or ACT as well, and will use the student's best scores from either test. Science and Math SAT Subject Tests are recommended."

SELECTIVITY

Admissions Rating	**91**
# of applicants	3,708
% of applicants accepted	75
% of acceptees attending	28
# accepting a place on wait list	107
# of early decision applicants	165
% accepted early decision	84

FRESHMAN PROFILE

Range SAT Verbal	570-670
Average SAT Verbal	620
Range SAT Math	630-720
Average SAT Math	674
**TPR Projected Range SAT Writing*	*610-680*
Range ACT Composite	24-29
Average ACT Composite	29
Minimum Paper TOEFL	550
Minimum Computer Based TOEFL	213
Average HS GPA	3.6
% graduated top 10% of class	55
% graduated top 25% of class	86
% graduated top 50% of class	99

DEADLINES

Early decision application deadline	11/15
Early decision notification	12/15
Regular application deadline	2/1
Regular notification	4/1
Nonfall registration?	yes

APPLICANTS ALSO LOOK AT

AND OFTEN PREFER

California Institute of Technology, Cornell U., Massachusetts Institute of Technology

AND SOMETIMES PREFER

Carnegie Mellon U., Case Western Reserve U., Rensselaer Polytechnic Institutet

AND RARELY PREFER

Clarkson U., Drexel U., U. of Connecticut, U. of New Hampshire

FINANCIAL FACTS

Financial Aid Rating	**80**
Annual tuition	$31,390
Room & Board	$9,460
Books and supplies	$880
% frosh rec. need-based scholarship or grant aid	73
% UG rec. need-based scholarship or grant aid	71
% frosh rec. need-based self-help aid	58
% UG rec. need-based self-help aid	65
% frosh rec. any financial aid	91
% UG rec. any financial aid	89
Avg. frosh grant	$12,121
Avg. frosh loan	$4,620
Independent 529 member?	No

XAVIER UNIVERSITY (LA)

ONE DREXEL DRIVE, BOX 132, NEW ORLEANS, LA 70125-1098 • ADMISSIONS: 504-520-7388 • FAX: 504-520-7941

CAMPUS LIFE

Quality of Life Rating	**61**
Fire Safety Rating	**60**
Type of school	private
Affiliation	Roman Catholic
Environment	metropolis

STUDENTS

Total undergrad enrollment	3,290
% male/female	25/75
% from out of state	59
% from public high school	81
% live on campus	30
% in (# of) fraternities	1 (4)
% in (# of) sororities	3 (4)
% African American	82
% Asian	5
% Caucasian	2
% international	2
# of countries represented	8

SURVEY SAYS . . .

Class discussions are rare
Small classes
Great computer facilities
Great off-campus food
Frats and sororities dominate social scene
Student government is popular
Very little drug use

ACADEMICS

Academic Rating	**72**
Calendar	semester
Student/faculty ratio	16:1
Profs interesting rating	72
Profs accessible rating	68
% profs teaching UG courses	98
% classes taught by TAs	0
Most common lab size	20-29 students
Most common reg class size	20-29 students

MOST POPULAR MAJORS

Pre-pharmacy studies
psychology

Academics

Xavier University of Louisiana, the nation's only historically black Catholic college or university, excels in a number of areas, most famously in premedical and pharmacy studies. Xavier promotional literature justifiably boasts of its accomplishments in these fields: of all American schools, Xavier confers the most biology and life sciences degrees to African Americans; awards the greatest number of Doctor of Pharmacy degrees to African Americans; and places the most African Americans into medical schools. Given these achievements, it should surprise no one that students here must survive a tough curriculum; "Xavier wears you out so that the real world will not," is how one student puts it. Fortunately, undergrads receive plenty of support from a faculty and staff who "provide a family-like atmosphere for students and lay a strong foundation for those who want to pursue positions of leadership and service." Professors here "are very knowledgeable and know a lot about their subjects. Most of them break material down really well so you can understand complex ideas." They are also "passionate about what they do," exuding an enthusiasm that inspires students. Xavier is also strong in business studies.

Life

To state the obvious, Xavier "is set in the middle of New Orleans, so there is plenty to do." Students tell us that "a lot of first years do a lot of partying," which explains why close to one in four doesn't return for sophomore year. Those who manage to stick around for the duration tell us that "during the week, everyone is mostly focused on schoolwork. For the weekend, people like to chill at home and watch movies or go out to parties." Since campus policies impose strict restrictions on noise, dorm visitation, and drinking, parties usually occur off campus, either at one of the many other area colleges or at clubs in town. Students also like to "just go to the French Quarter and walk around" or hit the many music clubs and fine eateries that distinguish the Crescent City. When hanging on campus, students praise the student government's efforts to "provide wonderful activities for students living on and off campus" but dis the campus itself, telling us that "Xavier could improve on the atmosphere of the campus. Sure, it's an old school, but the grounds could still be more appealing."

Student Body

"Xavier is a historically black college, so there is a majority of black students on campus," students explain, but they also point out that "we do have students of other racial and ethnic backgrounds who also attend." Observes one undergrad, "I have personally seen a great interaction with the student population, but there is still some segregation among the students sometimes, which doesn't go unnoticed." The typical Xavier undergrad is "black, smart, sometimes a little too hard on themselves," and "strives for success and wants to further her education through a graduate/professional program." Undergraduates here are typically studious, occasionally to the point of being "stress worshippers."

Financial Aid: 504-520-7517 • E-mail: apply@xula.edu • Website: www.xula.edu

ADMISSIONS

Very important factors considered include: Recommendations, secondary school record, standardized test scores. *Important factors considered include:* Class rank. *Other factors considered include:* Alumni/ae relation, character/personal qualities, essays, extracurricular activities, interview, minority status, talent/ability, volunteer work, work experience. SAT Reasoning or ACT required; TOEFL required of all international applicants. High school diploma is required and GED is accepted. *Academic units required:* 4 English, 2 math, 1 science, 1 social studies, 8 academic electives. *Academic units recommended:* 4 math, 3 science, 1 foreign language, 2 social studies, 1 history.

Inside Word

This school is a prestigious pipeline for those committed to a career in both natural and hard sciences. Xavier is best known for its identity as a Catholic institution with a predominantly African American student body and its reputation as a great premed school.

FINANCIAL AID

Students should submit: FAFSA. The Princeton Review suggests that all financial aid forms be submitted as soon as possible after January 1. *Need-based scholarships/grants offered:* Pell, SEOG, state scholarships/grants, private scholarships, the school's own gift aid, United Negro College Fund. *Loan aid offered:* Direct Subsidized Stafford, Direct Unsubsidized Stafford, Direct PLUS, FFEL Subsidized Stafford, FFEL Unsubsidized Stafford, FFEL PLUS, Federal Perkins. Applicants will be notified of awards on a rolling basis beginning or about April 1. Federal Work-Study Program available. Institutional employment available. Off-campus job opportunities are good.

FROM THE ADMISSIONS OFFICE

"SAT and ACT scores are used as a factor in admission decisions at Xavier University of Louisiana. Effective for the fall 2006, applicants should take the new SAT or the ACT with Writing component. In addition to being used for admission decisions, the scores and sub scores are used for course placement purposes at Xavier."

SELECTIVITY

Admissions Rating	**78**
# of applicants	4,248
% of applicants accepted	83
% of acceptees attending	28
# accepting a place on wait list	76
% admitted from wait list	7

FRESHMAN PROFILE

Range SAT Verbal	440-470
Average SAT Verbal	492
Range SAT Math	430-540
Average SAT Math	487
**TPR Projected Range SAT Writing*	*510-530*
Range ACT Composite	18-24
Average ACT Composite	21
Minimum Paper TOEFL	550
Average HS GPA	3.06
% graduated top 10% of class	30
% graduated top 25% of class	55
% graduated top 50% of class	83

DEADLINES

Regular application deadline	7/1
Regular notification	4/15
Nonfall registration?	yes

FINANCIAL FACTS

Financial Aid Rating	**64**
Annual tuition	$11,300
Room & Board	$7,100
Books and supplies	$1,000
Required fees	$900
% UG rec. need-based self-help aid	44
% frosh rec. any financial aid	79
% UG rec. any financial aid	84
Avg. frosh grant	$3,215
Independent 529 member?	No

XAVIER UNIVERSITY (OH)

3800 VICTORY PARKWAY, CINCINNATI, OH 45207-5311 • ADMISSIONS: 513-745-3301 • FAX: 513-745-4319

CAMPUS LIFE

Quality of Life Rating	**81**
Fire Safety Rating	**77**
Type of school	private
Affiliation	Roman Catholic-Jesuit
Environment	metropolis

STUDENTS

Total undergrad enrollment	3,770
% male/female	44/56
% from out of state	37
% live on campus	48
% African American	10
% Asian	2
% Caucasian	84
% Hispanic	2
% international	1
# of countries represented	38

SURVEY SAYS

Small classes
Students are happy
Everyone loves the Musketeers
Frats and sororities are unpopular or nonexistent
Lots of beer drinking

ACADEMICS

Academic Rating	**81**
Calendar	semester
Student/faculty ratio	13:1
Professors interesting rating	81
Professors accessible rating	86
% professors teaching UG courses	87
% classes taught by TAs	0
Most common lab size	10-19 students
Most common regular class size	10-19 students

MOST POPULAR MAJORS

Education
liberal arts and sciences/liberal studies
marketing/marketing management

STUDENTS SPEAK OUT

Academics

At Xavier University, students claim that "the academic experience is so fulfilling because of the rigorous core curriculum—every student and alum has studied Plato, great art, literature, chemistry, etc." In fact, one proud student credits Xavier with having "the hardest core curriculum of all 28 Jesuit universities in the United States." "Professors are better than I could have ever imagined. I truly love going to my classes just to hear them speak," raves an enamored student. The university's religious affiliation is fundamental to its academics: "The Jesuits have a strong commitment to students developing morally, intellectually, and spiritually, and helping make the society around us a better place to live." Students do complain about the registration process and the fact there is "always some construction [on campus] (but the end result is worth it!)." The administration is highly accessible; as one student boasts, "I have had the opportunity to interact one-on-one with the dean of students, the VP of student affairs, the dean of social sciences, and the president of our university, and I am not alone in these bragging rights, by any means." And when problems arise, as they inevitably do, students can go to "'The Man,' Adrian Schiess, who is a student advocate and will fix the problem whether it is financial aid, bursar, or housing."

Life

"There's always SOMETHING to do" in Cincinnati, students say, "whether that be a concert or a baseball game or going out to dinner or going to see a movie or a play." There are also "opportunities to see live music at a local music spot called Bogart's, which attracts some good bands," and "Main Street is a lot of fun." On Xavier's campus, there's "always something going on." One student notes that there are "always nonalcoholic activities on campus." "Xavier just opened up the Cintas Center, a 10,000-seat arena that now hosts concerts, comedy fests, and ESPN sports events," reports one student; although entertaining, some feel that "we have gotten very commercialized since the building of the 'almighty Cintas Center'—our small shrine to materialism and basketball here on campus." Some other facilities are lacking, as students wish Xavier "could improve our on-campus library." For those with philanthropic sensibilities, "service is HUGE here so a lot of people join forces to go out into the community to make a difference or to travel to third-world countries to spend a semester in service learning."

Students

Students at Xavier love being here. "I know this is really cheesy, but I always joke that Xavier, and not Disney World, is the happiest place on earth," enthuses one student. "The students at Xavier are one big family," adds another. "It's almost sickening how happy all of us are." Students feel their "fellow students are much smarter than the average person," and they're "incredibly friendly"—"everyone says 'hi' to everyone!" Another student tempers this assessment and admits that "it's not that we really have cliques, but we certainly have comfort zones." On account of these comfort zones, perhaps, little intermingling occurs. Apparently, much of the student body looks "like they stepped off a page from an Abercrombie and Fitch catalog." Still, another student suggests that "while it may appear to be a largely white university, the student body is very social-justice oriented and works for equality for members of all races."

XAVIER UNIVERSITY (OH)

FINANCIAL AID: 513-745-3142 • E-MAIL: XUADMIT@XAVIER.EDU • WEBSITE: WWW.XAVIER.EDU

ADMISSIONS

Very important factors considered include: Secondary school record. *Important factors considered include:* Character/personal qualities, class rank, essays, recommendations, standardized test scores. *Other factors considered include:* Alumni/ae relation, extracurricular activities, talent/ability, volunteer work, work experience. SAT Reasoning or ACT required. TOEFL required of all international applicants. High school diploma is required, and GED is accepted. *Academic units recommended:* 4 English, 3 math, 3 science, 2 foreign language, 3 social studies, 5 academic electives, 1 health/physical education.

The Inside Word

Xavier passes the test for many students who arrive for their freshman year expecting an accommodating place that provides all the hallmarks of a big school, academically and socially. Applicants who intend to enact a finely specialized course load must be prepared for the core courses as well.

FINANCIAL AID

Students should submit: FAFSA. The Princeton Review suggests that all financial aid forms be submitted as soon as possible after 1/1. *Need-based scholarships/grants offered:* Pell, SEOG, state scholarships/grants, private scholarships, the school's own gift aid. *Loan aid offered:* FFEL Subsidized Stafford, FFEL Unsubsidized Stafford, FFEL PLUS, Federal Perkins. Applicants will be notified of awards on or about 3/1. Federal Work-study Program available. Institutional employment available. Off-campus job opportunities are excellent.

FROM THE ADMISSIONS OFFICE

"Founded in 1831, Xavier University is the fourth oldest of the 28 Jesuit colleges and universities in the United States. The Jesuit tradition is evident in the university's core curriculum, degree programs, and opportunities for involvement. Xavier is home to 6,600 total students; 3,700 degree-seeking undergraduates. The student population represents more than 45 states and 38 foreign countries.

"The university offers 69 academic majors and concentrations and 42 minors in the colleges of arts and sciences, business, and social sciences. The most popular majors include business, communication arts, education, psychology, and sport management/marketing, as well as pre-professional areas of study. Other programs of note include university scholars, honors AB, army ROTC, study abroad, service learning, service fellowship, and our newest honors program-philosophy, politics, and the public.

"There are more than more than 100 academic clubs, social and service organizations, and recreational sports activities on campus. Students participate in groups such as student government, campus ministry, performing arts, and intramural sports teams. Xavier is a member of the Division I Atlantic 10 Conference and fields teams in men's and women's basketball, cross-country, golf, soccer, swimming, and tennis as well as men's baseball and women's volleyball.

"The university is situated on more than 140 acres in a residential area of Cincinnati, Ohio. The face of Xavier has continued to change with the addition of a 10,000-seat arena and convocation center, a complex that includes banquet facilities and a student dining hall. Recent additions to campus include a recreation park, apartments for upperclassmen, and a new $18 million student center with a performing arts theater.

"Applicants for fall 2006 must submit results from the SAT or ACT. Xavier will accept results from the old or new SAT/ACT, and the student's best score(s) from either test will be used. The Writing portion of the SAT/ACT is not required and will not be used in admission and scholarship decisions."

SELECTIVITY

Admissions Rating	**86**
# of applicants	4,764
% of applicants accepted	74
% of acceptees attending	25
# accepting a place on wait list	149
% admitted from wait list	1

FRESHMAN PROFILE

Range SAT Verbal	530-640
Average SAT Verbal	583
Range SAT Math	530-650
Average SAT Math	588
**TPR Projected Range SAT Writing*	*580-660*
Range ACT Composite	23-28
Average ACT Composite	26
Minimum Paper TOEFL	500
Minimum Computer Based TOEFL	173
Average HS GPA	3.57
% graduated top 10% of class	29
% graduated top 25% of class	58
% graduated top 50% of class	89

DEADLINES

Regular notification	3/15
Nonfall registration?	yes

APPLICANTS ALSO LOOK AT

AND OFTEN PREFER
University of Notre Dame

AND SOMETIMES PREFER
Miami University
Ohio State University—Columbus
University of Dayton

AND RARELY PREFER
University of Cincinnati

FINANCIAL FACTS

Financial Aid Rating	**74**
Annual tuition	$21,250
Room & Board	$8,640
Books and supplies	$950
Required fees	$580
% frosh rec. need-based scholarship or grant aid	61
% UG rec. need-based scholarship or grant aid	50
% frosh rec. need-based self-help aid	44
% UG rec. need-based self-help aid	38
% frosh rec. any financial aid	95
% UG rec. any financial aid	98
Avg. frosh grant	$9,777
Avg. frosh loan	$3,625
Independent 529 member?	No

YALE UNIVERSITY

PO BOX 208234, NEW HAVEN, CT 06520-8234 • ADMISSIONS: 203-432-9316 • FAX: 203-432-9392

CAMPUS LIFE

Quality of Life Rating	**93**
Fire Safety Rating	**60**
Type of school	private

STUDENTS

Total undergrad enrollment	5,294
% male/female	50/50
% from out of state	87
% from public high school	53
% live on campus	87
% African American	8
% Asian	13
% Caucasian	52
% Hispanic	6
% Native American	1
% international	9
# of countries represented	82

SURVEY SAYS

Registration is a breeze
Great library
Musical organizations are popular
Student publications are popular

ACADEMICS

Academic Rating	**97**
Calendar	semester
Student/faculty ratio	6:1
Professors interesting rating	84
Professors accessible rating	81
% classes taught by TAs	12
Most common regular class size	10-19 students

STUDENTS SPEAK OUT

Academics

"There are too many strengths to name" at Yale University, one of the nation's top undergraduate and graduate institutions, but that doesn't stop undergrads here from trying; they identify "the resources, of course, the marvelous professors, and the students themselves" as some of Yale's biggest assets. As one student puts it, "Coming to Yale means that you will be able to do anything you want to do at the highest caliber. They will make it as easy as they can for you to learn what you want." If the experience sounds a little daunting, that's because it is. Explains one undergrad, "It's intimidating, Yale University. You feel like you have something to prove. Were you the 'mistake' who got in? You challenge yourself for the sake of learning and for the sake of being the best." (And it's comforting to note that "faculty tries to ensure that no one is lost in the wash.") Students' burdens are somewhat lessened by the fact that "you don't really have to deal with the highest levels of the administration, because every residential college has a Master (for residential issues) and a Dean (for academic issues), who you can easily discuss things with, and who will generally help you take care of things in the most efficient way possible."

Life

Yale is extremely demanding academically, but students here still find time for plenty of extracurricular enrichment and fun. Reports one student, "People generally study Monday through Thursday, and oftentimes have extracurriculars in the evenings. On the weekends, people tend to study during the day and go out at night." Undergrads tell us that "art, music, theater, and sports are huge, loved, and well-funded, as are organizations such as the Yale Daily News, the Slavic Chorus (a cappella is huge here), Just Add Water (a comedy troupe), and the fire-juggling club (best Halloween show in the world!)." The campus also sustains "an absolutely ridiculous amount of theatrical and musical events." Students also love the traditional "Masters' Teas, of which there are several every week, with everyone from the Swiss delegate to the United Nations to Eric Schlosser (author of Fast Food Nation) to biomedical engineers coming to share their life experiences over tea and chocolates." Yale's campus is "gorgeous" with "jaw-dropping architecture and awesome dorms and dining halls." While New Haven is not held in especially high regard, students appreciate that "there are some excellent clubs and restaurants in town" and that "the city provides easy access to New York," which can be reached by train in about 90 minutes.

Student Body

While "there is no typical Yale student," most agree that "there are two overarching characteristics that everyone here has been blessed with: talent and motivation." Notes one student, "Though we come from different backgrounds and have different interests, it's easy to look around and imagine your classmates being the leaders of the next generation." Professors and peers alike never cease to surprise you and just completely blow you away with their talent and knowledge and personality. Yet at the same time, everyone is down-to-earth. Very few people flaunt their abilities, though they have every right to." Students "tend to have a liberal bent, although any political affiliation (just like any background) is welcomed, and politics carry over from mere discussion into real action: Community programs, public-health advocacy and work, and political campaigns are all vital to campus life." Undergrads are also typically "noncompetitive and very supportive of each other academically and socially." Explains one student, "If I have to miss lecture, I know that first, I can always e-mail my professor and ask for help and second, any one of a dozen friends will gladly not only share notes, but also go over them with me to make sure that I understand them." Thanks to need-blind admissions and generous financial aid, "the economic backgrounds of students are very diverse."

FINANCIAL AID: 203-432-2700 • E-MAIL: UNDERGRADUATE.ADMISSIONS@YALE.EDU • WEBSITE: WWW.YALE.EDU/ADMIT

ADMISSIONS

Very important factors considered include: Character/personal qualities, class rank, essays, extracurricular activities, recommendations, secondary school record, standardized test scores, talent/ability. *Other factors considered include:* Alumni/ae relation, geographical residence, interview, minority status, state residency, volunteer work, work experience. TOEFL required of all international applicants. High school diploma or equivalent is not required.

The Inside Word

There is no grey area; Yale is ultra-selective with growing applicant pools each year. And there's nothing to be gained by appealing a denial here—the admissions committee considers all of its decisions final. Yale uses a regional review process that serves as a preliminary screening for all candidates, and only the best-qualified, well-matched candidates actually come before the admissions committee.

FINANCIAL AID

Students should submit: FAFSA, CSS/Financial Aid PROFILE, state aid form, noncustodial (divorced/separated) parents' statement, business/farm supplement, tax returns. Regular filing deadline is 3/1. The Princeton Review suggests that all financial aid forms be submitted as soon as possible after 1/1. *Need-based scholarships/grants offered:* Pell, SEOG, state scholarships/grants, private scholarships, the school's own gift aid, United Negro College Fund, Alumni Club Awards. *Loan aid offered:* FFEL Subsidized Stafford, FFEL Unsubsidized Stafford, FFEL PLUS, Federal Perkins, state loans, college/university loans from institutional funds. Applicants will be notified of awards on or about 4/1. Federal Work-study Program available. Institutional employment available. Off-campus job opportunities are good

FROM THE ADMISSIONS OFFICE

"The most important questions the admissions committee must resolve are 'Who is likely to make the most of Yale's resources?' and 'Who will contribute significantly to the Yale community?' These questions suggest an approach to evaluating applicants that is more complex than whether Yale would rather admit well-rounded people or those with specialized talents. In selecting a class of 1,300 from approximately 19,700 applicants, the admissions committee looks for academic ability and achievement combined with such personal characteristics as motivation, curiosity, energy, and leadership ability. The nature of these qualities is such that there is no simple profile of grades, scores, interests, and activities that will assure admission. Diversity within the student population is important, and the admissions committee selects a class of able and contributing individuals from a variety of backgrounds and with a broad range of interests and skills.

"Applicants for the entering class fall 2006 may take either version of the SAT. In addition, applicants will be required to take three SAT Subject Tests of their choice. Applicants may take the ACT, with the Writing component, as an alternative to the SAT and SAT Subject Tests."

SELECTIVITY

Admissions Rating	**99**
# of applicants	17,735
% of applicants accepted	11
% of acceptees attending	68
# accepting a place on wait list	998
% admitted from wait list	1
# of early decision applicants	646
% accepted early decision	16

FRESHMAN PROFILE

Range SAT Verbal	690-790
Range SAT Math	690-790
**TPR Projected Range SAT Writing*	*690-750*
Range ACT Composite	30-34
Minimum Paper TOEFL	600
% graduated top 10% of class	95
% graduated top 25% of class	99
% graduated top 50% of class	100

DEADLINES

Early decision application deadline	11/1
Early decision notification	12/15
Regular application deadline	12/31
Regular notification	4/1
Nonfall registration?	no

APPLICANTS ALSO LOOK AT AND SOMETIMES PREFER

Harvard College
Massachusetts Institute of Technology
Stanford University

AND RARELY PREFER

Amherst College
Brown University
University of Pennsylvania
Wesleyan University
Williams College

FINANCIAL FACTS

Financial Aid Rating	**97**
Annual tuition	$29,820
Room & Board	$9,030
Books and supplies	$2,650
% frosh rec. need-based scholarship or grant aid	43
% UG rec. need-based scholarship or grant aid	40
% frosh rec. need-based self-help aid	43
% UG rec. need-based self-help aid	40
Independent 529 member?	No

PART 4

“MY ROOMMATE’S FEET REALLY STINK.”

Our survey has seven questions that allow students to answer in narrative form. We tell students that we don't care *what* they write: if it is "witty, informative, or accurate," we try to get it into this book. We use all the informative and accurate essays to write the "Students Speak Out" sections; below are excerpts from the wittiest, pithiest, and most outrageous narrative responses to our open-ended questions.

LITERARY ALLUSIONS...

"To study at this school is to have infinite control over your destiny: You can crouch in your room like Gregor Samsa transformed into a dung beetle, or you can plunge into the infinite sea of faces that each year flood OSU like a tidal wave."

— A.W., Ohio State University

"Two jokes about St. John's College students:
1. *Q: How many Johnnies does it take to change a light bulb?*
   A: Let's define 'change' before we go any further.
2. *Q: What did the Chorus say to Creon after Oedipus poked out his eyes?*
   A: Now that's a face only a mother could love."

— April W., St. John's College

"'Prosperity unbruised cannot endure a single blow, but a man who has been at constant feud with misfortunes develops a skin calloused by time...and even if he falls he can carry the fight upon one knee.' —Seneca on Providence."

— Matthew D., U. of Connecticut

"Very definitely a love/hate relationship here. This is the level of hell that Dante missed."

—Amy P., Caltech

"The Deep Springs Experience is like working in an atrophy factory. Much of what you do in labor and government is fixing, improving, or replacing what came before you. No matter what frame of reference you use—daily, monthly, or yearly—you still feel like Sisyphus. The joy and value comes in building your muscles on so many different rocks."

—Whet M., Deep Springs College

"Lewd quotes on the bathroom walls at least come from great authors."

—Matt J., Simon's Rock College of Bard

FOOD...

"The food here is really bad; it's either bland or sickening. You're lucky if they don't screw up the bread."

— Scott P., Bentley College

"If you're looking for gray skies, a gray campus, and gray food, then Albany is the place to be!"

— Michele G., SUNY at Albany

"When students first arrive, they call the Observatory Hill Dining Facility 'O-Hill.' They soon learn to call it 'O-Hell,' because the food here is beyond revolting."

— Greg F., U. of Virginia

"The food isn't that bad, if you don't mind varying shades of brown. On a good day the food on your tray will remind you of the brown paint sampler at your local Sherwin-Williams dealer."

— Rob P., College of the Holy Cross

"If I had known that I'd be rooming with roaches and poisoned by the cafeteria staff I would have gone to Wayne State. I really can't complain, though, because I have met my husband here, like my mom did 20 years before."

— M.L.P., Fisk University

"You should mention Lil', the lady who has worked in the dining hall for fifty years and who everyone loves. She plays the spoons all the time and runs around."

— Aaron R., Tufts University

"The food here has particularly fancy names, and it seems as though they spend more time thinking of these names than they spend on making decent food."

— Andrew Z., Wheaton College

"We spend more time at the lunch table than George, Jerry, Elaine, and Kramer, except that our cafeteria workers aren't as good looking."

—Chris D., Wake Forest University

HOMETOWN...

"People ask me, 'Mike Z., why did you come to NYU?' I tell them, 'I didn't come to NYU, I came to New York City.'"

— Mike Z., NYU

"Change the name of UC—Irvine to UC—Newport Beach and we would have more girls."

— Pat M., UC—Irvine

"As this school is located in a tiny Texas town, a favorite activity is called 'rolling.' Rolling entails piling into a car with many drinks and driving the back country roads. Very slowly."

— Anonymous, Southwestern University

"Connecticut is a cute state. It's a great place to go to school, but I wouldn't want to live here."

— Claire S., NJ native, Fairfield University

"Binghamton is always gray. The two days a week we have sun, it's beautiful, but otherwise, sunglasses are not a must unless you're an artsy-fartsy pseudo-chic literature and rhetoric/ philosophy major."

— Deborah C., SUNY at Binghamton

"Socially, the surrounding area is so dead that the Denny's closes at night."

— Thomas R., UC—Riverside

"The local liquor stores and towing companies make a lot of money."

— Katherine R., U. of Rhode Island

"Davis is boring; you need a lot of drugs."

— Anonymous, UC—Davis

"It is definitely important to have a car, as the population of Canton frequently matches our winter temperature. 'Canton gray,' our perennial sky color, is one Crayola missed."

— Daniel R., St. Lawrence University

"Contrary to popular belief, cow tipping is definitely passé here."

— Anonymous, U. of Connecticut, Storrs

"Life in New Orleans—'And the people sat down to eat and to drink, and rose up to play.'—Exodus 32:6."

— Theresa W., Tulane University

"Fredericksburg is boring if one is not amused by the simple pleasures of existence such as breathing, sleep, and other things."

— Rich W., Mary Washington College

"I love escaping from Claremont. I wish I had a car! Claremont seems to be stuck in a white, bureaucratic, conservative nightmare. I feel cut off from the rest of the world, like I've fallen into Wonderland—the rules of the outside world don't apply here. However, I do feel like I've gotten and am getting a good education."

— Anonymous, Scripps College

"What do we do for fun? Danville is small, so we go on raids to Wal-Mart. It never fails, no matter what time of day or night that you go to Wal-Mart, you will always run into at least two separate groups of people you know. Plus, Wal-Mart is just a cool place to play around in. Where else can you find [everything from] toy footballs and bikes to goofy hats, clothes, shoes? And let me tell you, those aisles make for a good game of hide and seek."

—Anonymous, Centre College

SECURITY...

"Campus security is made up of a bunch of midget high school dropouts with Napoleonic complexes who can spot a beer can from a mile away."

— Anonymous, UC—San Diego

"For fun we try to ski around campus on the snow, but campus safety must feel that we should be smoking weed because they allow that more than outdoor activities."

—Male Junior, Clarkson University

"Public safety here is a joke. The public safety officers are like the Keystone Kops on Thorazine."

— Anonymous, Bryn Mawr College

"No doors are locked here—<u>none</u>—but you have to notice the doorknob."

—Female Senior, Simon's Rock College of Bard

CLASSMATES...

"Sure, our campus is diverse if you call diverse a campus full of white kids looking to make 30 to 50 grand after graduation."

— Joseph M. C., Davidson College

"If you're thinking of applying to MIT, go ahead. Because, believe it or not, most people here are at least as stupid as you are."

— Patrick L., MIT

"My 'life' at school revolves around devising new methods in which to escape and to get away from the nagging, 'supportive' women's environment."

—Caitlin B., Mount Holyoke College

"Students here mostly get along and since it is a business school we all have a common goal of being rich."

—Female Sophomore, Babson College

"People who go to school here are all pretty good-looking, especially the women. It should be renamed UKB, the University of Ken and Barbie."

— Tony H., Arizona State University

"Wesleyan is not only the 'diversity university' but also the 'controversy university,' the 'fight adversity university,' and the 'if we keep trying we might have some unity' university. We satisfy all types."

— John P., Wesleyan University

"Mt. Holyoke students are friendly and respectful with the exception of the occasions when the entire campus gets PMS."

—Abigail K., Mount Holyoke College

"Everyone walks too fast around here. You try to say 'hi' to someone, you've got to time it just right 'cause they aren't going to stop to talk to you. Plus, everyone wears the same clothes!"

— Terry B., Wittenberg University

"Girls over 5'8", watch out—for some reason, guys here have munchkin blood in them or something."

— Robyn A., Tufts University

"A school can be defined by its graffiti and its level of cleverness. Three quarters of our school graffiti is pro- or anti- a specific fraternity, with the other one quarter devoted to homophobic or misogynist theories."

— Matthew E., College of William and Mary

"This is a great university if you're not studying sciences involving animal research, politics, teacher education (certification), or anything that offends any long-haired leftist who's a vegetarian."

— Brock M., U. of Oregon

"This school is filled with wealthy, well-dressed egomaniacs who are about as socially conscious as Marie Antoinette."

— Anonymous, Hofstra University

"For self-absorbed artists my peers are all surprisingly good dancers."

—Jackie G., Bennington College

"When you first come here, you think everybody's really strange. Over time, though, you realize everybody is, and so are you. No big deal."

— Josh B., St. John's College

"University of Chicago's reputation is not entirely deserved. It's not true the place is completely full of nerds. It's only partially completely full of nerds."

— David G., U. of Chicago

"I have this really big booger in my nose that I can't quite handle. What do I do? Pick it in public and look like a typical Brown freak, or just deal with it?"

—"Optional," Brown University

"Don't let anyone try to tell you that this is a diverse but close-knit atmosphere. The people here are about as diverse as a box of nails."

— Cari L., College of the Holy Cross

"UNH is about as diverse as the NHL."

— Curtis E., U. of New Hampshire

"We are cheeseballs, but rather enlightened; thus we condescendingly tolerate almost everyone."

—Cache M., Lawrence U.

"Denison has attempted to lose the 'rich kid party school' image and expand the diversity of the student body, but now it is becoming the 'I wish this were still a rich kid party school.' There is an awful lot available here, but students seem unmotivated and lazy."

— Anonymous, Denison University

"Most of my peers are narrow-minded morons who seem to live in the fifties. Because of this constant annoyance, the rest of us have a camaraderie that allows us to see how the other half lives."

—Gary A., LSU

"Everyone here is too smart for their [sic] own good. As one upper-level executive in the Houston area put it, 'The students at Rice know how to make it rain, but they don't know to come in out of it.'"

— John B., Rice U.

"My roommate's feet really stink."

— Anonymous, Claremont McKenna

"Kids at Bard are like fish in a fish bowl, no blinking but always hitting the glass."

—Zak V., Bard College

"Sometimes people complain about the lack of student involvement. I think someone should really do something about the apathy at St. Lawrence."

— Bill P., St. Lawrence University

"Bates is so diverse! Yesterday I met somebody from Connecticut!"

— Ellen H., Bates College

"Most are either Bible-thumping, goodie-goodie, white, stuck-up, right-wing, straight-A losers or work hard, play harder and party hardy, willing-to-try-anything cool people."

—Male Sophomore, Colorado School of Mines

"Rose-Hulman is one of the few places where it's safer to leave a $20 bill on your desk than it is to forget to log out of the computer network."

— Zac C., Rose-Hulman Institute of Technology

"Wabash College is an all-male institution, so all of my classmates are men."

—Anonymous, Wabash College

"People at F&M are about as original and colorful as the pages of the Encyclopedia Britannica, with different numbers so you can tell them apart, but otherwise arranged much around the same old dull principles."

—Anonymous, Franklin and Marshall College

"I am constantly impressed with the creativity of hell-raisers on campus. One day I walked past the Manor House to find a dozen plastic babies climbing all over the roof! Right before Parents' Weekend, some people hung up signs saying 'Princeton Review reports: "LC students ignore herpes on a regular basis." Please visit the health clinic!'"

—Anonymous, Lewis and Clark College

"I have not met anyone who was horrible."

—Anonymous, UMBC

"When I first visited this campus, I thought, 'Wow, people here are mean. They walk around like they're cold and empty and can't see anyone.' And then I came here and I realized that I was mostly right; people will run right into you and not even turn around."

—Anonymous, University of California—Irvine

ADMINISTRATION...

"The only thing the administration does well is tasks involving what Kenneth Boulding would call 'suboptimization.' Give them something that really doesn't need doing and it will be accomplished efficiently."

— Dana T., U. of Minnesota—Twin Cities

"Our business office may be the smoothest running machine since the Pinto!"

— Robert C., University of Dallas

"Despite the best efforts of the administration to provide TCNJ students with an inefficient, cold-hearted, red-tape infested, snafu-riddled Soviet-style administrative bureaucracy, The College of New Jersey is a pretty decent place to go for a fairly reasonable amount of money."

— Anonymous, The College of New Jersey

"The admissions office tries to make you apply based on, 'Well, we're very old and . . . and . . . well, we look nice. We'll do whatever it takes to make you happy! Really! I mean it. See my honest smile?' If you visit the school, ditch the tour and the gimmicks and talk to the professors."

— Anonymous, Southwestern University

"Going to a school as small as Emerson means that instead of saying 'screw you, Mr. 90803,' the administration will say, 'screw you, Joe.'"

— "Joe Bloggs," Emerson College

"The administration runs a wonderful school, and the students and teachers have a wonderful school. Fortunately, these are not the same school."

—Male Freshman/Sophomore, Bard College

"Administration is like the stock market, you invest time and money, sometimes you get a return, other times you don't."

—J.W.R., Albertson College of Idaho

"The bursar's office and financial aid are slightly retarded when it comes to communication. The daily walk between the two offices might have contributed to my not gaining 'The Freshman 15.'"

—Brittany R., Wesleyan College

"Columbia is like a fruit truck. It picks up varied and exotic fruits and deposits them rotten at their destination."

— Paul L., Columbia University

"The U. of Minnesota is a huge black hole of knowledge. It sucks things into it from far and wide, compressing to the essence. Unfortunately, it is very hard to get anything out of a black hole. What I have managed to eke out has been both rewarding and depressing."

— James McDonald, U. of Minnesota

"The strangest incident I've ever had in class was when one of my journalism profs burnt our tests in the microwave. But, he decided to give everyone in the class an A, instead of retesting."

—Ashlea K., Ohio University

"Boulder is the world in a nutshell, served with alfalfa sprouts."

— Glenn H., U. of Colorado, Boulder

"Going to Northwestern is like having a beautiful girlfriend who treats you like crap."

— Jonathan J. G., Northwestern University

"Unless you are totally committed to science, do not come. Caltech has as much breadth as a Russian grocery store."

— Daniel S., Caltech

"Being at Marlboro is like having a recurring bizarre dream. You're not quite sure what it all means, but it happens a lot. If it stopped you'd probably wonder why, but then you'd just eat breakfast."

— Mark L., Marlboro College

"Life at school is an oxymoron."

—Dave G., UC—Davis

"One other thing I LOVE about NYU: online registration! God bless the NYU registrar!"

—Timothy A., New York University

"Vassar is like a sexual disease: once you've accepted it, it's great, but when you realize you've got another three years to put up with it, you go see a medical adviser immediately."

— Henry R., Vassar College

"Vassar is like a big walrus butt: lots of hair, but also very moist."

— Calder M., Vassar College

"I feel that this school is a maze with snakes and bulls. If you live with a raised fist or a raised phallus, it is easy. If you are earthly, bound to do nothing, come."

— Anonymous, U. of Oregon

"Getting an education from MIT is like getting a drink from a firehose."

— Juan G., MIT

"Financial Aid office needs a complete overhaul. An atom bomb would suffice."

—Male Senior, Duquesne University

"My life here is as the torrential rains of Dhamer upon the Yaktong Valley. I bleat like a llama shedding out of season."

— Ronald M., James Madison University

"This school is like a tight anus: there's tremendous pressure to come out straight and conformed."

— Stephen J., Washington and Lee University

"Intro classes have the consistency of Cheez Whiz: they go down easy, they taste horrible, and they are not good for you."

— Pat T., U. of Vermont

"This school was founded by Jesuits . . . . However, I believe that it has been hijacked by yuppie prisses."

—Anonymous, Loyola Marymount University

SEX, DRUGS, ROCK & ROLL...

"This school is no good for people who like art, music, and Sonic Youth. 'Society is a hole.' There's a quote by Sonic Youth."

— Meghan S., Lake Forest College

"Montreal is the city of festivals. It is the party-central of Canada. McGill is located right in the middle of it all."

—Female, McGill University

"The university tries to offer activities as an alternative to alcohol on the weekends. Those are not heavily attended. The weekends are for drinking."

—Maura G., Ohio University

"Beam, Bud, beer, babes—the four essential B's."

— "Jim Beam," Wittenberg University

"William and Mary: where you can drink beer and have sex in the same place your forefathers did."

— Adam L., College of William and Mary

"Yeah, there aren't any guys, but who doesn't like doing homework on a Saturday night?"

— Nicole C., Wellesley College

"UCSB is the only place where U Can Study Buzzed and still ace an exam the next day."

— Tracy B., UC—Santa Barbara

"The dances here are a riot because I love watching nerds and intellectuals dance."

—Male Senior, Columbia University

"When I visited schools, I went to Brown and Northwestern on the same trip. I went to NU on a Wednesday and Thursday night. I partied like a champ. At Brown on Friday I was invited to two parties (I should be psyched) but they were both for NUDE people. AUGH YUCK!"

— Silvy N., Northwestern University

"A Denison student might be quoted as saying, 'Life is a waste of time, and time is a waste of life; so get wasted all the time, and have the time of your life.'"

— Katherine H., Denison University

"This campus is an extremely great place to spend four college years, but it is still plagued, as all other campuses are, including Christian colleges, with sin. Therefore, this campus needs to come under submission to Jesus Christ."

— Laura D., James Madison University

"I have been around the block, you know, sex, drugs, and rock and roll. . . . I was in a sorority . . . . I tend to sleep around, too, but I basically think like a guy, so guys don't disrespect me. I am very picky in who I sleep with, only the best-bodied, best-looking dudes. They feel privileged, and I give them a hell of a time. I am quite the hottie, and I know it, so anyone who has a problem can just stay away."

—Anonymous, University of South Dakota

"St. Mary's College of Maryland Poem:

We are located on the H2O
We get blazed up where ever we go.
You throw your shoes around the tree
When you lose your virginity.
Parties here are just like heaven,
'Cause were all boozed up 24/7.
The girls are cute; the guys are hot,
If you open your window you are bound to smell pot.
If you visit my school I can promise you this,
You'll get so finagled you'll wake up in piss."

—Anonymous, St. Mary's College of Maryland

NEANDERTHALS

"If U R looking to settle down with an unattractive big woman, Hofstra is the place."

— Anonymous, Hofstra University

"There are lots of complaints about the attractiveness of the female students, but we females have our own saying about the guys at CMU—'The odds are good, but the goods are odd.'"

—Beth M., Carnegie Mellon University

"Girls at BYU are like parking spaces: the good ones are taken, the close ones are handicapped or reserved, and the rest are too far out!"

— Todd P., Brigham Young University

"In Rolla, we have tons of women, but not many of them!"

— Todd O., U. of Missouri—Rolla

"The faculty is great, academics are challenging, but the women are liberated and become difficult to live with. To sum it all up, Hendrix is so cool."

— Mike S., Hendrix College

"The students seem to have serious problems in general, perhaps they all need a little Viagra to perk things up a bit."

—Female Freshman, Albertson College

"UCSD rages—NOT! If you like the ocean and the library and have a fear of parties and girls without facial hair, you've hit the jackpot!!!"

— Spencer M., UC—San Diego

"There's a saying I've heard around: nine out of ten girls in California look good, the tenth goes to UCSD."

— Michael K., UC—San Diego

"U of C is OK if all you want to do is work, but if you are looking for a good social scene or a hot stinkin' babe, go to California, young man!"

—Benjamin D., University of Chicago

"Doesn't matter that we got no women. I'm never in bed anyway."

—Male Sophomore, California Institute of Technology

"Beer, football, and boobies are what Clemson is all about!"

— Paul S., Clemson University

"The men here often complain that there are too few women here; if they took a look in the mirror, maybe they'd realize why girls don't come here!"

— Tara L., Stevens Institute of Technology

"I would have sex more often but the girls are nasty!"

—Anonymous, St. Bonaventure University

"We need some more hot girls. Tell hot girls to come here."

—Anonymous, Macalester College

SCHOOL VS. THE "REAL WORLD"...

"College is the best time of your life. Never again will you be surrounded by people the same age as you, free from grown-ups and the threat of working in the real world. Your parents give you money when you ask for it, and all you have to do is learn!"

— Jennifer F., Syracuse University

"Real life experience in such concepts—alienation, depression, suppression, isolationism, edge of racial tension, apathy, etc.—before the 'Real World.'"

— Anonymous, NYU

"When we lose a football game to a college with lower academic standards, we console ourselves by saying that one day they will work for us and then we'll get even!"

— Michael J., Sewanee—University of the South

"Going to Chem. review is like masturbating with sandpaper: it's just a bad idea."

—Robby M., California Institute of Technology

SCHOOLS THAT ARE ALL THAT & A BAG OF CHIPS

"I like Duquesne because it has a mission beyond just educating students—it tries also to educate the heart and soul—and that makes for better students, a better university, and a better world."

—Female Senior, Duquesne University

"For the first time in my life I am allowed to think for myself. . . . This is an environment where one can proclaim in class that Socrates is a bastard and, if able to support the statement, be respected for it."

—Female Freshman, Simon's Rock College of Bard

"Best ever dude! Nobody complains if I leave the toilet seat up."

—Derek L., Deep Springs College

"We're small enough that you'll probably hug a significant portion of the population by the time you graduate."

—Male Junior, Bard College

"We play dodge ball at recess and think what it would be like if we could fly."

—Joseph W., Beloit College

"The students here are as diverse as their views and backgrounds. My friends are mostly thespians and lesbians, and they rock!"

—Female Junior, Bennington College

IN CASE YOU WERE WONDERING...

"You forgot to ask the most pertinent question, which is: 'Have you ever seen Elvis teach your 100 level courses?'"

— Adam L., Alfred University

"I was smart once. I used to sleep. Then I majored in chemical engineering."

— C. C. Smith, Clemson University

"There's about 15 too many classes along the lines of 'Talking Heads: The Politics of Cabbage in 19th Century Guam.'"

—Sarah G., Bennington College

"Classes are hard to get. Usually you have to cheat and just add the class, telling them you are a graduating senior. I've done that for the last three years and it works!"

—Anonymous, UC—Davis

"I am a hermit who enjoys Ramen noodles and skin flicks. In the winter, I sit in a yoga position by a patch of ice on the sidewalk and mock people as they fall. I often bend spoons with my mind."

—Junior, Indiana University of Pennsylvania

"When I'm not trying to free Mumia, experience non-gender orgasm/transgender interpretive dance, contracting any number of venereal diseases, or trying to be hopelessly unique, I obsess to no end in trying to reconcile my existentialist beliefs with paying $30,000 a year to attend this socially legitimizing institution."

—Katherine S., Bard College

"Those who oppose the Dark Lord will be crushed, but those who are its friend will receive rewards beyond the dreams of avarice."

— Anonymous, Sarah Lawrence College

"There is a real problem with moles on this campus; no one is willing to talk about them."

— Alexander D., Bates College

"Bates College is a phallocentric, logocentric, Greco-Roman, linear-rational, ethnocentric, homophobic, patriarchal institution. How's that for a list of catchwords?"

— Stephen H., Bates College

"I think if our generation's parents knew how consumptive, ill-informed, and drug-addicted their children were, they'd suffer a collective nervous breakdown."

— Anonymous, U. of Denver

"Our school is the school of the future and always will be."

— Chuck C., Rhodes College

"To begin, there's an apartment complex on a main road in my college city, and one of the apartments has put up a sign a few times this year that reads 'Honk for a drink.' So anytime someone drives by and honks his/her horn, the guys on the balcony take a swig of beer. I have also heard a story of a guy who turned 21 here and his buddies had a beer tube made that went from the third floor apartments down to the ground filled with beer for the guy to drink . . . . Someone like me would never survive an ordeal like that given my stature. Also, because Interstate 81 cuts through our campus, many drunk girls, especially on homecoming, enjoy giving the truck drivers a little peep show either day or night . . . . One of the great things about our school, though, is that we have a bus service called 'Ride with Len.' This man had a relative die from a drunk driver, and so on the weekends he takes to driving a huge bus around our town to take college kids to their prospective places safely. He has gotten so popular, that more buses and drivers have been added. ***So I'd say that although many people drink here, they drink responsibly."***

—Anonymous, James Madison University

CONFUSED PEOPLE...

"A crust of bread is better than nothing. Nothing is better than true love. Therefore, by the transitive property, a crust of bread is better than true love."

—Jason G., Gettysburg College

"Bentley College has fulfilled all and more of my expectations than I ever imagined."

— Dawn T., Bentley College

"Everyone seems to be really into political correctness, but in the wake of the recent Supreme Court decision, I don't see that lasting very long."

—John R., Birmingham Southern College

"Sarah Lawrence is a haven of unity and acceptance. Every morning at sunrise the entire campus gathers around the flagpole, holds hands, and sings 'We Are The World.' If you're really lucky, you get to be Dionne Warwick or Willie Nelson. If you show up late you have to be Bob Dylan. But everyone gets free doughnuts, and it's the happiest time of the day for most students. One morning I went hung over and threw up in the middle of the circle. I was so ashamed, but then I looked around at the diverse group of smiling faces from all over the country and the world and suddenly I felt better. I went home and threw up some more, thankful to live in the world of love that is Sarah Lawrence."

— Matt F., Sarah Lawrence College

(On the Academics/Administration) "They think they know a lot but they actually don't know anything, but some of them know that, so they know everything."

—Male Junior, College of the Atlantic

PART 5

INDEXES

INDEPENDENT COUNSELING

Currently, there are two professional organizations for independent counselors, Higher Education Consultants Association (HECA) and Independent Educational Consultants Association (IECA). Counselors affiliated with both groups provide varied and detailed services to students and families exploring future educational opportunities. You may find out more information about each group by visiting their individual websites. Each site provides a searchable database of member counselors, as well as clear descriptions of their qualifications. As a courtesy, below you will find a list of IECA Counselors and their contact information. Should you consider the services of an independent counselor, I encourage you to visit both the HECA and IECA websites for up to date information and listings.

Sincerely,
Robert Franek
Author—*The Best 361 Colleges*
VP—Publisher
The Princeton Review

HECA—Higher Education Consultants Association is an organization for independent educational consultants, educational services and other professionals. HECA is a non-profit, educational association comprised of professionals dedicated to helping students and families explore higher education options and opportunities.

www.hecaonline.org

IECA—The Independent Educational Consultants Association (IECA) is a national non-profit professional association of independent consultants.

www.iecaonline.com

INDEX OF IECA COLLEGE COUNSELORS

Alabama

Rosalind P. Marie,
Marie Associates
2759A Jeff Road
Harvest, AL 35749
256-852-4688
consultrm@aol.com
www.educationalavenues.com

Paulette R. Pearson,
Paulette Pearson Consulting Inc.
537 Oakline Drive
Hoover, AL35226
205-978-4090
ppearson@bellsouth.net

Arizona

Christopher Covert
The Ceel Kenny Group, LLC
11 Sundial Circle,
PO Box 2475
Carefree, AZ 85377
480-575-1535
CCovert915@aol.com
www.sedonaed.com

Rusty Haynes
CollegeMasters, Inc.
PO Box 12127
Scottsdale, AZ 85267
480-342-8304
collegemasters@cox.net
www.collegemasters.org

Nancy P. Masland
Nancy P. Masland & Associates
PO Box 30248
Tucson, AZ 85751
520-749-4220
nancy@nancypmasland.com
www.nancypmasland.com

W. Judge Mason
Educational Consultant
150 Devils Kitchen Drive
Sedona, AZ 86351
928-284-5719
judge@judgemason.org
www.judgemason.org

Adrianne G. Selbst
College Quest
21826 N. Calle Royale
Scottsdale, AZ 85255
480-585-7993
AdrianneG@cox.net
www.azcollegequest.com

Arkansas

Thomas A. Eppley, Jr.,
Thomas A. Eppley & Associates
2901 N. Grant
Little Rock, AR 72207
501-223-8949

California

Diane Grant Albrecht
Cathedral Hill Office Building
1255 Post Street, Suite 1001
San Francisco, CA 94109
415-928-1562
DGA84@aol.com

Miriam I. Bodin
Bodin Associates/Educ. Alternatives
5050 El Camino Real, Suite 101
Los Altos, CA 94022
650-937-1111
mbodin@bodinassociates.com
www.bodinassociates.com

Karen A. Curreri
IvyWise
9744 Wilshire Boulevard #312
Beverly Hills, CA 90212
310-246-0406
kcurreri@ivywise.com
www.ivywise.com

Kay Davison
National Institute for Educ. Planning
2042 Business Center Drive, Suite 200
Irvine, CA 92612
949-833-7899
kdavisonca@earthlink.net

David Denman
Educational Consultant
3030 Bridgeway Avenue, Suite 233
Sausalito, CA 94965
415-332-1831

Diane Geller
DeFelice & Geller, Inc.
2999 Overland Avenue, Suite 217
Los Angeles, CA 90064
310-202-0838
dhgeller@aol.com

Lynn Hamilton
PO Box 50724
Santa Barbara, CA 93150
805-969-1177
l.hamilton@cox.net
www.schoolfinders.com

Melissa Mose
Marriage & Family Therapist
18663 Ventura Blvd. #201
Tarzana. CA 91356
818-222-6340
mlmose@pacbell.net

Jill Q. Porter
Educational Consultant
1850 Castellana Road
La Jolla, CA 92037-3840
619-284-7277
porters@electriciti.com

Virginia Reiss
Licensed Educational Psychologist
980 Magnolia Avenue, Suite 8
Larkspur, CA 94939
415-461-4788
vreiss2@earthlink.net

Barbara E. Stahl, MA, CEP
1675 Scott Blvd. #321
Santa Clara, CA 95050
408-244-9540

Toby Waldorf
Educational Consultant
212 S. Woodburn Dr.
Los Angeles, CA 90049
310-476-2762
twaldorf@twaldorf.com
www.destination-u.com/toby

Rachel Winston
Educators With A Vision
7700 Irvine Center Drive, #800
Irvine, CA 92618
949-833-7706
rwinston@cerrocoso.edu

Colorado

Steven R. Antonoff
Antonoff Associates, Inc.
1241 South Parker Road, Suite 203
Denver, CO 80231
303-745-5577
schoolbuff@aol.com

Diane E. Arnold
Arnold Educational Consultants, LLC
2733 Big Horn Circle
Lafayette, CO 80026
303-604-2339
Darnold64@aol.com

Shirley Burr Darling
Educational Consulting Service
1355 S. Colorado Boulevard, Suite 300
Denver, CO 80222
303-757-3010
SBDarling@aol.com

Jana P. Lynn
Lynn Associates
6249 Songbird Circle
Boulder, CO 80303
303-443-7845
drjanalynn@comcast.net

Estelle R. Meskin
Educational Consultant
282 Monroe Street
Denver, CO 80206
303-394-3291
EMeskin@aol.com

Connecticut

Camille M. Bertram
Camille M. Bertram Educational Cons., LLC
120 Riders Lane
Fairfield, CT 06824
203-255-2577
CMBert@aol.com
www.cmbconsultants.com

Virginia J. Bush
Educational Consultant
15 Agawam Avenue, Fenwick
Old Saybrook, CT 06475
860-388-1242

Adrienne A. DuBois
DuBois & Associates
15 E. Putnam Avenue
Greenwich, CT 06830
203-629-2566
AADuBois@aol.com

Donald M. Dunbar
Dunbar Educational Consultants
191 Elm Street
New Canaan, CT 06840
203-259-4123
DunbarEd@optonline.net

Susan B. Edwards
Susan B. Edwards Associates
10 Pennoyer Street
Rowayton, CT 06853
203-866-2692
SusanBEdwards@att.net
www.susanbedwards.com

John M. Greenwood
Dunbar Educational Consultants
191 Elm Street
New Canaan, CT 06840
203-966-5454
dunbedc@aol.com

Alan Haas
Educational Futures
191 Main Street
New Canaan, CT 06840
203-966-6993
EduFutures@aol.com
www.educationalfutures.com

Emilie K. Hinman
Dunbar Educational Consultants, Inc.
10 Indian Chase Drive
Greenwich, CT 06830
203-625-6344
EKHDunbar@aol.com

Margaret M. King
Margaret King & Associates
1895 Post Road
Fairfield, CT 06824
203-255-5511
mkingec@aol.com

Carol A. Loewith
Educational Consultant
191 Fairfield Woods Road
Fairfield, CT 06825
203-372-4222
CALEdCon@aol.com

William M. Morse
William Morse Associates, Inc.
260 Riverside Avenue
Westport, CT 06880-4804
203-222-1066
wmmorse@aol.com

James P. Robinson
Robinson/Scholastic Objectives
281 Loon Meadow Drive,
PO Box 628
Norfolk, CT 06058
860-542-1300
jrobinson@scholasticobjectives.net
www.scholasticobjectives.net

Daria M. Rockholz
The College Connection
PO Box 539
Ridgefield, CT 06877
203-438-2469
drockholz@aol.com

Jan Rooker
College Coach
6 Prides Crossing
New Canaan, CT 06840
203-972-3487
rookerj@msn.com

Marcia B. Rubinstien
EDUFAX
345 North Main Street, Suite 317
West Hartford, CT 06117
860-233-3900
edufax@edufax.com
www.edufax.com

Amy Sack, PhD
101 Oakland Drive
Trumbull, CT 06611
203-261-8068
asack2@aol.com
www.admissionsaccomplished.com

Alison Pedicord Schleifer
Educational Consultant
220 Alston Avenue
New Haven, CT 06515
203-387-3454
hs32@mindspring.com

Laura Seese
Educational Advancement Associates
14 Old Farms Lane, Suffield, CT 06093
860-254-5451
LauraSeese@edadvancement.com
www.edadvancement.com

Mary Spiegel
Spiegel Educational Consulting, LLC
16 Plumb Creek Road
Trumbull, CT 06611
203-261-3299
spiegels2@juno.com

Susan Wexler
Educational Consultant
14 Bushy Ridge Road
Westport, CT 06880
203-341-0599
susanwex@aol.com

Delaware

Bettina G. Heiman
CollegeChoice
2408 Driftwood Drive
Wilmington, DE 19810
302-475-7912
collegechoice@comcast.net

District of Columbia

Kpakpundu Ezeze
Future Quest, Inc.
1346 Ritchie Place, NE
Washington, DC 20017
202-832-6339
kezeze@aol.com

Steven Roy Goodman
Tilden Gardens 502
3020 Tilden Street NW
Washington, DC 20008-3081
202-986-9431
steve@topcolleges.com
www.topcolleges.com

Florida

Robin G. Abedon
12904 Mizner Way
Wellington, FL 33414
561-790-5462
rabedon@takingtheNextStep.com
www.takingtheNextStep.com

Betty Jean Arsenault, Ed.D.
Arsenault Educational Consultants LLC
801 International Parkway, 5th Fl.
Heathrow, FL 32746
407-562-1800
DrBetty@bellsouth.net
www.ArsenaultEducationalConsultants.com

Sandy Bercu
College Consulting Services
14043 Shady Shores Drive
Tampa, FL 33613
813-963-6342
sbercu@aol.com

Shirley H. Grate
SG, Inc. (GRES)
PO Box 17623
West Palm Beach, FL 33406-7623
561-906-9715
sgrate@aol.com

Janet Greenwood
Greenwood Associates, Inc.
310 S. Brevard Avenue
Tampa, FL 33606
813-254-5303
JGreenwd@GreenwdAssoc.com
www.GreenwdAssoc.com

Martha Moses
Martha Moses & Associates
8100 SW 81 Drive, Suite 277
Miami, FL 33143
305-273-0014
mmoses@gate.net

Judi Robinovitz
Judi Robinovitz Associates
3010 N. Military Trail, Suite 220
Boca Raton, FL 33431
561-241-1610 or 888-GET-1600
JudiRobino@aol.com
www.ScoreAtTheTop.com

Georgia

Leonard A. Buccellato
Licensed Psychologist
3340 Peachtree Road, NE, Suite 1125
Atlanta, GA 30326
404-231-9925
Lenbuccellato@mindspring.com

Mark L. Fisher
Fisher Educational Consultants, Inc.
10 Glenlake Pway-S. Turnpike, #130-182
Atlanta, GA 30328
678-222-3444
mfisher@mindspring.com

Jean P. Hague
400 Colony Square
1201 Peachtree, NE #200
Atlanta, GA 30361
404-872-9128
jeanhague@aol.com

B.J. Hopper
B.J. Hopper & Associates
3400 Peachtree Road, Suite 1539
Atlanta, GA 30326
404-814-1394
BHopper719@aol.com

George G. Kirkpatrick
The George G. Kirkpatrick Co.
3210 Peachtree Road, NE, Suite 12
Atlanta, GA 30305-2400
404-233-3989
kirkeducon@aol.com
www.theggkco.com

Sandra G. Lawrence
Independent College Consultant
2952 Foxhall Circle
Augusta, GA 30907
706-860-9517
MrsL31747@aol.com

Mary M. Poe
Educational Consultant
501 Manor Ridge Drive
Atlanta, GA 30305
404-351-9557
teedmp@att.net

J. Victor Spigener, III
Educational Consultant
8045 Sandorn Drive
Roswell, GA 30075
770-650-1962
spigenerv@bellsouth.net

Leigh Anne Spraetz
Greenwood Associates, Inc.
730 Mallory Manor Court
Alpharetta, GA 30022
678-336-3265
laspraetz@comcast.net
www.greenwdassoc.com

Illinois

Susan J. Bigg
Educational Consultant
1410 Wrightwood Avenue #K
Chicago, IL 60614-1140
773-404-1699
wbyeats@megsinet.net

Jill Burstein
Jill Burstein Educational Consulting
30 W. St. Andrews
Deerfield, IL 60015
847-940-8090
collegefinderjb@aol.com
www.college-finder.org

Harriet R. Gershman
Access Education International
1800 Sherman Avenue, Suite 203
Evanston, IL 60201
847-492-3434
ACSGersh@aol.com

Nancy Gore Marcus
333 Rosewood Avenue
Winnetka, IL 60093
847-446-7557
ngmadvise@aol.com

Imy F. Wax
Licensed Clinical Prof. Counselor
1320 Carol Lane
Deerfield, IL 60015
847-945-0913
ImyWax@aol.com

Kentucky

Paul Levitch
Levitch Associates, LLC
7508 New LaGrange Rd., Suite 9
Louisville, KY 40222
502-412-7244
paul@levitch.net
www.levitch.net

Louisiana

Nancy W. Cadwallader
Collegiate Advisory Placement Services
PO Box 66371
Baton Rouge, LA 70896
225-928-1818
cadwallader@worldnet.att.net

Kathie Livaudais Carnahan
Carnahan & Associates
4904 Magazine Street
New Orleans, LA 70115
504-269-6449
collegepro@bellsouth.net

Maryland

Judith Bass
Bass Educational Services
4229 Cherry Valley Drive
Olney, MD 20832
240-606-4996
judy@collegeconsulting.info

Diane E. Epstein
College Planning Service, Inc.
6704 Pawtucket Road
Bethesda, MD 20817-4836
301-320-5311
dianecps@comcast.net

Charlotte Klaar
College Consulting Services
14 Fiona Way
Brunswick, MD 21758
301-834-6888
CKlaar@ccs4college.com
www.ccs4college.com

Shirley Levin
College Bound
6809 Breezewood Terrace
Rockville, MD 20852
301-468-6668
lev4advice@verizon.net

Irena S.M. Makarushka, PhD
School Search Group, LLC
502 Baltimore Avenue
Towson, MD 21204
410-494-0209
makarushka@ssgllc.com

Lori Potts-Dupré
7006 Carroll Avenue, Suite 202
Takoma Park, MD 20912
301-891-8866
LNPD@aol.com

Nancy Rosenberg
Specialized College Counseling
6412 Kenhowe Drive
Bethesda, MD 20817
301-320-5652
nancy@specialcc.com
www.specialcc.com

Gail H. Ross
College Admissions Consultant
6128 Durbin Road
Bethesda, MD 20817
301-229-7005
gailhross@hotmail.com

Virginia Reynolds Vogel
Educational Guidance Service
85 Bay Drive
Annapolis, MD 21403
301-469-6973
jhvogs@aol.com

Massachusetts

Peter D. Adams
Educational Counseling
295 Bug Hill Road
Ashfieldl, MA 01330
413-628-4791
padamsec@rcn.com

Edward L. Bigelow
Dunbar Educational Consultants, Inc.
16 Prescott Street, #300
Wellesley Hills, MA 02481
781-263-9992
nbigelow@dunbarconsultants.com
www.dunbarconsultants.com

Susan Bisson, Ed.M.
Advocates for Human Potential, Inc.
490-B Boston Post Road, Suite 200

Sudbury, MA 01776
978-261-1433
sbisson@ahpnet.com
www.ahpnet.com

Joan H. Bress
College Resource Associates
12 Southwood Road
Worcester, MA 01609
508-757-8920
jbress@aol.com
www.CollegeResourceAssociates.com

Stella Christine Chapman
Starr Education Services
1073 Long Pond Road
Plymouth, MA 02360
617-938-3595
chapman_christine@yahoo.com
www.starreducation.com

Marilyn F. Engelman
Educational Directions
57 East Main Street, Suite 224
Westborough, MA 01581
508-870-1515
marilyn171@aol.com

Leslie S. Goldberg
Leslie S. Goldberg & Associates, LLC
15 Sentinel Road
Hingham, MA 02043
781-749-2074
leslie@edconsult.org
www.edconsult.org

Renee LeWinter Goldberg
Options in Education
175 Beacon Street, #309
Somerville, MA 02143
617-864-8864
Renee@optionsined.com
www.optionsined.com

Adam R. Goldberg
Leslie S. Goldberg & Associates
33 Clark St., Suite 1
Newton Centre, MA 02459
617-969-5151
adam@edconsult.org
www.edconsult.org

Louise Kreiner
Kreiner Associates
PO Box 5217
Bradford, MA 01835-0217
978-373-9561
KreinerCon@aol.com
www.louisekreiner.com

Timothy B. Lee
Advocates for Human Potential, Inc.
490-B Boston Post Road, #200
Sudbury, MA 01776-3365
978-261-1412
tlee@ahpnet.com
www.ahpnet.com

Priscilla B. Lewis
Educational Consultant
PO Box 128 (Barnstable)
Cummaquid, MA 02637
508-362-9697
rblewis@attbi.com

Midge Lipkin
Schoolsearch
127 Marsh Street
Belmont, MA 02478
617-489-5785
mlipkin@schoolsearch.com
www.schoolsearch.com

Mary Mansfield
Mansfield Associates
20 Lincoln Lane
Sudbury, MA 01776
978-443-4404
rsmansfie@aol.com

Sarah M. McGinty
McGinty Consulting Group
322 Marlborough Street
Boston, MA 02116
617-262-3435
sarahmcginty@att.net
www.mcgintyconsulting.com

Adam S. Metsch
The College Advisor of N. England, Inc.
94 Shaker Road
East Longmeadow, MA 01028
413-525-9595
Adam@College-Advisor.com
www.College-Advisor.com

Bonny C. Musinsky
Musinsky & Associates
49 Kendall Common Road
Weston, MA 02493
781-899-5759
bonny@musinskyassociates.com
www.musinskyassociates.com

Laurie H. Nash
Educational Consultant
24 Cross Hill Road
Newton Centre, MA 02459
617-332-2794
Laurie@LaurieNash.com

Cornelia Nicholson
Educational Consultant
44 Fairwinds Drive
Osterville, MA 02655
508-420-3085
cdnicholson@comcast.net

Michael W. Spence
Howland & Spence, Inc.
262 Beacon Street
Boston, MA 02116
617-536-4319
mspence@howlandspence.com

Michigan

Teresa S. Lloyd, Ed.S.
Grosse Point College Administration Consulting
1020 Bishop Rd.
Grosse Point Park, MI 48230
313-882-2526
tslloyd@comcast.net
www.gpcollegeconsulting.com

Lynn B. Luckenbach
Lynn B. Luckenbach, Inc.
111 S. Old Woodward, Suite 214
Birmingham, MI 48009
248-644-0749
lynnluck@aol.com

Minnesota

Janine Braman
Braman Educational Consulting
2243 Fairmount Avenue
St. Paul, MN 55105
651-308-2111
janinebraman@comcast.net

Valerie J. Broughton
Educational Consulting Services
208 Portland Ave. So.
Minneapolis, MN 55401
612-251-1978
valerie@ecsminnesota.com
www.ecsduluth.com

Nicky B. Carpenter
Educational Consultants
1001 Twelve Oaks Center Drive, Suite 1020
Wayzata, MN 55391
952-475-0330
NCARPEN635@aol.com

Deborah Landon, MBA
Educational Advisory Services
4549 Abbott Avenue S.
Minneapolis, MN 55410
612-922-5888
landoneducation@yahoo.com
www.susanmspain.com

Suzanne Luse
Suzanne Luse & Associates
3588 Woodland Trail
Eagan, MN 55123
651-688-0595
sueluse@comcast.net

Susan F. Sykes
Educational Consultant
19 Hawthorne Road
Hopkins, MN 55343
763-218-1030
ssadvisor@winternet.com

Missouri

James C. Heryer
College Guidance & Placement
705 Brush Creek Blvd.
Kansas City, MO 64110
816-531-2706
jheryer@aol.com

Rosalyn S. Lowenhaupt
Indep. School Placement Service
7710 Carondelet, #101
St. Louis, MO 63105
314-727-4909
isps-rsl@att.net

Jane Schoenfeld
Indep. School Placement Serv.
7710 Carondelet, #101
St. Louis, MO 63105
314-727-4909
isps-jbs@att.net

New Hampshire

Peter P. Drake
Drake Associates Educational Planners, LLC
195 Old Dublin Road
PO Box 355
Hancock, NH 03449
603-525-3232
ppdnhd@aol.com

Mei-Ling Henrichson
Mei-Ling Henrichson Educational Consulting
PO Box 138
Winchester, NH 03470
603-239-8189
mlhedcon@ix.netcom.com

New Jersey

Judith Berg
Judith Berg Associates
257 Monmouth Street, Building B #1
Oakhurst, NJ 07755
732-531-1300
jberg@monmouth.com

Barbara A. Fallon
Educational Consultant
PO Box 200
Saddle River, NJ 07458
201-488-9547
barbarafallon1@yahoo.com

Barbara Hannmann
Licensed Professional Counselor
325 Springhouse Lane
Moorestown, NJ 08057
609-458-2928
bobbihann@aol.com

Leonard Krivy
Educational Consultant
1765 Fireside Lane
Cherry Hill, NJ 08003
856-428-1282
LPKPHD@aol.com

Ronna Morrison
Ronna Morrison Associates
11 Maple Avenue
Demarest, NJ 07627
201-768-8250
RonnaCEP@aol.com

Marylou Schaffer
Crossroads Youth Counseling
17 Hathaway Lane
Verona, NJ 07044
973-857-1251
MLSCROSS@aol.com

Anita Targan
Anita Targan Associates
2 Gloucester Place
Morristown, NJ 07960
973-538-7607
atargan@earthlink.net

New Mexico

Whitney Laughlin
Educational Consultant
18 Cougar Ridge Road
Santa Fe, NM 87505
505-690-9054
laughlin@rt66.com
www.whitneylaughlin.com

Kim A. Rubin
Academic Consultants
1800 Old Pecos Trail, Suite J
Santa Fe, NM 87505
505-989-8910
generalinfo@academicconsultants.com
www.academicconsultants.com

New York

Noreen Cambria
Cambria Associates, Inc.
58 New Street
Huntington, NY 11743
631-424-6450
contact@guidancepro.com
www.guidancepro.com

Kyung Yo Cho
North Shore Educational Consultants
318 Hillside Drive South
New Hyde Park, NY 11040
516-294-3337
winnercircle123@hotmail.com

Katherine Cohen
IvyWise, LLC
140 West 57th Street, Suite 3D
New York, NY 10019
212-262-3500
kcohen@ivywise.com
www.ivywise.com

Marilyn G.S. Emerson
College Planning Services, Inc.
84 Old Farm Road, N.
Chappaqua, NY 10514
914-747-1760
mgse@collplan.com
www.collplan.com

Robert Franek
Educational Consultant
403 West 21st Street, Suite 3W
New York, NY 10011
212-367-9334
robertfranek@earthlink.net

Geraldine C. Fryer
Educational Advisor
1066 Boston Post Road
Rye, NY 10580-2902
914-967-7952
gcfryer@aol.com

Patricia B. Gildersleeve
The College Advisory Service
16 Harrogate Road
New Hartford, NY 13413
315-732-9001
pbgilder@aol.com

Carol Gill
Carol Gill Associates
369 Ashford Avenue
Dobbs Ferry, NY 10522
914-693-8200
carolgill@aol.com
www.collegesplus.com

Carole Gitnik
College Admission Advisor
7 Yale Drive
Manhasset, NY 11030
516-625-9678
CLG8640@yahoo.com

Pearl Glassman
Pearl Glassman Counseling, Inc.
30 White Birch Road
Pound Ridge, NY 10576
914-764-5153
glassman@cloud9.net

Barbara Ann Kenefick
Educational Advisor
PO Box 247
Chatham, NY 12037-0247
518-392-4753
bkenefick@berkshireschool.org

Jane E. Kolber
Educational Consultant
142 East 71 Street
New York, NY 10021
212-734-1704
JEKWFK@aol.com

Joette Krupa
College Placement Consultants
2330 Shirl Lane
Niskayuna, NY 12309
518-346-1095
hjkrupa@nycap.rr.com

Yong Moon, M.S.
Empire College Bound Counseling Company
63-10 Northern Boulevard #311
Flushing, NY1358
718-661-4936
gt1976@aol.com

Mike Musiker
Musiker Associates
1326 Old Northern Blvd.
Roslyn Village, NY 11576
516-621-3713
mike@summerfun.com
www.summerfun.com

Suzan Reznick
The College Connection
39 Roma Orchard Road
Peekskill, NY 10566
914-734-8440
asksuzan@optonline.net

Jill Rifkin
College Options
145 Darroch Road
Delmar, NY 12054
518-439-1843
jrrif@aol.com

Christine J. Scott
Scott-Deutsch Associates
PO Box 586
Ardsley, NY 10502
917-519-2900
cscottub@aol.com

Joan Tager
Educational Consultant
577 Old Montauk Highway
Montauk, NY 11954
631-668-4239
capstager1@aol.com

Sally M. Ten Eyck
College Assistance Plus
43 Tygert Road
Altamont, NY 12009
518-765-3288
smteneyck@yahoo.com

North Carolina

R. Gordon Bingham
Bingham Associates
173 Tullyries Lane
Lewisville, NC 27023
336-946-2819
gbingham2@triad.rr.com

Mary Jane Freeman
Davidson Center for Learning
& Academic Planning
PO Box 550,
452 S. Main Street
Davidson, NC 28036-0550
704-892-4533
MaryjaneF@aol.com
www.davidsoncenter.com

Linda McMullen
Licensed Professional Counselor
3435 Lakeview Trail,
PO Box 6278
Kinston, NC 28501
252-523-2769
mcmullen@eastlink.net

Ann Crandall Sloan
Triangle Educational Planners
3820 Merton Drive, Suite 215
Raleigh, NC 27609
919-828-2828
acsloan@bellsouth.net
www.triangleeducationalplanners.com

Ohio

Arline Altman
College-Career Planning Consulting
6050 Cranberry Court
Columbus, OH 43213
614-864-0356
collegecareerplan@insight.rr.com

Toni DiPasquale
Partners in Educational Planning
7353 Old Stable Lane
Dayton, OH 45459-4210
937-435-0621 or 888-664-0621
pepservice@aol.com

Bill Kellerman, MA
College 101
6467 Oregon Pass
West Chester, OH 45069
513-379-9521
wlk@cinci.rr.com

Phyllis G. Kozokoff
Licensed Professional Counselor
23811 Chagrin Blvd., Suite 307
Cleveland, OH 44122
216-464-3686
Pkozokoff@aol.com

Oregon

Marilyn Petrequin
Petrequin College Consulting
2455 NW Marshall St., Suite 6
Portland, OR 97210
503-223-4429
mpetrequin@yahoo.com
www.home.earthlink.net/
~mzpetrequin

Nancy E. Smith
11235 SW Lynnvale Drive
Portland, OR 97225
503-520-9666
dekesmith@aol.com

Pennsylvania

Peggy Baker
Educational Consultant
1934 Whiteacre Drive North
Bethlehem, PA 18015
610-867-2477
Pegedu@yahoo.com

Laurie Crockett Barclay
College Planning Associates
912 W. Fourth Street
Williamsport, PA 17701
570-322-1313
lbarclay@suscom.net

Grant Calder
Bennett Educational Resources, Inc.
310 North High StreetWest
Chester, PA 19380
610-692-9096
gcalder@schoolplacement.com
www.schoolplacement.com

Robert Cohen
College Admissions Services
65 E. Elizabeth Ave., Suite 612
Bethlehem, PA 18018
610-867-1818
rdcollege@enter.net
www.collegeplan.com

Dodge Johnson
College Planning
547 Sugartown Road
Malvern, PA 19355
610-647-6755
dodge.johnson@comcast.net

James A. Nolan
Access Education International
1062 Lancaster Avenue, #22
Rosemont, PA 19010
610-527-9242
NolEduIntl@aol.com

Lloyd R. Paradiso
Sage Education Resource Group
Cresslund Farm, Box 459
Blue Bell, PA 19422
267-975-7580
lparadiso@sageeducation.com
www.sageeducation.com

Luisa M. Rabe
Pruett Rabe Associates
112 Buck Lane
Haverford, PA 19041
610-896-9522
luisa@pruettrabe.com

Suzanne F. Scott
Licensed/Certified School Psychologist
681 Meetinghouse Road–1
Elkins Park, PA 19027
215-887-2201
scottaas@comcast.net
www.IECAonline.com/suzannescott

Susan Strom
College Selection Consultants
680 Long Acre Lane
Yardley, PA 19067
215-321-7019
susanstrom@comcast.net

Barry Sysler
Academic Directions
509 Coachwood Court
Newtown, PA 18940
866-496-8733
bsysler@aol.com
www.academicdirections.com

Rhode Island

Susan M. Hanflik
Educational Consultant
170 Summit Drive
Cranston, RI 02920
401-944-4315
smhanflik@cox.net

C. Claire Law
Educational Avenues
65 Osprey Drive, Suite 100
E. Greenwich, RI 02818
401-885-7682
clairelaw@cox.net
www.educationalavenues.com

Ruth Lipka
Academic Admissions Consultants, LLC
430 Old River Road
Lincoln, RI 02838
401-762-3675
alllipka@cox.net

Andrea C. O'Hearn
Academic Answers
PO Box 96
Barrington, RI 02806
401-246-2511
acanswers@aol.com

Patricia A. Zito
White Water Consulting, LLC
264 Bonnet Point Road
Narragansett, RI 02882
401-789-7760
Pat.Zito@cox.net

South Carolina

William S. Dingledine, Jr.
Educational Directions, Inc.
PO Box 5249
Greenville, SC 29606
864-467-1838
WSDingle@bellsouth.net
www.educdir.com

Ann Carol Price
Educational Planning Services
3104 Devine Street
Columbia, SC 29205
803-252-5777
anncarolprice@yahoo.com
www.thepricegroup.com

Tennessee

Mary B. Consoli
Mary B. Consoli Associates
624 Reliability Circle
Knoxville, TN 37932
865-675-1997
mbconsoli@aol.com
www.mbconsoli.com

Farron G. Peatross
Educational Placement Services, Inc.
5130 Greenway Cove
Memphis, TN 38117
901-685-3156
peatross@bellsouth.net

Bunny Porter-Shirley
Educational Planning Services
801 Lynnbrook Road
Nashville, TN 37215
615-269-3322
eduplanners@comcast.net
www.eduplanners.com

Anne Thompson
Educational Consultant
3978 Central Avenue
Memphis, TN 38111
901-458-6291, ext. 1812
athompson@cpcmemphis.net
www.cpcmemphis.net

Texas

Carol G. Cohen
Cohen's College Connection
4950 Keller Springs Road, Suite 160
Addison, TX 75001-6205
972-381-9990
carolgene@cohenscc.com

Elizabeth Hall
Education Consulting Services
2509 Hartford Road
Austin, TX 78703
512-476-5082
ehh@mail.utexas.edu

Lindy Kahn
Lindy Kahn Associates, Inc.
6717 Vanderbilt
Houston, TX 77005
713-668-2609
lindyk23@hotmail.com
www.educationalconsulting.com

Ceel Kenny
The Ceel Kenny Group, LLC
531 Rockhill Drive
San Antonio, TX 78209
210-804-0600
sea@sedona.net
www.sedonaed.com

Peggy D. Manley, M.Ed.
Educational Search & Placement
2902 Bowman Avenue
Austin, TX 78703
512-481-0717
espsat@austin.rr.com

Londa May
Campus Selection
2 Dunloggin Lane
The Woodlands, TX 77380
281-364-9700
londa@houston.rr.com

Marsha R. Meyers
Cohen's College Connection
6705 Regalbluff
Dallas TX 75248-5433
mmeyers@ev1.net
www.cohenscc.com

Ann Montgomery
Woodfin & Associates
4545 Post Oak Place, Suite 110
Houston, TX 77027
713-942-0345
wyndhover@aol.com
www.bestschoolforyou.com

Judy W. Muir, M.Ed.
6162 San Felipe Rd.
Houston, TX 77057
713-819-5400
judywmuir@yahoo.com

Mary Jo O'Neal
Greenwood Associates, Inc.
9 Diamond Oak Court
The Woodlands, TX 77381
281-298-8180
mjoneal@greenwdassoc.com
www.greenwdassoc.com

Marshall E. Shumsky, PhD
Cognitive, Adolescent,
& Child Development
7887 San Felipe Road, Suite 101
Houston, TX 77063-1620
713-784-6610
shumsky@shumsky.net
www.theeducationdoctor.com

Elissa Sommerfield
School Placement Services
9636 Hollow Way
Dallas, TX 75220
214-363-7043
esom@techrack.com

Rhea M. Wolfram
Rhea M. Wolfram Associates
13928 Hughes Lane
Dallas, TX 75240-3510
972-233-1115
rwolframsis@airmail.net

Christie Theriot Woodfin
Christie Woodfin & Associates
4545 Post Oak Place, Suite 110
Houston, TX 77027
713-439-1300
CWOODFINEd@aol.com
www.bestschoolforyou.com

Vermont

Lora K. Block
College Advisory Services
34 McIntosh Lane
Bennington, VT 05201
802-447-0776
lblock@sover.net

Robert M. Kantar
Educational Resources
1041 Brown Farm Road
Lyndonville, VT 05851
802-626-4620
RKantar@aol.com
www.bobkantar.com

Benjamin L. Mason
Mason & Associates
PO Box 59
2687 Greenbush Road
Charlotte, VT 05445
802-425-7600
BEEMASON@aol.com

Virginia

Samuel Barnett
SchoolFutures
227 Nutley Street, NW
Vienna, VA 22180
703-938-1787
schoolfutures@earthlink.net
www.schoolfutures.com

Shirley A. Bloomquist
A Second Opinion
11136 Rich Meadow Drive
Great Falls, VA 22066
703-406-8034
sbloomqu@aol.com

Leslie A. Kent, MA
Leslie Kent Consulting
2713 Verily Court
Oakton, VA 22124
703-620-9297
lakent@cox.net

Joan E. Levin, LCSW, M.Ed.
A+ College Counseling
2026 Rhode Island Avenue
McLean, VA 22101
703-359-0202
joanendow@hotmail.com

Emily A. Snyder, MA
Know Your Options
12731 Lady Somerset Lane
Fairfax, VA 22033
703-817-0797
emily@knowyouroptions.net
www.knowyouroptions.net

Washington

Andrew Bryan
O'Shaughnessy & Bryan Associates
13400 NE 20th Street, Suite 47
Bellevue, WA 98005
888-385-2877
ABryanEdPlan@aol.com
www.academicinstitute.com

Linda Jacobs
Linda Jacobs & Associates
5508 35th Ave. NE, Suite 104
Seattle, WA 98105
206-323-8902
LinJacobs@aol.com

Kiersten A. Murphy
Murphy Educational Consulting
7221 Laurel Avenue, SE
Snoqualmie, WA 98065
425-396-5618
kiersten@schoolconsultant.com
www.schoolconsultant.com

Sherrill O'Shaughnessy
O'Shaughnessy & Bryan Associates
The Academic Institute, Inc.
13400 NE 20th Street, Suite 47
Bellevue, WA 98005
425-401-6844
EdPlan@aol.com
www.academicinstitute.com

Pauline B. Reiter, PhD
College Placement Consultants
40 Lake Bellevue, Suite 100
Bellevue, WA 98005
425-453-1730
preiter@qwest.net

West Virginia

Jamie Dickenson
The Collegiate Advisor
1596 Kanowha Boulevard E.
Charleston, WV 25311
304-556-4807
jamie@jamiedickenson.com
www.jamiedickenson.com

Wisconsin

Laurie A. Bookstein
College Placement Services
9596 N. Regent Road
Milwaukee, WI 53217
414-351-6801
cpsinclab@aol.com

Joanne Hytken
Educational Consulting
7114 North Lake Drive
Milwaukee, WI 53217
414-351-1271
jhytken@aol.com

Gisela Terner
Special Ed. Consulting & College Planning
1009 West Glen Oaks Lane, Suite 208
Mequon, WI 53092
262-240-2213
gterner@execpc.com

INTERNATIONAL

Jamaica

Sandra Bramwell-Riley, MPA
Versan Educational Services
2 Richings Avenue #13
Kingston 6, Jamaica BWI
876-946-0500
versanedu@jamweb.net
www.versan-edu.com

Greece

Christine Jackson Counelis
Carpe Diem International
Amalias 2
Kifissia 145 61 Greece
3021.080.82.997
carpedm@otenet.gr

Japan

Makiko Kashikura
Educational Information & Consultants
Le Chateau de Fontaine 2F, 1-10-23 Jingumae
Shibuya-ku, Tokyo 150-0001 Japan
81.3.3408.2901
makiko@edictoday.co.jp
www.edictoday.co.jp

Kyomi Kumehara
Educational Information & Consultants
Le Chateau de Fontaine 2F, 1-10-23 Jingumae
Shibuya-ku, Tokyo 150-0001 Japan
81.3.3408.2901
kyomi@edictoday.co.jp
www.edictoday.co.jp

Tamiko Nakamura
Educational Information & Consultants
Le Chateau de Fontaine 2F, 1-10-23 Jingumae
Shibuya-ku, Tokyo 150-0001 Japan
81.3.3408.2901
tamiko@edictoday.co.jp
www.edictoday.co.jp

South Korea

Yung Oh
Starr Education Services, Inc.
2nd floor, Jinyoung Bldg, 909-3
Daechidong Kangnam-ku, Seoul
South Korea
82.2.561.8191
starr_ses@yahoo.com

Ock Kyung Chun
Seoul Academy for Foreign Studies
5th floor, Dongyang Bl. 1331
Seochodong
Seocho-Ku, 137-860 Seoul, Korea
822.3473.6561
ok@seoulacademy.org
www.seoulacademy.org

Turkey

H. Nazan Kabatepe
Adnan Saygun Cad. Gundes Bloklari
Selin Apt. Kat: 2D
10 Ulus/Istanbul Turkey
90.212.2637560
nazankabatepe@erkagroup.com
www.nazankabatepe.com

INDEX OF SCHOOLS

A

Agnes Scott College 46
Albertson College 48
Albion College 50
Alfred University 52
Allegheny College 54
American University 56
Amherst College 58
Arizona State University 60
Auburn University 62
Austin College 64

B

Babson College 66
Bard College 68
Barnard College 70
Bates College 72
Baylor University 74
Bellarmine University 76
Beloit College 78
Bennington College 80
Bentley College 82
Berea College 84
Birmingham-Southern College 86
Boston College 88
Boston University 90
Bowdoin College 92
Bradley University 94
Brandeis University 96
Brigham Young University (UT) 98
Brown University 100
Bryant University 102
Bryn Mawr College 104
Bucknell University 106

C

Cal Poly—San Luis Obispo 108
California Institute of Technology 110
Calvin College 112
Carleton College 114
Carnegie Mellon University 116
Case Western Reserve University 118
Catawba College 120
Catholic University of America, The 122
Centenary College of Louisiana 124
Centre College 126
Chapman University 128
City University of New York—Brooklyn College 130
City University of New York—Hunter College 132
City University of New York—Queens College 134
Claremont McKenna College 136
Clark University 138
Clarkson University 140
Clemson University 142
Coe College 144
Colby College 146
Colgate University 148
College of the Atlantic 150
College of Charleston 152
College of the Holy Cross 154
College of New Jersey, The 156
College of the Ozarks 158
College of Saint Benedict/Saint John's University 160
College of William and Mary 162
College of Wooster, The 164
Colorado College 166
Colorado School of Mines 168
Colorado State University 170
Columbia University—Columbia College 172
Connecticut College 174
Cooper Union 176
Cornell College 178
Cornell University 180
Creighton University 182

D

Dartmouth College 184
Davidson College 186
Deep Springs College 188
Denison University 190
DePaul University 192
DePauw University 194
Dickinson College 196
Drew University 198
Drexel University 200
Duke University 202
Duquesne University 204

E

Earlham College 206
Eckerd College 208
Elon University 210
Emerson College 212
Emory University 214
Eugene Lang College 216
Evergreen State College, The 218

F

Fairfield University 220
Fisk University 222
Flagler College 224
Florida State University 226
Fordham University 228
Franklin & Marshall College 230
Franklin W. Olin College of Engineering 232
Furman University 234

G

George Mason University 236
George Washington University, The 238
Georgetown University 240
Georgia Institute of Technology 242
Gettysburg College 244
Gonzaga University 246
Goucher College 248
Grinnell College 250
Grove City College 252
Guilford College 254
Gustavus Adolphus College 256

H

Hamilton College 258
Hampden-Sydney College 260
Hampshire College 262

Hampton University 264
Hanover College 266
Harvard College 268
Harvey Mudd College 270
Haverford College 272
Hendrix College 274
Hillsdale College 276
Hiram College 278
Hobart and William Smith Colleges 280
Hofstra University 282
Hollins University 284
Howard University 286

I

Illinois Institute of Technology 288
Illinois Wesleyan University 290
Indiana University—Bloomington 292
Indiana University of Pennsylvania 294
Iowa State University 296
Ithaca College 298

J

James Madison University 300
Johns Hopkins University 302
Juniata College 304

K

Kalamazoo College 306
Kansas State University 308
Kenyon College 310
Knox College 312

L

Lafayette College 314
Lake Forest College 316
Lawrence University 318
Lehigh University 320
Lewis & Clark College 322
Louisiana State University 324
Loyola University New Orleans 326
Loyola College in Maryland 328
Loyola Marymount University 330
Loyola University of Chicago 332
Lynchburg College 334

M

Macalester College 336
Manhattanville College 338
Marist College 340
Marlboro College 342
Marquette University 344
Massachusetts Institute of Technology 346
McGill University 348
Mercer University—Macon 350
Miami University 352
Michigan State University 354
Michigan Technological University 356
Middlebury College 358
Mills College 360
Millsaps College 362
Monmouth University (NJ) 364
Montana Tech of the University of Montana 366
Moravian College 368
Mount Holyoke College 370
Muhlenberg College 372

N

New College of Florida 374
New Jersey Institute of Technology 376
New Mexico Institute of Mining & Technology 378
New York University 380
North Carolina State University 382
Northeastern University 384
Northwestern University 386

O

Oberlin College 388
Oglethorpe University 390
Ohio Northern University 392
Ohio State University—Columbus 394
Ohio University—Athens 396
Ohio Wesleyan University 498

P

Pennsylvania State—University Park 400
Pepperdine University 402
Pitzer College 404
Pomona College 406
Princeton University 408
Providence College 410
Purdue University—West Lafayette 412

Q

Quinnipiac University 414

R

Randolph-Macon College 416
Randolph-Macon Woman's College 418
Reed College 420
Rensselaer Polytechnic Institute 422
Rhodes College 424
Rice University 426
Rider University 428
Ripon College 430
Rochester Institute of Technology 432
Rollins College 434
Rose-Hulman Institute of Technology 436
Rutgers, The State University of New Jersey—
New Brunswick/Piscataway Campus 438

S

Saint Anselm College 440
Saint Louis University 442
Saint Mary's College of California 444
Saint Mary's College of Maryland 446
Saint Michael's College 448
Saint Olaf College 450
Salisbury University 452
Samford University 454
Santa Clara University 456
Sarah Lawrence College 458
Scripps College 460
Seattle University 462
Seton Hall University 464
Sewanee—The University of the South 466
Siena College 468
Simmons College 470
Simon's Rock College of Bard 472
Skidmore College 474
Smith College 476
Sonoma State University 478

Southern Methodist University 480
Southwestern University 482
Spelman College 484
St. Bonaventure University 486
St. John's College (MD) 488
St. John's College (NM) 490
St. John's University 492
St. Lawrence University 494
Stanford University 496
State University of New York at Albany 498
State University of New York at Binghamton 500
State University of New York at Buffalo 502
State University of New York at Stony Brook 504
State University of New York College at Geneseo 506
State University of New York College at Purchase 508
Stephens College 510
Stevens Institute of Technology 512
Suffolk University 514
Susquehanna University 516
Swarthmore College 518
Sweet Briar College 520
Syracuse University 522

T

TCU 524
Temple University 526
Texas A&M University—College Station 528
Transylvania University 530
Trinity College (CT) 532
Trinity University 534
Truman State University 536
Tufts University 538
Tulane University 540

U

Union College (NY) 542
United States Air Force Academy 544
United States Coast Guard Academy 546
United States Merchant Marine Academy 548
United States Military Academy 550
United States Naval Academy 552
University of Alabama—Tuscaloosa, The 554
University of Arizona 556
University of Arkansas—Fayetteville 558
University of California—Berkeley 560
University of California—Davis 562
University of California—Los Angeles 564
University of California—Riverside 566
University of California—San Diego 568
University of California—Santa Barbara 570
University of California—Santa Cruz 572
University of Central Florida 574
University of Chicago 576
University of Colorado—Boulder 578
University of Connecticut 580
University of Dallas 582
University of Dayton 584
University of Delaware 586
University of Denver 588
University of Florida 590
University of Georgia 592
University of Hawaii—Manoa 594
University of Idaho 596
University of Illinois—Urbana-Champaign 698
University of Iowa 600
University of Kansas 602
University of Kentucky 604
University of Louisiana at Lafayette 606
University of Maine 608
University of Mary Washington 600
University of Maryland—Baltimore County 612
University of Maryland—College Park 614
University of Massachusetts—Amherst 616
University of Miami 618
University of Michigan—Ann Arbor 620
University of Minnesota—Twin Cities 622
University of Mississippi 624
University of Missouri—Rolla 626
University of Montana—Missoula 628
University of Nebraska—Lincoln 630
University of New Hampshire 632
University of New Mexico 634
University of New Orleans 636
University of North Carolina at Asheville 638
University of North Carolina—Chapel Hill 640
University of North Carolina—Greensboro 642
University of North Dakota 644
University of Notre Dame 646
University of Oklahoma 648
University of Oregon 650
University of the Pacific 652
University of Pennsylvania 654
University of Pittsburgh—Pittsburgh 656
University of Puget Sound 658
University of Redlands 660
University of Rhode Island 662
University of Richmond 664
University of Rochester 666
University of San Diego 668
University of San Francisco 670
University of Scranton, The 672
University of South Carolina—Columbia 674
University of South Dakota, The 676
University of South Florida 678
University of Southern California 680
University of Tennessee—Knoxville 682
University of Texas—Austin, The 684
University of Toronto 686
University of Tulsa, The 688
University of Utah 690
University of Vermont 692
University of Virginia 694
University of Washington 696
University of Wisconsin—Madison 698
University of Wyoming 700
Ursinus College 702

V

Valparaiso University 704
Vanderbilt University 706
Vassar College 708
Villanova University 710
Virginia Tech 712

W

Wabash College 714
Wagner College 716
Wake Forest University 718
Warren Wilson College 720
Washington and Lee University 722

Washington State University 724
Washington University in St. Louis 726
Webb Institute 728
Wellesley College 730
Wells College 732
Wesleyan College 734
Wesleyan University 736
West Virginia University 738
Westminster College (PA) 740
Wheaton College (IL) 742
Wheaton College (MA) 744
Whitman College 746
Whittier College 748
Willamette University 750
William Jewell College 752
Williams College 754
Wittenberg University 756
Wofford College 758
Worcester Polytechnic Institute 760

X

Xavier University of Louisiana 762
Xavier University (OH) 764

Y

Yale University 766

INDEX OF SCHOOLS BY LOCATION

UNITED STATES

ALABAMA

Auburn University 62
Birmingham-Southern College 86
Samford University 454
University of Alabama—Tuscaloosa, The 555

ARKANSAS

Hendrix College 274
University of Arkansas—Fayetteville 558

ARIZONA

Arizona State University 60
University of Arizona 556

CALIFORNIA

Cal Poly—San Luis Obispo 108
California Institute of Technology 110
Chapman University 128
Claremont McKenna College 136
Harvey Mudd College 270
Loyola Marymount University 330
Mills College 360
Pepperdine University 402
Pitzer College 404
Pomona College 406
Saint Mary's College of California 444
Santa Clara University 456
Scripps College 460
Sonoma State University 478
Stanford University 496
University of California—Berkeley 560
University of California—Davis 562
University of California—Los Angeles 564
University of California—Riverside 566
University of California—San Diego 568
University of California—Santa Barbara 570
University of California—Santa Cruz 572
University of Redlands 660
University of San Diego 668
University of San Francisco 670
University of Southern California 680
University of the Pacific 652
Whittier College 748

COLORADO

Colorado College 166
Colorado School of Mines 168
Colorado State University 170
United States Air Force Academy 544
University of Colorado—Boulder 578
University of Denver 588

CONNECTICUT

Connecticut College 174
Fairfield University 220
Quinnipiac University 414
Trinity College (CT) 532
United States Coast Guard Academy 546
University of Connecticut 580
Wesleyan University 736
Yale University 766

DELAWARE

University of Delaware 586

DISTRICT OF COLUMBIA

American University 56
Catholic University of America, The 122
George Washington University, The 238
Georgetown University 240
Howard University 286

FLORIDA

Eckerd College 208
Flagler College 224
Florida State University 226
New College of Florida 374
Rollins College 434
University of Central Florida 574
University of Florida 590
University of Miami 618
University of South Florida 678

GEORGIA

Agnes Scott College 46
Emory University 214
Georgia Institute of Technology 242
Mercer University—Macon 350
Oglethorpe University 390
Spelman College 484
University of Georgia 592
Wesleyan College 734

HAWAII

University of Hawaii—Manoa 594

IDAHO

Albertson College 48
University of Idaho 596

ILLINOIS

Bradley University 94
DePaul University 192
Illinois Institute of Technology 288
Illinois Wesleyan University 290
Knox College 312
Lake Forest College 316
Loyola University of Chicago 332
Northwestern University 386
University of Chicago 576
University of Illinois—Urbana-Champaign 598
Wheaton College (IL) 742

INDIANA

DePauw University 194
Earlham College 206
Hanover College 266
Indiana University—Bloomington 292
Purdue University—West Lafayette 412
Rose-Hulman Institute of Technology 436
University of Notre Dame 646
Valparaiso University 704
Wabash College 714

IOWA

Coe College 144
Cornell College 178
Grinnell College 250
Iowa State University 296
University of Iowa 600

KANSAS

Kansas State University 308
University of Kansas 602

KENTUCKY

Bellarmine University 76
Berea College 84
Centre College 126
Transylvania University 530
University of Kentucky 604

LOUISIANA

Centenary College of Louisiana 124
Louisiana State University 324
Loyola University New Orleans 326
Tulane University 540
University of Louisiana at Lafayette 606
University of New Orleans 636
Xavier University of Louisiana 762

MAINE

Bates College 72
Bowdoin College 92
Colby College 146
College of the Atlantic 150
University of Maine 608

MARYLAND

Goucher College 248
Johns Hopkins University 302
Loyola College in Maryland 328
Saint Mary's College of Maryland 446
Salisbury University 452
St. John's College (MD) 488
United States Naval Academy 552
University of Maryland—Baltimore County 612
University of Maryland—College Park 614

MASSACHUSETTS

Amherst College 58
Babson College 66
Bentley College 82
Boston College 88
Boston University 90
Brandeis University 96
Clark University 138
College of the Holy Cross 154
Emerson College 212
Franklin W. Olin College of Engineering 232
Hampshire College 262
Harvard College 268
Massachusetts Institute of Technology 346
Mount Holyoke College 370
Northeastern University 384
Simmons College 470
Simon's Rock College of Bard 472
Smith College 476
Suffolk University 514
Tufts University 538
University of Massachusetts—Amherst 616
Wellesley College 730
Wheaton College (MA) 744
Williams College 754
Worcester Polytechnic Institute 760

MICHIGAN

Albion College 50
Calvin College 112
Hillsdale College 276
Kalamazoo College 306
Michigan State University 354
Michigan Technological University 356
University of Michigan—Ann Arbor 620

MINNESOTA

Carleton College 114
College of Saint Benedict/Saint John's University 160
Gustavus Adolphus College 256
Macalester College 336
Saint Olaf College 450
University of Minnesota—Twin Cities 620

MISSISSIPPI

Millsaps College 362
University of Mississippi 622

MISSOURI

College of the Ozarks 158
Saint Louis University 442
Stephens College 510
Truman State University 536
University of Missouri—Rolla 626
Washington University in St. Louis 726
William Jewell College 752

MONTANA

Montana Tech of the University of Montana 366
University of Montana—Missoula 628

NEBRASKA

Creighton University 182
University of Nebraska—Lincoln 630

NEVADA

Deep Springs College 188

NEW HAMPSHIRE

Dartmouth College 184
Saint Anselm College 442
University of New Hampshire 632

NEW JERSEY

College of New Jersey, The 156
Drew University 198
Monmouth University (NJ) 364
New Jersey Institute of Technology 376
Princeton University 408
Rider University 428
Rutgers, The State University of New Jersey—
New Brunswick/Piscataway Campus 438
Seton Hall University 464
Stevens Institute of Technology 512

NEW MEXICO

New Mexico Institute of Mining & Technology 378
St. John's College (NM) 490
University of New Mexico 634

NEW YORK

Alfred University 52
Bard College 68
Barnard College 70
City University of New York—Brooklyn College 130
City University of New York—Hunter College 132
City University of New York—Queens College 134
Clarkson University 140
Colgate University 148
Columbia University—Columbia College 172
Cooper Union 176
Cornell University 180
Eugene Lang College 216
Fordham University 228
Hamilton College 258
Hobart and William Smith Colleges 280
Hofstra University 282
Ithaca College 298
Manhattanville College 338
Marist College 340
New York University 380
Rensselaer Polytechnic Institute 422
Rochester Institute of Technology 432
Sarah Lawrence College 458
Siena College 468
Skidmore College 474
St. Bonaventure University 486
St. John's University 492
St. Lawrence University 494
State University of New York at Albany 498
State University of New York at Binghamton 500
State University of New York at Buffalo 502
State University of New York at Stony Brook 504
State University of New York College at Geneseo 506
State University of New York College at Purchase 508
Syracuse University 522
Union College (NY) 542
United States Merchant Marine Academy 548
United States Military Academy 550
University of Rochester 666
Vassar College 708
Wagner College 716
Webb Institute 728
Wells College 732

NORTH CAROLINA

Catawba College 120
Davidson College 186
Duke University 202
Elon University 210
Guilford College 254
North Carolina State University 382
University of North Carolina at Asheville 638
University of North Carolina—Chapel Hill 640
University of North Carolina—Greensboro 642
Wake Forest University 718
Warren Wilson College 720

NORTH DAKOTA

University of North Dakota 644

OHIO

Case Western Reserve University 118
College of Wooster, The 164
Denison University 190
Hiram College 278
Kenyon College 310
Miami University 352
Oberlin College 388
Ohio Northern University 392
Ohio State University—Columbus 394
Ohio University—Athens 396
Ohio Wesleyan University 398
University of Dayton 584
Wittenberg University 756
Xavier University (OH) 764

OKLAHOMA

University of Oklahoma 648
University of Tulsa, The 688

OREGON

Lewis & Clark College 322
Reed College 420
University of Oregon 650
Willamette University 750

PENNSYLVANIA

Allegheny College 54
Bryn Mawr College 104
Bucknell University 106
Carnegie Mellon University 116
Dickinson College 196
Drexel University 200
Duquesne University 204
Franklin & Marshall College 230
Gettysburg College 244
Grove City College 252
Haverford College 272
Indiana University of Pennsylvania 294
Juniata College 304
Lafayette College 314
Lehigh University 320
Moravian College 368
Muhlenberg College 372
Pennsyvania State—University Park 400
Susquehanna University 516
Swarthmore College 518
Temple University 526
University of Pennsylvania 654
University of Pittsburgh—Pittsburgh 656
University of Scranton, The 672
Ursinus College 702
Villanova University 710
Westminster College (PA) 740

RHODE ISLAND

Brown University 100
Bryant University 102
Providence College 410
University of Rhode Island 662

SOUTH CAROLINA
Clemson University 142
College of Charleston 152
Furman University 234
University of South Carolina—Columbia 674
Wofford College 758

SOUTH DAKOTA
University of South Dakota, The 676

TENNESSEE
Fisk University 222
Rhodes College 424
Sewanee—The University of the South 466
University of Tennessee—Knoxville 682
Vanderbilt University 706

TEXAS
Austin College 64
Baylor University 74
Rice University 426
Southern Methodist University 480
Southwestern University 482
TCU 524
Texas A&M University—College Station 528
Trinity University 534
University of Dallas 582
University of Texas—Austin, The 684

UTAH
Brigham Young University (UT) 98
University of Utah 690

VERMONT
Bennington College 80
Marlboro College 342
Middlebury College 358
Saint Michael's College 448
University of Vermont 692

VIRGINIA
College of William and Mary 162
George Mason University 236
Hampden-Sydney College 260
Hampton University 264
Hollins University 284
James Madison University 300
Lynchburg College 334
Randolph-Macon College 416
Randolph-Macon Woman's College 418
Sweet Briar College 520
University of Mary Washington 610
University of Richmond 664
University of Virginia 694
Virginia Tech 712
Washington and Lee University 722

WASHINGTON
Evergreen State College, The 218
Gonzaga University 246
Seattle University 462
University of Puget Sound 658
University of Washington 696
Washington State University 724
Whitman College 746

WEST VIRGINIA
West Virginia University 738

WISCONSIN
Beloit College 78
Lawrence University 318
Marquette University 344
Ripon College 430
University of Wisconsin—Madison 698

WYOMING
University of Wyoming 700

CANADA
McGill University 348
University of Toronto 686

ABOUT THE AUTHORS

Robert Franek is a graduate of Drew University and Vice President & Publisher for The Princeton Review. He has proudly been a part of the company for five years. Robert comes to The Princeton Review with an extensive admissions background. In addition, he owns a walking tour business, leading historically driven, yet not boring, walking tours of his favorite town, New York City!

Tom Meltzer is a graduate of Columbia University. He has taught for The Princeton Review since 1986 and is the author or coauthor of seven Princeton Review titles, the most recent of which is *Illustrated Word Smart*, which Tom cowrote with his wife, Lisa. He is also a professional musician and songwriter. A native of Baltimore, Tom now lives in Hillsborough, North Carolina.

Christopher Maier is a graduate of Dickinson College. During the past five years, he's lived variously in New York City, coastal Maine, western Oregon, central Pennsylvania, and eastern England. Now he's at an oasis somewhere in the midwestern cornfields—the University of Illinois—where he's earning his MFA in fiction. Aside from writing for magazines, newspapers, and The Princeton Review, he's worked as a radio disc jockey, a helping hand in a bakery, and a laborer on a highway construction crew. He's trying to avoid highway construction these days.

Carson Brown graduated from Stanford University in 1998, and after getting paid too much for working for various Internet companies for several years, sold her BMW and moved to Mexico. She has now overstayed her welcome south of the border and is returning to San Francisco to be responsible and further her career working as a writer and editor.

Julie Doherty is a freelance writer, Web designer, and preschool teacher. She lives in Mexico City.

Andrew Friedman graduated in 2003 from Stanford University, where he was a President's Scholar. He lives in New York City.

Counselor Order Form

The Princeton Review

AME:________________ TITLE:________________

ompany or School Name:________________

illing Address:________________ City:________________ State:________ Zip Code:________

hipping Address: (If different from billing)________________

ity:________________ State:________ Zip Code:________

hone:________ Fax:________ Email Address:________________

ILLING INFORMATION: *Check one of the following*

☐ Enclosed a check for the sum of:________________

☐ Please send me a bill with a Purchase Order #________________

☐ Please charge my credit card for the sum of:________________

redit Card # and type:________________ Expiration Date:______

lame on the Card:________________ Signature:________________ Date:______

RDERING INSTRUCTIONS:

he Essential Package includes 1 of each book listed in the Essential Package column. There is no limit to the quantity you may order.

		Essential Package	Single Books	Your Price	Total Price
Your Educator DISCOUNT		30%	15%	15%	
Essential Package Price		$150			$150
TITLE	ISBN	Quantity	Quantity		
The Best 361 Colleges, 2006 Edition	0375764836	Included		$18.66	
Complete Book of Colleges, 2006 Edition	0375764828	Included		$22.91	
Colleges With a Conscience	0375764801	Included		$14.41	
Eye on Apply: Six True Stories of College Admissions	0375764267	Included		$13.56	
College Essays that Made a Difference	0375763449	Included		$11.86	
Guide to College Majors 2005 Edition	0375764690	Included		$17.85	
Visiting College Campuses 7th Edition	0375764003	Included		$17.00	
Taking Time Off 2nd Edition	0375763031	Included		$11.05	
The K&W Guide to Colleges for Students with Learning Disabilities, 8th Edition	037576495X	Included		$22.95	
Paying for College Without Going Broke	0375765026	Included		$17.00	
America's Best Value Colleges, 2006 Edition	0375764674	Included		$13.56	
SUB-TOTAL Books					$

The Princeton Review College data Set CDs	CD	Price	Total Price
Full Data Set (all regions in one CD)		$49.00	
Mid-Atlantic Regional Data Set		$20.00	
Midwestern Regional Data Set		$20.00	
Northeastern Regional Data Set		$20.00	
Southeastern Regional Data Set		$20.00	
Western Regional Data Set		$20.00	
SUB-TOTAL CDs			$

✔ Don't Forget Shipping & Handling

Books & CDs: $2.95 for 1, $9.95 for 2 or more

Total (Books, CDs, and Shipping and Handling)

$________________

Please fax this order form to
attn: Book Orders, 212-874-1754
or mail to
The Princeton Review attn: Book Orders
2315 Broadway, New York, NY 10024
Please call or Email with questions
212-874-8282 x1687 or TPRBooks@Review.com

NOTES

College Money

Crisis Planning: Where's The Money?

Congratulations! You have just undertaken a very important step in taking control of your future. This is a great book, filled with invaluable information that will help you choose the college that is best for you.

It should now be clear to you, how absolutely critical college selection is going to be for your success. You need to find the best fit for you from an academic standpoint, but don't underestimate the importance of a good fit from a social and geographic standpoint.

Once you have found a list of schools that you think will serve you well, you also need to put a financial filter on the list, because no matter how you look at it, college is going to be expensive, and sooner or later the bills will have to be paid.

To avoid conflict and disappointment, to do some crisis college planning. College is looming in the near future and there isn't enough money in the family coffers to pay for it all. You and your parents need to discuss your college budget. Face it, your college education will probably put a strain on the family finances, and if you have brothers and sisters, your parents have to factor their future college educations into the mix as well. On top of that, they cannot ignore the fact that their retirement years are not too far off, and they cannot afford to saddle themselves with huge education debt.

But don't despair. Just because the family cannot pay the entire cost of college doesn't mean that you can't go. You and your parents need to examine all of the resources available and you might need to be creative in crafting a solution.

Consider:

- Parent contributions—Have they accumulated any savings for college? Are they able to come up with additional money out of current income during the college years that can be funneled toward college? Do they have an idea of exactly how much they are prepared to spend each year on college?
- Student contributions—Do you have college savings set aside? Are you willing to work during the college years to help supplement? What kinds of student loans are available to you?
- Financial aid—Look for colleges that have money to give you. Don't forget, in addition to federal and state aid, many colleges have other money to help you out. Are you willing to do your homework to find the colleges that will find you attractive as a potential student and give you money to convince you to go there?
- Loans—Often, loans are part of a financial aid package. However, there are also private loans available for students as well as parents. How much debt are all of you willing to take on?
- Non-need based scholarships—There are many scholarships that are awarded for reasons other than financial need. Often they are awarded as a prize in an essay contest or some other type of competition. Are you willing to do the work that is necessary to win this "free" money? Don't forget, these scholarships are usually only good for one year so you will have to do this every year if it is part of your plan.
- Other sources—Would you consider military training to get money for college? Reserve Officer Training Corps (ROTC) is a way of getting financial help with college. You will have to give part of your time both during college and after to military service in return for financial assistance.

So you see, there are options, and the sooner you examine your choices the better. These choices are directly affected by a key factor—need-based financial aid. If your family can qualify for need-based financial aid, be sure to look for the colleges that have the money to meet your need. In this not-so-perfect world, not all colleges have unlimited funds and you may find that you have to ante up more than expected.

Furthermore, some college financing strategies could actually reduce the amount of need-based financial aid that you are entitled to receive. So it is important to know pretty early in the college selection game whether financial aid is going to be in your future.

A professional evaluation of your family's ability to qualify for need-based financial aid can be the most important thing you do in the entire college selection process. It can tell you whether you can expect it, or whether you should just forget about it and look for other sources of non-need aid. To learn more about these issues and what to do, you and your parents should visit *http://www.collegemoney.com/howplan_cp.asp*.

When your child is ready for private college, you will be, too.

Lock in tomorrow's tuition at less than today's price with Independent 529 Plan.

It's never too late to start saving for your child's future. But since private college tuition costs go up every year, the sooner you lock in prices with Independent 529 Plan the more prepared you'll be. Along with protection against tuition inflation, you'll enjoy freedom from market risk and federal taxes.* Plus, the comfort of knowing how your child will benefit from your foresight—with a private college education.

Open an account today at www.ind529best361.org
or call 1-888-718-7878.

TIAA CREF
FINANCIAL SERVICES FOR THE GREATER GOOD℠

Independent 529 Plan
TOMORROW'S TUITION AT LESS THAN TODAY'S PRICE

*As of June 2005. Participation in Independent 529 Plan does not guarantee admission to any college or university, nor does it affect the admissions process. Owning a certificate may have an adverse impact on financial aid determinations. The law allowing for federal income tax-free qualified withdrawals is set to expire on December 31, 2010. Congress may or may not extend this law beyond this date. Future changes in the law may create adverse tax consequences, or lead to termination of the Plan. TIAA-CREF and its affiliates do not provide tax advice. Please consult your tax advisor. Purchasers should read the Disclosure Booklet, including the Enrollment Agreement, carefully before making purchase decisions. Teachers Personal Investors Services, Inc. and TIAA-CREF Individual and Institutional Services, LLC Distributors. As of September 2004. Tutition Plan Consortium, LLC is the program sponsor and TIAA-CREF Tuition Financing, Inc. is the program manager.

se Independent 529 Plan funds at 250* of the nation's leading private colleges, with more joining all the time.

abama
rmingham-Southern College
ulkner University
mford University
niversity of Mobile

kansas
endrix College
on College

alifornia
alifornia Lutheran University
napman University Claremont
cKenna College
arvey Mudd College
ills College
ount St. Mary's College
ccidental College
epperdine University
tzer College
oint Loma Nazarene University
omona College
aint Mary's College of California
tanford University
niversity of LaVerne
niversity of Redlands
niversity of San Diego
niversity of the Pacific
estmont College
hittier College

olorado
olorado College
egis University

onnecticut
airfield University
esleyan University

istrict of Columbia
merican University
atholic University of America
eorge Washington University

orida
acksonville University
ollins College
aint Leo University
niversity of Miami

eorgia
gnes Scott College
erry College
lark Atlanta University
mory University
aGrange College
ercer University
glethorpe University
pelman College
esleyan College

awaii
haminade University
f Honolulu

daho
lbertson College of Idaho
orthwest Nazarene University

linois
ugustana College
radley University
lmhurst College
linois Institute of Technology
nox College
ake Forest College
onmouth College
orth Central College
livet Nazarene University
niversity of Chicago

ndiana
utler University
DePauw University
Earlham College
Franklin College of Indiana
Rose-Hulman Institute of Technology
Saint Mary's College
University of Evansville
University of Notre Dame
Valparaiso University
Wabash College

Iowa
Buena Vista University
Central College
Clarke College
Dordt College
Grinnell College
Graceland University
Loras College
Luther College
Northwestern College
Waldorf College
Wartburg College

Kentucky
Centre College
Transylvania University

Louisiana
Centenary College of Louisiana
Dillard University
Tulane University

Maryland
College of Notre Dame of Maryland
Goucher College
Loyola College in Maryland
McDaniel College
Mount Saint Mary's College

Massachusetts
Amherst College
Berklee College of Music
Boston University
Clark University
Gordon College
Hampshire College
Massachusetts Institute of Technology
Mount Holyoke College
Smith College
Springfield College
Wellesley College
Wheaton College

Michigan
Albion College
Hope College
Kalamazoo College

Minnesota
Carleton College
Gustavus Adolphus College
Hamline University
Macalester College
St. Olaf College

Missouri
Culver-Stockton College
Drury University
Hannibal-LaGrange College
Maryville University of Saint Louis
Rockhurst University
Saint Louis University
Stephens College
Washington University in St. Louis
Webster University
Webster University Conservatory
Westminster College

Nebraska
Creighton University
Doane College

New Hampshire
Franklin Pierce College

New Jersey
Centenary College
Drew University
Princeton University
Rider University
Stevens Institute of Technology

New Mexico
College of Santa Fe

New York
Bard College
Canisius College
Daemen College
Elmira College
Hartwick College
Hobart & William Smith Colleges
Ithaca College
Marist College
Medaille College
Nazareth College
Niagara University
Pace University
Roberts Wesleyan College
Rochester Institute of Technology
Skidmore College
Syracuse University
University of Rochester
Vassar College
Wells College

North Carolina
Catawba College
Greensboro College
Guilford College
Lenoir Rhyne College
Methodist College
Salem College
Wake Forest University

Ohio
Ashland College
Capital University
Case Western Reserve University
College of Wooster
Denison University
Hiram College
John Carroll University
Kenyon College
Mount Vernon Nazarene University
Muskingum College
Oberlin College
Ohio Wesleyan University
Tiffin University
University of Dayton
Wittenberg University

Oklahoma
Oklahoma Christian University
Southern Nazarene University
University of Tulsa

Oregon
George Fox University
Lewis & Clark College
Linfield College
Pacific University
Reed College
Willamette University

Pennsylvania
Allegheny College
Alvernia College
Arcadia University
Carnegie Mellon University
Chatham College
Dickinson College
Drexel University
Franklin & Marshall College
Gettysburg College
Grove City College
Immaculata University
Juniata College
Keystone College
La Salle University
Marywood University
Moravian College
Muhlenberg College
Saint Francis University
Susquehanna University
Thiel College
Ursinus College
Waynesburg College
Westminster College
York College of Pennsylvania

South Carolina
Charleston Southern University
Columbia College
Converse College
Furman University
Presbyterian College
Wofford College

South Dakota
Augustana College

Tennessee
Belmont University
Carson-Newman College
Lambuth University
Rhodes College
Trevecca Nazarene University
University of the South
Vanderbilt University

Texas
Abilene Christian University
Austin College
Baylor University
Dallas Baptist University
Hardin-Simmons University
Lubbock Christian University
Rice University
St. Edward's University
St. Mary's University
Southern Methodist University
Southwestern University
Texas Christian University
Trinity University
University of Dallas
University of Mary Hardin-Baylor

Vermont
Middlebury College
Saint Michael's College

Virginia
Bridgewater College
Eastern Mennonite University
Hampden-Sydney College
Hollins University
Mary Baldwin College
Randolph-Macon Woman's College
Shenandoah University
Sweet Briar College
University of Richmond
Virginia Wesleyan College

Washington
Pacific Lutheran University
Seattle Pacific University
Whitworth College

West Virginia
West Virginia Wesleyan College

Wisconsin
Lakeland College
Lawrence University
Ripon College

Our Books Help You Navigate the College Admissions Process

Find the Right School

Best 361 Colleges, 2006 Edition
0-375-76483-6 • $21.95/C$29.95
Previous Edition: 0-375-76405-4

Complete Book of Colleges, 2006 Edition
0-375-76482-8 • $26.95/C$37.95
Previous Edition: 0-375-76406-2

America's Best Value Colleges,
2006 Edition
0-375-76467-4 • $15.95/C$22.95

Visiting College Campuses, 7th Edition
0-375-76400-3 • $20.00/C$30.00

Get In

Cracking the New SAT, 2006 Edition
0-375-76485-2 • $19.95/C$27.95

Cracking the New SAT with CD-ROM,
2006 Edition
0-375-76486-0 • $31.95/C$44.95

Math Workout for the New SAT
0-375-76433-X • $16.00/C$23.00

Reading and Writing Workout for the New SAT
0-375-76431-3 • $16.00/C$23.00

11 Practice Tests for the New SAT & PSAT,
2nd Edition
0-375-76516-6 • $19.95/C$27.95

Cracking the ACT, 2005 Edition
0-375-76454-2 • $19.00/C$27.00

Cracking the ACT with Sample Tests on CD-ROM, 2005 Edition
0-375-76455-0 • $31.95/C$44.95

Crash Course for the ACT, 2nd Edition
0-375-76364-3 • $9.95/C$14.95

Crash Course for the New SAT
0-375-76461-5 • $9.95/C$13.95

Get Help Paying for It

Paying for College Without Going Broke,
2005 Edition
0-375-76421-6 • $20.00/C$27.00

Paying for Graduate School Without Going Broke, 2005 Edition
0-375-76422-4 • $20.00/C$27.00

How to Save for College
0-375-76425-9 • $14.95/C$21.00

WE KNOW APPLYING TO COLLEGES IS STRESSFUL.

Why Not Win $500 for It?

Yeesh. Everyone around you may be weary of your obsessing over every detail of your (or your child's) college search. You know the angst. Location? Academic reputation? Tuition? Majors? Dream school? Safety school? But we're into this stuff even more than you are. So much so that we've created our College Hopes Survey, an opportunity for you to tell us how your search and application experience is going. Our survey's a heck of a lot shorter than any college app you'll face (it's just 10 questions). And it'll only take about five minutes to complete.

But wait, there's more. We're giving a $500 scholarship to one lucky participant (at random). Ten questions. Five minutes. Chance for $500 bucks. You do the math.

Complete this form and mail or fax it back to us. Or visit us at *www.PrincetonReview.com/go/survey* and submit your survey to us online.

In March 2006, we'll post our survey findings on our website, www.PrincetonReview.com and give one participant the happy news that they've won the $500 scholarship. Right about the time you'll be receiving those fat (or not-so-fat) letters from colleges. Hope springs eternal.

Official Rules:

We will conduct a random drawing in February 2006 to select a winner. The winner of the drawing will receive a $500 scholarship. Your odds of winning depend upon the number of entries received. If you win, you must redeem the scholarship within twelve months of notification. This promotion is not open to employees of The Princeton Review or Random House and is, of course, void where prohibited by law. All taxes are the sole responsibility of the winners. No purchase necessary: if you choose not to buy this book (big mistake!) or fill out the survey (bad decision!), you may enter this drawing by going to our website at: *www.PrincetonReview.com/go/survey* or by sending a postcard with your name, address, and phone number to The Princeton Review, c/o Robert Franek - College Hopes Survey, 2315 Broadway, New York, New York, 10024-4332. You may also write us to get a listing of the prize winner. By the way, we are not responsible for failures in electronic transmission or lost, misdirected, illegible, or mutilated entries.

The Princeton Review
www.PrincetonReview.com

College Hopes Survey

Fill out online at *www.PrincetonReview.com/go/survey*

or tear out and snail mail to Robert Franek at The Princeton Review, 2315 Broadway, New York, NY 10024

or fax to Robert Franek at 212-874-0775.

Name ____________________

Address (optional) ____________________

City / State / Zip ____________________

Daytime phone ____________________

E-mail address ____________________

I am ___ a parent of a student ___ a student applying to attend college beginning in

___ Fall or Spring 2005 ___ Fall or Spring 2006 ___ Later (indicate year: ________).

1 What would be your "dream college?" What college would you most like to attend (or see your child attend) if chance of being accepted or cost were not an issue?

____

2 Which of the following would describe your "safety" school? What type of college are you (or your child) applying to that you think you (or your child) will be most likely to get into and afford? (Choose one.)

___ Private College in my state

___ State or Public College in my state

___ Private College in another state

___ State or Public College in another state

3 How would you gauge your stress level about the college application process? (Choose one.)

___ Very High

___ High

___ Average

___ Low

___ Very Low

4. What has been, or what do you think will be the toughest part of your (your child's) college application experience? (Choose one.)

___ Deciding which colleges to apply to

___ Taking standardized tests such as the SAT, ACT, APs or SAT Subject Tests

___ Writing college essays

___ Deciding which college to attend

5. What's your biggest concern about applying to or attending college? (Choose one.)

___ Won't get into first-choice college

___ Will get into first choice college, but won't be able to attend (due to insufficient savings or financial aid)

___ Will attend a college I (or my child) may regret

___ Amount of education loan debt I (or my child) will take on to pay for the college I (my child) attend(s)

6. When it comes to choosing the actual college you (or your child) will attend, which of the following do you think it is most likely to be? (Choose one.)

___ College with the best academic reputation

___ College that will be the most affordable (with either lowest costs and/or best financial aid package)?

___ College with the best program for my (my child's) career interests and prospects.

___ College that will be the best overall fit

7. What do you estimate your (or your child's) college degree will cost, including four years of tuition, room & board, fees, books and other miscellaneous costs? (Choose one.)

___ Up to $25,000

___ $25,000 to $50,000

___ $50,000 to $75,000

___ More than $75,000

8. What do you (or your child) most want to get out of attending college? (Choose one.)

___ A great overall education

___ A great education in a specific field or career area

___ A better-paying job upon graduation

___ A well-rounded, maturing life experience

9. Ideally, how far from home would you like the college you (your child) attend(s) to be? (Choose one)

___ 0–100

___ 100–500

___ 500–1,000

___ 1,000 or more